EMPLOYMENT
&
LABOR LAW

SEVENTH EDITION

EMPLOYMENT & LABOR LAW

PATRICK J. CIHON

Law and Public Policy, Management Department, Whitman School of Management, Syracuse University

JAMES OTTAVIO CASTAGNERA

Associate Provost/Associate Counsel, Rider University

Australia • Brazil • Japan • Korea • Mexico • Singapore • Spain • United Kingdom • United States

Employment & Labor Law, 7th Edition

Patrick J. Cihon and James Ottavio Castagnera

Vice President of Editorial, Business: Jack W. Calhoun

Editor-in-Chief: Rob Dewey

Senior Acquisitions Editor: Vicky True

Developmental Editor: Krista Kellman

Editorial Assistant: Nicole Parsons

Marketing Director: Lisa Lysne

Marketing Manager: Jennifer Garamy

Marketing Coordinator: Heather Mooney

Content Project Manager: Pre-Press PMG

Production Manager: Jennifer Ziegler

Senior Media Editor: Kristen Meere

Senior Manufacturing Buyer: Kevin Kluck

Production Service and Compositor: Pre-Press PMG

Senior Art Director: Michelle Kunkler

Production Technology Analyst: Jeff Weaver

Permissions Acquisitions Manager: Roberta Broyer

Cover Designer: Tin Box Studio, Inc.

Cover Image: © Victor Melniciuc/iStockphoto

Library of Congress Control Number: 2009937736

ISBN-13: 978-1-4390-3727-0

ISBN-10: 1-4390-3727-2

South-Western Cengage Learning
5191 Natorp Boulevard
Mason, OH 45040
USA

Cengage Learning products are represented in Canada by Nelson Education, Ltd.

Printed in the United States of America
1 2 3 4 5 6 7 13 12 11 10 09

BRIEF CONTENTS

CONTENTS

Chapter 7 Gender and Family Issues: Title VII and Other Legislation 147

Chapter 8 Discrimination Based on Religion and National Origin & Procedures Under Title VII 197

PREFACE

A quarter century ago, when we first undertook the writing of an employment and labor law textbook, we had no notion that our creative effort would carve itself such a long-lasting niche in higher education. Clearly, however, the release of this 7th Edition, as well as accolades like those below, confirm that *Employment & Labor Law* is now firmly established. Lest this sound as if we were resting on our laurels, allow us to hastily add that this new edition has been significantly revised and updated. A source of particular pride is Part One, which contains three entirely new chapters, expressly intended to bring our "old standard" firmly into the employment and labor firmament of the 21st century. Three issues of critical importance in the new millennium—privacy, globalization, and immigration—are treated specifically and in-depth for the first time in our long run. Additionally, numerous new cases, case problems, hypotheticals, and "The Working Law" features ensure that every chapter of this new volume is on the cutting edge of the topic it covers.

> I have practiced labor and employment law for over twenty years and I think this is the best text for a basic labor and employment law class… It's simple to read and straightforward. I tell my students to keep the book and not sell it because it is quite helpful for the basic questions they will be asked in the work world.
>
> Maris Stella (Star) Swift
> *Grand Valley State University*

> The text is well laid-out, and is written in language that is appropriate for the students; there is no reason for the students to not read the text. The questions that follow the edited cases help to focus the student's analysis of the case in question, its relevance to the topic, and introduce the student to legal concepts and outcomes they tend to neglect or may not fully understand…"
>
> Curt M. Weber
> *University of Wisconsin – Whitewater*

> [*Employment & Labor Law* has an] excellent balance of in-depth case-law readings, related ethical considerations, Internet resources and foundational materials for the non-lawyer audience.
>
> Susan F. Alevas
> *New York University*

Hallmark Features

In the constantly changing, often controversial areas of employment and labor law, the 7th edition of this textbook provides current information in a way that highlights critical thinking, ethical decision-making, and relevance to the business world. The unique hallmark features of this text that have been retained include:

Current and Balanced Coverage

This text offers a comprehensive balance of both employment law and labor law topics and includes up-to-date information regarding the ADA Amendments Act, the 2008 Amendments to ERISA under ARRA, the Lilly Ledbetter Act, the new FMLA regulations, coverage of The Genetic Information Nondiscrimination Act, and more.

Readability

In no other area of the law are nonlawyer professionals exposed to such legal regulation, and in no other area do they experience the need for "lawyer-like" skills to the extent that human resources directors and industrial relations specialists do. This book is therefore written to help business and management students, not necessarily lawyers. The straightforward writing style clarifies complex concepts, while pedagogical features help readers develop the legal reasoning and analysis skills that are vital for success in the business world.

The Working Law

Connecting legal concepts and cases to our everyday environment, The Working Law feature highlights the relevancy of the law while sparking student interest and bringing concepts to life. Cutting-edge topics like emotional distress via social networking websites and increasing age discrimination claims in today's tough ecomony as well as controversial discussions about sweatshops and the "don't ask, don't tell" policy are just a few of those considered in this edition.

Ethical Dilemma

What is the extent of global corporate social responsibility? Can employers use genetic information in hiring decisions? What are the boundaries regarding religion and harassment in the workplace? Questions like these, presented in the Ethical Dilemma features in each chapter, address the increasing need for ethical behavior in decision-making. These features can be used to encourage debates in lecture or as assignments that consider the differences between what is legal and what is ethical.

Full Text of Statues in Appendices

To better familiarize students with the provisions of relevant statues, a number of important employment and labor law statutes are provided in the appendices.

New for This Edition

After speaking with over 100 professors teaching employment and labor law, we've tailored this edition of *Employment & Labor Law* to meet the specific needs of this course. The following new features have been added:

NEW Guide to Briefing Cases

Students will find the new Guide to Briefing Cases, which gives a quick overview of how to read a case citation and outlines what information to provide in a brief, to be a valuable reference. While offering an excellent refresher for students who have already taken legal environment or business law courses, it also gives students with no previous legal background an introduction to the basics of case analysis.

NEW Overview of Employment Law Chapter

In order to provide students with a better foundation, this new chapter details how employment law has developed over time and where it's heading under the Obama Administration.

NEW Privacy Chapter

Of growing interest to both students and instructors, this new chapter explores the often controversial issues of employee privacy—including the recent *Quon* case regarding text-messaging.

NEW International Law and Immigration Chapter

As business models shift to being more and more global, this new chapter explores the increasingly important issues of international law and immigration.

Expanded Discrimination Chapters

The chapter on age and disability discrimination has been split into two chapters to accommodate the significant changes in these areas and to allow professors more time to devote to discussing these topics.

Streamlined Labor Law Coverage

While organized labor remains an important player in the workplace arena, some labor law chapters have been reorganized and streamlined in order to better present the material without sacrificing topical coverage. In the 7th edition, the chapters on ERISA and employee welfare programs have been combined into one chapter, as have the chapters on the development of unions and the NLRA and NLRB.

NEW Case Treatment

New summarized cases, in which the authors outline the facts, issue, and decision of a real case in their own words, have been added to provide more case illustrations that are concise and student-friendly. However, as learning to interpret cases in the language of the court is crucial in developing analytical and critical thinking skills, half of the cases in the text remain excerpted in the words of the court. These case extracts have been crisply edited to focus attention on the relevant concept, while including occasional dissents and/or concurring opinions, which allow the reader to experience the fact that law develops from the resolution—or at least the accommodation—of differing views. These two different types of case treatment allow for flexibility in approach and depth of coverage.

NEW Concept Summaries

The 7th edition of *Employment & Labor Law* now offers Concept Summaries throughout each chapter to reinforce the legal concepts illustrated in applicable sections and to provide students with a quick outline to ensure that they understand what they have read.

NEW Key Terms

To help students master the specialized legal terminology and easily identify integral ideas, a new Key Terms section has been added to the end of each chapter. Page references direct students back to the relevant chapter content and marginal definitions.

NEW End-of-Chapter Problem Types

Each chapter now contains nearly 50 percent more problems—including five short answer questions regarding basic chapter comprehension, ten case problems based on real cases, and five hypothetical scenarios to provide students an opportunity to critically analyze real-life situations without a case citation reference. This increased versatility in the end-of-chapter assignments offers instructors a variety of ways in which to engage students and measure comprehension.

Significant Revisions

Some of the highlights of the revised contents of this edition include:

- **Chapter 1**: This brand-new chapter provides a broad overview of the employment and labor law landscape covered in the subsequent chapters. *Gilbert & Sullivan* notwithstanding, the law is not a seamless web. However, the American mosaic of employment and labor laws does present a public-policy picture, which ought to be perceived and considered before embarking on in-depth considerations of its many and diverse pieces.
- **Chapter 4**: Perhaps no issue is of greater concern to employees—after compensation and benefits—than personal privacy in this so-called Information Age. From the possibility of genetic testing for latent medical defects to the ability to monitor our e-mail, our Internet usage, indeed our every move, privacy rights are in jeopardy, while litigation nonetheless increases. Sure to encourage lively debates, this new chapter brings privacy issues to the forefront.
- **Chapter 5**: "The world is flat," to quote *New York Times* columnist Thomas Friedman. Employers and employees alike compete against their counterparts in regions of the globe. No longer is it enough for students of employment and labor law to grasp the major tenets of American statutory and common law. Furthermore, in a 21st century society that has moved way beyond America's traditional melting pot, knowledge of the rules and regulations applying to immigrants, international students, and foreign workers is critical. This new chapter explores these issues.
- **Chapter 7**: This chapter includes coverage of the Lilly Ledbetter Fair Pay Act of 2009, the first act of Congress signed by President Obama, and the amended FMLA military leave and caregiver leave regulations.

- **Chapter 8**: Bringing sensitive ethical issues to the forefront, this chapter more closely examines religious discrimination issues regarding Islam and national origin discrimination against persons from the Middle East.
- **Chapter 9**: Previously combined with coverage of discrimination based on disability, age discrimination now stands as its own chapter with expanded content and related end-of-chapter assignments to highlight the importance of this topic for those who wish to cover it in greater detail.
- **Chapter 10**: Material on the new ADA Amendments Act of 2008 (ADAAA) and the Genetic Information Nondiscrimination Act (GINA) is included in this chapter, which has been expanded and written as a standalone chapter instead of being combined with age discrimination coverage (as in the prior edition).
- **Chapter 11**: Violence in the workplace is a topic sure to ignite lively debate. This chapter now offers a new section to cover the controversial state laws regarding guns in the workplace.
- **Chapter 12**: Adopting a market-tested approach, the chapters on the development of labor unions and the NLRA and the organization, procedures, and jurisdiction of the NLRB have been streamlined into one chapter to better suit the way in which instructors prefer to teach this course without sacrificing topical coverage.
- **Chapter 13**: This chapter presents material regarding the hotly debated Employee Free Choice Act, which would change the face of how workforces organize under current labor laws if passed.
- **Chapter 14**: Employee use of employer e-mail systems, something that all employees or future employees will be able to relate to, is now covered in this chapter.
- **Chapter 17**: To address the significant impact our current economy has had on all aspects of business, this chapter now includes substantial new material on the General Motors and Chrysler bankruptcy and reorganization as well as retiree benefits obligations.
- **Chapter 18**: President Obama signed four executive orders in the beginning of his term that strongly favor organized labor. These include the new Executive Order 13496 regarding notification of employee rights, which is covered in this chapter.
- **Chapter 19**: View significant labor law issues in an everyday, easy-to-relate-to setting with this chapter's updated material on national security and collective bargaining rights for federal employees and TSA airport screens.
- **Chapter 21**: Following market preferences, this chapter now combines content on ERISA with that of employee welfare programs like social security, workers' compensation, and unemployment compensation.
- **Appendix G**: Text of the Genetic Information Nondiscrimination Act of 2008, which prohibits employers and health insurance companies from using genetic information when making decisions regarding hiring, firing, job placement, promotion, health plan coverage, and health plan premium amounts, has been added as an Appendix to the text.

If you have used the previous edition of this textbook and would like to map the course materials you've already developed to the new edition, please visit the website at www.cengage.com/cihon for a ***Table of Contents Correlation Guide.***

Instructor Resources

Instructor's Manual with Test Bank

www.cengage.com/blaw/cihon

The Instructor's Manual provides an overview of the chapter, a lecture outline with page references, case synopses for each excerpted case, answers to the case questions, and answers to the end-of-chapter questions, case problems, and hypothetical scenarios. The Test Bank includes true/false, multiple choice, short answer, and essay questions ready to use for creating tests.

PowerPoint Slides

www.cengage.com/blaw/cihon

NEW FOR THIS EDITION, PowerPoint slides have been created to highlight the key learning objectives in each chapter—including slides summarizing each legal case, The Working Law, and Ethical Dilemma feature. These PowerPoint slides offer a basic chapter outline to accompany class lecture.

Textbook Companion Website

www.cengage.com/blaw/cihon

The companion website for this edition of *Employment & Labor Law* has been enhanced to streamline necessary resources. In addition to providing access to the Instructor's Manual, Test Bank, PowerPoint slides, and Court Case Updates, the website now also offers links to the following: important labor and employment law sites, labor and employment law blogs, legal forms and documents, free legal research sites (comprehensive and circuit-specific), help in the classroom, labor and employment law directories, departments, agencies, associations, and organizations. Also, NEW TO THIS EDITION, interactive quiz questions test basic student comprehension of the concepts illustrated in the chapter.

Business Law Digital Video Library

www.cengage.com/blaw/dvl

The Business Law Digital Video Library has fourteen videos that address employment law topics (like employment-at-will, employment discrimination, employee privacy, etc.) in addition to other topics. Access to these videos is FREE for your students when bundled with a new textbook. Please be sure to let your sales representative know if you would like temporary access to demo this product, which offers a total of over sixty-five clips with instructor resources (like discussion questions).

Court Case Updates

www.cengage.com/blaw/cases

South-Western's Court Case Updates provide monthly summaries of the most important legal cases happening around the country. Access to these cases is free for textbook adopters.

Business Law Case Database

www.textchoice.com
Wondering what happened to your favorite case? The Business Law Case Database is a robust case library that houses over 700 cases. You can now hand-pick the cases you want, making it easy to create customizable casebooks. Start by searching the Business Law Custom Case Database by state or topic for a complete list of offerings.

Westlaw Access

www.westlaw.com
Westlaw, West Group's vast online source of value-added legal and business information, contains over 15,000 databases of information spanning a variety of jurisdictions, practice areas, and disciplines. Qualified instructors may receive ten complimentary hours of Westlaw for their course. Certain restrictions apply; contact your South-Western sales representative for details.

Acknowledgments

The authors wish to thank the many people who contributed to the completion of this book. Pat Cihon wishes to acknowledge the contributions of his research assistant Jonathan Terracciano.

We also would like to thank all those who have contributed to the preparation and production of this 7th edition. In particular, we wish to acknowledge the contribution and assistance of our editors at South-Western Publishing, a part of Cengage Learning: Editor-in-Chief, Rob Dewey; Acquisitions Editor, Vicky True; Marketing Manager, Jennifer Garamy; Content Project Manager, Patrick Franzen; and Developmental Editor, Krista Kellman, for her guidance and insights during the revision of this edition.

In addition, we appreciate the efforts of Cynthia P. Letsch, J.D., S.P.H.R., who prepared the Instructor's Manual and ANSR Source India Pvt. Ltd., who revised the Test Bank and created PowerPoint slides and online quiz questions.

We wish to thank the following reviewers, whose helpful comments and suggestions were used during the preparation of this edition of the book:

Susan F. Alevas
New York University

Bruce-Alan Barnard
Davenport University

Curtiss K. Behrens
Northern Illinois University

Helen Bojarczyk.
Baker College - Auburn Hills

Colette Borom Carpenter
Mercy College

Terry Conry
Ohio University

Larry G. Covell
Jefferson Community College

Sandra J. Defebaugh
Eastern Michigan University

Ronald L. Foster
Cornerstone University, Davenport University

John L. Gilbert
Southern Illinois University – Edwardsville

Diane M. Pfadenhauer
St. Joseph's College

Veena P. Prabhu
California State University – Los Angeles

JoDee Salisbury
Baker College

Stephanie R. Sipe
Georgia Southern University

Joe Stauffer
University of Texas of the Permian Basin

Byron Stuckey
Dallas Baptist University

Maris Stella (Star) Swift
Grand Valley State University

Patsy Thimmig
Mount Mercy College

Donald Lee Vardaman, Jr.
Troy University

Janette C. Waterhouse
University of Iowa

Curt M. Weber
University of Wisconsin – Whitewater

Kelly Collins Woodford
University of South Alabama

Lastly, the authors wish to rededicate the book to the memory of their parents, John E. and Marian M. Cihon and James Ottavio and Catherine L. Castagnera.

Professor Patrick J. Cihon
Law and Public Policy
Management Department,
Whitman School of Management
Syracuse University

Dr. James Ottavio
Associate Provost & Associate Counsel for Academic Affairs
Rider University

GUIDE TO BRIEFING CASES

You will be required to read and understand cases in order to understand and analyze the legal decisions forming the basis of the law. A case is a bit like a parable or a fable. It presents a set of facts and events that led two opposing parties into a conflict requiring resolution by a court or agency. The judge or adjudicator is guided by legal principles developed from statutes or prior cases in the resolution of the dispute. There may be competing legal principles that must be reconciled or accommodated. The case is a self-contained record of the resolution of the dispute between the parties, but it is also an incremental step in the process of developing legal principles for resolution of future disputes.

It is the legal principles—their reconciliation and development—and the reasoning process involved that justify the inclusion of the cases we have selected. The critical task of the reader, therefore, is to sift through the facts of a case and to identify the legal principles underlying that case. In analyzing a case you may find it helpful to ask, after reading the case, "Why was this particular case included at this point in the chapter? What does this case add to the textual material immediately preceding it?"

In analyzing the cases, especially the longer ones, you may find it helpful to "brief" them. Case briefing is a highly useful corollary to efficient legal research. A case brief is nothing more than a specialized outline. As such, a brief summarizes the main feature of a court opinion. A group of briefs, accurately and lucidly constructed, often form the bridge between the relevant decisions identified by a lawyer's research, on one hand, and the memorandum of law, which is his/her final work product, on the other. The following template should prove useful in outlining the case excerpts published in this textbook.

How to Brief a Case

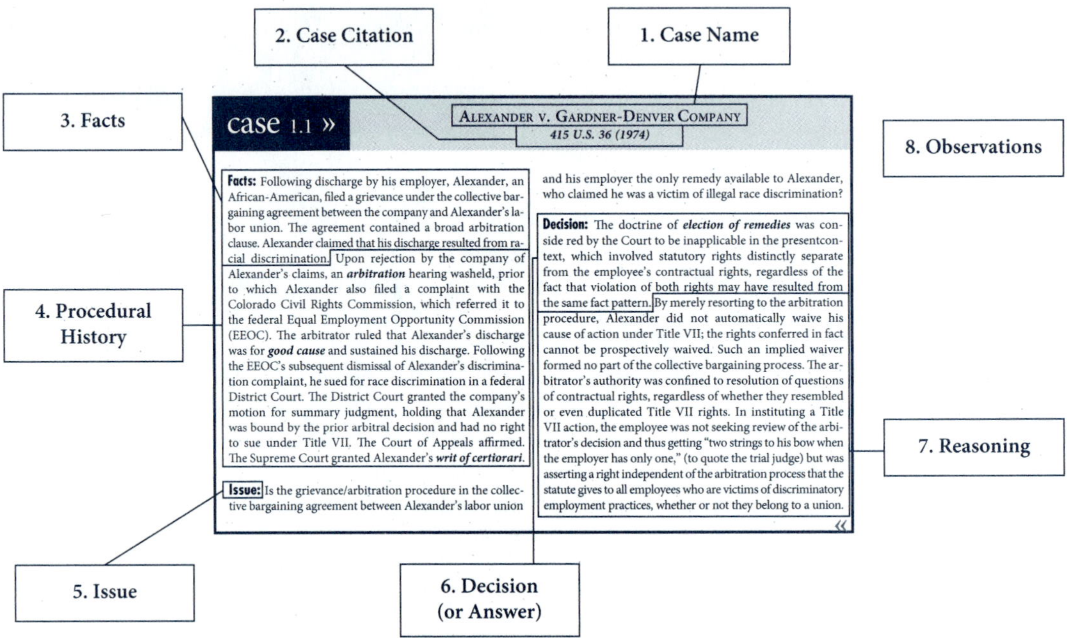

1. **Case Name:** The case name need not include a complete list of all the plaintiffs and defendants, where multiple parties were involved. Typically, a decision is identified by the last name of the first-named plaintiff and the last name of the first-named defendant. Organizations, which are parties, should be identified by their full names, except that terms such as "Corporation" may be abbreviated, i.e., "Corp."

   For the *Alexander* case presented on page 7, the case name would be *Alexander v. Gardner-Denver Company.*

2. **Case Citation:** Published decisions are identified by the reporters in which they are published. Typical citations begin with the volume number, followed by the name of the reporter, and then the page number where the case begins. Following this information will be the date of the decision in parentheses.

   For example, the very first case in this text is *Alexander v. Gardner Denver Company*. The citation is 415 U.S. 36 (1974). This tells the reader that the case appears in volume 415 of the official Supreme Court reporter, starting on page 36, and that the Court announced this decision in 1974.

   Citations come in a dizzying variety of forms. They all have one thing in common: a proper citation provides sufficient information for the reader to know the precise place where the full text can be located, the court which issued the decision, and the date it was announced. The "Bible" of case citations is *The Bluebook: A Uniform System of Citation,* published by the editors of the *Harvard Law Review*. It is now available online at http://www.law.harvard.edu/news/2008/02/25_bluebook.php.

3. **Facts:** Here a concise summary of the main facts of the case are presented in no more than a couple of paragraphs. Only facts relevant and material to the court's decision should be included.

   In the *Alexander* case, the full legal case has been summarized into relevant facts for you already.

4. **Procedural History:** In a sentence or two the briefer presents an explanation of how the case made its way to the appeals court in which it is now under consideration.

   In the *Alexander* case, the history has been summarized for you already.

5. **Issue:** A critical portion of the brief, this section identifies the precise question that *this* court is being asked to answer. The issue is usually expressed in the form of a question. That question seldom is the ultimate question in the underlying case, such as whether the defendant in a criminal case is guilty, or whether the plaintiff in a civil suit should is entitled to damages. Rather the issue before the appellate court is usually a more narrow legal point that is an essential step toward enabling the trial judge or jury to reach a correct decision on the ultimate issues of the lawsuit. The issue on appeal is almost always a question of law, not fact.

   For example, in *Alexander v. Gardner Denver Company*, the U.S. Supreme Court was required to tell the lower federal courts whether a union member (Alexander) was required to submit his discrimination case to a labor arbitrator exclusively, or whether he could also pursue his rights under the federal anti-discrimination statutes. The Court was not asked to decide the ultimate issue of whether or not the plaintiff had meritorious discrimination claim.

6. **Decision (or Answer):** Here in a very few words, the briefer records how the court answered the question that was posed to it.

7. **Reasoning:** The analysis underlying the court's decision should be summarized here. As with the "Facts," this analysis should be no more than a couple of paragraphs in length.

8. **Observations:** This optional section is where the briefer may choose to add his/her own reaction to the court's opinion, some notes on decisions which closely agree or sharply disagree with the outcome of the case, or any other observations that he/she thinks may be useful when it comes time to write the research paper, memorandum of law, or other work product at the end of this research product.

PART 1

COMMON-LAW EMPLOYMENT ISSUES

First the Forest, then the Trees: *An Overview of Employment and Labor Law*

Employment and labor are, arguably, as old as recorded history. In the New Testament's parable of the laborers in the vineyard, we find those workers who began picking grapes at dawn complaining to the owner, because those he hired at noon received the exact same wage as they got. "What business is it of yours, if I choose to be generous?" he inquires rhetorically.

The parable is a rare recorded case of employer largesse. More often workers' complaints have involved too little pay, lack of benefits, unreasonably long hours, or unsafe workplace conditions. These complaints typically have been addressed—when at all—by worker self-help or government intervention.

For example, in the Middle Ages, craftsmen formed guilds according to their respective trades. But by the 14th century, as one famous historian has explained, "Once united by a common craft, the guild masters, journeymen, and apprentices had spread apart into entrepreneurs and hired hands divided by class hatred. The guild was now a corporation in which the workers had no voice."[1] Dissatisfaction led to working-class revolts, which in turn resulted in brutal reprisals by the upper classes.[2]

The Black Death, a plague which first decimated Europe's population in the mid-14th century, actually benefited those workers who survived. The labor shortage encouraged demands for higher wages and better conditions. Rulers' responses were swift and severe. In 1339, Britain's king issued a proclamation which required everyone to accept the same wages that they had received two years earlier. The new labor law also established stiff penalties for refusing to work, for leaving a job in search of higher pay, and for an offer of higher wages by an employer. Parliament reissued the proclamation as the Statute of Laborers in 1351, denouncing not only workers who had the temerity to demand higher wages, but

---

[1]Barbara W. Tuchman, *A Distant Mirror: The Calamitous 14th Century* (New York: Alfred A. Knopf, 1978), p. 39.

[2]*Ibid.*, pp. 383–91.

especially decrying those who chose "rather to beg in idleness than to earn their bread in labor."[3]

Employment-at-Will
Both the employee and the employer are free to unilaterally terminate the relationship at any time and for any legally permissible reason, or for no reason at all.

Common Law
Judge-made law as opposed to statutes and ordinances enacted by legislative bodies.

The Industrial Revolution in 19th century England and America witnessed the rise of the ***employment-at-will*** doctrine in the ***common law***. At-will employment—covered in depth in Chapter 2—meant, in theory, that either the employer or the worker could terminate their relationship at any time for any reason. In reality, the employers had all the bargaining power; real negotiation of terms and conditions of employment was, for the most part, a myth.

To put the relationship more nearly into balance, workers banded together into labor unions. The reaction of the American judiciary, drawn almost exclusively from the upper, propertied class, was negative. Early court cases concluded that labor organizations were criminal conspiracies.[4]

Labor, however, persisted. The unions' first breakthrough came in 1842, when the Supreme Judicial Court of Massachusetts held that unionized workers could only be indicted if either their means or their ends were illegal and that the "tendency" of organized labor to "diminish [the employer's] gains and profits" was not in itself a crime.[5] Progress was slow but more or less steady thereafter, highlighted by such federal legislation as the Federal Employers Liability Act (1908) and the Railway Labor Act (1926), which allowed for alternative methods of dispute resolution, first in the railroad, and later in the airline industry.

The New Deal and the Rise of the Modern American Union

Still, nearly a century would elapse before the Great Depression and the subsequent New Deal of President Franklin D. Roosevelt resulted in the enactment of the major federal employment and labor laws, which govern the fundamental features of the employment relationship and unionization to this very day. These statutes include:

- The Social Security Act (1935), which provides modest pensions to retired workers
- The National Labor Relations Act (1935), which sets the ground rules for the give and take between labor unions and corporate managers
- The Walsh-Healy Act (1936), the first of several statutes to set the terms and conditions of employment to be provided by government contractors
- The Merchant Marine (Jones) Act (1936), which provides remedies for injured sailors
- The Fair Labor Standards Act (1938), which sets minimum wages, mandates overtime pay, and regulates child labor

---

[3] *Ibid.*, pp. 125–26.

[4] See, *e.g.*, *Commonwealth v. Pullis*, 3 Commons & Gilmore (Philadelphia Mayor's Court 1806).

[5] *Commonwealth v. Hunt*, 44 Mass. (4 Met.) 111 (1842).

Before these statutes could revolutionize the American workplace, FDR's New Deal had to survive constitutional challenge in the Supreme Court. In the early years of Roosevelt's presidency (1933–1936) the Justices repeatedly refused to enforce New Deal legislation, consistently declaring the new laws unconstitutional. Only after FDR threatened to "pack" the court with new appointments from the ranks of his New Deal Democrats did the high court reverse course and declare a piece of labor legislation to be constitutionally legitimate.

In *West Coast Hotel Company v. Parrish*,[6] the challenged law was actually a state statute. Elsie Parrish, a chambermaid working at the Cascadian Hotel in Wenatchee, Washington (owned by the West Coast Hotel Company), sued her employer for the difference between what she was being paid, and the $14.50 per 48-hour work week mandated by the state's Industrial Welfare Committee and the Supervisor of Women in Industry, pursuant to a state law. The trial court held for the defendant. The Washington Supreme Court, taking the case on a direct appeal, reversed the trial court and found in favor of Mrs. Parrish. The hotel appealed to the U.S. Supreme Court. In a decision, which clever pundits labeled "the switch in time that saved the nine" (because it forestalled the president's court-packing plan), the justices asked, "What can be closer to the public interest than the health of women and their protection from unscrupulous and overreaching employers? And if the protection of women is a legitimate end of the exercise of state power, how can it be said that the requirement of the payment of a minimum wage fairly fixed in order to meet the very necessities of existence is not an admissible means to that end?"

The Court majority answered those questions by stating that the legislature of the state was clearly entitled to consider the situation of women in employment, that they were in the class receiving the least pay, that their bargaining power was relatively weak, and that they were the ready victims of those who would take advantage of their necessitous circumstances. Furthermore, continued the Court, the legislature was entitled to adopt measures to reduce the evils of what was known as "the sweating system," which referred to the exploiting of workers at wages so low as to be insufficient to meet the bare cost of living. Deferring to the judgment of the state lawmakers, the Court majority conceded that the legislature had the right to consider that its minimum wage requirements would be an important component of its policy of protecting these highly vulnerable workers. The opinion pointed to the prevalence of similar laws in a growing number of states as evidence of a broadening national consensus that (1) sweatshops were evil and (2) these kinds of laws significantly contributed to their eradication.

While this ruling was directly applicable only to state minimum wage laws—and arguably, only to such statutes as they applied to women—the broader impact was essentially to sweep away judicial opposition to the flood of legislation at both the federal and state levels, which was overwhelmingly favorable to workers and their labor organizations. One result was a rush by workers to join labor unions, which organized with legal impunity. Corporations which resisted were charged with unfair labor practices under the National Labor Relations Act—covered in depth in Part 3—and compelled by the National Labor Relations Board to recognize and bargain with organized labor.

[6] 300 U.S. 379 (1937).

Concept *Summary* » 1.1

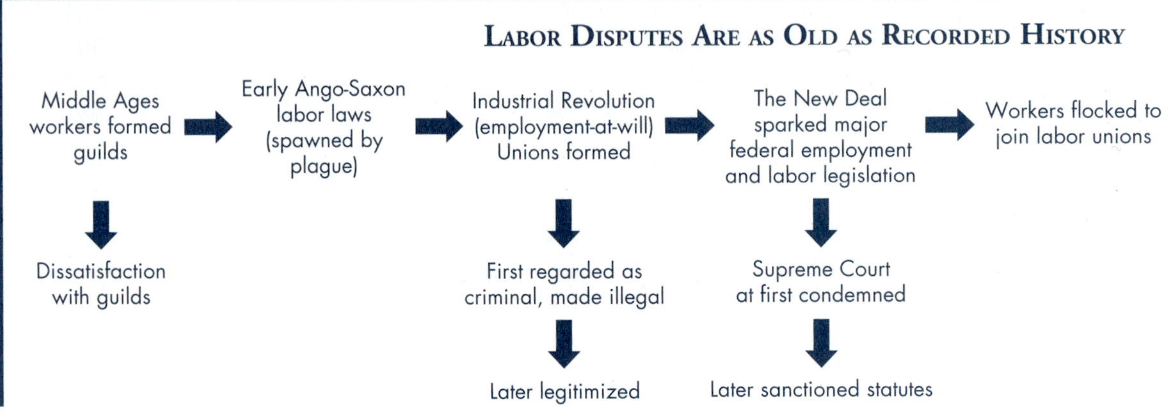

The Post-War Decline of Organized Labor

Several significant issues and trends combined to cause the gradual decline of organized labor in America from its peak in the 1950s, when one in three private-sector employees belonged to a union, to fewer than one in ten eligible private-sector workers being affiliated with a labor organization in this first decade of the 21st century.

One of the worst abuses of union power occurred when John L. Lewis, president of the United Mine Workers, violated a "gentlemen's agreement" with the Roosevelt Administration during WWII. Sullivan called a strike at the height of the war, making his miners look unpatriotic and selfish in the public eye. Critics, especially political conservatives aligned with "Big Business," believed the combined American Federation of Labor/Congress of Industrial Organizations (AFL-CIO) had grown to be far too powerful. The upshot in 1947 was the Taft-Hartley Act, a federal statute which enacted unfair labor practices for which unions might be charged and punished, such as coercing workers to join against their will.

Globalization
The integration of national economies into a worldwide economy, due to trade, investment, migration and information technology.

Individual Employee Rights
Rights enjoyed by workers as individuals, as against collective rights secured by unionization; sources are statutes and court decisions.

Arbitration
The settlement of disputes by a neutral adjudicator chosen by the parties.

As the Cold War developed between the U.S. and the U.S.S.R., perceived Communist influences in such large and powerful unions as the International Longshoremen's Association placed organized labor in the gun sights of such so-called "Red Hunters" as the infamous Senator Joseph McCarthy. Similarly, alleged organized-crime ties of other huge unions, notably the Teamsters, attracted the attention of politicians, ranging from Senator Estes Kefauver in the 1950s to Attorney General Robert F. Kennedy in the early 1960s.

Most destructive of all to organized labor, however, has been ***globalization***. American industry's stranglehold on major manufacturing sectors, such as autos and steel, was successfully challenged immediately after WWII—first by a reconstructed Japan, then subsequently by many other Asian and European competitors. The manufacturing sector was the bedrock of unionism. When it declined, organized labor inevitably followed.

Meanwhile, among the many political and social trends of the 1960s was the rise of ***individual employee rights***. Leading the way was the Civil Rights Act of 1964.

Good Cause
A substantial reason, not arbitrary or capricious or illegally discriminatory.

Writ of Certiorari
A court order requiring the court below to certify the record of a case and send it up on appeal.

Election of Remedies
A litigant's choice of solutions for a perceived wrong; for example, a plaintiff may have a choice between money damages and a court order of restitution.

Title VII[7]—covered in detail in Part 2—declared employment discrimination based on race, sex, religion, and several other "protected categories" illegal. Other laws and court decisions followed in relatively quick succession, seemingly in inverse proportion to the steady decline of collective bargaining under the auspices of organized labor. Other major examples of individual-employee-rights laws and legal concepts include the Age Discrimination in Employment Act (1967) and the generalized recognition of theories of wrongful discharge (see Chapter 2) and related employment-related torts (see Chapter 3) in the American common law.

These new laws and common-law legal theories have often supplanted labor unions as the main source of legal protection for American workers. In fact, sometimes they actually have conflicted with the legal remedies available to workers under collective bargaining agreements. For example, under Title VII, an employee alleging illegal discrimination has the right to file a complaint with the Equal Employment Opportunity Commission (EEOC). If he or she is a union member, that same employee has not only a right, but an obligation, to pursue any such wrong as a grievance under the grievance, apparently as his or her exclusive remedy. In *Alexander v. Gardner-Denver Company*, the Supreme Court was called upon to reconcile

case 1.1 »

Alexander v. Gardner-Denver Company

415 U.S. 36 (1974)

Facts: Following discharge by his employer, Alexander, an African-American, filed a grievance under the collective bargaining agreement between the company and Alexander's labor union. The agreement contained a broad arbitration clause. Alexander claimed that his discharge resulted from racial discrimination. Upon rejection by the company of Alexander's claims, an ***arbitration*** hearing was held, prior to which Alexander also filed a complaint with the Colorado Civil Rights Commission, which referred it to the federal Equal Employment Opportunity Commission (EEOC). The arbitrator ruled that Alexander's discharge was for ***good cause*** and sustained his discharge. Following the EEOC's subsequent dismissal of Alexander's discrimination complaint, he sued for race discrimination in a federal District Court. The District Court granted the company's motion for summary judgment, holding that Alexander was bound by the prior arbitral decision and had no right to sue under Title VII. The Court of Appeals affirmed. The Supreme Court granted Alexander's ***writ of certiorari***.

Issue: Is the grievance/arbitration procedure in the collective bargaining agreement between Alexander's labor union and his employer the only remedy available to Alexander, who claimed he was a victim of illegal race discrimination?

Decision: The doctrine of ***election of remedies*** was considered by the Court to be inapplicable in the present context, which involved statutory rights distinctly separate from the employee's contractual rights, regardless of the fact that violation of both rights may have resulted from the same fact pattern. By merely resorting to the arbitration procedure, Alexander did not automatically waive his cause of action under Title VII; the rights conferred in fact cannot be prospectively waived. Such an implied waiver formed no part of the collective bargaining process. The arbitrator's authority was confined to resolution of questions of contractual rights, regardless of whether they resembled or even duplicated Title VII rights. In instituting a Title VII action, the employee was not seeking review of the arbitrator's decision and thus getting "two strings to his bow when the employer has only one," (to quote the trial judge) but was asserting a right independent of the arbitration process that the statute gives to all employees who are victims of discriminatory employment practices, whether or not they belong to a union. «

[7] 42 U.S.C. Sec. 2000e *et seq.*

this clash between individual and collective worker rights within a decade of Title VII's enactment. The employer wanted to limit the aggrieved employee's remedy to the grievance/arbitration procedures in the collective bargaining agreement that Gardner-Denver had with Alexander's union. More to the point, the company wanted to cut off Alexander's access to Title VII.

In this decision, the Supreme Court established a critical distinction between individual and collective employee rights. Perhaps it was not the Court's intention, but the decision had the effect of further undermining the eroding influence of labor unions in the American workplace. If the union member is able to effectively pursue his rights outside of the labor-management relationship, then why should he bother to pay dues to a labor organization?

The Resurrection of the Arbitration Remedy

The proliferation of individual employee rights soon swamped the state and federal courts. By the 1980s, for example, employment law cases dominated the federal District Court dockets across the country. In their heyday, labor unions diverted much of this court business into their grievance/arbitration processes. The decline of organized labor combined with the Supreme Court's ruling that individual rights—at least those derived from antidiscrimination, ***whistleblower***, and other such statutes—could not be automatically ceded to the labor-management dispute-resolution process contributed significantly to the litigation deluge.

Whistleblowers
Employees who report or attempt to report employer wrongdoing or actions threatening public health or safety to government authorities.

In 1991, the Supreme Court revisited the issue of whether an agreement to arbitrate employment disputes could ever trump an employee's right to pursue his or her claims under a federal statute that enabled the aggrieved employee to file a complaint with an agency and/or in court. The case involved a standard employment contract that almost all employees in the financial-services industry are required to sign.

case 1.2 »

Gilmer v. Interstate/Johnson Lane Corporation

500 U.S. 20 (1991)

Facts: Gilmer was required by his employer to register as a securities representative with, among others, the New York Stock Exchange (NYSE). His registration application contained an agreement to arbitrate, when required to by NYSE rules. NYSE Rule 347 provided for arbitration of any controversy arising out of a registered representative's employment or termination of employment. The company terminated Gilmer's employment at age 62. He filed a charge with the Equal Employment Opportunity Commission (EEOC) and brought suit in the District Court, alleging that he had been discharged in violation of the Age Discrimination in Employment Act of 1967 (ADEA). The company moved to compel arbitration, relying on the agreement in Gilmer's registration application. The court denied the company's motion, based on *Alexander v. Gardner-Denver Co.* In *Alexander*, the court held that an employee's suit under Title VII of the Civil Rights Act of 1964 was not foreclosed by the prior submission of his claim to arbitration under the terms of a collective bargaining agreement. It concluded that Congress intended to protect ADEA claimants from a waiver of the judicial forum. The Court of Appeals reversed the decision and the company took the case to the Supreme Court, which agreed to hear it.

Issue: Should the rule of *Alexander v. Gardner-Denver Co.* apply to an arbitration provision in an individual contract as opposed to a collective bargaining contract?

Decision: In the opinion, which took many knowledgeable observers by surprise, the Court said it saw no inconsistency between the important social policies furthered by the ADEA and enforcing agreements to arbitrate age discrimination claims. While arbitration focuses on specific disputes between the parties involved, so too does judicial resolution of claims. Just the same, both can further broader social purposes, and with equal force. The justices pointed out that various other laws, including antitrust and securities laws and the civil provisions of the ***Racketeer Influenced and Corrupt Organizations Act (RICO)***, are designed to advance equally important public policies, and yet claims under them are considered by Congress to be appropriate for arbitration. Nor were the majority of justices persuaded that allowing arbitration would somehow undermine the EEOC's role in ADEA enforcement, since an ADEA claimant remained free under the Court's holding to file an EEOC charge. However, he was precluded from instituting suit—not an insignificant limit on the rights he would otherwise have had under the statute. This limitation didn't trouble the Court, primarily because it perceived that the ADEA already reflected a flexible approach to claims resolution, such as by permitting the EEOC to pursue informal resolution methods. This suggested to the justices that out-of-court dispute resolution is consistent with the statutory scheme, and that arbitration is consistent with Congress' grant of concurrent jurisdiction over ADEA claims to state and federal courts.

«

Racketeer Influenced and Corrupt Organizations Act (RICO)
A federal law designed to criminally penalize those that engage in illegal activities as part of an ongoing criminal organization (e.g., the mafia).

The WORKING Law

Supreme Court Upholds Arbitration Clause

On April 1, 2009, by a vote of 5–4, the U.S. Supreme Court held that, where a provision of a collective bargaining agreement clearly and unmistakably requires union members to arbitrate Age Discrimination in Employment (ADEA) claims, this provision will be enforced by the federal courts. Writing in dissent, Justice Stevens complained, "Notwithstanding the absence of change in any relevant statutory provision, the Court has recently retreated from, and in some cases reversed, prior decisions based on its changed view of the merits of arbitration.... [T]he Court in *Gardner-Denver* held that a clause of a collective bargaining agreement (CBA) requiring arbitration of discrimination claims could not waive an employee's right to a judicial forum for statutory claims.... Today the majority's preference for arbitration again leads it to disregard our precedent."

Note: *14 Penn Plaza L.L.C. v. Pyett*[8] is excerpted and discussed in greater depth in Chapter 9.

[8]2009 WL 838159, 186 LRRM (BNA) 2065, 105 FEP Cases (BNA) 1141 (U.S.S.C. 2009).

Concept *Summary* » 1.2

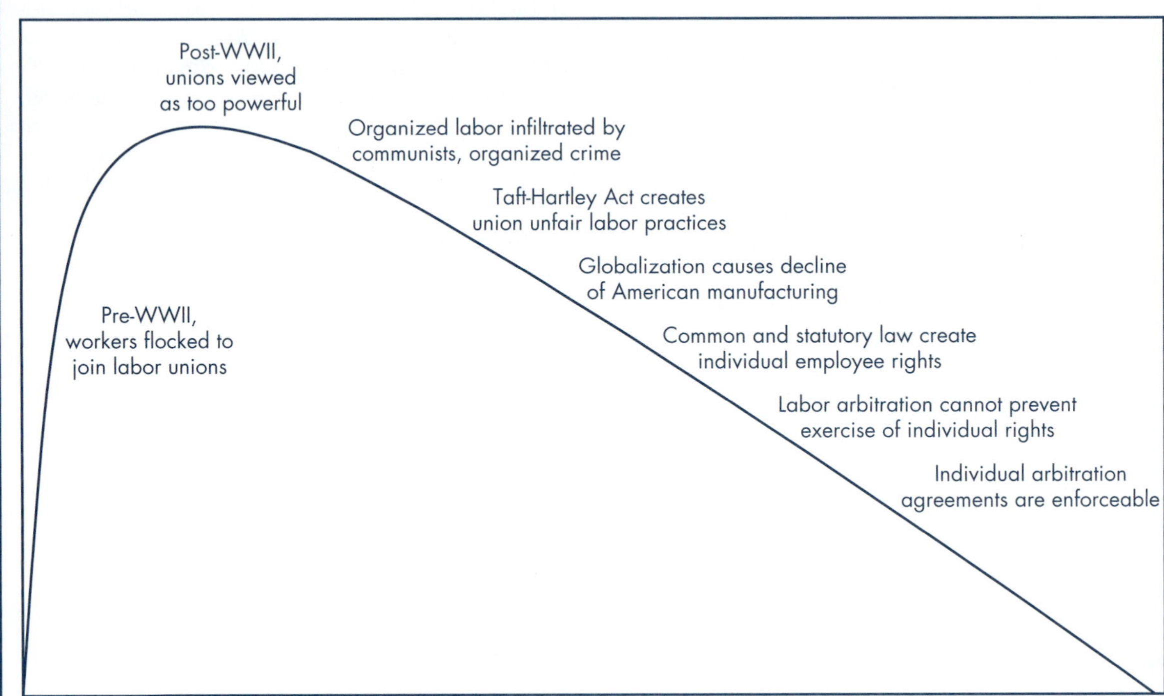

Employee Health, Safety, and Welfare

In the preceding section, we charted a sort of "bell curve" in the rise and fall of labor unions. American workers first banded together to increase their bargaining power and improve their working and living conditions. They then turned increasingly away from unions and toward a panoply of individual rights, ranging from statutory prohibitions of employment discrimination to common-law wrongful discharge decisions, all of which is discussed in detail in the chapters that follow.

Also covered thoroughly in their own sections of this text are the major aspects of employee health, safety, and welfare, as they are embodied in our federal and state laws. These include:

- The federal Occupational Safety and Health Act (OSHA) and its many state-law counterparts
- Workers' compensation and unemployment insurance statutes, which are a part of virtually every state's statutory safety net for injured and out-of-work workers
- The U.S. Social Security system, which includes both pensions and support payments for permanently disabled workers who are still too young to retire

- The Employee Retirement Income Security Act (ERISA), which is intended to protect and preserve employee pensions
- The Family and Medical Leave Act (FMLA) and its numerous state and local counterparts, which increasingly require employers to grant paid leaves of absence for an ever-increasing range of personal issues
- Worker Adjustment and Retraining (WARN) Acts, both federal and state, which are aimed at letting employees know when a plant closing or mass layoff is in the offing

As extensive as this web of federal, state, and local laws may seem to be, some notable—and for many, very troubling—gaps remain in the American labor and employment law system. No national statute requires private employers to provide their employees with either health insurance or a pension plan, for example.

The WORKING Law

Medical Tourism Soars as Americans Seek Major Savings on Health Care April 1, 2008

By Laurie Goering

Apr. 1, 2008 (McClatchy-Tribune News Service delivered by Newstex)—NEW DELHI—When James Payne found out he needed a liver transplant, he first tried to arrange the surgery at a top local hospital in south Florida. Doctors there told him that they couldn't schedule the procedure for a few months and that it would cost $450,000, a fortune for the uninsured former investment banker.

So the fifty-five-year-old and his wife, who planned to donate half of her own liver to her husband, bought plane tickets to India instead. There, at one of New Delhi's premiere hospitals, a transplant specialist carried out the surgery for $58,000—a price tag that included their 10-week hospital stay.

"If you want to live, this is where you come," said a smiling Payne, who planned to return home to Florida last month and said he would recommend his experience to anyone suffering similar problems.

The number of Americans heading abroad for medical procedures is surging as the country's 46 million people without health insurance look for treatment they can afford and cash-strapped U.S. companies struggle to find cheaper ways to provide high-quality medical care to their employees, according to the American Medical Association.

Mexico has long attracted American travelers looking for cut-rate cosmetic surgery or dental work, and countries like Malaysia, Thailand, and the Philippines continue to lure medical tourists, as well. But India—15 hours away from the U.S. by plane—is fast becoming the destination of choice for patients seeking risky high-end procedures they can't afford or can't manage to schedule with a doctor they trust at home. These include things such as heart surgery, organ transplants and orthopedic procedures such as knee replacement or hip resurfacing.

Last year, the South Asian giant attracted 150,000 medical tourists from the United States, Britain, Africa, and elsewhere in South Asia, largely by offering an enticing trio of advantages: highly trained English-speaking doctors, quick appointments, and bargain-basement prices. In India, a heart bypass goes for $10,000 and a hip replacement for $9,000, compared with $130,000 and $43,000 respectively in the United States, the AMA said.

India's initial rush of patients, however, may be nothing compared with what is to come. According to the AMA, major U.S. employers and insurers are exploring whether they could hold down soaring health-care costs by shipping their workers halfway across the world for elective surgery.[1]

[1]http://www.bcbs.com/news/national/medical-tourism-soars-as-americans-seek-major-savings-on-health-care.html

The 2008–2009 Economic Crisis

Recessions
Periodic economic downturns.

Depressions
Severe declines in economic activity.

Capitalism has always been subject to cycles. Boom times are invariably followed by busts. Usually such cycles have happened "naturally." Periodic downturns, called ***recessions***, and even severe downturns, called ***depressions***, have ended, as the economy enjoyed a new growth spurt. During the 1930s, a time remembered as the Great Depression, some sensed that the world economy had become flat. Guided by the theories of British economist John Maynard Keynes, the New Deal administration of President Franklin Roosevelt engaged in deficit spending and government intervention to jump start the stalled national economy. Despite these radical reforms—including the new labor laws discussed earlier in this chapter—recovering remained uncertain, until World War II revived American manufacturing and carried it to unheard-of heights of productivity and profitability.

Many expected a deep recession following WWII, as wartime production of armaments ceased and millions of returning veterans simultaneously sought employment. However, Big Business, Big Labor, and Big Government teamed up to help prevent such an economic decline. A veterans' education bill placed tens of thousands of vets in college classrooms, both delaying their demands for immediate employment and training them for more sophisticated, higher paying positions. The Cold War kept arms production and military service at higher levels than were anticipated. And the virtual devastation of Europe and much of Asia forestalled serious competition to American manufacturers.

As noted above, beginning in the 1970s and continuing down to the present day, American manufacturing has experienced a steady decline. However, widespread availability of higher education has insured that Americans by and large are well trained to participate in the new, high-paying careers of the digital (or information) age. True, many workers, who once enjoyed high-pay, big-benefits jobs on unionized assembly lines, are now stuck in dead-end jobs in convenience stores, retail establishments, and the like. But the financial, computer, health care, and high-tech industries have enabled many Americans to maintain the high quality of life once secured by the unionized manufacturing sector.

At least this was the case until the fall of 2008, when an economic meltdown—largely precipitated by the collapse of a house of cards in the home-mortgage and insurance industries—drove major American corporations to the brink—and some over the brink—of bankruptcy. In the face of this crisis, the U.S. Congress enacted a series of bailout bills, which made billions and billions of dollars available to beleaguered companies ranging from General Motors to insurance giant AIG. As these funds were scattered about, inevitable accusations of abuse proliferated.

ethical DILEMMA

White House Blog (March 16, 2009): Help for Small Business, Condemnation for AIG Bonuses

This morning, the President [Obama] discussed a sharp contrast. On the one hand, he invited hard working small-business owners to the East Wing of the White House to discuss ways in which the government could help them stay above water. He lightheartedly lavished praise on the sandwich made for him by Marco Lentini, the owner of a small food company, and commended Cynthia L. Blankenship, a community bank owner who has not only been responsible, but has helped keep credit flowing to other small businesses even as it dries up elsewhere.

But the inspiration of the dozens of small-business owners who joined the president stood against a backdrop of the greed and excess displayed in reports of tens of millions of dollars in bonuses being given out to employees of AIG, one of the largest recipients of taxpayer rescue dollars. Obama condemned this recklessness is no uncertain terms, and pledged to fight it:

"I've asked Secretary Geithner to use that leverage and pursue every single legal avenue to block these bonuses and make the American taxpayers whole. (Applause.) I want everybody to be clear that Secretary Geithner has been on the case. He's working to resolve this matter with the new CEO, Edward Liddy—who, by the way, everybody needs to understand came on board after the contracts that led to these bonuses were agreed to last year.

"But I think Mr. Liddy and certainly everybody involved needs to understand this is not just a matter of dollars and cents. It's about our fundamental values. All across the country, there are people who are working hard and meeting their responsibilities every day, without the benefit of government bailouts or multimillion dollar bonuses. You've got a bunch of small-business people here who are struggling just to keep their credit line open—that they are foregoing pay, as one of our entrepreneurs talked about, they are in some cases mortgaging their homes, and doing a whole host of things just in order to keep things afloat. All they ask is that everyone, from Main Street to Wall Street to Washington, play by the same rules. And that is an ethic that we have to demand.

"And what this situation also underscores is the need for overall financial regulatory reform, so we don't find ourselves in this position again, and for some form of resolution mechanism in dealing with troubled financial institutions, so that we've got greater authority to protect American taxpayers and our financial system in cases such as this."[1]

[1] http://www.whitehouse.gov/blog/09/03/16/Help-for-small-business-condemnation-for-AIG-bonuses/

Concept *Summary* » 1.3

Employee Health, Safety, and Welfare

- Web of federal and state laws include:
  - OSHA
  - ERISA
  - FMLA
  - WARN
- Gaps:
  - Pensions
  - Health care
- What about workers who are left behind?
  - Creative solutions, e.g., "medical tourism"
- Economic cycles:
  - Booms and busts
  - Recessions
  - Depressions
- Workforce development:
  - From a manufacturing to an information economy

Brave New World

As the first decade of the 21st century comes to a close, you—especially those of you in the midst of your college educations—may well wonder what the world holds in store for you in terms of potential career opportunities. Worth wondering, too, is what changes in American employment and labor law might be anticipated, and how might these shifts in law and policy impact our career aspirations.

Lilly Ledbetter Fair Pay Act
Statute that extends time in which an employee may file suit under several federal employment statutes.

Employee Free Choice Act
Bill which, if enacted, will make it easier for unions to organize workers.

Health-Insurance Reform
Effort by the Obama Administration and Congress to solve the problems of high cost and limited coverage of the US health insurance system.

Federal Employment and Labor Law

With the Obama Administration and a Democratic Congress in Washington in 2010, the federal legislative agenda includes the following:

- The ***Lilly Ledbetter Fair Pay Act***, passed in 2009, seeks to ensure equal pay for all workers, primarily by enhancing workers' ability to collect damages for every occasion on which a federal antidiscrimination law is violated.
- The ***Employee Free Choice Act***, if it becomes federal law, will make it much easier for labor unions to organize workers, perhaps ushering in a new era of organized-labor ascendancy in the American workplace.
- President Obama has promised major ***health-insurance reform*** to rectify the plight of tens of millions of Americans, including millions of so-called "working poor," who lack such coverage.

Additionally, American immigration law, which has not experienced a major overhaul since 1986, is deemed by many lawmakers and government officials to be long overdue for radical revisions. With an estimated 12 million illegal immigrants living and working in the U.S., some frustrated states and cities have taken the matter into their own hands, enacting laws and ordinances aimed at controlling or punishing employment of undocumented aliens.

North American Free Trade Agreement (NAFTA)
Treaty among Canada, the US and Mexico to foster free trade across their national borders.

In the international arena, a resurrection of organized labor is likely to lead to challenges being leveled at such international free-trade accords as the ***North American Free Trade Agreement (NAFTA)***. As the policy director of the AFL-CIO told a Congressional committee in 2006, "The North American Free Trade Agreement (NAFTA) was sold to the American public and American workers as a market-opening agreement that would create high-paying export-related jobs here in the United States, bring prosperity to Mexico, and spur economic growth and political stability throughout North America. The outcome has been quite different. While it is true that the trade and investment that flows between the three North American countries have grown rapidly since NAFTA was implemented in 1994, on measures of much more importance to the average North American citizen, NAFTA has been a dismal failure. Workers in all three NAFTA countries have seen their wages fall or stagnate (failing to keep pace with productivity increases), as job insecurity and inequality have grown. At the same time, NAFTA rules have disadvantaged North American family farmers, many small businesses, consumers, and the environment relative to multinational corporate interests."[9] The Obama Administration and the Democratic-controlled Congress can expect increased pressure from Big Labor to back away from such free-trade agreements.

All of these issues are covered in the chapters that follow. One thing is certain: as you undertake your study of employment and labor in 2010 and beyond, you can count on witnessing dramatic changes in the world of work and the laws which strive to regulate it. We predict, in fact, that this may well be the most exciting era of employment and labor law evolution since the New Deal, some 75 years ago.

[9]http://www.aflcio.org/issues/jobseconomy/globaleconomy/upload/LeeTestimony2006-0911.pdf

CHAPTER REVIEW

» Key Terms

- *employment-at-will* « 4
- *common law* « 4
- *globalization* « 6
- *individual employee rights* « 6
- *arbitration* « 7
- *good cause* « 7
- *writ of certiorari* « 7
- *election of remedies* « 7
- *whistleblowers* « 8
- *Racketeer Influenced and Corrupt Organizations Act (RICO)* « 9
- *recessions* « 12
- *depressions* « 12
- *Lilly Ledbetter Fair Pay Act* « 14
- *Employee Free Choice Act* « 14
- *health-insurance reform* « 14
- *North American Free Trade Agreement (NAFTA)* « 15

» Summary

- Anglo-American labor and employment law can be traced back at least to 14th century England. Laws tended to be heavily pro-employer well into the 19th century, when courts decriminalized labor unions and workers were able to combine and thus counter-balance corporate power.
- While some federal and state labor and employment reforms occurred prior to 1930, the first era of significant pro-employee legislation was the New Deal of the Great Depression. The National Labor Relations Act and the Fair Labor Standards Act were among the many statutes enacted by the Congress during the 1930s. As a result, labor unions proliferated and prospered.
- After World War II, unions went into a slow but inexorable decline due to unfavorable legislation, the decline of American manufacturing, and the rise of individual employee rights. The Supreme Court decided in the 1970s that union grievance/arbitration procedures could not strip union members of their individual rights, especially where federal antidiscrimination laws were concerned.
- In the 1980s, as the federal court were deluged with employment cases, the Supreme Court reversed course somewhat, endorsing the use of arbitration clauses individual employment contracts.
- Employee health, safety and welfare laws have proliferated at the federal and state levels, notably OSHA, ERISA, FMLA, and WARN. But gaps remain, notably in the areas of mandatory pension and health insurance benefits, which are not required under U.S. law.
- The Obama Administration and the Democrat-dominated Congress in 2010 share a large agenda of pro-labor and pro-employee legislation, some of which—notably the Lilly Ledbetter Fair Pay Act—have been enacted, some of which—notably the Employee Free Choice Act—are pending, and some of which—notably universal health care—remain under discussion.

» Problems

Questions

1. Can you think of any public policy reasons why the courts developed the concept of employment at will in 19th century America? In thinking about this question, consider that the U.S. Congress made huge land grants to companies willing to undertake the building of the nation's railroads. Can you see how both employment at will and public financial support of private enterprise might rise from the same underlying policy considerations?
2. How did new technologies combine with the arrival of millions of unskilled immigrants from Ireland, and later southern and eastern Europe, impact the relative bargaining power of capitalists and workers in 19th century America? What do you think were some reasons why the courts at first tended to support capital against labor? Why do you think that view gradually changed?
3. Imagine that the Supreme Court during the 1930s had staunchly refused to change its view and continued to declare almost all New Deal labor and employment laws to be unconstitutional, as the Court did at first. What do you think might have been some of the results of such intransigence on the Court's part?
4. Granting that organized labor has been guilty of abusing its power, and that when it was on top, some unions were aligned at times with the Mafia or with the American Communist Party, on balance do you think that labor unions are a blessing or a curse to American society?
5. Explain the Supreme Court's attempts in the *Alexander* and *Gilmer* cases to balance private arbitration with public legal remedies, such as government agency and court cases. Do you think the Court has struck the right balance? If not, then what changes would you make?
6. Although many federal (and state) laws, such as OSHA and ERISA, establish important rights for all American workers, we've noted some significant gaps, such as the absence of universal health care and mandated pension plans. Do you think the Congress should pass laws to fill these gaps? Or, alternatively, do you believe that Uncle Sam has intruded far enough—or even too far—into the realm of free enterprise already?
7. Does the prevalence of medical tourism suggest that the United States and/or American business have let down the American worker?
8. Do you agree with the decision of the federal government, first under the Bush Administration and then under President Obama, to bail out failing financial companies? Did the behavior of companies such as AIG, either before or after the bailout, suggest that they deserved to be rescued? If not, why were they? Are you as future workers and taxpayers better off as a result?
9. Explain the roles that the courts play in creating and/or implementing labor and employment law. Do any of the roles you can identify amount to unreasonable intrusions into the roles of Congress and the state legislatures? Private enterprise?
10. Of the legislative goals of the Obama administration identified above, which ones do you support and which do you oppose? Why?
11. Are there any laws not on the Obama agenda that you would like to put there?
12. Do you believe that free trade is a benefit or a detriment to American workers in the long run? To organized labor?

Employment Contracts and Wrongful Discharge

Common Law
Judge-made law as opposed to statutes and ordinances enacted by legislative bodies.

This chapter and the one that follows are a survey of several major areas of the law where the federal and state legislatures have not fully populated the field with statutes and, therefore, the courts are still, by and large, sovereign. This type of law is referred to as ***common law***. These include employment-at-will and wrongful discharge, as well as express and implied employment contracts.

Employment-at-Will and Its Exceptions

Employment-at-Will
Both the employee and the employer are free to unilaterally terminate the relationship at any time and for any legally permissible reason, or for no reason at all.

Whistleblowers
Employees who report or attempt to report employer wrongdoing or actions threatening public health or safety to government authorities.

To appreciate how far the courts have come, it is necessary to look back to where they were just decades ago. In the 19th century, virtually every state court subscribed to the doctrine of ***employment-at-will***. In its raw form, employment-at-will holds that an employee who has not been hired for an express period of time (say a year) can be fired at any time for any reason—or for no reason at all.

State and federal laws have narrowed this sweeping doctrine in many ways. The National Labor Relations Act (NLRA) forbids firing employees for engaging in protected concerted activities. Title VII forbids discharge on the basis of race, color, gender, creed, or national origin. The Age Discrimination in Employment Act (ADEA) protects older workers from discriminatory discharge. The Occupational Safety and Health Act (OSHA) makes it illegal to fire an employee in retaliation for filing a safety complaint.

Although employers may complain that employment regulation is pervasive, these laws leave broad areas of discretion for private sector employers to discharge at-will employees. Except in a minority (but growing number) of states and cities that have adopted ordinances to the contrary, the law allows an employer to discharge homosexuals and transvestites if the company does not approve of such sexual preferences.

Whistleblowers—employees who bring intraorganizational wrongdoing to the attention of the authorities—have often been fired for their trouble (frequently despite ostensible legal protection, although, as we shall see later in this chapter, much tougher protections were put into place by the U.S. Congress in the wake of one of the financial-industry debacles of the 21st century). Sometimes employees get fired simply because the boss does not like them. In such situations, these employees are not covered by any of the federal and state labor laws previously discussed. Should they be protected? If so, how?

Advocates of the employment-at-will doctrine defend it by pointing out that:

- the employee is likewise free to sever the working relationship at any time; and
- in a free market, the worker with sufficient bargaining power can demand an employment contract for a set period of time if so desired.

The trouble with the second point, in the view of most workers, is that as individuals they lack the bargaining power to command such a deal. This is one reason that in this age of globalization, labor unions continue to claim a role in securing workers' rights and job security, despite a plethora of federal and state statutes. Unless and until a federal statute creates a "just cause" requirement (see below) for all employment terminations—something which is not even on the national agenda—many workers' best bet for job security is unionization. Indeed, making unionization easier is a priority item on the Obama Administration's legislative agenda (see Chapter 13).

The first of these arguments is not so easily dismissed. If the employee is free to quit at any time with or without notice, why should the employer be denied the same discretion in discharging employees? One answer to this troublesome question—an answer given by a majority of the state courts at this time—is, "The firing of an at-will employee is permitted, except if the discharge undermines an important public policy."

Wrongful Discharge Based on Public Policy

Public Policy Exception
Although the employee is employed at-will, termination is illegal if a clear and significant mandate of law (statutory or common) is damaged if the firing is permitted to stand unchallenged.

The most commonly adopted exception to the pure employment-at-will rule (the employee can be fired at any time for any reason) is the ***public policy exception***. If a statute creates a right or a duty for the employee, he or she may not be fired for exercising that legal right or fulfilling that legal duty. A widely adopted example is jury duty. The courts of most states agree that an employer cannot fire an employee who misses work to serve on a jury (provided, of course, that the employee gives the employer proper notice).

Many courts accepting this exception, however, have kept it narrow by holding that the right or duty must be clearly spelled out by statute. For instance, in the seminal case of *Geary v. United States Steel Corporation*,[1] the Pennsylvania Supreme Court upheld the dismissal of a lawsuit brought by a salesman who was fired for refusing to sell what he insisted to management was an unsafe product. The court noted, "There is no suggestion that he possessed any expert qualifications or that his duties extended to making judgments in matters of product safety." Most courts applying *Geary* have required the plaintiff-employee to point to some precise statutory right or duty before ruling the discharge wrongful.

Additionally, if the statute itself provides the employee with a cause of action, the courts are reluctant to recognize an alternative remedy in the form of a lawsuit for wrongful discharge. Thus, several Pennsylvania courts agree that an employee fired on the basis of gender or race discrimination in Pennsylvania has, as his or her exclusive state law remedy, the Pennsylvania Human Relations Act (PHRA), which requires that the employee initially seek redress with the

[1]456 Pa. 171, 319 A.2d 174, 115 L.R.R.M. (BNA) 4665, Pa., March 25, 1974.

Dicta
Opinions of a judge or appellate panel of judges that are tangential to the rule, holding, and decision which are at the core of the judicial pronouncement.

Tort
A private or civil wrong or injury, caused by one party to another, either intentionally or negligently.

commission created by that act. If the employee fails to file with the commission, thus losing the right of action under the PHRA, that person cannot come into court with the same grievance claiming wrongful discharge. Many other states' courts have reached similar conclusions regarding their states' antidiscrimination, workers' compensation, and work safety laws.

Pennsylvania has demonstrated a strong reluctance to depart from the ancient and time-tested rule of employment-at-will. In the 1970s, the Pennsylvania Supreme Court published ***dicta*** in one or two of its decisions that seemed to suggest that the ***tort*** of wrongful discharge was about to blossom in that commonwealth's common law. Taking their lead from this dicta, the federal district courts and the U.S. Court of Appeals for the Third Circuit, sitting in Pennsylvania, developed and shaped this cause of action. Then, perhaps to these federal judges' dismay, in the 1990s, the high court of Pennsylvania issued opinions that virtually took these legal developments back to square one. However, where the state legislature made its intent to supercede the at-will doctrine, the high court acquiesced to the lawmakers' decision.

case 2.1 » Knox v. Board of School Directors of Susquenita School District

585 Pa. 171, 888 A.2d 640 (2005)

Justice Castille

The parties stipulated to the following facts: On September 15, 1987, appellant became the business manager of the Susquenita School District in Perry County ("School District" or "District"), a position that the parties agreed falls within the Code's definition of "business administrator." On March 16, 1988, the District's Board of School Directors ("Board" or "appellee") formally notified appellant by letter that he had been elected to a three-year term of employment, commencing the prior September 15, and running to September 15, 1990. Appellant was advised to sign and return an attachment to the letter, but neither party was able to locate such a document and appellant could not recall if he had signed it. At the end of the original three-year term of employment, the Board took no further action to define the term of appellant's position, or the conditions of renewal, but appellant continued to serve as the District's business manager.

Some seven years later, on June 10, 1997, the Board passed a resolution stating that appellant's term of employment would expire on June 30, 1997, and that the Board would not extend or renew appellant's term of employment beyond that date. The resolution directed the School Superintendent to notify appellant of the decision and also announced that the Board would seek a new business manager. On June 11, 1997, Susquenita School Superintendent Mark T. Dietz sent a Memo to appellant advising him of the Board's determination "that your term of employment will expire as of June 30, 1997."

By counseled letter dated June 23, 1997, appellant attempted to appeal the Board's decision, requesting a hearing and a bill of particulars concerning the reasons for the Board's determination. The Board refused to provide a hearing or a bill of particulars. In the meantime, on or about June 20, 1997, appellant applied to the Public School Employees Retirement System for a lump sum retirement payment. Thereafter, in May of 1998, the School District formally abolished the position of business manager; from July 1, 1997, until September of 2000, the duties of the business manager were performed by an outside consultant.

On July 9, 1997, appellant filed a petition for review of the School Board's job termination action in the Court of Common Pleas. Following a hearing on September 18, 2000, the trial court filed an order and memorandum opinion in which it concluded, *inter alia*, that appellant had a property interest in his job as business manager in light of Section 10-1089 of the Code. Section 10-1089, which is entitled simply, "Business Administrator," provides as follows:

(a) A governing board of a school entity may employ or continue to employ a person serving in the function of business administrator of the school entity who shall perform such duties as the governing board may determine, including, but not limited to, the business responsibilities specified in section 433 of this act.

(b) The governing board may enter into a written employment agreement with a person hired after the effective date of this section to serve as a business administrator or into an amended or renewed agreement with a person serving in that function as of such effective date. The agreement may define the period of employment, salary, benefits, other related matters of employment and provisions of renewal and termination of the agreement.

(c) Unless otherwise specified in an employment agreement, the governing board shall, after due notice, giving the reasons therefore, and after hearing if demanded, have the right at any time to remove a business administrator for incompetency, intemperance, neglect of duty, violation of any of the school laws of this Commonwealth, or other improper conduct.

(d) A person serving as business administrator shall not be a member of the governing board of the school entity.

(e) A person serving as business administrator may serve as secretary or treasurer of the governing board.

(f) For purposes of this section, the term "school entity" shall mean a school district, intermediate unit, or an area vocational-technical school. The term "governing board" shall mean the board of directors or joint board of such entity.

24 P.S. § 10-1089. The trial court determined from the stipulated facts that appellant was a business administrator as defined in the statute, and that even though there was no written employment agreement in effect at the time of his termination, the due process protections governing "removal" which are set forth in Section 10-1089(c) were applicable. Accordingly, the trial court ordered that the Board, "schedule a hearing … and make a determination as to whether or not the business manager should be dismissed for cause."

Thereafter, the parties filed a joint request for reconsideration, asking that the court issue a final order, and suggesting four issues to be addressed in that final order: (1) whether appellant had a term of employment which expired on June 30, 1997; (2) whether appellant had a property interest in continued employment under Section 10-1089; (3) whether appellant's retirement barred his claim; and (4) whether the Board's subsequent determination on May 8, 1998 to abolish the business manager position barred any remedy to appellant for periods after that date. On December 11, 2001, the trial court issued a final order in which it concluded that: appellant's term of employment did not expire on June 30, 1997; appellant had a property interest in continued employment by virtue of Section 10-1089; and appellant's retirement did not bar his claim because he had only applied for retirement because of the sudden termination of his job, and he needed the money. With respect to the fourth question, the trial court found that appellant's property interest in the business manager position ended when the District formally abolished it on May 4, 1998. Addressing the possible scope of damages, the trial court noted that appellant was theoretically entitled to back pay from June 30, 1997 to either September 15, 1997 or September 15, 1999, depending upon whether his continuing appointment was deemed to extend for a one-year or a three-year term. Rather than resolve this employment duration issue, the court determined that a "fair resolution" was to deem appellant's entitlement to benefits to have expired as of May 4, 1998, when the business manager position was formally abolished.

The parties cross-appealed. Appellant challenged the trial court's conclusion that any remedy was limited to the period from June 30, 1997 through May 4, 1998, and the Board challenged whether, under Section 10-1089(c), appellant had a cognizable property interest in continued employment at all after June 30, 1997 and whether, in any event, his retirement barred his claim.

On appeal, a divided panel of the Commonwealth Court reversed in an unpublished decision. The panel majority framed the controlling issue as whether, under the statute, a school district business administrator who does not have a written employment agreement has a property right in continued employment. The majority rejected appellant's argument that the statute mandates that a business administrator without an employment contract may only be removed from the position for the specific causes stated in Section 10-1089(c). To the contrary, the majority found that the statute grants school boards the option of entering into employment agreements with business administrators, thereby creating a property right via written contract, but that no such property right exists in circumstances where the business administrator and the school board have not entered into a written employment agreement. Section 10-1089(c), the majority reasoned, only addresses the process required when a school board seeks to remove from office a business administrator who has a written employment agreement; but, if there is no written employment agreement, the administrator is an employee at-will who is subject to dismissal at any time and for any reason. The majority further reasoned that the General Assembly's failure expressly to include business administrators without written employment agreements in Section 10-1089(c) indicates that it did not intend to establish an expectation of continued employment for such school employees. Because there was no evidence that the Board here chose to enter into a formal, written employment agreement with appellant beyond the first three years he was actually employed, the panel majority held that appellant was an at-will employee subject to summary dismissal. In light of its conclusion in this regard, the majority did not address the Board's alternate argument respecting the effect of appellant's retirement, nor did it address appellant's scope-of-remedy claim on his cross-appeal.

Analysis

Pennsylvania has long subscribed to the at-will employment doctrine. Exceptions to the doctrine have generally been limited to instances where a statute or contract limits the power of an employer unilaterally to terminate the employment relationship:

Generally, an employer "may discharge an employee with or without cause, at pleasure, unless restrained by some contract." *Henry v. Pittsburgh & Lake Erie Railroad Co.*, 139 Pa. 289, 297 21 A. 157 (1891). "Absent a statutory or contractual provision to the contrary, the law has taken for granted the power of either party to terminate an employment relationship for any or no reason." *Geary v. U.S. Steel Corporation*, 456 Pa. 171, 175, 319 A.2d 174, 176 (1974).

Shick v. Shirey, 552 Pa. 590, 716 A.2d 1231, 1233 (1998). See also *McLaughlin v. Gastrointestinal Specialists, Inc.*, 561 Pa. 307, 750 A.2d 283, 286 (2000). Further, "[t]his general rule is not abrogated just because the employee is a governmental worker since one does not have a per se *right in governmental employment." Pipkin v. Pennsylvania State Police*, 548 Pa. 1, 693 A.2d 190, 191 (1997) (citing *Commonwealth, Office of Administration v. Orage*, 511 Pa. 528, 515 A.2d 852, 853 (1986)). Nearly a half century ago, in *Scott v. Philadelphia Parking Authority*, 402 Pa. 151, 166 A.2d 278 (1961), this Court outlined the parameters of tenure in public employment, as follows:

> Without more, an appointed public employee takes his job subject to the possibility of summary removal by the employing authority. He is essentially an employee-at-will. As we said in *Mitchell v. Chester Housing Authority*, [132 A.2d 873, 880 (1957)], with reference to a state agency employee but applicable in general, "... good administration requires that the personnel in charge of implementing the policies of an agency be responsible to, and responsive to those charged with the policy-making function, who in turn are responsible to a higher governmental authority, or to the public itself, whichever selected them. This chain of responsibility is the basic check on government possessed by the public at large." The power to dismiss summarily is the assurance of such responsibility.

Tenure in public employment, in the sense of having a claim to employment which precludes dismissal on a summary basis, is, where it exists, a matter of legislative grace. It represents a policy determination that regardless of personality or political preference or similar intangibles, a particular job, to be efficiently fulfilled, requires constant and continuous service despite changes in political administration. In general, the legislature has conferred tenure as an integral part of a comprehensive governmental employment scheme such as those embodied in the Civil Service Act or the Teacher Tenure Acts. These legislative directives, and regulations promulgated thereunder, set forth in great detail the minimal requirements an employee must meet in order to secure initially governmental employment, the standards for advancement of such an employee, job classifications for remunerative purposes, and the requisites for discharge. Importantly, it is not until an employee has qualified under the systems that he is entitled to his tenure rights. See *Templeton Appeal,* [399 Pa. 10, 159 A.2d 725 (1960)].

166 A.2d at 280–81 (footnotes omitted).

As the parties have noted, the General Assembly has adopted measures in the Public School Code that serve to limit the application of the at-will employment doctrine and to protect certain school employees from summary removal. First, Section 5-514 offered a measure of job protection to school "officers, employees, [and] appointees," setting forth the grounds for removal and the right to notice and a hearing. See *Coleman v. Board of Ed. of School Dist. of Philadelphia*, 477 Pa. 414, 383 A.2d 1275, 1280 (1978) ("Section 514 establishes rights in a School District employee not to be dismissed without specific cause and not to be dismissed without due notice and a statement of reasons, and it establishes corresponding duties in the School District"). In nearly identical language, and just as unambiguously, Section 10-1089(c) adopted protections for school business administrators during the terms of their employment: "(c) Unless otherwise specified in an employment agreement, the governing board shall, after due notice, giving the reasons therefore, and after hearing if demanded, have the right at any time to remove a business administrator for incompetency, intemperance, neglect of duty, violation of any of the school laws of this Commonwealth, or other improper conduct."

[4] We agree with appellant and amicus that the plain language of the statute encompasses all school business administrators, and not just those subject to written employment agreements. By its terms, subsection (c) neither limits its application to written employment relationships, nor purports to exclude those administrators working without the benefit of a written contract. Additionally, the introductory caveat ("Unless otherwise specified in an employment agreement") itself is not limited to written agreements, nor does that caveat advert to the "written employment agreement" addressed in subsection (b)'s recognition of the authority of the governing board to enter into such written agreements: instead, subsection (c), at least, is open-ended. This construct suggests that the protections offered in the provision were intended to be applicable so long as there is not some other agreement between the parties addressing the subject of the statute. Furthermore, we deem it significant that Section 10-1089(c), which is *in pari materia* with Section 5-514 of the public school code, indeed appears intended merely to extend to business administrators the very same protections that had long been afforded to those school employees governed by Section 5-514, and with the same lack of qualification. Accordingly, we hold that the protections offered by Section 10-1089 apply equally to business administrators with or without written employment agreements, and that the Commonwealth Court panel majority erred in concluding otherwise.

[5] Our holding that the Commonwealth Court erred in its broad determination that Section 10-1089(c) applies only to written employment agreements, however, does not entirely resolve this appeal. The Board is correct that this statute, again by its plain terms, is addressed only to the "removal" of school business administrators. The statute does not purport to confer any extra-contractual right to continued employment or tenure beyond what the parties may have agreed to in writing, orally, or as a matter of history and experience. Thus, Section 10-1089(c) does not provide a school business administrator with employment for life absent misconduct falling into one of the enumerated statutory circumstances. As this Court noted in Scott, "where the legislature has intended that tenure should attach to public employment, it has been very explicit in so stating." *Scott,* 166 A.2d at 281. To read into Section 10-1089(c) any such explicit legislative grant of tenure in the position of school business administrator is to go beyond what the statute provides.

Rather, Section 10-1089(c) merely provides a business administrator with a certain degree of job security against removal during the term of his employment, whatever that term, as established by the agreement of the parties, might be. In this case, the Board appeared to concede below that appellant's employment was not entirely "at will," but that his expectations were tied into the school district's fiscal year and budgeting, i.e., that his employment was subject to yearly renewal. Even in the absence of a written, contractually specified term of employment, appellant's long-term relationship with his employer no doubt provided some indicia of his expected term of employment.

The question of whether appellant in fact was "removed" during his contractual term of employment, such that Section 10-1089(c) is implicated, or whether that term ended on June 30, 1997, when he was not reappointed or rehired, was not specifically addressed by the Commonwealth Court panel, given its broader conclusion that the removal protections simply do not apply in the absence of a written agreement. It is also a question which was neither accepted for review, nor briefed before this Court. In these circumstances, the Court having answered the overarching question of statutory interpretation, the better course is to simply vacate the order below and remand the matter to the Commonwealth Court for further consideration in light of this Opinion.

Vacated and remanded.

Case Questions

1. Explain the Pennsylvania Supreme Court's ruling. Does it ensure the plaintiff's continued employment with the school district?
2. If your answer for question 1 above, was "no," what must the plaintiff still prove, when his case is reconsidered by the trial judge?
3. What is meant by teacher tenure? Is the plaintiff claiming that he holds the equivalent of tenure in the school district? What does the Supreme Court say on this issue?
4. How are "continued employment" and "removal" from employment different legal issues in the high court's view?
5. Does the court's decision in this case suggest a liberalization of historic position on employment-at-will, or is the decision essentially limited to its particular facts?

Concept *Summary* » 2.1

EMPLOYMENT-AT-WILL AND WRONGFUL DISCHARGE

Justifications for at-will employment:

- Freedom of contract
- Free enterprise in a competitive marketplace

Problems with at-will employment:

- Disparities of bargaining power between employer and employee
- Potential for unfair treatment falling outside statutory protections

Exceptions to at-will employment:

- Statutory exceptions, such as antidiscrimination laws
- Employment contracts containing set lengths of employment
- Public policy exception

Express and Implied Contracts of Employment

Express Contract
A contract in which the terms are explicitly stated, usually in writing but perhaps only verbally, and often in great detail. In interpreting such a contract, the judge and/or the jury is asked only to determine what the explicit terms are and to interpret them according to their plain meaning.

Implied Contract
A contractual relationship, the terms and conditions of which must be inferred from the contracting parties' behavior toward one another.

Some employees have express contracts of employment, usually for a definite duration. Others fall within the coverage of a collective bargaining agreement negotiated for them by their union. Most workers, however, have no express agreement as to the term of their employment, and some were given an oral promise of a fixed term in a state in which the statute of frauds requires that contracts for performance extending for a year or more be written. Such employees have sometimes tried to convince the courts that they have been given implied promises that take them outside the ranks of their at-will co-workers. An ***express contract*** has terms spelled out by the parties, usually in writing. ***Implied contracts*** are contracts that the courts infer from company policies (such as those published in employee handbooks) and the behavior of the parties or that are implied from the law.

If a company provides its employees with a personnel handbook, and that handbook says that employees will be fired only for certain enumerated infractions of work rules or that the firm will follow certain procedures in disciplining them, a worker may later argue that the manual formed part of his or her employment contract with the firm. An increasing number of state and federal courts agree.

Many employers in turn have responded by adding clauses to their employee handbooks that reserve the firm's right to make unilateral changes or to vary the application of particular policies to fit the unique circumstances of each new situation. The following cases involves determinations of if and when an employer can withdraw a unilaterally promulgated policy and replace it with another, thus unilaterally altering the employment relationship, or deviate from a policy's particular terms in a specific instance.

case 2.2 »

Asmus v. Pacific Bell

23 Cal. 4th 1 (Cal. Supreme Ct. 2000)

Facts: In 1986, Pacific Bell issued the following "Management Employment Security Policy" (MESP):

> It will be Pacific Bell's policy to offer all management employees who continue to meet our changing business expectations employment security through reassignment to and retraining for other management positions, even if their present jobs are eliminated. This policy will be maintained so long as there is no change that will materially affect Pacific Bell's business plan achievement.

Nevertheless, in 1992 the company terminated the policy.

Plaintiffs were sixty former Pacific Bell management employees who were affected by the MESP cancellation. They chose to remain with the company for several years after the policy termination and received increased pension benefits for their continued employment while working under the new Management Force Adjustment Program. All but eight of them signed releases waiving their right to assert claims arising from their employment under the MESP or its termination.

Issue: Once an employer's unilaterally adopted policy—which requires employees to be retained so long as a specified condition does not occur—has become a part of the employment contract, may the employer thereafter unilaterally terminate the policy, even though the specified condition has not occurred?

Decision: The court concluded that the answer was "yes," an employer may unilaterally terminate a policy that contains a specified condition, if the condition is one of indefinite duration, and the employer effects the change after a reasonable time, on reasonable notice, and without interfering with the employees' vested benefits.

case 2.3 »

Marcus v. KFG Employment Services, INC.

2009 WL 1167849 (Michigan Ct. App.)

Facts: On July 25, 2005, defendant entered into an employment contract with plaintiff when defendant hired plaintiff as a staff assistant at a pay rate of $10 per hour. Plaintiff's duties consisted of driving trucks and making deliveries of defendant's products. In addition, plaintiff was provided an employee handbook. The handbook contained defendant's employee policies and outlined benefits to be provided and procedures to be followed with respect to performance evaluations and raises. Plaintiff contended that he was an "excellent" and "superior" employee, but he was never given a raise.

After nearly two years, plaintiff's employment with defendant ended on July 5, 2007. Several months later, plaintiff filed a complaint alleging breach of contract. According to plaintiff, defendant breached the employment contract because defendant failed to provide plaintiff with any performance evaluations during his two years of employment and did not give plaintiff a five-dollar raise.

Issue: Did the defendant breach the employment contract by failing to provide the plaintiff with performance evaluations and a five-dollar raise?

Decision: Plaintiff's argument that the employment contract incorporated certain segments of the employee handbook was unavailing, because the employment agreement contained an "integration clause" that declared in express terms that the contract contained the entire agreement between the parties. When parties indicate in a contract that the contract is to be a full and complete integration of their agreement, the courts of have given this expressed declaration full effect.

case 2.4 »

Kritzer v. Curators of University of Missouri

2009 WL 1286027 (Missouri Ct. App.)

Facts: The University terminated Kritzer on December 6, 2004, for alleged misconduct related to maintenance of patient records. Kritzer appealed her termination. The University had a regulation and a human resources policy manual containing provisions pertaining to appealing termination from employment. Included were provisions governing grievance procedures and prescribing several steps in the grievance process. The first three steps are entirely informal:

(1) after discussion with immediate supervisor, the aggrieved former employee may file a written grievance with a supervisor, department head, or designated University representative, with a copy to the Campus Grievance Representative;

(2) the aggrieved former employee may appeal to the Campus Grievance representative; and

(3) the aggrieved former employee may appeal to the University Grievance Representative.

(4) The fourth and fifth steps are more formal. The fourth step of the grievance procedure allows the aggrieved former employee to a hearing before a formal "grievance committee," composed in accordance with procedures established in the policy.

(5) The fifth step involves a review of the decision of the grievance committee by the Board of Curators in the event of appeal by either party from the grievance committee determination.

The policy expresses no limitations on the review authority of the Board of Curators, although it appears that if there is no appeal to the Curators by either side, the ruling or recommendation of the grievance committee becomes the final decision. The grievance committee, in a decision authored by the professional arbitrator, found that Kritzer should not be terminated but, instead, should be reinstated to employment, subject to a two-week suspension. The University appealed the grievance committee's decision to the Board of Curators. The Curators, after review of the matter, rejected the recommendation of the grievance committee. The Curators upheld Kritzer's termination on the grounds asserted.

Issue: Was the Curators decision to terminate Kritzer invalid because the Curators were bound by an arbitration award resulting from step four of the grievance procedure?

Decision: The fact that Kritzer was entitled to a hearing before the grievance committee and an appeal to the Board of Curators did not change her status as an at-will employee. The Board of Curators retained the ultimate decision-making authority and was not required to follow the grievance committee's findings.

«

These three decisions, viewed together, indicate that the employer retains considerable control over the terms of the employment relationship and that American courts, by and large, remain reluctant at the end of this first decade of the new century to read into employment contracts and employee handbooks implied rights which are not expressly stated.

The WORKING Law

Model Employment Termination Act

The National Conference of Commissioners on Uniform State Laws was organized in the 1890s as part of a movement in the American Bar Association for the reform and unification of American law. Currently, the conference's list comprises ninety-nine uniform acts and twenty-four model acts, which the states are encouraged to adopt. In 1987, the conference established a drafting committee to create a Uniform Employment Termination Act to provide employees with statutory protection against wrongful discharge. By 1991, the conference had approved a "model" act. However, division among the commissioners has prevented the act from achieving the status of "uniform." Consequently, states are encouraged to modify the model to suit each jurisdiction's particular social, economic, and legal needs. So far, only a handful of states have done so.[1]

The heart and soul of the Model Employment Termination Act (META) in its present form is Section 3(a), which states that "an employer may not terminate the employment of an employee without good cause."

Section 3(b) limits application of the "good cause" limitation on employment-at-will to workers who have been with the particular employer for at least one year. Section 4(c) adds another possible exception, stating that employer and employee may substitute a severance pay agreement for the good cause standard, and the good cause standard is inapplicable to situations where termination comes at the expiration of an express oral or written contract containing a fixed duration for the employment relationship.

The META suggests that claims under it be subject to binding arbitration with arbitral awards being issued within thirty days of hearings. Section 10 forbids retaliation against employees who make claims or who testify under the procedural provisions of the META.

---

[1] See, e.g., Montana Wrongful Discharge from Employment Act, Mont. Code Ann. Sections 39-2-901 through 39-2-915.

Concept *Summary* » 2.2

Employment Contracts and Employee Handbooks

- Common law presumption of at-will employment can be overcome by and express contract or by implication, e.g., based on a policy in an employee handbook
- American courts remain reluctant to infer terms and conditions of employment, when the employer has not expressly awarded the right to its employees, or where the relevant employment documents, or even the reasonable passage of time, indicate the employer set limits on its obligations to the employee(s)

Protection for Corporate Whistleblowers

On July 30, 2002, Congress passed and the president signed the Sarbanes-Oxley Act (SOX). SOX amended the creaky Securities and Exchange Acts of 1933 and 1934, as well as the more recent-vintage Employee Retirement Income Security Act (ERISA), plus the Investment Advisers Act of 1940 and the U.S. Criminal Code. SOX includes two provisions, one criminal and the other civil, for the protection of employees who report improper conduct by corporate officials concerning securities fraud and corruption.

Dozens of federal laws, such as Occupational Safety and Health Act (OSHA) and Title VII, protect employees who blow the whistle on illegal practices or who cooperate in investigations and testify at hearings from employer retaliation, such as employment termination. Dozens of states have jumped on the whistleblower bandwagon, adding a dizzying variety of whistleblower laws to the panoply of rules and regulations that human resource managers and employment lawyers must consider before initiating "industrial capital punishment" (i.e., firing a miscreant worker). In those increasingly rare jurisdictions or circumstances in which no federal or state antiretaliation rule is implicated, the courts often have shown themselves willing to carve out a public policy exception to employment-at-will, where the plaintiff provides proof that he or she was fired for reporting or restricting illegal supervisory activity. But the proliferation of such laws and court rulings have often fallen short of protecting whistleblowers, either because of poor enforcement procedures or ineffectual remedies. SOX is unique in making whistleblower retaliation a federal crime that can result in officer/director defendants actually going to prison.

Perhaps the scariest aspect of SOX's criminal provision is that it can be used to punish retaliation against persons who provide information to law enforcement officials relating to the possible commission of any federal offense, not just securities fraud, albeit securities fraud was the catalyst for the legislation. The provision makes it a crime to "knowingly, with the intent to retaliate, take ... any action harmful to any person, including interference with lawful employment or livelihood of any person, for providing a law enforcement officer any truthful information relating to the commission or possible commission of any Federal offense." Individuals found guilty under this proviso may be fined up to a quarter-million dollars and imprisoned up to ten years. Corporate defendants can face up to a half-million dollar fine if convicted.

Civil Liability Under SOX

A child of corporate greed and accounting scandals, SOX's legislative history indicates that its whistleblower provisions are intended primarily to protect employees of publicly traded companies acting in the public interest to try to prevent officer/director wrongdoing and "to encourage and protect those who report fraudulent activity that can damage innocent investors in publicly traded companies." The following case exemplifies the limits of this new federal whistleblower cause of action.

case 2.5 » Brady v. Calyon Securities (USA)

406 F. Supp.2d 307 (S.D.N.Y. 2005)

Lynch, District Judge

The facts stated below are taken from plaintiff's complaint, the allegations of which must be accepted as true for purposes of this motion.

Plaintiff Charles J. Brady ("Brady") is a 52-year-old graduate of the United States Military Academy at West Point, and a "Vietnam War Era Veteran." (Am.Compl.§ 1.) After his military service, he earned an MBA degree from the University of Chicago School of Business. Brady currently holds multiple licenses to work in the securities industry, and is registered with and licensed by both the New York Stock Exchange ("NYSE") and National Association of Securities Dealers ("NASD"). (*Id.* at §§ 17, 18.) In February 1999, Brady was hired by Calyon Securities (USA) as an equity analyst. (*Id.* at 19.)

Calyon Securities (USA) is a broker-dealer incorporated in New York, and an indirect wholly owned subsidiary of the French company, Calyon. Until a recent corporate acquisition, Calyon Securities (USA) was known as a Credit Lyonnais Securities (USA), Inc. and was a wholly owned subsidiary of Credit Agricole. (D.Mem.2.) Francois Pages was the Chief Executive Officer of Credit Lyonnais Securities (USA)/ Calyon Securities (USA), and Eric Schindler was the Head of Investment Banking. (Am.Compl.§§ 8-9.)

In 2001, Brady was promoted and began reporting to Schindler. Brady objected to reporting directly to Schindler, who was the head of the investment banking department, because both NASD and NYSE rules and the Sarbanes-Oxley Act ("Sarbanes-Oxley") forbid a research analyst from being supervised or controlled by an employee in the investment banking department. (*Id.* at § 31.) Brady informed various supervisors and compliance officers of his objections.

In the summer of 2003, Brady met with Pages and again complained about the company's failure to comply with the NYSE and NASD rules. Because Brady felt that his complaints were not adequately addressed, he approached Pages to submit his resignation. Pages informed Brady that he was aware of the problem and that it would be corrected immediately. (*Id.* at § 88.) Brady turned down another job elsewhere, but his employer continued to require Brady to report to Schindler in the investment banking department. (*Id.* at §§ 89, 92.)

Plaintiff alleges that Schindler subsequently began to berate Brady for his rigid "military-like" approach to following the NYSE and NASD rules. (*Id.* at § 43.) During Brady's last employee review in February 2004, Schindler told Brady that he rated him poorly, not for his actual job performance, but for getting in the way of the investment banking department, and that he no longer needed "an old wise man to run research." (*Id.* at § 42.) He then repeatedly described Brady as the "old man with all the wisdom" and "the old man that is so knowledgeable in research." (*Id.* at § 44.)

On July 1, 2004, Brady gave the Head of Compliance a letter, complaining again about the research department being controlled and supervised by the head of investment banking. Brady was terminated that day. (*Id.* at §§ 47, 48.)

• • •

In Count Ten, Brady brings a claim under Section 806 of the Sarbanes-Oxley Act, 18 U.S.C. 1514A, which protects employees of public companies from retaliation by the companies for engaging in certain whistleblowing activities. Brady fails to assert a valid claim under that statute.

Section 806 specifically states that (1) public companies that are issuers of a class of securities registered under Section 12 of the Securities Exchange Act of 1934, 15 U.S.C. § 781, (2) public companies that are issuers of securities required to file reports under Section 15(d) of the Securities Exchange Act of 1934, 15 U.S.C. 78o(d) or (3) officers, employees, contractors, subcontractors, or agents of such companies, may not "discharge, demote, suspend, threaten, harass, or in any other manner discriminate against an employee in the terms and conditions of employment because of any lawful act done by the employee...." 18 U.S.C. 1514A(a). A specific requirement, therefore, is that defendant be a publicly traded company. See *Getman v. Southwest Sec., Inc.*. No.2003-SOX-8, at 18 (ALJ Feb. 2, 2004) (Administrative Review Board of the Department of Labor finding employer potentially liable under Sarbanes-Oxley for retaliating against an employee who refused to participate in alleged misconduct because employer was a "publicly traded company"). See also *Collins v. Beazer Homes USA, Inc.*, 334 F.Supp.2d 1365, 1368 n. 1 (N.D.Ga. 2004) (specifically noting that defendant employer was a "*publicly traded company* with a class of securities registered under section 12 of the Securities Exchange Act of 1934" in a whistleblower case brought pursuant to Sarbanes-Oxley) (emphasis added, internal quotations omitted).

In this case, plaintiff has not alleged that any of the defendants are publicly traded companies, and he does not dispute their contentions that they are neither publicly traded companies nor "issuers of securities" as defined by Sarbanes-Oxley. Instead, plaintiff alleges that defendants have acted as "agents and/or underwriters of numerous public companies." (Am.Compl.§ 100.) This argument misses the mark.

The mere fact that defendants may have acted as an agent for certain public companies in certain limited financial contexts related to their investment banking relationship does not bring the agency under the employment protection provisions of Sarbanes-Oxley. Section 806's reference to "any officer, employee, contractor, subcontractor, or agent of such company," 18 U.S.C. 1514A(a), "simply lists the various potential actors who are prohibited from engaging in discrimination on behalf of a covered employer." *Minkina v. Affiliated Physicians Group*. No.2005-SOX-19, at 6 (ALJ Feb. 22, 2005), *appeal dismissed,* (ARB July 29, 2005). The Act makes plain that neither publicly traded companies, nor anyone acting on their behalf, may retaliate against qualifying whistleblower employees. Nothing in the Act suggests that it is intended to provide general whistleblower protection to the employees of any employer whose business involves acting in the interests of public companies. On plaintiff's theory, the Sarbanes-Oxley Act, by its use of the word "agent," adopted a general whistleblower protection provision governing the employment relationships of any privately-held employer, such as a local realtor or law firm, that has ever had occasion, in the normal course of its business, to act as an agent of a publicly traded company, even as to employees who had no relation whatsoever to the publicly traded company.

Therefore, as an employee of non-publicly traded companies, Brady is not covered by Sarbanes-Oxley, and Count Ten must be dismissed.

Case Questions

1. Why did the trial judge dismiss the plaintiff's whistleblower claim?
2. What was plaintiff's argument for the application of Sarbanes-Oxley's whistleblower protections to him?
3. Whose position do you favor on the basis of the law as it is written?
4. Whose position do you favor on the basis of the Congressional policy underlying the Sarbanes-Oxley Act?
5. Whose position furthers the interests of the investing public the most?

ethical DILEMMA

When the Whistleblower Is a Lawyer

A young attorney asserts that certain partners of the law firm asked him to research the firm's obligations upon inadvertently finding possible child pornography on the computer of an important client or the computer of an executive of an important client. The young lawyer researched the issue and advised the partners that they were obligated to report the materials to law enforcement authorities. Unhappy with this news, the firm sought an opinion from outside counsel who orally provided the same advice. Rather than report the material to law enforcement, the partners instructed the plaintiff to find an entity that could permanently erase the images. Although the young associate attorney proceeded to contact such a company, he admittedly failed to have the images at issue promptly erased, hoping to convince the partners to report the images to authorities. Some months later, in December 2005, the partners discovered that the images had not been erased and terminated his employment.

The lawyer sued the firm for wrongful discharge, contending that his termination violated a clear mandate of public policy, namely strict federal laws requiring prompt reporting of instances of child pornography. The firm's partners sought to have his lawsuit dismissed, contending that he couldn't prove his case without violating equally stringent mandates of attorney–client privilege, since winning would require that he prove the underlying child-pornography violations.

Which policy do you think is more important, the federal law against child pornography or the rules of attorney–client privilege? Is there any way for a judge to balance these two competing public policies?

Concept *Summary* » 2.3

Whistleblowers

- A whistleblower is an employee who calls attention to the employer's illegal or unethical activities
- Many federal and state statutes seek to protect whistleblowers by making retaliation an illegal act
- The most significant whistleblower-protection law of the 21st century is the federal Sarbanes-Oxley Act, which protects employees who blow the whistle on illegal financial transactions
- Whistleblowers' rights may conflict with the privacy rights of others

CHAPTER REVIEW

» Key Terms

common law	« 19	*public policy exception*	« 20	*express contract*	« 25
employment-at-will	« 19	*dicta*	« 21	*implied contract*	« 25
whistleblowers	« 19	*tort*	« 21		

» Summary

- The employment-at-will doctrine became the norm in 19th century American common law. The at-will doctrine holds that, unless the parties expressly agree on a specific duration, the employment relationship may be severed by either the employee or the employer at any time and for any reason.
- During the second half of the 20th century, American courts narrowed the at-will doctrine by carving out several common-law exceptions. The most common of these is the public policy exception, which holds that an employer cannot fire an employee if that termination would undermine a clear mandate of public policy. For example, many states have punished employers for firing workers who were absent from work because they had been called to jury duty.
- Another exception to the at-will rule is the legal doctrine of an implied contract. While the parties may not have agreed expressly to a duration of the employment relationship, an employee handbook or other employer policy may state that employees will not be fired except for good cause. Or such a company document may accord employees certain procedural rights, such as arbitration, before a job termination becomes final.
- Under the doctrine of good faith and fair dealing, which only a minority of American courts have adopted as a limitation on at-will employment, a terminated worker may bring a wrongful discharge action whenever the employer has failed to deal in good faith. For instance, an employer who fires a salesperson simply to escape paying commissions might run afoul of this common-law rule.
- The Model Employment Termination Act seeks to make "good cause" the basis for all employment terminations and to provide the parties with arbitration as their remedy when the propriety of a firing is in dispute. So far, only a handful of states have adopted all or some of the model act.
- Whistleblowers, who are ostensibly protected from retaliation under many federal and state laws, nevertheless have often been victimized by their employers, discovering too late that the laws on which they relied lacked the teeth to properly protect them. The federal Sarbanes-Oxley Act of 2002 makes such retaliation against those reporting a federal crime itself a crime that can result in the imprisonment of corporate officers.

» Problems

Questions

1. What were some of the socioeconomic conditions in 19th century America that led the majority of state courts to adopt the legal principle of employment-at-will?
2. What changes occurred in American society during the 20th century that may have encouraged the majority of state courts to carve out exceptions to the pristine employment-at-will doctrine?
3. Of the three most widely adopted exceptions to the employment-at-will doctrine—public policy, implied contract, good faith and fair dealing—which would you accept and which would you reject if you were a Supreme Court justice in your state? Why?
4. Is it preferable to change the law by enacting a statute, such as the Model Employment Termination Act, or for a state's Supreme Court to make the change by judicial fiat in a court decision?
5. Given that under the Sarbanes-Oxley Act a corporate official who retaliates against a whistleblower may be put in prison, what penalties should be imposed upon a so-called "whistleblower" who turns out to be a liar?

Case Problems

6. The company's employee handbook stated clearly that employment at the firm was strictly on an at-will basis. However, at other spots, the same handbook laid out policies for progressive disciplinary action when employees violated company rules and procedures that the company said it would follow whenever a reduction in force was required by financial circumstances, included a letter from the company president saying that the company's general practice was to terminate employees only when there existed "good cause," and stated a policy of reassigning laid off employees who were performing satisfactorily.

   Pursuant to a reduction in force, the chief financial officer terminated the financial reports supervisor after twenty-two years of good performance. Does the supervisor have a cause of action for breach of his employment contract under the employee handbook as it is described to you above? See *Guz v. Bechtel National, Inc.* [24 Cal. 4th 317, 8 P.3d 1089 (2000)].
7. An at-will employee was fired for taking unpaid medical leave while his physician was trying to determine whether he had contracted tuberculosis. The employee claimed that the company's human resources director had told him that he "needed to take time off from work" pending the outcome of the tests. The company retorted that, while it did not dispute that the statement was made by the human resources director, the employee handbook stated that medical leaves and other unpaid leaves could only be granted in writing by enumerated company officials, specifically "by one of the principals, vice president of finance, or vice president of personnel."

   The employee contended that because the human resources director told him to stay home until he had the test results, the company was stopped from asserting the handbook provision in support of its subsequent decision to terminate his employment for failing to get written leave authorization. Is the employee right? See *Honorable v. American Wyott Corporation* [11 P.3d 928 (Wyoming Supreme 2000)].
8. The corporation's vice president complained to the board of directors about what she perceived to be potential violations of state and federal antitrust laws by the corporation. The CEO, on learning of this, fired the vice president, who sued claiming that termination of her at-will employment amounted to violation of a clear mandate of public policy. While conceding that state and federal antitrust laws are significant expressions of public policy, the company contended that for the vice president to win her wrongful discharge lawsuit, she must be able to prove that the firm actually was guilty of antitrust violations.

   Is the company correct in taking this position? Or should it be enough that the vice president can prove she held a good faith belief in the existence of such violations at the time that she circumvented the "chain of command" and complained to the board about the perceived violations? See *Murcott v. Best*

Western International, Inc. [9 P.3d 1088 (Arizona App. 2000)].

9. The in-house legal counsel for a corporation, like all top members of management, signed an employment contract when he came to work for the company. The contract stated, among other things, that any disputes arising under the contract would be submitted to binding arbitration. Some time later, when the attorney's employment was terminated, he sought to institute a breach of contract claim in state court. The company moved to have the case dismissed on the basis of the provision in the contract that all disputes would be submitted to a private arbitrator.

   The attorney countered that since his cause of action was for a material breach of the contract, and that a material breach of the contract rendered it null and void, he had no obligation to abide by the arbitration clause and subject himself to binding arbitration. Is he right? What public policy considerations should the court take into account in deciding this issue? See *Burkhart v. Semitool, Inc.* [5 P.3d 1031 (Montana Supreme 2000)].

10. Wisconsin statute prohibits corporate employees from falsifying business records. A company's CEO requested that the company's payroll clerk cut her a bonus check without making any payroll deductions. The payroll clerk countered that in his opinion the IRS Code required that payroll deductions be taken out of the bonus check. The CEO countered that she would be personally responsible for any tax liability that resulted from the clerk's issuing a lump sum payment. The clerk refused and was fired.

    Does the payroll clerk, who was an at-will employee, have a cause of action for wrongful discharge under Wisconsin law? On what legal theory? See *Strozinsky v. School District of Brown Deer* [237 Wis. 2d 19, 614 N.W.2d 443 (2000)].

11. The Iowa Civil Rights Act prohibits firing an employee in retaliation for opposing a discriminatory practice. The plaintiff in this case was fired not for opposing any such prohibited, discriminatory employment practice by the defendant company. Rather, he was terminated for voicing his opposition to the termination of a second employee, who had been previously fired for testifying against the employer's position in a discrimination case.

    While the plaintiff concedes that he does not have a direct cause of action for retaliatory discharge under the Iowa antidiscrimination statute, he contends that he should have a wrongful discharge claim for violation of a clear mandate of public policy based upon the intent of the legislature as implied by the antiretaliatory provision of that statute. What do you think? See *Fitzgerald v. Salsbury Chemical, Inc.* [No. 52/98-1492 (Iowa Supreme 2000)].

12. The Oklahoma State Insurance Fund (SIF) hired the consulting firm of Alexander & Alexander to review the SIF's operations and recommend a reorganization plan. Ultimately, the consultants recommended a reduction in force of 145 employees and the outsourcing of some of the SIF's functions. Some seven state employees who lost their jobs in the SIF filed suit against the state, alleging that the real reason they were selected for termination was their report that an SIF employee working on the reorganization had taken kickbacks from vendors who hoped to participate in the outsourcing part of the plan. The state of Oklahoma had a whistleblower statute that protected public employees who reported "mismanagement" to the state's civil service agency. The seven plaintiffs in this case admitted that they had not availed themselves of this statute, but had limited their alleged whistleblowing activities to reporting their suspicions internally to other SIF employees. Consequently, it was undisputed that they could not avail themselves of the protections of the state statute. Furthermore, the statute did not define what was encompassed by the term mismanagement.

    Based on these facts, should the courts accord the plaintiffs a common-law cause of action for wrongful discharge? If so, under which of the three major theories of common-law wrongful dismissal should they be permitted to proceed? See *Barker v. State Insurance Fund*, 2001 WL 1383604 (Okla. Supreme).

13. A secretary employed by a local branch of the United Food and Commercial Workers Union was a vocal supporter of California Proposition 226, a statewide

ballot initiative which, if enacted, would prohibit unions from expending dues contributions for political purposes. When she was fired by her union, she sued, claiming that terminating her because of her political position violated a clear mandate of public policy. The union moved to dismiss her state law action on the ground that union misconduct is regulated in great detail by the federal Labor Management Reporting and Disclosure Act (LMRDA—see Chapter 18).

The relevant common-law rule is: "A state action is preempted when it is an obstacle to the accomplishment and execution of the purposes and objectives of the Congress." Applying this rule to the facts above, and assuming that the LMRDA does in fact prohibit such actions as the firing of a union employee for espousing a political position, should the state court dismiss the plaintiff's suit against the union? See *Thunderburk v. United Food and Commercial Workers Local* 324, 168 LRRM (BNA) 2623 (Cal. Ct. App. 2001).

14. The plaintiff alleged that she had been fired for refusing to have sex with her supervisor. Unfortunately for her, because the firm she worked for was tiny, it did not fall under the jurisdiction of Title VII of the federal 1964 Civil Rights Act (see Chapter 3), which covers employers with at least fifteen workers. Her alternative, the Utah Antidiscrimination Act (UADA), also exempted small businesses, having adopted the federal law's fifteen-employee threshold. She therefore contended that she should be entitled to sue under the state's common-law tort of wrongful discharge on the basis of a public policy against sexual harassment reflected in the decisions interpreting both Title VII and the UADA.

    How should the court rule on her claim? Are there competing public policies at issue here? See *Gottling v. P.R., Inc.*, 2002 WL 31055952, 2002 UT 95 (Utah Supreme).

15. Assume that the defendant in Case Problem 14 is a law firm and the alleged harasser is an attorney practicing before the Utah bar. Assume further that the state Supreme Court has enacted a code of conduct covering attorneys licensed to practice in the state's courts and that this code contains a canon to the effect that all licensed Utah attorneys are required to live up to "commonly-recognized community standards of moral conduct" and to avoid acts of "moral turpitude."

    Should the Utah bar association act upon a complaint of misconduct and consider disbarring the attorney if the plaintiff files a complaint with its ethics panel? Should the court's ruling on the existence or nonexistence of a cause of action in the preceding case problem have any impact upon the ethics panel's decision to initiate disciplinary proceedings?

Hypothetical Scenarios

16. Deborah, a registered nurse, was a member of the "Blue Team" in the ER of her hospital. The team's supervising physician believed strongly that team cohesion and *esprit de corps* were essential to the efficient and safe functioning of the team, as if it were a well-oiled machine. To help foster this attitude among team members, the doctor annually organized an overnight outdoor "adventure." This year she arranged for the team members to go whitewater rafting together on a nearby river. During the overnight campout, the alcohol flowed liberally and teammates took part in impromptu Karaoke and skits. Deborah was dragged up from the campfire to participate with two other female team members in a raucous rendition of "Moon River," which ended with the singers "mooning" their colleagues seated around the fire. Deborah refused to bare her bottom. Not much was said that night or the next day, but in the weeks that followed the outing, her supervisor was markedly chilly toward her. When it was time for her annual review, Deborah found that she was given a less-than-satisfactory score for "cooperation"; a few months later she was denied a promotion she expected to receive. Furthermore, her colleagues took their lead from the supervisor and became generally unfriendly to Deborah, making her day-to-day work experience highly unpleasant. She took the hint and updated her résumé. She found a job at another hospital, albeit at a reduced salary.

    Does Deborah have a claim of constructive discharge (i.e., that her treatment at the hands of her employer was so intolerable as to leave her no choice but to resign, thus amounting in effect to a wrongful discharge)? If so, what public policy can she claim was violated by her constructive discharge? Does the employer have a *bona fide* business reason with which to counter Deborah's claim?

17. Boris was a physician on the staff of a city hospital. He was an at-will employee. He was a recent immigrant from an East European country which had a health-care system that was years behind that of the U.S. in terms of technology and equipment. Consequently, equipment which was deemed to be obsolete in Boris's hospital was often considered to be nearly state-of-the-art in his homeland. A number of such pieces of lab equipment were targeted for disposal by his department at the hospital. Without seeking permission, Boris rented a truck and with the help of a friend, took the equipment from the hospital's rear loading dock and, easily finding a buyer, shipped the equipment off to a health-care facility in his homeland. When the hospital learned what Boris had done, he was fired. The hospital also called the police and filed a criminal complaint. However, when the local DA studied the police report, she determined that the equipment had been abandoned by the hospital and therefore no crime had been committed.

    Does Boris have a claim of wrongful discharge? Does your answer change if the hospital's employee handbook said that employees would only be fired for "good cause"?

    Does your answer change if Boris had salvaged equipment like this before, but with the advance permission of the head of his department, and he assumed that he had standing permission to continue doing so?

18. Stanley sold prefabricated steel sheds. One day he learned that a shed similar to those he sold had collapsed, killing a worker who was inside the structure at the time. Stanley went to his supervisor and indicated his concern that he was selling an unsafe product. The supervisor assured him that the shed in question had collapsed because the buyer's employees had assembled it incorrectly. Not satisfied with this answer, Stanley went over his boss's head to the vice president of sales, who likewise assured him that the sheds were safe and even gave him a copy of a report that seemed to confirm this. Still unsatisfied, Stanley attempted to see the president of the company. At this point, out of patience with Stanley, his supervisor and the vice president conferred with HR and fired him.

    Does Stanley have a claim of wrongful discharge? If the federal Occupational Safety and Health Act has regulations relating to the safe construction of steel sheds, might these regulations help strengthen Stanley's case?

19. Mindy and Fred work for a large retail chain. The chain's billionaire owner is a staunch fundamentalist Christian. He requires his stores to enforce rules of conduct that include forbidding adultery between members of the sales staff. As sales associates, Mindy and Fred ran afoul of this rule when they began a relationship while Mindy's divorce was still pending. When word got around about their affair, both sales associates were fired. Do Mindy and Fred have wrongful discharge claims against the company?

    If they were unaware of the rule against adultery, would your answer be any different?

20. Janice signed an employment contract under which she agreed to be the CEO of a new company, which planned to provide some very advanced software programs to the financial services industry. She also signed a shareholders' agreement, which provided her with a substantial number of stock options, which could be exercised "at such time as the company surpassed $100 million in annual sales" provided "said employee is at that time an active member of the management team." The contract was for a term of three years, renewable by mutual agreement of the parties. At the end of the three-year term, the company notified Janice that it had decided not to renew her contract. Three months after Janice involuntarily left the company, a huge software deal with Wells Fargo pushed sales for the year past the $100 million mark.

    Does Janice have a breach of contract claim against her former employer? Does she have a wrongful discharge claim against the company?

Commonly Committed Workplace Torts

With increased frequency in the final decades of the 20th century, legal actions for wrongful termination were embellished by accompanying counts accusing employers of (and seeking additional damages for) defamation, invasion of privacy, infliction of emotional distress, and other forms of alleged improper conduct. Less frequently, employers and their defense counsels encountered such claims standing on their own. This trend has not diminished in the first decade of the new century. In this chapter and the next (which focuses on employee privacy rights, a matter of special concern in our Internet age), we look at some of the major personal injury claims that plaintiff-employees pursue.

Tort
A private or civil wrong or injury, caused by one party to another, either intentionally or negligently.

The word ***tort*** derives from the French influence upon the English language and the English common law. It means a civil wrong not based upon a preexisting contractual relationship. By and large, tort law is the law of personal injury. Its application to employer–employee relationships is affected by workers' compensation insurance (see Chapter 21), which immunizes the employer from some tort liabilities. The extent of this immunity varies widely from state to state. In an effort to circumvent such employer immunity and defeat that affirmative defense, plaintiffs sometimes contend that they were not employees at all, but rather independent contractors not covered by state worker compensation statutes.

Additionally, where the work force is unionized (see Chapters 12–18) or where the employer is a public entity (see Chapter 19), the employee/plaintiff's right to bring a common-law tort action against the employer may be subject to significant restrictions. These may include National Labor Relations Act preemption, a requirement to submit the claim to binding arbitration (even nonunionized companies may add arbitration clauses to their employment contracts to ward off these proliferating claims), and sovereign immunity, where public employers are targeted.

Furthermore, employers are turning the tables and using the tort of trade secret theft as a means of guarding their valuable intellectual property from misappropriation by disgruntled, departing employees.

Defamation: Libel and Slander

Defamation
An intentional, false, and harmful communication.

One of the most commonly committed workplace torts is ***defamation***. The tort of defamation has been defined as follows:

> A communication is defamatory if it tends so to harm the reputation of another as to lower him in the estimation of the community or to deter third persons from associating or dealing with him.[1]

Expanding on this bare-bones definition, it is said that language is defamatory:

> … if it tends to expose another to hatred, shame, obloquy, contempt, ridicule, aversion, ostracism, degradation, or disgrace, or to induce an evil opinion of one in the minds of right-thinking persons and to deprive him of their confidence and friendly intercourse in society.[2]

Libel
A written falsehood.

Slander
A spoken falsehood.

Defamation is subdivided into the torts of ***libel*** and ***slander***, the former being defamation by writing and the latter defamation through speech. These two torts may be further divided into the libel or slander that is per se and the libel or slander that is not per se. What makes this distinction critical in some cases is that libel/slander per se requires no showing of specific damages for the plaintiff to recover a judgment, whereas libel/slander that is not per se demands such a showing from the injured party. The term "per se" connotes that the third person to whom the defamation is communicated (and indeed the court) can recognize the damaging nature of the communication without being apprised of the contextual setting (innuendo) in which the communication was made. Professor Prosser has identified the commonly recognized forms of per se defamation as:

> … the imputation of crime, of a loathsome disease, and those affecting the plaintiff in his business, trade, profession, office or calling.…[3]

Business defamation thus may be defined as defamation per se having the following characteristics:

> False spoken or written words that tend to prejudice another in his business, trade, or profession are actionable without proof of special damage if they affect him in a manner that may, as a necessary consequence, or do, as a natural consequence, prevent him from deriving there from that pecuniary reward which probably otherwise he might have obtained.[4]

Strict Liability
Plaintiff prevails without proving negligence.

This definition leaves the door to the courtroom wide open to the defamed employee, whose job is his or her "business, trade, or profession." Indeed, since business defamation is a per se tort, it can amount to strict liability once the plaintiff has proved that the damaging statement was published. This use of the words ***strict liability*** is not to say that no defenses are available. On the contrary, it is possible to identify several. One can dispute the contention that one published the statement or that it is defamatory. Or one can try to prove that the statement is true. Failing these, the defendant may be able to argue successfully that the statement was made from behind the shield of a privilege.

---

[1] *Black's Law Dictionary*, 6th ed. (St. Paul, MN: West, 1991), p. 288.

[2] *Ibid.*

[3] *Ibid.*

[4] *Ibid.*

Qualified Privilege Immunity from a suit in the absence of malice.

The law recognizes ***qualified privilege***. When a person is protected by qualified privilege, the remarks made will be immune from a defamation suit if the person made them in good faith. If the remarks were made with malice, or in bad faith, they will not be privileged. The law generally recognizes a qualified privilege where one person communicates with another who has a legitimate need to know the information. For example, comments concerning an employee's performance made to a supervisor, and communicated through the organizational structure, are privileged if made in good faith. In addition, assessments of an employee, communicated by a former employer to a prospective employer, made in good faith, are privileged. But comments or remarks, if not made in good faith and/or communicated to persons who have no legitimate need to know, are subject to a defamation action.

The following case is a good example of a dilemma that has become all too common in the American workplace: An employer attempting to avoid liability by prompt investigation of a sexual harassment claim finds itself the target of a defamation suit by the accused supervisor.

case 3.1 »

Olaes v. Nationwide Mutual Insurance Company

135 Cal. App. 4th 1501, 38 Cal. Rptr. 3d 467 (Cal. App. 3d Dist. 2006)

Raye, Justice

Factual and Procedural Background

In 2001 a Nationwide employee complained about Olaes's unwelcome comments and touching. An investigation that followed revealed other complaints. In May 2003 another woman complained about unwanted touching by Olaes. Nationwide discharged Olaes. Olaes filed a complaint alleging Nationwide falsely accused him of sexual harassment and failed to adequately investigate prior to his termination. Nationwide filed a motion to strike....

Discussion

I

On appeal from an order denying a motion [to strike a pleading], we engage in a two-step process. First, we determine whether the defendant made a threshold showing that the cause of action triggers the statute. If this condition is met, we consider whether the plaintiff has demonstrated a probability of prevailing on the claim. We review each step of the process independently.

II

We begin by determining whether Olaes's cause of action arose from acts "in furtherance of defendants' right of petition or free speech ... in connection with a public issue." Nationwide bears the burden on this issue.

As used in *section 425.16, subdivision (e)* [of the California Strategic Lawsuit Against Public Participation statute] a protected act includes: "(1) any written or oral statement or writing made before a legislative, executive, or judicial proceeding, or any other official proceeding authorized by law; (2) any written or oral statement or writing made in connection with an issue under consideration or review by a legislative, executive, or judicial body, or any other official proceeding authorized by law; (3) any written or oral statement or writing made in a place open to the public or a public forum in connection with an issue of public interest; (4) or any other conduct in furtherance of the exercise of the constitutional right of petition or the constitutional right of free speech in connection with a public issue or an issue of public interest." To fall within the purview of *section 425.16,* Nationwide must demonstrate that the speech Olaes complains injured him falls within one of these four categories.

III

The parties offer differing interpretations of the language of *section 425.16, subdivision (e)* defining a protected act as any written or oral statement made before, or in connection with an issue under consideration or review by, "a legislative, executive, or judicial proceeding or body, or any other official proceeding authorized by law." It is the latter clause, "any other official proceeding authorized by law," that forms the heart of this dispute. Nationwide contends its procedure for investigating employee sexual harassment complaints qualifies as an official proceeding authorized by law. Defamatory statements made in the course of the proceeding are privileged. Olaes claims a private workplace investigation is not an official proceeding as delineated by *section 425.16.*

To resolve this conflict, we must ascertain the meaning of "official proceeding authorized by law" as used in *section 425.16.* The objective of statutory interpretation is to ascertain and effectuate legislative intent. In determining this intent, we first look to the language of the statute, giving effect to its plain meaning. Where the words of the statute are clear, we may not add to or alter them to accomplish a purpose that does not appear on the face of the statute or from its legislative history. We possess no power to rewrite the statute so as to make it conform to a presumed intent that is not expressed. . . .

Helpfully, the Supreme Court and the statute itself provide us with the basic legislative intent underlying *section 425.16. Section 425.16* codifies the Legislature's desire to encourage continued participation in matters of public significance, a participation that should not be chilled through abuse of the judicial process. To effectuate this goal, the Legislature instructs that *section 425.16* "shall be construed broadly."

With these precepts in mind, we turn to the language "official proceeding authorized by law." Nationwide argues the phrase "under consideration or review by a legislative, executive, or judicial body, or any other official proceeding authorized by law" explicitly includes nongovernmental proceedings. In support, Nationwide cites a definition of "official" as "belonging or relating to the discharge of duties" and "authorized by a government." According to Nationwide, its sexual harassment procedure is authorized and required by the Legislature.

Olaes counters with a definition of "official" as "of or relating to" a "duty, charge, or position conferred by an exercise of governmental authority and for a public purpose." Olaes argues the usual and ordinary meaning of "official" connotes governmental or public, not private or nongovernmental.

Nationwide also contends the phrase "any other official proceeding authorized by law" as used in *section 425.16, subdivision (e)(1) and (2)* is meaningless and surplusage if it does not refer to private proceedings. According to Nationwide, to give meaning to the phrase the statute must be construed to apply to nongovernmental proceedings. Nationwide reads "legislative, executive, or judicial" as encompassing the entire universe of "governmental," leaving nongovernmental proceedings as the "other official proceedings" authorized by law.

We find this construction tortuous at best and illogical at worst. *Section 425.16* represents the Legislature's effort to protect and encourage participation in matters of public interest. Defamation suits aimed at chilling speech on such matters run afoul of *section 425.16* and are subject to a motion to strike. The Legislature carefully delineated the forums in which speech is to be encouraged and protected: legislative, executive, or judicial proceedings, or any other official proceeding authorized by law. Reading "any other official proceeding" in context reveals the Legislature intended to protect speech concerning matters of public interest in a governmental forum, regardless of label.

Our analysis of cases construing the phrase "other official proceedings" as used in *Civil Code section 47,* former *subdivision 2* (now *subdivision (b)*) bolsters this interpretation. Prior to its amendment in *1979, Civil Code section 47, subdivision (b)* provided for an absolute privilege for publications made "in any (1) legislative or (2) judicial proceeding, or (3) in any other official proceeding authorized by law." In *Hackethal v. Weissbein (1979) 24 Cal.3d 55* (Hackethal), the Supreme Court considered the phrase "other official proceeding" and determined the use of "official" was probably intended to deny application of the absolute privilege to nongovernmental proceedings. *(Id. at p. 60.)* The court found statements made in a hospital peer review proceedings were not absolutely privileged. . . .

As Olaes points out, the Legislature, in drafting *Code of Civil Procedure section 425.16,* employed language identical to that in *Civil Code section 47, subdivision (b)* to delineate acts "in furtherance of defendants' right of petition or free speech . . . in connection with a public issue." However, the Legislature chose not to include *section 47, subdivision (b)*'s category of nongovernmental proceedings reviewable by mandate. The Legislature is deemed to be aware of statutes and judicial decisions already in existence and to have enacted or amended a statute in light thereof. (*Leake v. Superior Court (2001) 87 Cal. App.4th 675, 680*).

Nationwide attempts to come within the purview of *section 425.16* by arguing its sexual harassment procedure is a legally required dispute resolution proceeding. Nationwide describes the process by which employees report harassment and the employer conducts an investigation and takes prompt corrective action. According to Nationwide, "Because an employer's proceedings for resolving sexual harassment complaints are legally required—as well as being the first step in the process of instituting a civil action—they are 'other official proceedings authorized by law'. . . ."

We disagree. Despite Nationwide's attempt to cast its sexual harassment procedure as a quasi-governmental proceeding, the procedure involved was designed and instituted by a private company. Although, as Nationwide suggests, employers must take all reasonable steps necessary to prevent harassment from occurring under *Government Code section 12940, subdivision (k),* such a duty does not automatically transform a private employer into an entity conducting "official" proceedings.

As Olaes notes, a private employer possesses neither the powers nor the responsibilities of a government agency. Instead, each private employer develops its own idiosyncratic methods of handling employee harassment complaints. The corporate individuals implementing those procedures do not act in the capacity of governmental officials performing an official duty. Nor are the resulting proceedings reviewable by writ of mandate.

Despite Nationwide's claims to the contrary, we cannot view a corporation's sexual harassment procedure as a "quasi-judicial proceeding." Nationwide argues that, as a general rule, the absolute privilege under *Civil Code section 47, subdivision (b)* is applicable to defamatory statements made in quasi-judicial proceedings. Therefore, Nationwide argues, since "other official proceeding s authorized by law" embraced in *section 47, subdivision (b)* encompasses quasi-judicial proceedings, *Code of Civil Procedure section 425.16* should also include quasi-judicial proceedings.

Nationwide cites criteria for determining whether an administrative body possesses a quasi-judicial power to fall under *Civil Code section 47, subdivision (b)*'s definition of "official proceeding": (1) whether the administrative body is vested with discretion based upon investigation and consideration of evidentiary facts, (2) whether it is entitled to hold hearings and decide the issue by the application of rules of law to the ascertained facts, and (3) whether its power affects the personal or property rights of private persons. According to Nationwide, its harassment procedure, as implemented by its human resource specialist, meets all three criteria.

However, the fact that the private company's personnel department is charged with implementing a harassment policy and establishes procedures that mimic those of a governmental agency does not transform it into an "administrative body." Nationwide's human resource specialist may indeed be vested with discretion, apply California law regarding harassment, and make decisions affecting the personal and property rights of the accused harasser. Still, the human resource specialist is not an administrative body possessing quasi-judicial powers.

Nationwide also contends *Code of Civil Procedure section 425.16* should be construed to avoid the "anomaly" that would result if statements made in sexual harassment investigations were protected under *Civil Code section 47, subdivision (b)* but not under *section 425.16*. The authorities cited by Nationwide do not support the proposition that statements made in sexual harassment proceedings are protected under *section 47, subdivision (b)*.

In *Cruey v. Gannett Co. (1998) 64 Cal.App.4th 356 14 IER Cases 66 (Cruey)*, the appellate court reversed the trial court's grant of summary judgment in favor of a defendant employee in a defamation action based on her written complaint of sexual harassment to the employer's human resources department. The court noted the employer was a private entity and the employee's complaint did not fall within the official duty privilege of *Civil Code section 47, subdivision (b)* since the privilege does not apply to private individuals. (*Cruey, supra, 64 Cal.App.4th at p. 368.*) The employee's accusation was "at best ... conditionally privileged." (*Id. at p. 369.*) Summary judgment was inappropriate because the plaintiff raised a triable issue of fact as to malice. (*Id. at p. 370.*) The appellate court did not hold, as Nationwide claims, that speech made in the course of an employer's harassment investigation is privileged. None of the authorities cited by Nationwide stand for this proposition.

IV

In the alternative, Nationwide argues its alleged conduct was in furtherance of its exercise of the constitutional rights of petition and free speech in connection with a public issue or an issue of public interest. *Section 425.16, subdivision (e)* considers "any other conduct in furtherance of the exercise of the constitutional right of petition or the constitutional right of free speech in connection with a public issue or an issue of public interest" a protected act.

Nationwide contends eradicating sexual harassment from the workplace is a fundamental public interest. According to Nationwide, "if would-be complainants and employers can be subjected to costly lawsuits simply because they exercised their civil right to complain of harassment and complied with their legal obligation to investigate such complaints, they will be discouraged from doing so." This behavior, Nationwide argues, is exactly what *section 425.16* was designed to prevent.

The public interest in the fair resolution of claims of sexual harassment is undeniable. However, we agree with Olaes that this general public interest does not bring a complaint alleging defamation during a sexual harassment investigation into *section 425.16*'s ambit.

In *Weinberg, supra, 110 Cal.App.4th 1122,* this court considered what constitutes an issue of public interest under *section 425.16*. After reviewing applicable case law, we ascertained five guiding principles: (1) public interest does not equate with mere curiosity; (2) a matter of public interest should be a matter of concern to a substantial number of people, not to a relatively small, specific audience; (3) there should be some degree of closeness between the statements at issue and the asserted public interest; (4) the focus of the speaker's conduct should be the public interest rather than an effort to "'gather ammunition' for a private controversy"; and (5) those charged with defamation cannot, by their own conduct, create their own defense by making the claimant a public figure. (*Weinberg, at pp. 1132–1133.*)

In *Weinberg*, a dispute between two token collectors resulted in one collector's working to discredit the other in the eyes of a relatively small group of fellow collectors. (*Weinberg, supra, 110 Cal.App.4th at p. 1135.*) We held that statements by the publisher of an advertisement in a token collecting newsletter that a token collector had stolen a valuable item from the publisher did not involve a matter of public interest as defined in *section 425.16.*

In a similar vein, in *Rivero v. American Federation of State, County and Municipal Employees, AFL-CIO (2003) 105 Cal. App.4th 913 (Rivero)*, the court considered a defamation suit by the supervisor of janitors at a public university against the union that publicly accused him in newsletters of solicitation of bribes and favoritism. The court found such statements did not concern a "public issue" under *section 425.16:* "If the union were correct, discussion of nearly every workplace dispute would qualify as a matter of public interest. We conclude, instead, that unlawful workplace activity below some threshold level of significance is not an issue of public interest, even though it implicates a public policy." (*Rivero, at p. 924.*)

Here, although we agree the elimination of sexual harassment implicates a public interest, an investigation by a private employer concerning a small group of people does not rise to a public interest under *section 425.16.* We do not minimize the significance of the underlying investigation; we merely find a dispute among a small number of people in a workplace does not implicate a broader public interest subject to a motion to strike under *section 425.16, subdivision (e).*

Since Olaes's defamation complaint does not implicate statements made during a legislative, executive, or judicial proceeding and does not concern a matter of public interest, the trial court correctly found *section 425.16* does not apply.

Case Questions

1. What are the social and economic policies that underlie the creation by the courts of a qualified privilege in the business environment?
2. Are there any additional policy considerations that courts need to consider, such that a sexual harassment investigation "implicates a public interest" and therefore the employer is entitled to even broader immunity from suit than under traditional common-law principles of "qualified privilege" in a business environment?
3. Do you agree with the California appeals court that the defendant's sexual harassment investigation "does not concern a matter of public interest," or do you think that the court should have defined "public interest" more broadly?

Concept *Summary* » 3.1

DEFAMATION

- Two types:
  - Libel: written lies
  - Slander: spoken lies
- Defamation gives rise to damages if the lies harm, among other things, the plaintiff's career
- Defenses include:
  - Truth
  - Privilege
  - Immunity
- Privilege can be absolute or qualified
  - Public employers may enjoy an absolute privilege or sovereign immunity from suite
  - Private employers have a qualified privilege, meaning they are protected from suite if they speak without malice

Tortious Infliction of Emotional Distress

Intentional Infliction of Emotional Distress Purposely outrageous conduct causing emotional harm.

The elements of a prima facie case of ***intentional infliction of emotional distress*** are:

- extreme and outrageous conduct by the defendant;
- the defendant's intention of causing, or reckless disregard of the likelihood of causing, emotional distress;
- the plaintiff's suffering of severe emotional distress; and
- as a direct result of the defendant's extreme and outrageous conduct.

Negligent Infliction of Emotional Distress Carelessly outrageous conduct causing emotional harm.

A minority of jurisdictions also recognize the tort of ***negligent infliction of emotional distress***. In these states, a defendant may be liable in damages for unreasonable behavior that results in severe emotional harm to the plaintiff, even though the defendant never meant to inflict any harm.

The following case involves claims of both intentional and negligent infliction of emotional distress, which arose in the context of a sexually hostile work environment. The negligence variety of the tort is even more difficult to establish than intentional infliction, albeit mere negligence is usually a lower level of culpability than intentional conduct. As you read the opinion, see if you can discern why this is so.

case 3.2 »

SIMPSON v. OHIO REFORMATORY FOR WOMEN

2003 WL 758486 (Ohio Court of Appeals 2003)

McCormac, J.

Plaintiff-appellant, Susan Simpson, appeals from a judgment of the Ohio Court of Claims ruling in favor of defendant-appellee, the Ohio Reformatory for Women ("ORW"), on her claims for negligent infliction of emotional distress, negligent supervision, and constructive discharge.

This action arises out of plaintiff's employment with ORW. From August 1996 until November 1999, plaintiff was employed at ORW in the medical records department as an "office assistant 3." According to plaintiff's trial testimony, from December 1996, until she resigned from her position at ORW in November 1999, plaintiff was subjected to almost continuous harassment by one or more unidentified coworkers. As a result of the continual workplace harassment, plaintiff claimed that she suffered severe emotional distress and was forced to quit her job with ORW.

Plaintiff's testimony reveals that the bulk of the incidents of harassment directed at her involved tampering with her work area, office equipment, or work product. For example, plaintiff testified that on various occasions when she arrived at work in the morning she found documents which she had left on her desk the night before soiled or crumpled up, all of her office equipment and supplies distributed around the office or on the floor next to her desk, her desk chair adjusted to the lowest possible level, or her desk covered in debris, including one time in which it appeared that someone had emptied the "dots" from all the office hole punches onto her desk....

Plaintiff also described several incidents in which offensive or inappropriate comments were made about her. For example, plaintiff described an incident in which a "Far Side" cartoon, that had been altered such that the names of the characters in the cartoon were changed to the names of several ORW employees, including plaintiff, was placed on her chair. As altered, the cartoon suggested plaintiff was receiving favorable treatment from ORW's deputy warden. On another occasion, while plaintiff was away from her desk, someone wrote "nasty bitch" across the bottom of a document that was on plaintiff's desk.

Plaintiff testified that she reported almost every incident of harassment to Mary Miller, ORW's healthcare administrator ... [and] to ORW's chief institutional investigator, James Hoffman, and on several occasions made her complaints known to ORW's deputy warden. Despite plaintiff's complaints, ORW did nothing to stop the harassment. In fact, plaintiff testified, after she started to complain about the harassment, the situation actually got worse.

According to plaintiff, the stress caused by the constant harassment at work eventually caused her to suffer from panic attacks, constant headaches, stomach problems, heart palpitations, anxiety, and depression. As a result of these symptoms and the fact that ORW refused to take any action to stop the workplace harassment directed at her, she resigned her position with ORW in November 1999....

In pursuing her claim for intentional infliction of emotional distress against ORW, plaintiff did not seek to establish that ORW's conduct was itself "extreme and outrageous." Rather, plaintiff sought to hold ORW vicariously liable for the extreme and outrageous harassment allegedly perpetrated against her by one or more unidentified ORW employees. Ordinarily, an employer is not liable for the intentional torts of its employees unless it can be shown that the intentional tort was in the furtherance of the employer's business.... [T]he Ohio Supreme court held that, where an employer knows or has reason to know that an employee is sexually harassing another employee, but fails to take corrective action against the harassing employee, the employer can be held liable for the sexual harassment, even if the harassment was not in furtherance of the employer's business. In seeking to hold ORW liable on her claim for intentional infliction of emotional distress, plaintiff sought to extend the [Supreme Court's] holding to allegations of non-sexual harassment. The trial court allowed plaintiff to proceed on this theory....

The record contains evidence that both plaintiff's immediate superior, Miller, and ORW's lead investigator, Hoffman, looked into plaintiff's complaints....

ORW took steps to alleviate plaintiff's discomfort by allowing her to lock her office supplies up in the evening and asking other office employees to refrain from using her desk or equipment. In the sole incident in which the perpetrator was identified, the case of the altered "Far Side" cartoon, the perpetrator was required to apologize to plaintiff.

Finally, Miller testified that it was possible that one of the inmate clerks who worked in the medical records office was responsible for some of the incidents ..., as plaintiff had angered several inmate clerks by treating them poorly....

While ORW did not conduct a full-blown investigation, ... the actions taken by ORW in response to plaintiff's complaint satisfy the requirements of [our Supreme Court]....

Case Questions

1. As the court analyzes the facts of the case, are negligent infliction of emotional distress and vicarious employer liability treated as the same thing?
2. If plaintiff's immediate supervisor were responsible for the harassing activities, how would the court's analysis of the employer's liability have been different?
3. Was the harassing conduct alleged by the plaintiff so extreme and outrageous as to support a claim of either intentional or negligent infliction of emotional distress?
4. If the harassing conduct had more blatant sexual overtones, would the court's decision on the negligent infliction/vicarious liability issue have been different?
5. If you were the prison warden, would you have required a greater effort on the part of plaintiff's supervisor and the chief investigator to find and punish the people harassing the plaintiff?

The WORKING Law

Infliction of Emotional Distress via Social Networking Sites

On April 19, 2006, Anna Draker, a vice-principal at Clark High School in Texas, was advised by a co-worker that some students had created a website on MySpace.com. The website, which appeared to have been created by Draker, contained her name, photo, and place of employment, as well as explicit and graphic sexual references. It was subsequently discovered that Benjamin Schreiber and Ryan

Todd, at the time both minors and students at Clark High School, were responsible for creating the website. Draker sued the students and their parents, alleging among other things intentional infliction of emotional distress.

The Texas Court of Appeals said of her emotional distress claim, "The Internet capabilities of modern society present numerous opportunities for individuals to engage in extreme and outrageous conduct that can produce severe emotional distress.[1] There appears to be little civil remedy for the injured targets of these internet communications. Intentional infliction of emotional distress would seem to be one option. But as it has developed, the tort is nearly impossible to establish. The citizens of Texas would be better served by a fair and workable framework in which to present their claims, or by an honest statement that there is, in fact, no remedy for their damages."

See *Draker v. Schreiber*, 271 SW 3d 318 (Tex. App. 2008).

---

[1] See *Layshock v. Hermitage Sch. Dist.*, 496 F. Supp.2d 587, 590-91 (W.D.Pa. 2007) (discussing a student's creation of a false MySpace profile of his high school principal); David L. Hudson, Jr., *Taming the Gossipmongers*, 94 A.B.A. J. 19 (2008) (reviewing the use of the 1996 Communications Decency Act to protect Web publishers, such as juicycampus.com, from liability for content created by third parties); John Seigenthaler, Op-Ed, "A False Wikipedia 'Biography,'" *USA Today*, November 29, 2005, available at http://www.usatoday.com/news/opinion/editorials/2005-11-29-wikipedia-edit-_x.htm (detailing the "Internet character assassination" of a former government official with an Internet "biography" reference, indicating that the official was suspected of involvement in the assassinations of President John Kennedy and Attorney General Robert Kennedy); Linda Deutsch, "Woman Pleads Not Guilty in Internet Suicide Case," *USA Today*, June 16, 2008, available at http://www.usatoday.com/news/nation/2008-06-16-327594069_x.htm (discussing a 13-year-old girl's suicide after receiving more than a dozen cruel messages from a nonexistent teen boy via a false MySpace profile).

Concept *Summary* » 3.2

Infliction of Emotional Distress

- May be intentionally or negligently inflicted
  - Intentional infliction requires outrageous conduct by defendant with the intent and result of causing severe emotional distress to the plaintiff
  - Negligent infliction requires similarly extreme behavior by the defendant, who, though lacking a bad intent, carelessly causes severe emotional harm to the plaintiff
- Many courts shy away from this tort, particularly the negligent variety, because of problems of proving the extent of the plaintiff's suffering and/or the causal connection, particularly where the defendant never intended to cause the harm
- Social networking sites, such as Facebook and Myspace, have vastly expanded the potential for causing harm, since the hapless target potentially may be exposed to the entire universe of cyberspace

Tortious Interference with Contract

Tortious Interference with Contract
Unprivileged intrusion into a contractual relationship.

Another tort worth noting, based upon its common occurrence in the context of employment law, is ***tortious interference with contract.*** It is a claim that is sometimes available to plaintiff-employees against third parties, who sometimes are named as additional defendants along with the plaintiff's employer in cases of alleged wrongful termination or breach of an employment contract. Following are some recent examples of how this tort plays out in real-world situations.

case 3.3 »

Mattesich v. Hayground Cove Asset Management, LLC
876 N.Y.S.2d 405 (N.Y. Supreme Ct., App. Div. 2009)

Facts: The plaintiff's termination agreement with his former employer contained a clause which said that neither party to the contract would ever disparage the other. Subsequently, the plaintiff applied for a position with a prospective employer. When he failed to get the job, he claimed that it was because the defendant breached the nondisparagement provision of their severance agreement and thus tortiously interfered with the plaintiff's prospective employment prospects.

Issue: Is the former employer liable to the plaintiff for beach of the severance contract and/or for tortuous interference with his prospective employment agreement with a possible new employer?

Decision: The former employer has no liability to the plaintiff because, while the defendant may have acted wrongly, the plaintiff can't prove that he would have gotten the new job in the absence of the defendant's alleged interference. «

case 3.4 »

Zarr v. Washington Tru Solutions, L.L.C.
208 P.3d 919, 2009 WL 1404700 (N.M.App. 2009)

Facts: Washington Tru Solutions was a contractor for the United States Department of Energy (DOE). WTS subcontracted with NCI to perform the information technology (IT) functions of WTS's DOE project. Zarr was employed by NCI to head the IT project for WTS and her responsibilities included oversight of expenditures and forecasting NCI's annual budget. Zarr's position required interaction with Haug, WTS's chief executive at the DOE project site.

NCI was satisfied with Zarr's work performance during her employment. Haug, however, apparently experienced difficulties with Zarr throughout her involvement on the project. Areas of contention between Zarr and Haug included NCI's budget projections and personality-based friction. The situation culminated in August 2003 when Zarr took her concern about a WTS proposal directly to DOE personnel without first going through WTS. Haug was angry that Zarr had not gone through the proper channels and requested that Zarr be removed from the project. At the time, no other positions within NCI were available to Zarr, although she was offered a consulting contract. On August 19, pursuant to WTS's request, Zarr was released from her position at NCI. Zarr filed a complaint against NCI, WTS, and two individual employees of WTS in April 2004.

Issue: Does Zarr have a tortuous interference with contract claim against WTS, because the defendant's employee, Haug, had her removed from the DOE project?

Decision: The defendant contended it requested Zarr's removal from the project because of ongoing problems with the budget forecast and because Zarr did not follow procedure when she took her concerns about an expenditure directly to DOE instead of going through WTS. Zarr argued that WTS's stated reasons for firing her were entirely pretextual. In support of her position, Zarr pointed to the timing of her release from employment, her lack of any disciplinary record regarding the budget issues, and the fact that another employee involved in budgeting was retained and given additional responsibilities.

The court acknowledged that the timing of Zarr's release from employment supported her own argument, but then went on to say that WTS's argument that she was released because in going to DOE with her concerns, she chose a different chain of command at WTS than was acceptable to Haug. The record also revealed to the appellate panel that WTS had previously expressed concerns about Zarr resolving issues directly with DOE instead of going through WTS. Although Zarr did not have a record of discipline with regard to the budget forecast issues, all parties agreed NCI's estimates were over budget due to labor costs, the estimates fluctuated from month to month, and confusion existed about which party was responsible for various expenditures. That one of Zarr's subordinates was retained and given additional responsibilities, although he too worked on the budget, was not viewed to be a convincing argument that Zarr's dismissal was due to an improper motive because Zarr was the person ultimately responsible for providing budget forecasts.

In the final analysis the court ruled that, even though one of WTS's motives may have been improper, the company also indisputably had a legitimate reason for requiring her release from employment. Consequently, under the state's common law on tortuous interference with contract, WTS had no liability to the plaintiff.

«

case 3.5 »

Rice v. Meriden Housing Authority

2009 WL 1143075 (Conn. Super. 2009)

Facts: When the plaintiff was convicted of driving under the influence (DUI), his employer—the Meriden Connecticut Housing Authority—voted to fire him. Challenging his termination of employment, he also sued the housing authority's attorney, who admittedly held a great deal of animosity toward the plaintiff. And, in fact, the attorney did speak at the meeting in which authority's board voted in favor of firing the plaintiff.

Issue: Was the attorney liable for tortiously interfering with Rice's employment relationship with the housing authority?

Decision: The court held that, while there certainly was an employment contract, and there was great ill will on the part of the defendant attorney toward Rice, and no doubt he would have liked to see Rice terminated, and a jury could find he acted solely out of ill will, and it could even find the defendant prepared his report and his testimony at the termination on hearing with the purpose of having Rice terminated—despite all of this, a jury could not properly find that the attorney had any liability for his actions.

The problem, concluded the court, was that, even given all of those suppositions and the obvious fact that Rice certainly suffered an actual loss in losing his job, it was the commission which voted to terminate Rice, not the lawyer. He was present as a witness during the termination hearings but not during the deliberative process. Rice was terminated for the DUI conviction, the existence of which was never disputed by the plaintiff, and he was unable to present any evidence that the board would have voted any differently in the absence of the lawyer's report and testimony. Therefore, Rice had no tortuous interference claim against the attorney.

«

Concept *Summary* » 3.3

Tortious Interference with Contract

- A cause of action aimed at a third party who allegedly causes the plaintiff to be fired or interferes with his/her ability to get a job
- Third party must interfere for an improper reason, such as animosity toward the plaintiff, and not for a valid business reason, in order to be held responsible for this tort
- In at least some jurisdictions, if the third party acts out of mixed motives, such as both malice and a legitimate business reason, the plaintiff will not have a cause of action for tortuous interference

Retaliatory Demotion

Retaliatory Demotion Reduction in rank, salary, or job title as a punishment.

Students also should alert themselves to the emerging cause of action called ***retaliatory demotion***, a tort that echoes the wrongful discharge cause of action considered in Chapter 2. The elements of the tort are much the same as with a wrongful discharge. Consequently, if firing the employee would be illegal under the circumstances, the chances are good that a demotion is equally illegitimate in the eyes of the courts.

ethical DILEMMA

When an Employee–Lawyer Sues Her Own Employer–Client

A senior attorney at a corporation filed a claim for an on-the-job injury with her firm's risk management department, but the company refused to pay most of her medical bills. For more than two years, she repeatedly attempted to resolve her claim, but her employer refused to discuss her claim and continued to refuse to pay most of her medical bills. On several occasions, the lawyer spoke to the senior litigation attorney, her supervisor, and told him that she would be forced to hire counsel, to which he responded, "You have to do what you have to do."

The aggrieved attorney finally retained counsel and filed a lawsuit, claiming that her employer was negligent in allowing the electrical sockets to protrude from the floor, the condition that had caused her to fall and get hurt, and that its actions violated the regulations promulgated under the Occupational Safety and Health Act of 1970 (OSHA).[1]

A short time later, she received her annual performance review. Although she had always received annual bonuses for her performance, and had continued to perform in an exemplary fashion, this time her boss told her that he did not believe she deserved a bonus. As a result, for that year she was the only attorney at the firm who did not receive an annual bonus.

Additionally, she was told that, because she filed the lawsuit, she had committed ethical violations and could therefore no longer represent the company in important cases. She was demoted, her caseload was subjected to "extraordinary scrutiny," and she was criticized for her performance and lack of professionalism.

Was the lawyer justified in suing her employer? Was the company within its rights in subsequently demoting her? Can you think of any legitimate business reasons for doing so?

Could the company have fired her, if it had wanted to do so? Does the fact that she was an attorney make any difference to your answer?

---

[1] 29 U.S.C. § 651 *et seq.* (2000).

Concept *Summary* » 3.4

RETALIATORY DEMOTION

- The rules governing wrongful discharge (Chapter 2) generally apply with equal force to retaliatory demotions
- Retaliatory demotion cases are somewhat more delicate than wrongful discharge suits, since the plaintiff remains an employee of the defendant-firm, unless the latter takes the next step and actually fires him/her
  - This fact creates complex ethical issues for the parties and the courts to sort out

Theft of Trade Secrets

Trade Secrets Proprietary information protected by common law or state statute.

In all of the foregoing cases, the plaintiffs were employees and former employees, while the defendants were companies that were accused by these plaintiffs of tortious behavior that allegedly injured these workers. Less frequently, employers sue their own employees. One area of tort law in which such suits are becoming increasingly more common is ***trade secrets***. In this Information Age, a knowledgeable and unscrupulous employee can walk off the employer's premises with immensely valuable trade secrets encapsulated on a single compact disc. The common law will protect employers from such misappropriations by allowing judges to issue injunctions and award damages. Sometimes employers reinforce their common law rights by requiring employees to sign confidentiality and noncompetition agreements at time of hire. These latter agreements expressly forbid such employees from joining a competitor for a specified period of time after leaving the company. In some states, such illicit employee behavior is also a crime.

case 3.6 » L-3 COMMUNICATIONS CORP. v. KELLY
809 N.Y.S.2d 482 (2005)

Elizabeth Hazlitt Emerson, J.

This decision is rendered with respect to plaintiff L-3 Communications Corporation's (hereinafter referred to as "*L-3*" or "*Plaintiff*") Order to Show Cause for a Temporary Restraining Order and Preliminary Injunction dated July 14, 2005 ("*Order to Show Cause*"), in which plaintiff requests that Alexander Kelly, Mark D-Squared, Mark Dsquared, Inc. (collectively, the "*Defendants*") be restrained and enjoined from:

a. Providing any information received from Plaintiff, or arising out of Defendants' services to Plaintiff, in whole or in part, to any other individual or entity;
b. Disclosing and/or utilizing Plaintiff's trade secrets and proprietary information, including but not limited, to customer preferences, vendor lists, pricing information, design techniques and strategies, and configuration techniques and strategies; and
c. Providing services of any nature, directly or indirectly, to Datapath, Inc., or to any other individual or entity, *only* with respect to the GMT Satellite Project.

After conducting several conferences attended by representatives of the Plaintiff, the Defendants and their respective attorneys, the Court directed that an immediate hearing be held. Such hearing was conducted over a period of four days:

July 27, 2005, August 1, 2005, August 4, 2005 and August 9, 2005. The Court also addressed Plaintiff's request for discovery contained in the Order to Show Cause by directing that the Defendants produce copies of all documents in Defendants' possession containing information belonging to Plaintiff. The Defendant complied with the Court's direction and produced such documents, together with an affidavit of Defendant Alexander Kelly dated July 21, 2005, describing the production. In addition, given the serious nature of the allegations, the Court directed that limited depositions be conducted. A deposition of Defendant Alexander Kelly was conducted on July 22, 2005, and a deposition of Robert A. Koelzer, Vice President of Engineering at L-3 Narda Satellite Networks, was also conducted on July 22, 2005.

As previously stated, the Court took testimony over a period of four full days. As such, the Court had an opportunity to consider and evaluate the testimony of a variety of witnesses including, without limitation, Julius Asmus, Director of Government Sales for L-3; Robert Koelzer, Vice President of Engineering at L-3 Narda Satellite Networks; and the Defendant Alexander Kelly. In addition, the Court carefully reviewed numerous documents included in the record and legal memoranda submitted to the Court in connection with this application for emergency relief.

Facts

Briefly, this matter arises in connection with a request by a branch of the U.S. military (the "*Customer*") for proposals for the manufacture of a satellite system (the "*Project*") that meets certain objectives and specifications set forth by such Customer. L-3, or more specifically its Narda Satellite Division, is in the process of developing a system that responds to the Customer's request and is preparing its bid for the Project. As is clear from the record, the Project will be awarded pursuant to a competitive bid process and is an extremely important contract for L-3. In fact, L-3 began to prepare for its bid many months before any formal request was received from the Customer. The record also demonstrates that the process for obtaining such contract is extremely competitive and that the contents of each potential bidder's proposal remains at all times confidential and contains proprietary information. In fact, many aspects of a bidder's proposal will remain confidential and will not be disclosed to other competitors even after the contract has been awarded and a system is in production. As of the date of this decision, each potential bidder is preparing to participate in the demonstration phase of the process.

Plaintiff's request for a Preliminary Injunction arises from its assertion that "a very real possibility exists that defendants are in fact using information that they received in confidence from plaintiff to further the commercial interests of other competing aerospace contractors." (See Levitt Affidavit paragraph 9.) As previously noted, Plaintiff seeks to prevent not only the disclosure of confidential or proprietary information, but to prevent the Defendants from providing services of any nature to Datapath or any other entity with respect to the Project. As the record demonstrates, from the period of 1999 until June 2005, the Defendant performed services for Plaintiff as an independent contractor. During this period, the relationship between Plaintiff and Defendants was set forth in a Professional Services Agreement (the "*Agreement*") dated December 10, 2001 (See Plaintiff's Exhibit 1). Paragraph 6(c) of the Agreement clearly provides that "information made available to independent contractor or produced by or for him pursuant to this agreement not clearly within the public domain shall be considered proprietary and shall not be disclosed to others or used for manufacture without prior written permission by L-3." The Agreement, however, also clearly provides in paragraph 4 thereof that "independent contractor may be employed by other persons, firms or corporations *engaged* in the same or similar business as that of L-3 Satellite Networks, provided however, that the provisions of section 6 hereof shall be strictly observed by the independent contractor with respect to such other persons, firms or corporations." The Agreement does not contain a restrictive covenant or other similar provision that limits the ability of the Defendants to work for competitors or on competing projects.

The record demonstrates that, during the period from 1999 to 2005, Defendant Alexander Kelly was given a variety of projects, assignments, or significant responsibility for systems that were produced by L-3. In fact, many of these projects led to the development or formed the basis for the development of the system that may be proposed to the Customer in connection with its request for bids for the Project. The record also shows that Defendant Kelly had access to a great deal of proprietary, confidential, or sensitive information during the time he worked at L-3. It is also apparent that, as late as June 2005, he e-mailed such material to his home computer. Although Plaintiff's witnesses testified that it was not the practice of the engineering department to send material home, such witnesses could not point to a policy that would prohibit the practice. Finally, notwithstanding Defendant Kelly's work on confidential or sensitive systems for L-3, the witnesses acknowledged that, while working for L-3, he also rendered services to competitors of L-3, including Datapath. However, such services did not relate to projects for which these companies might be competitively bidding.

Turning to the Project in question, when L-3 began work on its proposal, it conducted three "Roadmap" meetings. These meetings were attended by a group of L-3 employees including Mr. Koelzer and Mr. Asmus. Mr. Kelly also attended these three meetings at the request of Mr. Asmus. Minutes prepared by Mr. Asmus reflect that certain aspects of the Project were discussed, but the witnesses differ sharply as to the level of detail and significance of this discussion.

As L-3 began to prepare its response to the proposal, Mr. Kelly was asked by Mr. Jeff Okwit to work on L-3's proposal. Before Defendant Kelly could begin work in response to Mr. Okwit's request, he was informed that he would not be working for L-3 on the Project. Thereafter, Defendant Kelly went to Mr. Asmus to request additional assignments, and the record indicates that Mr. Asmus responded that he would see what he could do. It appears, however, that no significant assignments were given to Defendant Kelly after this time and that his work for L-3 continued to decline.

Defendant Kelly testified that, in late March, he was asked by Datapath, an important competitor of L-3 and potential bidder on the Project, to work on a matter unrelated to the Project. Mr. Kelly further testified that, in late May, he was asked by Datapath to work on the Project for Datapath. Sometime thereafter, Mr. Kelly was asked by Mr. Asmus to work on a back-up proposal for L-3's main proposal for the Project, but the record indicates that Defendant Kelly declined to do so.

In June of 2005, L-3 witnesses testified that they were made aware by a supplier that Defendant Kelly was working for Datapath on the Project. Although Defendant Kelly did not advise L-3 prior to taking on his assignment for Datapath, he did confirm his work when confronted by employees of L-3. However, citing confidentiality, Defendant Kelly declined to describe in detail the nature of his responsibilities or his assignment for Datapath. In connection with the hearing, Defendant Kelly was questioned extensively about his assignment for Datapath. Although he declined to give specific details, again citing the confidential nature of the process, Kelly stated that he was involved in writing Datapath's proposal for the Project. He also acknowledged during his testimony that, although he was not involved in developing Datapath's design for the Project, he was called upon from time to time to offer technical advice.

• • •

Turning to the case at bar, the Court finds that Plaintiff has failed to make the evidentiary showing necessary to support its request for injunctive relief precluding the Defendant's from providing services of any nature to Datapath or any other entity with respect to the Project. Notwithstanding the foregoing, the Court notes that Plaintiff has demonstrated that Defendants have retained proprietary information obtained by Defendants while performing services for L-3. The Court notes that, although Plaintiff did not make a specific demand for such information, Plaintiff has the right to expect that such information will not be retained by Defendants. Accordingly, Defendants are directed to return all information made available to or produced by them pursuant to the Agreement and shall be enjoined from retaining any such information.

Turning next to Plaintiff's request regarding Defendants ability to work for Datapath, it is clear that Plaintiff's witnesses expressed a sincere concern that Defendants' work might lead to disclosure of L-3's proprietary information. However, the record is devoid of any specific facts that would support this concern. Plaintiff, though sincere in its belief, relies upon possibility, conjecture, and speculation to make its argument. Instead of supporting Plaintiff's argument, the facts argue against such a broad and powerful injunction. The Defendants are and have been for some time operating as independent contractors, not as employees. Their arrangements are governed by the Agreement, which does not contain restrictive covenant and, in fact, expressly permits Defendants to work for competitors. The record shows that, from time to time, Defendant performed services for competitors of Plaintiff with Plaintiff's knowledge. In fact, it is clear that Defendant Kelly has worked in the industry for many different companies and has successfully handled the confidentiality concerns of many competing clients. The only restriction on Defendants is with respect to the use and/or disclosure by them of Plaintiff's proprietary information and there was no evidence presented that Defendants actually disclosed, or even threatened to disclose, such information. The Court has considered carefully the various arguments offered by Plaintiff that, because Defendants had knowledge of Plaintiff's business, it would be impossible for Defendants to perform work on the Project for Datapath without disclosing its proprietary information. However, for the foregoing reasons, the Court finds that Plaintiff has failed to meet its burden of proof.

Case Questions

1. What remedies does the plaintiff request against its former employee? Do these remedies seem like reasonable requests?

2. What problems will the defendant encounter if the court agrees with his former employer and enters the order against him that it requests?

3. Do you think the court set the right balance between the employer's interests and the employee's needs in making its decision?

4. What more might the plaintiff proven that would have persuaded the court to come out the other way?

5. Can you conceive of a middle ground that could have set a better balance between the parties' conflicting interests?

Concept *Summary* » 3.5

Theft of Trade Secrets

- This is a rare area in which the employer or former employer appears in the guise of plaintiff, rather than defendant
- The term "trade secrets" often is synonymous with "proprietary information"
- The common law of most states imposes an obligation upon employees to respect and protect the trade secrets of their employers
  - Confidentiality and noncompetition agreements often are required by employers at the time of hire in order to bolster their common law protections
  - In some states, such misappropriation of trade secrets also is a crime
- Employers, whose employees misappropriate trade secrets for their own use or for the benefit of a new employer, are entitled to obtain an injunction (court order) putting a stop to such illegal behavior

CHAPTER REVIEW

» Key Terms

tort	« 37	*qualified privilege*	« 39	*tortious interference with contract*	« 46
defamation	« 38	*intentional infliction of emotional distress*	« 43	*retaliatory demotion*	« 48
libel	« 38	*negligent infliction of emotional distress*	« 43	*trade secrets*	« 49
slander	« 38				
strict liability	« 38				

» Summary

- Defamation can be verbal (slander) or written (libel). Many states recognize a qualified business privilege—that commercial efficiency demands that employers be able to share information about employees and applicants without undue fear of litigation. The qualified privilege requires the plaintiff-employee, who claims employer defamation, to prove the employer spoke falsely out of malice—that is, knew or should have known what was communicated was false.
- Infliction of emotional distress is a tort which usually requires proof by the plaintiff/employee that the employer's actions, which caused severe emotional distress, were outrageous. The normal stress involved in being fired from one's job, without something more, normally will not support this tort claim.
  - Third parties are sometimes named as defendants in wrongful discharge suites, where the plaintiff-employee claims that the third party maliciously interfered with his/her employment contract or future job opportunities.
  - Closely affiliated with wrongful discharge is the lesser offense of retaliatory demotion. Most courts approach the latter tort similarly to assessing the merits of a wrongful termination claim. However, these cases are often somewhat trickier than wrongful firings, since the parties typically remain in an employment relationship while the suite proceeds. This situation sometimes causes the employer-defendant to give in to the urge to convert the demotion into an actual job termination. Complex ethical issues, such as the plaintiff's duty of loyalty to his/her employer, make the decisions of both employer and employee extremely difficult.
- In this Information Age, not only are employees suing their employers for a variety of alleged torts, but increasingly, employers are suing their former employees, accusing them of theft of the company's trade secrets. Some states treat misappropriation as garden-variety theft, whereas others have criminal statutes expressly directed to this particular offense. Either way, such theft is also a subset of the tort of conversion of another's property. Because the employer usually alleges irreparable harm, injunctions are a typical part of the court's remedy when the plaintiff/employer prevails.

» Problems

Questions

1. Define defamation. When is language defamatory? Into what two torts is defamation divided?
2. Give some examples of absolute and qualified privilege with regard to invasion of privacy and defamation as they may occur in the workplace.
3. Explain the differences between intentional and negligent infliction of emotional distress. How are they handled differently by the courts and why?
4. How is tortious interference with a contract different from breach of contract? Do the two concepts come together in a case of wrongful discharge?
5. Are there circumstances in which a demotion could constitute a breach of contract, whether or not the demotion is retaliatory?

Case Problems

6. A regional vice president directly supervised thirty-four employees and had indirect supervision of more than 400 others. She also managed an annual budget of $20 million and made company policy in her regional facility. When offered a vice presidency at a higher salary with her employer's competitor, the vice president not only jumped ship, but she also induced seventeen key employees, who reported to her, to go along with her. Because she was well aware of all their compensation packages, she was able to help the competitor carefully tailor its counteroffers for maximum efficiency of results in luring them away.

   Do you believe the vice president owed a fiduciary duty or other duty of loyalty to her employer, such that she should be enjoined from stealing away those seventeen key employees? If so, should the injunction extend to the competitor, or is the competitor merely an innocent bystander?

   Is the salary information available to the departing vice president a trade secret of her current employer? If so, how should the court prevent her from taking unfair advantage of this knowledge when seeking to hire away other employees to the competitor? See *GAB Business Services, Inc. v. Lindsey & Newsom Claim Services, Inc.* [83 Cal. App. 4th 409 (2000)].
7. A popular disc jockey signed a three-year contract with a radio station under which she agreed that if she quit her job at the station, she would not go on the air with any competing station for at least six months. A year into the relationship, she left for a higher paying position with a competing station. However, for the first six months, she did not broadcast any shows for her new employer. Instead, she engaged in promotional activities and winning over advertisers from her former station, which sued her and her new affiliation.

   Do you think the disc jockey should be forbidden by court order from working in promotional and sales activities for the new station? Should the court find that her knowledge of her former employer's relationships with its advertisers is a trade secret? See *Saga Communications of New England v. Voornas* [No. 2000 ME 156 (Maine Supr. 2000)].
8. Assume that in problem 7, the disc jockey's contract with her former employer contained a provision that all disputes will be subject to arbitration. Should this provision prevent the radio station from going to court and seeking an injunction to enforce its noncompetition and trade secret rights?

   Should the court in deciding this question distinguish between the noncompetition promise, which is an express part of the disc jockey's employment contract, and the trade secret issue, which is really a tort claim under the common law? If the court decides to order an arbitration, should it dismiss the case or merely stay proceedings pending the arbitration? Do you think an arbitrator has the right to issue an "injunction" enforcing the noncompete agreement and protecting the radio station's trade secrets? Or should the arbitrator be limited to awarding money damages? (Note: You may also want to review the discussion of employment arbitration in Chapter 1, as you formulate your answer here.) See *Saga Communications of New England v. Voornas* [No. 2000 ME 156 (Maine Supr. 2000)].

9. A physician at the University of California was removed from the chairmanship of the university hospital's radiology department in the wake of accusations of financial improprieties. A quarter million dollars, obtained chiefly in the form of rebates from medical equipment vendors allegedly had been inappropriately placed in the department's operating accounts. No allegations were ever made that the plaintiff had made any personal use of the funds, only that he had inappropriately deposited them in the department's accounts rather than in the medical center's general fund. The university, after learning of this, took action to reallocate the funds and also dismissed the plaintiff as chair. But he retained his tenured teaching position and his status as a staff physician.

   If the plaintiff believes that he was guilty of no wrongdoing on these facts, does he have a cause of action for defamation against the university? Does he have a cause of action for retaliatory demotion? If the loss of the chairmanship occurred without a hearing, does he have a constitutional tort claim under the due process clause of the Fourteenth Amendment of the U.S. Constitution? If the plaintiff is in the right, what remedy or remedies should the court award him? Money damages? Reinstatement? Both? See *Katzberg v. Regents of University of California* [29 Cal.4th 300, 58 P.3d 339 (Cal. Supreme Ct. 2002)].

10. A supervisor was accused of sexual harassment by one of his subordinates. After an investigation, the company fired him. Contending that he was innocent, the supervisor sued his former employer, contending among other things that, since his efforts to find a new job required him to "self-publicize" the company's stated reason for his termination and that reason (sexual harassment) was false, his former employer was guilty of the tort of defamation.

   Can the tort of defamation lie against an employer when it is the plaintiff/employee who is communicating the defamatory information to third parties? Assuming that as a technical matter the elements of the tort of defamation are all present in such a case, are there any public policy reasons you can think of that argue against a state supreme court recognizing a cause of action for defamation based upon admitted "self-publication" by the plaintiff/employee? See *Gonsalves v. Nissan Motor Corp.* [2002 WL 31670451 (Hawaii Supreme Ct. 2002)].

11. Randy Curtis worked for St. Onge Livestock Company as a field man, soliciting customers to sell livestock through St. Onge. In time, he worked his way up to manager of the company. Twice he discussed incentive pay plans with the company's owner. The idea behind the incentive pay plans was to enable Curtis to eventually buy the business. An agreement was worked out, including a noncompete provision, under which Curtis received some $20,000 in incentive pay over the next four years. Then, along came the owner of a rival sale-barn, who approached Curtis about managing the competing operation. Curtis advised the rival of his noncompete agreement, and the rival's attorney opined that the noncompete was valid and enforceable. All the same, Curtis and the rival decided that Curtis would "jump ship" and manage the rival firm. Once Curtis switched employers, twenty-three customers did likewise. St. Onge not only sued Curtis for breach of contract but also sued the rival for tortious interference with Curtis's St. Onge contract.

   Is the rival company guilty of tortious interference with contract? If so, is there any excuse for its tortious conduct? If not, what remedy or remedies should the court accord St. Onge against the rival firm? See *St. Onge Livestock Co., Ltd. v. Curtis* [2002 WL 1870449 (S.D. Supreme Ct. 2002)].

12. The employer was in the business of transporting developmentally disabled adults and children from their homes and care providers to various day-care centers and schools. Over a three-year period, no fewer than three male drivers filed reports of misbehavior by a male adult customer named Ernest Rocha. In one report, Rocha was alleged to have refused to remain seated and to have brandished a knife. Additionally, three female drivers had filed reports during the same general time frame, all of which alleged that Rocha had exposed himself while on the buses. The plaintiff/driver was hired in the wake of these half-dozen reports and was required to deal with Rocha, who allegedly touched her, grabbed her purse, demanded

money, refused to remain in his seat, and exposed himself to her. These repeated incidents, reported by plaintiff to her dispatcher, culminated in an incident in which Rocha allegedly touched the plaintiff "all over" and shoved his hands under her shirt. She in turn scratched his face and kicked and pushed him.

Based on these facts, should the employer be vicariously liable for Rocha's sexual harassment and tortious battering of the plaintiff? If the employer should be held vicariously liable, should that liability include intentional infliction of emotional distress upon the plaintiff? See *Salazar v. Diversified Paratransit, Inc.* [126 Cal. Rptr.2d 475, (Cal. App. Ct. 2002)].

13. Faquir began working for the Los Angeles Bureau of Sanitation in 1979, as a sewer maintenance laborer. By 1992, he was a wastewater collection supervisor and seeking a promotion to wastewater collection manager. Failing to receive a promotion and concluding that the process had been discriminatory, Faquir and another supervisor brought suit against the city for race discrimination and retaliation. In 1994, while his action was pending, Faquir went on an extended leave of absence due to stress associated with workplace discrimination. Faquir's lawsuit was successful. In 1997, judgment was entered in his favor in an amount exceeding $800,000. In 2001, Faquir attempted to return to work as a wastewater collection supervisor and again sought to promote to wastewater collection manager. His immediate supervisor, wastewater collection manager Barry Berggren, refused to allow him to return to work. As a result, Faquir filed a second lawsuit. This suit was resolved prior to trial, and Faquir returned to work on September 23, 2001, as a wastewater collection manager. Faquir was a wastewater collection manager I, the lowest grade of the then-existing class. When the class consolidation went into effect in March 2003, Faquir became a sanitation wastewater manager (SWM) I, effective retroactive to September 2002. Subsequently, he applied for several SWM III positions, but was never successful. He then applied for open SWM II positions. While at first not being selected, he persisted and eventually received an SWM II position.

If Faquir can prove that he was qualified for the SWM III rank, should he be entitled to sue for wrongful failure to promote him? If so, can he argue that his promotion to SWM II was in effect a retaliatory demotion, since he was qualified for one of the open SWM III positions? If he does file such a suit, should the company be permitted to lay him off, pending its resolution? See *Faquir v. City of Los Angeles* [2007 WL 2052146 (Cal. App. 2007)].

14. Trosper filed a complaint alleging the following: Bag 'N Save employed her as a "deli manager." During the course of her employment, she suffered a work-related injury which required medical treatment. When she reported her injury to her employers, the company demoted her from "deli manager" to "deli clerk," and her annual salary decreased from $30,100 to $22,500. Trosper's complaint does not allege that she filed for workers' compensation. Bag 'N Save, however, acknowledges that Trosper filed a workers' compensation claim and that she reported the injury under the Nebraska Workers' Compensation Act.

Does Trosper seem to have a prima facie case of retaliatory demotion? What legitimate business reasons might the company have for demoting Trosper in the wake of her injuries? If the company has mixed motives in demoting her, what should be the result? See *Trosper v. Bag N Save* [273 Neb. 855, 734 N.W.2d 704 (2007)].

15. Around July 2002, defendants' computer technician, Tom Foster, informed the defendants that he believed someone was accessing pornographic websites at night from some of defendants' computers, including the one in plaintiffs' office. Defendants and various department heads and administrative staff members decided to conduct surveillance in areas where the illicit computer access had taken place. At approximately 4:30 in the afternoon on Friday, October 25, 2002, the plaintiffs noticed a red light on a shelf in their office blinking when there was movement in front of it. They looked more closely and discovered a camera. They followed the cord attached to the camera and discovered that it was plugged in and that the plug was hot to the touch. Plaintiffs notified their supervisor, who called IT technician Hitchcock at his home to report the

discovery. Hitchcock, who had not been to the facility that day, called plaintiff Hernandez in her office to explain the surveillance and assure her that the camera had not been installed to observe plaintiffs. Plaintiffs were extremely upset by their discovery and did not return to work until Wednesday, October 30, 2005. When they returned, the plaintiffs asked to view the surveillance tape. Plaintiffs were shown a tape containing scenes of their empty office, Hitchcock adjusting the camera, and about five minutes of static. In his deposition, Hitchcock stated that he had been planning to remove the camera the very weekend plaintiffs found it, because there had been no pornographic websites accessed from the computer in plaintiffs' office in the three-week period during which he had been periodically "recording" their office.

Do the plaintiffs have a cause of action for negligent infliction of emotional distress? See *Hernandez v. Hillsides, Inc.* [48 Cal Rptr. 3d 780 (Cal. App. 2006)].

Hypothetical Scenarios

16. Fred, an off-duty police officer, became a bit intoxicated in his local bar one Saturday evening, and shot off his mouth. Among other things, he told everyone within hearing distance that his precinct captain was "probably on the take, just like every other hotshot on the force." When this comment got back to his captain, the captain reported it to the police commissioner. Fred was given a written reprimand and demoted from sergeant to corporal, and the captain filed a lawsuit for defamation.

    Based on these facts, was Fred actually guilty of defaming his captain? What obstacles to proving a case of defamation and recovering money from Fred does the captain face? If Fred is a member of a police officers' union and could be disciplined only for good cause, what arguments does the union have in a grievance situation to contest Fred's drop in rank?
17. Super Saver is a convenience store chain. Maggie Jones is a clerk who works the night shift in one of the company's many stores. She and other employees who work nights have often asked to have hidden alarms placed under the front counter in case of robberies. The company, not wanting to spend the money, has never complied with the request.

    Last Saturday night, an armed robber entered the store while Maggie was working the night shift alone. He put a loaded revolved directly in her face and ordered her to lie on the floor. He then tied her hands behind her back and shouted, "One peep out of you, girl, and I'll blow whatever brains you have right out of your head!" He then robbed the register, loaded a trash bag with cigarettes and exited the store. Maggie lay on the floor, weeping hysterically, until a customer came in a half-hour later and called the police on his cell phone. Although physically unharmed, Maggie was hospitalized overnight. At the hospital, she was sedated. Since the incident, she has been unable to work in a convenience store and has been under the care of a psychologist.

    Does Maggie have a viable cause of action for infliction of emotional distress against her former employer?
18. Barney is the winningest basketball coach in the history of Central State University. His five-year contract is set to expire at the end of this season. The university's athletic director (AD) has been authorized by the board to offer Barney a new five-year contract with a substantial salary increase, plus greater flexibility is cutting his own deals for product endorsements. Having reviewed and signed the new contract, Barney stopped by the AD's office to drop it off. But before he can remove the signed contract from his briefcase, he's told by the AD that the latter had a conversation with his counterpart at Eastern State, and that Eastern State really wants to hire Barney for their own floundering program. Barney asked his AD what he thought he should do. The AD relied, "If I were you, I'd hold onto that contract and give Eastern a call." Barney followed that advice, was subsequently offered a better deal, and signed with Eastern.

    Is Central's athletic director guilty of tortuous interference with Barney's contract with the university? If so, what should Central's remedy be?
19. Dana was a highly conscientious environmental health and safety manager at Fiberoptics Corporation. One day a janitorial employee reported to Dana that

he found a brown paper bag in a corner of the men's changing room inside the plant. Dana went to the changing room and confirmed the presence of the bag. She called the local fire department, which sent a first-responder unit to the plant. The plant was shut down and evacuated, while the first responders examined the mysterious parcel. It turned out to contain a bagel with cream cheese and a latte. The company lost more than $10,000 due to lost employee time and lost production, and the fire company sent the firm a bill for $2,000. The CEO told Dana, "I know you meant well, but you clearly overreacted. I'm not firing you, but I am demoting you to a position in the HR department. You'll keep your salary."

Is Dana the victim of a retaliatory demotion? If so, what are her damages?

20. Nancy Drew worked for Sam Spade as an assistant private detective. Sam generously taught her everything he knew about good detective work. He also allowed her to handle assignments for some of his best corporate clients. Fly By Night, Inc., a local airline company loved Nancy's work. The commercial carrier also realized that as a hungry young neophyte, she would work more cheaply than Sam. Management therefore told her that they would lend her some seed money to start her own agency and that they would give her a three-year contract to work on retainer for the airline. Nancy submitted her resignation to Sam. A week later, he heard from Fly By Night that his services were no longer needed.

    Does Sam have an action against Nancy for theft of trade secrets? How about for tortuous interference with contract?

Employee Privacy Rights in the 21st Century

Do we, as workers, have privacy rights in our places of employment? We often ask our students, most of whom hold part-time jobs, this question. Instinctively, they answer "yes," but seem unsure about the accuracy of their answer or their support of it.

The idea of a right to privacy originated in America. Louis Brandeis (later a Supreme Court Justice) and another young lawyer, Samuel D. Warren, published an article called "The Right to Privacy" in the *Harvard Law Review* in 1890, in which they argued that the Constitution and the common law implied a general "right to privacy." Their efforts were never entirely successful. It took the renowned tort scholar Dean Prosser to postulate some decades later that the "privacy" umbrella covered four separate torts, the only unifying element of which is "the right to be left alone." These four elements of common-law privacy are:

- Appropriating the plaintiff's identity for the defendant's benefit
- Placing the plaintiff in a false light in the public eye
- Publicly disclosing private facts about the plaintiff
- Unreasonably intruding upon the seclusion or solitude of the plaintiff

In *Griswold v. Connecticut*,[1] the Supreme Court for the first time expressly acknowledged a right of privacy implicit in the Constitution. Griswold was executive director of the Planned Parenthood League of Connecticut. Fellow-appellant Buxton was a licensed physician and a professor at the Yale Medical School, and served as medical director for the League at its center in New Haven. The center operated from November 1 to November 10, 1961, when the two appellants were arrested. They gave information, instruction, and medical advice to *married persons* as to the means of preventing conception. They examined the woman and prescribed the best contraceptive device or material for her use. Fees were usually charged, although not always.

---

[1]381 U.S. 479, 85 S.Ct. 1678, 14 L.Ed.2d 510 (1965).

The statutes constitutionality involved in the case provided:

> Any person who uses any drug, medicinal article or instrument for the purpose of preventing conception shall be fined not less than fifty dollars or imprisoned not less than sixty days nor more than one year or be both fined and imprisoned.
>
> Any person who assists, abets, counsels, causes, hires or commands another to commit any offense may be prosecuted and punished as if he were the principal offender.

The appellants were found guilty as accessories and fined $100 each. They appealed, contending that the accessory statute as so applied violated the Fourteenth Amendment. They argued that their services concerned a relationship (marriage) that lay within the zone of privacy created by several fundamental constitutional guarantees. In forbidding the use of contraceptives rather than merely regulating their manufacture or sale, they claimed that the law sought to achieve its goals by having a maximum destructive impact upon that relationship. Such a law, they said, could not stand in light of the principle that a governmental purpose to control or prevent activities constitutionally subject to state regulation may not be achieved by means which sweep unnecessarily broadly and thereby invade the area of protected freedoms.

Justice William O. Douglas, writing for the majority of the Court, asked the rhetorical question, "Would we allow the police to search the sacred precincts of marital bedrooms for telltale signs of the use of contraceptives?" His answer: "The very idea is repulsive to the notions of privacy surrounding the marriage relationship."

Declaring the law unconstitutional and reversing the convictions, he wrote, "We deal with a right of privacy older than the Bill of Rights—older than our political parties, older than our school system. Marriage is a coming together for better or for worse, hopefully enduring, and intimate to the degree of being sacred. It is an association that promotes a way of life, not causes; a harmony in living, not political faiths; a bilateral loyalty, not commercial or social projects. Yet it is an association for as noble a purpose as any involved in our prior decisions."

While this decision had the marital bed as its focus, its impact has been far broader, as it has claimed to find a generalized right of privacy between the lines of the Bill of Rights.

Privacy Rights in the Employment Area

Clearly, public employees enjoy the protection accorded to all of us by the Fourth Amendment of the U.S. Constitution against unreasonable searches and seizures by governmental entities. This important Constitutional right is extended to state and municipal employees by the Fourteenth Amendment's "due process" clause. Public employers, unquestionably, are state actors for the purposes of the Fourth and Fourteenth Amendments' restrictions.

What about employees working for private firms? Labor lawyers commonly counsel their clients that "the Bill of Rights stops at the factory door." This is generally true. All the same, employees of private corporations do have significant common law and statutory privacy protections. In the words of one widely read employment law expert, "The most common way employers invade their employees' privacy is to intrude on their seclusion, solitude, or private affairs. There is a delicate balance between the employer's legitimate need for the intrusion versus the employees' legitimate expectations of privacy regarding the intrusion."[2] This expert suggests that the common ways in which employers (both public and private) intrude upon their employees' privacy include surveillance and eavesdropping; monitoring and reviewing computer information and use; requests for information from third parties; requests for medical information; and conducting internal investigations.[3]

Surveillance and Eavesdropping

Surveillance
Monitoring of behavior.

Eavesdropping
Surreptitiously listening to others' conversations.

The word ***surveillance*** is commonly used to describe "observation from a distance by means of electronic equipment or other technological means. However, surveillance also includes simple, relatively no- or low-technology methods such as direct observation, observation with binoculars, postal interception, or similar methods."[4] ***Eavesdropping***, on the other hand, is "the act of surreptitiously listening to a private conversation."[5] Both techniques are commonly associated with police, spies, and military intelligence. As such, they are the subjects of many laws and much controversy, especially in our post-9/11 world of international terrorism, the USA Patriot Act, and the Department of Homeland Security.

Employers often are tempted to observe and eavesdrop on employees to insure quality of customer service; to prevent inventory and intellectual property thefts; and to discourage wasting time on Internet abuses—to name just a few motives. Not surprisingly, such activities have generated much litigation, especially when the employer's intrusion on employee privacy resulted in employee discipline. Following are several cases which exemplify the types of incidents that give rise to privacy-based lawsuits.

case 4.1 »

Anderson v. City of Columbus, Georgia

374 F. Supp. 2d 1240 (E.D. GA 2005)

Facts: The city of Columbus maintained a call center. Operators who worked at the call center were on notice that calls would be monitored for quality of service. A recording system was installed to facilitate monitoring. Operators discovered that the system recorded anything and everything that was said while they wore their headsets, even when they weren't handling outside calls, such as after the called had been disconnected.

One operator complained about her supervisor after a call had been terminated. The boss later listened to her grumbling on the recording monitor and fired the operator for her disparaging observations of him.

Issue: When are invasions of privacy intentional?

Decision: The trial judge ruled that for such a cause of action to be cognizable, the plaintiff had to prove that the intrusion was intentional, and not just the inadvertent offshoot of the vagaries of the recording system. The former operator's invasion of privacy claim, therefore, was dismissed.

«

---

[2]Labor lawyer Mark R. Filipp in Filipp & Castagnera, *Employment Law Answer Book*, 6th ed. (N.Y.: Aspen Law and Business, 2006), pp. 5–13.

[3]*Ibid.*, pp. 5–15.

[4]http://en.wikipedia.org/wiki/Surveillance

[5]http://en.wikipedia.org/wiki/Eavesdropping

case 4.2 »

Williams v. City of Tulsa

393 F. Supp. 2d 1124 (N.D. OK 2005)

Facts: The city of Tulsa equipped its underground sewage system with an elaborate array of surveillance equipment, including closed-circuit TV cameras. Numerous signs warned workers that "the premises are videotaped 24 hours a day." The camera primarily at issue here was pointed at the restroom door. Though the camera wasn't actually inside the restroom, whenever the door was open, the camera could see inside the restroom.

Issue: When are invasions of privacy intentional?

Decision: The court dismissed the privacy cause of action because the intrusion was inadvertent and incidental.

«

case 4.3 »

Quon v. Arch Wireless Operating Co., Inc.

445 F. Supp. 2d 1116 (N.D. CA 2006)

Facts: The defendant was contracted to audit the use of city-owned cell phone/pager devices for text-messaging by police department employees. The audit resulted in the review of personal text messages, often including messages sent by employees when they were off duty and away from work. The employees were required to carry the devices at all times and were permitted to make private use of them, provided they reimbursed the city for such uses.

Issue: When are invasions of privacy intentional?

Decision: The plaintiff-employees were permitted to proceed with their privacy action, since they had a reasonable expectation that the city and its private auditing firm would not pry into the plaintiffs' personal communications.

«

In *Anderson* and *Williams*, the judges dismissed the privacy claims, because the intrusions were unintentional. The call-center supervisor didn't purposely tap his employees' phones. The video camera wasn't placed directly in the restroom and its purpose was to protect, not to spy on, the employees. By contrast, when an employer deliberately intrudes on employee privacy, where the target employees could reasonably expect to have their privacy respected, as in *Quon*, a different outcome can be anticipated. Under such circumstances, employers may expect to be sued successfully.

Concept *Summary* » 4.1

Surveillance and Eavesdropping

- **Surveillance**: Monitoring of behavior
- **Eavesdropping**: Surreptitiously listening to others' conversations
  - Can include:
    - E-mail
    - Instant messages
    - Text messages

Monitoring and Reviewing Computer Information and Use

Information Technology
The study, design, development, implementation, support or management of computer-based information systems.

Although private employers, and even public employers with an appropriate notice that trumps employees' privacy expectations, are free to monitor and review employee use of employer-owned computers, some employers have voluntarily—or under pressure from a labor union—limited their own access to such devices and the information stored in them. The policy below, adopted by a northeastern university, where the faculty and clerical staff are both represented by labor unions, seeks a balance between protecting the integrity of the institution's ***information technology*** and the employees' (especially the tenured faculty's) privacy interests.

The WORKING Law

Rights and Responsibilities of Users of the Rider University Computer Network

Networks
Group of computers, all inter-connected to one another.

This policy governs the use of computers and networks at Rider University. As a user of these resources, you are responsible for reading and understanding this document. This policy exists to protect the users of computing resources, computing hardware and ***networks***, system administrators, other University employees and the University itself. The University reserves the right to change this policy in accordance with applicable University procedures....

Rider University is committed to protecting the rights of students, faculty, and staff to freedom of expression and to free academic inquiry and experimentation. Concomitantly, users must respect the rights of other users, respect the integrity of the systems and related physical resources, and observe all relevant laws, regulations, and contractual obligations....

While users do not own their accounts on the University computer network, they are granted the exclusive use of those accounts. Users therefore are entitled to privacy regarding computer communication and stored data. Subject to the exceptions set out below, users have reason to expect the same level of privacy for their files on the University's computer (i.e., files in a user's home directory) as users have in any space under their personal control. Private communications by computer (e-mail) will be treated to the same degree of privacy as any private communication. Users should note that by adopting this policy the University does not assume an affirmative responsibility of insuring the privacy or integrity of users' e-mail....

System Administrators
Persons employed by an organization's IT department to manage and oversee a network of computers.

System administrators or other University employees will access user files without permission of the user only when immediate action is necessary to protect the integrity of the computer network or when subject to a search by law enforcement agencies acting under the order of a court of appropriate jurisdiction. In the event of an order by a court, or a governmental agency with subpoena authority, the user of that file will be notified of that order prior to the University providing access to those files to the extent permitted by applicable law. Copies of all user files stored on the network may be routinely backed up for disaster recovery purposes. Such copying shall not be considered to be in violation of this policy as long as such operations are purely mechanical and do not involve the viewing of those files. However, ultimate responsibility for the back-up of files in personal accounts, local disks, and personal computers, lies with the account holder.

Academic Freedom
The college professors' right to take unpopular positions in the classroom and in scholarly work without fear of reprisals by the university.

While Rider University is committed to intellectual and ***academic freedom*** and to the application of those freedoms to computer media and facilities, the University is also committed to protecting the privacy and integrity of computer data belonging to the University and to individual users....

This policy sets a balance that tips in favor—some would say heavily in favor—of the employee. As such, it reflects the power that the employee unions, especially the faculty union, wielded at the institution. Most organizations have not gone so far in according their employees such a broad expectation of privacy with regard to their workplace computers ... and for good reason. Such a policy as this can make it difficult for an organization not only to investigate allegations of employee wrongdoing, but also even to defend itself under some circumstances, such as where the computer files of a hostile ex-employee are required and the disgruntled individual refuses to cooperate.

Concept *Summary* » 4.2

Monitoring Computer Information and Use

- **Information technology**: The study, design, development, implementation, support or management of computer-based information systems
- **Networks**: Group of computers, all inter-connected to one another
- **System administrators**: Persons employed by an organization's IT department to manage and oversee a network of computers
- **Sources of employee privacy rights/computers:**
  - Public employees: First and Fourteenth Amendments
  - College professors: Academic freedom
  - Private employees: Tort of invasion of privacy
  - Unionized employees: Collective bargaining agreement

Requests for Information from Third Parties

Malice
Knowledge or reckless disregard of the falsity of a communication.

Privacy concerns arise in the context of third-party information requests primarily at the hiring stage. Communications between employers regarding a former/prospective employee typically are protected by a qualified privilege, provided such communications are conducted in the absence of malice. While malice in the generic sense usually implies animosity toward somebody, ***malice*** in the context of defamation[6] and invasion of privacy means knowledge that your statement is false or a reckless disregard of its truth or falsity.

[6]See Chapter 3, "Commonly Committed Workplace Torts."

Some employers, often on the advice of legal counsel, have opted in recent years to limit responses to reference requests to confirming the dates of the former employee/applicant's employment, his/her salary or wage rate, and job title. While this approach generally is the safest, it inhibits the free-flow of information required for the hiring employer to make an informed and intelligent decision. And, while this policy may protect the former employer from tort liability in most circumstances, where the former employee was fired for serious cause, withholding this knowledge from a potential new employer may actually open the former employer to more significant liability than if he or she had spoken up.

The following is an actual reference policy adopted by an organization in the health care industry. Try to articulate reasons why this organization chose to institute this policy.

> When you terminate employment, you may use this hospital as a reference when seeking other employment. However, by law we can only give limited information from your file to your prospective employer unless you sign a release form. Letters of recommendation for terminating employees, therefore, cannot be given. We recommend that you retain your personal copies of your [evaluation forms] to share with prospective employers.

Negligent Hiring
When an employer hires an employee that the employer knows (or should have known through reasonable checks) could cause injury to others.

Faced with such restrictive reference policies, employers often take it upon themselves to learn as much as they can about prospective employees. Increases in incidents of workplace violence and concomitant increases in ***negligent hiring*** lawsuits, by customers and co-workers of violent employees, have added urgency to this effort. Applicants, therefore, are often asked to authorize extensive background investigations before they are offered employment. A typical authorization policy looks something like this:

Background Screening Policy

ABC Company is committed to providing a safe and secure working environment for its employees, vendors, and customers. To this end, the company's selection process includes background checks of all potential employees. ABC Company will follow all applicable state, federal, and local laws governing employment and background screening in all respects. The following procedures will be followed to ensure compliance with our background screening policy:

Applicants

As part of the selection process, all applicants will be required to sign a release for the completion of a background check when being considered for potential employment. The following information will be verified:

- Social Security trace
- Criminal search
- Employment verification
- Education verification
- Motor vehicle report (if the position requires a valid driver's license)

Procedures

1. The Human Resources Department will initiate background checks at the time a CONTINGENT employment offer is made to an applicant. No offer of employment is binding until completion of a background check and notification from HR to the hiring manager that a final offer can be made.
2. Human Resources will confirm to the hiring manager that the background screen is complete and that the applicant meets ABC Company's criteria for employment. In the event that adverse information is discovered, the offer will be retracted and the selection process and next steps will be determined on a case-by-case basis.
3. The external vendor will notify the applicant of any information that cannot be verified through customary search methods to obtain another source of verification such as W2s, paycheck stubs, or diploma. Any material information that cannot be verified will result in a disposition of "not recommended."
4. Any prospective employee who receives a "not recommended" result will receive communications consistent with Fair Credit Reporting Act (FCRA) requirements. Should you have any questions regarding this process, please feel free to contact your recruiting consultant.

Background checks, especially of the criminal variety, are a sore point for many employees and labor unions. With regard to criminal background investigations, unions often observe that in the absence of a unified national clearinghouse, investigators are limited to checking the records of the states and counties where the applicant admits to having previously resided. This means that less than full disclosure by the applicant can result in a serious offense being entirely overlooked. Employees and labor organizations also object to the discretion that is often exercised by HR professionals in determining whether a revealed offense will disqualify the applicant. That determination is necessarily a judgment call, taking into consideration the seriousness of the crime, the recency or remoteness of the conviction, and the direct or indirect relationship of the crime to the employer's business.

Concept *Summary* » 4.3

Requests for Information from Third Parties

- Types of privileges:
  - Absolute: Congress; courtroom testimony
  - Qualified: Business privilege; journalist's privilege
- Elements of qualified privilege:
  - Bona fide reason
  - Absence of malice

Requests for Medical Information

Protected Health Information (PHI)
Information specifically identified by federal law as subject to privacy protection.

The federal Health Insurance Portability and Accountability Act (HIPAA), enacted in 1998 and having taken full effect some five years later, mandates—among other things[7]—stringent policies and procedures aimed at preventing the unauthorized use or disclosure of health and medical information, commonly called ***protected health information (PHI)*** in the relevant regulations. In general, the privacy regulations promulgated pursuant to HIPAA apply to health care and health insurance providers. Covered entities include:

- Health care plans
- Health care clearing houses
- Health care providers

The regulations are aimed at restricting access to health care information, and tracking the use and disclosure of such information.

The Department of Health and Human Services' Office of Civil Rights 2002 Guidelines pointed out that the regulations address disclosure of information by covered entities to non-covered entities.[8] As a matter of fact, one of the express purposes of HIPAA's privacy provisions is to prevent employers from using PHI for personnel decisions. Furthermore, if an employer, as the sponsor of an employee health insurance plan, wants to receive PHI from covered health care providers in order to administer the plan, then the employer has to place itself under the HIPAA umbrella. Consequently, many thousands of private employers are subject to HIPAA and its implementing regulations. Employers subject to HIPAA must:

- Create a "firewall" between employees who administer health insurance plans and all other employees to prevent illegal dissemination of PHI
- Amend health insurance plan documents to describe how PHI will be handled and by whom
- Certify in writing that they will comply with HIPAA's regulations
- Designate a privacy official who will be specifically responsible for policing compliance
- Notify plan participants of the company's use and disclosure policies under HIPAA

Additionally, The Americans with Disabilities Act (ADA) also protects employees and applicants, who may suffer from physical and mental disabilities, from discriminatory use of their medical records to deny them employment and advancement. Jose Rosenberg, director of the Greensboro Office of the U.S. Equal Employment Opportunity Commission, drew a distinction between offering someone a job contingent on his passing a physical, which is legal, and asking for medical information in general, which is not.[9]

[7]Not least among these other things is the worker's ability to maintain health insurance coverage between and among different employers.

[8]45 C.F.R. Section 164.504(f)(3)(iv).

[9]http://blog.news-record.com/staff/health/privacy/

ethical DILEMMA

One of the most pressing ethical dilemmas facing employers today is if, and if so how, to use genetic information that is readily available. DNA testing can tell an employer and/or its health and life insurance carriers the likelihood that an employee or applicant will contract a wide range of serious medical conditions, which pose potentially catastrophic claims under the firm's health and life insurance plans. However, ***genetic testing*** is undoubtedly among the most serious intrusions into an employee's privacy that an employer might make. Below is a policy aimed at addressing this issue. Do you think it balances the two parties' interests?

Genetic Testing
Examination of chromosomes, genes and proteins in human cells in a search for defects.

Policy Against Use of Genetic Information

[Company Name] does not collect, consider or make employment or benefit decisions based on genetic information.

[Company Name] does not use genetic information or genetic testing to identify individuals (applicants or employees) who are especially susceptible to general workplace risks, who may become unable to work, or who are likely to incur significant health care costs for either themselves or their dependents.

Accordingly, applicants for employment or employees of [Company Name] will not be required to undergo any genetic testing or reveal genetic information to [Company Name].

Limited Toxic Chemicals Exception

Testing prior to exposure. There is only one exception to our "no genetic information" policy. Employees may be asked to submit to genetic testing before working around certain toxic chemicals in the workplace. [Company Name] may require genetic testing to determine the individual's susceptibility to or level of exposure of certain toxic chemicals that occur in the workplace. Work in a specified toxic area will not be permitted until testing demonstrates that the individual does not have sensitivity to the chemicals.

Informed, written consent required. Although genetic testing may be required, it will only be conducted after the individual's informed, written consent has been obtained. If testing consent is not obtained, the individual will not be permitted to work in the specified area.

No retaliation. No adverse reaction may be taken against an employee as a result of the genetic test; however, the genetic test may disqualify the individual from work in the toxic area.

There will be no retaliation against any applicant or employee who refuses to take a genetic test or refuses to reveal the results of a genetic test to [Company Name].

Confidentiality. Any genetic information obtained for this purpose will be stored in confidential files, not in the employee's regular employment record. [Company Name] will not, except upon the individual's informed, written consent, give the results to anyone else.

A number of state EEO laws prohibit use of genetic testing and also "predisposing genetic characteristics" as a basis of employment decisions.[10] Genetic testing raises the specter of eugenics, the now-discredited science that sought to control the direction of human evolution. In the infamous case of *Buck v. Bell*,[11] in which no less a liberal jurist than Oliver Wendell Homes, declaring Virginia's compulsory-sterilization law constitutional, infamously wrote, "Three generations of imbeciles are enough." Any tattered shred of credibility eugenics still had was destroyed by the revelations of ghastly medical experiments carried out by Nazi doctors in the Third Reich's concentration camps. Novels like Aldous Huxley's *Brave New World*, which postulated a future in which humans were designed and engineered in labs, also helped discredit eugenics.

On the other hand, as medical science learns more about our DNA, the possibility for the prevention or cure of many horrible diseases, including cancer, makes the science of genetics a valuable area of human knowledge. Therefore, genetic testing is an area of increased interest to many people. However, employers who seek to forestall costly medical claims by identifying genetically vulnerable applicants up front are unlikely to find much sympathy in American courtrooms.

Concept *Summary* » 4.4

Requests for Medical Information

- Relevant laws:
  - HIPAA
  - ADA
  - Genetic-testing statutes

- Covered entities:
  - Health care plans
  - Health care clearing houses
  - Health care providers
  - Employers

Internal Investigations

Drug Testing
Testing of human blood and/or urine for the presence of controlled/illegal substances.

Perhaps the aspect of internal investigation that has instigated the greatest amount of litigation is ***drug testing***. The federal Drug-Free Workplace Act[12] mandates drug testing for employers receiving federal funding. Yet, in all cases, drug testing raises significant privacy issues. One way to insulate an organization from liability is to promulgate a reasonable policy. Read the following example of a substance abuse policy, consider the reasoning behind its provisions, and evaluate its potential effectiveness in solving the problem(s) it is intended to address while avoiding employer liability.

---

[10] See NY Human Rights Law, [NY Exec. Law, s. 296(1)(a)].

[11] 274 U.S. 200 (1927).

[12] 41 U.S.C. Section 702 *et seq.* P.L. 100-690 (1988).

Active Employee Substance Abuse Testing Policy

Reasonable Suspicion
Justifiably suspecting a person, based on facts or circumstances, of inappropriate or criminal activities.

Substance Abuse
Long-term use or dependance on alcohol or drugs.

Employee Assistance Program (EAP)
Includes a range of psychological, health, fitness and legal services aimed at helping employees solve problems that interfere with job performance.

Employees may be required to submit to drug and/or alcohol testing at a laboratory chosen by the company if there is a cause for ***reasonable suspicion*** of substance abuse.

Whenever possible, the supervisor should have the employee observed by a second supervisor or manager before requiring testing. Employees who refuse substance testing under these circumstances will be terminated.

Circumstances that could be indicators of a ***substance abuse*** problem and considered reasonable suspicion are:

1. Observed alcohol or drug abuse during work hours on company premises.
2. Apparent physical state of impairment.
3. Incoherent mental state.
4. Marked changes in personal behavior that are otherwise unexplainable.
5. Deteriorating work performance that is not attributable to other factors.
6. Accidents or other actions that provide reasonable cause to believe the employee may be under the influence.

If the test results are positive, the employee may be administratively referred to the ***Employee Assistance Program (EAP)***. If the employee refuses treatment, or does not comply with the treatment recommended by the EAP, termination will result.

If the tests are positive and if an employee is granted a leave of absence for substance abuse rehabilitation, he or she will be required to participate in all recommended after-care and work rehabilitation programs. Upon successful completion of all or part of these required programs, the employee may be released to resume work but must agree to random substance abuse testing and close performance monitoring to ensure that he or she remains drug free.

Likewise, many employers mandate a preemployment drug, ultimate employment being contingent upon success passing of the test:

Pre-Employment Drug Testing Policy

All job applicants at this company will undergo screening for the presence of illegal drugs or alcohol as a condition for employment.

Applicants will be required to voluntarily submit to a urinalysis test at a laboratory chosen by the company, and by signing a consent agreement, will release the company from liability.

Any applicant with positive test results will be denied employment at that time, but may initiate another inquiry with the company after six months.

The company will not discriminate against applicants for employment because of past abuse of drugs or alcohol. It is the current abuse of drugs or alcohol which prevents employees from properly performing their jobs that the company will not tolerate.

Another area fraught with landmines is employer investigation of sexual harassment litigation. While employers are obligated to promptly and thoroughly investigate allegations of sexual harassment, and remedy them where they are well founded, accused supervisors sometimes fight back, claiming innocence and leveling charges of defamation and invasion of privacy. The following case illustrates this dilemma.

case 4.4 » MASSEY v. ROTH

290 Ga.App. 496, 659 S.E.2d 872 (2008)

BARNES, Chief Judge

Marguerite Massey and Wesley J. Kolar appeal the denial of their motion to dismiss an invasion of privacy claim brought against them by Stella M. Roth, contending that, as state employees who were acting within the scope of their employment, these claims are barred by the Georgia Tort Claims Act and sovereign immunity. We agree, and therefore reverse. . . .

Roth supervised Massey and Kolar at the University of Georgia Environmental Protection Division (EPD) until May 2006. Roth, Massey, and Kolar were subordinates of Kenneth Scott, who was the Associate Vice President for Environmental Safety and who, as their supervisor, had the capacity to make decisions affecting the employees' compensation, evaluations, and employment conditions. Roth and Scott, who was married to someone else, began a sexual relationship in 2003, which violated the University's Non-Discrimination and Anti-Harassment (NDAH) policy. Other employees became aware of the relationship, and some feared for their jobs due to favoritism or retaliation. On at least one occasion Scott terminated an employee upon Roth's recommendation during their affair.

In summer 2003 Massey found an intimate letter with references to a sex manual and sexual activity from Roth to Scott, inside a Valentine's Day card located in a canvas bag in a communal office supply closet. Massey had observed a pattern of intimidation at the EPD by Roth and Scott, and in January 2004, Massey took a copy of the card and letter to the UGA Office of Legal Affairs to complain about the relationship between Roth and Scott. According to NDAH policy, a supervisor should not have relations with a subordinate the supervisor evaluates for performance and raises, as Scott was doing. The legal affairs director, Stephen Shewmaker, questioned Scott, who initially denied the affair but eventually admitted it and claimed the affair had ended. Both Roth and Scott were reprimanded, but the affair continued.

Kolar and Roth began to experience work-related conflicts, and Kolar feared Roth would use her influence with Scott to have him fired. Massey gave Kolar a copy of the card and letter for his protection, as evidence of the improper relationship between Roth and Scott if Roth tried to have him fired. In explaining why she did so, Massey said:

"I thought that Wes [Kolar] was going to lose his job because of his relationship—his working relationship with [Stella] Roth, who was involved in an illegal relationship with the divisional vice president. And there have been many other people at that division who have been treated the same way for the same reasons who have quit because they were intimidated into it or have been terminated. And there have been legal procedures by some of those people. And I thought that if Wes [Kohler] was terminated that if he needed to go through a grievance procedure he would need to know that [Stella Roth] and Ken [Scott] were violating that policy."

Roth admits that Massey acted within University policy by taking the card and letter to the Office of Legal Affairs, admits that neither defendant circulated untrue statements about her, and admits that she has no evidence that Massey gave the card and letter to anyone other than Kolar and the Office of Legal Affairs or that Kolar gave a copy to anyone besides a single fellow employee, Dennis Widner. Ultimately, a copy of the letter was mailed anonymously to several newspapers, university organizations, and Scott's wife. Roth admits that she has no proof that either Massey or Kolar took part in these anonymous mailings.

If Massey and Kolar were acting within the scope of their employment when they shared the card and letter with another employee, this suit is barred by the Georgia Torts Claims Act. The Act provides:

> This article constitutes the exclusive remedy for any tort committed by a state officer or employee. A state officer or employee who commits a tort while acting within the scope of his or her official duties or employment is not subject to lawsuit or liability therefore. However, nothing in this article shall be construed to give a state officer or

> employee immunity from suit and liability if it is proved that the officer's or employee's conduct was not within the scope of his or her official duties or employment. OCGA § 50-21-25(a)

Massey and Kolar argue that their conduct in sharing the card and letter fell within the scope of their employment in light of the harassment they underwent due to Roth and Scott's affair, and in light of the University's NDAH policy. Regarding sexual relationships between employees, the policy provides:

> When one party has a professional relationship towards the other, or stands in a position of authority over the other, even an apparently consensual sexual relationship may lead to sexual harassment or other breaches of professional obligations.... The University also strongly discourages sexual relationships between faculty or administrators and graduate/professional students and/or employees whose work they supervise. Anyone involved in a sexual relationship with someone over whom he or she has supervisory power must recuse himself or herself from decisions that affect the compensation, evaluation, employment conditions, instruction, and/or the academic status of the subordinate involved.

In his affidavit in this case, legal affairs director Shewmaker stated that Scott had supervisory power over Roth, Massey, Kolar, and Widner that allowed him to make decisions affecting their compensation, evaluations, and employment conditions. Shewmaker also stated that the sexual relationship between Roth and Scott violated the school's NDAH policy. While Roth said she terminated the relationship in January 2004, her deposition testimony in this case established to the contrary that the affair had continued through the present. This lack of candor upon being confronted by the legal affairs office caused delay in addressing the personnel issues surrounding the relationship, which could have reasonably caused unease among the employees subordinate to Scott. The University has adopted policy standards set out in federal law, including EEOC guidelines on employer liability under Title VII for sexual favoritism. According to Shewmaker:

> "The EEOC guidelines explicitly state that actions of sexual favoritism which affect third party employment are violations if the conduct is "sufficiently severe or pervasive 'to alter the conditions of [third party employees] employment and create an abusive working environment'". Under this interpretation, a class of individuals could be considered third party victims of sexual harassment in that their employment conditions could be affected by a sexual relationship between a supervisor and another employee."

Thus, Massey, Kolar, and Widner could be potential victims of sexual harassment, who would be expected to share among themselves any material that could be evidence of a violation of the NDAH policy.

While Roth and the trial court correctly note that Shewmaker's legal conclusions are not binding, his description of Massey and Kolar's actions and analysis of the University policies and framework are more than legal conclusions and constitute evidence that Massey and Kolar acted within the scope of their employment.

Massey and Kolar presented evidence that they distributed the card and letter so that the subordinates would be able to defend themselves in the event of sanctions or termination. Actions taken by employees to defend themselves and enforce university policies can reasonably be construed as actuated by a purpose to serve the employer, and thus fall within the scope of their employment. Therefore, the trial court erred in denying the motion to dismiss.

Judgment reversed.

Case Questions

1. What was the university's rationale for its prohibition of intimate relationships between supervisors and subordinates? Does this policy impinge upon their privacy rights and, if so, does the university's rationale outweigh those privacy rights, in your opinion?
2. Why would a state provide immunity from suit to public employees acting in the course of their employment? Are there both pros and cons to such a shield from liability?
3. At what point, if any, in the factual scenario of this case, do you think the distribution of the card and letter extend beyond the limits of the immunity afforded the defendants by the state statute?
4. The opinion indicates that the card and letter eventually fell into the hands of news media and university organizations. When public employees behave the way the plaintiff did, does the public have a right to know?

As demonstrated in the *Massey* case, supervisors who engage in intimate relationships with their subordinates can set in motion a variety of distinct but closely related legal problems. Whenever a power relationship in the workplace is combined with a private sexual relationship, a tacit implication of *quid pro quo* harassment enters the scenario. This takes two forms: potential favoritism by the supervisor towards his/her paramour and (at a minimum) a perception by the subordinate's co-workers that he/she is gaining benefits that they are denied. As these workplace dynamics generate gossip, the potential for defamation and invasion of privacy come onto the stage. In our age of easily replicable communications (photocopying, email, etc.), rumors, once at large, are often impossible to contain. At this stage in the drama, HR and legal counsel are faced with a damage-control challenge of highly complex dimensions. As the internal investigation and disciplinary process proceed, these professionals must exercise every reasonable effort, while balancing the accused's and accuser's due-process rights, to maintain confidentiality and protect the privacy of all parties.

Concept *Summary* » 4.5

INTERNAL INVESTIGATIONS

- Reasons for drug tests:
  - Required by law in some industries
  - Reasonable suspicion
  - Random
  - Prior history (e.g., return to work)
  - Workplace accident

Personnel Files

Personnel files pose two major issues for employers regarding what should be placed and retained in the employee's file and which employees should have access to personnel files. Typical items in a personnel fell include applications, references and letters of recommendation, performance evaluations, disciplinary actions, and attendance records. (Health records usually are maintained in separate HR files, as is appropriate under HIPAA and the ADA, as noted above.) Access to such files should be limited to HR and legal department employees, direct supervisors and senior management. "Need to know" is the operative principle here.

So, what about the employee's access to his/her own personnel file? A typical company policy might look something like this:

POLICY: EMPLOYEE ACCESS TO THEIR PERSONNEL FILES

Employee files are maintained by the Human Resources department and are considered confidential. Managers and supervisors other than Human Resources may only have access to personnel file information on a need-to-know basis. A manager or supervisor considering the hire of a former employee or transfer of a current employee may be granted access to the file.

[Company Name] shall provide access to personnel files by current or former employees in accordance with applicable laws.

Representatives of government or law enforcement agencies, in the course of their business, may be allowed access to file information. This decision will be made at the discretion of the Human Resources department in response to the request, a legal subpoena, or court order.

Many states have statutes dealing with access by current and former employees to their files. Pennsylvania's law is a good example:

> An employer shall, at reasonable times, upon request of an employee, permit that employee or an agent designated by the employee to inspect his or her own personnel files used to determine his or her own qualifications for employment, promotion, additional compensation, termination or disciplinary action. The employer shall make these records available during the regular business hours of the office where these records are usually and ordinarily maintained, when sufficient time is available during the course of a regular business day, to inspect the personnel files in question. The employer may require the requesting employee or the agent designated by the employee to inspect such records on the free time of the employee or agent. At the employer's discretion, the employee may be required to file a written form to request access to the personnel file or files or to indicate a designation of agency for the purpose of file access and inspection. This form is solely for the purpose of identifying the requesting individual or the designated agent of the requesting individual to avoid disclosure to ineligible individuals. To assist the employer in providing the correct records to meet the employee's need, the employee shall indicate in his written request, either the purpose for which the inspection is requested, or the particular parts of his personnel record which he wishes to inspect or have inspected by the employee's agent.[13]

Note, too, that the sample policy in the adjoining box allows access to "government or law enforcement agencies." Who else should be entitled to access an employee's personnel file and under what circumstances? Company HR, legal, and management employees are often confronted with process servers delivering subpoenas related to everything from personal injury actions to child-support orders to criminal cases. How should employee privacy interests be balanced with the justice system's interest in fair and expeditious processes? In the *Commonwealth* case that follows, a defendant on trial for murder attempted to obtain access to the personnel files of the arresting officers for purposes of cross-examination at trial.

[13]43 Pa. Stat. Section 1322.

case 4.5 »

COMMONWEALTH V. BLAKENEY

596 Pa. 510, 946 A.2d 645 (2008)

Chief Justice CASTILLE:

[After a jury trial in the Dauphin County Court of Common Pleas, Herbert Blakeney was found guilty of the murder of Basil Blakeney and of attempted murder and aggravated assault of Duana Swanson. Prior to the trial, the defendant, Herbert Blakeney, sought to subpoena the entire personnel files of Officers Vernouski and Painter, who responded to the victims' police call and were involved in arresting the defendant. Blakeney stated that he wanted to view their files in the hope of finding some "prior involvement with tampering with evidence or other relevant evidence of misconduct." After a hearing, the trial court refused to allow the subpoena of the personnel files on grounds of irrelevance. Blakeney then appealed his conviction because of the denial of access to the personnel files.]

. . . Appellant [Herbert Blakeney] now claims that the trial court abused its discretion when it denied him access to the personnel files. Appellant argues that this ruling deprived him of a fair opportunity to examine the officers' truthfulness. Appellant ... argues that because he was questioning the truthfulness of the two officers, any allegations that the officers had fabricated, lied, or perjured themselves in the past would be relevant. Appellant argues that, at the very least, the trial court should have conducted an *in camera* review of the officers' personnel files.

The Commonwealth responds that appellant did not articulate any reasonable basis to support his request at trial, and had nothing more than a "blind hope" that inspection of the records would unveil some piece of information that would aid appellant's defense....

Appellant's unfounded speculation concerning Officers Vernouski and Painter is not a reasonable basis that would justify inspection, either by appellant or by the court *in camera*. Appellant presented no evidence that such an inspection would lead to any relevant evidence. In contrast, the defendant in *Mejia-Arias*, the case upon which appellant relies, articulated a reasonable basis justifying inspection because the officers who were to testify against the defendant were recently suspected of lying in connection with prior search warrants.

Appellant's motion sought nothing more than a "wholesale inspection" of personnel files, which should certainly require a greater showing of basis and necessity than simply unsupported speculation concerning investigatory files pertaining to a defendant's prosecution. Furthermore, as the Commonwealth notes, the strong public interest in protecting the privacy and safety of law enforcement officers requires a narrowly targeted and supported request for relevant documents. A defendant has no right to obtain or review personnel records in the mere hope that he might uncover some collateral information with which to challenge the credibility of a police officer. Consequently, appellant's claim that the trial court abused its discretion in rejecting his request for access to the officers' personnel files lacks merit.

Case Questions

1. As a general proposition, which legal interest should outweigh the other in a case like this: the employees' privacy interests or the defendant's right to a fair trial?
2. Does the fact that the employees, whose personnel files were sought here, were police officers change your answer to question 1?
3. Assuming the court was corrected in denying the defendant's request for access to the personnel files, what more, if anything, might the defendant have alleged that could have tipped the balance in his favor. Persuading the judge to grant access?
4. Suppose that, instead of being a defendant in a murder case, Blakeney was a plaintiff suing the same officers for police brutality. Would that change the balance between his due-process rights and their privacy interests? If so, how?
5. Assuming that the judge had ruled the other way and granted Blakeney access to the officers' personnel files, should they have been afforded an opportunity to review their files first and/or request that certain materials be redacted from the files?

«

Concept *Summary* » 4.6

PERSONNEL FILES

- Issues:
  - What should be in a personnel file?
  - Who can see the file?
  - Who can make copies?
  - Who can take notes?
  - When is information released to third parties?

- Factors:
  - Federal and state laws
  - Qualified privilege
  - Legal process (e.g., subpoena)
  - Collective bargaining agreement
  - Company policies

CHAPTER REVIEW

» Key Terms

eavesdropping	« 61	*academic freedom*	« 64	*drug testing*	« 69
surveillance	« 61	*malice*	« 64	*substance abuse*	« 70
information technology	« 63	*negligent hiring*	« 65	*reasonable suspicion*	« 70
networks	« 63	*protected health information (PHI)*	« 67	*Employee Assistance Program (EAP)*	« 70
system administrators	« 63	*genetic testing*	« 68		

» Summary

- The tort of invasion of privacy is a relatively recent addition to American common law. A broad and generalized privacy right grounded in the U.S. Constitution's Bill of Rights is an even more recent arrival on the American legal scene.
- The four general grounds for an invasion of privacy lawsuit recognized by most American courts today are:
  - Appropriating the plaintiff's identity for the defendant's benefit
  - Placing the plaintiff in a false light in the public eye
  - Publicly disclosing private facts about the plaintiff
  - Unreasonably intruding upon the seclusion or solitude of the plaintiff.
- The major areas where an employer is likely to risk liability for invading the privacy of its employees in the modern U.S. workplace are:
  - Surveillance and eavesdropping
  - Monitoring and reviewing computer information and use
  - Requests for information from third parties
  - Requests for medical information, and
  - Conducting internal investigations.

» Problems

Questions

1. What is the most important factor which distinguishes the tort of invasion of privacy from the tort of defamation?
2. Taking into account all the new technologies in the workplace, as compared to even fifteen or twenty years ago, and considering the events of September 11, 2001, in general, is employee privacy or workplace safety the more important consideration for the average employer today?

3. Does genetic testing have any legitimate place in a company's human resource policies today?
4. When should an employer refer the investigation of alleged employee wrongdoing to outside experts, such as attorneys, HR consultants, or private investigators? When should the matter be referred to a law enforcement agency?
5. What are the pros and cons of placing a written record of every counseling session between a supervisor and his/her subordinate into the subordinate's personnel file?

Case Problems

6. In this chapter, we briefly examined several cases in which the employer's surveillance was challenged as an alleged invasion of employees' privacy. Are there circumstances under which an employer's failure to provide surveillance will support tort liability? In one recent case, Dean, a mentally disabled but "very dedicated" Whataburger employee of fourteen years, was murdered when he was shot in the face by Marshall, who was, at the direction of Love, attempting to rob the Whataburger restaurant at which Love served as manager. In the wrongful death suit brought by Dean's estate against Whataburger, the plaintiffs' expert "emphasized that Whataburger was the only fast-food chain of which he was aware that had 'failed to develop a comprehensive robbery prevention program to protect its employees.'" At the time of the capital murder of Dean, Whataburger had no security manual or methodology in place. There were no minimum standards published or training provided to managers, and "Whataburger's conduct of not addressing workplace violence and robbery prevention fell below the standard of care and constituted malice or conscious indifference to the magnitude of the risk of harm and disregard for the safety of its employees. This conduct was a proximate cause of Christopher Dean's death." The expert focused in particular on the "lack of security guards, alarms, bullet-resistant barriers, and surveillance equipment," and cited "a combination of surveillance camera and hold-up alarm system as significant deterrents." Should Whataburger be found liable for Dean's death? See *Barton v. Whataburger, Inc.*, 2009 WL 417292 (Tex. App., February 13, 2009).
7. What if the plaintiff-employee, who is suing her employer, is guilty of eavesdropping? In a recent case, female firefighters filed employment discrimination action against city and individual defendants, asserting claims include hostile-environment sexual harassment and disparate-treatment discrimination. One plaintiff alleged that while assigned to a fire station, she became the object of severe harassment, consisting of repeated verbal assault and sexual innuendo. When she reported this harassment to her superiors, she was rebuked for her part in precipitating trouble in the work environment. Subsequent complaints about what she perceived as demeaning and hostile statements in her presence resulted in her being accused by the employer of eavesdropping. If the plaintiff is guilty of eavesdropping on her coworkers and/or supervisors, (1) should her testimony about what she heard be admitted at trial; and (2) if she was disciplined for eavesdropping, should this discipline be admitted as evidence of employer retaliation? See *Stachura v. Toledo*, 177 Ohio App.3d 481, 895 NE2d 202 (2008).
8. Television writers filed class-action lawsuits against studios, networks, production companies and talent agencies, asserting an industry-wide pattern and practice of age discrimination. The writers served subpoenas on third parties, including the Writers Guild of America, seeking data on Writers Guild members from which they could prepare a statistical analysis to support their claims of age discrimination. A privacy notice was sent to 47,000 Writers Guild members, advising them of their right to object to disclosure of personal information on privacy grounds. Some 7,700 individuals filed objections. The writers moved to overrule the objections. The trial court sustained the objections in their entirety. The writers sought a writ directing the trial court to vacate its order and allow access to certain of the requested information, arguing the information was critical to proving their claims and privacy concerns were minimal. On balance, who has the stronger claim, the TV writers who want the information, or the companies and the union who want to keep the information confidential? See *Alch v. Superior Court*, 165 Cal.App.4th 1412, 82 Cal. Rptr.3d 470 (2008).

9. Two employees sued an employer, who had placed a surveillance video camera in an office that employees shared, for invasion of privacy, intentional infliction of emotional distress, and negligent infliction of emotional distress. The employer, a facility for abused children, defended on the grounds that (1) the plaintiffs were not recorded or viewed by the surveillance equipment defendants placed in their office; and (2) all employees of the facility had a diminished expectation of privacy that was overcome by defendants' need to protect the children residing at their facility. Does the fact that the employees were never actually recorded let the employer off the liability hook? Did the nature of the employer's business diminish the employees' expectation of privacy to the point where their privacy interest could not support an invasion of privacy lawsuit? See *Hernandez v. Hillsides, Inc.*, 48 Cal. Rptr. 3d 780 (Cal. App. 2006).
10. On February 6, 1991, the decedent Daniel Boyle, a police officer for the city of Philadelphia, died as a result of a gunshot wound to the head, sustained in the course and scope of his employment. On March 17, 1992, Patricia Rossa filed a fatal-claim petition on behalf of her daughter with the state's workers' compensation board, and the matter was assigned to Workers' Compensation Judge Lundy, who placed the matter in indefinite postponement status to allow the parties the opportunity to file a paternity claim in the court of common pleas. The claimant presented the testimony of Rossa, Patricia J. Ranalli, Claimant's grandmother and Rossa's mother, Raymond Ranalli, Rossa's stepfather, Louis Rossa, Rossa's brother, and Ethel Weir, Rossa's grandmother, all to the effect that Officer Boyle was the father of her daughter. The employer—the City of Philadelphia—petitioned to do genetic testing before the workers' comp claim was allowed. Should the court order such genetic tests? See *Rossa ex rel. Rossa v. W.C.A.B. (City of Philadelphia)*, 794 A.2d 919 (Pa. Commonwealth Ct. 2002).
11. Wahkiakum School District required its student athletes to refrain from using or possessing alcohol or illegal drugs. Beginning in 1994, the school district implemented myriad ways to combat drug and alcohol use among the student population. Nevertheless, drug and alcohol problems persisted. Acting independently of the school district, the Wahkiakum Community Network (community network) began surveying district students. From these surveys, the community network ranked teen substance abuse as the number one problem in Wahkiakum County. The community network's surveys showed that in 1998, 40 percent of sophomores reported previously using illegal drugs and 19 percent of sophomores reported illegal drug use within the previous 30 days, while 42 percent of seniors reported previously using illegal drugs and 12.5 percent reported illegal drug use within the previous 30 days. As a result, the school district decided to implement random drug testing, where all students may be tested initially and then subjected to random drug testing during the remainder of the season. The school district formed the Drug and Alcohol Advisory Committee (now the "Safe and Drug Free Schools Advisory Committee") to help deal with the student substance abuse problems. The committee evaluated the effectiveness of its previous programs, and contemplated adopting Policy 3515, which would require random drug testing of student athletes. Parents sued to block the policy. On balance, which concern should be accorded greater judicial weight, preventing drug abuse or student-athletes' privacy rights? Does the balance change if the athletes are NCAA Division I athletes at a major university? Does the balance change if the athletes are professional athletes employed by major league teams? See *York v. Wahkiakum School District*, 163 Wash.2d 297, 178 P.3d 995 (2008).
12. The University of Wyoming employed Corrine Sheaffer for more than twenty-five years. However, in February 2004, UW terminated Sheaffer from her position as transportation and parking services manager. UW's position was that Sheaffer was terminated "for cause" for her role in a secret audiotape recording of a meeting of the UW Traffic Appeals Committee (TAC). Sheaffer's reason for taping the meeting was centered on the number of appeals that were being granted and a general lack of consistency in the handling of the appeals. There was a generalized perception by Sheaffer that the

members of the TAC were biased in favor of faculty, administration, and student athletes. Sheaffer believed that the only way to get the upper administration to sit up and take notice was to make them hear exactly what went on in the meetings. She also complained that the language used in the hearings created an abusive work environment amounting to sexual harassment. When she was fired, she charged retaliatory discharge. Absent any justification for the eavesdropping, was Sheaffer guilty of an invasion of her colleagues' privacy that was deserving of employer discipline? If she was trying to collect evidence of a sexually hostile work environment, did this justify her conduct? If Wyoming has a whistleblower statute, do you think she should qualify as a protected whistleblower? See *Sheaffer v. State ex rel. University of Wyoming*, 2009 WL 387269 (Wyoming Supreme Court, February 18, 2009).

13. The State of Vermont appealed the Vermont Labor Relations Board's decision, reinstating grievant Lawrence Rosenberger to his position as a game warden and awarding him back pay after he was discharged for falsifying a time report to obtain compensation for work not done. One of the main issues for the Board to resolve at the grievance hearing in this case was how to remedy the employer's violation of a collective bargaining agreement provision requiring state employers to inform employees of their right to union representation before being called to a meeting that might lead to disciplinary action. The state argued that the board erred by adopting the criminal law doctrines—the exclusionary rule and its companion fruit-of-the-poisonous-tree corollary—to exclude from the grievance hearing not only the grievant's admissions during an initial interview without union representation, but also his admissions during later investigative interviews when accompanied by a union representative. Should the employer's error invalidate the results of its internal investigation? See *In re Rosenberger, 2009* WL 350631 (Vermont Supreme Court, February 13, 2009).

14. Plaintiff Richard and three other Lafayette police officers had performed authorized off-duty security work at Club 410, a nightclub located in downtown Lafayette, Louisiana, for some time. Richard in fact was head of security at Club 410. On the night that other police raided the club and confiscated illegal drugs, Richard received a phone call from the club. On the basis of that call, the ten-year veteran was subjected to a non-random drug test, which revealed the use of steroids. He was fired. Did the employer-police department have sufficient reasonable suspicion, based upon the occurrence of the phone call on the night of the raid, to subject Richard to the non-random drug test? See *Richard v. Lafayette Fire and Police Civil Service Board*, 2009 WL 307145 (Louisiana Supreme Court, February 6, 2009).

15. This action arose from a dispute between political opponents. The plaintiff Derith Smith alleged that Charles Stewart, the village manager, wrongfully terminated her during her employment with the Village of Suttons Bay. However, she did not file suit against the village because she obtained other employment as the elected supervisor of Elmwood Township. On May 17, 2005, the plaintiff received an anonymous mailing while serving as Elmwood Township supervisor. This mailing consisted of a document written by Stewart that was contained in her personnel file, but was never brought to her attention or discussed during her employment. The document raised various issues regarding the plaintiff's employment, such as whether she inappropriately paid herself a higher wage and whether she misrepresented her status as an employee when she was in fact an independent contractor. Someone had added a caption to the document that read, "Attention: Suttons Bay Villagers Alledged (sic) Misuse of Village Taxpayer Funds?" and "Subject: Personnel meeting scheduled for August 10, 2004…." The plaintiff sued, alleging that the mailing defamed her, invaded her privacy, constituted an injurious falsehood, and was a violation of her free speech rights. What do you think are her chances of prevailing on the invasion of privacy count in the complaint? If she has a valid cause of action, against whom does she have it? See *Smith v. Anonymous Joint Enterprise*, 2009 WL 249415 (Mich. Ct. App., February 3, 2009).

Hypothetical Scenarios

16. Assume that an employer's computer-use policy permits employees to use their company-owned

laptops for personal e-mails and Web searches, provided such use does not interfere with company business. Assume further that, when members of the company's outside sales force have their laptops collected and replaced by newer models, the IT department in the act of inspecting the old computers and sweeping their hard drives for redistribution to clerical workers, discovers Internet pornography on a salesman's hard drive. If, as is the case with some corporations such as Wal-Mart, the company has a policy against pornography entering its premises, should the salesman be reported to HR and disciplined? Suppose that some of the material appears to be "kiddy porn" that violates federal law. Does this change your answer? If the salesman is fired, does he have the basis for a wrongful discharge action? If he is prosecuted for possessing "kiddy porn," does he have a viable Fourth/Fourteenth Amendment search-and-seizure defense?

17. Suppose that a 25-year-old woman, whose mother and aunts all were afflicted with breast cancer by the time they were 45, has a genetic test conducted at her own expense. The test reveals that she has inherited her mother's genetic susceptibility to breast cancer. After applying for employment and being given the position, her HR orientation includes registration for employer-paid health insurance. The insurance questionnaire asks if she suffers from any preexisting medical condition. What should the new employee answer? Suppose that, later on, she desires to take advantage of the employer's wellness program. This includes free annual breast examinations. Should she reveal to the health care provider that she has a genetic susceptibility to breast cancer? If she does so, what obligations does the health care provider have (1) to the employee, (2) to the employer, and (3) to the insurance carrier?

18. A web site reads as follows: "Need to pass a Drug test? Our detox online store is here to help you! Pass a drug test now! Results are guaranteed!!! Our drug detoxification products are produced by the best manufactures and based on alternative or herbal methods of flushing toxins from your system. Nowadays, popular trade publications such as *Men's Health, Glamour, Muscle Media, Whole Foods*, and many others have mentioned these cleansing products as very effective and safe. Pass your drug test with rapid detox now. We take care of our customers and respect privacy! All products will be shipped in plain boxes. Just to let you know—You are not alone!!! Shop with confidence. Do not be afraid to log in and create an account. Overnight shipping is available. Place your order by 2 pm EST and your order will be shipped the same day!" How can an employer guard against employee use of such products to defeat the employer's drug-testing program? Be sure to consider whether your proposed solution(s) themselves create additional privacy concerns for the employer. *See* http://www.stardetox.com/.

19. Beginning a mere week after the terrorist attacks of September 11, 2001, envelopes packed with anthrax spores started turning up in people's mailboxes. Two of those people were sitting U.S. Senators Tom Daschle of South Dakota and Patrick Leahy of Vermont. The *National Enquirer* in Florida and TV network offices in New York also were targeted. The envelopes were all postmarked in the Trenton/Princeton (NJ) area. The FBI visited the biology labs on every college campus along the Route One corridor between New York and Philadelphia. The bureau also intensely investigated Uncle Sam's own bio-weapons facilities, including Fort Detrick in Frederick, Maryland. The investigation proved to be one of needles and haystacks. Eventually, FBI suspicions focused on a bio-weapons researcher named Steven Hatfill. Indeed, after years of investigating, the agency's only "person of interest" was this Fort Detrick alumnus. Although never indicted, Hatfill's POI status was enough to make him a leper to his profession, essentially unemployable. Hatfill eventually was cleared and suspicion shifted to another scientist at the same government facility. That suspect actually committed suicide before being indicted and tried. Should Hatfill be permitted to sue his former employer, the federal government? If so, what legal theories presented in this chapter might apply? On balance, whose interests were more important here, Hatfill's or Uncle Sam's? Did both parties have important privacy interests in this case? At some point in the FBI's investigation, did the balance shift from one of them to other?

20. Pat was a certified registered nurse anesthetist who worked at a hospital. Pat met with his supervisor regarding his job performance. His supervisor told

Pat of complaints he had received from members of the hospital staff, including complaints that Pat was often late for surgeries, did not make proper patient status reviews, and failed to review EKG and lab results in a timely manner. The supervisor warned Pat that his repeated failure to perform patient work-ups in advance of surgery and his careless attitude would no longer be tolerated. No mention of the meeting was placed in Pat's personnel file. Should Pat have a right to see the written records of the alleged complaints? Does your answer change if the complaints are placed in Pat's personnel file? Does your answer to this second question depend in any way upon applicable state law(s)?

The Global Perspective: *International Employment Law and American Immigration Policy*

Before 1964, an American labor lawyer need only have known the National Labor Relations Act to practice competently. Beginning in that fateful year, nearly a half-century ago, federal and state statutory and common law greatly complicated the employment and labor law landscape. Still, a competent employment law lawyer's expertise had no need to extend beyond U.S. borders. As the first decade of the new century draws to a close, employment lawyers and HR executives must be versed in both international law and the employment laws and policies of the world's major nations. Additionally, a working knowledge of U.S. immigration law is virtually a "must," as new arrivals and employees of overseas subsidiaries increasingly figure into the work forces of American-based firms.

International Employment Law and Policy

The ***International Labor Organization (ILO)*** is the branch of the United Nations charged with developing and promulgating uniform labor and employment standards internationally, encouraging member nations to adopt those universal standards, and monitoring compliance by those nations which have adopted them. The ILO, which is based in Geneva, has promulgated a vast scheme of labor and employment laws, regulations, and guidelines. These ILO "laws" cannot supersede an individual nation's sovereignty unless that nation affirmatively adopts any such laws. The United States is not a signatory to many ILO enactments or pronouncements; however, U.S. labor and employment laws in many instances are equal or superior to the ILO scheme in according rights and remedies to workers within our borders (exceptions involve labor organization rights and employment security versus employment at will). However, Americans doing business globally must be mindful of ILO legal principles adopted by the nations in which they are operating and employing personnel. United States embassies and consulates should be consulted not only about the labor and employment laws of the host nation but also about any relevant ILO rules and regulations.

Conventions
International laws, usually sponsored by the United nations or other multi-national organizations, to which a number of nations agree to adhere.

Conventions are "pacts or agreements between states or nations in the nature of a treaty."[1] In the context of international employment law, conventions are the uniform codes of procedure and standards of conduct that the ILO seeks to promulgate and enforce in order to establish international standards for the fair treatment of workers among all member-nations of the United Nations. International conventions to which the United States is a signatory that should be noted when doing business abroad, and that can affect international labor relations and employment litigation, include:

- *Convention on the Service Abroad of Judicial and Extrajudicial Documents in Civil or Commercial Matters.* Facilitates and standardizes the service of legal processes, such as complaints, summons, and subpoenas, in pursuit of litigation, including labor and employment litigation.
- *Convention on the Recognition and Enforcement of Foreign Arbitral Awards.* Assures that signatory states will enforce arbitral awards, including labor and employment arbitration awards, against parties found within their jurisdictions.
- *Convention on the Taking of Evidence Abroad in Civil or Commercial Matters.* A judicial authority (*e.g.*, a court) in one contracting state may request its counterpart in another contracting state to facilitate such discovery activities as the taking of depositions or sworn statements in support of litigation, including labor and employment litigation.
- *Convention on the Civil Aspects of International Child Abduction.* Aims to control and eliminate exploitation of child labor.

The major conventions on labor and employment, adopted under the auspices of the United Nations and the ILO, most of which have not been signed by the United States (primarily because they may conflict with existing U.S. labor and employment laws), involve the abolition of forced labor (signed by the U.S.), employment discrimination, and collective bargaining.

Global Corporate Responsibility
Philosophy which says that corporations should behave as good global citizens.

The fact that more and more business is being conducted across borders has lead to a growing concern about how companies with differing policies should act. ***Global corporate responsibility*** signifies the notion, held by many advocates of workers' rights and environmental issues, that multinational corporations have the ethical obligation to behave in fair and humane ways toward their workers and to pursue "green" policies and practices to protect the environments in which they operate.

ethical DILEMMA

Should Multinational Corporations Be Required to Act According to Ethical Standards in Their Labor and Employment Relations?

According to Senior Fellow and Director of Globalization Studies Susan Aaronson of the Kenan Institute, Washington Center, global corporate social responsibility is:

- A foreign policy issue in that corporations are ambassadors of their nation's values;
- An economic issue in that America's future markets are overseas; and

[1] *Black's Law Dictionary*

- A moral issue on which the reputation of the corporation, its management, and shareholders depends on doing business abroad.

Whether corporate social responsibility extends to treatment of foreign employees may depend upon the policies and laws of the host nation. For example, in a vigorous effort to eradicate child labor and slavery, Brazil has enacted a "National Pact" which includes placing firms profiting from child and slave workers on a so-called "Dirty List."

In the United Kingdom, a nation characterized in the recent past by protection and encouragement of labor unions, a minister of corporate social responsibility was appointed for the first time in 2000. The United Kingdom, Germany, and Belgium require private pension funds to report on the social responsibility performances of the companies in which they have invested their members' contributions. Because of their historically protective attitudes toward their labor forces, it must be noted that private pensions constitute only small fractions of the overall retirement schemes in these nations. Since 2001, the Dutch government has required all firms seeking taxpayer-funded export credits to attest to their adherence to specified social responsibility guidelines. In 2002, France for the first time mandated disclosure of corporate social and environmental performance.

In the United States, the mission of promoting "labor and corporate social responsibility falls to a unit of the Department of State" (DOS). Strengthening respect for worker rights and promoting corporate social responsibility around the world contributes to the U.S. foreign policy goals of democracy promotion, free trade, international development, and human rights.

The State Department's Office of International Labor and Corporate Social Responsibility, part of the Bureau of Democracy, Human Rights and Labor, promotes these issues in partnership with the private sector, organized labor, NGOs, intergovernmental organizations, international organizations, and other U.S. federal agencies.

Key priority areas include:

- Promoting organized labor and their role as reformers in developing countries;
- Partnering with the private sector to protect human rights, including workers' rights, and to promote good governance, transparency, and the rule of law;
- Promoting labor rights through free trade agreements and other international negotiations; and
- Combating child labor, forced labor, and trafficking in persons.

The State Department supports projects that promote these goals, including an antisweatshop initiative to fund the development of approaches to combat sweatshop labor in overseas factories. Since 2000, nearly $18 million in projects have been funded through this initiative.[1]

[1] See http://www.state.gov/g/drl/lbr/

The Alien Tort Claims Act and International Workers' Rights

Alien Tort Claims Act Federal statute which provides a cause of action for aggrieved aliens in U.S. courts.

The ***Alien Tort Claims Act***[2] was enacted in 1789 as part of the original Judiciary Act. In its original form, it simply said that "[t]he district courts shall have original jurisdiction of any civil action by an alien for a tort only, committed in violation of the law of nations or a treaty of

[2] 28 USC 1350.

the United States." For almost two centuries, the statute lay relatively dormant, supporting jurisdiction in only a handful of cases. In recent years, however, the statute has been rediscovered by attorneys seeking to vindicate the rights of foreign workers allegedly oppressed by U.S. multinational corporations.

For example, two United States Courts of Appeals decisions were announced in December, 2008, interpreting the Alien Tort Claims Act as it may or may not apply to labor-related claims. The two decisions offer mixed messages but, by and large, bode well for multinational corporate-defendants.

case 5.1 » Sarei v. Rio Tinto, PLC

2008 WL 5220286 (9th Cir. 2008)

Facts: Bougainville is an island in the South Pacific located just off the main island of Papua New Guinea (PNG). Rich in natural resources, including copper and gold, the island was targeted as a prime mining site by defendants Rio Tinto, PLC, a British and Welsh corporation, and Rio Tinto Limited, an Australian corporation (collectively "Rio Tinto"). Rio Tinto was part of an international mining group that operated more than 60 mines and processing plants in 40 countries, including the United States. To operate a mine on Bougainville, Rio Tinto required and received the assistance of the PNG government. According to the plaintiffs' complaint, beginning in the 1960s Rio Tinto displaced villages, razed massive tracts of rain forest, intensely polluted the land, rivers, and air (with extensive collateral consequences including fatal and chronic illness, death of wildlife and vegetation, and failure of farm land), and systematically discriminated against its Bougainvillian workers, who lived in slave-like conditions.

In November 1988, some Bougainville residents revolted; they sabotaged the mine and forced its closure. After Rio Tinto demanded that the PNG government quash the uprising, the government complied and sent in troops. PNG forces used helicopters and vehicles supplied by Rio Tinto. On February 14, 1990, the country descended into a civil war after government troops slaughtered many Bougainvillians in what has come to be known as the "St. Valentine's Day Massacre."

Unable to resume mining, Rio Tinto threatened to abandon its operations and halt all future investment in PNG unless the government took military action to secure the mine. In April 1990, the PNG government imposed a military blockade on the island that lasted almost a decade. The blockade prevented medicine, clothing, and other necessities from reaching the residents. Under further pressure from Rio Tinto, according to the complaint, the government engaged in aerial bombardment of civilian targets, wanton killing and acts of cruelty, village burning, rape, and pillage. As a result, an estimated 15,000 Bougainvillians, including many children, died. Of the survivors, tens of thousands are displaced and many suffer health problems. In March 2002, the PNG Parliament formalized a peace accord that ended the civil war.

In November 2000, nearly a year and a half before the civil war formally ended, the plaintiffs filed their class action, raising numerous claims under the Alien Tort Statute, 28 U.S.C. Section 1350:

- crimes against humanity resulting from the blockade;
- war crimes for murder and torture;
- violation of the rights to life, health, and security of the person resulting from the environmental damage;
- racial discrimination in destroying villages and the environment, and in working conditions;
- cruel, inhuman, and degrading treatment resulting from the blockade, environmental harm, and displacement;
- violation of international environmental rights resulting from building and operating the mine; and
- a consistent pattern of gross violations of human rights resulting from destruction of the environment, racial discrimination, and PNG military activities. The plaintiffs also raised various non-ATS claims ranging from negligence to public nuisance.

A model of brevity, the Alien Tort Act says, simply, "The district courts shall have original jurisdiction of any civil action by an alien for a tort only, committed in violation of the law of nations or a treaty of the United States." In *Sosa v. Alvarez-Machain*,[1] the high court held, "Though the Alien Tort Statute (ATS) … is a jurisdictional statute, which does not create a statutory cause of action for aliens, it was not intended to lie fallow until specific causes of action were authorized by further legislation, but was meant to have practical effect from the moment that it became law, by providing a basis for district courts to exercise jurisdiction over a modest number of causes of action recognized under the law of nations, such as for offenses against ambassadors, violations of safe conduct, and possibly for piracy." The Court also indicated that plaintiffs should first exhaust causes of action available to them under local law.

Issue: Should the plaintiffs be required to exhaust their other available remedies before being permitted to sue in a U.S. court under the Alien Tort Statute?

Decision: In *Sarel,* the Ninth Circuit, sitting *en banc*, considered the significance of this exhaustion requirement. The plurality opinion noted that, "As the Supreme Court directed in *Sosa,* exhaustion of local remedies should 'certainly' be considered in the 'appropriate case' for claims brought under the ATS.[2] This is an appropriate case for such consideration under both domestic prudential standards and core principles of international law."

Six judges then went on to hold, "As a preliminary matter, to 'exhaust,' it is not sufficient that a plaintiff merely initiate a suit, but rather, the plaintiff must obtain a final decision of the highest court in the hierarchy of courts in the legal system at issue, or a show that the state of the law or availability of remedies would make further appeal futile.... Another basic element is that the remedy must be available, effective, and not futile. To measure effectiveness, a court must look at the circumstances surrounding the access to a remedy and the ultimate utility of the remedy to the petitioner. In addition, '[w]hen a person has obtained favorable decision in a domestic court, but that decision has not been complied with, no further remedies need be exhausted.' A judgment that cannot be enforced is an incomplete, and thus ineffective, remedy. The adequacy determination will also necessarily include an assessment of any delay in the delivery of a decision. We remand to the district court for the limited purpose to determine in the first instance whether to impose an exhaustion requirement on plaintiffs."

---

[1]124 S.Ct. 2739, 542 U.S. 692, 159 L.Ed.2d 718 (2004) This colorful case concerned a Mexican physician accused by U.S. authorities of participating in the torture and death of a U.S. Drug Enforcement Agency officer south of the border. The doctor was kidnapped by the famous bounty hunter Duane "Dog" Chapman—http://www.dogthebountyhunter.com/—and brought back to Texas to stand trial.

[2]542 U.S. at 733 n. 21.

case 5.2 » Romero v. Drummond Company, Inc.

2008 WL 5274192 (11th Cir. 2008)

A Colombian labor union sued executives of Drummond, Ltd., the Colombian subsidiary of an American coal mining company located principally in Alabama, paid paramilitary operatives to torture and assassinate leaders of the union, SINTRAMIENERGETICA. In 2002 and 2003, the union and several of its leaders and relatives of deceased leaders sued Drummond and its parent company and executives under the Alien Tort Statute and the Torture Victim Protection Act of 1991. The Torture Act establishes a separate cause of action for victims of torture and extrajudicial killing. The district court consolidated the complaints and later granted partial summary judgment against them; one claim for relief—that Drummond aided and abetted the killings, which were war crimes—remained. At a trial of that claim, the jury returned a verdict for Drummond. The plaintiffs appealed the partial summary judgment and a series of discovery and evidentiary rulings made before and during the trial. Long after the discovery deadline had been extended and later expired, the plaintiffs moved for continuances and the admission of the testimonies of several new witnesses, and some of those requests were denied. Drummond challenged the subject-matter jurisdiction of the district court.

In the underlying complaints in this case, the union, its leaders, and relatives of its leaders complained that Augusto Jimenez, the president of the mining operations of Drummond, Ltd., with the knowledge of company executives in the United States, hired paramilitaries affiliated with the United Self-Defense Forces of Colombia to torture union leaders Juan Aquas Romero, Jimmy Rubio Suarez, and Francisco Ruiz Daza, and to kill union leaders Valmore Locarno Rodriquez, Victor Hugo Orcasita Amaya, and Gustavo Soler Mora. The complaints included claims of torture, extrajudicial killing, and denials of the right to associate, lodged under the Alien Tort Statute, claims of torture and extrajudicial killing, grouped under the

Torture Act, a claim of wrongful death under Colombian law, and claims for assault, intentional infliction of emotional distress, negligent infliction of emotional distress, negligent supervision, and false imprisonment under Alabama law.

On these complex facts and complicated legal issues, the appellate court held:

(1) Torture Victim Protection Act allows suits against corporate defendants;
(2) Alien Tort Statute contains no express exception for corporations, and the statute grants jurisdiction over complaints of torture against corporate defendants;
(3) plaintiffs failed to satisfy "state action" requirement of the Torture Victim Protection Act;
(4) district court did not abuse its discretion in refusing to exercise supplemental jurisdiction over plaintiffs' wrongful death claim under Colombian law;
(5) district court did not abuse its discretion in denying plaintiffs' motion for additional continuance when they were not able to complete letter rogatory process to secure witness' testimony for rescheduled trial date;
(6) district court did not abuse its discretion in excluding testimony of late-disclosed witnesses; and
(7) district court did not abuse its discretion in refusing to allow plaintiffs' proffered experts to testify.

In sum, the panel affirmed the district judge, essentially defeating the plaintiffs' claims.

Case Questions

1. Why didn't the plaintiffs seek to secure justice in their own countries?
2. In *Romero*, the plaintiffs sought to have the U.S. federal judge take jurisdiction of their wrongful death claim, brought under Colombian law. Wouldn't a Colombian court be better equipped to adjudicate this claim? Why did they prefer to bring it into an American courtroom?
3. If a multinational corporation strictly abides by the laws of each country in which it does business, affording its workers in each country whatever rights and benefits are required by local law, shouldn't this be sufficient to insulate such company from legal liability? Don't the shareholders of such a corporation have the right to expect management to take advantage of business-favorable laws and policies to maximize the firm's profits?
4. In these two cases, are the unions' and workers' grievances so closely connected to the fundamental labor-relations policies of the their respective countries that a U.S. court would be intruding upon foreign policy issues, which are the exclusive realm of the executive branch of our government, if it were to adjudicate these cases?
5. Why does the court in *Sarei* suggest that the plaintiffs should first have to exhaust their local (i.e., home country) remedies before coming into a U.S. courtroom?

One knowledgeable observer, viewing the two circuit court decisions with an eye fixed on the potential of the two federal statutes' applicability in the global environmental arena, commented, "Like the earlier 9th Cir. case, this [11th Circuit] case demonstrates that the use of the Alien Tort Statute to establish jurisdiction and the use of the Torture Act will be difficult in the context of environmental and toxic tort matters occurring in third countries."[3] Given that each case enjoys a strong nexus to labor and employment law, we must conclude that this commentator's conclusion applies with equal force to foreign labor unions and labor leaders, as well as classes of workers, who had hopes of bringing tort claims into American federal courts against multinational corporations headquartered in the U.S. Like the ILO conventions, most of which the U.S. has declined to sign, and the idealistic

[3]Thomas H. Clarke, Jr., "Like the earlier reported 9th Circuit case, this recent 11th Circuit case shows that using the Alien Tort Statute or the Torture Act in an environmental context will be quite difficult," Lexis-Nexis Environmental & Climate Change Center, December 26, 2008, http://law.lexisnexis.com/practiceareas/Torts/General-Interest

concept of corporate responsibility, discussed earlier (see the Ethical Dilemma), the Alien Tort Statute is unlikely to have a high impact upon the way U.S. corporations deal with their overseas employees. For workers and reformers seeking to impact American multinationals, especially in nations which lack meaningful human rights and labor legislation, global labor organizations may present the highest prospect of success.

Global Labor Unions

Global Unions
International labor organizations, which typically attempt to organize employees of globalized industries.

Recently the international trade union movement has begun to use the term ***Global Unions*** as an umbrella designation. The components of Global Unions include the International Confederation of Free Trade Unions, which represents national trade union centers around the globe and the Union Network International.

Union Network International (UNI)

Union Network International (UNI) is an organization aimed at meeting the globalization of corporations, trade, and manufacturing head on. Reasoning that the global labor market no longer recognizes or is confined within the borders of traditional nation-states, UNI seeks to organize workers on an international scale. The organization targets multinational corporations, seeking to apply global pressure in order to organize local and regional corporate facilities. "When companies are local, unions can be local; when companies are national, unions must be national; when companies are global, unions must be global. Our aim is to build more effective alliances in multinationals," UNI explains.[4]

At its August 2005 Chicago convention, UNI announced that signing global agreements with targeted companies would be that organization's focus going forward. In 2007, UNI expanded its attention to monitoring private equity funds. In a March 2007 press release, UNI stated:

> "In the furor that has enveloped private equity these past weeks, one of the criticisms of their way of doing business is the absence of any regard to corporate social responsibility (CSR). UNI Global Union has had a look at the websites of a range of the key private equity funds and has found precious few, if any, references to CSR, to the ILO core conventions, the UN Global Compact or the UN Principles for Responsible Investment (UNPRI). We are struck by the lack of any commitment to these global principles, which have been forged to improve the accountability and responsibility of the business community to all shareholders.... It is challenging to find even a minor reference to CSR matters among fund managers or those who spend time assessing trends in private equity funds. Issues of human rights, labor standards, environment and even corporate governance are seldom discussed as pros and cons of private equity. The fact that private equity funds closely guard their information represents a substantial impediment to actively analyzing the CSR performance of companies they hold. In the weeks to come, we will be keeping a close watch on whether there will be a shift towards more transparency, disclosure or any commitment to CSR principles."

[4]www.union-network.org

UNI claims to hold the allegiance of approximately 15 million workers in 900 unions in 150 countries, representing employees in the following economic sectors:

- Commerce
- Electricity
- Finance
- Gaming
- Graphical
- Hair and beauty
- IBITS (industry, business services, information and computer technology)
- Media, entertainment, and the arts
- Postal
- Property services (cleaning and security)
- Social insurance
- Telecom
- Tourism[5]

UNI has targeted a list of 100 multinational employers. As of early 2009, UNI had achieved labor contracts with the following targeted corporations:

- Carrefour (a Paris-based food retailer)
- Hennes & Mauritz of Sweden (trading as H&M stores in the United States)
- Falck (a Danish rescue, health care, and safety-training organization)
- Internet Security Systems (based in Atlanta, GA)
- Metro AG of Germany
- OTE (Greek telecommunications company)
- Telefónica (the Spanish telecom provider)[6]

In total, according to UNIs General Secretary Philip Jennings, the organization now boasts 50 signed collective agreements and another 50 in various stages of negotiation.[7]

---

[5]http://www.union-network.org

[6]http://www.union-network.org/UNIsite/In_Depth/Multinationals/Multinationals.html

[7]UNI's contact information is as follows:
Union Network International
8–10 Avenue Reverdil
CH-1260 Nyon, Switzerland
Tel. +41 22 365 21 00
Fax: +41 22 365 21 21
E-mail: contact@union-network.org
Website: www.union-network.org

The WORKING Law

Global Unions Seek to Organize American Workers Through the "Back Door"

A good example of how this "back door" organizing can happen—offered by President Andy Stern of the Service Employees International Union (SEIU)—was the acquisition of three well-known U.S. security firms by Sweden-based Securitas. The American companies were Pinkerton, Burns International Services, and Loomis Fargo. At about the same time, Group 4 Securicor, a British-Danish outfit, picked up Wackenhut. "All of a sudden," commented Stern, "we found ourselves needing to talk more to CEOs in Europe than in America."

Attorney Gerald Hathaway of the New York firm Littler Mendelson noted that labor organizations are woven into the socioeconomic fabric of continental nations such as Germany, where union leaders commonly serve on boards of directors. Unions such as the SEIU are finding that they can deal with these parent corporations, imposing terms and conditions upon their U.S. subsidiaries.

UNI and similar international labor organizations seek to sign so-called "global framework agreements" capable of following the corporation to wherever it establishes operations around the world. The concept of a global agreement is well known in American labor relations, with unions hoping to represent a single employer's employees at multiple locations negotiating for an umbrella agreement that will apply wherever the union later achieves majority support from a location's workforce.[1]

See http://www.workforce.com/archive/feature/24/26/53/index.php?ht5labor%20unions%20labor%20unions

---

[1]See, e.g., *Raley's and United Food and Commercial Workers*, 336 NLRB 374 (2001). (The parties attempted to negotiate a global agreement that would cover any future demands for recognition by Local 588. They subsequently signed two separate agreements under which the Respondent recognized Local 588, pursuant to a card check, as the representative of its employees at the Yreka store and at one of the Redding stores.)

Concept *Summary* » 5.1

International Labor and Employment Law and Policy

- Sources:
  - Corporate responsibility: Ethical principle incorporated into some nations' law and policy
  - International Labor Organization: UN agency that promulgates international conventions
  - Alien Tort Claims Act: Old U.S. statute subject to 21st century interpretations
  - Global Labor Unions: Seek to foster workplace justice through collective bargaining agreements (labor contracts)

Immigration Law and Policy

The fundamental U.S. immigration statute is the Immigration and Nationality Act (INA) of 1952. Prior to its passage, U.S. immigration was governed by a variety of federal statutes, which were not collected under a single title of the U.S. Code.

Immigration Reform and Control Act of 1986

Immigration Reform and Control Act (IRCA) of 1986
The most recent major overhaul of U.S immigration law.

The last major overhaul of the U.S. immigration statutory scheme, founded upon the 1952 law, occurred more nearly a quarter of a century ago. The purposes of the ***Immigration Reform and Control Act (IRCA) of 1986*** were to:

- Provide a solution for controlling illegal immigration to the United States;
- Make some changes in the U.S. system of legal immigration; and
- Provide a controlled legalization program for undocumented aliens who entered the United States before 1982.

Primarily by the creation of civil and criminal penalties for employers who hire undocumented (illegal) aliens, IRCA intended to stem the flow of illegal immigrants. IRCA altered several immigration provisions of the INA of 1952. First, a new immigrant category for dependents of employees of international organizations was created. IRCA recognized the unique position of children and spouses of long-term international organization employees when those employees die, transfer, or retire. It is often difficult for children and spouses to become reoriented to their original society and culture. For all purposes, these individuals are "Americanized." The special immigrant category recognizes their Americanization and allows the individuals to remain in this country if they meet certain residence requirements.

Second, IRCA restricted the ability of many foreign students to adjust their status to that of lawful permanent resident aliens. This modification was aimed at reducing the number of foreign students who remain in the United States. IRCA also altered the allocation of visas and created a visa waiver program.

Finally, IRCA modified the former H-2 program for temporary workers by adding the H-2A program for temporary agricultural workers. It also established a mechanism by which "special agricultural workers" are admitted to perform field work in perishable crops. Under this mechanism, agricultural workers move freely between employers without penalty and are fully protected under all federal, state, and local labor laws. This mechanism creates a legal workforce without decreasing the number of workers available to harvest perishable crops.

IRCA also provided a one-shot amnesty program under which illegal aliens who entered the United States before January 1, 1982, could become legalized. Applications for the amnesty program were accepted for an 18-month period that ended in April 1988. IRCA "grandfathered" workers hired prior to November 6, 1986; however, although the employers were not subject to sanctions, the grandfather provisions of IRCA did not make it lawful for an unauthorized alien to accept employment. Consequently, the alien was (and is) still subject to deportation for accepting employment.

Today, experts estimate that more than 12 million illegal aliens are living in the U.S., and some pundits predict that the number is substantially higher.

Employer Compliance with IRCA

Employers must verify the employment eligibility of any employee hired. The preemployment question that must be asked is: Is the employee a U.S. citizen or lawfully authorized to work in the United States? To comply with verification requirements, an employer must show that it has examined documents that establish both:

- the employment authorization; and
- the identity of the employee.

A U.S. passport, certificate of U.S. citizenship, certificate of naturalization, or certain resident alien cards establish both. Employment authorization documents include a Social Security card or a birth certificate. Identity documents include a driver's license, other state-issued card, or under certain circumstances, other documentation approved by the Attorney General.

One of the proposals afloat in the Congress for immigrant verification and control is an electronic employment-verification system aimed at screening approximately 54 million new hires annually. The Government Accountability Office estimates that creation, dissemination, and operation of this proposed system could cost $11.7 billion. Employer cost per employee is expected to run somewhere between $10 and $50. One thing seems certain: the seldom-enforced requirement of the Immigration Reform and Control Act of 1986 (passed the last time the United States granted amnesty to its illegal aliens) that employers verify the legitimacy of their workers will no longer be winked at by the federal government, regardless of what other provisions a new immigration statute may contain.

Documents HR Offices May Use to Verify New Employees' Eligibility

For identity:

- Driver's license
- Other state-issued I.D. card (e.g., a Pennsylvania Liquor Control Board I.D. card)

For employment authorization:

- Social Security card
- Birth certificate

For satisfaction of both categories:

- U.S. passport
- Certificate of U.S. citizenship
- Certificate of naturalization
- Certain resident-alien cards
- Unexpired foreign passport with attached visa authorizing U.S. employment
- Alien registration card with photo

The employer is expected to examine the proffered documents. If they appear reasonably on their face to be genuine and to relate to the person presenting them, they are to be accepted. To refuse to accept such documents, in fact, may be viewed by the INS as an unfair immigration-related employment practice. On the other hand, if the document does not appear reasonably on its face to be genuine or to relate to the person presenting it, the employer is expected to refuse to accept it. Instead, that employer should contact the local INS office closest to the employer's facility and request assistance. Under these circumstances, that employer will not be guilty of a verification violation and, all else being equal, should not be charged. If charged, the employer can raise the "good faith" defense, since the employer did not knowingly hire an illegal alien. Only original documents are acceptable. The one exception to this hard-and-fast rule is a certified copy of a birth certificate.

An employee who fails to provide required documentation within three business days of being hired may be terminated from employment. If the employee claims the documents were lost or stolen, a receipt for a request for replacement documents will suffice for the time being. In that case, the employee has an additional 90 days in which to present those replacement documents to the employer, whose human resources department should make sure that there is a follow-up request should the employee fail to proffer the replacement documents within the time allotted by law. Remember, these policies must be applied uniformly to all employees in order to avoid a charge of immigrant-related discrimination.

Who Enforces U.S. Immigration Laws?

- **U.S. Citizenship and Immigration Services:** On March 1, 2003, service and benefit functions of the U.S. Immigration and Naturalization Service (INS) transitioned into the Department of Homeland Security (DHS) as the U.S. Citizenship and Immigration Services (USCIS). The president nominated Eduardo Aguirre to lead the USCIS; he was confirmed by the Senate on June 19, 2003. The USCIS is responsible for the administration of immigration and naturalization adjudication functions and establishing immigration services policies and priorities. These functions include:
    - adjudication of immigrant visa petitions;
    - adjudication of naturalization petitions;
    - adjudication of asylum and refugee applications;
    - adjudications performed at the service centers, and
    - all other adjudications performed by the INS.[8]
- **U.S. Immigration and Customs Enforcement:** Created in March 2003, Immigration and Customs Enforcement (ICE) is the largest investigative branch of the Department of Homeland Security (DHS). The agency was created after [September 11, 2001] by combining the law enforcement arms of the former [INS] and the former U.S. Customs Service, to more effectively enforce our immigration and customs laws so as to protect the United States against terrorist attacks. ICE does this by targeting illegal immigrants: the

[8]http://www.uscis.gov/graphics/aboutus/index.htm

people, money, and materials that support terrorism and other criminal activities. ICE is a key component of the DHS "layered defense" approach to protecting the nation.[9]

- **U.S. Department of Justice:** The DOJ mission statement provides this list of responsibilities: "to enforce the law and defend the interests of the United States according to the law; to ensure public safety against threats foreign and domestic; to provide federal leadership in preventing and controlling crime; to seek just punishment for those guilty of unlawful behavior; and to ensure fair and impartial administration of justice for all Americans."[10]

  The Office of Special Counsel for Immigration-Related Unfair Employment Practices (OSC), in the Civil Rights Division, is responsible for enforcing the antidiscrimination provisions of the Immigration and Nationality Act (INA), 8 U.S.C. § 1324b, which protect U.S. citizens and legal immigrants from employment discrimination based upon citizenship or immigration status and national origin, from unfair documentary practices relating to the employment eligibility verification process, and from retaliation.[11]
- **U.S. Social Security Administration:** The Social Security Administration (SSA) is headquartered in Baltimore, Maryland, and has ten regional offices and 1,300 local offices nationwide. [The agency] pays retirement, disability, and survivors benefits to workers and their families and administers the Supplemental Security Income program. [It] also issues Social Security numbers.[12]
- **Federal Bureau of Investigation:** Since the tragic events of September 11, 2001, one week into [its new director's] term, the Bureau became responsible for spearheading what is perhaps the most extensive reorganization the FBI has experienced since its conception. By May 2002, the director articulated ten top FBI priorities:
  - protecting the United States from terrorist attacks, from foreign intelligence operations, and from cyber-based attacks and high-technology crimes;
  - combating public corruption at all levels;
  - protecting civil rights;
  - combating international and national organized crime, major white-collar crime, and significant violent crime;
  - supporting our law enforcement and intelligence partners; and
  - upgrading FBI technology.

  "While we remain committed to our other important national security and law enforcement responsibilities, the prevention of terrorism takes precedence in our thinking and planning; in our hiring and staffing; in our training and technologies; and, most importantly, in our investigations," the Director has said.[13]

---

[9]http://www.ice.gov/about/index.htm

[10]http://www.usdoj.gov/02organizations/

[11]http://www.usdoj.gov/crt/osc/htm/WebOverview2005.htm

[12]http://www.ssa.gov/aboutus/

[13]http://www.fbi.gov/aboutus.htm

- **U.S. Department of Labor:** The Department of Labor fosters and promotes the welfare of the job seekers, wage earners, and retirees of the United States by improving their working conditions, advancing their opportunities for profitable employment, protecting their retirement and health care benefits, helping employers find workers, strengthening free collective bargaining, and tracking changes in employment, prices, and other national economic measurements. In carrying out this mission, the Department administers a variety of federal labor laws, including those that guarantee workers' rights to safe and healthful working conditions; a minimum hourly wage and overtime pay; freedom from employment discrimination; unemployment insurance; and other income support.[14]

  The Immigration and Nationality Act (INA) sets forth the conditions for the temporary and permanent employment of aliens in the United States and includes provisions that address employment eligibility and employment verification. These provisions apply to all employers. DOL provides a wide variety of resources to aid employers with compliance.[15]
- **U.S. Department of State:** The Department of State's mission statement reads as follows: "Create a more secure, democratic, and prosperous world for the benefit of the American people and the international community."[16] The Bureau of Consular Affairs within the State Department manages the visa process.[17]

Anatomy of an ICE Raid

During the first week of March 2007, ICE agents raided a leather factory in New Bedford, Massachusetts. Supported by local law enforcement, ICE arrested 361 workers. Most were female sewing-machine operators from Guatamala or El Salvador. The Michael Bianco plant employed a total of 500 workers, who made backpacks and vests for the U.S. military under an $83 million federal contract.

The detainees were taken to Fort Devens, a former Army base near Ayer, Massachusetts. The following day, some 60 women, sole caretakers of their children, were released. The remaining workers were dispersed to detention centers and jails for processing of their cases.

Also arrested were factory-owner Francesco Insolia and four plant managers. They were soon released on bail.

The arrests were hardly completed before the public relations war commenced. In a public statement, the U.S. attorney characterized the illegals as "exploited workers with low-paying jobs and horrible working conditions." At a gathering in a local church, relatives of those arrested confirmed the U.S. attorney's claims of exploitative conditions in the factory. One speaker was quoted in the media as saying, "They are only allowed two minutes to use the bathrooms and threatened with a fine of $20 if they return late to the job."

Ultimately, the war of words made its way into a federal courthouse. By November 2007, the detainees' main case had climbed all the way up into the lofty realm of the U.S. Court of Appeals for the Second Circuit, sitting in Boston:

---

[14]http://www.dol.gov/opa/aboutdol/mission.htm

[15]http://www.dol.gov/compliance/laws/comp-ina.htm

[16]http://www.state.gov/s/d/rm/rls/dosstrat/2004/23503.htm

[17]Information on all types of visas can be found at http://travel.state.gov/visa/visa_1750.html

case 5.3 » AGUILAR V. U.S. IMMIGRATION AND CUSTOMS ENFORCEMENT

2007 WL 4171244 (U.S. Ct. App. 1st Cir.)

On March 6, 2007, federal officers conducted a raid as part of "Operation United Front." The raid targeted Michael Bianco, Inc., a Department of Defense contractor suspected of employing large numbers of illegal aliens. Immigration and Customs Enforcement (ICE) agents, armed with search and arrest warrants, appeared unannounced at the factory, arrested five executives on immigration-related criminal charges, and took more than 300 rank-and-file employees into custody for civil immigration infractions. The ICE agents cast a wide net and paid little attention to the detainees' individual or family circumstances.

The government's subsequent actions regarding the undocumented workers who were swept up in the net lie at the epicenter of this litigation. After releasing dozens of employees determined either to be minors or to be legally residing in the United States, ICE transported the remaining detainees to Fort Devens (a holding facility in Ayer, Massachusetts). Citing a shortage of available bed space in Massachusetts, ICE then began transferring substantial numbers of aliens to faraway detention and removal operations centers (DROs). For example, on March 7, 90 detainees were flown to a DRO in Harlingen, Texas, and the next day 116 more were flown to a DRO in El Paso, Texas.

ICE attempted to coordinate its maneuvers with the Massachusetts Department of Social Services (DSS) to ensure the proper care of family members. It took steps to address concerns about child welfare and released several detainees for humanitarian reasons. Still, the petitioners allege (and, for present purposes, we accept) that ICE gave social welfare agencies insufficient notice of the raid, that caseworkers were denied access to detainees until after the first group had been transferred, and that various ICE actions temporarily thwarted any effective investigation into the detainees' needs. As a result, a substantial number of the detainees' minor children were left for varying periods of time without adult supervision.

With respect to the detainees themselves, the petitioners averred that ICE inhibited their exercise of the right to counsel. According to the petitioners, a squad of volunteer lawyers who had offered to provide the detainees with guidance was turned away from Fort Devens on March 7. The next day, the lawyers were allowed to meet with those detainees (some thirty in number) who had expressly requested legal advice. The petitioners allege that, notwithstanding this largesse, some detainees were denied access to counsel after they arrived in Texas.

On the afternoon of March 8, the Guatemalan consul, acting as next friend of the detainees (many of whom were Guatemalan nationals), filed a petition for a writ of habeas corpus and a complaint for declaratory and injunctive relief in the United States District Court for the District of Massachusetts. The action sought the detainees' immediate release or, in the alternative, a temporary restraining order halting further transfers. The district court enjoined ICE from moving any of the remaining detainees out of Massachusetts pending further order of the court....

The district court patiently sorted through them and, in a thoughtful rescript, eventually dismissed the action for want of subject matter jurisdiction.... We have scoured the case law for any authority suggesting that claims similar to those asserted here are actionable under the substantive component of the Due Process Clause, and we have found none. That chasm is important because, given the scarcity of 'guideposts for responsible decision-making in this uncharted area,' courts must be 'reluctant to expand the concept of substantive due process.'[1]

This unfortunate case is a paradigmatic example of an instance in which the prudential principle announced by the *Collins* Court should be heeded. Accordingly, we dismiss the petitioners' substantive due process claims for failure to satisfy the prerequisites of Federal Rule of Civil Procedure 12(b)(6)....

We are sensitive to the concerns raised by the petitioners and are conscious that undocumented workers, like all persons who are on American soil, have certain inalienable rights. But in the first instance, it is Congress—not the judiciary—that has the responsibility of prescribing a framework for the vindication of those rights. When Congress speaks clearly and formulates a regime that satisfies constitutional imperatives, the courts must follow Congress's lead. In that sense, it does not matter whether a court approves or disapproves of an agency's *modus operandi.*

We add only two comments. First, we applaud the able district judge for the skill and sensitivity with which he handled this highly charged case. Second, we express our hope that ICE, though it has prevailed, nonetheless will treat this chiaroscuro series of events as a learning experience in order to devise better, less ham-handed ways of carrying out its important responsibilities.

Case Questions

1. The due process clauses of the Fifth and Fourteenth Amendments decree that "no person" may be deprived of life, liberty or property without due process of law. If the detainees in this case, who clearly are persons if not U.S. citizens, cannot secure their due process rights in a federal court, where do you think they will be secured?
2. Assuming that, following dismissal of their federal court case, the detainees are afforded an opportunity to be heard in some other forum, such as in front of an immigration judge,[2] do you think it would be more fair to place the burden of proving their right to stay in the U.S., or lack of such a right, upon the detainees or the ICE agency?
3. In what ways, if any, do you think that the ICE agency (in the words of the court) was "ham-handed"?
4. If the detainees ultimately are found to be illegal aliens, what penalty should be imposed upon them? What if some of them are found to be repeat offenders? What if they can prove they have children who were born in the United States?
5. Does this case suggest to you that the U.S. system for dealing with illegal-alien workers requires reforming? If so, what policy recommendations would you make to President Obama, if asked?

[1] *Washington v. Glucksberg*, 521 U.S. 702, 720, 117 S.Ct. 2258, 138 L.Ed.2d 772 (1997) (*quoting Collins v. Harker Heights*, 503 U.S. 115, 125, 112 S.Ct. 1061, 117 L.Ed.2d 261 (1992)).

[2] See http://www.usdoj.gov/eoir/ocijinfo.htm

Aftermath

On November 4, 2007, the *Boston Globe* reported, "The New Bedford leather goods company that helped push deportation methods into the national spotlight when it was raided by federal immigration agents in March has been sold to a Missouri-based manufacturer of military and law enforcement gear. Michael Bianco Inc., whose top officers were indicted in August for allegedly taking overt steps to shield illegal workers from authorities and help them stay in this country, was sold to Eagle Industries Inc., a longtime competitor, according to David Costello, the buyer's Boston-based spokesman." The *Globe* added, "Following the raid, the federal Occupational Safety and Health Administration fined Bianco $45,000 after identifying 15 violations, including chemical, mechanical, and electrical hazards."[18]

The U.S. attorney's press release, announcing the indictments of the managers, stated, "If convicted, INSOLIA, COSTA and MELO each face a maximum sentence of 10 years in prison, a $250,000 fine, a $100 special assessment, and at least two years of supervised release on the charge of conspiring to harbor illegal aliens; and 6 months in prison, a $100 special assessment, and $10,000 fine for each illegal alien hired by MBI on the conspiracy to hire illegal aliens charge."

State and Local Involvement with Illegal Immigrants

As a general proposition, immigration law and policy are deemed to be the exclusive provinces of the federal government. State and local governments are usually deemed to be preempted from intruding into this area of the law. However, in recent years, many state and local governments have become frustrated with federal inaction or ineffectiveness in the face of rapidly rising numbers of illegal-immigrant workers, who make claims upon public services and, allegedly, increase crime rates in communities where they settle.

[18] http://boston.com/news/local/articles/2007/11/04/new_bedford_factory_is_sold_was_site_of_ immigration_raid/

In early 2006, the tiny Pennsylvania town of Hazleton, sitting atop the state's central-eastern anthracite coal fields, made national and international news by enacting a statute aimed as punishing, among others, employers who hired illegal aliens. Although the Hazleton ordinance was soon stymied by a federal court injunction on the ground that it is preempted by federal immigration and labor laws, more than 100 U.S. municipalities in twenty-seven states have taken up consideration of ordinances aimed at dealing with illegal aliens. Among the early entrants in this controversial legal arena were:

California

On October 4, 2006, the city of Escondido passed an ordinance by a city council vote of 3–2. According to the *San Diego Union Tribune*, "Under the ordinance, residents, businesses and city officials can file written complaints with the city if they suspect a landlord is renting to illegal immigrants. Complaints based 'solely or primarily on the basis of national origin, ethnicity, or race shall be deemed invalid,' the ordinance says. After complaints are filed, landlords would have to provide documentation to the city of their tenants' immigration status. The city would then ask the federal government to verify the documents. If tenants are found to be illegal immigrants, landlords would be given 10 days to evict them or face suspension of their business licenses. Repeat offenders could face misdemeanor charges and fines."

Missouri

During the summer of 2006, the alderman of Valley Park passed an ordinance which said that landlords could be fined for renting to illegal immigrants, and businesses could lose their licenses for five years for hiring them. In March 2007, the ordinance was declared illegal by a state court. According to the *St. Louis Post-Dispatch*, the judge ruled that the ordinances conflicted with state landlord-tenant laws—which spell out precise rules for how tenants can be evicted—and that a city of Valley Park's size cannot levy such damaging penalties against businesses.

The Board of Aldermen has tinkered with the ordinances. Instead of fining landlords, the new version says landlords can lose their occupancy permits if they are found renting to illegals. Another change: businesses caught employing illegals can lose their licenses for up to 20 days, instead of five years.

Texas

In November 2006, the city council of Farmers Branch unanimously passed an ordinance authorizing fines for landlords who rent to illegal aliens and also declared English to be the official language of the community. The council indicated at time of passage its expectation of litigation challenging the law.

Virtually all such ordinances, after enactment, have been challenged by the ACLU and/or proimmigration interest groups. So far as we are aware, none was being actively enforced at the time this supplement went to press. The successful challenge of Valley Park, Missouri's ordinance in state court on the basis of conflict with statewide landlord–tenant laws is the exception. In most cases, challenges are grounded upon conflicts with the U.S. Constitution and/or federal statutory law. Typically, courtroom challenges revolve around the Fourteenth Amendment to the U.S. Constitution, which requires among other things that all persons be accorded due process of law. For instance, in the Hazleton [PA] case itself, U.S. District Judge James M. Munley reportedly ruminated on the record about due process, where the ordinance refers appeals to a local District Justice … an official deemed by the Plaintiff ACLU to be too lowly and uninformed on immigration law to determine such appeals. Other challenges are grounded upon notions of federal preemption. These cases contend that the Congress has co-opted the field of immigration law, as is appropriate for an issue which affects all areas of the U.S. and implicates our national borders.

The Legal Arizona Workers Act

One state statute, which stands out from the crowd by virtue of having so far survived all legal challenges is the Legal Arizona Workers Act.[19] In December 2007, a federal judge considered whether or not the new law could withstand a typical constitutional challenge.

case 5.4 » ARIZONA CONTRACTORS ASSOCIATION, INC. v. NAPOLITANO

2007 WL 4293641 (D. AZ 2007)

Facts: When the plaintiffs initiated their challenge to the statute, the judge initially held that, since county prosecutors were charged with enforcing the law, they were the proper defendants in the suit. The plaintiffs, therefore, were dismissed for lacking standing. Undeterred, they returned to court, seeking to cure the standing issue and obtain a temporary restraining order. The court this time ordered a hearing on the motion for a temporary restraining order (TRO), which would prevent enforcement of the law pending a final resolution of their constitutional challenge. The federal judge declined to issue the TRO.

Issue: Is the Legal Arizona Workers Act Preempted by federal immigration law?

Decision: During the subsequent 12 months, the matter proceeded to hearing, and the district court dismissed the Arizona attorney general for lack of subject matter jurisdiction, because he lacked the authority to bring enforcement actions. The court ruled in favor of the remaining defendants on the merits. It held that the act is not expressly preempted by IRCA because the act is a licensing law within the meaning of the federal statute's savings clause. It held that neither the act's sanction provisions, nor the provision mandating use of the federal government's E-Verify identification system, was inconsistent with federal policy, and thus they were not impliedly preempted. Finally, the court held that the act did not, on its face, violate due process because employers' due process rights were adequately protected.

The plaintiffs appealed. Thus, at last, the Ninth Circuit confronted the case on its merits. In September, the appeals court issued its decision. The appeals panel held:

> "(1) Act was licensing measure that fell within savings clause of Immigration Reform and Control Act's (IRCA) preemption provision;
> (2) Act was not impliedly preempted by IRCA; and
> (3) Act did not, on its face, violate employers' right to procedural due process."[1]

[1]Chicanos Por La Causa, Inc. v. Napolitano, 544 F.3d 976 (9 Cir. 2008).

«

In the wake of the Ninth's Circuit's blessing on the act, the Arizona Attorney general has moved forward with its implementation.[20] According to the official legislative notice to employers, "A judicial determination of a violation of this new state law will subject the employer to probation, and may subject the employer to a suspension or revocation of all licenses as defined in section 23-211, Arizona Revised Statutes depending on the following conditions:

[19]Ariz.Rev.Stat. §§ 23–211 to 23–216.

[20]See http://www.azag.gov/LegalAZWorkersAct/FAQ.html

- For a first violation of an employer *knowingly* hiring an unauthorized alien, the court shall order mandatory three years' probation and may suspend all licenses held by the employer for a maximum of ten days. The employer must file a signed sworn affidavit with the county attorney within three business days, stating that the employer has fired all unauthorized aliens and that the employer will not intentionally or knowingly employ any unauthorized alien.
- For a first violation of an employer *intentionally* hiring an unauthorized alien, the court shall order a mandatory five years' probation and order the appropriate licensing agencies to suspend all licenses held by the employer for a minimum of ten days. The employer must file a signed sworn affidavit, stating that the employer has fired all unauthorized aliens and that the employer will not intentionally or knowingly employ any unauthorized alien with the county attorney. A license that is suspended will remain suspended until the employer files a signed sworn affidavit.
- For a second violation of this new state law committed during a period of probation, the court will order the appropriate licensing agencies to permanently revoke all licenses that are held by the employer."[21]
- Licenses that can be lost under the law include, "any agency permit, certificate, approval, registration, charter or similar form of authorization that is required by law and that is issued by any agency for the purposes of operating a business in this state."[22]

Concept *Summary* » 5.2

IMMIGRATION LAW AND ENFORCEMENT

- Major federal statutes:
  - Immigration and Nationality Act of 1952 is the foundational statute upon which U.S. immigration policy, following the Second World War, was built.
  - Immigration Reform and Control Act of 1986 is the single most sweeping revision of the 1952 statute. Significantly, it was intended to stem the flow of illegal immigrants into the U.S. labor market.
- Major federal agencies:
  - Department of Homeland Security
    - U.S. Immigration and Customs Enforcement (ICE): the immigration police
    - U.S. Citizenship and Immigration Service (USCIS): processes applications for immigrant and nonimmigrant presence in the U.S.
  - Department of Justice
    - Federal Bureau of Investigation (FBI): Assists Home Security with domestic law enforcement, e.g., terrorists
    - Drug Enforcement Agency: Assists where drug smuggling is a factor
  - Department of Labor: Processes labor determinations related to temporary worker visas
  - Department of State: Issues visas, supervises exchange-visitor programs

---

[21]Notice available at http://www.azleg.gov/Employer_Notice.asp

[22]Ariz. Rev. Stats. 23-211 (9)(a).

CHAPTER REVIEW

» Key Terms

International Labor Organization (ILO)	« 83	***global corporate responsibility***	« 84	***Global Unions***	« 89
conventions	« 84	***Alien Tort Claims Act***	« 85	***Immigration Reform and Control Act (IRCA) of 1986***	« 92

» Summary

- The principle source of international labor and employment law is the International Labor Organization (ILO), which develops conventions covering significant topics in labor and employment law and policy. Sovereign nations are free to adopt or decline to adopt these conventions. The United States has adopted some, but far from all, the ILO's conventions. In some areas, the U.S. decision not to sign onto particular conventions is grounded in the belief that U.S. labor law and policy are superior to the international options.
- Corporate social responsibility is more of an aspiration or ideal than it is an actual example of international employment law. However, some nations have incorporated notions of corporate social responsibility into their laws.
- The Alien Tort Claims Act is one of the oldest U.S. statutes on the books and for many, many years was little used. However, in the 21st century workers and labor unions in foreign countries have rediscovered the statute and are attempting to use it—with mixed results—against U.S.-based multinational companies.
- International labor unions are attempting to organize the employees of multinational corporations on a global scale.
- U.S. immigration law's most recent major overhaul took place in 1986. A major goal of Congress at that time was to staunch the flow of illegal immigrants into the country. However, limited resources and lack of will resulted in only limited, spotty enforcement of the new statutory scheme. The result has been an enormous influx of illegal aliens into the U.S. during the past two decades.
- After September 11, 2001, the Department of Homeland Security was created and the Immigration and Naturalization Service (INS) was split into an enforcement branch, Immigration and Customs Enforcement (ICE), and a services-oriented branch, the Citizenship and Immigration Service (USCIS). ICE has been more active than the predecessor INS in enforcing the laws, including increased raids of workplaces known to employ numerous undocumented immigrants.

- Nevertheless, many states and municipalities, frustrated by the failure of the federal government to staunch the flow and employment of illegal immigrants, have enacted their own statutes and ordinances to deal with the problem on the local level. These laws have been subjected to court challenges. Recently some of them have survived these challenges and remain in effect.

» Problems

Questions

1. Can an argument be made that even underpaid and exploited workers in so-called sweatshops in underdeveloped nations are better off than if no such sweatshops existed?
2. If your answer to (1), above, is "yes," does this justify the exploitation of these workers?
3. If a foreign nation chooses not to enact or enforce humane wage and hour, health and safety, and other HR laws for the benefit of its citizens, why should an American company, doing business in that nation, be expected to do any better?
4. If menial and dirty jobs which American citizens have no interest in performing are filled primarily by illegal aliens, isn't the best policy for all concerned to ignore the presence of these workers in the U.S.?
5. Granting that it is probably unrealistic to round up and deport the estimated 12 million illegal immigrants in the U.S., what social services should these illegal residents in the U.S. be permitted to have: Welfare and/or unemployment compensation when they are out of work? Emergency room services? Public school for their children? The right to join a labor union? The right to file a health and safety complaint with an appropriate federal or state agency? The right to sue for unpaid wages or job-related injury?

Case Problems

6. The plaintiff, a private citizen, sought to obtain for Native Americans "just compensation for the minerals mined in the Black Hills of South Dakota." He averred that the Black Hills belonged to Native Americans and were taken from them in violation of the Fifth Amendment of the U.S. Constitution. He also asserted in one of several consolidated complains that American companies that operate sweatshops "should not be allowed to enter into international trade with the United States," and asked that the court enjoin such trade. Additionally, he contended that the "globalization of the auto industry violate[s] the Sherman Anti-Trust Act." In yet another complaint, he contended that the U.S. Food and Drug Administration is "in violation of the Treaty of Unification of Pharmacopeial Formulas for Patent Drugs." Finally, he pled that the "U.S.A.," presumably the federal government, is "trading in fur seals in violation of [a] treaty." How should the federal district judge assigned to these consolidated cases resolve them? Why? See *Demos v. U.S.*, 2007 WL 1492413 (CIT), 29 ITRD 1926 (U.S. Court of International Trade 2007).
7. The plaintiffs, current and former residents of the Republic of the Sudan a class action suit against Talisman Energy, Inc. and Sudan, alleging violations of international law stemming from oil exploration activities conducted in that country. Specifically, the plaintiffs alleged that the defendants collaborated to commit gross human rights violations, including extrajudicial killing, forcible displacement, war crimes, confiscation and destruction of property, kidnapping, rape, and enslavement for forced labor. Collectively, the plaintiffs claimed that these activities amounted to genocide. Talisman moved to dismiss this action on the basis of lack of subject matter jurisdiction, lack of personal jurisdiction, lack of plaintiffs' standing, *forum non conveniens*, international comity, act of state doctrine, political question doctrine, failure to join necessary and indispensable parties, and because equity does not require a useless act. Based upon what you have read in this chapter, is there a basis in U.S. law for the plaintiffs to proceed with their case? See *Presbyterian Church of Sudan v. Talisman Energy, Inc.*, 244 F. Supp. 2d 289 (S.D.N.Y. 2003).

8. The plaintiffs were seven Guatemalan citizens currently residing in the United States. Del Monte is a Delaware company; its principal place of business is in Coral Gables, Florida. In Guatemala, the plaintiffs were officers in SITRABI, a national trade union of plantation workers. At the time in question, they represented workers on a Bandegua banana plantation that was a wholly owned subsidiary of Del Monte. SITRABI and Bandegua were negotiating a new collective bargaining agreement for workers at the plantation. While those negotiations were ongoing, Bandegua terminated 918 workers. SITRABI responded by filing a complaint in the Labor Court of Guatemala. The plaintiffs allege that on October 13, 1999, Bandegua hired a private, armed security force. (Private security forces are permitted and regulated in Guatemala.) According to the plaintiffs, Del Monte agents met with the security force "to plan violent action against the Plaintiffs and other SITRABI leaders." According to the plaintiffs, at 5:45 p.m., the security force, which is described as "a gang of over 200 heavily armed men," arrived at SITRABI's headquarters. There, the security force held two plaintiffs hostage, threatened to kill them, and shoved them with guns. Throughout the evening, other SITRABI leaders were lured, abducted, or otherwise forced to the headquarters and similarly detained. The plaintiffs, at gunpoint, announced the labor dispute was over and that they were resigning. Do the plaintiffs have a cause of action against Del Monte in federal court? See *Aldana v. Del Monte Fresh Produce, NA, Inc.*, 416 F.3d 1242 (11th Cir. 2005).

9. San Juan Pueblo is a federally recognized Indian tribe, which is to say an independent Indian nation, located in New Mexico. Most of its 5,200 members live on tribal lands that are held in trust by the United States for the Pueblo. The Pueblo is governed by a tribal council, which is vested with legislative authority over tribal lands. Through federally approved leases, the Pueblo leases portions of its tribal land to nontribal businesses as a source of generating tribal income and as a means of employment for tribal members. On November 6, 1996, the San Juan Pueblo Tribal Council enacted Tribal Ordinance No. 96-63. The ordinance in substance is a so-called "right-to-work" measure (see Chapter 14). The Pueblo asserts that the ordinance is a valid exercise of its inherent sovereign authority. As amended, the ordinance prohibits the making of agreements containing union-security clauses covering any employees, whether tribal members or not. Section 6(a) of the ordinance reads:

> No person shall be required, as a condition of employment or continuation of employment on Pueblo lands, to: (i) resign or refrain from voluntary membership in, voluntary affiliation with, or voluntary financial support of a labor organization; (ii) become or remain a member of a labor organization; (iii) pay dues, fees, assessments or other charges of any kind or amount to a labor organization; (iv) pay to any charity or other third party, in lieu of such payments any amount equivalent to or a pro-rata portion of dues, fees, assessments or other charges regularly required of members of a labor organization; or (v) be recommended, approved, referred or cleared through a labor organization.

Should the tribal law be considered preempted by the National Labor Relations Act, or should the tribal council be recognized as a sovereign government body outside the reach of the NLRA? What policy reasons can you think of, that favor one or the other of these outcomes? See *NLRB v. Pueblo of San Juan*, 276 F.3d 1186 (10th Cir. 2002).

10. During August to October 2002, Cianbro Corporation applied to the United States Department of Labor and the Maine Department of Labor for H-2B temporary labor certifications for as many as 120 foreign workers to be employed as structural and pipe welders on two giant oil rigs known as the Amethyst 4 and 5 that were under construction in the harbor of Portland, Maine. To make their determinations, the DOL and the Maine DOL were required to calculate prevailing wages and working conditions for the jobs for which Cianbro sought temporary labor certifications pursuant to a DOL regulation, 20 C.F.R. § 656.40. Federal regulations (8 C.F.R. § 214.2(h)(6)(iii)(A)) provided that before filing a petition with the INS (now USCIS) director in whose jurisdiction a petitioning employer intends to employ an H-2B nonagricultural temporary worker, the employer must apply for a temporary labor certification with

the Secretary of Labor. The Secretary of Labor's temporary labor certification provided advice to the INS director on "whether or not United States workers capable of performing the temporary services or labor are available and whether the alien's employment will adversely affect the wages and working conditions of similarly employed United States workers." Many qualified and available U.S. workers applied for positions with Cianbro as structural and pipe welders during the period when the DOL was supposed to be reevaluating the matter after receipt of the relevant union's letter, opposing the company's application; however, none was offered employment by Cianbro. Meanwhile the federal and state agencies proposed to issue more than 50 H-2B visas. On March 21, 2003 the relevant unions filed an application for a temporary restraining order. Should the court grant this TRO, blocking the issuance of the H-2B visas, pending resolution of the unions' objections? What policy considerations should the judge take into account on both sides of the controversy when making this decision? See *Maine State Building and Construction Council v. Chao*, 265 F. Supp.2d 105 (D. Maine 2003).

11. JAL was a Japanese commercial air carrier based in Tokyo. HACS, a Hawaii corporation with its principal place of business in Honolulu, provided contract flight crews to JAL. Plaintiffs Ventress and Crawford were employed by HACS to perform services for JAL flights. The plaintiffs' employment agreements with HACS contained mandatory arbitration provisions. In December 2002, Ventress and Crawford jointly filed a complaint against JAL and HACS in the U.S. District Court for the Central District of California, alleging that JAL required a seriously ill pilot to fly in June 2001, in violation of American and Japanese aviation laws as well as JAL's own operations manual. Crawford expressed his concern to a JAL official in Honolulu in July 2001. Afterward, he experienced harassment from his superiors, including repeated performance checks, questions, and homework assignments. In December 2001, HACS informed Crawford that his assignment to JAL was cancelled because of unsatisfactory performance. That same month, Ventress submitted reports on the June incidents to JAL, HACS, and aviation regulators. Ventress claimed repeated harassment from JAL thereafter, including demands to undergo psychiatric evaluations. Ventress was not allowed to fly after September 2001. The complaint sought recovery for violation of California's whistleblower statute, wrongful termination in violation of the public policy protecting whistleblowers and emotional distress. The California whistleblower law states in pertinent part, "An employer may not retaliate against an employee for disclosing information to a government or law enforcement agency, where the employee has reasonable cause to believe that the information discloses a violation of state or federal statute, or a violation or noncompliance with a state or federal regulation." Cal. Labor Code § 1102.5(b). The defendant claimed that the plaintiffs' claims were preempted by the Friendship, Commerce, and Navigation Treaty (U.S.-Japan, April 2, 1953). The treaty was primarily designed to protect the right of employers on both sides of the Pacific to "utilize the services of their own nationals in managerial, technical, and confidential capacities to be critical." The court here was faced with three choices:

    (1) dismiss the case as preempted by the treaty;
    (2) stay the proceedings and require the plaintiffs to pursue arbitration under the express terms of their employment contracts; or
    (3) permit the action to proceed under the California Whistleblower Law.

    What policy considerations can you come up with in favor of or against each of these options? See *Ventress v. Japan Airlines*, 486 F.3d 1111 (9th Cir. 2007).

12. The governor of Missouri issued a press release which included the following announcements:

    > KINGSTON—Gov. Matt Blunt today highlighted his tough new directives in the fight against illegal immigration in Missouri in a visit to the Caldwell County Sheriff's Office, where on an average day the facility holds approximately 55 immigration detainees. "With Washington failing to enact policies to enforce our federal immigration laws it is necessary for our state to take action," Gov. Blunt said. "We support and welcome lawful immigrants into Missouri but will also continue to take a tough stand against illegal immigration in our state."

Gov. Blunt has offered his support to local prosecutors in their efforts in the fight against illegal immigration and reminds prosecutors that state law makes the receipt of tax credits by employers of illegal aliens who are ineligible for state tax credits, tax abatements, or loans a class A misdemeanor, punishable by up to a year in prison. In a letter to prosecutors, the governor notes that since the attorney general has yet to bring a case to enforce this law, it is left to them to enforce the law in their counties.

Gov. Blunt also called on his administration to work with ICE for authority under Section 287g of the Immigration and Nationality Act that would deputize state law enforcement officers to enforce federal laws and protect Missourians against illegal immigration. The agreement will allow select troopers, capitol police, and water patrol officers to help enforce immigration laws. The governor has directed his staff to examine the costs associated with the 287g designation and plans to seek funding in next year's budget to help state and local law enforcement agencies pursue the cooperative agreement and help enhance public safety.

The governor also directed state law enforcement agencies to verify the immigration status of every criminal presented for incarceration.

In addition, he took significant steps to shield taxpayers' money from supporting building projects that employ illegal workers including:

- Conducting random on-site inspections of all projects accompanied by the tax credit recipient to monitor and retrieve documentation regarding the legal status of all workers on the job. The inspections will include direct employees of the tax credit recipient, contracted or subcontracted agents, and both general contractors and their subcontractors.
- Performing a Compliance by Written Demand action for all tax credit recipients that requires all workers' proof of legal status, including contractors and subcontractors to be submitted within 30 days of the date of the receipt of the written request.

Based upon what you have learned in this chapter, evaluate the legality of the governor's various proposals in light of (1) federal preemption and (2) due process of law considerations.

13. David Rodriguez, a citizen of Mexico, entered the United States without inspection at El Paso, Texas, on or about July 22, 1996. During his time in the United States, he lived in Minnesota and fraudulently obtained a Texas birth certificate, a Minnesota driver's license and a social security card in the name of Oscar Martinez, and a social security card and legal resident card in the name of David Rodriguez Silva. He sought to obtain employment with a private employer by checking a box on a Form I-9 indicating that he was a "citizen or national of the United States" and by submitting the fraudulent Martinez driver's license and social security card as support for his claim. On April 19, 2001, Rodriguez married Veronica Vazquez, a United States citizen. On April 24, 2001, he submitted an immediate relative immigrant visa petition, which the Immigration and Naturalization Service (now the USCIS) approved. The INS informed Rodriguez that he would be considered for lawful permanent residence status subject to his application for adjustment of status. On February 26, 2002, Rodriguez and his wife appeared for an interview with a district adjudications officer as part of the process to adjust his status. Rodriguez brought the fraudulent documents. After the interview, the adjudications officer prepared a sworn statement that included the questions and answers from the interview. Rodriguez reviewed and signed the statement. In the interview and in his resulting sworn statement, Rodriguez admitted that he knew that with the use of the fraudulent documents he had made a claim to a government agency that he was a citizen of the United States. The INS denied Rodriguez's application for adjustment of status because he had made a false claim that he was a United States citizen. On appeal of the agency's decision, the court can either affirm the decision—in which case Rodriguez will be deported back to Mexico—or overlook his earlier employment history and order his change of status based upon his

marriage to an American citizen. What are the ethical considerations favoring each of these outcomes? What would you do, if you were the judge and had discretion to rule either way? See *Rodriguez v. Mukasey*, 519 F.3d 773 (8th Cir. 2008).

14. Petitioner Agri Processor Co. was a wholesaler of kosher meat products based in Brooklyn, New York. In September 2005, the company's employees voted to join the United Food and Commercial Workers union. When the company refused to bargain, the union filed an unfair labor practice charge with the National Labor Relations Board. The company defended its refusal, arguing that most of those who voted were undocumented aliens. The company argues that undocumented aliens are prohibited from unionizing because they do not qualify as "employees" protected by the National Labor Relations Act. The NLRA states, "The term 'employee' shall include any employee . . ., but shall not include any individual employed as an agricultural laborer, or in the domestic service of any family or person at his home, or any individual employed by his parent or spouse, or any individual having the status of an independent contractor, or any individual employed as a supervisor, or any individual employed by an employer subject to the Railway Labor Act . . ., or by any other person who is not an employer as herein defined." How should the court rule in this case? Does the statutory definition compel an outcome, or is there sufficient ambiguity for the court to go either way? If so, what are the public policy considerations that the court ought to weigh in reaching a determination of the case? See *Agri Processor, Inc. v. NLRB*, 514 F.3d 1 (D.C. Cir. 2008).

15. Yu owned and operated the Great Texas Employment Agency along with his girlfriend, Ya Cao. Great Texas was in the business of supplying Chinese restaurants in several states with immigrant workers. Yu advertised Great Texas to Chinese restaurant owners through direct mailings and in the Midwest edition of a Chinese periodical, agreeing to supply "Hispanic and Middle Southern American workers" for "odd jobs" or positions such as "dishwashers" or "busboys." Upon receiving an order from a restaurant owner, Great Texas would recruit immigrant workers from Texas, and arrange for their transportation to the restaurants.

    Authorities began investigating Yu after a border patrol agent encountered two men riding bicycles on Interstate 29 in North Dakota in June 2004. The two men admitted that they were Mexican citizens who were in the country illegally and who had been working at a Chinese restaurant in Grand Forks, North Dakota. One of the men had an employment contract, written in both Chinese and Spanish, which provided that the employee would receive a salary of $1,000 per month. The contract also listed a 312 area code telephone number for an employment agency. Agents asked to interview Yu, and he consented. After receiving his *Miranda* warnings, Yu explained that he lived at the residence with Ya Cao (whom he referred to as Lily) and that Ya Cao and a Spanish-speaking recruiter would go to street corners to find workers to fill requests. He said that he paid $20 for each worker recruited. Yu admitted that some of the workers were illegal but said that he assumed most were legal and that the restaurants would check on the workers' immigration status. After he was indicted, he contested the charges and sought to have his statement excluded on the ground that the spoke poor English and did not understand what rights he was giving up. If you were the trial judge, how would you rule on Yu's motion to suppress the confession? See *U.S. v. Shan Wei Yu*, 484 F.3d 979 (8th Cir. 2007).

Hypothetical Scenarios

16. One well-known approach to corporate responsibility is the so-called "triple bottom line." Traditionally, a corporation's bottom line referred to the company's net profits. "In practical terms, triple-bottom-line accounting means expanding this traditional reporting framework to take into account ecological and social performance in addition to financial performance. The phrase was coined by John Elkington in 1994. It was later expanded and articulated in his 1998 book *Cannibals with Forks: The Triple Bottom Line of* 21st *Century Business.* Sustainability, itself, was first defined by the

Brundtland Commission of the United Nations in 1987. The concept of TBL demands that a company's responsibility be to stakeholders rather than shareholders. In this case, "stakeholders" refers to anyone who is influenced, either directly or indirectly, by the actions of the firm. According to the stakeholder theory, the business entity should be used as a vehicle for coordinating stakeholder interests, instead of maximizing shareholder (owner) profit." [http://en.wikipedia.org/wiki/Triple_bottom_line] Assume that an American corporation decides to adopt the triple-bottom-line approach with regard to its environmental and labor relations policies worldwide. What are the pros and cons of this decision for the firm's traditional bottom line? What response should shareholders make to this decision? Does your answer to the second question depend upon whether the particular shareholder happens to be

(1) an individual investor,
(2) a university endowment fund, or
(3) an employee pension fund?

17. Villagers from Myanmar's Tenasserim region, the rural area through which an American oil company built a new pipeline, alleged that the Myanmar Military forced them, under threat of violence, to work on and serve as porters for the project. For instance, John Doe IX testified that he was forced to build a helipad near the pipeline site in 1994 that was then used by company officials who visited the pipeline during its planning stages. John Doe VII and John Roe X described that the construction of helipads at Eindayaza and Po Pah Pta, both of which were near the pipeline site, were used to ferry executives and materials to the construction site, and were constructed using the forced labor of local villagers, including Plaintiffs John Roes VIII and IX, as well as John Does I, VIII and IX, who testified that they were forced to work on building roads leading to the pipeline construction area. Finally, John Does V and IX testified that they were required to serve as "pipeline porters"—workers who performed menial tasks such as such as hauling materials and cleaning the army camps for the soldiers guarding the pipeline construction. Plaintiffs also alleged, in furtherance of the forced labor program just described, that the Myanmar Military subjected them to acts of murder, rape, and torture. For instance, Jane Doe I testified that after her husband, John Doe I, attempted to escape the forced labor program, he was shot at by soldiers, and, in retaliation for his attempted escape; that she and her baby were thrown into a fire, resulting in injuries to her and the death of the child. Other witnesses described the summary execution of villagers who refused to participate in the forced labor program, or who grew too weak to work effectively. Several Plaintiffs testified that rapes occurred as part of the forced labor program. For instance, both Jane Does II and III testified that while conscripted to work on pipeline-related construction projects, they were raped at knife-point by Myanmar soldiers who were members of a battalion that was supervising the work. Plaintiffs finally allege that American firm's conduct gives rise to liability for these abuses. What must these plaintiffs prove in order to pursue an Alien Tort Claims Act case against the U.S. oil company? What must the U.S. try to show in order to successfully defend itself? Should the law impose an obligation on the oil company to "police" how the host country's military fulfills a national agreement to assist the oil company in building the pipeline?

18. A European labor union succeeded in organizing the workers at a facility in Germany that was owned and operated by a U.S.-headquartered and incorporated multinational corporation. After successfully negotiating a first contract for the German workers, the union presented the corporation's board of directors with a demand that they recognize the union as the collective bargaining representative for all workers holding similar rank-and-file jobs worldwide. Without trying to deal with the National Labor Relations Act, which you'll learn about further on in this book, what are the equitable considerations that, let's say, a world court should consider in deciding whether or not the multinational corporation ought to be required to recognize the union globally? Are there any possible advantages to the corporation in voluntarily agreeing to do so?

19. In a U.S. ICE raid on a Midwestern meat packing plant, federal agents round up dozens of illegal aliens

employed at the plant. Assuming that an immigration judge has the authority to do, how much weight should he/she give to the following factors in deciding whether to repatriate these illegal workers to their countries of origin:

(1) length of time in the U.S.;

(2) children born in the U.S.;

(3) clean criminal and credit records;

(4) skill level and value to the employer; and

(5) membership in a U.S, labor union?

20. In assessing penalties against the employer in hypothetical number (19) above, and again assuming that the court has broad discretion whether to impose severe or mild penalties, what weight should a judge give each of the following factors in determining punishment:

(1) availability or lack of American workers to fill the jobs held by the alien workers;

(2) level of compensation and benefits provided to the illegal workers;

(3) the health and safety conditions to which the illegal workers were subjected; and

(4) the handling of payroll deductions or lack of such payroll "formalities"?

PART 2

EQUAL EMPLOYMENT OPPORTUNITY

CHAPTER 6

Title VII of the Civil Rights Act and Race Discrimination

Ideally, employers should hire those employees best qualified for the particular job being filled; an employee should be selected because of his or her ability to perform the job. Determining the qualifications required for the job, however, may be difficult. In fact, required qualifications that have no relationship to job performance may disqualify prospective employees who are capable of performing satisfactorily. In addition, some employers may be influenced in their selection of employees by their biases—conscious or unconscious—regarding certain groups of people. All of these factors are part of the problem of discrimination in employment.

Discrimination in employment, whether intentional or unintentional, has been a major concern of many people who believe that our society has not lived up to its ideals of equality of opportunity for all people. The glaring inequities in our society sparked violent protests during the civil rights movement of the 1960s. African Americans, Hispanic Americans, and Native Americans constituted a disproportionate share of those living in poverty. Women of all races and colors found their access to challenging and well-paying jobs limited; they were frequently channeled into lower paying occupations traditionally viewed as "women's work."

Title VII of the Civil Rights Act of 1964

To help remedy these problems of discrimination, Congress passed the Civil Rights Act of 1964, which was signed into law by President Johnson on July 2, 1964. The Civil Rights Act was aimed at discrimination in a number of areas of our society: housing, public accommodation, education, and employment. Title VII of the Civil Rights Act deals with discrimination in employment. It became the foundation of modern federal equal employment opportunity (EEO) law.

Title VII has been amended several times since its passage; the amendments made in 1968, 1972, and 1991 were substantial. The 1991 amendments, made by the Civil Rights Act of 1991, were intended to reverse several U.S. Supreme Court decisions that were perceived as making it more difficult for plaintiffs to bring suit under Title VII. Congress again amended

Title VII in 2009 to reverse another Supreme Court decision dealing with the time limit for bringing pay discrimination claims.

This part of the book focuses on the statutory provisions requiring equal opportunity in employment. This chapter deals with the provisions of Title VII, as amended, prohibiting employment discrimination based on race. Chapter 7 will discuss the Title VII provisions regarding employment discrimination based on gender, as well as other gender-related EEO legislation. Chapter 8 will discuss discrimination based on religion and national origin, the enforcement of Title VII, and the remedies available under it. Chapter 9 will discuss the Age Discrimination in Employment Act and EEO laws dealing with discrimination based on disability. Finally, Chapter 10 will focus on other federal and state EEO legislation.

Coverage of Title VII

Title VII of the Civil Rights Act of 1964
Legislation that outlawed discrimination in terms and conditions of employment based on race, color, sex, religion or national origin.

Title VII of the Civil Rights Act of 1964 took effect on July 2, 1965. It prohibits the refusal or failure to hire any individual, the discharge of any individual, or the discrimination against any individual with respect to compensation, terms, conditions, or privileges of employment because of that individual's race, color, religion, sex, or national origin.

Title VII, as amended, applies to employers, labor unions, and employment agencies. An employer under Title VII is defined as a person, partnership, corporation, or other entity engaged in an industry affecting commerce that has fifteen or more employees. In *Walters v. Metropolitan Educational Enterprises, Inc.*,[1] the Supreme Court held that the "payroll method" is used to determine the number of employees for coverage of Title VII. The criterion requires that the employer have at least fifteen employees on its payroll, whether they actually worked or not, for each working day of twenty or more calendar weeks in the current or preceding calendar year. According to the Supreme Court decision in *Clackamas Gastroenterology Associates, P.C. v. Wells*,[2] common-law principles should be applied in determining whether managing directors or physician-shareholders of professional corporations are employees for the purpose of determining coverage under Title VII. Such common-law principles include:

- whether the organization can hire or fire the individual or set the rules and regulations of the individual's work;
- whether, and to what extent, the organization supervises the individual's work;
- whether the individual reports to someone higher in the organization;
- whether, and to what extent, the individual is able to influence the organization;
- whether the parties intended that the individual be an employee, as expressed in written agreements or contracts; and
- whether the individual shares in the profits, losses, and liabilities of the organization.

The question of whether the employer meets the fifteen-employee requirement is an element of the plaintiff's claim for relief under the statute; an employer that fails to raise the issue during the trial cannot seek to raise it after the trial is completed.[3]

---

[1]519 U.S. 202 (1997).

[2]538 U.S. 440 (2003).

[3]*Arbaugh v. Y & H Corporation*, 546 U.S. 500 (2006).

State and local governments are also covered by Title VII; the federal government and wholly owned U.S. government corporations are covered under separate provisions of Title VII. Subsequent legislation extended the coverage of Title VII to other federal employees: (1) The Congressional Accountability Act of 1995[4] extended the coverage of Title VII of the Civil Rights Act of 1964, as amended, to the employees of the House of Representatives, the Senate, the Capitol Guide Service, the Capitol Police, the Congressional Budget Office, the Office of the Architect of the Capitol, the Office of the Attending Physician, and the Office of Technology Assessment; and (2) The Presidential and Executive Office Accountability Act[5] extended the coverage of Title VII to the Executive Office of the President, the Executive Residence at the White House, and the official residence of the Vice President. Title VII does not apply to tax-exempt bona fide private membership clubs.

The 1991 amendments to Title VII extended the coverage of the Act to American employers that employ U.S. citizens abroad. Foreign corporations that are controlled by American employers are also covered with regard to the employment of U.S. citizens. For such employers, compliance with Title VII is not required if this compliance would force the employer to violate the law of the country where the workplace is located. The effect of this amendment was to overturn the Supreme Court decision in *EEOC v. Arabian American Oil Co.*[6] Labor unions with at least fifteen members or that operate a hiring hall are subject to Title VII. Unions are prohibited from discriminating in employment opportunities or status against their members or applicants on the basis of race, color, religion, gender, or national origin. Employment agencies violate Title VII by discriminating on prohibited bases in announcing openings, interviewing applicants, or referring applicants to employers.

Administration of Title VII

Title VII is administered by the Equal Employment Opportunity Commission (EEOC), a five-member commission appointed by the president that works with the commission's Office of General Counsel. The EEOC is empowered to issue binding regulations and nonbinding guidelines in its responsibility for administering and enforcing the act. Although the EEOC generally responds to complaints of discrimination filed by individuals, it can also initiate an action on its own if it finds a "pattern or practice" of discrimination in employment.

The regulations and guidelines under Title VII require that employers, unions, and employment agencies post EEOC notices summarizing the act's requirements. Failure to display such notices is punishable by a fine of not more than $100 per violation. The act further requires that those covered keep records relevant to the determination of whether unlawful employment practices have been, or are being, committed. Covered employers must maintain payroll records and other records relating to applicants and to employee promotion, demotion, transfer, and discharge.

[4] 2 U.S.C. §1301.

[5] 3 U.S.C. §§402, 411.

[6] 499 U.S. 244 (1991).

The WORKING Law

$200 Million Discrimination Suit Filed Against Catering Group

A group of African-American catering workers who are employed at Philadelphia's Comcast Center by Compass, a British firm that is the world's largest catering group, have filed a suit alleging race discrimination, harassment, and unlawful retaliation. The employees complained that they were subjected to racial abuse by the executive chef at the Comcast Center, and that the employer failed to stop it. The employees also alleged that the African-American employees had to eat lunch in the locker room and clean up after white workers. The suit also alleged that African-American employees were not allowed to work in front of guests during private functions, but were required to work in the kitchen, out of view of the guests. Comcast issued a statement disputing the claims of the lawsuit, and emphasized that the firm "has strong and clear policies that embrace diversity, inclusion, and respect in the workplace, and prohibit any sort of behavior that is contrary to these values.

Sources: "$200M Suit Claims Discrimination by Compass in Philadelphia Complex," *The Guardian*, Dec. 2, 2008, p. 28; "$200 Million Race-Bias Suit Filed Against Food Firm," *The Philadelphia Inquirer*, Dec. 2, 2008, p. C1.

Discrimination Under Title VII

Section 703 of Title VII states that it shall be an unlawful employment practice for an employer "to fail or refuse to hire or to discharge any individual, or otherwise to discriminate against an individual with respect to his compensation, terms, condition, or privileges of employment, because of such individual's race, color, religion, sex or national origin." It should be clear from the wording of Section 703 that Title VII prohibits intentional discrimination in employment on the basis of race, color, religion, sex, or national origin. An employer who refuses to hire African Americans, or who will only hire women for clerical positions rather than for production jobs, is in violation of Title VII. Likewise, a union that will not accept Hispanic Americans as members, or that maintains separate seniority lists for male and female members, violates the act. Such intentional discrimination, called **disparate treatment**, means the particular employee is subject to different treatment because of that employee's race, color, gender, religion or national origin.

Disparate Treatment
When an employee is treated differently from others due to race, color, religion, gender or national origin.

In the years immediately following the passage of Title VII, some people believed that the act was intended to protect only minority or female employees. That idea was specifically rejected by the Supreme Court in the 1976 case of *McDonald v. Santa Fe Trail Transportation Co.*[7] The case arose when three employees of a trucking company were caught stealing cargo from the company. Two of the employees, who were white, were discharged; the third, an African American, was given a suspension but was not discharged. The employer justified the difference

[7]427 U.S. 273 (1976).

in disciplinary penalties on the ground that Title VII protected the African American employee. The white employees filed suit under Title VII. The Supreme Court emphasized that Title VII protects all employees; every individual employee is protected from any discrimination in employment because of race, color, sex, religion, and national origin. The employer had treated the white employees differently because of their race, and the employer was therefore in violation of Title VII.

Concept *Summary* » 6.1

Showing Disparate Treatment

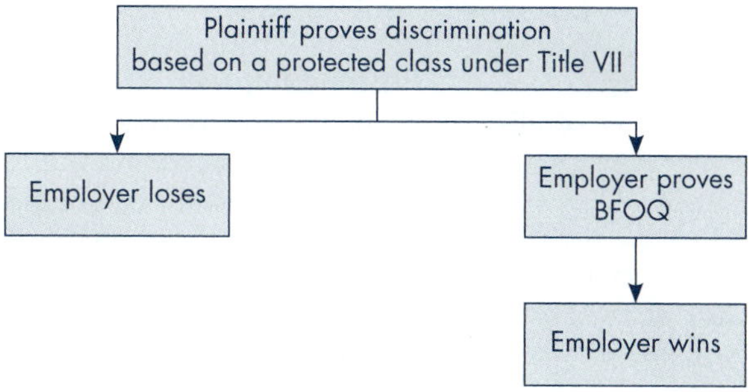

Plaintiff proves discrimination based on a protected class under Title VII
→ Employer loses
→ Employer proves BFOQ → Employer wins

Bona Fide Occupational Qualification (BFOQ) An exception to the civil rights law that allows an employer to hire employees of a specific gender, religion, or national origin when business necessity—the safe and efficient performance of the particular job—requires it.

Business Necessity The safe and efficient performance of the business or performance of a particular job requires that employees be of a particular sex, religion or national origin.

Bona Fide Occupational Qualifications (BFOQs)

Although Title VII prohibits intentional discrimination in employment, it does contain a limited exception that allows employers to select employees on the basis of gender, religion, or national origin when the employer can establish that being of a particular gender, religion, or national origin is a ***bona fide occupational qualification (BFOQ)***. To establish that a particular characteristic is a BFOQ, the employer must demonstrate that ***business necessity***—the safe and efficient operation of the business—requires that employees be of a particular gender, religion, or national origin. Employer convenience, customer preference, or coworker preference will not support the establishment of a BFOQ. Title VII recognizes BFOQs only on the basis of gender, religion, and national origin; the act provides that race and color can never be used as BFOQs. (BFOQs will be discussed in more detail in the next chapter.)

Unintentional Discrimination: Disparate Impact

It should be clear that intentional discrimination in employment on the basis of race, religion, gender, color, or national origin (the "prohibited grounds"), apart from a BFOQ, is prohibited, but what about unintentional discrimination? An employer may specify certain requirements for a job that operate to disqualify otherwise capable prospective employees.

Disparate Impact
The discriminatory effect of apparently neutral employment criteria.

Although the employer is allowed to hire those employees best able to do the job, what happens if the specified requirements do not actually relate to the employee's ability to perform the job but do have the effect of disqualifying a large proportion of minority applicants? This discriminatory effect of apparently neutral requirements is known as a ***disparate impact***. Should the disparate impact of such neutral job requirements be prohibited under Title VII?

Concept *Summary* » 6.2

Discrimination Under Title VII

Disparate Treatment	Disparate Impact
Intentional discrimination in terms or conditions of employment	The discriminatory effect of apparently neutral employment criteria or selection devices; does not require intention to discriminate on the part of the employer
The employer intentionally treats employees or applicants differently because of their race, color, sex,* religion,* or national origin*	The employment criteria or selection device disproportionately disqualifies employees based on race, color, sex, religion, or national origin

*May be subject to BFOQ exception

Frequently, the neutral requirement at issue may be a test used by the employer to screen applicants for a job. Title VII does allow the use of employment testing. Section 703(h) provides, in part,

> … [i]t shall not be an unlawful employment practice for an employer to give and act upon the results of any professionally developed ability test provided that such test, its administration or action upon the results is not designed, intended or is used to discriminate because of race, color, religion, sex, or national origin.

The effect of that provision and the legality of using job requirements that have a disparate impact were considered by the Supreme Court in the following case.

case 6.1 » Griggs v. Duke Power Company

401 U.S. 424 (1971)

Background

Duke Power Company is an electrical utility company operating in North Carolina. Prior to July 2, 1965, the effective date of Title VII of the Civil Rights Act of 1964, the Company discriminated on the basis of race in the hiring and assigning of employees at its Dan River plant. The plant was organized into five operating departments: (1) Labor, (2) Coal Handling, (3) Operations, (4) Maintenance, and (5) Laboratory and Test. African Americans were only employed in the Labor Department where the highest paying jobs paid less than the lowest paying jobs in the other four operating departments in which only whites were employed.

Promotions were normally made within each department on the basis of job seniority. Transferees into a department usually began in the lowest position. In 1955 the Company instituted a policy of requiring a high school education for initial assignment to any department except Labor, and for transfer from the Coal Handling to any "inside" department (Operations, Maintenance, or Laboratory). When the Company abandoned its policy of restricting African Americans to the Labor Department in 1965, it instituted a requirement of having a high school diploma in order to transfer from the Labor Department to any other department. However, the white employees hired before the adoption of the high school diploma requirement continued to perform satisfactorily and achieve promotions in the various operating departments. The U.S. Census Bureau data from the 1960 census indicated that approximately 34 percent of white males in North Carolina had a high school diploma, compared to about 12 percent of African American males in North Carolina who had completed high school. The Company added a further requirement for new employees on July 2, 1965, the date on which Title VII became effective. To qualify for placement in any but the Labor Department it became necessary to register satisfactory scores on two professionally prepared aptitude tests, as well as to have a high school education. However, employees with a high school diploma who had been hired prior to the adoption of the aptitude test requirements were still eligible for transfer to the four desirable departments from which African Americans had been excluded. In September 1965 the Company began to permit incumbent employees who lacked a high school education to qualify for transfer from Labor or Coal Handling to an "inside" job by passing two tests—the Wonderlic Personnel Test, which purports to measure general intelligence, and the Bennett Mechanical Comprehension Test. Neither was directed or intended to measure the ability to learn to perform a particular job or category of jobs. The requisite scores used for both initial hiring and transfer approximated the national median for high school graduates. For the employees who took the tests, the pass rate for white employees was 58 percent, while the pass rate for African American employees was 6 percent.

Griggs and a group of other African-American employees brought suit against Duke Power, alleging that the high school diploma requirement and the aptitude test requirements violated Title VII because they made it more difficult for African-American employees to be promoted from the Labor Department, and had the effect of continuing the previous job segregation. The District Court had found that while the Company previously followed a policy of overt racial discrimination prior to the passage of Title VII, such conduct had ceased. The District Court also concluded that Title VII was intended to be prospective only and not retroactive, and therefore, the impact of prior discrimination was beyond the reach of the Act. On appeal, the U.S. Court of Appeals for the Fourth Circuit concluded that the intent of the employer should govern, and that in this case there was no showing of intentional discrimination in the company's adoption of the diploma and test requirements. The Court of Appeals concluded there was no violation of the Act. Griggs then appealed to the U.S. Supreme Court.

Burger, Chief Justice

We granted the [appeal] in this case to resolve the question whether an employer is prohibited by ... Title VII from requiring a high school education or passing of a standardized general intelligence test as a condition of employment in or transfer to jobs when (a) neither standard is shown to be significantly related to successful job performance, (b) both requirements operate to disqualify Negroes at a substantially higher rate than white applicants, and (c) the jobs in question formerly had been filled only by white employees as part of a longstanding practice of giving preference to whites....

The objective of Congress in the enactment of Title VII ... was to achieve equality of employment opportunities and remove barriers that have operated in the past to favor an identifiable group of white employees over other employees. Under the Act, practices, procedures, or tests neutral on their face, and even neutral in terms of intent, cannot be maintained if they operate to "freeze" the status quo of prior discriminatory employment practices.

The Court of Appeals' opinion ... agreed that, on the record in the present case, "whites register far better on the Company's alternative requirements" than Negroes. This consequence would appear to be directly traceable to race. Basic intelligence must have the means of articulation to manifest itself fairly in a testing process. Because they are Negroes, petitioners have long received inferior education in segregated schools and this Court expressly recognized these differences ... Congress did not intend by Title VII, however, to guarantee a job to every person regardless of qualifications. In short, the Act does not command that any person be hired simply because he was formerly the subject of discrimination, or because he is a member of a minority group.... What is required by Congress is the removal of artificial, arbitrary, and unnecessary barriers to employment when the barriers operate invidiously to discriminate on the basis of racial or other impermissible classification.

Congress has now provided that tests or criteria for employment or promotion may not provide equality of opportunity merely in the sense of the fabled offer of milk to the stork and the fox. On the contrary, Congress has now required that the posture and condition of the job-seeker be taken into account. It has—to resort again to the fable—provided that the vessel in which the milk is proffered be one all seekers can use. The Act proscribes not only overt discrimination but also practices that are fair in form, but discriminatory in operation. The touchstone is business necessity. If an employment practice which operates to exclude Negroes cannot be shown to be related to job performance, the practice is prohibited.

On the record before us, neither the high school completion requirement nor the general intelligence test is shown to bear a demonstrable relationship to successful performance of the jobs for which it was used. Both were adopted, as the Court of Appeals noted, without meaningful study of their relationship to job-performance ability. Rather, a vice president of the Company testified, the requirements were instituted on the Company's judgment that they generally would improve the overall quality of the work force.

The evidence, however, shows that employees who have not completed high school or taken the tests have continued to perform satisfactorily and make progress in departments for which the high school and test criteria are now used. The promotion record of present employees who would not be able to meet the new criteria thus suggests the possibility that the requirements may not be needed even for the limited purpose of preserving the avowed policy of advancement within the Company....

The Court of Appeals held that the Company had adopted the diploma and test requirements without any "intention to discriminate against Negro employees." We do not suggest that either the District Court or the Court of Appeals erred in examining the employer's intent; but good intent or absence of discriminatory intent does not redeem employment procedures or testing mechanisms that operate as "built-in headwinds" for minority groups and are unrelated to measuring job capability.

... Congress directed the thrust of the Act to the consequences of employment practices, not simply the motivation. More than that, Congress has placed on the employer the burden of showing that any given requirement must have a manifest relationship to the employment in question....

The Company contends that its general intelligence tests are specifically permitted by § 703(h) of the Act. That section authorizes the use of "any professionally developed ability test" that is not "designed, intended or used to discriminate because of race...."

The Equal Employment Opportunity Commission, having enforcement responsibility, has issued guidelines interpreting § 703(h) to permit only the use of job-related tests. The administrative interpretation of the Act by the enforcing agency is entitled to great deference.... Since the Act and its legislative history support the Commission's construction, this affords good reason to treat the guidelines as expressing the will of Congress.

... Nothing in the Act precludes the use of testing or measuring procedures; obviously they are useful. What Congress has forbidden is giving these devices and mechanisms controlling force unless they are demonstrably a reasonable measure of job performance.... Far from disparaging job qualifications as such, Congress has made such qualifications the controlling factor, so that race, religion, nationality, and sex become irrelevant. What Congress has commanded is that any tests used must measure the person for the job and not the person in the abstract.

The judgment of the Court of Appeals ... is reversed.

Case Questions

1. What is the significance of the fact that Duke Power had intentionally discriminated against African Americans in hiring prior to the passage of Title VII?
2. Why did the high school diploma requirement and the aptitude tests requirement operate to disqualify African Americans from eligibility for transfer at a greater rate than whites? Explain your answer.
3. Why does the court say that the high school diploma requirement and the aptitude test requirements were "unrelated to measuring job capability"?
4. Does Title VII allow an employer to use applicants' scores on professionally developed aptitude tests as criteria for hiring? Explain your answer.
5. What is the fable of the stork and the fox that Chief Justice Burger refers to? How does it relate to this case?

The *Griggs* case dealt with objective employment selection requirements—a high school diploma and passing two aptitude tests—but in *Watson v. Fort Worth Bank & Trust*,[8] the Supreme Court held that a claim of disparate impact discrimination may be brought against an employer using a subjective employment practice, such as an interview rating. The plaintiff alleging a disparate impact claim must identify the specific employment practice being challenged, and the plaintiff must offer statistical evidence sufficient to show that the challenged practice has a disparate impact on applicants for hiring or promotion because of their membership in a protected group.

Section 703(K) and Disparate Impact Claims

The 1991 amendments to Title VII added Section 703(k), which deals with disparate impact claims. Section 703(k) requires that the plaintiff demonstrate that the employer uses a particular employment practice that causes a disparate impact on one of the bases prohibited by Title VII. If such a showing is made, the employer must then demonstrate that the practice is job related for the position in question and is consistent with business necessity. Even if the employer makes such a showing, if the plaintiff can demonstrate that an alternative employment practice—one without a disparate impact—is available, and the employer refuses to adopt it, the employer is still in violation of the act. Section 703(k) states that a plaintiff shall demonstrate that each particular employment practice that is challenged causes a disparate impact unless the plaintiff can demonstrate that the elements of the decision-making process are not capable of separation for analysis. If the employer demonstrates that the challenged practice does not have a disparate impact, then there is no need to show that the practice is required by business necessity. Work rules that bar the employment of individuals using or possessing illegal drugs are exempt from disparate impact analysis; such rules violate Title VII only when they are adopted or applied with an intention to discriminate on grounds prohibited by Title VII.

If the employment practice at issue is shown to be sufficiently job related, and the plaintiff has not shown that alternative practices without a disparate impact are available, then the employer may continue to use the challenged employment practice because it is necessary to perform the job. Nothing in Title VII prohibits an employer from hiring only those persons who are capable of doing the job. The 1991 amendments to Title VII added Section 703(k)(2), which states that demonstrating that an employment practice is required by business necessity is not a defense to a claim of intentional discrimination under Title VII. Most of the cases dealing with disparate impact discrimination involve race, gender, or national origin discrimination, although the language of Section 703(k) is not limited to only those bases of discrimination.

Uniform Guidelines on Employee Selection
Regulations adopted by the EEOC and other federal agencies that provide for methods of demonstrating a disparate impact and for validating employee selection criteria.

The Uniform Guidelines on Employee Selection

How can a plaintiff demonstrate a claim of disparate impact? How can an employer demonstrate that a requirement is job-related? The ***Uniform Guidelines on Employee Selection Procedures***,[9] a series of regulations adopted by the EEOC and other federal agencies, provide some answers to those questions.

---

[8] 487 U. S. 977 (1988).

[9] 29 C.F.R. Part 1607 (1978).

Showing a Disparate Impact

The Supreme Court held in *Watson v. Fort Worth Bank & Trust* that a plaintiff must "offer statistical evidence of a kind and degree sufficient to show that the practice in question has caused the exclusion of applicants for jobs or promotions because of their membership in a protected group." In *Wards Cove Packing Co. v. Atonio*,[10] the Supreme Court described one way to demonstrate that hiring practices had a disparate impact on nonwhites by comparing the composition of the employer's work force with the composition of the labor market from which applicants are drawn:

> The "proper comparison [is] between the racial composition of [the at-issue jobs] and the racial composition of the qualified … population in the relevant labor market." It is such a comparison—between the racial composition of the qualified persons in the labor market and the persons holding at-issue jobs—that generally forms the proper basis for the initial inquiry in a disparate impact case. Alternatively, in cases where such labor market statistics will be difficult if not impossible to ascertain, we have recognized that certain other statistics—such as measures indicating the racial composition of "otherwise-qualified applicants" for at-issue jobs—are equally probative for this purpose.

Four-Fifths Rule
A mathematical formula developed by the EEOC to demonstrate disparate impact of a facially neutral employment practice on selection criteria.

The Uniform Guidelines, adopted before the *Watson and Wards Cove* decisions, set out another way to demonstrate the disparate impact of a job requirement. This procedure, known as the ***Four-Fifths Rule***, compares the selection rates (the rates at which applicants meet the requirements or pass the test) for the various protected groups under Title VII. The Four-Fifths Rule states that a disparate impact will be demonstrated when the proportion of applicants from the protected group with the lowest selection rate (or pass rate) is less than 80 percent of the selection rate (pass rate) of the group with the highest selection rate.

For example, a municipal fire department requires that applicants for firefighter positions be at least five feet, six inches tall and weigh at least 130 pounds. Of the applicants for the positions, five of twenty (25 percent) of the Hispanic applicants meet the requirements, while thirty of forty (75 percent) of the white applicants meet the requirements. To determine whether the height and weight requirements have a disparate impact on Hispanics, the pass rate for Hispanics is divided by the pass rate for whites. Since .25/.75 = .33, or 33 percent, a disparate impact according to the Four-Fifths Rule exists. Stating the rule in equation form, disparate impact exists when:

$$\frac{\text{Pass rate for group with lowest pass rate}}{\text{Pass rate for group with highest pass rate}} < .80$$

Using the numbers from our example:

$$\frac{.25\ \text{(Hispanic pass rate)}}{.75\ \text{(White pass rate)}} = .33; .33 < .80$$

Therefore, a disparate impact exists, establishing a prima facie case of employment discrimination. To continue using such a test, the employer must satisfy the court that the test is sufficiently job related.

---

[10]490 U.S. 642 (1989).

Validating Job Requirements

The fire department must demonstrate that the height and weight requirements are job related in order to continue using them in selecting employees. The Uniform Guidelines provide several methods to show that the height and weight requirements are job related. The Uniform Guidelines also require a showing of a statistical correlation demonstrating that the requirements are necessary for successful job performance. In our example, the fire department would have to show that the minimum height and weight requirements screen out those applicants who would be unable to perform safely and efficiently the tasks or duties of a firefighter.

When the job requirements involve passing an examination, it must be shown that a passing score on the exam has a high statistical correlation with successful job performance. The Uniform Guidelines set out standards for demonstrating such a correlation (known as test validity) developed by the American Psychological Association. The standards may be classified into three types: content validity, construct validity, and criterion-related validity.

Content Validity

Content Validity
A method of demonstrating that an employment selection device reflects the content of the job for which employees are being selected.

Content validity is a means of measuring whether the requirement or test actually evaluates abilities required on the job. The fire department using the height and weight requirements would have to show that the requirements determine abilities needed to do the job—that anyone shorter than five feet, six inches or weighing less than 130 pounds would be unable to do the job. That would be difficult to do, but to validate the requirements as job related, such a showing is required by the Uniform Guidelines. If the job of firefighter requires physical strength, then using a strength test as a selection device would be valid. (Height and weight requirements are sometimes used instead of a physical strength test, but they are much more difficult to validate than strength tests.) The strength test used to screen applicants should reflect the actual tasks of the job—for example, carrying large fire hoses while climbing a ladder. For the job of typist, a spelling and typing test would likely have a high content validity because these tests measure abilities actually needed on the job. A strength test for a typist, on the other hand, would have a low content validity rating because physical strength has little relationship to typing performance. The Uniform Guidelines set out statistical methods to demonstrate the relationship (if any) of the requirements to job performance. An employer seeking to validate such requirements must follow the procedures and conditions in the Uniform Guidelines.

Construct Validity

Construct Validity
A method of demonstrating that an employment selection device selects employees based on the traits and characteristics that are required for the job in question.

Construct validity is a means of isolating and testing for specific traits or characteristics that are deemed essential for job performance. Such traits, or constructs, may be based on observations but cannot be measured directly. For example, a teacher may be required to possess the construct "patience," or an executive may be required to possess "leadership" or "judgment." Such traits, or constructs, cannot be measured directly, but they may be observed based on simulations of actual job situations. The Uniform Guidelines set out procedures and methods for demonstrating that certain constructs are really necessary to the job and that means used to test for or identify these constructs actually do measure them.

Criterion-Related Validity

Criterion-Related Validity
A method of demonstrating that an employment selection device correlates with the skills and knowledge required for successful job performance.

Criterion-related validity concerns the statistical correlation between scores received on tests ("paper-and-pencil" tests) and job performance. An employer who administers an IQ test to prospective employees must establish that there is a high statistical correlation between successful performance on the test and successful performance on the job. That correlation may be established by giving the test to current employees and comparing their test scores with their job performance; the correlation coefficient so produced is then used to predict the job performance of other current or prospective employees taking the same test. The Uniform Guidelines provide specific procedures and requirements for demonstrating the criterion-related validity of tests used for employment selection. Failure to comply with the requirements of the Uniform Guidelines will prevent an employer from establishing that a test is job related. If the test has not been validated, its use for employment purposes will violate Title VII if such a test has a disparate impact. Furthermore, a test validated for one group, such as Hispanic Americans, may have to be separately validated for one or more other groups, such as African Americans or Asian Americans.

Concept *Summary* » 6.3

PROVING JOB RELATEDNESS

Content Validity Studies	**Construct Validity Studies**	**Criterion-Related Validity Studies**
Is the selection device or test an accurate sample of the job's requirements?	Does the selection device test for traits or characteristics essential for job performance?	Does the employment test identify skills or knowledge necessary for successful job performance?
Employers need to show that the selection device or test reflects important tasks or aspects of the job	Employers must show that they are accurately screening for constructs identified as essential for successful job performance	Employers must show that the test has a high statistical correlation between success on the test and success on the job

In *Ricci v. DeStefano,*[11] the New Haven Fire Department administered an exam to candidates for promotion, but decided not to use the exam results because of a perceived disparate impact on African Americans. A group of white firefighters who would have been promoted based on the exam results filed suit, claiming that the employer's action was race-based discrimination against them. A divided Supreme Court held that the employer had violated Title VII because it did not have a "strong basis in evidence" to justify taking race-conscious action to reject the exam results. Justice Kennedy, writing for the majority, held that the exam was job related, and that fear of litigation alone was not a sufficient reason for setting aside the exam results.

[11]129 S.Ct. 2658 (2009).

In light of the *Ricci* case, employers should ensure that any exams or other employment selection devices have been validated as being job related. If the exam or selection device is job related, employers may continue to use it even if the exam has a disparate impact on a protected group (as long as there is no available alternative exam or selection device that does not have a disparate impact).

The following case deals with an employer's attempt to justify a strength test used to select applicants for hiring in a meat packing plant.

case 6.2 » Equal Employment Opportunity Commission v. Dial Corp.

469 F.3d 735 (8th Cir. 2006)

Facts: A Dial plant located in Fort Madison, Iowa, produces canned meats. Entry-level employees at the plant are assigned to the sausage packing area, where workers daily lift and carry up to 18,000 pounds of sausage, walking the equivalent of four miles in the process. They are required to carry approximately thirty-five pounds of sausage at a time and must lift and load the sausage to heights between thirty and sixty inches above the floor. Employees who worked in the sausage packing area experienced a disproportionate number of injuries as compared to the rest of the workers in the plant. Dial implemented several measures to reduce the injury rate starting in late 1996. In 2000, Dial also instituted a strength test used to evaluate potential employees, called the Work Tolerance Screen (WTS). In this test, job applicants were asked to carry a thirty-five pound bar between two frames, approximately thirty and sixty inches off the floor, and to lift and load the bar onto these frames. The applicants were told to work at their "own pace" for seven minutes. An occupational therapist watched the process, documented how many lifts each applicant completed, and recorded her own comments about each candidate's performance. Starting in 2001, the plant nurse, Martha Lutenegger, also watched and documented the process. Lutenegger reviewed the test forms and had the ultimate hiring authority.

Women and men had worked together, doing the same jobs, in the sausage packing area for years. In the three years before the WTS was adopted, 46 percent of the new hires were women, but the number of female hires dropped to 15 percent after the WTS test was implemented. The percentage of women who passed the test decreased each year the TWS was used, with only 8 percent of the women applicants passing in 2002. Overall, 38 percent of female applicants passed, while 97 percent of the male applicants passed. While injuries among sausage workers declined consistently after 2000 when the WTS was adopted, the downward trend in injuries had begun in 1998 after the company had instituted other measures to reduce injuries.

Paula Liles applied to Dial in January 2000 and was one of the first applicants to take the WTS test. She was not hired, even though the occupational therapist administering the WTS test told her that she had passed. Liles filed a discrimination complaint with the EEOC in August 2000. On September 24, 2002, EEOC brought this action on behalf of Liles and fifty-three other women who had applied to work at Dial and were denied employment after taking the WTS. The EEOC claimed that the use of the WTS test had an unlawful disparate impact on female applicants.

At the trial, the EEOC presented an expert on industrial organization who testified that the WTS was significantly more difficult than the actual job that workers performed at the plant. He explained that although workers did 1.25 lifts per minute on average and rested between lifts, applicants who took the WTS performed six lifts per minute on average, usually without any breaks. He also testified that in two of the three years before Dial had implemented the WTS, the women's injury rate had been lower than that of the male workers. EEOC's expert also analyzed the company's written evaluations of the applicants and testified that more men than women were given offers of employment even when they had received similar comments about their performance on the WTS. EEOC also introduced evidence that the occupational nurse marked some women as failing despite their having completed the full seven-minute test.

Dial presented an expert in work physiology, who testified that in his opinion the WTS effectively tested skills which were representative of the actual job, and an industrial and organizational psychologist, who testified that the WTS measured the requirements of the job and that the decrease in injuries could be attributed to the test. Dial also called plant nurse Martha Lutenegger who testified that although she and other Dial managers knew the WTS was screening out more women than men, the decrease in injuries warranted its continued use.

The trial court held that Dial was in violation of Title VII because the WTS had a discriminatory effect on female applicants, that Dial had not demonstrated that the WTS was a business necessity or shown either content or criterion validity, and that Dial had not effectively controlled for other variables that may have caused the decline in injuries, including other safety measures that Dial had implemented starting in 1996. Dial was ordered to pay back pay and benefits to the female applicants.

Dial appealed to the U.S. Court of Appeals for the Eighth Circuit. Dial attacked the trial court's findings of disparate impact, and claimed that it had proved that the WTS was a business necessity.

Issue: Has Dial proven that use of the WTS to screen applicants for employment was a business necessity because it reduced the number of injuries in the sausage production area?

Decision: In a disparate impact case, once the plaintiff establishes a prima facie case, the employer must then show the challenged practice is "related to safe and efficient job performance and is consistent with business necessity." An employer using the business necessity defense must prove that the practice was related to the specific job and the required skills and physical requirements of the position. Although a validity study of an employment test can be sufficient to prove business necessity, it is not necessary if the employer demonstrates the procedure is sufficiently related to safe and efficient job performance. If the employer demonstrates business necessity, the plaintiff can still prevail by showing that there is a less discriminatory alternative available.

Dial claimed that the WTS was shown by its experts to have both content and criterion validity. Under EEOC's Uniform Guidelines, "A content validity study should consist of data showing that the content of the selection procedure is representative of important aspects of performance on the job for which the candidates are to be evaluated." Dial's physiology expert testified that the WTS was highly representative of the actions required by the job. The trial court was persuaded by the testimony of the EEOC's expert in industrial organization "that a crucial aspect of the WTS is more difficult than the sausage-making jobs themselves" and that the average applicant had to perform four times as many lifts as current employees and had no rest breaks. There was also evidence that in a testing environment where hiring is contingent upon test performance, applicants tend to work as fast as possible during the test in order to outperform the competition.

Dial argued that the WTS had criterion validity because both overall injuries and strength-related injuries decreased dramatically following the implementation of the WTS. The Uniform Guidelines establish that criterion validity can be shown by "empirical data demonstrating that the selection procedure is predictive of or significantly correlated with important elements of job performance." Despite Dial's claims that the decrease in injuries showed that the WTS enabled it to predict which applicants could safely handle the strenuous nature of the work, the evidence showed that the sausage plant injuries started decreasing before the WTS was implemented. Moreover, the injury rate for women employees was lower than that for men in two of the three years before Dial implemented the WTS. The evidence did not require the district court to find that the decrease in injuries resulted from the implementation of the WTS instead of the other safety mechanisms Dial started to put in place in 1996.

Dial also argued that the district court improperly gave it the burden to establish that there was no less discriminatory alternative to the WTS, instead of holding that the EEOC had the burden as part of the burden-shifting framework in disparate impact cases. Because Dial failed to demonstrate that the WTS was a business necessity, however, the EEOC never was required to show the presence of a nondiscriminatory alternative. Part of the employer's burden to establish business necessity is to demonstrate the need for the challenged procedure, and the court found that Dial had not shown that its other safety measures could not produce the same results.

The Court of Appeals upheld the district court findings of a disparate impact on female applicants and that Dial had not shown that the WTS was required as business necessity. The court affirmed the trial court finding that Dial was liable for back pay and benefits.

Concept *Summary* » 6.4

Showing Disparate Impact

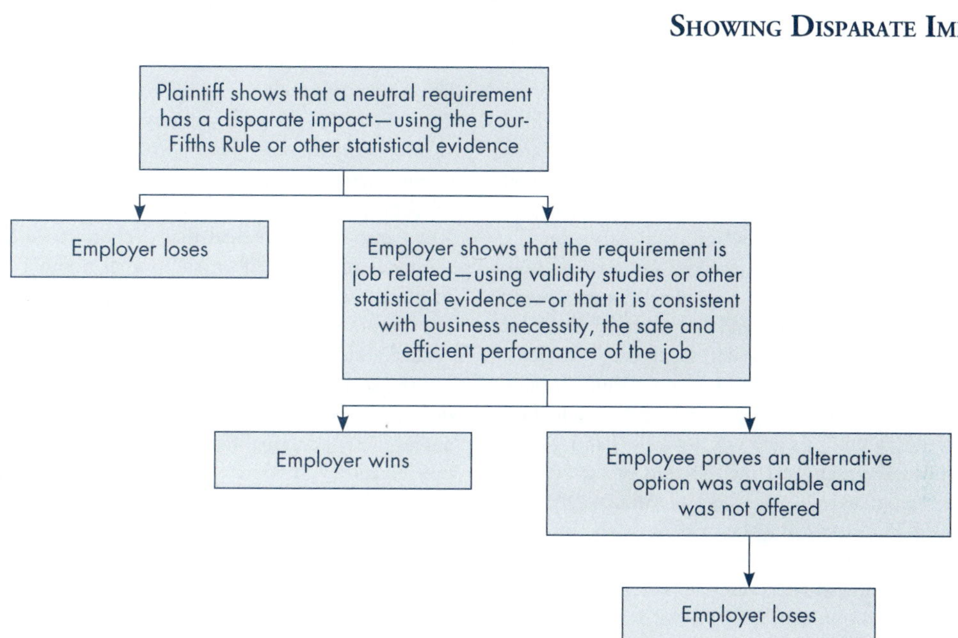

The "Bottom Line" and Discrimination

Does the fact that an employer's work force contains a higher percentage of minority employees than does the general population of the surrounding area serve to insulate the employer from claims of discrimination in employment? The following case involves a similar issue. The employer argues that the "bottom line"—the number of minority employees promoted—disproves any claim of discrimination. The claimants argue that the employer used a discriminatory exam (one with a disparate impact on minorities) to select those eligible for promotion. Was Title VII violated?

case 6.3 » Connecticut v. Teal

457 U.S. 440 (1982)

Facts: This case addresses the question of whether an employer sued for violation of Title VII of the Civil Rights Act of 1964 may assert a "bottom-line" theory as a defense. Under the "bottom-line" theory, an employer's acts of racial discrimination in promotions—by using an examination having disparate impact—would not render the employer liable for the racial discrimination suffered by employees disqualified from consideration for promotion by the examination if the "bottom-line" result of the promotional process were an appropriate racial balance.

Winnie Teal, Rose Walker, Edith Latney, and Grace Clark were African-American employees of the Department of Income Maintenance of the state of Connecticut. Each was promoted provisionally to the position of welfare eligibility supervisor and served in that capacity for almost two years. However, to gain permanent status as supervisors, they had to go through a selection process that required, as the first step, a passing score on a written examination. This written test was administered to 329 candidates on December 2, 1978. Of these candidates, 48 identified themselves as African American and 259 identified themselves as white. The results of the examination were announced in March 1979. With the passing score set at 65, 54.17 percent of the identified African-American candidates passed. The pass rate for African-American candidates was approximately 68 percent of the passing rate for the candidates. Teal, Walker, Latney, and Clark [the respondents] were among those who failed the examination, and they were excluded from further consideration for permanent supervisory positions. They filed suit against the state of Connecticut, claiming that the use of the exam that disqualified African Americans in disproportionate numbers and was not job related. Meanwhile, based on the exam and the selection process results, Connecticut promoted 11 of the 48 African-American employees and 35 of the 259 white employees who took the test. The overall result of the selection process was that, of the 48 identified African-American candidates who participated in the selection process, 22.9 percent were promoted, and of the 259 identified white candidates, 13.5 percent were promoted. Connecticut argued this "bottom-line" result, more favorable to blacks than to whites, should be a complete defense to the suit. The trial court held that the "bottom-line" promotion percentages here were a defense, and that Connecticut's use of the exam was not a violation of Title VII. But on appeal, the U.S. Court of Appeals for the Second Circuit reversed the trial court decision. The court of appeals held that when an exam used to screen out applicants from proceeding to the next step in the selection process had a disparate impact on minority candidates, the employer must show that the exam was job related. Connecticut then appealed to the U.S. Supreme Court.

Issue: Is the "bottom line"—the fact that an employer promoted a greater percentage of minority employees than nonminorities—a defense to the claim of using an exam that had a disparate impact on African-American candidates for promotion?

Decision: Justice Brennan, writing the majority opinion for the Court, noted that the literal language of Section 703(a)(2), as interpreted by *Griggs,* speaks, not in terms of jobs and promotions, but in terms of *limitations and classifications* that would deprive any individual of employment opportunities. When an employer uses a screening exam that has not been shown to be job related and operates as a barrier to deny a minority or woman applicant employment or promotion, and that barrier has a significant adverse effect on minorities or women, then the applicant has been deprived of an employment *opportunity* "because of … race, color, religion, sex, or national origin." Section 703(a)(2) prohibits discriminatory "artificial, arbitrary, and unnecessary barriers to employment," that "limit … or classify … applicants for employment … in any way which would deprive or tend to deprive any individual of employment *opportunities.*" The Court has never held that Section 703(a)(2) required the focus to be placed on the overall number of minority or female applicants actually hired or promoted instead of on the promotion requirements or selection process that created a discriminatory bar to employment opportunities.

The suggestion that disparate impact should be measured only at the bottom line ignores the fact that Title VII guarantees these individual respondents the *opportunity* to compete equally with white workers on the basis of job-related criteria. Title VII strives to achieve equality of opportunity by rooting out "artificial, arbitrary, and unnecessary" employer-created barriers to professional development that have a discriminatory impact upon individuals. Therefore, the respondents' rights under Section 703(a)(2) have been violated unless Connecticut can demonstrate that the examination was job related; that is, demonstrate that it measured skills related to effective performance in the role of welfare eligibility supervisor.

The respondents' claim of disparate impact from the examination, which operated as a pass–fail barrier to employment opportunity, stated a prima facie case of employment discrimination under Section 703(a)(2) despite the employer's nondiscriminatory "bottom-line" promotions. The "bottom-line" is no defense to their prima facie case under Section 703(h).

Those claiming that the "bottom line" may be a defense to a charge of discrimination against an individual employee appear to confuse unlawful discrimination with discriminatory intent. But the factual question of discriminatory intent is not what is at issue in this case. Here petitioners seek simply to justify discrimination against respondents on the basis of their favorable treatment of other members of respondents' racial group. Under Title VII, "A racially balanced work force cannot immunize an employer from liability for specific acts of discrimination." *Furnco Construction Corp. v. Waters* (1978).

Every *individual* employee is protected against both discriminatory treatment and against "practices that are fair in form, but discriminatory in operation." Requirements and tests that have a discriminatory impact are merely some of the more subtle, but also more pervasive "practices and devices which have fostered racially stratified job environments to the disadvantage of minority citizens."

The Supreme Court held that Connecticut's nondiscriminatory "bottom line" for promotions was not a defense to respondents' prima facie claim of employment discrimination by using an exam that had a disparate impact on minority candidates and was not shown to be job related. The Court affirmed the judgment of the Court of Appeals for the Second Circuit.

«

Seniority and Title VII

Seniority
The length of service on the job.

Seniority, the length of service on the job, is frequently used to determine entitlement to employment benefits, promotions, or transfers, and even job security itself. Seniority systems usually provide that worker layoffs be conducted on the basis of inverse seniority; those with the least length of service, or seniority, are laid off before those with greater seniority. Seniority within a department may also be used to determine eligibility to transfer to a different department.

Seniority may have a discriminatory effect when an employer, prior to the adoption of Title VII, refused to hire women or minority workers. If, after Title VII's adoption, the employer does hire them, those workers will have the least seniority. In the event of a layoff, the workers who lose their jobs will be women and minorities, whereas white males will retain their jobs. The layoffs by inverse seniority have a disparate impact on women and minorities. Does this mean the seniority system is in violation of Title VII, as in *Griggs*?

Section 703(h) of Title VII contains an exemption for bona fide seniority systems. That section states, in part,

> Notwithstanding any other provision of this title, it shall not be an unlawful employment practice for an employer to apply different standards of compensation or different terms, conditions, or privileges of employment pursuant to a bona fide seniority or merit system provided that such differences are not the result of an intention to discriminate because of race, color, religion, sex or national origin.

What is the effect of Section 703(h) on a seniority system that has a disparate impact or that operates to perpetuate the effects of prior discrimination? In several cases decided shortly after the adoption of Title VII, courts held that departmental seniority systems that operated to deter minority employees from transferring out of low-paying and inferior jobs were in violation of Title VII because they perpetuated prior discrimination. The issue reached the Supreme Court in the case of *International Brotherhood of Teamsters v. United States*. The Court had to address the question of whether a seniority system that perpetuated the effects of prior discrimination was bona fide under Section 703(h).

case 6.4 » International Brotherhood of Teamsters v. United States

431 U.S. 324 (1977)

Stewart, J.

This litigation brings here several important questions under Title VII of the Civil Rights Act of 1964.... The issues grow out of alleged unlawful employment practices engaged in by an employer and a union. The employer [T.I.M.E.-DC] is a common carrier of motor freight with nationwide operations, and the union represents a large group of its employees. The district court and the court of appeals held that the employer had violated Title VII by engaging in a pattern and practice of employment discrimination against Negroes and Spanish-surnamed Americans, and that the union had violated the Act by agreeing with the employer to create and maintain a seniority system that perpetuated the effects of past racial and ethnic discrimination....

... The central claim ... was that the company had engaged in a pattern or practice of discriminating against minorities in hiring so-called line drivers. Those Negroes and Spanish-surnamed persons who had been hired, the Government alleged, were given lower paying, less desirable jobs as servicemen or local city drivers, and were thereafter discriminated against with respect to promotions and transfers. In this connection the complaint also challenged the seniority system established by the collective-bargaining agreements between the employer and the union. The Government sought a general injunctive remedy and specific "make whole" relief for all individual discriminatees, which would allow them an opportunity to transfer to line-driver jobs with full company seniority for all purposes.

The cases went to trial and the district court found that the Government had shown "by a preponderance of the evidence that T.I.M.E.-D.C. and its predecessor companies were engaged in a plan and practice of discrimination in violation of Title VII...." The court further found that the seniority system contained in the collective-bargaining contracts between the company and the union violated Title VII because it "operate[d] to impede the free transfer of minority groups into and within the company." Both the company and the union were enjoined from committing further violations of Title VII....

... The union further contends that the seniority system contained in the collective-bargaining agreements in no way violated Title VII. If these contentions are correct, it is unnecessary, of course, to reach any of the issues concerning remedies that so occupied the attention of the court of appeals.

... The district court and the court of appeals, on the basis of substantial evidence, held that the Government had proved a prima facie case of systematic and purposeful employment discrimination, continuing well beyond the effective date of Title VII. The company's attempts to rebut that conclusion were held to be inadequate. For the reasons we have summarized, there is no warrant for this Court to disturb the findings of the district court and the court of appeals on this basic issue....

The district court and the court of appeals also found that the seniority system contained in the collective-bargaining agreements between the company and the union operated to violate Title VII of the Act.

For purposes of calculating benefits, such as vacations, pensions, and other fringe benefits, an employee's seniority under this system runs from the date he joins the company, and takes into account his total service in all jobs and bargaining units. For competitive purposes, however, such as determining the order in which employees may bid for particular jobs, are laid off, or are recalled from layoff, it is bargaining-unit seniority that controls. Thus, a line driver's seniority, for purposes of bidding for particular runs and protection against layoff, takes into account only the length of time he has been a line driver at a particular terminal. The practical effect is that a city driver or serviceman who transfers to a line-driver job must forfeit all the competitive seniority he has accumulated in his previous bargaining unit and start at the bottom of the line drivers' "board."

The vice of this arrangement, as found by the district court and the court of appeals, was that it "locked" minority workers into inferior jobs and perpetuated prior discrimination by discouraging transfers to jobs as line drivers. While the disincentive applied to all workers, including whites, it was Negroes and Spanish-surnamed persons who, those courts found, suffered the most because many of them had been denied the equal opportunity to become line drivers when they were initially hired, whereas whites either had not sought or were refused line-driver positions for reasons unrelated to their race or national origin.

The linchpin of the theory embraced by the district court and the court of appeals was that a discriminatee who must forfeit his competitive seniority in order finally to obtain a line-driver job will never be able to "catch up" to the seniority level of his contemporary who was not subject to discrimination. Accordingly, this continued, built-in disadvantage to the prior discriminatee who transfers to a line-driver job was held to constitute a continuing violation of Title VII, for which both the employer and the union who jointly created and maintained the seniority system were liable.

The union, while acknowledging that the seniority system may in some sense perpetuate the effects of prior discrimination, asserts that the system is immunized from a finding of illegality by reason of Section 703(h) of Title VII....

It argues that the seniority system in this case is "bona fide" within the meaning of Section 703(h) when judged in light of its history, intent, application, and all of the circumstances under which it was created and is maintained. More specifically, the union claims that the central purpose of Section 703(h) is to ensure that mere perpetuation of *pre-Act* discrimination is not unlawful under Title VII. And, whether or not Section 703(h) immunizes the perpetuation of *post-Act* discrimination, the union claims that the seniority system in this case has no such effect. Its position in this Court, as has been its position throughout this litigation, is that the seniority system presents no hurdles to post-Act discriminatees who seek retroactive seniority to the date they would have become line drivers but for the company's discrimination. Indeed, the union asserts that under its collective-bargaining agreements the union will itself take up the cause of the post-Act victim and attempt, through grievance procedures, to gain for him full "make whole" relief, including appropriate seniority.

The Government responds that a seniority system that perpetuates the effects of prior discrimination—pre- or post-Act—can never be "bona fide" under Section 703(h); at a minimum Title VII prohibits those applications of a seniority system that perpetuate the effects on incumbent employees of prior discriminatory job assignments.

The issues thus joined are open ones in this Court....

Because the company discriminated both before and after the enactment of Title VII, the seniority system is said to have operated to perpetuate the effects of both pre- and post-Act discrimination. Post-Act discriminatees, however, may obtain full "make whole" relief, including retroactive seniority under *Franks v. Bowman*. without attacking the legality of the seniority system as applied to them. *Franks* made clear and the union acknowledges that retroactive seniority may be awarded as relief from an employer's discriminatory hiring and assignment policies even if the seniority system agreement itself makes no provision for such relief. Here the Government has proved that the company engaged in a post-Act pattern of discriminatory hiring, assignment, transfer, and promotion policies. Any Negro or Spanish-surnamed American injured by those policies may receive all appropriate relief as a direct remedy for this discrimination.

What remains for review is the judgment that the seniority system unlawfully perpetuated the effects of pre-Act discrimination. We must decide, in short, whether Section 703(h) validates otherwise bona fide seniority systems that afford no constructive seniority to victims discriminated against prior to the effective date of Title VII, and it is to that issue that we now turn.

... Were it not for Section 703(h), the seniority system in this case would seem to fall under the *Griggs* rationale. The heart of the system is its allocation of the choicest jobs, the greatest protection against layoffs, and other advantages to those employees who have been line drivers for the longest time. Where, because of the employer's prior intentional discrimination, the line drivers with the longest tenure are without exception white, the advantages of the seniority system flow disproportionately to them and away from Negro and Spanish-surnamed employees who might by now have enjoyed those advantages had not the employer discriminated before the passage of the Act. This disproportionate distribution of advantages does in a very real sense "operate to 'freeze' the status quo of prior discriminatory employment practices." But both the literal terms of Section 703(h) and the legislative history of Title VII demonstrate that Congress considered this very effect of many seniority systems and extended a measure of immunity to them....

In sum, the unmistakable purpose of Section 703(h) was to make clear that the routine application of a bona fide seniority system would not be unlawful under Title VII. This was the intended result even where the employer's pre-Act discrimination resulted in whites having greater existing seniority rights than Negroes. Although a seniority system inevitably tends to perpetuate the effects of pre-Act discrimination in such cases, the congressional judgment was that Title VII should not outlaw the use of existing seniority lists and thereby destroy or water down the vested seniority rights of employees simply because their employer had engaged in discrimination prior to the passage of the Act.

To be sure, Section 703(h) does not immunize all seniority systems. It refers only to "bona fide" systems, and a proviso requires that any differences in treatment not be "the result of an intention to discriminate because of race ... or national origin...." But our reading of the legislative history compels us to reject the Government's broad argument that no seniority system that tends to perpetuate pre-Act discrimination can be "bona fide." ... Accordingly, we hold that an otherwise neutral, legitimate seniority system does not become unlawful under Title VII simply because it may perpetuate pre-Act discrimination. Congress did not intend to make it illegal for employees with vested seniority rights to continue to exercise those rights, even at the expense of pre-Act discriminatees....

The seniority system in this case is entirely bona fide. It applies equally to all races and ethnic groups. To the extent that it "locks" employees into nonline-driver jobs, it does so for all. The city drivers and servicemen who are discouraged from transferring to line-driver jobs are not all Negroes or Spanish-surnamed Americans; to the contrary, the overwhelming majority are white. The placing of line drivers in a separate bargaining unit from other employees is rational, in accord with the industry practice, and consistent with NLRB precedents. It is conceded that the seniority system did not have its genesis in racial discrimination, and that it was negotiated and has been maintained free from any illegal purpose. In these circumstances, the single fact that the system extends no retroactive seniority to pre-Act discriminatees does not make it unlawful.

Because the seniority system was protected by Section 703(h), the union's conduct in agreeing to and maintaining the system did not violate Title VII. On remand, the district court's injunction against the union must be vacated.

... **So ordered.**

Case Questions

1. How does the seniority system in this case operate to deter minority employees from transferring? Does it affect white employees the same way?
2. Was the Teamsters Union guilty of intentional discrimination in this case? Was the union guilty of disparate impact discrimination? What is the relevance of Section 703(h) to this case? Explain your answer.
3. When is a seniority system "bona fide" under Section 703(h)?

In *American Tobacco Co. v. Patterson*,[12] the Supreme Court ruled that Section 703(h) applies to seniority systems that were adopted after the passage of Title VII as well as to those in operation at the time Title VII was adopted. The protection of Section 703(h) extends to rules that determine entry into seniority classifications, according to the 1980 Supreme Court decision in *California Brewers Association v. Bryan*.[13] That case involved the rule that an employee had to have worked at least forty-five weeks in a calendar year to be classified as a "permanent employee." Permanent employees were given preference in layoffs and transfers over temporary employees (those not meeting the forty-five-week rule). An African American employee claimed that the forty-five-week rule had a disparate impact on minority workers. The Court, rejecting the claim, held that the forty-five-week rule was within the Section 703(h) exemption for bona fide seniority systems.

According to *Teamsters*, a seniority system is bona fide within the meaning of Section 703(h) when it is neutral on its face (it applies equally to all employees) and it is not intentionally used to discriminate. Furthermore, the court will consider whether the system had its origin in discrimination, whether it has been negotiated and maintained free from discriminatory intent, and whether the basis of the seniority system is reasonable in light of industry practice.

Section 706(e)(2), added to Title VII by the 1991 amendments, addresses the time limits for a challenge to a seniority system that allegedly is used intentionally to discriminate in violation of Title VII. According to that section, a claim may be filed after the allegedly discriminatory seniority system is adopted, after the plaintiff becomes subject to the seniority system, or after the plaintiff is injured by the application of the seniority system. Section 706(e)(2) was intended to reverse the Supreme Court decision in *Lorance v. AT&T Technologies, Inc.*,[14] which held that the time limit for challenging a seniority system ran from the date on which the system was adopted, even if the plaintiff was not subjected to the system until five years later.

---

[12] 456 U.S. 63 (1982).

[13] 444 U.S. 598 (1980).

[14] 490 U.S. 900 (1989).

Concept *Summary* » 6.5

BONA FIDE SENIORITY SYSTEM

- Section 703(h) immunizes employment actions taken pursuant to a bona fide seniority system.
- To be bona fide within the meaning of Section 703(h), the seniority system:
  - Must be neutral on its face—apply equally to all groups
  - Must have its origin free from intentional discrimination
  - Must have been negotiated and maintained free from intentional discrimination
  - Must have its basis be reasonable in light of industry practice

Mixed-Motive Cases Under Title VII

In *Price Waterhouse v. Hopkins*,[15] the Supreme Court held that when a plaintiff shows that the employer has considered an illegal factor under Title VII (race, sex, color, religion, or national origin) in making an employment decision, the employer must demonstrate that it would have reached the same decision if it had not considered the illegal factor. According to the Supreme Court, if the employer can show this, the employer can escape liability under Title VII; that is, it will not have violated the statute.

The 1991 amendments to Title VII addressed this "mixed-motive" situation and partially overruled the *Price Waterhouse* decision. Section 703(m) now states that "an unlawful employment practice is established when the complaining party demonstrates that race, color, religion, sex, or national origin was a motivating factor for any employment practice, even though other factors also motivated the practice." That is, the employer violates Title VII when an illegal factor is considered, even though there may have been other factors also motivating the decision or practice. If the employer is able to show that it would have reached the same decision in the absence of the illegal factor, then the employer's liability for remedy under Title VII is reduced under Section 706(g)(2)(B). Section 706(g)(2)(B), also added by the 1991 amendments, states that the employer is subject to a court order to cease violating Title VII and is liable for the plaintiff's legal fees but is not required to pay damages or to reinstate or hire the plaintiff. In *Desert Palace, Inc. v. Costa*,[16] the Supreme Court held that a plaintiff need only "demonstrate" that the defendant used a prohibited factor (race, color, gender, religion, or natural origin) as one of the motives for an employment action. That demonstration can be made either by circumstantial evidence or direct evidence; the act does not require direct evidence to raise the mixed motive analysis under Section 703(m).

---

[15] 490 U.S. 228 (1989).

[16] 539 U.S. 90 (2003).

Retaliation Under Title VII

Section 704(a) of Title VII prohibits retaliation by an employer, union, or employment agency against an employee or applicant because that person has opposed any practice that is prohibited by Title VII (known as the "opposition clause") or because that person has taken part in or assisted any investigation, hearing, or proceeding under Title VII (known as the "participation clause"). To demonstrate a case of retaliation under Section 704(a), plaintiffs must demonstrate that:

(1) they were engaged in an activity or activities protected under Title VII;

(2) they suffered an adverse employment decision or action; and

(3) there was a causal link between the protected activity and the adverse employment decision.

The "protected activity" must be related to either the participation clause or the opposition clause of Section 704. An employee who voluntarily cooperated with an employer's internal investigation of a sexual harassment complaint was protected under the opposition clause of Section 704 even though she did not make a complaint to the employer or file a formal charge under Title VII; the Supreme Court held that her subsequent discharge by the employer violated Title VII, according to *Crawford v. Metropolitan Govt. of Nashville & Davidson City.*[17] In *Burlington Northern & Santa Fe Railroad Co. v. White,*[18] the U.S. Supreme Court held that retaliation under Title VII is not limited to ultimate employment decisions such as promotion or termination, but rather includes any action that a reasonable employee would find to be materially adverse—such that it might dissuade a reasonable worker from making or supporting a charge under Title VII. Section 704(a) also protects former employees from retaliation, according to *Robinson v. Shell Oil Company.*[19] In that case, an employer gave a former employee a negative reference because the employee had filed a Title VII charge against the employer; the Supreme Court ruled that giving the negative reference was retaliation in violation of Section 704(a).

Concept Summary » 6.6

Retaliation Under Title VII

- To demonstrate retaliation under Title VII, plaintiffs must show the following:
  - They were engaged in an activity protected under Title VII or opposed a practice prohibited by Title VII;
  - They suffered an adverse employment decision or employment action;

AND

  - There was a casual link between the protected activity and the adverse employment decision.

---

[17]129 S.Ct. 846 (2009).

[18]548 U.S. 53 (2006).

[19]519 U.S. 337 (1997).

Affirmative Action and Title VII

Affirmative action has been an extremely controversial and divisive legal and political issue since Title VII was enacted in 1964. Critics of affirmative action argue that it benefited individuals who were not, themselves, victims of illegal discrimination, and operated to discriminate against persons (usually white males) who were not personally guilty of illegal discrimination. Supporters argue that affirmative action is necessary to overcome the legacy of prior discrimination and that our society is still not free from racism and sexism.

Affirmative action programs in employment involve giving some kind of preference in hiring or promotion to qualified female or minority employees. Employees who are not members of the group being accorded the preference (usually white males) may therefore be at a disadvantage for hiring or promotion. Recall that *McDonald v. Santa Fe Trail* held that Title VII protected every individual employee from discrimination because of race, sex, color, religion, or national origin. Is the denial of preferential treatment to employees not within the preferred group (defined by race or sex) a violation of Title VII? Affirmative action programs by public sector employers raise legal issues under the U.S. Constitution as well as under Title VII: Does the affirmative action program violate the constitutional prohibitions against intentional discrimination contained in the Equal Protection Clause? The discussion of affirmative action in this chapter focuses mainly on affirmative action under Title VII. Chapter 11 will also discuss affirmative action under the Constitution.

Title VII does not require employers to enact affirmative action plans; however, the courts have often ordered affirmative action when the employer has been found in violation of Title VII. The courts have consistently held that remedial affirmative action plans—plans set up to remedy prior illegal discrimination—are permissible under Title VII because such plans may be necessary to overcome the effects of the employer's prior illegal discrimination. But if the plan is a voluntary one and the employer has not been found guilty of prior discrimination, does it violate Title VII by discriminating on the basis of race or gender?

This question was addressed by the U.S. Supreme Court in the next case.

case 6.5 »

United Steelworkers of America v. Weber

443 U.S. 193 (1979)

Facts: Weber, a white employee, was excluded from a training program that was run by the employer and the union and designed to create more skilled craftworkers. Under a voluntary affirmative action program, 50 percent of the spaces in the training program were reserved for minority employees, while admission to the other 50 percent of the spaces was based on seniority. The affirmative action plan was temporary and would cease when the percentage of skilled craftworkers who were minorities was similar to the percentage of minority workers in the local labor market. Weber was not senior enough to qualify for the seats not reserved for minority employees, but he did have more seniority than the minority employees who were admitted under the affirmative action program. Weber filed a complaint with the EEOC, and ultimately sued the employer and the union, arguing that excluding him from the training program while admitting less senior minority employees was race discrimination prohibited by Title VII.

Issue: Did the voluntary affirmative action plan adopted by the employer and union violate Title VII because it excluded more senior white employees while admitting minority employees with less seniority?

Decision: The Supreme Court held that the voluntary affirmative action program was legal under Title VII. The Court's majority opinion stated that Title VII's prohibition in Sections 703(a) and (d) against racial discrimination does not condemn all private, voluntary, race-conscious affirmative action plans. The Court stated that the purpose of the affirmative action plan was consistent with the purposes of Title VII bothwere designed to break down old patterns of racial segregation and hierarchy, and both were intended to open employment opportunities for African Americans in occupations that have been traditionally closed to them.

As well, the plan did not unnecessarily trammel the interests of the white employees. The plan did not require the discharge of white workers and their replacement with new African Americans, and. the plan did not create an absolute bar to the advancement of white employees because half of those trained in the program will be white. The plan was a temporary measure and was not intended to maintain racial balance, but simply to eliminate a manifest racial imbalance. Preferential selection of craft trainees at the Gramercy plant will end as soon as the percentage of black skilled craftworkers in the Gramercy plant approximates the percentage of blacks in the local labor force.

The Court in *Weber* upheld the legality of a voluntarily adopted affirmative action program by an employer who had not been found guilty of prior discrimination. When is an employer justified in initiating a voluntary affirmative action program? What kind of evidence must the employer demonstrate to support the adoption of the affirmative action plan? What evidence must an individual who alleges discriminatory treatment by an employer acting pursuant to an affirmative action program demonstrate to establish a claim under Title VII?

In *Johnson v. Transportation Agency, Santa Clara County, California*,[20] the U.S. Supreme Court held that an employer can justify the adoption of an affirmative action plan by showing that "a conspicuous … imbalance in traditionally segregated job categories" exists in its work force. A plaintiff challenging an employment decision based on an affirmative action plan has the burden of showing that the affirmative action plan is not valid. In *Johnson*, the Court upheld the legality of an affirmative action plan that granted a relative preference to women and minorities in hiring for positions in traditionally male-dominated jobs. The fact that the employer's plan had no definite termination date was not a problem, according to the court, because it did not set aside a specific number of positions. The plan used a flexible, case-by-case approach and was designed to attain a more balanced work force. The affirmative action plan, therefore, met the criteria set out in *Weber:* It furthered the purposes of Title VII by overcoming a manifest imbalance in traditionally segregated job categories, and it did not "unnecessarily trammel" the interests of the nonpreferred employees.

Both *Weber* and *Johnson* involved suits under Title VII. When considering the legality of affirmative action programs under the U.S. Constitution, the approach used by the courts is slightly different from the approach used in Title VII cases. In *Wygant v. Jackson Board of Education*[21] and in *Adarand Constructors, Inc. v. Pena,*[22] the U.S. Supreme Court held that affirmative action plans by public sector employers must pass the strict scrutiny test under the U.S. Constitution. The strict scrutiny test, a two-part test, requires that (1) the affirmative action plan must serve a "compelling governmental interest," and (2) it must be "narrowly tailored" to further that compelling interest. Although the language of the test for the legality of affirmative action under Title VII and the test under the Constitution is similar, the Supreme Court has

[20] 480 U.S. 616 (1987).

[21] 476 U.S. 267 (1986).

[22] 515 U.S. 200 (1995).

emphasized that the tests are distinct and different. In two cases that dealt with the constitutionality of using affirmative action criteria for admissions to the University of Michigan, and not with employment, *Grutter v. Bollinger*[23] and *Gratz v. Bollinger*,[24] a majority of the Supreme Court held that achieving the educational benefits of a diverse student body was a compelling governmental interest.[25] Those cases indicate that achieving the benefits of a diverse work force may be a sufficiently compelling governmental interest to justify the use of affirmative action programs for hiring or promotion decisions by public sector employers.

But in addition to being justified by a compelling governmental interest, the affirmative action program must also be narrowly tailored to achieve that purpose. The courts have held that affirmative action programs that give a relative preference rather than an absolute one—race or gender is used as a "plus factor" rather than as the determinative factor—are narrowly tailored. Programs that are temporary and that will cease when the employer achieves a more diverse work force have also been held to be narrowly tailored. However, an affirmative action program that required laying off or firing nonminority employees was held to be unconstitutional in *Wygant v. Jackson Board of Education*.

The following case discusses the legality of an affirmative action plan under both Title VII and the Constitution.

case 6.6 » UNIVERSITY AND COMMUNITY COLLEGE SYSTEM OF NEVADA V. FARMER

113 Nev. 90, 930 P.2d 730 (Nev. Sup. Ct. 1997), cert. denied, 523 U.S. 1004 (March 9, 1998)

Background

Between 1989 and 1991, only one percent of the University of Nevada's full-time faculty were black, while eighty-seven to eighty-nine percent of the full-time faculty were white; twenty-five to twenty-seven percent of the full-time faculty were women. In order to remedy this racial imbalance, the University instituted the "minority bonus policy," an unwritten amendment to its affirmative action policy which allowed a department to hire an additional faculty member following the initial placement of a minority candidate.

In 1990, the University advertised for an impending vacancy in the sociology department. The announcement of the position vacancy emphasized a need for proficiency in social psychology and mentioned a salary range between $28,000.00 and $34,000.00, dependent upon experience and qualifications. The University's hiring guidelines require departments to conduct more than one interview; however, this procedure may be waived in certain cases. Yvette Farmer was one of the three finalists chosen by the search committee for the position but the University obtained a waiver to interview only one candidate, Johnson Makoba, a black African male emigrant. The department chair recalled that the search committee ranked Makoba first among the three finalists. Because of a perceived shortage of black Ph.D. candidates, coupled with Makoba's strong academic achievements, the search committee sought approval to make a job offer to Makoba at a salary of $35,000.00, with an increase to $40,000.00 upon completing his Ph.D. This initial offer exceeded the advertised salary range for the position; even though Makoba had not accepted any competing offers, the University justified its offer as a method of preempting any other institutions from hiring Makoba. Makoba

[23]539 U.S. 306 (2003).

[24]539 U.S. 244 (2003).

[25]However, in the 2007 decision of *Parents Involved in Community Schools v. Seattle School Dist. No.1*, 127 S.Ct. 2738 (2007), the Supreme Court held that a public school system's goal of achieving racial diversity in schools did not justify the use of race as a factor in assigning pupils to a particular school.

accepted the job offer. Farmer was subsequently hired by the University the following year; the position for which she was hired was created under the "minority bonus policy." Her salary was set at $31,000.00 and a $2,000.00 raise after completion of her dissertation.

Farmer sued the University and Community College System of Nevada ("the University") claiming violations of Title VII of the Civil Rights Act, the Equal Pay Act and for breach of an employment contract. Farmer alleged that despite the fact that she was more qualified, the University hired a black male (Makoba) as an assistant professor of sociology instead of her because of the University's affirmative action plan. After a trial on her claims, the trial court jury awarded her $40,000 in damages, and the University appealed to the Supreme Court of Nevada. The issue on appeal was the legality of the University's affirmative action plan under both Title VII and the U.S. Constitution.

Steffen, Chief Justice

... Farmer claims that she was more qualified for the position initially offered to Makoba. However, the curriculum vitae for both candidates revealed comparable strengths with respect to their educational backgrounds, publishing, areas of specialization, and teaching experience. The search committee concluded that despite some inequalities, their strengths and weaknesses complemented each other; hence, as a result of the additional position created by the minority bonus policy, the department hired Farmer one year later....

The University contends that the district court made a substantial error of law by failing to enter a proposed jury instruction which would have apprised the jury that Title VII does not proscribe race-based affirmative action programs designed to remedy the effects of past discrimination against traditionally disadvantaged classes. The University asserts that the district court's rejection of the proposed instruction left the jury with the impression that all race-based affirmative action programs are proscribed....

Farmer ... asserts that the University's unwritten minority bonus policy contravenes its published affirmative action plan. Finally, Farmer alleges that all race-based affirmative action plans are proscribed under Title VII of the Civil Rights Act as amended in 1991; therefore, the University discriminated against her as a female, a protected class under Title VII.

Tension exists between the goals of affirmative action and Title VII's proscription against employment practices which are motivated by considerations of race, religion, sex, or national origin, because Congress failed to provide a statutory exception for affirmative action under Title VII. Until recently, the Supreme Court's failure to achieve a majority opinion in affirmative action cases has produced schizophrenic results....

United Steelworkers of America v. Weber is the seminal case defining permissible voluntary affirmative action plans [under Title VII].... Under *Weber*, a permissible voluntary affirmative action plan must: (1) further Title VII's statutory purpose by "break[ing] down old patterns of racial segregation and hierarchy" in "occupations which have been traditionally closed to them"; (2) not "unnecessarily trammel the interests of white employees"; (3) be "a temporary measure; it is not intended to maintain racial balance, but simply to eliminate a manifest racial imbalance." ...

Most recently, in *Adarand Constructors, Inc. v. Pena*, the Supreme Court revisited [the issue of the constitutionality of] affirmative action in the context of a minority set-aside program in federal highway construction. In the 5–4 opinion, the Court held that a reviewing court must apply strict scrutiny analysis for all race-based affirmative action programs, whether enacted by a federal, state, or local entity.... [T]he Court explicitly stated "that federal racial classifications, like those of a State, must serve a compelling governmental interest, and must be narrowly tailored to further that interest." ...

Here, in addition to considerations of race, the University based its employment decision on such criteria as educational background, publishing, teaching experience, and areas of specialization. This satisfies [the previous cases'] commands that race must be only one of several factors used in evaluating applicants. We also view the desirability of a racially diverse faculty as sufficiently analogous to the constitutionally permissible attainment of a racially diverse student body....

The University's affirmative action plan conforms to the *Weber* factors [under Title VII]. The University's attempts to diversify its faculty by opening up positions traditionally closed to minorities satisfies the first factor under *Weber*. Second, the plan does not "unnecessarily trammel the interests of white employees." The University's 1992 Affirmative Action Report revealed that whites held eighty-seven to eighty-nine percent of the full-time faculty positions. Finally, with blacks occupying only one percent of the faculty positions, it is clear that through its minority bonus policy, the University attempted to attain, as opposed to maintain, a racial balance.

The University's affirmative action plan ... [also] passes constitutional muster. The University demonstrated that it has a compelling interest in fostering a culturally and ethnically diverse faculty. A failure to attract minority faculty perpetuates the University's white enclave and further limits student exposure to multicultural diversity. Moreover, the minority bonus policy is narrowly tailored to accelerate racial and gender diversity. Through its affirmative action policies, the University achieved greater racial and gender diversity by hiring Makoba and Farmer. Of note is the fact that Farmer's position is a direct result of the minority bonus policy.

Although Farmer contends that she was more qualified for Makoba's position, the search committee determined that Makoba's qualifications slightly exceeded Farmer's. The record, however, reveals that both candidates were equal in most respects. Therefore, given the aspect of subjectivity involved in choosing between candidates, the University must be given the latitude to make its own employment decisions provided that they are not discriminatory.

[The court then rejected Farmer's claim that the 1991 amendments to Title VII prohibit affirmative action.]

... we conclude that the jury was not equipped to understand the necessary legal basis upon which it could reach its factual conclusions concerning the legality of the University's affirmative action plan. Moreover, the undisputed facts of this case warranted judgment in favor of the University as a matter of law. Therefore, even if the jury had been properly instructed, the district court should have granted the University's motion for judgment notwithstanding the [jury's] verdict. Reversal of the jury's verdict on the Title VII claim is therefore in order.

The University ... has adopted a lawful race-conscious affirmative action policy in order to remedy the effects of a manifest racial imbalance in a traditionally segregated job category....

The University has aggressively sought to achieve more than employment neutrality by encouraging its departments to hire qualified minorities, women, veterans, and handicapped individuals. The minority bonus policy, albeit an unwritten one, is merely a tool for achieving cultural diversity and furthering the substantive goals of affirmative action.

For the reasons discussed above, the University's affirmative action policies pass constitutional muster. Farmer has failed to raise any material facts or law which would render the University's affirmative action policy constitutionally infirm....

Young and Rose, JJ., concur.

Springer, J., dissenting [omitted]

Case Questions

1. Why did the University adopt its affirmative action plan and the "minority bonus policy"?
2. How was Farmer injured or disadvantaged under the University's affirmative action plan?
3. How does the Court here apply the Weber test for legality of affirmative action under Title VII to the facts of this case? Explain your answer.
4. According to the Court here, how does the constitutional "strict scrutiny" test apply to the facts of the case here? Explain your answer.

The affirmative action plan in the previous case was a voluntary plan; that is, it was not imposed upon the employer by a court to remedy a finding of illegal discrimination. The affirmative action plans in the *Weber, Johnson*, and *Wygant* cases were also voluntary plans. Title VII specifically mentions affirmative action as a possible remedy available under §706(g)(1). In *Local 28, Sheet Metal Workers Int. Ass'n. v. EEOC,*[26] the Supreme Court held that Title VII permits a court to require the adoption of an affirmative action program to remedy "persistent or egregious discrimination." The Court in *U.S. v. Paradise,*[27] upheld the constitutionality of a judicially imposed affirmative action program to remedy race discrimination in promotion decisions by the Alabama State Police.

[26] 478 U.S. 421 (1986).

[27] 480 U.S. 149 (1987).

ethical DILEMMA

You are the human resource manager for Wydget Corporation, a small manufacturing company. Wydget's assembly plant is located in an inner-city neighborhood, and most of its production employees are African Americans and Hispanics, as well as some Vietnamese and Laotians who live nearby. Wydget's managers are white males who sometimes have difficulty relating to the production workers. The board of directors of Wydget is considering whether to establish a training program to groom production workers for management positions, targeting women and minorities in particular. The CEO has asked you to prepare a memo to guide the board of directors in its decision about the training program. Should you establish such a program? How can you encourage minority employees to enter the program without discouraging the white employees? What criteria should be used for determining admission into the training program? Address these issues in a short memo, explaining and supporting your position.

Other Provisions of Title VII

The 1991 amendments to Title VII added two other provisions to the act. One addresses the ability to challenge affirmative action programs and other employment practices that implement judicial decisions or result from consent decrees. Section 703(n) now provides that such practice may not be challenged by any person who had notice of such decision or decree and had an opportunity to present objections or by any person whose interests were adequately represented by another person who had previously challenged the judgment or decree on the same legal ground and with a similar factual situation. Challenges based on claims that the order or decree was obtained through fraud or collusion, is "transparently invalid," or was entered by a court lacking jurisdiction are not prevented by Section 703(n).

The other added provision deals with the practice known as "race norming." Race norming refers to the use of different cutoff scores for different racial, gender, or ethnic groups of applicants or adjusting test scores or otherwise altering test results of employment-related tests on the basis of race, color, religion, sex, or national origin. Section 703(l) makes race norming an unlawful employment practice under Title VII.

CHAPTER REVIEW

» Key Terms

Title VII of the Civil Rights Act of 1964	« 114	***business necessity***	« 117	***Four-Fifths Rule***	« 122
disparate treatment	« 116	***disparate impact***	« 118	***content validity***	« 123
bona fide occupational qualification (BFOQ)	« 117	***Uniform Guidelines on Employee Selection Procedures***	« 121	***construct validity***	« 123
				criterion-related validity	« 124

» Summary

- Equal employment opportunity (EEO) legislation represents a statutory limitation on the employment-at-will doctrine. The EEO laws prohibit termination and other forms of employment discrimination because of an employee's race, color, gender, religion, or national origin. Title VII of the Civil Rights Act of 1964, as amended, protects all individuals from intentional discrimination (known as disparate treatment) as well as the unintentionally discriminatory effect of apparently neutral criteria that are not job related (known as disparate impact).
- Employers are free to hire employees who can effectively perform the job. The Uniform Guidelines on Employee Selection define methods for employers to demonstrate that employment selection criteria are job related; employers can use content-related, criterion-related, or construct-related validity studies to meet the requirements of Section 703(k). Employers are also free to use seniority for employment decisions, as long as the seniority system is bona fide under Section 703(h) of Title VII.
- Affirmative action, giving some employees preferential treatment because of their race, color, or gender, has become more controversial in recent years. Remedial affirmative action, designed to remedy the lingering effects of prior illegal discrimination, has been endorsed by the courts; the *Weber* and *Johnson* decisions allow voluntary affirmative action under Title VII when it is consistent with the purposes of the act and does not unduly harm those persons who are not of the preferred group. More recent decisions of the U.S. Supreme Court indicate that the Court will look very closely at an employer's justification for adopting an affirmative action program.

» Problems

Questions

1. What are the main provisions of Title VII of the Civil Rights Act? Which employers are subject to Title VII? What employees or applicants are protected from employment discrimination by Title VII?
2. What is meant by a bona fide occupational qualification (BFOQ)? What must be shown to establish that job-selection requirements are a BFOQ?
3. What is meant by disparate treatment? What is meant by disparate impact? What is the difference between disparate treatment and disparate impact? How can a claim of disparate impact be demonstrated?
4. When is a seniority system protected against challenge under Title VII? When is a seniority system bona fide under Title VII?
5. What are the Uniform Guidelines for Employee Selection? What is the Four-Fifths Rule, and how is it used?

Case Problems

6. Southeastern Pennsylvania Transportation Authority [SEPTA] is a regional mass transit authority in the Philadelphia area. SEPTA sought to upgrade the fitness level of its transit police by adopting a requirement that, in order to be hired as transit police, job applicants must be able to run 1.5 miles in twelve minutes or less.

   The requirement was developed by a consultant to SEPTA, Dr. Paul Davis, after he studied the job of transit officer for several days. He felt that completion of the 1.5 mile run within the required time would ensure that the applicant possessed sufficient aerobic capacity to perform the job. SEPTA also tested transit officers hired prior to the adoption of the 1.5-mile run requirement, and discovered that a significant percentage of the incumbents could not complete the run within the required time limit. Some of the incumbent employees who failed the run requirement had been awarded special recognition and commendations for their job performance. One female employee, hired by mistake after she had failed the requirement, was nominated for Officer of the Year awards because of her job performance.

   After the adoption of the 1.5-mile run requirement, only 12 percent of the female applicants successfully passed it, while 56 percent of the male applicants passed it; SEPTA employed 234 transit police officers, but only sixteen of the officers were female. A group of female applicants who failed the 1.5-mile run requirement filed suit against SEPTA under Title VII, alleging that the 1.5-mile run requirement had a disparate impact on women. SEPTA argued that the more physically fit officers are, the better they are able to perform their job. Will the plaintiffs be successful in their suit, or can SEPTA establish that the 1.5-mile run requirement is job related? Explain your answer. See *Lanning v. Southeastern Pennsylvania Transportation Authority* [181 F.3d 478 (3d Cir. 1999), *cert. denied*, 528 U.S. 1131 (Mem.) (2000)].
7. The city of Montgomery, Alabama, had a policy for its fire department that any firefighter convicted of a felony would be discharged. In August 1998, two white firefighters were fired after being convicted of felonies. However, on appealing their discharges to the Montgomery City-County Personnel Board, they were reinstated. In November 1999, Tate Williams, an African American man, was discharged, and on appeal, the board refused reinstatement.

   Was this refusal race discrimination? Does your answer depend on whether the white firefighters had committed less serious felonies than Williams? Should the board have considered each man's overall record in rendering its decisions? Are there any other factors the board should have taken into account? See *Williams v. City of Montgomery* [742 F.2d 586, 37 F.E.P. Cases 52 (11th Cir. 1984)].
8. In November 1997, a supervisor saw white employee Bill Peterson accept from an employee of another company on the same construction site what appeared to be a marijuana cigarette. Peterson subsequently confessed to taking a few puffs from the "joint," and he was fired. A day later, the company

put out a general hiring call; Peterson applied and was rehired. In August 1998, the company promulgated a new rule that anyone fired could not be rehired for at least thirty days. In October 1998, Albert Leonard, an African American man, was hired as a laborer. During a routine lunchbox check by a security guard at the gate that very day, Leonard was found to be in possession of marijuana. He was fired the next day, and his termination notice contained a notation "not for rehire." Leonard was never rehired, either within or after thirty days from his discharge.

Is he a victim of race discrimination? Explain your answer. See *Leonard v. Walsh Construction Co.* [37 F.E.P. Cases 60 (U.S. Dist. Ct. S.D. Ga. 1985)].

9. Sue Bedean, an engineer, was hired by the Tennessee Valley Authority under a voluntarily adopted affirmative action plan designed to bring females into traditionally male technical jobs. After a few months on the job, Bedean was laid off because of economic conditions; the other two engineers in her department, who were both male, were not laid off. The employer asserted that the two male engineers were more qualified than Bedean. Bedean filed suit under Title VII, arguing that the employer's failure to give her preference on layoff was a violation of the affirmative action program and of Title VII.

   Is the employer required by Title VII to continue to give preference to Bedean, after hiring her under an affirmative action program? Is a violation of the affirmative action program a violation of Title VII? Explain your answer. See *Liao v. TVA* [867 F.2d 1366 (11th Cir. 1989)].

10. Chaline, a white male, was employed as a production manager at an African American–oriented radio station in Houston. Chaline had previously worked as a disc jockey at other radio stations. The radio station manager, for financial reasons, decided to combine the production manager position with that of a part-time disc jockey. Chaline desired to remain as production manager and to assume the disc jockey duties. However, the station manager told him that he lacked the proper "voice" to serve as disc jockey on the station and that he was not sensitive to the listening tastes of the African American audience. The radio station had never had a white disc jockey. The station manager asked Chaline to transfer to a position in the sales department; Chaline refused and was discharged. Chaline filed a complaint with the EEOC challenging his discharge on grounds of race discrimination.

    If the complaint results in a suit in federal court, will Chaline be successful? Explain your answer. See *Chaline v. KCOH, Inc.* [693 F.2d 477 (5th Cir. 1982)].

11. The city of South Bend, Indiana, adopted an affirmative action plan to give preference to minorities in hiring and promotion for police and firefighter positions. The affirmative action plan was adopted voluntarily by the city in response to the marked disparity between the percentage of African American employees in the police and fire departments with the percentage of African Americans in the general population of the city. Janowiak, a white, filed suit challenging the affirmative action plan; he argued that the city should have compared the percentage of African-American employees in the police and fire departments with the percentage of African Americans in the qualified area labor pool to determine whether the affirmative action plan was necessary.

    How will the court rule on his challenge? What is the proper comparison to determine whether the affirmative action plan is justified? See *Janowiak v. Corporate City of South Bend* [836 F.2d 1034 [PN (7th Cir. 1987), *cert. denied*, 489 U.S. 1051 (1989)].

12. Crystal Chambers, a twenty-two-year-old unmarried African American woman, was employed by the Girls Club of Omaha, Nebraska. The club, whose membership was more than half African American, had as its stated goal to "provide a safe alternative from the streets and to help girls take care of themselves." Because of two incidents of unwed motherhood among staff members, the club's directors passed a Negative Role Model Policy, which stated that any unwed employee who became pregnant would be terminated. Pursuant to this policy, Chambers was fired when she became pregnant.

    Can you suggest a theory under which Chambers could challenge her discharge based on race discrimination? Can the Girls Club articulate a bona fide business reason sufficient to overcome a finding of race discrimination? See *Chambers v. Omaha Girls Club* [834 F.2d 697 (8th Cir. 1987)].

13. King was hired by the University of Minnesota as a full, tenured professor in 1990. He was appointed to the Afro-American Studies Department and later became chairman. Four years later, he was asked to step down as chairman. The university alleged it had received many complaints from King's students and colleagues concerning poor teaching, absence from class, low enrollment, and undocumented research. Consequently, the university repeatedly denied King salary increases and ultimately approved a 9–2 vote in his department to fire him, pursuant to the complex procedures in the school's tenure code.

    Assuming that King was guilty as charged, what arguments, if any, remain available to him if he tries to challenge his dismissal on the basis of race discrimination? See *King v. University of Minnesota* [774 F.2d. 224 (8th Cir. 1985), *cert. denied*, 475 U.S. 1095 (1986)].

14. Since his childhood, Dennis Walters, a white man, had dreamed of becoming director of the Atlanta Cyclorama, a gigantic display depicting a famous Civil War battle. Before ever applying for this position, Walters gained experience in historical preservation with the Georgia Historical Commission and the North Carolina Museum of History. Despite this experience, every time he applied for the post (which became available in 1996), he was rejected. First, an African American female who had been a campaign aide to Atlanta's mayor was selected. When she left the job a year later, Walters reapplied. He was judged qualified, but when an African American applicant was ruled unqualified, the position was reannounced rather than being offered to Walters or any other white candidate. Next, an African-American male was hired. When he was fired a short time later, Walters again applied. This time a white female was hired. Walters filed a race discrimination charge with the EEOC.

    Was Walters a victim of race discrimination? Does it matter whether the white female who ultimately got the job was better qualified than Walters? If Walters wins, what remedy should he receive? See *Walters v. City of Atlanta* [803 F.2d 1135 (11th Cir. 1986)].

15. Wal-Mart's Transportation Division includes approximately 8,000 drivers in forty-seven field transportation offices nationwide. The hiring process for drivers at every transportation office is identical. First, new drivers are recruited almost exclusively through the "word of mouth" referral by current Wal-Mart drivers. Wal-Mart provides current drivers with a "1-800 card" to pass out to prospective applicants. The card lists the minimum driver qualifications and a 1-800 number drivers can call to request an application. Wal-Mart does little advertising of its OTR driver positions in addition to the 1-800 cards. Potential applicants who call the 1-800 number, regardless of the transportation office to which they wish to apply, are initially processed and screened at Wal-Mart's Bentonville headquarters. An application is then sent to the potential applicant. The applicant is instructed to return the completed application to the Bentonville headquarters. If the application is completed and the applicant meets the minimum requirements, and if the applicant's preferred transportation office is currently hiring, the application is then forwarded to the appropriate transportation office. Sometimes an applicant submits an application directly to a transportation office. After the application is forwarded from the Bentonville headquarters to the appropriate transportation office, a screening committee, consisting of current drivers at the transportation office, decides which applicants will be granted an interview, and then interviews those applicants. A management committee then interviews applicants who successfully complete the screening committee interview.

    Wal-Mart has no written or objective criteria to guide the driver screening committees when those committees analyze applicants during the hiring process. Wal-Mart does require each driver screening committee to be 50 percent diverse, but that does not guarantee that any member of the screening committee is African American.

    Tommy Armstrong and Darryl Nelson are African-American truck drivers who applied for positions as over-the-road ("OTR") truck drivers at transportation offices operated by Wal-Mart; their applications were rejected. They discover that

African Americans represent 8.4 percent of Wal-Mart's OTR drivers nationwide; a study prepared for the American Trucking Association using U.S. Census Bureau data indicates that African Americans represent about 15 percent of persons employed as "driver/sales workers or truck drivers" in the "truck transportation" industry nationwide in the U.S. Armstrong and Nelson decide to file a suit under Title VII against Wal-Mart. Would their claim involve disparate impact or disparate treatment discrimination? What problems may be raised by the "word of mouth" referral system for recruiting new drivers? What defenses could Wal-Mart raise in response to their suit? See *Nelson v. Mal-Mart Stores, Inc.* [2009 WL 88550 (E.D. Ark. Jan. 13, 2009)].

Hypothetical Scenarios

16. Cantor Enterprises is a public relations and advertising agency; its clerical and administrative staff are represented by a union. A number of the clerical staff are college graduates with marketing or advertising degrees who hope to be promoted into a copywriter or account manager position; however, such workers become discouraged if there are no higher positions open, and their job performance deteriorates or they quit. The result is a high turnover rate for the clerical and administrative positions. Cantor and the union decide that the company will no longer hire college graduates for entry-level clerical and administrative positions. Does this "no college degree" rule violate Title VII? Explain your answer.
17. Stith, Inc. operates a small manufacturing plant. In order to upgrade its workforce, Stith's H.R. manager decides as of January 1, 2009, to adopt a requirement that the company will only hire applicants with a high school diploma or equivalent. Previously, Stith had only required applicants to complete a simple aptitude test, and a number of current employees are not high school graduates. Does the new requirement raise any problems under Title VII? Explain.
18. Cratchit worked as a staff accountant for Scrooge & Partners. Scrooge asks Cratchit to interview the applicants for an administrative assistant position, but tells him not to hire any African-American applicants. Cratchit reminds Scrooge that Title VII prohibits race discrimination, and Scrooge immediately removes Cratchit from the interview process and cuts his working hours from forty hours per week to thirty hours per week. Has Scrooge violated Title VII? Why? Is Cratchit protected by Title VII in this situation? Explain.
19. A local call center is seeking to expand its work force. Because of the nature of its work, the call center decides to hire only persons who speak perfect English and not to hire any person who has a noticeable accent or, in the words of the call center manager, "who sounds too much like a minority." Does the call center hiring policy violate Title VII? Explain your answer.
20. HomeCare provides healthcare aides who work in the homes of its clients, who are generally elderly or disabled persons. Some of the clients are bedridden and require total personal care. HomeCare screens applicants for employment by using a strength test—the applicants must be able to lift a dummy weighing 150 pounds. The strength test disqualifies most female applicants, as well as a majority of Asian and Hispanic male applicants. What must HomeCare do to show that the strength test has validity under the Uniform Guidelines? Should HomeCare use a construct validity, a content validity, or a criterion-related validity approach for the strength test? Explain.

Gender and Family Issues: *Title VII and Other Legislation*

The preceding chapter introduced Title VII of the Civil Rights Act of 1964 and discussed its prohibitions on employment discrimination based on race. This chapter focuses on discrimination based on gender, family-related issues, and the relevant provisions of Title VII and other legislation.

Gender Discrimination

Title VII prohibits any discrimination in terms or conditions of employment because of an employee's sex; it also prohibits limiting, segregating, or classifying employees or applicants in any way that would deprive individuals of employment opportunities or otherwise adversely affect their status as employees because of their sex. (While some people may argue that sex is a biological or physical construct and gender is a psychological and sociological construct, the courts have generally treated the terms "sex" and "gender" as interchangeable.) Title VII protects all individuals from employment discrimination based on sex or gender; this means both men and women are protected from sex discrimination in employment. Employers who refuse to hire an individual for a particular job because of that individual's gender violate Title VII, unless the employer can demonstrate that being of a particular gender is a ***bona fide occupational qualification (BFOQ)*** for that job. The act also prohibits advertising for male or female employees in help-wanted notices (unless it is a BFOQ) or maintaining separate seniority lists for male and female employees. Unions that negotiate such separate seniority lists or refuse to admit female members also violate Title VII.

Bona Fide Occupational Qualification (BFOQ)
An exception to the civil rights law that allows an employer to hire employees of a specific gender, religion, or national origin when business necessity—the safe and efficient performance of the particular job—requires it.

Dress Codes and Grooming Requirements

The act prohibits imposing different working conditions or requirements on similarly situated male and female employees because of the employee's gender. Some cases have involved employer dress codes and grooming standards. Employers need not have identical dress code or grooming requirements for men and women. For example, men may be required to wear a necktie while women are not, *Fountain v. Safeway Stores, Inc.*;[1] men may be required to wear suits while women must wear "appropriate business attire," *Baker v. California Land Title Co.*;[2] or women may be permitted to wear long hair while males are not permitted to have hair below the collar, *Willingham v. Macon Tel. Publishing Co.*[3] The key is that the standards are related to commonly accepted social norms and are reasonably related to legitimate business needs; however, an employer who requires women to wear a uniform but has no such requirement for men violates Title VII, *Carroll v. Talman Federal Savings & Loan Assoc.*[4]

Gender as a BFOQ

As mentioned in Chapter 6 the act does allow employers to hire only employees of one sex, or of a particular religion or national origin, if that trait is a BFOQ; most BFOQ cases involve BFOQs based on gender. Section 703(e)(1), which defines the BFOQ exemption, states that

> ... it shall not be an unlawful employment practice for an employer to hire and employ employees, for an employment agency to classify, or refer for employment any individual, for a labor organization to classify its membership or to classify or refer for employment any individual ... on the basis of his religion, sex, or national origin in those certain instances where religion, sex, or national origin is a bona fide occupational qualification reasonably necessary to the normal operation of that particular business or enterprise....

The statute requires that an employer justify a BFOQ on the basis of business necessity. In other words, the safe and efficient performance of the job in question requires that the employee be of a particular gender, religion, or national origin. Employer convenience, customer preference, or co-worker preference is not sufficient to support a BFOQ. The additional costs to provide bathroom facilities for female workers was also not a sufficient basis to establish a BFOQ. What must an employer demonstrate to establish a claim of business necessity? The following case illustrates the approach taken by the courts when an employer claims a BFOQ based on gender.

case 7.1 »

Diaz v. Pan American World Airways

442 F.2d 385 (U.S. Court of Appeals for the Fifth Circuit, 1971)

Facts: Diaz, a male, applied for a job as flight cabin attendant with Pan American Airlines [Pan Am] but was rejected because Pan Am had a policy of only hiring females for that position. He then filed charges with the Equal Employment Opportunity Commission (EEOC), alleging that Pan Am had unlawfully discriminated against him on the grounds of sex. EEOC efforts to resolve the complaint were unsuccessful, and Diaz then filed a class action suit on behalf of himself and others similarly situated, alleging that Pan Am had violated Section 703 of Title VII. The trial court also found that Pan Am's passengers overwhelmingly preferred to be served by female flight attendants, and that given the unique environment of an aircraft cabin, female flight attendants were better able to attend to the special psychological needs of the passengers. Pan Am did not claim that there were no males with the necessary qualities to perform these functions, but

[1] 555 F.2d 753 (9th Cir. 1977).

[2] 507 F.2d 895 (9th Cir. 1974), *cert. denied*, 422 U.S. 1046 (1975).

[3] 507 F.2d 1084 (5th Cir. 1975).

[4] 604 F.2d 1028 (7th Cir. 1979), *cert. denied*, 445 U.S. 929 (1980).

the trial court found that the actualities of the hiring process would make it more difficult to find these few males. The trial court held that hiring females only was the best method for screening out applicants likely to be unsatisfactory, and to require Pan Am to hire male flight attendants would likely reduce the average level of flight attendant performance. The trial court held that hiring only female flight attendants was a "bona fide occupational qualification (BFOQ) reasonably necessary to the normal operation" of Pan Am's business. The trial court ruled in favor of Pan Am, and Diaz appealed to the U.S. Court of Appeals for the Fifth Circuit.

Issue: Did Pan Am demonstrate that being female is a bona fide occupational qualification for the job of flight cabin attendant?

Decision: The court of appeals held that the BFOQ provision, Section 703(e), should be read narrowly; the test for a BFOQ is business *necessity*, not business *convenience*. Discrimination based on sex under a BFOQ is valid only when the *essence* of the business operation would be undermined by not hiring members of one sex exclusively. The primary function of an airline is to transport passengers safely from one point to another. While a pleasant environment—enhanced by the obvious cosmetic effect that female flight attendants provide as well as their apparent ability to perform the nonmechanical functions of the job in a more effective manner than most men—may be important, it is tangential to the essence of the business involved. Pan Am did not show that having male flight attendants so seriously affected the operation of an airline as to jeopardize or even minimize its ability to provide safe transportation from one place to another. Indeed, the evidence disclosed that many airlines, including Pan Am, had hired both men and women flight attendants in the past, and Pan Am did use male flight attendants on some of its foreign flights. When hiring, Pan Am could consider the ability of *individuals* to perform the nonmechanical functions of the job. However, because the nonmechanical aspects of the job of flight cabin attendant were not "reasonably necessary to the normal operation" of Pan Am's business, Pan Am could not exclude all males from the job simply because most males may not have performed as adequately as most females. Pan Am had not shown that "all or substantially all men" were unable to perform the requirements of the job properly. Pan Am claimed that the customers preferred female flight attendants because they could better perform the nonmechanical aspects of the job, but those aspects were tangential to the business, and customer preference cannot justify a BFOQ.

The court of appeals reversed the judgment of the trial court, and held that Pan Am had not established that hiring only females as flight attendants was a BFOQ.

«

In *Dothard v. Rawlinson*,[5] the U.S. Supreme Court held that the dangers presented by the conditions in Alabama maximum security prisons, characterized as "rampant violence" and "a jungle atmosphere," would reduce the ability of female guards to maintain order and would pose dangers to the female guards and to other prisoners. The Court therefore upheld as a BFOQ an Alabama state regulation restricting guard positions in maximum security prisons to persons of the same gender as the prisoners being guarded.

The courts will also allow claims of a BFOQ based on gender when community standards of morality or propriety require that employees be of a particular gender. Examples include hiring females only to work as attendants in the fitting rooms of a women's dress shop and hiring males as locker-room attendants for the men's locker rooms in an athletic club.

Gender Stereotyping

If an employer refuses to promote a female employee because, despite her excellent performance, she is perceived as being too aggressive and unfeminine, has the employer engaged in sex discrimination in violation of Title VII? This question was addressed by the Supreme Court in the following case.

[5] 433 U.S. 321 (1977).

case 7.2 » PRICE WATERHOUSE v. ANN B. HOPKINS

490 U.S. 228 (1989)

[Ann Hopkins, a senior manager in an office of Price Waterhouse, was proposed for partnership in 1982. She was neither offered nor denied admission to the partnership; instead, her candidacy was held for reconsideration the following year. When the partners in her office later refused to repropose her for partnership, she sued under Title VII of the Civil Rights Act of 1964, charging that the firm had discriminated against her on the basis of sex in its decisions regarding partnership. The trial court ruled in her favor on the question of liability and the U.S. Court of Appeals for the District of Columbia Circuit affirmed. Price Waterhouse then appealed to the U.S. Supreme Court, which granted *certiorari* to hear the appeal.]

Brennan, J.

At Price Waterhouse, a nationwide professional accounting partnership, a senior manager becomes a candidate for partnership when the partners in her local office submit her name as a candidate. All the other partners in the firm are then invited to submit written comments on each candidate—either on a "long" or a "short" form, depending on the partner's degree of exposure to the candidate. Not every partner in the firm submits comments on every candidate. After reviewing the comments and interviewing the partners who submitted them, the firm's Admissions Committee makes a recommendation to the Policy Board. This recommendation will be either that the firm accept the candidate for partnership, put her application on "hold," or deny her the promotion outright. The Policy Board then decides whether to submit the candidate's name to the entire partnership for a vote, to "hold" her candidacy, or to reject her. The recommendation of the Admissions Committee, and the decision of the Policy Board, are not controlled by fixed guidelines: a certain number of positive comments from partners will not guarantee a candidate's admission to the partnership, nor will a specific quantity of negative comments necessarily defeat her application....

Ann Hopkins had worked at Price Waterhouse's Office of Government Services in Washington, D.C. for five years when the partners in that office proposed her as a candidate for partnership. Of the 662 partners at the firm at that time, 7 were women. Of the 88 persons proposed for partnership that year, only 1—Hopkins—was a woman. Forty-seven of these candidates were admitted to the partnership, 21 were rejected, and 20—including Hopkins—were "held" for reconsideration the following year. Thirteen of the 32 partners who had submitted comments on Hopkins supported her bid for partnership. Three partners recommended that her candidacy be placed on hold, eight stated that they did not have an informed opinion about her, and eight recommended that she be denied partnership.

In a jointly prepared statement supporting her candidacy, the partners in Hopkins' office showcased her successful 2-year effort to secure a $25 million contract with the Department of State, labeling it "an outstanding performance" and one that Hopkins carried out "virtually at the partner level." ... Judge Gesell specifically found that Hopkins had "played a key role in Price Waterhouse's successful effort to win a multi-million dollar contract with the Department of State." Indeed, he went on, "[n]one of the other partnership candidates at Price Waterhouse that year had a comparable record in terms of successfully securing major contracts for the partnership." The partners in Hopkins' office praised her character as well as her accomplishments, describing her in their joint statement as "an outstanding professional" who had a "deft touch," a "strong character, independence and integrity." Clients appear to have agreed with these assessments.... Evaluations such as these led Judge Gesell to conclude that Hopkins "had no difficulty dealing with clients and her clients appear to have been very pleased with her work" and that she "was generally viewed as a highly competent project leader who worked long hours, pushed vigorously to meet deadlines and demanded much from the multidisciplinary staffs with which she worked."

On too many occasions, however, Hopkins' aggressiveness apparently spilled over into abrasiveness. Staff members seem to have borne the brunt of Hopkins' brusqueness. Long before her bid for partnership, partners evaluating her work had counseled her to improve her relations with staff members. Although later evaluations indicate an improvement, Hopkins' perceived shortcomings in this important area eventually doomed her bid for partnership. Virtually all of the partners' negative remarks about Hopkins—even those of partners supporting her—had to do with her "interpersonal skills." Both "[s]upporters and opponents of her candidacy," stressed Judge Gesell, "indicated that she was sometimes overly aggressive, unduly harsh, difficult to work with and impatient with staff."

There were clear signs, though, that some of the partners reacted negatively to Hopkins' personality because she was a woman. One partner described her as "macho"; another suggested that she "overcompensated for being a woman";a third advised her to take "a course at charm school." Several partners criticized her use of profanity; in response, one partner suggested that those partners objected to her swearing only "because it[']s a lady using foul language." Another supporter explained that Hopkins "ha[d] matured from a tough-talking somewhat masculine hard-nosed mgr to an authoritative, formidable, but much more appealing lady ptr candidate." But it was the man who, as Judge Gesell found, bore responsibility for explaining to Hopkins the reasons for the Policy Board's decision to place her candidacy on hold who delivered the *coup de grace*: in order to improve her chances for partnership, Thomas Beyer advised, Hopkins should "walk more femininely, talk more femininely, dress more femininely, wear make-up, have her hair styled, and wear jewelry."

Dr. Susan Fiske, a social psychologist and Associate Professor of Psychology at Carnegie-Mellon University, testified at trial that the partnership selection process at Price Waterhouse was likely influenced by sex stereotyping. Her testimony focused not only on the overtly sex-based comments of partners but also on gender-neutral remarks, made by partners who knew Hopkins only slightly, that were intensely critical of her. One partner, for example, baldly stated that Hopkins was "universally disliked" by staff, and another described her as "consistently annoying and irritating"; yet these were people who had had very little contact with Hopkins. According to Fiske, Hopkins' uniqueness (as the only woman in the pool of candidates) and the subjectivity of the evaluations made it likely that sharply critical remarks such as these were the product of sex stereotyping....

In previous years, other female candidates for partnership also had been evaluated in sex-based terms. As a general matter, Judge Gesell concluded "[c]andidates were viewed favorably if partners believed they maintained their femin[in]ity while becoming effective professional managers"; in this environment, "[t]o be identified as a 'women's lib[b]er' was regarded as [a] negative comment." In fact, the judge found that in previous years "[o]ne partner repeatedly commented that he could not consider any woman seriously as a partnership candidate and believed that women were not even capable of functioning as senior managers—yet the firm took no action to discourage his comments and recorded his vote in the overall summary of the evaluations."

Judge Gesell found that Price Waterhouse legitimately emphasized interpersonal skills in its partnership decisions, and also found that the firm had not fabricated its complaints about Hopkins' interpersonal skills as a pretext for discrimination. Moreover, he concluded, the firm did not give decisive emphasis to such traits only because Hopkins was a woman; although there were male candidates who lacked these skills but who were admitted to partnership, the judge found that these candidates possessed other, positive traits that Hopkins lacked.

The judge went on to decide, however, that some of the partners' remarks about Hopkins stemmed from an impermissibly cabined view of the proper behavior of women, and that Price Waterhouse had done nothing to disavow reliance on such comments. He held that Price Waterhouse had unlawfully discriminated against Hopkins on the basis of sex by consciously giving credence and effect to partners' comments that resulted from sex stereotyping. Noting that Price Waterhouse could avoid equitable relief by proving by clear and convincing evidence that it would have placed Hopkins' candidacy on hold even absent this discrimination, the judge decided that the firm had not carried this heavy burden....

Congress' intent to forbid employers to take gender into account in making employment decisions appears on the face of the statute.... We take these words [of Title VII] to mean that gender must be irrelevant to employment decisions.... The critical inquiry, the one commanded by the words of Section 703(a)(1), is whether gender was a factor in the employment decision *at the moment it was made*. Moreover, since we know that the words "because of" do not mean "solely because of," we also know that Title VII meant to condemn even those decisions based on a mixture of legitimate and illegitimate considerations. When, therefore, an employer considers both gender and legitimate factors at the time of making a decision, that decision was "because of" sex and the other, legitimate considerations—even if we may say later, in the context of litigation, that the decision would have been the same if gender had not been taken into account....

... The central point is this: while an employer may not take gender into account in making an employment decision (except in those very narrow circumstances in which gender is a BFOQ), it is free to decide against a woman for other reasons.... the employer's burden is most appropriately deemed an affirmative defense: the plaintiff must persuade the factfinder on one point, and then the employer, if it wishes to prevail, must persuade it on another.

... our assumption always has been that if an employer allows gender to affect its decisionmaking process, then it must carry the burden of justifying its ultimate decision....

In saying that gender played a motivating part in an employment decision, we mean that, if we asked the employer at the moment of the decision what its reasons were and if we received a truthful response, one of those reasons would be that the applicant or employee was a woman. In the specific context of sex stereotyping, an employer who acts on the basis of a belief that a woman cannot be aggressive, or that she must not be, has acted on the basis of gender....

As to the existence of sex stereotyping in this case, we are not inclined to quarrel with the District Court's conclusion that a number of the partners' comments showed sex stereotyping at work. As for the legal relevance of sex stereotyping, we are beyond the day when an employer could evaluate employees by assuming or insisting that they matched the stereotype associated with their group, for "[i]n forbidding employers to discriminate against individuals because of their sex, Congress intended to strike at the entire spectrum of disparate treatment of men and women resulting from sex stereotypes." An employer who objects to aggressiveness in women but whose positions require this trait places women in an intolerable and impermissible Catch-22: out of a job if they behave aggressively and out of a job if they don't. Title VII lifts women out of this bind.

Remarks at work that are based on sex stereotypes do not inevitably prove that gender played a part in a particular employment decision. The plaintiff must show that the employer actually relied on her gender in making its decision. In making this showing, stereotyped remarks can certainly be evidence that gender played a part. In any event, the stereotyping in this case did not simply consist of stray remarks. On the contrary, Hopkins proved that Price Waterhouse invited partners to submit comments; that some of the comments stemmed from sex stereotyping; that an important part of the Policy Board's decision on Hopkins was an assessment of the submitted comments; and that Price Waterhouse in no way disclaimed reliance on the sex-linked evaluations. This is not, as Price Waterhouse suggests, "discrimination in the air"; rather, it is, as Hopkins puts it, "discrimination brought to ground and visited upon" an employee....

In finding that some of the partners' comments reflected sex stereotyping, the District Court relied in part on Dr. Fiske's expert testimony....

Indeed, we are tempted to say that Dr. Fiske's expert testimony was merely icing on Hopkins' cake. It takes no special training to discern sex stereotyping in a description of an aggressive female employee as requiring "a course at charm school." Nor, turning to Thomas Beyer's memorable advice to Hopkins, does it require expertise in psychology to know that, if an employee's flawed "interpersonal skills" can be corrected by a soft-hued suit or a new shade of lipstick, perhaps it is the employee's sex and not her interpersonal skills that has drawn the criticism.

... Hopkins showed that the partnership solicited evaluations from all of the firm's partners; that it generally relied very heavily on such evaluations in making its decision; that some of the partners' comments were the product of stereotyping; and that the firm in no way disclaimed reliance on those particular comments, either in Hopkins' case or in the past. Certainly a plausible—and, one might say, inevitable—conclusion to draw from this set of circumstances is that the Policy Board in making its decision did in fact take into account all of the partners' comments, including the comments that were motivated by stereotypical notions about women's proper deportment....

... The District Judge acknowledged that Hopkins' conduct justified complaints about her behavior as a senior manager. But he also concluded that the reactions of at least some of the partners were reactions to her as a woman manager. Where an evaluation is based on a subjective assessment of a person's strengths and weaknesses, it is simply not true that each evaluator will focus on, or even mention, the same weaknesses. Thus, even if we knew that Hopkins had "personality problems," this would not tell us that the partners who cast their evaluations of Hopkins in sex-based terms would have criticized her as sharply (or criticized her at all) if she had been a man. It is not our job to review the evidence and decide that the negative reactions to Hopkins were based on reality; our perception of Hopkins' character is irrelevant. We sit not to determine whether Ms. Hopkins is nice, but to decide whether the partners reacted negatively to her personality because she is a woman.

[The Supreme Court affirmed the trial court and court of appeals' decision that employment decisions based on sex stereotypes may constitute sex discrimination in violation of Title VII.]

Case Questions

1. Was Hopkins qualified for promotion to partner? Explain your answer. What reasons did Price Waterhouse offer for its refusal to promote Hopkins to partner?
2. How did the partners' comments about Hopkins reflect gender stereotyping? What was the relevance of those comments? Does it matter that Price Waterhouse also had legitimate reasons for its reluctance to promote Hopkins?
3. Does an employer action based upon mixed motives, some of which include sex or race discrimination, violate Title VII? What defenses can an employer offer under such circumstances?

On remand from the Supreme Court, the District Court in *Hopkins* found that Ann Hopkins had been a victim of sex discrimination and ordered that Price Waterhouse make her a partner.[6] Following the Supreme Court decision in *Price Waterhouse v. Hopkins*, the federal courts of appeals have held that discrimination against a male employee with gender identity disorder because he did not conform to the employer's expectations of how a male should act and behave was discrimination based on stereotypical gender norms and violated Title VII.[7] In *Nichols v. Azteca Restaurant Enterprises, Inc.*[8] the court held that abuse and ridicule by co-workers and managers directed at a male employee because he appeared effeminate and did not conform to a male stereotype was discrimination "because of sex" for the purposes of establishing a claim under Title VII.

"Gender-Plus" Discrimination

An employer who places additional requirements on employees of a certain gender but not on employees of the opposite gender violates Title VII. For example, an employer who refuses to hire females having preschool-aged children but who does hire males with preschool-aged children is guilty of an unlawful employment practice under Title VII.[9] Such discrimination is known as gender-plus discrimination. The additional requirement (no preschool-aged children) becomes an issue only for employees of a certain gender (female). Because similarly situated employees (men and women both with preschool-aged children) are treated differently because of their gender, the employer is guilty of gender discrimination.

[6]See *Hopkins v. Price Waterhouse*, 737 F. Supp. 1202, (D.D.C. 1990); *aff'd.*, 920 F.2d 967 (D.C. Cir. 1990).

[7]*Smith v. City of Salem, Ohio*, 369 F.3d 912 (6th Cir. 2004).

[8]256 F.3d 864 (9th Cir. 2001).

[9]*Phillips v. Martin Marietta Corp.*, 400 U.S. 542 (1971).

Concept *Summary* » 7.1

Gender Discrimination

- Gender discrimination
  - Title VII prohibits discrimination because of sex
    - Applies to both men and women
  - Examples of gender discrimination
    - Advertising for male/female employees in help-wanted ads
    - Maintaining separate male/female seniority lists
    - Requiring dress codes that are not equally enforced
      - Note that dress codes need not be identical for men and women
  - Exceptions
    - If sex is a BFOQ for a job
- Gender stereotyping
  - Occurs when a person is treated differently because he/she does not conform to the typical social norms expected of his/her gender
  - Examples of gender stereotyping
    - Overly aggressive women
    - Effeminate men
- Sex-plus discrimination
  - Occurs when a person is treated differently because of additional requirements beyond gender
  - Examples of gender-plus discrimination
    - Refusing to hire women with preschool-aged children, but hiring men with preschool-aged children

Gender Discrimination in Pay

Both Title VII and the Equal Pay Act apply to gender discrimination in pay. There is some overlap between Title VII and the Equal Pay Act, which was passed in 1963, a year before the passage of Title VII. There are also some differences in coverage, procedures, and remedies. This section discusses both the Equal Pay Act and the Title VII provisions relating to gender-based pay differentials.

Equal Pay Act of 1963
Federal legislation that requires that men and women performing substantially equal work be paid equally.

The Equal Pay Act

The ***Equal Pay Act of 1963*** requires that men and women performing substantially equal work be paid equally. The act does not reach other forms of gender discrimination or discrimination on grounds other than gender.

Coverage

The Equal Pay Act was enacted as an amendment to the Fair Labor Standards Act, which regulates minimum wages and maximum hours of employment. The Equal Pay Act's coverage is therefore similar to that of the Fair Labor Standards Act. The act applies to all employers "engaged in commerce (interstate commerce)," and it applies to all employees of an "enterprise engaged in commerce." Virtually all substantial business operations are covered.

The act also covers state and local government employees. The Congressional Accountability Act of 1995[10] extended the coverage of Fair Labor Standards Act, including the Equal Pay Act, to federal employees of these offices:

- House of Representatives
- Senate
- Capitol Guide Service
- Capitol Police
- Congressional Budget Office
- Office of the Architect of the Capitol
- Office of the Attending Physician
- Office of Technology Assessment

The Equal Pay Act coverage does not depend on a minimum number of employees. Hence, the act may apply to firms having fewer than the fifteen employees required for Title VII coverage.

There are some exceptions to the coverage of the Equal Pay Act. These exceptions deal with operations that are exempted from the Fair Labor Standards Act. For example, certain small retail operations and small agricultural operations are excluded. Seasonal amusement operations and the fishing industry are also exempted from the act.

Provisions

The Equal Pay Act prohibits discrimination by an employer:

> between employees on the basis of sex by paying wages to employees in such establishment at a rate less than the rate at which he pays wages to employees of the opposite sex … for equal work on jobs the performance of which requires equal skill, effort, and responsibility, and which are performed under similar working conditions.

A plaintiff claiming violation of the Equal Pay Act must demonstrate that the employer is paying lower wages to employees of the opposite sex who are performing equal work in the same establishment. Note that the act does not require paying equal wages for work of equal value, known as comparable worth. The act requires only "equal pay for equal work." Work that is equal, or substantially equivalent, involves equal skills, effort, and responsibilities and is performed under similar working conditions.

[10] 2 U.S.C. §1301.

Equal Work When considering whether jobs involve substantially equivalent work under the Equal Pay Act, the courts do not consider job titles, job descriptions, or job classifications to be controlling. Rather, they evaluate each job on a case-by-case basis, making a detailed inquiry into the substantial duties and facts of each position.

Effort Equal effort involves substantially equivalent physical or mental exertion needed for performance of the job. If an employer pays male employees more than female employees because of additional duties performed by the males, the employer must establish that the extra duties are a regular and recurring requirement and that they consume a substantial amount of time. Occasional or infrequent assignments of extra duties do not warrant additional pay for periods when no extra duties are performed. The employer must also show that the extra duties are commensurate with the extra pay. The employer who assigns extra duties only to male employees may face problems under Title VII unless the employer can demonstrate that being male is a BFOQ for performing the extra duties. Unless the employer can make the requisite showing of business necessity to justify a BFOQ, the extra duties must be available to both male and female employees.

Skill Equal skill includes substantially equivalent experience, training, education, and ability. The skill, however, must relate to the performance of actual job duties. The employer cannot pay males more for possessing additional skills that are not used on the job. The act requires equal or substantially equivalent skills, not identical skills. Differences in the kinds of skills involved will not justify differentials in pay when the degree of skills required is substantially equal. For example, male hospital orderlies and female practical nurses may perform different duties requiring different skills, but if the general nature of their jobs is equivalent, the degree of skills required by each is substantially equal according to *Hodgson v. Brookhaven General Hospital.*[11]

Responsibility Equal responsibility includes a substantially equivalent degree of accountability required in the performance of a job, with emphasis on the importance of the job's obligations. When work of males and females is subject to similar supervisory review, the responsibility of males and females is equal. But when females work without supervision, whereas males are subject to supervision, the responsibility involved is not equal.

When considering the responsibility involved in jobs, the courts focus on the economic or social consequences of the employee's actions or decisions. Minor responsibility such as making coffee or answering telephones may not be an indication of different responsibility. The act does not require identical responsibility, only substantially equivalent responsibility. For instance, if a male employee is required to compile payroll lists and a female employee must make and deliver the payroll, the responsibilities may be substantially equivalent.

[11]436 F.2d 719 5th Cir. (1972).

Working Conditions The act requires that the substantially equivalent work be performed under similar working conditions. According to the 1974 Supreme Court decision in *Corning Glass Works v. Brennan*,[12] working conditions include the physical surroundings and hazards involved in a job. Exposures to heat, cold, noise, fumes, dust, risk of injury, or poor ventilation are examples of working conditions. Work performed outdoors involves different working conditions from work performed indoors. Work performed during the night shift, however, is not under different working conditions from the performance of the same work during the day.

The Equal Pay Act does not reach pay differentials for work that is not substantially equal in skill, effort, responsibility, and working conditions.

Defenses Under the Equal Pay Act

Although a plaintiff may establish that an employer is paying different wages for men and women performing work involving equivalent effort, skills, responsibility, and working conditions, the employer may not be in violation of the Equal Pay Act because the act provides several defenses to claims of unequal pay for equal work. When the pay differentials between the male and female employees are due to a seniority system, a merit pay system, a productivity-based pay system, or "a factor other than sex," the pay differentials do not violate the act.

Employers justifying pay differentials on seniority systems, merit pay systems, or production-based pay systems must demonstrate that the system is bona fide and applies equally to all employees. A merit pay system must be more than an *ad hoc* subjective determination of employees' merit, especially if there is no listing of criteria considered in establishing an employee's merit. Any such systems should be formal and objective to justify pay differentials.

The "factor other than sex" defense covers a wide variety of situations. A "shift differential," for example, involves paying a premium to employees who work during the afternoon or night shift. If the differential is uniformly available to all employees who work a particular shift, it qualifies as a "factor other than sex." But if females are precluded from working the night shift, a night-shift pay differential is not defensible under the act. A training program may be the basis of a pay differential if the program is bona fide. Employees who perform similar work but are in training for higher positions may be paid more than those not in the training program. The training program should be open to both male and female employees, unless the employer can establish that gender is a BFOQ for admission to the program. In *Kouba v. Allstate Insurance Co.*,[13] the U.S. Court of Appeals for the Ninth Circuit held that using an employee's prior salary to determine pay for employees in a training program was not precluded by the Equal Pay Act.

The following case is a good illustration of the court's inquiry into the alleged equality of jobs involved in an Equal Pay Act complaint.

---

[12]417 U.S. 188 (1974).

[13]691 F.2d 873 (1982).

case 7.3 »

LAFFEY V. NORTHWEST AIRLINES

567 F.2d 429 (U.S. Court of Appeals, District of Columbia Circuit, 1976)

Facts: Between 1927 and 1947, all flight attendants employed on NWA's flights were women; NWA classified them as "stewardesses." In 1947, NWA started international flights and created a new cabin-attendant position of "purser" and adopted a policy of only hiring men for purser positions. NWA created another strictly all-male cabin-attendant classification—"flight service attendant"—to serve as a training and probationary position for future pursers. It was not until 1967 that a new collective bargaining agreement allowed stewardesses to apply for purser positions.

The company also imposed other restrictions on stewardesses seeking to become pursers that were not imposed on the male flight service attendants. In 1970, after three years of allowing women to become pursers, NWA had 137 male cabin attendants—all as pursers—and 1,747 female cabin attendants—all but one as stewardesses. The only female purser was Mary P. Laffey, who bid for a purser vacancy in 1967, after nine years' service as a stewardess. NWA delayed acting on her application and began to administer new tests to purser applicants. These tests had never previously been used in selecting pursers, and during the time between Laffey's application and her appointment as a purser, NWA hired two male pursers without benefit of any tests. Finally, in June, 1968, Laffey became a purser, but was placed on the bottom rung of the purser-salary schedule and was paid less than she had been paid as a senior stewardess. She was paid less than male pursers with equivalent seniority and cabin attendant service. NWA's pay scale for pursers ranged from 20 to 55 percent higher than salaries paid to stewardesses of equivalent seniority. NWA also paid female stewardesses lower salaries and pensions than male pursers, provided female cabin attendants with less expensive and less desirable layover accommodations than male cabin attendants, and paid male pursers a uniform-cleaning allowance that was not paid to female attendants.

Laffey filed a class action suit against NWA, claiming that the refusal to hire females as pursers violated Title VII and that the differential pay scale and allowances for male pursers and female attendants violated Title VII and the Equal Pay Act. The trial court held that NWA had violated Title VII and the Equal Pay Act. NWA appealed only on Equal Pay Act holdings, claiming that the trial court erred by holding that the purser and stewardess positions were equivalent.

Issue: Are the jobs of purser and stewardess equivalent in terms of the skills, effort, responsibilities, and working conditions for the purposes of the Equal Pay Act?

Decision: The court made extensive findings comparing the work actually done by pursers and stewardesses and held it to be essentially equal when considered as a whole. The duties performed do not differ significantly in nature between pursers and stewardesses: both must check cabins before departure, greet and seat passengers, prepare for take-off, and provide in-flight food, beverage, and general services. Both must complete required documentation, maintain cabin cleanliness, and ensure that passengers comply with regulations. The primary responsibility of any cabin attendant is to insure the safety of passengers during an emergency, and cabin attendants all must possess a thorough knowledge of emergency equipment and procedures on aircraft, must know first aid techniques, and must be able to handle the myriad of medical problems that arise in flight. Food service varies greatly between flights, but pursers do not engage in any duties that are not performed on the same or another flight by the stewardesses. Stewardesses and pursers have different documentation responsibilities, but the court held that those duties were comparable.

Senior cabin attendants—either purser or stewardess—have a number of supervisory duties. These include monitoring and, where necessary, correcting the work of other cabin attendants; determining the times of meals and movie showings; shifting cabin attendants from section to section to balance workloads; and giving predeparture briefings on emergency equipment and procedures. On large planes, even if a purser in the first-class section is designated the senior cabin attendant, the senior in tourist shoulders these same burdens in her section of the aircraft—overseeing the great majority of passengers and cabin attendants. Stewardesses and pursers alike are subject to disciplinary action if they fail to carry out their "supervisory responsibilities."

Once a plaintiff showed that NWA had discriminated against women cabin attendants on the basis of sex by paying stewardesses less than pursers performing jobs requiring equivalent skill, effort, and responsibility and which are performed under similar working conditions, the employer had the burden of showing that the wage differential was justified under one of the four exceptions in the Act:

- a seniority system;
- a merit pay system;
- a pay system which measures earnings by quantity or quality of production; or
- a differential based on any other factor other than sex.

Both the trial court and the court of appeals both held that NWA had failed to show that the differences in pay and benefit allowances were justified under any of the four exceptions in the Equal Pay Act.

The court of appeals affirmed the trial court decision that the purser and stewardess positions were substantially equal within the meaning of the Equal Pay Act, and that NWA's differential pay and benefit allowances violated the Equal Pay Act.

«

Concept *Summary* » 7.2

The Equal Pay Act

- Requires employers to pay equal wages for equal work
- Work is equal when male and female employees perform work involving equivalent:
  - Skill
  - Effort
  - Responsibilities
  - Working conditions
- Unless the pay differentials are due to:
  - Seniority system
  - Merit pay system
  - Productivity-based pay system
  - A "factor other than sex"

Procedures Under the Equal Pay Act

The Equal Pay Act is administered by the Equal Employment Opportunity Commission (EEOC). Prior to 1979, it was administered by the Department of Labor, but in July 1979, the EEOC became the enforcement agency. The act provides for enforcement actions by individual employees (Section 16), or by the U.S. Secretary of Labor (Section 17), who has transferred that power to the EEOC.

There is no requirement that an individual filing a suit under the Equal Pay Act must file first with the EEOC. If the EEOC has filed a suit, it precludes individual suits on the same complaint. An individual suit must be filed within two years of the alleged violation. An Equal Pay Act violation will be held to be continuing for each payday in which unequal pay is received for equal work.

In a case decided under Title VII, *Ledbetter v. Goodyear Tire & Rubber Co.*,[14] a divided Supreme Court held that the receipt of individual paychecks reflecting a discriminatory performance evaluation system did not constitute a separate violation of Title VII, but rather simply reflected the effects of the discriminatory evaluation system. The *Ledbetter* decision meant that an employee alleging sex discrimination in pay would have to file suit within 180 days (or, in some cases, 300 days) from the employer's adoption of the discriminatory pay policies. If the employee did not become aware of the discriminatory pay practice or policy until a year or more after it was adopted, it was too late to file suit under Title VII. However, *Ledbetter* was overruled by legislation signed into law by President Obama in early 2009. The ***Lilly Ledbetter Fair Pay Act***[15] amended Title VII (and the Age Discrimination in Employment Act, the Americans with Disabilities Act, and the Rehabilitation Act) to provide that the time limit for filing suit alleging discrimination in pay begins either:

Lilly Ledbetter Fair Pay Act
Statute that extends time in which an employee may file suit under several federal employment statutes.

- when the discriminatory pay practice or policy is adopted;
- when the employee becomes subject to the discriminatory pay policy or practice; or
- when the employee is affected by the application of the discriminatory pay practice or policy.

The act makes it clear that each payment of wages, benefits, or other compensation (that is, each time the employee receives the discriminatory pay) are paid under the discriminatory pay practice or policy is a separate violation. Employees filing pay discrimination suits under Title VII can recover back pay for up to two years prior to the date they filed a complaint with the Equal Employment Opportunity Commission.

Remedies

An individual plaintiff's suit under the Equal Pay Act may recover the unpaid back wages due and may also receive an amount equal to the back wages as liquidated damages under the act. The trial court has discretion to deny recovery of the liquidated damages if it finds that the employer acted in good faith. An employer claiming to act in good faith must show some objective reason for its belief that it was acting legally.

The back pay recovered by a private plaintiff can be awarded for the period from two years prior to the suit. However, if the court finds the violation was "willful," it may allow recovery of back pay for three years prior to filing suit. According to *Laffey*, a violation is willful when the employer was aware of the appreciable possibility that its actions might violate the act. A successful private plaintiff also is awarded legal fees and court costs.

The remedies available under a government suit include injunctions and back pay with interest. The act does not provide for the recovery of liquidated damages in a government suit.

Unlike Title VII, the Equal Pay Act does not allow recovery of punitive damages. However, the potential recovery of liquidated damages for up to three years (in the case of willful violations) may offer recovery beyond that available under Title VII because of its limitations on punitive damages. Therefore, in certain cases, the remedies available under the Equal Pay Act may exceed those recoverable under Title VII.

---

[14]550 U.S. 618 (2007).

[15]P.L. 111-2 (January 29, 2009).

Title VII and the Equal Pay Act

As in *Laffey*, plaintiffs often file suit under both Title VII and the Equal Pay Act. Generally, conduct that violates the Equal Pay Act also violates Title VII. However, Title VII's coverage extends beyond that of the Equal Pay Act.

An employer paying different wages to men and women doing the same job is violating the law unless the pay differentials are due to a bona fide seniority system, a merit pay system, a productivity-based pay system, or a "factor other than sex." The Equal Pay Act prohibits paying men and women different rates if they are performing substantially equivalent work, unless the difference in pay is due to one of the four factors just listed. Section 703(h) of Title VII also allows pay differentials between employees of different sexes when the differential is due to seniority, merit or productivity-based pay systems, or a factor other than sex. That provision of Section 703(h) is known as the ***Bennett Amendment***.

Bennett Amendment
The provision of Section 703(h) that allows pay differentials between employees of different sexes when the pay differential is due to seniority, merit pay, productivity-based pay, or a factor other than sex.

The Equal Pay Act applies only when male and female employees are performing substantially equivalent work. Can Title VII be used to challenge pay differentials between men and women when they are not performing equal work? What is the effect of the Bennett Amendment?

In *County of Washington v. Gunther*,[16] the Supreme Court held that the Bennett Amendment incorporates the defenses of the Equal Pay Act into Title VII. In other words, pay differentials due to a seniority system, merit-pay system, productivity-based pay system, or a factor other than sex do not violate Title VII.

The *Gunther* case also held that Title VII prohibits intentional gender discrimination in pay even when the male and female employees are not performing equivalent work. In *Gunther*, the plaintiffs were able to establish a prima facie case of intentional discrimination by the employer in setting pay scales for female employees. In *Spalding v. University of Washington*[17] and *A.F.S.C.M.E. v. State of Washington*,[18] the U.S. Court of Appeals for the Ninth Circuit held that a plaintiff bringing a *Gunther*-type claim under Title VII must establish evidence of intentional discrimination (known as disparate treatment). The court held that statistical evidence purporting to show gender-based disparate salary levels for female professors, standing alone, was not sufficient to establish intentional discrimination as required by *Gunther*.

Comparable Worth

Comparable Worth
A standard of equal pay for jobs of equal value; not the same as equal pay for equal work.

Some commentators felt that the *Gunther* decision was, in effect, an endorsement of the idea of ***comparable worth***—that is, that employees should receive equal pay for jobs of equal value. Notice that comparable worth is different from the equal-pay-for-equal-work requirements of the Equal Pay Act. The Supreme Court in *Gunther* emphasized that it was not endorsing comparable worth; it held simply that Title VII prohibited intentional discrimination on the basis of gender for setting pay scales. The courts of appeals have consistently maintained that Title VII does not require comparable worth standards. An employer need not pay equal wages for work of equal value as long as the pay differential is not due to intentional gender

[16]452 U.S. 161 (1981).

[17]740 F.2d 686 (1984).

[18]770 F.2d 1401 (1985).

discrimination by the employer. In *Lemons v. Denver*,[19] the U.S. Court of Appeals for the Tenth Circuit held that Title VII did not prohibit a public employer from paying public health nurses salaries based on the private sector wage rates for nurses, even though the public health nurses were paid less than the predominantly male jobs of garbage collector or tree trimmer. The employer was not guilty of gender discrimination simply by following the "market," even if the "market" wages for nurses reflected the effects of historical discrimination against women. Several states, however, have adopted laws requiring comparable worth pay for public sector employees.

Gender-Based Pension Benefits

Women, on the average, live longer than men. Such differences in life expectancy are used by actuaries in determining the premium and benefit levels for annuities purchased by individuals. Gender-based actuarial tables used to determine premiums and benefits for pensions would require that women pay higher premiums to receive the same levels of benefits as men of the same age. Does an employer who uses gender-based actuarial tables to determine entitlement to pensions offered as an employment benefit violate Title VII? This question was addressed by the Supreme Court in the following case.

case 7.4 »

City of Los Angeles v. Manhart
435 U.S. 702 (1978)

[As a class, women live longer than men. The Los Angeles Department of Water and Power [Department] administered its own retirement, disability and death benefit programs for its employees. Because women, as a class, live longer than men, the Department required its female employees to make larger contributions to its pension fund than its male employees. Upon retirement, male and female employees of the same age, seniority and salary received the same monthly pension benefits, but before retirement the female employees were required to pay contributions to the pension fund that were 14.84 percent higher than those paid by males. This differential was based on actuarial mortality tables and the experience of the Department, which indicated that women on average live longer than men and thus would receive more retirement benefit payments. A group of female employees filed suit against the Department, alleging that the practice of making female employees pay higher contributions to receive equal benefits upon retirement violated Title VII. The trial court held for the employees, ruling that the Department's practice was illegal sex discrimination; upon appeal, the U.S. Court of Appeals for the Ninth Circuit affirmed the trial court's verdict. The Department then appealed to the U.S. Supreme Court.]

Stevens, J.:

The Department … [contends] that … the differential in take-home pay between men and women was not discrimination within the meaning of Section 703(a)(1) because it was offset by a difference in the value of the pension benefits provided to the two classes of employees … [and] in any event, the retroactive monetary recovery is unjustified. We consider these contentions in turn.…

It is now well recognized that employment decisions cannot be predicated on mere "stereotyped" impressions about the characteristics of males or females.… This case does not, however, involve a fictional difference between men and women. It involves a generalization that the parties accept as unquestionably true: women, as a class, do live longer than men. The Department treated its women employees differently from its men employees because the two classes

[19] 620 F.2d 228 (1980).

are in fact different. It is equally true, however, that all individuals in the respective classes do not share the characteristic that differentiates the average class representatives. Many women do not live as long as the average man and many men outlive the average woman. The question, therefore, is whether the existence or nonexistence of "discrimination" is to be determined by comparison of class characteristics or individual characteristics. A "stereotyped" answer to that question may not be the same as the answer which the language and purpose of the statute command.

The statute makes it unlawful "to discriminate against any *individual* with respect to his compensation, terms, conditions, or privileges of employment, because of such *individual's* race, color, religion, sex, or national origin." [emphasis added] The statute's focus on the individual is unambiguous. It precludes treatment of individuals as simply components of [a] racial, religious, sexual, or national class. If height is required for a job, a tall woman may not be refused employment merely because, on the average, women are too short. Even a true generalization about the class is an insufficient reason for disqualifying an individual to whom the generalization does not apply.

That proposition is of critical importance in this case because there is no assurance that any individual woman working for the Department will actually fit the generalization on which the Department's policy is based. Many of those individuals will not live as long as the average man. While they were working, those individuals received smaller paychecks because of their sex, but they will receive no compensating advantage when they retire.

It is true, of course, that while contributions are being collected from the employees, the Department cannot know which individuals will predecease the average woman. Therefore, unless women as a class are assessed an extra charge, they will be subsidized, to some extent, by the class of male employees. It follows, according to the Department, that fairness to its class of male employees justifies the extra assessment against all of its female employees.

But the question of fairness to various classes affected by the statute is essentially a matter of policy for the legislature to address. Congress has decided that classifications based on sex, like those based on national origin or race, are unlawful. Actuarial studies could unquestionably identify differences in life expectancy based on race or national origin, as well as sex. But a statute that was designed to make race irrelevant in the employment market, ... could not reasonably be construed to permit a take-home pay differential based on a racial classification.

Even if the statutory language were less clear, the basic policy of the statute requires that we focus on fairness to individuals rather than fairness to classes. Practices which classify employees in terms of religion, race, or sex tend to preserve traditional assumptions about groups rather than thoughtful scrutiny of individuals. The generalization involved in this case illustrates the point. Separate mortality tables are easily interpreted as reflecting innate differences between the sexes; but a significant part of the longevity differential may be explained by the social fact that men are heavier smokers than women.

Finally, there is no reason to believe that Congress intended a special definition of discrimination in the context of employee group insurance coverage. It is true that insurance is concerned with events that are individually unpredictable, but that is characteristic of many employment decisions. Individual risks, like individual performance, may not be predicted by resort to classifications proscribed by Title VII. Indeed, the fact that this case involves a group insurance program highlights a basic flaw in the Department's fairness argument. For when insurance risks are grouped, the better risks always subsidize the poorer risks. Healthy persons subsidize medical benefits for the less healthy; unmarried workers subsidize the pensions of married workers; persons who eat, drink, or smoke to excess may subsidize pension benefits for persons whose habits are more temperate. Treating different classes of risks as though they were the same for purposes of group insurance is a common practice that has never been considered inherently unfair. To insure the flabby and the fit as though they were equivalent risks may be more common than treating men and women alike; but nothing more than habit makes one "subsidy" seem less fair than the other.

An employment practice which requires 2,000 individuals to contribute more money into a fund than 10,000 other employees simply because each of them is a woman, rather than a man, is in direct conflict with both the language and the policy of the Act. Such a practice does not pass the simple test of whether the evidence shows "treatment of a person in a manner which but for the person's sex would be different." It constitutes discrimination and is unlawful unless exempted by the Equal Pay Act or some other affirmative justification.... The Department argues that the different contributions exacted from men and women were based on the factor of longevity rather than sex. It is plain, however, that any individual's life expectancy is based on a number of factors, of which sex is only one. The record contains no evidence that any factor other than the employee's sex was taken into account in calculating the 14.84 percent differential between the respective contributions by men and women. We agree with Judge Duniway's observation that one cannot "say that an actuarial distinction based entirely on sex is 'based on any other factor other than sex.' Sex is exactly what it is based on."

• • •

[W]e recognize that in a case of this kind it may be necessary to take special care in fashioning appropriate relief.... Although Title VII was enacted in 1964, this is apparently the first litigation challenging contribution differences based on valid actuarial tables. Retroactive liability could be devastating for a pension fund. The harm would fall in large part on innocent third parties. If, as the courts below apparently contemplated, the plaintiffs' contributions are recovered from the pension fund, the administrators of the fund will be forced to meet unchanged obligations with diminished assets. If the reserve proves inadequate, either the expectations of all retired employees will be disappointed or current employees will be forced to pay not only for their own future security but also for the unanticipated reduction in the contributions of past employees....

[The practice of requiring female employees to pay more into the pension system in order to receive the same benefits upon retirement violated Title VII's prohibition on sex discrimination in pay, but the Supreme Court directed that its decision would not have retroactive effect.]

So ordered.

Case Questions

1. What factors determine a person's longevity? What factors did the department's pension plan take into consideration in determining premiums employees had to pay?
2. Does Title VII allow a "reasonable cost differential" defense to a charge of gender discrimination?
3. How can an employer comply with *Manhart*'s requirement of equal treatment between male and female employees for pensions? If women live longer than men, won't men be paid less under a unisex pension? Would that violate Title VII? Explain.

The Supreme Court noted in *Manhart* that it did not want to revolutionize the insurance industry. In the subsequent case of *Arizona Governing Committee v. Norris*,[20] the Supreme Court held that a deferred compensation plan for state employees, administered by a private insurance company that used gender-based actuarial tables to determine monthly benefit payments, violated Title VII. The Court held that its ruling would apply prospectively only, not retroactively.

Pregnancy Discrimination

Pregnancy Discrimination Act of 1978
An act that amended Title VII to include pregnancy discrimination in the definition of sex discrimination.

In *General Electric v. Gilbert*[21] the Supreme Court held that General Electric's refusal to cover pregnancy or related conditions under its sick-pay plan, even though male-specific disabilities such as vasectomies were covered, did not violate Title VII. In response to the *General Electric v. Gilbert* decision, Congress passed the ***Pregnancy Discrimination Act of 1978***, which amended Title VII by adding Section 701(k) to Title VII. Section 701(k) provides:

> The terms "because of sex" or "on the basis of sex" include, but are not limited to, because of or on the basis of pregnancy, childbirth, or related medical conditions; and women affected by pregnancy,

[20] 463 U.S. 1073 (1983).

[21] 429 U.S. 125 (1976).

childbirth, or related medical conditions shall be treated the same for all employment-related purposes, including receipt of benefits under fringe benefit programs, as other persons not so affected but similar to their ability or inability to work....

Simply stated, the amendment to Title VII requires that an employer treat a pregnant employee the same as any employee suffering a nonpregnancy related, temporary disability (unless in a relatively rare instance, the employer can establish a BFOQ for pregnancy-related discrimination). If the employer's sick-leave pay benefits cover temporary disabilities, it must also provide coverage for pregnancy-related leaves. In *Newport News Shipbuilding and Dry Dock Co. v. EEOC*,[22] the Supreme Court held that an employer's medical insurance plan covering 80 percent of the cost of hospital treatment for employees' spouses or dependents, but which limited coverage of spouses' pregnancy-related costs to $500, was in violation of the pregnancy discrimination provisions of Title VII. Title VII required the employer to provide coverage for spouses' pregnancy-related conditions equal to the coverage of spouses' or dependents' other medical conditions.

Employers who fire pregnant employees are clearly in violation of Title VII, as are employers who fire pregnant employees because of the assumption that the employees will likely be absent from work for lengthy periods.[23] Discriminating against an employee who has had an abortion, or who is contemplating having an abortion, is also prohibited by Title VII.[24] The act also prohibits discharging an employee because of her efforts to become pregnant by in-vitro fertilization.[25] An employer that transferred a successful sales representative to an undesirable sales territory because of her desire to start a family despite having several miscarriages was held to have violated Title VII in *Goss v. Exxon Office Systems Co.*[26] The exclusion of prescription contraceptives from an employer's otherwise comprehensive prescription drug plan has also been held to violate Title VII.[27]

Pregnancy and Hazardous Working Conditions

On-the-job exposure to harsh substances or potentially toxic chemicals may pose a hazard to the health of employees. The risk of such hazards may be greatly increased when pregnant employees are exposed to them; the hazards may also affect the health of the fetus carried by the pregnant employee. An employer wishing to avoid potential health problems for female employees and their offspring may prohibit women of childbearing age from working in jobs that involve exposure to hazardous substances. Do such restrictions violate Title VII, or may they be justified as BFOQs?

---

[22]462 U.S. 669 (1983).

[23]*Maldonado v. U.S. Bank*, 186 F.3d 759 (7th Cir.1999).

[24]*Turic v. Holland Hospitality*, 85 F.3d 1211 (6th Cir. 1996).

[25]*Pacourek v. Inland Steel Co.*, 858 F.Supp. 1393 (N.D. Ill. 1994).

[26]33 B.N.A. FEP Cas. 21 (E.D. Pa. 1983).

[27]*Erickson v. The Bartell Drug Co.*, 141 F.Supp.2d 1266 (W.D. Wash. 2001); *EEOC v. United Parcel Service, Inc.*, 141 F.Supp.2d 1216 (D. Minn. 2001).

The U.S. Supreme Court in *U.A.W. v. Johnson Controls, Inc.*[28] held that the employer's restrictions were gender discrimination in violation of Title VII. For an employer to establish a BFOQ would require showing that the employee's pregnancy interfered with the employee's ability to perform the job. The Court noted:

> ... women as capable of doing their jobs as their male counterparts may not be forced to choose between having a child and having a job.... Johnson Controls' professed moral and ethical concerns about the welfare of the next generation do not suffice to establish a BFOQ of female sterility. Decisions about the welfare of future children must be left to the parents who conceive, bear, support, and raise them rather than to the employers who hire those parents.... Johnson Controls has attempted to exclude women because of their reproductive capacity. Title VII (and the pregnancy discrimination amendments) simply do not allow a woman's dismissal because of her failure to submit to sterilization.

The Family and Medical Leave Act

The Family and Medical Leave Act[29] signed into law by President Clinton in 1993, allows eligible employees to take up to twelve weeks unpaid leave in any twelve months because of:

- the birth, adoption, or foster care of a child;
- the need to care for a child, spouse, or parent with a serious health condition; or
- the employee's own serious health condition makes the employee unable to perform functions of his or her job.

The FMLA was amended in 2008 and 2009 to allow employees to take up to twenty-six weeks' leave to care for members of the armed forces and recent veterans who have a serious injury or illness, or twelve weeks' leave to deal with situations arising from the fact that a child, spouse, or parent is called to active military duty or is deployed to a foreign country.

FMLA Coverage

The FMLA applies to private sector employers with fifty or more employees; public sector employers are covered without regard to the number of employees. Employees employed at worksites with less than fifty employees may still be covered if the employer employs at least fifty employees within seventy-five miles of the work site. In *Hackworth v. Progressive Casualty Insurance Co.*,[30] the Department of Labor's interpretation that the seventy-five miles should be measured in surface miles (using surface transportation over public streets and roads) rather than linear miles ("as the crow flies") was upheld. In *Nevada Dept. of Human Resources v. Hibbs*,[31] the Supreme Court held that the Eleventh Amendment of the Constitution does not grant the states immunity from suits for damages by employees under the FMLA.

---

[28] 499 U.S. 187 (1991).

[29] 29 U.S.C. §2611 *et seq.*

[30] 468 F.3d 722 (10th Cir. 2006).

[31] 538 U.S. 721 (2003).

Employees of covered employers are eligible for leave under the act if they have been employed by the employer for at least twelve months and must have worked at least 1,250 hours of the twelve-month period immediately preceding commencement of the leave. The employer may designate "key employees" who may be denied leave under the act; key employees are those whom it would be necessary for the employer to replace in order to prevent substantial and grievous economic injury to the operation of business. The employer must give written notice to key employees at the time such employees give notice of leave and may deny reinstatement to key employees who take leave. Key employees must be salaried employees and must be among the highest paid 10 percent of the employees at the work site. No more than 10 percent of the employees at a work site can be designated key employees.

Entitlement to Medical Leave

Serious Health Condition

The regulations under the FMLA[32] define "serious health condition" as:

- an illness, injury, or condition that requires inpatient hospital care, or
- that lasts more than three days and requires continuing treatment by a health-care provider, or
- that involves pregnancy, or
- a long-term or permanently disabling health condition, or
- absences for receiving multiple treatments for restorative surgery, or
- for a condition that would likely result in a period of incapacity of more than three days if it were not treated.

An employee's food poisoning that required one visit to a doctor but did not require hospitalization was not a serious health condition under the FLMA, nor was a child's ear infection that lasted only one day and required only a single visit to the doctor. However, a child's throat and upper respiratory infection that incapacitated the child for more than three days did qualify as a serious health condition under the FLMA.

Leave Provisions

The leave may be taken all at once, or in certain cases, intermittently, or the employee may work at a part-time schedule. An employee or the employer may choose to substitute paid leave such as vacation or sick leave for part or all of the FMLA leave if the employee is entitled to such paid leave. The employee's ability to substitute paid leave is determined by the terms of the employer's normal leave policy. Under certain circumstances, the employee may take the leave on an intermittent basis—that is, taking the leave in separate blocks of time or through a reduced work schedule for the employee. If the leave is for planned medical treatment, the employee must make a reasonable effort to schedule the medical treatment so not to unduly disrupt the employer's operation. If both parents are employed by the same employer, the leave because of childbirth or to care for a sick child may be limited to a total of twelve weeks between both parents. The employee's health benefits must be maintained during leave if the health coverage was provided to the employee before the leave; if the employee fails to return to

---

[32] 29 C.F.R. §825.100 *et seq.*

work after the leave, the employer may recover the premiums it paid to maintain the employee's health benefits. The employee has the right to return to the same or equivalent position, and the leave cannot result in the loss of any benefit by the employee. In *Ragsdale v. Wolverine World Wide, Inc.*,[33] the employer granted an employee a medical leave of thirty weeks, but the employer failed to notify the employee that the leave would count against the employee's FMLA leave. According to a regulation under the FMLA, adopted by the Department of Labor, the employer's failure to provide such a notice would require the employer to grant the employee an additional twelve-week leave. The Supreme Court held that the regulation was invalid because it was contrary to the FMLA legislation and it went beyond the authority of the Secretary of Labor under the FMLA.

Military Leave Provisions

The 2008 National Defense Authorization Act[34] amended the FMLA to allow employees to take up to twelve weeks of unpaid leave during a twelve-month period for "qualifying exigencies" arising out of an employee's spouse, child, or parent being on active duty service or deployed to a foreign country, or called to active duty service as a member of the National Guard or Reserves. The amended FMLA also allows employees to take "military caregiver leave" of up to 26 weeks of unpaid leave to care a child, spouse, parent, or next of kin who is a current member of the armed forces (including the National Guard or Reserves) or a veteran within five years of discharge and who suffers a serious illness or injury.

Qualified Exigencies

An employer covered by the FMLA must grant employees eligible under the FMLA an unpaid leave of up to twelve weeks during a twelve-month period for qualified exigencies arising out of the fact that an employee's spouse, child, or parent is a member of the National Guard or Reserves is either on active duty or has been notified of an impending call to active duty. Note that this qualifying exigency leave is also available to employees whose family members (child, spouse, or parent) are members of the regular armed forces and are deployed to a foreign country. The regulations under the amended FMLA define qualifying exigencies as including:

- issues arising from a family member's short notice deployment—deployment on notice of seven days or less;
- military events and related activities such as official ceremonies, programs, or events sponsored by military or family support or assistance programs sponsored or promoted by the military, military service organizations, or the American Red Cross that are related to the active duty or call to active duty status of a family member;
- certain child care and related activities, such as providing for, or arranging for alternative childcare, or enrolling or transferring a child to a new school or day-care facility, when such activities arise from the call to active duty of a family member;
- making or updating financial or legal arrangements to address a family member's absence due to the call to active duty;

[33]535 U.S. 81 (2002).

[34]P.L. 110-181 (2008).

- attending counseling (provided by someone other than a health-care provider) for the employee, the family member called to active duty, or a child of the person called to active duty, when the need for counseling arises from the call to active duty or the active duty status of the family member;
- taking up to five days of leave to spend time with a family member who is on short-term, temporary rest and recuperation leave during deployment;
- attending certain postdeployment activities such as arrival ceremonies, reintegration briefings and events, or other official ceremonies or programs sponsored by the military for a period of ninety days following the termination of the family member's active duty status, or addressing issues arising from the death of a family member in the military;
- "any other event that the employer and employee agree is a qualifying exigency."

Military Caregiver Leave

Under this provision of the FMLA, an employee may take up to twenty-six weeks of unpaid leave to care for a family member (child, spouse, parent, or next of kin) who is a member of the armed forces (including the Reserves or National Guard) and who is undergoing medical treatment, recuperation, therapy, or who is otherwise in outpatient status or is on the temporary disability retired list because of a serious illness or injury. The caregiver leave is also available to care for a veteran who undergoes medical treatment within five years of being discharged. For the purposes of this provision, a serious illness or injury is one that was incurred by the service member in the line of active duty and that will render the service member medically unfit to perform the duties of his or her office, grade, rank, or rating. The definition of serious illness also includes the aggravation of existing or pre-existing injuries incurred while on active duty. Spouses who work for the same employer are limited to a combined total of twenty-six weeks in a single twelve-month period if the leave is to care for a service member with a serious illness or injury. Note that the military caregiver leave is available to care for family members ("next of kin") beyond those family members (child, spouse, or parent) for whose care leave may be taken under the other the provisions of the FMLA.

Notice Requirements for FMLA Leave

Employees seeking to take a leave under any provisions of the FMLA must give notice of the leave to their employer at least thirty days in advance of the leave when the need for the leave is foreseeable. If the need for the leave becomes foreseeable less than thirty days in advance of the beginning of the leave, the employee is to give notice as soon as it is practical—usually the same or the next business day the need for the leave arises. When the need for the leave is not foreseeable, the employee must provide the employer with notice as soon as it is practical under the facts and circumstances of the particular case. Employees requesting leave, or notifying the employer of the need for leave, must provide the employer with information sufficient for the employer to determine whether the FMLA applies to the leave request.

When employers are given a request for a leave under the FMLA, they must notify the employee of the employee's eligibility for the leave within five days of the request; if the employer determines that the employee is not eligible for leave, the employer must give the reason that the employee is not eligible. Reasons for noneligibility may include:

- That the employer is not covered by the FMLA
- That the employee has been designated as a "key employee"

- That the employee has not worked for the employer for twelve months or has not worked the required 1,250 hours in the twelve-month period immediately preceding the request for leave
- That the employee has already used up her or his leave entitlement within the preceding twelve months

If the employee is eligible for leave under the FMLA, the employer must inform the employee that the leave is designated as, and will be counted as, FMLA leave. The notice that the leave will be counted as FMLA leave must be given in writing within five business days of the employer's determination. The employer must also notify the employee of the number of hours, days, or weeks that will be counted against the employee's FFMLA entitlement.

Certification Requirements

Employers may require that employees requesting leave due to a serious health condition affecting the employee or a covered family member be supported by a certification from a health care provider. An employer may also require a second or third medical opinion, at the employer's expense. Employers may also require that requests for FMLA military leave be supported by an appropriate certification. For requests for "qualifying exigency" leave, the employer may require that a copy of the military member's active duty orders or other such information providing appropriate facts related to the particular qualifying exigency. For requests for leave to care for an injured or ill service member, the employer may require that the employee provide a certification completed by an authorized health care provider or by a copy of the Invitational Travel Order or Invitational Travel Authorization issued to any member of the service member's family. Note that an employer may not require a second or third medical opinion for leaves for qualifying exigencies or to care for injured or ill service members.

Job Restoration Requirements

The employer may require that an employee on leave seeking to return to work provide medical certification that the employee is capable of returning to work. When the employee returns from FMLA leave, the employer must restore the employee to her or his original job or to an equivalent job with equivalent pay, benefits, and other terms and conditions of employment. An employee's use of FMLA leave must not result in the loss of any employment benefit that the employee had earned or had become entitled to before taking the leave. If the employer pays a bonus based on achievement of a specified goal such as hours worked, products sold, or perfect attendance, and the employee has not met that goal because of the FMLA leave, the employer need not pay the bonus to the employee unless it would be paid to an employee on equivalent leave status for a reason not qualifying for FMLA leave. FMLA leave may not be counted against the employee under a "no fault" attendance policy.

The following case deals with the issue of whether an employee's absences qualified for FMLA leave or could be counted against the employee under the employer's attendance policy.

case 7.5 »

Novak v. MetroHealth Medical Center

503 F.3d 572 (6th Cir. 2007)

Facts: Donna Novak was employed by MetroHealth Medical Center. MetroHealth maintained a "point-based" attendance policy that assigned points to employees based on the number of hours of unexcused absence. Employees were terminated if they accumulated 112 points during a twelve-month period (leave authorized under the FMLA was not included in the point total). Novak was absent from work a number of times in late March 2004. She called MetroHealth each day that she was absent to provide an explanation. Some absences were because she was experiencing back pain; others were because she was helping care for her eighteen-year-old daughter, Victoria, who had recently given birth. She said that her daughter was suffering from "postpartum depression" and that she had to help her care for the baby (Novak's grandson).

Novak's absences resulted in her accumulating more than 112 points, and she faced termination. She requested that MetroHealth grant her leave under the FMLA. Novak consulted a Dr. Patil about her back pain, but she had been treated by a Dr. Wloszek in the past. MetroHealth required Novak to submit a FMLA certification form that was to be completed by the physician of record, Dr. Wloszek, and not by Dr. Patil. Dr. Wloszek completed the form, but because she had not examined Novak since October 2003, Dr. Wloszek omitted information on the description of the medical facts and the likely duration of Novak's condition. Novak then asked Boda, Wloszek's assistant, to complete the remainder of the form and fax it to MetroHealth. MetroHealth questioned the authenticity of Dr. Wloszek's certification forms, and contacted Dr. Wloszek, who told them that she completed the form based on secondhand information from Novak about her condition. Novak also submitted certification forms for her absences to help her daughter care for the baby.

On April 16, 2004, MetroHealth determined that Novak's March absences did not qualify for the FMLA leave. Her absences were not authorized and, as a result, MetroHealth terminated her employment. Novak filed suit against MetroHealth, alleging interference with her FMLA rights and retaliation under the FMLA. The trial court held that there was no basis for the FMLA claims, and dismissed them with prejudice. Novak appealed to the U.S. Court of Appeals for the Sixth Circuit.

Issue: Was Novak entitled to FMLA leave because of her back pain and/or her caring for her daughter and her grandson?

Decision: An employer may require an employee requesting FMLA leave to provide a doctor's certification confirming the existence of a serious health condition. A doctor's certification of a serious health condition is sufficient if it states:

- the date on which the serious health condition began;
- the probable duration of the condition;
- the appropriate medical facts within the health care provider's knowledge; and
- a statement that the employee is unable to perform her job duties.

An employer may show that the certification is invalid or inauthentic.

The court of appeals agreed that Novak's certification forms from Dr. Wloszek were insufficient to establish the existence of a serious health condition for purposes of the FMLA. MetroHealth had established that the certification was unreliable and it acted reasonably in refusing to grant FMLA leave on that basis.

Novak also claimed that she was entitled to FMLA leave to care for her daughter, who was suffering from short-term postpartum depression. The FMLA permits an employee to take leave to care for a parent, spouse, or child suffering from a serious health condition. However, the FMLA authorizes leave to care for a child eighteen years of age or older only if that child is "disabled" within the definition of the Americans with Disabilities Act. Because Novak did not establish that her adult daughter suffered from a disability, the FMLA did not authorize Novak's leave to care for her. Novak offered evidence about her daughter's difficulty in caring for the baby and Novak's need to help with the care of her grandchild. But the FMLA does not entitle an employee to take leave to care for a grandchild, only for a parent, spouse, or child.

The court of appeals held that Novak was not entitled to FMLA leave. The court therefore affirmed the dismissal of Novak's FMLA claims.

«

Concept *Summary* » 7.3

THE FMLA

Family and Medical Leave Act

- Qualified employees may take up to twelve weeks' unpaid leave for:
  - Birth and care of a child
  - Adoption or placement of a child into foster care
  - Care for self or spouse, child, or parent with a serious health condition
  - Qualifying exigencies arising from the call to active military duty of a spouse, child, or parent
- Qualified employees may take up to twenty-six weeks' unpaid leave for:
  - Care for a spouse, child, parent, or next of kin who suffers a serious illness or injury in the line of active military duty

Effect of Other Laws on the FMLA

The FMLA does not preempt or supersede any state or local law that provides for greater family or medical leave rights than those granted under the FMLA. In addition, employers are required to comply with any collective bargaining agreement or employee benefit program that provides for greater rights than those given under the FMLA.

State Legislation

The California Fair Employment and Housing Act Law requires employers to provide pregnant employees up to four months of unpaid pregnancy leave and to reinstate female employees returning from pregnancy leave to the job they held prior to the leave.

However, if the job is unavailable due to business necessity, the employer is required to make a good-faith effort to provide a substantially similar job. The California law does not require the employer to offer such treatment to employees returning from other temporary disability leaves. California Federal Savings and Loan, a California bank, alleged that the California law violated the Pregnancy Discrimination Act because it required the employer to treat pregnant employees differently from other temporarily disabled employees. In *California Federal Savings and Loan v. Guerra*,[35] the Supreme Court upheld the California law. The majority reasoned that the Pregnancy Discrimination Act amendments to Title VII were intended merely to create a minimum level of protection for pregnant employees that could be supplemented by state legislation as long as the state laws did not conflict with the terms or policies of Title VII. The Court also noted that the California law did not prevent employers from extending the right of reinstatement to employees on other temporary disability leaves; hence, the law did not require that pregnant employees be treated more generously than nonpregnant employees on temporary disability leave.

[35] 479 U.S. 272 (1987).

The WORKING Law

California Provides for Paid Family Leave

As of July 1, 2004, the state of California provides for temporary paid family leave through the state's disability insurance program. Workers who take time off to care for a seriously ill child, spouse, domestic partner, or who take time off to bond with a newborn child, adopted child or child, placed through foster care are eligible for up to six weeks of "family temporary disability insurance benefits." The worker must make a claim for the benefits with the state Disability Insurance Program, and will begin receiving benefits after a seven-day waiting period. No more than six weeks of benefits may be received within any twelve-month period. Workers who are already receiving unemployment compensation, state disability benefits, or any other temporary disability benefits under state or federal law are not eligible to receive family temporary disability insurance benefits. Workers who are entitled to a leave under the federal Family and Medical Leave Act or the California Family Rights Act must take the family temporary disability insurance leave at the same time as the leave under those laws.

Source: California's Unemployment Insurance Code, §§ 3300–3303.

Sexual Harassment

Sexual harassment is one of the most significant employment problems facing our society. It imposes significant costs on both employers and employees. Victims of sexual harassment may experience severe emotional anguish, physical and mental stress, frustration, humiliation, guilt, withdrawal and dysfunction in family and social relationships, medical expenses, loss of sick leave and vacation, and litigation costs. Employers suffer from absenteeism, higher turnover of employees, replacement and retraining costs, morale problems, losses in productivity, and of course, litigation expenses and damages.

Sexual Harassment
Unwelcome sexual advances, requests for sexual favors, or other verbal or physical conduct of a sexual nature that the employee is required to accept as a condition of employment, the employee's response to such conduct is used as a basis for employment decisions, or such conduct creates a hostile working environment.

The language of Title VII does not specifically mention sexual harassment, and in some early cases, the courts had difficulty determining whether sexual harassment was within the Title VII prohibition on gender discrimination. Now, however, the courts are clear on the position that sexual harassment is gender discrimination prohibited by Title VII. The EEOC has issued guidelines defining sexual harassment and declaring that sexual harassment constitutes gender discrimination in violation of Title VII. ***Sexual harassment*** is defined as unwelcome sexual advances, requests for sexual favors, or other verbal or physical conduct of a sexual nature, where the employee is required to accept such conduct as a condition of employment, the employee's response to such conduct is used as a basis for employment decisions such as promotion, bonuses, or retention, or such conduct unreasonably interferes with the employee's work performance or creates a hostile working environment. The Title VII protections against sexual harassment apply to all individuals—both men and women—covered by Title VII. (Note that Title VII also prohibits harassment based on race, color, religion, or national origin.)

Quid Pro Quo Harassment
Harassment where the employee's response to the harassment is considered in granting employment benefits.

Hostile Environment Harassment
Harassment which may not result in economic detriment to the victim, but which subjects the victim to unwelcome conduct or comments and may interfere with the employee's work performance.

The EEOC Guidelines and the courts have recognized two general categories of sexual harassment: quid pro quo harassment and hostile environment harassment. In ***quid pro quo harassment***, the employee's response to the request for sexual favors is considered in granting employment benefits, such as a male supervisor promising a female employee that she will be promoted or receive a favorable performance rating if she sleeps with him. Such harassment was held to violate Title VII in *Barnes v. Costle*.[36] In ***hostile environment harassment***, an employee may not suffer any economic detriment but is subjected to unwelcome sexual comments, propositions, jokes, or conduct that have the effect of interfering with the employee's work performance or creating a hostile work environment. The Supreme Court held hostile environment sexual harassment was prohibited by Title VII in *Meritor Savings Bank, FSB v. Vinson*.[37]

EEOC Guidelines on Sexual Harassment

Section 1604.11 Sexual Harassment

(a) Harassment on the basis of sex is a violation of § 703 of Title VII.[1] Unwelcome sexual advances, requests for sexual favors, and other verbal or physical conduct of a sexual nature constitute sexual harassment when (1) submission to such conduct is made either explicitly or implicitly a term or condition of an individual's employment; (2) submission to or rejection of such conduct by an individual is used as the basis for employment decisions affecting such individual; or (3) such conduct has the purpose or effect of unreasonably interfering with an individual's work performance or creating an intimidating, hostile, or offensive working environment.

(b) In determining whether alleged conduct constitutes sexual harassment, the Commission will look at the record as a whole and at the totality of the circumstances, such as the nature of the sexual advances and the context in which the alleged incidents occurred. The determination of the legality of a particular action will be made from the facts, on a case-by-case basis.

(c) Applying general Title VII principles, an employer, employment agency, joint apprenticeship committee or labor organization (hereinafter collectively referred to as "employer") is responsible for its acts and those of its agents and supervisory employees with respect to sexual harassment regardless of whether the specific acts complained of were authorized or even forbidden by the employer and regardless of whether the employer knew or should have known of

[1]The principles involved here continue to apply to race, color, religion, or national origin.

[36]561 F.2d 983 (D.C. Cir. 1977).

[37]477 U.S. 57 (1986).

their occurrence. The Commission will examine the circumstances of the particular employment relationship and the job functions performed by the individual in determining whether an individual acts in either a supervisory or agency capacity.

(d) With respect to conduct between fellow employees, an employer is responsible for acts of sexual harassment in the workplace where the employer (or its agents or supervisory employees) knows or should have known of the conduct, unless it can show that it took immediate and appropriate corrective action.

(e) An employer may also be responsible for the acts of nonemployees with respect to sexual harassment of employees in the workplace, where the employer (or its agents or supervisory employees) knows or should have known of the conduct and fails to take immediate and appropriate corrective action. In reviewing these cases, the Commission will consider the extent of the employer's control and any other legal responsibility which the employer may have with respect to the conduct of such nonemployees.

(f) Prevention is the best tool for the elimination of sexual harassment. An employer should take all steps necessary to prevent sexual harassment from occurring, such as affirmatively raising the subject, expressing strong disapproval, developing appropriate sanctions, informing employees of their rights and procedures for raising the issue of harassment under Title VII, and developing methods to sensitize all concerned.

(g) Other related practices: Where employment opportunities or benefits are granted because of an individual's submission to the employer's sexual advances or requests for sexual favors, the employer may be held liable for unlawful sex discrimination against other persons who were qualified for but denied that employment opportunity or benefit.

Quid Pro Quo Harassment

To establish a case of quid pro quo harassment, a plaintiff must show five things:

- She or he belongs to a protected group
- She or he was subject to unwelcome sexual harassment
- The harassment was based on sex
- Job benefits were conditioned on the acceptance of the harassment, and if appropriate
- There is some basis to hold the employer liable

The essence of quid pro quo harassment is that the employee's submission to such conduct is made either explicitly or implicitly a term or condition of an individual's employment or that submission to or rejection of such conduct by the employee is used as the basis for employment decisions affecting the employee.

The case of *Tomkins v. Public Service Electric & Gas Co.*[38] is a classic example of quid pro quo sexual harassment. Tomkins was told by her male supervisor that she should have sex with

[38]568 F.2d 1044 (3d Cir. 1977).

him if she wanted him to give her a satisfactory evaluation and recommend her for promotion. When she refused, she was subjected to a demotion, negative evaluations, disciplinary suspensions, and was ultimately fired. The U.S. Court of Appeals held that Title VII is violated when a supervisor makes sexual advances or demands toward a subordinate employee and conditions the employee's continued employment or possible promotion on a favorable response to those advances or demands.

The EEOC Guidelines on sexual harassment also provide that when an employer rewards one employee for entering a sexual relationship, other employees denied the same reward or benefit may have a valid harassment complaint. In *King v. Palmer*,[39] a supervisor promoted a nurse with whom he was having an affair rather than one of several more qualified nurses. The court held that the employer was guilty of gender discrimination against the superior nurses who were denied the promotion.

Hostile Environment Harassment

Unlike quid pro quo harassment, hostile environment harassment does not involve the conditioning of any job status or benefit on the employee's response to the harassment. Rather, the unwelcome harassment has the effect of interfering with the employee's work performance or creating a hostile work environment for the employee. Because no employment consequences are conditioned on the employee's response to the harassing conduct, some courts refused to hold that hostile environment harassment violated Title VII. The Supreme Court rejected that approach and upheld the EEOC Guidelines that declare hostile environment harassment to be sex discrimination in violation of Title VII in the case of *Meritor*. After that decision, the lower courts addressed the question of just how severe the harassing conduct has to be, and how hostile the work environment must become, before such harassment is found to violate Title VII. That issue was finally settled by the Supreme Court in the following decision.

case 7.6 »

Harris v. Forklift Systems, Inc.

510 U.S. 17 (1993)

O'Connor, J.:

Teresa Harris worked as a manager at Forklift Systems, Inc., an equipment rental company, from April 1985 until October 1987. Charles Hardy was Forklift's president.... [T]hroughout Harris' time at Forklift, Hardy often insulted her because of her gender and often made her the target of unwanted sexual innuendos. Hardy told Harris on several occasions, in the presence of other employees, "You're a woman, what do you know" and "We need a man as the rental manager"; at least once, he told her she was "a dumbass woman." Again in front of others, he suggested that the two of them "go to the Holiday Inn to negotiate [Harris'] raise." Hardy occasionally asked Harris and other female employees to get coins from his front pants pocket. He threw objects on the ground in front of Harris and other women, and asked them to pick the objects up. He made sexual innuendos about Harris' and other women's clothing.

[39] 778 F.2d 878 (D.C. Cir. 1985).

In mid-August 1987, Harris complained to Hardy about his conduct; Hardy said he was surprised that Harris was offended, claimed he was only joking, and apologized. He also promised he would stop, and based on this assurance Harris stayed on the job. But in early September, Hardy began anew: While Harris was arranging a deal with one of Forklift's customers, he asked her, again in front of other employees, "What did you do, promise the guy … some [sex] Saturday night?" On October 1, Harris collected her paycheck and quit.

Harris then sued Forklift, claiming that Hardy's conduct had created an abusive work environment for her because of her gender. The [trial] Court found this to be a "close case," but held that Hardy's conduct did not create an abusive environment. The court found that some of Hardy's comments "offended [Harris], and would offend the reasonable woman," but that they were not "so severe as to be expected to seriously affect [Harris'] psychological well being." [On appeal, the U.S. Court of Appeals for the Sixth Circuit affirmed the trial court decision. Harris then appealed to the U.S. Supreme Court.] We granted certiorari to resolve a conflict among [the federal courts of appeals] … on whether conduct, to be actionable as "abusive work environment" harassment (no quid pro quo harassment issue is presented here), must "seriously affect [an employee's] psychological well-being" or lead the plaintiff to "suffer injury" ….

Title VII of the Civil Rights Act of 1964 makes it "an unlawful employment practice for an employer … to discriminate against any individual with respect to his compensation, terms, conditions, or privileges of employment, because of such individual's race, color, religion, sex, or national origin." As we made clear in *Meritor Savings Bank v. Vinson* … this language "is not limited to 'economic' or 'tangible' discrimination. The phrase 'terms, conditions, or privileges of employment' evinces a congressional intent 'to strike at the entire spectrum of disparate treatment of men and women' in employment," which includes requiring people to work in a discriminatorily hostile or abusive environment. When the workplace is permeated with "discriminatory intimidations, ridicule, and insult," that is "sufficiently severe or pervasive to alter the conditions of the victim's employment and create an abusive working environment," Title VII is violated….

But Title VII comes into play before the harassing conduct leads to a nervous breakdown. A discriminatorily abusive work environment, even one that does not seriously affect employees' psychological well-being, can and often will detract from employees' job performance, discourage employees from remaining on the job, or keep them from advancing in their careers. Moreover, even without regard to these tangible effects, the very fact that the discriminatory conduct was so severe or pervasive that it created a work environment abusive to employees because of their race, gender, religion, or national origin offends Title VII's broad rule of workplace equality.

… We therefore believe the District Court erred in relying on whether the conduct "seriously affected plaintiff's psychological well-being" or led her to "suffer injury." Such an inquiry may needlessly focus the factfinder's attention on concrete psychological harm, an element Title VII does not require. Certainly Title VII bars conduct that would seriously affect a reasonable person's psychological well-being, but the statute is not limited to such conduct. So long as the environment would reasonably be perceived, and is perceived, as hostile or abusive, there is no need for it also to be psychologically injurious.

This is not, and by its nature cannot be, a mathematically precise test. We need not answer today all the potential questions it raises, nor specifically address the EEOC's new regulations on this subject … But we can say that whether an environment is "hostile" or "abusive" can be determined only by looking at all the circumstances. These may include the frequency of the discriminatory conduct; its severity; whether it is physically threatening or humiliating, or a mere offensive utterance; and whether it unreasonably interferes with an employee's work performance. The effect on the employee's psychological well-being is, of course, relevant to determining whether the plaintiff actually found the environment abusive. But while psychological harm, like any other relevant factor, may be taken into account, no single factor is required.

Forklift, while conceding that a requirement that the conduct seriously affect psychological well being is unfounded, argues that the District Court nonetheless correctly applied the *Meritor* standard. We disagree. Though the District Court did conclude that the work environment was not "intimidating or abusive to [Harris]," it did so only after finding that the conduct was not "so severe as to be expected to seriously affect plaintiff's psychological well-being" and that Harris was not "subjectively so offended that she suffered injury." The District Court's application of these incorrect standards may well have influenced its ultimate conclusion, especially given that the court found this to be a "close case."

We therefore reverse the judgment of the Court of Appeals, and remand the case for further proceedings consistent with this opinion.

So ordered.

Case Questions

1. How did the harassment directed against Harris affect her economically? How did the harassment directed against Harris affect her emotionally? Did it interfere with her work performance? Explain your answers.

2. How severe must "hostile environment" sexual harassment be before it violates Title VII?

3. Is the standard used to determine when sexual harassment becomes severe enough to create a "hostile environment" a subjective or an objective standard? Explain your answer.

Reasonable Person or Reasonable Victim?

In cases involving claims of hostile environment harassment, the courts have dealt with the question of which standard should be used to determine whether the challenged conduct was sufficiently severe and hostile. Most courts have used the "reasonable person" standard. That is, would a reasonable person find the conduct to be offensive and severe enough to create a hostile environment or to interfere with the person's work performance? The EEOC issued a policy statement declaring that courts should also consider the perspective of the victim to avoid perpetuating stereotypical notions of what behavior was acceptable to persons of a specific gender.

In response to that, some courts adopted the "reasonable victim" or "reasonable woman" standard, recognizing that men and women were likely to perceive and react differently to certain behaviors. In *Ellison v. Brady*,[40] the court held that the reasonable woman standard should be used to determine whether a series of unsolicited love letters sent to a female employee by a male co-worker had the effect of creating a hostile work environment. Even when courts did adopt the reasonable woman standard, they emphasized that the standard was not totally subjective, but was to be based on whether an objective reasonable woman would find the conduct offensive or would have been detrimentally affected.

The Supreme Court, although not specifically addressing the issue of whether to use the reasonable person or reasonable woman standard, used the reasonable person standard in *Harris v. Forklift Systems, Inc.*

Employer Liability for Sexual Harassment

The EEOC Guidelines state that employers are liable for sexual harassment by supervisory or managerial employees and may also be liable for harassment by co-workers or even nonemployees under certain circumstances. The Supreme Court in *Meritor* rejected the EEOC Guidelines' position on employer liability for supervisors or managerial employees and instead held that employer liability should be determined according to traditional common-law agency principles; that is, was the harasser acting as an agent of the employer?

[40] 924 F.2d 872 (9th Cir. 1991).

Concept *Summary* » 7.4

Sexual Harassment

- Sexual harassment is:
  - Unwelcome:
    - Sexual advances
    - Requests for sexual favors
    - Verbal or physical conduct of a sexual nature
  - Where the employee is required to accept such conduct as a condition of employment
- Quid pro quo harassment
  - The employee's response to sexual harassment is used as a basis for employment decisions
    - Examples: A male supervisor promising a female employee a promotion if she sleeps with him
- Hostile work environment
  - Sexual harassment unreasonably interferes with the employee's work performance or creates a hostile working environment
    - Example: Co-workers or supervisors continually subject an employee to unwelcome sexual comments or requests for sexual favors.

Agency Relationships

Whether an agency relationship is created is a question of fact to be determined on the specifics of a particular situation. Supervisors or managerial employees, acting in the course of their employment, are generally held to be agents of the employer; that is, they act with the actual, or apparent, authorization of the employer. An agency relationship can also be created by an employer's acceptance of, tolerance of, acquiescence to, or after-the-fact ratification of an employee's conduct, such as when the employer becomes aware of harassment and fails to take action to stop it.

Employer Liability for Supervisors

When is an employer liable under Title VII for sexual harassment by a supervisor or managerial employee? The courts have consistently held an employer liable for quid pro quo sexual harassment by a manager or supervisor because such conduct is related to the supervisor's or manager's job status. But courts have differed over holding an employer liable for hostile environment harassment by a supervisor or manager. Some courts held an employer liable only when the harassment was somehow aided by the supervisor's job status, while other courts held that the employer was liable when it knew or should have known of the harassment. The U.S. Supreme Court settled the issue of employer liability for hostile environment harassment by a supervisor or manager in the following case.

case 7.7 »

Faragher v. City of Boca Raton
524 U.S. 775 (1998)

[Beth Ann Faragher worked as an ocean lifeguard for the Marine Safety Section of the Parks and Recreation Department of the City of Boca Raton, Florida (City), from 1985 to 1990. Her immediate supervisors were Bill Terry, David Silverman, and Robert Gordon. During her employment, Terry repeatedly touched the bodies of female employees without invitation, made contact with another female lifeguard in a motion of sexual simulation, and made crudely demeaning remarks about women generally. During a job interview with a woman he hired as a lifeguard, Terry said that the female lifeguards had sex with their male counterparts and asked whether she would do the same. Silverman behaved in similar ways: he made frequent, vulgar references to women and sexual matters, commented on the bodies of female lifeguards and beachgoers, and at least twice told female lifeguards that he would like to engage in sex with them.

Faragher and other female lifeguards did not complain to higher management about Terry or Silverman, although they did have informal talks with Gordon. Gordon did not feel that it was his place to report these complaints to Terry, his own supervisor, or to any other city official. In April 1990, a former lifeguard formally complained to the City's Personnel Director about Terry's and Silverman's harassment of her and other female lifeguards. The City investigated the complaint and found that Terry and Silverman had behaved improperly; the City reprimanded them, and required them to choose between a suspension without pay or the forfeiture of annual leave.

Faragher resigned in June 1990, and in 1992 filed a suit against Terry, Silverman, and the City, alleging violations of Title VII and other federal and state laws. She claimed that the harassment by Terry and Silverman created a "sexually hostile atmosphere." Because Terry and Silverman were agents of the City, and their conduct amounted to discrimination in the terms, conditions, and privileges of her employment, Faragher sought to hold the City liable for damages, court costs, and attorney's fees. The federal trial court ruled that the conduct of Terry and Silverman was discriminatory harassment sufficiently serious to alter the conditions of Faragher's employment and constitute an abusive working environment, and held the City liable for the harassment of its supervisory employees. The trial court awarded Faragher one dollar in nominal damages on her Title VII claim. The City appealed, and the Court of Appeals for the Eleventh Circuit reversed the judgment against the City, ruling that Terry and Silverman were not acting within the scope of their employment when they engaged in the harassment, that they were not aided in their actions by the agency relationship, and that the City had no constructive knowledge of the harassment by virtue of its pervasiveness or Gordon's actual knowledge. Faragher appealed to the U.S. Supreme Court.]

Souter, J.:

Since our decision in *Meritor,* Courts of Appeals have struggled to derive manageable standards to govern employer liability for hostile environment harassment perpetrated by supervisory employees.

In the case before us, a justification for holding the offensive behavior within the scope of Terry's and Silverman's employment was well put in Judge Barkett's dissent [in the Court of Appeals]: "[A] pervasively hostile work environment of sexual harassment is never (one would hope) authorized, but the supervisor is clearly charged with maintaining a productive, safe work environment. The supervisor directs and controls the conduct of the employees, and the manner of doing so may inure to the employer's benefit or detriment, including subjecting the employer to Title VII liability." It is by now well recognized that hostile environment sexual harassment by supervisors (and, for that matter, co-employees) is a persistent problem in the workplace. An employer can, in a general sense, reasonably anticipate the possibility of such conduct occurring in its workplace, and one might justify the assignment of the burden of the untoward behavior to the employer as one of the costs of doing business, to be charged to the enterprise rather than the victim.

We ... agree with Faragher that in implementing Title VII it makes sense to hold an employer vicariously liable for some tortious conduct of a supervisor made possible by abuse of his supervisory authority. Several courts, indeed, have noted what Faragher has argued, that there is a sense in which a harassing supervisor is always assisted in his misconduct by the supervisory relationship. The [supervisor's] agency relationship affords contact with an employee subjected to a supervisor's sexual harassment, and the victim may well be reluctant to accept the risks of blowing the whistle on a superior. When a person with supervisory authority discriminates in the terms and conditions of subordinates' employment, his actions necessarily draw upon his superior position over the people who report to him, or those under them, whereas an employee generally cannot check a supervisor's abusive conduct the same way that she might deal with abuse from a co-worker. When a fellow employee harasses, the victim can walk away or tell the offender where to go, but it may be difficult to offer such responses to a supervisor, whose "power to supervise—[which may be] to hire and fire, and to set work schedules and pay rates—does not disappear … when he chooses to harass through insults and offensive gestures rather than directly with threats of firing or promises of promotion." Recognition of employer liability when discriminatory misuse of supervisory authority alters the terms and conditions of a victim's employment is underscored by the fact that the employer has a greater opportunity to guard against misconduct by supervisors than by common workers; employers have greater opportunity and incentive to screen them, train them, and monitor their performance.

In sum, there are good reasons for vicarious liability for misuse of supervisory authority. That rationale must, however, satisfy one more condition. We are not entitled to recognize this theory under Title VII unless we can square it with *Meritor's* holding that an employer is not "automatically" liable for harassment by a supervisor who creates the requisite degree of discrimination, and there is obviously some tension between that holding and the position that a supervisor's misconduct aided by supervisory authority subjects the employer to liability vicariously; if the "aid" may be the unspoken suggestion of retaliation by misuse of supervisory authority, the risk of automatic liability is high….

The … basic alternative to automatic liability would … allow an employer to show as an affirmative defense to liability that the employer had exercised reasonable care to avoid harassment and to eliminate it when it might occur, and that the complaining employee had failed to act with like reasonable care to take advantage of the employer's safeguards and otherwise to prevent harm that could have been avoided….

In order to accommodate the principle of vicarious liability for harm caused by misuse of supervisory authority, as well as Title VII's equally basic policies of encouraging forethought by employers and saving action by objecting employees, we adopt the following holding in this case and in *Burlington Industries Inc. v. Ellerth* [decided the same day]. An employer is subject to vicarious liability to a victimized employee for an actionable hostile environment created by a supervisor with immediate (or successively higher) authority over the employee. When no tangible employment action is taken, a defending employer may raise an affirmative defense to liability or damages, subject to proof by a preponderance of the evidence. The defense comprises two necessary elements: (a) that the employer exercised reasonable care to prevent and correct promptly any sexually harassing behavior, and (b) that the plaintiff employee unreasonably failed to take advantage of any preventive or corrective opportunities provided by the employer or to avoid harm otherwise. While proof that an employer had promulgated an anti-harassment policy with complaint procedure is not necessary in every instance as a matter of law, the need for a stated policy suitable to the employment circumstances may appropriately be addressed in any case when litigating the first element of the defense. And while proof that an employee failed to fulfill the corresponding obligation of reasonable care to avoid harm is not limited to showing an unreasonable failure to use any complaint procedure provided by the employer, a demonstration of such failure will normally suffice to satisfy the employer's burden under the second element of the defense. No affirmative defense is available, however, when the supervisor's harassment culminates in a tangible employment action, such as discharge, demotion, or undesirable reassignment….

Applying these rules here, we believe that the judgment of the Court of Appeals must be reversed. The District Court found that the degree of hostility in the work environment rose to the actionable level and was attributable to Silverman and Terry. It is undisputed that these supervisors "were granted virtually unchecked authority" over their subordinates, "directly controll[ing] and supervis[ing] all aspects of [Faragher's] day-to-day activities." It is also clear that Faragher and her colleagues were "completely isolated from the City's higher management." … The judgment of the Court of Appeals for the Eleventh Circuit is reversed, and the case is remanded for reinstatement of the judgment of the District Court.

It is so ordered.

Case Questions

1. Why should an employer be liable for the actions of a supervisor? Does the same reasoning apply in the case of sexual harassment by a supervisor?
2. What actions can an employer take to avoid being held liable for sexual harassment by a supervisor?
3. What are the requirements of the defense for employers set out by the Supreme Court in this case? Could the City of Boca Raton use that defense here? Explain your answers.

Employer Liability for Co-Workers and Nonemployees

For both quid pro quo harassment and hostile environment harassment by nonsupervisory or nonmanagerial employees, an employer will be liable if it knew of, or should have known of, the harassing conduct and failed to take reasonable steps to stop it. An employer may even be liable for harassment by nonemployees if the employer had some control over the harasser and failed to take reasonable steps to stop it once the employer became aware of, or should have been aware of, the harassment.

Individual Liability

The courts have held that individual employees are not liable for damages under Title VII; this means that the employee doing the harassing will not be held personally liable for damages under Title VII. They are subject to court injunctions to cease and desist from such conduct. But harassers or potential harassers should be aware that they may be held personally liable under the various state EEO laws or under common-law tort claims. The damages under state EEO laws and tort claims may include compensatory and punitive damages in addition to employment-related damages and legal fees.

Public employees who engage in sexual harassment may, in addition to the foregoing remedies, be subject to suits for damages under 42 U.S.C. §1983 and criminal prosecution under 18 U.S.C. §242.

Concept *Summary* » 7.5

LIABILITY FOR SEXUAL HARASSMENT

- Employer liability
  - Employers are liable for employees acting in the course of their employment, including:
    - Managerial/supervisors
    - Co-workers—if the employer knows or should have known about the harassment and fails to take action to stop it
    - Nonemployees—if the employer knows or should have known about the harassment and fails to take action to stop it
- Individual liability
  - Individual harassers are not liable for damages under Title VII
  - Individuals may face damages under certain state EEO laws or common-law tort claims
  - Public employees may also be subject to criminal prosecution

Employer Responses to Sexual Harassment Claims

Employers have several defenses to raise against claims of sexual harassment. Prevention is probably the best defense to stop sexual harassment before any legal problems develop.

Prevention

As the Supreme Court decision in *Faragher* stated, the best way for an employer to avoid liability for sexual harassment is to take active steps to prevent it. Both the EEOC Guidelines and the Supreme Court emphasize the importance of having a policy against sexual harassment and of following that policy whenever a complaint arises. According to the EEOC Guidelines and court decisions, the sexual harassment policy should define sexual harassment and give practical, concrete examples of such conduct. The policy must also make it very clear that such conduct by anyone in the organization will not be tolerated, and it should specify the penalties, up to and including termination, for violations of the policy. The policy should spell out the procedures for filing complaints of sexual harassment, designate specific (preferably managerial) employees who are responsible for receiving and investigating complaints, and should include reassurances that employees who file complaints will be protected from retaliation or reprisals.

The policy must be communicated to all employees, who should be educated about the policy through training and workshops; all employees must understand the policy and be aware of the employer's commitment to the policy. Above all, the employer must take steps to enforce the policy immediately upon receipt of a complaint of sexual harassment because the policy is effective only if it is followed. If the employer acts promptly to enforce the policy whenever a complaint of sexual harassment is received, it will generally avoid liability for such conduct according to *Faragher*.

Defenses

In addition to the preventive approach and the defense set out in *Faragher*, employers have a few other defenses to raise when faced with charges of sexual harassment. The definition of sexual harassment indicates that the conduct complained of must be unwelcome and of a sexual nature, and it must either be *quid pro quo* or serious enough to create a hostile working environment. Generally, the courts will not consider isolated incidents or trivial comments to constitute sexual harassment. As the Supreme Court indicated in *Harris v. Forklift Systems*, factors to consider in determining whether the challenged conduct amounts to sexual harassment include its frequency, severity, whether it is physically threatening or humiliating or a mere offensive utterance, and whether it unreasonably interferes with an employee's work performance. In *Scott v. Sears, Roebuck & Co.*,[41] the court held that one pat on the buttocks, winks, one dinner invitation, and an offer by one employee to give a female employee a "rubdown" did not create a hostile environment. In *Rabidue v. Osceola Refining Co.*[42] the court held that the display of pin-up photos and posters of nude or scantily clad women did not seriously affect female employees; but in *Barbetta v. Chemlawn Services Corp.*[43] the court held that a proliferation of pornographic material featuring nude women did create a hostile working environment for female employees.

The fact that the harassed employee failed to file a complaint through the employer's sexual harassment complaint procedure does not automatically protect the employer from liability. The employer may still be held liable if it knew of, or had reason to know of, the harassment.[44]

---

[41]798 F.2d 210 (7th Cir. 1986).

[42]805 F.2d 611 (6th Cir. 1986).

[43]669 F.Supp. 569 (W.D. N.Y. 1987).

[44]*Burlington Industries, Inc. v. Ellerth*, 542 U.S. 742 (1998).

Unwelcome

Conduct of a sexual nature must be unwelcome to be sexual harassment; the target of the harassment must indicate that it is unwelcome. In *Meritor*, the Supreme Court held that as long as the victim indicates that the conduct is unwelcome, it is still sexual harassment, even if the victim voluntarily complies with the harassment. A consensual sexual relationship, instigated by a female employee in an attempt to advance in her job, was held not to be sexual harassment in *Perkins v. General Motors Corporation.*[45]

Provocation

Meritor also indicated that the employer can raise the defense of provocation by the victim: Did the victim instigate the allegedly harassing conduct through her or his own style of dress, comments, or conduct? The issue of provocation goes to whether the conduct was unwelcome: If the victim has encouraged the allegedly harassing conduct, is it really unwelcome? In *McLean v. Satellite Technology Services, Inc.*,[46] where a female employee regularly offered to engage in sexual acts with other employees and often lifted her skirt to show her supervisor that she was not wearing undergarments, a single attempt by her supervisor to hug and kiss her was held not to be sexual harassment. However, the fact that an employee had posed nude for a national magazine did not automatically mean that she would find her boss's sexual advances welcome,[47] nor did the fact that a female employee swore "like a drunken sailor" mean that she welcomed harassing conduct.[48]

Conduct of a Sexual Nature

In order to be sexual harassment, the conduct complained of must be based on the employee's sex. Tasteless comments or jokes or annoying behavior, while offensive, may not be sexual harassment. A supervisor who is obnoxious and verbally abusive to all employees is not guilty of sexual harassment as long as the abuse is not based on sex. In *Holman v. State of Indiana*,[49] the U.S. Court of Appeals for the Seventh Circuit held that a supervisor's harassment and solicitation of sexual favors of both male and female employees was not conduct "because of sex."

---

[45] 709 F.Supp. 1487 (W.D. Mo. 1989).

[46] 673 F.Supp. 1458 (E.D. Mo. 1987).

[47] *Burnes v. McGregor Electronic Industries, Inc.*, 989 F.2d 959 (8th Cir. 1993).

[48] *Steiner v. Showboat Operating Co.*, 25 F.3d 1459 (9th Cir. 1994).

[49] 211 F.3d 399 (7th Cir. 2000).

Concept *Summary* » 7.6

DEFENSES TO SEXUAL HARASSMENT CLAIMS

- Prevention
  - Employers should have a policy that:
    - Defines harassment
    - Outlines penalties and procedures for filing complaints
    - Protects employees who file complaints from retaliation
- Defenses
  - Conduct was isolated incident—not frequent or severe enough to cause unreasonable interference with work performance
  - Employee did not indicate that conduct was unwelcome
  - "Victim" provoked harassment through his/her own conduct

Same-Sex Harassment

The Supreme Court decision in *Oncale v. Sundowner Offshore Services, Inc.*[50] resolved a split among the Courts of Appeals regarding whether same-sex harassment was prohibited by the sexual harassment prohibition of Title VII. The Supreme Court held that Title VII prohibits discrimination because of sex in terms or conditions of employment, including sexual harassment by employees of the same sex as the victim of the harassment. Oncale, a worker on an offshore oil platform, alleged that his male co-workers had subjected him to sexual assault and sex-related humiliating actions and had threatened him with rape. His supervisors failed to take any remedial action when he complained. The Supreme Court decision emphasized that Title VII does not reach conduct tinged with offensive sexual overtones but does forbid conduct of a sexual nature that creates a hostile work environment, conduct so severe as to alter the conditions of the victim's employment. The Court stated:

> We see no justification in the statutory language or our precedents for a categorical rule excluding same-sex harassment claims from the coverage of Title VII. As some courts have observed, male-on-male sexual harassment in the workplace was assuredly not the principal evil Congress was concerned with when it enacted Title VII. But statutory prohibitions often go beyond the principal evil to cover reasonably comparable evils, and it is ultimately the provisions of our laws rather than the principal concerns of our legislators by which we are governed. Title VII prohibits "discriminat [ion] ... because of ... sex" in the "terms" or "conditions" of employment. Our holding that this includes sexual harassment must extend to sexual harassment of any kind that meets the statutory requirements.
>
> We have emphasized, moreover, that the objective severity of harassment should be judged from the perspective of a reasonable person in the plaintiff's position, considering "all the circumstances." [citing *Harris*] In same-sex, (as in all) harassment cases, that inquiry requires careful consideration of the social context in which particular behavior occurs and is experienced by its target. A professional football player's working environment is not severely or pervasively abusive, for example, if the coach smacks him on the buttocks as he heads onto the field—even if the same

[50] 523 U.S. 75 (1998).

> behavior would reasonably be experienced as abusive by the coach's secretary (male or female) back at the office. The real social impact of workplace behavior often depends on a constellation of surrounding circumstances, expectations, and relationships which are not fully captured by a simple recitation of the words used or the physical acts performed. Common sense, and an appropriate sensitivity to social context, will enable courts and juries to distinguish between simple teasing or roughhousing among members of the same sex, and conduct which a reasonable person in the plaintiff's position would find severely hostile or abusive.

According to *Hamner v. St. Vincent Hospital and Health Care Center, Inc.*,[51] Title VII's prohibition on sexual harassment does not include harassment based on sexual orientation or sexual preference. However, a male employee who was harassed by managers and co-workers because he was perceived as being effeminate and did not conform to a male stereotype established a case of hostile environment sexual harassment.[52]

Remedies for Sexual Harassment

Remedies for sexual harassment available under Title VII include injunctions to stop the harassment and to refrain from such conduct in the future, lost wages and benefits, compensatory and punitive damages for intentional conduct, and legal fees and reinstatement (if appropriate). Employment-related damages, such as back pay, benefits, seniority, and so on, are recoverable in their entirety. Compensatory damages (such as damages for emotional trauma and/or medical expenses) and punitive damages are available in cases of intentional violations of Title VII. Sexual harassment is generally held to be intentional conduct, so such damages are generally available to successful plaintiffs; however, there are statutory limits on the amount of compensatory and punitive damages under Title VII based on the size of the employer. In addition to Title VII, sexual harassment may also be challenged under state EEO laws and common-law torts such as intentional infliction of emotional distress, invasion of privacy, battery, and assault. Compensatory and punitive damages may be available under the various state EEO laws and are usually available under tort law; there are generally no statutory limitations on such damages available under state EEO laws and tort claims.

In addition to Title VII, state EEO laws, and tort claims, federal and state constitutional provisions may also apply to public sector employers guilty of sexual harassment. Public employees who engage in sexual harassment may be subject to suits for damages under 42 U.S. C. §1983, which allows civil suits for damages against persons who act, under the color of law, to deprive others of legally protected rights. In *United States v. Lanier*,[53] the Supreme Court upheld the criminal prosecution of a public employee guilty of sexual harassment under 18 U.S.C. §242, which provides for criminal penalties of fines and prison terms of up to ten years for persons who, under the color of law, willfully subject another person to the deprivation of legally protected rights.

---

[51]224 F.3d 701 (7th Cir. 2000).

[52]*Nichols v. Azteca Restaurant Enterprises, Inc.*, 256 F.3d 864 (9th Cir. 2001).

[53]520 U.S. 259 (1997).

ethical DILEMMA

Your office cubicle is next to that of Mona Leslie, a newly hired female employee in your department. Her male supervisor seems to be devoting a lot of attention to her, and drops by her cubicle many times a day. You can hear the supervisor's conversations—and they include some off-color jokes and comments. You have also heard, on several occasions, the supervisor ask Mona to go to lunch with him, or to go out for a drink after work. Mona always politely declines his invitations, but at times she appears to be distressed and agitated after the supervisor's visits. In a conversation with Mona, you inform her that you believe that the supervisor's conduct is in violation of the company's sexual harassment policy. She responds that she is a new employee and doesn't want to "make waves" because she really needs her job. What should you do—inform the HR Department of the supervisor's behavior? Explain your response.

Sexual Orientation, Sexual Preference, and Sexual Identity Discrimination

Title VII and Other EEO Legislation

Prior to the U.S. Supreme Court decision in *Price Waterhouse v. Hopkins*, the federal courts had consistently held that Title VII's prohibition of discrimination based on gender does not extend to discrimination against homosexuals or lesbians.[54] Similar decisions held that Title VII did not protect transvestites and transsexuals from employment discrimination.[55] As well, the Rehabilitation Act and the Americans with Disabilities Act specifically exclude homosexuality, bisexuality, transvestism, transsexualism, and other sexual behavior conditions from their protection against discrimination based on disability or handicap as well. Recall, however, that in *Price Waterhouse*, the U.S. Supreme Court held that Title VII's prohibition of sex discrimination included discrimination based on sex stereotypes. In light of that decision, could a male transsexual bring a claim of sex discrimination against the employer who fired him because he did not meet the employer's perceptions of how a male should look and behave? That is the issue addressed in the following case.

---

[54] *DeSantis v. Pacific Telephone and Telegraph Co.*, 608 F.2d 327 (9th Cir. 1979); *Williamson v. A.G. Edwards & Sons, Inc.*, 876 F.2d 69 (8th Cir. 1989).

[55] *Holloway v. Arthur Andersen & Co.*, 566 F.2d 659 (9th Cir. 1977); *Sommers v. Budget Marketing Inc.*, 667 F.2d 748 (8th Cir. 1982); *Ulane v. Eastern Airlines, Inc.*, 742 F.2d 1081 (7th Cir. 1984).

case 7.8 »

Smith v. City of Salem, Ohio

378 F.3d 566 (6th Cir. 2004)

Facts: Smith had been a lieutenant in the Salem Fire Department for seven years. His service had been without any negative incidents. Smith, a male by birth, was a transsexual and had been diagnosed with gender identity disorder ("GID"), which the American Psychiatric Association characterizes as a disjunction between an individual's sexual organs and sexual identity. After being diagnosed with GID, Smith began expressing a more feminine appearance on a full-time basis, including at work, in accordance with international medical protocols for treating GID. As a result, Smith's co-workers began questioning him about his appearance and commenting that his appearance and mannerisms were not "masculine enough." Smith notified his supervisor, Eastek, about his GID diagnosis and treatment. He also informed Eastek of the likelihood that his treatment would eventually include a complete physical transformation from male to female. Smith had approached Eastek in order to answer any questions Eastek might have concerning his appearance and manner and so that Eastek could address Smith's co-workers' comments and inquiries. Smith specifically asked Eastek not to divulge the conversation to any of his superiors, particularly to Greenamyer, chief of the Fire Department. However, Eastek told Greenamyer about Smith's behavior and his GID.

Greenamyer then met with other city officials and arranged a meeting of the City's executive body to discuss Smith and devise a plan for terminating his employment. During the meeting, Greenamyer and the mayor agreed to arrange for the Salem Civil Service Commission to require Smith to undergo three separate psychological evaluations. They hoped that Smith would either resign or refuse to comply. If he refused, they could terminate his employment for insubordination. Another official who attended the meeting telephoned Smith afterwards to inform him of the plan.

Two days later, Smith's lawyer telephoned the mayor to advise him of Smith's legal representation and the potential legal problems for the City if it followed through on the plan. Four days later, Greenamyer suspended Smith for one twenty-four hour shift, based on his alleged infraction of a City and/or Fire Department policy. Smith challenged his suspension to the City's Civil Service Commission, and ultimately before the county court, which reversed the suspension because the regulation Smith was alleged to have violated was not in effect.

Smith had previously filed a complaint under Title VII with the EEOC, which granted him a "right to sue" letter. Smith filed suit in the federal district court alleging sex discrimination and retaliation in violation of Title VII. The trial court dismissed Smith's suit on the ground that he failed to state a claim for sex stereotyping pursuant to *Price Waterhouse v. Hopkins*. The trial court held that his claim was really based upon his transsexuality and that Title VII does not prohibit discrimination based on an individual's transsexualism. Smith then appealed to the U.S Court of Appeals for the Sixth Circuit, claiming that he was a victim of sex discrimination both because of his gender nonconforming conduct and because of his identification as a transsexual.

Issue: Has Smith established a claim of sex discrimination because of sex stereotyping, under the Supreme Court decision in *Price Waterhouse*?

Decision: Smith claimed that *Price Waterhouse* applied to his case. He stated that his conduct and mannerisms did not conform to his employers' and co-workers' sex stereotypes of how a man should look and behave and the discrimination he experienced was a direct result of this. The court of appeals held that Smith had established claims of sex stereotyping and gender discrimination and that the trial court erred in relying on a series of pre-*Price Waterhouse* cases holding that transsexuals were not protected by Title VII.

The Supreme Court decision in *Price Waterhouse* held that Title VII protected a woman who failed to conform to social expectations concerning how a woman should look and behave and established that Title VII's reference to "sex" encompasses both the biological differences between men and women, and gender discrimination based on a failure to conform to stereotypical gender norms. It follows that employers who discriminate against men because they *do* wear dresses and makeup, or otherwise act femininely, are also engaging in sex discrimination, because the discrimination would not occur except for the victim's sex. Sex stereotyping based on a person's gender nonconforming behavior is discrimination in violation of Title VII.

The court of appeals held that Smith had stated a claim of sex discrimination under Title VII. The court reversed the trial court decision and remanded the case back to that court.

Other courts have taken the same approach as the Sixth Circuit did in *Smith*. In *Nichols v. Azteca Restaurant Enterprises, Inc.*,[56] the U.S. Court of Appeals for the Ninth Circuit held that a male employee who was subjected to abuse and ridicule by managers and co-workers because of his effeminate appearance had established a claim under Title VII.

State EEO Legislation

While no federal legislation expressly protects homosexuals, a number of state EEO laws, including those of California, Colorado, Connecticut, Delaware, Hawaii, Illinois, Iowa, Maine, Maryland, Massachusetts, Minnesota, Nevada, New Hampshire, New Jersey, New Mexico, New York, Oregon, Rhode Island, Vermont, Washington, Wisconsin, and the District of Columbia, prohibit discrimination based on sexual preference or sexual orientation. Other states, including Louisiana, Michigan, Ohio, and Pennsylvania prohibit sexual orientation or sexual preference discrimination by public sector employers under executive orders issued by the governor. In addition, some large cities such as New York City and San Francisco have human rights ordinances that prohibit discrimination based on sexual orientation or sexual preference The state EEO laws of California, Colorado, Minnesota, New Jersey, New Mexico, Oregon, Rhode Island, Washington, and the District of Columbia also prohibit employment discrimination based on gender identity or gender expression, which means that transsexuals and persons who have undergone sex change operations are protected from discrimination on those grounds.

There are some limits to the coverage of the state laws against discrimination based on sexual orientation or sexual preference. In *Boy Scouts of America v. Dale*,[57] the U.S. Supreme Court held that applying the New Jersey Law Against Discrimination's prohibition of discrimination based on sexual orientation to the Boy Scouts violated their constitutional right of expressive association under the First Amendment. The Court stated that prohibiting the Boy Scouts from dismissing a gay assistant scoutmaster would undermine the Boy Scouts' mission of instilling values in young people.

Constitutional Protection

Public employers who discriminate on the basis of homosexuality are subject to the equal protection provisions of the U.S. Constitution, which prohibit arbitrary or "invidious" discrimination. However, that has not stopped public employers from discriminating against homosexuals. The courts have generally allowed public employers to refuse to hire homosexuals when the employer can show that the ban on homosexuals has some legitimate relationship to valid employment-related concerns. In *Doe v. Gates*,[58] the court upheld the CIA's dismissal of a gay clerk typist because he "posed a threat to national security" based on the fact that he hid information about his homosexuality. The FBI's refusal to hire a lesbian as a special agent was upheld because homosexual conduct was illegal in the country in which she would have worked, and the agent would have been subject to blackmail to protect herself or

---

[56]256 F.3d 864 (9th Cir. 2001).

[57]530 U.S. 640 (2000).

[58]981 F.2d 1316 (D.C. Cir. 1993).

her partner.[59] The Georgia state attorney general's refusal to hire a lesbian as a staff attorney was affirmed on similar grounds in *Shahar v. Bowers*.[60]

A number of cases dealing with discrimination against homosexuals have involved the armed services' refusal to admit homosexuals. In several decisions, the courts have upheld this general policy, but have required the military to demonstrate that an individual has engaged in homosexual conduct in order to bar that person from military service.[61] Under President Clinton, the military adopted a "don't ask, don't tell" policy, under which persons will be barred from service if they engage in homosexual conduct or demonstrate a propensity to engage in such conduct. The policy focuses on conduct rather than a person's status. A person's declaration about his or her sexual orientation alone is not sufficient to bar that person from the military. The "don't ask, don't tell" policy has been upheld in several decisions, such as *Phillips v. Perry*[62] and *Thomasson v. Perry*.[63] It must be noted that the constitutional cases discussed above were decided prior to the Supreme Court decision in *Lawrence v. Texas*.[64] In *Lawrence*, which was a criminal law case and not an employment case, the Court, by a 6–3 vote, declared unconstitutional state laws making it a crime for adults of the same sex to engage in consensual sexual activity in the privacy of their home. The majority held that such laws infringed upon the constitutionally protected liberty interests of homosexuals. Some commentators argue that the *Lawrence* case may signal the end of government discrimination against homosexuals. Others claim that the case is more limited and deals only with laws that criminalized private, consensual sexual conduct between adults.

A related case was triggered by a number of law schools that refused to allow military recruiters access to their campuses as a protest over the military's policies regarding homosexuals. Congress reacted by passing legislation (known as the Solomon Amendment) that would cut off federal funds to schools if they did not allow military recruiters campus access. Several of the schools involved filed suit, challenging the Solomon Amendment. The Supreme Court held that the Solomon Amendment did not violate law schools' First Amendment freedom of expressive association.[65]

Other Gender-Discrimination Issues

Section 712 of Title VII states that:

> [n]othing contained in this title shall be construed to repeal or modify any Federal, State, territorial, or local law creating special rights or preference for veterans.

---

[59] *Padula v. Webster*, 822 F.2d 97 (D.C. Cir. 1987).

[60] 114 F.3d 1097 (11th Cir. 1997).

[61] *Watkins v. U.S. Army*, 875 F.2d 699 (9th Cir. 1989); *Meinhold v. United States Dept. of Defense*, 34 F.3d 1469 (9th Cir. 1994).

[62] 106 F.3d 1420 (9th Cir. 1997).

[63] 80 F.3d 915 (4th Cir. 1996).

[64] 539 U.S. 558 (2003).

[65] *Rumsfeld v. Forum for Academic and Institutional Rights, Inc.*, 547 U.S. 47 (U.S. 2006).

Because most veterans are male, any preference in employment according to veteran status will have a disparate impact on women. The effect of Section 712 is to allow such preference regardless of its disparate impact. In *Personnel Administrator of Massachusetts v. Feeney*,[66] the Supreme Court held that Section 712 was permissible under the Constitution because it was not specifically aimed at discriminating against women and did not involve intentional gender discrimination. Feeney had challenged a Massachusetts law that gave combat-era veterans an absolute preference over nonveterans for state civil service jobs. Feeney alleged that the preference and Section 712, which allowed it, violated the equal protection clause of the Constitution.

[66] 442 U.S. 256 (1979).

CHAPTER REVIEW

» Key Terms

bona fide occupational qualification (BFOQ) « 147

Equal Pay Act of 1963 « 154

Lilly Ledbetter Fair Pay Act « 160

Bennett Amendment « 161

comparable worth « 161

Pregnancy Discrimination Act of 1978 « 164

sexual harassment « 173

quid pro quo harassment « 174

hostile environment harassment « 174

» Summary

- Title VII allows employers to select employees based on their gender, religion, or national origin when these criteria are bona fide occupational qualifications (BFOQs) that are necessary for the safe and efficient operation of the business. The courts will look closely at the particular job in question and the employer's justification for the BFOQ. Title VII does not allow the use of race or color as a BFOQ.
- Employers need to ensure that all aspects of the employment process are free from gender discrimination. Promotions and work assignments must not be based on stereotypical assumptions about men's and women's roles or capabilities. Pay and benefits must comply with the Equal Pay Act and with Title VII, and employers must not restrict the job opportunities of females because of concerns about potential hazards to pregnant women or their children. The Family and Medical Leave Act requires larger employers to allow employees unpaid leave for childbirth, adoption, and medical conditions; for issues arising from the call to active military service; and to care for injuries or illness suffered during military service.
- Sexual harassment in the workplace can pose serious legal and morale problems; employers should take positive steps to inform employees that sexual harassment will not be tolerated and that the employer has a policy in place to resolve sexual complaints fairly and effectively. Title VII does not prohibit discrimination based on sexual orientation or sexual preference, but some states do outlaw such discrimination. The equal protection clause of the U.S. Constitution may restrict sexual orientation or sexual preference discrimination by public sector employers.

» Problems

Questions

1. Can customer preference be used to support a restaurant's decision to hire only male waiters? What must an employer demonstrate to justify using gender as a BFOQ for hiring?
2. Must an employer offer paid pregnancy leave for employees under Title VII? How do the Pregnancy Discrimination Act provisions of Title VII affect employment benefits?
3. Under what circumstances can an employer be held liable for a supervisor's sexual harassment of another employee? For sexual harassment by a co-worker? For sexual harassment by a nonemployee?
4. When can Title VII be used to challenge gender-based pay differentials for jobs that are not equivalent? Is there a difference between coverage of the Equal Pay Act and that of the pay discrimination prohibitions of Title VII? Explain your answers.
5. Are all employees entitled to take leave under the Family and Medical Leave Act? Explain.

Case Problems

6. Anderson, a female attorney, was hired as an associate in a large law firm in 2001. She had accepted the position based on the firm's representations that associates would advance to partnership after five or six years and that being promoted to partner "was a matter of course" for associates who received satisfactory evaluations. The firm also maintained that promotions were made on a "fair and equal basis." Anderson consistently received satisfactory evaluations, yet her promotion to partnership was rejected in 2007. She again was considered and rejected in 2008. The firm's rules state that an associate passed over for promotion must seek employment elsewhere. Anderson was therefore terminated by the firm on December 31, 2008. The firm, with more than fifty partners, has never had a female partner. Anderson filed a complaint alleging gender discrimination against the firm. The firm replied that the selection of partners is not subject to Title VII because it entails a change in status "from employee to employer."

   Does Title VII apply to such partnership selection decisions? Does Anderson's complaint state a claim under Title VII? See *Hishon v. King & Spaulding* [467 U.S. 69 (U.S. Sup. Ct. 1984)].
7. John Plebani had worked as a waiter at the Cabaret Restaurant in Binghamton, New York. He was discharged when the restaurant manager decided that business would improve if the image of the restaurant was changed to that of a "gentlemen's club" featuring female staff in skimpy uniforms. Cabaret hired females for all positions involving customer contact; males were limited to kitchen positions. For a few weeks after the change, there was a slight improvement in the restaurant's business, but there was no significant long-term change. Plebani filed charges under Title VII and the New York State Human Rights Law, alleging his discharge was due to gender discrimination.

   How should the court rule on Plebani's complaint? Why? What defenses can the restaurant claim? See *Guardian Capital Corp. v. N.Y.S. Human Rights Division* [46 A.D.2d 832, 360 N.Y. S.2d 937 (N.Y. App. Div. 1974)].
8. A group of nurses employed by the state of Illinois filed a complaint charging the state with gender discrimination in classification and compensation of employees. The nurses alleged that the state had refused to implement the changes in job classifications and wage rates recommended by an evaluation study conducted by the state. The study suggested that changes in pay and classification for some female-dominated job classes should be more equitable.

   Does the nurses' complaint state a claim under Title VII? Explain your answer. See *American Nurses Association v. Illinois* [783 F.2d 716 (7th Cir. 1986)].

9. Baker, a female, was employed as a history teacher by More Science High School for three years. Although she received good evaluation reviews for her first two years, her third-year review was poor. Her contract of employment was not renewed after the end of her third year. During Baker's third year, the coach of the boys' basketball team had given notice of his resignation, which was effective at the end of that school year. Baker was replaced by Dan Roundball, who was also hired as the coach of the boys' basketball team. Baker filed a complaint with the EEOC, alleging that her contract was not renewed because the school wanted to replace her with a man who would also coach the basketball team.

   Is More Science High School guilty of violating Title VII's prohibition on gender discrimination? Explain your answer. See *Carlile v. South Routt School Dist.* [739 F.2d 1496 (10th Cir. 1984)].

10. Linda Collins worked for Bowers Corp. for several years; in the past year, she had received twelve informal and four formal warnings for deficient attendance. Shortly after receiving the latest warning, she called in sick for two days. She simply informed her employer that she was "sick"; she did not provide any additional information or describe the nature of her sickness. Because of her prior attendance problems, Collins's employer fired her. She then filed suit under the FMLA, offering evidence that she suffered from depression and was being treated by Dr. Ronald K. Leonard. Dr. Leonard testified that Collins is incapacitated by depression between 10 percent and 20 percent of the time, and that episodes may occur without warning. The employer claimed that the notice given by Collins was not adequate to trigger protection under the FMLA. Has the employer violated the FMLA by firing Collins? Explain your answer. See *Linda S. Collins v. NTN-Bower Corp.* [272 F.3d 1006 (7th Cir. 2001)].

11. In October 2006, Rebecca Thomas was hired as a personnel assistant by Cooper Industries, a plant that manufactures hammers and axes and other hand tools. In February 2007, Thomas was promoted to personnel supervisor. Her boss, the plant's employee relations manager, was fired in March 2007, whereupon she filled his job in an acting capacity. The plant manager gave her the highest possible rating on her performance evaluation, but corporate officials repeatedly refused to interview her for permanent award of the position. According to testimony, the plant manager was told by the company vice president that there was "no way" a female employee relations manager could stand up to the union. A male was ultimately hired to fill the job on a permanent basis.

   Is this an example of gender discrimination? Explain your answer. See *Thomas v. Cooper Industries, Inc.* [627 F. Supp. 655 (W.D. N.C. 1986)].

12. Alvie Thompkins was employed as a full-time instructor of mathematics at Morris Brown College. Her classes were scheduled in academic year 2007–08 in such a way that she was able to hold down a second full-time post as a math instructor at Douglas High School. Only one other faculty member, Thompkins's predecessor at Morris Brown College, ever held down two concurrent full-time jobs, and the college's vice president for academic affairs testified that he had never been aware of this earlier situation. Some male "part-time" faculty of the college were employed full-time elsewhere. Although labeled "part-timers," some of these faculty sometimes taught nine- to twelve-credit hours per semester, which was about the same as many "full-time" faculty. Thompkins was told to choose between her two full-time jobs. When she refused to make a choice, she was fired.

   Is this a case of gender discrimination? Explain your answer. See *Thompkins v. Morris Brown College* [752 F.2d 558 37 F.E.P. Cases 24 (11th Cir. 1985)].

13. Diane L. Matthews served in the U.S. Army for four years as a field communication equipment mechanic. She received numerous awards and high performance ratings and ultimately was promoted to sergeant. After she was honorably discharged, she enrolled in the University of Maine and joined the Reserve Officers Training Corps program on campus. Her ROTC instructor learned that she had attended a student senate meeting, which had been called to discuss the budget for the WildeStein Club. Upon inquiring as to the nature of the club, he was told by Matthews that it was the campus homosexual organization. On further inquiry, she

told the officer she was a lesbian. Although her commander did not attempt to interfere with Matthews's continued membership in the club, he reported Matthews's disclosure to his supervisor. An investigation was conducted and she was disenrolled from the ROTC program.

Was Matthews a victim of gender discrimination? Explain your answer. See *Matthews v. Marsh* [755 F.2d 182, 37 F.E.P. Cases 126 (1st Cir. 1985)].

14. Wilson, a male, applied for a job as a flight attendant with Southwest Airlines. Southwest refused to hire him because the airline hires only females for those positions. Southwest, a small commuter airline in the southwestern United States must compete against larger, more established airlines for passengers. Southwest, which has its headquarters at Love Field in Dallas, decided that the best way to compete with those larger airlines was to establish a distinctive image. Southwest decided to base its marketing image as the "Love Airline"; its slogan is, "We're spreading love all over Texas." Southwest requires its flight attendants and ticket clerks, all female, to wear a uniform consisting of a brief halter top, hot pants, and high boots. Its quick ticketing and check-in flight counters are called "quickie machines," and the in-flight snacks and drinks are referred to as "love bites" and "love potions." Southwest claims that it is identified with the public through its "youthful, feminine" image; it cites surveys of its passengers to support its claim that business necessity requires it to hire only females for all public contact positions. The surveys asked passengers the reasons that they chose to fly with Southwest; the reason labeled "courteous and attentive hostesses" was ranked fifth in importance, after reasons relating to lower fares, frequency of flights, on-time departures, and helpful reservations personnel.

    Has Southwest established that its policy of hiring only females in flight attendant and ticket clerk positions is a bona fide occupational qualification? See *Wilson v. Southwest Airlines Co.* [517 F. Supp. 292 (N.D. Texas 1981)].

15. George Vorman was being recruited by the National Aeronautics and Space Administration (NASA) as a defense intelligence coordinator; that position involved access to classified intelligence and national security information. After the preliminary round of interviews, NASA required him to undergo extensive psychological testing and expanded security clearance investigation far beyond those normally required of recruits. Vorman was informed that the expanded investigation and testing were required because he was suspected of being homosexual. Vorman refused to either affirm or deny that he was homosexual because he felt that it was irrelevant to his qualifications for the job. NASA ultimately refused to hire Vorman; he filed suit claiming he was discriminated against because of NASA's perception of his sexual orientation.

    On what legal provisions can Vorman base his suit? Is he likely to win? Would the outcome be different if Vorman applied for a flight engineer position that did not involve classified national security information? Explain your answers. See *Norton v. Macy* [417 F.2d 1161 (D.C. Cir. 1969)] and *High Tech Gays v. Defense Industry Security Clearance Office* [895 F.2d 563 (9th Cir. 1990)].

Hypothetical Scenarios

16. Carol Lee was a local sales representative for CableCo, a national cable TV network. When a vacancy in the position of regional sales manager arose, Carol applied for the job. Her supervisor told her that the job involved a lot of overnight travel, and because she had small children, it "wouldn't be right" for her. The position was given instead to Tom Matthews, a single male with no children. Has Lee's employer violated Title VII's prohibitions against sex discrimination? Explain.

17. When Tom Berks asks his employer if the firm's health insurance benefits cover same-sex partners, he is fired. Under what laws, if any, does Berks have a legal claim? Why?

18. Nancy Carter's son, a soldier stationed in Afghanistan, was injured in combat and will have to undergo a lengthy rehabilitation. Carter asks her employer, the Denver Public School District, for a leave to help her son during his rehabilitation. Is Carter entitled to such leave? Explain. What must Carter provide the employer to support her request for the leave?

19. Mark Morris is a professor at Enormous State University. Every morning he greets the department secretary, Mollie Bloom, by saying, "Hello, sexy!" Bloom has become increasingly annoyed by Morris's comments, but whenever she complains to Gilman, the department chair, he ignores her complaints or tells her she needs to develop a sense of humor. Does Bloom have a legitimate complaint of sexual harassment? What must she show to establish such a claim? Would the university be held liable for Morris's conduct? How would your answer change if Bloom were Morris's graduate student instead of an employee of the university?

20. Linda Brown and Ralph Williams are recent law school graduates hired as first-year associates by Dewey, Cheatem, and Howe, a large Boston law firm. Brown graduated from Suffolk Law School, while Williams graduated from Harvard Law School. Over coffee one day, Brown discovers that Williams is being paid $20,000 more than she is. Is Dewey, Cheatem, and Howe violating the law by paying Brown less than Williams? Explain.

Discrimination Based on Religion and National Origin & Procedures Under Title VII

The preceding chapters dealt with Title VII of the Civil Rights Act of 1964 and its prohibitions on employment discrimination based on race and sex. This chapter deals with the Title VII provisions and procedures regarding discrimination based on religion and national origin.

Discrimination on the Basis of Religion

Title VII prohibits employment discrimination because of religion. The definition of religion under Title VII is fairly broad; it includes "… all aspects of religious observance and practice, as well as belief…." Harassment because of an individual's religious beliefs (or lack thereof) that creates a hostile work environment is also prohibited under Title VII. Title VII protection extends to the beliefs and practices connected with organized religions but also includes what the EEOC Guidelines[1] define as a person's "moral or ethical beliefs as to what is right and wrong which are sincerely held with the strength of traditional religious views." Such personal moral or ethical beliefs are protected even if the beliefs are not connected with any formal or organized religion. Atheism is included under the Title VII definition of religion according to *Young v. Southwestern Savings & Loan Association*,[2] but personal political or social ideologies are not protected. The racist and anti-Semitic beliefs of the Ku Klux Klan do not fall under the definition of religion[3] and harassment of an individual because of that person's self-identification as a member of the Ku Klux Klan was not harassment because of religion and did not give rise to a claim under Title VII.[4]

[1] 29 C.F.R. §1605.1.

[2] 509 F.2d 140 (5th Cir. 1975).

[3] *Bellamy v. Mason's Stores, Inc.*, 368 F.Supp. 1025 (W.D. Va. 1973), *aff'd on other grounds* 508 F.2d (4th Cir. 1974).

[4] *Swartzentruber v. Gunite Corp.*, 99 F.Supp.2d 976 (N.D. Ind. 2000).

Exceptions for Religious Preference and Religious Employers

Constitutional Issues

Government action involving religion raises issues under the First Amendment of the U.S. Constitution. The U.S. Constitution regulates the relationship between the government and the governed. That means that public sector employers, in addition to being covered by Title VII, are also subject to the constitutional protections for freedom of religion under the First Amendment of the U.S. Constitution. The First Amendment prohibits the establishment of religion by government (generally interpreted as government conduct favoring or promoting religion) and also prohibits undue government interference with the free exercise of religion. The Supreme Court has broadly interpreted religion in determining the scope of protection under the First Amendment, requiring only that the plaintiff demonstrate that her belief is "religious" in her own scheme of things and that it is sincerely held with the strength of traditional religious beliefs.[5] The case of *Lemon v. Kurtzman*[6] (discussed in the *Amos* case, below) set out a three-part test to determine if government action affecting religion violates the First Amendment:

- Does the government action have a secular purpose?
- Does the action neither advance nor inhibit religion?
- Does the government action involve "entanglement" of church and state?

In *Estate of Thornton v. Caldor, Inc.*[7] the Supreme Court held that a Connecticut statute requiring employers to allow employees to take off work on their religious Sabbath was unconstitutional. That statute violated the First Amendment because it advanced a religious purpose: It gave Sabbath observers an unqualified right not to work, and it ignored the interests and convenience of the employer and other employees who did not observe a Sabbath.

Ministerial Exemption under Title VII

Religious organizations, like individuals, enjoy the right of free exercise of religion under the First Amendment. Subjecting the actions of religious organizations to the provisions of Title VII could involve "excessive entanglement" of the government into the affairs of the religious organization. To avoid such constitutional concerns, and to avoid government interference with the free exercise rights of the religious organization, the federal courts have created a "ministerial exemption" under Title VII when a discrimination complaint involves personnel decisions of religious organizations regarding who would perform spiritual functions and about how those functions would be organized. For example, in *Petruska v. Gannon University*,[8] a female chaplain of a private Catholic university was removed from her position and replaced by a male. She claimed that the action was prompted by her gender and by the

---

[5] *Welsh v. United States*, 398 U.S. 333 (1970); *United States v. Seeger*, 380 U.S. 163 (1965); and *Frazee v. Illinois Dept. of Employment Security*, 489 U.S. 829 (1989).

[6] 403 U.S. 602 (1971).

[7] 472 U.S. 703 (1985).

[8] 462 F.3d 294 (3d Cir. 2006).

fact that she had complained about the university's response to sexual harassment claims. The U.S. Court of Appeals for the Third Circuit held that university's actions were protected by the "ministerial exception" because the position of chaplain served a spiritual function, and the religious institution was free to determine how to structure or reorganize that spiritual position. Most courts have limited the ministerial exemption to employment decisions of the religious employer—such as the Catholic Church's ban on female priests. Actions such as sexual harassment or retaliation by a religious employer may not be exempt because they do not involve protected employment decisions, according to *Elvig v. Calvin Presbyterian Church.*[9]

Statutory Provisions for Religious Preference

In addition to the ministerial exemption created by the courts under Title VII, the act contains several statutory provisions that allow employers to exercise religious preference in certain situations.

Religion as a BFOQ Section 703(e)(1) of Title VII includes religion within the BFOQ exception. Religion, as with gender or national origin, may be used as a BFOQ when the employer establishes that business necessity (the safe and efficient performance of the job) requires hiring individuals of a particular religion. Only rarely will a private sector business be able to establish a BFOQ based on religion. For example, an employer who is providing helicopter pilots under contract to the Saudi Arabian government to fly Muslim pilgrims to Mecca may require that all pilots be of the Muslim religion because Islamic law prohibits non-Muslims from entering the holy areas of the city of Mecca. The penalty for violating the prohibition is beheading. The employer could therefore refuse to hire non-Muslims or require all pilots to convert to Islam.[10]

Educational Institutions Under Section 703(e)(2)

Religiously affiliated schools, colleges, universities, or other educational institutions are permitted to give preference to members of their particular religion in hiring. This exception is broader than that available under the BFOQ provisions. Under Section 703(e)(2), the educational institution does not have to demonstrate business necessity to give preference to members of its religion when hiring employees. Therefore, a Hebrew day school can require that all of its teachers be Jewish, and a Catholic university like Notre Dame can require that the university president be Catholic.

Section 702(a)

In addition to the exception granted to religious schools or colleges under Section 703(e)(2), Section 702(a) provides an exception under Title VII to all

- religious societies;
- religious corporations;
- religious educational institutions; or
- religious associations.

---

[9]375 F.3d 951 (9th Cir. 2004).

[10]See the case of *Kern v. Dynalectron Corp.*, 577 F. Supp. 1196 (N.D. Texas 1983).

This exception covers all religious entities and is wider than that under Section 703(e)(2), which is limited to religious educational institutions. Section 702(a) states:

> This Title shall not apply to … a religious corporation, association, educational institution, or society with respect to the employment of individuals of a particular religion to perform work connected with the carrying on by such corporation, association, educational institution or society of its activities.

But how broad is the scope of the exemption under Section 702(a)? Does it extend to all activities of a religious corporation, even those that are not really religious in character? The Supreme Court considered that question in the next case.

case 8.1 » Corporation of the Presiding Bishop of the Church of Jesus Christ of Latter-Day Saints v. Amos

483 U.S. 327 (1987)

[Note that this case was decided prior to the 1991 amendments to Title VII, when Section 702(a) was simply Section 702.]

White, J.

Section 702 of the Civil Rights Act of 1964, as amended, exempts religious organizations from Title VII's prohibition against discrimination in employment on the basis of religion. The question presented is whether applying the Section 702 exemption to the secular nonprofit activities of religious organizations violates the Establishment Clause of the First Amendment. The District Court held that it does, and the case is here on direct appeal.

The Deseret Gymnasium (Gymnasium) in Salt Lake City, Utah, is a nonprofit facility, open to the public, run by the Corporation of the Presiding Bishop of The Church of Jesus Christ of Latter-day Saints (CPB), and the Corporation of the President of The Church of Jesus Christ of Latter-day Saints (COP). The CPB and the COP are religious entities associated with The Church of Jesus Christ of Latter-day Saints (Church), an unincorporated religious association sometimes called the Mormon or LDS Church.

Mayson worked at the Gymnasium for some 16 years as an assistant building engineer and then building engineer. He was discharged in 1981 because he failed to qualify for a temple recommend; that is, a certificate that he is a member of the Church and eligible to attend its temples.

Mayson and others purporting to represent a class of plaintiffs brought an action against the CPB and the COP alleging, among other things, discrimination on the basis of religion in violation … of the Civil Rights Act of 1964.… The defendants moved to dismiss this claim on the ground that Section 702 shields them from liability. The plaintiffs contended that if construed to allow religious employers to discriminate on religious grounds in hiring for nonreligious jobs, Section 702 violates the Establishment Clause [of the First Amendment].

The District Court first considered whether the facts of this case require a decision on the plaintiffs' constitutional argument. Starting from the premise that the religious activities of religious employers can permissibly be exempted under Section 702, the court developed a three-part test to determine whether an activity is religious. Applying this test to Mayson's situation, the court found: first, that the Gymnasium is intimately connected to the Church financially and in matters of management; second, that there is no clear connection between the primary function which the Gymnasium performs and the religious beliefs and tenets of the Mormon Church or church administration; and third, that none of Mayson's duties at the Gymnasium are "even tangentially related to any conceivable religious belief or ritual of the Mormon Church or church administration," … The court concluded that Mayson's case involves nonreligious activity.

The court next considered the plaintiffs' constitutional challenge to Section 702. Applying the three-part test set out in *Lemon v. Kurtzman*…, the court first held that Section 702 has the permissible secular purpose of "assuring that the government remains neutral and does not meddle in religious affairs by interfering with the decision-making process in religions.…" The court concluded, however, that Section 702 fails the second part of the *Lemon* test because the provision has the primary effect of advancing religion. Among the considerations mentioned by the court were: that

Section 702 singles out religious entities for a benefit, rather than benefiting a broad grouping of which religious organizations are only a part; that Section 702 is not supported by long historical tradition; and that Section 702 burdens the free exercise rights of employees of religious institutions who work in nonreligious jobs. Finding that Section 702 impermissibly sponsors religious organizations by granting them "an exclusive authorization to engage in conduct which can directly and immediately advance religious tenets and practices," the court declared the statute unconstitutional as applied to secular activity. The court entered summary judgment in favor of Mayson and ordered him reinstated with backpay. Subsequently, the court vacated its judgment so that the United States could intervene to defend the constitutionality of Section 702. After further briefing and argument the court affirmed its prior determination and reentered a final judgment for Mayson....

We find unpersuasive the District Court's reliance on the fact that Section 702 singles out religious entities for a benefit. Although the Court has given weight to this consideration in its past decisions, it has never indicated that statutes that give special consideration to religious groups are *per se* invalid. That would run contrary to the teaching of our cases that there is ample room for accommodation of religion under the Establishment Clause.

Where, as here, government acts with the proper purpose of lifting a regulation that burdens the exercise of religion, we see no reason to require that the exemption come packaged with benefits to secular entities. We are also unpersuaded by the District Court's reliance on the argument that Section 702 is unsupported by long historical tradition. There was simply no need to consider the scope of the Section 702 exemption until the 1964 Civil Rights Act was passed, and the fact that Congress concluded after eight years that the original exemption was unnecessarily narrow is a decision entitled to deference, not suspicion.

Appellees argue that Section 702 offends equal protection principles by giving less protection to the employees of religious employers than to the employees of secular employers.

... In a case such as this, where a statute is neutral on its face and motivated by a permissible purpose of limiting governmental interference with the exercise of religion, we see no justification for applying strict scrutiny to a statute that passes the *Lemon* test. The proper inquiry is whether Congress has chosen a rational classification to further a legitimate end. We have already indicated that Congress acted with a legitimate purpose in expanding the Section 702 exemption to cover all activities of religious employers.... it suffices to hold—as we now do—that as applied to the nonprofit activities of religious employers, Section 702 is rationally related to the legitimate purpose of alleviating significant governmental interference with the ability of religious organizations to define and carry out their religious missions.

It cannot be seriously contended that Section 702 impermissibly entangles church and state; the statute effectuates a more complete separation of the two and avoids the kind of intrusive inquiry into religious belief that the District Court engaged in this case. The statute easily passes muster under the third part of the *Lemon* test.

The judgment of the District Court is reversed, and the case is remanded for further proceedings consistent with this opinion.

It is so ordered.

Brennan, J., with whom Marshall, J. joins (concurring)

... my concurrence in the judgment rests on the fact that this case involves a challenge to the application of Section 702's categorical exemption to the activities of a nonprofit organization. I believe that the particular character of nonprofit activity makes inappropriate a case-by-case determination whether its nature is religious or secular....

... I concur in the Court's judgment that the nonprofit Deseret Gymnasium may avail itself of an automatic exemption from Title VII's proscription on religious discrimination.

O'Connor, J. (concurring)

... I emphasize that under the holding of the Court, and under my view of the appropriate Establishment Clause analysis, the question of the constitutionality of the Section 702 exemption as applied to for-profit activities of religious organizations remains open.

Case Questions

1. What is the relevance of the three-part test set out in *Lemon v. Kurtzman* to a claim under Title VII?
2. What, according to the Supreme Court, was the rationale for the enactment of the Section 702(a) exemption for religious organizations? How does that purpose relate to the three-part test from *Lemon v. Kurtzman*?
3. Does the Section 702(a) exemption apply to all activities of religious organizations, even to commercial activities? Does the exemption allow religious organizations to discriminate on the basis of race or gender? Explain your answers.

Reasonable Accommodation

Even when religion is not a BFOQ and the employer is not within the Section 702 exemption, the prohibition against discrimination on the basis of religion is not absolute. Section 701(j) defines religion as:

> includ[ing] all aspects of religious observance and practice, as well as belief, unless an employer demonstrates that he is unable to reasonably accommodate to an employee's religious observance or practice without undue hardship on the conduct of the employer's business.

An employer must make reasonable attempts to accommodate an employee's religious beliefs or practices, but if such attempts are not successful or involve undue hardship, the employer may discharge the employee. The following case explores the extent to which an employer is required to accommodate an employee's beliefs.

case 8.2 »

Trans World Airlines v. Hardison

432 U.S. 63 (1977)

White, J.

Petitioner Trans World Airlines (TWA) operates a large maintenance and overhaul base in Kansas City, Mo. On June 5, 1967, respondent Larry G. Hardison was hired by TWA to work as a clerk in the Stores Department at its Kansas City base. Because of its essential role in the Kansas City operation, the Stores Department must operate 24 hours per day, 365 days per year, and whenever an employee's job in that department is not filled, an employee must be shifted from another department, or a supervisor must cover the job, even if the work in other areas may suffer.

Hardison, like other employees at the Kansas City base, was subject to a seniority system contained in a collective-bargaining agreement which TWA maintains with petitioner International Association of Machinists and Aerospace Workers (IAM). The seniority system is implemented by the union steward through a system of bidding by employees for particular shift assignments as they become available. The most senior employees have first choice for job and shift assignments, and the most junior employees are required to work when the union steward is unable to find enough people willing to work at a particular time or in a particular job to fill TWA's needs.

In the spring of 1968 Hardison began to study the religion known as the Worldwide Church of God. One of the tenets of that religion is that one must observe the Sabbath by refraining from performing any work from sunset on Friday until sunset on Saturday. The religion also proscribes work on certain specified religious holidays.

When Hardison informed Everett Kussman, the manager of the Stores Department, of his religious conviction regarding observance of the Sabbath, Kussman agreed that the union steward should seek a job swap for Hardison or a change of days off; that Hardison would have his religious holidays off whenever possible if Hardison agreed to work the traditional holidays when asked; and that Kussman would try to find Hardison another job that would be more compatible with his religious beliefs. The problem was temporarily solved when Hardison transferred to the 11 P.M.–7 A.M. shift. Working this shift permitted Hardison to observe his Sabbath.

The problem soon reappeared when Hardison bid for and received a transfer from Building 1, where he had been employed, to Building 2, where he would work the day shift. The two buildings had entirely separate seniority lists; and while in Building 1 Hardison had sufficient seniority to observe the Sabbath regularly, he was second from the bottom on the Building 2 seniority list.

In Building 2 Hardison was asked to work Saturdays when a fellow employee went on vacation. TWA agreed to permit the union to seek a change of work assignments for Hardison, but the union was not willing to violate the seniority provisions set out in the collective-bargaining contract, and Hardison had insufficient seniority to bid for a shift having Saturdays off.

A proposal that Hardison work only four days a week was rejected by the company. Hardison's job was essential, and on weekends he was the only available person on his shift to perform it. To leave the position empty would have impaired Supply Shop functions, which were critical to airline operations; to fill Hardison's position with a supervisor or an employee from another area would simply have undermanned another operation; and to employ someone not regularly assigned to work Saturdays would have required TWA to pay premium wages.

When an accommodation was not reached, Hardison refused to report for work on Saturdays.... [Hardison was fired by TWA.]

The Court of Appeals found that TWA had committed an unlawful employment practice under Section 703(a)(1) of the Act....

In 1967 the EEOC amended its guidelines to require employers "to make reasonable accommodations to the religious needs of employees and prospective employees where such accommodations can be made without undue hardship on the conduct of the employer's business." The Commission did not suggest what sort of accommodations are "reasonable" or when hardship to an employer becomes "undue."

This question—the extent of the required accommodation—remained unsettled.... Congress [then] included the following definition of religion in its 1972 amendments to Title VII:

> The term "religion" includes all aspects of religious observance and practice, as well as belief, unless an employer demonstrates that he is unable to reasonably accommodate to an employee's or prospective employee's religious observance or practice without undue hardship on the conduct of the employer's business. [Section 701(j)] ...

The Court of Appeals held that TWA had not made reasonable efforts to accommodate Hardison's religious needs....

We disagree....

... As the record shows, Hardison himself testified that Kussman was willing, but the union was not, to work out a shift or job trade with another employee.

... it appears to us that the [seniority] system itself represented a significant accommodation to the needs, both religious and secular, of all of TWA's employees. As will become apparent, the seniority system represents a neutral way of minimizing the number of occasions when an employee must work on a day that he would prefer to have off....

We are also convinced, contrary to the Court of Appeals, that TWA cannot be faulted for having failed itself to work out a shift or job swap for Hardison. Both the union and TWA had agreed to the seniority system; the union was unwilling to entertain a variance over the objections of men senior to Hardison....

Had TWA nevertheless circumvented the seniority system by relieving Hardison of Saturday work and ordering a senior employee to replace him, it would have denied the latter his shift preference so that Hardison could be given his. The senior employee would also have been deprived of his contractual rights under the collective-bargaining agreement.

Title VII does not contemplate such unequal treatment.... we conclude that Title VII does not require an employer to go that far.

... [T]he Court of Appeals suggested that TWA could have replaced Hardison on his Saturday shift with other available employees through the payment of premium wages. Both of these alternatives would involve costs to TWA, either in the form of lost efficiency in other jobs or as higher wages.

To require TWA to bear more than a *de minimis* cost in order to give Hardison Saturdays off is an undue hardship....

As we have seen, the paramount concern of Congress in enacting Title VII was the elimination of discrimination in employment. In the absence of clear statutory language or legislative history to the contrary, we will not readily construe the statute to require an employer to discriminate against some employees in order to enable others to observe their Sabbath.

Reversed.

Case Questions

1. Did Hardison's religious beliefs present a scheduling problem when he was hired? Is the employer required to accommodate religious beliefs if a conflict arises only after the employee has been hired? Explain your answers.
2. Did the union's refusal to grant Hardison a variance from the seniority requirements of the collective bargaining agreement violate the union's duty to accommodate Hardison's beliefs under Title VII? Explain.
3. Why was TWA unwilling to pay some other employee overtime to work for Hardison on Saturdays? Was TWA required to do so under Title VII? Explain.

The Duty of Reasonable Accommodation

As the *Hardison* case illustrates, the prohibition of religious discrimination under Title VII is not absolute. An employee may not be protected under Title VII if the employer is unable to make reasonable accommodation to the employee's religious beliefs or practices without undue hardship to the employer's business. The determination of what accommodation is reasonable, and whether it would impose an undue hardship on the employer, is to be based on each individual case and the facts of each situation. The EEOC Guidelines indicate that the following factors will be considered in determining what a reasonable accommodation is and whether it results in undue hardship:

- The size of the employer's work force and the number of employees requiring accommodation
- The nature of the job or jobs that present a conflict
- The cost of the accommodation
- The administrative requirements of the accommodation
- Whether the employees affected are under a collective bargaining agreement
- What alternatives are available and have been considered by the employer.

The employee seeking accommodation must first inform the employer of the conflict with his or her religious beliefs or practices and must request accommodation. The employee is also required to act reasonably in considering the alternative means of accommodation available.[11]

case 8.3 »

WEBB V. CITY OF PHILADELPHIA
562 F.3d 256 (3d Cir. 2009)

Facts: Kimberlie Webb, a practicing Muslim, was a police officer for the City of Philadelphia. She requested permission to wear a traditional headscarf (known as a *khimar* or *hijaab*) with her uniform while on duty. The commanding officer denied the request because of Philadelphia Police Department Directive 78, which defines the approved Philadelphia police uniforms and prohibits the wearing of any religious symbols or garb as part of the uniform. Webb then filed a complaint of religious discrimination under Title VII with the Pennsylvania Human Relations Commission and the federal Equal Employment Opportunity Commission. While her complaint was pending before the EEOC, Webb arrived for work wearing the headscarf. She refused requests to remove it, and was sent home for failing to comply with Directive 78. The department ultimately suspended her for thirteen days for insubordination. Webb filed suit against the City of Philadelphia, alleging violations of Title VII because of religious discrimination, hostile work environment, and retaliation. The trial court granted the City's motion for summary judgment. The court stated that Directive 78 prevents any accommodation for religious symbols and attire not only because of the need for uniformity, but also to enhance cohesiveness, cooperation, and the *esprit de corps* of the police force. The court also held that the city would suffer an undue hardship if forced to permit officers to wear religious symbols or clothing or ornamentation with their uniforms. Webb appealed to the U.S. Court of Appeals for the Third Circuit.

Issue: Would allowing Webb to wear a headscarf while on duty constitute an undue hardship on the Philadelphia Police Department?

[11] *Jordan v. North Carolina National Bank*, 565 F.2d 72 (4th Cir.1977).

Decision: Once the plaintiff has established a *prima facie* case, the employer then has the burden to show that it made a good faith effort to accommodate the employee's religious belief, or that such an accommodation would work an undue hardship upon the employer's business. According to *Trans World Airlines, Inc. v. Hardison*, an accommodation would cause an undue hardship if it imposes more than a *de minimis* cost on the employer. Noneconomic costs such as violations of the seniority provisions of a collective agreement or the threat of possible criminal sanctions could also pose an undue hardship on employers. The U.S. Supreme Court has considered the importance of dress regulations for law enforcement personnel and for the military in *Goldman v. Weinberger*.[1] The Court there stated that the standardization of uniforms encourages "the subordination of personal preferences and identities in favor of the overall group mission." In *Daniels v. City of Arlington*,[2] the court held that a police department could refuse to allow a police officer to wear a gold cross on his uniform, in violation of an official "no pins" policy. The court held that the department's uniform standards were proper and that an accommodation of the officer's religious belief would have imposed an undue hardship. Here, the city demonstrated that the strict enforcement of Directive 78 was essential to the values of impartiality, religious neutrality, uniformity, and the subordination of personal preference necessary to the proper functioning of the police department.

The Third Circuit held that the uniform requirements were crucial to the safety of officers, to their morale and *esprit de corps*, and to public confidence in the police. The court of appeals therefore affirmed the trial court grant of summary judgment to the city.

[1]475 U.S. 503 (1986).

[2]246 F.3d 500 (5th Cir. 2001).

Some employees may find a co-worker's exercise of his or her religious beliefs offensive. How should the employer accommodate the employee's right to express her or his religious beliefs with the concerns of the co-workers? Must the employer allow an employee continually to ask co-workers if they "have been born again" or to invite them to attend religious services, when the co-workers have made it clear that they find such conduct offensive? In *Wilson v. U.S. West Communications*,[12] an employee insisted on wearing an antiabortion button featuring a color photo of a fetus as an expression of her religious beliefs. She also occasionally wore a T-shirt with a color image of a fetus. Other employees found the button and the T-shirt offensive or disturbing. Their reactions to the button and T-shirt caused disruptions at work, and the employer documented a 40 percent decline in productivity of the unit after the employee began wearing the button. The employer offered the employee three choices:

- she could wear the button while she was in her cubicle, but must take it off when she moved around the office;
- she could cover the button while at work; or
- she could wear a different antiabortion button without the photograph.

The employee refused, insisting that she had to wear the button to be a "living witness" to her religious beliefs. The employer ultimately fired the employee, and the former employee filed suit under Title VII, alleging religious discrimination. She argued that the disruption in the workplace was caused by the reaction of the co-workers, not by her wearing the button. The court of appeals held that the employer did not violate Title VII by firing the employee. Title VII requires that an employer reasonably accommodate an employee's religious beliefs but does not require that the employer allow that employee to impose her or his religious views on others.

[12]58 F.3d 1337 (8th Cir. 1995).

If there are several ways to accommodate the employee's religious beliefs, is the employer required to provide the accommodation that is preferred by the employee? In *Ansonia Board of Education v. Philbrook*,[13] the Supreme Court held the following:

> ... We find no basis in either the statute or its legislative history for requiring an employer to choose any particular reasonable accommodation. By its very terms the statute directs that any reasonable accommodation by the employer is sufficient to meet its accommodation obligation. The employer violates the statute unless it "demonstrates that [it] is unable to reasonably accommodate ... an employee's ... religious observance or practice without undue hardship on the conduct of the employer's business." Thus, where the employer has already reasonably accommodated the employee's religious needs, the statutory inquiry is at an end. The employer need not further show that each of the employee's alternative accommodations would result in undue hardship. As *Hardison* illustrates, the extent of undue hardship on the employer's business is at issue only where the employer claims that it is unable to offer any reasonable accommodation without such hardship. Once the Court of Appeals assumed that the school board had offered to Philbrook a reasonable alternative, it erred by requiring the board to nonetheless demonstrate the hardship of Philbrook's alternatives.... We accordingly hold that an employer has met its obligation under Section 701(j) when it demonstrates that it has offered a reasonable accommodation to the employee.

ethical DILEMMA

Allah in the Workplace?

A small group of employees at Wydget are Muslims; some wear turbans and burkas (robes covering their body). They have asked you, the human resource manager, to allow them to conduct religious prayer services in the plant cafeteria during their morning and afternoon coffee breaks and their lunch break. In general, those employees are good workers, and you do not want to do anything that would undermine their morale. However, a number of other Wydget employees have complained to you that they are suspicious of such meetings, which they fear may be a cover for terrorist or subversive activities. You are concerned that if you allow the lunchtime prayer services, other employees who are Buddhists, Hindus, or Christians may also seek to conduct religious or prayer services.

Should you allow the Muslim employees to hold the prayer services? What arguments can you make in favor of allowing the services? What arguments can you make against allowing them? How should you respond to the fears and perceptions of the other employees? Can Wydget allow the prayer services for the Muslims while refusing other employees the right to hold their own prayer services? Prepare a memo for the CEO on this question. The memo should list the arguments in favor of, and against, allowing the prayer services and should recommend a decision, with appropriate explanation and justification, for the CEO.

See the EEOC's "Questions and Answers About Employer Responsibilities Concerning the Employment of Muslims, Arabs, South Asians and Sikhs" at http://www.eeoc.gov/facts/backlash-employer.html.

[13] 479 U.S. 60 (1986).

Concept *Summary* » 8.1

Discrimination Based on Religion

- Religion includes:
  - All aspects of religious observance, practice, and belief
- Exceptions:
  - Constitutional protections (First Amendment)
    - *Lemon* test
  - Religion as a BFOQ (Section 703(e)(1))
  - Religious organizations (Section 702 (a))
  - Religiously affiliated educational institutions (Section 703(e)(2))
  - Religious societies, corporations, associations (Section 702 (a))
- Employer's duty of reasonable accommodation of religion:
  - Employee must inform employer of religious belief or conduct in conflict with work requirement
  - Employer must then attempt to make reasonable accommodation to belief or conduct—or show that accommodation would impose undue hardship
  - Undue hardship—employer not required to:
    - Pay more than minimal costs
    - Regularly pay overtime or premium wages
    - Act in violation of the seniority provisions of a collective agreement

Discrimination Based on National Origin

Title VII prohibits employment discrimination against any applicant or employee because of national origin, although it does recognize that national origin may be a BFOQ, where the employer demonstrates that hiring employees of a particular ethnic or national origin is a business necessity for the safe and efficient performance of the job in question. The government's response to the terrorist attacks on the World Trade Center and the Pentagon on September 11, 2001, and the public's heightened awareness regarding security and fear of potential threats led to increased scrutiny of individuals who appeared to be Muslims or of Middle Eastern origin. Incidents of "ethnic profiling" were common; persons (primarily males) perceived to be from Middle Eastern countries were subjected to security checks, searches, interrogation by authorities, and general public suspicion. Is such ethnic profiling permissible under Title VII? In general, no. Any employment discrimination against an individual because of that individual's (actual or perceived) national origin, ethnicity, or religion is a violation of Title VII unless it is justified by a BFOQ.

Following the events of September 11, 2001, the EEOC reported an increase in complaints alleging discrimination against individuals because they were perceived as being Muslim, Arabic, Middle Eastern, South Asian, or Sikh. More than 800 complaints of "backlash" discrimination were filed by individuals who alleged that they were discriminated against because of their religion or national origin. Most of the complaints involved discharge or harassment. EEOC enforcement efforts have resulted in nearly 100 individuals receiving over $1.45 million in benefits as resolution of employment discrimination complaints related to the September 11 attacks. The EEOC has also conducted numerous outreach and education efforts for employers to promote voluntary compliance with Title VII.[14] In recent years, the number of national origin discrimination complaints filed with the EEOC has been increasing, from 8,025 in its fiscal year 2001, to 10,601 in FY 2008. The EEOC recovered damage settlements of $22.8 million for national origin discrimination claims in FY 2007, and $25.4 million in FY 2008.[15]

Definition

National origin discrimination includes any discrimination based upon the place of origin of an applicant or employee or his or her ancestor(s) and any discrimination based upon the physical, cultural, or linguistic characteristics of an ethnic group. Title VII's prohibition on national origin discrimination includes harassment of employees because of their national origin and extends to discrimination based upon reasons related to national origin or ethnic considerations, such as:

- a person's marriage to a person of, or association with persons of, an ethnic or national origin group;
- a person's membership in, or association with, an organization identified with or seeking to promote the interests of any ethnic or national origin group;
- a person's attendance or participation in schools, churches, temples, or mosques generally used by persons of an ethnic or national origin group; or
- a person's name, or the name of the person's spouse, which is associated with an ethnic or national origin group.

An employer may violate the statute by discriminating against an applicant or employee whose education or training is foreign or, conversely, by requiring that training or education be done abroad. Title VII does allow employers to hire employees based on legitimate business, safety, or security concerns. Employers may impose heightened background screening for employees or applicants, as long as such requirements are related to legitimate job concerns and are applied uniformly to the employees in similar situations or job classes. Section 703(g) states that it is not a violation of Title VII for an employer to refuse to hire or to discharge an employee who is unable to meet the requirements for a national security clearance where federal law or regulations require such a clearance for the job in question.

As the following case illustrates, employers must also ensure that employees are not subjected to harassment based on their national origin.

---

[14] EEOC Press Release, 7/17/2003, "Muslim Pilot Fired Due to Religion and Appearance, EEOC Says in Post-9/11 Backlash Discrimination Suit," http://www.EEOC.gov/press/7-17-03a.html.

[15] "National Origin-Based Charges FY 1997–FY 2008." http://www.eeoc.gov/stats/origin.html.

case 8.4 »

Equal Employment Opportunity Commission v. WC&M Enterprises, Inc.

496 F.3d 393 (5th Cir. 2007)

[Mohommed Rafiq was born in India and was a practicing Muslim. He was a car salesman at WC&M Enterprises' Honda dealership in Conroe, Texas. After the September 11, 2001 terrorist attacks, Rafiq began to be subjected to ongoing harassment based on his religion and national origin by his managers and co-workers. When Rafiq arrived at work for his afternoon shift on 9/11, a number of his co-workers and managers, including Matthew Kiene (a co-worker), Kevin Argabrite (a finance manager), Jerry Swigart (Rafiq's direct supervisor), and Richard Burgoon (the general manager of the dealership), were watching television coverage of the attacks. Upon seeing Rafiq, Kiene called out, "Hey, there's Mohommed," and Argabrite said, "Where have you been?" in a mocking way, at which point everyone began to laugh. Rafiq inferred from these comments that the supervisors and colleagues were implying that he had participated in the terrorist attacks. After the U.S. began military action against Afghanistan, his co-workers and some managers began calling Rafiq "Taliban." Rafiq repeatedly asked them to stop calling him "Taliban," to no avail. He also complained a number of times to the managers without any real success.

Co-workers and some managers also ridiculed and harassed Rafiq in other ways, such as asking him, "Why don't you just go back where you came from since you believe what you believe?" and mocking Rafiq's religious dietary restrictions and his need to pray during the workday. They also often referred to Rafiq as an "Arab," even though Rafiq told them on numerous occasions that he was from India. This harassment continued through the end of his employment.

On October 16, 2002, Rafiq got into a dispute with his manager, Swigart, after being told that it was mandatory for all employees to attend a United Way meeting. When Rafiq questioned what, if any, connection there was between the United Way and his job, Swigart said, "This is America. That's the way things work over here. This is not the Islamic country where you come from." After the confrontation, Swigart issued Rafiq a written warning, which stated that Rafiq "was acting like a Muslim extremist" and that he could not work with Rafiq because of his "militant stance." On October 26, 2002, Argabrite "banged" on the partition separating Rafiq's office space from the sales floor; Argabrite did this to try to startle Rafiq whenever he walked by his office. This time, however, Rafiq responded by banging on the partition himself and saying, "Don't do that." Argabrite then confronted Rafiq and told Rafiq that he was a manager, so Rafiq could not tell him what to do. Rafiq later complained to Burgoon about Argabrite's continual harassment.

Two days later, Rafiq was fired. Rafiq filed a charge of discrimination with the EEOC, and the EEOC filed suit against the employer, alleging that WC&M subjected Rafiq to a hostile work environment on the basis of his religion and national origin, in violation of Title VII. The district court granted summary judgment to the employer, stating that the EEOC could not establish that Rafiq was harassed on the basis of his national origin, that the EEOC did not establish the existence of severe and pervasive harassment, and the EEOC had not shown that Rafiq's emotional distress or mental anguish from the harassment was so severe that it interrupted his daily life. The EEOC appealed to the U.S. Court of Appeals for the Fifth Circuit.]

Dennis, Circuit Judge

In this case involving allegations of a hostile work environment, the Equal Employment Opportunity Commission ("EEOC") appeals the district court's decision to enter summary judgment in favor of the defendant-appellee, WC&M Enterprises, Inc....

...the district court made two findings that essentially disposed of the EEOC's hostile work environment claim on the merits: (1) that the EEOC had not shown that Rafiq lost sales as a result of the alleged harassment that he suffered; and (2) that the EEOC could not bring a claim based on Rafiq's national origin because none of the harassing comments specifically referred to the fact that Rafiq was from India. The EEOC argues that the district court erred in each respect....

The Supreme Court has emphasized that Title VII's prohibition "is not limited to 'economic' or 'tangible' discrimination." Rather, "[w]hen the workplace is permeated with 'discriminatory intimidation, ridicule, and insult' that is 'sufficiently severe or pervasive to alter the conditions of the victim's employment and create an abusive working environment,' Title VII is violated." [*Harris v. Forklift Sys.*] ...

For harassment to be sufficiently severe or pervasive to alter the conditions of the victim's employment, the conduct complained of must be both objectively and subjectively offensive.... As the Supreme Court stated, "even without regard to ... tangible effects, the very fact that the discriminatory conduct was so severe or pervasive that it created a work environment abusive to employees because of their race, gender, religion, or national origin offends Title VII's broad rule of workplace equality."

Under the totality of the circumstances test, a single incident of harassment, if sufficiently severe, could give rise to a viable Title VII claim as well as a continuous pattern of much less severe incidents of harassment....

Here, the district court held that even if Rafiq could prove that any harassment occurred, "he has not shown that it was so severe that it kept him from doing his job." In so holding, the district court applied an incorrect legal standard. Whether Rafiq lost sales as a result of the alleged harassment is certainly relevant to his hostile work environment claim; but it is not, by itself, dispositive. The district court erred in concluding otherwise.

Applying the totality of the circumstances test, we conclude that the EEOC has presented sufficient evidence to create an issue of fact as to whether the harassment that Rafiq suffered was so severe or pervasive as to alter a condition of his employment. The evidence showed that Rafiq was subjected to verbal harassment on a regular basis for a period of approximately one year. During that time, Rafiq was constantly called "Taliban" and referred to as an "Arab" by Kiene and Argabrite, who also mocked his diet and prayer rituals. Moreover, Rafiq was sporadically subjected to additional incidents of harassment ...

Although no single incident of harassment is likely sufficient to establish severe or pervasive harassment, when considered together and viewed in the light most favorable to the EEOC, the evidence shows a long-term pattern of ridicule sufficient to establish a claim under Title VII....

In addition, the evidence is sufficient to show that the harassment Rafiq suffered was based on his religion and national origin.

Indeed, the EEOC's guidelines on discrimination define "discrimination based on national origin" broadly, to include acts of discrimination undertaken "because an individual has the physical, cultural or linguistic characteristics of a national origin group." Nothing in the guidelines requires that the discrimination be based on the victim's actual national origin. The EEOC's final guidelines make this point clear:

> In order to have a claim of national origin discrimination under Title VII, it is not necessary to show that the alleged discriminator knew the particular national origin group to which the complainant belonged .... [I]t is enough to show that the complainant was treated differently because of his or her foreign accent, appearance, or physical characteristics....

... In this case, the evidence that the EEOC presented supports its claim that Rafiq was harassed based on his national origin. Indeed, several of the challenged statements refer to national origin generally (even though they do not accurately describe Rafiq's actual country of origin): (1) Kiene's comment to Rafiq, "Why don't you just go back where you came from since you believe what you believe?"; (2) Swigart's statement, "This is America. That's the way things work over here. This is not the Islamic country where you come from."; and (3) Kiene's and Argabrite's practice of referring to Rafiq as "Taliban" and calling him an "Arab."

Accordingly, we conclude that the EEOC has submitted sufficient evidence to support its claim that Rafiq was subjected to a hostile work environment both on the basis of religion and on the basis of national origin.

... Rafiq testified at his deposition that the alleged harassment caused problems with his family life that led him to seek counseling from several mosques, that he had difficulty sleeping, lost 30 pounds, and suffered gastrointestinal problems. Although Rafiq equivocated about whether his gastrointestinal problems were attributable to the harassment, the record evidence is sufficient to show that the harassment caused some discernible injury to his mental state even when those symptoms are not considered. Accordingly, the district court erred in concluding that the EEOC could not recover for any mental anguish that Rafiq suffered.

... [W]e reverse the district court's grant of summary judgment in favor of the defendant... and remand this matter to the district court for proceedings consistent with this opinion.

Reversed and Remanded.

Case Questions

1. On what basis was Rafiq being harassed? What evidence supports his claim that the harassment was based on national origin and religion?
2. How did the harassing conduct here affect Rafiq? Must Rafiq show that the harassment caused him to lose sales or otherwise affected his work performance? Explain.
3. What is an employer's obligation under Title VII to prevent workplace harassment based on race, color, sex, national origin, or religion? What had the employer done in this case to stop the harassment?

Disparate Impact

Employers should avoid arbitrary employment criteria, such as height or weight requirements, for applicants or employees because such requirements may have a disparate impact on national origin. They have the effect of excluding large numbers of certain ethnic groups. For example, height requirements may exclude most persons of Asian or Hispanic origin and the refusal to recognize educational qualifications from foreign institutions may exclude foreign-born applicants. If such requirements or practices have a disparate impact, they constitute discrimination in violation of Title VII, unless they can be shown to be required for the effective performance of the job in question.

The WORKING Law

Ceisel Masonry to Pay $500,000 for Harassment of Hispanic Workers

EEOC Settles National Origin and Race Bias Class Suit on Eve of Trial

CHICAGO—Ceisel Masonry will pay half a million dollars to settle a race and national origin discrimination lawsuit brought by the U.S. Equal Employment Opportunity Commission (EEOC), the agency announced today. The EEOC's suit charged that the north suburban construction company violated federal anti-discrimination laws by subjecting its Hispanic workers to harassment based upon their race and national origin.

The EEOC brought its suit on behalf of a class of 10 Hispanic workers, charging that Ceisel's foremen and former superintendent would refer to the company's Latino employees with derogatory terms such as "f—ing Mexicans," "pork chop," "Julio," "spics," "chico," and "wetback." In addition, the EEOC and the former employees alleged that Hispanic workers were routinely exposed to racist graffiti, which the company never addressed. The case was scheduled for a two-week jury trial to start on May 4, 2009.

"No employee should have to trade his or her dignity for the right to work, and no employer should permit this type of verbal abuse of employees," said EEOC Acting Chairman Stuart J. Ishimaru. "We take allegations of racial or ethnic harassment very seriously and will pursue these cases vigorously."...

The consent decree settling the suit, signed by Judge Harry D. Leinenweber today, provides that the defendants will pay $500,000 to resolve this matter. The three-year decree enjoins the company from future discrimination on the basis of race or national origin and from any retaliation. It mandates that the company will provide all of its employees with training on how to prevent discrimination, as well as revise its policies on harassment and how to conduct harassment investigations. The decree also requires the company to hold its supervisors accountable if they do not comply with the company's new anti-harassment and investigation policies.

"This settlement is important vindication for those Hispanic employees who suffered harassment by their supervisors," said Richard J. Mrizek, the EEOC trial attorney who led the government's litigation of this case with EEOC Trial Attorney

Laurie Elkin. "The consent decree entered in this case will ensure that the company prevents harassment from taking place on its job sites."

John Hendrickson, regional attorney for the Chicago District Office, which oversees EEOC litigation in a six-state region, said, "This case is a reminder that the federal laws against discriminatory harassment on the job have broad, general application. They apply not only to race and sexual harassment but also to harassment on the basis of national origin. Employers must act decisively against harassment, especially when it comes from supervisors or foremen who have great power over workers, or pay the consequences."

The EEOC enforces federal laws prohibiting employment discrimination. Further information about the EEOC is available on the agency's website at www.eeoc.gov.

Source: EEOC press release of May 22, 2009.

English-Only Rules

English-Only Rules
Employer work rules requiring that employees speak English in the workplace during working hours.

An employer may violate Title VII by denying employment opportunities because of an applicant's or employee's foreign accent or inability to communicate well in English, unless the job in question involves public contact (such as sales clerks or receptionists). One issue of specific concern to the EEOC is the use by employers of ***English-only rules***, which prohibit employees from speaking any language but English at work. Absolute or "blanket" English-only rules, requiring employees to speak English exclusively during all their time in the workplace, are generally more difficult to justify than more limited English-only rules, which require employees to speak English only at certain times—such as when they are with customers—or in certain places—such as the sales floor or other "public contact" areas. The employer must clearly notify the employees of when and where the restriction applies.

The EEOC Guidelines on Discrimination Because of National Origin[16] take the position that blanket English-only rules violate Title VII unless they are required by business necessity. The EEOC believes that such rules may create an "atmosphere of inferiority, isolation, and intimidation" based on an employee's ethnicity, which could result in a discriminatory working environment and tend to be "a burdensome term and condition of employment." However, not all courts have agreed with the EEOC position on blanket English-only rules, as the following case illustrates.

case 8.5 »

GARCIA V. SPUN STEAK COMPANY

998 F.2d 1480 (9th Cir. 1993),* rehearing denied, *13 F.3d 296,
cert. denied, *512 U.S.1228 (1994)*

Facts: Spun Steak Company operates a meat processing plant in San Francisco. Spun Steak employs 33 workers, 24 of whom are Spanish-speaking. Prior to September 1990, these Spun Steak employees spoke Spanish freely to their co-workers during work hours. However, after receiving complaints that some of the Spanish-speaking employees made derogatory, racist comments in Spanish about African-American and Chinese-American co-workers, the company's

[16] 29 C.F.R. §1606

president concluded that an English-only rule would promote racial harmony in the workplace; enhance worker safety, because some employees who did not understand Spanish claimed that the use of Spanish distracted them while they were operating machinery; and enhance product quality, because the U.S.D.A. inspector in the plant spoke only English and could not understand if a product-related concern was raised in Spanish. The company adopted an "English-only" rule, requiring employees to speak English in connection with work. Employees were free to speak Spanish during lunch and breaks. Spun Steak also adopted a rule forbidding offensive racial, sexual, or personal remarks of any kind. Spun Steak did issue written exceptions to the policy, allowing its clean-up crew to speak Spanish because some members of the clean-up crew could only speak Spanish. Other employees who did not work on the clean-up crew were issued warning letters for speaking Spanish during working hours. Those employees, and the union representing the workers at Spun Steak, filed charges of discrimination against Spun Steak with the U.S. Equal Employment Opportunity Commission. The EEOC conducted an investigation and determined that there was reasonable cause to believe that Spun Steak violated Title VII. The employees and the union then filed suit against Spun Steak, alleging that the English-only policy violated Title VII. The trial court granted summary judgment for the Spanish-speaking employees, concluding that the English-only policy had a disparate impact on Hispanic workers and was not supported by sufficient business justification, and thus violated Title VII. Spun Steak appealed to the U.S. Court of Appeals for the Ninth Circuit.

Issue: Does the "English only" rule violate Title VII?

Decision: The plaintiffs claimed that the policy had a discriminatory impact on them because it imposed a burdensome term or condition of employment exclusively upon Hispanic workers by denying them the ability to express their cultural heritage on the job. The court of appeals held that Title VII does not protect the ability of workers to express their cultural heritage at the workplace, but rather is concerned only with disparities in the treatment of workers. There is nothing in Title VII that requires an employer to allow employees to express their cultural identity.

The Spanish-speaking employees also argued that the English-only policy had a disparate impact on them because it deprived them of a privilege given by the employer to native-English speakers: the ability to converse on the job in the language with which they feel most comfortable. It is undisputed that Spun Steak allows its employees to converse on the job. The ability to converse—especially to make small talk—is a privilege of employment, but a privilege is by definition given at the employer's discretion; an employer has the right to define its contours. Thus, an employer may allow employees to converse on the job, but only during certain times of the day or during the performance of certain tasks. The employer may proscribe certain topics as inappropriate during working hours or may even forbid the use of certain words, such as profanity. Here the employer has defined the privilege narrowly, but the plaintiffs, who can speak English, can readily comply with the English-only rule. The court held that there was no disparate impact regarding a privilege of employment if the affected employees can readily observe and comply with the rule and nonobservance is a matter of individual preference. Title VII protects against only those policies that have a significant impact, not against rules or policies that may inconvenience employees. The fact that employees may have to catch themselves from occasionally slipping into Spanish does not impose a burden significant enough to amount to a violation of Title VII.

With regard to the employee's claim that the "English-only" rule created an atmosphere of inferiority, isolation, and intimidation because it caused the work environment to become infused with ethnic tensions, the court held that the employees had not presented any evidence to show that the rule contributed to an atmosphere of isolation, inferiority, or intimidation. The bilingual employees were able to comply with the rule, and there was substantial evidence in the record demonstrating that the policy was enacted to prevent the employees from intentionally using their fluency in Spanish to isolate and to intimidate members of other ethnic groups. The court did note that in some circumstances English-only rules could exacerbate existing tensions, or, when combined with other discriminatory behavior, could contribute to an overall environment of discrimination. In such cases, the court must look to the totality of the circumstances in the particular factual context in which each claim arises.

The court of appeals held that the employees had failed to establish a case of national origin discrimination in violation of Title VII. Because the employees had failed to establish such a case, the court did not need to consider whether the rule was sufficiently supported by business justification. The court of appeals reversed the trial court grant of summary judgment for the employees, and remanded the case back to the trial court for reconsideration.

Citizenship

Title VII protects all individuals, both citizens and noncitizens, who reside in or are employed in the United States from employment discrimination based on race, color, religion, sex, or national origin. However, the Supreme Court in *Espinoza v. Farah Mfg. Co.*[17] held that Title VII's prohibition on national origin discrimination does not include discrimination on the basis of citizenship. Section 703(g) of Title VII also allows employers to refuse to hire applicants who are denied national security clearances for positions subject to federal security requirements.

The Immigration Reform and Control Act of 1986 and Discrimination Based on National Origin or Citizenship

The Immigration Reform and Control Act of 1986 (IRCA) prohibits employment discrimination because of national origin or citizenship against applicants or employees, other than illegal aliens, with respect to hiring, recruitment, discharge, or referral for a fee. Employers may, however, discriminate based upon citizenship when it is necessary to comply with other laws or federal, state, or local government contracts or when determined by the attorney general to be essential for an employer to do business with a government agency. Employers are permitted under the IRCA to give a U.S. citizen preference over an alien when both the citizen and the alien are "equally qualified" for the job for which they are being considered.

The Immigration Act of 1990 expanded the protection of the IRCA to cover seasonal agricultural workers. It is unlawful to intimidate, threaten, coerce, or retaliate against any person for the purpose of interfering with the rights secured under the IRCA's antidiscrimination provisions. Employers are also prohibited from requesting more or different employment-eligibility documents than are required under the IRCA and from refusing to honor documents that reasonably appear to be genuine.

The IRCA is enforced by the Department of Justice through the Special Counsel for Immigration-Related Unfair Employment Practices, a position created by the act. The non-discrimination provisions of the IRCA apply to employers with more than three employees, but they do not extend to national origin discrimination that is prohibited by Title VII. Consequently, employers who are subject to Title VII (those with fifteen or more employees) are not subject to the IRCA's provisions on national origin discrimination. However, because Title VII does not expressly prohibit discrimination based upon citizenship, all employers with more than three employees are covered by the IRCA's provisions against discrimination based upon citizenship.

[17]414 U.S. 86 (1973).

Concept *Summary* » 8.2

Discrimination Based on National Origin

- National origin discrimination includes discrimination based upon:
  - The place of origin of an applicant/employee (or his/her ancestors)
  - The physical, cultural, linguistic characteristics of an ethnic group
  - Associating with persons of a particular ethnic group or membership in organizations associated with particular ethnic groups
  - Refusal to recognize or credit foreign education or professional credentials
- Language
  - Title VII prohibits discrimination based on accents/fluency unless job requires public contact
  - English-only rules allowed if required for business necessity
  - Employers can refuse to hire persons denied national security clearances (Section 703(g))
- Coverage
  - Title VII—Discrimination based on national origin
    - Employers with at least fifteen employees
    - Citizens and noncitizens residing/working in the United States
    - Hiring, harassment
  - IRCA—Discrimination based on national origin or citizenship
    - Employers with more than three employees
    - Hiring, recruitment, discharge, or referral for a fee
    - Employers may set citizenship requirements if required by other laws, government contracts, or government agency

Enforcement of Title VII

This section focuses on the procedures for filing and resolving complaints of employment discrimination that arise under Title VII.

The Equal Employment Opportunity Commission

Title VII is administered and enforced by the Equal Employment Opportunity Commission (EEOC). The EEOC is headed by a five-member commission; the commissioners are appointed by the president with Senate confirmation. The general counsel of the EEOC is also appointed by the president, also with Senate confirmation.

Unlike the National Labor Relations Board (NLRB; another federal enforcement agency discussed in Chapter 12) the EEOC does not adjudicate, or decide, complaints alleging violations of Title VII, nor is it the exclusive enforcement agency for discrimination complaints. The EEOC staff investigates complaints filed with it and attempts to settle such complaints voluntarily. If a settlement is not reached voluntarily, the EEOC may file suit against the alleged discriminator in the federal courts.

The EEOC also differs from the NLRB in that the EEOC may initiate complaints on its own when it believes a party is involved in a "pattern or practice" of discrimination. In these cases, the EEOC need not wait for an individual to file a complaint with it. When a complaint alleges discrimination by a state or local government, Title VII requires that the Department of Justice initiate any court action against the public sector employer.

Procedures Under Title VII

Filing a Complaint

Title VII, unlike the National Labor Relations Act (discussed in Chapter 12), does not give the federal government exclusive authority over employment discrimination issues. Section 706(c) of Title VII requires that an individual filing a complaint of illegal employment discrimination must first file with a state or local agency authorized to deal with the issue, if such an agency exists. The EEOC may consider the complaint only after the state or local agency has had the complaint for sixty days or ceased processing the complaint, whichever occurs first.

State Agency Role

A number of states and municipalities have created equal employment opportunity agencies, also known as "fair employment" or "human rights" commissions. Some state agencies have powers and jurisdiction beyond those given to the EEOC. The New York State Human Rights Division enforces the New York State Human Rights Law. In addition to prohibiting discrimination in employment on the basis of race, color, religion, gender, and national origin, the New York legislation also prohibits employment discrimination on the basis of age, marital status, disability, and criminal record. The Pennsylvania Human Relations Act established the Human Rights Commission, which is empowered to hold hearings before administrative law judges to determine whether the act has been violated. The Pennsylvania legislation goes beyond Title VII's prohibitions by forbidding employment discrimination on the basis of disability.

Filing with the EEOC

When the complaint must first be filed with a state or local agency, Section 706(e) requires that it be filed with the EEOC within 300 days of the act of alleged discrimination. If there is no state or local agency, the complaint must be filed with the EEOC within 180 days of the alleged violation. By contrast, the limitation for filing a complaint under the New York State Human Rights Law is one year and under the Pennsylvania Human Relations Act is ninety days.

As noted earlier, an individual alleging employment discrimination must first file a complaint with the appropriate state or local agency, if such an agency exists. Once the complaint is filed with the state or local agency, the complainant must wait sixty days before filing the complaint with the EEOC. If the state or local agency terminates proceedings on the complaint prior to the passage of sixty days, the complaint may then be filed with the EEOC. This means that the individual filing the complaint with the state or local agency must wait for that agency to terminate proceedings or for sixty days, whichever comes first. *Mohasco Corp. v. Silver*[18]

[18] 447 U.S. 807 (1980).

involved a situation in which an individual filed a complaint alleging that he was discharged because of religious discrimination with the New York Division of Human Rights 291 days after the discharge. The state agency began to process and investigate the complaint; the EEOC began to process the complaint some 357 days after the discharge. The Supreme Court held that the complaint had not been properly filed with the EEOC within the 300-day limit. The Court held that the EEOC has a duty, under the statute, to begin processing a complaint within 300 days of the alleged violation. In order to allow the state agency the required sixty days for processing, the complaint must have been filed with the state agency within 240 days so that, when the EEOC began to process the complaint, it would be within the 300-day limit. However, as noted, when the state or local agency terminates proceedings on the complaint before sixty days have passed, the EEOC may begin to process the complaint upon the other agency's termination.

EEOC Procedure and Its Relation to State Proceedings

The EEOC has entered into "work-sharing" agreements with most state equal employment opportunity agencies to deal with the situation that arose in the *Mohasco* decision. Under such agreements, the agency that initially receives the complaint processes it. When the EEOC receives the complaint first, it refers the complaint to the appropriate state agency. The state agency then waives its right to process the complaint and refers it back to the EEOC. The state agency does retain jurisdiction to proceed on the complaint in the future, after the EEOC has completed its processing of the complaint. The EEOC treats the referral of the complaint to the state agency as the filing of the complaint with the state agency, and the state's waiver of the right to process the complaint is treated as termination of state proceedings, allowing the filing of the complaint with the EEOC under Section 706(c) of Title VII.

In *EEOC v. Commercial Office Products Co.*[19] the complainant filed a sex discrimination complaint with the EEOC on the 289th day after her discharge. The EEOC, under a work-sharing agreement, sent the complaint to the state agency, which returned the complaint to the EEOC after indicating that it waived its right to proceed on the complaint. The EEOC then began its investigation into the complaint and ultimately brought suit against the employer. The trial court and the court of appeals held that Section 706(c) required that either sixty days must elapse from the filing of the complaint with the state agency, or the state agency must both commence and terminate its proceedings, before the complaint could be deemed to have been filed with the EEOC. The Supreme Court, on appeal, reversed the court of appeals. The Supreme Court held that the state agency's waiver of its right to proceed on the complaint constituted a termination of the state proceedings under Section 706(c), allowing the EEOC to proceed with the complaint. As a result of this decision, in states where the EEOC and the state agency have work-sharing agreements, a complaint filed with the EEOC anytime within the 300-day time limit will be considered properly filed, and the EEOC can proceed with its processing of the complaint.

When Does the Violation Occur?

Because the time for filing a complaint under Title VII is limited, it is important to determine when the alleged violation occurred. In most situations, it is not difficult to determine the date

---

[19]486 U.S. 107 (1988).

Concept *Summary* » 8.3

Filing a Charge of Discrimination

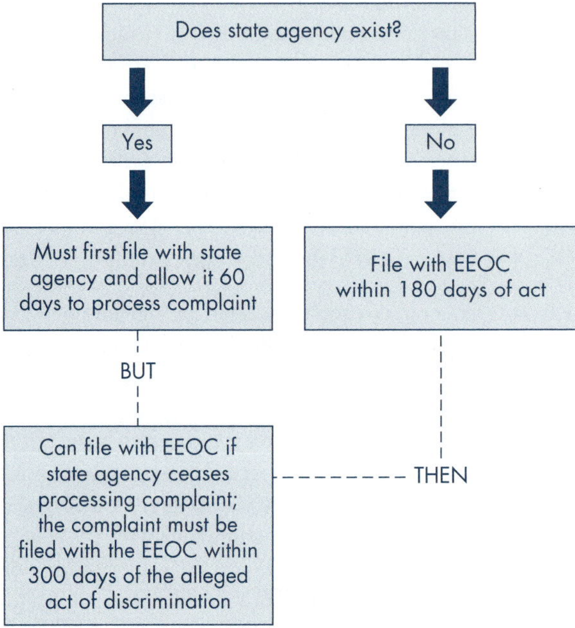

of the violation from which the time limit begins to run, but in some instances, it may present a problem. The Supreme Court, in *Delaware State College v. Ricks*,[20] held that the time limit for a Title VII violation begins to run on the date that the individual is aware of, or should be aware of, the alleged violation, not on the date that the alleged violation has an adverse effect on the individual. Following the rationale in the *Ricks* decision, the Supreme Court in *Ledbetter v. Goodyear Tire and Rubber Co.*[21] held that the time limit to challenge pay discrepancies based on a sexually discriminatory performance evaluation begins when the evaluation is made, not when paychecks reflecting that discriminatory evaluation are received. However, Congress overruled the *Ledbetter* decision by legislation signed into law by President Obama in 2009. The ***Lilly Ledbetter Fair Pay Act*** of 2009[22] added Section 706(e)(3)(A) to Title VII,[23] which states:

Lilly Ledbetter Fair Pay Act
Statute that extends time in which an employee may file suit under several federal employment statutes.

> For purposes of this section, an unlawful employment practice occurs, with respect to discrimination in compensation in violation of this subchapter, when a discriminatory compensation decision or other practice is adopted, when an individual becomes subject to a discriminatory compensation decision or other practice, or when an individual is affected by application of a discriminatory compensation decision or other practice, including each time wages, benefits, or other compensation is paid, resulting in whole or in part from such a decision or other practice.

---

[20] 449 U.S. 250 (1982).

[21] 550 U.S. 618 (2007).

[22] 2009 Pub. L. 111-2, § 3(A), 123 Stat. 5-6.

[23] 42 U.S.C. § 2000e-5(e)(3)(A).

The effect of the Lilly Ledbetter Fair Pay Act is to allow an employee to file a complaint with the EEOC within 180 days (or 300 where a state or local EEO agency exists) from the latest of three dates:

- when the discriminatory pay policy is adopted;
- when the employee becomes subject to the discriminatory pay policy; or
- when the employee is affected by the policy.

The act also specifies that each time the employee receives a paycheck reflecting the discriminatory pay policy, it is a new violation of Title VII. In deciding *Ledbetter v. Goodyear Tire and Rubber Co.*, the Supreme Court majority relied upon *Lorance v. AT&T Technologies, Inc.*[24] (see Chapter 6), where the Supreme Court ruled that the time limit for filing a complaint against an allegedly discriminatory change to a seniority system begins to run at the time the actual change is made—not when the employee becomes subject to the system, or when the seniority system has an adverse effect on the employee. But just as was the case with the *Ledbetter*, the decision in *Lorance* was reversed by Congress as part of the 1991 amendments to Title VII. Section 706(e)(2) now provides that for claims involving the adoption of a seniority system for allegedly discriminatory reasons, the violation can occur when the seniority system is adopted, when the complainant becomes subject to the seniority system, or when the complainant is injured by the application of the seniority system.

Continuing Violation

In *Bazemore v. Friday*,[25] the plaintiffs challenged a pay policy that discriminated against African-American employees. The pay policy had its origins in the era of racial segregation, prior to the date that Title VII applied to the employer, but the Supreme Court held that the violation was a continuing one—a new violation occurred every time the employees received a paycheck based on the racially discriminatory policy. Where the plaintiff alleges a continuing violation of Title VII, the plaintiff need only file within 180 or 300 days (depending on whether there is an appropriate local or state agency involved) of the latest incident of the alleged continuing violation. As noted above, the Lilly Ledbetter Fair Pay Act reaffirms the decision in *Bazemore* by stating that each paycheck reflecting the discriminatory pay policy is a new and separate violation of Title VII.

Hostile Environment Harassment

Employees alleging harassment creating a hostile environment in violation of Title VII must file their complaint with the EEOC within 180 days (if there is no state or local agency involved) or 300 days (it there is an appropriate state and local agency) of the most recent discrete incident of harassment, according to *National Railroad Passenger Corp. v. Morgan*.[26]

---

[24] 490 U.S. 900 (1989).

[25] 478 U.S. 385 (1986).

[26] 536 U.S. 101 (2002).

EEOC Procedure for Handling Complaints

Upon receipt of a properly filed complaint, the EEOC has ten days to serve a notice of the complaint with the employer, union, or agency alleged to have discriminated (the respondent). Following service upon the respondent, the EEOC staff conducts an investigation into the complaint to determine whether reasonable cause exists to believe it is true. If no reasonable cause is found, the charge is dismissed. If reasonable cause to believe the complaint is found, the commission will attempt to settle the complaint through voluntary conciliation, persuasion, and negotiation. If the voluntary procedures are unsuccessful in resolving the complaint after thirty days from its filing, the EEOC may file suit in a federal district court.

If the EEOC dismisses the complaint or decides not to file suit, it notifies the complainant that he or she may file suit on his or her own. The complainant must file suit within ninety days of receiving the right-to-sue notice.

When the EEOC has not dismissed the complaint but has also not filed suit or acted upon the complaint within 180 days of its filing, the complainant may request a right-to-sue letter. Again, the complainant has ninety days from the notification to file suit. The suit may be filed:

- in the district court in the district where the alleged unlawful employment practice occurred;
- where the relevant employment records are kept; or
- where the complainant would have been employed.

In *Yellow Freight System, Inc. v. Donnelly*,[27] the Supreme Court held that the federal courts do not have exclusive jurisdiction over Title VII claims; state courts are competent to adjudicate claims based on federal law such as Title VII. This means that the individual may file suit in either the federal or appropriate state court.

Because the complainant may be required to file first with a state or local agency and may file his or her own suit if the EEOC has not acted within 180 days, several legal proceedings involving the complaint may occur at the same time. What is the effect of a state court decision dismissing the complaint on a subsequent suit filed in federal court? In *Kremer v. Chemical Construction Co.*,[28] the U.S. Supreme Court held that a plaintiff who loses a discrimination suit in a state court is precluded from filing a Title VII suit based on the same facts in federal court. According to *Kremer*, the complainant who is unsuccessful in the state courts does not get a second chance to file a suit based on the same facts in federal court because of the full-faith-and-credit doctrine. However, the holding in Kremer was limited only to the effect of a state court decision.

What is the effect of a negative determination by a state administrative agency on the complainant's right to sue in federal court? In *University of Tennessee v. Elliot*,[29] the Supreme Court held that the full-faith-and-credit doctrine did not apply to state administrative agency decisions. Hence, a negative determination by the state agency would not preclude the complainant from suing in federal court under Title VII. (The Court in *Elliot* did hold that the findings of fact made by the state agency should be given preclusive effect by the federal courts in suits filed under 42 U.S. 1981 and 1983.)

---

[27] 494 U.S. 820 (1990).

[28] 456 U.S. 461 (1982).

[29] 478 U.S. 788 (1986).

Concept *Summary* » 8.4

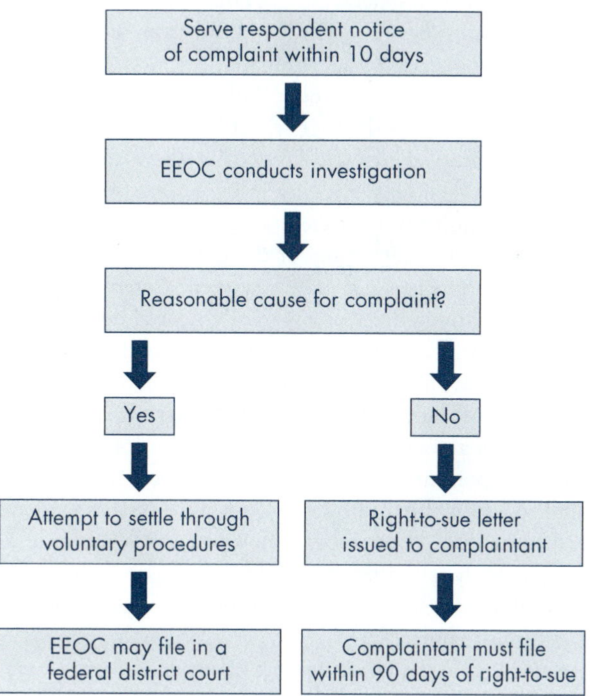

The Relationship Between Title VII and Other Statutory Remedies

In *Tipler v. E. I. du Pont de Nemours*,[30] the U.S. Court of Appeals for the Sixth Circuit held that the NLRB's rejection of an unfair labor practice charge alleging racial discrimination does not preclude the filing of a Title VII suit growing out of the same situation. However, if an employee had voluntarily accepted reinstatement with back pay in settlement of his or her grievance against the employer, the U.S. Court of Appeals for the Fifth Circuit held that the employee had waived his or her right to sue under Title VII on the same facts.[31]

In the case of *Johnson v. Railway Express Agency*,[32] the Supreme Court held that an action under Title VII is separate and distinct from an action alleging race discrimination under the Civil Rights Act of 1866, 42 U.S.C., Section 1981 (see Chapter 11).

---

[30] 433 F.2d 125 (1971).

[31] *Strozier v. General Motors*, 635 F.2d 424 (1981).

[32] 421 U.S. 454 (1975).

Burdens of Proof: Establishing a Case

Once the complaint of an unlawful employment practice under Title VII has become the subject of a suit in a federal district court, the question of the burden of proof arises. What must the plaintiff show to establish a valid claim of discrimination? What must the defendant show to defeat a claim of discrimination?

The plaintiff in a suit under Title VII always carries the burden of proof; that is, the plaintiff must persuade the trier of fact (the jury or the judge if there is no jury) that there has been a violation of Title VII. To do this, the plaintiff must establish a ***prima facie case*** of discrimination—enough evidence to raise a presumption of discrimination. If the plaintiff is unable to establish a prima facie case of discrimination, the case will be dismissed. The specific elements of a prima facie case, or the means to establish it, will vary depending on whether the complaint involves disparate treatment (intentional discrimination) or disparate impact (the discriminatory effects of apparently neutral criteria).

Prima Facie Case
A case "on the face of it" or "at first sight"; often used to establish that if a certain set of facts is proven, then it is apparent that another fact is established.

The plaintiff may use either anecdotal evidence or statistical evidence to establish the prima facie case. In *Bazemore v. Friday*, the plaintiffs offered a statistical multiple-regression analysis to demonstrate that pay policies discriminated against African-American employees. The employer argued that the multiple-regression analysis did not consider several variables that were important in determining employees' pay. The trial court and the court of appeals refused to admit the multiple-regression analysis as evidence because it did not include all relevant variables. On appeal, however, the Supreme Court held that the multiple-regression-analysis evidence should have been admitted. The failure of the analysis to include all relevant variables affects its probative value (the weight given to it by the trier of fact), not its admissibility.

According to the U.S. Supreme Court decision in *Desert Palace, Inc. v. Costa*,[33] a plaintiff seeking to establish a mixed-motive case under Section 703(m) of Title VII need only demonstrate that the defendant used a prohibited factor (race, color, gender, religion, or natural origin) as one of the motives for an employment action. That demonstration can be made either by circumstantial evidence or direct evidence. The act does not require direct evidence to raise the mixed-motive analysis under Section 703(m).

Disparate Treatment Claims

Claims of disparate treatment involve allegations of intentional discrimination in employment. A plaintiff alleging disparate treatment must establish that he or she was subjected to less favorable treatment because of his or her race, color, religion, gender, or national origin. The specific elements of a prima facie case of disparate treatment under Title VII are discussed in the following case.

[33] 539 U.S. 90 (2003).

case 8.6 » McDonnell Douglas Corp. v. Green

411 U.S. 792 (1973)

Powell, J.

The case before us raises significant questions as to the proper order and nature of proof in actions under Title VII of the Civil Rights Act of 1964.

Petitioner, McDonnell Douglas Corporation, is an aerospace and aircraft manufacturer headquartered in St. Louis, Missouri, where it employs over 30,000 people. Respondent, a black citizen of St. Louis, worked for petitioner as a mechanic and laboratory technician from 1956 until August 28, 1964 when he was laid off in the course of a general reduction in petitioner's work force.

Respondent, a long-time activist in the civil rights movement, protested vigorously that his discharge and the general hiring practices of petitioner were racially motivated. As part of this protest, respondent and other members of the Congress on Racial Equality illegally stalled their cars on the main roads leading to petitioner's plant for the purpose of blocking access to it at the time of the morning shift change. The District Judge described the plan for, and respondent's participation in, the "stall-in" as follows:

> ... five teams, each consisting of four cars, would "tie-up" five main access roads into McDonnell at the time of the morning rush hour. The drivers of the cars were instructed to line up next to each other completely blocking the intersections or roads. The drivers were also instructed to stop their cars, turn off the engines, pull the emergency brake, raise all windows, lock the doors, and remain in their cars until the police arrived. The plan was to have the cars remain in position for one hour....

... On July 2, 1965, a "lock-in" took place wherein a chain and padlock were placed on the front door of a building to prevent the occupants, certain of petitioner's employees, from leaving. Though respondent apparently knew beforehand of the "lock-in," the full extent of his involvement remains uncertain.

Some three weeks following the "lock-in," on July 25, 1965, petitioner publicly advertised for qualified mechanics, respondent's trade, and respondent promptly applied for reemployment. Petitioner turned down respondent, basing its rejection on respondent's participation in the "stall-in" and "lock-in." Shortly thereafter, respondent filed a formal complaint with the Equal Employment Opportunity Commission, claiming that petitioner had refused to rehire him because of his race and persistent involvement in the civil rights movement in violation of Sections 703(a)(1) and 704 (a).... The former section generally prohibits racial discrimination in any employment decision while the latter forbids discrimination against applicants or employees for attempting to protest or correct allegedly discriminatory conditions of employment.

The Commission made no finding on respondent's allegation of racial bias under Section 703(a)(1), but it did find reasonable cause to believe petitioner had violated Section 704(a) by refusing to rehire respondent because of his civil rights activity. After the Commission unsuccessfully attempted to conciliate the dispute, it advised respondent in March 1968, of his right to institute a civil action in federal court within 30 days.

On April 15, 1968, respondent brought the present action, claiming initially a violation of Section 704(a) and, in an amended complaint, a violation of Section 703(a)(1) as well. The District Court dismissed the latter claim of racial discrimination in petitioner's hiring procedures.... The District Court also found that petitioner's refusal to rehire respondent was based solely on his participation in the illegal demonstrations and not on his legitimate civil rights activities. The court concluded that nothing in Title VII or Section 704 protected "such activity as employed by the plaintiff in the 'stall-in' and 'lock-in' demonstrations."

... On appeal, the Eighth Circuit affirmed that unlawful protests were not protected activities under Section 704(a), but reversed the dismissal of respondent's Section 703(a)(1) claim relating to racially discriminatory hiring practices ... The court ordered the case remanded for trial of respondent's claim under Section 703(a)(1).

... The critical issue before us concerns the order and allocation of proof in a private, single-plaintiff action challenging employment discrimination. The language of Title VII makes plain the purpose of Congress to assure equality of employment opportunities and to eliminate those discriminatory practices and devices which have fostered racially stratified job environments to the disadvantage of minority citizens.

As noted in [*Griggs v. Duke Power Co.*]:

> Congress did not intend Title VII, however, to guarantee a job to every person regardless of

qualifications. In short, the Act does not command that any person be hired simply because he was formerly the subject of discrimination, or because he is a member of a minority group. Discriminatory preference for any group, minority or majority, is precisely and only what Congress has proscribed. What is required by Congress is the removal of artificial, arbitrary, and unnecessary barriers to employment when the barriers operate invidiously to discriminate on the basis of racial or other impermissible classification....

There are societal as well as personal interests on both sides of this equation. The broad, overriding interest shared by employer, employee, and consumer, is efficient and trustworthy workmanship assured through fair and racially neutral employment and personnel decisions. In the implementation of such decisions, it is abundantly clear that Title VII tolerates no racial discrimination, subtle or otherwise.

In this case, respondent, the complainant below, charges that he was denied employment "because of his involvement in civil rights activities" and "because of his race and color." Petitioner denied discrimination of any kind, asserting that its failure to re-employ respondent was based upon and justified by his participation in the unlawful conduct against it. Thus, the issue at the trial on remand is framed by those opposing factual contentions....

The complainant in a Title VII trial must carry the initial burden under the statute of establishing a prima facie case of racial discrimination. This may be done by showing (i) that he belongs to a racial minority; (ii) that he had applied and was qualified for a job for which the employer was seeking applicants; (iii) that, despite his qualifications, he was rejected; and (iv) that, after his rejection, the position remained open and the employer continued to seek applicants from persons of complainant's qualifications. In the instant case, we agree with the Court of Appeals that respondent proved a prima facie case.... Petitioner sought mechanics, respondent's trade, and continued to do so after respondent's rejection. Petitioner, moreover, does not dispute respondent's qualifications and acknowledges that his past work performance in petitioner's employ was "satisfactory."

The burden then must shift to the employer to articulate some legitimate, nondiscriminatory reason for respondent's rejection. We need not attempt in the instant case to detail every matter which fairly could be recognized as a reasonable basis for a refusal to hire. Here petitioner has assigned respondent's participation in unlawful conduct against it as the cause for his rejection. We think that this suffices to discharge petitioner's burden of proof at this stage and to meet respondent's prima facie case of discrimination.

The Court of Appeals intimated, however, that petitioner's stated reason for refusing to rehire respondent was a "subjective" rather than objective criterion which "carries little weight in rebutting charges of discrimination." Regardless of whether this was the intended import of the opinion, we think the court below seriously underestimated the rebuttal weight to which petitioner's reasons were entitled. Respondent admittedly had taken part in a carefully planned "stall-in," designed to tie up access and egress to petitioner's plant at a peak traffic hour. Nothing in Title VII compels an employer to absolve and rehire one who has engaged in such deliberate, unlawful activity against it....

... Petitioner's reason for rejection thus suffices to meet the prima facie case, but the inquiry must not end here. While Title VII does not, without more, compel rehiring of respondent, neither does it permit petitioner to use respondent's conduct as a pretext for the sort of discrimination prohibited by Section 703(a)(1). On remand, respondent must, as the Court of Appeals recognized, be afforded a fair opportunity to show that petitioner's stated reason for respondent's rejection was in fact pretextual. Especially relevant to such a showing would be evidence that white employees involved in acts against petitioner of comparable seriousness to the "stall-in" were nevertheless retained or rehired. Petitioner may justifiably refuse to rehire one who was engaged in unlawful, disruptive acts against it, but only if this criterion is applied alike to members of all races.

Other evidence that may be relevant to any showing of pretextuality includes facts as to the petitioner's treatment of respondent during his prior term of employment, petitioner's reaction, if any, to respondent's legitimate civil rights activities, and petitioner's general policy and practice with respect to minority employment. On the latter point, statistics as to petitioner's employment policy and practice may be helpful to a determination of whether petitioner's refusal to rehire respondent in this case conformed to a general pattern of discrimination against blacks. In short, on the retrial respondent must be given a full and fair opportunity to demonstrate by competent evidence that the presumptively valid reasons for his rejection were in fact a coverup for a racially discriminatory decision....

Case Questions

1. How can a plaintiff establish a prima facie case of disparate treatment discrimination?

2. What was McDonnell Douglas's reason for refusing to rehire Green? Why did Green argue that the reason was a pretext for illegal discrimination?

3. How could Green convince the Court that McDonnell Douglas's reason was a pretext? What evidence would be relevant to such a showing? What would be the effect of such a showing?

Defendant's Burden

If the plaintiff is successful in establishing a prima facie case of disparate treatment, the defendant must then try to overcome the plaintiff's claims. Is the defendant required to disprove those claims, prove that there was no discrimination, or merely explain the apparent discrimination? What is the nature of the defendant's burden in a disparate treatment case? In *Texas Department of Community Affairs v. Burdine*,[34] the U.S. Supreme Court stated:

> The nature of the burden that shifts to the defendant should be understood in light of the plaintiff's ultimate and intermediate burdens. The ultimate burden of persuading the trier of fact that the defendant intentionally discriminated against the plaintiff remains at all time with the plaintiff.... The burden that shifts to the defendant, therefore, is to rebut the presumption of discrimination by producing evidence that the plaintiff was rejected, or someone else was preferred, for a legitimate, nondiscriminatory reason. The defendant need not persuade the court that it was actually motivated by the proffered reasons. It is sufficient if the defendant's evidence raises a genuine issue of fact as to whether it discriminated against the plaintiff. To accomplish this, the defendant must clearly set forth, through the introduction of admissible evidence, the reasons for the plaintiff's rejection. The explanation provided must be legally sufficient to justify a judgment for the defendant. If the defendant carries this burden of production, the presumption raised by the prima facie case is rebutted....

According to *Burdine*, the defendant need only "articulate" some legitimate justification for its actions; the burden of proof—of persuading the trier of fact—remains with the plaintiff. Although the defendant need not *prove* that there was no discrimination, the nondiscriminatory justification or explanation offered by the defendant must be believable. Obviously, if the defendant's justification is not credible, then the plaintiff's prima facie case will not be rebutted, and the plaintiff will prevail.

Plaintiff's Burden of Showing Pretext

After the defendant has advanced a legitimate justification to counter, or rebut, the plaintiff's prima facie case, the focus of the proceeding shifts back to the plaintiff. The plaintiff, as was discussed in the *McDonnell Douglas* case, must be afforded an opportunity to show that the employer's justification is a mere pretext, or cover-up. This can be shown either directly, by persuading the court that a discriminatory reason likely motivated the defendant, or indirectly, by showing that the offered justification is not worthy of credence. The burden of showing that the defendant's offered justification is a pretext for discrimination is a very difficult one. According to the Supreme Court decision in *St. Mary's Honor Center v. Hicks*,[35] the plaintiff,

[34] 450 U.S. 248 (1979).

[35] 509 U.S. 502 (1993).

in addition to demonstrating that the defendant's justification is false, still has to convince the trier of fact that the defendant was motivated by illegal discrimination. In *Reeves v. Sanderson Plumbing Products, Inc.*,[36] when the plaintiff has established a prima facie case of discrimination, and in doing so has provided enough evidence for the trier of fact (jury or judge) to reject the employer's offered excuse as false, there was sufficient evidence to support a finding that the employer had intentionally discriminated against the plaintiff. (Note that the Reeves case involved a claim under the Age Discrimination in Employment Act, which is discussed in the next chapter, but the burden of proof analysis is also applicable under Title VII.)

Disparate Impact Claims

Unlike a disparate treatment claim, a claim of disparate impact does not involve an allegation of intentional discrimination. Rather, as in *Griggs v. Duke Power Co.*, it involves a claim that neutral job requirements have a discriminatory effect. The plaintiff, in order to establish a prima facie case, must show that the apparently neutral employment requirements or practices have a disproportionate impact upon a class protected by Title VII.

The Supreme Court in the *Wards Cove Packing Co. v. Atonio* and *Watson v. Fort Worth Bank & Trust* decisions (see Chapter 6) held that a plaintiff alleging a disparate impact claim must "offer statistical evidence of a kind and degree sufficient to show that the practice in question has caused the exclusion of applicants for jobs or promotions because of their membership in a protected group."

Four-Fifths Rule

As discussed in Chapter 6, one way to establish proof of a disproportionate impact is by using the Four-Fifths Rule from the EEOC Guidelines. The rule states that a disparate impact will be presumed to exist when the selection or pass rate for the protected class with the lowest selection rate is less than 80 percent of the selection or pass rate of the protected class with the highest rate. The Four-Fifths Rule is used primarily when challenging employment tests or requirements such as a high school diploma or minimum height and weight requirements.

Using Statistics

Another method of establishing a disparate impact may be by making a statistical comparison of the minority representation in the employers' work force and the minority representation in the population as a whole (or in the relevant area or labor market). When a job requires specific skills and training, the population used for comparison with the work force may be limited to available qualified individuals within the relevant area or labor market. The court may require specific demographic and geographic comparisons when using statistical evidence, as demonstrated in *Hazelwood School Dist. v. U.S.*[37]

---

[36]530 U.S. 133 (2000).

[37]433 U.S. 299 (1977).

Defendant's Burden

When the plaintiff has established a prima facie case of disparate impact, the defendant has two methods of responding. The defendant may challenge the statistical analysis, the methods of data collection, or the significance of the plaintiff's evidence. The defendant may also submit alternative statistical proof that leads to conclusions that contradict those of the plaintiff's evidence.

Rather than attacking the plaintiff's statistical evidence, the defendant alternatively may show that the employment practice, test, or requirement having the disparate impact is job related.

Although the Supreme Court decisions in *Watson v. Fort Worth Bank & Trust* and *Wards Cove Packing Co. v. Atonio* both held that the employer need only show some business justification for the challenged practice, and the plaintiff has the burden of persuasion for showing that the challenged practice is not job related, the 1991 amendments to Title VII overruled those cases. Section 703(k) requires that, once the plaintiff has demonstrated that the challenged practice has a disparate impact, the employer has the burden of persuasion for convincing the court that the practice is job related.

A defense of job relatedness can be established by using the methods of demonstrating validity set out in the Uniform Guidelines for Employee Selection. (The methods of demonstrating that a test or requirement is content valid, construct valid, or criterion valid are described in Chapter 6.)

If the defendant establishes that the practice, requirement, or test is job related, the plaintiff may still prevail by showing that other tests, practices, or requirements that do not have disparate impacts on protected classes are available and would satisfy the defendant's legitimate business concerns. The plaintiff may also try to show that the job-related justification is really just a pretext for intentional discrimination.

Concept *Summary* » 8.5

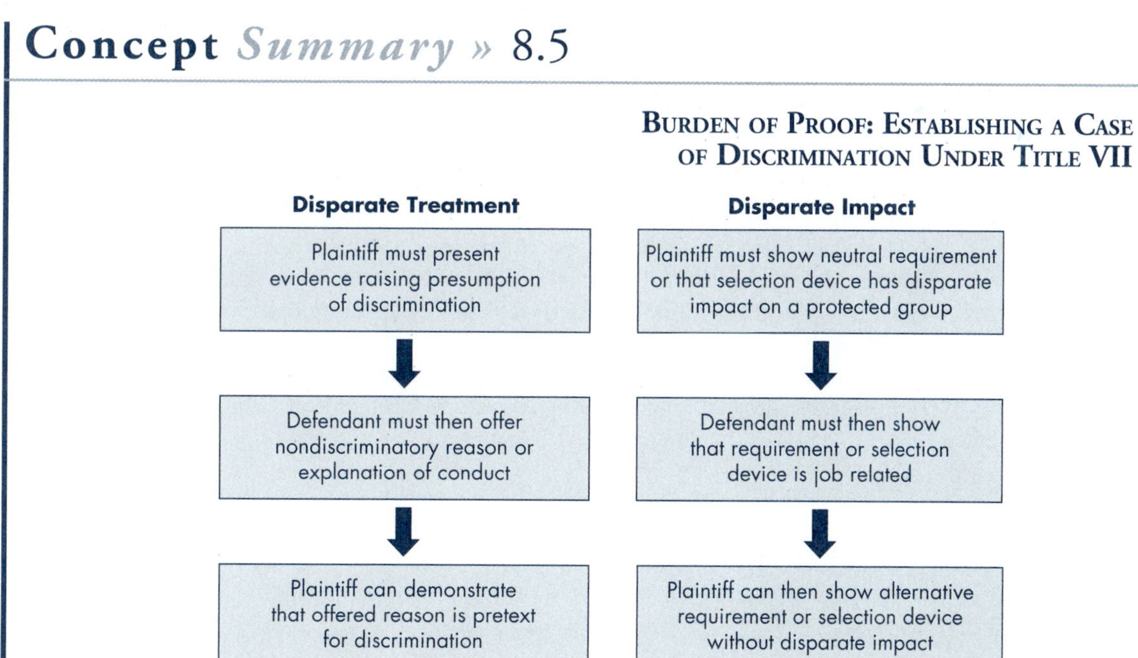

After-Acquired Evidence

After-Acquired Evidence
Evidence, discovered after an employer has taken an adverse employment action, that the employer uses to justify the action taken.

What happens when the employer, after an employee who was allegedly fired for discriminatory reasons has filed a Title VII claim, discovers that the employee had falsified credentials on the application for employment? Does the evidence of the plaintiff employee's misconduct (known as ***after-acquired evidence***) preclude the right of the plaintiff to sue? In *McKennon v. Nashville Banner Publishing Co.*,[38] the Supreme Court held that the after-acquired evidence does not preclude the plaintiff's suit, but rather goes to the issue of the remedies available. If the employer can demonstrate that the employee's wrongdoing is severe enough to result in termination had the employer known of the misconduct at the time the alleged discrimination occurred, the court must then consider the effect of the wrongdoing on the remedies available to the plaintiff. In such a case, the Supreme Court held that reinstatement would not be appropriate, and back pay may be awarded from the date of the alleged discrimination by the employer to the date upon which the plaintiff's misconduct was discovered. *McKennon* involved a suit under the Age Discrimination in Employment Act, but the after-acquired evidence rule has also been applied in Title VII suits, like *Wallace v. Dunn Construction Co.*[39] Evidence of the plaintiff's misconduct that occurs after the plaintiff was terminated was not relevant to the plaintiff's claim of discrimination and was excluded by the court in *Carr v. Woodbury County Juvenile Detention Center.*[40]

Arbitration of Statutory EEO Claims

Unions and employers generally agree that any disputes arising under their collective agreements will be settled through arbitration. More recently, an increasing number of employers whose employees are not unionized are requiring their employees to agree to settle any employment disputes through arbitration rather than litigation in the courts. Employers tend to favor arbitration because it is generally quicker than litigation, is confidential while court decisions are public, and the remedies available under arbitration may be less generous than those available through the courts. What is the effect of such arbitration agreements on the employee's ability to bring a suit under Title VII or other EEO legislation?

In *Alexander v. Gardner Denver Co.*,[41] the Supreme Court held that an arbitration proceeding under a collective agreement did not prevent an employee from filing suit alleging a violation of Title VII. The employee had lost in an arbitration challenging his discharge under the collective agreement but was still permitted to bring a Title VII suit in court. The Supreme Court held that the arbitration dealt with the employee's rights under the collective agreement, which were distinct from the employee's statutory rights under Title VII.

Seventeen years later, in *Gilmer v. Interstate/Johnson Lane Corp.*,[42] the Supreme Court held that a securities broker was required to arbitrate, rather than litigate, his age discrimination claim because he had signed an agreement to arbitrate all disputes arising from his

[38]513 U.S. 352 (1995).

[39]62 F.3d 374 (11th Cir. 1995).

[40]905 F. Supp. 619 (N.D. Iowa 1995), *aff'd by* 97 F.3d 1456 (8th Cir. 1996).

[41]415 U.S. 147 (1974).

[42]500 U.S. 20 (1991).

employment. The arbitration agreement was included in Gilmer's registration with the New York Securities Exchange, which was required for him to work as a broker. The Supreme Court in *Gilmer* held that the individual agreement to arbitrate, voluntarily agreed to by *Gilmer*, was enforceable under the Federal Arbitration Act (FAA) and required Gilmer to submit all employment disputes, including those under EEO legislation, to arbitration. The agreement to arbitrate did not waive Gilmer's rights under the statutes but simply required that those rights be determined by the arbitrator rather than the courts. The Court in Gilmer emphasized that it involved a different situation from *Alexander v. Gardner Denver*, which continued to apply when arbitration under a collective agreement was involved.

The distinctions between the *Alexander* case and the *Gilmer* case need to be emphasized. In *Gilmer*, the individual employee had agreed, as part of an agreement connected with his employment, to arbitrate all disputes growing out of that employment. In *Alexander*, the union and the employer had agreed, as part of a collective agreement, to arbitrate employment disputes arising under that collective agreement. The individual employee, while subject to the collective agreement, had not personally agreed to arbitrate any disputes.

Arbitration Clauses in Collective Agreements

The U.S. Supreme Court took a step toward resolving the distinction between *Gilmer* and *Alexander* when it decided the case of *14 Penn Plaza v. Pyett*.[43] That case involved age discrimination claims filed by employees covered by a collective agreement that included an arbitration clause that specifically covered any claims under Title VII, the Age Discrimination in Employment Act, and other EEO legislation. The Court held that the employees were required to arbitrate their age discrimination claims. The Court noted that *Alexander* rationale that arbitration dealt with contractual rights while litigation dealt with the employee's statutory rights did not apply where the collective bargaining agreement's arbitration provision expressly includes statutory claims as well as contractual claims arising under the terms of the collective agreement. The effect of the decision in *14 Penn Plaza v. Pyett* may not be to completely overrule *Alexander*, however, because the Court specifically refrained from holding that employees must arbitrate their statutory EEO claims when the union controls access to arbitration and may prevent the employees from pursuing their EEO claims through arbitration.

Individual Agreements to Arbitrate Employment Discrimination Disputes

The *Gilmer* case involved a claim of age discrimination under the Age Discrimination in Employment Act, but courts soon applied its reasoning to discrimination claims under Title VII and other federal and state employment discrimination legislation.

The FAA requires federal courts to enforce agreements to arbitrate if they are voluntary and knowing. However, Section 1 of the FAA states that it does not apply to "contracts of employment of seamen, railroad employees, or any other class of workers engaged in foreign or interstate commerce." How broadly should the courts read the exception for "contracts of employment" in Section 1 of the FAA? Does it encompass all employment contracts or is it limited to the specific kinds of contracts mentioned? This issue, which was not directly addressed by the *Gilmer* case,

---

[43] 129 S.Ct. 1456 (2009).

was decided by the U.S. Supreme Court in the case of *Circuit City Stores, Inc. v. Adams.*[44] The Supreme Court held that Section 1 of the FAA excludes only contracts of employment of the specific classes of workers listed in the statute. In *Circuit City*, the employer's application for employment contained a Dispute Resolution Agreement requiring employees to submit all employment disputes to binding arbitration. Applicants who refused to sign the Dispute Resolution Agreement were not hired. The Supreme Court held that such an agreement is enforceable under the FAA and that employees signing the agreement are precluded from suing the employer over employment disputes. While individual employees may be bound by arbitration agreements in their contracts of employment, the individual arbitration agreements do not prevent the EEOC from bringing suit against an employer to enforce EEO laws according to *EEOC v. Waffle House, Inc.*[45] The EEOC can bring legal action to enforce the EEO statutes, and may also seek individual remedies (such as back pay and reinstatement) for the employee who had signed the arbitration agreement.

Challenges to the Enforceability of Agreements to Arbitrate

The *Circuit City* decision means that employers may insist upon employees agreeing to arbitrate employment disputes as a condition of employment; applicants or employees who refuse to agree to such provisions will not be hired or will be fired. Because employers can force such arbitration agreements upon employees, a court asked to enforce an agreement to arbitrate must be satisfied that the agreement is knowing and reasonable. In *Brisentine v. Stone & Webster Engineering Corp.*,[46] the U.S. Court of Appeals for the Eleventh Circuit stated that, for an arbitration agreement to be enforced, it must meet three requirements:

- The employee must have individually agreed to the arbitration provision
- The arbitration must authorize the arbitrator to resolve the statutory EEO claims
- The agreement must give the employee the right to insist on arbitration if the statutory EEO claim is not resolved to his or her satisfaction in any grievance procedure or dispute resolution process of the employer

Most courts now take the position that an agreement to arbitrate, knowingly and voluntarily agreed to by an employee, is binding and requires the employee to arbitrate EEO claims instead of taking them to court. Arbitration agreements that were not knowingly agreed to will not be enforced, as shown in *Prudential Insurance Co. v. Lai*,[47] nor will the courts enforce agreements that are not binding upon the employer or that are unfair to the employee, according to *Hooters of America, Inc. v. Phillips*[48] and *Floss v. Ryan's Family Steak Houses.*[49] The courts will also refuse to enforce arbitration agreements that restrict remedies available to employees less than those remedies available under the appropriate EEO statute.[50] The

[44]532 U.S. 105 (2001).

[45]534 U.S. 279 (2003).

[46]117 F.3d 519 (11th Cir. 1997).

[47]42 F.3d 1299 (9th Cir. 1994).

[48]173 F.3d 933 (4th Cir. 1999).

[49]211 F.3d 306 (6th Cir. 2000).

[50]*Circuit City Stores, Inc. v. Adams*, 279 F.3d 889 (9th Cir. 2002), *cert. denied*, 535 U.S. 1112 (2002).

California Supreme Court, in the case of *Armendariz v. Foundation Health Psychcare Services, Inc.*,[51] set out requirements for enforcing agreements requiring arbitration of claims under California state employment discrimination legislation:

- the arbitration must be by a neutral arbitrator;
- the arbitration procedures must allow the parties access to witnesses and essential documents;
- the arbitrator must provide a written decision;
- the remedies available under the arbitration must be similar to those available in court; and
- the employee may not be required to pay any arbitrators' fees or expenses or any unreasonable costs as a condition of going to arbitration.

While *Armendariz* deals with state law, some federal courts have adopted its analysis with regard to enforcing mandatory agreements to arbitrate.

Costs of Arbitration

Some challenges to the enforceability of arbitration agreements involve the question of cost: Does the arbitration agreement require the employee to bear unreasonable costs? As mentioned in *Armendariz*, arbitration agreements that impose excessive costs on employees could operate to deter those employees from bringing complaints of employment discrimination. Because the employees may be required to arbitrate rather than litigate their claims, they are effectively denied the protection of the EEO laws. As a result, the courts have refused to enforce arbitration agreements that require the employee to bear unreasonable expenses associated with the arbitration. In *Green Tree Financial Corp. v. Randolph*,[52] which was not an employment case, the Supreme Court held that the party seeking to invalidate an arbitration agreement because it would be prohibitively expensive has the burden of demonstrating the likelihood of incurring such costs.

After *Green Tree*, the federal courts have struggled with the question of when the cost requirements of arbitration become prohibitively or unreasonably expensive. Plaintiffs who file EEO suits in the federal courts are required to pay a filing fee (currently less than $300) and must also bear the cost of legal representation. Attorneys for plaintiffs are likely to take such cases on a contingency basis (they will only charge legal fees if the plaintiff wins the suit). Title VII also provides that successful plaintiffs may recover legal fees as part of the statutory remedies available. In contrast, the employee filing for arbitration will be required to pay a filing fee and will also generally be held to pay at least half of the arbitrator's fees and expenses. There may be additional fees for administrative costs, for discovery proceedings, and for subpoenas of witnesses. One study estimated that the costs of filing for arbitration (based on holding three days of hearings) ranged between $3,950 and $10,925.[53] Requiring an employee to pay such expenses to pursue an employment discrimination claim may have the effect of deterring the employee from doing so. Some employers may have an incentive to impose arbitration requirements with high costs to prevent employees from filing employment discrimination claims. As a result, the

---

[51] 99 Cal. Rptr.2d 745, 24 Cal.4th 83 (2000).

[52] 531 U.S. 79 (2000).

[53] "The Costs of Arbitration," Public Citizen, April 2002.

courts have been sensitive to claims that the arbitration agreement imposes unreasonable costs on the employee.

In *Armendariz v. Foundation Health Psychcare Services, Inc.*, the California Supreme Court held that an arbitration agreement that required the employee to pay any expenses beyond that which would be required to file a suit in court would be unreasonable and not enforceable. In *Morrison v. Circuit City Stores, Inc.*,[54] the court held that a "fee-splitting" clause (which required the employee and the employer to split the costs of the arbitration and the arbitrator's fees) would be unreasonable and unenforceable when it would deter a substantial number of potential claimants from exerting their statutory rights.

The court, in making such a determination, should consider the employee's income and resources available, the potential costs of arbitration, and the costs of litigation as an alternative to arbitration. Such an approach may yield different results for different employees: For highly paid executive employees, fee-splitting requirements would be affordable and therefore enforceable, but for lower level employees, such cost requirements would not be enforceable. In the *Morrison* case, the court required the employee to arbitrate her claim but held that the employer had to pay the costs of the arbitration. Other courts have held fee-splitting clauses unreasonable per se. Such requirements are unenforceable because, by requiring the employee to pay at least some of the costs of arbitration, they automatically limit the remedies that would be available to the employee under Title VII.[55]

Remedies Under Title VII

Plaintiffs under Title VII are entitled to a jury trial on their claims. The remedies available to a successful plaintiff under Title VII are spelled out in Section 706(g). These remedies include:

- Judicial orders requiring hiring or reinstatement of employees
- Awarding of back pay and seniority
- Injunctions against unlawful employment practices
- "Such affirmative action as may be appropriate"

Section 706(k) provides that the court, in its discretion, may award legal fees to a prevailing party other than the EEOC or the United States. The Civil Rights Act of 1991 added the right to recover compensatory and punitive damages for intentional violations of Title VII. Individual employees, even those in supervisory or managerial positions, are not personally liable under Title VII.[56]

Back Pay

Section 706(g) states that the court may award back pay to a successful plaintiff. Back-pay orders spelled out by that section have some limitations, however. Section 706(g) provides that no back-pay order shall extend to a period prior to two years before the date of the filing of a complaint

---

[54]317 F.3d 646 (6th Cir. 2003)(*en banc*).

[55]*Perez v. Globe Airport Security Services*, 253 F.3d 1280 (11th Cir. 2001); *Circuit City Stores, Inc. v. Adams*, 279 F.3d 889 (9th Cir. 2002), *cert. denied*, 535 U.S. 1112 (2002); and *Ingle v. Circuit City Stores, Inc.*, 328 F.3d 1165 (9th Cir. 2003).

[56]*Tomka v. The Seiler Corp.*, 66 F.3d 1295 (2d Cir. 1995).

with the EEOC. It also provides that "Interim earnings or amounts earnable with reasonable diligence by the person or persons discriminated against shall operate to reduce the back pay otherwise allowable." That section imposes a duty to mitigate damages upon the plaintiff.

Although Section 706(g) states that a court may award back pay, it does not require that such an award always be made. What principles should guide the court on the issue of whether to award back pay?

According to the Supreme Court in *Albemarle Paper Co. v. Moody*,[57] Title VII is remedial in nature and is intended to "make whole" victims of discrimination. Therefore, a successful plaintiff should be awarded back pay as a matter of course. Back pay should be denied only in exceptional circumstances, such as when it would frustrate the purpose of Title VII.

In *Ford Motor Co. v. EEOC*,[58] the Supreme Court held that an employer's back-pay liability may be limited to the period prior to the date of an unconditional offer of a job to the plaintiff, even though the offer did not include seniority retroactive to the date of the alleged discrimination. The plaintiff's rejection of the offer, in the absence of special circumstances, would end the accrual of back-pay liability of the employer.

In addition, Section 706(g)(2)(B), added by the 1991 amendments to Title VII, limits an employer's liability in mixed-motive cases, provided that the employer can demonstrate that it would have reached the same decision even without consideration of the illegal factor. In these situations, the employer is subject to the court's injunctive or declaratory remedies and is liable for legal fees but is not liable for back pay or other damages, nor is the employer required to hire or reinstate the complainant.

Front Pay

Front Pay
Monetary damages awarded to a plaintiff instead of reinstatement or hiring.

In some cases, if a hiring or reinstatement order may not be appropriate or if there is excessive animosity between the parties, the court may award the plaintiff ***front pay***—monetary damages in lieu of reinstatement or hiring. The question of whether front pay is appropriate is a question for the judge, as is the determination of the amount of front pay. The amount of front pay depends upon the circumstances of each case. The court will consider factors such as the employability of the plaintiff and the likely duration of the employment. Any front pay awarded to the plaintiff by the court is separate from any compensatory and punitive damages awarded. The front-pay award is not subject to the statutory limits (discussed below) placed on the compensatory and punitive damages awards according to the Supreme Court decision in *Pollard v. E. I. du Pont de Nemours & Co.*[59]

Compensatory and Punitive Damages

The right to recover compensatory and punitive damages for intentional violations of Title VII was created by the Civil Rights Act of 1991, which amended Title VII. The 1991 act allows claims for compensatory and punitive damages, in addition to any remedies recoverable under Section 706(g) of Title VII, to be brought under 42 U.S.C. Section 1981, as amended by the 1991 act. Section 1981 (discussed in detail in Chapter 11) allows recovery of damages for

---

[57]422 U.S. 405 (1975).

[58]456 U.S. 923 (1982).

[59]532 U.S. 843 (2001).

intentional race discrimination. The Civil Rights Act of 1991 added a section to 42 U.S.C. Section 1981 that allows damages suits for intentional discrimination in violation of Title VII, for which the plaintiff could not recover under Section 1981 (that is, discrimination because of gender, religion, or national origin).

If the plaintiff can demonstrate that a private sector defendant (not a governmental unit, agency, or other public sector entity) has engaged "in a discriminatory practice or discriminatory practices with malice or with reckless indifference to the federally protected rights of an aggrieved individual," the plaintiff can recover compensatory and punitive damages. Punitive damages are not recoverable against public sector defendants. The compensatory and punitive damages are separate from, and in addition to, any back pay, interest, front pay, legal fees, or other remedies recovered under Section 706(g) of Title VII.

The compensatory and punitive damages recoverable under the amended Section 1981 are subject to statutory limits, depending on the number of employees of the defendant/employer:

- For employers with more than fourteen but fewer than 101 employees, the damages recoverable are limited to $50,000
- For defendants with more than 100 but fewer than 201 employees, the limit is $100,000
- For more than 200 but fewer than 501 employees, it is $200,000
- For employers with more than 500 employees, the limit is $300,000

The number of people employed by a defendant/employer is determined by considering the number employed in each week of twenty or more calendar weeks in the current or preceding year.

Plaintiffs bringing a claim for damages under the amended Section 1981 have the right to a jury trial. As noted, punitive and compensatory damages are not recoverable against a public sector employer; punitive and compensatory damages are only recoverable for intentional discrimination and not for claims of disparate impact discrimination. Punitive and compensatory damages under the amended Section 1981 are also recoverable for intentional violations of the Americans with Disabilities Act of 1990 (discussed in Chapter 10.)

When an employee has convinced the court that there was hostile environment harassment (based on race, sex, religion, or national origin) in violation of Title VII, the employer may be held liable for damages for all the acts that contributed to the hostile environment, even though some of those acts may have occurred more than 300 days (or 180 days, if appropriate) prior to the date on which the employee filed the complaint according to *National Railroad Passenger Corp. v. Morgan.*[60]

The federal courts of appeals have split on the question of whether a plaintiff who prevails under state law in a state agency and state court can file suit in federal court under Title VII to recover remedies that were not available under state law. In *Nestor v. Pratt & Whitney,*[61] the U.S. Court of Appeals for the Second Circuit allowed a plaintiff alleging sex discrimination to bring a suit under Title VII to recover compensatory and punitive damages. The plaintiff had been awarded back pay under Connecticut legislation, which did not provide for compensatory and punitive damages. The U.S. Court of Appeals for the Eighth Circuit, in *Jones v. American*

[60]536 U.S. 101 (2002).

[61]466 F.3d 65 (2d Cir. 2006).

State Bank,[62] and the U.S. Court of Appeals for the Seventh Circuit, in *Patzer v. Board of Regents*,[63] have also allowed such suits. However, the U.S. Court of Appeals for the Fourth Circuit has held a plaintiff who is successful before a state administrative agency may not file suit under Title VII to recover remedies that were not available under the state law.[64]

Limitations on Remedies for Mixed-Motive Discrimination

In cases involving mixed-motive discrimination claims under Section 703(m) of Title VII [see the discussion of the *Hopkins* case and Section 703(m) in Chapter 6], Section 706(g)(2) (B) provides that an employer will not be liable for damages when the employer can demonstrate that it would have reached the same decision even without consideration of the illegal factor. Where the employer has met the "same decision" test, the court will only issue a declaration or injunction and award the plaintiff legal fees. The plaintiff is not entitled to be hired, reinstated, or receive back pay, front pay, or compensatory and punitive damages.

Employer Liability for Punitive Damages Under Title VII

Prior to being amended in 1991, Title VII did not provide for the recovery of punitive or compensatory damages. Successful plaintiffs were limited to recovering wages, benefits, and legal fees. The Civil Rights Act of 1991 amended Title VII to allow recovery of punitive damages in cases in which the employer has engaged in intentional discrimination and has done so "with malice or with reckless indifference to the federally protected rights of an aggrieved individual." Under what circumstances should employers be held liable for punitive damages under Title VII? Are there any defenses that employers may raise to avoid liability for punitive damages? In *Kolstad v. American Dental Association*,[65] the Supreme Court answered those questions:

> The employer must act with "malice or with reckless indifference to [the plaintiff's] federally protected rights." The terms "malice" or "reckless indifference" pertain to the employer's knowledge that it may be acting in violation of federal law, not its awareness that it is engaging in discrimination.... An employer must at least discriminate in the face of a perceived risk that its actions will violate federal law to be liable in punitive damages. There will be circumstances where intentional discrimination does not give rise to punitive damages liability under this standard. In some instances, the employer may simply be unaware of the relevant federal prohibition. There will be cases, moreover, in which the employer discriminates with the distinct belief that its discrimination is lawful. The underlying theory of discrimination may be novel or otherwise poorly recognized, or an employer may reasonably believe that its discrimination satisfies a bona fide occupational qualification defense or other statutory exception to liability.... Holding employers liable for punitive damages when they engage in good faith efforts to comply with Title VII, however, is in some tension with the very principles underlying common law limitations on vicarious liability for punitive damages—that it is "improper ordinarily to award punitive damages against one who himself is personally innocent and therefore liable only vicariously." Where an employer has undertaken such good faith efforts at Title VII compliance, it "demonstrat[es] that it never acted in reckless disregard of federally protected rights."

---

[62] 857 F.2d 494 (8th Cir. 1988).

[63] 763 F.2d 851 (7th Cir. 1985).

[64] *Chris v. Tenet*, 221 F.3d 648 (4th Cir. 2000).

[65] 527 U.S. 526 (1999).

> … We agree that, in the punitive damages context, an employer may not be vicariously liable for the discriminatory employment decisions of managerial agents where these decisions are contrary to the employer's "good-faith efforts to comply with Title VII."

Remedial Seniority

The *Teamsters* case, discussed in Chapter 6, held that a bona fide seniority system is protected by Section 703(h), even when it perpetuates the effects of prior discrimination. If the court is prevented from restructuring the bona fide seniority system, how can the court remedy the prior discrimination suffered by the plaintiffs? In *Franks v. Bowman Transportation Co.*,[66] the Supreme Court held that remedial seniority may be awarded to the victims of prior discrimination to overcome the effects of discrimination perpetuated by the bona fide seniority system. The Court stated that "the denial of seniority relief to victims of illegal … discrimination in hiring is permissible 'only for reasons which, if applied generally, would not frustrate the central statutory purposes of eradicating discrimination … and making persons whole for injuries suffered through past discrimination….'"

The granting of remedial seniority may be necessary to place the victims of discrimination in the position they would have been in had no illegal discrimination occurred.

Legal Fees

Section 706(k) provides that the court, in its discretion, may award "reasonable attorney's fees" under Title VII. The section also states that the United States or the EEOC may not recover legal fees if they prevail, but shall be liable for costs "the same as a private person" if they do not prevail.

In *New York Gaslight Club v. Carey*,[67] the Supreme Court held that an award of attorney's fees under Section 706(k) can include fees for the legal proceedings before the state or local agency when the complainant is required to file with that agency by Section 706(c).

Section 706(k) does not require that attorney's fees be awarded to a prevailing party; the award is at the court's discretion. In *Christianburg Garment Co. v. EEOC*,[68] the Supreme Court held that a successful plaintiff should generally be awarded legal fees except in special circumstances. A prevailing defendant should be awarded legal fees only when the court determines that the plaintiff's case was frivolous, unreasonable, vexatious, or meritless. A case is meritless, according to the Court, not simply because the plaintiff lost, but where the plaintiff's case was "groundless or without foundation." Why should prevailing defendants be treated differently than prevailing plaintiffs under Title VII?

Class Actions

The rules of procedure for the federal courts allow an individual plaintiff to sue on behalf of a whole class of individuals allegedly suffering the same harm. Rule 23 of the Federal Rules of Civil Procedure allows such suits, known as *class actions*, when several conditions are met. First, the number of members of the class is so numerous that it would be "impracticable" to

---

[66] 424 U.S. 747 (1976).

[67] 447 U.S. 54 (1980).

[68] 434 U.S. 412 (1978).

have them join the suit individually. Second, there must be issues of fact or law common to the claims of all members. Third, the claims of the individual seeking to represent the entire class must be typical of the claims of the members of the class. Finally, the individual representative must fairly and adequately protect the interests of the class.

When these conditions are met, the court may certify the suit as a class-action suit on behalf of all members of the class. Individuals challenging employment discrimination under Title VII may sue on behalf of all individuals affected by the alleged discrimination by complying with the requirements of Rule 23. In *General Telephone Co. of the Southwest v. Falcon,*[69] the Supreme Court held that an employee alleging that he was denied promotion due to national origin discrimination is not a proper representative of the class of individuals denied hiring by the employer due to discrimination. The plaintiff had not suffered the same injuries allegedly suffered by the class members.

The EEOC need not seek certification as a class representative under Rule 23 to seek classwide remedies under Title VII according to the Supreme Court decision in *General Telephone v. EEOC.*[70] The EEOC, said the Court, acts to vindicate public policy and not just to protect personal interests.

Remedies in Class Actions

Classwide remedies are appropriate under Title VII according to the Supreme Court's holding in *Franks v. Bowman Transportation Co.*,[71] which authorized such classwide "make whole" orders. In *Local 28, Sheet Metal Workers v. EEOC* (see Chapter 6), the Supreme Court upheld court-ordered affirmative action to remedy prior employment discrimination. The Court specifically said affirmative relief may be available to minority group members who were not personally victimized by the employer's prior discrimination. Additionally, in *Local 93, Int'l Ass'n. of Firefighters v. Cleveland* (see Chapter 11), the Supreme Court approved a consent decree that imposed affirmative action to remedy prior discrimination, again upholding the right of nonvictims to benefit from the affirmative remedy.

Public Employees Under Title VII

Title VII was amended in 1972 to cover the employees of state and local employers. These employees are subject to the same procedural requirements as private employees. However, Section 706(f)(1) authorizes the U.S. Attorney General, rather than the EEOC, to file suit under Title VII against a state or local public employer.

Most federal employees are covered by Title VII but are subject to different procedural requirements. Section 701(b) excludes the United States, wholly owned federal government corporations, and any department or agency of the District of Columbia subject to civil service regulations from the definition of "employer" under Title VII. Section 717 of the act does provide, however, that "All personnel actions affecting employees or applicants for employment ... in positions under the federal civil service, the D.C. Civil Service and the U.S. Postal Service ... shall be made free from any discrimination based on race, color, religion, sex or national origin."

---

[69]457 U.S. 147 (1982).

[70]446 U.S. 318 (1980).

[71]424 U.S. 747 (1976).

Section 717 also designated the federal Civil Service Commission as the agency having jurisdiction over complaints of discrimination by federal employees. However, that authority was transferred to the EEOC under Reorganization Plan No. 1 of 1978. The EEOC adopted procedural regulations regarding Title VII complaints by federal employees. A federal employee alleging employment discrimination must first consult with an Equal Employment Opportunity (EEO) counselor within the employee's own agency. If the employee is not satisfied with the counselor's resolution of the complaint, the employee can file a formal complaint with the agency's designated EEO official. The EEO official, after investigating and holding a hearing, renders a decision. That decision can be appealed to the head of the agency. If the employee is not satisfied with that decision, he or she can either seek judicial review of it or file an appeal with the EEOC. If the employee chooses to file with the EEOC, the complaint is subject to the general EEOC procedures. The employee has ninety days from receiving notice of the EEOC taking final action on the complaint to file suit. The employee may file suit, as well, when the EEOC has not made a decision on the complaint after 180 days from its filing with the EEOC.

Employees of Congress and the White House

The Civil Rights Act of 1991 extended the coverage of Title VII to employees of Congress. Employees of the following offices are subject to Title VII through the Congressional Accountability Act of 1995:

- House of Representatives
- Senate
- Capitol Guide Service
- Capitol Police
- Congressional Budget Office
- Office of the Architect of the Capitol
- Office of the Attending Physician
- Office of Technology Assessment

Those employees can file complaints of illegal discrimination with the Office of Compliance, created by the act, within 180 days of the alleged violation. The Office of Compliance initially attempts to resolve the complaint through counseling and mediation. If the complaint is still unresolved after the counseling and mediation period, the employee may either seek administrative resolution of the complaint through the Office of Compliance or file suit in federal court. Employees of the executive office of the president, the executive residence at the White House, and the official residence of the vice president are subject to Title VII through the Presidential and Executive Office Accountability Act. Complaints by those employees of violations of Title VII are subject to an initial counseling and mediation period. The employee may then choose to pursue the complaint with the EEOC or file suit in federal court.

CHAPTER REVIEW

» Key Terms

English-only rules	« 212	*prima facie case*	« 222	*front pay*	« 233
Lilly Ledbetter Fair Pay Act	« 218	*after-acquired evidence*	« 228		

» Summary

- The protection that Title VII provides for employees from religious discrimination is not absolute. Religion may be a BFOQ, and the employer is not required to accommodate an employee's religious beliefs or practices if doing so would impose undue hardship on the employer, as defined in the *Hardison* case. Religious corporations and religiously affiliated educational institutions may give preference in employment to members of their particular religion according to Section 702(a) of Title VII and the *Amos* decision. Public sector employers are also subject to the First Amendment of the U.S. Constitution, which may further restrict their dealings with employees' religious beliefs and practices.
- Title VII prohibits employment discrimination based on national origin, although national origin may be used as a BFOQ when necessary for safe and efficient performance of the particular job. Employer English-only rules may also present problems under Title VII, unless supported by specific business justification. Title VII does not prohibit discrimination based on citizenship, but the Immigration Reform and Control Act of 1986 prohibits employment discrimination based on citizenship or national origin.
- The enforcement procedures under Title VII require that individuals claiming illegal discrimination go first to the appropriate state or local agency and then file their complaint with the Equal Employment Opportunity Commission (EEOC) after sixty days or the termination of proceedings at the state or local level, whichever comes first. The EEOC may decide to file suit on the complaint, and if it chooses not to sue, the individual may do so. Title VII suits can be brought in either federal or state courts. The plaintiff in a suit under Title VII must establish a prima facie case of discrimination; the defendant must then offer some legitimate explanation for the apparently discriminatory action to rebut the plaintiff's claims. If the defendant does offer a legitimate explanation for the challenged conduct, the plaintiff still has the opportunity to demonstrate that the employer's explanation was a pretext for illegal discrimination. Successful plaintiffs under Title VII may get an order of reinstatement, may recover back pay and benefits, legal fees, and in cases of intentional discrimination, can recover compensatory and punitive damages up to the appropriate statutory limit. Prevailing defendants may recover legal fees if the plaintiff's case was frivolous, groundless, or brought in bad faith. Plaintiffs claiming discrimination may be required to take their cases to arbitration rather than sue in court if they have knowingly and voluntarily agreed to arbitrate such complaints.

» Problems

Questions

1. How does Title VII's prohibition of religious discrimination differ from the prohibition of discrimination based on race or color? Explain your answer.
2. What is meant by national origin under Title VII? Does Title VII prohibit discrimination based on ancestry? Explain.
3. What is the effect of a state court's dismissal of a discrimination complaint on the complainant's right to file suit in federal court? What is the effect of a state EEO agency dismissal of a discrimination complaint on the right of the complainant to file suit in federal court?
4. What remedies are available to a successful plaintiff under Title VII? When are punitive damages recoverable?
5. Must a complainant always file a complaint of illegal discrimination with the relevant state or local agency before filing a complaint with the EEOC? Explain.

Case Problems

6. Morgan was an untenured faculty member at Ivy University. In February 1995, he was informed that the Faculty Tenure Committee recommended that he not be offered a tenured position with the university. Failure to achieve tenure requires that the faculty member seek employment elsewhere. The university offers such faculty members a one-year contract following denial of tenure. At the expiration of the one-year contract, the faculty member's employment is terminated.

   Morgan appealed to the tenure committee for reconsideration. The committee granted him a one-year extension for reconsideration. In February 1996, the committee denied Morgan tenure at Ivy University. The university board of trustees affirmed the committee's decision. Morgan was informed of the trustees' decision and offered a one-year contract on June 26, 1996.

   Morgan accepted the one-year contract, which would expire on June 30, 1997. On June 1, 1997, Morgan filed charges with the EEOC alleging race and sex discrimination by Ivy University in denying him tenure. The one-year contract expired on June 30, 1997, and Morgan's employment was terminated.

   Assuming no state or local EEOC agency is involved, is Morgan's complaint validly filed with the EEOC? What employment practice is he challenging? When did it occur? See *Delaware State College v. Ricks* [449 U.S. 250 (1980)].
7. Cohen, a college graduate with a degree in journalism, applied for a position with *The Christian Science Monitor*, a daily newspaper published by the Christian Science Publishing Society, a branch of the Christian Science Church. The church board of directors elects the editors and managers of the *Monitor* and is responsible for the editorial content of the *Monitor.* The church subsidizes the *Monitor*, which otherwise would run at a significant loss. The application for employment at the *Monitor* is the same one used for general positions with the church. It contains many questions relating to membership in the Christian Science Church and to its religious affiliation.

   Cohen, who is not a member of the Christian Science Church, was rejected for employment with the *Monitor.* He filed a complaint with the EEOC alleging that his application was not given full consideration by the *Monitor* because he is not a member of the Christian Science Church. The *Monitor* claimed that it can apply a test of religious qualifications to its employment practices.

   Is the *Monitor* in violation of Title VII? Explain your answer. See *Feldstein v. Christian Science Monitor* [555 F.Supp. 974 (D.C. Mass. 1983)].
8. Dewhurst was a female flight attendant with Sub-Central Airlines. Sub-Central's employment policies prohibited female attendants from being married, but married male employees were employed by Sub-Central. Dewhurst was married on June 15, 1980. She was discharged by Sub-Central the next day.

Sub-Central, under pressure from the EEOC, eliminated the "no-married females" rule in March 1982.

Dewhurst was rehired by Sub-Central on February 1, 1983. Sub-Central refused to recognize her seniority for her past employment with Sub-Central as the company's policy is to refuse to recognize prior service for all former employees who are rehired. Dewhurst filed a complaint with the EEOC on March 1, 1983, alleging that Sub-Central's refusal to credit her with prior seniority violated Title VII.

Is her complaint validly filed with EEOC? See *United Airlines v. Evans* [431 U.S. 553 (1977)].

9. Smith, Washington, and Bailey are African-American bricklayers. They had applied for work with Constructo Co., a brick and masonry contractor. Constructo refused their applications for the reason that company policy is to hire only bricklayers referred by Constructo employees. The three filed charges with the EEOC, which decided not to file suit against Constructo. The bricklayers then filed suit in federal court against Constructo, alleging race discrimination in hiring.

   At the trial, the three presented evidence of their rejection by Constructo. Constructo denied any racial discrimination in hiring and introduced evidence showing that African Americans make up 13 percent of its work force. Only 5.7 percent of all certified bricklayers in the greater metropolitan area are African American.

   Has Constructo met its burden under Title VII? Have the three African Americans met their burden under Title VII? See *Furnco Construction Co. v. Waters* [438 U.S. 567 (1978)].

10. Walker is a clerk with the U.S. Postal Service. The Postal Service distributes the materials for the draft registration required of young men. Walker, although not a formal member of the Society of Friends (known as Quakers), had a long history of involvement with the Quakers. She therefore refused to distribute draft registration materials when she was working. The Postal Service fired her.

    Is Walker's refusal to distribute the draft registration materials protected by Title VII? Explain your answer. See *McGinnis v. U.S. Postal Service* [512 F.Supp. 517 (U.S. Dist. Ct., N.D. Cal. 1980)].

11. Kim Cloutier was employed by Costco Corp. When she was hired, she had several tattoos and wore multiple earrings. When she was transferred to Costco's deli department, she was informed that Costco's dress code prohibited food handlers, including deli workers, from wearing any jewelry. Her supervisor instructed her to remove her earrings. Cloutier refused to do so, and requested a transfer to a cashier position. She was transferred and worked as a cashier for several years. During her time as a cashier, she underwent several facial and eyebrow piercings, and wore various types of facial jewelry. In 2001, Costco revised its dress code to prohibit all facial jewelry except earrings. Cloutier continued to wear her facial jewelry for several months. In June, 2001, Costco began enforcing its ban on facial jewelry. Cloutier's supervisor informed her that she must remove her facial jewelry and eyebrow piercing. Cloutier returned to work the next day wearing the facial jewelry and eyebrow piercing, and when confronted by her supervisor, she insisted that she was a member of the Church of Body Modification [see http://www.uscobm.com] and wearing the facial jewelry was part of her religion. Costco then offered to let her wear plastic retainers (to keep her piercings open) or to cover the eyebrow piercing with a band-aid. Cloutier rejected that offer, stating that her beliefs required her to display all of her facial piercings at all times. She maintained that the only acceptable accommodation would be to excuse her from Costco's dress code and allow her to wear facial jewelry while at work. Costco replied that such an accommodation would interfere with its ability to maintain a professional appearance and would thus create an undue hardship on Costco's business. Cloutier filed a complaint with the EEOC, alleging religious discrimination in violation of Title VII. After receiving a right to sue letter from the EEOC, Cloutier filed suit against Costco under Title VII. How should the court rule on her suit? Explain your answer. See *Cloutier v. Costco Wholesale Corp.* [390 F.3d 126 (1st Cir. 2004)].

12. Elizabeth Westman was employed by Valley Technologies as an engineering technician. On June 15, 1997, she was terminated after being informed by her supervisor that the company was

experiencing financial difficulties and could no longer afford to employ her. Westman subsequently learned, on May 15, 1998, that she was terminated so that her supervisor could hire a less qualified male technician in her place. Upon learning of the real reason for her discharge, Westman immediately filed a complaint with the EEOC. The employer argued that her complaint should be dismissed because it was not filed within the time limit required under Title VII.

Will her complaint be dismissed or was it properly filed? Explain your answer. See *Reeb v. Economic Opportunity Atlanta, Inc.* [516 F.2d 924 (5th Cir. 1975)].

13. S. A. Bouzoukis was employed as a member of the faculty of Enormous State University. She was denied tenure and offered a one-year terminal contract. Bouzoukis alleged that she was denied tenure because of gender discrimination, and she retained an attorney to pursue her claim against the university. Her attorney met with university officials to discuss the complaint, and the university requested that Bouzoukis allow the university time to conduct an investigation into her complaint. The university officials stated that if Bouzoukis agreed to delay filing her complaint with the EEOC, they would not raise the issue of time limits as a defense if the complaint could not be settled through negotiations. The university's investigation and subsequent negotiations dragged on for ten months and no settlement was reached. Bouzoukis then filed the complaint with the EEOC. She later filed suit in federal court. The university argued in court that the suit should be dismissed because the complaint was not filed with the EEOC within 300 days of the alleged violation.

    How should the court rule on the time limit issue? Explain your answer. See *Leake v. University of Cincinnati* [605 F.2d 255 (6th Cir. 1979)].

14. Bernardo Huerta, an employee of the Adams Corp., was transferred to a position that prevented him from being eligible for overtime work. Huerta filed a complaint with the EEOC alleging that he had been discriminated against because of his national origin. After negotiations subsequent to the filing of the complaint, Huerta and the Adams Corp. reached a settlement agreement on his complaint. A year later, Huerta claimed that Adams had broken the settlement agreement, and he filed suit in federal court. The court granted judgment for Huerta, and he asked the court to award him legal fees. Adams Corp. argued that the action to enforce the settlement agreement was not the same as an action under Title VII. Therefore, Huerta should not be awarded legal fees as a prevailing party under Title VII. Should the court award Huerta legal fees? Explain your answer. See *Robles v. United States* [54 Emp. Prac. Dec. (CCH) P 40, 193 (D.D.C. 1990)].

15. Marjorie Reiley Maguire was a professor in the theology department at Marquette University, a Roman Catholic institution. Approximately half of the twenty-seven members of the department were Jesuits, and only one other member was female at the time Maguire came up for tenure. The school denied her tenure because of her pro-choice view on the abortion issue—that is, because she favored personal choice rather than the Church's strict ban on abortions.

    Was she a victim of gender discrimination? See *Maguire v. Marquette University* [814 RRF. 2d 1213 (7th Cir. 1987)].

Hypothetical Scenarios

16. Covert Communications provides interpreters and linguistic analysts to federal law enforcement agencies on a contract basis. Much of the work performed for its government clients by Covert involves national security matters, and the clients require that the Covert employees must have government security clearances. Because of the security clearance requirement, Covert will not hire applicants who are not U.S. citizens. Farik Al Quran speaks Arabic and Pashto fluently, but is refused a job with Covert because he is not a U.S. citizen. Does Covert's refusal to hire Al Quran violate Title VII? Explain.

17. Raji Gobendar is a practicing Sikh, an Asian religion that requires adult males to wear a turban on their head and to grow beards. He is hired by Security Systems as a private security guard. Security Systems requires its security guards to wear a uniform, including a hat, and company policy prohibits facial

hair and beards. Gobendar is told that he must shave his beard and must wear the uniform hat rather than his turban when he is on duty. Security Systems refuses to allow any exceptions to its uniform and facial hair policies and violations of the policies could result in termination. Must Security Systems grant an exception to its policies because of Gobendar's religious beliefs? Explain.

18. Your boss, the HR manager for Springfield Enterprises, asks you to research and prepare a report on whether the company should require employees to sign an agreement to arbitrate all employment disputes that might arise. Would such a requirement be acceptable under Title VII? How would the arbitration requirement benefit the employer? What would be the effect of the requirement on the employees?

19. Wang's Mandarin Palace is a Chinese restaurant in Rochester, New York. The restaurant only hires persons of Chinese ancestry as employees because the owner believes that customers would be uncomfortable with employees who are not of Chinese origin. Does the restaurant's hiring policy qualify as a BFOQ under Title VII? Explain.

20. Thrivent Financial for Lutherans is a fraternal benefit society that provides financial services and offers service and educational programs to members of the Lutheran Church. Harris is a CPA who applies for a job with Thrivent Financial. Thrivent Financial refuses to hire Harris because he is a member of the Southern Baptist Church, and Thrivent Financial only hires Lutherans. Which, if any, provisions of Title VII can Thrivent Financial use to justify its hiring policy? Explain.

Discrimination Based on Age

Title VII of the Civil Rights Act, which was discussed in the preceding chapters, prohibits employment discrimination based on race, color, religion, gender, or national origin. In addition to Title VII, other federal legislation deals with employment discrimination because of other factors. This chapter covers the Age Discrimination in Employment Act, which prohibits employment discrimination based on age.

The Age Discrimination in Employment Act

Discrimination in terms or conditions of employment because of age is prohibited by the Age Discrimination in Employment Act of 1967 (ADEA). The act's prohibitions, however, are limited to age discrimination against employees aged forty and older. It was intended to protect older workers who were more likely to be subjected to age discrimination in employment. (Although the ADEA's protection is limited to older workers, state equal employment opportunity laws may provide greater protection against age discrimination. The New York Human Rights Law, for example, prohibits age discrimination in employment against persons eighteen and older.)

Coverage

The ADEA applies to employers, labor unions, and employment agencies. Employers involved in an industry affecting commerce, with twenty or more employees, are covered by the act. U.S. firms that employ American workers in a foreign country are subject to the ADEA. Labor unions are covered if they operate a hiring hall or if they have twenty-five or more members and represent the employees of an employer covered by the act.

The definition of employer under the ADEA includes state and local governments; the U.S. Supreme Court upheld the inclusion of state and local governments under the ADEA in

EEOC v. Wyoming.[1] However, in the case of *Kimel v. Florida Board of Regents,*[2] decided in January 2000, the Supreme Court held that the Eleventh Amendment of the U.S. Constitution provides state governments with immunity from suits by private individuals under the ADEA.

Concept *Summary* » 9.1

The Age Discrimination in Employment Act

- The ADEA prohibits discrimination in employment based on age against employees aged forty or older
- ADEA coverage:
  - Employers with twenty or more employees
  - Labor unions operating a hiring hall or with twenty-five or more members
  - Employment agencies
  - Federal government employees

Provisions

The ADEA prohibits the refusal or failure to hire, the discharge, or any discrimination in compensation, terms, conditions, or privileges of employment because of an individual's age (forty and older). The act applies to employers, labor unions, and employment agencies. The main effect of the act is to prohibit the mandatory retirement of employees. The act does not affect voluntary retirement by employees. It does provide for some limited exceptions and recognizes that age may be a bona fide occupational qualification (BFOQ).

A plaintiff alleging a violation of the ADEA must establish a prima facie case that the employer has discriminated against the employee because of age. The plaintiff must demonstrate that age was " the determining factor" in the employer's action. In *Gross v. FBL Financial Services, Inc.*,[3] the Supreme Court held that the language of the ADEA does not allow for "mixed motive" cases–rather than showing that age was "a determining factor," the plaintiff must show that age was the "but-for cause" of the employer's action. The Court in *Gross* specifically rejected the "mixed motive" approach used under Title VII (see Chapter 6).

The process for establishing a claim under the ADEA is as follows: the plaintiff must establish a prima facie case of age discrimination; the employer defendant must then offer a legitimate justification for the challenged action; and if the defendant offers such a justification, the plaintiff can still show that the offered justification is a pretext for age discrimination.

Examples of violations of the ADEA include:

- The mandatory retirement of workers over age fifty-five while allowing workers under fifty-five to transfer to another plant location or
- The denial of a promotion to a qualified worker because the employee is over fifty

---

[1]460 U.S. 226 (1983).

[2]528 U.S. 62 (2000).

[3]129 S.Ct. 2343 (2009).

While discrimination against older workers is prohibited by the ADEA, according to *General Dynamics Land Systems, Inc. v. Cline*,[4] an employer that eliminated health insurance for workers under fifty but continued health insurance for the employees over fifty was held not to have violated the ADEA. What must a plaintiff alleging that he was fired because of his age show to establish a prima facie case of age discrimination? Must the employee demonstrate that the employer replaced him with a person under forty (that is, someone not protected by the ADEA). The U.S. Supreme Court addressed that question in the following case.

case 9.1 »

O'Connor v. Consolidated Coin Caterers Corp.

517 U.S. 308 (1996)

Facts: James O'Connor was employed by Consolidated Coin Caterers Corporation and was fired at age fifty-six. He filed suit under the ADEA, alleging that he was fired because of his age. The trial court granted the employer's motion for summary judgment, and O'Connor appealed. The U.S. Court of Appeals for the Fourth Circuit held that in order to establish a prima facie case, a plaintiff must prove that: (1) he was in the age group protected by the ADEA (aged forty or older); (2) he was discharged or demoted; (3) at the time of his discharge or demotion, he was performing his job at a level that met his employer's legitimate expectations; and (4) following his discharge or demotion, he was replaced by someone, of comparable qualifications outside the ADEA's protection (someone under forty). Because O'Connor was replaced by a person who was forty years old, the court of appeals concluded that the last element of the prima facie case had not been established, and affirmed the trial court's grant of summary judgment. O'Connor then appealed to the U.S. Supreme Court.

Issue: Must an employee demonstrate that he was replaced by someone under the age of forty in order to establish a prima facie case of age discrimination in violation of the ADEA?

Decision: The courts have applied the basic evidentiary framework set forth in *McDonnell Douglas* to age discrimination claims under the ADEA. There must be a logical connection between each element of the prima facie case and the illegal discrimination for which it establishes a legally mandatory, rebuttable presumption. The ADEA prohibits discrimination because of an individual's age. The language of the ADEA does not ban discrimination against employees because they are aged forty or older; it bans discrimination against employees because of their age, but limits the protected class to those employees who are forty or older. The fact that the plaintiff has lost out to another person in the protected class (another person over forty) is thus irrelevant, as long as the plaintiff has lost out because of his age. For example, there can be no greater inference of age discrimination (as opposed to discrimination directed at a person forty or over) when a forty-year-old is replaced by a thirty-nine-year-old than when a fifty-six-year-old is replaced by a forty-year-old. The fact that an ADEA plaintiff was replaced by someone outside the protected class lacks probative value and therefore is not a proper element of the prima facie case. Rather than requiring a plaintiff to show that he was replaced by someone under forty, the plaintiff must provide evidence adequate enough to establish a presumption that an employment decision was based on age. Because the ADEA prohibits discrimination on the basis of age, the fact that a replacement is substantially younger than the plaintiff is a far more reliable indicator of age discrimination than is the fact that the plaintiff was replaced by someone outside the class protected by the ADEA (someone under forty).

In this case, the Supreme Court reversed the judgment of the Fourth Circuit. A plaintiff under the ADEA does not have to show that he was replaced by someone under forty.

«

[4]540 U.S. 581 (2004).

The WORKING Law

Age Discrimination Claims Increase

The Equal Employment Opportunity Commission reported that age discrimination complaints increased by 29 percent over last year. The EEOC received 24,582 claims in its fiscal year that ended September 30, 2008. The increase suggests that older workers may have been disproportionately affected by the economic downturn, with employers taking the opportunity to shed older workers, who are more likely to have higher salaries than younger workers. Older workers are also likely to have difficulty finding a job in a difficult job market—and may have trouble adjusting to a digital job search process vastly different from what they had experienced before. Employers do not necessarily view years of experience as an asset, and may feel that older workers are "overqualified," while viewing younger workers as being more "flexible." Employers may also assume that the older workers applying for jobs paying less than their previous positions paid may be more likely to leave if and when the economy improves.

Statistics from the Bureau of Labor Statistics indicate that the unemployment rate for those fifty-five and older rose to 6.2 percent in April 2009, up from 3.3 percent a year earlier.

Sources: Jennifer Levitz, "More Workers Cite Age Bias After Layoffs," *The Wall Street Journal Abstracts*, March 11, 2009; "In Brief," *New York Newsday*, March 12, 2009; Dana Mattioli, "With Jobs Scarce, Age Becomes an Issue," *The Wall Street Journal*, May 19, 2009.

Defenses

When the plaintiff has established a prima facie case of age discrimination, the defendant must articulate some legitimate justification for the challenged action. The ADEA provides some specific exemptions and defenses on which the defendant may rely. The following are not violations:

- actions pursuant to a bona fide seniority system, retirement, pension or benefit system,
- for good cause, or
- for a "reasonable factor other than age."

The act also recognizes that age may be a BFOQ, and permits the mandatory retirement of certain executive employees at age sixty-five.

The ADEA was amended in 1990 to provide an additional defense for employers: Where the employer employs American workers in a foreign country and compliance with the ADEA would cause the employer to violate foreign law, the employer is excused from complying with the ADEA. In *Mahoney v. RFE/RL Inc.*,[5] the employer's compliance with German law requiring employees to enforce a labor contract setting retirement age at sixty-five was held to be a defense under the foreign law exception of the ADEA.

[5]47 F.3d 447 (D.C. Cir. 1995).

Bona Fide Seniority or Benefit Plan

The ADEA allows an employer to observe the terms of a bona fide seniority system or employee benefit plan, such as a retirement or pension plan, as long as the plan or system is not "subterfuge to evade the purpose of this Act." The ADEA provides, however, that no seniority system or benefit plan "shall require or permit the involuntary retirement of any individual."

In *Public Employees' Retirement System of Ohio v. Betts,*[6] the Supreme Court held that the ADEA exception protected any age-based decisions taken pursuant to a bona fide benefit plan as long as the plan did not require mandatory retirement. In response to that decision, Congress passed the Older Workers Benefit Protection Act, which became law in October 1990. The law amended the ADEA to require that any differential treatment of older employees under benefit plans must be "cost-justified." That is, the employer must demonstrate that the reduction in benefits is only to the extent required to achieve approximate cost equivalence in providing benefits to older and younger employees. General claims that the cost of insuring individuals increases with age are not sufficient; the employer must show that the specific level of reductions for older workers in a particular benefit program is no greater than necessary to compensate for the higher cost of providing such benefits for older workers.

Reasonable Factor Other Than Age

The ADEA allows employers to differentiate between employees when the differentiation is based on a reasonable factor other than age. For example, an employer may use a productivity-based pay system, even if older employees earn less than younger employees because they do not produce as much as younger employees. The basis for determining pay would be the employees' production, not their age. Similarly, when a work force reduction is carried out pursuant to an objective evaluation of all employees, it does not violate the act simply because a greater number of older workers than younger workers were laid off according to *Mastie v. Great Lakes Steel Co.*[7] As well, the employer is permitted to discipline or discharge employees over forty for good cause. In *Hazen Paper Co. v. Biggins,*[8] the Supreme Court held that discrimination directed against an employee because of his years of service is not the same as discrimination because of age; hence, the employer's conduct in allegedly firing an employee to prevent him from becoming eligible for vesting under the pension plan was based on a factor other than age.

The Supreme Court's decision in *Hazen Paper* was based on the fact that the ADEA has a specific exemption for employer actions based on a factor other than age. The Court did not decide the question of whether a disparate impact claim may be brought under the ADEA. Disparate impact claims, you recall, involve challenges to apparently neutral employment criteria that have a disproportionate impact on a protected group of employees—in the case of the ADEA, employees forty and older. After the *Hazen Paper* decision, the federal courts of appeals have differed on the question of whether an age discrimination claim based on the disparate impact theory is possible. In the following decision, the Supreme Court considered whether a disparate impact claim of age discrimination is available under the ADEA.

---

[6]492 U.S. 158 (1989).

[7]424 F. Supp. 1299 (E.D. Mich. 1976).

[8]507 U.S. 604 (1993).

case 9.2 » Smith v. City of Jackson, Mississippi

544 U.S. 228 (2005)

[The City of Jackson, Mississippi adopted a pay plan in May 1999 that was intended to bring the starting salaries of police officers up to the average of other police departments in the region. The city granted raises to all police officers, but the officers with less than five years of tenure received proportionately greater raises than officers with more than five years of tenure. Most of the officers who were older than forty years of age had more than five years tenure. A group of older officers filed suit against the city, alleging that the differential raise policy violated the Age Discrimination in Employment Act. They alleged that the city had engaged in intentional age discrimination, and also that the pay raise policy had a disparate impact against the older officers. The trial court dismissed the suit, and the U.S. Court of Appeals affirmed the dismissal. The officers then appealed to the U.S. Supreme Court.]

Stevens, J.

… [This] suit raises the question whether the "disparate-impact" theory of recovery announced in *Griggs v. Duke Power Co.* for cases brought under Title VII of the Civil Rights Act of 1964, is … [available] under the ADEA….

As enacted in 1967, § 4(a)(2) of the ADEA … provided that it shall be unlawful for an employer "to limit, segregate, or classify his employees in any way which would deprive or tend to deprive any individual of employment opportunities or otherwise adversely affect his status as an employee, because of such individual's age…." Except for substitution of the word "age" for the words "race, color, religion, sex, or national origin," the language of that provision in the ADEA is identical to that found in § 703 (a)(2) of the Civil Rights Act of 1964 (Title VII). Other provisions of the ADEA also parallel the earlier statute. Unlike Title VII, however, § 4(f)(1) of the ADEA contains language that significantly narrows its coverage by permitting any "otherwise prohibited" action "where the differentiation is based on reasonable factors other than age" [the RFOA provision].

In determining whether the ADEA authorizes disparate-impact claims, we begin with the premise that when Congress uses the same language in two statutes having similar purposes, particularly when one is enacted shortly after the other, it is appropriate to presume that Congress intended that text to have the same meaning in both statutes…. In *Griggs*, a case decided four years after the enactment of the ADEA, we considered whether § 703 of Title VII prohibited an employer "from requiring a high school education or passing of a standardized general intelligence test as a condition of employment in or transfer to jobs when (a) neither standard is shown to be significantly related to successful job performance, (b) both requirements operate to disqualify Negroes at a substantially higher rate than white applicants, and (c) the jobs in question formerly had been filled only by white employees as part of a longstanding practice of giving preference to whites." Accepting the Court of Appeals' conclusion that the employer had adopted the diploma and test requirements without any intent to discriminate, we held that good faith "does not redeem employment procedures or testing mechanisms that operate as 'built-in headwinds' for minority groups and are unrelated to measuring job capability."

We explained that Congress had "directed the thrust of the Act to the *consequences* of employment practices, not simply the motivation." … We thus squarely held that § 703(a) (2) of Title VII did not require a showing of discriminatory intent…. While our opinion in *Griggs* relied primarily on the purposes of the Act, buttressed by the fact that the EEOC had endorsed the same view, we have subsequently noted that our holding represented the better reading of the statutory text as well. Neither § 703(a)(2) nor the comparable language in the ADEA simply prohibits actions that "limit, segregate, or classify" persons; rather the language prohibits such actions that "deprive any individual of employment opportunities or *otherwise adversely affect* his status as an employee, because of such individual's" race or age…. Thus the text focuses on the *effects* of the action on the employee rather than the motivation for the action of the employer.

Griggs, which interpreted the identical text at issue here, thus strongly suggests that a disparate-impact theory should be cognizable under the ADEA. Indeed, for over two decades after our decision in *Griggs*, the Courts of Appeal uniformly interpreted the ADEA as authorizing recovery on a "disparate-impact" theory in appropriate cases. IT WAS ONLY AFTER our decision in *Hazen Paper Co. v. Biggins* that some of those courts concluded that the ADEA did not authorize a disparate-impact theory of liability. Our opinion in *Hazen Paper*, however, did not address or comment on the issue we decide today. In that case, we held that an employee's allegation that he was discharged shortly before his pension would have vested did not state a cause of action under a *disparate-treatment* theory. The motivating factor was not, we held, the employee's age, but rather his years of service, a factor that the ADEA did not prohibit an employer from considering when terminating an employee. While we noted that disparate-treatment "captures the essence of what Congress sought to prohibit in the ADEA," we were careful to explain that we were not deciding "whether a disparate impact theory of liability is available under the ADEA.... In sum, there is nothing in our opinion in *Hazen Paper* that precludes an interpretation of the ADEA that parallels our holding in *Griggs*.

The Court of Appeals' categorical rejection of disparate-impact liability [in this case] ... rested primarily on the RFOA provision and the majority's analysis of legislative history. As we have already explained, we think the history of the enactment of the ADEA ... supports the pre-*Hazen Paper* consensus concerning disparate-impact liability. And *Hazen Paper* itself contains the response to the concern over the RFOA provision.

The RFOA provision provides that it shall not be unlawful for an employer "to take any action otherwise prohibited under subsectio[n] (a) ... where the differentiation is based on reasonable factors other than age discrimination...." In most disparate-treatment cases, if an employer in fact acted on a factor other than age, the action would not be prohibited under subsection (a) in the first place....

In disparate-impact cases, however, the allegedly "otherwise prohibited" activity is not based on age.... It is, accordingly, in cases involving disparate-impact claims that the RFOA provision plays its principal role by precluding liability if the adverse impact was attributable to a nonage factor that was "reasonable." Rather than support an argument that disparate impact is unavailable under the ADEA, the RFOA provision actually supports the contrary conclusion.

The text of the statute, as interpreted in *Griggs*, the RFOA provision, and the EEOC regulations all support petitioners' view. We therefore conclude that it was error for the Court of Appeals to hold that the disparate-impact theory of liability is categorically unavailable under the ADEA.

Two textual differences between the ADEA and Title VII make it clear that even though both statutes authorize recovery on a disparate-impact theory, the scope of disparate-impact liability under ADEA is narrower than under Title VII. The first is the RFOA provision, which we have already identified. The second is the amendment to Title VII contained in the Civil Rights Act of 1991. One of the purposes of that amendment was to modify the Court's holding in *Wards Cove Packing Co. v. Atonio*, a case in which we narrowly construed the employer's exposure to liability on a disparate-impact theory. While the relevant 1991 amendments expanded the coverage of Title VII, they did not amend the ADEA or speak to the subject of age discrimination. Hence, *Wards Cove's* pre-1991 interpretation of Title VII's identical language remains applicable to the ADEA.

Congress' decision to limit the coverage of the ADEA by including the RFOA provision is consistent with the fact that age, unlike race or other classifications protected by Title VII, not uncommonly has relevance to an individual's capacity to engage in certain types of employment....

Turning to the case before us, we initially note that petitioners have done little more than point out that the pay plan at issue is relatively less generous to older workers than to younger workers. They have not identified any specific test, requirement, or practice within the pay plan that has an adverse impact on older workers. As we held in *Wards Cove*, it is not enough to simply allege that there is a disparate impact on workers, or point to a generalized policy that leads to such an impact. Rather, the employee is "'responsible for isolating and identifying the *specific* employment practices that are allegedly responsible for any observed statistical disparities.'" Petitioners have failed to do so.... In this case not only did petitioners thus err by failing to identify the relevant practice, but it is also clear from the record that the City's plan was based on reasonable factors other than age.

The plan divided each of five basic positions—police officer, master police officer, police sergeant, police lieutenant, and deputy police chief—into a series of steps and half-steps. The wage for each range was based on a survey of comparable communities in the Southeast. Employees were then assigned a step (or half-step) within their position that corresponded to the lowest step that would still give the individual a 2% raise. Most of the officers were in the three lowest ranks; in each of those ranks there were officers under age 40 and officers over 40. In none did their age affect their compensation. The few officers in the two highest ranks are all over 40. Their raises, though higher in dollar amount than the raises given to junior officers, represented a smaller percentage of their salaries, which of course are higher than the salaries paid to their juniors. They are members of the class complaining of the "disparate impact" of the award.

Petitioners' evidence established two principal facts: First, almost two-thirds (66.2%) of the officers under 40 received raises of more than 10% while less than half (45.3%) of those over 40 did. Second, the average percentage increase for the entire class of officers with less than five years of tenure was somewhat higher than the percentage for those with more seniority. Because older officers tended to occupy more senior positions, on average they received smaller increases when measured as a percentage of their salary. The basic explanation for the differential was the City's perceived need to raise the salaries of junior officers to make them competitive with comparable positions in the market.

While there may have been other reasonable ways for the City to achieve its goals, the one selected was not unreasonable. Unlike the business necessity test, which asks whether there are other ways for the employer to achieve its goals that do not result in a disparate impact on a protected class, the reasonableness inquiry includes no such requirement.

Accordingly, while we do not agree with the Court of Appeals' holding that the disparate-impact theory of recovery is never available under the ADEA, we affirm its judgment.

It is so ordered.

Case Questions

1. How did the city's pay raise plan affect older police officers? Why did the city adopt such a pay raise plan?
2. According to Justice Stevens, what provisions of the ADEA allow plaintiffs to bring a disparate impact claim of age discrimination?
3. How does a claim of disparate impact age discrimination under the ADEA differ from a claim of disparate impact discrimination under Title VII of the Civil Rights Act of 1964?
4. Why did the Supreme Court dismiss the plaintiff's disparate impact age discrimination claim fail here? Explain.

In *Meacham v. Knolls Atomic Power Laboratory,*[9] a case decided following *Smith*, the Supreme Court held that an employer raising the "reasonable factor other than age" defense has to demonstrate that it relied on the "factor other than age," and has the burden of persuading the court that the factor was "reasonable."

Executive Exemption

Section 631(c) of the ADEA allows the mandatory retirement of executive employees who are over the age of sixty-five. To qualify under this exemption, the employee must have been in a bona fide executive or high policy-making position for at least two years and, upon retirement, must be entitled to nonforfeitable retirement benefits of at least $44,000 annually. An employee who is within the executive exemption can be required to retire upon reaching age sixty-five; mandatory retirement of such executives prior to sixty-five is still prohibited.

State or Local Government Firefighters or Law Enforcement Officers

Section 623(j) of the ADEA allows state and local governments to set, by law, retirement ages for firefighters and law enforcement officers. Where the state or local retirement age law was in effect as of March 3, 1983, the retirement age set by that law may be enforced. Where the state or local legislation setting the retirement age was enacted after September 30, 1996, the retirement age must be at least fifty-five. This original version of this exception was inserted into the ADEA in response to the Supreme Court decision in *Johnson v. Mayor and City Council of Baltimore,*[10] but that provision expired at the end of 1993. The current version of this exception was added to the ADEA in 1996.

---

[9]128 S.Ct. 2395 (2008).

[10]472 U.S. 353 (1985).

Bona Fide Occupational Qualification (BFOQ)

The ADEA does recognize that age may be a BFOQ for some jobs. The act states that a BFOQ must be reasonably necessary to the normal operation of the employer's business. In *Hodgson v. Greyhound Lines, Inc.*,[11] the court held that Greyhound could refuse to hire applicants for bus driver positions if the candidates were over thirty-five years old because of passenger safety considerations. However, a test pilot could not be mandatorily retired at age fifty-two according to *Houghton v. McDonnell Douglas Corp.*[12]

The Supreme Court considered the question of what is required to qualify as a BFOQ under the ADEA in the following case.

case 9.3 »

Western Air Lines v. Criswell

472 U.S. 400 (1985)

Facts: Western Air Lines [Western] is a commercial airline. Its flights involve a variety of aircraft that require three crew members in the cockpit: a captain, a first officer, and a flight engineer. The captain is the pilot and is responsible for all phases of the operation of the aircraft. The first officer is the copilot and assists the captain. The flight engineer usually monitors a side-facing instrument panel, and does not operate the flight controls unless the captain and the first officer become incapacitated. A Federal Aviation Administration (FAA) regulation requires that persons serving as a pilot or first officer on commercial flights must retire upon reaching the age of sixty. The FAA justifies the mandatory retirement for pilots and first officers because of the increasing risk of incapacitating medical events and adverse changes as a consequence of aging, and the inability to detect or predict an individual's risk of sudden or subtle incapacitation; therefore ensuring passenger safety requires caution in avoiding known age-related risks. The FAA regulation does not apply to flight engineers, but Western requires its flight engineers also to retire at age sixty. Criswell was a pilot who applied to transfer to a flight engineer position just prior to his 60th birthday. Western refused the transfer because, even as a flight engineer, he would be required to retire at sixty. Criswell filed suit against Western Air Lines for violating the ADEA; Western claimed the mandatory retirement age for flight engineers was a BFOQ "reasonably necessary to the normal operation of the particular business." Following the trial, the jury concluded that Western's mandatory retirement rule did not qualify as a BFOQ even though it purportedly was adopted for safety reasons. On appeal, the court of appeals affirmed the trial verdict. Western then appealed to the U.S. Supreme Court.

Issue: What must an employer demonstrate to support a claim of a BFOQ based on safety considerations?

Decision: Western argued that the age-sixty retirement rule is reasonably necessary to the safe operation of the airline. The evidence at trial established that the flight engineer's normal duties were less critical to the safety of flight than those of a pilot. The flight engineer does have critical functions in emergency situations and might cause considerable disruption in the event of his own medical emergency. Criswell's expert witness testified that physiological deterioration is caused by disease, not aging, and that it was possible to use individual medical examinations to determine whether flight crew members, including those over age sixty, were physically qualified to continue to fly. Several other commercial airlines allow flight engineers over age sixty to continue flying without any noticeable reduction in their safety records. Western argued that the court should defer to Western's judgment of legitimate concerns for passenger safety. The court emphasized that the ADEA requires that age qualifications must be something more than "convenient" or "reasonable"; they must be "reasonably necessary to the particular business," such

[11] 499 F.2d 859 (7th Cir. 1974).

[12] 553F.2d 561 (8th Cir. 1977).

as when the employer is compelled to rely on age as a proxy for the valid safety-related job qualifications. The employer could demonstrate that it had a reasonable factual basis to believe that all or substantially all persons over age sixty would be unable to perform the duties of the job safely and efficiently. The employer could also establish that age was a legitimate proxy for the safety-related job qualifications by proving that it would be "impossible or highly impractical" to deal with older employees on an individualized basis. Western argued that because flight engineers must meet the same stringent qualifications as pilots, it was logical to extend to the FAA requirement of retirement at sixty to flight engineers. The evidence here clearly established that the qualifications for a flight engineer were less rigorous than those for a pilot. Even where public safety is involved, the ADEA requires that a court make its own determination of what is reasonably necessary for the safe and efficient performance of the job requirements, including passenger safety, rather than deferring to the judgment of the employer regarding a BFOQ.

The Supreme Court affirmed the court of appeals' decision that Western had not established the mandatory retirement of flight engineers was a BFOQ.

«

Early Retirement and Work Force Reductions

The ADEA does not prohibit voluntary retirement as long as it is truly voluntary. The Older Workers Benefit Protection Act of 1990, which amended the ADEA, contained several provisions concerning work force reductions. Employers seeking to reduce their work force may offer employees early retirement incentives, such as subsidized benefits for early retirees or paying higher benefits until retirees are eligible for social security, as long as the practice is a permanent feature of a plan that is continually available to all who meet eligibility requirements and participation in the early retirement program is voluntary. Severance pay made available because of an event unrelated to age (such as a plant closing or work force reduction) may be reduced by the amount of health benefits or additional benefits received by individuals eligible for an immediate pension.

Waivers

Employers may require employees receiving special benefits upon early retirement to execute a waiver of claims under the ADEA if the waiver is knowing and voluntary and the employees receive additional compensation for the waiver, over and above that to which they are already entitled. The waivers must be in writing and must specifically refer to rights under the ADEA. The waivers do not operate to waive any rights of the employee that arise after the waiver was executed. The employees required to execute a waiver must be advised, in writing, to consult an attorney about the waiver and must be given at least twenty-one days to consider the matter before deciding whether to execute the waiver. The employees must also be allowed to revoke the waivers up to seven days after signing. If the waivers are part of a termination incentive program offered to a group or class of employees, the employer must give the employees forty-five days to consider the waiver. If the early retirement and waiver are offered to a class of employees, the employer must provide employees with the following information:

- A list of the class eligible for early retirement
- The factors to determine eligibility for early retirement
- The time limits for deciding upon early retirement

- Any possible adverse action if the employee declines to accept early retirement and the date of such possible action

For any waiver involving a claim that is already before the Equal Employment Opportunity Commission (EEOC) or a court, employees must be given "reasonable time" to consider the waiver. No waiver affects an employee's right to contact the EEOC or the EEOC's right to pursue any claim under the ADEA. In any suit involving a waiver of ADEA rights, the burden of proving that the waiver complies with ADEA requirements is on the person asserting that the waiver is valid (usually the employer).

When an employee accepts an employer's offer of severance benefits in return for signing a waiver that does not comply with the waiver requirements set out in the ADEA, does the employee's retention of those benefits operate to "ratify" the waiver and make it effective? The U.S. Supreme Court addressed that question in the following case.

case 9.4 » Oubre v. Entergy Operations, Inc.

522 U.S. 422 (1998)

Kennedy, Justice

Petitioner Dolores Oubre worked as a scheduler at a power plant in Killona, Louisiana, run by her employer, respondent Entergy Operations, Inc. In 1994, she received a poor performance rating. Oubre's supervisor met with her on January 17, 1995, and gave her the option of either improving her performance during the coming year or accepting a voluntary arrangement for her severance. She received a packet of information about the severance agreement and had 14 days to consider her options, during which she consulted with attorneys. On January 31, Oubre decided to accept. She signed a release, in which she "agree[d] to waive, settle, release, and discharge any and all claims, demands, damages, actions, or causes of action … that I may have against Entergy.…" In exchange, she received six installment payments over the next four months, totaling $6,258.

The Older Workers Benefit Protection Act (OWBPA) imposes specific requirements for releases covering ADEA claims. In procuring the release, Entergy did not comply with the OWBPA in at least three respects: (1) Entergy did not give Oubre enough time to consider her options, (2) Entergy did not give Oubre seven days after she signed the release to change her mind, and (3) the release made no specific reference to claims under the ADEA.

Oubre filed a charge of age discrimination with the Equal Employment Opportunity Commission, which dismissed her charge on the merits but issued a right-to-sue letter. She filed this suit against Entergy in the United States District Court for the Eastern District of Louisiana, alleging constructive discharge on the basis of her age in violation of the ADEA and state law. Oubre has not offered or tried to return the $6,258 to Entergy, nor is it clear she has the means to do so. Entergy moved for summary judgment, claiming Oubre had ratified the defective release by failing to return or offer to return the monies she had received. The District Court agreed and entered summary judgment for Entergy. The Court of Appeals affirmed.…

The employer rests its case upon general principles of state contract jurisprudence. As the employer recites the rule, contracts tainted by mistake, duress, or even fraud are voidable at the option of the innocent party. The employer maintains, however, that before the innocent party can elect avoidance, she must first tender back any benefits received under the contract. If she fails to do so within a reasonable time after learning of her rights, the employer contends, she ratifies the contract and so makes it binding. The employer also invokes the doctrine of equitable estoppel. As a rule, equitable estoppel bars a party from shirking the burdens of a voidable transaction for as long as she retains the benefits received under it. Applying these principles, the employer claims the employee ratified the ineffective release (or faces estoppel) by retaining all the sums paid in consideration of it. The employer, then, relies not upon the execution of the release but upon a later, distinct ratification of its terms.…

In 1990, Congress amended the ADEA by passing the OWBPA. The OWBPA provides: "An individual may not waive any right or claim under [the ADEA] unless the waiver is knowing and voluntary.... [A] waiver may not be considered knowing and voluntary unless at a minimum" it satisfies certain enumerated requirements....

The statutory command is clear: An employee "may not waive" an ADEA claim unless the waiver or release satisfies the OWBPA's requirements. The policy of the Older Workers Benefit Protection Act is likewise clear from its title: It is designed to protect the rights and benefits of older workers. The OWBPA implements Congress' policy via a strict, unqualified statutory stricture on waivers, and we are bound to take Congress at its word. Congress imposed specific duties on employers who seek releases of certain claims created by statute. Congress delineated these duties with precision and without qualification: An employee "may not waive" an ADEA claim unless the employer complies with the statute. Courts cannot with ease presume ratification of that which Congress forbids.

The OWBPA sets up its own regime for assessing the effect of ADEA waivers, separate and apart from contract law. The statute creates a series of prerequisites for knowing and voluntary waivers and imposes affirmative duties of disclosure and waiting periods. The OWBPA governs the effect under federal law of waivers or releases on ADEA claims and incorporates no exceptions or qualifications. The text of the OWBPA forecloses the employer's defense, notwithstanding how general contract principles would apply to non-ADEA claims.

The rule proposed by the employer would frustrate the statute's practical operation as well as its formal command. In many instances a discharged employee likely will have spent the monies received and will lack the means to tender their return. These realities might tempt employers to risk noncompliance with the OWBPA's waiver provisions, knowing it will be difficult to repay the monies and relying on ratification. We ought not to open the door to an evasion of the statute by this device.

Oubre's cause of action arises under the ADEA, and the release can have no effect on her ADEA claim unless it complies with the OWBPA. In this case, both sides concede the release the employee signed did not comply with the requirements of the OWBPA. Since Oubre's release did not comply with the OWBPA's stringent safeguards, it is unenforceable against her insofar as it purports to waive or release her ADEA claim. As a statutory matter, the release cannot bar her ADEA suit, irrespective of the validity of the contract as to other claims....

It suffices to hold that the release cannot bar the ADEA claim because it does not conform to the statute. Nor did the employee's mere retention of monies amount to a ratification equivalent to a valid release of her ADEA claims, since the retention did not comply with the OWBPA any more than the original release did. The statute governs the effect of the release on ADEA claims, and the employer cannot invoke the employee's failure to tender back as a way of excusing its own failure to comply.

We reverse the judgment of the Court of Appeals and remand for further proceedings consistent with this opinion.

It is so ordered.

Appendix to Opinion of the Court

Older Workers Benefit Protection Act, §201, 104 Stat. 983, 29 U.S.C. §626(f)

(f) Waiver

(1) An individual may not waive any right or claim under this chapter unless the waiver is knowing and voluntary. Except as provided in paragraph (2), a waiver may not be considered knowing and voluntary unless at a minimum—

(A) the waiver is part of an agreement between the individual and the employer that is written in a manner calculated to be understood by such individual, or by the average individual eligible to participate;

(B) the waiver specifically refers to rights or claims arising under this Act;

(C) the individual does not waive rights or claims that may arise after the date the waiver is executed;

(D) the individual waives rights or claims only in exchange for consideration in addition to anything of value to which the individual already is entitled;

(E) the individual is advised in writing to consult with an attorney prior to executing the agreement;

(F) (i) the individual is given a period of at least 21 days within which to consider the agreement; or

(ii) if a waiver is requested in connection with an exit incentive or other employment termination program offered to a group or class of employees, the individual is given a period of at least 45 days within which to consider the agreement;

(G) the agreement provides that for a period of at least 7 days following the execution of such agreement, the individual may revoke the agreement, and the agreement shall not become effective or enforceable until the revocation period has expired;

(H) if a waiver is requested in connection with an exit incentive or other employment termination program offered to a group or class of employees, the employer (at the commencement of the period specified in subparagraph (F)) informs the individual in writing in a manner calculated to be understood by the average individual eligible to participate, as to—

(i) any class, unit, or group of individuals covered by such program, any eligibility factors for such program, and any time limits applicable to such program; and

(ii) the job titles and ages of all individuals eligible or selected for the program, and the ages of all individuals in the same job classification or organizational unit who are not eligible or selected for the program.

(2) A waiver in settlement of a charge filed with the Equal Employment Opportunity Commission, or an action filed in court by the individual or the individual's representative, alleging age discrimination of a kind prohibited under section 4 or 15 may not be considered knowing and voluntary unless at a minimum—

(A) subparagraphs (A) through (E) of paragraph (1) have been met; and

(B) the individual is given a reasonable period of time within which to consider the settlement agreement.

(3) In any dispute that may arise over whether any of the requirements, conditions, and circumstances set forth in subparagraph (A), (B), (C), (D), (E), (F), (G), or (H) of paragraph (1), or subparagraph (A) or (B) of paragraph (2), have been met, the party asserting the validity of a waiver shall have the burden of proving in a court of competent jurisdiction that a waiver was knowing and voluntary pursuant to paragraph (1) or (2).

(4) No waiver agreement may affect the Commission's rights and responsibilities to enforce this Act. No waiver may be used to justify interfering with the protected right of an employee to file a charge or participate in an investigation or proceeding conducted by the Commission.

Case Questions

1. Why was the waiver signed by Oubre not valid under the ADEA?
2. Did Entergy argue that the waiver did comply with the ADEA? Why did Entergy argue that the waiver should be binding on Oubre?
3. Must Oubre return the money Entergy gave her for signing the waiver before she can sue Entergy under the ADEA? Explain your answer.

ethical DILEMMA

You are the manager of a small financial planning and consulting firm in Little Rock, Arkansas. The firm has been experiencing a slowdown in business lately, and because of the decline in business, you are forced to eliminate one of two financial planner positions. One of the financial planners is fifty-five and has been with the company for years. She is one of the highest paid employees. She is married and has two children in college. Because her husband has severe medical problems, he is unable to work and depends on her medical benefits for his medical treatment. The other financial planner is twenty-seven. He is single and lives with his parents. You must choose which of the two financial planners to lay off. How should you make the decision? What criteria should you use in making the decision? Note that Arkansas does not have any state law prohibiting age discrimination by private sector employers, but your firm is subject to the federal Age Discrimination in Employment Act.

Concept *Summary* » 9.2

EXCEPTIONS UNDER THE ADEA

- Exceptions under the ADEA:
  - Age as a BFOQ
  - Actions under a bona fide seniority system or benefit plan
  - Actions based on a "reasonable factor other than age"
  - Executive exemption:
    - Employees in bona fide executive position for at least two years
    - Entitled to retirement benefits of at least $44,000
    - Can be required to retire at age sixty-five
  - State or local government firefighters or law enforcement officers can be required to retire at age fifty-five

Procedures Under the ADEA

The ADEA is enforced and administered by the EEOC. The EEOC acquired the enforcement responsibility from the Department of Labor pursuant to a reorganization in 1978. The ADEA allows suits by private individuals as well as by the EEOC.

An individual alleging a violation of the ADEA must file a written complaint with the EEOC and with the state or local equal employment opportunity (EEO) agency if one exists. Unlike Title VII, however, the individual may file simultaneously with both the EEOC and the state or local agency. There is no need to go to the state or local agency prior to filing with the EEOC. The complaint must be filed with the EEOC within 180 days of the alleged violation if no state or local agency exists. If such an agency does exist, the complaint must be filed with the EEOC within thirty days of the termination of proceedings by the state or local agency, and it must be filed no later than 300 days from the alleged violation.

After filing with the EEOC and the state or local EEO agency, the individual must wait sixty days before filing suit in federal court. Although there is no requirement that the individual wait for a right-to-sue notice from the EEOC, the sixty-day period is to allow time for a voluntary settlement of the complaint. If the EEOC dismisses the complaint or otherwise terminates proceedings on the complaint, it is required to notify the individual filing the complaint. The individual then has ninety days from receipt of the notice to file suit. Even though the individual must wait at least sixty days from filing with the agencies before bringing suit in court, the court suit must be filed no later than ninety days from receiving the right-to-sue notice from the EEOC. An individual can file an age discrimination suit in federal court even if the state or local EEO agency has ruled that the employee was not the victim of age discrimination according to the Supreme Court decision in *Astoria Federal Savings & Loan v. Solimino*.[13] If the EEOC files suit under the ADEA, the EEOC suit supersedes any ADEA suit filed by the individual or any state agency. As with Title VII, the ADEA allows for a jury trial.

[13] 501 U.S. 104 (1991).

After-Acquired Evidence

After-Acquired Evidence
Evidence, discovered after an employer has taken an adverse employment action, that the employer uses to justify the action taken.

In *McKennon v. Nashville Banner Publishing Co.*,[14] the employer discovered that an employee allegedly fired because of her age had copied confidential documents prior to her discharge. The employer argued that the evidence of the plaintiff/employee's misconduct (known as ***after-acquired evidence***) precluded the right of the plaintiff to sue under the ADEA. The Supreme Court held that the after-acquired evidence does not preclude the plaintiff's suit but rather goes to the issue of what remedies are available. If the employer can demonstrate that the employee's wrongdoing was severe enough to result in termination had the employer known of the misconduct at the time the alleged discrimination occurred, the court must then consider the effect of the wrongdoing on the remedies available to the plaintiff. In such a case, reinstatement might not be appropriate, and back pay could be awarded only from the date of the alleged discrimination by the employer to the date upon which the plaintiff's misconduct was discovered.

Arbitration of ADEA Claims

In *Gilmer v. Interstate/Johnson Lane Corp.*,[15] the Supreme Court held that a securities broker was required to arbitrate, rather than litigate, his age discrimination claim because he had signed an agreement to arbitrate all disputes arising from his employment. The individual agreement to arbitrate, voluntarily agreed to by Gilmer, was enforceable under the Federal Arbitration Act and required Gilmer to submit all employment disputes, including those under EEO legislation, to arbitration. The agreement to arbitrate did not waive Gilmer's rights under the statutes but simply required that those rights be determined by the arbitrator rather than the courts. In general, agreements to arbitrate ADEA claims will be enforced when they were voluntarily and knowingly agreed to by the employees, but such arbitration agreements do not prevent the EEOC from bringing a suit on behalf of the individual employees subject to the arbitration agreements. The employees covered by a collective agreement that contained an arbitration clause that specifically included age discrimination claims were required to arbitrate their ADEA claims rather than litigate them, according to the Supreme Court decision in *14 Penn Plaza v. Pyett.*[16] (See the discussion of the arbitration of EEO claims in Chapter 8).

Suits by Federal Employees

Despite the fact that the federal government is not included in the ADEA's definition of employer, Section 15 of the act provides that personnel actions in most federal government positions shall be made free from discrimination based on age. The ADEA protects federal workers "who are at least 40 years of age."

Complaints of age discrimination involving federal employees are now handled by the EEOC. A federal employee agency must file the complaint with the EEOC within 180 days of the alleged violation. The employee may file suit in federal court after thirty days from filing with the EEOC. The ADEA provides only for private suits in cases involving complaints by federal employees. No provision is made for suits by the EEOC.

---

[14] 513 U.S. 352 (1995).

[15] 500 U.S. 20 (1991).

[16] 129 S.Ct. 1456 (2009).

Government Suits

In addition to private suits, the ADEA provides for suits by the responsible government agency (now the EEOC, formerly the secretary of labor) against nonfederal employers. The EEOC must attempt to settle the complaint voluntarily before filing suit. There is no specific time limitation for this required conciliation effort. Once conciliation has been attempted, the EEOC may file suit.

The 1991 amendments to the ADEA eliminated the previous time limits spelled out for suits by the EEOC. As a result, at present, the courts are split on the question of when the EEOC suit must be filed. Some courts have held that there is no specific statute of limitations on ADEA suits filed by the EEOC, as with *EEOC v. Tire Kingdom*;[17] other courts have held that the EEOC is also subject to the ninety-day limitation, as with *McConnell v. Thomson Newspapers, Inc.*[18]

Concept *Summary* » 9.3

Procedures Under the ADEA

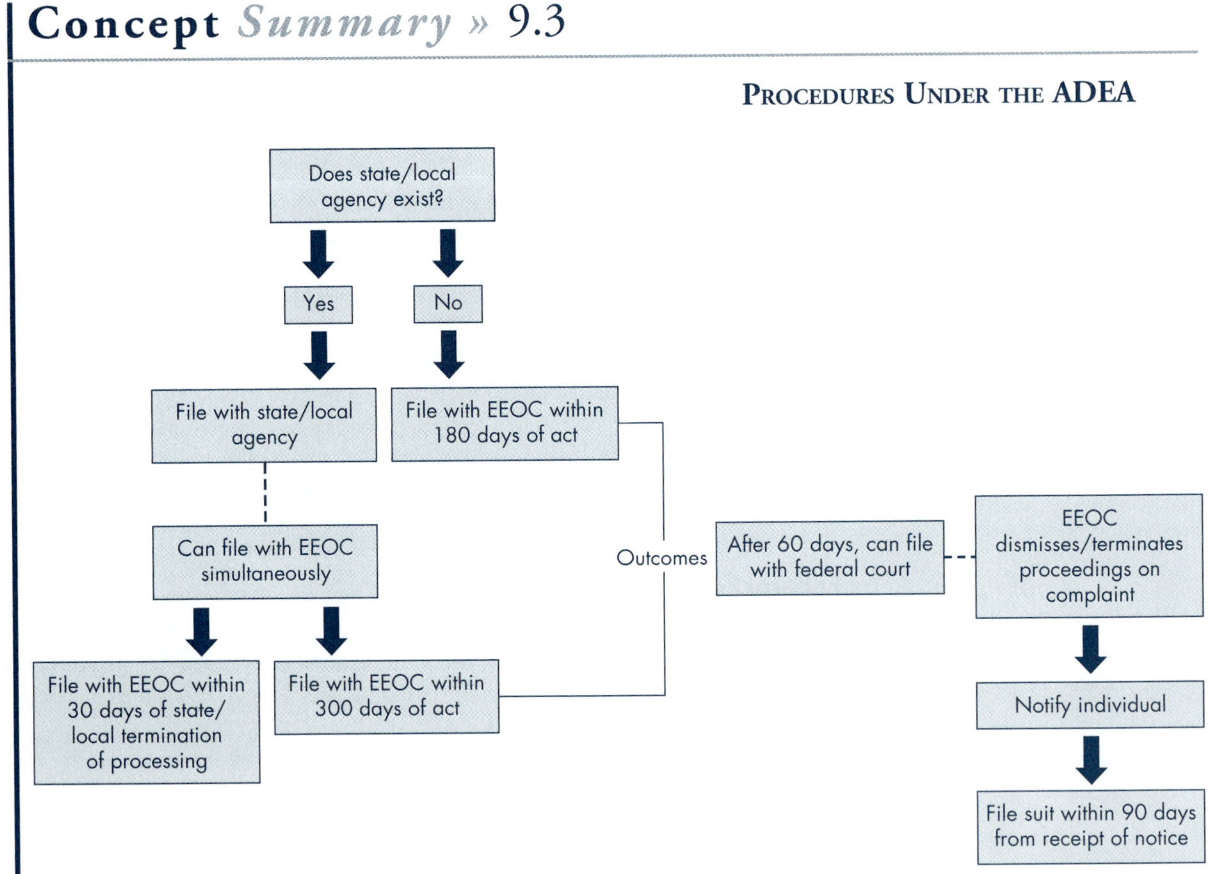

[17]80 F.3d 449 (11th Cir. 1996).

[18]802 F.Supp. 1484 (E.D.Tex. 1992).

Remedies Under the ADEA

The remedies available under the ADEA are similar to those available under the Equal Pay Act. Successful private plaintiffs can recover any back wages owing and legal fees. They may also recover an equal amount as liquidated damages if the employer acted "willfully." The Supreme Court, in the 1985 case of *Trans World Airlines, Inc. v. Thurston*,[19] held that an employer acts willfully when "the employer either knew or showed reckless disregard for the matter of whether its conduct was prohibited by the ADEA." Injunctive relief is also available, and legal fees and costs are recoverable by the successful private plaintiff. Back pay and liquidated damages recovered under the ADEA are subject to income taxation according to *Commissioner of IRS v. Schleier*.[20] Remedies in suits by the EEOC may include injunctions and back pay. Liquidated damages, however, are not available in such suits.

[19] 469 U.S. 111 (1985).

[20] 515 U.S. 323 (1995).

CHAPTER REVIEW

» Key Terms

after-acquired evidence « 259

» Summary

- The Age Discrimination in Employment Act (ADEA) prohibits discrimination in employment based on age. The ADEA protects only employees aged forty and older from such discrimination, but some state laws protect employees aged eighteen and older. Mandatory retirement is prohibited, except where age is a BFOQ necessary for the safe and efficient performance of the job in question; the *Western Air Lines* case interprets the BFOQ provisions of the ADEA. Exceptions under the ADEA allow certain executives to be retired at age sixty-five and allow public sector employers to establish retirement ages for law enforcement officers and firefighters. Employers may differentiate among employees because of age in the provision of employment benefits, as long as the differentiation is cost justified and pursuant to a bona fide benefits plan. Voluntary early retirement is not prohibited, and employers may offer supplemental benefits as an inducement for early retirement. The ADEA imposes certain requirements on employers who require employees to sign a waiver as a condition of receiving early retirement incentives.

» Problems

Questions

1. What, if any, incentives can an employer offer employees to retire voluntarily? Can an employer require employees to waive their rights under the ADEA as a condition of receiving such incentives? Explain your answers.
2. What must an employer show to establish a BFOQ under the ADEA? What other defenses are available to an employer under the ADEA?
3. Many ADEA suits arise from workforce reductions. What factors should an employer consider to determine which employees to be laid off?
4. When can an employer institute a mandatory retirement age for employees?
5. What must a plaintiff demonstrate to make a disparate impact claim under the ADEA? What defense can an employer raise in an ADEA disparate impact case?

Case Problems

6. Springfield Power Co. lost a major electricity customer when General Motors closed several auto factories in Springfield's service area. Because of the loss of business, Springfield decided to reduce its workforce. Managers were instructed to rate their workers on the factors of "performance, flexibility, and critical skills." Using those discretionary ratings, combined with points for years of service, the company then decided which workers would be laid

off. Of the thirty-one workers who were laid off, thirty of them were over the age of forty. Several of the employees who were laid off file suit against Springfield under the ADEA. Can the workers establish a prima facie case of age discrimination? What defense can the employer raise here? See *Meacham v. Knolls Atomic Power Lab.* [128 S.Ct. 2395 (2008)].

7. Davis, an Indiana State Police officer, resigned to take another job when he was aged forty-two. Two months later he asked to be reinstated to his old position. The Indiana State Police refused because of its policy that ex-troopers seeking reinstatement must meet all the requirements for new applicants. The Indiana State Police required that applicants be over the age of twenty-one and under forty—no applicant forty or over will be hired. Davis points out that the Indiana State Police allows officers to work until age sixty-five, so that had he not resigned, he would have been able to continue working at age forty-three, or fifty-five, or even sixty-four. However, because of a two month break in his service, he is now disqualified from serving because of his age. He files suit, alleging that refusal to rehire him violates the ADEA. Is Indiana's policy of not rehiring officers over the age of forty in violation of the ADEA? Explain. See *Davis v. Indiana State Police* [541 F.3d 760 (7th Cir. 2008)].
8. Wholesale Grocers, Inc. is shutting down several warehouses in upstate New York. The company's pension plan provides that employees are entitled to a nonforfeitable pension upon retirement after working for the company for five years. When closing the warehouses, the company decided to offer severance pay to workers under the age of fifty-five, while workers aged fifty-five or older were offered early retirement but no severance pay. Does the denial of severance pay violate the ADEA? Explain. See *E.E.O.C. v. Great Atlantic and Pacific Tea Co.* [618 F.Supp. 115 (D.C. Ohio 1985)].
9. Burns, aged sixty-four, and Smithers, aged thirty-eight, were applicants for the position of postmaster at the Shelbyville Post Office. Burns had been the assistant postmaster for several years, and was seeking promotion to postmaster as the final step in his career. After interviewing both candidates, the Postal Service Management Selection Board decided to promote Smithers because they felt he had "management potential to advance beyond Shelbyville." Can Burns establish a prima facie case of age discrimination under the ADEA? What defenses are available to the employer? Explain. See *Smithers v. Bailar* [629 F.2d 892 (3d Cir. 1980)].
10. The city of Memphis is experiencing a budget shortfall. By abolishing the rank of captain, the chief of police demonstrates that the Memphis Police Department will save $1,400,000. Unlike promotion to other ranks, which is based on merit, officers are promoted to captain automatically when they achieve thirty years of service with the department. Captains perform the same duties as lower ranked officers, but receive higher pay because of their rank as captain. Officers who are captains were given the choice of returning to their prior lower rank and having their pay reduced, or retiring. Several officers who had been captains file suit against the city, alleging age discrimination. What must they show to establish a claim of disparate impact age discrimination? What defenses are available to the city? Explain. See *Aldridge v. City of Memphis* [2007 WL 4370707 (W.D. Tenn. Dec. 10, 2007)].
11. Ann Lindsey and Linda York, both over forty years old, were employed as head waitresses shortly after the opening of the Cabaret Royale, an upscale gentlemen's club in Dallas. Its facilities include a gourmet restaurant, conference room with office services, a boutique, wide-screen viewing of sports events, and topless dancing. Lindsey was hired in January 1989. Two months later, she sought promotion to dancer. She spoke with one of the managers, and that same evening, she was summoned into the office of the general manager, Brian Paul, and told that she was "too old" to be a dancer. York was present at the time. In ensuing weeks, several younger waitresses were promoted to dancer. Finally, on May 8, 1989, Lindsey resigned and immediately became employed as a dancer at the Million Dollar Saloon. Cabaret Royale contends that Lindsey was not qualified to be one of its dancers because she failed to meet its attractiveness standard; specifically, she was not "beautiful, gorgeous, and sophisticated." York also began working as a waitress in January 1989. On May 8,

1989, she left work around 1:30 A.M. claiming to be ill. As she left, she saw a regular customer, Kevin Hale, waiting for a cab and she gave him a ride home. When she returned to work two days later, she was informed that she was fired. She maintains that no reasons were assigned for her dismissal. Cabaret Royale responds that she was terminated because she violated the club's prohibition against leaving with customers. York counters that younger waitresses were not disciplined for the identical behavior. The Cabaret employed only one other nonmanagement female over age forty, Joy Tarver, a dancer who also was terminated at the same time. York and Lindsey filed suit under the ADEA.

Can they establish a prima facie case of age discrimination? Are they likely to be successful in their claim? Explain your answers. See *Lindsey v. Prive Corp.* [987 F.2d 324 (5th Cir. 1993)].

12. The El Paso Natural Gas Company had a rule that pilots of the company's private planes must either accept ground jobs or retire at age sixty. Pilots' duties included night flying, visual flying, and instrument flying. Transfer to a ground job at age sixty was permitted if one was available. Otherwise, the pilot was forced to retire. El Paso argued that it was impractical for the company to try to monitor the health of a pilot after age sixty and that the FAA regulation requiring retirement of commercial pilots after age sixty was prima facie proof of the legality of the company's rule under the ADEA BFOQ provisions.

    Do you agree? Explain your answer. See *EEOC v. El Paso Natural Gas Co.* [626 F. Supp. 182 (W. D. Tex. 1985)].

13. Giles Parkinson had been Chief General Counsel for Cordmaker, Inc. for a number of years. He was nearly sixty years old. After experiencing financial difficulties and a severe downturn in business, Cordmaker eliminated Parkinson's position and informed him that he was being terminated. Most of his duties were reassigned to other employees, including a thirty-seven-year-old attorney. Parkinson informed the board of directors of Cordmaker that he believed their decision to fire him was illegal and that he would file suit. Parkinson was then placed on a leave of absence and paid full salary for six months and 70 percent of his salary for three months thereafter. He requested that he be able to use his former office, and the company's phones and computers, to conduct a job search but was barred from using any company facilities. Parkinson filed suit under the ADEA and the New York Human Rights Law, alleging that Cordmaker had discriminated against him because of his age and had retaliated against him for complaining of age discrimination by denying him use of company facilities.

    How should the court rule on his suit? Explain your answer. See *Wanamaker v. Columbian Rope Co.* [108 F.3d 462 (2d Cir. 1997)].

14. Gerald Woythal was Chief Engineer for Tex-Tenn Corp. He was one of the company's original employees and sixty-two years old. His boss was Operating Manager James Carico. Carico found it difficult to communicate with Woythal, whom he characterized as having a negative attitude, being apathetic about the company's future and sometimes unavailable when Carico needed to talk to him. The company was experiencing rapid growth, and Carico was concerned about the Engineering Department's ability to meet the increased demands placed upon it. He decided to hire an additional engineer to serve as Woythal's assistant. Woythal showed no interest in the hiring decision or in recruiting the new engineer. When Carico asked Woythal about his plans for the future and what he wanted to do for Tex-Tenn, Woythal simply replied that he would work until he was seventy. When Carico pressed Woythal about his plans for the Engineering Department, Woythal was uninterested and evasive. Carico then called Woythal into his office for a discussion and told him that "the company needed his participation, and if he chose not to participate, he would not be needed." Carico then asked Woythal if he intended to be an active participant in the company and told him to make his mind up by the end of the month. Woythal interpreted Carico's remarks to mean that he was fired, and he left the company at the end of the month. Tex-Tenn hired a younger engineer to replace Woythal. Woythal then filed suit under the ADEA, alleging age discrimination.

Can Woythal establish a legitimate claim of age discrimination? What defenses can Tex-Tenn raise? How should the court rule on the suit? Explain your answers. See *Woythal v. Tex-Tenn Corp.* [112 F.3d 243 (6th Cir. 1997)].

15. Ralph Sheehan was an assistant editor at Racing Form, Inc., a publisher that prints horse racing newsletters, programs, and tout sheets. Racing Form decided to computerize its operations, which would eliminate several jobs. The company human resources manager prepared a list of the jobs to be eliminated and the employees occupying those jobs, the jobs to be retained and the employees filling those jobs, and the birth dates of those employees. Sheehan, age fifty, was informed that his job would be eliminated. He noticed from the listing that most of the employees losing their jobs were older, while those being retained were younger. Sheehan filed an age discrimination complaint and argued that including the employees' birth dates was evidence of age discrimination. Is the court likely to agree with Sheehan? Are there other legitimate reasons for including the employees' birth dates on the listing? Explain. See *Sheehan v. Daily Racing Form* [104 F.3d 940 (7th Cir. 1997)].

Hypothetical Scenarios

16. DeLormer is sales manager for Fast Freddy's Auto Sales, a local car dealer selling Kia, Hyundai, and Subaru cars. Fred Fischer, the owner of Fast Freddy's, decides to reorganize his workforce due to slumping auto sales. Fischer tells DeLormer, who is sixty, that his job will be eliminated and the position's duties will be consolidated with those of the service manager position. Fischer also tells DeLormer that the new position will be filled by Gaines, the current service manager, who is forty-two. DeLormer feels that he is being terminated because of his age. Can DeLormer establish a prima facie case of age discrimination based on these facts? Explain.

17. Rotert, age fifty-nine, worked as a mortgage processing officer. Her manager told her that her duties were being changed to those of a loan consultant and that she would be transferred to another, more distant branch office. The manager told Rotert that her salary would be the same. Rotert protested the new work assignment and resigned. She filed a claim for unemployment benefits, which was denied because she was not "constructively discharged" due to the new assignment. Rather, the state agency held, she had voluntarily quit. When Rotert filed an ADEA complaint, again stating that she was constructively discharged in favor of a younger employee who took her former job as mortgage processing officer, the company argued for dismissal because the issue of "constructive discharge" had already been decided against her by the state agency. How should the court rule? Why?

18. The City of Rochester will not accept applications for positions with the city's fire department and police department from persons over the age of thirty. The city also has a mandatory retirement age for police officers and firefighters of age fifty-five. The city maintains that the strenuous nature of the work of the firefighters and police officers requires that employees be in good physical shape, and that experience on the job can help offset the effects of aging on the employees up until about the age of fifty-five. However, after age fifty-five, the effects of aging on the cardiovascular system are more likely to cause potential problems for the employees. Has the city established that the age limit for applicants and the mandatory retirement age are BFOQ's under the ADEA? Explain.

19. Kentucky's state pension system requires that police officers who are disabled after reaching the age of fifty-five to retire and receive normal retirement benefits, while officers who become disabled prior to age fifty-five receive disability benefits until they reach the normal retirement age of sixty, and then begin receiving pension benefits. Officer Wiggums and his partner are injured after crashing their patrol car during a high speed chase. Wiggums, aged fifty-six, is required to retire and take his pension, while his partner, aged fifty-three, will receive disability benefits until he reaches the age of sixty, and then will begin receiving his pension. Does Kentucky's pension system violate the ADEA? Explain.

20. Watkins Co. was looking to hire an administrative secretary, and after viewing the applications of various candidates, selected two applicants for personal interviews. When the manager interviewed Sue Phillips, aged forty-seven, he asked her how comfortable she felt working with computers, using various software programs and the internet. The manager also made a note on Phillips' application that she "seemed too old and inflexible." The same manager next interviewed Sonya Glass, aged thirty-three, but simply asked her about her prior work experience. The manager decided to hire Glass for the position. Does Phillips have a claim under the ADEA? Explain.

Discrimination Based on Disability

The legislation prohibiting employment discrimination because of disability is more recent than the other equal employment opportunity legislation. The Rehabilitation Act of 1973 prohibits discrimination because of disability by the federal government, by government contractors, and by recipients of federal financial assistance. The Americans with Disabilities Act of 1990 (ADA) also prohibits discrimination in employment because of disability. The ADA is patterned after the Civil Rights Act of 1964. The coverage of the ADA is much broader than the Rehabilitation Act. The ADA covers all employers with fifteen or more employees. This chapter discusses both the ADA and the Rehabilitation Act.

The Americans with Disabilities Act

The ADA is a comprehensive piece of civil rights legislation for individuals with disabilities. Title I of the act, which applies to employment, prohibits discrimination against individuals who are otherwise qualified for employment. The act became law on July 26, 1990, effective two years after that date for employers with twenty-five or more employees and three years from that date for employers with fifteen or more employees.

Coverage

The ADA applies to both private and public sector employers with fifteen or more employees but does not apply to most federal government employers, American Indian tribes, or bona fide private membership clubs. The Congressional Accountability Act of 1995[1] extended the coverage of the ADA and the Rehabilitation Act to the employees of the following offices:

- House of Representatives
- Senate

[1]Pub. L. 104-1, 109 Stat. 3.

- Capitol Guide Service
- Capitol Police
- Congressional Budget Office
- Office of the Architect of the Capitol
- Office of the Attending Physician
- Office of Technology Assessment

The Presidential and Executive Office Accountability Act[2] extended coverage of the ADA and the Rehabilitation Act to:

- the executive office of the president;
- the executive residence at the White House; and
- the official residence of the vice president.

U.S. employers operating abroad or controlling foreign corporations are covered with regard to the employment of U.S. citizens, unless compliance with the ADA would cause the employer to violate the law of the foreign country in which the workplace is located.

In *Board of Trustees of the University of Alabama v. Garrett*,[3] the U.S. Supreme Court, in a 5–4 decision, ruled that the Eleventh Amendment of the U.S. Constitution gave the states immunity from individual suits for damages under the ADA. The Court's reasoning in *Garrett* was consistent with its earlier decision in *Kimel v. Florida Board of Regents*.[4]

Provisions

The ADA prohibits covered employers from discriminating in any aspect of employment because of disability against an otherwise qualified individual with a disability. Illegal discrimination under the ADA includes:

> … limiting, segregating, or classifying employees or applicants in a way that adversely affects employment opportunities because of disability, using standards or criteria that have the effect of discriminating on the basis of disability or perpetuating discrimination against others, excluding or denying jobs or benefits to qualified individuals because of the disability of an individual with whom a qualified individual is known to associate, failing to make reasonable accommodation to the known limitations of an otherwise qualified individual unless such accommodation would impose an undue hardship, failing to hire an individual who would require reasonable accommodation, and failing to select or administer employment tests in the most effective manner to ensure that the results reflect the skills of applicants or employees with disabilities.

The ADA also prohibits retaliation against any individual because the individual has opposed any act or practice unlawful under the ADA or because the individual has filed a charge or participated in any manner in a proceeding under the ADA. The act also prohibits coercion or intimidation of, threats against, or interference with an individual's exercise of or enjoyment of any rights granted under the act.

---

[2]Pub. L. 104-331, 110 Stat. 4053.

[3]531 U.S. 356 (2001).

[4]528 U.S. 62 (2000).

Qualified Individual with a Disability

Qualified Individual with a Disability
An individual with a disability who is able to perform, with reasonable accommodation, the requirements of the job in question, despite the disability.

The ADA and the Rehabilitation Act impose obligations not to discriminate against an otherwise ***qualified individual with a disability***. According to the Supreme Court decision in *Southeastern Community College v. Davis*,[5] a person is a qualified individual with a disability if the person "is able to meet all … requirements in spite of his disability." The individual claiming to be qualified has the burden of demonstrating his or her ability to meet all physical requirements legitimately necessary for the performance of duties. An employer is not required to hire a person with a disability who is not capable of performing the duties of the job. However, the regulations under the act require the employer to make "reasonable accommodation" to the disabilities of individuals.

The ADA defines "qualified individual with a disability" as "an individual with a disability who, with or without reasonable accommodation, can perform the essential functions of the employment position that such individual holds or desires." When determining the essential functions of a job, the court or the EEOC, which administers and enforces the ADA, is to consider the employer's judgment as to what is essential. If a written job description is used for advertising the position or interviewing job applicants, that description is to be considered evidence of the essential functions of the job.

In *Cleveland v. Policy Management Systems*,[6] the Supreme Court held that an individual who applies for Social Security disability benefits may still be a "qualified individual with a disability" within the meaning of the ADA. In *Albertsons, Inc. v. Kirkingburg*,[7] the Supreme Court held that a truck driver who was not able to meet federal safety standards for commercial motor vehicle operators was not "a qualified individual with a disability" under the ADA. The employer was not required to participate in an experimental program that would have waived the safety standards.

Definition of Disability

The ADA defines "individual with a disability" very broadly. Disability means, with respect to an individual:

(a) a physical or mental impairment that substantially limits one or more of the major life activities of such individual;

(b) a record of such an impairment; or

(c) being regarded as having such an impairment.

---

[5]442 U.S. 397 (1979).

[6]526 U.S. 795 (1999).

[7]527 U.S. 555 (1999).

The ADA Amendments Act of 2008

The ADA was amended, effective January 1, 2009,[8] to indicate that the definition of disability should be construed in favor of broad coverage of individuals under the ADA. Specifically, the amendments expanded the definition of "major life activities" to include, but not limited to:

- Caring for oneself
- Performing manual tasks
- Seeing
- Hearing
- Eating
- Sleeping
- Walking
- Standing
- Lifting
- Bending
- Speaking
- Breathing
- Learning
- Reading
- Concentrating
- Thinking
- Communicating
- Working

The amended ADA also states that "major life activity" also includes the operation of a major bodily function, including but not limited to:

- Functions of the immune system
- Normal cell growth
- Digestive
- Bowel
- Bladder
- Neurological
- Brain
- Respiratory
- Circulatory
- Endocrine
- Reproductive functions

Individuals can establish that they are "regarded as having such an impairment" if they show that they have been subjected to discriminatory treatment because of an actual or perceived physical or mental impairment, whether or not the impairment limits or is perceived to limit a major life activity.

In cases decided before the 2009 amendments, the Supreme Court restricted the scope of the ADA's definition of disability. In *Sutton v. United Air Lines, Inc.*,[9] the court held that when determining whether an individual has a disability that substantially limits one or more major life activities, a court must also consider the existence of corrective, mitigating, or remedial measures that may reduce the effect of the disability. In *Toyota Motor Manufacturing, Kentucky, Inc. v. Williams*,[10] the Court stated that when assessing the impact of a disability of the major life activity of performing manual tasks, the central inquiry must be whether the individual is unable to perform the variety of tasks central to most people's daily lives, not whether the individual is unable to perform the tasks associated with her specific job.

---

[8]Pub. L. 110-325, 122 Stat. 3553.

[9]527 U.S. 471 (1999).

[10]534 U.S. 184 (2002).

The 2009 amendments specifically overrule those two decisions, and set out rules of construction for the definition of disability. The ADA now provides that "[a]n impairment that substantially limits one major life activity need not limit other major life activities in order to be considered a disability" and that "[a]n impairment that is episodic or in remission is a disability if it would substantially limit a major life activity when active." The amendments also state that when determining whether an impairment substantially limits a major life activity, the court is not to consider the ameliorative effects of mitigating measures, assistive devices or aids, other than eyeglasses or contact lenses.

Employees who use illegal drugs are not protected by the ADA, nor are alcoholics who use alcohol at the workplace or who are under the influence of alcohol at the workplace. Individuals who are former drug users or recovering drug users, including persons participating in a supervised rehabilitation program and individuals "erroneously regarded" as using drugs but who do not use drugs, are under the ADA's protection.

The definition of disability under the ADA includes infectious or contagious diseases, unless the disease presents a direct threat to the health or safety of others and that threat cannot be eliminated by reasonable accommodation. Temporary or short-term nonchronic conditions, with little or no long-term or permanent impact, are usually not considered disabilities. The 2009 amendments to the ADA specifically state that the "being regarded as having an impairment" aspect of the definition of disability shall not apply to impairments that are transitory (defined as an impairment with an actual or expected duration of six months or less) and minor. The act's protection does not apply to an individual who is a transvestite, nor are homosexuality, bisexuality, or sexual behavior disorders such as exhibitionism or transsexualism considered disabilities. Compulsive gambling, kleptomania, pyromania, and psychoactive substance use disorders resulting from current illegal use of drugs are also not within the definition of disability.

The WORKING Law

THE GENETIC INFORMATION NONDISCRIMINATION ACT

Congress passed the Genetic Information Nondiscrimination Act (GINA) in 2008; its employment-related provisions took effect in November, 2009. The legislation prohibits discrimination based on genetic information by employers with 15 or more employees, employment agencies, labor organizations and joint labor-management committees. GINA defines genetic information as an individual's genetic tests, the genetic tests of an individual's family members, and the "manifestation of a disease or disorder." Discrimination in hiring, firing, compensation or any other terms of employment based on genetic information is prohibited. Labor unions cannot exclude, expel, or otherwise discriminate against individuals based on genetic information. Employers are prohibited from inquiring about genetic information of applicants or employees, and from requesting or requiring, collecting or purchasing genetic information regarding an individual or an individual's family members. Employers must maintain the confidentiality of any genetic information. Employers may ask employees to provide genetic information as part of a voluntary wellness program and employers that are forensic laboratories for law enforcement purposes may require employees to provide genetic information only to be used to detect sample contamination for analysis of DNA identification markers. Voluntary wellness programs may not require employee participation nor may the employee be penalized for not participating. The employee must give written authorization describing the genetic information to be obtained, the general purposes for which it will be used, and the restrictions on disclosure of the information. Employers may conduct genetic monitoring of the biological effects of toxic substances in the workplace, if the employer gives written notice of the monitoring, the employee gives written authorization, the employee is given the individual monitoring results, and the employer receives only aggregate monitoring results not identifying individuals.

case 10.1 »

CHALFANT V. TITAN DISTRIBUTION, INC.

475 F.3d 982 (8th Cir. 2007)

Facts: Titan Distribution had contracted with Quintak, Inc. to run its tire mounting and distribution operation. Quintak employees worked at Titan's building using Titan's equipment. In July 2002, Titan decided to end the contract with Quintak and run the operation itself. Titan announced it would hire some of Quintak's employees, but they would have to apply and have a qualifying physical. Titan managers Barucic and Luthin were in charge of the application process.

Robert Chalfant had worked for Quintak as a second shift supervisor. His duties included loading trucks with a forklift. Chalfant had been working for Quintak for five years. In the past, Chalfant had suffered a heart attack and had undergone carpal tunnel surgery and heart bypass surgery, and he had arthritis in his back, neck, ankle, and hands. He applied for the same position with Titan that he had had with Quintak, second shift supervisor. In his application, Chalfant stated that he was physically handicapped.

The physical examination was conducted by Dr. Anthony Sciorrota, who determined that Chalfant could work in his current capacity, including driving a forklift. Dr. Sciorrota also wrote on the exam record that Chalfant would need to have a functional capacity examination if he was required to do heavy lifting. Barucic received the exam record and wrote "OK for lift driving" on the top of the record and sent it to Luthin with the application. While his application was pending, Chalfant continued working as a second shift supervisor in the tire and wheel mounting division as an employee of Labor Ready, a temporary work service used by Titan during the application period.

During the first week of August 2002, Chalfant was told by a Titan manager that he was included in a list of Quintak employees to be retained by Titan, but on August 8, 2002, he was told that he had failed the physical and would not be hired. Within two months, Chalfant took a job with AMPCO Systems, a parking ramp management company. At AMPCO, Chalfant performed general service work. His job there involved walking up to five miles a day and lifting more than he did as a Quintak employee.

Chalfant sued Titan for disability discrimination under the Americans with Disabilities Act. After a trial, the jury found for Chalfant on the disability discrimination claims and awarded $60,000 in back pay and $100,000 in punitive damages. The district court then awarded $18,750 in front pay. Titan appealed.

Issue: Has Chalfant demonstrated sufficient evidence to establish that Titan regarded him as disabled under the ADA?

Decision: Titan regarded Chalfant as disabled because it mistakenly believed that his physical ailments substantially limited his ability to work in a broad range of jobs. Chalfant wrote in his application packet that he considered himself physically handicapped because of his ailments. Titan therefore knew about the ailments. The physician who conducted the physical exam did not find that Chalfant had failed the physical and that he could operate a forklift. The doctor did recommend that Chalfant undergo a functional capacity examination if he was required to do heavy lifting. Chalfant applied for the second shift supervisor position, a position that did not require unique or strenuous lifting. Titan employees testified that there was no lifting requirement, or even a job description, for the second shift supervisor position. Chalfant also testified that he had not been required to do any heavy lifting when he was the second shift supervisor for Quintak and Labor Ready.

The court of appeals held that there was sufficient evidence for a reasonable jury to conclude that Titan believed Chalfant's impairments substantially restricted his ability to work in a class of jobs or a broad range of jobs despite the fact that he was able to perform the essential functions of the second shift supervisor position. Titan accepted that Chalfant passed his physical, notified him that he would be hired, then changed the results of his physical to "failed" and notified him that he would not be hired. Titan's inconsistent behavior could lead a reasonable jury to infer that Titan knew it might be acting in violation of federal law. There was sufficient evidence to support the submission of the issue of punitive damages to the jury.

The court of appeals affirmed the trial court verdict and the award of punitive damages to Chalfont.

«

Medical Exams and Tests

The ADA limits the ability of an employer to test for or inquire into the disabilities of job applicants and employees. Employers are prohibited from asking about the existence, nature, or severity of a disability. However, an employer may ask about the individual's ability to perform the functions and requirements of the job. Employers are likewise not permitted to require preemployment medical examinations of applicants. However, once an offer of a job has been extended to an applicant, employers can require a medical exam, provided that such an exam is required of all entering employees. Current employees are similarly protected from inquiries or exams, unless those requirements can be shown to be "job-related and consistent with business necessity." The act does not consider a drug test to be a medical examination, and it does not prohibit an employer from administering drug tests to its employees or from making employment decisions based on the results of such tests.

Reasonable Accommodation

The definition of a "qualified individual with a disability" includes the individual who is capable of performing the essential functions of a job with reasonable accommodation on the part of the employer. The ADA and the Rehabilitation Act impose on employers the obligation to make reasonable accommodations for such individuals or employees, unless the accommodation would impose "undue hardship" on the employer. Examples of accommodations listed in the ADA include:

- Making facilities accessible to disabled individuals
- Restructuring jobs
- Providing part-time or modified work schedules
- Acquiring or modifying equipment

- Adjusting or modifying examinations, training materials, or policies
- Providing qualified readers or interpreters

Failure to make such reasonable accommodation (which would not impose an undue hardship), or failure to hire an individual because of the need to make accommodation for that individual, is included in the definition of illegal discrimination under the act. Employers are not required to create a new position for the disabled applicant or employee, nor are they required to offer the individual the most expensive means of accommodation.

A number of courts have held that extending a medical leave beyond the twelve-week leave available under the Family and Medical Leave Act (discussed in Chapter 7) can be a reasonable accommodation to an employee's disability under the ADA. The courts have considered whether the extended leave would create an undue hardship for the employer, and whether the leave would permit the employee eventually to perform the essential functions of her or his job, as in *Nunes v. Wal-Mart Stores*[11] and *Cehrs v. Northeast Ohio Alzheimer's Research Center.*[12] According to *Smith v. Blue Cross/Blue Shield of Kansas, Inc.*,[13] an accommodation that would eliminate an essential function of the employee's job is not reasonable, and an employer is not required to wait indefinitely for an employee to return to work.

When an employee requests an accommodation that conflicts with the seniority provisions of a collective bargaining agreement, the employer ordinarily need only demonstrate the conflict to establish that the accommodation is unreasonable. However, according to the Supreme Court decision in *U.S. Airways, Inc. v. Barnett,*[14] the employee may present evidence of special circumstances that would make an exception to the seniority rules reasonable under the particular facts.

Reasonable accommodations may include the minimal realignment or assignment of job duties or the provision of certain assistance devices. For example, an employer could reassign certain filing or reception duties from the requirements of a typist position to accommodate an individual confined to a wheelchair. An employer could also be required to equip telephones with amplifiers to accommodate an employee's hearing disability. Although the extent of accommodation required must be determined case by case, drastic realignment of work assignments or the undertaking of severe financial costs by an employer would be considered "unreasonable" and would not be required. In *PGA Tour, Inc. v. Martin,*[15] (which involved the public accommodation provisions of Title III of the ADA and not the ADA's employment-related provisions under Title I), the Court held that allowing a disabled golfer to ride in a golf cart, rather than walk during a golf tournament, was a reasonable accommodation that did not fundamentally alter the nature of the event.

How should an employer respond to an employee's request for reasonable accommodation? This is discussed in the following case.

---

[11]164 F.3d 1243 (9th Cir. 1999).

[12]155 F.3d 775 (6th Cir. 1998).

[13]102 F.3d 1075 (10th Cir. 1996), *cert. denied,* 522 U.S. 811 (1997).

[14]535 U.S. 391 (2002).

[15]532 U.S. 661 (2001).

case 10.2 » HUMPHREY V. MEMORIAL HOSPITALS ASSOCIATION

239 F.3d 1128 (9th Cir. 2001)

Background

[Carolyn Humphrey worked for Memorial Hospitals Association (MHA) as a medical transcriptionist from 1986 until her termination in 1995. Humphrey's transcription performance was generally evaluated as excellent. In 1989, she began to experience problems getting to work on time or at all. She began engaging in a series of obsessive rituals that prevented her from arriving at work on time. She felt compelled to wash, rinse and brush her hair for up to three hours. She would also feel compelled to dress very slowly, to repeatedly check for papers she needed, and to pull out strands of her hair and examine them closely because she felt as though something was crawling on her scalp.

MHA gave Humphrey a disciplinary warning in June 1994 because of her tardiness and absenteeism, but her obsessions and peculiar rituals grew worse after the warning, and her attendance record did not improve. In December 1994, she received a "Level III" warning, because she was tardy four days and absent one day in a two-week period. Humphrey began to suspect that her debilitating symptoms and inability to get to work on time might be related to a medical condition.

In May 1995, after a diagnostic evaluation and psychological testing, Dr. John Jacisin diagnosed her with obsessive-compulsive disorder (OCD). He sent a letter explaining that diagnosis to her supervisor on May 18, 1995, telling her that Humphrey's OCD "is directly contributing to her problems with lateness." The letter also stated that Jacisin would like to see Humphrey continue to work, but it may be necessary for her to take some time off until her symptoms are under better control.

On June 7, 1995, Humphrey met with her supervisor to review Dr. Jacisin's letter. What happened at this meeting is disputed: MHA claimed that Humphrey rejected the leave of absence alluded to in the doctor's letter, but Humphrey claimed that she was never offered a leave of absence and never rejected one. Humphrey wanted to try to keep working, if possible, and the supervisor told her that she could have an "accommodation" that would allow her to do so. The supervisor suggested a flexible start time arrangement, and Humphrey accepted, but she continued to miss work. MHA never suggested modifying the accommodation.

On September 18, 1995, Humphrey sent her supervisor an e-mail request that she be allowed to work from her home as a new accommodation. MHA did allow some medical transcriptionists to work out of their homes, but MHA denied Humphrey's request because of her disciplinary warnings for tardiness and absenteeism. The supervisor did not suggest an alternative accommodation or reassess its arrangements to accommodate Humphrey in light of the failure of the flexible work schedule arrangement.

Sometime later Humphrey asked about working at home but was told that she would have to be free of attendance problems for a year before she could be considered for an at-home transcriptionist position. Humphrey was absent two more times, and was fired on October 10, 1995 because of her history of tardiness and absenteeism. Humphrey testified that after learning of her termination, she went across the hall to her supervisor's office and asked if she might take a leave of absence instead, but her request was refused. MHA concedes that it would have granted the request if Humphrey had asked for a leave of absence prior to her termination, as MHA had a policy of permitting medical leaves of absence to employees with disabilities.

Humphrey filed suit against MHA under the ADA. The district court granted MHA's motion for summary judgment, and Humphrey appealed to the U.S. Court of Appeals for the Ninth Circuit.]

Reinhardt, Circuit Judge

Humphrey contends that MHA violated the ADA and the FEHA by failing to reasonably accommodate her disability and by terminating her because of that disability.... To prevail on a claim of unlawful discharge under the ADA, the plaintiff must establish that he is a qualified individual with a disability and that the employer terminated him because of his disability.... It is undisputed that Humphrey had the skills, training, and experience to transcribe medical records.... Humphrey is a "qualified individual" under the ADA so long as she is able to perform the essential functions of her job "with or without reasonable accommodation." Either of two potential reasonable accommodations might have made it possible for Humphrey to perform the essential functions of her job: granting her a leave of absence or allowing her to become a "home-based transcriptionist." ...

Working at home is a reasonable accommodation when the essential functions of the position can be performed at home and a work-at-home arrangement would not cause undue hardship for the employer. [EEOC Enforcement

Guidance: Reasonable Accommodation and Undue Hardship Under the Americans with Disabilities Act, FEP (BNA) 405:7601, at 7626 (March 1, 1999).] Humphrey does not dispute that regular and predictable performance of the job is an essential part of the transcriptionist position because many of the medical records must be transcribed within twenty-four hours, and frequent and unscheduled absences would prevent the department from meeting its deadlines. However, physical attendance at the MHA offices is not an essential job duty; in fact ... MHA permits some of its medical transcriptionists to work at home.

MHA denied Humphrey's application for a work-at-home position because of her disciplinary record, which consisted of ... warnings for tardiness and absenteeism prior to her diagnosis of OCD. It would be inconsistent with the purposes of the ADA to permit an employer to deny an otherwise reasonable accommodation because of past disciplinary action taken due to the disability sought to be accommodated. Thus, Humphrey's disciplinary record does not constitute an appropriate basis for denying her a work-at-home accommodation....

... We conclude, as a matter of law, that ... MHA had an affirmative duty under the ADA to explore further methods of accommodation before terminating Humphrey.

Once an employer becomes aware of the need for accommodation, that employer has a mandatory obligation under the ADA to engage in an interactive process with the employee to identify and implement appropriate reasonable accommodations. "An appropriate reasonable accommodation must be effective, in enabling the employee to perform the duties of the position." The interactive process requires communication and good-faith exploration of possible accommodations between employers and individual employees, and neither side can delay or obstruct the process. Employers, who fail to engage in the interactive process in good faith, face liability for the remedies imposed by the statute if a reasonable accommodation would have been possible.

Moreover, we have held that the duty to accommodate "is a 'continuing' duty that is 'not exhausted by one effort.'" ... the employer's obligation to engage in the interactive process extends beyond the first attempt at accommodation and continues when the employee asks for a different accommodation or where the employer is aware that the initial accommodation is failing and further accommodation is needed. This rule fosters the framework of cooperative problem-solving contemplated by the ADA, by encouraging employers to seek to find accommodations that really work, and by avoiding the creation of a perverse incentive for employees to request the most drastic and burdensome accommodation possible out of fear that a lesser accommodation might be ineffective.

... Even if we assume that Humphrey turned down the leave of absence in June in favor of a flexible start-time arrangement, her attempt to perform her job functions by means of a less drastic accommodation does not forfeit her right to a more substantial one upon the failure of the initial effort.

By the time of her annual performance review in September, it was abundantly clear to MHA that the flexible start time accommodation was not succeeding; Humphrey had accumulated six unreported absences in each of the months of August and September, and her evaluation stated that her attendance record was "unacceptable." At this point, MHA had a duty to explore further arrangements to reasonably accommodate Humphrey's disability.

Humphrey also realized that the accommodation was not working, and requested a work-at-home position. When it received that request, MHA could have either granted it or initiated discussions with Humphrey regarding other alternatives. Instead, MHA denied her request without suggesting any alternative solutions, or exploring with her the possibility of other accommodations. Rather than fulfill its obligation to engage in a cooperative dialogue with Humphrey, Pierson's e-mail suggested that the matter was closed: "During our 6/7/95 meeting, you requested to be accommodated for your disability by having a flexible start-time, stating that you would have no problems staying for a full shift once you arrived. You were given this flexible start time accommodation which continues to remain in effect." ... [A]n employer fails to engage in the interactive process as a matter of law where it rejects the employee's proposed accommodations by letter and offers no practical alternatives. Similarly, MHA's rejection of Humphrey's work-at-home request and its failure to explore with Humphrey the possibility of other accommodations, once it was aware that the initial arrangement was not effective, constitutes a violation of its duty regarding the mandatory interactive process.

Given MHA's failure to engage in the interactive process, liability is appropriate if a reasonable accommodation without undue hardship to the employer would otherwise have been possible. As we have already discussed, a leave of absence was a reasonable accommodation for Humphrey's disability. Ordinarily, whether an accommodation would pose an undue hardship on the employer is a factual question. Here, however, MHA has conceded that granting a leave of absence would not have posed an undue hardship.

MHA had a policy of granting leaves to disabled employees, and admits that it would have given Humphrey a leave had she asked for one at any time before her termination. MHA's ultimate position, therefore, is simply that Humphrey is not entitled to a leave of absence because she failed to ask for one before she was fired. As we have explained, however, MHA was under a continuing duty to offer a reasonable accommodation. Accordingly, we hold as a matter of law ... that MHA violated the ADA's reasonable accommodation requirement.

Unlike a simple failure to accommodate claim, an unlawful discharge claim requires a showing that the employer terminated the employee because of his disability.... In this case, MHA's stated reason for Humphrey's termination was absenteeism and tardiness. For purposes of the ADA, with a few exceptions, conduct resulting from a disability is considered to be part of the disability, rather than a separate basis for termination. The link between the disability and termination is particularly strong where it is the employer's failure to reasonably accommodate a known disability that leads to discharge for performance inadequacies resulting from that disability.... Humphrey has presented sufficient evidence to create a triable issue of fact as to whether her attendance problems were caused by OCD. In sum, a jury could reasonably find the requisite causal link between a disability of OCD and Humphrey's absenteeism and conclude that MHA fired Humphrey because of her disability.

For the foregoing reasons, the district court's grant of summary judgment to MHA on Humphrey's ADA and FEHA claims is hereby REVERSED and the case is REMANDED for proceedings consistent with this opinion.

It is so ordered.

Case Questions

1. How did Humphrey's condition affect her ability to perform her job? Was Humphrey "an otherwise qualified individual with a disability" under the ADA? Explain your answers.
2. What accommodation did the employer initially offer to Humphrey? Was the accommodation effective? Explain.
3. What accommodation did Humphrey then request from her employer? How did the employer respond to her request? Why?
4. Was the employer's decision to terminate Humphrey a violation of the ADA? Explain your answer.

A court's consideration of what would be a reasonable accommodation to the individual's disability is to be done on a case-by-case basis. What may be a reasonable accommodation in one situation may not be reasonable under differing circumstances. In *Vande Zande v. State of Wisconsin Dept. of Administration*,[16] the court held that an employer's refusal to allow a disabled employee to work at home was not a violation of the ADA. The court there stated:

> Most jobs in organizations public or private involve teamwork under supervision rather than solitary unsupervised work, and teamwork under supervision generally cannot be performed at home without a substantial reduction in the quality of the employee's performance. This will no doubt change as communications technology advances, but is the situation today. Generally, therefore, an employer is not required to accommodate a disability by allowing the disabled worker to work, by himself, without supervision, at home.... An employer is not required to allow disabled workers to work at home, where their productivity inevitably would be greatly reduced.

Undue Hardship
An accommodation that requires significant difficulty or expense for the employer.

Undue Hardship

An employer is not required to make accommodation for an individual if that accommodation would impose "undue hardship on the operation of the business of the covered entity." The ADA provides a complex definition of what constitutes an ***undue hardship***, including a list of

[16] 44 F.3d 538 (7th Cir. 1995).

factors to be considered in determining the impact of the accommodation on the employer. An accommodation imposes an undue hardship if it requires significant difficulty or expense when considered in light of the following factors:

- the nature and cost of the accommodation needed under this act;
- the overall financial resources of the facility or facilities involved in the provision of the reasonable accommodation; the number of persons employed at such facility; the effect on expenses and resources, or the impact otherwise of such accommodation upon the operation of the facility;
- the overall financial resources of the covered entity; the overall size of the business of a covered entity with respect to the number of its employees; the number, type, and location of its facilities; and
- the type of operation or operations of the covered entity, including the composition, structure, and functions of the work force of such entity; the geographic separateness, administrative, or fiscal relationship of the facility or facilities in question to the covered entity.

It should be obvious that the definition of undue hardship is intended to be flexible. What would be a reasonable accommodation for Microsoft could be a significant expense or difficulty for a much smaller employer.

Concept *Summary* » 10.1

Discrimination Based on Disability

- The Americans with Disabilities Act (Title I) prohibits employment discrimination based on disability against otherwise qualified individuals with a disability
- ADA applies to public and private sector employers with fifteen or more employees
- ADA requires employers to make reasonable accommodation to otherwise qualified individuals with a disability, unless accommodation would impose undue hardship on employer

Defenses Under the ADA

In addition to the defense of undue hardship, the ADA sets out four other possible defenses for employers.

Direct Threat to Safety or Health of Others

Employers may refuse to hire or accommodate an individual if that individual's condition poses a "direct threat" to the health or safety of others in the workplace. Direct threat is defined as a "significant risk to the health or safety of others that cannot be eliminated by reasonable accommodation." The definition of disability under the act includes infectious or contagious diseases. According to *School Board of Nassau County, Florida v. Arline*,[17] in determining if such a disease presents a direct threat to others, the employer's considerations must be based on objective and accepted public health guidelines, not on stereotypes or public attitudes or fears. An employer would probably not be required to hire an individual with an active case of hepatitis or tuberculosis, but could not discriminate against an individual who has been treated for cancer, exposed to the HIV virus (associated with AIDS), or has had a history of mental illness. According to *Chevron, U.S.A. v. Echazabal*,[18] an employer may refuse to hire an individual when performance of the job would endanger the individual's own health due to an existing disability.

Job-Related Criteria

Employers may hire, select, or promote individuals based on tests, standards, or criteria that are job related or are consistent with business necessity. Employers could refuse to hire or promote individuals with a disability who are unable to meet such standards, tests, or criteria or when performance of the job cannot be accomplished by reasonable accommodation. For example, an employer would be justified in refusing to hire a blind person for a bus driver position.

Food Handler Defense

An employer in the food service industry may refuse to assign or transfer to a job involving food handling any individual who has an infectious or communicable disease that can be transmitted to others through the handling of food, when the risk of infection cannot be eliminated by reasonable accommodation. The ADA requires the secretary of Health and Human Services to develop a list of diseases that can be transmitted through food handling. Only the diseases on that list (which is to be updated annually) may be used as a basis for refusal under this defense. The secretary of Health and Human Services has stated that HIV infection (associated with AIDS) cannot be transmitted through food handling.[19]

Religious Entities

Title I of the ADA does not prohibit a religious corporation, association, educational institution, or society from giving preference in employment to individuals of a particular religion to perform work connected with the carrying on by such corporation, association, educational institution, or society of its activities. Thus, as in the *Amos* case (see Chapter Eight, a gymnasium operated by the Church of Jesus Christ of Latter-day Saints may refuse to hire an individual with a disability who is not a member of that church.

---

[17] 480 U.S. 273 (1987).

[18] 536 U.S. 73 (2002).

[19] See "How to Comply with the Americans with Disabilities: A Guide for Restaurants and Other Food Service Employers," [accessible at http://www.eeoc.gov/facts/restaurant_guide.html].

Concept *Summary* » 10.2

Defenses Under the ADA

- Defenses under the ADA:
  - Individual's condition poses a direct threat to the health or safety of the individual or others in the workplace
  - Employers can hire based on job-related criteria
  - Employers in the food service industry can refuse to hire individuals with diseases that can be communicated through handling of food
  - Religious entities can give preference to members of a particular religion.

Enforcement of the ADA

The ADA is enforced by the EEOC. The act specifically provides that the procedures and remedies under Title VII of the Civil Rights Act of 1964 shall be those used or available under the ADA. This means that an individual must first file a complaint with a state or local agency, where appropriate, and then with the EEOC. The EEOC, or the individual if the EEOC declines, may file suit against an employer. Remedies available include injunctions, hiring or reinstatement order (with or without back pay), and attorney fees. The Civil Rights Act of 1991 amended 42 U.S.C. Section 1981A to allow suits for compensatory and punitive damages against parties accused of intentional discrimination in violation of the ADA.

Such damages are not available where the alleged discrimination involves provision of a reasonable accommodation of an individual's disability and the employer demonstrates that it made a good-faith effort to accommodate the individual's disability. Punitive damages are not available against public sector employers. The ADA also directs the EEOC to develop and issue regulations to enforce the act.

The Rehabilitation Act

The Rehabilitation Act of 1973 protects the employment rights of individuals with a disability. The act's provisions prohibit discrimination against otherwise qualified individuals with a disability. The definition of "individual with a disability" under the Rehabilitation Act is similar to that under the ADA:

> any person who (a) has a physical or mental impairment, which substantially limits one or more of such person's major life activities, (b) has a record of such an impairment, or (c) is regarded as having such an impairment.

The Supreme Court decision in *School Board of Nassau County, Fla. v. Arline*[20] held that the definition of disability under the Rehabilitation Act included contagious diseases; the employee with an infectious disease is "otherwise qualified" within the meaning of the act if the threat posed to others by the disease can be eliminated or avoided through reasonable accommodation by the employer.

The Civil Rights Restoration Act of 1988, passed by Congress over President Reagan's veto, amended the definition of "individual with a disability" under the Rehabilitation Act to exclude a person with:

> a currently contagious disease or infection and who, by reason of such disease or infection, would constitute a direct threat to the health or safety of other individuals or who, by reason of the currently contagious disease or infection, is unable to perform the duties of the job.

Provisions

The Rehabilitation Act imposes obligations not to discriminate against otherwise qualified individuals with a disability. According to *Southeastern Community College v. Davis*, a person is "an otherwise qualified individual with a disability" under the Rehabilitation Act (as with the ADA) if the person is able to meet the requirements of the position in spite of the disability or with reasonable accommodation of the disability. The individual claiming to be qualified has the burden of demonstrating her or his ability to meet all physical requirements legitimately necessary for the performance of the duties of the position. An employer is not required to hire a person with a disability who is not capable of performing the duties of the position. However, the employer is required to make reasonable accommodation to the disability of the individual if such accommodation will allow the individual to perform the job and does not impose undue hardship on the employer.

Three main provisions of the Rehabilitation Act deal with discrimination against otherwise qualified individuals with a disability:

- Section 501 prohibits such discrimination by federal government employers
- Section 503 prohibits such discrimination by employers with federal contracts
- Section 504 prohibits the denial of participation in, or the benefits of, any federally funded activity to an otherwise qualified individual with a disability

Section 501: Federal Government Employers

Section 501 of the Rehabilitation Act prohibits discrimination on the basis of disability by federal executive agencies, departments, and instrumentalities. It also requires them to develop affirmative action plans for the hiring, placement, and advancement of individuals with disabilities. The plans are to be updated annually and reviewed and approved by the EEOC.

Enforcement of Section 501

Section 505(a) of the act provides that Section 501 is enforced through the provisions under Title VII of the Civil Rights Act of 1964, as amended. While federal executive employees with complaints of alleged violations may bring a private suit, they must first seek review of the

[20] 480 U.S. 273 (1987).

alleged violation with their agency's Equal Employment Opportunity (EEO) counselor, whose decision is subject to a formal review through the agency's EEO complaint procedures. The employee can then either seek judicial review of the final decision of the agency or appeal the action to the EEOC. If the employee elects to seek judicial review, a civil action may be filed in federal court within ninety days of receipt of notice of the agency's final decision or within 180 days of filing with the agency if there has been no decision. Employees choosing to refer the complaint to the EEOC may file a civil action within ninety days of receipt of the EEOC's notice of final action or within 180 days of filing with the EEOC if there has been no EEOC decision within that time.

Remedies available include injunctions, orders directing hiring or reinstatement, with or without back pay and interest, attorney fees, and expert witness fees. In addition to the remedies under the Civil Rights Act, plaintiffs alleging intentional discrimination in violation of Section 501 can bring an action seeking compensatory damages under 42 U.S.C. Section 1981A. Such damages are not available when the alleged discriminatory practice involves reasonable accommodation and the respondent showed good-faith efforts. Punitive damages under 42 U.S.C. Section 1981A are not available against public sector employers.

Section 503: Federal Contractors

Section 503 of the Rehabilitation Act prohibits discrimination on the basis of disability by federal contractors with annual contracts in excess of $10,000. Federal contractors with contracts of $50,000 or more are also required to develop affirmative action plans as to the hiring of otherwise qualified individuals with a disability. Enforcement of Section 503 is through the administrative procedures of the Office of Federal Contract Compliance Programs (OFCCP) under the Department of Labor. Aggrieved individuals must file a complaint with the OFCCP. There is no individual right to file suit under Section 503. Employers found in violation of Section 503 may be subject to injunctions, withholding of progress payments under the contract, termination of the contract, or debarment from future contracts. Remedies available under the administrative procedures for individuals who are victims of discrimination in violation of Section 503 include hiring or reinstatement, back pay, and benefits.

Section 504: Federally Assisted Programs

Section 504 of the Rehabilitation Act prohibits discrimination on the basis of disability against otherwise qualified individuals with a disability by persons or entities operating or administering any federally funded programs. To be covered by Section 504, the entities must be the direct recipient of federal financial assistance. According to *U.S. Department of Transportation v. Paralyzed Veterans of America*,[21] indirect beneficiaries are not recipients within the meaning of the section. The statutory language provides that "No otherwise qualified individual with a disability … shall … (solely by reason of the disability) be excluded from participation in, be denied the benefits of, or be subjected to discrimination under …" any program receiving federal financial assistance. If any part of the entity receives any federal

[21]477 U.S. 597 (1986).

funding, the nondiscrimination requirement applies to the entire entity. There is no minimum funding amount required for coverage under Section 504. While the language of Section 504 does not specifically refer to employment, its prohibition against discrimination extends to employment discrimination, even though the primary purpose of the federal financial assistance is not providing employment, according to the Supreme Court decision in *Consolidated Rail Corp. v. Darrone.*[22]

Employers are required to make reasonable accommodation to the otherwise qualified employee's or applicant's condition. Any employment requirements that adversely affect disabled persons must be directly and substantially related to business necessity and safe job performance. In *Southeastern Community College v. Davis*, the Supreme Court upheld the college's refusal to admit a woman with a severe hearing disability to the registered nurses training program. The woman's disability was not correctable with a hearing aid and would create problems in carrying out her duties during the clinical portions of her training. The college was not required to redesign the program to accommodate her disability because the components of the nursing program were required by state law.

Enforcement of Section 504

The regulations under Section 504 make the agencies administering the funding the primary enforcement authority for complaints against the recipients of such funding. Most agencies have developed their own administrative procedures for investigating and adjudicating claims of discrimination. The federal Department of Education coordinates and oversees enforcement of Section 504 by the other federal agencies. Unlike Section 503, there is an individual right to sue under Section 504. Persons claiming a violation of Section 504 may seek equitable relief and recover back pay, monetary damages, and legal fees; they are not required to pursue the agency's administrative procedures before filing suit. Punitive damages are not recoverable in private suits brought under Section 504, according to *Barnes v. Gorman.*[23]

Concept *Summary* » 10.3

THE REHABILITATION ACT

- Section 501 prohibits disability discrimination by federal government employers
- Section 503 prohibits disability discrimination by federal contractors with annual contracts over $10,000
- Section 504 prohibits disability discrimination by persons or entities operating any program receiving federal financial assistance

[22]465 U.S. 624 (1984).

[23]536 U.S. 181 (2002).

AIDS and the Disability Discrimination Legislation

Recall that the definition of disability under both the ADA and the Rehabilitation Act includes contagious diseases, such as AIDS. Although AIDS is contagious, medical authorities agree that it is not transmitted through the casual contact likely to occur in the workplace. The courts have consistently held that persons who are HIV-positive suffering from AIDS or AIDS-related conditions are individuals with a disability under the Rehabilitation Act and the ADA. Therefore, employers are required to make reasonable accommodation for employees with AIDS or related conditions, as long as the employees are capable of performing the essential functions of the job and do not present a direct threat to the health or safety of others.

The nature of the risk posed by the employee's HIV-positive status, or AIDS infection, depends on the nature of the job in question. In *Chalk v. U.S. District Court,*[24] a teacher who was diagnosed with AIDS was granted an injunction against transfer to an administrative position because the risk of AIDS transmission in the classroom was minimal. However, in *Doe v. University of Md. Medical Systems Corp.*,[25] an HIV-positive neurosurgeon was not entitled to continue his residency because he posed a significant risk to his patients, and in *Doe v. Washington University,*[26] an HIV-positive dental student was not permitted to continue his dental education. *Severino v. North Fort Meyers Fire Control Dist.*[27] held that a firefighter who was HIV-positive was reasonably accommodated under the Rehabilitation Act by being reassigned to light duties because the medical evidence indicated a risk of transmission of his disease to others during rescue operations. In *Leckelt v.Board of Comm. of Hosp. District No. 1,*[28] a licensed practical nurse who refused to report the results of an HIV test was legally discharged for violating a hospital policy requiring employees to report any infectious disease to protect patients, coworkers, and the infected employees themselves.

Because the definition of individual with disability under both the ADA and the Rehabilitation Act includes an individual regarded as having a physical or mental condition that impairs a major life activity, an employee who is discharged because of a false and unfounded rumor that he or she was infected with HIV is protected as an individual with a disability. Do individuals who are HIV positive, but who do not present any evidence of impairment and who suffer from no ailments that affect the manner in which they live, fall under the definition of "individual with a disability" under the ADA or the Rehabilitation Act? The U.S. Supreme Court, in *Bragdon v. Abbott,*[29] held that asymptomatic HIV was a disability within the meaning of the ADA because it was a medical condition that impaired the major life activity of reproduction.

---

[24] 840 F.2d 701 (9th Cir. 1988).

[25] 50 F.3d 1261 (4th Cir. 1995).

[26] 780 F. Supp. 628 (E.D. Mo. 1991).

[27] 935 F.2d 1179 (11th Cir. 1991).

[28] 909 F.2d 820 (5th Cir. 1990).

[29] 524 U.S. 624 (1998).

State Disability Discrimination Legislation

All fifty states have laws that prohibit discrimination against individuals with disabilities. The coverage of such laws varies; some cover both private and public sector employers, while others apply only to the public sector. The provisions of such laws generally parallel those of the ADA but in some instances go beyond the ADA protections. The California Fair Employment and Housing Act requires only that physical and mental disabilities place a "limitation" on a major life activity, rather than the "substantial limitation" required under the ADA. Some states have specific legislation prohibiting discrimination against individuals with specific conditions, such as the sickle cell trait, Tay-Sachs disease, HIV, or AIDS. Kentucky, for example, prohibits employers from requiring that applicants or employees take an HIV test, unless the employer can establish that the absence of HIV infection is a BFOQ for the job in question. New York, New Jersey, and North Carolina prohibit discrimination against applicants or employees because of genetic traits or conditions and prohibit requiring individuals to undergo genetic testing as a condition of employment.

Drug Abuse and Drug Testing

Neither the ADA nor the Rehabilitation Act prohibits drug testing by employers. The ADA specifically states that drug tests are not considered medical exams under its provisions. Section 104 of the ADA specifically excludes from the definition of "qualified individual with a disability" any persons who are currently engaged in the illegal use of drugs and allows employers to prohibit the use of alcohol and illegal drugs at the workplace. The Rehabilitation Act also excludes from its protection individuals who are alcoholics or drug abusers whose current use of alcohol or drugs prevents them from performing the duties of the job or whose employment constitutes a direct threat to the property or safety of others. Note that the ADA and the Rehabilitation Act refer to the current use of drugs or alcohol. Both laws specifically protect:

- former drug users who have successfully been rehabilitated;
- persons who are participating in or have completed a supervised drug rehabilitation program and who no longer use drugs; and
- persons who are "erroneously regarded" as using illegal drugs but who do not actually use such drugs.

The following case deals with the question of whether an employee who was addicted to cocaine and who voluntarily entered a drug rehabilitation program is protected under the ADA.

case 10.3 »

Brown v. Lucky Stores, Inc.

246 F.3d 1182 (9th Cir. 2001)

[Karen Brown was employed by Lucky Stores. She was arrested for drunk driving, possession of methamphetamine, and being under the influence of an illegal controlled substance. Because she could not post bail, she remained in jail from November 10 to November 15, 1996. She then appeared in court and was convicted of driving under the influence of intoxicants and possession of methamphetamine. The court conditioned suspension of her sentence on her participation in a round-the-clock 90-day drug and alcohol rehabilitation program. She attended the rehabilitation program from November 15, 1996 to February 12, 1997.

On the day of her arrest, Brown called Rebecca Caldeira, her sister-in-law, and asked her to inform John Hunt, Brown's manager at Lucky Stores, that she was in jail and could not make it to work that day. Caldeira called Hunt on November 10 and informed him of Brown's incarceration. Brown did not report for work on Nov. 10th, 11th, and 16th because she was either in jail or attending the rehabilitation program. Lucky Stores fired Brown for abandoning her job. The collective bargaining agreement ("CBA") governing Brown's employment authorized the discharge of an employee for "improper conduct," and a company policy provided that an employee who misses three consecutive shifts for an unauthorized reason will be terminated from employment.

Brown filed suit against Lucky Stores and Hunt alleging discrimination based on her alcoholism under the ADA, Rehabilitation Act, FEHA and various state tort and contract claims. The trial court granted summary judgment in favor of Lucky Stores and Hunt on the ADA, Rehabilitation Act and FEHA claims. The court concluded that an employer is permitted to terminate an alcoholic employee for violating a rational rule of conduct even if the misconduct was related to the employee's alcoholism. The court further concluded Lucky Stores did not have a duty to accommodate Brown because she never requested an accommodation.]

FISHER, Circuit Judge

Karen L. Brown appeals the district court's grant of summary judgment in favor of Lucky Stores and John Hunt on her claims that she was terminated because of her alcoholism in violation of the Americans with Disabilities Act ("ADA"), the Rehabilitation Act and California's Fair Employment and Housing Act ("FEHA").... This appeal requires us to address the scope of the ADA's so-called "safe harbor" provision [42 U.S.C. § 12114(b)(2)] which extends the Act's protections to an individual "participating in a supervised rehabilitation program, and ... no longer engaging in" the illegal use of drugs. We hold that the "safe harbor" provision applies only to employees who have refrained from using drugs for a significant period of time....

Although alcoholism is a protected disability under the ADA,... Brown has not presented any evidence that she was terminated because of her status as an alcoholic, as is required to prove her ADA claim. Rather, the evidence shows that Lucky Stores terminated her pursuant to its general policy under which three consecutive unexcused absences from work warrant termination. The ADA clearly states that an employer:

> may hold an employee who engages in the illegal use of drugs or who is an alcoholic to the same qualification standards for employment or job performance and behavior that such entity holds other employees, even if any unsatisfactory performance or behavior is related to the drug use or alcoholism of such employee. [42 U.S.C. § 12114(c)(4)]

Thus, Lucky Stores' termination of Brown did not violate the ADA.

Brown argues that her absence from work on November 16 was protected by 42 U.S.C. § 12114(b)(2). Section 12114(a) of the statute specifies that an employee or applicant "currently engaging in the use of illegal drugs" is not covered by the ADA, while section 12114(b) clarifies that section (a) does not apply to an individual who "has successfully completed a supervised drug rehabilitation program and is no longer engaging in the illegal use of drugs, or has otherwise been rehabilitated successfully and is no longer engaging in such use," [42 U.S.C. § 12114(b)(1)], nor to one who "is participating in a supervised rehabilitation program and is no longer engaging in such use" [§ 12114(b)(2)]. Mere participation in a rehabilitation program is not enough to trigger the protections of § 12114(b); "refraining from illegal use of drugs also is essential. Employers are entitled to seek reasonable assurances that no illegal use of drugs is occurring or has occurred recently enough so that continuing use is a real and ongoing problem." Brown's continuing use of drugs and alcohol was clearly an ongoing problem at least until November 10, as demonstrated by her incarceration for driving while intoxicated and possession of methamphetamine. Because she had not refrained from the use of drugs and alcohol for a sufficient length of time, she was not entitled to the protections of the ADA's safe-harbor provision.

Brown also claims that Lucky Stores had a duty to provide a reasonable accommodation for her disability by excusing her absence from her November 16 shift in order to attend the rehabilitation program.... Neither Brown nor her sister-in-law asked for an accommodation, however. Brown testified that she never believed she needed rehabilitation while working for Lucky Stores. That, coupled with the absence of evidence that she ever requested an accommodation, leads us to conclude Lucky Stores was under no affirmative obligation to provide an accommodation for her.

Barnett v. U.S. Air, Inc. [228 F.3d 1105 (9th Cir. 2000)] does not alter our conclusion. In *Barnett,* we held that the interactive process for finding a reasonable accommodation may be triggered by the employer's recognition of the need for such an accommodation, even if the employee does not specifically make the request. The exception to the general rule that an employee must make an initial request applies,

however, only when the employer "(1) knows that the employee has a disability, (2) knows, or has reason to know, that the employee is experiencing workplace problems because of the disability, and (3) knows, or has reason to know, that the disability prevents the employee from requesting a reasonable accommodation." *Barnett* went on to explain that the employer is required to initiate the interactive process only when "an employee is unable to make such a request" and "the company knows of the existence of the employee's disability." The record does not show that Brown was unable to request a reasonable accommodation, or that Lucky Stores knew or had reason to know that Brown had a disability preventing her from making such a request.

In sum, we conclude that Lucky Stores did not terminate Brown in violation of the ADA, she was not entitled to the protections of the ADA's "safe harbor" provision and Lucky Stores had no duty to provide an accommodation for her, given that she never requested one.

The Rehabilitation Act is restricted in application to "any program or activity receiving Federal financial assistance or under any program or activity conducted by any Executive agency or by the United States Postal Service." [29 U.S.C. § 794(a)] Plaintiff has made no showing that Lucky Stores receives federal funds or is otherwise under executive agency control. Accordingly, her Rehabilitation Act claim fails....

We affirm the district court's judgment as to Brown's ADA, FEHA and Rehabilitation Act claims and its dismissal of the state law tort claims without prejudice....

Case Questions

1. What is the "safe harbor" provision of the ADA that Brown claims should apply to her case? How does the court of appeals interpret that provision—does it provide protection for Brown? Explain why or why not.
2. Did Brown's participation in a drug rehabilitation program shield her from adverse employment action by her employer? Explain.
3. Must employers treat alcoholic employees the same as employees who use illegal drugs for purposes of the ADA? Are there some reasons that might justify treating alcoholic employees differently? Explain.

An employer's policy against rehiring former employees discharged for workplace misconduct was a legitimate, nondiscriminatory reason for refusing to rehire a former employee who was discharged after testing positive for cocaine use, and was not a violation of the ADA, according to *Raytheon Co. v. Hernandez.*[30]

Federal Drug Testing Legislation

Drug testing by employers is not generally prohibited by any federal legislation. Indeed, federal laws or regulations may require that certain employees, such as those in the airline or transportation industry, undergo periodic or random drug testing. The Drug-Free Workplace Act, passed by Congress in 1988, requires that government contractors doing more than $25,000 of business annually and recipients of federal grants of more than $25,000 establish written drug-free workplace policies and establish drug-free awareness programs.

State Drug Testing Legislation

A number of states have passed legislation regarding drug testing of employees. Most such laws set mandatory procedural requirements for employers who subject employees or applicants to drug testing. In general, these laws require that employers:

- provide employees with a written statement of their drug testing policy;
- require confirmatory tests in the case of an initial positive test result;

[30] 540 U.S. 44 (2003).

- allow employees or applicants who have tested positive to have the sample retested at their own expense;
- offer employees who test positive the opportunity to enroll in a drug rehabilitation program; and
- allow termination of employees testing positive only when they refuse to participate in such a program, fail to complete such a program, or violate the terms of the rehabilitation program.

Several states, including Connecticut and West Virginia, require employers to have reasonable grounds to suspect that employees are using drugs before subjecting employees (other than employees in safety-sensitive positions or subject to federal drug testing requirements) to drug tests.

Drug Testing by Private Sector Employers

As noted, neither the ADA nor the Rehabilitation Act prohibits drug testing by employers. Private sector employers may be subject to federal laws or regulations that require drug testing of certain employees and may be required by the Drug-Free Workplace Act to establish a drug-free workplace policy. In general, federal and state laws do not prohibit drug testing by private sector employers, though such testing may be subject to the procedural requirements of any relevant state laws. Employers whose work forces are unionized are required to bargain in good faith with the union representing their employees before instituting a drug testing program for those employees.

Drug Testing by Public Sector Employers

In addition to the legal issues that may arise under specific drug testing laws, drug testing of employees or applicants by a public sector employer could raise questions of its legality under the Constitution. In *New York City Transit Authority v. Beazer*,[31] a case that arose prior to the passage of the ADA, the Supreme Court upheld the constitutionality of a New York City Transit Authority rule prohibiting the employment of persons using methadone. The rule was held to serve the purposes of safety and efficiency and was a policy choice that the public sector employer was empowered to make.

The constitutional challenges to public sector drug testing are based on the Fourth Amendment, which forbids unreasonable searches or seizures by the government. Drug testing is considered a search. The general requirement under the Fourth Amendment is that the government must show some reasonable cause to justify the drug testing. In *Skinner v. Railway Labor Executives' Association*,[32] the Supreme Court upheld the constitutionality of Federal Railroad Administration regulations that required drug tests of all railroad employees involved in accidents, regardless of whether there was any reason to suspect individual employees of drug use. The Supreme Court held that the testing program served a compelling government interest by regulating conduct of railroad employees to ensure public safety, and that interest outweighed the privacy concerns of the employees. The fact that the employees had been involved in an accident was sufficient reason to subject them to drug testing.

---

[31] 440 U.S. 568 (1979).

[32] 489 U.S. 602 (1989).

In *National Treasury Employees Union v. Von Raab,*[33] the Supreme Court upheld rules of the U.S. Customs Service that required drug tests of all employees in, or applicants for, positions that involved the interdiction of drug smuggling, carrying a firearm, or access to classified materials. The government interest in public safety and in preventing law enforcement officials from being subjected to bribery or blackmail because of their own drug use justified the drug testing program under the Fourth Amendment. The unique mission of the Customs Service and the important government interests served by the testing justified the testing of all employees in the particular positions even without any showing of individualized suspicion that they were using drugs.

Subsequent to its decisions in *Skinner* and *Von Raab,* the Supreme Court held in *Chandler v. Miller*[34] that a Georgia law that required all candidates for state political offices to pass a drug test was unconstitutional because there was no evidence of a drug problem among elected officials, and the political offices did not involve high risk or safety-sensitive positions or drug-interdiction efforts.

A number of lower federal court decisions have also dealt with drug testing by public sector employers. In *American Fed. of Govt. Employees v. Thornburgh (INS),*[35] the court confined drug testing by the Immigration and Naturalization Service to the job classes specified in *Von Raab*: those employees involved directly in drug interdiction, carrying firearms, and with access to classified information. In *AFGE v. Thornburgh (Bureau of Prisons),*[36] the court enjoined the Bureau of Prisons' program of mandatory random testing of all employees, regardless of their job function, because the employer had failed to demonstrate a special need for the testing, as required by the Supreme Court decisions. *NTEU v. Watkins*[37] upheld the Department of Energy's drug testing of employees in "sensitive" positions:

- Those with access to sensitive information
- Presidential appointees
- Law enforcement officers
- Those whose duties pertain to law enforcement or national security or to protection of lives or property
- Those occupied with public health or safety
- Those positions involved with a high degree of trust

The court in *Watkins* also held that testing employees carrying firearms was not justified unless they also had law enforcement duties, and merely holding a security clearance does not decrease one's privacy expectation to justify testing with no other justification present.

---

[33]489 U.S. 656 (1989).

[34]520 U.S. 305 (1997).

[35]713 F. Supp. 359 (N.D.Cal. 1989).

[36]720 F. Supp. 154 (N.D.Cal. 1989).

[37]722 F. Supp. 766 (D.D.C. 1989).

In *Harmon v. Thornburgh*,[38] the court held that the *Von Raab* and *Skinner* public safety rationale to justify testing focuses on the immediacy of the threat posed. Therefore, the Department of Justice program of random drug testing of prosecutors, those with access to grand jury proceedings, and those with top-secret security clearances was not justified here. The court did allow the testing of employees with access to top-secret national security information. In *AFGE v. Skinner*,[39] the Department of Transportation's drug testing of employees in jobs with a direct impact on public health, safety, or national security, such as air traffic controllers, safety inspectors, aircraft mechanics, and motor vehicle operators, was upheld by the court of appeals.

In the case of *Georgia Association of Educators v. Harris*,[40] a federal court in Georgia issued an injunction against the enforcement of Georgia legislation requiring drug tests of all applicants for state employment. The court held that the testing requirement could not stand under the standards set out in *Von Raab*.

ethical DILEMMA

To Test or Not to Test?

You are the HR director of Cantor, Inc., a firm that provides counseling and therapy services for children and adolescents with emotional problems. Some of the clients also have drug abuse problems. While there is no evidence that any Cantor employees are using illegal drugs, you are considering instituting a drug testing program for the employees because of the symbolic value of having the employees serve as role models for the clients. On the other hand, requiring employees to undergo random drug testing could adversely affect their morale, and comprehensive drug testing would cost up to $300 per employee tested. Should you require all employees (including yourself) to be tested for drug use? Does the fact that the firm is funded by financial grants from the state and federal governments affect your decision? How would you explain your decision to Cantor's Board of Directors?

Drug Testing and the NLRB

A number of National Labor Relations Board (NLRB) decisions have dealt with drug testing. An employer's mandatory drug testing program for all employees who suffered work-related injuries was held to be a mandatory bargaining subject in *Johnson–Bateman Co.*,[41] requiring that employers must bargain in good faith with the union(s) representing their employees before instituting drug testing requirements. In *Oil, Chemical and Atomic Workers Int. Union,*

---

[38] 878 F.2d 484 (D.C. Cir. 1989).

[39] 885 F.2d 884 (D.C. Cir. 1989).

[40] 749 F. Supp. 1110 (N.D.Ga., 1990).

[41] 295 NLRB No. 26, 131 L.R.R.M. 1393 (1989).

Local 2-286 v. Amoco Oil Co.,[42] the court of appeals issued an injunction to prevent an employer from unilaterally implementing a drug testing program, pending the outcome of arbitration over whether the collective agreement gave the employer the right to institute such a program. However, drug testing of job applicants is not a mandatory bargaining subject according to *Star Tribune*,[43] which means that employers may unilaterally adopt drug testing for applicants for employment.

Concept Summary » 10.4

Drug Abuse and Drug Testing

- Coverage
  - The ADA and Rehabilitation Act do not cover individuals currently using drugs or alcohol
  - The acts do cover:
    - Former drug users who have been successfully rehabilitated
    - Persons participating in or who have completed a supervised drug rehabilitation program and no longer use drugs
    - Persons erroneously regarded as using illegal drugs
- Testing
  - Drug testing is not prohibited by federal or state legislation or the ADA or Rehabilitation Act
  - Public employers requiring drug testing may face problems under the Fourth Amendment
  - Private sector employers requiring drug testing may be subject to state laws
- Legislation
  - Drug-Free Workplace Act requires government contractors with contracts of more than $25,00 and recipients of federal grants of more than $25,000 to establish drug-free workplaces
  - State drug testing laws require that employers:
    - Provide written statement of drug testing policy
    - Require confirmatory tests if initial test result is positive
    - Allow employees/applicants who have tested positive to have the sample retested at their own expense
    - Offer employees who test positive the opportunity to enroll in a drug rehabilitation program
    - Allow termination of employees testing positive only when they refuse to participate in, fail to complete, or violate the terms of such a program

---

[42] 885 F.2d 697 (10th Cir. 1989).

[43] 295 NLRB No. 63, 131 L.R.R.M. 1404 (1989).

CHAPTER REVIEW

» Key Terms

qualified individual with a disability « 269

undue hardship « 277

» Summary

- Both the Americans with Disabilities Act (ADA) and the Rehabilitation Act prohibit employment discrimination against otherwise qualified individuals with a disability. Both acts have the same broad definition of disability. Persons otherwise qualified, but who are perceived by others as having a disability, are protected under both acts. Persons with AIDS or who are HIV-positive have generally been held to be protected from employment discrimination under both acts. The Rehabilitation Act covers only employers who are government contractors or who operate or administer federally funded activities. The ADA covers both public and private employers with fifteen or more employees. Both acts require employers to make reasonable accommodation to the conditions of otherwise qualified individuals with a disability, as discussed in the *Humphrey* case.
- Neither the ADA nor the Rehabilitation Act requires or forbids drug testing of employees, although the ADA does protect employees who have successfully completed a drug rehabilitation program or who are "erroneously regarded as using drugs." Public employers who require employees to be tested for drugs may face problems under the Fourth Amendment of the U.S. Constitution. Private sector employers who impose drug testing programs may be subject to appropriate state laws.

» Problems

Questions

1. How does the coverage of the Americans with Disabilities Act differ from that of the Rehabilitation Act? Is there any overlap between the coverage of the acts? Explain your answers.
2. What constitutes a disability under the ADA? Are all individuals with disabilities protected under the ADA?
3. Under what circumstances can public sector employers require their employees to take drug tests? How do the circumstances under which private sector employers may require employees to take drug tests differ from those of public sector employers?
4. What are the differences in the procedures for filing complaints under Section 503 and Section 504 of the Rehabilitation Act?
5. Is alcoholism a disability under the ADA? Are alcoholics protected under the ADA? Explain.

Case Problems

6. When Finan began to have seizures, his employer, Good Earth Tools, temporarily suspended him from his sales position because it required him to drive. Finan's doctor diagnosed him as having epilepsy, but determined that his seizures could be controlled with proper medication. The doctor also told Finan that he would be able to drive after he had been free from seizures for six months. Good Earth restored Finan to the sales position, but restricted him to telephone and Internet sales rather than driving. Because of the restrictions on his sales activity, Finan's sales performance declined significantly. After six months, he was permitted to make sales calls in person, but one month later Good Earth placed him on probation because of poor sales performance. Two months later, Good Earth fired him. Finan sued Good Earth under the ADA. Can Finan establish a *prima facie* case of disability discrimination under the ADA? What, if any, defenses can Good Earth raise here? Explain. See *Finan v. Good Earth Tools, Inc.* [2009 WL 1375135 (8th Cir, May 19, 2009)].
7. Michael Mengine was employed by the United States Postal Service (USPS) as a letter carrier. Following hip surgery, he was no longer able to perform the duties of a letter carrier, which required prolonged walking and substantial lifting. Mengine went on sick leave, but after exhausting his leave, he requested assignment to light duty work. The USPS assigned him to temporary light duty work for a month, but after the expiration of that temporary position, the Postal Service informed him that there were no permanent light duty positions available. Mengine asked the USPS to create a permanent light duty position for him, but that request was refused and Mengine ultimately took disability retirement. He then filed suit under the ADA, alleging that the USPS refused to offer him a reasonable accommodation. Has the USPS violated the ADA? Explain. See *Mengine v. Runyon* [114 F.3d 415 (3d Cir. 1997)].
8. Allan Peden, a Detroit police officer, suffered a heart attack and underwent successful heart surgery. His physician approved his return to work on indefinite restricted duty conditions, and for ten years he continued working in clerical positions with the police department's Crime Analysis Unit (CAU). The Detroit Police Department decided to update the written job description for police positions based on a list of "24 Essential Job Functions of a Law Enforcement Officer" developed by the Michigan Law Enforcement Officers Training Council. The list included such tasks as pursuing suspects in foot chases, engaging in vehicle pursuits, effecting forcible arrests, overcoming violent resistance, and qualifying with a firearm. The Police Department described the duties of police officers as including patrolling an assigned post, enforcing laws, apprehending violators of the law, transporting sick and injured people to hospitals, and serving warrants. The Police Department physicians reviewed Peden's medical records and determined that he was unable to perform the required tasks on the job description. The Police Department then placed Peden on involuntary disability retirement. The Department claimed that he was incapable of performing the essential functions of a police officer position, but Peden argued that the job description did not accurately reflect the nature of his previous position. Will the court rule for Peden or the Police Department? Why? See *Peden v. City of Detroit* [470 Mich. 195, 680 N.W.2d 857 (Mich. 2004)].
9. Gaul worked for AT&T as Senior Technical Associate. He was diagnosed as suffering from depression and anxiety-related disorders, but was able to control his condition for more than a year with antidepressant drugs. He then suffered a nervous breakdown and was hospitalized for several weeks. He was absent from work for approximately three months. After receiving treatment, his condition appeared under control, but he later suffered a relapse after an unfavorable performance review from his manager and again went out on disability leave. Gaul asked that AT&T assign him to a "low stress" position, but AT&T ignored his request and Gaul was placed on disability retirement. Is Gaul a "qualified individual with a disability" within the meaning of the ADA? Does AT&T have a duty to accommodate Gaul's condition? Explain. See *Gaul v. Lucent Technologies, Inc.* [134 F.3d 576 (3d Cir. 1998)].

10. Steven Anders was a waste hauler employed by Waste Management. When he arrived at work one morning, he had a disagreement with his supervisor over the route he was assigned for the day. He decided to leave work, claiming that he felt sick. Rather than going to his home, Anders went to the employer's regional office to speak to the managers there. Anders entered the office, but while waiting to speak to a manager, he began to shake, and his head and chest ached, so he went outside to get some fresh air. The managers then went outside to get Anders, but when they talked to him, Anders began to pound his fists on his car and smashed his cell phone on the ground. Anders became short of breath, and the managers tried to escort him back into the building. Anders then attempted to attack one of the managers, but was restrained. He calmed down, but then became violent and threatened the manager again. Anders was terminated by the employer; he then filed suit under the ADA, claiming that he suffered from "panic disorder" which caused his behavior. He had previously asked for time off work under the Family and Medical Leave Act, but was denied such leave. How should the court rule on Anders' ADA claim? Explain. See *Anders v. Waste Management of Wisconsin* [463 F.3d 670 (7th Cir. 2006)].

11. Alan Labonte was hired as executive director of the Hutchins & Wheeler law firm in June 1992. In his first year in the position, he created a timekeeping system that saved the firm $13,000 per month, negotiated leases to lower rental payments by $43,000, lowered client disbursement costs by $200,000, and reduced overtime costs by $40,000. The firm's partners gave him a performance evaluation stating that they were "very satisfied" with his performance and he received a raise of $4,600. After about a year, Labonte developed a limp. When he consulted a doctor about the problem, he was informed that he had multiple sclerosis. After his diagnosis, he informed the firm and requested that the partners meet with his doctors to determine what measures could be taken to accommodate his condition. One partner had a brief lunch meeting with one doctor, who suggested that the firm limit the amount of walking that Labonte would be required to do.

The firm made no effort to limit Labonte's walking, to move his office, or to rearrange his job. Instead, the firm assigned additional duties to him and pressured him to cancel a personal trip to Florida that he had planned. On one occasion, a partner told him to go home if he was tired, so he wouldn't wear himself out and become ineffective. In January 1994, the firm terminated Labonte because his condition affected his performance. The firm claimed that his thinking was "not as crisp as it needed to be." After he was terminated, Labonte applied for, and was granted, disability benefits under the firm's insurance policy, stating that he was "unable to work long hours in a stressful job" and "needed a flexible work schedule." He then worked as a consultant and enrolled in a graduate program at a local university. Labonte brought a claim of disability discrimination against the firm under both state and federal law. After following the administrative procedures, he filed suit in federal court. The firm argued that Labonte was precluded from bringing suit because he accepted disability benefits.

How should the court rule on his claim? Can he pursue the suit despite accepting disability benefits? Why should that matter for his claim? Explain your answers. See *Labonte v. Hutchins & Wheeler* [424 Mass. 813, 678 N.E.2d 853 (Mass. Sup. Ct., 1997)].

12. Dura Automotive Systems operates a factory manufacturing auto glass window units through a manufacturing process involving high temperature injection molds and cutting machines. Lately there had been a high rate of workplace accidents at the facility and managers suspect that drug use by the workers was the cause. Dura hired FFS, a consulting firm, to implement a comprehensive drug testing program. The program would test for twelve substances which the parties believed could create a safety risk in a manufacturing facility. Some of the substances were found in legal prescription drugs. The drug testing involved an initial screening test of urine samples provided by the employees. If the initial screen tested positive for one of the banned substances, the employee's sample was then subjected to a confirmatory test. The results of the confirmatory test were then reviewed by a licensed medical review officer, who

would contact the employee to determine if there was a medical explanation for the positive result. If the employee provided a valid medical explanation and documentation—such as a medical prescription for a drug containing one of the banned substances—the medical review officer would change the test results from "positive" to "negative" and forward the results to FFS, who then relayed the results to Dura.

Dura management, however, regarded the confirmatory testing as irrelevant—they required any employee whose initial test result was positive to provide a list of all the medications that the employee was taking. Dura then sent letters to the employees taking such medications, informing them that they were placed on thirty-day leave to allow them to transition to a different medication or to stop using the medication altogether. Dura ignored letters from employees' physicians stating that the medications would not affect the employees' performance and were necessary for the employees' health. Employees who failed the initial drug test were permitted to take another test within thirty days—and if the second test was negative, the employee was allowed to return to work. But if the second test was positive, the employee was placed on indefinite layoff and was terminated after six months. Dura also implemented random and "post layoff return" drug testing, and any employee failing such test could be terminated immediately.

Several Dura employees who failed an initial drug test because they were taking legally prescribed medications containing one of the banned substances had their initial "positive" results changed to "negative" by the medical review officer after documenting their medical need for the prescription drug; however, Dura would not allow them to return to work, and they were ultimately terminated by Dura. Those seven employees file suit against Dura under the ADA. Is Dura's drug testing policy a violation of the ADA? Explain. See *Bates v. Dura Automotive Systems, Inc.*, 2009 WL 1108479 [M.D. Tenn. April 23, 2009].

13. Bonnie Cook applied for employment as an attendant at a Rhode Island hospital for the developmentally disabled. She had previously worked at the hospital and had a good work record but left voluntarily. She was not rehired because she was extremely obese. She was five feet two inches tall and weighed more than 320 pounds. The hospital's human resources director stated that she felt Cook's obesity would limit her ability to evacuate patients in case of an emergency and make her more susceptible to developing serious health problems. Cook sued the hospital under the ADA.

    Is Cook's obesity a disability under the ADA? Does her obesity prevent her from being an "otherwise qualified individual with a disability" under the ADA? Does it matter that Cook's weight may change? How should the court decide this case? Explain your answers. See *Cook v. State of Rhode Island Dept. of Mental Health, Retardation and Hospitals* [10 F.3d 17 (1st Cir. 1993)].

14. Bultemeyer was a custodian for the Fort Wayne Community Schools (FWCS), but he developed serious mental illnesses, including bipolar disorder, anxiety attacks, and paranoid schizophrenia. Bultemeyer went on disability leave for several months while undergoing treatment for his condition. He was then contacted by the employee relations director of FWCS to see if he was ready to return to work. When he answered that he was, she told him that there was an open position at Northrop School, the largest of the schools operated by FWCS. She told him that in order to begin working again, he would have to take a physical examination that was required of all employees returning from disability leave. She then informed him that he would not receive any special accommodations. He was directed to work at Northrop, and told that if he did not, his employment would be terminated. Bultemeyer reported as directed, but after touring Northrop School with the custodial foreman, he told the employee relations director that he could not work at Northrop; however, he also told her that he was not resigning. Bultemeyer was also afraid to take the physical exam, because he thought that if he passed, he would have to work at Northrop, and if he worked there, he would be unable to perform his tasks and would get fired. So Bultemeyer did not take the physical, and he did not report for work as

directed. He did contact his psychiatrist, who wrote a letter to FWCS stating that it would be in Bultemeyer's best interest to return to a school that might be less stressful than Northrop School. In response, FWCS notified him that his employment with FWCS was terminated because he had not reported for work and had not taken the physical. Bultemeyer filed suit against FWCS, alleging that FWCS had violated the ADA by failing to make reasonable accommodations for his mental disability. Has FWCS violated the ADA? Explain. See *Bultemeyer v. Fort Wayne Community Schools* [100 F.3d 1281 (7th Cir. 1996)].

15. The administrators at Wayzatta Central High School, in Wayzatta, Mississippi, were concerned about rumors of illegal drug use by the high school students. The school administrators decided to require all high school varsity athletes to undergo drug tests. Although there was no specific evidence that the athletes were using drugs, the administration reasoned that athletes tend to be role models and opinion leaders for the student body. Hence, requiring them to take drug tests would also send a strong antidrug message to the rest of the students. When some students complained that the faculty were not subject to the drug testing, the administration adopted a policy that also required all faculty and staff at the school to take drug tests, despite the fact that there was no evidence of drug use by the faculty. Anyone testing positive would be discharged. The teachers protested the drug testing policy and decided to file suit to challenge it.

    On what grounds can the teachers challenge the drug testing policy? Is their legal challenge likely to be successful? Is the drug testing of the student athletes legal? Explain. See *Board of Education of Indpt. School Dist. No. 92 of Pottawatomie County v. Earls* [536 U.S. 822 (2002)], *Georgia Assoc. of Educators v. Harris* [749 F.Supp. 1110 (N.D. Ga. 1990)], and *Vernonia School Dist. v. Acton* [515 U.S. 646 (1995)].

Hypothetical Scenarios

16. The City of Auburn, a public employer, decides that it wants its employees to participate in a health risk assessment program as a condition of being eligible for the employer's health plan. The program involves the employees filling out a health-related questionnaire, taking a blood pressure test, and giving a blood sample for screening. The results of the tests were only given to the employees, and the employer only received aggregate results. Employees who did not participate in the assessment were not eligible for coverage under the employer's health plan. Does the employer violate the ADA by requiring participation in the health risk assessment as a condition of participating in the health plan? Explain.

17. Zenor worked as a pharmacist at El Paso Medical Center. Her job requires that she work with restricted narcotics, sedatives, pain relievers, and other prescription medications. Zenor had developed an addiction to cocaine, and on the night of August 15, after injecting herself with cocaine, she suffered a mild seizure and was unable to report for work the next morning. She called the pharmacy manager and told him she was unable to work because of a "drug reaction." When asked what drug was involved, she admitted that it was cocaine. The manager reminded her of the employer's drug-free policy and advised her to check into a rehabilitation program. Zenor made arrangements to enroll on a residential ninety-day rehabilitation program. She notified the manager of her participation in the rehabilitation program, and the manager promised to arrange a medical leave to cover the time in the rehabilitation program. After Zenor completed half of the rehabilitation program, her manager informed her that her employment would be terminated at the end of the rehabilitation program. Is Zenor protected under the ADA? Has her employer violated the ADA? Explain.

18. Bonds tested positive for cocaine and was fired by Selig, Inc. for violating its drug-free workplace policy. Bonds then enrolled in a drug rehabilitation program and was able to end his drug abuse. He was drug-free for over two years, and reapplied to Selig to be rehired. To support his application, he provided letters from his pastor about his active church participation and from an Alcoholics Anonymous counselor about his regular attendance at meetings and his recovery. Selig refused to rehire

Bonds because of its policy against rehiring employees who are terminated for workplace misconduct. Bonds claims the "no rehire" policy violates the ADA. Does it? Explain.

19. Deborah Friend applied to enroll in the nursing program at Rockland Community College, a public college that received financial aid funding from the federal government. In addition to the academic courses, the nursing program also required students to complete a clinical program. After being notified that she was accepted into the nursing program, Friend was asked by the director of the nursing program to list any medical conditions that might affect her ability to complete the clinical portions of the nursing program. Friend suffers from diminished hearing, but she has a cochlear implant that allows her to hear normally. She informed the director of her condition, who told her that her admission into the program was withdrawn because her condition would prevent her from performing the clinical requirements. Has Rockland Community College violated the Rehabilitation Act? Explain.

20. Rosen had worked for many years as a waiter at Café Boeuf, an elegant French restaurant in Minneapolis. When Rosen was interviewed on a community television program about living with HIV, he admitted that he was HIV-positive but was asymptomatic. Upon learning about his TV appearance, the restaurant fired him. Rosen filed suit against the Café Boeuf under the ADA. Is Rosen protected by the ADA? Has Café Boeuf violated the ADA? Explain.

Other EEO and Employment Legislation: *Federal and State Laws*

In addition to the legislation discussed in the preceding chapters, there are other legal provisions that can be used to attack discrimination in employment. Those other provisions include the Civil Rights Acts of 1866 and 1870, Executive Order 11246, the Uniformed Services Employment and Reemployment Act, the National Labor Relations Act, the Constitution, and the various state EEO laws. This chapter discusses these provisions in some detail.

The Civil Rights Acts of 1866 and 1870

The Civil Rights Acts of 1866 and 1870 were passed during the Reconstruction era immediately following the Civil War. They were intended to ensure that the newly freed slaves were granted the full legal rights of U.S. citizens. The acts are presently codified in Sections 1981, 1983, and 1985 of Chapter 42 of the U.S. Code (referred to as 42 U.S.C. Sections 1981, 1983, 1985).

Section 1981

Section 1981 provides, in part, that:

> All persons within the jurisdiction of the United States shall have the same right in every State and Territory to make and enforce contracts ... as is enjoyed by white citizens....

The Supreme Court held in *Jones v. Alfred H. Mayer Co.*[1] that the acts could be used to attack discrimination in private employment. Following *Jones*, Section 1981 was increasingly used, in addition to Title VII, to challenge employment discrimination. In *Johnson v. Railway Express Agency*,[2] the Supreme Court held that Section 1981 provided for an independent cause of action (right to sue) against employment discrimination. A suit under Section 1981 was separate and distinct from a suit under Title VII.

[1] 392 U.S. 409 (1968).

[2] 421 U.S. 454 (1975).

In the 1989 decision of *Patterson v. McLean Credit Union*,[3] the Supreme Court held that Section 1981 covered only those aspects of racial discrimination in employment that related to the formation and enforcement of contracts and did not cover harassment based on race. The Civil Rights Act of 1991 amended Section 1981 and effectively overturned the *Patterson* decision by adding Section 1981(b), which states:

> For the purposes of this section, the term "make and enforce contracts" includes the making, performance, modification, and termination of contracts, and the enjoyment of all benefits, privileges, terms and conditions of the contractual relationship.

The 1991 act also added Section 1981A, which gives the right to sue for compensatory and punitive damages to victims of intentional discrimination in violation of Title VII, the Americans with Disabilities Act of 1990, and the Rehabilitation Act.

The wording of Section 1981 ("... as is enjoyed by white citizens ...") seems to indicate a concern with racial discrimination. In *Saint Francis College v. Al-Khazraji*,[4] a college professor alleged that he was denied tenure because he was an Arab. The college argued that Arabs are members of the Caucasian (white) race and that the professor was therefore not a victim of race discrimination subject to Section 1981. In determining whether Section 1981 applied to the professor's claim, the Supreme Court held that:

> Based on the history of Section 1981, we have little trouble in concluding that Congress intended to protect from discrimination identifiable classes of persons who are subjected to intentional discrimination solely because of their ancestry or ethnic characteristics. Such discrimination is racial discrimination that Congress intended Section 1981 to forbid, whether or not it would be classified as racial in terms of modern scientific theory. The Court of Appeals was thus quite right in holding that Section 1981, "at a minimum," reaches discrimination against an individual "because he or she is genetically part of an ethnically and physiognomically distinctive sub-grouping of *homo sapiens*." It is clear from our holding, however, that a distinctive physiognomy is not essential to qualify for Section 1981 protection. If respondent on remand can prove that he was subjected to intentional discrimination based on the fact that he was born an Arab, rather than solely on the place or nation of his origin, or his religion, he will have made out a case under Section 1981.

Based on *Saint Francis College v. Al-Khazraji*, the courts now interpret "race" under Section 1981 broadly to include claims of ethnic discrimination that are racial in character, such as claiming that an individual was treated differently because he was Hispanic rather than "Anglo," as in *Lopez v. S. B. Thomas, Inc.*[5] Plaintiffs may bring suits under Section 1981 to challenge racial or ethnic harassment or retaliation, according to *Manatt v. Bank of America, N.A.*[6]

Section 1983

Section 1983 of 42 U.S.C. provides that:

> Every person who, under the color of any statute, ordinance, regulation, custom or usage, of any State or Territory, subjects, or causes to be subjected, any citizen of the United States or other person within the jurisdiction thereof to the deprivation of any rights, privileges, or immunities

[3] 491 U.S. 164 (1989).

[4] 481 U.S. 604 (1987).

[5] 831 F.2d 1184 (2d Cir. 1987).

[6] 339 F.3d 792 (9th Cir. 2003).

secured by the Constitution and laws, shall be liable to the party injured in an action at law equity, or other proper proceeding for redress.

As with Section 1981, Section 1983 is restricted to claims of intentional discrimination. But unlike Section 1981, the prohibitions of Section 1983 extend to the deprivation of any rights guaranteed by the Constitution or by law. In *Maine v. Thiboutot*,[7] the Supreme Court held that Section 1983 encompasses claims based on deprivation of rights granted under federal statutory law. This means that claims alleging discrimination on grounds prohibited by federal law, such as gender, age, religion, national origin, and so forth, can be brought under Section 1983. But because of the wording of Section 1983 ("... under the color of any statute, ... of any state"), claims under Section 1983 are restricted to cases in which the alleged discrimination is by someone acting (or claiming to act) under government authority. That means employment discrimination by public employers is subject to challenge because such employers act under specific legal authority. In general, claims against private sector employers can rarely be filed under Section 1983. Any claims against private employers under Section 1983 must establish that the employer acted pursuant to some specific government authority; this is the "state action" requirement. In addition, in *Brown v. GSA*,[8] the Supreme Court held that the only remedy available to federal government employees complaining of race discrimination in employment is provided by Section 717 of Title VII.

Section 1985(c)

Section 1985(c) of 42 U.S.C. prohibits two or more persons from conspiring to deprive a person or class of persons "of the equal protection of the laws, or of equal privileges and immunities under the law." The provision was enacted in 1871 to protect African Americans from the violent activities of the Ku Klux Klan.

In *Griffin v. Breckenridge*,[9] the Supreme Court held that a group of African Americans alleging that they were attacked and beaten by a group of whites could bring suit under Section 1985(c). It appeared that the provision could be used to attack intentional discrimination in private employment when two or more persons were involved in the discrimination. But in 1979, the Supreme Court held in *Great American Federal Savings & Loan Ass'n. v. Novotny*[10] that Section 1985(c) could not be used to sue for violation of a right created by Title VII. Relying on *Novotny*, lower courts have held that Section 1985(c) cannot be used to challenge violations of the Equal Pay Act or the Age Discrimination in Employment Act.

Procedure Under Sections 1981 and 1983

A suit under Section 1981 is not subject to the same procedural requirements as a suit under Title VII. There is no requirement to file a claim with any administrative agency, such as the Equal Employment Opportunity Commission (EEOC), before filing suit under Section 1981 or Section 1983. The plaintiff may file suit in federal district court and is entitled to a jury trial;

---

[7]448 U.S.1 (1980).

[8]425 U.S. 820 (1976).

[9]403 U.S. 88 (1971).

[10]442 U.S. 366 (1979).

a successful plaintiff may recover punitive damages in addition to compensatory damages such as back pay, benefits, and legal fees.

The right to sue under Section 1981A for compensatory and punitive damages for intentional violations of Title VII and the Americans with Disabilities Act of 1990 was added by the Civil Rights Act of 1991. The act also set upper limits on the amount of damages recoverable based on the size of the employer (as discussed in Chapter 8). Punitive damages are not recoverable against public sector employers. For claims arising under the provisions added by the 1991 amendments, the limitations period for filing suit is four years, according to *Jones v. R. R. Donnelley & Sons Co.*[11]

Concept *Summary* » 11.1

The Civil Rights Acts of 1866 and 1870

- The Civil Rights Acts of 1866 and 1870
  - 42 U.S.C. Section 1981: Allows for individual suits for damages for intentional discrimination based on race or color
    - Section 1981A: Provides for compensatory and punitive damages for intentional violations of Title VII, the Americans with Disabilities Act, and the Rehabilitations Act
  - Section 1983: Allows for individual suits for intentional action "under color of state law" causing deprivation of any rights guaranteed by law
  - Section 1985(c): Allows for suits against persons conspiring to deprive persons of rights protected by law
    - Does not apply for suits claiming deprivation of rights under Title VII
- Enforcement by individual suits; no administrative enforcement

Executive Order No. 11246

Contract Compliance Program
Regulations which provide that all firms having federal government contracts or subcontracts exceeding $10,000 must include a no-discrimination clause in the contract.

Executive Order No. 11246, originally signed by President Johnson in 1965 and amended by President Nixon in 1969, provides the basis for the federal government contract compliance program. Under that executive order, as amended, firms doing business with the federal government must agree not to discriminate in employment on the basis of race, color, religion, national origin, or gender.

Equal Employment Requirements

The ***contract compliance program*** is administered by the U.S. Secretary of Labor through the Office of Federal Contract Compliance Programs (OFCCP).[12] The OFCCP has issued

[11] 541 U.S. 369 (2004).

[12] See "Compliance Assistance by Law—the Executive Order No. 11246," accessible at http://www.dol.gov/compliance/laws/comp-eeo.htm.

extensive regulations spelling out the requirements and procedures under the contract compliance program. The regulations provide that all firms having contracts or subcontracts exceeding $10,000 with the federal government must agree to include a no-discrimination clause in the contract. The clause, which is binding on the firm for the duration of the contract, requires the contractor to agree not to discriminate in employment on the basis of race, color, religion, gender, or national origin. The contractor also agrees to state in all employment advertisements that all qualified applicants will be considered without regard to race, color, religion, gender, or national origin and to inform each labor union representing its employees of its obligations under the program. The contracting firm is also required to include the same type of no-discrimination clause in every subcontract or purchase order pursuant to the federal contract.

The Secretary of Labor, through the OFCCP, may investigate any allegations of violations by contracting firms. Penalties for violation include the suspension or cancellation of the firm's government contract and the disbarment of the firm from future government contracts.

Affirmative Action Requirements

Affirmative Action Plans
Programs which involve giving preference in hiring or promotion to qualified female or minority employees.

In addition to requiring the no-discrimination clause, the OFCCP regulations may require that a contracting firm develop a written plan regarding its employees. Firms with contracts of services or supply for over $50,000 and having fifty or more employees are required to maintain formal written programs, called ***affirmative action plans***, for the utilization of women and minorities in their work force. Affirmative action plans, which must be updated annually, must contain an analysis of the employer's use of women and minorities for each job category in the work force. When job categories reveal an underutilization of women and minorities—that is, fewer women or minorities employed than would reasonably be expected based on their availability in the relevant labor market—the plan must set out specific hiring goals and timetables for improving the employment of women and minorities. The firm is expected to make a good-faith effort to reach those goals; the goals set are more in the nature of targets than hard-and-fast "quotas." The firms must submit annual reports of the results of their efforts to meet the goals set out in the affirmative action plan.

Firms holding federal or federally assisted construction contracts or subcontracts over $10,000 are also subject to affirmative action requirements. The contracting firm must comply with the goals and timetables for employment of women and minorities set periodically by the OFCCP. Those construction industry goals are set for "covered geographic areas" of the country based on census data for the areas. The "goals and timetables" approach to affirmative action for construction industry employees was held to be constitutional and legal under Title VII in *Contractors Ass'n. of Eastern Pennsylvania v. Shultz.*[13]

Procedure Under Executive Order No. 11246

Individuals alleging a violation of a firm's obligations under Executive Order No. 11246 may file complaints with the OFCCP within 180 days of the alleged violation. The OFCCP may refer the complaint to the EEOC for investigation, or it may make its own investigation. If it makes its own investigation, it must report to the director of the OFCCP within sixty days.

[13] 442 F.2d 159 (3d Cir. 1971).

If there is reason to believe that a violation has occurred, the firm is issued a show-cause notice, directing it to show why enforcement proceedings should not be instituted; the firm has thirty days to provide such evidence. During this thirty-day period, the OFCCP is also required to make efforts to resolve the violation through mediation and conciliation.

If the firm fails to show cause or if the conciliation is unsuccessful, the director of the OFCCP may refer the complaint to the Secretary of Labor for administrative enforcement proceedings or to the Department of Justice for judicial enforcement proceedings. The individual filing the complaint may not file suit privately against the firm alleged to be in violation, but the individual may bring suit to force the OFCCP to enforce the regulations and requirements under the Executive Order.[14] Administrative enforcement proceedings involve a hearing before an administrative law judge (ALJ). The ALJ's decision is subject to review by the Secretary of Labor; the secretary's decision may be subjected to judicial review in the federal courts.[15]

Firms found to be in violation of the obligations under the Executive Order, either through the courts or the administrative proceedings, may be subject to injunctions and required to provide back pay and grant retroactive seniority to affected employees. The firm may also have its government contract suspended or canceled and may be declared ineligible for future government contracts. Firms declared ineligible must demonstrate compliance with the Executive Order's requirements to be reinstated by the director of the OFCCP.

Concept *Summary* » 11.2

E.O. 11246

- Federal Contractors (>$10K) must agree not to discriminate on race, color, religion, sex, or national origin
- Contractors with >$50K and 50+ employees must have a written affirmative action plan that:
  - Assesses diversity of workforce
  - Sets goals and timetables to remedy any underutilization of women and minorities

Employment Discrimination Because of Military Service: The Uniformed Services Employment and Reemployment Rights Act

During the recent U.S. military actions in Afghanistan and Iraq, many persons who were members of the National Guard or military reserves were called to active duty; in some instances, the tour of active duty lasted more than one year. What are the legal rights of employees who are called to active duty? Do they have the right to return to their job after their active duty service is over? Federal legislation protects the reemployment rights of employees who serve in the military services or who are members of the reserves and are called into active duty.

---

[14] *Legal Aid Society v. Brennan*, 608 F.2d 1319 (9th Cir. 1979).

[15] *Firestone Co. v. Marshall*, 507 F. Supp. 1330 (E.D. Texas 1981).

The Uniformed Services Employment and Reemployment Rights Act

The Uniformed Services Employment and Reemployment Rights Act (USERRA),[16] enacted in 1994, replaced the Veterans' Reemployment Rights Act. USERRA covers both private and public sector employers, including the federal government; it prohibits employers from discriminating against employees because of their service in the military. USERRA applies only to noncareer military service—that is, to employees who are called to active duty from their civilian jobs. It does not apply to career military service, according to *Woodman v. Office of Personnel Management.*[17]

Employees who are absent from employment because they were ordered to active military service are entitled to reinstatement and employment benefits if they meet the following requirements:

- They gave the employer notice of the period of military service
- They are absent for a cumulative total of less than five years
- They submitted an application for reemployment within the designated time period

The time period for submitting the notice of reemployment to the employer depends on the length of the military service. For military service less than thirty-one days, the employee need only report to work on the first full workday after completion of the service and transportation to the employee's residence. For service longer than thirty days but less than 181 days, the notice must be submitted not later than fourteen days after completing the period of military service. For service longer than 180 days, the notice must be submitted not later than ninety days after completion of the period of military service.

Employers are not required to reinstate employees after their military service if:

- the employer's circumstances have changed so that reemployment would be unreasonable or impossible;
- the reemployment would cause undue hardship in accommodation, training, or effort; or
- the initial employment was for a brief, nonrecurring period.

In any such case, the employer has the burden of proving that the denial of reemployment was permissible under the act.

Employees reemployed after military service are entitled to the seniority, rights, and benefits they had as of the date the military service began, plus any seniority, rights, and benefits that they would have received had they remained continuously employed. Persons who are reemployed under the act after military service of more than 180 days may not be discharged without cause within one year of reemployment; persons reemployed after military service of more than thirty days but less than 180 days may not be discharged without cause within 180 days of reemployment. Persons who are affected by alleged violations of the USERRA must file written complaints with the federal Secretary of Labor; the Secretary will

---

[16] 38 U.S.C. § 4301 *et seq.*

[17] 258 F.3d 1372 (Fed. Cir. 2001).

investigate any complaint and make reasonable attempts to settle it. If such attempts are unsuccessful, affected persons may request that the secretary refer a complaint to the U.S. Attorney General to take court action to enforce the act or may file legal action themselves in the appropriate federal district court.

Remedies available under such a suit include ordering the employer to comply with the act and compensation for lost wages, benefits, and legal fees. Liquidated damages are available where the employer's violation was willful. According to *Gummo v. Village of Depew, N.Y.*,[18] the employee only needs to show that the military service was a substantial or motivating factor in the employer's decision to discharge the employee; it need not be the sole reason. An employer can escape liability by showing that the employee *would* have been discharged even if the employee had no military service.[19]

The following case involves a claim of termination of a reservist in violation of USERRA, and discusses the allocation of the burden of proof under the statute.

case 11.1 » VELÁZQUEZ-GARCÍA V. HORIZON LINES OF PUERTO RICO, INC.

473 F.3d 11 (1st Cir. 2007)

[Velázquez was employed by Horizon, an ocean shipping and transport business. Velázquez supervised the stevedores at its marine terminal in San Juan, Puerto Rico. Velázquez enlisted in the U.S. Marine Corps Reserves in December 2002, and reported for six months of basic training. He returned to his job after basic training, but continued to report for monthly weekend training sessions, as well as annual two-week more intensive training sessions. Velázquez was a shift employee at Horizon and often had to work weekends, so Horizon needed to adjust his work hours to accommodate his military schedule. Velázquez claimed that his superiors complained and pressured him about the difficulty of rescheduling his shifts. He also stated that he was frequently the butt of jokes at work, being referred to as "G.I. Joe,""little lead soldier," and "Girl Scout."]

Stahl, Senior Circuit Judge

This case presents an issue of the proper allocation of the burden of proof in cases of alleged discriminatory treatment under the Uniformed Services Employment and Reemployment Rights Act of 1994 ("USERRA")....

During Velázquez's periods of military service, Horizon continued to pay his full salary. As a result, when Velázquez returned to work, Horizon would deduct from his paycheck amounts necessary to offset Velázquez's military income for those days in which he received both a military and a civilian paycheck.

During this same time period, Velázquez began operating a side business cashing the checks of Horizon employees. Before 2001, Horizon had paid its stevedores' daily wages in cash. In 2001, Horizon began paying daily wages by check instead. Seeing a business opportunity, around February 2004, Velázquez began cashing these employee checks for a fee. He did this almost exclusively during off-duty hours, though he testified to cashing "one or two" checks while on duty. He performed the service primarily outside Horizon's gate or in its parking lot.

Around September 2004, Horizon finished recouping the salary that it was owed for the periods when Velázquez was performing his military duties. On September 21, 2004, seven months after he began his side business, Velázquez was observed cashing checks by Horizon's operations manager, Roberto Batista, one of Velázquez's supervisors and one of the people Velázquez described as having trouble with his military schedule. Batista reported this to

---

[18] 75 F.3d 98 (2d. Cir. 1996).

[19] *Dean v. Consumer Product Safety Comm.*, 548 F.3d 1370 (Fed. Cir. 2008).

several other Horizon managers, and on September 23, 2004, Batista fired Velázquez. The termination letter did not state a reason, but Velázquez was told that his check-cashing side business was in violation of Horizon's Code of Business Conduct ("Code"). He was given no warnings or other prior discipline, and had an otherwise clean record as a good employee.

Velázquez brought suit under USERRA, alleging that his firing constituted illegal discrimination due to his military service. Horizon moved for summary judgment, which the district court granted. The district court held that Velázquez had not shown sufficient discriminatory animus, nor had he shown that the stated reason for his firing, the Code violation, was mere pretext. This appeal followed.

We have not previously addressed the mechanism of proving discrimination claims under USERRA. Thus, we first turn to the statute and its history.... The language of the statute and the legislative history make clear that the employee need only show that military service was "a motivating factor" in order to prove liability, unless "the employer can prove that the [adverse employment] action would have been taken" regardless of the employee's military service. (emphasis added). Therefore, we hold that "in USERRA actions there must be an initial showing by the employee that military status was at least a motivating or substantial factor in the [employer] action, upon which the [employer] must prove, by a preponderance of evidence, that the action would have been taken despite the protected status."

... under USERRA, the employee does not have the burden of demonstrating that the employer's stated reason is a pretext. Instead, the employer must show, by a preponderance of the evidence, that the stated reason was *not* a pretext; that is, that "the action *would* have been taken in the absence of [the employee's military] service." (emphasis added).

The district judge ... ruled that Velázquez was unable to show that Horizon at least partially based its decision to fire him on his military service. The district judge gave three principal reasons for this ruling. First, he discounted Velázquez's testimony of anti-military remarks made by his co-workers, in part because he had not reported any harassment to Horizon. Second, he said that the evidence of the timing of his firing close to a return from training was of no probative value because he had returned from several other training sessions without being fired. Third, he noted that other Horizon employees in the military had not been demoted or fired.

... we believe, after carefully reviewing the record, that the judge committed error on each of these three points. First, the court discounted Velázquez's testimony of anti-military remarks because it was his own self-serving testimony and because he had not previously reported it or made a formal complaint....

On appeal, Horizon argues that the anti-military comments were just "stray remarks," and as such cannot be sufficient evidence of discriminatory animus. If true, that would undermine Velázquez's argument that the issues raised are "genuine." ... Here, Velázquez points not only to the remarks by co-workers, but also to complaints by Batista and others about the difficulty of adjusting Velázquez's work schedule, and to the timing of his firing (which we address below).... At least one such speaker, Juan Carrero, was shift marine manager and appears to be superior to Velázquez. Carrero was also in part responsible for scheduling, which was the source of Horizon's problems with Velázquez.... Here, the remarks that Velázquez describes in his testimony are clearly anti-military.... The district judge next discounted the timing of Velázquez's firing, saying that the fact that he was fired after returning from his military service is of no probative value, given that he had returned from other periods of service without being fired. But the emphasis of Velázquez's argument is elsewhere. The important factor, he argues, is not the time of his return from service, but rather the time of his final recoupment of the salary differential that he owed to Horizon. Horizon, according to Velázquez, waited until Velázquez had paid back the money he owed Horizon for the periods when his civilian salary was supplemented by his military salary. Once he had repaid the overage, he claims, Horizon then found the pretext to fire him.

Such facts, if true, could be considered evidence of discriminatory animus. The other USERRA cases that address the timing of firing look at "proximity in time between the employee's military activity and the adverse employment action." But that is not an exclusive test, and there is no reason to limit ourselves to looking only at the proximity of the adverse employment action to military activity. The proximity to other military-related events may also be probative. If what Velázquez alleges is true, Horizon should not escape liability for making the tactical decision to wait until it recouped the salary it was owed before using a pretext to fire Velázquez.

Finally, the district judge held that the fact that the company had not fired other employees who served in the military demonstrated that they did not fire Velázquez for discriminatory reasons.... The district court failed to address Velázquez's argument that the other employees were not shift employees, and that therefore their military service did not cause as much scheduling conflict as his did. A reasonable jury could conclude that the different situations of these employees could result in Horizon firing Velázquez for his military service, while tolerating the other employees serving in the military.

For these reasons, we find that Velázquez has presented sufficient facts to withstand summary judgment on the question of whether his military status was at least a motivating factor in his dismissal. The issue is one for a jury.

After holding that Velázquez had not provided sufficient evidence to show that his military status was a motivating factor in his dismissal, the district judge held further that, even if he had, Horizon had adequately demonstrated that it had a non-pretextual reason for firing Velázquez.... The issue under USERRA is not whether an employer is "entitled" to dismiss an employee for a particular reason, but whether it would have done so if the employee were not in the military. Here, Velázquez's violation of the Code may well be a fireable offense under Horizon's policies, but that is only the beginning of the analysis. Horizon must go further and demonstrate, by a preponderance of the evidence, that it *would* indeed have fired Velázquez, regardless of his military status.

There is sufficient doubt on this issue to make it a jury question. Velázquez points out that he never received a copy of the Code, nor any warnings to stop his check-cashing business, both of which one might have expected to occur before a firing, particularly in a case where the Code is arguably ambiguous as to whether something like check-cashing is in fact a violation. Furthermore, some other employees who had similar Code violations were not summarily fired, as Velázquez was. Also questionable is the fact that Velázquez had been cashing checks for Horizon employees adjacent to Horizon property for seven months before Horizon claimed to discover these acts. A reasonable jury could question the truth of that claim, given that the alleged discovery occurred so close to the final recoupment of salary. Given this, Horizon has not met its burden at summary judgment of showing that no reasonable jury could find that Velázquez's check-cashing business was a mere pretext for his dismissal. Horizon points only to the Code violation and, under USERRA, that is not enough.

For the forgoing reasons we *reverse* the district court's grant of summary judgment and *remand* for further proceedings consistent with this opinion.

Case Questions

1. What is the significance of the timing of Velázquez's termination by Horizon?
2. What evidence did Velázquez show to support his claim that Horizon fired him because of his reserve service? What reason did Horizon offer for firing him?
3. According to the Court of Appeals, who has the burden of showing that Horizon's alleged reasons for firing Velázquez are a pretext? What must they show in order to meet that burden? Have they done so here? Explain.

Concept *Summary* » 11.3

Uniformed Services Employment and Reemployment Rights Act

- USERRA prohibits employers from discriminating against employees because of their (noncareer) service in the military
- To qualify, employees must:
  - give the employer notice of the period of military service;
  - be absent for a cumulative total of less than five years; and
  - submit an application for reemployment within the designated time period.
- Employers are not required to reinstate employees if:
  - the employer's circumstances have changed so that reemployment would be unreasonable or impossible;
  - the reemployment would cause undue hardship in accommodation, training, or effort; or
  - the initial employment was for a brief, nonrecurring period.

The National Labor Relations Act

The unfair labor practice prohibitions of the National Labor Relations Act (NLRA) may be used to attack discrimination in employment in some instances. In *United Packinghouse Workers Union v. NLRB*,[20] the court held that race discrimination by an employer was an unfair labor practice in violation of Section 8(a)(1) of the NLRA. Retaliation against employees who filed charges with the EEOC, by refusing to recall them from layoff, was held to violate Section 8(a)(1) in *Frank Briscoe Inc. v. NLRB.*[21]

Unions that discriminate against African Americans in membership or in conditions of employment are in violation of Section 8(b)(1)(A) and their duty of fair representation of all employees in the bargaining unit according to the Supreme Court decision of *Syres v. Oil Workers.*[22] (See the *Steele v. Louisville & Nashville R.R.* case in Chapter 18.) In *Hughes Tool Co.*[23] the NLRB held that a union's refusal to represent African-American workers violated Section 8(b)(1)(A) and was grounds to rescind the union's certification as bargaining agent. Discrimination against female employees by a union also violates Section 8(b)(1)(A) as held in *NLRB v. Glass Bottle Blowers Local 106.*[24] (See Chapter 18 for a discussion of the duty of fair representation.)

Employers and unions that negotiate, or attempt to negotiate, discriminatory provisions in seniority systems, pay scales, or promotion policies may commit unfair labor practices in violation of Section 8(a)(5) or Section 8(b)(3) by refusing to bargain in good faith.

Constitutional Prohibitions Against Discrimination

Certain provisions of the U.S. Constitution may be used by public sector employees to challenge discrimination in their employment. The Constitution regulates the relationship between the government and individuals; therefore, the Constitution's prohibitions against discrimination apply only to government employers and to private employers acting under government support or compulsion (state action).

Due Process and Equal Protection

The primary constitutional provisions used to attack discrimination are the guarantees of due process of law and equal protection found in the Fifth and Fourteenth Amendments. The Fifth Amendment applies to the federal government, and the Fourteenth Amendment

[20] 416 F.2d 1126 (D.C. Cir. 1969).

[21] 637 F.2d 946 (3d Cir. 1981).

[22] 350 U.S. 892 (1955).

[23] 56 L.R.R.M. 1289 (1964).

[24] 520 F.2d 693 (6th Cir. 1975).

applies to state and local governments. In addition, specific enactments such as the First Amendment guarantee of freedom of religion may be used to challenge discrimination. In *Brown v. GSA*,[25] the Supreme Court held that the only remedy available to persons complaining of race discrimination in federal government employment is provided by Section 717 of Title VII. However, not all federal employees are covered by Title VII. For example, members of the armed forces or the personal staff members of elected officials, who are not covered by Title VII, could file constitutional challenges to alleged discrimination.

In the case of *Davis v. Passman*,[26] the Supreme Court held that a member of a congressman's staff, who was not covered by Title VII, could bring a suit under the Fifth Amendment against her employer for discharging her because of intentional gender discrimination.

Challenges to employment discrimination under the due process and equal protection guarantees involve claims that the discriminatory practices deny the victims of the discrimination rights equal, or treatment equal, to those who are not targets of the discrimination. Blanket prohibitions on employment of females, or of members of a minority group, deny those employees due process of law by presuming that all women, or members of the minority group, are unable to perform the requirements of a particular job.

In *Washington v. Davis*,[27] the Supreme Court held that the constitutional prohibitions applied only to invidious, or intentional, discrimination; claims alleging disparate impact could not be brought under the constitutional provisions.

Not all intentional discrimination on the basis of race, gender, and so on is unconstitutional, however. In considering claims of discrimination under the Constitution, the court will first consider the basis of discrimination. Some bases of discrimination, or "classifications" by government action, will be considered ***suspect classes***. That is, there is little justification for treating persons differently because they fall within a particular class. For example, racial discrimination involves classifying, and treating differently, employees by race. Such conduct can rarely be justified. The court will strictly scrutinize any offered justification for such conduct. The government must show that such classification, or treatment, is required because of a compelling government interest, and no less discriminatory alternatives exist. For example, classifying employees by race, while discriminatory, may be justified if the reason is to compensate employees who had been victims of prior racial discrimination.

Suspect Class
A basis of discrimination, classification, or differential treatment—such as race, color, gender, religion or national origin—by government action, for which there is little legitimate justification for treating persons because of such characteristics.

Affirmative Action and the Constitution

Affirmative action has become an extremely controversial issue in recent years (see the discussion in Chapter 6). The courts have been growing more skeptical about the legality of affirmative action requirements imposed by government entities.

---

[25] 425 U.S. 820 (1976).

[26] 442 U.S. 228 (1979).

[27] 426 U.S. 229 (1976).

Strict Scrutiny Test
A constitutional analysis used by courts hearing equal protection claims involving governmental discrimination based on a "suspect class." This test requires the government to demonstrate that the discriminatory treatment was necessary to achieve a compelling government purpose and that the governmental action was "narrowly tailored" to achieve the compelling purpose.

The U.S. Supreme Court, in the 1995 decision *Adarand Constructors, Inc. v. Pena,*[28] held that federal government affirmative action programs giving preferential treatment based on race or color must be justified under the ***strict scrutiny test***. This test requires the government to demonstrate that the affirmative action program was necessary to achieve a compelling government purpose and that the program was "narrowly tailored" to achieve the compelling purpose. It must also show that it did not unduly harm those who were not given the preferential treatment.

A majority of the Supreme Court upheld the use of affirmative action in admissions by a public university, the University of Michigan, in two cases, *Grutter v. Bollinger*[29] and *Gratz v. Bollinger*.[30] In these cases, which did not deal with employment, the Supreme Court held that achieving the educational benefits of a diverse student body was a compelling governmental interest. However, in a more recent case dealing with public schools, *Parents Involved in Community Schools v. Seattle School Dist. No. 1*,[31] the Supreme Court held that diversity in education was not a sufficient justification for the schools' use of racial classifications in assigning students to particular schools.

Extending the rationale of these cases to employment would indicate that achieving the benefits of a diverse work force may be a sufficiently compelling governmental interest to justify the use of affirmative action programs for hiring or promotion decisions by public sector employers. However, an affirmative action program must also be narrowly tailored to achieve the compelling governmental purpose. The courts have held that affirmative action programs that give a relative preference rather than an absolute one—race or gender is used as a "plus factor" rather than as the determinative factor—are narrowly tailored. Programs that are temporary and that will cease when the employer achieves a more diverse work force have also been held to be narrowly tailored.

Wygant v. Jackson Board of Education[32] involved an affirmative action program that was not narrowly tailored. In this case, the collective bargaining agreement between a public school board and the teachers' union contained an affirmative action program in the event that layoffs of teachers were necessary. Layoffs would be based on seniority ("last hired, first fired") unless the effect of the seniority-based layoffs would reduce the percentage of minority teachers at a given school below the percentage of minority students in that school. If that were the case, the affirmative action program would require the layoff of senior nonminority teachers ahead of minority teachers with less seniority. The purpose of the plan was to ensure the presence of minority teachers in the schools so that the minority teachers could serve as role models for minority students and encourage them to get an education. Wygant, a white teacher who lost her job under the affirmative action plan, brought suit, arguing that the plan calling for race-based layoffs was in violation of the Equal Protection Clause of the Fourteenth Amendment. The Supreme Court held that although providing role models for minority students might be a

[28]515 U.S. 200 (1995).

[29]539 U.S. 306 (2003).

[30]539 U.S. 244 (2003).

[31]551 U.S. 701 (2007).

[32]476 U.S. 267 (1986).

compelling governmental purpose, a plan requiring the layoff of teachers because of their race was "not sufficiently narrowly tailored" to the achievement of that purpose. The Court stated "the … selection of layoffs as the means to accomplish even a valid purpose cannot satisfy the demands of the Equal Protection Clause."

Remedial affirmative action programs—that is, programs adopted to remedy illegal discrimination—have generally been held to be constitutional. In *Local 28, Sheet Metal Workers Int. Ass'n. v. EEOC*,[33] the U.S. Supreme Court held that courts may impose affirmative action programs to remedy "persistent or egregious discrimination," even if the affirmative action plan had the effect of benefiting individuals who were not themselves victims of discrimination. The Court emphasized that affirmative action programs should be imposed by a court only as a last resort and such programs should be "tailor[ed] … to fit the nature of the violation" the court seeks to remedy. In *Local 93, Int. Ass'n. of Firefighters v. Cleveland*,[34] the Supreme Court held that the parties in an employment discrimination suit may enter into a settlement agreement (known as a consent decree) requiring an affirmative action program where the employer has been found guilty of discrimination. The consent decree's affirmative action program may benefit minority employees who were not personally victims of illegal employment discrimination.

In *U.S. v. Paradise*,[35] the Supreme Court upheld a court-ordered affirmative action plan that required the Alabama Public Safety Department to promote to corporal one African-American state trooper for every white trooper promoted, until either African Americans occupied 25 percent of the corporal positions or until the department instituted a promotion policy that did not have an adverse impact on African-American troopers. The majority held that the order was necessary to remedy past "pervasive, systematic and obstinate" discrimination by the department.

Other Constitutional Issues

Nonsuspect Class
A basis of discrimination, classification, or differential by government action which is neutral with regard to race, color, gender, religion or national origin, and which is related to legitimate government interests. Examples of nonsuspect classes are age, veteran status, or personal achievement.

Some forms of discrimination involve classifications that may be more neutral than racial classifications. The courts refer to such classifications as ***nonsuspect classes***. When discrimination is based on nonsuspect classes, the court will consider whether the discriminatory classification bears a reasonable relationship to a valid state interest. For example, in *Personnel Administrator of Massachusetts v. Feeney*,[36] the Supreme Court upheld a Massachusetts law that required all veterans to be given preference for state civil service positions over nonveterans, even though the law had the effect of discriminating against women because veterans were overwhelmingly male. The classification of applicants on the basis of veteran status was reasonably necessary for the valid government objective of rewarding veterans for the sacrifices of military service.

---

[33] 478 U.S. 421 (1986).

[34] 478 U.S. 501 (1986).

[35] 480 U.S. 149 (1987).

[36] 442 U.S. 256 (1979).

In *Cleveland Board of Education v. LaFleur*,[37] the Supreme Court struck down a rule imposing a mandatory maternity leave on teachers reaching the fifth month of pregnancy on grounds that it violated the due process rights of the teachers. The rule denied the teachers the freedom of personal choice over matters of family life, and it was not shown to be sufficiently related to the school-board interests of administrative scheduling and protecting the health of teachers. The rule had the effect of classifying every teacher reaching the fifth month of pregnancy as being physically incapable of performing the duties of the job, when such teacher's ability or inability to perform during pregnancy is an individual matter.

Personal grooming requirements and restrictions on hair length and facial hair for police officers were upheld by the Supreme Court in *Kelley v. Johnson*[38] because they were reasonably related to the maintenance of discipline among members of the police force. In *Goldman v. Weinberger*,[39] the Supreme Court dismissed a challenge under the First Amendment to an Air Force uniform regulation that prevented an Orthodox Jew from wearing his yarmulke while on duty. Despite the fact that the yarmulke was unobtrusive, the regulations were justified by the Air Force interest in maintaining morale and discipline, which were held to be legitimate military ends. As discussed in Chapter 7, the courts have consistently upheld the constitutionality of the military's "don't ask, don't tell" policy barring persons from serving in the military if they engage in homosexual conduct or demonstrate a propensity to engage in such conduct, as in *Phillips v. Perry*[40] and *Thomasson v. Perry*.[41]

The WORKING Law

U.S. Supreme Court Declines to Hear Constitutional Challenge to "Don't Ask, Don't Tell"

The U.S. Supreme Court declined to grant leave to appeal on a constitutional challenge to the military's "don't ask, don't tell" policy. The case involved a request for the Court to review a suit initially filed by twelve persons who were dismissed from the armed services under the policy, which requires that persons who have engaged in, or attempted to engage in homosexual acts, or who have effectively identified themselves as homosexual, be excluded from service in the armed forces. The suit challenged the policy on constitutional grounds, but the trial court held that the policy did not violate the due process right, the equal protection rights, or the First Amendment rights of the plaintiffs. The plaintiffs appealed, but the U.S. Court of

(continued)

[37]414 U.S. 632 (1974).

[38]425 U.S. 238 (1976).

[39]475 U.S. 503 (1976).

[40]106 F.3d 1420 (9th Cir. 1997).

[41]80 F.3d 915 (4th Cir. 1996).

Appeals for the First Circuit affirmed the trial court decision. Pietrangelo, one of the plaintiffs, then sought leave to appeal to the U.S. Supreme Court. Most of the other plaintiffs from the original suit asked the Supreme Court not to review the case, preferring instead to have the Obama Administration address the situation. President Obama had made a campaign pledge to end the policy, and he has asked the Pentagon to review the implications of repealing the policy. Geoff Morrell, spokesman for Defense Secretary Robert Gates, stated in May 2009 that "President Obama ... is committed to repeal the Don't Ask, Don't Tell policy ... he is committed to do it in a way that is at [sic] least disruptive to our troops, especially given that they have been simultaneously waging two wars for six years now."

In a decision from May 2008, the U.S. Court of Appeals for the Ninth Circuit has allowed another challenge to the policy based on due process grounds to go forward. That case involves a suit by a former Air Force flight nurse, Major Margaret Witt, who had been awarded numerous medals for her service but was dismissed because she was involved in a long-term relationship with a female civilian. The Ninth Circuit held that the Air Force must demonstrate that the application of the "don't ask, don't tell" policy to Major Witt significantly furthers the interest of troop readiness and unit cohesion, and that no other "less intrusive means" would substantially achieve those interests. The Servicemembers Legal Defense Network, an organization assisting servicemembers affected by the "don't ask, don't tell" policy, view the Witt case as a better vehicle to bring the issue before the Supreme Court.

A bill that would repeal the policy was introduced in the House of Representatives in early 2009 by Rep. Ellen Tauscher of California, and has about 150 co-sponsors.

Sources: Cook v. Rumsfeld, 429 F. Supp.2d 385 (D. Mass. 2006), *affirmed by, Cook v. Gates,* 528 F.3d 42 (1st Cir. 2008), *certiorari denied, sub nom. Pietrangelo v. Gates,* 2009 WL 1576585 (June 8, 2009); *Witt v. Dept. of the Air Force,* 527 F.3d 806 (9th Cir. 2008); Gordon Lubold, "Supreme Court Rejects Challenge to 'Don't Ask, Don't Tell,'" *Christian Science Monitor,* June 8, 2009; William Branigin, "Supreme Court Turns Down 'Don't Ask' Challenge," *The Washington Post,* June 8, 2009.

Concept *Summary* » 11.4

CONSTITUTIONAL PROHIBITIONS AGAINST DISCRIMINATION

- U.S. Constitution
  - Due process of law and equal protection under the Fifth and Fourteenth Amendments
  - Basis of discrimination considered first
- Affirmative action
  - Strict scrutiny test: Requires the government to demonstrate that an affirmative action plan is necessary to achieve a compelling government purpose and is narrowly tailored to achieve that purpose
  - Remedial affirmative action programs: Programs adopted to remedy illegal discrimination; should be tailored to fit the nature of the violation

State EEO and Employment Laws

The discussion of EEO law in this and preceding chapters has focused mainly on federal legislation. In addition to the various federal laws, most states also have their own equal employment opportunity legislation or regulations. State laws figure into the enforcement of federal laws. Recall that under Title VII, persons complaining of employment discrimination must file with the appropriate state or local EEO agency before taking their complaint to the federal Equal Employment Opportunity Commission. Such state or local EEO laws may provide greater protection than the federal legislation does. For example, the Michigan Civil Rights Act specifically prohibits discrimination based on height or weight, and the District of Columbia Human Rights Law prohibits discrimination based on personal appearance or political affiliation. The New York State Human Rights Law prohibits age discrimination in employment against employees aged eighteen or older (unless age is a bona fide occupational qualification [BFOQ]).

Gender Discrimination

All state EEO laws prohibit gender discrimination in terms or conditions of employment, except in those instances where sex may be a BFOQ. Most state laws interpret gender discrimination as including sexual harassment, but some state laws, such as Minnesota's Human Rights Act, specifically prohibit sexual harassment in addition to the general prohibition on gender discrimination. Maine law requires employers to post a notice in the workplace informing employees that sexual harassment is illegal and describing how to file a complaint of sexual harassment with the Maine Human Rights Commission.

Sexual Orientation Discrimination

Although federal law does not prohibit discrimination because of sexual orientation or sexual preference, a number of states have legislation prohibiting such discrimination. California, Colorado, Connecticut, Delaware, Hawaii, Illinois, Iowa, Maine, Maryland, Massachusetts, Minnesota, Nevada, New Hampshire, New Jersey, New Mexico, New York, Oregon, Rhode Island, Vermont, Washington, Wisconsin, and the District of Columbia prohibit employment discrimination based on sexual orientation or sexual preference by public and private sector employers. Several other states, including Louisiana, Michigan, Ohio and Pennsylvania, prohibit public sector employers from discriminating because of sexual orientation or sexual preference through executive orders issued by the governor. In some large cities, including New York City and San Francisco, local ordinances prohibit employment discrimination because of sexual orientation or sexual preference.

Family Friendly Legislation

A number of states have legislation similar to the federal Family and Medical Leave Act, which allows employees to take unpaid leave for childbirth, adoption, or serious illness of a child, parent, or spouse. California's Fair Employment and Housing Act requires that an employer reinstate an employee returning from pregnancy leave to her previous job, unless that job was unavailable because of business necessity. In that case, an employer is required to make a reasonable, good-faith effort to provide a similar position for the employee. New Jersey law allows employees to take up to six weeks of paid medical or family care leave under the state's disability insurance program. The District of Columbia requires employers to provide paid medical or family care leave; the amount of leave that employees accrue depends upon the size of the employer and the number of hours worked by the employees.

New York law protects the right of a mother to breast-feed her child in any public or private place where she is authorized to be, and allows employees who are nursing mothers to take reasonable unpaid break time to express breast milk; employers are to make reasonable efforts to provide a room where an employee may express breast milk in privacy. Several states require that employers allow employees time off (without pay) to attend their children's school meetings or conferences if held during normal working hours. The number of hours allowed per year varies by state, and Nevada simply prohibits an employer from discharging an employee for absences due to school conferences or meetings. In each case, the employee is required to give appropriate advance notice to the employer. New York requires employers with twenty or more employees to allow employees leave time to donate blood; such employees may take up to three hours' leave in any twelve-month period.

Other Employment Legislation

Whistleblower Laws

Whistleblowers
Employees who report or attempt to report employer wrongdoing or actions threatening public health or safety to government authorities.

A number of federal and state laws provide some protection for ***whistleblowers***—employees who report employer wrongdoing or actions threatening public health or safety. The federal Civil Service Reform Act[42] provides general protection for civil service workers from any discipline or retaliation because they have disclosed a violation of laws or regulations, gross mismanagement or a gross waste of funds, or a substantial and specific danger to the public health or safety. The federal Office of Special Counsel is responsible for investigating and pursuing claims of whistleblowers. A number of specific federal laws provide protection from retaliation for employees who report violations of those laws. Examples include the Safe Drinking Water Act, which protects employees who report illegal pollution of water, and the Federal Mine Health and Safety Act, which protects employees reporting mine safety violations.

The Sarbanes-Oxley Act of 2002,[43] which was passed in response to the corporate scandals involving Enron and WorldCom, imposes both civil and criminal penalties for employers who take adverse employment actions against whistleblowers. The legislation applies to corporations whose shares are publicly traded in the U.S. The criminal provisions make it a federal crime to retaliate knowingly against persons who provide information to law enforcement officials relating to the possible commission of any federal offense. Penalties include fines of up to $250,000 and imprisonment of up to ten years for individual violators and fines of up to $500,000 for corporations. The civil provisions allow suits by employees allegedly retaliated against by their employers for providing information or cooperating in investigations related to violations of specified securities laws, SEC rules or regulations, or any

[42]5 U.S.C. § 2303.

[43]Pub.L. No. 107-204, 116 Stat. 745.

other provision of federal law relating to shareholder fraud.[44] The civil whistleblower provisions are administered by the Department of Labor, and provide for remedies including

- Reinstatement
- Back pay
- Legal fees and costs
- Compensatory damages

The whistleblower provisions of Sarbanes-Oxley do not apply to foreign citizens working abroad for foreign subsidiaries of U.S. corporations.[45]

All fifty states and the District of Columbia have some form of whistleblower laws. Some state laws, such as those of Connecticut, Florida, Hawaii, and Maine, cover both private and public sector employees; most such laws, however, cover only public sector workers. In California, Louisiana, and New Jersey, both public and private sector employees who reasonably believe that an employer is acting illegally are protected if they report such actions to the authorities. New York has separate legislation for public and private employers. In New York, public sector employees who reasonably believe that their employer has violated the law, and that the violation poses a "substantial and specific danger" to public health or safety, are protected. However, according to *Green v. Saratoga A.R.C.*,[46] the private sector whistleblower law requires that the conduct employees report must be an actual violation of a law, rule or regulation; a reasonable belief that the conduct was illegal is not sufficient to state a claim under the law.

The following case involves the question of whether testimony in a civil suit is protected activity under the Michigan Whistleblower Protection Act.

case 11.2 »

Henry v. City of Detroit

234 Mich.App. 405, 594 N.W.2d 107 (Mich. Ct. App. 1999), appeal denied, 461 Mich. 937, 606 N.W.2d 24 (Mich. 1999)

Facts: Henry was a commander in the Detroit Police Department. After the death of a suspect (Green) in police custody, the department formed a board of review to investigate the death and to recommend whether any officers should be criminally charged. Henry was the chairman of the board of review. McKinnon, the police chief, gave orders that effectively precluded the board of review from performing its obligations. As a result, some innocent officers were falsely accused and disciplined by the police department.

One of those officers, Lessnau, was acquitted of killing Green and then filed a civil suit against the police department. During the trial of Lessnau's suit, Henry was called as a witness and testified that the department rules concerning the board of review were violated and the board of review was not allowed to perform its duties. Henry also testified before the Michigan Employment Relations Commission (MERC) in an unrelated matter.

Less than four months after plaintiff's testimony in the civil suit and less than one month following his testimony

[44] *Livingston v. Wyeth, Inc.*, 520 F.3d 344 (4th Cir. 2008).

[45] *Carnero v. Boston Scientific Corp.*, 433 F.3d 1 (1st Cir. 2006).

[46] 233 A.D.2d 821, 650 N.Y.S.2d 441 (N.Y. App. Div. 1996).

before the MERC, Henry was given the choice of taking an early retirement or a demotion. He claimed the forced retirement was in retaliation for his testimony in the civil suit and before the MERC. The city claimed that he was being demoted because of poor job performance and for being out of his precinct during the middle of several work days. Henry filed suit under Michigan's Whistleblower's Protection Act [MWPA, MCL 15.362; MSA 17.428(2)].

After a trial, the jury found that defendants city of Detroit and Police Chief McKinnon retaliated against plaintiff for his testimony in the civil suit and awarded him $1.08 million in damages. The defendants appealed to the Michigan Court of Appeals.

Issue: Has Henry established a prima facie case of retaliation because of his whistleblowing?

Decision: To establish a prima facie violation of the WPA, a plaintiff must show (1) that the plaintiff was engaged in a protected activity as defined by the WPA, (2) that the plaintiff was discharged, and (3) a causal connection existed between the protected activity and the discharge. The plain language of the statute provides protection for two types of "whistleblowers": (1) those who report, or are about to report, violations of law, regulation, or rule to a public body; and (2) those who are requested by a public body to participate in an investigation held by that public body or in a court action. "Type 1" whistleblowers are persons who takes it upon themselves to communicate the employer's wrongful conduct to a public body in an attempt to bring the violation to light to remedy the situation or harm done by the violation. "Type 2" who participate in a previously initiated investigation or hearing at the behest of a public body. If the plaintiff falls under either category, then that plaintiff has engaged in "protected activity" for purposes of presenting a prima facie case under the MWPA.

Henry testified that the internal procedures governing the board of review were not followed here. Because the board of police commissioners, pursuant to the city charter, drafted the police manual that set forth the procedures governing the board of review, the board of review was a public body within the meaning of the MWPA. The court held that Henry presented a prima facie case of a violation of the MWPA as a Type 2 whistleblower. By giving a deposition in a civil case, Henry clearly participated in a "court action." The court held that Henry's testimony was activity protected by the MWPA—his attendance and testimony were compelled under state law, and "compelled" is a higher standard than the "requested" language of the MWPA. There was also evidence to support the claim that Henry's testimony was causally connected to his demotion or forced retirement: 1) he was a veteran of the Detroit Police Department and had received several honors and citations; 2) prior to his testimony, he had never been reprimanded or subject to any disciplinary action; and 3) less than four months after his testimony, he was forced to choose between a demotion or retirement.

A reasonable jury could conclude that Henry was subjected to such action because he testified in the *Lessnau* case. The court therefore held that Henry had presented a prima facie violation of the MWPA for consideration by the jury. The court affirmed the trial court's award of damages to Henry.

Criminal Record

Federal EEO laws do not specifically prohibit employment discrimination based on criminal record. However, refusing to hire applicants because of their arrest records (as opposed to convictions) may constitute disparate impact discrimination in violation of Title VII.[47] Some states have specific prohibitions on discrimination because of criminal records. The New York State Human Rights Law prohibits employment discrimination because of prior criminal convictions, unless such convictions have a direct and specific relationship to the job being sought or when granting employment to the individual would involve an unreasonable risk to the property or safety of others or the general public. The New York Human Rights Law also specifically prohibits employers from seeking information about arrests that did not result in a

[47] *Green v. Missouri Pacific Railroad Co.*, 523 F.2d 1290 (8th Cir. 1975).

conviction; this restriction does not apply to applicants for employment as law enforcement officers or to governmental bodies that grant licenses for guns or firearms.

Some states require that employers conduct criminal record background checks on applicants for certain positions:

- Tennessee law requires applicants for jobs with public schools to disclose any prior convictions
- Texas law allows institutions of higher education to obtain background checks on applicants for security-sensitive positions
- Vermont requires persons employed as private security officers, armed guards or couriers, guard dog handlers, and applicants for private detective licenses to undergo background checks for prior convictions
- Missouri requires criminal background checks for persons working as home care providers, youth service workers, school bus drivers, and nursing home workers
- North Carolina requires a background check for applicants and employees in nuclear power plants
- Indiana law requires criminal background checks for employees of the state Lottery Commission

A growing number of states, including Delaware, Florida, Hawaii, Indiana, Missouri, Nebraska, New York, and Virginia, require criminal background checks for employees involved in child care or day care.

Polygraph Testing

The federal Employee Polygraph Protection Act of 1988 (EPPA)[48] severely restricts the right of private employers to require employees to take polygraph, or "lie detector," tests; many states have similar laws. The EPPA does not apply to public sector employers; it prohibits private sector employers, unless they fall under one of four exceptions, from requiring employees or applicants to submit to polygraph tests as a condition of employment. Employers are also prohibited from disciplining or discharging any employees because they refused to submit to a polygraph test. The exceptions under the EPPA allow polygraph testing under the following circumstances:

- Private employees who are working as consultants to, or employees of, firms that are contractors to federal national security intelligence operations
- Employers engaged in the provision of private security services, armored car services, or the installation and maintenance of security alarm systems may require polygraph testing of certain prospective employees
- Employers whose business involves the manufacture, sale, or distribution of controlled substances (drugs) are authorized to test employees who have direct access to the controlled substances

[48] 29 U.S.C. § 2001 - § 2009.

- Employers who have a reasonable basis to suspect that employees may have been involved in an incident that resulted in economic loss to the employer may request that those employees take polygraph tests

The EPPA requires that any polygraph test must be administered by a validly licensed examiner. An employer that requests employees to submit to a polygraph test under the fourth exception (ongoing investigation into an economic loss) must meet specific procedural requirements:

- The employer must provide the employees with a written statement describing the incident being investigated, specifically identifying the economic loss and the reason for testing the particular employees
- The employees must be given a written notice of the date, time, and location of the test
- The employees must read, and sign, a written notice that they cannot be required to submit to the test as a condition of employment
- The employees have the right to review all questions that will be asked during the test and are informed that they have the right to terminate the test at any time

The EPPA specifically forbids the polygraph operator from asking any questions relating to religious beliefs, beliefs or opinions on racial matters, political beliefs or affiliations, any questions relating to sexual behavior, and any questions relating to beliefs, affiliations, or lawful activities of labor unions.

After the test has been administered, the employer must furnish the employees with a written copy of the examiner's conclusions regarding their test, a copy of questions asked, and their charted responses. The polygraph examiner may only disclose information acquired through the test to the employer requesting the test and to the employees subjected to the test; the employer may only disclose information to the employees involved.

Even when an employer may legally administer a polygraph test under the EPPA, and the employer has complied with the procedural requirements, the employer may not discharge, discipline, or otherwise deny employment to an individual solely on the basis of the polygraph test results. The employer must have additional evidence to support any employment action taken against the tested employees. The EPPA is enforced by the federal Secretary of Labor, who may assess civil penalties of up to $10,000 against violators. In addition, individual employees or applicants who allege violations of the EPPA may bring a civil suit for damages, reinstatement, back pay, benefits, and legal fees. The time limit for bringing such suits is three years from the alleged violation. *Rubin v. Tourneau, Inc.*[49] held that the company performing the polygraph test may be sued, along with the employer, by an employee alleging violations of the EPPA. Failure to comply with the EPPA's procedural requirements is a violation subject to civil suit according to *Mennen v. Easter Stores*[50] and *Long v. Mango's Tropical Cafe, Inc.*[51] The following case addresses the question of whether the employer's actions fall under the exceptions of the EPPA.

---

[49]797 F. Supp. 247 (S.D.N.Y. 1992).

[50]951 F. Supp. 838 (N.D. Iowa 1997).

[51]958 F. Supp. 612 (S.D. Fla. 1997).

case 11.3 » Polkey v. Transtecs Corporation

404 F.3d 1264 (11th Cir. 2005)

Before BLACK, BARKETT and PRYOR, Circuit Judges

PER CURIAM

Transtecs Corporation appeals the district court's award of summary judgment to Sabrina Polkey on her claim that Transtecs requested her to take a polygraph exam, in violation of the Employee Polygraph Protection Act ("EPPA"). Transtecs argues that summary judgment was inappropriate because the district court erred as a matter of law in concluding that a request to take a polygraph exam alone constitutes an EPPA violation. Transtecs further contends that its polygraph request falls within two of the EPPA's exemptions: (i) the national defense and security exemption; (ii) the ongoing investigation exemption....

[Transtecs performed mailroom services at the Pensacola Naval Air Station ("NAS") under contract with the Department of Defense. Transtecs employees do not have access to most forms of classified material, but do handle "official use only" material. Polkey worked in the NAS mailroom as mailroom supervisor for Transtecs since October 1, 2000; there were also five other clerks at the NAS mailroom.]

On Friday, January 11, 2002, after the mailroom had closed for the day, Polkey returned to the mailroom to retrieve an item she had forgotten in the refrigerator. She then discovered that the front desk computer had been left on. When she turned it off, she discovered fourteen opened and undelivered Christmas cards in the wastebasket near the front computer. Polkey immediately contacted her supervisor, Carl Kirtley, and requested that he come to the mailroom. Polkey told Kirtley that mailroom employee Ronnie Cole had been primarily assigned to the front desk that day. In the wastebasket, Kirtley found Cole's pay stub along with the undelivered mail.

After discussing the matter with DOD personnel and Transtecs' management, both Kirtley and a civilian investigator questioned the six mailroom employees, each of whom denied opening the mail. Nonetheless, Kirtley suspected that Cole was responsible, though he hadn't eliminated the other employees.

After consulting with Transtecs' management, Kirtley arranged for polygraph testing of all the mailroom employees at Transtecs' expense. Transtecs contends that it had already determined that all the mailroom employees would be fired unless one admitted to the wrongdoing, but arranged for polygraph exams to absolve the company of any wrongdoing in the event the DOD pursued charges against the perpetrator.

Kirtley held a meeting with the mailroom employees, during which he requested that each of them submit to a polygraph exam. He explained that the examination was voluntary, and asked each to sign a general release form. The form did not contain information about the mail tampering incident, did not state the basis for testing each employee, and was not signed by any Transtecs official. Each employee signed the form. Kirtley scheduled Cole for a polygraph test that same afternoon.

The following day, Kirtley received an oral report of the polygraph exam results that indicated deception when Cole denied opening the mail. According to Kirtley, he conveyed this information to Godwin Opara, Transtecs' president. Opara denies this, claiming that Kirtley told him the test results were inconclusive. While Kirtley claims he could not rule out any employee positively, he concedes that after learning of Cole's test results, he had no reason to suspect that Polkey was involved in any way with the opening of the mail. Kirtley then scheduled another meeting with the mailroom employees and encouraged each of them to take the optional polygraph exam to clear their name. Polkey and other employees expressed concern over the reliability of polygraph exams, fearing that the exam might inaccurately implicate them. All the employees ultimately refused to submit to the exam. Kirtley informed Opara of this decision.

Less than one week later, Polkey was fired, ostensibly for permitting package deliveries through the mailroom's back door, in contravention of NAS security procedures. [Polkey then filed suit alleging Transtecs violated the EPPA by unlawfully requesting that she take a polygraph exam and discharging her because she refused to submit to a polygraph exam. The trial court granted summary judgment to Polkey on the "request" claim, and the parties then settled the remaining counts, and stipulated to nominal damages on Polkey's "request" claim. On appeal, the court only considered the legality of the request that she take the polygraph exam.]

Under the EPPA, it is unlawful for a covered employer to "directly or indirectly, require, *request, suggest, or* cause any employee ... to take or submit to any lie detector test." (emphasis added). Because the statute is phrased in the alternative, its plain language prohibits an employer from requesting or suggesting that an employee submit to a polygraph exam, even where the test is ultimately not administered and no adverse employment action is taken as a consequence.... Because the statute's meaning on this point is clear and unambiguous, its plain language controls our analysis.

Transtecs urges an alternative construction of the EPPA, one which would essentially read the "request or suggest" language out of the statute. In Transtecs' view, the EPPA should not be interpreted to prohibit polygraph exam requests, for such a construction would render superfluous the statute's separate prohibitions on requiring employee polygraphs or using the results to take adverse employment action. Transtecs further argues that the paucity of reference to the "request or suggest" language in the EPPA's legislative history supports its interpretation.... Because the statutory text clearly prohibits a covered employer's request or suggestion that an employee submit to a lie detector exam, the EPPA's language both begins and ends our inquiry. Thus, the district court did not err in concluding that Transtecs violated the EPPA by "requesting" or "suggesting" that Polkey take a polygraph test.

The EPPA provides that its prohibitions will not be "construed to prohibit the administration, by the Federal Government, in the performance of any counterintelligence function, of any lie detector test" to an employee of a contractor of the Department of Defense ("DOD"). Transtecs argues that as it operated the mailroom where Polkey worked under a DOD contract that provided for a "secret" clearance level, it was engaging in "counterintelligence operations" that triggered the national defense exemption.

Transtec's argument fails because the national defense exemption applies, by its own terms, *only* to the federal government. The statute does not purport to allow defense contractors to administer or request polygraph exams from their employees; rather, the national defense exemption extends only to the federal government. Indeed, any hint of ambiguity on this point is resolved by the regulations implementing the EPPA, which explicitly state that the national security exemptions "apply only to the federal government; they do not allow private employers/contractors to administer such [lie detector] tests." [29 C.F.R. § 801.11(a) (emphasis added)]. As a private contractor, Transtecs' attempted reliance on the national security exemption is thus misplaced.

The EPPA's prohibitions do not prohibit a covered employer from requesting a polygraph exam, where the employer demonstrates that: (i) the test is administered in connection with an ongoing investigation involving economic loss or injury to the employer's business; (ii) the employee had access to the subject of the investigation; (iii) the employer has a reasonable suspicion as to the employee's involvement in the loss; and (iv) the employer provides the employee with a signed written notice that specifically identifies the economic loss at issue, indicates that the employee had access to the property being investigated, and describes the basis for the employer's reasonable suspicion. [29 U.S.C. § 2006(d)(1-4)]. As the statute is phrased in the conjunctive, an employer must comply with each of these requirements for the ongoing investigation exemption to apply.... It is undisputed that Transtecs' polygraph request satisfied the first two elements of the exemption, as it was conducting an ongoing investigation into the Christmas card tampering incident, and Polkey did have access to those cards and the receptacle in which they were discovered. Transtecs' entitlement to the exemption thus rests on its compliance with the reasonable suspicion and written notice requirements.

As an initial matter, we agree with the district court's holding that Transtecs was not required to provide Polkey with the signed written notice required by § 2006(d)(4) at the time of its polygraph request. The statute requires only that the statement be "provided to the examinee before the test." [29 U.S.C. § 2006(d)(4).] The implementing regulations have interpreted this provision to require at least 48 hours between the time the examinee is provided with the statement and the test administration. [29 C.F.R. § 801.12(g)(2)]. The statute differentiates between "employees" and "examinees": while the other elements of the ongoing investigation exemption apply to "employees" more broadly, only "examinees" must be provided with a signed written notice. Because Polkey ultimately refused the polygraph exam, she never became an "examinee", and Transtecs accordingly never became obligated to provide her with the signed written notice required by § 2006(d)(4).

Nonetheless, Transtecs' reliance on the ongoing investigation exemption fails because it cannot satisfy its burden of establishing reasonable suspicion of Polkey's responsibility for the Christmas card incident. While the statute does not clarify what constitutes a "reasonable suspicion," the regulations define it as "an observable, articulable basis in fact which indicates that a particular employee was involved in, or responsible for, an economic loss." [29 C.F.R. § 801.12(f)(1)]. Access to the property and potential opportunity, standing alone, cannot constitute reasonable suspicion. By the time Transtecs' made its second polygraph request of Polkey, Polkey's supervisor conceded that he had no reason to suspect that Polkey was involved in the mail opening incident. Instead, at the time of Transtecs' second request, the company aimed to test all of its employees only in order to absolve the company of any responsibility for the theft. To allow such blanket testing under the ongoing investigation exemption would vitiate § 2006(d)(3)'s requirement of reasonable suspicion as to each individual employee. We thus agree with the district court that Polkey was entitled to summary judgment on Transtecs' second polygraph request, as at the time the company lacked reasonable suspicion as to her involvement in the mail incident.

AFFIRMED.

Case Questions

1. May an employer voluntarily request that an employee take a polygraph test?
2. Can Transtecs rely on the EPPA exception for government contractors engaged in national security work? Explain.
3. What are the EPPA requirements for the exception allowing an employer with a reasonable suspicion that employees are involved in an incident resulting in economic loss? Did Transtecs comply with those requirements? Explain.

Honesty Testing

Honesty Tests
Employment tests used by employers as a screening device to evaluate employees or applicants on various workplace behaviors such as truthfulness, perceptions about employee theft, admissions of theft, and drug use.

Because federal and state legislation generally prohibits employers from requiring employees to take polygraph tests, some employers have turned to other ***honesty tests*** in an attempt to evaluate employees or applicants. These are usually "paper-and-pencil" tests and may include psychological profile testing. (Most psychological profile tests are generally not intended to be used as an employment screening device, but employers may choose to use them as part of the hiring process.) The honesty tests seek to measure various workplace behaviors such as

- Truthfulness
- Perceptions about the pervasiveness of employee theft
- Illegal drug use
- Admissions of theft

There is some controversy over the validity of honesty tests: A 1990 study by the federal Office of Technology and Assessment found research on the effectiveness of such tests inconclusive, but a 1991 study by the American Psychological Association was much more positive and favorable.

The federal EPPA does not prohibit honesty testing, and neither does most state legislation. However, Massachusetts specifically prohibits employers from using honesty tests; Rhode Island bars using honesty tests as the primary basis of employment decisions, and Wisconsin also limits the use of honesty tests by employers. The use of psychological profile tests as an employee selection device could possibly raise issues under the Americans with Disabilities Act or state antidiscrimination legislation (see Chapter 10). Employers desiring to use psychological profile tests should have a legitimate, work-related rationale for the testing.

Off-Duty Conduct

A number of states protect employees from employment discrimination because of their lawful, off-the-job conduct. This legislation is mainly designed to protect smokers or tobacco users from employment discrimination as long as their tobacco use is off duty. Tennessee law protects the off-duty use of "agricultural products not regulated by the alcoholic beverage commission." New York and Minnesota protect the "legal use of consumable products" off duty, covering alcohol as well as tobacco. States such as Illinois, Minnesota, Montana, New York, North Carolina, South Dakota, West Virginia, Wisconsin, and Wyoming protect off-duty smokers from employment discrimination but do allow employers to differentiate between smokers and nonsmokers in the costs of insurance and medical benefits, as long as the cost differential reflects the actual difference in the cost of coverage. In states such as Michigan that do not have such protective legislation, it is legal for employers to fire or refuse to hire smokers.

ethical DILEMMA

An Additional Charge for Smokers?

As the Employee Benefits Manager at Immense Multinational Business (IMB), you are responsible for trying to hold down the cost of employee medical insurance while still providing comprehensive quality medical care to IMB employees. Lately, you have noticed that some employees, usually those who smoke, have significantly higher medical claims than nonsmokers. Studies indicate that employees who smoke a pack of cigarettes a day have claims that are 18 percent higher than those of nonsmokers; smokers are 29 percent more likely than nonsmokers to have annual medical claims over $5,000. Estimates by the American Lung Association indicate that the medical benefits for smokers cost at least $1,000 more per year than for nonsmokers.

Based on such information, you are considering whether IMB should impose an additional annual charge of $500 for medical benefits and insurance coverage on employees who are smokers. Would such an additional charge for smokers be legal? What arguments can you make for imposing the additional charge on smokers? What arguments can you make for not imposing the additional charge? Should IMB impose the additional charge? Explain your answers.

Section 201-d of the New York State Labor Law probably goes the furthest in protecting off the-job activities. It prohibits employers from discriminating against employees because of their legal off-duty recreational or political activities. On the question of whether an employee's affair with a co-worker was protected "recreational activity" under the legislation, a split developed among various courts. A state appellate court, in the case of *NYS v. Wal-Mart Stores,*[52] held that

[52]207 A. D.2d 150, 621 N.Y.S.2d 158 (N.Y.A.D. 1995). See also *Carey v. de Souza*, 254 A.D.2d 119, 678 N.Y.S.2d 264 (N.Y.A.D. 1998) (the court assumed that dating is a protected recreational activity for purposes of the decision but did not consider the issue on its merits); and *Bilquin v. Roman Catholic Church, Diocese of Rockville Centre,* No. 0118588/99 (Sup.Ct. Nassau County, Sept. 12, 2000) (the definition of "recreational activities" does not include "personal relationships).

dating a co-worker was not protected under the legislation, while the Federal District Court for the Southern District of New York in two separate cases, *Pasch v. Katz Media Corp.*[53] and *Aquilone v. Republic Nat'l Bank of New York*,[54] held that dating and co-habitation with a co-worker were protected. In the following case, the U.S. Court of Appeals for the Second Circuit resolved the split.

case 11.4 »

McCavitt v. Swiss Reinsurance America Corporation

237 F.3d 166 (2d Cir. 2001) (per curiam)

Facts: McCavitt was employed as an executive by Swiss Reinsurance America Corporation (Swiss Re). He had been involved in a personal relationship with Diane Butler, who was also an executive with Swiss Re. Swiss Re had no formal antifraternization policy, but McCavitt claimed that he was initially denied a promotion and ultimately discharged by Swiss Re because of he was dating Butler. McCavitt filed suit against Swiss Re, alleging that his discharge was in violation of New York Labor Law Section 201-d. The trial court dismissed McCavitt's complaint for failure to state a legal claim. McCavitt appealed to the U.S. Court of Appeals for the Second Circuit.

Issue: Is McCavitt protected under New York Labor Law § 201-d from being discharged for dating a co-worker?

Decision: The provisions of § 201-d of New York Labor Law that relate to the issue here state:

> 2. Unless otherwise provided by law, it shall be unlawful for any employer or employment agency to refuse to hire, employ or license, or to discharge from employment or otherwise discriminate against an individual in compensation, promotion or terms, conditions or privileges of employment because of:...c. an individual's legal recreational activities outside work hours, off of the employer's premises and without use of the employer's equipment or other property.

The statute defines "recreational activities" as:

> any lawful, leisure-time activity, for which the employee receives no compensation and which is generally engaged in for recreational purposes, including but not limited to sports, games, hobbies, exercise, reading and the viewing of television, movies and similar material.

While the New York Court of Appeals has not ruled on the question of whether dating was a "recreational activity" protected by § 201-d, several lower courts have. The Appellate Division of the New York Supreme Court held that dating was not a protected activity in *State v. Wal-Mart Stores, Inc.* In *Carey v. de Souza*, the Appellate Division assumed that dating is a protected recreational activity for purposes of the decision but did not consider the issue on its merits. A Nassau County New York Supreme Court in *Bilquin v. Roman Catholic Church, Diocese of Rockville Centre* determined that "recreational activities" did not include "personal relationships."

However, the U.S. District Court for the Southern District of New York has taken the opposite position in two cases. In *Pasch v. Katz Media Corp.*, it held that the New York Court of Appeals would deem co-habitation to be a protected recreational activity under § 201-d; and in *Aquilone v. Republic Nat'l Bank of New York*, it held that an employee's friendship with another person, where contacts between them took place off the employer's premises and not on the employer's time, was protected recreational activity under § 201-d.

The district court here held that it was bound to follow the Third Department's decision in *Wal-Mart*. With regard to interpreting and applying New York state law, the federal courts are bound to apply New York law as interpreted by New York's intermediate appellate courts, unless there is persuasive evidence that the New York Court of Appeals, which has not ruled on this issue, would reach a different conclusion. The court of appeals therefore held that dating a co-worker was not protected "recreational activity" under § 201-d. The court overruled the *Pasch* and *Aquilone* cases, and affirmed the trial court's dismissal of McCavitt's suit. «

[53] 1995 WL 469710, 1995 U.S. Dist. LEXIS 11153 (S.D.N.Y. Aug.8, 1995).

[54] 1998 WL 872425, 1998 U.S. Dist. LEXIS 19531(S.D.N.Y. Dec.15, 1998).

In the absence of specific legislative provisions, state tort laws may provide some protection for employees' off duty conduct. In *Rulon-Miller v. IBM*,[55] the court awarded an employee damages for invasion of privacy and intentional infliction of emotional distress for her discharge because she was dating an employee of a competitor. But in *Barbee v. Household Automotive Finance Corporation*,[56] the court held that a supervisor discharged for dating a subordinate did not have a claim for invasion of privacy because he had been repeatedly warned against such conduct, and therefore had no reasonable expectation of privacy regarding such conduct.

Guns at Work Laws

In *Hansen v. America Online, Inc.*,[57] the Utah Supreme Court rejected a wrongful termination suit brought by several employees who were discharged for violating an employer's policy prohibiting possession of a firearm on the employer's property. The court held that the discharge of the employees was not in violation of public policy, and that the private property rights of the employer allowed the employer to ban firearms from its property.

In response the *Hansen* decision, the National Rifle Association began a lobbying campaign at the state legislature level. As a result of that campaign, a number of states have passed laws that allow employees to bring firearms onto their employer's property, as long as the weapons are kept locked in the employee's vehicle.[58] Oklahoma passed such a law[59] in 2005, making it a criminal offense for any "person, property owner, tenant, employer, or business entity" to prohibit any person, except a convicted felon, from transporting and storing firearms locked in a motor vehicle on "any property set aside for any motor vehicle." The law also provides that property owners who attempt to bar guns from their property are subject to a civil suit to enforce the law, and are liable for court costs and legal fees. The law was challenged by a number of employers on the grounds that requiring employers to allow guns on their property would violate the employers' general duty under the federal Occupational Safety and Health Act (OSHA) to provide a safe workplace. The U.S. District Court for the Northern District of Oklahoma agreed with the employers and granted an injunction against enforcement of the law,[60] but on appeal, the U.S. Court of Appeals for the 10th Circuit reversed the trial court and held that the Oklahoma law was valid and was not in conflict with federal law.[61]

---

[55] 162 Cal. App.3d 241, 208 Cal.Rptr. 524 (Cal. Ct. App. 1984).

[56] 113 Cal. App.4th 525, 6 Cal.Rptr.3d 406 (Cal. Ct. App. 2003).

[57] 96 P.3d 950 (Utah 2004).

[58] States with such laws include Oklahoma, Florida, Georgia, Kansas, Kentucky, Alaska, Minnesota, Mississippi, and Nebraska.

[59] 21 Okla. Stat. § 1289.7a and § 1290.22.

[60] *ConocoPhillips Co. v. Henry*, 520 F. Supp.2d 1282 (N.D. Ok. 2007).

[61] *Ramsey Winch, Inc. v. Henry*, 555 F.3d 1199 (10th Cir. 2009).

CHAPTER REVIEW

» Key Terms

contract compliance program « 302
affirmative action plans « 303
suspect classes « 310
strict scrutiny test « 311
nonsuspect classes « 312
whistleblowers « 316
honesty tests « 323

» Summary

- In addition to the primary EEO laws at the federal level, other legislation protects employees from some other forms of discrimination in employment. The Civil Rights Acts of 1866 and 1870 allow persons who are victims of intentional discrimination to sue for damages: 42 U.S.C. Section 1981 can be used against intentional race or national origin discrimination, and 42 U.S.C. Section 1983 can be used for intentional discrimination by public sector employers.
- Government contractors are subject to the affirmative action requirements of Executive Order 11246, and employees who serve in the military are protected from employment discrimination by the Uniformed Services Employment and Reemployment Rights Act. The National Labor Relations Act may provide employees with legal remedies against employment discrimination.
- Public sector employers are subject to the constitutional equal protection and due process provisions that prohibit intentional discrimination. The federal courts are becoming increasingly skeptical about governmental affirmative action programs, which entail preferential discrimination based on race or gender. State employment discrimination and employment laws supplement federal legislation and provide additional protection for employees.

» Problems

Questions

1. Against which kinds of discrimination can 42 U.S.C. Section 1981 be used? What remedies are available to plaintiffs under 42 U.S.C. Section 1981? Against which kinds of discrimination can 42 U.S.C. Section 1983 be used? What remedies are available under 42 U.S.C. Section 1983?
2. When are employees protected from discrimination because of their service in the U.S. military forces? What must the employees do to receive such protection? What remedies are available under the USERRA?
3. When are employers subject to the obligations of E.O. 11246? What does E.O. 11246 require of employers?

4. Can a public sector employer use affirmative action to give hiring preference to female applicants? Can that public sector employer give females preference when deciding which employees to lay off? Explain your answers.
5. Does the U.S. Constitution prohibit all employment discrimination based on race? Explain your answer.

Case Problems

6. Keller worked for the Maryland Department of Social Services. She sued both the department and the state after she was denied promotion to case worker associate III. She argued that the state had violated Title VII and Section 1983 by refusing to promote her because she was African American. The state moved for dismissal of Keller's Section 1983 count, arguing that Title VII provides a concurrent and more comprehensive remedy and, therefore, preempts Keller from coming under Section 1983.

   How should the court rule? See *Keller v. Prince George's County Department of Social Services* [616 F. Supp. 540 (D. Md. 1985)].
7. Marta Davis sued her employer under Section 1981 of the 1866 Civil Rights Act, claiming she was discriminated against because of her Hispanic ancestry. The company contended that Section 1981 was passed in 1866 in response to the enactment of "black codes" in several states, which prevented African Americans from exercising fundamental rights to which they were entitled as part of their newly acquired citizenship. The company asserts that because this was the clear congressional purpose for passing Section 1981, it cannot be stretched to cover national origin discrimination.

   Do you agree? See *Davis v. Boyle-Midway, Inc.* [615 F. Supp. 560 (N.D. Ga. 1985)].
8. Alice Bobo, an African-American woman, was employed by Continental Baking Company in a production position. She was fired because she refused to wear a hat as part of her uniform; she claimed that her male co-workers were not required to wear such hats. She filed suit against Continental Baking under 42 U.S.C. Section 1981, alleging that her discharge was due to gender and race discrimination.

   Can she pursue her claims under 42 U.S.C. Section 1981? Explain your answer. See *Bobo v. Continental Baking Co.* [662 F.2d 340 (5th Cir. 1981)].
9. Rita Novak was employed by Dakota Industries as general manager: she was also a member of the U.S. Army Reserves. Her reserve unit was called up to active duty in Bosnia for six months in December 1996, and she gave the employer appropriate notice of her need to be absent from her job for that period. Upon completion of her duty in Bosnia, she returned to the job at Dakota Industries on July 7, 1997. She was reemployed at the same rate of pay as she received prior to leaving for Bosnia, but the employer did not give her the general pay increase granted by Dakota to all employees in May 1997. Novak informed the employer that she was entitled to receive the May 1997 pay increase, but the employer refused and told her she was lucky to have a job at all. Three weeks later, Novak informed her employer that she was required to attend a two-day training program for the Reserves and that she would be absent from work on August 14 and 15, 1997. The employer complained about the disruption caused by her absence during her service in Bosnia and informed her that her Reserve duty was "too much trouble" and that she was needed on the job. Novak then presented a copy of her reserve orders to report for the training session, along with a written request for a two-day leave; the employer told her that if she went, she "shouldn't come back." When Novak did not appear for work on August 14, the employer prepared a check for her, with the notation "final pay owing as of termination date, August 14, 1997." The employer presented the check to Novak when she reported for work August 18, told her she was fired, and asked for her keys.

   What legal remedies can Novak pursue against Dakota Industries? What steps should she take to pursue a claim, and what is her likelihood of success? What remedies can she recover? Explain your answers. See *Novak v. Mackintosh* [937 F. Supp. 873 (D.S.D. 1996)].
10. Porter, an African-American male, was rejected as an applicant for the Washington, D.C., Police Department because he failed to pass Test 21, a

verbal facility and reading comprehension test. Porter discovered that African Americans fail Test 21 at a rate four times higher than that of Caucasian applicants. Porter files suit against the D.C. Police Department, alleging that the use of Test 21 constitutes race discrimination in violation of the Constitution's Equal Protection clause.

How should the court rule on his claim? Can Porter bring any other legal challenges to the use of Test 21? Explain. See *Washington v. Davis* [426 U.S. 229 (1976)].

11. Joseph K. Bonacorsa had been involved in the harness racing industry for a number of years; he was licensed by the New York State Racing and Wagering Board as both a harness owner and a driver. He had been convicted of perjury for lying under oath that he and his wife owned several horses. These horses were in fact owned by Gerald Forrest, who had previously been found guilty of conspiring to fix races at harness tracks and was therefore legally barred from owning licensed race horses. When Bonacorsa was convicted of perjury, the New York State Racing and Wagering Board revoked his harness owner and driver license. Bonacorsa served two years in prison and was on probation for a number of years. When his probation period ended, he was issued a certificate of good conduct by the N.Y. Board of Parole. Upon receiving the certificate, Bonacorsa applied to the State Racing and Wagering Board to reinstate his harness owner and driver license. The Racing and Wagering Board refused to reinstate his license because his prior conviction was conduct that "impugned the integrity of racing within the state." Bonacorsa decided to pursue a legal challenge to the board's refusal to grant him a license.

    Under what legal provisions can he sue to challenge the refusal to grant him a license? What is his likelihood of success? Explain. See *Bonacorsa v. Lindt* [129 A.D.2d 518, 514 N.Y.S.2d 370 (N.Y. A. D. 1987)].

12. Christine Noland was employed as an administrative assistant in the County Assessor's Office in Comanche County, Oklahoma. Her immediate supervisor was Robert McAdoo; McAdoo was initially the county deputy assessor and was later promoted to the assessor position. Throughout the period of her employment, Noland claims that McAdoo subjected her to unwelcome sexual advances, remarks, and physical contact. McAdoo would put his arm around her waist or neck despite the fact that she continually told him to stop. McAdoo would also stand in a doorway so that Noland had to rub against him to pass through. When Noland refused McAdoo's request that he and she attend an out-of-town conference, she was fired. Noland filed suit under 42 U.S.C. Section 1983 against both the county and McAdoo personally, alleging sexual harassment.

    Can Noland bring a sexual harassment claim under 42 U.S.C. Section 1983? Can McAdoo personally be held liable under 42 U.S.C. Section 1983? Does Noland have any other statutory remedies available? Explain your answers. See *Noland v. McAdoo* [39 F.3d 269 (10th Cir. 1994)],

13. Madden, a member of the U.S. Air Force Reserves, was hired for a temporary ninety-day position of process engineer by Rolls-Royce Data Systems at its Indiana facilities. Madden claimed to be have an engineering degree from Purdue, but he never graduated. Madden made a number of mistakes on the job, and he was terminated at the end of the ninety-day period. When he was told that he would not be considered for a permanent position, his supervisor did not mention Madden's performance, but instead referred to Madden's impending call-up to active duty service with the Air Force. Madden later applied for another position with Rolls-Royce, but the H.R. manager was unable to verify Madden's degree credentials, and he was not hired. Madden filed suit against Rolls-Royce under USERRA, claiming that his temporary position was not renewed and he was not hired for the other position because of his military service obligations. What must he demonstrate in order to establish a claim under USERRA? What defenses can the employer raise? Is Madden likely to succeed? Explain. See *Madden v. Rolls Royce Corp.*, 563 F.3d 636 (7th Cir. 2009).

14. Green, an African-American male, applied for a clerical position with the Missouri-Pacific Railroad but was not hired because he had a criminal record.

Green had been convicted of refusing to report for induction into the armed forces in 1971 and had served four years in federal prison. Green's refusal to report for induction was based on his religious beliefs. After serving his sentence, he had been employed by a public service agency for eighteen years; his work record was excellent. Green had no other arrests or convictions on his record. Missouri-Pacific had a policy of refusing to hire any person convicted of a criminal offense.

What, if any, legal remedies can Green pursue against Missouri-Pacific? Would he have any additional remedies if the office where he applied was located in Alabama? In New York? Explain your answers. See *Green v. Missouri-Pacific Railroad* [549 F.2d 1158 (8th Cir. 1977)].

15. A New York State constitutional provision and a civil service statute required that military veterans with wartime service be granted extra points on competitive exams for state civil service jobs. Wartime vets received a five-point bonus on the exam, and disabled vets received an extra ten points. However, this bonus was limited to veterans who were New York residents at the time they entered military service.

    Is this affirmative action program permissible under the Constitution and federal statutory law? See *Attorney General of the State of New York v. Soto-Lopez* [476 U.S. 898 (1986)].

Hypothetical Scenarios

16. You are a member of the local health food cooperative retail store (co-op) in Detroit. At the co-op's monthly membership meeting, the manager says the store has adopted a new policy to prohibit hiring any person who smokes. The co-op already prohibits smoking in the workplace (as required by the state's "Clean Indoor Air Act"). The new policy would bar hiring smokers even if they don't smoke during working hours. Is the proposed policy legal—can the co-op refuse to hire anyone who smokes? Would your answer be different if the co-op was in Buffalo, N.Y.? Explain.
17. Fahran Al Muhammed applied unsuccessfully for a job with the federal Department of Housing and Urban Development (HUD). He believes he was not hired because he is of Iranian descent. He files suit against HUD under 42 U.S.C. § 1981. Is his case likely to succeed? Explain.
18. You work for the local Honda dealership as a sales associate. You love to play softball, but your employer refuses to sponsor a team in the local recreation league. The Ford dealership across the street from your employer has a team and lets you join. When your manager learns that you are playing on the Ford team, he tells you that "it's a conflict of interest" and that you must quit the team or lose your job. Can the manager legally fire you for playing on the Ford softball team? Does your answer depend upon where your employer is located? Explain.
19. As the new audit manager at Immense Multilateral Business, you are responsible for supervising the work of the audit division, and for preparing quarterly reports to be filed with the Securities and Exchange Commission (SEC). You discover that the company accounting practices are not consistent with Generally Accepted Accounting Principles (GAAP), as required by the SEC regulations, and that the quarterly reports contain inaccurate information. When you inform the CEO about the problem, he tells you to ignore it. When you persist, he asks you "Do you like your job? Do you want to keep your job?" If you choose to inform the SEC of the problem, what, if any, legal provisions may apply to your situation? Explain.
20. You are the assistant HR manager at the regional office of Quickie-Mart, Inc., a chain of convenience stores. The store manager at the Dover store informs you that she has noticed a decline in cash receipts of several cashiers over the last month or two. She wants to force the cashiers to take polygraph tests to "see which ones are stealing from us." Can you require the cashiers to take a polygraph test? Can the cashiers who refuse to take a polygraph test be fired? Under what circumstances, if any, can the cashiers be subjected to polygraph testing? Explain.

PART 3

LABOR RELATIONS LAW

The Rise of Organized Labor and Its Regulatory Framework

The Industrial Revolution brought about the rise of centralized manufacturing, with factories replacing the cottage industry in which craftsmen produced their own goods. These factories required laborers, who were subjected to harsh conditions and long hours. Despite the hardships that the new Industrial Age presented, it also carried the promise of a vast increase both in wealth and in mass-produced consumer goods. That increase would be sufficient to make possible a greatly improved standard of living for all classes, including the factory workers. It would be necessary, however, for laborers to join together to ensure that they would get their share of the increasing wealth of the nation. Employers reacted to the collective action of the workers by turning to the courts in an attempt to prevent the laborers from improving their lot in life at the expense of the landed class, or the employers. Although labor's initial attempts at joining together were held illegal as combinations or conspiracies, the ruling class and public opinion gradually came to recognize the legitimacy of joint action by workers.

Labor Development in America

The craftsmen and journeymen of late eighteenth- and early nineteenth-century America recognized the importance of organized activity to resist employer attempts to reduce wages. The American courts initially reacted to these activities with hostility.

One of the earliest recorded American labor cases is the *Philadelphia Cordwainers* case, decided in 1806. The cordwainers, or shoemakers, formed a club and presented the master cordwainers, their employers, with a rate schedule for production of various types of shoes. The wage increases they demanded ranged from twenty-five to seventy-five cents per pair. The employers, however, who were attempting to compete with shoe producers in other cities, sought to lower prices to compete more effectively. The employers took their complaint to the public prosecutor and the workers were charged with "contriving and intending unjustly and oppressively, to increase and augment the prices and rates usually paid to them" and with preventing, by "threats, menaces, and other unlawful means" other journeymen from working for lower wages. They were also accused of conspiring to refuse to work for any master who employed workers who did not abide by the club's rules.

In directing the jury to consider the case, the judge noted that "… A combination of workmen to raise their wages may be considered in a two fold point of view: one is to benefit themselves … the other is to injure those who do not join their society. The rule of law condemns both…." The jury found the defendants guilty of conspiracy to raise their wages. The effect of the decision was to render combinations of workers for the purpose of raising wages illegal. The case produced a public outcry by the Jeffersonians and in the press.

Not all of labor's activities were held illegal. For example, in *People v. Melvin,*[1] a New York cordwainers' case decided in 1809, the charge of an illegal combination to raise wages was dismissed. The court declared that the journeymen were free to join together, but they could not use means "of a nature too arbitrary and coercive, and which went to deprive their fellow citizens of rights as precious as any they contended for."

Although that language may have sounded promising, the law remained in a most unsettled state. In 1835, the New York Supreme Court in *People v. Fisher*[2] found unionized workers guilty of ***criminal conspiracy*** under a statute that vaguely stated, "If two or more persons shall conspire … to commit any act injurious to the public health, to public morals, or to trade or commerce; or for the perversion or obstruction of justice or the due administration of the laws—they shall be deemed guilty of a misdemeanor." The workers—again shoemakers organized into a club—had struck to force the discharge of a co-worker who had accepted wages below the minimum set by the club. The defendants were guilty of conspiring to commit an act "injurious to trade or commerce," the court reasoned. Artificially high wages meant correspondingly higher prices for boots, which prevented local manufacturers from selling as cheaply as their competitors elsewhere. Furthermore, the court observed, the community was deprived of the services of the worker whose discharge was procured by the shoemakers' union.

Criminal Conspiracy
A crime that may be committed when two or more persons agree to do something unlawful.

Such decisions provoked outrage among workers in the eastern states. In the wake of these trials, mobs of workers sometimes held their own mock trials and hanged unpopular judges in effigy. Despite such popular sentiments, the courts and the law remained major obstacles to organized labor's achieving a legitimate place in society. The first step toward that achievement was the law's recognition that a labor organization was not per se an illegal conspiracy. That legal development came in the landmark decision of the Massachusetts Supreme Court in 1842 in the case of *Commonwealth v. Hunt,*[3] which held that union activities were not illegal conspiracies as long as the objectives of those activities, and the means employed to achieve those objectives, were not illegal.

Although *Commonwealth v. Hunt* did not abolish the doctrine of criminal conspiracy with regard to unions, it did make it extremely difficult to apply the doctrine to labor activities. After 1842, the legality of labor unions was accepted by mainstream judicial opinion. Furthermore, in the post-Civil War period, most state appellate courts accepted the legality of peaceful strikes, provided that the purpose of the work stoppage was determined by the court to be legal.

The Post–Civil War Period

After *Commonwealth v. Hunt,* the courts grudgingly accorded labor unions a measure of legitimacy, but the labor movement was forced to struggle—sometimes violently—with

[1]2 Wheeler C.C. 262, Yates Sel. Cas. 112 (1809).

[2]14 Wend. 9 (1835).

[3]45 Mass. (4 Met.) 111 (Mass. 1842).

employers for recognition. The years following the Civil War were a turbulent period for the American labor movement. Those years saw not only a great increase in the growth and development of unions, but they were also marked by violent strikes in several industries.

The last decades of the nineteenth century saw three centers of labor activity: the Knights of Labor, the Socialists, and the American Federation of Labor. Each group sought to rejuvenate organized labor after the declines suffered during the 1870s.

The Knights of Labor

The Noble Order of the Knights of Labor, first developed in Philadelphia in 1869, sought to organize both skilled and unskilled workers. Following the violent Railway Strike of 1877, workers rushed to join the Knights, which became a national organization. From 1878 to 1884, they conducted a large number of strikes, but their focus on industry-wide organizations rather than craft unions posed problems because the unskilled workers could easily be replaced during a strike. Membership in the Knights grew but turnover was high, as members were suspended for nonpayment of dues, usually in the wake of unsuccessful strikes. Some locals disbanded when employers, following unsuccessful strikes, forced workers to sign ***yellow-dog contracts*** (in which they agreed not to join any union). After suffering defeats in a number of strikes, by 1886 the Knights sought to form a political alliance with the agrarian reform movement and the socialists. This turn to political action had only moderate success. The skilled trades unions within the Knights came to believe that they could more effectively achieve their goals through narrowly based organizations emphasizing labor actions rather than political efforts. Those unions pulled out of the Knights of Labor, causing its decline.

Yellow-Dog Contracts
Employment contracts requiring employees to agree not to join a union.

The Socialists

The establishment of the International Workingmen's Association (the First International) by Karl Marx in London in 1864 stirred interest in socialism in the United States. In 1865, the German Workingmen's Union was formed in New York City.[4] The socialist movement initially sought to organize unions, but it turned to political activities in the aftermath of the Railway Strike of 1877, with its political arm becoming the Socialist Labor Party. The public outcry following the Haymarket Riot in 1886, during which a bomb killed eleven persons, served to undercut the public acceptance and legitimacy of the socialist movement.

The labor activities of the socialist movement came to be represented by the Industrial Workers of the World (the IWW, or "Wobblies") during the early decades of the twentieth century. The Wobblies were a radical union that engaged in a number of violent strikes. Their counterpart in the western United States was the Western Federation of Miners, led by William "Big Bill" Haywood, a socialist labor leader. Following the Russian Revolution in 1917, the Wobblies were eclipsed by the American Communist Party, which emphasized political activities. The influence of the Communist Party in labor activities, although important during the Depression, declined during World War II and the late 1940s; the Cold War and the McCarthy "red hunts" in the late 1940s and early 1950s effectively brought an end to organized labor's links to the American Communist Party.

[4]It was later reorganized as the Social Party and ultimately became known as Section 2 of the First International.

The American Federation of Labor

The American Federation of Labor (AFL), which ultimately became the dominant organization of the American labor movement, was the rival of both the Socialists and the Knights of Labor. The AFL emphasized union activities in contrast to the political activities of the Knights and the Socialists. This "pure and simple" trade union movement was started by Samuel Gompers and Adolph Strasser of the Cigarmakers' Union. The AFL adopted a pattern of union organization based on the British trade union system:

- local unions were to be organized under the authority of a national association;
- dues were to be raised to create a large financial reserve; and
- sick and death benefits were to be provided to members.

The national organization's focus was on wages and practical, immediate goals rather than on the ideological and political aims of the Knights of Labor and the Socialists. A federation of trade unions developed. Although the federation was open to unskilled workers, it was dominated by unions representing the skilled trades or crafts. The federation's unions initially faced stiff rivalry from the Knights of Labor but as the Knights declined, the AFL grew in size and importance. By 1900, organized labor was largely composed of the 500,000 skilled workers in AFL-affiliated unions. For the next few decades, the AFL and its affiliated craft unions dominated the organized labor movement in America.

The Congress of Industrial Organizations

The Congress of Industrial Organizations (CIO) was a federation of unions that sought to organize the unskilled production workers largely ignored by the AFL. It grew out of a renewed interest in industry-wide organizing activity led by the autoworkers, steel workers, and the mine workers under John L. Lewis. The AFL opposed the new organization and in 1938 expelled all unions associated with the CIO. The CIO, which emphasized political activity as well as organizing activity, had spectacular success in organizing the workers of the steel, automobile, rubber, electrical, manufacturing, and machinery industries. After years of bitter rivalry, the AFL was finally forced to recognize the CIO; the AFL (with 10.5 million members) merged with the CIO (with 4.5 million members) in 1955. The resulting organization, the AFL-CIO, was the dominant body in the American labor movement.

The Change to Win Coalition

In 2005, seven major unions accounting for nearly six million members broke away from the AFL-CIO to form the Change to Win Coalition:

- The International Brotherhood of Teamsters
- The Service Employees International Union
- The Laborers' International Union of North America
- The United Brotherhood of Carpenters and Joiners of America
- The United Farm Workers of America
- The United Food and Commercial Workers International Union
- Unite Here

The coalition seeks to revitalize the labor movement by putting greater efforts into organizing and adapting to the changing attitudes of twenty-first century American workers.

Concept *Summary* » 12.1

Labor Development in America

- Nineteenth century views:
  - Courts initially reacted to attempts to organize labor with hostility
    - Formation viewed as a criminal conspiracy
  - Legality of labor unions eventually accepted (*Commonwealth v. Hunt*)
- Post–Civil war:
  - Labor unions develop and grow in reaction to the political, social, and economic environment
    - Knights of Labor
    - Socialists
    - American Federation of Labor (AFL)
    - Congress of Industrial Organizations (CIO)
    - Change to Win Coalition

Recent Trends in the Labor Movement

The years following World War II were boom years for the labor movement. Unions grew in strength in the manufacturing industries until approximately one-third of the American labor force was unionized. Union membership in the private sector reached a peak in the early 1950s and has been slowly declining since then; by 2009, only about 12 percent of the work force (public and private sector) were unionized. Since the 1960s, unionized employers have faced increasing competition from domestic nonunion firms and foreign competitors. The "oil-induced" inflation of the 1970s also increased the economic pressures on manufacturers and employers, making them very sensitive to production costs—of which labor costs are a significant component. The manufacturing sector of the U.S. economy, in which the labor movement's strength was concentrated, has been hit hardest by the changing economic conditions and global competition.

The late 1970s and the 1980s were marked by the "restructuring" of American industry. Mergers, takeovers, plant relocations to the mostly nonunion Sun Belt and overseas, and plant closings all became common occurrences, as did collective bargaining, where the employer asked the union for "give backs"—reductions in wages and benefits and relaxation of restrictive work rules. The mid-1980s were characterized by the decline of the manufacturing sector and the rise of the service economy, the indifference (or hostility) of the Reagan Administration toward organized labor, and an aggressiveness toward unions on the part of management. The decline of manufacturing in the U.S., and the outsourcing of jobs to low-wage countries continued through the 1990s and into the first decade of the twenty-first century, and the economic recession that began in late 2007 resulted in the loss of huge numbers of jobs. The dramatic decline of the U.S. auto industry, marked by General Motors and Chrysler filing for bankruptcy, and the drastic wage and benefits cuts forced upon the

United Auto Workers were stark evidence of the decline of organized labor. As of 2009, less than 8 percent of U.S. private sector workers were union members.

While private sector unions have been in decline, unions in the public sector have been growing since the 1960s; by 2009, about 36 percent of government employees were union members. The 1980s were difficult for public sector unions—the "tax revolts" by American voters and the antigovernment attitude of the Reagan and George H. W. Bush Administrations put limits on the ability of government employers to improve wages and benefits for public sector employees. The Clinton Administration provided unions with a sympathetic ear at the White House, but the Republican-controlled Congress blocked Clinton's ability to make legislative changes and limited the extent to which organized labor could take advantage of the Democratic president's years in office. What political influence labor enjoyed during the Clinton Administration vanished during the eight years of the George W. Bush Administration. The election of Barack Obama, and the control of both houses of Congress by the Democrats, brought a renewed hope to the U.S. labor movement, and union officials look forward to more political influence and the passage of worker-friendly legislation.

The WORKING Law

Packing Plant Workers Ratify First Union Contract After Bitter Organizing Campaign

Smithfield Packing Co. and the United Food and Commercial Workers Union agreed on a collective agreement covering the workers at the company's plant in Tar Heel, North Carolina. The plant, one of the world's largest pork packing plants, had been the location of a hard-fought organizing campaign by the union. The workers had voted against union representation in 1994 and in 1997, but the National Labor Relations Board and the federal courts held that the company had engaged in unfair labor practices by making threats to fire workers, freeze wages, and close the plant if the workers voted for the union. The company agreed to pay $1.1 million in back wages and interest to workers fired during the union's organizing campaign. Union supporters held marches and prayer meetings and organized a boycott of Smithfield products. Smithfield claimed that the negative publicity created by the union campaign cost the company nearly $900 million; the company filed a lawsuit against the union. The company and union agreed to settle the suit and hold an election in December, 2008. The union won the election, and contract negotiations lasted four months. The new contract, which took effect July 1, 2009, provided for wage increases of $1.50 per hour over four years, continued company-provided family healthcare coverage, improved sick leave and vacation benefits, protected and extended the pension plan, and created a worker-management safety committee and company-funded safety training.

Sources: Emery P. Dalesio, "Smithfield Packing, Union Agree on NC Contract," *Associated Press Online*, June 26, 2009; "Worker at World's Largest Pork Plant Ratify First-ever Union Contract," United Food and Commercial Workers International Union Press Release, July 1, 2009.

Legal Responses to the Labor Movement

While judicial hostility against union formation decreased over time, employers facing threats of strikes or boycotts by unions sought new legal weapons to use against labor activists. The development of the labor injunction in the late 1880s provided a powerful weapon for use against the activities of organized labor.

Injunctions

Injunction
A court order to provide remedies prohibiting some action or commanding the righting of some wrongdoing.

An ***injunction*** is a court order directing a person to do, or to refrain from doing, specific actions. Injunctions are available whenever monetary damages alone are inadequate and when the plaintiff's interests are facing irreparable harm from the defendant's actions. A defendant who violates the court order is subject to fines and can be jailed for contempt of the court.

Throughout the last decade of the nineteenth century and the first two decades of the twentieth century, the courts willingly granted injunctions against actual or threatened strikes or boycotts by unions. The courts did not require any showing that the strike or boycott actually harmed the employer's business. The courts were also willing to assume that legal remedies such as damage awards were inadequate. Generally, the injunctions granted were written in very broad terms and directed against unnamed persons. The injunctions were often granted in ***ex parte proceedings***, so-called because they occurred without any representative of the union present.

Ex Parte Proceedings
Court hearings in which one party, usually the defendant, is not present and is not able to take part.

Once an injunction had been granted, court officers would enforce it against the union. Union members who resisted risked jail terms and/or fines for being in contempt of the court order. In the face of such threatened sanctions, union leaders generally had to comply by stopping the strike or boycott. Therefore, the labor injunction became a potent weapon for management to use against any union pressure tactics.

Yellow-Dog Contracts

In addition to securing labor injunctions against union activities, employers were able to use the courts to enforce yellow-dog contracts, or contracts of employment that required employees to agree not to join a union. By incorporating the antiunion promise in the contract, employers could legally make nonmembership in unions a condition of employment. Employees who joined a union could be fired for breach of their employment contract.

In the 1917 case of *Hitchman Coal Co. v. Mitchell*,[5] the Supreme Court upheld an injunction against a strike that was intended to force the employer to abandon the yellow-dog contracts. The majority of the Court held that the union, by inducing the workers to break their contracts, was guilty of wrongly interfering with contractual relations. The Court's decision confirmed the importance of the yellow-dog contract as another weapon in the employers' legal arsenal against unions.

[5] 245 U.S. 229 (1917).

Antitrust Laws

In addition to labor injunctions and yellow-dog contracts, antitrust laws provided yet another legal weapon for employers. Congress passed the Sherman Antitrust Act in 1890 in response to public agitation against such giant business monopolies as the Standard Oil Company and the American Tobacco Company. The act outlawed restraints of trade and monopolizing of trade. Section 1 stated "Every contract, combination in the form of trust or otherwise, or conspiracy, in restraint of trade or commerce among the several states, or with foreign nations, is hereby declared to be illegal." It provided for criminal penalties—fines and imprisonment—for violations.

Other provisions of the act allowed private parties to sue for damages if they were injured by restraints of trade, and gave the federal courts power to issue injunctions against violators of the act. Most observers assumed the act was limited to business trusts and predatory corporate behavior. *Loewe v. Lawlor*, known as the *Danbury Hatters'* case, however, made it clear that organized labor activities were also subject to the Sherman Act.

case 12.1 »

Loewe v. Lawlor
208 U.S. 274 (1908)

Facts: The *Danbury Hatters'* case grew out of an AFL boycott of the D. E. Loewe Company of Danbury, Connecticut, that was called to assist efforts by the United Hatters' Union to organize the Loewe workers. The company responded by filing a suit under the Sherman Act in 1903. The company alleged that the boycott was a conspiracy to restrain trade, and it sought damages totaling $240,000 against the individual union members. The district court, rejecting the union's argument that the boycott did not interfere with "trade or commerce among the states," found the defendants liable for damages. The union appealed to the U.S. Supreme Court.

Issue: Are union boycotts attempts to restrain or interfere with trade in violation of the Sherman Act?

Decision: The Supreme Court held that the boycott was a combination in restraint of trade within the meaning of the Sherman Act. The Court refused to read into the act an exemption for labor activities, citing the words of Section 1 that "every … combination or conspiracy in restraint of trade" was illegal.

«

After the Supreme Court's decision in the *Danbury Hatters'* case, other employers also successfully attacked union boycotts under the Sherman Act. In the face of such actions, the AFL lobbied Congress for legislative relief. The passage of the Clayton Act in 1914 appeared to provide the relief sought by labor.

The key provisions of the Clayton Act, which also amended the Sherman Act, were Sections 6 and 20. Section 6 stated:

> the labor of a human being is not a commodity or article of commerce. Nothing contained in the antitrust laws shall be construed to forbid the existence and operation of labor … organizations, … nor shall such organizations, or the members thereof, be held or construed to be illegal combinations or conspiracies in restraint of trade, under the antitrust laws.

Section 20 restricted the issuance of labor injunctions. It provided that no injunction could be issued against employees unless irreparable harm to the employer's property or property rights was threatened and the legal remedy of monetary damages would be inadequate. Samuel Gompers of the AFL declared those sections to be "labor's Magna Carta."

The effect of those sections was the subject of the following 1921 Supreme Court decision.

case 12.2 » Duplex Printing Press Company v. Deering
254 U.S. 443

Facts: The Machinists' Union at the Duplex Printing Press Company organized a strike to force the employer to agree to a closed-shop provision, to accept an eight-hour workday, and to adopt a union-proposed wage scale. When the strike proved unsuccessful, the union called for a national boycott of Duplex products. Duplex responded by filing suit for an injunction under the Clayton Act against the officers of the New York City Local of the Machinists' Union. The union argued that Sections 6 and 20 of the Clayton Act prevented the issuance of an injunction against the union and its officers.

Issue: Do Sections 6 and 20 of the Clayton Act are exempt labor union activities from the prohibitions of the Sherman Act?

Decision: A majority of the Supreme Court held that Section 6:

> assumes the normal objects of a labor organization to be legitimate, and declares that nothing in the antitrust laws shall be construed to forbid the existence and operation of such organizations or to forbid their members from lawfully carrying out their legitimate objects.... But there is nothing in the section to exempt such an organization or its members from accountability where it or they depart from its normal and legitimate objects and engage in actual combination of conspiracy in restraint of trade. And by no fair or permissible construction can it be taken as authorizing any activity otherwise unlawful, or enabling a normally lawful organization to become a cloak for an illegal combination or conspiracy in restraint of trade as defined by the antitrust laws.

The Court found that Congress did not intend for Section 6 or Section 20 to be a general grant of immunity for conduct that would otherwise violate the antitrust laws, and upheld the injunction against the union and its officers. The Court's decision effectively gutted the Clayton Act provisions that had been hailed by Gompers.

«

The effects of the labor injunction and the *Danbury Hatters'* and *Duplex* cases continued to make things extremely difficult. Labor would have to wait for the effects of the Great Depression, as well as the accession of the Democratic Party to national power, before the legal and judicial impediments to its activities would be removed.

Concept *Summary* » 12.2

Legal Responses to the Labor Movement

- Injunctions: Court orders requiring or prohibiting certain actions
  - Employers used injunctions to prevent strikes or boycotts
- Yellow-dog contracts: Employment contracts requiring employees not to join a union
  - Employers could make nonunion membership a condition of employment
- Antitrust laws: Designed to protect free trade and competition
  - Employers used them to challenge union boycotts by seeking damages for interference with trade
    - Sherman Antitrust Act
    - Clayton Act

The Development of the National Labor Relations Act

Organized labor reacted to the judicial endorsement of employer antiunion tactics by engaging in coordinated political pressure for legislative controls on judicial involvement in labor disputes. This political activity yielded results in 1932 when a federal anti-injunction act, sponsored by Senator Norris and Congressman La Guardia, was enacted.

The Norris–La Guardia Act

Common Law
Judge-made law as opposed to statutes and ordinances enacted by legislative bodies.

The Norris–La Guardia Act, in effect, was a legislative reversal of the prevailing view of the judiciary that economic injury inflicted by unions pursuing their economic self-interest was unlawful both at ***common law*** and under antitrust laws. The act created a laissez-faire environment for organized labor's self-help activities.

Provisions

Section 1 of the Norris–La Guardia Act prohibit the federal courts from issuing injunctions in labor disputes except in strict conformity with the provisions set out in the act. Those provisions, contained in Section 7, require the following:

- The court must hold an open-court hearing, with opportunity for cross-examination of all witnesses and participation by representatives of both sides to the controversy.
- The court can issue an injunction only if the hearing has established that unlawful acts have actually been threatened or committed and will be committed or continue to be committed unless restraints were ordered.
- The party seeking the injunction has to establish that substantial and irreparable injury to its property will follow and that it has no adequate remedy at law.
- The court has to be convinced that the public officials charged with the duty to protect the threatened property are unable or unwilling to provide adequate protection.

Only after complying with this procedure and making such findings can the court issue an injunction in a labor dispute.

Section 4 of the act sets out a list of activities that are protected from injunctions, even when the foregoing safeguards might be observed. The section states that:

> [n]o court of the United States shall have jurisdiction to issue any restraining order or temporary or permanent injunction in any case involving or growing out of any labor dispute to prohibit any person or persons participating or interested in such dispute (as these terms are herein defined) from doing, whether singly or in concert, any of the following acts:
>
> (a) Ceasing or refusing to perform any work or to remain in any relation of employment;
>
> (b) Becoming or remaining a member of any labor organization or of any employer organization, regardless of any such undertaking or promise as is described in Section 3 of this act;
>
> (c) Paying or giving to, or withholding from, any person participating or interested in such labor dispute, any strike or unemployment benefits or insurance, or other moneys or things of value;
>
> (d) By all lawful means aiding any person participating or interested in any labor dispute who is being proceeded against in, or is prosecuting, any action or suit in any court of the United States or of any State;
>
> (e) Giving publicity to the existence of, or the facts involved in, any labor dispute, whether by advertising, speaking, patrolling, or by any other method not involving fraud or violence;

(f) Assembling peaceably to act or to organize to act in promotion of their interests in a labor dispute;

(g) Advising or notifying any person of an intention to do any of the acts heretofore specified;

(h) Agreeing with other persons to do or not to do any of the acts heretofore specified; and

(i) Advising, urging, or otherwise causing or inducing without fraud or violence the acts heretofore specified, regardless of any such undertaking or promise as is described in Section 3 of this act.

The term *labor dispute* was defined in Section 13(c) of the act, which states:

> The term "labor dispute" includes any controversy concerning the terms or conditions of employment, or concerning the association or representation of persons in negotiating, fixing, maintaining, changing, or seeking to arrange terms or conditions of employment, regardless of whether or not the disputants stand in the proximate relation of employer and employee.

Finally, Section 3 of the act declares that yellow-dog contracts are contrary to public policy of the United States and are not enforceable by any federal court. Nor can the courts use such contracts as the basis for granting any legal or equitable remedies (such as injunctions).

State Anti-Injunction Laws

Although the Norris–La Guardia Act applies only to the federal courts, a number of states passed similar legislation restricting their court systems in issuing labor injunctions. These acts are known as "little Norris–La Guardia Acts." The Supreme Court upheld the constitutionality of Wisconsin's little Norris–La Guardia Act in the 1937 decision of *Senn v. Tile Layers' Protective Union.*[6] Although the case did not involve the federal act, it did raise the same legal issues as would an attack on the constitutionality of the federal act; the decision in *Senn* was regarded as settling the question of the federal act's constitutionality.

Validity and Scope of the Norris–La Guardia Act

The following case illustrates the judicial approach to the validity and the broad scope of the provisions of the Norris–La Guardia Act.

case 12.3 »

Utilities Services Engineering, Inc v. Colorado Building & Construction Trades Council

549 F.2d 173 (10th Cir. 1977)

McWilliams, Circuit Judge

The issue is whether the district court had jurisdiction to enjoin certain picketing. The district court concluded that under the several provisions of the Norris-LaGuardia Act, it had no jurisdiction to enjoin peaceful picketing which arose out of a "labor dispute." This appeal followed.

The action was brought by Utilities Services Engineering, Inc. and Blackinton & Decker, Inc. against the Colorado Building & Construction Trades Council. Both plaintiffs are contractors engaged in the building and construction industry. The defendant is an unincorporated association comprised of various labor unions whose members are engaged in the building and construction industry.

... Utilities is presently under contract with Johns-Manville Corporation to perform certain electrical maintenance work at the Johns-Manville Research and Development Center.... Decker is also presently under contract with Johns-Manville to perform certain construction work in progress.... Utilities

[6] 301 U.S. 468 (1937).

is not a signatory to any collective bargaining agreements with any labor organization.

On or about April 5, 1976, the Trades Council threatened in writing to picket Utilities unless and until Utilities entered into an agreement with the Trades Council concerning the subcontracting of work.... Utilities declined to sign the agreement tendered it by the Trades Council, and the latter, on April 22 and 23, 1976, true to its promise, picketed Utilities at the Research and Development Center and distributed handbills to the public in support of its effort to obtain Utilities' signature on the aforementioned agreement. As a result of this picket line at the Utilities job site ... about 450 union craftsmen employed by Decker ... refused to work and brought construction at that particular job site to a complete halt.

It was in this general setting that Utilities and Decker brought the present action against the Trades Council.... It was alleged in the complaint that the proposed agreement under its "literal wording" represents an attempt on the part of the Trades Council to engage in a combination or conspiracy which is illegal under the Sherman Act....

In addition to seeking monetary damages the plaintiffs also asked for a temporary restraining order enjoining the Trades Council from further picketing of Utilities and a preliminary and permanent injunction enjoining such continued picketing. When the request for a temporary restraining order came on for hearing the trial judge ... was of the firm view that under the Norris-LaGuardia Act he was without jurisdiction to enjoin the Council's picketing. On this basis, then, he denied the request for a temporary restraining order. Being of the view that he had no jurisdiction to enjoin, the trial judge similarly denied plaintiffs' request for a preliminary injunction hearing. From these rulings the plaintiffs appeal....

As indicated, then, the basis for the trial court's denial of the plaintiffs' request for a preliminary injunction was that it lacked jurisdiction under the Norris-LaGuardia Act to enjoin the Council's picketing. We conclude that the trial court was correct in so holding. The trial court expressed doubt that the proposed agreement offended the antitrust provisions of the Sherman Act, but made no express holding on that particular matter.

The pertinent parts of the Norris-LaGuardia Act provide as follows: (1) No court of the United States shall have jurisdiction to issue any restraining order or temporary or permanent injunction in a case involving or growing out of a labor dispute except in strict conformity with the several provisions of the Act; (2) No court of the United States shall have jurisdiction to issue any restraining order or temporary or permanent injunction in any case involving or growing out of any labor dispute to prohibit any person or persons from giving publicity to the facts involved in the labor dispute by advertising, speaking, patrolling or by any other method not involving fraud or violence; and (3) No court of the United States shall have jurisdiction to issue any temporary or permanent injunction in any case arising out of a labor dispute, except after hearing and after a finding of fact by the court that unlawful acts have been threatened and will be committed unless restrained.

Utilities initially argues that there is no "labor dispute" between it and the Trades Council, and therefore the Council is not entitled to the immunity granted by the Act. In arguing that there is no existing labor dispute between the parties, Utilities seizes on paragraph 8 in the proposed agreement. We do not read paragraph 8 as being an admission by the Trades Council that there is no labor dispute between it and Utilities. Though by that paragraph the Council did indeed disavow that it was acting as a bargaining agent for Utilities' employees or that it sought to establish terms of employment, other than the payment of the prevailing rate of wages, such is not the equivalent of a concession that the Council does not have a labor dispute with Utilities. Paragraph 8 is just what it purports to state, and nothing more. Utilities attempts to read too much into the language contained in paragraph 8.

The term "labor dispute" is defined at [Sec. 13 of the Norris-LaGuardia Act]. Without setting forth that statute verbatim, we conclude that this is a case growing out of a labor dispute by reason of each of the following, any one of which is sufficient to bring the instant controversy under the Norris-LaGuardia Act: (1) Each of the parties in this case is engaged in the construction industry, or has a direct or indirect interest therein; (2) each of the plaintiffs is an employer and the Union is an association of employees; and (3) there is a controversy concerning a condition of employment of workers employed by subcontractors of Utilities, although the parties to this case do not "stand in the proximate relation of employer and employee."

In determining whether there is a labor dispute in the instant case, *New Negro Alliance v. Sanitary Grocery Co.* (1938) has particular applicability. There members of a black mutual improvement association picketed a grocery store that discriminated against blacks in its employment practices. The Supreme Court held that there was a labor dispute and that the members of the association were interested persons in that dispute to the end that under the Norris-LaGuardia Act the district court was without jurisdiction to enjoin the picketing....

As indicated above, it is to us evident that the instant controversy as described in the complaint itself does grow out of a labor dispute under the statutory definition of that term.... The Trades Council has an obvious and legitimate interest of its own in seeing that employees of subcontractors, even though nonunion, are nonetheless paid the prevailing rate of wage. Subcontractors paying substandard wages would tend to have an edge in any competitive bidding. Understandably, then, the Council sought to have contractors enter into an agreement whereby their subcontractors would be required to pay their employees prevailing wages. The contention by Utilities that the immunities of the Norris-LaGuardia Act do not apply because there is no labor dispute is without merit. There being, then, a labor dispute between Utilities and the Trades Council, it would appear that under [the Norris-LaGuardia Act] the district court had no power to issue an injunction enjoining the Trades Council from continued picketing which admittedly did not involve fraud or violence....

Judgment affirmed.

Case Questions

1. Why was the Colorado Building & Construction Trades Council picketing the construction site?
2. Did the contractors here have a contract with any union? How could this dispute be characterized as a "labor dispute" within the Norris–La Guardia Act?
3. What is the significance of the court's determination that the picketing here was part of a labor dispute under the Norris–La Guardia Act?
4. Under the Norris–La Guardia Act, can a federal court ever issue an injunction in a labor dispute? If so, what must be shown to support issuing such an injunction?

«

The Railway Labor Act

The Railway Labor Act, passed in 1926, allowed railroad employees to designate bargaining representatives of their own choosing, free from employer interference. This legislation introduced some of the ideas and approaches later incorporated in the National Labor Relations Act (NLRA).

The railroads were one of the earliest industries in which employees were unionized. As noted earlier, the railroads were the target of several violent strikes during the late nineteenth century. The importance of the railroads for the nation's economic development and the railroads' position as essentially being public utilities made the disruptive effects of labor disputes involving the railroads a subject for government concern. Congress passed several laws aimed at minimizing or avoiding labor strife in the railroad industry.

The Railway Labor Act established a three-step procedure for settling disputes.

- The first step involved using a federal mediation board to attempt to facilitate negotiation of the parties' differences.
- If that failed, the board would then try to induce the parties to arbitrate the dispute. Although not compelled to submit the dispute to arbitration, the parties would be legally bound by the results if they agreed to arbitration.
- Finally, if arbitration was refused, the board could recommend to the president that an emergency board of investigation be created. If the president created the emergency board, the parties in dispute were required to maintain the status quo for thirty days while the investigation proceeded. Even if an emergency board was not appointed, the parties were still required to maintain the status quo for thirty days. This mandatory cooling-off period was designed to allow the dispute to be settled through negotiation. The union retained its right to strike, and the employer could lock out once the cooling-off period expired.

The act also provided that both labor and management had the right to designate bargaining representatives without the "interference, influence or coercion" of the other party. That provision was the subject of the Supreme Court's 1930 decision of *Texas & New Orleans Railroad v. Brotherhood of Railway Clerks.*[7] The union had sought, and was granted, an injunction against employer interference with the employees' designation of a bargaining representative under the act. The railroad argued that the act did not create any legally enforceable right of free choice for employees and that the act's provisions were an unconstitutional interference with management's right to operate the railroad. The Supreme Court upheld the injunction and the constitutionality of the Railway Labor Act, rejecting the railroad's challenges.

The Railway Labor Act was amended by Congress in 1934, 1936, 1951, and 1966. The act was extended to cover airline employees, and a duty to bargain with the duly designated representative of each side was spelled out. The amendments also provided that unions representing the airline or railway employees could bargain for a union shop provision. The National Railroad Adjustment Board was created to arbitrate disputes involving the railroads and unions; its awards are final and binding upon the parties. The amendments also created sanctions for enforcement of the act by declaring violations to be misdemeanors. Such violations included the interference with the designation of representatives by either party, the use of yellow-dog contracts, and the changing of any terms or conditions of employment without complying with the provisions of a collective agreement.

The amendments creating the duty to bargain with representatives of the employees were the subject of a challenge in the 1937 Supreme Court case of *Virginia Railway Co. v. System Federation No. 40.*[8] The Supreme Court held that the act created a mandatory requirement of recognizing and negotiating with the bargaining representatives duly designated by the parties and that this requirement could be enforced by court order.

The National Industrial Recovery Act

The other statutory predecessor of the National Labor Relations Act was the National Industrial Recovery Act (NIRA), the centerpiece of President Franklin D. Roosevelt's New Deal. Roosevelt took office in 1933, the fourth year of the Great Depression. Some 15 million people were unemployed, and there was a widespread belief that the nation's economic growth had come to a permanent halt. Roosevelt proposed his New Deal program to pull the nation out of the Depression. It involved government working closely and actively with business to revive the economy.

The NIRA set up a system in which major industries would operate under codes of fair competition, which would be developed by trade associations for each industry. These associations would be under the supervision and guidance of the National Recovery Administration (NRA). The NIRA, in Section 7(a), also provided that the codes of fair competition contain the following conditions:

> (1) That employees shall have the right to organize and bargain collectively through representatives of their own choosing, and shall be free from interference, restraint, or coercion of employers of

---

[7]281 U.S. 548 (1930).

[8]300 U.S. 515 (1937).

> labor, or their agents, in the designation of such representatives or in self-organization or in other concerted activities for the purpose of collective bargaining or other mutual aid or protection; (2) that no employee . . . shall be required as a condition of employment to join any company union or to refrain from joining, organizing, or assisting a labor organization of his own choosing; and (3) that employers shall comply with the maximum hours of labor, minimum rates of pay, and other conditions of employment, approved or prescribed by the President.

The NRA, responsible for administering the codes of fair competition under the NIRA, had to rely on voluntary cooperation from the industries being regulated. The NRA announced that codes containing provisions concerning hours, rates of pay, and other conditions of employment would be subject to NRA approval, although such conditions had not been arrived at through collective bargaining. The practical effect of this announcement was to allow industry to develop such codes unilaterally, without input from organized labor. While employees rushed to join unions, employers refused to recognize and bargain with the unions. A wave of strikes resulted.

President Roosevelt issued a plea for industrial peace and created the National Labor Board to "consider, adjust and settle differences and controversies that may arise through differing interpretations" of the NIRA provisions.

The National Labor Board

The National Labor Board (NLB) was created in August 1933. It was composed of seven members; three representatives each would be chosen by the NRA's Industrial Advisory Board and Labor Advisory Board. The seventh member was Senator Robert Wagner of New York, who was chairman. The NLB initially functioned as a mediation board, seeking to persuade the parties to settle their differences peacefully.

The weakness of enforcement powers given to the NLB was its most serious drawback. The NLB relied mainly on the power of persuasion, which was effective only as long as an employer was not overtly antagonistic to organized labor. When, in 1934, the nation's automobile manufacturers all refused to recognize the United Automobile Workers Union or to allow the NLB to conduct a representative election, President Roosevelt had General Hugh Johnson, head of the NRA, negotiate a settlement rather than stand behind the NLB order. That decision destroyed what little effectiveness the NLB retained.

Despite its short tenure, the NLB did make several contributions to modern labor law. It evolved from a mediation service into an adjudicative body akin to the present National Labor Relations Board (NLRB). It also established the principles of majority rule and exclusive representation of the employees in a particular bargaining unit. In addition, the Board developed other rules that have come to be basic principles of labor relations law, among them the following:

- An employer was obligated to bargain with a union that had been chosen as representative by a majority of employees;
- Employers had no right to know of an employee's membership in, or vote for, a union when a secret ballot representation election was held; and
- Strikers remained employees while on strike and were entitled to displace any replacements hired if the strike was the result of employer violations of the NIRA.

The "Old" National Labor Relations Board

In June 1934, President Roosevelt formulated Public Resolution No. 44. This resolution, which was then passed by Congress, authorized the President to establish a "board or boards" empowered to investigate disputes arising under Section 7(a) of the NIRA and to conduct secret ballot representation elections among employees. Enforcement of Board decisions would remain with the NRA and the Department of Justice. Roosevelt then abolished the NLB and transferred its funds, personnel, and pending cases to the National Labor Relations Board (the "old" NLRB). The NLRB was denied all jurisdiction over disputes in the steel and auto industries. The NLRB reaffirmed the key rulings of the NLB; it also issued guidelines to assist regional offices in handling common types of cases and began organizing its decisions into a body of precedents guiding future action.

When the Supreme Court declared the NIRA to be unconstitutional in its 1935 *Schechter Poultry Corp. v. U.S.*[9] decision, it also destroyed the "old" NLRB.

Concept *Summary* » 12.3

The Development of the National Labor Relations Act

- The Railway Labor Act: Established dispute settlement procedures for the railroad industry; it was later extended to the airline industry
- The National Industrial Recovery Act (NIRA): Provided protection for employees organizing unions and encouraged collective bargaining
- The National Labor Board (NLB): Mediated labor disputes, but had no legal authority
- The "Old" National Labor Relations Board ("old" NLRB): Replaced the NLB, but was dissolved after the Supreme Court declared the NIRA unconstitutional
- The Norris-La Guardia Act: Limited the use of labor injunctions by employers and outlawed yellow-dog contracts

The National Labor Relations Act

Senator Wagner introduced a proposed National Labor Relations Act (NLRA) in the Senate in 1935. Despite initial stiff opposition, the NLRA was passed by Congress and enacted into law in 1935. Because of the doubts over the NLRA's constitutionality, President Roosevelt had difficulty finding qualified people willing to be appointed to the National Labor Relations Board (NLRB) established under the NLRA. The main concern over the constitutionality of the NLRA was whether it was a valid exercise of the interstate commerce power given to Congress under the commerce clause of the Constitution. In *Schechter Poultry,* the Supreme Court had held that the NIRA was not within the federal government power to regulate interstate commerce. In passing the NLRA, Congress had relied on the power to regulate

[9] 295 U.S. 495 (1935).

commerce among the states given to it under the commerce clause. The findings of fact incorporated in Section 1 of the NLRA contained the following statement:

> The denial by employers of the right of employees to organize and the refusal by employers to accept the procedure of collective bargaining lead to strikes and other forms of industrial strife or unrest, which have the intent or the necessary effect of burdening or obstructing commerce. . . .

For more than a year after the passage of the NLRA, there was only limited activity by the NLRB. The Board set out to develop economic data supporting the findings of fact in Section 1 of the NLRA. It also sought the best possible case to take to the Supreme Court to settle the constitutionality issue.

Finally, the NLRB brought five cases to the federal courts of appeals. The cases involved an interstate bus company, the Associated Press news service, and three manufacturing firms. The Board lost all three of the manufacturing company cases in the courts of appeals on the interstate commerce issue. All five of the cases were taken to the Supreme Court and were heard by the Court in February 1937. The NLRB developed its arguments in the *Jones & Laughlin Steel* case, one of the manufacturing cases, almost entirely on the interstate commerce issue. That case became the crucial litigation in the test of the NLRA's constitutionality.

The Supreme Court in its 1937 decision in *NLRB v. Jones & Laughlin Steel Corp.*[10] upheld the constitutionality of the NLRA by a 5–4 vote. The majority opinion, by Chief Justice Hughes, held that the disruption of operations of Jones & Laughlin due to industrial strife would have a serious and direct effect on interstate commerce. In the words of the Court,

> When industries organize themselves on a national scale, making their relation to interstate commerce the dominant factor in their activities, how can it be maintained that their industrial labor relations constitute a forbidden field into which Congress may not enter when it is necessary to protect interstate commerce from the paralyzing consequences of industrial war?

By the slimmest of margins, the Supreme Court had upheld the validity of the National Labor Relations Act. The decision also meant that a labor relations board effectively empowered to deal with disputes between labor and management had finally been established.

Overview of the National Labor Relations Act

The passage of the National Labor Relations Act, or the Wagner Act, constituted a revolutionary change in national labor policy. Workers were now legally protected by the federal government in their rights to organize for mutual aid and security and to bargain collectively through representatives of their own choice.

The purpose of the act, as stated in Section 1, was to:

> eliminate the causes of certain substantial obstructions to the free flow of commerce … by encouraging the practice and procedure of collective bargaining and by protecting the exercise by workers of full freedom of association, self-organization, and designation of representatives of their own choosing, for the purpose of negotiating the terms and conditions of their employment or other mutual aid or protection.

---

[10]301 U.S. 1 (1937).

The basis of the act was the protection of the rights of employees, defined by Section 7:

> Employees shall have the right to self-organization, to form, join, or assist labor organizations, to bargain collectively through representatives of their own choosing, and to engage in concerted activities for the purpose of collective bargaining or other mutual aid or protection.

To protect these basic rights of employees, the act prohibited certain practices of employers that would interfere with or prevent the exercise of such rights. Those practices were designated unfair labor practices, and the act listed five of them:

1. interference with, or restraint or coercion of, employees in the exercise of their Section 7 rights;
2. domination of, or interference with, a labor organization (including financial or other contributions to it);
3. discrimination in terms or conditions of employment of employees for the purpose of encouraging or discouraging union membership;
4. discrimination against an employee for filing a charge or testifying in a proceeding under the act and;
5. refusal to bargain collectively with the employees' legal bargaining representative.

The act reconstituted the National Labor Relations Board to enforce and administer the statute. The Board created a nationwide organization, developed a body of legal precedents (drawing heavily upon decisions of its predecessors), and developed and refined its procedures. In its efforts to carry out the policies of the legislation, the Board was frequently criticized for being too pro-union. At the same time, unions were accused of abusing their newly gained power under the act. A 1946 strike by the United Mine Workers, in defiance of a Supreme Court order to remain on the job, seemed to crystallize public opinion that unions had grown too powerful.

This public concern was reflected in congressional action to limit unions' abuse of their powers. Congressional critics were especially concerned over jurisdictional disputes, in which two unions claimed the right to represent the workers of an employer, leaving the employer "trapped" between them, and recognitional picketing, which was aimed at forcing an employer to recognize the union regardless of the sentiments of the employees. These kinds of congressional concerns resulted in the passage of the Taft-Hartley Act in 1947. The Taft-Hartley Act outlawed the ***closed shop***, a term describing an employer who agrees to hire only employees who are already union members. It also added a list of unfair labor practices by unions and emphasized that employees had the right, under Section 7, to refrain from collective activity as well as engage in it. The purpose and effect of the Taft-Hartley Act were to balance the rights and duties of both unions and employers.

Closed Shop
An employer who agrees to hire only those employees who are already union members.

After Taft-Hartley, the National Labor Relations Act[11] was amended several times, the most significant version being the Landrum-Griffin Act of 1959. Landrum-Griffin was passed in response to concerns about union racketeering and abusive practices aimed at union members. The act set out specific rights for individual union members against the union, and

[11]The Taft-Hartley Act incorporated the National Labor Relations Act. Scholars and labor lawyers differ over whether the modern act should be referred to as the NLRA or the Labor Management Relations Act, or both. For convenience, and since the enforcing agency is still called the NLRB, we will continue to refer to the act as the National Labor Relations Act.

it proscribed certain kinds of conduct by union officials, such as financial abuse, racketeering, and manipulation of union-election procedures.

The National Labor Relations Board

Unless otherwise specified, the discussion throughout this and subsequent chapters will focus on the current National Labor Relations Act and the present National Labor Relations Board's organization, jurisdiction, and procedure.

Organization

Because the Wagner Act gave little guidance concerning the administrative structure of the newly created agency, the NLRB adopted an administrative organization that made it prosecutor, judge, and jury with regard to complaints under the act. The Board investigated charges of unfair labor practices, prosecuted complaints, conducted hearings, and rendered decisions. Pursuant to its statutory authority, the Board did appoint a general counsel to serve as legal adviser and direct litigation, but the general counsel was subordinate to the Board in virtually all matters.

The combination of prosecutorial and judicial functions was one of the major criticisms leveled by commentators and attorneys against the Board in the years prior to the passage of the Taft-Hartley Act. This issue, not surprisingly, was addressed by Taft-Hartley in 1947. Although retaining the concept of a single enforcement agency, Taft-Hartley made the Office of the General Counsel an independent unit to direct the administrative and enforcement efforts of the NLRB regional offices. The Board itself was expanded from three to five members. It continued to exercise the judicial function of deciding complaints filed under the act.

The newly organized NLRB represented a unique type of administrative agency structure in that it was bifurcated into two independent authorities within the single agency: the five-member Board and the general counsel. Exhibit 12.1 depicts the organization of the two authorities of the bifurcated agency.

The Board

The Board itself is the judicial branch of the agency. The five members of the Board are nominated by the U.S. president and must be confirmed by the Senate. They serve five-year terms. Members of the Board can be removed from office by the president only for neglect of duty or malfeasance in office. One member is to be designated by the president as chairperson. Members have a staff of about twenty-five legal clerks and assistants to help in deciding the numerous cases that come before them. The executive secretary of the Board is the chief administrative officer, charged with ruling on procedural questions, assigning cases to members, setting priorities in case handling, and conferring with parties to cases that come before the Board. There is also a solicitor, whose function is to advise members on questions of law and policy. Finally, an information director assists the Board on public relations issues.

Administrative Law Judges (ALJs) Formerly called trial examiners, these judges are independent of both the Board and the general counsel.

The NLRB also has a branch called the Division of Judges. These ***administrative law judges (ALJs)***, formerly called trial examiners, are independent of both the Board and the general counsel. Appointed for life, they are subject to the federal Civil Service Commission rules governing appointment and tenure. This organizational independence is necessary because the ALJs conduct hearings and issue initial decisions on unfair labor practice

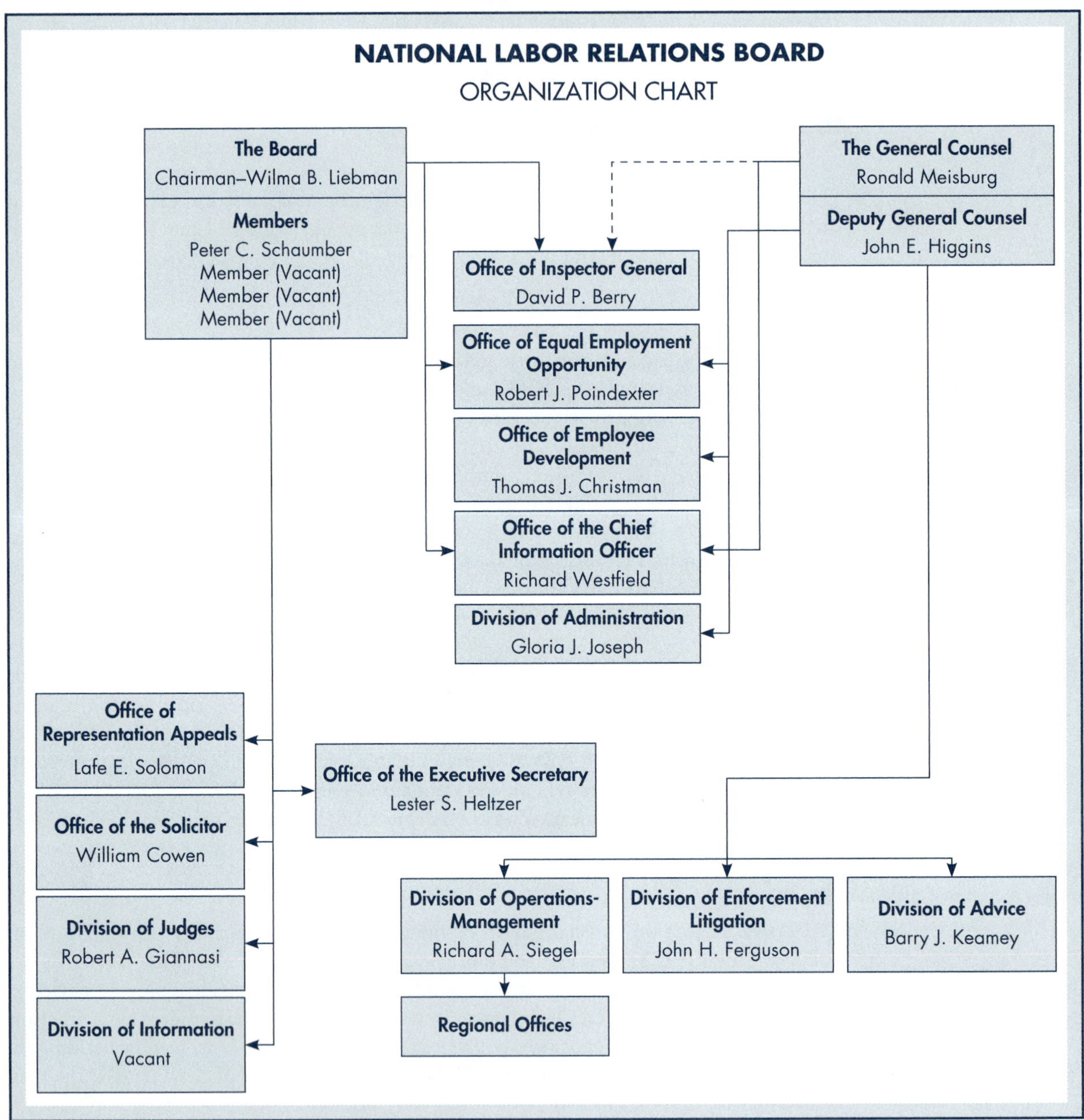

Exhibit 12.1 The National Labor Relations Board

complaints issued by regional offices throughout the United States, under the authority delegated to these offices by the general counsel.

The Board is prohibited by law from reviewing an ALJ's findings or recommendations before the issuance of the ALJ's formal report. The ALJ's function is that of a specialized trial court judge: to decide unfair labor practice complaints. ALJ decisions may be appealed to the Board, which functions as a specialized court of appeal. After rendering their initial decisions, ALJs (like trial court judges) have nothing to do with the disposition of the case if it is appealed to the Board.

Current Members of the NLRB

The current (July 2009) members of the NLRB are:

- Wilma B. Liebman was designated as chairman of the NLRB by Barack Obama on January 20, 2009. She was appointed to the NLRB initially by Bill Clinton and reappointed by George W. Bush; her current term expires in August 2011. She previously served as special assistant to the director of the Federal Mediation and Conciliation Service and was legal counsel to the Bricklayers and Allied Craftsmen union and the International Brotherhood of Teamsters union. Liebman is a graduate of Barnard College and the George Washington University Law Center.
- Peter C. Schaumber was appointed to the NLRB by George W. Bush; his current term expires August 27, 2010. He previously served as chairman of the NLRB from March 19, 2008 until January 19, 2009. Schaumber was previously in private practice in Washington, D.C., and was associate director of a law department division in the Office of the Comptroller of the Currency, an assistant United States attorney for the District of Columbia, and assistant corporation counsel for the District of Columbia. Schaumber is a graduate of Georgetown University and the Georgetown University Law Center.
- There are currently three vacant positions; President Obama has announced his intention to nominate Craig Becker, Mark Pearce, and Brian Hayes to fill those positions. Becker is currently associate general counsel to the Service Employees International Union and to the AFL-CIO. Pearce is a labor lawyer and partner with the Buffalo firm of Creighton, Pearce, Johnsen & Giroux. Hayes is currently the Republican labor policy director for the U.S. Senate Committee on Health, Education, Labor, and Pensions.

The current general counsel of the NLRB is Ronald Meisburg, who was appointed by George W. Bush and confirmed by the Senate in August 2006. He previously served as a member of the NLRB and was in private practice in Washington, D.C. He is a graduate of Carson-Newman College and the University of Louisville Brandeis School of Law.

Source: NLRB Web site, www.nlrb.gov/about_us/overview/index.aspx

The General Counsel

The Office of the General Counsel is the prosecutorial branch of the NLRB and is also in charge of the day-to-day administration of the NLRB regional offices. The general counsel is nominated by the president, with Senate confirmation for a four-year term. The structure of this branch of the NLRB is more complex than that of the Board (see Exhibit 12.1). The Office of the General Counsel has four divisions:

- *Division of Operations Management*: Supervises operations of field offices and the management of all cases in the Washington, D.C., divisions

- *Division of Advice*: Oversees the function of legal advice to the regional offices, the injunction work of the district court branch, and the legal research and special projects office
- *Division of Enforcement Litigation*: Responsible for the conduct of agency litigation enforcing or defending Board orders in the federal courts of appeal or the Supreme Court
- *Division of Administration*: Directs the management, financial, and personnel work of the Office of the General Counsel

The NLRB has thirty-four regional offices and a number of subregional offices. The staff of each regional office consists of a regional director, regional attorney, field examiners, and field attorneys. Although Section 3(d) of the act gives the general counsel "final authority, on behalf of the Board, in respect of investigation of charges and issuance of complaints ... and in respect of the prosecution of such complaints before the Board," the Office of General Counsel has exercised its statutory right to delegate this power to the regional directors, who make most of the day-to-day decisions affecting enforcement of the act.

Procedures

The NLRB handles two kinds of legal questions:

- those alleging that an unfair labor practice has taken place in violation of the act and
- representation questions concerning whether, and if so how, employees will be represented for collective bargaining.

In either type of case, the NLRB does not initiate the proceeding; rather, it responds to a complaint of unfair practice or a petition for an election filed by a party to the case. (The Board refers to unfair practice cases as C cases and to representation cases as R cases.)

Unfair Labor Practice Charges

The filing of an unfair practice charge initiates NLRB proceedings in unfair labor practice cases. The act does not restrict who can file a charge; the most common charging parties are employees, unions, and employers. However, in *NLRB v. Indiana & Michigan Electric Co.,*[12] the Supreme Court held that an individual who was a "stranger" to the dispute could file an unfair labor practice charge. The NLRB has adopted a special form for the filing of unfair practice charges (see Exhibit 12.2). In its fiscal year 2008, there were 22,501 unfair labor practice charges filed with the NLRB.

Section 10(b) of the act requires that unfair practice charges must be filed within six months of the occurrence of the alleged unfair practice. Once a charge has been timely filed, the procedure is as follows:

- The charge is investigated by a field examiner. A charge can be resolved at this stage through mutual adjustment, voluntary withdrawal, or agency dismissal for lack of merit.
- If the charge is found to have merit and the case has not been settled by adjustment, a formal complaint is issued by the regional director. (In recent years, approximately one-third of all charges filed were voluntarily withdrawn, another one-third were dismissed as having no merit, and approximately one-third were found to have merit. Of the charges having merit, approximately 60 percent were settled with no formal complaint being

[12]318 U.S. 9 (1943).

INTERNET
FORM NLRB-501
(11-94)

UNITED STATES OF AMERICA
NATIONAL LABOR RELATIONS BOARD
CHARGE AGAINST EMPLOYER

FORM EXEMPT UNDER 44 U.S.C. 3512

DO NOT WRITE IN THIS SPACE	
Case	Date Filed

INSTRUCTIONS:
File an original and 4 copies of this charge with NLRB Regional Director for the region in which the alleged unfair labor practice occurred or is occurring.

1. EMPLOYER AGAINST WHOM CHARGE IS BROUGHT

a. Name of Employer		b. Number of Workers Employed
c. Address *(street, city, State, ZIP, Code)*	d. Employer Representative	e. Telephone No. Fax No.
f. Type of Establishment *(factory, mine, wholesaler, etc.)*	g. Identify Principal Product or Service	

h. The above-named employer has engaged in and is engaging in unfair labor practices within the meaning of Section 8(a), subsections (1) and *(list subsections)* ______ of the National Labor Relations Act, and these unfair labor practices are unfair practices affecting commerce within the meaning of the Act.

2. Basis of the Charge *(set forth a clear and concise statement of the facts constituting the alleged unfair labor practices.)*

By the above and other acts, the above-named employer has interfered with, restrained, and coerced employees in the exercise of the rights guaranteed in Section 7 of the Act.

3. Full name of party filing charge *(if labor organization, give full name, including local name and number)*

4a. Address *(street and number, city, State, and ZIP Code)*	4b. Telephone No. Fax No.

5. Full name of national or international labor organization of which it is an affiliate or constituent unit *(to be filled in when charge is filed by a labor organization)*

6. DECLARATION
I declare that I have read the above charge and that the statements are true to the best of my knowledge and belief.

By ______________________ ______________________
(Signature of representative or person making charge) *(Title, if any)*

Fax No. ______________

Address ______________________ ______________ ______________
(Telephone No.) *Date*

WILLFUL FALSE STATEMENTS ON THIS CHARGE CAN BE PUNISHED BY FINE AND IMPRISONMENT (U.S. CODE, TITLE 18, SECTION 1001)

Exhibit 12.2 Unfair labor practice charge form
Source: NLRB Web site at http://www.nlrb.gov/e-gov/online_forms.aspx

issued. Thus, approximately 86 percent of all charges filed were disposed of before reaching the hearing stage in the procedure.)

- A public hearing on the complaint is held in front of an ALJ. (The Taft-Hartley amendments added the requirement that "so far as practicable" this hearing shall be conducted in accordance with the rules of evidence applicable to federal district courts.) At the conclusion of the hearing, the ALJ issues a report with findings of fact and recommendations of law.
- The ALJ's report is served on the parties and forwarded to the Board in Washington, D.C. Each party then has twenty days to file exceptions to the report. These exceptions are in effect an appeal to the Board. If no exceptions are taken, the ALJ's report is automatically accepted by the Board as a final order.
- If exceptions have been filed to the ALJ's report by one or more parties, the Board reviews the case and issues a decision and remedial order. The parties will normally have filed briefs with the Board, explaining their respective positions on the exceptions. Sometimes (although rarely) a party will also request and be granted the opportunity to make oral arguments before the Board. Normally, a three-member panel of the Board handles any single case at this stage. (In 40 percent of all the "appeals," the Board approves the ALJ's report in its entirety.)

See Exhibit 12.3 for a summary of unfair labor practice procedures. Orders of the Board are not self-enforcing; if a party against whom an order is issued refuses to comply, the NLRB must ask the appropriate federal circuit court of appeals for a judgment enforcing the order. In addition, any party to the case may seek review of the Board's decision in the appropriate federal court of appeal. The scope of this judicial review of the Board's order is not the same as an appeal from the verdict of a federal trial court; the appeals court is required to accept the Board's findings of fact provided that the findings are supported by substantial evidence in the case record. Any party to the case decided by the federal circuit court of appeals may petition the U.S. Supreme Court to grant certiorari to review the appellate court's decision. The Supreme Court generally restricts its review to cases in which a novel legal issue is raised or in which there is a conflict among the courts of appeal. (Only a minuscule percentage of labor cases reach this final step of the procedure.)

If the regional director refuses to issue a complaint after investigating a charge that decision can be appealed to the Office of Appeals of the General Counsel in Washington, D.C. Approximately 30 percent of the charges dismissed by the regional offices are appealed to the Office of Appeals of the General Counsel. The Office of Appeals reverses the dismissal by the regional offices only rarely—in less than 10 percent of the cases appealed. The courts have upheld the general counsel's absolute discretion in these decisions; a conclusion that the charge lacks significant merit to issue a complaint cannot be appealed beyond the General Counsel's Office of Appeals. As such, the charging party's statutory rights have been procedurally exhausted and terminate without any hearing or judicial review.

Representation Elections

The other type of cases coming before the NLRB involves representation questions—employees choosing whether or not to be represented by a labor union as their exclusive bargaining agent. In fiscal year 2008, 3,400 representation cases were filed with the NLRB. Although the issues and procedures involved in representation questions are discussed in detail in Chapter 13, a few points are highlighted in this discussion of NLRB procedures.

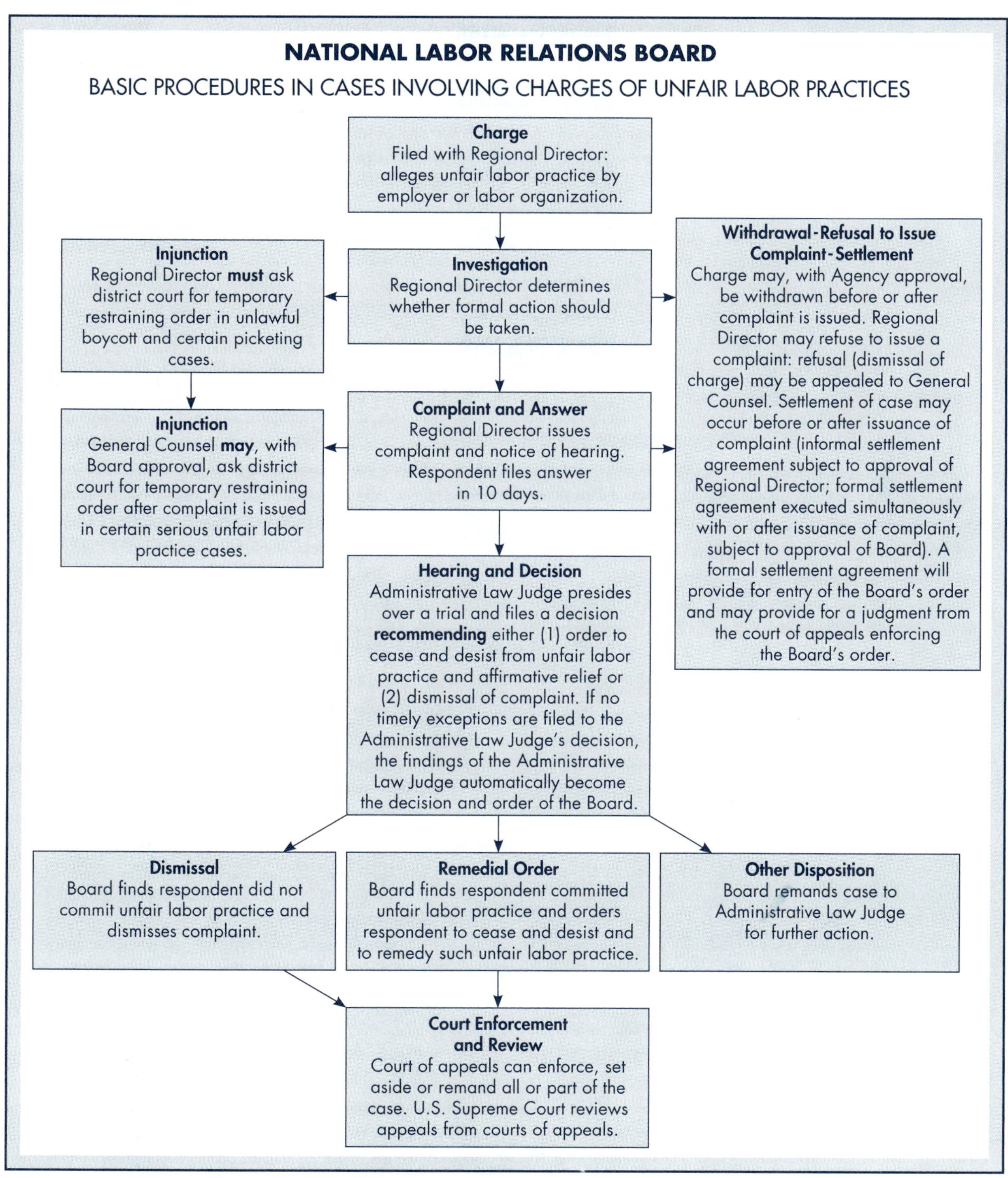

Exhibit 12.3 NLRB Procedures for Unfair Labor Practice Charges
Source: Exhibit C, "Justification of Performance for Committee on Appropriations. F.Y. 2010," available at http://www.nlrb.gov/publications/reports/Justification_Document.aspx

Representation proceedings are at the very heart of the NLRA because the acceptance or rejection of a union as bargaining agent by a group of employees is the essence of the exercise of the rights guaranteed by Section 7 of the act—to engage in, or refrain from, concerted activity for purposes of collective bargaining or mutual aid or protection. Section 9 of the act outlines the procedures available to employees for exercising their rights under Section 7.

For nearly twenty-five years, the Board had primary responsibility for the conduct of all representation elections. Then, in 1959, Congress decided that election procedures were sufficiently settled that the Board could delegate its duties in this area to the regional directors. The Board did so in 1961. Specifically, the regional directors are authorized by the Board to

- decide whether a question concerning representation exists;
- determine the appropriate collective bargaining unit;
- order and conduct an election;
- certify the election's results and;
- resolve challenges to ballots by making findings of fact and issuing rulings.

The Board has retained limited review, as the statute suggests, to ensure uniform and consistent application of its interpretation of law and policy. There are four grounds on which the Board will review an election:

- if a significant issue of law or policy is raised due to an absence of or departure from reported Board precedent;
- if the regional director has made a clear error regarding some factual issue and this error is prejudicial to the rights of one of the parties;
- if the procedure involved some error that prejudiced a party and;
- if the Board believes that one of its rules or policies is due for a reconsideration.

Ordinarily, once the regional director has decided that a representation election should be held involving a particular unit of employees, a Notice and a Direction of Election are issued by the regional office, even though one of the parties has appealed some aspect of the director's decision to the Board in Washington. However, unless the parties have waived their right to request Board review, the director will set the election date no earlier than twenty-five days from the notices. On the other hand, the date will usually not be set any later than thirty days after the director's decision to proceed.

Jurisdiction

Under the NLRA, the NLRB is given authority to deal with labor disputes occurring "in commerce" or "affecting commerce" [as defined in Section 2(7) of the act]. Consistent with the federal courts' traditional view of the scope of federal commerce clause powers, the Supreme Court has held that the NLRB can regulate labor disputes in virtually any company, unless the firm's contact with interstate commerce is de minimus (minuscule and merely incidental).

Rather than exercise its jurisdiction to the full extent of the federal commerce power, the NLRB has chosen to set certain minimum jurisdictional standards. These standards specify the limits beyond which the NLRB will decline jurisdiction over any labor dispute. The Landrum-Griffin Act recognized this policy by providing that the NLRB may decline jurisdiction over any labor dispute that would have been outside the NLRB's minimum jurisdictional standards as of August 1, 1959. The NLRB may expand its jurisdictional standards, but it cannot contract them beyond their position as of August 1, 1959. The 1959 amendments to the act also provide that the states under certain circumstances may assert jurisdiction over labor disputes on which the NLRB declines to assert jurisdiction.

General Jurisdictional Standards

The NLRB jurisdictional standards are set in terms of the dollar volume of business that a firm does annually. The current NLRB jurisdictional standards are as follows:

- *General Nonretail Firms*. Sales of goods to consumers in other states, directly or indirectly (termed outflow) or purchases of goods from suppliers in other states, directly or indirectly (termed inflow) of at least $50,000 per year.
- *Retail Businesses*. Annual volume of business of at least $500,000, including sales and excise taxes.
- *Combined Manufacturing and Retail Enterprises*. When an integrated enterprise manufactures a product and sells it directly to the public, either the retail or the nonretail standard can be applied.
- *Combined Wholesale and Retail Companies*. When a company is involved in both wholesale and retail sales, the nonretail standard is applicable.
- *Instrumentalities, Channels, and Links of Interstate Commerce*. Annual income of at least $50,000 from interstate transportation services or the performing of $50,000 or more in services for firms that meet any of the other standards, except indirect inflow and outflow established for nonretail businesses.
- *National Defense*. Any enterprise having a substantial impact on the national defense. *U.S. Territories and the District of Columbia*. Same standards are applied to the territories as to enterprises operating in the fifty states; plenary (total) jurisdiction is exercised in the District of Columbia.
- *Public Utilities*. At least $250,000 total annual volume of business.
- *Newspapers*. At least $200,000 total annual volume of business.
- *Radio, Telegraph, Telephone, and Television Companies*. At least $100,000 total annual volume of business.
- *Hotels, Motels, and Residential Apartment Houses*. At least $500,000 total annual volume of business.
- *Taxicab Companies*. At least $500,000 total annual volume of business.
- *Transit Systems*. At least $250,000 total annual volume of business.
- *Privately Operated Health-Care Institutions*. Nursing homes, visiting nurses' associations, and similar facilities and services, $100,000; all others, including hospitals, $250,000 total annual volume of business.
- *Nonprofit, Private Educational Institutions*. $1 million annual operating expenditures. U.S. Postal Service. The Board was empowered to assert jurisdiction under the Postal Reorganization Act of 1970.
- *Multiemployer Bargaining Associations*. Regarded as a single employer for the purpose of totaling up annual business with relation to the above standards.

- *Multistate Establishments.* Annual business of all branches is totaled with regard to the Board's standards.
- *Unions as Employers.* The appropriate nonretail standard.

Exempted Employers

Not all employers—or employees of such employers—meeting the NLRB jurisdictional standards are subject to the provisions of the NLRA. Certain kinds of employers have been excluded from coverage of the act by specific provisions in the act; other employers have been exempted as a result of judicial decisions interpreting the act.

Section 2(2) of the act defines the term *employer* as "including any person acting as an agent of an employer, directly or indirectly," but not including:

- the federal government or any wholly owned government corporation;
- any state or political subdivision thereof (county, local, or municipal governments); railroads, airlines, or related companies that are subject to the Railway Labor Act (In 1996, Congress amended the Railway Labor Act to include Federal Express under its jurisdiction, rather than under the NLRA; United Parcel Service, however, remains under the NLRA.); and
- labor organizations in their representational capacity. (Unions are covered by the act in the hiring and treatment of their own employees.)

In addition to these statutory exclusions, judicial decisions have created other exclusions. The NLRB will usually refuse to exercise jurisdiction over an employer that has a close relationship to a foreign government, even if such employers would otherwise come under its jurisdiction. In *Incres S.S. v. Maritime Workers,*[13] the Supreme Court held that the act does not apply to labor disputes of foreign crews on foreign flag vessels temporarily in U.S. ports, even if such ships deal primarily in American contracts. However, when the dispute involves American residents working while the vessel is in port, the dispute is subject to the act. In *Int. Longshore Assoc. v. Allied International, Inc.*,[14] the Supreme Court held that a politically motivated refusal by American longshoremen to service American ships carrying Russian cargo, to protest the Soviet invasion of Afghanistan, was subject to the jurisdiction of the NLRB.

The Supreme Court has also held in *NLRB v. Catholic Bishop*[15] that the NLRB lacked jurisdiction over a parochial high school. The Court stated that its holding was necessary to avoid excessive government entanglement with religion, as prohibited by the First Amendment. The NLRB has taken the position that the Court's decision exempts from NLRB jurisdiction only those organizations devoted principally to the promulgation of the faith of a religion. For example, the NLRB has refused jurisdiction over a television station owned by a church in which more than 90 percent of the station's broadcasts were religious in nature. However, hospitals operated by religious organizations, or religious charity services providing aid to the elderly, have been held subject to NLRB jurisdiction because they were not principally involved with promulgating the religion's faith.

---

[13]372 U.S. 24 (1963).

[14]456 U.S. 212 (1982).

[15]440 U.S. 490 (1979).

Exempted Employees

Just as with employers, not all employees employed by employers in or affecting commerce are subject to the provisions of the NLRA. These exclusions from coverage are the result of both statutory provisions and judicial decisions.

Statutory Exemptions Section 2(3) of the NLRA, in its definition of "employee," expressly excludes:

- individuals employed as agricultural laborers;
- individuals employed as domestics within a person's home;
- individuals employed by a parent or spouse;
- independent contractors;
- supervisors; and
- individuals employed by employers subject to the Railway Labor Act.

Several of these statutory exclusions require some discussion. For example, the NLRA does not specifically define the term "agricultural laborer"; rather, Congress has directed the NLRB to consider the definition of "agriculture" found in Section 3(f) of the Fair Labor Standards Act,[16] which is very broad. It includes cultivating, tilling, growing, dairying, producing, or harvesting any agricultural commodity, raising livestock, or any operations or practices performed by a farmer or on a farm as incident to, or in conjunction with such farming operations. The NLRB considers the facts of each case, looking to the specific duties and the time spent at the duties to determine whether persons are agricultural laborers within the meaning of the NLRA.

In *Holly Farms Corp. v. NLRB*,[17] the Supreme Court (by a 5–4 decision) held that the "live haul" crews of a poultry processor, who drive from the processor's location to independent farms and there collect and cage chickens, lift the cages on a truck, and transport them back to the processor, were not agricultural laborers within the meaning of Section 2(3) and were therefore covered by the NLRA. Agricultural employees exempted from the NLRA may be covered by state legislation; several states, such as California and Arizona, have created agricultural labor relations boards to cover the labor disputes of agricultural laborers.

Independent Contractor
A person working as a separate business entity.

An ***independent contractor*** is a person working as a separate business entity; these individuals are not subject to the direction and control of an employer. For example, a person who owns and operates a dump truck and who contracts to provide rubbish disposal service to a firm might be an independent contractor and not an employee of the firm. If the firm used its own truck and directed a worker to haul away its rubbish, the worker would be an employee and not an independent contractor. The NLRB looks to the degree of control and direction exercised by the firm over the worker to determine whether the worker is an employee or an independent contractor.

Supervisor
Person with authority to direct, hire, fire, or discipline employees in the interests of the employer.

The term ***supervisor*** is defined in Section 2(11) of the NLRA as someone who, in the interests of the employer, has the authority to direct, hire, fire, discipline, transfer, assign, reward, responsibly direct, suspend, or adjust the grievances of other employees and who uses independent judgment in the exercise of such authority. The NLRB, applying Section 2 (11)

---

[16] 29 U.S.C. § 203(f).

[17] 517 U.S. 392 (1996).

to nurses in the health-care industry, held that nurses who directed other employees in patient care were not acting in the interests of their employer and therefore were not supervisors within the meaning of Section 2(11). The Supreme Court rejected the NLRB's decision in *NLRB v. Health Care & Retirement Corporation of America.*[18] The NLRB then held that nurses did not exercise "independent judgment" within the meaning of Section 2(11) because the nurses were exercising "ordinary professional or technical judgment" in directing other employees to deliver patient care in accordance with employer-specified standards.

The following case involves the Supreme Court's consideration of the NLRB's determination that those nurses were not supervisors under the NLRA.

case 12.4 » National Labor Relations Board v. Kentucky River Community Care, Inc.

532 U.S. 706 (2001)

[Kentucky River Community Care, Inc. (Kentucky River) operates a residential care facility for persons suffering from mental retardation and mental illness. The facility, Caney Creek, employs approximately 110 professional and nonprofessional employees and about 12 managerial or supervisory employees. In 1997, the Carpenters Union petitioned the NLRB to represent a single unit of all 110 potentially eligible employees at Caney Creek. At the hearing on the petition, Kentucky River objected to the inclusion of Caney Creek's six registered nurses in the bargaining unit, arguing that they were supervisors under §2(11) of the Act and therefore were excluded from the class of employees covered by the NLRA and included in the bargaining unit. The Board's regional director initially held that Kentucky River had the burden of proving supervisory status; the regional director then held that Kentucky River had not carried that burden and therefore included the nurses in the bargaining unit. The regional director directed an election to determine whether the union would represent the unit; the union won the election and was certified as the representative of the Caney Creek employees.

Kentucky River then refused to bargain with the union in order to get judicial review of the certification decision. The NLRB's general counsel filed an unfair labor practice complaint under §§8(a)(1) and 8(a)(5) of the Act. The Board granted summary judgment to the general counsel, holding Kentucky River had violated the NLRA. Kentucky River then petitioned the U.S. Court of Appeals for the Sixth Circuit. The Sixth Circuit held that the Board had erred in placing the burden of proving supervisory status on respondent rather than on its general counsel, and it also rejected the Board's determination that the registered nurses did not exercise "independent judgment." The court stated that the Board had erred by classifying the nurses' supervision of nurse's aides in administering patient care as "routine" because the nurses have the ability to direct patient care by virtue of their training and expertise, not because of their connection with management. The NLRB then appealed to the U.S. Supreme Court.]

Scalia, J.

Under the National Labor Relations Act, employees are deemed to be "supervisors" and thereby excluded from the protections of the Act if, *inter alia,* they exercise "independent judgment" in "responsibly ... direct[ing]" other employees "in the interest of the employer." This case presents two questions: which party in an unfair-labor-practice proceeding bears the burden of proving or disproving an employee's supervisory status; and whether judgment is not "independent judgment" to the extent that it is informed by professional or technical training or experience....

The Act expressly defines the term "supervisor" in §2(11) ... [but] does not, however, expressly allocate the burden of proving or disproving a challenged employee's supervisory status. The Board therefore has filled the statutory gap with the consistent rule that the burden is borne by the party claiming that the employee is a supervisor....

The Board argues that the Court of Appeals for the Sixth Circuit erred in not deferring to its resolution of the statutory ambiguity, and we agree. The Board's rule is supported by "the general rule of statutory construction that the burden of proving justification or exemption under a special exception

[18] 511 U.S. 571 (1994).

to the prohibitions of a statute generally rests on one who claims its benefits. The burden of proving the applicability of the supervisory exception ... should thus fall on the party asserting it. In addition, it is easier to prove an employee's authority to exercise 1 of the 12 listed supervisory functions than to disprove an employee's authority to exercise any of those functions, and practicality therefore favors placing the burden on the party asserting supervisory status. We find that the Board's rule for allocating the burden of proof is reasonable and consistent with the Act....

The text of §2(11) of the Act ... sets forth a three-part test for determining supervisory status. Employees are statutory supervisors if (1) they hold the authority to engage in any 1 of the 12 listed supervisory functions, (2) their "exercise of such authority is not of a merely routine or clerical nature, but requires the use of independent judgment," and (3) their authority is held "in the interest of the employer." [*NLRB v. Health Care & Retirement Corp. of America*] The only basis asserted by the Board, before the Court of Appeals and here, for rejecting respondent's proof of supervisory status with respect to directing patient care was the Board's interpretation of the second part of the test—... to wit that employees do not use "independent judgment" when they exercise "ordinary professional or technical judgment in directing less-skilled employees to deliver services in accordance with employer-specified standards." The Court of Appeals rejected that interpretation....

The Board ... argues further that the judgment even of employees who are permitted by their employer to exercise a sufficient *degree* of discretion is not "independent judgment" if it is a particular *kind* of judgment, namely, "ordinary professional or technical judgment in directing less-skilled employees to deliver services." ... The text, by focusing on the "clerical" or "routine" (as opposed to "independent") nature of the judgment, introduces the question of degree of judgment.... But the Board's categorical exclusion turns on factors that have nothing to do with the degree of discretion an employee exercises. Let the judgment be significant and only loosely constrained by the employer; if it is "professional or technical" it will nonetheless not be independent. The breadth of this exclusion is made all the more startling by virtue of the Board's extension of it to judgment based on greater "experience" as well as formal training. What supervisory judgment worth exercising, one must wonder, does not rest on "professional or technical skill or experience"? If the Board applied this aspect of its test to every exercise of a supervisory function, it would virtually eliminate "supervisors" from the Act.

As it happens, though, only one class of supervisors would be eliminated in practice, because the Board limits its categorical exclusion with a qualifier: Only professional judgment that is applied "in directing less-skilled employees to deliver services" is excluded from the statutory category of "independent judgment." This second rule is no less striking than the first, and is directly contrary to the text of the statute. *Every* supervisory function listed by the Act is accompanied by the statutory requirement that its exercise "requir[e] the use of independent judgment" before supervisory status will obtain, but the Board would apply its restriction upon "independent judgment" to just 1 of the 12 listed functions: "responsibly to direct." There is no apparent textual justification for this asymmetrical limitation, and the Board has offered none. Surely no conceptual justification can be found in the proposition that supervisors exercise professional, technical, or experienced judgment only when they direct other employees. Decisions "to hire, ... suspend, lay off, recall, promote, discharge, ... or discipline" other employees, must often depend upon that same judgment, which enables assessment of the employee's proficiency in performing his job.... Yet in no opinion that we were able to discover has the Board held that a supervisor's judgment in hiring, disciplining, or promoting another employee ceased to be "independent judgment" because it depended upon the supervisor's professional or technical training or experience. When an employee exercises one of these functions with judgment that possesses a sufficient degree of independence, the Board invariably finds supervisory status.

The Board's refusal to apply its limiting interpretation of "independent judgment" to any supervisory function other than responsibly directing other employees is particularly troubling because just seven years ago we rejected the Board's interpretation of part three of the supervisory test that similarly was applied only to the same supervisory function. [*NLRB v. Health Care & Retirement Corp. of America*] In *Health Care*, the Board argued that nurses did not exercise their authority "in the interest of the employer," as §2(11) requires, when their "independent judgment [was] exercised incidental to professional or technical judgment" instead of for "disciplinary or other matters, i.e., in addition to treatment of patients." It did not escape our notice that the target of this analysis was the supervisory function of responsible direction. "Under §2(11)," we noted, "an employee who in the course of employment uses independent judgment to engage in 1 of the 12 listed activities, including responsible direction of other employees, is a supervisor. Under the Board's test, however, a nurse who in the course of employment uses independent judgment to engage in responsible direction of other employees is not a supervisor." We therefore rejected the Board's analysis as "inconsistent with ... the statutory language," because it "rea[d] the responsible direction portion of §2(11) out of the statute in nurse cases." It is impossible to avoid the conclusion that the Board's interpretation of "independent judgment," applied to nurses for the first time after our decision in *Health Care*, has precisely the same object.... The Labor Management Relations Act, 1947 (Taft-Hartley Act) expressly excluded "supervisors" from the definition of "employees" and thereby from the protections of the Act. §2(3) ... The term "supervisor" means any individual having authority ... "to hire, transfer, suspend, lay off, recall, promote, discharge, assign, reward, or discipline other employees, or responsibly to direct them, or to adjust their grievances." Moreover, the Act assuredly did not incorporate the Board's current interpretation of the term "independent judgment" as applied to the function of responsible direction ... because it had limited the category of supervisors more directly, by requiring functions in *addition* to responsible direction.

... What is at issue is the Board's contention that the policy of covering professional employees under the Act justifies the categorical exclusion of professional judgments from a term, "independent judgment," that naturally includes them. And further, that it justifies limiting this categorical exclusion to the supervisory function of responsibly directing other employees. These contentions contradict both the text and structure of the statute, and they contradict as well the rule of *Health Care* that the test for supervisory status applies no differently to professionals than to other employees. We therefore find the Board's interpretation unlawful....

... the Board's error in interpreting "independent judgment" precludes us from enforcing its order.... Our conclusion that the Court of Appeals was correct to find the Board's test inconsistent with the statute ... suffices to resolve the case. The judgment of the Court of Appeals is affirmed.

It is so ordered.

Case Questions

1. What test determines whether an employee is a supervisor under the NLRA?
2. What is the basis of the NLRB position that nurses who direct other employees in delivering patient care are not exercising independent judgment within the meaning of Section 2(11)? Is the NLRB's position based upon the language of the NLRA? Explain your answers.
3. What is the significance of the determination that the staff nurses are supervisors under the NLRA? What implications does this case have for other professional employees? Explain.

In light of the Supreme Court decision in *NLRB v. Kentucky River Community Care*, the NLRB again considered whether charge nurses were supervisors within the meaning of Section 2(11) in its decision in *Oakwood Healthcare, Inc.*[19] The NLRB majority opinion defined the following terms:

- *Assign*: "... the act designating an employee to a place (such as a location, department, or wing) appointing an employee to a time (such as a shift or overtime period), or giving significant overall duties, i.e., tasks, to an employee.... In the health care setting, the term 'assign' encompasses the charge nurses' responsibility to assign nurses and aides to particular patients."
- *Responsibly to direct*: whether the "... 'alleged supervisor is held fully accountable and responsible for the performance and work product of the employees' he directs...."
- *Independent judgment*: "professional or technical judgments involving the use of independent judgment are supervisory if they involve one of the 12 supervisory functions of Section 2(11).... Whether the registered nurse is a [Section] 2(11) supervisor will depend on whether his or her responsible direction is performed with the degree of discretion required to reflect independent judgment.... We find that a judgment is not independent if it is dictated or controlled by detailed instructions, whether set forth in company policies or rules, the verbal instructions of a higher authority or in the provisions of a collective bargaining agreement."

[19] 348 NLRB 686 (2006).

In the *Oakwood Healthcare case*, the majority held that employees who permanently served as charge nurses were supervisors under Section 2(11) and were excluded from the bargaining unit, but that the employees who only served as charge nurses when the permanent charge nurses were absent or on vacation were not supervisors under the NLRA and were not excluded from the bargaining unit.

Managerial Employees
Persons involved in the formulation or effectuation of management policies.

Judicial Exemptions In addition to the statutory exclusions of employees from NLRA coverage, the U.S. Supreme Court has created other exemptions. ***Managerial employees***, persons whose positions involve the formulation or effectuation of management policies, were held to be excluded from NLRA coverage in *NLRB v. Textron*.[20] In the 1980 decision in *NLRB v. Yeshiva University*,[21] the Supreme Court held that faculty at a private university, who play a significant role in developing and implementing university academic policies, were managerial employees and thus excluded from the protection of the NLRA. Following *Yeshiva*, the U.S. Court of Appeals for the First Circuit held in *Boston Univ. Chapter, AAUP v. NLRB*[22] that faculty at Boston University were managerial employees. However, where faculty do not have input in developing or implementing policy and exercise no supervisory duties, they have been held to be employees under the coverage of the NLRA, as in *Stevens Inst. v. NLRB*[23] and *Bradford College*.[24]

The NLRB recently reversed its position on the question of whether graduate students, who teach classes, and medical residents and interns, are employees under the NLRA. In *Brown University*,[25] the NLRB reversed its previous decisions in *Boston Medical Center*[26] and *New York University*.[27] Those decisions had held that medical residents and interns and university graduate teaching assistants were employees under the NLRA. The *Brown University* decision means that medical residents and interns, and graduate assistants are not protected by the NLRA in their efforts to unionize, and their employers are under no legal obligation to recognize and bargain with them if they do form a union.

Employees excluded from the act's coverage are not prevented from organizing and attempting to bargain collectively with their employer. There is nothing in the NLRA to prohibit such action. Exclusion means that those employees cannot invoke the act's protection for the exercise of rights to organize and bargain. There is no requirement that their employer recognize or bargain with their union or even tolerate such activity. Because those employees are denied the act's protections, the employer is free to discipline or discharge excluded employees who attempt to organize and bargain. Therefore, the faculty members in *Boston University* and the graduate assistants in *New York University* may attempt to organize and bargain with their employer, but the university need not recognize and bargain with them.

---

[20] 416 U.S. 267 (1974).

[21] 444 U.S. 672 (1980).

[22] 835 F.2d 399 (1987).

[23] 620 F.2d 720 (9th Cir. 1980).

[24] 261 NLRB 565 (1982).

[25] 342 NLRB 483 (2004).

[26] 330 NLRB 152 (1999).

[27] 332 NLRB 1205 (2000).

ethical DILEMMA

Faculty Consultation Rights at Prestigious University?

You are the vice president for faculty relations at Prestigious University, a private university in New Jersey. The major portion of your duties involves negotiation and communication with the Prestigious University chapter of the American Association of University Professors (AAUP). The Prestigious chapter of the AAUP has functioned as the representative of the faculty for discussions over salary, benefits, and working conditions for a number of years. Although there is no formal collective agreement between the university administration and the AAUP chapter, the administration has never instituted any policies or changes to benefits or working conditions without first getting the approval of the AAUP chapter.

Because of declining enrollment, increased building maintenance costs, and the expenses of updating computer facilities all across the campus, the university is experiencing financial difficulties. The administration decides to freeze faculty salaries and reduce its contribution to the faculty's medical insurance and pension plans. The AAUP chapter strongly objects to such actions and will not cooperate with the university administration to implement them. The great majority of the faculty at Prestigious University supports the AAUP's position.

Should the university administration continue to work with the AAUP in its capacity as faculty representative, or should the administration impose its financial proposals over the AAUP's objections? The university president has asked you to prepare a memo that outlines the advantages and disadvantages of the two approaches and recommends a course of action. Which approach would you recommend? Why? Prepare the requested memo and explain your position.

Confidential Employees
Persons whose job involves access to confidential labor relations information.

Confidential employees are neither supervisors nor managerial employees, but those persons whose position involves access to confidential labor relations information. The following case discusses the scope of the confidential employee exemption.

case 12.5 » NLRB v. Meenan Oil Co., L.P.

139 F.3d 311 (2d Cir. 1998)

Jacobs, Circuit Judge

The National Labor Relations Board (the "Board") petitions for enforcement of its order finding that Meenan Oil Co., L.P. ("Meenan" or the "Company") violated Sections 8 (a) (1) and (5) of the National Labor Relations Act (the "NLRA"), by refusing to bargain with a properly certified union and requiring Meenan to bargain with the union on demand. Meenan contends that the two collective bargaining units at issue were improperly certified because they include employees who are outside the protection of the NLRA. Specifically, Meenan asserts that ... its administrator for payroll and personnel matters is ... a confidential employee; and the executive secretary to its general manager is a confidential employee....

Rosemary Gould is [General Manager] Zaweski's executive secretary. She sits outside his office and spends most of her time answering telephones, typing, filing, and performing other clerical tasks. She also opens Zaweski's mail, including items marked "confidential." Gould types documents dealing with employee discipline, including disciplinary notices, termination notices, minutes of union grievance meetings, and grievance settlement documents. Ordinarily, she prepares the documents after a decision has been made, and often after their contents have been disclosed to the relevant employees or union representatives, or discussed with them; copies are generally sent to the employees and union immediately after they are produced. Gould also types some internal memoranda dealing with various personnel issues. These memoranda give her access to intra-management communications that affect union employees generally, even if they do not specifically concern labor issues or strategies. Thus Gould is responsible for typing the Company's annual profit plan, which forecasts the salary increase or decrease planned for every Meenan employee. Meenan asserts that her access to all of these materials makes Gould a confidential employee, and that it was error to include her in a collective bargaining unit.

Angela Gabriel, the Company's payroll/personnel administrator, had worked for the Company for about twelve years at the time of the election.... Gabriel reports to the Company's accounting supervisor on most matters, but reports to Zaweski on issues of personnel. Her primary responsibility is to handle the paperwork for payroll and personnel matters. Specifically, she: prepares the weekly payroll figures; collects personnel forms when new employees are hired; receives and files copies of insurance claims, disciplinary notices, and other notices; maintains a complete set of personnel files; calculates and fills out the forms for employees' benefit fund contributions; helps managers keep track of employees' absences and overtime, and is expected to point out any discrepancies she observes; fills out unemployment compensation forms using information provided by the Company's managers; and occasionally copies documents from an employee's file in order to assist a manager who is testifying at an unemployment hearing.

... Gabriel's duties give her access to potentially sensitive information about the Company. Copies of all employees' personnel files are filed in Gabriel's office. She receives employees' drug-test results, though she plays no role in deciding what to do about the results. Gabriel is privy to some union-related information (such as impending layoffs), but she generally acquires that information only when it is in the process of being forwarded to the union. Most important for present purposes, she assists Zaweski with the preparation of the Company's annual profit plan, and in that way has access to the current salary as well as salary changes forecast by the Company for all employees and supervisors, and at least some managers. Because she has access to all of this information, Meenan contends that Gabriel, like Gould, is a confidential employee who for that reason must be excluded from any bargaining unit....

The Board excludes from collective bargaining units individuals who fit the definition of "confidential employees." *NLRB v. Hendricks County Rural Elec. Membership Corp.*, 454 U.S. 170, 189 (1981)....

The Supreme Court has identified two categories of confidential employees who are excluded from the NLRA's protection: (i) employees who "assist and act in a confidential capacity to persons who formulate, determine, and effectuate management policies in the field of labor relations," and (ii) employees who "regularly have access to confidential information concerning anticipated changes which may result from collective bargaining negotiations."

There are arguably some confidential aspects to many employment relationships, but the Board (for that reason) hews strictly to a narrow definition of a confidential employee.... *In Hendricks County*, the Supreme Court approved the Board's use of this "labor nexus" test; so employees who have access to confidential business information are not for that reason excludible from collective bargaining units. The Board looks to "the confidentiality of the relationship between the employee and persons who exercise managerial functions in the field of labor relations." Moreover, the confidential labor-related information available to the employee must be information that is not already known to the union or in the process of being disclosed to it.

The rationale for the exclusion of confidential employees (as so defined) is that management should not be forced to negotiate with a union that includes employees "who in the normal performance of their duties may obtain advance information of the [c]ompany's position with regard to contract negotiations, the disposition of grievances, and other labor relations matters." An individual who routinely sees data which would enable the union to predict, understand or evaluate the bargaining position of the employer is therefore excluded from union membership.

We conclude that Angela Gabriel, the payroll/personnel administrator, and Rosemary Gould, the executive secretary to the general manager, are confidential employees. Both are in a confidential employment relationship with General Manager Zaweski, who is largely responsible for conducting Meenan's labor relations. Both women fit neatly within the category of confidential employee, identified by the Supreme Court in *Hendricks County*, as those who "assist and act in a confidential capacity to persons who formulate, determine, and effectuate management policies in the field of labor relations."

Zaweski has responsibility for preparing the Company's annual profit plan. Gabriel assists him in that project by filling out forms that show the current salaries and most recent pay raises of the Company's employees, including supervisors and at least some members of management. The forms containing this information, as prepared by Gabriel, are forwarded to the Company's managers, who apply corporate salary increase guidelines to arrive at a recommendation for the timing and size of each employee's next raise, and review these recommendations with Zaweski. A copy of the revised recommendations is then sent to the Company's corporate department, and a copy is retained by Gabriel. If the corporate department revises the figures, Gabriel receives a copy of the updated document. Gabriel thus has knowledge of the proposed salary increase—or decrease—of every Meenan employee. Often she learns of these proposed changes six to seven months before they are implemented.

Zaweski's executive secretary, Rosemary Gould, types the initial draft of the annual profit plan, and in so doing she gets to see the proposed wage and salary figures before they are sent to the corporate department and to Gabriel. Gould testified that she, Gabriel and Zaweski are the only non-corporate employees who see this document.

Because Gabriel and Gould assist Zaweski with the preparation of the Company's annual profit plan, they have access to projected wage and salary data for both union and non-union employees. This information, in the hands of the Union, would give it a significant strategic advantage in negotiations. The Union could predict the size of the raises that management already planned to give both union and non-union employees, prior to any collective bargaining session, and use that level of compensation as a floor for its demands. At the same time, information about the present and projected compensation of managers would afford leverage in bargaining for comparable raises for union members. Even if this information is never mentioned, it would enable the Union to anticipate and gauge management's resistance to its demands.

In summary, the projected wage and salary data contained in the profit plan influences and signals "the [c]ompany's position with regard to contract negotiations." Meenan is not required to bargain with a union whose members have this advantage.

The Board's finding that Gabriel and Gould are not confidential employees is unsupported by substantial evidence, and we therefore decline to enforce the Board's order insofar as Gabriel and Gould are included in the Office Clerical collective bargaining unit....

For the foregoing reasons, we modify the Board's order to remove Meenan's "payroll/personnel administrator" and its "executive secretary" from the Office Clerical collective bargaining unit. The order as modified is enforced.

Case Questions

1. What is the rationale for the exclusion of confidential employees?
2. Does the confidential employee exclusion apply to all employees who have access to the employer's confidential information? What is the "labor nexus" test?
3. What are the key features of Gould's and Gabriel's job duties for the purposes of the "labor nexus" test? Would including Gabriel and Gould in the bargaining unit place the employer at a disadvantage when dealing with the union? Explain.

Although managerial employees are excluded from the act's coverage, it is not clear whether "confidential" employees are excluded from the act's coverage or are simply excluded from bargaining units with other employees. If confidential employees, like managers, are excluded from the act's coverage, they are denied the protections of the act. If, however, they are excluded only from bargaining units, they remain employees under the act and are entitled to its statutory protection. The Supreme Court did not specifically address this question in *Hendricks*, nor did the court in *Meenan Oil Co.*

Unions in the construction industry often try to organize a contractor's work force by getting some of their organizers to be hired by the contractor. Can persons who are on the payroll of a union as organizers also be employees under the meaning of Section 2(3)? The following case involves that question in the context of the legality of an employer's refusal to hire persons who are also on the union payroll as organizers.

case 12.6 »

NLRB v. Town & Country Electric, Inc.

516 U.S. 85 (1995)

Facts: Town & Country Electric, Inc., a nonunion electrical contractor, advertised for job applicants, but it refused to interview ten of eleven union applicants who responded to the ad. Its employment agency hired the one union applicant whom Town & Country interviewed, but he was dismissed after only a few days on the job. Those rejected applicants were members of the International Brotherhood of Electrical Workers, Locals 292 and 343; they filed a complaint with the National Labor Relations Board (NLRB), claiming that Town & Country and the employment agency had refused to interview (or retain) them because of their union membership, a violation of the National Labor Relations Act (NLRA).

An administrative law judge ruled in favor of the union members, and the NLRB affirmed that ruling. The NLRB determined that all eleven job applicants were "employees," as the Act defines that word. The Board recognized that under well-established law, it made no difference that the ten applicants were never hired; nor did it matter that the union members intended to try to organize the company if they were hired, and that the union would pay them for their organizing. The NLRB held that the company had committed unfair labor practices by discriminating against them on the basis of union membership.

The United States Court of Appeals for the Eighth Circuit reversed the NLRB. It held that the NLRB had incorrectly interpreted the word "employee," and that term "employee" did not include those persons who work for a company while simultaneously being paid by a union to organize that company. The decision of the court of appeals meant that the applicants here were not protected by the NLRA from discrimination because of their union membership. The court refused to enforce the Board's order, and the NLRB appealed to the U.S. Supreme Court.

Issue: Does the definition of "employee" under the NLRA include persons working for a company and, at the same time, being paid by a union to help the union organize the company?

Decision: The National Labor Relations Act definition of "employee" [Section 2(3)] is as follows:

> The term "employee" shall include any employee, and shall not be limited to the employees of a particular employer, unless this subchapter explicitly states otherwise, and shall include any individual whose work has ceased as a consequence of, or in connection with, any current labor dispute or because of any unfair labor practice, and who has not obtained any other regular and substantially equivalent employment, but shall not include any individual employed as an agricultural laborer, or in the domestic service of any family or person at his home, or any individual employed by his parent or spouse, or any individual having the status of an independent contractor, or any individual employed as a supervisor, or any individual employed by an employer subject to the Railway Labor Act, as amended from time to time, or by any other person who is not an employer as herein defined.

The NLRB interpretation of this language to include company workers who are also paid union organizers is consistent with the broad language of the Act itself. That language is broad enough to include those company workers whom a union also pays for organizing. The ordinary dictionary definition of "employee" includes any "person who works for another in return for financial or other compensation." The NLRB's broad, literal interpretation of the word "employee" is consistent with the NLRA's purposes of protecting "the right of employees to organize for mutual aid without employer interference," and "encouraging and protecting the collective bargaining process."

Town & Country argues that a worker also being paid as a union organizer is sometimes acting adversely to the company, and the organizer may stand ready to leave the company if so requested by the union. Town & Country claims that means that the union, not the company, would have "the right to control the conduct of the employee," and therefore the worker must be the employee of the union alone. Town & Country's argument fails because the NLRB correctly found that it was not supported by common law. The NLRB concluded that service to the union for pay does not involve abandonment of service to the company. Common sense suggests that a worker going about the ordinary tasks during a working day is subject to the control of the company, whether or not the worker is also paid by the union. The fact that union and company interests may sometimes differ does not matter. The union organizers may limit their organizing to nonwork hours. If that is so, union organizing, when done for pay but during nonwork hours, would be equivalent to "moonlighting," a practice wholly consistent with a company's control over its workers as to their assigned duties. There are legal remedies for Town & Country's concerns, other than excluding paid or unpaid union organizers from protection under the NLRA. If the company is concerned about employees quitting without notice, it can offer its employees fixed-term contracts rather than hiring them "at will," or it can negotiate with its workers for a notice period. A company faced with unlawful activity by its workers can discipline or dismiss those workers, or file a complaint with the NLRB, or notify law enforcement authorities.

The Supreme Court held the NLRB's interpretation of the word "employee" was lawful, and that the statutory definition of the term does not exclude paid union organizers. The Supreme Court vacated the judgment of the court of appeals, and remanded the case is remanded for further proceedings consistent with its opinion.

In *Toering Electric Co.*,[28] the NLRB held that when an employer is charged with discriminatorily failing to hire an applicant for employment, the NLRB General Counsel has the burden of proving that the applicant was genuinely interested in working for the employer. The employer can defend itself against the unfair labor practice charge by raising a reasonable question as to the applicant's actual interest in working for the employer. If the employer puts forward such evidence, then the general counsel must establish, by a preponderance of evidence, that the applicant was interested in establishing an employment relationship with the employer. If the general counsel fails to make such a showing, then the employer's refusal to hire the applicant is lawful. This approach has been criticized as not being consistent with the Supreme Court's opinion in *NLRB v. Town & Country Electric, Inc.*

Jurisdiction over Labor Organizations

Section 2(5) of the NLRA defines *labor organization* as:

> any organization of any kind, or any agency or employee representation committee or plan, in which employees participate and which exists for the purpose, in whole or in part, of dealing with employers concerning grievances, labor disputes, wages, rates of pay, hours of employment, or conditions of work.

NLRB and Supreme Court decisions have held that the words "dealing with" are broad enough to encompass relationships that fall short of collective bargaining. For example, in *NLRB v. Cabot Carbon,*[29] the Supreme Court held that the act encompassed employee committees that functioned merely to discuss with management, but not bargain over, such matters of mutual interest as grievances, seniority, and working conditions. There is also case law to suggest that a single individual cannot be considered a labor organization "in any literal sense."[30]

Preemption and the NRLA

Because of the broad reach of NLRB jurisdiction under the federal commerce power, it is important to consider whether the states have any authority to legislate regarding labor relations in the private sector. Although state laws that conflict with federal laws are void under

[28] 351 N.L.R.B. No. 18 (2007).

[29] 360 U.S. 203 (1959).

[30] See *Bonnaz v. NLRB*, 230 F.2d 47 (D.C. Cir. 1956).

the supremacy clause of Article VI of the Constitution, the Supreme Court has consistently held that states may regulate activities involving interstate commerce where such regulation is pursuant to a valid state purpose. In such situations, the states have concurrent jurisdiction with the federal government: The regulated firm or activity is subject to both the state and federal regulations. But where an activity is characterized by pervasive federal regulation, the Supreme Court has held that Congress has, under the supremacy clause powers, "occupied the field" so that the federal law preempts any state regulation. One example of such preemption is the regulation of radio and television broadcasting by the Federal Communications Commission. Has Congress, through the enactment of the NLRA, preempted state regulation of private sector labor disputes?

The Supreme Court tried to answer this question in two leading decisions. In *San Diego Building Trades Council v. Garmon*,[31] the Supreme Court held that state and federal district courts are deprived of jurisdiction over conduct that is "arguably subject" to Section 7 or Section 9 of the NLRA. In *Sears Roebuck v. San Diego County District Council of Carpenters*,[32] the Supreme Court held that state courts may deal with matters arising out of a labor dispute when the issue presented to the state court is not the same as that which would be before the NLRB. The Court said it would consider the nature of the particular state interests being asserted and the effect on national labor policies of allowing the state court to proceed. *Sears* involved a trespassing charge filed against picketing by the carpenters; no unfair practice charges were filed with the NLRB by either party to the dispute. The Court upheld the right of the state court to order the picketers to stop trespassing on Sears's property, recognizing that Congress did not preempt all state regulation of matters growing out of a labor dispute.

In *Wisconsin Dept. of Industry, Labor & Human Relations v. Gould*,[33] the Supreme Court held that the NLRA preempted a Wisconsin law that barred any firm violating the NLRA three times within five years from doing business with the state. The Court held that the law sought to supplement the sanctions for violations of the NLRA and so was in conflict with the NLRB's comprehensive regulation of industrial relations.

The Supreme Court summarized the principles of the preemption of state laws by federal labor relations law in the 1993 case of *Building & Construction Trades Council of the Met. Dist. v. Assoc. Builders and Contractors of Mass.*,[34] which upheld a state regulation requiring contractors working on public contracts to abide by the terms of a collective agreement. The Court noted that federal labor relations law preempts state regulation of activities that are protected by Section 7 or are defined as unfair labor practices by the NLRA (as in *San Diego Building Trades v. Garmon*), and state regulation of areas left to the control of market and economic forces (as in *Wisconsin Dept. of Industry, Labor & Human Relations v. Gould*).

President Clinton's Executive Order No. 12954 disqualified firms that hired permanent replacement workers during lawful strikes from federal contracts over $100,000. This order, however, was held to be preempted by the NRLA, which allows employers to hire permanent replacements in economic strikes, according to *Chamber of Commerce v. Reich*.[35]

---

[31] 359 U.S. 236 (1959).

[32] 436 U.S. 180 (1978).

[33] 475 U.S. 282 (1986).

[34] 507 U.S. 218, (1993).

[35] 74 F.3d 1322 (D.C. Cir. 1996), *rehearing denied*, 83 F.3d 439 (D.C. Cir. 1996).

Federal legislation may also expressly preserve the right of the states to regulate activities. For example, Section 103 of the Labor-Management Reporting and Disclosure Act, dealing with internal union affairs, states that "Nothing contained in this title shall limit the rights and remedies of any member of a labor organization under any State ... law or before any court or other tribunal...." Because of this provision, states are free to legislate greater protection for union members vis-à-vis their unions, and state courts are free to hear suits that may arise under such laws.

Concept *Summary* » 12.4

The National Labor Relations Board

- Organization
  - Five-member board
  - Division of judges (ALJs)
  - General counsel
- Types of cases
  - Unfair labor practices (ULPs)
  - Representation elections
- Jurisdiction
  - Exempted employers
    - Federal government/government-owned corporations
    - Railroads, airlines, or other companies subject to RLA
    - Representational labor organizations
  - Statutorily exempted employees: The NLRA excludes persons who are:
    - Employed as agricultural laborers
    - Employed in the domestic service of any person or family in a home
    - Employed by a parent or spouse
    - Employed as an independent contractor
    - Employed as a supervisor
    - Employed by an employer subject to the Railway Labor Act, such as railroads and airlines
    - Employed by federal, state, or local government
    - Employed by any other person who is not an employer as defined in the NLRA
  - Judicially exempted employees: The courts have also held the following persons are also excluded from the NLRA:
    - Managerial employees
    - Confidential employees

CHAPTER REVIEW

» Key Terms

criminal conspiracy	« 334	*common law*	« 342	*independent contractor*	« 361
yellow-dog contracts	« 335	*closed shop*	« 350	*supervisor*	« 361
injunction	« 339	*administrative law judges (ALJs)*	« 351	*managerial employees*	« 365
ex parte proceedings	« 339			*confidential employees*	« 366

» Summary

- Organized labor developed slowly in the United States, with the post–Civil War industrialization spurring the rise of the Knights of Labor, the socialists, and the American Federation of Labor (AFL). The AFL ultimately developed into the dominant organization of the American labor movement; its merger with the CIO in 1955 marked the high point for organized labor in the United States. Since the mid-1950s, the percentage of the American work force that is unionized has steadily dwindled, from around 35 percent to the current level of approximately 12 percent. Unions still exert political influence, but there has been no resurgence of the labor movement since the mid-1950s. The U.S. legal system responded to organized labor by initially trying to suppress it through the use of the conspiracy doctrine, the labor injunction, and yellow-dog contracts. The antitrust laws, intended to attack anticompetitive business practices, were also used against union strikes and boycotts.
- It was not until the Great Depression of the 1930s that organized labor received legislative protection. The Norris–La Guardia Act, passed in 1932, greatly limited the use of labor injunctions by the federal courts. The National Industrial Recovery Act, the centerpiece of Franklin Roosevelt's New Deal, provided protection for employees organizing unions and encouraged collective bargaining. The National Labor Board (NLB) was created in 1933 to mediate labor disputes, but it had to rely on persuasion rather than legal authority. The NLB was replaced by the "old" National Labor Relations Board in 1934. When the Supreme Court declared the National Industrial Recovery Act unconstitutional in 1935, it meant the end of the old NLRB.
- Congress passed the Wagner Act shortly thereafter; the NLRA, and the NLRB it created, survived a constitutional challenge in the 1937 decision of *NLRB v. Jones & Laughlin Steel Corp.* The Wagner Act became the foundation for the development of the current National Labor Relations Act, the legal framework for labor relations in the United States.
- The National Labor Relations Act (NRLA) regulates private sector labor relations; the NLRA is administered by the National Labor Relations Board (NLRB). The NLRA defines the basic rights of employees and prohibits actions by employers or

unions that interfere with or restrict those rights—defined as unfair labor practices. The NLRB adjudicates complaints of unfair labor practices under the NLRA and conducts representation elections.

- The NLRA excludes public sector employers, railroads, and airlines subject to the Railway Labor Act from its definition of employer; and the NLRB has adopted guidelines to define the scope of its jurisdiction over private sector employers. The NRLA also excludes certain employees from the act's coverage: agricultural laborers, persons employed as domestics in the homes of others, individuals employed by parents or spouses, independent contractors, supervisors, and employees of Railway Labor Act employers. In addition to the statutory exclusions, the courts have excluded managerial employees and confidential employees.
- The NLRA preempts state laws that purport to regulate conduct protected by or prohibited by the NLRA and that seek to regulate areas left by the NLRA to the market and economic forces.

» Problems

Questions

1. Why was the labor injunction an effective weapon against union activities?
2. How were the antitrust laws used to deter union activities?
3. What were the main provisions of the Norris–La Guardia Act? How did the Norris–La Guardia Act affect union activities?
4. What were the major provisions of the Wagner Act? What were the effects of this act? What factors led to the passage of the Taft-Hartley Act? What were the effects of this act?
5. Which employers are covered by the NLRA? Which employers are exempt from NLRA coverage? Which employees are excluded from NLRA coverage?

Case Problems

6. The legislature of West Virginia enacted a law in 1983 (effective July 1, 1984) requiring that at least 40 percent of the board of directors of all nonprofit and local government hospitals in the state be composed of an equal proportion of "consumer representatives" from "small businesses, organized labor, elderly persons, and persons whose income is less than the national median income." The American Hospital Association joined with a number of West Virginia hospitals in seeking an injunction against enforcement of the law and a declaratory judgment that, among other things, the law interfered with bargaining rights between the hospitals and their employees and was therefore preempted by federal labor law.

   If you were arguing for the plaintiff hospitals, how would you contend that this West Virginia law might interfere with the collective bargaining relationship? If you were the federal judge hearing the case, how would you rule and why? See *American Hospital Association v. Hansbarger* [600 F. Supp. 465, 118 L.R.R.M. 2389 (N.D. W.Va. 1984)].

7. Spring Valley Farms, Inc. supplied poultry feed to farmers who raised broiler and egg-laying poultry. Sarah F. Jones had the title of feed delivery manager with the company in Cullman, Alabama, and she dispatched the drivers who delivered the feed. Drivers could earn more money on "long hauls" (more than fifty miles from the mill) than on "short hauls." Therefore, Spring Valley Farms instructed Jones to "equalize" the number of long and short hauls so that all drivers would earn approximately the same wages. The company also instructed her to work the drivers as close to forty hours per week as possible and then to "knock them off" by seniority. It was left to Jones's discretion to devise methods for accomplishing these objectives.

   Does Spring Valley Farms fall under the jurisdiction of the NLRB? Is Jones as manager excluded from the Board's jurisdiction? See *Spring Valley Farms* [272 NLRB No. 205, 118 L.R.R.M. 1015 (1984)].

8. In 1976, the citizens of New Jersey amended their state constitution to permit the legislative authorization of casino gambling in Atlantic City. Determined to prevent the infiltration of organized crime into its nascent casino industry, the New Jersey legislature enacted the Casino Control Act, which provides for the comprehensive regulation of casino gambling, including the regulation of unions representing industry employees. Sections 86 and 93 of the act specifically impose certain qualification criteria on officials of labor organizations representing casino industry employees. (Section 86, for example, contains a list of crimes, conviction of which disqualifies a union officer from representing casino employees.) A hotel employees' union challenged the state law, arguing that it was preempted by the NLRA, which gives employees the right to select collective bargaining representatives of their own choosing. The case reached the U.S. Supreme Court.

   How should the Supreme Court have ruled? Why? See *Brown v. Hotel Employees Local 54* [468 U.S. 491116 L.R.R.M. 2921 (1984)].

9. The Volunteers of America (VOA) is a religious movement founded in New York City in 1896. Its purpose is "to reach and uplift all segments of the population and to bring them to a knowledge of God." The Denver Post of the VOA, founded in 1898, is an unincorporated association operated under the direction of the national society. It maintains three chapels in the Denver area, at which it conducts regular religious services and Bible study groups. The VOA also operates a number of social programs in Denver, including temporary care, shelter, and counseling centers for women and children.

   The United Nurses, Professionals and Health Care Employees Union filed a petition with the NLRB to represent the counselors at these shelters. The VOA argued it was not subject to the Board's jurisdiction because (1) the First Amendment to the U.S. Constitution precludes NLRB jurisdiction over a religious organization, and (2) it received partial funding from the city and county governments under contracts specifying the services it was to perform so that the government, not the VOA, was the true employer. The case reached the Tenth Circuit Court of Appeals.

   How should the court have ruled on these two arguments? See *Denver Post of VOA v. NLRB* [732 F.2d 769 (10th Cir. 1984)] and *Aramark Corp. v. NLRB* [179 F.3d 872 (10th Cir. 1999)].

10. The *Alcoa Seaprobe* was a U.S.-flagged oceangoing vessel engaged in offshore geophysical and geotechnical research. While berthed in Woods Hole, Massachusetts, its owner, Alcoa Marine Corporation (a Delaware corporation headquartered in Houston, Texas), had contracted with Brazil's national oil company to use *Alcoa Seaprobe* for offshore exploration of Brazil's continental shelf. When Alcoa sent the Seaprobe to Brazil, it did not intend to return the vessel to the United States.

    The Masters, Mates & Pilots Union (International Longshoremen) filed a petition to represent the crew of *Alcoa Seaprobe*. Alcoa Marine Corporation argued that since *Seaprobe* was not expected to operate in U.S. territorial waters, the NLRA did not apply.

    How should the NLRB have ruled? See *Alcoa Marine Corp.* [240 NLRB No. 18, 100 L.R.R.M. 1433 (1979)].

11. National Detective Agencies, Inc., of Washington, D.C., provided security officers to various clients in the District of Columbia. Among these clients was the Inter-American Development Bank, "an international economic organization whose purpose is to aid in the economic development and growth of its member nations, who are primarily members of the Organization of American States." The Federation of Special Police petitioned the NLRB to represent National's employees, including those who worked at the bank.

    National argued that the bank could require National to issue orders and regulations to its guards and to remove any guard the bank considered unsatisfactory. The bank had the right to interview all job applicants and to suggest wage scales. Consequently, National argued, the bank was a joint employer of the guards and, as an international organization, enjoyed "sovereign immunity" from NLRA jurisdiction. Therefore, these guards should not be included in the proposed bargaining unit.

How do you think the NLRB ruled on this argument? Is this case conceptually distinguishable from the *Alcoa Seaprobe* case in problem 10? See *National Detective Agencies* [237 NLRB No. 72, 99 L.R.R.M. 1007 (1978)].

12. Dudczak was employed as a production supervisor at VPA, Inc. until he was fired because his brother and cousin had led a union organizing campaign among the workers at VPA. Dudczak filed an unfair labor practice complaint with the NLRB, alleging that his discharge was a violation of Section 8(a)(1). Subsequent to the firing of Dudczak, VPA agreed to recognize the union as the exclusive bargaining agent of its employees.

    How should the NLRB rule on Dudczak's complaint? Explain your answer. See *Kenrich Petrochemicals v. NLRB* [893 F.2d 1468 (3d Cir. 1990)].

13. The faculty at the Universidad Central de Bayamon in Puerto Rico seek to unionize in order to bargain collectively with the university over wages, working conditions, and so on. The university, which describes itself as a "Catholic-oriented civil institution," is governed by a board of trustees, of whom a majority are to be members of the Dominican religious order.

    Is the Universidad subject to NLRB jurisdiction, or is it exempt under the Catholic Bishop doctrine? See *Universidad Central de Bayamon* [273 NLRB No. 138 (1984); 778 F.2d 906 (1st Cir.) *rev'd. on rehearing*, 793 F.2d 383 (1985)].

14. Callaghan, an employee of Smith Transportation, is one of the leaders of an effort to unionize the Smith employees. Biggins, the personnel manager of Smith, suspects Callaghan is involved in the organizing campaign and decides to fire him. Callaghan is given notice on January 15, 2001, that his employment will be terminated on January 31, 2001. On July 20, 2001, Callaghan files a complaint with the appropriate regional office of the NLRB, alleging that he was fired in violation of Sections 8(a)1 and 3 of the NLRA. Smith Transportation argues that the complaint was not filed within the required six-month limitations period.

    Was the complaint filed in a timely fashion? Does the time limit run from when the employee is notified of the impending discharge or from when the discharge becomes effective? See *United States Postal Service* [271 NLRB No. 61, 116 L.R.R.M. 1417 (1984)].

15. Speedy Clean Service, Inc. provides janitorial services for office buildings; a number of its employees are Hispanics who have entered the United States illegally. When several employees try to organize a union to represent them, Speedy Clean fires all of its workers. The discharged employees file unfair labor practice charges with the NLRB; the employer argues that the illegal aliens are not entitled to protection under the act.

    Are illegal aliens included within the definition of "employee" under Section 2(3)? Explain your answer. See *Hoffman Plastic Compounds, Inc. v. NLRB* [535 U.S. 137 (2002)].

Hypothetical Scenarios

16. The part-time faculty at Farber College are disturbed by the college administration's decision to freeze their pay. They are paid a flat fee for each course they teach, and that fee has not been raised for the last five years. The part-time faculty do not play any role in developing college policies or in deciding curriculum matters. The part-time faculty do not have permanent offices, and must meet with students in the campus cafeteria or coffee shop. The part-time faculty decide to form a union to bargain with the college administration. Are the part-time faculty "employees" under the NLRA? Why? Would your answer change if Farber were a public college? Why?

17. Betty Suarez is the administrative assistant for the manager at Mode, Inc., a small fashion design house. She prepares the payroll for the firm, and assists the manager with some personnel decisions. The office staff at Mode, Inc. seek to form a union, and Betty is interested in being a part of the union. Are there any legal restrictions on Betty being a member of the bargaining unit? Explain.

18. Cantor, Inc. is a firm that provides counseling and therapy services for children and adolescents with emotional problems. The firm is funded primarily by financial grants from state and local government agencies and charitable foundations, although it does receive a small amount of income from fees paid by clients (or the clients' insurance company). The

funding agencies do require that Cantor, Inc. meet certain performance standards, but do not have any role in determining Cantor's employment policies. Is Cantor, Inc. an employer under the NLRA? Explain.

19. The taxi drivers at 4-Star Cabs pay the company a daily rental fee for the use of the company cabs, but get to keep all the fares that they earn during their driving shifts. The drivers determine their working hours, and must pay for the gas they use during their shifts. The company carries an "umbrella" auto insurance policy that covers the drivers, but it does not provide any benefits to the drivers. Are the drivers "employees" under the NLRA? Explain.

20. Your roommate is a medical resident at St. Olaf's Hospital, which is run by the Lutheran Church. She tells you that the residents are interested in forming a union because they are forced to work long hours for low pay. The residents have graduated from medical school, but must complete a certain number of years as residents before they can be certified as licensed medical practitioners. What rights do the residents have under the NLRA? Can they require the hospital administration to discuss working conditions with them? Explain.

The Unionization Process

In the preceding chapter, we discussed briefly the National Labor Relations Board's (NLRB) administrative structure and procedures in representation (R) cases. In this chapter, we consider in greater detail the mechanisms created by the Board for determining whether a company's employees will be represented by a union for purposes of collective bargaining.

Exclusive Bargaining Representative

We have seen that Section 7 of the NLRA entitles employees "to bargain collectively through representatives of their own choosing." Section 9(a) adds that:

> Representatives designated or selected for the purposes of collective bargaining by the majority of the employees in a unit appropriate for such purposes, shall be the exclusive representatives of all the employees in such unit for the purposes of collective bargaining in respect to rates of pay, wages, hours of employment, or other conditions of employment.

The position of the union as exclusive bargaining agent supersedes any individual contracts of employment made between the employer and the unit employees. Any dealings with individual unit employees must be in accordance with the collective bargaining agreement.

The Taft-Hartley Act added some protection for minority factions within bargaining units by adding to Section 9(a) the stipulation that:

> any individual or a group of employees shall have the right at any time to present grievances to their employer and to have such grievances adjusted, without the intervention of the bargaining representative, as long as the adjustment is not inconsistent with the terms of a collective bargaining contract or agreement then in effect.

The extent to which this provision allows the employer to deal with individual employee grievances, and its effect on the union's position as exclusive bargaining agent, will be discussed in Chapter 15.

Employees' Choice of Bargaining Agent

Although the most common method of determining the employees' choice of a bargaining representative is to hold a secret ballot election, the NLRA does not require such procedures. Employers confronted by a union claiming to have the support of a majority of their employees may recognize the union as the exclusive bargaining agent for those employees. Section 9(a) requires only that the union, in order to become the exclusive bargaining agent, be designated or selected by a majority of the employees. It does not require that an election be held to determine employee choice. The propriety of this method of recognition, called a ***voluntary recognition***, is well established, provided that the employer has no reasonable doubt of the employees' preference and that recognition is not granted for the purpose of assisting one particular union at the expense of another seeking to represent the same employees.

Voluntary Recognition
An employer agreeing to recognize a union with majority support as the exclusive bargaining agent for the workers in the bargaining unit, without holding a certification election.

Bargaining status achieved through a voluntary recognition imposes on the employer the duty to bargain with the union in good faith, just the same as with a union victory in a representation election conducted by the Board. But the representation election method has several advantages over the voluntary recognition method. The representation election procedures involve the determination of the bargaining unit—that is, which of the employer's workers should be grouped together for purposes of representation and bargaining. Following a union victory in an election, the employer is obligated to recognize and bargain with the union for at least twelve months following the election. No petitions seeking a new representation (or decertification) election can be filed for that unit of employees during the twelve-month period. For a voluntary recognition, the employer is obligated to recognize and bargain with the union only for a "reasonable length" of time, unless a collective bargaining agreement is agreed upon. In the absence of an agreement, the voluntary recognition does not prevent the filing of a petition seeking a representation election for that same group of employees. In addition, an employer who voluntarily recognizes a union claiming to have majority support commits an unfair labor practice if the union does not actually have the support of a majority of the employees in the bargaining unit. Thus, a representation election conducted by the Board is the method of recognition preferred by the parties in most cases.

Just as filing a charge initiates the administrative process in an unfair labor practice (C) case, so too a petition from an interested party is needed to initiate a Board-sponsored election under Section 9(c)(1)(A). Any employee, group of employees, or labor organization can file such a petition seeking a representation election or a decertification election on behalf of the employees as a whole (see Figure 13.1). An employer is entitled to file a petition only after one or more individuals or unions present that employer with a claim for recognition as the bargaining representative according to Section 9(c)(1)(B).

If it is a union or employees who file a petition with the appropriate regional office of the Board, the NLRB will not proceed with the election until the petitioning union or employee group presents evidence that at least 30 percent of the employee group support the election request. (If an employer files the petition under the circumstances outlined above, this rule does not apply.) Usually, this showing of support is reflected in signed and dated ***authorization cards*** obtained by the union from the individual employees. These cards may simply state that the signatories desire an election to be held, or they may state that the signing employee authorizes the union to be his or her bargaining representative (see Figure 13.2). Other acceptable showings of employee interest can include a letter or similar informal document bearing a list of signatures and applications for union membership.

Authorization Cards
Cards signed by employees indicating that they authorize the union to act as the employees' bargaining agent and to seek an election on behalf of the employees.

FORM NLRB-502 (3-96)

UNITED STATES GOVERNMENT
NATIONAL LABOR RELATIONS BOARD
PETITION

FORM EXEMPT UNDER 44 U.S.C. 3512

DO NOT WRITE IN THIS SPACE	
Case No.	Date Filed

INSTRUCTIONS: Submit an original and 4 copies of this Petition to the NLRB Regional Office in the Region in which the employer concerned is located. If more space is required for any one item, attach additional sheets, numbering item accordingly.

The Petitioner alleges that the following circumstances exist and requests that the National Labor Relations Board proceed under its proper authority pursuant to Section 9 of the National Labor Relations Act.

1. **PURPOSE OF THIS PETITION** *(If box RC, RM, or RD is checked and a charge under Section 8(b)(7) of the Act has been filed involving the Employer named herein, the statement following the description of the type of petition shall not be deemed made.)* **(Check One)**

☐ **RC-CERTIFICATION OF REPRESENTATIVE** - A substantial number of employees wish to be represented for purposes of collective bargaining by Petitioner and Petitioner desires to be certified as representative of the employees.

☐ **RM-REPRESENTATION (EMPLOYER PETITION)** - One or more individuals or labor organizations have presented a claim to Petitioner to be recognized as the representative of employees of Petitioner.

☐ **RD-DECERTIFICATION (REMOVAL OF REPRESENTATIVE)** - A substantial number of employees assert that the certified or currently recognized bargaining representative is no longer their representative.

☐ **UD-WITHDRAWAL OF UNION SHOP AUTHORITY (REMOVAL OF OBLIGATION TO PAY DUES)** - Thirty percent (30%) or more of employees in a bargaining unit covered by an agreement between their employer and a labor organization desire that such authority be rescinded.

☐ **UC-UNIT CLARIFICATION** - A labor organization is currently recognized by Employer, but Petitioner seeks clarification of placement of certain employees: *(Check one)* ☐ In unit not previously certified. ☐ In unit previously certified in Case No. ______

☐ **AC-AMENDMENT OF CERTIFICATION** - Petitioner seeks amendment of certification issued in Case No. ______
Attach statement describing the specific amendment sought.

2. Name of Employer	Employer Representative to contact	Telephone Number
3. Address(es) of Establishment(s) involved *(Street and number, city, State, ZIP code)*		Telecopier Number (Fax)
4a. Type of Establishment *(Factory, mine, wholesaler, etc.)*	4b. Identify principal product or service	

5. Unit involved *(In UC petition, describe* **present** *bargaining unit and attached description of proposed clarification.)*	6a. Number of Employees in Unit:
Included	Present
	Proposed *(By UC/AC)*
Excluded	6b. Is this petition supported by 30% or more of the employees in the unit?* ☐ Yes ☐ No *Not applicable in RM, UC, and AC
(If you have checked box RC in 1 above, check and complete EITHER item 7a or 7b, whichever is applicable.)	

7a. ☐ Request for recognition as Bargaining Representative was made on *(Date)* ______ and Employer declined recognition on or about *(Date)* ______ *(If no reply received, so state.)*

7b. ☐ Petitioner is currently recognized as Bargaining Representative and desires certification under the Act.

8. Name of Recognized or Certified Bargaining Agent *(If none, so state.)*	Affiliation
Address, Telephone No. and Telecopier No. (Fax)	Date of Recognition or Certification
9. Expiration Date of Current Contract. If any *(Month, Day, Year)*	10. If you have checked box UD in 1 above, show here the date of execution of agreement granting union shop *(Month, Day, and Year)*
11a. Is there now a strike or picketing at the Employer's establishment(s) involved? Yes ______ No ______	11b. If so, approximately how many employees are participating?

11c. The Employer has been picketed by or on behalf of *(Insert Name)* ______, a labor organization, of *(Insert Address)* ______ Since *(Month, Day, Year)* ______

12. Organizations or individuals other than Petitioner *(and other than those named in items 8 and 11c)*, which have claimed recognition as representatives and other organizations and individuals known to have a representative interest in any employees in unit described in item 5 above. *(If none, so state.)*

Name	Affiliation	Address	Date of Claim
			Telecopier No. (Fax)

13. Full name of party filing petition (If labor organization, give full name, including local name and number)

14a. Address *(street and number, city, state, and ZIP code)*	14b. Telephone No.
	14c. Telecopier No. (Fax)

15. Full name of national or international labor organization of which it is an affiliate or constituent unit *(to be filled in when petition is filed by a labor organization)*

I declare that I have read the above petition and that the statements are true to the best of my knowledge and belief.

Name *(Print)*	Signature	Title *(if any)*
Address *(street and number, city, state, and ZIP code)*		Telephone No.
		Telecopier No. (Fax)

WILLFUL FALSE STATEMENTS ON THIS PETITION CAN BE PUNISHED BY FINE AND IMPRISONMENT (U.S. CODE, TITLE 18, SECTION 1001)

FIGURE 13.1 Petition to Initiate NLRB Election
Source: NLRB web site at http://www.nlrb.gov/nlrb/shared_files/forms/nlrbform502.pdf.

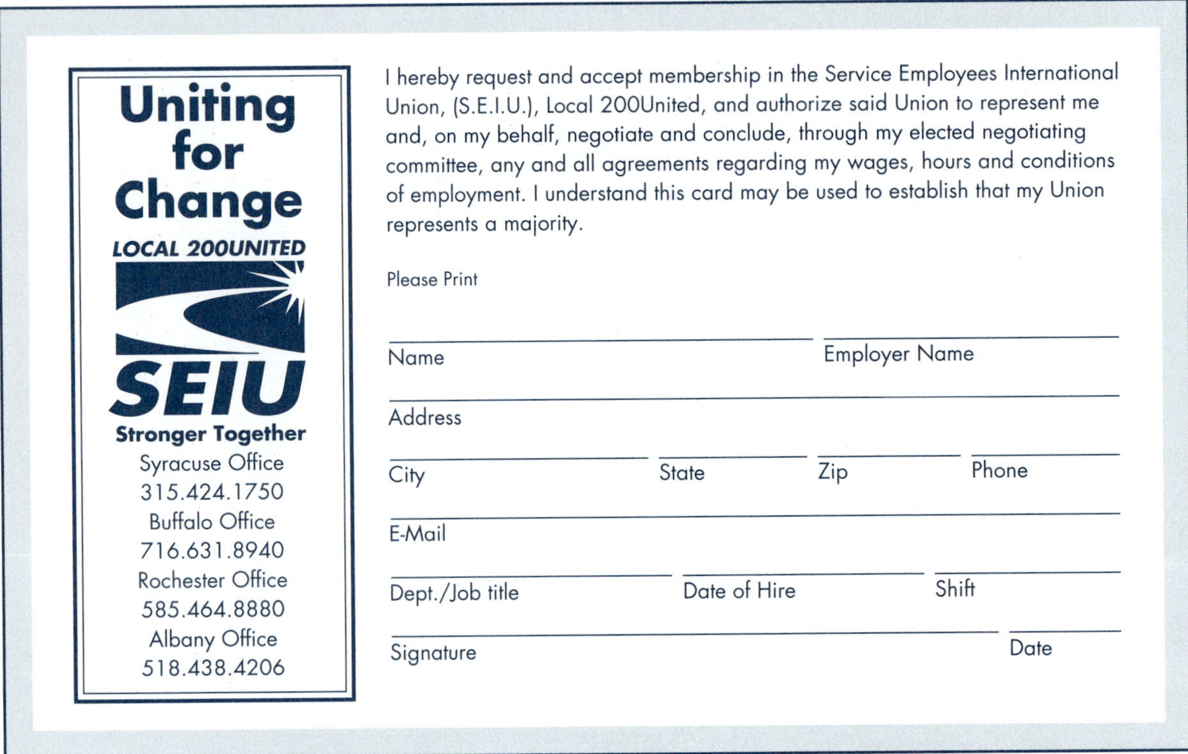
Uniting for Change
LOCAL 200UNITED
SEIU
Stronger Together
Syracuse Office
315.424.1750
Buffalo Office
716.631.8940
Rochester Office
585.464.8880
Albany Office
518.438.4206

I hereby request and accept membership in the Service Employees International Union, (S.E.I.U.), Local 200United, and authorize said Union to represent me and, on my behalf, negotiate and conclude, through my elected negotiating committee, any and all agreements regarding my wages, hours and conditions of employment. I understand this card may be used to establish that my Union represents a majority.

Please Print

Name ______ Employer Name ______

Address ______

City ______ State ______ Zip ______ Phone ______

E-Mail ______

Dept./Job title ______ Date of Hire ______ Shift ______

Signature ______ Date ______

FIGURE 13.2 Union Authorization Card

Forty-Eight-Hour Rule
NLRB requirement that a party filing a petition for a representation election must provide evidence to support the petition within 48 hours of the filing.

Under the Board's ***forty-eight-hour rule***, an employer who files a petition must submit to the regional office proof of a union's recognition demand within two days of filing the petition. Likewise, a petitioning union or employee group has forty-eight hours after filing in which to proffer authorization cards or other proof of 30 percent employee support for the requested election. Upon the docketing (logging in) of a petition, a written notification of its filing is sent by the regional director to the employer and any labor organizations claiming to represent any employees in the proposed unit or known to have an interest in the case's disposition. Employers are asked to submit the following:

- A payroll list covering the proposed bargaining unit
- Data showing the nature and volume of the company's business for jurisdictional purposes
- A statement of company position on the appropriateness of the requested bargaining unit

The new R case is then assigned to a Board agent, who investigates to determine whether the following conditions exist:

- The employer's operations affect commerce within the act's meaning.
- A question about representation really exists (that is, no union presently represents the employees and is shielded by the election bar rule, or some similar impediment to the election).

- The proposed bargaining unit is appropriate.
- The petitioning union, if any, has garnered a 30 percent showing of interest among the employees.

If the agent finds some impediment to an election, the regional director can dismiss the petition. The decision to dismiss can be appealed to the Board in Washington, D.C. Conversely, the petitioning party may choose to withdraw the petition. The usual penalty for withdrawal is imposition of a six-month waiting period before the same party can petition again. (If the employer has submitted the petition, the named union may disclaim interest, also leading to dismissal.)

If the petition survives this initial investigation, the parties may still require the resolution of issues raised by the petition. Questions such as the definition of the bargaining unit, the eligibility of certain employees to participate in the election, and the number of polling places need to be settled prior to holding the election. The parties may agree to waive their rights to a hearing on these issues and proceed to a ***consent election***. In so doing, they may either agree that all rulings of the regional director on these questions are final and binding, or they may reserve the right to appeal the regional director's decisions to the Board.

Consent Election
Election conducted by the regional office giving the regional director final authority over any disputes.

If the parties fail to agree on some of these issues and have not agreed to a consent election, then a representation hearing will be held before a presiding officer, who may be a Board attorney, field examiner, or ALJ. The act does not prescribe rules of evidence to be used in this proceeding (in contrast to the C case hearing); indeed, the Board's rules and regulations state that federal court rules of evidence shall not be controlling.

A second union, with a 10 percent showing of interest from among the employees, is entitled to intervene and participate in the hearing. Such an intervention can also block a consent election and compel a hearing to take place.

Shortly after the hearing, the hearing officer will submit a report to the director, who will then render a decision either to hold an election or to dismiss the petition. This decision can be appealed by a party to the Board in Washington only on the following grounds:

- A Board legal precedent was not followed or should be reconsidered.
- A substantial factual issue is clearly erroneous in the record.
- The conduct of the hearing was prejudicial to the appealing party.

The Board will act expeditiously on the appeal. Meanwhile, the regional director will proceed with plans for the election, which usually occurs twenty-five to thirty days after it has been ordered.

Rules that Bar Holding an Election

The philosophy of the NLRB and the courts is that a Board-sponsored election is a serious step, which the affected employees should not be permitted to disavow or overrule frivolously or hastily. Furthermore, the newly certified bargaining agent should be given a reasonable opportunity to fulfill its mandate by successfully negotiating a collective bargaining agreement with the company. If the Board failed to protect the successfully elected bargaining representative from worker fickleness or rival union challenges, the employer would be encouraged to avoid timely and sincere bargaining in an effort to erode the union's support before an agreement is reached. The Board has, therefore, fashioned several election bar rules.

Contract Bar Rule
A written labor contract bars an election during the life of the bargaining agreement, subject to the "open-season" exception.

Under the ***contract bar rule***, a written labor contract—signed and binding on the parties and dealing with substantial terms and conditions of employment—bars an election among the affected bargaining unit during the life of that bargaining agreement. This rule has two exceptions. First, the Board provides a window, or "open season," during which a rival union can offer its challenge by filing an election petition. This window is open between the ninetieth day and sixtieth day prior to the expiration of the current collective bargaining agreement. The rationale here is that a rival union should not be completely prevented from filing an election petition. Otherwise, the employer and incumbent union could continually bargain new contracts regardless of whether the employees wished to continue to be represented by the incumbent union.

If no new petition is filed during the open-season period, then the last sixty days of the contract provide a period during which the parties can negotiate a new agreement insulated from any outside challenges. If a petition is filed during this insulated period, it will be dismissed as untimely. In the event that the employer and the incumbent union fail to reach a new agreement and the old agreement expires, then petitions may be filed anytime after the expiration of the existing agreement.

The second exception to the contract bar rule is that a contract for longer than three years will operate only as a bar to an election for three years. In *American Seating Co.*,[1] the Board held that an agreement of excessive duration cannot be used to preclude challenges to the incumbent union indefinitely. Therefore, any contract longer than three years duration will be treated as if it were three years long for the purposes of filing petitions; that is, the open-season period would occur between the ninetieth and the sixtieth day prior to the end of the third year of the agreement.

Section 9(C)(3) of the NLRA provides that when a valid election has been held in a bargaining unit, no new election can be held for a twelve-month period for that unit or any subdivision of the unit. When the employees of a unit have voted not to be represented by a union, no other union may file for an election for those employees for twelve months. By the same token, when a union has been certified as the winner of the election, it is free from challenge to its status for at least twelve months. This twelve-month period usually runs from the date of certification, but when an employer refuses to bargain with the certified union, the Board may extend the period to twelve months from when good-faith bargaining actually commences. The twelve-month period under Section 9(C)(3) applies only when an election has been held.

The NLRB recently adopted a new rule regarding situations where the employer has voluntarily recognized a union, that is, where no recognition election has been held. In *Dana Corp.*,[2] the Board held that employees and rival unions have forty-five days to challenge the voluntary recognition of a union. Following a voluntary recognition, the employer and the union involved must notify the Board in writing of the voluntary recognition; the employer must then post in the workplace an official NLRB notice of the voluntary recognition. That notice indicates that the employees may file a decertification petition or a rival union may file a petition seeking an election within forty-five days from the posting of the notice. A petition may be filed during the forty-five day "window" period notwithstanding the fact that the

---

[1]106 NLRB 250 (1953).

[2]351 NLRB No. 28 (2007).

employer and union had executed a collective bargaining unit. If no petition has been filed during the forty-five day "window" period, then the NLRB will apply a nonrebuttable presumption that the union has majority support and that presumption will continue for a reasonable period of time. In addition, any collective bargaining agreement entered into after the date of the voluntary recognition will only operate to bar a petition for a representation or decertification election after the forty-five day period to challenge the voluntary recognition has expired and no such petition has been filed.

Concept *Summary* » 13.1

Restrictions on Holding Representation Elections

- A valid election was held within the last twelve months
- A written labor contract covering the terms and conditions of employment exists
  - However, a petition may be filed between the ninetieth and the sixtieth day prior to the expiration of the contract
  - For a contract longer than three years, a petition may be filed between the ninetieth and the sixtieth day prior to the expiration of the third year of the contract
- When the employer has voluntarily recognized a union, and no challenge to union's status has been filed during the forty-five-day notice period, the NLRB will not accept a petition for an election for a "reasonable period" of time

Defining the Appropriate Bargaining Unit

Bargaining Unit
Group of employees being represented by a union.

The ***bargaining unit*** is a concept central to labor relations under both the Railway Labor Act and the NLRA. The bargaining unit is the basic constituency of the labor union; it is the group of employees for which the union seeks to acquire recognition as bargaining agent and to negotiate regarding employment conditions. In order for collective bargaining to produce results fair to both sides, it is essential that the bargaining unit be defined appropriately. The bargaining unit should encompass all employees who share a community of interests regarding working conditions. It should not be so broad as to include divergent or antagonistic interests. Nor should it submerge the interests of a small yet well-defined group of employees within the larger unit.

Section 9(b) of the NLRA provides that the definition of an appropriate bargaining unit is a matter left to the Board's discretion. What constitutes an appropriate bargaining unit is the most commonly disputed issue in representative case hearings. It is also one of the most complex and difficult questions for the Board and the courts to resolve. The Supreme Court in *Packard Motor Car v. NLRB*[3] observed that "The issue as to what unit is appropriate is one for which no absolute rule of law is laid down by statute.... The decision of the Board, if not final, is rarely to be disturbed." This statement is a bit misleading because Section 9(b) of the NLRA does set out some guidelines for the Board in determining the appropriate unit. Section 9(b) states that the goal in defining a bargaining unit is to "assure the employees the fullest freedom

[3]330 U.S. 485 (1947).

in exercising the rights guaranteed by this Act." Section 9(b) also contains the following five provisions:

- The options open to the Board in determining a bargaining unit include an employerwide unit, a craft unit, a single-plant unit, or a subdivision thereof.
- The unit cannot contain both professional employees [as defined by Section 2(12) of the act] and nonprofessional employees, unless a majority of the professional employees have voted to be included in the unit.
- A craft unit cannot be found to be inappropriate simply on the ground that a different unit (e.g., a plantwide unit) was established by a previous Board determination, unless a majority of the employees in the proposed craft unit vote against representation in such a separate craft unit.
- A unit including nonguard or nonsecurity employees cannot include plant guards or security personnel; conversely, a union representing plant guards cannot be certified if it also includes workers other than guards as members or if it is directly or indirectly affiliated with a union representing persons other than guards.[4]
- The extent to which employees have already been organized at the time of the filing of the election petition is not to be controlling of the Board's definition of the appropriate bargaining unit.

In addition to the statutory commands, the Board has fashioned a number of other factors to be considered in determining the appropriate unit. Those factors include the following:

- the community of interest of included employees concerning wages, hours, working conditions, the nature of duties performed, and the skills, training, or qualifications required;
- geographical and physical proximity of included workers;
- any history of prior collective bargaining tending to prove that a workable relationship exists or can exist between the employer and the proposed unit;
- similarity of the unit to the employer's administrative or territorial divisions, the functional integration of the company's operations, and the frequency of employee interchange and;
- the desires of the employees concerning the bargaining unit, such as might be determined through a secret ballot among workers who have the statutory prerogative of choosing between a plantwide unit or a separate craft unit. (This right to self-determination by election is referred to as the *Globe* doctrine, after the case in which the standards for such elections were set out, *Globe Machine and Stamping*,[5] pursuant to Section 9(b)(2) of the act.)

Where a company employs temporary workers supplied by a personnel staffing agency in addition to its own employees, the NLRB will only include the temporary workers in a

---

[4]By requiring that guards and security personnel be organized in a separate bargaining unit and separate unions, Congress appears to hold the view that the normal duties of plant guards can create conflicts of interest with their union loyalties. Section 9(b) prohibits the NLRB from certifying a "mixed" bargaining unit—one containing guards and nonguards—but it does not preclude voluntary recognition of a union representing a mixed unit, *General Service Employees Union, Local No. 73 v. NLRB*, 230 F.3d 909 (7th Cir. 2000).

[5]3 NLRB 294 (1937).

bargaining unit with the firm's employees if both the employer and the staffing agency agree to the multiemployer bargaining unit, according to *Oakwood Care Center*.[6]

The following case illustrates the NLRB's application of the "community of interest" test, where the union seeks to represent maintenance workers while the employer argues that the bargaining unit should include both maintenance and production workers.

case 13.1 »

BUCKHORN, INC. AND INTERNATIONAL UNION OF INDUSTRIAL AND INDEPENDENT WORKERS

343 NLRB 201 (Sept. 30, 2004)

Decision On Review and Order by Chairman Battista and Members Schaumber and Meisburg

On December 4, 2003, the Acting Regional Director for Region 25 issued a Decision and Direction of Election in the above-entitled proceeding in which he found appropriate the petitioned-for unit of all maintenance employees employed by the Employer at its Bluffton, Indiana facility. Thereafter … the Employer filed a timely request for review of the Acting Regional Director's decision. The Employer contends that a separate maintenance unit is not an appropriate unit for bargaining and that the only appropriate unit must include production employees as well as maintenance employees.

On January 14, 2004, the Board granted the Employer's request for review….

Facts

The Employer manufactures plastic containers. All aspects of the production process are located within the same facility in Bluffton, Indiana. Manufacturing a container involves conveying plastic pellets from storage silos through an automated system that liquefies the pellets and then delivers the liquid plastic to one of nine presses. The liquefied plastic is poured through nozzles into an individual mold in the shape of a specific product that is installed in the press. After the product is molded, it is removed from the press and readied for shipment to the customer. The nine presses run automatically the majority of the time without the assistance of an employee. When the presses are run on a semi-automatic basis, an employee operates the controls to start the production cycle. The presses have a computerized robot affixed to them that assists in removing the molded product from the press and in placing the product on a conveyer belt, attached to the press, that takes the product to the shipping area. Molds are changed at the conclusion of a product run. Employees remove the existing mold and nozzles and install a new mold and new nozzles for the next product run. The removed mold and nozzles are cleaned, repaired if necessary, and stored…. The Employer operates around the clock, 7 days a week, with the majority of employees assigned to one of four rotating 12-hour shifts. A number of employees work an 8-hour shift, Monday through Friday.

There are approximately 100 hourly paid employees who work at the Bluffton facility, 19 of whom are the maintenance employees the Petitioner [the union] seeks to represent. The remaining employees are production and shipping/receiving/ warehouse employees…. The plant manager has overall responsibility for the operation of the plant. A production manager, who reports directly to the plant manager, is responsible for production operations. Reporting to the production manager are four production supervisors, each of whom is assigned to one of the four 12-hour shifts. The maintenance supervisor and the project engineer also report to the production manager.

The maintenance employees the [union] seeks to represent occupy one of five job classifications: skilled maintenance, set-up maintenance, tooling associate, tooling technician, and nozzle prep/build associate. The skilled maintenance employees are primarily responsible for the maintenance and upkeep/repair of the presses, as well as for programming the computerized robots. They spend approximately 90 percent of their time on the production floor working on the presses. Additionally, skilled maintenance employees are responsible for the upkeep of the production facility and the automated system that moves the plastic pellets from the storage silos to the presses. They may also help with mold changes. The skilled maintenance employees, currently five in number,

[6] 343 NLRB 659 (2004).

report directly to the maintenance supervisor. There is one skilled maintenance employee assigned to each of the four rotating shifts; the fifth skilled maintenance employee works the Monday through Friday schedule.

The remaining maintenance employees, in the job categories of set-up maintenance, tooling associate, tooling technician, and nozzle prep associate, spend the majority of their time performing a variety of functions related to changing molds on the presses. They remove, clean, lubricate, and repair the molds and nozzles which have been removed from the presses, and they install the new mold and nozzles required to produce a new product. These duties involve hydraulic and electrical work. Unlike the skilled maintenance employees, however, these maintenance employees, currently 14 in number, do not report to the maintenance supervisor. Rather, they report directly to the production supervisor responsible for the shift on which they work. Set-up maintenance employees and tooling associates work one of the rotating shifts, while the tooling technicians and the nozzle prep associates work the Monday through Friday schedule.

Production employees include production associates, team leaders, auditors, utility associates, and shipping/warehouse employees.... The production supervisor on each shift supervises the production associates, team leaders, and utility associates, as well as the 14 maintenance employees. Auditors and shipping/repair/warehouse associates have separate supervision.

Nine production employees designated as "helpers" work with the set-up maintenance employees and the tooling associates in the mold change process. These "helpers" regularly perform tasks performed by these maintenance employees, such as removing and installing nozzles, extension blocks, thermocouple wires and hydraulic hoses, as well as operating the crane to remove a mold from the press. Employees in all job classifications have frequent contact and interaction during the day, especially production employees and the skilled maintenance and set-up maintenance employees, who spend almost all their time on the production floor working on the presses doing repairs or production work. Thirteen of the current nineteen maintenance employees were originally hired as production associates, while four current production employees previously held maintenance positions.

The majority of production employees and maintenance employees work similar shifts....

Analysis

It is the Board's longstanding policy, as set forth in American Cyanamid Co. [131 NLRB 909 (1961)] to find petitioned-for separate maintenance department units appropriate where the facts of the case demonstrate the absence of a more comprehensive bargaining history and the petitioned-for maintenance employees have a community of interest separate and distinct from other employees. In determining whether a sufficient community of interest exists, the Board examines such factors as mutuality of interests in wages, hours, and other working conditions; commonality of supervision; degree of skill and common functions; frequency of contact and interchange with other employees; and functional integration. "While many factors may be common to most situations ... the effect of any one factor, and therefore the weight to be given it in making the unit determination, will vary from industry to industry and from plant to plant." [*American Cyanamid Co.*, 131 NLRB at 911]

In this case, the [union] contends that the maintenance employees constitute a distinct and homogeneous unit with interests different from those of the production employees. The [union] argues that maintenance employees are in a separate administrative department, are required to have, and do have, skills different from those of production employees, and receive higher wages. The [union] further asserts that there is little job interchange between maintenance and production employees, that maintenance employees are required to take their annual vacation during the summer plant shutdown, unlike other employees, and that they receive training from the Employer that other classifications of employees do not receive.

The Employer contends that a separate unit of maintenance employees is not appropriate, and that an all-inclusive unit of maintenance and production employees is appropriate. The Employer relies on the high degree of functional integration of its operations where, in the Employer's words, "employees work side by side and have daily interaction with each other." The Employer also states that there is a high degree of overlap in job functions. The Employer contends that production employees and maintenance employees throughout its facility share a community of interest based on their common supervision, comparable skills and job functions, frequent interchange, virtually identical terms and conditions of employment, and similar work schedules.

We agree with the Employer that the petitioned-for unit is not an appropriate unit for collective bargaining purposes. Contrary to the Acting Regional Director, we do not find that the petitioned-for maintenance employees constitute a distinct, homogeneous group of employees that would warrant granting the Petitioner's request for a separate unit.

We reach this conclusion based on a number of factors. First, the Employer's operations are highly integrated and there is a significant degree of contact and interaction among the maintenance employees and the production employees. For example, the skilled maintenance and set-up maintenance employees spend virtually all their working time on the production floor, working with production employees on the presses to produce a finished product, and to change the molds on the presses when required. Production employees seek out the assistance of maintenance employees when a mechanical problem arises and routinely perform the same duties as maintenance employees, especially during the mold change process.

Second, there is not a wide disparity in skill level between the maintenance employees and the production employees, except for the five skilled maintenance employees. Although the skilled maintenance position is the highest skilled position in the plant, there are no educational or certification requirements for the job. Further, maintenance employees regularly perform production work. In fact, set-up maintenance employees, who comprise one-half of the maintenance employees, work with and perform the same work as production employees during the mold change process. Both groups of employees regularly assist employees in the shipping/ receiving/warehouse area and employees from both groups routinely relieve each other during breaks and can fill in for one another on certain steps in the manufacturing process. Additionally, the production employees designated as "helpers" routinely do the same work as the set-up maintenance employees and tooling associates during the mold change process.

Third, there is evidence of permanent transfers between the two groups of employees. Two-thirds of the current maintenance employees were hired from the ranks of production employees, and four production employees were previously maintenance employees.

A fourth factor weighing against the appropriateness of a separate maintenance unit is that the 19 maintenance employees do not share common supervision: only the 5 skilled maintenance employees are supervised by the maintenance supervisor. Significantly, the maintenance supervisor is not available during all shifts when skilled maintenance employees work; he works Monday through Friday from 7 a.m. to 4 p.m. In his absence, the skilled maintenance employees receive their assignments from the shift production supervisor who has the authority to supersede directions left by the maintenance supervisor. The other classifications of maintenance employees are supervised by the shift production supervisor who also supervises production employees. The production supervisors function as the sole immediate supervisors of 14 of 19 maintenance employees, as well as approximately 70 production employees. While nominally within the maintenance department, 14 maintenance employees are supervised by production supervisors who have authority to hire and discipline them and direct their work.

Finally, in all significant respects, all maintenance employees and production employees share identical terms and conditions of employment, including work rules and policies, work schedules and vacations, lunch facilities, and fringe benefits. Although certain maintenance employees are paid at a higher level than production employees, largely because of their skill level, there is some overlap in wages, just as there is overlap among employees in the exercise of their job skills. While these two factors might appear to favor separate units, we find that the modest discrepancy in wage rates and skill levels is relatively insignificant and is outweighed by all the other factors that clearly demonstrate the broad community of interest that the maintenance employees share with production employees.

Order

Accordingly, we conclude that the petitioned-for unit limited solely to maintenance employees is not an appropriate unit for the purposes of collective bargaining.... We reverse the Acting Regional Director's finding and remand the case to the Regional Director for further appropriate action.

The Acting Regional Director's Decision and Direction of Election is reversed. This proceeding is remanded to the Regional Director for further appropriate action consistent with this Decision on Review and Order.

Case Questions

1. What are the factors that the NLRB considers in determining whether maintenance department employees should be in a bargaining unit separate from production employees? Why would the union seek a unit covering only the maintenance department employees? Why would the employer want a bargaining unit covering both maintenance and production employees?
2. Do the maintenance workers interact with the production employees? Are the maintenance employees subject to separate supervision and separate working conditions? Explain.
3. Did the NLRB decide that a separate unit or an integrated unit is the appropriate bargaining unit in this case? Which factors did the NLRB here consider decisive in making its decision?

Craft Unit Severance

One of the most complex issues in bargaining unit determination involves the questions of craft unit severance: When is it appropriate to certify a craft bargaining unit representing employees who were previously included in a larger bargaining unit? The NLRB decision *Mallinckrodt Chemical Works*[7] is the leading pronouncement on the matter. In that case, the NLRB indicated that it will look to the following factors:

- if the proposed craft unit consists of skilled crafts workers performing functions on a nonrepetitive basis, or if it is a functionally distinct department;
- the history of collective bargaining of the employees involved and other plants of the employer;
- the extent to which the employees in the proposed unit have established and maintained their separate identity during inclusion in the larger unit;
- the history and pattern of collective bargaining in the industry involved;
- the degree of integration of the employer's production processes;
- the qualifications of the union seeking to represent the separate craft unit; and
- the union's experience in representing employees like those in the proposed craft unit.

Bargaining Unit Definition in the Health-Care Industry

The 1974 amendments to the NLRA extended NLRB jurisdiction over nonprofit health-care institutions. The congressional committee reports accompanying the amending legislation stated that "Due consideration should be given by the Board to preventing proliferation of bargaining units in the health care industry." The Board issued its final rule for such determinations in 1989.[8] The rule states that the Board will recognize the following eight bargaining units for acute-care hospitals:

- Physicians
- Registered nurses
- Other professional employees
- Medical technicians
- Skilled maintenance workers
- Clerical workers
- Guards
- Other nonprofessional employees

No unit with fewer than six employees will be certified (except for guard units).

In *American Hospital Association v. NLRB*,[9] the U.S. Supreme Court upheld the NLRB's health-care industry bargaining unit rules and the power of the NLRB to establish bargaining units through its rule-making authority. In certain circumstances, such as where other bargaining units already exist at the health-care facility, or where there are fewer than six employees in any of the specific categories, the NLRB will apply the traditional "community of interest" test bargaining units, according to *Kaiser Foundation Hospitals*.[10]

---

[7]162 NLRB 387 (1966).

[8]The final rule was printed in 54 Federal Register 16336 (April 21, 1989).

[9]499 U.S. 606 (1991).

[10]312 NLRB 933 (1993).

Concept *Summary* » 13.2

BARGAINING UNIT ISSUES

Bargaining unit choices:

- Single employer or multiemployer unit
- Single plant or employerwide unit
- Industrial or craft unit

Restrictions on bargaining unit definition:

- Guards must be in a separate unit
- Professional employees can only be included in a unit with nonprofessionals if a majority of the professionals vote for inclusion

Voter Eligibility

Along with determining the appropriate bargaining unit, the question of which employees are actually eligible to vote in the election must be resolved. Factors to be considered are whether an employee is within the bargaining unit and whether striking employees are able to vote.

In general, when the election has been directed (or agreed to, for consent elections), the Board establishes an eligibility date—that is, the date by which an employee must be on the employer's payroll in order to be eligible to vote. The eligibility date is usually the end of the payroll period immediately preceding the direction of (or agreement to hold) the election. Employees must be on the payroll as of the eligibility date, and they must also continue to be on the payroll on the date the election is held. Employees hired after the eligibility date but before the election date are not eligible to vote.

Employees may be on strike when an election is held. This is most often the case in decertification elections, when the employees not striking seek to get rid of the union. Section 2(3) of the NLRA defines *employee* to include "any individual whose work has ceased as a consequence of … any current labor dispute … and who has not obtained any other regular and substantially equivalent employment." The Board has adopted several rules clarifying the voting rights of striking employees.

Unfair Labor Practice Strike
A strike to protest employer unfair practices.

Economic Strike
A strike over economic issues such as a new contract or a grievance.

The Board distinguishes whether the employees are on an unfair labor practice strike or an economic strike. An ***unfair labor practice strike*** is a strike by employees in protest of, or precipitated by, employer unfair labor practices. The Board holds that unfair labor practice strikers cannot be permanently replaced by the employer. Unfair labor practice strikers are eligible to vote in any election held during the strike.

Economic strikes are strikes over economic issues, such as grievances or a new contract. Unlike unfair labor practice strikers, economic strikers may be permanently replaced by the employer. Economic strikers who have not been permanently replaced may vote in any election during the strike, but economic strikers who have been permanently replaced may vote only in elections held within twelve months after the strike begins. After twelve months, they lose their eligibility to vote. The employees hired to replace economic strikers may vote if they are permanent replacements—that is, if the employer intends to retain them after the strike is over. Replacements hired on a temporary basis, who will not be retained after the strike ends, are not eligible to vote. As a result of these rules, during the first twelve months of a strike, permanent replacements and all economic strikers may vote. After twelve months, only the permanent replacements and those economic strikers who have not been permanently replaced may vote.

Economic strikers or unfair labor practice strikers who obtain permanent employment elsewhere and who abandon their prior jobs lose their eligibility to vote. Although the Board generally presumes that other employment by strikers during a strike is temporary, they will hold that a striker has lost eligibility to vote if it can be shown that he or she does not intend to return to the prior job. Also, strikers fired for wrongdoing during the strike are not eligible to vote.

According to *O. E. Butterfield, Inc.*,[11] when the eligibility of employees to vote is challenged, the NLRB holds that, in the case of both unfair labor practice strikes and economic strikes, the employer has the burden of proving that replacements hired during the strike are permanent employees in order for the replacements to be qualified to vote in a representation election. Although the Board prefers that challenges to voter eligibility be resolved at a hearing prior to the election, such challenges may also be raised at the time the challenged employee votes. When an employee's right to vote is challenged, the ballot at issue is placed in a sealed envelope rather than in the ballot box. After all employees have voted, the Board first counts the unchallenged ballots. If the results of the election will not be changed by the challenged ballots—because there are not enough of them to change the outcome—the Board will not rule on the challenges. However, if the challenged ballots could affect the election results, the Board will hold a hearing to resolve the challenges, count those ballots from the eligible voters, and then certify the election results.

Representation Elections

Excelsior List
A list of the names and addresses of the employees eligible to vote in a representation election.

Within seven days after the regional director approves a consent election or directs that an election be held, the employer must file an election eligibility list with the regional office. This list, called an ***Excelsior list*** after the decision in which the Board set out this requirement, *Excelsior Underwear, Inc.*,[12] contains the names and home addresses of all employees eligible to vote so that the union can contact them outside their work environment, beyond the boss's observation and control. A Board agent will then arrange a conference with all parties to settle the details of the election. According to *North Macon Health Care Facility*,[13] the NLRB will set aside elections won by the employer where the employer has failed to provide the union with an Excelsior list containing the full first and last names of all employees in the bargaining unit.

[11] 319 NLRB 1004 (1995).

[12] 156 NLRB No. 111 (1966).

[13] 322 NLRB No. 82 (1996).

The election is generally held on company premises; however, if the union objects, it can be held elsewhere. In *San Diego Gas & Electric*,[14] the NLRB held that the regional director may authorize the use of mail-in ballots in cases where:

- the eligible employees are scattered over a wide geographic area because of their job duties;
- the eligible employees are scattered because of their work schedules; or
- there is a strike, lockout, or picketing in progress at the employer's location.

Laboratory Conditions
The conditions under which a representative election is held; the NLRB tries to ensure that neither the employer nor the union unduly affects the employees' free choice.

The NLRB agent supervises the conduct of the election, and all parties are entitled to have observers present during the voting. All parties to the election will undoubtedly have engaged in an election campaign prior to the vote. The Board regards such an election as an experiment to determine the employees' choice. The Board therefore strives for ***laboratory conditions*** in the conduct of the election and requires that neither side engage in conduct that could unduly affect the employees' free choice.

The WORKING Law

Congress Debates the Employee Free Choice Act

Organized labor is pushing Congress to enact the Employee Free Choice Act, which would make it easier for employees to organize. The House of Representatives had passed similar legislation in 2007, but the bill died in the Senate in the face of a threatened Republican filibuster and promises by President George W. Bush to veto it if it passed. Now, with the Democrats enjoying control of both the House and the Senate, and a Democratic president in the White House, the bill's prospects are greatly improved.

The bill would amend the NLRA to allow workers to form a union if a majority of the employees signed authorization cards, rather than requiring that a secret-ballot election be held by the NLRB. The bill would also increase penalties for employers that engage in unfair employment practices during union organizing campaigns, and allow for binding arbitration in first contract negotiations. Organized labor claims that the current system of holding an election allows employers to intimidate and threaten workers into voting against the union. Employer groups argued that eliminating secret-ballot elections would subject workers to pressure and bullying from union supporters to sign cards.

The passage of the bill in its present form is not certain, despite the control of Congress by the Democrats—not all of the sixty Democratic Senators have expressed support for the bill, and there has been a strong campaign against the bill by employer groups.

Sources: "The Imperfect Union Bill: Employer Intransigence Makes Finding Common Ground More Difficult," *The Washington Post*, May 11, 2009, p. A-16; "Franken Sponsors 'Card Check'," *Supermarket News*, July 13, 2009, p. 6.

---

[14]325 NLRB 1143 (1998).

Captive-Audience Speeches
Meetings or speeches held by the employer during working hours, which employees are required to attend.

The laboratory conditions can be violated by unfair practices committed by either side. Conduct that does not amount to an unfair practice may also violate the laboratory conditions if the Board believes that wrongful misconduct will unduly affect the employees' choice. ***Captive-audience speeches*** given by representatives of the employers or mass meetings by the union within twenty-four hours of an election at which the union promises to waive initiation fees for members who join before the election are examples of such conduct. Elections have been set aside where a supervisor distributed antiunion hats to the employees, as in *Barton Nelson, Inc.*;[15] where the employer offered employees who were not scheduled to work two hours' pay to come in to vote, as in *Sunrise Rehabilitation Hospital*[16] and where the union used a sound truck to broadcast prounion songs into the plant on the day of the election, as in *Bro-Tech Corp. v. NLRB.*[17] A supervisor's comment that he would "kick [the employees'] asses" if they voted for the union was grounds to set aside an election according to *Medic One, Inc.*[18] However, according to *Lockheed Martin Skunk Works*,[19] an employer's failure to prevent employees urging decertification of the union from sending e-mail messages to the employees was not a reason to set aside the election when the union also had access to the employer's e-mail system.

In *Atlantic Limousine, Inc.*,[20] the NLRB adopted a rule barring employers and unions from conducting any election raffles where eligibility to participate in the raffle is tied in any way to voting in the election or being at the election site on election day, or if the raffle is conducted at any time during a period beginning twenty-four hours before the scheduled opening of the polls and ending with the closing of the polls. Violations of the rule will result in setting aside the election upon filing an objection. The rule against raffles includes announcing a raffle, distributing raffle tickets, identifying raffle winners, and awarding raffle prizes.

Actions by third parties, other than the employer and union, may also violate the laboratory conditions. In one case, the local newspaper in a small southern town printed racially inflammatory articles about the union attempting to organize the work force of a local employer. The Board held that the injection of racial propaganda into the election violated the laboratory conditions and was reason to invalidate the election, which the union lost.

A local pastor who met with employees and discussed possible plant closure if the union won the election was acting as an agent of the employer. In *Southern Pride Catfish*,[21] his comments were held to be an unfair labor practice and were grounds to set aside the election.

The Board will not monitor the truthfulness of the election propaganda of either side. Misrepresentations in campaign promises or propaganda will not, of themselves, be grounds to set aside the election results. The NLRB will intervene, however, if either party uses a forged document that renders the voting employees unable to recognize the propaganda for what it

[15] 318 NLRB 712 (1995).

[16] 320 NLRB 212 (1995).

[17] 105 F.3d 890 (3d Cir. 1997).

[18] 331 NLRB 464 (2000).

[19] 331 NLRB 852 (2000).

[20] 331 NLRB 1025 (2000).

[21] 331 NLRB 618 (2000).

Twenty-Four-Hour Silent Period
The twenty-four-hour period prior to the representation election, during which the parties must refrain from formal campaign meetings.

is, as in *NLRB v. St. Francis Healthcare Center.*[22] The Board requires that the parties in an election refrain from formal campaigning for twenty-four hours prior to the election. This ***twenty-four-hour silent period*** is intended to give the employees time to reflect upon their choice free from electioneering pressures. Any mass union rallies or employer captive-audience speeches during the silent period will be grounds to set aside the election results, according to *Comet Electric*[23] and *Bro-Tech Corp. v. NLRB.*[24]

Figure 13.3 shows a sample ballot for a representation election.

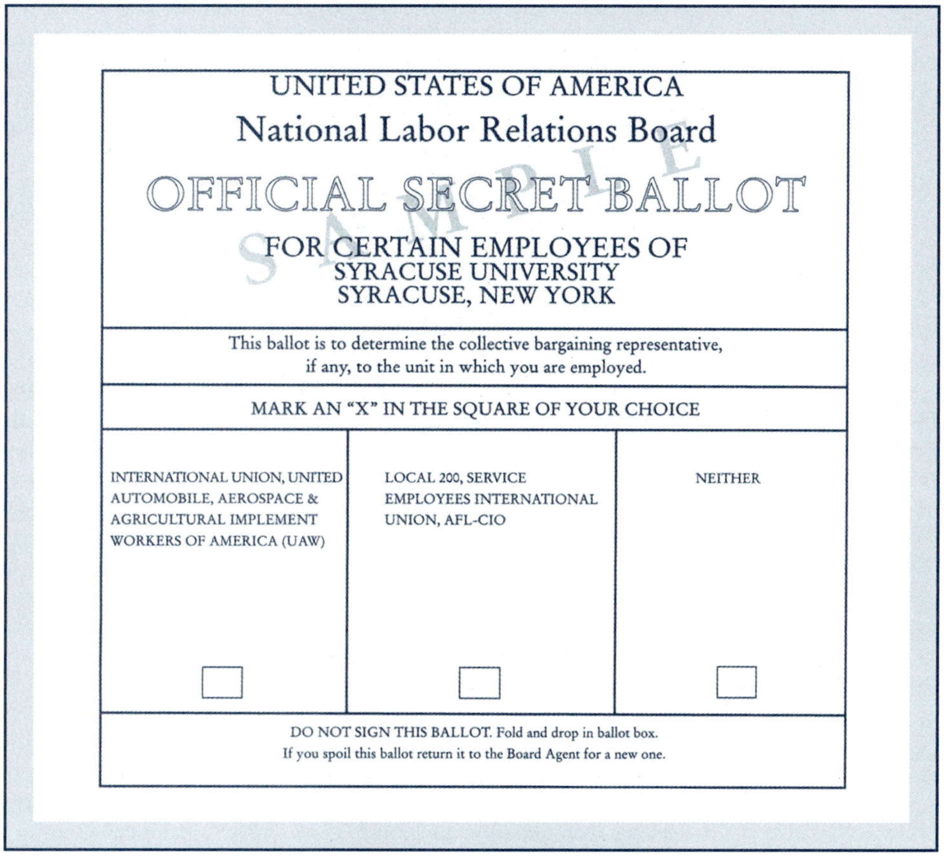

UNITED STATES OF AMERICA

National Labor Relations Board

OFFICIAL SECRET BALLOT

SAMPLE

FOR CERTAIN EMPLOYEES OF
SYRACUSE UNIVERSITY
SYRACUSE, NEW YORK

This ballot is to determine the collective bargaining representative, if any, to the unit in which you are employed.

MARK AN "X" IN THE SQUARE OF YOUR CHOICE

INTERNATIONAL UNION, UNITED AUTOMOBILE, AEROSPACE & AGRICULTURAL IMPLEMENT WORKERS OF AMERICA (UAW)	LOCAL 200, SERVICE EMPLOYEES INTERNATIONAL UNION, AFL-CIO	NEITHER
☐	☐	☐

DO NOT SIGN THIS BALLOT. Fold and drop in ballot box.
If you spoil this ballot return it to the Board Agent for a new one.

FIGURE 13.3 Sample NLRB Representation Election Ballot
Source: NLRB poster at 1979 Syracuse University representation election.

[22]212 F.3d 945 (6th Cir. 2000).

[23]314 NLRB 1215 (1994).

[24]105 F.3d 890 (3d Cir. 1997).

If either party believes the election laboratory conditions were violated, that party may file objections to the other party's conduct with the regional director within five days of the election. Post-election unfair labor practice charges could also result in the election results being set aside.

After the election is held, the parties have five days in which to file any objections with the regional director. If the director finds the objections to be valid, the election will be set aside. If the objections are held to be invalid, the results of the election will be certified. To be victorious, a party to the election must receive a majority of the votes cast; that is, either the union or the no-union choice must garner a majority of the votes cast by the eligible employees. If the election involved more than one union and no choice received a simple majority, the Board will hold a run-off election between the two choices getting the highest number of votes. If a union wins, it will be certified as the bargaining agent for all the employees in the bargaining unit.

Because the conduct of representation elections is a matter subject to the discretion of the regional directors and the Board, only limited judicial review of certification decisions is available. However, as a practical matter, an employer can obtain review of the Board's certification decision by refusing to bargain with the certified union and contesting the issue in the subsequent unfair labor practice proceeding.

Decertification of the Bargaining Agent

Decertification Petition
Petition stating that a current bargaining representative no longer has the support of a majority of the employees in the bargaining unit.

An employee or group of employees, or a union or individual acting on their behalf, may file a ***decertification petition*** under Section 9(c)(1) of the act, asserting that "the individual or labor organization, which has been certified or is being currently recognized by their employer as the bargaining representative" no longer enjoys the unit's support. The Board also requires the showing of 30 percent employee interest in support of a decertification petition to entertain it. This 30 percent rule has been criticized by some commentators in that the petition signifies nothing more than that fewer than half the employees are unhappy with their representative. Yet the mere filing of the petition can totally disrupt the bargaining process because the employer may refuse to bargain while the petition is pending.

An employer is not permitted to file a decertification petition; the Board will dismiss a decertification petition by employees if it discovers that the employer instigated the filing. However, a company can file an election petition if it can demonstrate by objective evidence that it has reasonable grounds for believing that the incumbent union has lost its majority status. Such petitions must be filed during the open-season periods, just as with petitions seeking representation elections.

Deauthorization Elections

Union Shop Clause
Clause in an agreement requiring all present and future members of a bargaining unit to be union members.

Section 9(e)(1) of the NLRA provides for the holding of a deauthorization election to rescind the union shop clause in a collective agreement. The ***union shop clause***, which may be included in a collective agreement, requires that all present and future members of the bargaining unit become, and remain, union members. They typically must join the union after thirty days from the date on which they were hired. Failure to join the union or to remain a union member is grounds for discharge. The provisions of Section 9(e)(1) state that a petition for a deauthorization election may be filed by an employee or group of employees.

The petition must have the support of at least 30 percent of the bargaining unit. If a valid petition is filed, along with the requisite show of support, the Board will conduct a secret ballot election to determine whether a majority of employees in the unit wish to remove the union shop clause from the agreement. As is the case with representation and decertification elections, no deauthorization election can be held for a bargaining unit (or subdivision of the unit) if a valid deauthorization election has been held in the preceding twelve-month period. Unlike representation elections and decertification elections, which are determined by a majority of the votes actually cast, deauthorization elections require that a majority of the members in the bargaining unit vote in favor of rescinding the union shop clause for it to be rescinded.

Acquiring Representation Rights Through Unfair Labor Practice Proceedings

Unfair labor practice charges filed with the Board while representation proceedings are pending may invoke the Board's blocking charge policy. The filing of such charges usually halts the representation case, and no election will be held pending the resolution of the unfair labor practice charges. An employer may wish to forestall the election and erode the union's support by committing various unfair labor practices, thereby taking unfair advantage of this policy.

A union may wish to proceed with the pending election despite the unfair labor practice charges. It can do so by filing a request-to-proceed notice with the Board. If the union proceeds and wins the election, then the effect of the unfair labor practice charges is not very important. However, if the union loses the election, it may be because of the effect of the employer's illegal actions. In that case, the union could file objections to the election and request that a new election be held. But how could the union overcome the lingering effects of the employer's unfair practices? Rather than seek a new election or proceed with the original election, the union may rely on the unfair practice charges and ask the Board, as a remedy for the unfair labor practices, to order the employer to recognize and bargain with the union without its ever winning an election.

In the case of *NLRB v. Gissel Packing Co.*,[25] the Supreme Court held that the NLRB may issue a bargaining order, requiring the employer to recognize and bargain with the union, as a remedy for the employer's unfair labor practices where those practices were pervasive, outrageous, and precluded the union from ever demonstrating majority support. The Court in *Gissel Packing* also held that a bargaining order might be an appropriate remedy where the employer's unfair labor practices, although not pervasive and outrageous, nevertheless had the effect of preventing any election from being a true demonstration of the employees' desires as to union representation; however, in such situations, a bargaining order should only be granted where the union, at some point during the organizing campaign, had majority support.

The following case illustrates the application of the *Gissel Packing* bargaining order remedy.

---

[25]395 U.S. 575 (1969).

case 13.2 »

National Steel Supply, Inc. and International Brotherhood of Trade Unions, Local 713

344 NLRB No. 121, 2005 WL 1564867 (N.L.R.B.) (2005)

Facts: In response to unfair labor practice charges filed by the union, Local 713, the Administrative Law Judge (ALJ) held that the employer had committed unfair labor practices during a union organizing campaign by unlawfully interrogating employees, discharging an employee because of his union activities, and unlawfully discharging and refusing to reinstate the twenty-seven employees (out of a bargaining unit of thirty-one employees) who engaged in a strike to protest the employer's illegal actions. The ALJ also recommended that the NLRB issue a bargaining order under *Gissel Packing* as a remedy for the unfair labor practices committed by the employer. The employer then sought review of the ALJ decision by the NLRB.

Issue: Is a bargaining order the appropriate remedy in light of the unfair labor practices committed by the employer here?

Decision: The NLRB agreed with the ALJ that the employer violated Section 8(a)(1) on August 13, 2004 by interrogating employee Eric Atalaya about union activities, and violated Section 8(a)(3) and (1) by terminating Atalaya. The NLRB also found that the employer violated Section 8(a)(3) and (1) by issuing a written warning to Atalaya and by refusing to reinstate, and subsequently discharging twenty-seven of the unfair labor practice strikers upon unconditional offer to return to work.

The NLRB agreed with ALJ that the Union had attained the support of a majority of the employees in the bargaining unit, as evidenced by authorization cards signed by the employees.

The Board will issue a *Gissel* bargaining order in two categories of cases, known as "category I" and "category II" cases. Category I involves "exceptional cases" marked by unfair labor practices so "outrageous" and "pervasive" that traditional remedies cannot erase their coercive effects, thus rendering a fair election impossible. Category II involves "less extraordinary cases marked by less pervasive practices which nonetheless still have the tendency to undermine majority strength and impede the election processes." The NLRB here held that the violations were sufficiently outrageous and pervasive to warrant a bargaining order under category I. The employer had interrogated and threatened employees and illegally discharged over 85 percent of the employees in the bargaining unit. Threats of job loss and the actual discharge of union adherents are "hallmark" violations, which are highly coercive because of their potentially long-lasting impact. Terminating a majority of the bargaining unit is unlawful conduct that "goes to the very heart of the Act" and is not likely to be forgotten. The impact of the violations was heightened by the small size of the unit and the direct involvement of the employer's highest officers. The NLRB held that there was a strong likelihood that the employer's unfair labor practices would have a pervasive and lasting effect on the employees' exercise of their Section 7 rights. The NLRB held that traditional unfair labor practice remedies cannot erase the coercive effects of the conduct, making the holding of a fair election impossible. The NLRB therefore ordered the employer to cease and desist from engaging in unfair labor practices, and to recognize and, on request, bargain with the Union as the exclusive representative of the employees in the bargaining unit.

«

Other Bargaining Order Remedy Issues

The Supreme Court's *Gissel Packing* decision indicated that the NLRB could issue a bargaining order to remedy outrageous and pervasive unfair labor practices by the employer, even if the union never had established majority support of the employees in the appropriate bargaining unit. The U.S. Court of Appeals for the Third Circuit held that the Board had the power to issue such an order in *United Dairy Farmers Co-op. Assoc. v. NLRB.*[26] However, in

[26] 633 F.2d 1054 (1980).

Conair Corp. v. NLRB,[27] the U.S. Court of Appeals for the D.C. Circuit held that it was inappropriate for the Board to issue a bargaining order where the union never established evidence of majority support. The NLRB now takes the position that it will not issue a bargaining order unless the union had, at some point, shown evidence of majority support during the organizing campaign, according to *Gourmet Foods, Inc.*[28]

A second area of dispute over bargaining order remedies is the question of whether the NLRB should consider subsequent events and changed circumstances when determining whether a bargaining order remedy is appropriate: Has the passage of time, the turnover of employees in the unit, or other factors limited the effects of the employer's unfair labor practices? The NLRB takes the position that it will not consider subsequent events or changed circumstances because to do so would allow the employer to capitalize on its misconduct. The courts of appeals have divided on this issue. The Seventh Circuit enforced a bargaining order despite a delay of four years and turnover of most the bargaining unit employees in *America's Best Quality Coatings v. NLRB,*[29] while the Sixth Circuit, the Second Circuit, and the D.C. Circuit held that the Board must consider subsequent events and the effect of the passage of time when deciding to issue a bargaining order in *DTR Industries v. NLRB,*[30] *Kinney Drugs, Inc. v. NLRB,*[31] and *Charlotte Amphitheater Corp. v. NLRB.*[32]

Employer Response to Union Recognition Demands

The *Gissel Packing* case involved an employer who committed unfair labor practices after the union claimed majority support. But what about the situation in which an employer, after being confronted by the union claiming recognition, simply refuses to recognize the union but refrains from committing any unfair labor practices? Is the employer required to petition for an election or recognize the union? Or is it up to the union to initiate the election process? In *Linden Lumber Div., Summer & Co. v. NLRB,*[33] the U.S. Supreme Court held that an employer who receives a request for voluntary recognition from a union claiming to have the majority support of the employer's employees is not required to recognize the union, provided that the employer has no knowledge of the union's support (independent of the union's claim to have majority support) and does not commit any unfair labor practices. Neither is the employer required to petition the NLRB for a representation election in response to the union's request for recognition; it is then up to the union either to file a petition for an election or to institute unfair labor practice charges. Of course, if the employer does engage in unfair labor practices after receiving the union's request for recognition, the union is free to seek a *Gissel*-type bargaining order from the NLRB as a remedy. Such bargaining orders, however, are granted infrequently.

---

[27]721 F.2d 1355 (1983), *cert. denied*, 467 U.S. 1241 (1984).

[28]270 NLRB 578 (1984).

[29]44 F.3d 106, *cert. denied*, 515 U.S. 1158 (1995).

[30]39 F.3d 106 (6th Cir. 1994).

[31]74 F.3d 1419 (2d Cir. 1996).

[32]82 F.3d 1074 (D.C. Cir. 1996).

[33]419 U.S. 301 (1974).

ethical DILEMMA

Employee Union Support: To Survey or Not to Survey?

You are the human resource manager at Southwestco, a small manufacturing company. The office clerical and technical employees at Southwestco are not unionized, but the production employees are. You have heard rumors that some clerical and technical employees are starting a campaign to become unionized, and several employees have specifically told you that they don't want to join. One morning, you receive a letter via certified mail from the union local representing the production workers. The union now claims to have the support of an overwhelming majority of the office clerical and technical employees and requests that the company recognize the union as the exclusive bargaining representative for all clerical and technical employees. How should you respond to the union demand?

You are considering whether to conduct a survey of the clerical and technical employees to determine whether a majority of them support the union. What arguments can you make in favor of conducting such a survey? What arguments can you make against it? Prepare a memo for the board of directors recommending (1) a response to the union demand for recognition and (2) whether to conduct a survey of the employees. Explain and support your positions.

Concept *Summary* » 13.3

Representation Elections

- Procedures for holding elections:
  - Employer must give union an Excelsior list to determine all employees eligible to vote in an election
  - Parties must maintain laboratory conditions to ensure that employees can exercise free choice
    - Violations of laboratory conditions include unfair labor practices, captive-audience speeches, incentives (such as raffles), threats, and extreme third-party propaganda
    - The parties must observe the twenty-four-hour silent period prior to the election
  - Decertification petitions can be filed by employees to determine if the union no longer has the majority's support
    - Petitions must meet the 30 percent rule
  - Deauthorization elections can rescind the agency shop clause in a collective agreement
- Unfair labor practice charges
  - Unfair labor practices by employers may delay or halt elections, but unions may choose to proceed despite unfair labor practice charges
  - Under the *Gissel Packing* decision, the NLRB may issue a bargaining order rather than proceed with the election if the unfair labor practices were pervasive and outrageous and the union had majority support at some point

CHAPTER REVIEW

» Key Terms

voluntary recognition	« 380	***bargaining unit***	« 385	***captive-audience speeches***	« 394
authorization cards	« 380	***unfair labor practice strike***	« 391	***twenty-four-hour silent period***	« 395
forty-eight-hour rule	« 382	***economic strikes***	« 391	***decertification petition***	« 396
consent election	« 383	***Excelsior list***	« 392	***union shop clause***	« 396
contract bar rule	« 384	***laboratory conditions***	« 393		

» Summary

- The NLRA gives employees the right to determine for themselves whether they wish to be represented by a union. If the majority of the employees in an appropriate bargaining unit indicate that they support a union, the NLRA provides that the union then becomes the exclusive bargaining representative of that bargaining unit. Although representation elections conducted by the NLRB are the most common means through which unions acquire representation rights, an employer may also voluntarily recognize a union as bargaining representative for a group of employees when the union demonstrates majority support.
- Unions, employees, or employers may file a petition with the NLRB seeking a representation election. Unions or employees may file a petition for a decertification election. When a petition is filed, the NLRB will determine whether the contract bar rule precludes holding an election; if not, the NLRB must then determine an appropriate bargaining unit. The NLRB uses the "community of interest" test to define the bargaining unit. While the bargaining unit determination depends on the facts of each case, in the health-care industry the NLRB will apply its rules for bargaining unit determination.
- The NLRB conducts representation elections under "laboratory conditions" to ensure that the election represents the free choice of the employees. Violations of the laboratory conditions or of the twenty-four-hour silent period rule may result in the NLRB invalidating the election results. Representation and decertification elections are by secret ballot, and the winner is determined by a majority of the votes cast. If no choice captures a majority of votes, a runoff election is held between the two choices getting the most votes. For deauthorization elections, which seek to rescind agency shop or union shop dues requirements, the result is determined by whether any choice gets a majority of the votes of all employees in the bargaining unit. Either party may file challenges to votes or to the election itself; valid challenges will be determined after a hearing by either the regional director or the NLRB itself.

- Unions may also acquire representation rights through unfair labor practice proceedings. The NLRB may issue a bargaining order when the effects of unfair labor practices by employers prevent a fair election from being held. Such remedies are the exception, with the NLRB and the courts preferring elections as the means to give effect to employees' right of free choice under the NLRA.

» Problems

Questions

1. What are the methods by which a union can acquire representation rights for a group of employees?
2. What is a bargaining unit? What factors does the NLRB consider in determining the appropriate bargaining unit?
3. What is the contract bar rule? What are the exceptions to it?
4. Under what conditions are economic strikers ineligible to vote in representation elections? Under what conditions are unfair labor practice strikers ineligible to vote in representation elections?
5. When must an employer recognize a union requesting voluntary recognition?

Case Problems

6. In 2000, employees of the Kent Corporation elected an independent union as their collective bargaining representative. A collective bargaining agreement was hammered out and ultimately ratified by the employees, effective until December 31, 2003. In November 2003, the two sides again negotiated, the result being a contract to be in effect until December 31, 2006. This agreement was signed by the association committee members but was never ratified by the rank and file. In fact, evidence showed there had been no association membership meetings, no election of officers, no dues ever collected, and no association treasury since 2000.

   In August 2004, the Steelworkers Union filed a representation petition. The NLRB regional director ruled that the association was a defunct union and that its current contract was no bar to an election. The company filed a request for review of the decision with the NLRB in Washington, D.C. The association vice president and a member of the bargaining committee attested to their willingness to continue representing the employees. There was no evidence that the association had ever failed to act on a bargaining unit member's behalf.

   How should the NLRB rule on the association's representative status? See *Kent Corporation* [272 NLRB No. 115, 117 L.R.R.M. 1333 (1984)].

7. L&J Equipment Company was engaged in the surface mining of coal, with its principal site in Hatfield, Pennsylvania, and six satellite sites in other parts of western Pennsylvania. In early 2001, the United Mine Workers of America began organizing L&J's mining employees. A few days after the first organizing meeting, a company-owned truck was destroyed by fire. Authorities determined the fire had been deliberately set. Three weeks later, the United Mine Workers filed a petition for an election. The date set for the election was November 4, 2001.

   During the intense election campaign, promanagement employees were threatened. A week before the election, a company-owned barn burned to the ground. The United Mine Workers won the election by a vote of 39–33.

   L&J refused to bargain. The union filed a Section 8(a)(5) charge, and the Board found that L&J was guilty of an unfair labor practice. L&J appealed to the U.S. Court of Appeals for the Third Circuit, claiming that the Board abused its discretion in certifying the union in light of its preelection improprieties.

   How should the appellate court have ruled on this challenge? See *NLRB v. L&J Equipment Co.* [745 F.2d 224, 117 L.R.R.M. 2592 (3d Cir. 1984)].

8. Action Automotive, Inc., a retail auto parts and gasoline dealer, had stores in a number of Michigan

cities. In March 2003, Local 40 of the Retail Store Employees Union filed a petition for a representation election. The union got a plurality of the unchallenged votes. But the challenged ballots could have made the difference.

The union challenged the ballots of the wife of the company's co-owner/president, who worked as a general ledger clerk at the company's headquarters, and of the mother of the three owner/ brothers, who worked as a cashier in one of the nine stores. The company argued that since neither received any special benefits, neither should be excluded from the employee unit or denied her vote.

The case reached the U.S. Supreme Court. What arguments could you make to the Court for the union's view? For the company's view? See *NLRB v. Action Automotive, Inc.* [469 U.S. 970 (1985)].

9. Micronesian Telecommunications Corporation (MTC) had its principal office on Saipan, a Pacific island held as a U.S. trust territory. Electrical Workers Local 1357 (IBEW) sought to represent the employees of MTC, including its employees on neighboring islands.

   What jurisdictional issues should the NLRB have addressed before asserting jurisdiction of the case? If the Board asserted jurisdiction, what factors should it have considered with respect to whether employees on the neighboring islands belonged in the same bargaining unit with the workers on Saipan? See *Micronesian Tel. Corp.* [273 NLRB No. 56, 118 L.R.R.M. 1067 (1984)].

10. Kirksville College in Missouri was a nonprofit corporation providing health-care services, medical education, and medical research. Service Employees Local 50 filed three representation petitions seeking to represent separate units composed, respectively, of all technical, all professional, and all service/ maintenance employees at the Kirksville Health Center, an unincorporated subsidiary of the college. The college also had several affiliated hospitals and rural clinics within a sixty-mile radius of the main campus.

    What factors should the NLRB consider in deciding whether technical, professional, and service employees should be in separate units? What factors must be looked at to decide whether clinic employees should properly have their own bargaining unit(s) or be part of a broader unit taking in (a) the college, (b) affiliated hospitals, and/or (c) satellite facilities? See *Kirksville College* [274 NLRB No. 121, 118 L.R.R.M. 1443 (1985)].

11. The Steelworkers Union sought to represent a unit composed of four occupational health nurses in an aluminum plant. The company argued that the nurses were managerial employees, exempt from the act, or in the alternative, professional employees who must be part of a bargaining unit of all the plant's professional employees. The nurses' primary responsibilities were treating employees' injuries and illnesses, administering routine physical examinations to applicants and employees, and maintaining logs and records.

    What additional facts did the NLRB need to decide the issues raised by the company? See *Noranda Aluminum Inc. v. NLRB* [751 F.2d 268, 118 L.R.R.M. 2136 (8th Cir. 1984)].

12. Because of the mixture of ethnic groups in the employer's factory, the NLRB conducted the election using a ballot translated from English into Spanish, Vietnamese, and Laotian. Food & Commercial Workers Local 34 won the election 119–112.

    The translations were line-by-line. Some English-reading employees claimed this made it difficult to read. Some of the translations were later found to be somewhat inaccurate. Neither side challenged any ballots.

    How should the NLRB have ruled on the company's challenge to the election outcome based on the flawed ballots? See *Kraft, Inc.* [273 NLRB 1484, 118 L.R.R.M. 1242 (1985)].

13. One employee ballot in a close election was marked with a large "X" in the "No Union" box and the word "Yes" written above the box.

    Should the NLRB count this ballot? If so, how? See *NLRB v. Newly Wed Foods Inc.* [758 F.2d 4, 118 L.R.R.M. 3213 (1st Cir. 1985)].

14. The International Brotherhood of Electrical Workers, Local Unions 605 and 985, AFL-CIO ("the union") have represented a bargaining unit comprised of MP&L's service and maintenance

employees since 1938. The most recent collective bargaining agreement concerning these employees is for the term of October 15, 2003, until October 15, 2005. That agreement does not include MP&L's storeroom and warehouse employees.

In January 2004, the union petitioned the NLRB for certification as bargaining representative of these storeroom and warehouse employees. MP&L opposed the petition, urging that the Board's contract bar rule barred the election required for the union to be certified. MP&L contended that the contract bar rule must be applied to employees intentionally excluded from an existing collective bargaining agreement.

The regional director rejected MP&L's contention. The Board affirmed this decision. An election was held, and a slim majority of the storeroom and warehouse employees voted to be represented by the union. The NLRB certified the results of the election.

To obtain judicial review of the Board's decision to permit a representation election, MP&L refused to bargain with the union on behalf of the newly represented employees. The union filed an unfair labor practice charge with the Board.

How should the Board have ruled on this challenge by MP&L? See *NLRB v. Mississippi Power & Light Co.* [769 F.2d 276 (5th Cir. 1985)].

15. The source of dispute was a representation election held at Kusan's Franklin, Tennessee, plant on October 19, 2002. The union won that election by a vote of 118–107. Kusan, however, filed objections with the Board over the conduct of the election. The objections charged that the union interfered with the election by conducting a poll of the employees and threatening and coercing employees during the course of the polling.

    In December 2002, the regional director of the NLRB investigated Kusan's objections and issued a report recommending that the objections be overruled. The results of the election were certified by the Board in April 2003.

    Kusan's objections centered on a petition that Kusan employees who supported the union circulated among their fellow workers prior to the election. The petition, which bore approximately 100 names, read as follows:

    > We, the undersigned, are voting YES for the IAM. We don't mind being on the firing line because we know it's something that has to be done. Please join with us. VOTE YES and help us to make Kusan, Inc. a better place to work and earn a living.

    Kusan contends that the circulation and distribution of the petition constituted impermissible "polling" of the employees by the union.

    How should the Board have ruled on Kusan's objections? See *Kusan Mfg. Co. v. NLRB* [749 F.2d 362, 117 L.R.R.M. 3394 (6th Cir. 1984)].

Hypothetical Scenarios

16. The employees in the Parking Services Department at Prestigious University, a large private university in upstate New York, are attempting to organize a union. Some of the Parking Services employees are clerical workers who work in the Parking Office located in the campus Administration Building, while others work as parking lot attendants. The parking lot attendants work out of kiosks located in the various parking lots around the campus. The parking lot attendants control access to the parking lots by checking for appropriate parking permits. They also issue parking tickets to enforce parking regulations and call for tow trucks to take away cars that are in violation of the parking regulations. The union organizing the workers seek to have all the parking employees in one bargaining unit. The university administration claims that the parking lot attendants are guards within the meaning of Section 9(b)(3) of the NLRA, and must be placed in a separate bargaining unit. Are the parking lot attendants guards within the meaning of Section 9(b)(3)? Should they be in a separate bargaining unit? Explain your answer.
17. The part-time faculty at Prestigious University are attempting to form a union to represent them in bargaining with the university. In order to get more of the part-time faculty to join, the union organizers promise that any faculty members who sign an authorization card before a representation election

is held will get a reduction in their union dues for the first year of membership. The union also holds a rally at a campus area pizza restaurant on the night before the representation election. Has the union violated the NLRB election conditions? Explain.

18. The maintenance and food service workers at Prestigious University are represented by the International Brotherhood of Teamsters Union. The union and the university administration have just agreed on a new collective bargaining agreement covering the next four years. A number of workers in the skilled maintenance department are dissatisfied with their union because they feel that the union accepted lower wage raises in return for getting a long-term contract. They contact a representative of the Service Employees International Union to discuss ousting the Teamsters as their bargaining representative. What must the workers do to get the NLRB to hold a decertification election?

19. Glassco manufactures glass containers—bottles and jars—for the food processing industry. Most of the employees work on production lines tending molding machines that extrude the containers. Glassco also employs some skilled glassblowers, who create crystal decanters. The glassblowers are skilled artisans who work in a separate area of the plant and fashion the decanters using molten glass and rudimentary hand tools. Because of their specialized skills, the pay scales for the glassblowers are higher than for the production workers.

    All the Glassco employees are represented by the International Molders Union, and are grouped together in one bargaining unit. The glassblowers feel that their interests are not being adequately represented by the union because there are only a few glassblowers, compared to the hundred or so production workers. The glassblowers file a petition with the NLRB to form their own union, the Glass Artisans Guild. Should the NLRB sever the glassblowers from the production bargaining unit? What factors will the NLRB consider in making its decision? Explain.

20. When the NLRB held a deauthorization election for the unionized employees at Shaw Manufacturing Co., only 60 of the 100 members of the bargaining unit actually voted. Of those voting, 25 voted to keep the union shop requirement, and 35 voted to eliminate it. Must the union and the employer rescind the union shop requirement of their collective agreement? Explain.

CHAPTER 14

Unfair Labor Practices by Employers and Unions

Unfair Labor Practices (ULPs) Actions by employers or unions that interfere with the rights of employees under the National Labor Relations Act.

The National Labor Relations Act (NLRA) defines a list of ***unfair labor practices (ULPs)*** by both employers and unions. Such unfair labor practices are various forms of conduct or activities that adversely affect employees in the exercise of their rights under Section 7 of the act. The unfair labor practices by employers in Section 8(a) were in the Wagner Act; the union unfair labor practices in Section 8(b) were added by the Taft-Hartley Act in 1947 and amended by the Landrum-Griffin Act of 1959.

Section 8(a) makes it illegal for an employer to engage in the following conduct:

- interfere with, restrain, or coerce employees in the exercise of rights guaranteed to them by Section 7 of the act;
- dominate, interfere with, or contribute financial or other support to a labor organization;
- discriminate in the hiring or terms or conditions of employment of employees in order to encourage or discourage membership in any labor organization;
- discharge or discriminate against an employee for filing charges or giving testimony under the NLRA; and
- refuse to bargain collectively with the bargaining representatives of the employees, as designated in Section 9(a).

Section 8(b) makes it illegal for unions to engage in the following conduct:

- restrain or coerce employees in the exercise of their rights under Section 7, or restrain or coerce an employer in the selection of a representative for collective bargaining purposes;
- cause or attempt to cause an employer to discriminate against an employee in terms or conditions of employment in order to encourage (or discourage) union membership;
- refuse to bargain collectively with an employer (when the union is the bargaining agent of the employees);
- engage in secondary picketing or encourage secondary boycotts of certain employers;
- require employees to pay excessive or discriminatory union dues or membership fees;

- cause an employer to pay for services that are not performed (feather-bedding); and
- picket an employer in order to force the employer to recognize the union as bargaining agent when the union is not entitled to recognition under the act (recognition picketing).

Because both employer and union unfair practices involve, for the most part, the same kinds of conduct, we examine them together in this chapter. The refusal to bargain by either employer or union will be discussed in Chapter 15, which deals with the duty to bargain in good faith. The union offenses of secondary picketing and recognition picketing will be discussed in Chapter 16, along with other forms of union pressure tactics.

Section 7: Rights of Employees

Because all unfair practices involve conduct that interferes with employees in the exercise of their rights under Section 7 of the NLRA, it is important to determine the exact rights granted employees by Section 7. Section 7 contains this statement:

> Employees shall have the right to self-organization, to form, join or assist labor organizations, to bargain collectively through representatives of their own choosing, and to engage in other concerted activities for the purpose of collective bargaining or other mutual aid or protection, and shall also have the right to refrain from any or all such activities....

The rights under Section 7 are given to all employees covered by the NLRA; the employees need not be organized union members to enjoy such rights. In addition, because the rights are given to the individual employee, they may not be waived by a union purporting to act on behalf of the employees.

For conduct of employees to be protected under Section 7, it must be concerted and it must be for the purpose of collective bargaining or other mutual aid or protection. A group of employees discussing the need for a union in order to improve working conditions is obviously under the protection of Section 7, as are employees who attempt to get their coworkers to join a union. But the protection of Section 7 also extends to activities not directly associated with formal unionization. For example, a group of nonunion employees who walked off the job to protest the extremely cold temperatures inside the shop were held to be exercising their Section 7 rights, as was an employee who circulated a petition about the management of the company's credit union. An employee collecting signatures of coworkers on a letter to management protesting the selection of a new supervisor was held to be engaged in protected activity in *Atlantic-Pacific Coast Inc. v. NLRB.*[1] In *NLRB v. Caval* Tool Div.,[2] an employee who challenged a new break policy announced at a company meeting was held to be engaged in concerted activity because she was acting in the interests of all the production workers. Section 7 protects employees in these situations from discipline or discharge for their conduct.

There are, of course, limits to the extent of Section 7 protection. Employees acting individually may not be protected; in addition, conduct not related to collective bargaining or

[1] 52 F.3d 260 (9th Cir. 1995).

[2] 262 F.3d 184 (2d Cir. 2001).

mutual aid or protection purposes is not protected. For example, an employee seeking to have a foreman removed because of a personal "grudge" was held not protected by Section 7; nor was a group of employees striking to protest company sales to South Africa protected.

Perhaps the most difficult aspect of determining whether conduct is protected under Section 7 deals with the "concerted action" requirement: When is an individual employee, acting alone, protected? The following Supreme Court decision addresses this question.

case 14.1 » NLRB v. City Disposal Systems

465 U.S. 822 (1984)

Brennan, J.

James Brown, a truck driver employed by respondent, was discharged when he refused to drive a truck that he honestly and reasonably believed to be unsafe because of faulty brakes. Article XXI of the collective-bargaining agreement between respondent and Local 247 of the International Brotherhood of Teamsters, Chauffeurs, Warehousemen and Helpers of America, which covered Brown, provides:

> [T]he Employer shall not require employees to take out on the street or highways any vehicle that is not in safe operating condition or equipped with safety appliances prescribed by law. It shall not be a violation of the Agreement where employees refuse to operate such equipment unless such refusal is unjustified.

The question to be decided is whether Brown's honest and reasonable assertion of his right to be free of the obligation to drive unsafe trucks constituted "concerted activit[y]" within the meaning of Section 7 of the NLRA. The National Labor Relations Board (NLRB) held that Brown's refusal was concerted activity within Section 7, and that his discharge was, therefore, an unfair labor practice under Section 8(a)(1) of the Act. The Court of Appeals disagreed and declined enforcement.

James Brown was assigned to truck No. 245. On Saturday, May 12, 1979, Brown observed that a fellow driver had difficulty with the brakes of another truck, truck No. 244. As a result of the brake problem, truck No. 244 nearly collided with Brown's truck. After unloading their garbage at the landfill, Brown and the driver of truck No. 244 brought No. 244 to respondent's truck-repair facility, where they were told that the brakes would be repaired either over the weekend or in the morning of Monday, May 14.

Early in the morning of Monday, May 14, while transporting a load of garbage to the landfill, Brown experienced difficulty with one of the wheels of his own truck—No. 245—and brought that truck in for repair. At the repair facility, Brown was told that, because of a backlog at the facility, No. 245 could not be repaired that day. Brown reported the situation to his supervisor, Otto Jasmund, who ordered Brown to punch out and go home. Before Brown could leave, however, Jasmund changed his mind and asked Brown to drive truck No. 244 instead. Brown refused explaining that "there's something wrong with that truck.... [S]omething was wrong with the brakes ... there was a grease seal or something leaking causing it to be affecting the brakes." Brown did not, however, explicitly refer to Article XXI of the collective-bargaining agreement or to the agreement in general. In response to Brown's refusal to drive truck No. 244, Jasmund angrily told Brown to go home. At that point, an argument ensued and Robert Madary, another supervisor, intervened, repeating Jasmund's request that Brown drive truck No. 244. Again, Brown refused, explaining that No. 244 "has got problems and I don't want to drive it." Madary replied that half the trucks had problems and that if respondent tried to fix all of them it would be unable to do business. He went on to tell Brown that "[w]e've got all this garbage out here to haul and you tell me about you don't want to drive." Brown responded, "Bob, what are you going to do, put the garbage ahead of the safety of the men?" Finally, Madary went to his office and Brown went home. Later that day, Brown received word that he had been discharged. He immediately returned to work in an attempt to gain reinstatement but was unsuccessful.

... Brown filed an unfair labor practice charge with the NLRB, challenging his discharge. The Administrative Law Judge (ALJ) found that Brown had been discharged for refusing to operate truck No. 244, that Brown's refusal was covered by Section 7 of the NLRA, and that respondent had therefore committed an unfair labor practice under

Section 8(a)(1) of the Act. The ALJ held that an employee who acts alone in asserting a contractual right can nevertheless be engaged in concerted activity within the meaning of Section 7....

The NLRB adopted the findings and conclusions of the ALJ and ordered that Brown be reinstated with back pay. On a petition for enforcement of the Board's order, the Court of Appeals disagreed with the ALJ and the Board. Finding that Brown's refusal to drive truck No. 244 was an action taken solely on his own behalf, the Court of Appeals concluded that the refusal was not a concerted activity within the meaning of Section 7.

Section 7 of the NLRA provides that "[e]mployees shall have the right to ... join or assist labor organizations, to bargain collectively through representatives of their own choosing, and to engage in other concerted activities for the purpose of collective bargaining or other mutual aid or protection." The NLRB's decision in this case applied the Board's longstanding "*Interboro* doctrine," under which an individual's assertion of a right grounded in a collective-bargaining agreement is recognized as "concerted activit[y]" and therefore accorded the protection of Section 7. The Board has relied on two justifications for the doctrine: First, the assertion of a right contained in a collective-bargaining agreement is an extension of the concerted action that produced the agreement; and second, the assertion of such a right affects the rights of all employees covered by the collective-bargaining agreement.

Neither the Court of Appeals nor respondent appears to question that an employee's invocation of a right derived from a collective-bargaining agreement meets Section 7's requirement that an employee's action be taken "for purposes of collective bargaining or other mutual aid or protection." As the Board first explained in the Interboro case, a single employee's invocation of such rights affects all the employees that are covered by the collective-bargaining agreement. This type of generalized effect, as our cases have demonstrated, is sufficient to bring the actions of an individual employee within the "mutual aid or protection" standard, regardless of whether the employee has his own interests most immediately in mind.

The term "concerted activit[y]" is not defined in the Act but it clearly enough embraces the activities of employees who have joined together in order to achieve common goals. What is not self-evident from the language of the Act, however, and what we must elucidate, is the precise manner in which particular actions of an individual employee must be linked to the actions of fellow employees in order to permit it to be said that the individual is engaged in concerted activity. We now turn to consider the Board's analysis of that question as expressed in the *Interboro* doctrine.

Although one could interpret the phrase, "to engage in concerted activities," to refer to a situation in which two or more employees are working together at the same time and the same place toward a common goal, the language of Section 7 does not confine itself to such a narrow meaning. In fact, Section 7 itself defines both joining and assisting labor organizations—activities in which a single employee can engage—as concerted activities. Indeed, even the courts that have rejected the *Interboro* doctrine recognize the possibility that an individual employee may be engaged in concerted activity when he acts alone. They have limited their recognition of this type of concerted activity, however, to two situations: (1) that in which the lone employee intends to induce group activity, and (2) that in which the employee acts as a representative of at least one other employee. The disagreement over the *Interboro* doctrine, therefore, merely reflects differing views regarding the nature of the relationship that must exist between the action of the individual employee and the actions of the group in order for Section 7 to apply. We cannot say that the Board's view of that relationship, as applied in the *Interboro* doctrine, is unreasonable.

The invocation of a right rooted in a collective-bargaining agreement is unquestionably an integral part of the process that gave rise to the agreement. That process—beginning with the organization of a union, continuing into the negotiation of a collective-bargaining agreement, and extending through the enforcement of the agreement—is a single, collective activity. Obviously, an employee could not invoke a right grounded in a collective-bargaining agreement were it not for the prior negotiating activities of his fellow employees. Nor would it make sense for a union to negotiate a collective-bargaining agreement if individual employees could not invoke the rights thereby created against their employer. Moreover, when an employee invokes a right grounded in the collective-bargaining agreement, he does not stand alone. Instead, he brings to bear on his employer the power and resolve of all his fellow employees. When, for instance, James Brown refused to drive a truck he believed to be unsafe, he was in effect reminding his employer that he and his fellow employees, at the time their collective-bargaining agreement was signed, had extracted a promise from City Disposal that they would not be asked to drive unsafe trucks. He was also reminding his employer that if it persisted in ordering him to drive an unsafe truck, he could reharness the power of that group to ensure the enforcement of that promise. It was just as though James Brown was reassembling his fellow union members to reenact their decision not to drive unsafe trucks. A lone employee's invocation of a right grounded in his collective-bargaining agreement is, therefore, a concerted activity in a very real sense....

... By applying Section 7 to the actions of individual employees invoking their rights under a collective-bargaining agreement, the *Interboro* doctrine preserves the integrity of the entire collective-bargaining process; for by invoking a right grounded in a collective-bargaining agreement, the employee makes that right a reality, and breathes life, not only into the promises contained in the collective-bargaining agreement, but also into the entire process envisioned by Congress as the means by which to achieve industrial peace.

To be sure, the principal tool by which an employee invokes the rights granted him in a collective-bargaining agreement is the processing of a grievance according to whatever procedures his collective-bargaining agreement establishes. ... Indeed, it would make little sense for Section 7 to cover an employee's conduct while negotiating a collective-bargaining agreement, including a grievance mechanism by which to protect the rights created by the agreement, but not to cover an employee's attempt to utilize that mechanism to enforce the agreement.

... As long as the employee's statement or action is based on a reasonable and honest belief that he is being, or has been, asked to perform a task that he is not required to perform under his collective-bargaining agreement, and the statement or action is reasonably directed toward the enforcement of a collectively bargained right, there is no justification for overturning the Board's judgment that the employee is engaged in concerted activity, just as he would have been had he filed a formal grievance....

In this case, the Board found that James Brown's refusal to drive truck No. 244 was based on an honest and reasonable belief that the brakes on the truck were faulty. Brown explained to each of his supervisors his reason for refusing to drive the truck. Although he did not refer to his collective-bargaining agreement in either of these confrontations, the agreement provided not only that "[t]he ... employer shall not require employees to take out on the streets or highways any vehicle that is not in safe operating condition," but also that "[i]t shall not be a violation of the Agreement where employees refuse to operate such equipment, unless such refusal is unjustified." There is no doubt, therefore, nor could there have been any doubt during Brown's confrontations with his supervisors, that by refusing to drive truck No. 244, Brown was invoking the right granted him in his collective-bargaining agreement to be free of the obligation to drive unsafe trucks.... Accordingly, we accept the Board's conclusion that James Brown was engaged in concerted activity when he refused to drive truck No. 244. We therefore reverse the judgment of the Court of Appeals and remand the case for further proceedings consistent with this opinion....

It is so ordered.

Case Questions

1. What is the relationship of the collective bargaining process to the right to refuse to operate unsafe equipment that was invoked by Brown? Did Brown mention the collective agreement when he refused to operate the truck?
2. How was Brown's individual refusal to operate the truck he felt was unsafe "concerted activity" within the meaning of Section 7 of the NLRA? Explain your answer.
3. Under what other circumstances, if any, can individual action be regarded as concerted within the meaning of Section 7?

In *Meyers Industries*,[3] a NLRB decision handed down before the Supreme Court decided *City Disposal Systems*, the Board held that in order for an individual employee's action to be concerted, it would require "that the conduct be engaged in with or on the authority of other

[3]268 NLRB 493 (1984).

employees, and not solely by and on behalf of the employee himself." The case involved an employee who was discharged after refusing to drive his truck and reporting safety problems with his truck to state transportation authorities; the employee had acted alone and the workers were not unionized. Is this holding consistent with the Supreme Court's decision in *City Disposal Systems*?

The U.S. Court of Appeals for the District of Columbia remanded the Board's decision in *Meyers Industries* to the Board for reconsideration.[4] On rehearing, the Board reaffirmed its decision that the employee had not been engaged in concerted activity. When the case again came before the court of appeals in *Prill v. NLRB*,[5] the D.C. Circuit Court upheld the Board's decision, holding that it was a reasonable interpretation of the act. In *Ewing v. NLRB*,[6] the court of appeals upheld the Board in a case similar to *Meyers Industries* on the Board's third try at justifying the conclusion that the employee did not engage in concerted activity.

Even though conduct may be concerted under Section 7, it may not be protected by the act. As noted in the *City Disposal Systems* decision, the employee may not act in an abusive manner. The Board has held that illegal, destructive, or unreasonable conduct is not protected, even if such conduct was concerted and for purposes of mutual aid or protection. For example, workers who engaged in on-the-job slowdowns by refusing to process orders were not protected because they could not refuse to work yet continue to get paid. Threats or physical violence by employees are not protected, nor is the public disparagement of the employer's product by employees or the referral of customers to competitors of the employer. The rights of employees under Section 7 are at the heart of the act; they are enforced and protected through unfair labor practice proceedings under Sections 8(a) and 8(b).

Concept *Summary* » 14.1

Protected Activity Under Section 7

Activity is protected under Section 7 if:

- It is concerted activity
- It is for collective bargaining or mutual aid and protection purposes
- It is not illegal, destructive, or unreasonable

[4] 755 F.2d 941 (1985).

[5] 835 F.2d 1481 (1987).

[6] 861 F.2d 353 (2d Cir. 1988).

Types of Unfair Labor Practices Alleged, Fiscal Year 2008

Number of Cases Showing Specific Allegations	Percent of Total Cases	
Subsections of Sec. 8(a): Total cases.................	16,179	100.0
8(a)(1)	2,643	16.3
8(a)(1)(2)	121	0.7
8(a)(1)(3)	4,747	29.3
8(a)(1)(4)	128	0.8
8(a)(1)(5)	6,643	41.1
8(a)(1)(2)(3)	69	0.4
8(a)(1)(2)(5)	104	0.6
8(a)(1)(3)(4)	341	2.1
8(a)(1)(3)(5)	1,217	7.5
8(a)(1)(4)(5)	14	0.1
8(a)(1)(2)(3)(4)	9	0.1
8(a)(1)(2)(3)(5)	48	0.3
8(a)(1)(2)(4)(5)	3	0
8(a)(1)(3)(4)(5)	80	0.5
8(a)(1)(2)(3)(4)(5)..	12	0.1
B. Charges filed against unions under Section 8(b)		
Subsections of Sec. 8(b): Total cases.................	6,210	100.0
8(b)(1)	4,864	78.3
8(b)(2)	33	0.5
8(b)(3)	268	4.3
8(b)(4)	487	7.8
8(b)(5)	3	0
8(b)(6)	1	0
8(b)(7)	54	0.9
8(b)(1)(2)	400	6.4
8(b)(1)(3)	70	1.1
8(b)(1)(5)	2	0
8(b)(2)(3)	4	0.1
8(b)(3)(5)	1	0
8(b)(3)(6)	4	0.1
8(b)(1)(2)(3)	16	0.3
8(b)(1)(2)(5)	1	0
8(b)(1)(3)(6)	1	0
8(b)(1)(2)(3)(5)(6)..	1	0

Source: *Seventy-Third Annual Report of the National Labor Relations Board, for Fiscal Year 2008*, Table 2, page 80.

Sections 8(A)(1) and 8(B)(1): Violation of Employee Rights by Employers or Unions

Interference with, coercion, or restraint of employees in the exercise of their Section 7 rights by employers or unions is prohibited by Section 8(a)(1) and Section 8(b)(1), respectively. While violations of other specific unfair labor practice provisions may also violate Sections 8 (a)(1) or 8(b)(1), certain kinds of conduct involve violations of Sections 8(a)(1) or 8(b)(1) only. This section discusses conduct that violates those specific sections only.

The NLRB has held that any conduct that has the natural tendency to restrain or coerce employees in the exercise of their Section 7 rights is a violation; actual coercion or restraint of the employees need not be shown. Intention is not a requirement for a violation of Sections 8(a)(1) and 8(b)(1); the employer or union need not have intended to coerce or restrain employees. All that is necessary is that they engage in conduct that the Board believes has the natural tendency to restrain employees in the exercise of their Section 7 rights.

Many employer violations of Section 8(a)(1) occur in the context of union organizing campaigns. Such violations usually involve restrictions on the soliciting activities of employees or coercive or threatening remarks made by the employer. The employer's ability to make antiunion remarks is discussed first.

Antiunion Remarks by Employer

During a union organizing campaign, the employer might attempt to persuade employees not to support the union. Such attempts may involve statements of opinion regarding the prospects of unionization and may also involve implicit promises or threats of reprisal. The extent to which the employer may communicate its position has been the subject of numerous Board and court decisions. Section 8(c) of the act states that:

> The expressing of any views, argument or opinion ... shall not constitute or be evidence of an unfair labor practice under any of the provisions of this Act, if such expression contains no threat of reprisal or force or promise of benefit.

It should be clear from the wording of Section 8(c) that explicit threats to fire union sympathizers are not protected by Section 8(c) and are therefore violations of Section 8(a)(1). The Board believes that because employees are economically dependent on the employer for their livelihood, they will be especially sensitive to the views explicitly or implicitly expressed by the employer. The Board will therefore examine closely the "totality of circumstances" of any employer's antiunion remarks to determine if they go beyond the protections of Section 8(c) and thus violate Section 8(a)(1).

In the *Gissel Packing* decision, mentioned in Chapter 13, the Supreme Court defined the limits to which an employer may predict the consequences of unionization. The employer may make a prediction based on objective facts to convey the employer's reasonable belief as to demonstrably probable effects or consequences, provided that such factors are beyond the employer's control. If the employer makes predictions about matters within the control of the employer, the Board is likely to view such statements as implicit threats because the employer is in a position to make those predictions come true. Statements such as, "The union almost put us out of business last time and the new management wouldn't hesitate to close this plant," have been held to be violations of Section 8(a)(1), whereas comments such as, "If the union gets in, it will have to bargain from scratch for everything it gets," have been held to be within Section 8(c)'s protection.

In *American Spring Wire Co.*,[7] the company's president made the following speech to employees in response to rumors that a union was trying to organize the workers:

> ... We have beaten the Union on two occasions in this plant by overwhelming majorities and I know the majority of us are tired of such activity. The majority of us do not deserve such continuing harassment. We have set up in this Company all the means of communication possible, and to those of you who still think you can win more with the Union than you have with us in the past nine years, well—you are dead wrong—leave us alone—get the hell out of our plant....
>
> I want to say something to you as clearly as I possibly can. Whether or not ASW has a union is really not significant to the Corporation's future, or to myself, Dave Carruthers, or other major employees of this Company. As far as I am concerned those of us who are loyal to each other as a group can make valve spring wire, music wire, alloy wire, in Moline, Illinois; Saskatchewan, Canada; Puerto Rico; or Hawaii. We don't need Cleveland, Ohio, or all this beautiful property. Remember nine years ago we had nothing. Today our Company has developed a certain amount of wealth and goodwill at the banks, a fantastic organization of people and friends who supply us goods, and above all a long and growing list of customers. These people do business with us, not with this building or this land. We do not intend to have this statement appear as a threat because it is not. It is a statement of fact. Facts are that our real concern regarding a union is with the majority of you who have opposed it in the past, and who would be locked into it should it come to this plant.
>
> With that in mind, I want to tell you that those of us in management do not wish to become involved in another election. We need the time to do the things that will continue to promote our Company, ourselves, and hopefully, you. I am asking you as your friend not to sign union cards, as we don't have the patience to put up with it again. This next battle is yours, not ours. It is up to each one of you who is against the union to stop the card signing before it gets started. I don't care how you do it. Organize yourselves and get it done....

The NLRB held that the statement directing union supporters to "... get the hell out of our plant" and telling those employees who opposed the union to "... stop the card signing before it gets started. I don't care how you do it...." were threatening and coercive. The statement that "We don't need Cleveland, Ohio...." was held to be a clear threat to close the plant if the employees joined a union. The remarks were held to be a violation of Section 8(a)(1). In *NLRB v. Exchange Parts*,[8] the Supreme Court held that the announcement of improved vacation pay and salary benefits during a union organizing campaign violated Section 8(a)(1). The Court reasoned that

[7] 237 NLRB 1551 (1978).

[8] 375 U.S. 405 (1964).

> The danger inherent in the well-timed increases in benefits is the suggestion of the fist inside the velvet glove. Employees are not likely to miss the inference that the source of benefits now conferred is also the source from which future benefits must flow and which may dry up if it is not obliged.

Why is the promise of benefits not protected under Section 8(c)? How does it interfere with the employees' exercise of Section 7 rights?

In *Heck's, Inc.*,[9] the Board declared that an employer did not commit an unfair labor practice by informing its unionized employees that it was opposed to their union and to unionization in general. However, the employer did commit an unfair labor practice by including its antiunion policy in its employee handbook and unilaterally requesting that all employees sign a statement agreeing to be bound by that policy.

Employer Limitations on Soliciting and Organizing

For employees to exercise their right, under Section 7, to choose their bargaining representative free from coercion, the employees must have access to information that will enable them to exercise this right intelligently. Such information may come from fellow employees who are active in union organizing attempts, or it may come from nonemployee union organizers. Although the union may attempt to reach the employees individually at their homes, it is more convenient and more effective to contact the employees at the work site when they are all assembled there. But organizing activities at the workplace may disrupt production and will certainly conflict with the employer's right to control and direct the work force. The employer's property rights at the workplace also include the right to control access to the premises. Clearly, then, the right of employees to organize is in conflict with the employer's property rights over the enterprise. How is such a conflict to be reconciled?

In *NLRB v. Babcock & Wilcox*,[10] the Supreme Court upheld a series of NLRB rules for employer restrictions upon nonemployee access to the premises and soliciting activity of employees. In the following case, the Supreme Court reconsidered the issues raised in *Babcock & Wilcox*.

case 14.2 »

Lechmere, Inc. v. NLRB

502 U.S. 527 (1992)

Facts: Local 919 of the United Food and Commercial Workers Union was attempting to organize the employees at a Lechmere retail store in Newington, Connecticut. The store was located at the south end of the Lechmere Shopping Plaza, while the main parking lot was to its north. The main entrance to the plaza was on the east side, off of the Berlin Turnpike, a four-lane divided highway. The parking lot is separated from the highway by a forty-six-foot-wide grassy strip, broken only by the Plaza's entrance. To begin the organizing campaign, the union ran a full-page advertisement in a local newspaper, but it drew little response. The union then sent nonemployee organizers into Lechmere's parking lot to place handbills on the windshields of cars parked in a corner of the lot used mostly by employees. Lechmere's manager immediately confronted the organizers, informed them that Lechmere prohibited solicitation or handbill distribution of any kind on its property, and asked them to leave. They left, and Lechmere personnel removed the handbills. The union organizers repeated the handbilling in the parking lot on several other occasions;

[9] 293 NLRB 1111, 131 L.R.R.M. 1281 (1989).

[10] 351 U.S. 105 (1956).

each time they were asked to leave and the handbills were removed. The organizers then relocated to the public grassy strip, from where they attempted to pass out handbills to cars entering the lot during hours (before opening and after closing) when the drivers were assumed to be primarily store employees. For one month, the union organizers returned daily to the grassy strip to picket Lechmere; after that, they picketed off and on for another six months. They also recorded the license plate numbers of cars parked in the employee parking area; with the cooperation of the Connecticut Department of Motor Vehicles, and managed to secure the names and addresses of some 41 nonsupervisory employees. The union sent four mailings to these employees and made some attempts to contact them by phone or home visits. These mailings and visits resulted in one signed union authorization card.

The union then filed an unfair labor practice charge with the NRLB, alleging that Lechmere violated the Section 8(a)(1) of NLRA by barring the nonemployee organizers from its property. An administrative law judge (ALJ) ruled in the union's favor, recommending that Lechmere be ordered to cease and desist from barring the union organizers from the parking lot.

On review the NLRB affirmed the ALJ's judgment and adopted the recommended order. Lechmere then sought judicial review, but the U.S. Court of Appeals for the First Circuit denied Lechmere's petition for review and enforced the Board's order. Lechmere then appealed to the U.S. Supreme Court.

Issue: Was Lechmere's refusal to allow nonemployee union organizers onto its property to attempt to organize the store's employees an unfair labor practice?

Decision: The NLRA confers rights on employees, not on unions or their nonemployee organizers; however, in *NLRB v. Babcock & Wilcox Co.*, the Supreme Court recognized that the employees' "right of self-organization depends in some measure on [their] ability ... to learn the advantages of self-organization from others." In that case, the Court held that Section 7 of the NLRA may, in certain circumstances, restrict an employer's right to exclude nonemployee union organizers from its property. As a rule, employers cannot be compelled to allow distribution of union literature by nonemployee organizers on their property. However, there are exceptions to that rule, such as where the location of a plant and the living quarters of the employees place the employees beyond the reach of reasonable union efforts to communicate with them; in such cases, employers' property rights may be "required to yield to the extent needed to permit communication of information on the right to organize." Under the *Babcock & Wilcox Co.* doctrine, the NLRB must accommodate the employees' Section 7 rights and the employer's property rights with as little destruction of the one as is consistent with the maintenance of the other. In *Babcock*, the Court distinguished between the union activities of employees and of nonemployees. In cases involving employee activities, the NLRB allows the employees to receive information on self-organization on the company's property from fellow employees during nonworking time; but Section 7 does not require that nonemployee organizers be granted access to the employer's property except in the rare case where "the inaccessibility of employees makes ineffective the reasonable attempts by nonemployees to communicate with them through the usual channels." Where reasonable alternative means of access exist, the employer does not have to allow the nonemployee organizers on its property.

In the case here, the ALJ held that reasonable alternative means of communicating with the Lechmere employees were available to the union. The NLRB, reviewing the ALJ's decision, however, held that there "was no reasonable, effective alternative means available for the Union to communicate its message" to the employees. The Supreme Court held that the NLRB decision was in error, because the exception to the *Babcock* rule is a narrow one. The employer does not have to allow nonemployees on its property whenever other means of access to employees may be cumbersome or less-than-ideally effective; the employer is required to allow the nonemployee organizers on its property only when "the location of a plant and the living quarters of the employees place the employees beyond the reach of reasonable union efforts to communicate with them." Classic examples include logging camps, mining camps, and mountain resort hotels. The union has the burden of establishing that the employees are inaccessible. Here, because the employees do not reside on Lechmere's property, they are presumed not to be beyond the reach of the union's message. The fact that the employees live in a large metropolitan area does not in itself render them "inaccessible" in the meaning of *Babcock*. The union tried advertising in local newspapers; the NLRB held that this was not reasonably effective because it was expensive and might not reach the employees. Whatever the merits of that conclusion, other alternative means of communication were readily available; access to employees, not success in winning them over, is the critical issue. The union here failed to establish the existence of any unique obstacles that frustrated its access to Lechmere's employees, and the NLRB erred in concluding that Lechmere committed an unfair labor practice by barring the nonemployee organizers from its property. The Supreme Court reversed the decision of the court of appeals, and denied enforcement of the NLRB order.

«

As the Supreme Court noted in *Lechmere*, under certain circumstances the employer may be required to allow union organizers access to its property when there are no other reasonable alternative means of access available. In *Thunder Basin Coal v. Reich*,[11] the Supreme Court stated that the employer's right to exclude union organizers comes from state property law, not from the NLRA; nothing in the NLRA requires that employers exclude organizers. Where the employer has no state law property right to exclude union organizers, *Lechmere* does not apply, and the employer may not prohibit access by the union, according to *NLRB v. Calkins*.[12] In *United Food and Commercial Workers v. NLRB*,[13] the U.S. Court of Appeals for the D.C. Circuit held that an employer leasing the property had no right, under state law, to deny access to union organizers. An employer's attempts to deny unions access to a temporary sidewalk in front of the employer's hotel and casino violated Section 8(a)(1) of the NLRA because the employer had no property rights to the sidewalk to allow it to exclude people from demonstrating on that sidewalk, as in *Venetian Casino Resort, L.L.C. v. NLRB*.[14]

Restrictions on Employees

Although nonemployees may be barred completely, an employer may place only "reasonable restrictions" on the soliciting activities of employees. Employer rules limiting soliciting activities must have a valid workplace purpose, such as ensuring worker safety or maintaining the efficient operation of the business, and must be applied uniformly to all soliciting, not just to union activities. The employer may limit the distribution of literature where it poses a litter problem. Employee soliciting activity may be limited to nonworking areas such as cafeterias, restrooms, or parking lots. Such activities may also be restricted to "nonworking times" such as coffee breaks and lunch breaks. However, an employer may not completely prohibit such activities. In the absence of exceptional circumstances, blanket prohibitions on soliciting have been held unreasonable and in violation of Section 8(a)(1). In *Martin Luther Mem. Home, Inc.*,[15] the Board set out a framework for determining whether an employer's restrictive work rule is in violation of Section 8(a)(1):

- if the work rule explicitly restricts protected activity under Section 7, it is a violation;
- if the rule does not explicitly restrict protected activity, it is still a violation of Section 8(a)(1) if the employees would reasonably construe the language of the rule to prohibit protected activity, or if the rule was promulgated in response to union activity, or if the rule has been applied to restrict the exercise of protected activity.

In *Northeastern Land Services, Inc. v. NLRB*,[16] the U.S. Court of Appeals for the First Circuit upheld the NLRB decision that an employer rule that prohibited employees from discussing terms of employment, including compensation, under penalty of dismissal, was overly restrictive of protected activity and was a violation of Section 8(a)(1). Employers may not

[11]510 U.S. 200 (1994).

[12]187 F.3d (9th Cir. 1999).

[13]222 F.3d 1030 (D.C. Cir. 2000).

[14]484 F.3d 601 (D.C. Cir. 2007).

[15]343 NLRB 646 (2004).

[16]560 F.3d 36 (2009).

restrict "visual-only" solicitations such as wearing hats, buttons, and so forth in the absence of exceptional circumstances. Employer rules requiring that employees get prior approval from the employer for solicitation are overly restrictive and violate section 8(a)(1) according to *Opryland Hotel*[17] and *Gallup, Inc. v. United Steelworkers of America.*[18] Employers have the right to restrict the use of company bulletin boards and telephones during working time and company email systems, but the employer may not enforce such rules in a discriminatory manner to exclude or restrict union activities. If the employer allows employees the occasional personal use of company telephones or email systems could it lawfully exclude use related to union matters? That is the question addressed in the following case.

case 14.3 » GUARD PUBLISHING COMPANY V. NATIONAL LABOR RELATIONS BOARD

571 F.3d 53 (D.C. Cir. 2009)

Facts: Guard Publishing Company publishes *The Register-Guard* (RG), a daily newspaper in the Eugene, Oregon, area. In 1996, the RG installed a new computer system and adopted a Communication Systems Policy (CSP) to govern use of communication systems, including email. The CSP provided that:

> Company communication systems and the equipment used to operate the communication systems are owned and provided by the Company to assist in conducting the business of The Register-Guard. Communication systems are not to be used to solicit or proselytize for commercial ventures, religious or political causes, outside organizations, or other non-job-related solicitations.

While RG employees used email regularly for work-related matters, the company was also aware that employees also used email to send and receive personal messages, such as baby announcements, party invitations, and the occasional offer of sports tickets or request for services such as dog walking. Managing editor Dave Baker admitted that he had received personal e-mail from employees and had not disciplined them. Baker himself sent at least two e-mails seeking volunteers for the newspaper's annual United Way campaign.

The RG employees were represented by the Eugene Newspaper Guild (ENG). The president of the ENG, Suzi Prozanski, sent an e-mail May 4, 2000, that corrected information about a union rally held the previous Monday afternoon. Before that rally, Baker had e-mailed employees advising them to leave work early because of a police warning that anarchists might attend the rally. Bishop, an employee and union member, sent an e-mail to the union indicating that it was the company that had warned the police about anarchists.

Prozanski's May 4th e-mail informed employees that the union had discovered that some of the information contained in earlier e-mails was incomplete, because the union had not been aware that the local police had initially contacted the company.

The next day, Baker sent Prozanski a disciplinary warning stating that she used the company's e-mail system for the express purpose of conducting union business, in violation of the company's CSP. In August, Prozanski sent employees two more emails. The first reminded employees to "wear green on Tuesday" to show support for the union's contract negotiations. The second asked for volunteers to help with the union's entry in a local parade. RG's director of human relations sent Prozanski another disciplinary warning, stating that she had violated the CSP by using the system for dissemination of union information.

In September, the union filed a charge with the NLRB alleging that the company committed an unfair labor practice by sending the disciplinary warnings. A NLRB administrative law judge (ALJ) found that RG did not violate the NLRA merely by maintaining the CSP, but did violate Section 8(a)(1) by discriminatorily enforcing the policy to prohibit union-related e-mails while allowing a variety of

[17] 323 NLRB 723 (1997).

[18] 349 NLRB 1213 (2007).

non-work-related e-mails. In particular, he found that *The Register-Guard* committed unfair labor practices by disciplining Prozanski for both the May and August e-mails.

On review by the NLRB, the NLRB agreed that the disciplinary warning for the May e-mail was an unfair labor practice, but that later e-mails were solicitations in violation of the CSP, for which RG could legally discipline Prozanski. Both the union and the company then sought review of the NLRB decision, and the NLRB sought enforcement of its order, before the U.S. Court of Appeals for the D.C. Circuit.

Issue: Did the employer commit an unfair labor practice by discriminatorily enforcing the CPS against the union?

Decision: The court noted that the NLRB held that the company had not violated Section 8(a)(1) when it issued a disciplinary warning to Prozanski for the second and third e-mails, because the NLRB stated that the CSP only prohibited non-job-related solicitations, and the August e-mails were solicitations. The NLRB noted that the company had tolerated personal employee e-mail messages, but that there was no evidence that the company permitted employees to use e-mail to solicit other employees to support any group or organization.

The Court of Appeals noted that the union did not challenge the legality of a company policy that bars union access to e-mail on a neutral basis, but that the company selectively enforced its e-mail policy against the union. The court stated that a valid no-solicitation rule applied in a discriminatory manner or maintained for discriminatory reasons against union solicitation was an unfair labor practice. The court held that substantial evidence supported the decision that the company's decision to discipline Prozanski was unlawfully discriminatory because the CSP did not cover such an e-mail. The CSP provided that company communication systems were not to be used "to solicit or proselytize for commercial ventures, religious or political causes, outside organizations, or other non-job-related solicitations;" it did not prohibit all non-job-related communications. The May e-mail was not a solicitation, it simply clarified the facts surrounding the Union's rally the day before. The only difference between Prozanski's May e-mail and the e-mails permitted by the employer was that Prozanski's e-mail was union-related. Baker's disciplinary notice admonished Prozanski for "us[ing] the company's e-mail system expressly for the purpose of conducting Guild business."

The court did not agree with the NLRB decision that the company acted lawfully in disciplining Prozanski for the August e-mails. The court agreed with the NLRB that those e-mails were solicitations calling for employees to take action in support of the Union. The NLRB noted that the company tolerated personal solicitations by employees, but did not permit employees to use e-mail to solicit other employees to support any group or organization. However, the CSP made no distinction between solicitations for groups and for individuals, mentioning solicitations for "outside organizations" as just one example of the forbidden category of all "non-job-related solicitations." As well, the company's August disciplinary warning, which explained the rationale for disciplining Prozanski, did not invoke the organization-versus-individual line drawn by the NLRB. To the contrary, the warning told Prozanski to "refrain from using the company's systems for union/*personal* business." The May disciplinary notice did not draw an organizational line either, but rather admonished Prozanski that it was impermissible "to use the company's e-mail for purposes other than company business."

The court held that the NLRB determination that the company legally disciplined Prozanski for the August emails was not supported by substantial evidence on the record. The court therefore granted the union's petition for review, set aside the NLRB's determination that the disciplining of Prozanski for her August emails was not an unfair labor practice, and remanded that issue to the NLRB for further proceedings consistent with the court's opinion.

When the workplace is a department store or hospital, "no-solicitation" rules may present particular problems. An employer will attempt to ensure that soliciting activity does not interfere with customer access or patient care, yet the Board will ensure that the employees are still able to exercise their Section 7 rights. In *Beth Israel Hospital v. NLRB*,[19] the U.S. Supreme

[19]437 U.S. 483 (1978). See "Case Handling Instructions for Cases Concerning Bill Johnson's Restaurant and *BE & K Construction Company v. NLRB*," Memorandum of the General Counsel, Memorandum 02-09, Sept. 20, 2002, available online at the NLRB website at http://www.nlrb.gov/research/memos/general_counsel_memos.aspx. Go to year 2002, and then click on the link for GC Memo 02-09.

Court upheld the Board order allowing a hospital to prohibit soliciting by employees in patient-care areas, but prohibiting the hospital from denying employees the right to solicit in the hospital cafeteria.

Other Section 8(A)(1) Violations

An employer filing an ultimately unsuccessful suit against unions engaged in protected activity is not automatically in violation of Section 8(a)(1) when there were reasonable grounds for the suit, *BE & K Construction Co. v. NLRB.*[20] Other employer practices likely to produce Section 8(a)(1) complaints may involve interrogation of employees regarding union sympathies and the denial of employee requests to have a representative present during disciplinary proceedings.

Polling and Interrogation

An employer approached by a union claiming to have the support of a majority of employees may wish to get some independent verification of the union's claim. In *Struknes Construction,*[21] the NLRB set out guidelines to reconcile the legitimate interests of an employer in polling employees regarding union support with the tendency of such a poll to restrain employees in the free exercise of their Section 7 rights. The NLRB requires that the employer have a "good faith reasonable doubt" about a union's claim of majority support in order to conduct a poll of employees regarding their support of a union. The Supreme Court upheld the Board's "good faith reasonable doubt" requirement in *Allentown Mack Sales and Service, Inc. v. NLRB.*[22] If the employer chooses to poll its employees, the poll must be conducted according to the following guidelines:

- It must be done in response to a union claim of majority support
- The employees must be informed of the purpose of the poll
- The employees must be given assurances that no reprisals will result from their choice
- The poll must be by secret ballot

In addition, the employer must not have created a coercive atmosphere through unfair labor practices or other behavior; and the poll must not be taken if a representation election is pending. Why should the Board preclude such a poll when an election is pending? In light of *Linden Lumber* (in Chapter 13), what happens when the poll by the employer discloses that the union has majority support?

The employer polling pursuant to the *Struknes* rules needs to be distinguished from the interrogation of employees regarding their union sympathies. Polling is to be done by secret ballot and only in response to a union claim for voluntary recognition. Interrogation may involve confronting individual employees and questioning them about their union sympathies. Such interrogation may be in response to a union organizing campaign or a request for

---

[20]536 U.S. 516 (2002).

[21]165 NLRB 1062 (1967).

[22]522 U.S. 359 (1998).

voluntary recognition, and, according to *Johnnie's Poultry Co.*[23] and *Wisconsin Porcelain Co.*,[24] must include reassurances that participation in the interrogation is voluntary and that there will be no reprisals taken against the employees.

The NLRB has held that interrogation of individual employees, even known union adherents, is not an unfair labor practice if it is done without threats or the promise of benefits by the employer in *Rossmore House*.[25] If the interrogation is accompanied by threats against the employees or other unfair labor practices by the employer, however, it may be a violation of Section 8(a)(1).

In *Alliance Rubber*,[26] the Board, in a 2–1 decision, held that two polygraph examiners, hired by the employer to help in an investigation of suspected plant sabotage and drug use, were acting as agents of the employer when they interrogated employees about union activities in the course of administering polygraph exams to the employees. The Board held that the questioning was made even more stressful because of its connection with the investigation into drug use and sabotage, and it implicitly gave the employees the message that engaging in union activity might result in their being suspected of engaging in unlawful activity in the plant. The company vice president's conduct reasonably led employees to believe that the examiners asked the questions about union activities on behalf of the employer; therefore, the employer and the polygraph operators were held to have violated Section 8(a)(1).

Weingarten Rights

In *NLRB v. Weingarten*,[27] an employer refused to allow an employee to have a union representative present during the questioning of the employee about thefts from the employer. The Supreme Court upheld the NLRB ruling that such a refusal violated Section 8(a)(1). The Court reasoned that "the action of an employee in seeking to have the assistance of his union representative at a confrontation with his employer clearly falls within the literal wording of Section 7 that '[e]mployees shall have the right … to engage in concerted activities for the purpose of … mutual aid or protection.'" Shortly after its decision in *Weingarten*, the Board extended ***Weingarten* rights** to nonunion employees as well, as in *Materials Research Corp.*[28] However, in *E. I. DuPont & Co.*,[29] the NLRB decided to restrict such rights to unionized employees only. In 2000, the NLRB again reversed that position and again held that nonunion employees are also entitled to have a representative present during investigatory interviews in *Epilepsy Foundation of Northeast Ohio*.[30] That decision was enforced by the U.S. Court of Appeals for the District of Columbia in *Epilepsy Foundation of Northeast Ohio v. NLRB*.[31]

Weingarten Rights
The right of employees to have a representative of their choice present at meetings that may result in disciplinary action against the employees.

---

[23]146 NLRB 770 (1964), *enforcement denied by NLRB v. Johnnie's Poultry Co.*, 344 F.2d 617 (8th Cir. 1965).

[24]349 NLRB No. 17 (2007).

[25]269 NLRB 1176 (1984), *affirmed sub nom Hotel & Restaurant Employees Local 11 v. NLRB*, 760 F.2d 1006 (9th Cir. 1985).

[26]286 NLRB 645 (1987).

[27]420 U.S. 251 (1975).

[28]262 NLRB 1010 (1982).

[29]289 NLRB 627 (1988).

[30]331 NLRB 676 (2000).

[31]268 F.3d 1095 (2001).

However, the NLRB once again reversed its position on the question of whether non-union employees are entitled to *Weingarten* rights; in *IBM Corp.*,[32] where the NLRB held that *Weingarten* rights are not available to nonunion workers.

Under present NLRB doctrine, unionized employees have a right to have a representative present applies whenever the meeting with management will have the "probable" result of the imposition of discipline or where such a result is "seriously considered." The NLRB also held that, absent extenuating circumstances, the employee is entitled to the union representative of his or her choice in *Anheuser-Busch v. NLRB*.[33] The Board has set the following two requirements on the exercise of *Weingarten* rights by employees: the employee must actually request the presence of a representative to have the right (see *Montgomery Ward & Co.*[34]) and an employer who violates an employee's *Weingarten rights* is not prevented from disciplining the employee, provided that the employer has independent evidence, not resulting from the "tainted" interview, to justify the discipline, (see *ITT Lighting Fixtures, Div. of ITT*[35]).

Violence and Surveillance

One last area of employer violations of Section 8(a)(1) involves violence and surveillance of employees. It should be clear from the wording of Section 8(a)(1) that violence or threats of violence directed against employees by the employer (or agents of the employer) violate Section 8(a)(1) because they interfere with the free exercise of the employees' Section 7 rights. Employer surveillance of employee activities, or even creating the impression that the employees are under surveillance, also violates Section 8(a)(1) because such a practice has the natural tendency to restrict the free exercise of the employees' Section 7 rights. An employer photographing or videotaping employees who are engaging in protected activity is a violation of Section 8(a)(1), according to *F. W. Woolworth Co.*[36] In *Allegheny Ludlum Corp. v. NLRB*,[37] an employer asking employees to agree to be filmed for use in an antiunion video was also in violation of Section 8(a)(1).

Union Coercion of Employees and Employers

Whereas Section 8(a)(1) prohibits employer interference with employees' Section 7 rights, Section 8(b)(1)(A) prohibits union restraint or coercion of the exercise of Section 7 rights by the employee. It is important to remember that Section 7 also gives employees the right to refrain from concerted activity. (There is an important qualification on the employees' right to refrain from union activities; Section 7 recognizes that a union shop or agency shop provision requiring employees to join the union or to pay union dues may be valid. We discuss these provisions later in this chapter.)

---

[32] 341 NLRB 1228 (2004).

[33] 363 F.3d 267 (4th Cir. 2003).

[34] 269 NLRB 904 (1984).

[35] 261 NLRB 229 (1982).

[36] 310 NLRB 1197 (1993).

[37] 301 F.3d 167 (3d Cir. 2002).

Section 8(b)(1)(A)

In *Radio Officers Union v. NLRB*,[38] the Supreme Court stated that the policy behind Section 7 and Section 8(b) was "to allow employees to freely exercise their right to join unions, be good, bad or indifferent members, or to abstain from joining any union, without imperiling their livelihood."

Union threats or violence directed at employees are clear violations of Section 8(b)(1)(A), as in *United Food and Commercial Workers, Local 7R (Conagra Foods, Inc.*,[39] because such actions tend to coerce or interfere with the employees' free choice of whether or not to support the union. But just as with employer actions under Section 8(a)(1), less blatant conduct may also be an unfair labor practice. Where the union has waived its initiation fees for employees who join prior to a representation election, the Board has found a Section 8(b)(1)(A) violation. By the same reasoning, union statements such as, "Things will be tough for employees who don't join the union before the election," were also held to violate Section 8(b)(1)(A). In *Local 466, Int. Brotherhood of Painters and Allied Trades (Skidmore College)*,[40] a union business agent's statement, in response to an internal union investigation into alleged financial improprieties initiated by other union members, which said, "when this is over with, someone's going to get hurt ...," was held to be a threat of reprisal violating Section 8(b)(1)(A), However, a union representative photographing employees distributing union literature outside the employer's facility is not per se a violation of Section 8(b)(1)(A), nor does it violate the laboratory conditions for holding a representation election according to *Randell Warehouse of Arizona, Inc.*[41]

Section 8(b)(1)(A) does recognize the need for unions to make rules regarding membership qualifications. A proviso to the section declares "[t]his paragraph shall not impair the right of a labor organization to prescribe its own rules with respect to the acquisition or retention of membership therein." The courts have tended to construe this provision liberally, provided that the union action does not affect the job tenure of an employee. The courts have allowed unions to fine members who refused to go on strike; they have also upheld the right of unions to file suit in state court to collect such fines. However, when a union has expelled a member for filing an unfair labor practice charge with the NLRB without exhausting available internal union remedies, the Supreme Court has found the union in violation of Section 8(b)(1)(A), as in *NLRB v. Industrial Union of Marine and Shipbuilding Workers*.[42] The Court reasoned, "Any coercion used to discourage, retard or defeat that access [to the NLRB] is beyond the legitimate interests of a labor organization."

Section 8(b)(1)(B)

Section 8(b)(1)(B) protects employers from union coercion in their choice of a representative for purposes of collective bargaining or the adjustment of grievances. The legislative history of this section suggests that it was intended to prevent unions from coercing firms into multiemployer bargaining units.

---

[38]347 U.S. 17 (1954).

[39]347 NLRB No. 97 (2006).

[40]332 NLRB 445 (2000).

[41]328 NLRB 1034 (1999).

[42]391 U.S. 418 (1968).

In a number of industries, employers bargain with a union on a multiemployer basis. This is particularly true in industries characterized by a number of small firms and a single large union. Examples are:

- Coal mining
- The trucking industry
- Construction
- The longshoring industry

Whipsaw Strikes Strikes by a union selectively pitting one firm in an industry against the other firms.

To offset the power of the large union, the employers join together and bargain through an employers' association or multiemployer bargaining unit. This joint bargaining by employers prevents the union from engaging in ***whipsaw strikes***—that is, strikes in which the union selectively strikes one firm in the industry. Because that firm's competitors are not struck, they can continue to operate and draw business from the struck firm. The struck firm is under great pressure to concede to union demands to regain lost business. When the firm capitulates, the union repeats the process against other firms. Multiemployer bargaining resists such efforts because all firms bargain together; if the union strikes one firm, the others can lock out their employees to undermine the union's pressure.

In addition to preventing whipsaw strikes, other reasons for engaging in multiemployer bargaining include the following:

- It eases each company's administrative burden by reducing the number of negotiating sessions and aiding information exchange.
- When one large company is the pacesetter in the industry and the union is likely to insist that other firms adopt approximately the same contract terms, smaller employers may have more input into the bargaining process by joining the leader in a multiemployer bargaining arrangement.
- Establishment of uniform wages, hours, and working conditions among the members of the bargaining group means firms will not have to engage in economic competition in the labor market.

Despite the legislative history of Section 8(b)(1)(B), the section does not mention multiemployer bargaining. The Board and the courts have taken the position that multi-employer bargaining cannot be demanded by the interested employers or by the relevant union; rather, it must be consented to by both sides.[43] The union need not agree to bargain with the employers' association, nor can it insist that any company or companies form or join such a bargaining group. However, once the parties have agreed to multiemployer bargaining and negotiations have begun, neither an employer nor the union may withdraw without the consent of the other side, except in the event of "unusual circumstances." This rule prevents one side from pulling out just because the bargaining has taken an undesirable turn. (The Board has held that an impasse, or deadlock in negotiations, does not constitute "unusual circumstances.")

Unions have been found guilty of violating Section 8(b)(1)(B) when they struck to force a company to accept a multiemployer association for bargaining purposes and when they tried

[43]See *Oakwood Care Center*, 343 NLRB 659 (2004).

to force a firm to enter an individual contract in conflict with the established multiemployer unit. In addition, unions that have insisted on bargaining with company executives rather than an attorney hired by management have been held to violate Section 8(b)(1)(B).

Section 8(A)(2): Employer Domination of Labor Unions

In-House Unions Unions created and controlled by the employer.

In the years just prior to and shortly after the passage of the Wagner Act in 1935, employer-formed and dominated unions were common. Firms that decided they could no longer completely resist worker demands for collective action created ***in-house unions***, or captive unions. Such unions or employee associations created an impression of collective bargaining while allowing management to retain complete control. This type of employer domination is outlawed by Section 8(a)(2). That section also outlaws employer interference in the formation or administration of a labor organization, as well as employer support (financial or otherwise) of the same.

As remedies for Section 8(a)(2) violations, the Board may order the employer to cease recognizing the union, to cancel any agreements reached with the union, to cease giving support or assistance to the union, or to disband an in-house or captive union.

Although in-house unions are not a common problem today, the problem of employer support is of continuing interest. Support such as secretarial help, office equipment, or financial aid is prohibited. An employer is permitted by Section 8(a)(2) to allow "employees to confer with him during working hours without loss of time or pay."

An employer who agrees to recognize a union that does not have the support of a majority of employees violates Section 8(a)(2); such recognition is a violation even if the employer acted on a good-faith belief that the union had majority support. An employer is also prohibited from recognizing one union while another union has a petition for a representation election pending before the NLRB. However, in *RCA del Caribe*,[44] the Board held that an employer may continue negotiations with an incumbent union even though a rival union had filed a petition for a representation election. Are these two positions consistent? How can they be reconciled?

In addition to being prohibited from recognizing a nonmajority union, the employer is forbidden from helping a union solicit membership or dues checkoff cards and from allowing a supervisor to serve as a union officer.

One area of interest under Section 8(a)(2) has developed recently as many employers initiated innovative work arrangements among employees. To improve productivity and worker morale, some employers have created autonomous work groups, quality circles, or work teams in which groups of employees are given greater responsibility for determining work schedules, methods, and so forth. When these work groups or teams discuss working conditions, pay, or worker grievances with representatives of the employer, they could be classified as labor organizations under the NLRA. Section 2(5) defines a labor organization as:

> any organization of any kind, or any agency or employee representation committee or plan, in which employees participate and which exists for the purpose, in whole or in part, of dealing with employers concerning grievances, labor disputes, wages, rates of pay, hours of employment, or conditions of work.

[44] 262 NLRB 963 (1982).

The following case deals with the question of whether employer-created "employee action committees" were employer dominated or controlled labor organizations in violation of Section 8(a)(2).

case 14.4 » ELECTROMATION, INC. v. NLRB

35 F.3d 1148 (7th Cir. 1994)

[Electromation, a manufacturer of small electrical components, employed approximately 200 employees; the employees were not represented by a union. In response to financial losses, the company decided to cut expenses by revising its employee attendance policy and replacing the scheduled wage increases with lump-sum payments based on the length of each employee's service at the company. When Electromation informed its employees of these changes, a number of employees signed a letter to the company expressing their dissatisfaction with the changes and asking the company to reconsider. The company president met with randomly selected employees to discuss wages, bonuses, incentive pay, tardiness, attendance programs, and bereavement and sick leave policy. Following this meeting, the president and supervisors concluded that the company would involve the employees to come up with solutions to these issues through the use of "action committees" of employees and management.

At a meeting to explain the action committees, the employees initially reacted negatively to the concept. They reluctantly agreed to the proposed committees and suggested that they be allowed to sign up for specific committees. The next day, the company informed the employees of the formation of five action committees and posted sign-up sheets for the following committees: (1) Absenteeism/Infractions; (2) No Smoking Policy; (3) Communication Network; (4) Pay Progression for Premium Positions; and (5) Attendance Bonus Program. Each committee was to consist of employees and one or two members of management, as well as the company's Employee Benefits Manager, Loretta Dickey, who was in charge of the coordination of all the committees. No employees were involved in the drafting of any aspect of the memorandum or the statement of subjects that the committees were to consider. The company then posted a memo announcing the members of each committee and dates of the initial committee meetings. The company's Employee Benefits Manager had determined which employees would participate on each committee. In late January and early February 1989, four of the action committees began to meet, but the No Smoking Policy Committee was never organized.

At the first meeting of the Attendance Bonus Program Committee, management officials solicited employee ideas regarding a good attendance award program. Through the discussions, the committee developed a proposal, but management declared it was too costly and it was not pursued further.

On February 13, 1989, the International Brotherhood of Teamsters, Local Union No. 1049 (the "union") demanded recognition from the company; the company had been unaware that any organizing efforts had occurred. In late February, the president informed Employee Benefits Manager Dickey of the union's demand. Upon the advice of counsel, Dickey announced at the next meeting of each committee that, due to the union demand, the company could no longer participate in the committees, but that the employee members could continue to meet if they so desired. Finally, on March 15, 1989, the president formally announced to the employees that "due to the Union's campaign, the Company would be unable to participate in the committee meetings and could not continue to work with the committees until after the union election."

The election was held on March 31, 1989; the employees voted 95-82 against union representation. On April 24, 1989, a regional director of the Board issued a complaint alleging that Electromation had violated the Act; the NLRB ultimately found that Electromation violated Sections 8(a)(2) and (1) of the NLRA through its establishment and administration of "action committees" consisting of employees and management. Electromation sought judicial review of the NLRB order.]

Will, J.

... In this appeal, we consider a petition to set aside and a cross-petition to enforce an order of the National Labor Relations Board.

... An allegation that Electromation has violated Section 8(a)(2) and (1) of the Act raises two distinct issues: first, whether the action committees in this case constituted "labor organizations" within the meaning of Section 2(5); and second, whether the employer dominated, influenced, or interfered with the formation or administration of the organization or contributed financial or other support to it, in violation of Section 8(a)(2) and (1) of the Act....

... Under [the] statutory definition [of labor organization,§2(5)] the action committees would constitute labor organizations if: (1) the Electromation employees participated in the committees; (2) the committees existed, at least in part, for the purpose of "dealing with" the employer; and (3) these dealings concerned "grievances, labor disputes, wages, rates of pay, hours of employment, or conditions of work."

In reaching its decision in this case, the Board also noted that "if the organization has as a purpose the representation of employees, it meets the statutory definition of 'employee representation committee or plan' under Section 2(5) and will constitute a labor organization if it also meets the criteria of employee participation and dealing with conditions of work or other statutory subjects." Because the Board found that the employee members of the action committees had acted in a representational capacity, it did not decide whether an employee group could ever be found to constitute a labor organization in the absence of a finding that it acted as a representative of the other employees....

With respect to the first factor, there is no question that the Electromation employees participated in the action committees. Turning to the second factor, which is the most seriously contested on appeal, the Board found that the activities of the action committees constituted "dealing with" the employer. In this appeal, the company primarily argues that the Board erred in finding that Section 8(a)(2) was violated. However, as an alternative ground for setting aside part of the Board's order, the company contends that there is not substantial evidence to support the finding that at least three of the action committees—the Absenteeism/Infractions Committee, the Communication Network Committee, and the Pay Progression for Premium Positions Committee—existed for the purpose of "dealing with" Electromation. Interestingly, the company concedes on appeal that there is enough evidence to support a finding that the fourth committee—the Attendance Bonus Program Committee—existed for the purpose of dealing with the company. The company argues that the other three action committees existed only as simple communication devices not engaged in collective bargaining of any sort, so they are not labor organizations under the statutory definition.

... Given the facts surrounding the formation and administration of all the action committees in this case, we cannot treat each committee separately. First, in their formation and administration, the individual committees were constituted as part of a single entity or program. They were initially conceived as an integrated employer response to deal with growing employee dissatisfaction. It was not until later that individual committee subject areas were identified and categorized by management. Also, a single management representative, Loretta Dickey, was assigned the responsibility for coordinating all action committee activities. The interrelatedness of these committees is further demonstrated by the company's determination that an employee could serve on only one committee at a time.

The company in fact posted only a single announcement identifying the members of each committee. Without consulting each committee individually, Dickey drafted a single statement summarizing the contemplated activities of all the committees. We agree with the Board that the action committees can be differentiated only in the specific subject matter with which each dealt. Each committee had an identical relationship to the company: the purpose, structure, and administration of each committee was essentially the same....

... even if the committees are considered individually, there exists substantial evidence that each was formed and existed for the purpose of "dealing with" the company. It is in fact the shared similarities among the committee structures which compels unitary treatment of them for the purposes of the issues raised in this appeal....

We have previously noted that the broad construction of [the definition of] labor organization applies not only with regard to the "absence of formal organization, [but also to] the type of interchange between parties which may be deemed 'dealing'" with employers. Moreover, an organization may satisfy the statutory requirement that it exists for the purpose in whole or in part of dealing with employers even if it has not engaged in actual bargaining or concluded a bargaining agreement.

... the Supreme Court [in *Cabot Carbon* (1959)] expressly rejected the contention that "dealing with" means "bargaining with," noting that Congress had declined to accept a proposal to substitute the phrase "bargaining with" for "dealing with" under Section 2 (5).... First, the Court found that nothing in the plain words of Section 2(5), its legislative history, or the decisions construing it, supported the contention that an employee committee which does not "bargain with" employers in the usual concept of collective bargaining does not engage in "dealing with" employers and, therefore, is not a labor organization.... According to the *Cabot Carbon* Court, by adopting the broader term "dealing with" and rejecting the more limited term "bargaining collectively," Congress clearly did not intend that the broad term "dealing with" should be limited to and mean only "bargaining with."

… Relying in large part on these principles, the Board here explained that "dealing with" is a bilateral mechanism involving proposals from the employee organization concerning the subjects listed in Section 2(5), coupled with real or apparent consideration of those proposals by management.…

Given the … holding in *Cabot Carbon* that "dealing with" includes conduct much broader than collective bargaining, the Board did not err in determining that the Electromation action committees constituted labor organizations within the meaning of Sections 2(5) and 8(a)(2) of the Act. Although it is true that [the company] … made no guarantees as to the results regarding the employee recommendations, the activities of the action committees nonetheless constituted "dealing with" the employer. Finally, with respect to the third factor, the subject matter of that dealing—for example, the treatment of employee absenteeism and employee bonuses—obviously concerned conditions of employment. We further agree with the Board that the purpose of the action committees was not limited to the improvement of company efficiency or product quality, but rather that they were designed to function and in fact functioned in an essentially representative capacity. Accordingly, given the statute's traditionally broad construction, there is substantial evidence to support the Board's finding that the action committees constituted labor organizations.…

… [W]e must next consider whether, through their creation and administration of the action committees, the company acted unlawfully in violation of Section 8(a)(2) and (1) of the Act.

… the Board focused its analysis on the relationship between Electromation's actions in creating and administering the action committees and the resulting effect upon its employees' rights under the Act.… The Board correctly focused on management's participation in the action committees and its effect on the employees and found domination in that the company defined the committee structures and committee subject matters, appointed a manager to coordinate and monitor the committee meetings, structured each committee to include one or two management representatives, and permitted those managers to review and reject committee proposals before they could be presented to upper level management. The Board's interpretation of Section 8(a)(2) simply does not contravene the statutory language.…

Electromation … also argues that Section 8(a)(2) requires proof of actual domination or interference with the employees' free choice.…

As the Board found, substantial evidence supports the finding of company domination of the action committees. First, the company proposed and essentially imposed the action committees upon its employees as the only acceptable mechanism for resolution of their acknowledged grievances regarding the newly announced attendance bonus policies.…

The record also clearly shows that the employees were initially reluctant to accept the company's proposal of the action committees as a means to address their concerns; their reaction was "not positive." Nonetheless, the company continued to press the idea until the employees eventually accepted. Moreover, although the company informed the employees that they could continue to meet on their own, shortly after Electromation removed its management representatives from the committees due to the union recognition demand and announced that it would not work with the committees until after the union election, several of the committees disbanded.…

The company played a pivotal role in establishing both the framework and the agenda for the action committees. Electromation unilaterally selected the size, structure, and procedural functioning of the committees; it decided the number of committees and the topic(s) to be addressed by each. The company unilaterally drafted the action committees' purposes and goal statements, which identified from the start the focus of each committee's work.

… Electromation actually controlled which issues received attention by the committees and which did not.…

Although the company acceded to the employees' request that volunteers form the committees, it unilaterally determined how many could serve on each committee, decided that an employee could serve on only one committee at a time, and determined which committee certain employees would serve on, thus exercising significant control over the employees' participation and voice at the committee meetings.… Also, the company designated management representatives to serve on the committees. Employee Benefits Manager Dickey was assigned to coordinate and serve on all committees. In the case of the Attendance Bonus Program Committee, the management representative … reviewed employee proposals, determined whether they were economically feasible, and further decided whether they would be presented to higher management. This role of the management committee members effectively put the employer on both sides of the bargaining table, an avowed proscription of the Act. Finally, the company paid the employees for their time spent on committee activities, provided meeting space, and furnished all necessary supplies for the committees' activities. While such financial support is clearly not a violation of Section 8(a)(2) by itself, ... in the totality of the circumstances in this case such support may reasonably be characterized to be in furtherance of the company's domination of the action committees. We therefore conclude that there is substantial evidence to support the Board's finding of unlawful employer domination and interference in violation of Section 8(a)(2) and (1).

... Accordingly, because we find that substantial evidence supports the Board's factual findings and that its legal conclusions have a reasonable basis in the law, we affirm the Board's findings and enforce the Board's order.

Enforced.

Case Questions

1. What was the purpose of the action committees created by Electromation? Did the committees constitute labor organizations within the meaning of Section 2(5) of the NLRA? Explain your answer.
2. When does a labor organization "deal with" an employer within the meaning of Section 2(5)? Did Electromation "deal with" the action committees? Explain.
3. On what basis did the NLRB and the court determine that Electromation dominated and controlled the action committees?

An employer-created group of managers and employees that discussed matters such as medical benefits, stock ownership plans, and termination policy was held to be an employer-dominated labor organization in violation of Section 8(a)(2) in *Polaroid Corp.*[45] However, an employee committee that exists for the purpose of sharing information with the employer and simply gathers information and makes no proposals to the employer, is not a labor organization, according to *NLRB v. Peninsula General Hospital Medical Center.*[46]

ethical DILEMMA

Employee Involvement Group for Wydget?

You are the human resources manager of Wydget Corporation, a small manufacturing firm. The employees of Wydget are not unionized. Because of difficult business conditions, the workers' wages have not increased in several years, and their medical insurance benefits have been reduced. As a result, morale among employees is low, and there has been high turnover in the work force. You are considering creating an employee involvement group to provide an opportunity for workers to share their concerns and ideas with management and to discuss production problems and working conditions. How can you structure the group to ensure that employees feel their role is effective, without running afoul of Section 8(a)(2)? What are the potential problems associated with the creation of such a group? Should you establish the employee involvement group? Explain the reasons for your opinion.

[45] 329 NLRB 424 (1999).

[46] 36 F.3d 1262 (4th Cir. 1994).

Sections 8(A)(3) and 8(B)(2): Discrimination in Terms or Conditions of Employment

Under Section 8(a)(3) of the NLRA, employers are forbidden to discriminate "in regard to hire or tenure or employment or any term or condition of employment to encourage or discourage membership in any labor organization." Unions, under Section 8(b)(2), are forbidden to:

> cause or attempt to cause an employer to discriminate against an employee in violation of Subsection 8(a)(3) or to discriminate against an employee with respect to whom membership in such organization has been denied or terminated on some ground other than ... failure to tender the periodic dues and the initiation fees uniformly required as a condition of ... membership....

The intent of these sections is to insulate an employee's employment from conditions based on his or her union sympathies or lack thereof. If an employee is to have the free choice, under Section 7, to join or refrain from joining a union, then that employee must not be made to suffer economically for his or her choice. The wording of Sections 8(a)(3) and 8(b)(2) indicates that a violation of these sections has two elements.

- First, there must be some discrimination in the terms or conditions of employment—either a refusal to hire, discharge, lay off, or discipline—or a union attempt to get the employer to so discriminate.
- Second, the discrimination or attempt to cause discrimination must be for the purpose of encouraging or discouraging union membership.

For example, in *USF Red Star, Inc.*,[47] a union's efforts to get the employer to discharge an employee because of his internal union activities violated Section 8(b)(2) [and Section 8(b)(1)(A)]; when the employer discharged the employee because of the union's demands, it violated Section 8(a)(3) [and Section 8(a)(1)].

Because the discrimination (or attempt to cause it) must be for the purpose of encouraging or discouraging union membership, intention is a necessary part of a violation of these sections. If an employer (or union) states that an employee should be fired because of participation in union activities (or lack of participation), demonstrating the requisite intention for a violation is no problem. But most complaints involving Section 8(a)(3) or Section 8(b)(2) are not as clear-cut. For example, what happens if an employee who supports the union's organizing campaign also has a poor work record? How should the Board and the courts handle a case in which the employer or union has mixed motives for its actions? That is the subject of the following case.

case 14.5 » NLRB v. Transportation Management Corp.

462 U.S. 393 (1983)

White, J.

The National Labor Relations Act makes unlawful the discharge of workers because of union activity, but employers retain the right to discharge workers for any number of other reasons unrelated to the employee's union activities. When the General Counsel of the National Labor Relations Board (Board) files a complaint alleging that an employee was discharged because of his union activities, the employer may assert

[47] 330 NLRB 53 (1999).

legitimate motives for his decision. In *Wright Line* … the National Labor Relations Board reformulated the allocation of the burden of proof in such cases. It determined that the General Counsel carried the burden of persuading the Board that an anti-union animus contributed to the employer's decision to discharge an employee, a burden that does not shift, but that the employer, even if it failed to meet or neutralize the General Counsel's showing, could avoid the finding that it violated the statute by demonstrating by a preponderance of the evidence that the worker would have been fired even if he had not been involved with the Union. The question presented in this case is whether the burden placed on the employer in *Wright Line* is consistent with Sections 8(a)(1) and 8(a)(3), as well as with Section 10(c) of the NLRA, which provides that the Board must prove an unlawful labor practice by a "preponderance of the evidence."

Prior to his discharge, Sam Santillo was a bus driver for respondent Transportation Management Corporation. On March 19, 1979, Santillo talked to officials of the Teamster's Union about organizing the drivers who worked with him. Over the next four days Santillo discussed with his fellow drivers the possibility of joining the Teamsters and distributed authorization cards. On the night of March 23, George Patterson, who supervised Santillo and the other drivers, told one of the drivers that he had heard of Santillo's activities. Patterson referred to Santillo as two-faced, and promised to get even with him.

Later that evening Patterson talked to Ed West who was also a bus driver for respondent. Patterson asked, "What's with Sam and the Union?" Patterson said that he took Santillo's actions personally, recounted several favors he had done for Santillo, and added that he would remember Santillo's activities when Santillo again asked for a favor. On Monday, March 26, Santillo was discharged. Patterson told Santillo that he was being fired for leaving his keys in the bus and taking unauthorized breaks.

Santillo filed a complaint with the Board alleging that he had been discharged because of his union activities, contrary to Sections 8(a)(1) and 8(a)(3) of the NLRA. The General Counsel issued a complaint. The administrative law judge (ALJ) determined by a preponderance of the evidence that Patterson clearly had an anti-union animus and that Santillo's discharge was motivated by a desire to discourage union activities. The ALJ also found that the asserted reasons for the discharge could not withstand scrutiny. Patterson's disapproval of Santillo's practice of leaving his keys in the bus was clearly a pretext, for Patterson had not known about Santillo's practice until after he had decided to discharge Santillo; moreover, the practice of leaving keys in buses was commonplace among respondent's employees. Respondent identified two types of unauthorized breaks, coffee breaks and stops at home. With respect to both coffee breaks and stopping at home, the ALJ found that Santillo was never cautioned or admonished about such behavior, and that the employer had not followed its customary practice of issuing three written warnings before discharging a driver. The ALJ also found that the taking of coffee breaks during working hours was normal practice, and that respondent tolerated the practice unless the breaks interfered with the driver's performance of his duties. In any event, said the ALJ, respondent had never taken any adverse personnel action against an employee because of such behavior. While acknowledging that Santillo had engaged in some unsatisfactory conduct, the ALJ was not persuaded that Santillo would have been fired had it not been for his union activities.

The Board affirmed, adopting with some clarification the ALJ's findings and conclusions and expressly applying its *Wright Line* decision. It stated that respondent had failed to carry its burden of persuading the Board that the discharge would have taken place had Santillo not engaged in activity protected by the Act. The First Circuit Court of Appeals, relying on its previous decision rejecting the Board's *Wright Line* test … refused to enforce the Board's order and remanded for consideration of whether the General Counsel had proved by a preponderance of the evidence that Santillo would not have been fired had it not been for his union activities....

As we understand the Board's decisions, they have consistently held that the unfair labor practice consists of a discharge or other adverse action that is based in whole or in part on anti-union animus—or as the Board now puts it, that the employee's protected conduct was a substantial or motivating factor in the adverse action. The General Counsel has the burden of proving these elements under Section 10(c). But the Board's construction of the statute permits an employer to avoid being adjudicated a violator by showing what his actions would have been regardless of his forbidden motivation. It extends to the employer what the Board considers to be an affirmative defense but does not change or add to the elements of the unfair labor practice that the General Counsel has the burden of proving under Section 10(c). The Board has instead chosen to recognize, as it insists it has done for many years, what it designates as an affirmative defense that the employer has the burden of sustaining. We are unprepared to hold that this is an impermissible construction of the Act. "[T]he Board's construction here, while it may not be required by the Act, is at least permissible under it …" and in these circumstances its position is entitled to deference.

The Board's allocation of the burden of proof is clearly reasonable in this context.... The employer is a wrongdoer; he has acted out of a motive that is declared illegitimate by the statute. It is fair that he bear the risk that the influence of legal and illegal motives cannot be separated, because he knowingly created the risk and because the risk was created not by innocent activity but by his own wrongdoing.

For these reasons, we conclude that the Court of Appeals erred in refusing to enforce the Board's orders, which rested on the Board's *Wright Line* decision.

The Board was justified in this case in concluding that Santillo would not have been discharged had the employer not considered his efforts to establish a union. At least two of the transgressions that purportedly would have in any event prompted Santillo's discharge were commonplace, and yet no transgressor had ever before received any kind of discipline. Moreover, the employer departed from its usual practice in dealing with rules infractions; indeed, not only did the employer not warn Santillo that his actions would result in being subjected to discipline, it never even expressed its disapproval of his conduct. In addition, Patterson, the person who made the initial decision to discharge Santillo, was obviously upset with Santillo for engaging in such protected activity. It is thus clear that the Board's finding that Santillo would not have been fired even if the employer had not had an anti-union animus was "supported by substantial evidence on the record considered as a whole".... Accordingly, the judgment is

Reversed.

Case Questions

1. What reasons did the employer offer to justify Santillo's discharge? What, according to Santillo, prompted his discharge?
2. What evidence did the NLRB present to challenge the employer's reasons for the discharge?
3. When does the NLRB's *Wright Line* test apply? What does it require? Does the Supreme Court uphold the *Wright Line* test?

Can an employer refuse to hire an applicant whom the employer suspects is really a union organizer (known as a "salt" or "union salt"), or is such a refusal to hire a violation of Section 8(a)(3)? In *Toering Electric Co.*[48] the NLRB held that when an employer is charged with discriminatorily failing to hire an applicant for employment, the employer can defend itself against the unfair labor practice charge by raising a reasonable question as to the applicant's actual interest in working for the employer. If the employer puts forward such evidence, then the general counsel must establish, by a preponderance of evidence, that the applicant was genuinely interested in establishing an employment relationship with the employer. If the general counsel fails to make such a showing, then the employer's refusal to hire the applicant is lawful; if the general counsel succeeds in making such a showing, then the employer is in violation of Sections 8(a)(3) and 8(a)(1).

Discrimination in Employment to Encourage Union Membership

Union Security Agreements

Union Security Agreements Contract provisions requiring employees to join the union or pay union dues.

Although Section 8(a)(3) and Section 8(b)(2) prohibit discrimination to encourage or discourage union membership, there is an important exception regarding the "encouragement" of union membership. That exception deals with ***union security agreements***—when an employer and union agree that employees must either join the union or at least pay union dues in order to remain employees. This exception requires some discussion.

[48] 351 NLRB No. 18 (2007).

Prior to the Taft-Hartley Act of 1947, unions and employers could agree that an employer would hire only employees who were already union members. These agreements, called closed shop agreements, had the effect of encouraging (or requiring) workers to join unions if they wished to get a job. Such agreements clearly restrict the employee's free exercise of Section 7 rights; for that reason, they were prohibited. But the Taft-Hartley amendments did not completely prohibit all "union security" arrangements. Section 8(a)(3), as amended by Taft-Hartley, contains the following provision:

> Provided, that nothing in this Act ... shall preclude an employer from making an agreement with a labor organization ... to require as a condition of employment membership therein on or after the thirtieth day following the beginning of such agreement, whichever is later....

Section 8(a)(3) also provides that an employer can justify discharging an employee for nonmembership in a union only if membership was denied or terminated because of the employee's failure to pay the dues and initiation fees required of all members.

Union Shop Agreement
Agreement requiring employees to join the union after a certain period of time.

Agency Shop Agreement
Agreement requiring employees to pay union dues, but not requiring them to join the union.

The effect of these provisions is to allow an employer and union to agree to a union shop or agency shop provision. A ***union shop agreement*** requires that all employees hired by the employer must join the union after a certain period of time, not less than thirty days. Although employees need not be union members to be hired, they must become union members if they are to remain employed past the specified time period. An ***agency shop agreement*** does not require that employees actually join the union, but they must at least pay the dues and fees required of union members.

Although Section 8(a)(3) states that an employer and a union can agree "to require as a condition of employment membership" in the union on or after thirty days of hiring, Section 8(b)(2) and the second proviso to Section 8(a)(3) state that an employee cannot be fired except for failure to pay dues and initiation fees. In effect, this latter language has the legal effect of reducing all union shops to the level of agency shops. Under an agency shop agreement, remember, employees need not become formal members of the union but must pay union dues. Under the language of Section 8(b)(2), formal union members cannot be fired for disobeying the union's internal rules or failing to participate in union affairs. The only difference is that they may be fined by the union for these infractions, and the fines may be enforceable in a state court. Furthermore, the law is clear that an employee who pays dues but refuses to assume full union membership cannot be held to these rules and sanctions.

Unions argue that union security provisions are needed to prevent "free riders"; since all members of the bargaining unit get the benefits of the union's agreement, whether or not they are union members, they should be required to pay the costs of negotiating and administering the agreement—union dues. Only by paying the costs of such union representation can free riders be prevented.

Although such agreements do prevent free riders, they are also coercive to the extent that they may override an employee's free choice of whether or not to join a union. For that reason, the act permits states to outlaw such union security agreements. Section 14(b) states that

> Nothing in this Act shall be construed as authorizing the execution or application of agreements requiring membership in a labor organization as a condition of employment in any state or territory in which such execution or application is prohibited by State or Territorial law.

Right-to-Work Laws
Laws which prohibit union security agreements.

This section allows for the passage of ***right-to-work laws***, which prohibit such union security agreements. In states that have passed such a law, the union shop and agency shop agreements are illegal. A number of states, mainly in the South and West (the Sun Belt) have passed such laws. It is also worth noting that Section 19 of the act was amended to allow employees with bona fide religious objections to joining unions or paying union dues to make arrangements to pay the required fees or dues to a charitable organization.

When a union security agreement is in effect, the employer must discharge an employee, upon the union's request, if the employee has been denied membership in or expelled from the union for failure to pay the required union dues or fees. Under Section 8(b)(2), the union cannot legally demand the discharge of an employee for refusing to pay "back dues" or "reinstatement fees" after a lapse of membership in a prior job. Other examples of union violations of Section 8(b)(2) include:

- Forcing an employer to agree to hire only applicants satisfactory to the union
- Causing an employee to be discharged for opposition to the manner in which internal union affairs are conducted
- Causing an employee to be discharged because the worker was disliked or considered a troublemaker by the union leadership

Hiring Halls

Hiring Halls
A job-referral mechanism operated by unions whereby unions refer members to prospective employers.

In some industries, employers rely on unions to refer prospective employees to the various employers. Such arrangements, known as ***hiring halls***, are common in industries such as trucking, construction, and longshoring. Hiring halls and other job-referral mechanisms operated by unions may have the effect of encouraging membership in the union because an employee must go through the union to get a job. The NLRB and the Supreme Court have held such hiring halls or referral mechanisms to be legal as long as they meet the following conditions:

- The union must not discriminate on grounds of union membership for job referrals
- The employer may reject any applicant referred by the union
- A notice of the nondiscriminatory operation of the referral service must be posted in the hiring hall

It is also legal for the union to set skill levels necessary for membership or for referral to employers through a hiring hall.

Preferential Treatment for Union Officers: Super Seniority

In some collective agreements, an employer will agree to give union officers or stewards preferential treatment in the event of layoffs or recall of employees. Such provisions, known as super seniority because layoff and recall are usually done on the basis of seniority, may have the effect of encouraging union membership. Yet they also serve to ensure that employees responsible for the enforcement and administration of the collective agreement remain on the job to ensure the protection of all employees' rights under the contract. However, preferential treatment that goes beyond layoff and recall rights is not so readily justified. For that reason, and because it clearly discriminates in employment conditions to encourage union activity, broad super seniority clauses may involve violations of Sections 8(a)(3) and 8(b)(2).

Discrimination in Employment to Discourage Union Membership

Just as discrimination in terms or conditions of employment to encourage union membership violates Section 8(a)(3), so does discrimination that is intended to discourage union membership or activities. Most complaints alleging discrimination to discourage such activities occur in the context of union organizing campaigns or strikes.

Activity protected under Section 7 includes union organizing activity as well as strikes over economic issues or to protest unfair labor practices. The employer that refuses to hire, or discharges, lays off, or disciplines an employee for such activity is in violation of Section 8(a)(3). Although the employer must have acted with the intention of discouraging union membership, the Board has held that specific evidence of such an intention need not be shown if the employer's conduct is inherently destructive of the employee's Section 7 rights.

As noted earlier, several reasons may be behind an employer's action; antiunion motives may play a part, along with legitimate work-related reasons. Recall that in *NLRB v. Transportation Management*, the Supreme Court upheld the Board practice of requiring the employer to show that the discipline or discharge would have occurred even without the employee's protected conduct. If the employer can meet that burden, then it is not a violation of Section 8(a)(3). However, if there are no legitimate business reasons for the employer's actions, then the conduct is a violation, according to *Huck Store Fixture Co. v. NLRB.*[49]

An employer who fires employees for engaging in a union organizing campaign is in violation of Section 8(a)(3). Firing employees for striking over economic demands is also a violation. Other examples of Section 8(a)(3) violations include:

- layoffs that violate seniority rules and that fall mainly upon union supporters;
- disproportionately severe discipline of union officers or supporters;
- discharging a union supporter without the customary warning prior to discharge;
- discharging a union supporter based on past misconduct that had previously been condoned; and
- selective enforcement of rules against union supporters.

Strikes as Protected Activity

Strikes by employees are the essence of concerted activity; workers agree to withhold their labor from the employer in order to pressure the employer to accept their demands. A strike for collective bargaining purposes or for purposes of mutual aid and protection comes under the protection of Section 7. However, despite the purposes of the strike, if it violates the collective agreement or if workers are attempting to strike while still collecting their pay, the strike may not be protected.

When discussing the rights of strikers under the NLRA and the employer's response to the strike, the Board and the courts distinguish between economic strikes and *unfair labor practice strikes*. As discussed in Chapter 13, *an economic strike* is called to pressure the employer to accept the union's negotiating demands. It occurs after the old collective agreement has expired and negotiations for a new agreement break down. By contrast, an unfair labor practice strike is called to protest an employer's illegal actions. It does not involve contract demands or negotiations. The rights of strikers thus may depend on whether the strike is an unfair labor practice or economic strike. An economic strike may be converted into an unfair labor practice

[49]327 F.3d 528 (7th Cir. 2003).

strike by an employer's unfair practices that are committed during the strike, as in *Ryan Iron Works, Inc.*[50]

Unfair Labor Practice Strikes

The Supreme Court has held, in *Mastro Plastics v. NLRB*,[51] that unfair labor practice strikes are protected activity under the act. This means that unfair labor practice strikers may not be fired for going on strike, nor may they be permanently replaced. Strikes that begin as economic strikes may become unfair labor practice strikes if the employer commits serious unfair labor practices during the strike. For example, if the employer refused to bargain with the union over a new agreement and discharged the strikers, the strike would become an unfair labor practice strike. An employer may hire workers to replace the strikers during an unfair labor practice strike, but the strikers must be reinstated when the strike is over. In *National Steel Supply, Inc.*,[52] an employer who terminated or permanently replaced workers striking to protest the illegal termination of an employee violated Section 8(a)(3). Although misconduct on the picket line may normally be a sufficient reason for an employer to discharge a striker, the Board has held in prior decisions that severe misconduct (such as physical assault) is needed to justify the discharge of an unfair labor practice striker.

However, in *Clear Pine Mouldings, Inc.*,[53] the Board held that the existence of an unfair labor practice strike:

> does not in any way privilege those employees [on strike] to engage in other than peaceful picketing and persuasion.... There is nothing in the statute to support the notion that striking employees are free to engage in or escalate violence or misconduct in proportion to their estimates of the degree of seriousness of an employer's unfair labor practices.

Economic Strikes

Economic strikes, as previously noted, are work stoppages by the employees designed to force the employer to meet their bargaining demands for increased wages or other benefits. As with unfair labor practice strikes, economic strikes are protected activity; however, the protections afforded economic strikers are not as great as those given unfair labor practice strikers. As mentioned earlier in the discussion of protected activity under Section 7, on-the job slowdowns are not protected, and employees who engage in such conduct may be discharged. In addition, economic strikes in violation of the collective agreement are not protected.

When the economic strike is protected, the striking employees may not be discharged for going on strike; however, the employer may hire permanent replacements for the striking employees. The right to hire permanent replacements was affirmed by the Supreme Court in 1938 in the case of *NLRB v. MacKay Radio & Telegraph*.[54] Replacement workers hired on an at-will basis may be considered permanent replacements by the NLRB where the employer explicitly indicated to them that the employer intended to hire them as permanent

---

[50] 332 NLRB 506 (2000).

[51] 350 U.S. 270 (1956).

[52] 344 NLRB 973 (2005).

[53] 268 NLRB 1044 (1984).

[54] 304 U.S. 333 (1938).

replacements, according to *Jones Plastic & Engineering Co.*[55] Although the striking employees may be permanently replaced, they still retain their status as "employees" under the act. [See the definition of employee in Section 2(3).] Because they retain their status as employees, the strikers are entitled to be reinstated if they make an unconditional application for reinstatement and if vacancies are available. If no positions are available at the time of their application, even if the lack of vacancies is due to the hiring of replacements, the employer need not reinstate the strikers. However, if the strikers continue to indicate an interest in reinstatement, the employer is required to rehire them as positions become available. This requirement was upheld by the Supreme Court in *NLRB v. Fleetwood Trailers Co.*[56]

In *Laidlaw Corp.*,[57] the NLRB held that economic strikers who had made an unconditional application for reinstatement and who continued to make known their availability for employment were entitled to be recalled by the employer prior to the employer's hiring of new employees.

In *David R. Webb Co., Inc. v. NLRB*,[58] the Court of Appeals held that the employer's duty to reinstate strikers continues until the strikers have been reinstated to their former positions or to substantially equivalent positions. Reinstating them to lower positions does not satisfy the employer's obligation. The following case discusses when, if ever, the employer may have a legitimate justification to refuse to reinstate strikers.

The NLRB has held that a union may waive the right of strikers to be reinstated with full seniority in exchange for an end to a strike, as in *Gem City Ready Mix*[59] and *NLRB v. Harrison Ready Mix Concrete.*[60] The following case deals with an employer's justification for refusing to reinstate strikers in their former positions or other available equivalent positions.

case 14.6 »

Diamond Walnut Growers, Inc. v. NLRB

113 F.3d 1259 (D.C. Cir. 1997) (en banc)

Facts: Following the expiration of their collective bargaining agreement, nearly 500 of Diamond Walnut Growers permanent and seasonal employees went on strike. Diamond hired replacement workers to continue operations. The strike was bitter, and the union encouraged a public boycott of Diamond's products to exert economic pressure on Diamond. The boycott included a well-publicized national bus tour during which union members publicly distributed leaflets describing Diamond's work force as "scabs" who packaged walnuts contaminated with "mold, dirt, oil, worms and debris."

One year into the strike, the NLRB held a representation election. The union lost but filed objections with the NLRB, and the NLRB ordered that a new election be held in October 1993. Two weeks prior to the new election, four striking employees approached Diamond with an unconditional offer to return to work. Because their former jobs and other substantially equivalent jobs were not available for three of the returning strikers at the time of their return, Diamond placed them in seasonal jobs. The union lost the rerun election.

---

[55] 351 NLRB No. 11 (2007).

[56] 389 U.S. 375 (1967).

[57] 171 NLRB 1366 (1968).

[58] 888 F.2d 501 (7th Cir. 1990).

[59] 279 NLRB 191, 116 L.R.R.M. 1266 (1984).

[60] 770 F.2d 78 (6th Cir. 1985).

The NLRB General Counsel then filed a complaint alleging that Diamond had violated Sections 8(a)(3) and 8(a)(1) of the National Labor Relations Act by unlawfully discriminating against the three reinstated strikers by refusing to put them in certain seasonal position because of their protected activity. After a hearing, the ALJ recommended that the charges be dismissed because, while he found that Diamond had discriminated against the employees, the discrimination was not unlawful because no vacancies in their former jobs or in substantially equivalent jobs were available when they sought reinstatement.

On review, the NLRB reversed the ALJ's decision. The Board held that, while Diamond was under no legal obligation to reinstate the strikers, once it decided to reinstate them, it was required to act in a nondiscriminatory fashion toward them. The NLRB held that Diamond had discriminated against the three strikers because of their union status and/or because of certain protected activity they engaged in while on strike. The Board rejected Diamond's justifications for placing the three returning strikers as it did: the employer's concern that the replacement workers might instigate violence against the three and that the placements were justified by their participation in the boycott and the circulation of disparaging leaflets. The NLRB held that Diamond had failed to justify its discrimination and was guilty of unfair labor practices. Diamond sought judicial review of the NLRB decision in the U.S. Court of Appeals for the D.C. Circuit.

Issue: Did the employer provide an adequate business justification for its refusal to reinstate the three strikers in their former, or equivalent, positions?

Decision: The court held that this case was governed by *Fleetwood Trailers*. The general counsel must make out a prima facie case that the employer discriminated in its treatment of the returning strikers because of their protected activity. A struck employer faced with an unconditional offer to return to work is obliged to treat the returning employee like any other applicant for work, unless the employee's former job or its substantial equivalent is available, in which case the employee is preferred to any other applicant. But here the returning strikers were not treated like any other applicants. Diamond admitted that it took into account the returnees' protected activity in choosing to place them in jobs that were objectively less desirable than those for which they were qualified.

Under *Fleetwood Trailers*, once discrimination is shown, the burden shifts to the employer to establish that its treatment of the employees has a legitimate and substantial business justification. Diamond declined to place the returnees in their former jobs or equivalent positions for which they were qualified because of two concerns: potential hostility against them by the replacements workers, and because the returnees had participated in the union boycott activities, they might be tempted to engage in sabotage or to let defective nuts get through inspection or to contaminate the packaged walnuts. The Board concluded that the possibility of the returnees engaging in future sabotage was simply not a sufficient risk to constitute a substantial business justification for their treatment. As for the employer's concern for the safety of a few returning strikers, put in the midst of a majority of replacements in a strike marked by violence, it may be genuine; but the Board insisted that the employer provide evidence of a concrete threat to those strikers. Otherwise, an employer's generalized concern could easily serve as a handy pretext for disfavoring returning strikers. If there were evidence of such a threat, the employer might well be obliged to take adequate preventative measures against those who threatened the violence, rather than against those who were threatened. Strikes tend to be hard struggles, and although this one may have been more bitter than most, there is always a potential danger that returning strikers may engage in some form of sabotage, especially while the strike is still in progress. There is undeniably some risk in employing returning strikers during a strike, but an employer is forced to assume such risk of sabotage, because otherwise, the employer would not be required to take back strikers at all. There may well be situations in which an employer could produce compelling grounds for a relatively unfavorable assignment of a returning striker. The Board here implied that a serious threat of violence against the striker might suffice. The Board must consider whatever special circumstances are presented by an employer asserting the defense of substantial justification, and it may not summarily reject an employer's specific and persuasive explanation.

«

Other Strike-Related Issues

Recall that under Section 7, employees have the right to refrain from concerted activity, which includes the right to remain working rather than go on strike. As noted in the discussion of Section 8(b)(2), a union may impose some disciplinary sanctions upon union members who refuse to go on strike, but they may not cause an employer to discriminate against such employees in terms or conditions of employment. Nor may the employer offer incentives or benefits to the replacements or those employees not going on strike when such benefits are not available to the strikers. In the case of *NLRB v. Erie Resistor Co.*,[61] the Supreme Court held that the employer's granting of twenty years' seniority to all replacements violated Section 8(a)(3). The effect of such seniority was to insulate the replacements from layoff, while exposing employees who went on strike to layoff. This effect would continue long after the strike was over; it would place the former strikers at a disadvantage simply because they went on strike. Although *Erie Resistor* involved rather severe actions by the employer, the NLRB has held that any preferential treatment in terms or conditions of employment accorded to the nonstrikers or replacements, and not to the strikers, violates Section 8(a)(3).

A 1983 Supreme Court decision involved the rights of the workers hired to replace economic strikers. In *Belknap v. Hale*,[62] the Court held that replacements hired under the promise of permanent employment could sue the employer for breach of contract if they were laid off at the end of the strike. Does *Belknap v. Hale* undermine the rights of strikers to be reinstated?

Employer Response to Strike Activity

Lockout
An employer's temporary withdrawal of employment to pressure employees to agree to the employer's bargaining proposals.

Just as employees are free to go on strike to promote their economic demands, employers are free to withdraw employment from employees to pressure them to accept the employer's demands. This tactic, called a ***lockout***, is the temporary withdrawal of employment to pressure employees to agree to the employer's bargaining proposals. A lockout needs to be distinguished from a permanent closure of a plant to avoid unionization.

When the employees have not gone on strike, the employer may be reluctant to "lock them out." But when the threat of a "quickie strike" or unannounced walkout poses the prospect of damage to equipment or disruption of business, the employer may lock out to avoid such problems. The Board has consistently held that such "defensive" lockouts are not unfair labor practices. Lockouts by the employers in a multiemployer bargaining unit, to avoid a whipsaw strike by the union, have been held legal by the Board and the Supreme Court. What about the situation in which an employer locks out the unionized employees and hires replacements? This issue is addressed in the following Supreme Court decision.

case 14.7 »

NLRB v. Brown

380 U.S. 278 (1965)

Facts: Five employers operated six retail grocery stores. The employers were members of a multiemployer bargaining unit that was represented by Local 462 of the Retail Clerks International Association. When the negotiations to renew the collective agreement covering the multiemployer unit stalled, the union went on strike against Food Jet, one of the five employers. The other four employers immediately locked out all their employees represented by the union, telling them and the Local that they would be recalled to work when the strike against Food Jet ended. All the employers continued to operate their businesses using temporary replacement workers. The replacement employees were told that

[61] 373 U.S. 221 (1963).

[62] 463 U.S. 491 (1983).

they were hired only as long as the union was on strike. A new agreement was reached and the strike ended, and the employers immediately released the temporary replacements and restored the strikers and the locked out employees to their jobs. The union filed a complaint with the NLRB over the lockout and hiring of replacement workers. The NLRB held that the employers violated Sections 8(a)(1) and (3) of the NLRA by locking out their regular employees and using temporary replacements to carry on business. The Court of Appeals for the Tenth Circuit disagreed and refused to enforce the Board's order. The NLRB then appealed to the U.S. Supreme Court.

Issue: Have the employers violated Sections 8(a)(1) and (3) of the NLRA by locking out their regular employees and hiring temporary replacements during the strike against one of the employers in the multiemployer bargaining unit?

Decision: Under the NLRA, there are a number of economic weapons the parties can use in seeking to force acceptance of their bargaining demands. Absent proof of unlawful motivation, employers may resort to various economic weapons to blunt the effectiveness of an anticipated strike by stockpiling inventories, readjusting contract schedules, or transferring work from one plant to another. Employers are also able to use a lockout as a legitimate economic weapon in various circumstances. The Court here held that the employers' continued operations and the use of temporary replacements did not demonstrate any hostile motivation, nor was it inherently more destructive of employee rights than the lockout itself. The lockout and use of temporary replacements was part of the employers' defensive measure to preserve the multiemployer group in the face of the whipsaw strike. Because Food Jet legitimately continued business operations during the strike, it was only reasonable to regard the employers' actions as an attempt to preserve the integrity of the multiemployer bargaining unit that was threatened unless they stayed open for business during the lockout. If Food Jet had been able to stay open for business while the other stores were closed, the whipsaw strike could succeed in breaking up the multiemployer bargaining unit. Given the very competitive nature of the retail grocery business, the employers' use of temporary replacements during the lockout was consistent with a legitimate business purpose.

In order to find that conduct violated Section 8(a)(3) there must be discrimination that would discourage union membership, but the added element of antiunion intent is also required. While the use of temporary replacement workers in preference to the locked-out union members was discriminatory, the Court here held that any resulting tendency to discourage union membership was comparatively remote, and that the use of temporary workers was reasonably related to a legitimate business purpose. The use of replacement workers was temporary, only for the duration of the strike; the replacements did not threaten the jobs of the striking employees. The striking employees could end the strike and terminate the lockout at any time simply by agreeing to the employers' contract terms and returning to work on a regular basis. As well, the new collective agreement contained a union-shop provision that had been carried forward from the prior agreement, so a union member would have nothing to gain and much to lose by quitting the union. Given those circumstances, the Court held that the employers' actions here did not tend to discourage union membership. The employers' attempt to remain open for business using temporary replacements was a measure reasonably related to the legitimate business purpose of preserving the integrity of the multiemployer bargaining unit. In the absence of any evidentiary findings of hostile motive, there is no support for the NLRB determination that the employers violated Section 8(a)(1) or 8(a)(3). The Supreme Court therefore affirmed the court of appeals' refusal to enforce the NLRB decision.

«

Whereas *Brown* dealt with a defensive lockout in response to a strike against one employer, the Supreme Court, in *American Shipbuilding Co. v. NLRB*,[63] held that an employer is free to lock out employees in anticipation of the union going on strike. That decision allows the employer to use a lockout as an offensive weapon to promote its bargaining position; the employer need not wait for the union to strike first. An employer may not engage in a lockout unless negotiations have reached an impasse, or deadlock, and exceptional circumstances are

[63]380 U.S. 300 (1965).

required by the Board to justify lockouts prior to a bargaining impasse. In *Ancor Concepts, Inc.*,[64] the NLRB held that the use of permanent replacements after a lockout was a violation of Section 8(a)(3). How does that situation differ from *NLRB v. Brown?* The NLRB upheld the use of temporary replacements after an offensive lockout in *Harter Equipment*.[65]

Plant Closing to Avoid Unionization

The preceding discussion dealt with an employer's response to the economic demands of organized workers; the employer is free to lock out to avoid union bargaining demands. But what about the situation in which the employees are just in the process of forming a union? Can the employer shut down the plant to avoid unionization? Recall that Section 8(a)(1) prohibits threats of closure or layoff to dissuade employees from joining a union. Should it make any difference whether the shutdown to avoid unionization is complete (the entire operation) or partial (only part of the operation)? In *Textile Workers Union v. Darlington Mfg. Co.*,[66] the Supreme Court held that a total shutdown of a business, even if done for anti-union motivation, was not an unfair labor practice, but that a partial shutdown, done with the intent to deter workers from forming a union, was a violation of Section 8(a)(3).

Runaway Shop
Situation in which an employer closes in one location and opens in another to avoid unionization.

The Court in *Darlington* noted that a complete shutdown to avoid unionization is different from a ***runaway shop***, in which the employer closes in one location and opens in another to avoid unionization. Such runaway conduct is in violation of Section 8(a)(3). However, the motive requirement under Section 8(a)(3) may pose a problem in determining whether the relocation of the operation violates the act. If the employer raises some legitimate business reasons for the relocation, the NLRB counsel must demonstrate that the runaway would not have happened except for the employees' unionizing efforts. (See the *Transportation Management* case discussed earlier in this chapter.)

As remedy for a runaway shop, the Board will order that the offending employer offer the old employees positions at the new location. The employer must also pay the employees' moving or travel expenses. If the employer has shut down part of the operation, the Board may order the employer to reopen the closed portion or to reinstate the affected employees in the remaining parts of the operation. The employees will also be awarded back pay lost because of the employer's violation. Remedies are discussed more fully later in this chapter.

Other Unfair Labor Practices

In addition to the unfair labor practices already discussed, the NLRA prohibits several other kinds of conduct. Refusing to bargain in good faith, the subject of Section 8(a)(5) and Section 8(b)(3), will be discussed in Chapter 15, and union unfair practices involving picketing and secondary boycotts will be dealt with in Chapter 16. The remaining unfair labor practices are the focus of this section.

[64] 323 NLRB 742 (1997), *enforcement denied*, 166 F.3d 55 (2d Cir. 1999).

[65] 280 NLRB 597 (1986).

[66] 380 U.S. 263 (1965).

Employer Reprisals Against Employees

Section 8(a)(4) prohibits an employer from discharging or otherwise discriminating against an employee who has filed charges or given testimony under the act. Because employees must be free to avail themselves of the act's procedures to give effect to their Section 7 rights, reprisals against employees for exercising their rights must also infringe on those rights. Violations of Section 8(a)(4) include the discharge or disciplining of an employee filing unfair practice charges and the layoff of such employees. Refusing to consider an employee for promotion because that employee filed unfair practice charges is also a violation. In *BE & K Construction Co.*[67] the NLRB held that it was not an unfair labor practice when an employer files a lawsuit against employees because they engaged in activity protected by the NLRA if the lawsuit had a reasonable basis in law, even if the employer's motivation for bringing the suit was a desire to retaliate against the employees. Section 8(a)(4) is directed only against employers; union reprisals against employees for exercising their statutory rights are dealt with under Section 8(b)(1)(A).

Excessive Union Dues or Membership Fees

Section 8(b)(5) prohibits a union from requiring excessive dues or membership fees of employees covered by a union security agreement. Because a union security agreement requires that employees join the union (or at least pay all dues and fees) to retain their jobs, some protection against union abuse or extortion must be given to the affected employees. In deciding a complaint under Section 8(b)(5), the Board is directed by the act to consider "the practices and customs of labor organizations in the particular industry, and the wages currently paid to the employees affected."

Featherbedding

Section 8(b)(6) makes it unfair labor practice for a union "to cause or attempt to cause an employer to pay or deliver or agree to pay or deliver any money or other thing of value, in the nature of an extraction, for services which are not performed or not to be performed." The practice of getting paid for services not performed or not to be performed is known as ***featherbedding***.

Featherbedding
The practice of getting paid for services not performed or not to be performed.

Although this statutory prohibition may seem straightforward, it may not be easy to discern featherbedding from legal activities. For instance, a union steward may be employed to run a drill press. In reality, she may be spending much of her time assisting co-workers for the union's benefit and may even draw additional compensation for this service from the union. If the collective bargaining agreement allows for this activity, then it is legal.

In another situation, the employer may pay for work that is not really needed— because, for instance, of technological innovations in the industry—but through industrial custom and usage, the work is still performed by union members. This, too, is legal under the NLRA.

In *American Newspaper Publisher's Assoc. v. NLRB*,[68] the Supreme Court held that Section 8(b)(6) is limited only to payment (or demanding of payment) for services not actually

[67] 351 NLRB No. 29 (2007).

[68] 345 U.S. 100 (1953).

rendered. In that case, the payment by the employers for the setting of type that was not needed did not violate the act because the services, although not needed, were actually performed. Because of increasing economic competition from nonunionized firms and because of labor-saving technological developments, complaints of union featherbedding under Section 8(b)(6) are relatively rare today.

Concept *Summary* » 14.2

Unfair Labor Practices

Activity	By Employers	By Unions
• Interfering with, coercing, or restraining employees in the exercise of Section 7 rights	S. 8(a)(1)	S. 8(b)(1)(A)
• Coercing or restraining an employer in the selection of a bargaining representative	X	S. 8(b)(1)(B)
• Discriminating in hiring or terms or conditions of employment to encourage or discourage union membership	S. 8(a)(3)	X
• Causing or attempting to cause an employer to discriminate against an employee to encourage or discourage union membership	X	S. 8(b)(2)
• Reprisals against employees for exercising rights under the NLRA	S. 8(a)(4)	S. 8(b)(1)(A)

Remedies for Unfair Labor Practices

Under Section 10 of the NLRA, the NLRB is empowered to prevent any person from engaging in any unfair labor practice. Section 10(a) authorizes the Board to:

- investigate charges;
- issue complaints; and
- order hearings in unfair labor practice cases.

If the ALJ (or the Board on review) finds that an employer or union has been or is engaging in unfair labor practices, the NLRB will so state in its findings and issue a cease-and-desist order with regard to those practices. If the employer (or union) chooses not to comply with the order, the Board will petition the appropriate federal court of appeals for enforcement of its order as provided in Section 10(e).

The Board may also order the offending party to take affirmative action in the wake of the unfair labor practices. For instance, when an employee has been discriminatorily discharged in violation of Section 8(a)(1), (3), or (4), the Board will commonly require that the employee be reinstated, usually with back pay.

Finally, under Section 10(j) of the act, the Board in its discretion may seek an injunction in a federal district court to put a halt to unfair labor practices while the parties to a dispute await its final resolution by the Board.[69] The purpose is to preserve the status quo while the adjudicative process works itself out. The NLRB obtained an injunction against the Major League Baseball owners for their refusal to bargain in good faith with the Major League Baseball Players' Association in 1995, in *Silverman v. Major League Baseball Player Relations Committee, Inc.*[70] That injunction forced the owners back to the bargaining table with the players' union and was instrumental in getting the parties to settle the baseball strike in April 1995. Section 10(l) requires the Board to seek a temporary restraining order from a court when a union is engaging in a secondary boycott, hot cargo agreements, recognitional picketing, or a jurisdictional dispute. (Those unfair practices will be discussed in Chapter 16.)

Reinstatement

When an employee has been discharged or laid off in violation of the act, the Board is empowered by Section 10(c) to order reinstatement with back pay. However, Section 10(c) also states that the Board shall not order reinstatement of, or back pay for, an employee who has been discharged "for cause." Therefore, an employee guilty of misconduct may not be entitled to reinstatement. This provision is of particular interest in strike situations. Employees on an economic strike may be discharged for misconduct such as violence, destruction of property, and so on. In a 1984 decision, the Board held that verbal threats alone may justify discharge when they "reasonably tend to coerce or intimidate employees in the exercise of rights protected under the Act." The Board had held that in the case of unfair practice strikers, more severe misconduct is required to justify discharge. But in *Clear Pine Mouldings*,[71] the Board stated that unfair practice strikers are not given any privilege to engage in misconduct or violence just because they are on strike over employer unfair labor practices. In any situation, physical assaults or violence will not be tolerated by the Board.

What should the NLRB do when an employee who was fired illegally by the employer has lied under oath in the NLRB hearing? Is the employee entitled to be reinstated, or should the misconduct of lying justify dismissal? That is the question in the following case.

case 14.8 »

ABF Freight System, Inc. v. NLRB

510 U.S. 317 (1994)

Stevens, J.

... Michael Manso gave his employer a false excuse for being late to work and repeated that falsehood while testifying under oath before an Administrative Law Judge (ALJ). Notwithstanding Manso's dishonesty, the National Labor Relations Board (Board) ordered Manso's former employer to reinstate him with back pay. Our interest in preserving the integrity of administrative proceedings prompted us to grant certiorari to consider whether Manso's misconduct should have precluded the Board from granting him that relief.

---

[69]See "Utilization of Section 10(j) Proceedings," Memorandum of the General Counsel, Memorandum GC02-07, Aug. 9, 2002, available online at the NLRB website at http://www.nlrb.gov/research/memos/general_counsel_memos.aspx. Go to year 2002, and then click on the link for GC Memo 02-07.

[70]67 F.3d 1054 (2d Cir. 1995).

[71]268 NLRB 1044 (1984).

Manso worked as a casual dockworker at petitioner ABF Freight's (ABF's) trucking terminal in Albuquerque, New Mexico, from the summer of 1987 to August 1989. He was fired three times. The first time, Manso was one of 12 employees discharged in June 1988 in a dispute over a contractual provision relating to so-called "preferential casual" dockworkers. The grievance Manso's union filed eventually secured his reinstatement; Manso also filed an unfair labor practice charge against ABF over the incident.

Manso's return to work was short-lived. Three supervisors warned him of likely retaliation from top management—alerting him, for example, that ABF was "gunning" for him, and that "the higher echelon was after [him]".... Within six weeks ABF discharged Manso for a second time on pretextual grounds—ostensibly for failing to respond to a call to work made under a stringent verification procedure ABF had recently imposed upon preferential casuals. Once again, a grievance panel ordered Manso reinstated.

Manso's third discharge came less than two months later. On August 11, 1989, Manso arrived four minutes late for the 5 A.M. shift. At the time, ABF had no policy regarding lateness. After Manso was late to work, however, ABF decided to discharge preferential casuals—though not other employees—who were late twice without good cause. Six days later Manso triggered the policy's first application when he arrived at work nearly an hour late for the same shift. Manso telephoned at 5:25 A.M. to explain that he was having car trouble on the highway, and repeated that excuse when he arrived. ABF conducted a prompt investigation, ascertained that he was lying, and fired him for tardiness under its new policy on lateness.

Manso filed a second unfair labor practice charge. In the hearing before the ALJ, Manso repeated his story about the car trouble that preceded his third discharge. The ALJ credited most of his testimony about events surrounding his dismissals, but expressly concluded that Manso lied when he told ABF that car trouble made him late to work. Accordingly, although the ALJ decided that ABF had illegally discharged Manso the second time because he was a party to the earlier union grievance, the ALJ denied Manso relief for the third discharge based on his finding that ABF had dismissed Manso for cause.

The Board affirmed the ALJ's finding that Manso's second discharge was unlawful, but reversed with respect to the third discharge. Acknowledging that Manso lied to his employer and that ABF presumably could have discharged him for that dishonesty, the Board nevertheless emphasized that ABF did not in fact discharge him for lying and that the ALJ's conclusion to the contrary was "a plainly erroneous factual statement of [ABF]'s asserted reasons." Instead, Manso's lie "established only that he did not have a legitimate excuse for the August 17 lateness." The Board focused primarily on ABF's retroactive application of its lateness policy to include Manso's first time late to work, holding that ABF had "seized upon" Manso's tardiness "as a pretext to discharge him again and for the same unlawful reasons it discharged him on June 19." In addition, though the Board deemed Manso's discharge unlawful even assuming the validity of ABF's general disciplinary treatment of preferential casuals, it observed that ABF's disciplinary approach and lack of uniform rules for all dockworkers "raise[d] more questions than they resolve[d]." The Board ordered ABF to reinstate Manso with back pay.

The Court of Appeals enforced the Board's order. Its review of the record revealed "abundant evidence of anti-union animus in ABF's conduct towards Manso," including "ample evidence" that Manso's third discharge was not for cause....

... We assume that the Board correctly found that ABF discharged Manso unlawfully in August 1989. We also assume, more importantly, that the Board did not abuse its discretion in ordering reinstatement even though Manso gave ABF a false reason for being late to work. We are concerned only with the ramifications of Manso's false testimony under oath in a formal proceeding before the ALJ. We recognize that the Board might have decided that such misconduct disqualified Manso from profiting from the proceeding, or it might even have adopted a flat rule precluding reinstatement when a former employee so testifies ... however, the issue is not whether the Board might adopt such a rule, but whether it must do so.

False testimony in a formal proceeding is intolerable. We must neither reward nor condone such a "flagrant affront" to the truthseeking function of adversary proceedings.

ABF submits that the false testimony of a former employee who was the victim of an unfair labor practice should always preclude him from winning reinstatement with back pay.... The Act expressly authorizes the Board "to take such affirmative action including reinstatement of employees with or without back pay, as will effectuate the policies of [the Act]." Only in cases of discharge for cause does the statute restrict the Board's authority to order reinstatement. This is not such a case.

When Congress expressly delegates to an administrative agency the authority to make specific policy determinations, courts must give the agency's decision controlling weight unless it is "arbitrary, capricious, or manifestly contrary to the statute." Because this case involves that kind of express delegation, the Board's views merit the greatest deference. This has been our consistent appraisal of the Board's remedial authority throughout its long history of administering the Act....

Notwithstanding our concern about the seriousness of Manso's ill-advised decision to repeat under oath his false excuse for tardiness, we cannot say that the Board's remedial order in this case was an abuse of its broad discretion or that it was obligated to adopt a rigid rule that would foreclose relief in all comparable cases. Nor can we fault the Board's conclusions that Manso's reason for being late to work was ultimately irrelevant to whether anti-union animus actually motivated his discharge and that ordering effective relief in a case of this character promotes a vital public interest. Notably, the ALJ refused to credit the testimony of several ABF witnesses ... and the Board affirmed those credibility findings. The unfairness of sanctioning Manso while indirectly rewarding those witnesses' lack of candor is obvious. Moreover, the rule ABF advocates might force the Board to divert its attention from its primary mission and devote unnecessary time and energy to resolving collateral disputes about credibility. Its decision to rely on "other civil and criminal remedies" for false testimony rather than a categorical exception to the familiar remedy of reinstatement is well within its broad discretion. The judgment of the Court of Appeals is affirmed.

It is so ordered.

Case Questions

1. What was ABF's justification for discharging Manso the third time? Did the ALJ find that discharge illegal under the NLRA? Did the ALJ order that Manso be reinstated? Why?
2. Did the NLRB agree with the ALJ's decision as to what remedy Manso is entitled? Why?
3. Why does the Supreme Court uphold the NLRB's decision? Does the Court's decision encourage or reward lying under oath? Explain.

Front Pay
Monetary damages awarded to a plaintiff instead of reinstatement or hiring.

While the NLRB generally seeks reinstatement for employees discharged illegally, there are some instances when it may seek ***front pay*** rather than reinstatement. Front pay is a monetary award for loss of anticipated future earnings because of the unfair labor practice. The Board's general counsel[72] has indicated that front pay may be appropriate where:

- the unfair labor practice has impaired the ability of the employee to return to work;
- the employer or other employees remain hostile to the discharged employee; or
- the discharged employee is close to retirement.

Front pay may also be used as a substitute for a "preferential hire" list.

Back Pay

When calculating back-pay awards due employees under Section 10(c), the Board requires that the affected employees mitigate their damages. The Board will deduct from the back-pay wages to reflect income that the employee earned or might have earned while the case was pending. (Welfare benefits and unemployment insurance payments are not deducted from back-pay awards by the Board.) When an employer challenges a proposed back-pay award on grounds that the affected employee had not made efforts to find other, equivalent,

[72]See "Guideline Memorandum Concerning Frontpay," Office of the General Counsel, Feb. 3, 2000, available online at the NLRB website at http://www.nlrb.gov/research/memos/general_counsel_memos.aspx. Go to year 2000, and then click on the link for GC Memo 00-01.

employment, the Board's general counsel has the burden of introducing evidence of the employee's job search efforts, according to the NLRB decision in *St. George Warehouse*.[73] The Board also requires that interest (at a rate based on the Treasury bills index) be paid on back-pay awards under the act.

The Internal Revenue Service considers back-pay awards to be taxable income for the year in which the award is received. In some instances, an employee receiving a lump-sum back-pay award representing more than one year's worth of pay may have increased income tax liability due to the award. In such cases, the NLRB has indicated that it will seek an additional monetary award to cover the additional income taxes owed by the employee because of the lump sum-award, plus interest.[74]

The NLRB is precluded by the Immigration Reform and Control Act of 1986 (discussed in Chapter 5) from awarding back pay to an undocumented alien who is not legally entitled to work in the United States, as in *Hoffman Plastic Compounds, Inc. v. NLRB*.[75]

The general wording of Section 10(c) allows the Board great flexibility in fashioning remedies in various unfair practice cases. Such flexibility is exemplified by the bargaining order remedy in *Gissel Packing*, considered in Chapter 13. Furthermore, the Board has required the guilty party to pay the legal fees of the complainant in cases involving severe or blatant violations. In one case involving an employer's unfair practices that destroyed a union's majority support, the Board ordered the employer to pay the union's organizing expenses for those employees.

Delay Problems in NLRB Remedies

Although the NLRB has rather broad remedial powers under the NLRA, the delays involved in pursuing the Board's remedial procedures limit somewhat the effectiveness of its powers. The increasing caseload of the Board has delayed the procedural process to the point at which a determined employer can dilute the effectiveness of any remedy in a particular case.

Because unfair practice cases take so long to resolve, the affected employees may be left financially and emotionally exhausted by the process. Furthermore, the remedy, when it comes, may be too little, too late. One study found that when reinstatement was offered more than six months after the violation of the act occurred, only 5 percent of those discriminatorily discharged accepted their old jobs back.

Indeed, the final resolution of the back-pay claims of the employees in the *Darlington* case (presented earlier) did not occur until 1980—twenty-four years from the closing of their plant—to avoid the union!

---

[73]351 NLRB No. 42 (2007).

[74]See "Reimbursement for Excess Federal and State Income Taxes which Discriminatees Owe as a Result of Receiving a Lump-sum Backpay Award," Office of the General Counsel, Sept. 22, 2000, available online at the NLRB website at http://www.nlrb.gov/research/memos/general_counsel_memos.aspx. Go to year 2000, and then click on the link for GC Memo 00-07.

[75]535 U.S. 137 (2002). See "Procedures and Remedies for Discriminatees Who May Be Undocumented Aliens after Hoffman Plastic Compounds, Inc.," Memorandum of the General Counsel, Memorandum GC02-06, July 19, 2002, available online at the NLRB website at http://www.nlrb.gov/research/memos/general_counsel_memos.aspx. Go to year 2002, and then click on the link for GC Memo 02-06.

Obviously, a firm that can afford the litigation expenses may find it advantageous to delay a representation election by committing unfair practices or refusing to bargain with a certified union in violation of Section 8(a)(5), reasoning that the lawyers' fees plus any back-pay awards will total less of a cost of doing business than will increased wages and fringes under a collective bargaining agreement.

An attempt to remedy the delay in processing unfair practice cases was made in 1978. The Labor Law Reform Bill would have expedited Board review of ALJ decisions and limited judicial review. That bill was passed by the House of Representatives but was the victim of a filibuster by opponents in the Senate. Although the NLRB has attempted to reduce the backlog of cases pending (and the attendant delay in the resolution process) by increasing the workloads of ALJs and Board members, the delay problem remains. That problem, with its effects on the rights of employees under the act, poses a serious threat to the effectiveness of our national labor relations policies.

The NLRB has made reducing the time needed to resolve unfair labor practice cases a priority. In its 2008 fiscal year, the NLRB median time for handling unfair labor practice complaints was 311 days from the filing of a charge with the NLRB until the issuance of a decision by the administrative law judge. When the ALJ decision is reviewed by the NLRB, the median time from the issuance of the ALJ decision until the issuance of the NLRB decision was 269 days.[76]

[76]These figures are from "Table 23.—Time Elapsed for Major Case Processing Stages Completed," Seventy-Third Annual Report of the NLRB for Fiscal Year Ending Sept. 30, 2008, p. 138, available online at http://www.nlrb.gov/publications/reports/annual_reports.aspx. Click on the link for the FY 2008 report.

CHAPTER REVIEW

» Key Terms

- *unfair labor practices (ULPs)* « 407
- *Weingarten rights* « 422
- *whipsaw strikes* « 425
- *in-house unions* « 426
- *union security agreements* « 433
- *union shop agreement* « 434
- *agency shop agreement* « 434
- *right-to-work laws* « 434
- *hiring halls* « 435
- *lockout* « 440
- *runaway shop* « 442
- *featherbedding* « 443
- *front pay* « 447

» Summary

- Section 7 of the NLRA provides protection for employees who engage in concerted activity for collective bargaining or for mutual aid and protection. All employees under the NLRA enjoy the right to engage in protected activity; conduct by employers or unions that undercuts or interferes with employees' Section 7 rights is an unfair labor practice.
- Section 8 of the NLRA defines a list of unfair labor practices by employers and by unions. Restrictions on employees' organizing or soliciting activity may violate Section 8(a)(1) or 8(b)(1); employer support, domination, or control of a labor organization [as defined by Section 2(5)] may be in violation of Section 8(a)(2). Employers that discriminate in terms or conditions of employment against employees either to encourage or discourage union membership violate Section 8(a)(3), and unions that attempt to get an employer to engage in such discrimination against employees violate Section 8(b)(2). The NLRA does allow employers and unions to adopt union security provisions such as an agency shop or union shop agreement; however, closed shop agreements, which require that a person be a union member to be hired, are prohibited under the NLRA.
- Economic strikes are protected activities under the NLRA, but economic strikers may be permanently replaced and are not guaranteed to get their jobs back after the strike. Unfair labor practice strikes are also protected activities, and unfair labor practice strikers may not be permanently replaced. An employer may lock out employees in a bargaining dispute but may not permanently replace the locked-out workers.
- The NLRB has broad powers to remedy unfair labor practices, but in practice, the procedures for resolving unfair labor practice complaints may take a long time. Such delays may operate to undermine the effectiveness of the remedies available and the intent of the NLRA in protecting the free choice of employees.

» Problems

Questions

1. What kind of activity is protected by Section 7 of the NLRA? What is the effect of such protection? When can an individual acting alone be considered to be engaged in concerted activity under Section 7 of the NLRA?
2. To what extent may an employer limit union soliciting by employees? By nonemployees?
3. What is the relevance of motive under Section 8(a)(1)? What is the relevance of motive under Section 8(a)(3)? Explain.
4. What are union security provisions? Why would unions want to negotiate such provisions? Why are closed shop agreements outlawed?
5. To what extent is an economic strike protected activity? To what extent is an unfair labor practice strike protected activity? What is the practical significance of the difference in the treatment of the different types of strikers under the NLRA?

Case Problems

6. Sandra Falcone was employed as a dental hygiene assistant. During a staff meeting, Dr. Trufolo discussed some work-related problems. Falcone and a co-worker interrupted the meeting several times to disagree with Dr. Trufolo's comments. After the meeting, the office manager reprimanded Falcone and her co-worker for disrupting the meeting by questioning Dr. Trufolo and by giggling and elbowing each other. On the following Monday, Falcone presented a list of grievances to the office manager, which Falcone had discussed with co-workers. Shortly thereafter, she was fired.

   Based on these facts, did the employer commit an unfair labor practice by discharging Falcone? Upon what facts should the NLRB determine the true motive for the discharge? See *Joseph DeRario, DMD, P.A.* [283 NLRB No. 86, 125 L.R.R.M. 1024 (1987)].
7. Potter Manufacturing Co. laid off fifteen employees because of economic conditions and lack of business. The union representing the employees at Potter subsequently discovered that the employer had laid off employees that the employer believed were most likely to honor a picket line in the event of a strike. The union filed an unfair labor practice complaint with the NLRB, alleging that the layoffs violated Sections 8(a)1 and 8(a)3.

   How should the NLRB rule on the complaint? See *National Fabricators* [295 NLRB No. 126, 131 L.R.R.M. 1761 (1989)].
8. Shortly after the union won a representation election in a Philadelphia-area hospital, the hospital fired the union steward, allegedly for failing to report to work. Some eighteen months after the discharge, and while the unfair labor practice charge was still in litigation, a majority of the bargaining unit presented the president of the hospital with a petition requesting that the president withdraw recognition from the union and cease bargaining with it. Pursuant to the petition, after confirming the authenticity of the signatures and that it contained a majority of the bargaining unit members, the president withdrew recognition. The union filed another unfair labor practice charge.

   If the hospital was found guilty of discriminatorily discharging the union steward, can you make an argument that it committed a second unfair labor practice by withdrawing recognition from the union while the unfair labor practice charge was pending? Do you reach a different result if at the time the petition was presented the hospital had been found guilty of the discriminatory discharge but was in the process of appealing the Board's decision? Would the result be different if the hospital had been found guilty but had immediately remedied the illegal action by reinstating the employee with back pay? See *Taylor Hospital v. NLRB* [770 F.2d 1075 (3d Cir. 1985)].
9. During a strike by the employees at Gillen, Inc., the picketers carried signs referring to the company and its president as "scabs." The president of Gillen, Inc., D. C. Gillen, filed a defamation suit against the union for its picketing and signs. Gillen sought $500,000 in damages, despite the fact that he could

identify no business losses because of the picketing and signs. Gillen's suit was dismissed by the court as "groundless." The union then filed an unfair labor practice complaint against Gillen, Inc., alleging that filing the suit against the picketing and signs served to coerce the employees in the exercise of their rights under Section 7.

How should the NLRB rule on the complaint? Explain your answer. See *H. S. Barss Co.* [296 NLRB No. 151, 132 L.R.R.M. 1339 (1989)].

10. Rubber Workers District No. 8 began an organizing campaign at Bardcor Corporation, a small manufacturing company in Guthrie, Kentucky, during the summer of 1981. Shortly after the campaign began, the president of the corporation began taking pictures of workers in the plant. Employee Maxine Dukes asked supervisor Mike Loreille why the pictures were being taken. Loreille responded that the president wanted something to remember the employees by after he fired them for union activity.

    A majority of the company's thirty-seven employees signed union authorization cards. The next day, the employer discharged eight workers, seven of whom had signed cards. After the discharge, the union filed a series of unfair labor practice charges. The company was able to justify the discharges for economic reasons and argued that the picture-taking incident and Loreille's comment were nothing but jokes.

    What provision of the NLRA did the company allegedly violate by the picture-taking incident and the supervisor's comment to Ms. Dukes? Try to formulate an argument for and against finding a violation of the act by the employer in one or both of these actions. Could the picture-taking incident alone violate the act? Did the supervisor's comment alone violate the act? See *Bardcor Corporation* [270 NLRB No. 157 (1984)].

11. Employees of New Hope Industries' Donaldsonville, Louisiana, plant went on strike to protest the company's failure to pay them on time and to force assurance that they would be paid on time in the future. Emil Thiac, the sole owner of this manufacturer of children's clothing, threatened to discharge the employees in the event of a strike and subsequently did fire them when they struck. Thiac later informed an NLRB attorney investigating the situation that he would close down the plant rather than reinstate or give back pay to the discharged strikers. He also informed the attorney that efforts to obtain back pay could be futile because the company's money was tied up in trust funds for his children. Thiac ultimately closed the plant and refused to give the NLRB his home address or provide the Board with any means to communicate with him.

    Based on these facts, do you think the Board has any way of preventing Thiac from dissipating or hiding the company's assets while the unfair labor practice charges are pending? See *Norton v. New Hope Industries, Inc.* [unpublished opinion (U.S. Dist. Ct., M.D. La., 1985)].

12. Handicabs, Inc. provides transportation services to disabled and elderly persons in the Minneapolis–St. Paul metropolitan area. Handicabs established a policy prohibiting the discussion of company-related problems with clients. The policy, addendum no. 2 in the employee handbook, states in relevant part:

    > Discussing complaints or problems about the company with our clients will be grounds for immediate dismissal. ... All of our clients are protected by the Vulnerable Adults Act. According to this law, you must not tease them, take monies (other than ride-fare or tip) from them, curse or use profanity while in their presence, or do anything verbal or physical or of a sexual nature. Also, you must not put these people in a threatening or uncomfortable position by discussing any personal or company-related problems that may make them feel coerced or obligated to act upon or react to.

    In addition, Handicabs maintained a company policy, addendum no. 1, that prohibited its employees from discussing their wages among themselves, violation of which was also grounds for immediate termination.

    On September 20, 1994, Handicabs discharged one of its drivers, Ronald F. Trail, after receiving a complaint that he had been "talking about the union" with his passengers. The complaint was made by Claudia Fuglie, a Handicabs employee and paying client. Fuglie is wheelchair bound and dependent on the handicapped-accessible transit service. Fuglie complained that the talk of unionization and potential work stoppage distressed her.

In response to his termination, Trail filed an unfair labor practice charge with the NLRB. How should the NLRB rule on his complaint? Which, if any, sections of the NLRA has Handicabs violated? Explain. See *Handicabs, Inc. v. NLRB* [95 F.3d 681 (8th Cir. 1996)].

13. In response to rumors that the employees of Tristeel Fabrication, Inc. were seeking to join a union, Strodel, the plant manager, held a meeting with the employees. Strodel informed them that if they voted to join a union, "things will no longer be the same—they could get stricter. Any collective bargaining would start from scratch, with no guarantee that the company would agree to continue any of the benefits the employees presently had. Everything will be conducted by the book (meaning the collective agreement)."

    Do Strodel's comments constitute an unfair labor practice? Explain. See *Jamaica Towing, Inc.* [236 NLRB No. 223 (1978)] and *Fidelity Telephone Co.*, [236 NLRB No. 26 (1978)].

14. Santos Diaz, Antonio Lopez, Rafael Naraes, and Jose Rivera worked on the dock crew for Mike Yurosek & Son, Inc., a vegetable packing company. Each had been employed by Yurosek for between nine and fifteen years. In early September 1990, warehouse manager Juan Garza announced to the dock crew members that he was reducing their hours to approximately thirty-six a week. Some of the employees complained that the new schedule would not provide enough time to finish their work. Garza apparently responded: "That's the way it's going to be.... You are going to punch [out] ... exactly at the time that I tell you."

    On September 24, pursuant to the new schedule, the crew was scheduled to work from 10:00 A.M. to 4:30 P.M. Shortly before 4:30, foreman Jaime Ortiz approached each of the four employees individually and instructed each to work an additional hour. All four employees refused to stay. They told Ortiz that they were required to follow the new schedule imposed by Garza. The employees then proceeded to punch out. Ortiz met them at the time clock and instructed them not to punch in the next morning but to meet him in the company dining hall.

    The following day, the four employees were asked to wait in the company waiting room. Each employee was then individually called in turn into the personnel office and questioned by Garza, Ortiz, and three other company officers. When each employee was asked why he did not work the extra hour, each responded that he was adhering to the new schedule posted by Garza. After the interviews, the employees waited while the company officials discussed the matter. Each employee was then individually called back into the office and terminated for insubordination. The employees filed an unfair labor practice complaint with the NLRB over their termination.

    Was their conduct protected under Section 7? Was it concerted? How should the NLRB rule on their complaint? Explain. See *NLRB v. Mike Yurosek & Son, Inc.* [53 F.3d 261 (9th Cir. 1995)].

15. Lawson runs 700 convenience food stores in Ohio, Indiana, Pennsylvania, and Michigan. Following the murder of an employee in a Lawson store, the United Food and Commercial Workers Union (UFCW) began to organize Lawson sales assistants in northeastern Ohio. Some employees refused to report to work for two days after the murder as a protest against lax security measures.

    In response to the complaints, Lawson installed outdoor lights at its stores, adopted a policy that no one would be required to work alone at night, and began paying overtime for work done after closing hours.

    Following the initiation of the UFCW campaign, Lawson placed no-solicitation signs in all its stores and told employees that anyone violating the no-solicitation rule would be subject to discharge.

    When the UFCW filed a representation petition with the NLRB, seeking an election, employees were told that the stores would close if they voted in the union. One store manager told employees not to discuss the union at work because Lawson planned to install listening devices in the stores.

What, if any, unfair labor practices has Lawson committed? See *The Lawson Co. v. NLRB* [753F.2d 471 (6th Cir. 1985)].

Hypothetical Scenarios

16. Citywatcher.com, a video surveillance company, has issued a work rule requiring its employees to have radio frequency identification chips embedded in their forearms, in order to monitor the employees' movements while they are working. The employees feel that such a rule is overly intrusive and would inhibit the employees' willingness to discuss working conditions among themselves. Does the new work rule violate Section 8(a)(1) of the NLRA? Would it make a difference if the employer adopted the rule because it was aware that the employees had been discussing joining a union? Explain.
17. Gonzales worked in the meat department of Groceries-R-Us, and also served as a union steward at the store. When he learned that he had been scheduled to work on Saturdays, Gonzales confronted his supervisor. During this confrontation, Gonzales angrily threw his meat hook over his shoulder, narrowly missing an employee. He also threw a 40-pound piece of meat into a saw (breaking its blade), threw his knife into a box, threatened his supervisor, and refused to follow the store manager's order to leave the store. The employer terminated Gonzales, based on his threatening and violent behavior. Gonzales filed a complaint with the NLRB alleging that he was subjected to a more severe disciplinary penalty because he was a union steward. How should the NLRB rule on his complaint? Explain.
18. Decker, the regional manager for Aquatics, Inc., called Ali, one of the company's sales representatives, into his office for a one-on-one meeting. Decker asked Ali how the local management was treating him. Ali responded that he was being treated fine but some of the managers needed to go back to training as they were treating the employees "real bad." Decker then told him that there was a rumor that the sales representatives were threatening to organize a union. Ali said he knew nothing about that. Decker then asked Ali if anyone had approached him with a card to sign and he said no. During the course of this meeting they also discussed an anticipated employee bonus that had been drastically reduced and Decker explained that this was dependent on how the Company performed. Near the end of the meeting, Decker asked Ali whether he, as a loyal employee, would he be willing to let management know if someone approached him to sign a union card. Decker stated that he was going to get to the "bottom" of the union campaign. He also took notes during the course of the meeting, and told Ali that anything they discussed would "have to stay in the room" and not to mention the meeting to anyone." Did Decker's meeting with Ali violate the NLRA? Explain.
19. St. Pancras Medical Center, an acute-care hospital, issued a memorandum prohibiting its nursing and patient care employees from wearing buttons which read "RNs Organized to Promote Patient Care." The buttons were an effort to show support for the nurses' union in contract negotiations with the hospital. The hospital directed the employees not to wear any buttons in any areas of the hospital where they might encounter patients or patients' family members. The hospital claimed that wearing the buttons could cause "unease and worry among patients and their families," and disturb the tranquil hospital atmosphere that is necessary for successful patient care. The union feels that the rule is overly restrictive, and files an unfair labor practice complaint with the NLRB. Under which section of the NLRA should the union file its complaint? Is the rule valid, or does it violate the NLRA? Why?
20. Watkins is a member of the bargaining unit at Stith, Inc., and has been very vocal in his criticism of the performance of the union's leadership in the last contract negotiations. Ronnie Elder, the union's chief steward, is fed up with Watkins' complaints, and meets with Kay Alston, Stith's HR director, to discuss terminating Watkins. Has Elder committed an unfair labor practice? If so, which section of the NLRA has Elder violated? If Alston fires Watkins, has she committed an unfair labor practice? If so, which section of the NLRA has Alston violated?

CHAPTER 15 Collective Bargaining

Collective Bargaining Process by which a union and employer meet and confer with respect to wages, hours, and other terms and conditions of employment.

Employees join unions to gain some influence over their working conditions and wages; that influence is achieved through the process called ***collective bargaining***. Section 8(d) of the National Labor Relations Act (NLRA) defines collective bargaining as

> [t]he performance of the mutual obligation of the employer and the representative of the employees to meet at reasonable times and confer in good faith with respect to wages, hours, and other terms and conditions of employment, or the negotiation of an agreement or any question arising thereunder....

This process of meeting and discussing working conditions is actually a highly stylized and heavily regulated form of economic conflict. Within the limits of conduct spelled out by the National Labor Relations Board (NLRB) under the NLRA, the parties exert pressure on each other to force some concession or agreement. The union's economic pressure comes from its ability to withhold the services of its members—a strike. The employer's bargaining pressure comes from its potential to lock out the employees or to permanently replace striking workers. The NLRB and the courts, through their interpretation and administration of the NLRA, have limited the kinds of pressure either side may exert and how such pressure may be applied. This chapter examines the collective bargaining process and the legal limits placed on that process.

The Duty to Bargain

An employer is required to recognize a union as the exclusive bargaining representative of its employees when a majority of those employees support the union. The union may demonstrate its majority support either through signed authorization cards or by winning a representation election. Once aware of the union's majority support, the employer must recognize and bargain with the union according to the process spelled out in Section 8(d). Section 8(a)(5) makes it an unfair labor practice for an employer to refuse to bargain with the representative of its employees, and Section 8(b)(3) makes it an unfair practice for a union representing a group of employees to refuse to bargain with their employer.

Although the NLRA imposes an obligation to bargain collectively upon both employer and union, it does not control the results of the bargaining process. Section 8(d) makes it clear that the obligation to bargain "does not compel either party to agree to a proposal or require the making of a concession." The act thus reflects an ambivalence regarding the duty to bargain in good faith. The parties, to promote industrial relations harmony, are required to come together and negotiate, but in deference to the principle of freedom of contract, they are not required to reach an agreement. This tension between the goal of promoting industrial peace and the principle of freedom of contract underlies the various NLRB and court decisions dealing with the duty to bargain. The accommodation of these conflicting ideas makes the area a difficult and interesting aspect of labor relations law.

If the parties are required to negotiate, yet are not required to reach an agreement or even to make a concession, how can the Board determine whether either side is bargaining in good faith? Section 8(d) requires that the parties meet at reasonable times to discuss wages, hours, and terms and conditions of employment. It also requires that any agreement reached must be put in writing if either party so requests. But Section 8(d) does not speak to bargaining tactics. Is either side free to insist upon its proposal as a "take-it-or-leave-it" proposition? Can either side refuse to make any proposal? These questions must be addressed in determining what constitutes bargaining in good faith.

Bargaining in Good Faith

Section 8(a)(5) requires that the employer bargain with a union that is the representative of its employees according to Section 9(a). Section 9(a) states that a union that has the support of a majority of employees in a bargaining unit becomes the exclusive bargaining representative of all employees in the unit. That section also states that the employer may address the grievances of individual employees as long as it is done in a manner consistent with the collective agreement and the union has been given an opportunity to be present at such adjustment. That provision raises the question of how far the employer can go in dealing with individuals rather than the union. In *J. I. Case Co. v. NLRB*,[1] the Supreme Court held that contracts of employment made with individual employees were not impediments to negotiating a collective agreement with the union. J. I. Case had made it a practice to sign yearly individual contracts of employment with its employees. When the union, which won a representation election, requested bargaining over working conditions, the company refused. The employer argued that the individual contracts covered those issues and no bargaining could take place until those individual contracts had expired. The Supreme Court held that the individual contracts must give way to allow the negotiation of a collective agreement. Once the union is certified as the exclusive bargaining representative of the employees, the employer cannot deal with the individual employees in a manner inconsistent with the union's status as exclusive representative. To allow individual contracts of employment to prevent collective bargaining would undercut the union's position.

[1]321 U.S. 332 (1944).

What about the situation in which individual employees attempt to discuss their grievances with the employer in a manner inconsistent with the union's role as exclusive representative? How far does the Section 9(a) proviso go to allow such discussion? That question is addressed in the following Supreme Court decision.

case 15.1 » Emporium Capwell Co. v. Western Addition Community Organization

420 U.S. 50 (1975)

[Emporium Capwell Co. operates a department store in San Francisco. The company had a collective bargaining agreement with the Department Store Employees Union. The agreement, among other things, included a prohibition of employment discrimination because of race, color, religion, national origin, age, or sex. The agreement also set up a grievance and arbitration process to resolve any claimed violation of the agreement, including a violation of the nondiscrimination clause.]

Marshall, J.

This litigation presents the question whether, in light of the national policy against racial discrimination in employment, the National Labor Relations Act protects concerted activity by a group of minority employees to bargain with their employer over issues of employment discrimination.....

On April 3, 1968, a group of Company employees covered by the agreement met with the Secretary-Treasurer of the Union, Walter Johnson, to present a list of grievances including a claim that the Company was discriminating on the basis of race in making assignments and promotions. The Union official agreed to take certain of the grievances and to investigate the charge of racial discrimination. He appointed an investigating committee and prepared a report on the employees' grievances, which he submitted to the Retailer's Council and which the Council in turn referred to the Company. The report described "the possibility of racial discrimination" as perhaps the most important issue raised by the employees and termed the situation at the Company as potentially explosive if corrective action were not taken. It offered as an example of the problem the Company's failure to promote a Negro stock employee regarded by other employees as an outstanding candidate but a victim of racial discrimination.

Shortly after receiving the report, the Company's labor relations director met with Union representatives and agreed to "look into the matter" of discrimination and see what needed to be done. Apparently unsatisfied with these representations, the Union held a meeting in September attended by Union officials, Company employees, and representatives of the California Fair Employment Practices Committee (FEPC) and the local antipoverty agency. The Secretary-Treasurer of the Union announced that the Union had concluded that the Company was discriminating, and that it would process every such grievance through to arbitration if necessary. Testimony about the Company's practices was taken and transcribed by a court reporter, and the next day the Union notified the Company of its formal charge and demanded that the joint union-management Adjustment Board be convened "to hear the entire case."

At the September meeting some of the Company's employees had expressed their view that the contract procedures were inadequate to handle a systemic grievance of this sort; they suggested that the Union instead begin picketing the store in protest. Johnson explained that the collective agreement bound the Union to its processes and expressed his view that successful grievants would be helping not only themselves but all others who might be the victims of invidious discrimination as well. The FEPC and antipoverty agency representatives offered the same advice. Nonetheless, when the Adjustment Board meeting convened on October 16, James Joseph Hollins, Tom Hawkins, and two other employees whose testimony the Union had intended to elicit refused to participate in the grievance procedure. Instead, Hollins read a statement objecting to reliance on correction of individual inequities as an approach to the problem of discrimination at the store and demanding that the president of the Company meet with the four protestants to work out a broader agreement for dealing with the issue as they saw it. The four employees then walked out of the hearing.

Hollins attempted to discuss the question of racial discrimination with the Company president shortly after the incidents of October 16. The president refused to be drawn into such a discussion but suggested to Hollins that he see the personnel director about the matter. Hollins, who had spoken to the personnel director before, made no effort to do so again. Rather, he and Hawkins and several other dissident employees held a press conference on October 22 at which they denounced the store's employment policy as racist, reiterated their desire to deal directly with "the top management" of the Company over minority employment conditions, and announced their intention to picket and institute a boycott of the store. On Saturday, November 2, Hollins, Hawkins, and at least two other employees picketed the store throughout the day and distributed at the entrance handbills urging consumers not to patronize the store. Johnson encountered the picketing employees, again urged them to rely on the grievance process, and warned that they might be fired for their activities. The picketers, however, were not dissuaded, and they continued to press their demand to deal directly with the Company president.

On November 7, Hollins and Hawkins were given written warnings that a repetition of the picketing or public statements about the Company could lead to their discharge. When the conduct was repeated the following Saturday, the two employees were fired.

Respondent Western Addition Community Organization, a local civil rights association of which Hollins and Hawkins were members, filed a charge against the Company with the National Labor Relations Board. After a hearing the NLRB Trial Examiner found that the discharged employees had believed in good faith that the Company was discriminating against minority employees, and that they had resorted to concerted activity on the basis of that belief. He concluded, however, that their activity was not protected by Section 7 of the Act and that their discharges did not, therefore, violate Section 8(a)(1).

The Board, after oral argument, adopted the findings and conclusions of its Trial Examiner and dismissed the complaint. Among the findings adopted by the Board was that the discharged employees' course of conduct:

> ... was no mere presentation of a grievance, but nothing short of a demand that the [Company] bargain with the picketing employees for the entire group of minority employees.

Central to the policy of fostering collective bargaining, where the employees elect that course, is the principle of majority rule. If the majority of a unit chooses union representation, the NLRA permits them to bargain with their employer to make union membership a condition of employment, thereby imposing their choice upon the minority.... In establishing a regime of majority rule, Congress sought to secure to all members of the unit the benefits of their collective strength and bargaining power, in full awareness that the superior strength of some individuals or groups might be subordinated to the interest of the majority.

In vesting the representatives of the majority with this broad power Congress did not, of course, authorize a tyranny of the majority over minority interests.... we have held, by the very nature of the exclusive bargaining representative's status as representative of all unit employees, Congress implicitly imposed upon [the union] a duty fairly and in good faith to represent the interests of minorities within the unit. And the Board has taken the position that a union's refusal to process grievances against racial discrimination, in violation of that duty, is an unfair labor practice.....

Plainly, national labor policy embodies the principles of nondiscrimination as a matter of highest priority ... These general principles do not aid respondent, however, as it is far from clear that separate bargaining is necessary to help eliminate discrimination. Indeed, as the facts of this case demonstrate, the proposed remedy might have just the opposite effect. The collective bargaining agreement in this case prohibited without qualification all manner of invidious discrimination and made any claimed violation a grievable issue. The grievance procedure is directed precisely at determining whether discrimination has occurred. That orderly determination, if affirmative, could lead to an arbitral award enforceable in court. Nor is there any reason to believe that the processing of grievances is inherently limited to the correction of individual cases of discrimination. The decision by a handful of employees to bypass the grievance procedure in favor of attempting to bargain with their employer, by contrast, may or may not be predicated upon the actual existence of discrimination. An employer confronted with bargaining demands from each of several minority groups would not necessarily, or even probably, be able to agree to remedial steps satisfactory to all at once. Competing claims on the employer's ability to accommodate each group's demands, e.g., for reassignments and promotions to a limited number of positions, could only set one group against the other even if it is not the employer's intention to divide and overcome them. Having divided themselves, the minority employees will not be in position to advance their cause unless it be by recourse seriatim to economic coercion, which can only have the effect of further dividing them along racial or other lines. Nor is the situation materially different where, as apparently happened here, self-designated representatives purport to speak for all groups that might consider themselves to be victims of discrimination. Even if in actual bargaining the various groups did not perceive their interests as divergent and further subdivide themselves, the employer would be bound to bargain with them in a field largely preempted by the current collective bargaining agreement with the elected bargaining representatives....

... The policy of industrial self-determination as expressed in Section 7 does not require fragmentation of the bargaining unit along racial or other lines in order to consist with the national labor policy against discrimination. And in the face of such fragmentation, whatever its effect on discriminatory practices, the bargaining process that the principle of exclusive representation is meant to lubricate could not endure unhampered....

Respondent objects that reliance on the remedies provided by Title VII is inadequate effectively to secure the rights conferred by Title VII....

Whatever its factual merit, this argument is properly addressed to the Congress and not to this Court or the NLRB. In order to hold that employer conduct violates Section 8(a)(1) of the NLRA because it violates Section 704(a) of Title VII, we would have to override a host of consciously made decisions well within the exclusive competence of the Legislature. This obviously, we cannot do.

Reversed.

Case Questions

1. What were the complaints of the minority employees against the company? How did the union respond to their complaints?
2. Why did the employees reject using the procedures under the collective bargaining agreement? What happened to them when they insisted on picketing the store to publicize their complaints?
3. Did the NLRB hold that their conduct was protected under Section 7? Why? Did the Supreme Court protect their conduct? Why?

Although the employer in *J. I. Case* and the employees in *Emporium Capwell* were held to have acted improperly, there is some room for individual discussions of working conditions and grievances. Where the collective agreement permits individual negotiation, an employer may discuss such matters with individual employees. Examples of such agreements are the collective agreements covering professional baseball and football players; the collective agreement sets minimum levels of conditions and compensation, while allowing the athletes to negotiate salary and other compensation on an individual basis.

Procedural Requirements of the Duty to Bargain in Good Faith

A union or employer seeking to bargain with the other party must notify that other party of its desire to bargain at least sixty days prior to the expiration of the existing collective agreement or, if no agreement is in effect, sixty days prior to the date it proposes the agreement to go into effect. Section 8(d) requires that such notice must be given at the proper time; failure to do so may make any strike by the union or lockout by the employer an unfair labor practice. Section 8(d) also requires that the parties must continue in effect any existing collective agreement for sixty days from the giving of the notice to bargain or until the agreement expires, whichever occurs later. Strikes or lockouts are prohibited during this sixty-day "cooling-off" period. Employees who go on an economic strike during this period lose their status as "employees" and the protections of the act. Therefore, if the parties have given the notice to bargain later than sixty days prior to the expiration of the contract, they must wait the full sixty days to go on strike or lockout, even if the old agreement has already expired.

When negotiations result in matters in dispute, the party seeking contract termination must notify the Federal Mediation and Conciliation Service (FMCS) and the appropriate state mediation agency within thirty days from giving the notice to bargain. Neither side may resort to a strike or lockout until thirty days after the FMCS and state agency have been notified.

The NLRA provides for longer notice periods when the collective bargaining involves the employees of a health-care institution. In that case, the parties must give notice to bargain at least ninety days prior to the expiration of the agreement. No strike or lockout can take place for at least ninety days from the giving of the notice or the expiration of the agreement, whichever is later. Furthermore, the FMCS and state agency must be notified sixty days prior to the termination of the agreement. Finally, Section 8(g) requires that a labor organization seeking to picket or strike against a health-care institution must give both the employer and the FMCS written notice of its intention to strike or picket at least ten days prior to taking such action. Why should a labor organization be required to give health-care institutions advance notice of any strike or picketing?

As noted, Section 8(d) prohibits any strike or lockout during the notice period. Employees who go on strike during that period are deprived of the protection of the act. In *Mastro Plastics Co. v. NLRB*,[2] the Supreme Court held that the prohibition applied only to economic strikes—strikes designed to pressure the employer to "terminate or modify" the collective agreement. Unfair labor practice strikes, which are called to protest the employer's violation of the NLRA, are not covered by the Section 8(d) prohibition. Therefore, the employees in *Mastro Plastics* who went on strike during the sixty-day cooling-off period to protest the illegal firing of an employee were not in violation of Section 8(d) and were not deprived of the protection of the act.

Concept *Summary* » 15.1

The Duty to Bargain in Good Faith

Procedural Requirements: Section 8(d)

- The party seeking to begin negotiations must give notice of desire to bargain at least 60 days prior to the expiration of the collective agreement, or sixty days prior to the date the agreement will go into effect
- Any existing agreement must be kept in effect for sixty days from giving notice, or until its expiry date (whichever occurs later)
- Strikes and lockouts are prohibited during the sixty-day notice period
- If the negotiations result in a dispute, the party seeking contract termination must notify the FMCS and state mediation agency within thirty days from giving the notice to bargain; no strike or lockout can occur until after thirty days from giving notice to the FMCS and state agency

Creation of the Duty to Bargain

As has been discussed, the duty to bargain arises when the union gets the support of a majority of the employees in a bargaining unit. When a union is certified as the winner of a representation election, the employer is required by Section 8(a)(5) to bargain with it. (An employer with knowledge of a union's majority support, independent of the union's claim of such support, must also recognize and bargain with the union without resort to an election.) Because the NLRA does not provide a means of having a court review a certification decision

---

[2] 350 U.S. 270 (1956).

by the NLRB, employers who seek to challenge a certification decision may refuse to bargain with the union, thereby forcing the union to file unfair labor practices under Section 8(a)(5). Because NLRB unfair labor practice decisions are subject to judicial review by the federal courts of appeals, the employer can then raise the issue of the union's improper certification as a defense to the charge of refusing to bargain in good faith with the union.

When an employer is approached by two unions, each claiming to represent a majority of the employees, how should the employer respond? One way would be to refuse to recognize either union (provided, of course, that the employer had no independent knowledge of either union's majority support) and to insist on an election. Can the employer recognize voluntarily one of the two unions claiming to represent the employees?

In *Bruckner Nursing Home*,[3] the NLRB held that an employer may recognize a union that claims to have majority support of the employees in the bargaining unit even though another union is also engaged in an organizing campaign, as long as the second union has not filed a petition for a representation election. The Board reasoned that the rival union, unable to muster even the support of 30 percent of the employees necessary to file a petition, should not be permitted to prevent the recognition of the union with majority support. If, however, a valid petition for a representation election has been filed, then the employer must refrain from recognizing either union and must wait for the outcome of the election to determine if either union has majority support.

The *Bruckner Nursing Home* decision dealt with a situation in which the employees were not previously represented by a union. When an incumbent union's status has been challenged by a rival union that has petitioned for a representation election, is the employer still required to negotiate with the incumbent union? In *RCA del Caribe*,[4] the Board held that:

> the mere filing of a representation petition by an outside, challenging union will no longer require or permit an employer to withdraw from bargaining or executing a contract with an incumbent union. Under this rule … an employer will violate Section 8(a)(5) by withdrawing from bargaining based solely on the fact that a petition has been filed by an outside union….
>
> If the incumbent prevails in the election held, any contract executed with the incumbent will be valid and binding. If the challenging union prevails, however, any contract executed with the incumbent will be null and void….

The *Bruckner Nursing Home* and *RCA del Caribe* decisions were departures from prior Board decisions, which required that an employer stay neutral in the event of rival organizing campaigns or when the incumbent union faced a petition filed by a challenging union. Which approach do you think is more likely to protect the desires of the individual employees? Do *Bruckner Nursing Home* and *RCA del Caribe* make it more difficult to unseat an incumbent union?

When craft employees who had previously been included in a larger bargaining unit vote to be represented by a craft union, and a smaller craft bargaining unit is severed from the larger one, what is the effect of the agreement covering the larger unit? In *American Seating Co.*,[5] the NLRB held that the old agreement no longer applies to the newly severed bargaining unit, and the old agreement does not prevent the employer from negotiating with the craft union on

---

[3] 262 NLRB 955 (1982).

[4] 262 NLRB 963 (1982).

[5] 106 NLRB 250 (1953).

behalf of the new bargaining unit. Is this decision surprising? [Recall the *J. I. Case* decision discussed earlier and reexamine the wording of Section 8(d) in its entirety.]

Duration of the Duty to Bargain

When the union is certified as bargaining representative after winning an election, the NLRB requires that the employer recognize and bargain with the union for at least a year from certification, regardless of any doubts the employer may have about the union's continued majority support. This one-year period applies only when no collective agreement has been made. When an agreement exists, the employer must bargain with the union for the term of the agreement. Unfair labor practices committed by the employer, such as refusal to bargain in good faith, may have the effect of extending the one-year period, as the Board held in *Mar-Jac Poultry.*[6]

When a union acquires bargaining rights by voluntary recognition rather than certification, the employer is required to recognize and bargain with the union only for "a reasonable period of time" if no agreement is in effect. What constitutes a reasonable period of time depends on the circumstances in each case. If an agreement has been reached after the voluntary recognition, then the employer must bargain with the union for the duration of the agreement.

After the one-year period or a reasonable period of time—whichever is appropriate—has expired, and no collective agreement is in effect, the employer may refuse to bargain with the union if the employer can establish that the union has lost the support of the majority of the bargaining unit, according to *Levitz Furniture Co. of the Pacific.*[7] The employer's evidence to support the fact that the union has lost majority support must have a reasonable basis in fact and, in the case of a certified union, must be based only on events that occur after the expiration of the one-year period from the certification of the union, as held in *Chelsea Industries.*[8] In a successorship situation (see Chapter 17), the incumbent union is entitled to a rebuttable presumption of continuing majority support; that presumption will not serve as a bar to an otherwise timely petition for a representation election or a decertification election, according to *MV Transportation.*[9] In *Allentown Mack Sales and Services, Inc. v. NLRB,*[10] the U.S. Supreme Court upheld the NLRB's requirement that the employer have a "good faith reasonable doubt" about the union's majority support in order to take a poll of employees about their support of the union. The Board held in *NLRB v. Flex Plastics.*[11] that filing a decertification petition alone does not suffice to establish a reason to doubt the union's majority support. When the employer can establish some reasonable factual basis for its claim that the union has lost majority support, it may refuse to negotiate with the union. To find a violation of Section 8(a)(5), the Board must then prove that the union in fact represented a majority of the employees on the date the employer refused to bargain.

---

[6]136 NLRB 785 (1962).

[7]333 NLRB 717 (2001).

[8]331 NLRB 1648 (2000).

[9]337 NLRB 770 (2002).

[10]522 U.S. 359 (1998).

[11]726 F.2d 272 (6th Cir. 1984).

What happens if the union employees go on strike and are permanently replaced by the employer? Must the employer continue to recognize and bargain with the union? In *Pioneer Flour Mills*,[12] the NLRB held that economic strikers must be considered members of the bargaining unit for the purpose of determining whether the union has majority support for the first twelve months of the strike. After twelve months, if they have been permanently replaced, the strikers need not be considered part of the bargaining unit by the employer. Unfair labor practice strikers may not be permanently replaced and must be considered members of the bargaining unit.

Where an employer has hired replacements during an economic strike and now seeks to determine whether the union still has majority support, can the employer presume that the replacement workers oppose the union? The NLRB takes the position that it will not presume the replacements oppose the union, but rather will consider each case on its own facts: Has the employer presented sufficient objective evidence to indicate that the replacements do not support the union? The NLRB's approach was upheld by the Supreme Court in *NLRB v. Curtin Matheson Scientific, Inc.*[13]

What happens if the employer agrees with the union on a contract but then tries to raise a claim that the union has lost majority support? That is the subject of the following case.

case 15.2 »

Auciello Iron Works, Inc. v. NLRB

571 U.S. 781 (1996)

Facts: Auciello Iron Works had twenty-three production and maintenance employees, all represented by the Shopmen's Local No. 501 of the International Association of Bridge, Structural, and Ornamental Iron Workers. When the collective bargaining agreement expired on September 25, 1988, and negotiations for a new one were unsuccessful, the employees went on strike. On November 17, 1988, Auciello presented the union with a contract proposal. The union stopped picketing the next day, and nine days later the union telegraphed its acceptance of the offer. The day after the union indicated its acceptance of the offer, Auciello told the union that it doubted that a majority of the bargaining unit's employees supported the union. Auciello disavowed the collective bargaining agreement and denied it had any duty to continue negotiating with the union. Auciello based its doubt about the union's majority support to knowledge acquired before the union accepted the contract offer, including the facts that nine employees had crossed the picket line, that thirteen employees had given it signed forms indicating their resignation from the union, and that sixteen had expressed dissatisfaction with the union.

The union filed unfair labor practice charges with the NLRB. An administrative law judge found that a contract existed between the parties and that Auciello's withdrawal from it violated Sections 8(a)(1) and (5) of the NLRA. The Board affirmed the administrative law judge's decision. The Board treated Auciello's claim of good faith doubt as irrelevant and ordered Auciello to reduce the collective bargaining agreement to a formal written instrument. The Court of Appeals enforced the order and Auciello appealed to the Supreme Court.

Issue: Can an employer disavow a collective bargaining agreement because of a good faith doubt about a union's majority status at the time the contract was made, when the doubt arises from facts known to the employer before its contract offer had been accepted by the union?

Decision: The NLRB has adopted several presumptions about the existence of majority support for a union within a bargaining unit, required for its status of exclusive

[12] 174 NLRB 1202 (1969).

[13] 494 U.S. 775 (1990).

bargaining representative. The first two are conclusive presumptions:

- a union "usually is entitled to a conclusive presumption of majority status for one year following" certification as such exclusive bargaining representative by the NLRB; and
- a union is also entitled to a conclusive presumption of majority status during the term of any collective bargaining agreement, up to three years in length.

The NLRB also has a third presumption, though it is not a conclusive one. At the end of the certification year or upon expiration of the collective bargaining agreement, the presumption of majority status becomes a rebuttable one. An employer may overcome that presumption (when, for example, defending against an unfair labor practice charge) by showing that, at the time of its refusal to bargain, either:

- the union did not in fact enjoy majority support; or
- the employer had a "good faith" doubt, founded on a sufficient objective basis, about the union's majority support.

Auciello has raised the "good faith doubt" defense after a collective bargaining contract was reached upon the union's acceptance of an employer's outstanding offer.

The NLRB rejected Auciello's claim of an exception for an employer with doubts arising from facts antedating the contract. The NLRB said that such an exception would allow an employer to control the timing of its assertion of good faith doubt and thus to "'sit' on that doubt and ... raise it after the offer is accepted." The Board held that giving employers such unilateral control over a vital part of the collective bargaining process would undermine the stability of the collective bargaining relationship. The NLRB presumptions generally allow companies an adequate chance to act on their preacceptance doubts before contract formation, just as Auciello could have acted effectively under the Board's rule in this case. Auciello knew that the picket line had been crossed and that a number of its employees had expressed dissatisfaction with the union at least nine days before the contract's acceptance, and all of the resignation forms Auciello received were dated at least five days before the acceptance date. Auciello had at least three alternatives to doing nothing:

- it could have withdrawn the outstanding offer and then petitioned for a representation election;
- following withdrawal, it could also have refused to bargain further on the basis of its good faith doubt, leaving it to the union to charge an unfair labor practice; and
- it could have withdrawn its offer to allow it time to investigate while it continued to fulfill its duty to bargain in good faith with the union.

The company thus had generous opportunities to avoid the presumption before the moment of acceptance.

The Supreme Court upheld the NLRB decision that an employer's pre-contractual, good faith doubt was inadequate to support an exception to the conclusive presumption that arises at the moment a collective bargaining contract offer has been accepted. The Court affirmed the judgment of the Court of Appeals for the First Circuit.

The Nature of the Duty to Bargain in Good Faith

After having considered how the duty to bargain in good faith arises and how long it lasts, we now turn to exactly what it means: What is "good faith" bargaining?

As we have seen, the wording of Section 8(d) states that making concessions or reaching agreement is not necessary to good faith bargaining. The imposition of such requirements would infringe upon either party's freedom of contract and would destroy the voluntary nature of collective bargaining, which is essential to its success. What is required for good faith bargaining, according to the NLRB, is that the parties enter negotiations with "an open and fair mind" and "a sincere purpose to find a basis of agreement."

As long as the parties bargain with an intention to find a basis of agreement, the breakdown or deadlock of negotiations is not a violation of the duty to bargain in good faith. When talks reach a deadlock—known as an ***impasse***—as a result of sincere bargaining, either side may break off talks on the deadlocked issue. In determining whether an impasse exists, the

Impasse
A deadlock in negotiations.

Board considers the totality of circumstances: the number of times the parties have met, the likelihood of progress on the issue, the use of mediation, and so on. The Board considers that a change in the position of either party or a change in the circumstances may break an impasse; in that case, the parties would not be able to break off all talks on the issue.

When the impasse results from a party's rigid insistence upon a particular proposal, it is not a violation of the duty to bargain if the proposal relates to wages, hours, or terms and conditions of employment. In *NLRB v. American National Insurance Co.*,[14] the Supreme Court held that the employer's insistence upon contract language giving it discretionary control over promotions, discipline, work scheduling, and denying arbitration on such matters was not in violation of the duty to bargain in good faith. In *NLRB v. General Electric Co.*,[15] the Court of Appeals held that "take-it-or-leave-it" bargaining is not, by itself, in violation of the duty to bargain. But when an employer engages in other conduct indicating lack of good faith—such as refusing to sign a written agreement, attempting to deal with individual employees rather than the union, and refusing to provide the union with information regarding bargaining proposals—then the combined effect of the employer's conduct is to violate the duty to negotiate in good faith. But hard bargaining, in and of itself, is not a violation. At some point in negotiations, either side may make a "final" offer and hold to it firmly.

While negotiations are being conducted, is either side free to engage in tactics designed to pressure the other into making a concession? Is such pressure during bargaining consistent with negotiating in good faith? In *NLRB v. Insurance Agents International Union*,[16] the U.S. Supreme Court held that the use of economic pressure such as "work to rule" and "on the job slow-downs" is not inconsistent with the duty of bargaining in good faith; indeed, the use of economic pressure is "part and parcel" of the collective bargaining process.

The duty to bargain in good faith under Section 8(d) also includes the obligation to execute a written contract incorporating any agreement, if requested by either party. An employer may not refuse to abide by the agreement because it objects to the ratification process used by the union, according to *Valley Central Emergency Veterinary Hospital.*[17]

Subject Matter of Bargaining

As the preceding cases indicate, the NLRB and the courts are reluctant to control the bargaining tactics available to either party. This reluctance reflects a philosophical aversion to government intrusion into the bargaining process. Yet some regulation of bargaining is necessary if the bargaining process is to be meaningful. Some control is required to prevent the parties from making a charade of the process by holding firmly to arbitrary or frivolous

[14] 343 U.S. 395 (1952).

[15] 418 F.2d 736 (2d Cir. 1969), *cert. denied,* 397 U.S. 965 (1970).

[16] 361 U.S. 477 (1960).

[17] 349 NLRB 1126 (2007).

positions. One means of control is the distinction between mandatory and permissive subjects of bargaining.

Mandatory Bargaining Subjects

Mandatory Bargaining Subjects
Those matters that vitally affect the terms and conditions of employment of the employees in the bargaining unit; the parties must bargain in good faith over such subjects.

Mandatory bargaining subjects, according to the Supreme Court decision in *Allied Chemical & Alkali Workers v. PPG*,[18] are those subjects that "vitally affect the terms and conditions of employment" of the employees in the bargaining unit. The Supreme Court in *PPG* held that changes in medical insurance coverage of former employees who were retired were not a mandatory subject, and the company need not bargain over such changes with the union. The fact that the company had bargained over these issues in the past did not convert a permissive subject into a mandatory one; the company was free to change the insurance policy coverage unilaterally.

The NLRB and the Court have broadly interpreted the matters subject to mandatory bargaining as being related to "wages, hours, terms and conditions of employment" specified in Sections 8(d) and 9(a). Wages have been held to include all forms of employee compensation and fringe benefits, including items such as pensions, stock options, annual bonuses, employee discounts, shift differentials, and incentive plans. Hours and terms and conditions of employment have received similar broadening. The Supreme Court, in *Ford Motor Co. v. NLRB*,[19] held that the prices of food sold in vending machines in the plant cafeteria were mandatory subjects for bargaining when the employer had some control over pricing. In *California Newspapers Partnership d/b/a ANG Newspapers*,[20] the Board held that an employer was required to bargain over the employer's revisions to the e-mail use policy for employees; the employer's unilateral implementation of the policy violated the duty to bargain in good faith under the NLRA.

The aspect of mandatory bargaining subjects that has attracted the most controversy has been the duty to bargain over management decisions to subcontract work or to close down a plant. In *Fibreboard Paper Products v. NLRB*,[21] the Supreme Court held that an employer must bargain with the union over a decision to subcontract out work previously done by bargaining unit employees. Later, NLRB and Court decisions held that subcontracting that had never been done by bargaining unit employees was not a mandatory issue. In addition, decisions to change the corporate structure of a business or to terminate manufacturing operations were not mandatory subjects but rather were inherent management rights. Even the decision to go out of business entirely is not a mandatory subject of bargaining. But while the employer need not discuss such decisions with the union, the Board has held that the effects of such decisions upon the employees are mandatory bargaining subjects. The employer must therefore discuss the effects of such decisions with the union, including matters such as:

- Severance pay
- Transfer policies

---

[18]404 U.S. 157 (1971).

[19]441 U.S. 488 (1979).

[20]350 NLRB 1175 (2007).

[21]379 U.S. 203 (1964).

- Retraining
- The procedure to be used for layoffs

The following case illustrates the test used to determine whether a managerial decision, such as the decision to close part of the firm's operations, is a mandatory bargaining subject.

case 15.3 » First National Maintenance Corp. v. NLRB

452 U.S. 666 (1981)

Blackmun, J.

Must an employer, under its duty to bargain in good faith "with respect to wages, hours, and other terms and conditions of employment," Sections 8(d) and 8(a)(5) of the National Labor Relations Act, negotiate with the certified representative of its employees over its decision to close a part of its business? In this case, the National Labor Relations Board (Board) imposed such a duty on petitioner with respect to its decision to terminate a contract with a customer, and the United States Court of Appeals, although differing over the appropriate rationale, enforced its order.

Petitioner, First National Maintenance Corporation (FNM), is a New York corporation engaged in the business of providing housekeeping, cleaning maintenance, and related services for commercial customers in the New York City area. It contracts for and hires personnel separately for each customer, and it does not transfer employees between locations.

During the spring of 1977, petitioner was performing maintenance work for the Greenpark Care Center, a nursing home in Brooklyn. Petitioner employed approximately 35 workers in its Greenpark operation.

Petitioner's business relationship with Greenpark, seemingly, was not very remunerative or smooth. In March 1977, Greenpark gave petitioner the 30 days' written notice of cancellation specified by the contract, because of "lack of efficiency." This cancellation did not become effective, for FNM's work continued after the expiration of that 30-day period. Petitioner, however, became aware that it was losing money at Greenpark. On June 30, by telephone, it asked that its weekly fee be restored at the $500 figure, and, on July 6, it informed Greenpark in writing that it would discontinue its operations there on August 1 unless the increase were granted. By telegram on July 25, petitioner gave final notice of termination.

While FNM was experiencing these difficulties, District 1199, National Union of Hospital and Health Care Employees, Retail, Wholesale and Department Store Union, AFLCIO (Union), was conducting an organization campaign among petitioner's Greenpark employees. On March 31, 1977, at a Board-conducted election, a majority of the employees selected the union as their bargaining agent. Petitioner neither responded nor sought to consult with the union.

On July 28, petitioner notified its Greenpark employees that they would be discharged three days later.

With nothing but perfunctory further discussion, petitioner on July 31 discontinued its Greenpark operation and discharged the employees.

The union filed an unfair labor practice charge against petitioner, alleging violations of the Act's Section 8(a)(1) and (5). After a hearing held upon the Regional Director's complaint, the Administrative Law Judge made findings in the union's favor.... [H]e ruled that petitioner had failed to satisfy its duty to bargain concerning both the decision to terminate the Greenpark contract and the effect of that change upon the unit employees.

The Administrative Law Judge recommended an order requiring petitioner to bargain in good faith with the union about its decision to terminate its Greenpark service operation and its consequent discharge of the employees, as well as the effects of the termination. He recommended, also, that petitioner be ordered to pay the discharged employees back pay from the date of discharge until the parties bargained to agreement, or the bargaining reached an impasse, or the union failed timely to request bargaining or the union failed to bargain in good faith.

The National Labor Relations Board adopted the Administrative Law Judge's findings without further analysis, and additionally required petitioner, if it agreed to resume its Greenpark operations, to offer the terminated employees reinstatement to their former jobs or substantial equivalents; conversely, if agreement was not reached, petitioner was ordered to offer the employees equivalent positions, to be made available by discharge of subsequently hired employees, if necessary, at its other operations.

The United States Court of Appeals for the Second Circuit, with one judge dissenting in part, enforced the Board's order....

Although parties are free to bargain about any legal subject, Congress has limited the mandate or duty to bargain to matters of "wages, hours, and other terms and conditions of employment." Congress deliberately left the words "wages, hours, and other terms and conditions of employment" without further definition, for it did not intend to deprive the Board of the power further to define those terms in light of specific industrial practices.

Nonetheless, in establishing what issues must be submitted to the process of bargaining, Congress had no expectation that the elected union representative would become an equal partner in the running of the business enterprise in which the union's members are employed.

Some management decisions, such as choice of advertising and promotion, product type and design, and financing arrangements, have only an indirect and attenuated impact on the employment relationship. Other management decisions, such as the order of succession of layoffs and recalls, production quotas, and work rules, are almost exclusively "an aspect of the relationship" between employer and employee. The present case concerns a third type of management decision, one that had a direct impact on employment, since jobs were inexorably eliminated by the termination, but had as its focus only the economic profitability of the contract with Greenpark, a concern under these facts wholly apart from the employment relationship. This decision, involving a change in the scope and direction of the enterprise, is akin to the decision whether to be in business at all, "not in [itself] primarily about conditions of employment, though the effect of the decision may be necessarily to terminate employment." At the same time this decision touches on a matter of central and pressing concern to the union and its member employees: the possibility of continued employment and the retention of the employees' very jobs.

Petitioner contends it had no duty to bargain about its decision to terminate its operations at Greenpark. This contention requires that we determine whether the decision itself should be considered part of petitioner's retained freedom to manage its affairs unrelated to employment. The aim of labeling a matter a mandatory subject of bargaining, rather than simply permitting, but not requiring, bargaining, is to "promote the fundamental purpose of the Act by bringing a problem of vital concern to labor and management within the framework established by Congress as most conducive to industrial peace." The concept of mandatory bargaining is premised on the belief that collective discussions backed by the parties' economic weapons will result in decisions that are better for both management and labor and for society as a whole. This will be true, however, only if the subject proposed for discussion is amenable to resolution through the bargaining process. Management must be free from the constraints of the bargaining process to the extent essential for the running of a profitable business. It also must have some degree of certainty beforehand as to when it may proceed to reach decisions without fear of later evaluations labeling its conduct an unfair labor practice. Congress did not explicitly state what issues of mutual concern to union and management it intended to exclude from mandatory bargaining. Nonetheless, in view of an employer's need for unencumbered decisionmaking, bargaining over management decisions that have a substantial impact on the continued availability of employment should be required only if the benefit, for labor-management relations and the collective-bargaining process, outweighs the burden placed on the conduct of the business.

Both union and management regard control of the decision to shut down an operation with the utmost seriousness. As has been noted, however, the Act is not intended to serve either party's individual interest, but to foster in a neutral manner a system in which the conflict between these interests may be resolved. It seems particularly important, therefore, to consider whether requiring bargaining over this sort of decision will advance the neutral purposes of the Act.

A union's interest in participating in the decision to close a particular facility or part of an employer's operations springs from its legitimate concern over job security. The Court has observed: "The words of [Section 8(d)] ... plainly cover termination of employment which ... necessarily results" from closing an operation. The union's practical purpose in participation, however, will be largely uniform: it will seek to delay or halt the closing. No doubt it will be impelled, in seeking these ends, to offer concessions, information, and alternatives that might be helpful to management or forestall or prevent the termination of jobs. It is unlikely, however, that requiring bargaining over the decision itself, as well as its effects, will augment this flow of information and suggestions. There is no dispute that the union must be given a significant opportunity to bargain about these matters of job security as part of the "effects" bargaining mandated by Section 8(a)(5). A union, pursuing such bargaining rights, may achieve valuable concessions from an employer engaged in a partial closing.

Management's interest in whether it should discuss a decision of this kind is much more complex and varies with the particular circumstances. If labor costs are an important factor in a failing operation and the decision to close, management will have an incentive to confer voluntarily with the union to seek concessions that may make continuing the business profitable. At other times, management may have great need for speed, flexibility, and secrecy in meeting business opportunities and exigencies. It may face significant tax or securities consequences that hinge on confidentiality, the timing of a plant closing, or a reorganization of the corporate structure. The publicity incident to the normal process of bargaining may injure the possibility of a successful transition or increase the economic damage to the business. The employer also may have no feasible alternative to the closing, and even good faith bargaining over it may both be futile and cause the employer additional loss.

There is an important difference, also, between permitted bargaining and mandated bargaining. Labeling this type of decision mandatory could afford a union a powerful tool for achieving delay, a power that might be used to thwart management's intentions in a manner unrelated to any feasible solution the union might propose.

We conclude that the harm likely to be done to an employer's need to operate freely in deciding whether to shut down part of its business purely for economic reasons outweighs the incremental benefit that might be gained through the union's participation in making the decision, and we hold that the decision itself is not part of Section 8(d)'s "terms and conditions," over which Congress has mandated bargaining....

Case Questions

1. Why did First National Maintenance decide to close its operations at Greenpark? Could bargaining with the union affect those reasons? Explain your answer.
2. What test does the Supreme Court use to determine whether the decision to close operations is a mandatory bargaining subject? How does that test apply to the facts of this case?
3. What is the significance of labeling a decision a mandatory bargaining subject? Is the employer completely prohibited from acting alone on a mandatory subject? Explain.

Subsequent to the *First National Maintenance* decision, the NLRB has interpreted the "balancing test" set out by the court as focusing on whether the employer's decision is based on labor costs. A decision to relocate production to another plant was not a mandatory subject because the decision did not turn on labor costs, according to *Local 2179, United Steelworkers of America v. NLRB.*[22]

In short, the question whether the employer must bargain with the union over a management decision such as plant closing, work relocation, or corporate reorganization is whether or not the decision is motivated by a desire to reduce labor costs or to escape the collective bargaining agreement. If the decision is based on other business considerations, apart from labor costs, then the employer's duty to bargain is limited to the effects of the decision on the employees rather than the decision itself.

What is the effect of labeling a subject as a mandatory bargaining issue upon the employer's ability to make decisions necessary to the efficient operation of the enterprise? The Supreme Court opinion in *First National Maintenance* was concerned about placing burdens on the employer that would interfere with the need to act promptly. But rather than preventing employer action over mandatory subjects, the duty to bargain requires only that the employer negotiate with the union. If the union agrees or makes concessions, then the

[22] 822 F.2d 559 (5th Cir. 1987).

employer is free to act. If the union fails to agree and an impasse results from good faith bargaining, the employer is then free to implement the decision. The duty to bargain over mandatory subjects requires only that the employer bargain in good faith to the point of impasse over the issue. Once impasse has been reached, the employer is free to act unilaterally. In the case of *NLRB v. Katz*,[23] the Supreme Court stated that an employer may institute unilateral changes on mandatory subjects after bargaining to impasse. However, when the impasse results from the employer's failure to bargain in good faith, any unilateral changes would be an unfair labor practice in violation of Section 8(a)(5). The following case involves the application of the *Katz* decision.

case 15.4 »

Visiting Nurse Services Of Western Massachusetts, Inc. v. NLRB

177 F.3d 52 (1st Cir. 1999), cert. denied, 528 U.S. 1074 (2000)

Facts: VNS is a corporation that provides home-based nursing services. The collective bargaining agreement between VNS and the union representing its employees expired on October 31, 1992. Negotiations for a new agreement continued through March 1997. VNS proposed a 2 percent wage increase and to change from a weekly to a biweekly payroll system, to become effective on November 6, 1995. The union rejected the proposal but expressed a willingness to bargain about various proposed changes to the job classifications for the firm's nurses.

VNS presented a substantially identical proposal on December 6, 1995, but this proposal also granted VNS the sole and unqualified right to designate job classifications as it deemed necessary based on operational needs. On February 29, 1996, VNS again offered the union a 2 percent wage increase, effective retroactively to November 6, 1995, in return for the union's agreement to its proposals for a biweekly payroll system and the job classification changes. The union again rejected the proposal. Nevertheless, on March 21, 1996, VNS notified the union that it intended to implement both the wage increase and the biweekly pay proposals. The union replied that it opposed the unilateral implementation of the biweekly payroll system. VNS implemented the wage increase on April 7, 1996, and the biweekly payroll system on May 3, 1996.

On June 18, 1996, VNS presented another proposal that included the proposed job classification changes and a second 2 percent wage increase, and two new provisions: on transforming three holidays into "floating" holidays to be taken at a time requested by the employee, and the implementation of a "clinical ladders" program. VNS also proposed a smaller, alternative package (the "mini package") that also included a second 2 percent wage increase along with the proposals on floating holidays and the clinical ladders program. The parties did not reach an agreement on either proposal, but VNS advised the union that it was contemplating implementing the "mini package." The union again informed VNS that it opposed the unilateral implementation of these proposals. VNS then sent a memo to the employees (but not to the union) informing them that it had implemented the mini package with the wage increase to be applied retroactively to July 7, 1996. Ten days later, VNS notified the union that the wage increase had already been implemented and that the floating holidays and clinical ladders were "already in process."

The union filed unfair labor practice charges with the NLRB, which ultimately found that VNS violated Sections 8(a)(1) and (5) of the NLRA by unilaterally implementing:

- a bi-weekly payroll system on or about May 3, 1996;
- changes in holidays on or about September 6, 1996;
- a clinical ladder program on or about September 6, 1996; and
- changes in job classifications at some time subsequent to May 3, 1996.

[23] 369 U.S. 736 (1962).

VNS made these changes to mandatory subjects while it was still bargaining with the union and had not yet reached an impasse. VNS then sought review of the NLRB decision with the U.S. Court of Appeals for the First Circuit.

Issue: Did VNS's unilateral changes to mandatory bargaining subjects violate Sections 8(a)(1) and 8(a)(5) of the NLRA?

Decision: Before the NLRB, VNS argued that once it had given the union notice of its position on a particular issue and an opportunity to respond, it was free to unilaterally declare impasse on specific issues and to take action. The NLRB held when parties are engaged in negotiations for a collective bargaining agreement, an employer has the obligation to refrain from unilateral changes in the absence of an impasse. There are two limited exceptions to that general rule:

- when a union, in response to an employer's diligent and earnest efforts to engage in bargaining, insists on continually avoiding or delaying bargaining; or
- when economic exigencies or business emergencies compel prompt action by the employer.

The NLRB found that neither exception applied. The Supreme Court decision in *NLRB v. Katz* held that an employer must bargain to impasse before making unilateral changes to mandatory bargaining subjects. In *Litton Financial Printing Div. v. NLRB*, the Court reaffirmed that "an employer commits an unfair labor practice if, without bargaining to impasse, it effects a unilateral change of an existing term or condition of employment."

The Court of Appeals rejected VNS's argument that parties are at impasse when the union rejects or does not accept the employer's position on a particular issue. Whether there is an impasse is an intensely fact-driven question, with the initial determination to be made by the NLRB. The Court of Appeals' role is to review the NLRB's factual determinations to determine whether they are supported by substantial evidence in the record as a whole. An impasse occurs when, after good faith bargaining, the parties are deadlocked so that any further bargaining would be futile. Collective bargaining involves give and take on a number of issues, and the effect of VNS's position would be to permit the employer to remove, one by one, issues from the table and impair the ability to reach an overall agreement through compromise on particular items. In addition, it would undercut the role of the union as the collective bargaining representative, effectively communicating that the union lacked the power to keep issues at the table. The Court of Appeals enforced the NLRB's order.

Even if an employer has bargained to impasse over a mandatory subject and is free to implement changes, the changes made must be consistent with the proposal offered to the union. To institute changes unilaterally that are more generous than the proposals the employer was willing to offer the union is a violation of Section 8(a)(5), according to the Supreme Court decision in *NLRB v. Crompton-Highland Mills.*[24] Thus, the employer is not free to offer replacements wages that are higher than those offered to the union before the union went on strike. In some very exceptional circumstances, when changes must be made out of business necessity, the employer may institute unilateral changes without reaching an impasse, but those changes must be consistent with the offers made to the union, as held in *Raleigh Water Heating.*[25]

Permissive Bargaining Subjects
Those matters that are neither mandatory or illegal; the parties may, but are not required to, bargain over such subjects.

Permissive Bargaining Subjects

The previous discussion dealt with mandatory bargaining subjects; the Supreme Court in *NLRB v. Wooster Div. of Borg-Warner Corp.*[26] also recognized that there are permissive subjects and prohibited subjects. ***Permissive bargaining subjects*** are those matters not directly related to wages, hours, terms and conditions of employment, and not prohibited. Either party may

[24] 337 U.S. 217 (1949).

[25] 136 NLRB 76 (1962).

[26] 356 U.S. 342 (1958).

raise permissive items in bargaining, but such matters cannot be insisted upon to the point of impasse. If the other party refuses the permissive-item proposal, it must be dropped. *Borg-Warner* held that insisting upon permissive items to impasse and conditioning agreement on mandatory subjects upon agreement to permissive items was a violation of the duty to bargain in good faith. An interest arbitration clause in the collective bargaining agreement, which would require that all future contract disputes be settled by an arbitrator rather than by a strike or lockout, was held to be a permissive bargaining subject. The employer's insistence that the union agree to the interest arbitration clause as a condition of the employer signing the collective bargaining agreement was a violation of Section 8(a)(5), according to *Laidlaw Transit, Inc.*[27] Other examples of permissive items are proposals regarding:

- Union procedure for ratifying contracts
- Attempts to modify the union certification
- Strike settlement agreements
- Corporate social or charitable activities
- Requiring a transcript of all bargaining sessions

Matters that are "inherent management rights" or "inherent union rights" are also permissive subjects. An employer is under no duty to bargain over changes in permissive subjects; according to the Supreme Court opinion in *Allied Chemical & Alkalai Workers v. PPG*, cited earlier, unilateral changes on permissive subjects are not unfair practices.

Prohibited Bargaining Subjects

Prohibited bargaining subjects are proposals that involve violations of the NLRA or other laws. Examples would be a union attempt to negotiate a closed shop provision or to require an employer to agree to a "hot cargo clause" prohibited by Section 8(e) of the act. Any attempt to bargain over a prohibited subject may violate Section 8(a)(5) or Section 8(b)(3); any agreement reached on such items is null and void. It should be clear that prohibited subjects may not be used to precipitate an impasse.

Concept *Summary* » 15.2

BARGAINING SUBJECTS

Mandatory Bargaining Subjects	Permissive Bargaining Subjects	Prohibited Bargaining Subjects
Matters related to wages, hours, terms and conditions of employment	Anything that is neither a mandatory nor a prohibited bargaining subject	Proposals that involve a violation of the NLRA or other laws
Parties cannot make a unilateral change of a mandatory subject until bargaining in good faith to impasse	Parties can not insist on permissive subjects to the point of impasse	Any attempt to bargain over a prohibited subject is a violation of the duty to bargain in good faith

[27] 323 NLRB 867 (1997).

Modification of Collective Agreements

Section 8(d) of the act prohibits any modifications or changes in a collective agreement's provisions relating to mandatory bargaining subjects during the term of the agreement unless both parties to the agreement consent to such changes. (When the agreement has expired, either party may implement changes in the mandatory subjects covered by the agreement after having first bargained, in good faith, to impasse.)

In *Milwaukee Spring Div. of Illinois Coil Spring,*[28] the question before the NLRB was whether the employer's action to transfer its assembly operations from its unionized Milwaukee Spring facility to its nonunion operations in Illinois during the term of a collective agreement was a violation of Sections 8(a)(1), 8(a)(3), and 8(a)(5). The transfer of operations was made because of the higher labor costs of the unionized operations. As a result of the transfer, the employees at Milwaukee Spring were laid off. Prior to the decision to relocate operations, the employer had advised the union that it needed reductions in wages and benefit costs because it had lost a major customer, but the union had rejected any concessions. The employer had also proposed terms upon which it would retain operations in Milwaukee, but again, the union had rejected the proposals and declined to bargain further over alternatives to transfer. The NLRB had initially held that the actions constituted a violation of Sections 8(a)(1), 8(a)(3), and 8(a)(5); but on rehearing, the Board reversed the prior decision and found no violation. The majority of the Board reasoned that the decision to transfer operations did not constitute a unilateral modification of the collective agreement in violation of Section 8(d) because no term of the agreement required the operations to remain at the Milwaukee Spring facility. Had there been a work-preservation clause stating that the functions the bargaining unit employees performed must remain at the Milwaukee plant, the employer would have been guilty of a unilateral modification of the collective agreement, in violation of Section 8(d). The employer's offers to discuss concessions and the terms upon which it would retain operations in Milwaukee satisfied the employer's duty to bargain under Section 8(a)(5). The majority also held that the layoff of the unionized employees after the operations were transferred did not violate Section 8(a)(3). The effect of their decision, reasoned the majority, would be to encourage "realistic and meaningful collective bargaining that the Act contemplates." The dissent argued that the employer was prohibited from transferring operations during the term of the agreement without the consent of the union. The Court of Appeals for the D.C. Circuit affirmed the majority's decision in *U.A.W. v. NLRB.*[29]

Plant Closing Legislation

Because of concerns over plant closings, Congress passed the Worker Adjustment and Retraining Act (WARN) in August 1988. The law, which went into effect February 4, 1989, requires employers with 100 or more employees to give sixty days' advance notice prior to any plant closings or mass layoffs. The employer must give written notice of the closing or mass layoff to the employees or their representative, to the state economic development officials, and to the chief elected local government official. WARN defines a plant closing as being when fifty or more employees lose their jobs during any thirty-day period, because of a permanent

[28] 268 NLRB 601 (1984).

[29] 765 F.2d 175 (1985).

Mass Layoffs
Layoffs creating an employment loss during any thirty-day period for 500 or more employees or for fifty or more employees who constitute at least one-third of the full-time labor force at a unit of the facility.

Failing Firm Exception
An exception to the WARN notice requirement for layoffs that occurs when the employer can demonstrate that giving the required notice would prevent the firm from obtaining capital or business necessary to maintain the operation of the firm.

plant closing, or a temporary shutdown exceeding six months. A plant closing may also occur when fifty or more employees experience more than a 50 percent reduction in the hours of work during each month of any six-month period. ***Mass layoffs*** are defined as layoffs creating an employment loss during any thirty-day period for 500 or more employees or for fifty or more employees who constitute at least one-third of the full-time labor force at a unit of the facility. The act also requires a sixty-day notice when a series of employment losses adds up to the requisite levels over a ninety-day period. The notice requirement has two exceptions. One exception is the so-called ***failing firm exception***, when the employer can demonstrate that giving the required notice would prevent the firm from obtaining capital or business necessary to maintain the operation of the firm. The other exception is when the work loss is due to "unforeseen circumstances."

Although the legislation speaks of plant closings, and Congress had industrial plant closings as a primary concern when passing WARN, the courts have held that it applies to employers such as law firms, brokerage firms, hotels, and casinos. The act imposes a penalty for failure to give the required notice; the employer is required to pay each affected employee up to sixty days' pay and benefits if the required notice is not given. The act also provides for fines of up to $500 for each day the notice is not given, up to a maximum of $30,000. However, the fines can be imposed only in suits brought by local governments against the employer. WARN does not create any separate enforcement agency, nor does it give any enforcement authority to the Department of Labor.

The act requires only that advance notice of the plant closings or mass layoffs be given; it does not require that the employer negotiate over the decision to close or lay off. To that extent, WARN does not affect the duty to bargain under the NLRA or the results of the *First National Maintenance* decision.

ethical DILEMMA

Possible Plant Closing—to Meet or Not to Meet?

You are the human resource manager at Immense Multinational Business's production facility located in Utica, New York. The Utica plant is seventy-five years old. The plant is profitable but barely so. Its production costs are the highest in the corporation's manufacturing division. The workers at the Utica facility are unionized, and the wages at Utica are higher than at most of the company's other manufacturing plants. But the utility costs, real estate taxes, and N.Y. workers' compensation and unemployment insurance payroll taxes at the Utica plant are very high and are the main reasons for the plant's high production costs.

The company has recently opened a manufacturing plant in Puerto Rico. Corporate headquarters is considering expanding the production at that facility by transferring production from the Utica plant. The Utica workers have heard rumors that the plant will be closed. The officials of the local union at the Utica plant offer to meet with you to discuss the plant closing rumors and concessions that they are willing to make to keep the Utica plant open. Should you meet with them to discuss the plant closing and possible concessions? What arguments can you make for meeting with the union? What arguments can you make for not meeting with the union? Would refusing to meet and discuss those matters with the union be an unfair labor practice? Prepare a memo for corporate headquarters addressing these questions.

The Duty to Furnish Information

In *NLRB v. Truitt Mfg.*,[30] the Supreme Court held that an employer that pleads inability to pay in response to union demands must provide some financial information in an attempt to support that claim. The Court reasoned that such a duty was necessary if bargaining was to be meaningful; the employer is not allowed to "hide behind" claims that it cannot afford the union's pay demands. The rationale behind this requirement is that the union will be able to determine if the employer's claims are valid. If so, the union will moderate its demands accordingly.

The *Truitt* requirement to furnish information is not a "truth-in-bargaining" requirement. It relates only to claims of financial inability to meet union proposals. If the employer pleads inability to pay, the union must make a good faith demand for financial information supporting the employer's claim. In responding to the union request, the employer need not provide all the information requested by the union, but it must provide financial information in a reasonably usable and accessible form.

While the *Truitt* duty relates to financial information when the employer has pleaded inability to pay, another duty to furnish information is far greater in scope. Information relating to the enforcement and administration of the collective agreement must be provided to the union. This information is necessary for the union to perform its role as collective representative of the employees. This duty continues beyond negotiations to cover grievance arbitration during the life of the agreement as well. Such information includes:

- Wage scales
- Factors entering into compensation
- Job rates
- Job classifications
- Statistical data on the employer's minority employment practices
- A list of the names and addresses of the employees in the bargaining unit

The employer's refusal to provide the union with a copy of the contract for the sale of the employer's business was a violation of Section 8(a)(5) when the union sought the contract to determine whether the employees were adequately provided for after the sale and the union had agreed to keep the sales information confidential and to allow the employer to delete the sale price from the contract, according to *NLRB v. New England Newspapers, Inc.*[31] Employers using toxic substances have been required to furnish unions with information on the generic names of substances used, their health effects, and toxicological studies. Employers are not required to turn over medical records of identified individual employees. To safeguard the privacy of individual employees, the courts have required that individual employees must

[30] 351 U.S. 149 (1956).

[31] 856 F.2d 409 (1st Cir. 1988).

consent to the disclosure of individual health records and scores on aptitude or psychological tests. An employer is entitled, however, to protect trade secrets and confidential information such as affirmative action plans or privately developed psychological aptitude tests.

Information provided to the union does not have to be in the exact format requested by the union, but it must be in a form that is not burdensome to use or interpret. An employer may not prohibit union photocopying of the information provided, according to *Communications Workers Local 1051 v. NLRB.*[32]

Bargaining Remedies

We have seen that the requirements of the duty to bargain in good faith reflect a balance between promoting industrial peace and recognizing the principle of freedom of contract. To preserve the voluntary nature of collective bargaining, the Board and the courts will not require either party to make a concession or agree to a proposal.

When the violation of Section 8(a)(5) or Section 8(b)(3) involves specific practices, such as the refusal to furnish information or the refusal to sign an already agreed-upon contract, the Board orders the offending party to comply. Likewise, when an employer has illegally made unilateral changes, the Board requires that the prior conditions be restored and any reduction in wages or benefits be paid back. However, if the violation of the duty to bargain in good faith involves either side's refusal to recognize or negotiate seriously with the other side, the Board is limited in remedies available. In such cases, the Board will issue a "cease-and-desist" order directing the offending party to stop the illegal conduct and a "bargaining order" directing the party to begin to negotiate in good faith. But the Board cannot require that the parties make concessions or reach an agreement; it can only require that the parties return to the bargaining table and make an effort to explore the basis for an agreement. The following case deals with the limits on the Board's remedial powers in bargaining-order situations.

case 15.5 »

H. K. PORTER Co. v. NLRB

397 U.S. 99 (1970)

Black, J.

After an election, respondent United Steelworkers Union was, on October 5, 1961, certified by the National Labor Relations Board as the bargaining agent for the employees at the Danville, Virginia, plant of the H. K. Porter Co. Thereafter negotiations commenced for a collective bargaining agreement. Since that time the controversy has seesawed between the Board, the Court of Appeals for the District of Columbia Circuit, and this Court. This delay of over eight years is not because the case is exceedingly complex, but appears to have occurred chiefly because of the skill of the company's negotiators in taking advantage of every opportunity for delay in an Act more noticeable for its generality than for its precise prescriptions. The entire lengthy dispute mainly revolves around the union's desire to have the company agree to "check off" the dues owed to the union by its members, that is, to deduct those dues periodically from the company's wage payments to the employees. The record shows, as the Board found, that the company's objection to a checkoff was not due to any general principle or policy

[32]644 F.2d 923 (1st Cir. 1981).

against making deductions from employees' wages. The company does deduct charges for things like insurance, taxes, and contributions to charities, and at some other plants it has a checkoff arrangement for union dues. The evidence shows, and the court below found, that the company's objection was not because of inconvenience, but solely on the ground that the company was "not going to aid and comfort the union." Based on this and other evidence the Board found, and the Court of Appeals approved the finding, that the refusal of the company to bargain about the checkoff was not made in good faith, but was done solely to frustrate the making of any collective bargaining agreement. In May 1966, the Court of Appeals upheld the Board's order requiring the company to cease and desist from refusing to bargain in good faith and directing it to engage in further collective bargaining, if requested by the union to do so, over the checkoff.

In the course of that opinion, the Court of Appeals intimated that the Board conceivably might have required petitioner to agree to a checkoff provision as a remedy for the prior bad-faith bargaining, although the order enforced at that time did not contain any such provision. In the ensuing negotiations the company offered to discuss alternative arrangements for collecting the union's dues, but the union insisted that the company was required to agree to the checkoff proposal without modification. Because of this disagreement over the proper interpretation of the court's opinion, the union, in February 1967, filed a motion for clarification of the 1966 opinion. The motion was denied by the court on March 22, 1967, in an order suggesting that contempt proceedings before the Board would be the proper avenue for testing the employer's compliance with the original order. A request for the institution of such proceedings was made by the union, and in June 1967, the Regional Director of the Board declined to prosecute a contempt charge, finding that the employer had "satisfactorily complied with the affirmative requirements of the Order." ... The union then filed in the Court of Appeals a motion for reconsideration of the earlier motion to clarify the 1966 opinion. The court granted that motion and issued a new opinion in which it held that in certain circumstances a "checkoff may be imposed as a remedy for bad-faith bargaining." The case was then remanded to the Board and on July 3, 1968, the Board issued a supplemental order requiring the petitioner to "[g]rant to the Union a contract clause providing for the checkoff of union dues." ... The Board had found that the refusal was based on a desire to frustrate agreement and not on any legitimate business reason. On the basis of that finding the Court of Appeals approved the further finding that the employer had not bargained in good faith, and the validity of that finding is not now before us. Where the record thus revealed repeated refusals by the employer to bargain in good faith on this issue, the Court of Appeals concluded that ordering agreement to the checkoff clause "may be the only means of assuring the Board, and the court, that [the employer] no longer harbors an illegal intent."

In reaching this conclusion the Court of Appeals held that Section 8(d) did not forbid the Board from compelling agreement. That court felt that "Section 8(d) defines collective bargaining and relates to a determination of whether a ... violation has occurred and not to the scope of the remedy which may be necessary to cure violations which have already occurred." We may agree with the Court of Appeals that as a matter of strict, literal interpretation of that section it refers only to deciding when a violation has occurred, but we do not agree that that observation justifies the conclusion that the remedial powers of the Board are not also limited by the same considerations that led Congress to enact Section 8(d). It is implicit in the entire structure of the Act that the Board acts to oversee and referee the process of collective bargaining, leaving the results of the contest to the bargaining strengths of the parties. It would be anomalous indeed to hold that while Section 8(d) prohibits the Board from relying on a refusal to agree as the sole evidence of bad faith bargaining, the Act permits the Board to compel agreement in that same dispute. The Board's remedial powers under Section 10 of the Act are broad, but they are limited to carry out the policies of the Act itself. One of these fundamental policies is freedom of contract. While the parties' freedom of contract is not absolute under the Act, allowing the Board to compel agreement when the parties themselves are unable to do so would violate the fundamental premise on which the Act is based—private bargaining under governmental supervision of the procedure alone, without any official compulsion over the actual terms of the contract.

In reaching its decision, the Court of Appeals relied extensively on the equally important policy of the Act that workers' rights to collective bargaining are to be secured. In this case the Court apparently felt that the employer was trying effectively to destroy the union by refusing to agree to what the union may have considered its most important demand. Perhaps the court, fearing that the parties might resort to economic combat, was also trying to maintain the industrial peace which the Act is designed to further. But the Act, as presently drawn, does not contemplate that unions will always be secure and able to achieve agreement even when their economic position is weak, nor that strikes and lockouts will never result from a bargaining to impasse. It cannot be said that the Act forbids an employer or a union to rely ultimately on its economic strength to try to secure what it cannot obtain through bargaining. It may well be true, as the Court of Appeals felt, that the present remedial powers of the Board are insufficiently broad to cope with important labor problems. But it is the job of Congress, not the Board or the courts, to decide when and if it is necessary to allow governmental review of proposals for collective bargaining agreements and compulsory submission to one side's demands. The present Act does not envision such a process.

The judgment is reversed and the case is remanded to the Court of Appeals for further action consistent with this opinion.

Reversed and remanded.

Case Questions

1. Had the employer agreed to the union dues checkoff clause? Why did the court of appeals hold that the NLRB had the power to impose a checkoff clause on the employer?
2. Does the Supreme Court agree that the NLRB has the power to impose the checkoff clause? Why?
3. In light of this Supreme Court decision, what is the extent of the NLRB's power to remedy violations of the duty to bargain in good faith?

Because of the limitations on the NLRB's remedial powers in bargaining cases, an intransigent party can effectively frustrate the policies of the NLRA. If a union or employer is willing to incur the legal expenses and possible contempt-of-court fines, it can avoid reaching an agreement with the other side. Although unions are occasionally involved in such situations, most often employers have more to gain from refusing to bargain. The legal fees and fines may amount to less money than the employer would be required to pay in wages under a collective agreement (and the legal expenses are tax deductible). Perhaps the most extreme example of such intransigence was the J. P. Stevens Company. In the late 1970s, the company was found guilty of numerous unfair practices and was subjected to a number of bargaining orders, yet in only one case did it reach a collective agreement with the union.

Extreme cases like J. P. Stevens are the exception, however. Despite the Board's remedial shortcomings, most negotiations culminate in the signing of a collective agreement. That fact is a testament to the vitality of the collective-bargaining process and a vindication of a policy emphasis on the voluntary nature of the process.

Antitrust Aspects of Collective Bargaining

When a union and a group of employers agree upon specified wages and working conditions, the effect may be to reduce competition among the employers with respect to those wages or working conditions. In addition, when the parties negotiate limits on subcontracting work or the use of prefabricated materials, the effect may be to reduce or prevent competition among firms producing these materials. Although the parties may be pursuing legitimate goals of collective bargaining, those goals may conflict with the policies of the antitrust laws designed to promote competition.

In the case of *U.S. v. Hutcheson*,[33] the Supreme Court held that a union acting in its self-interest, which does not combine with nonlabor groups, is exempt from the antitrust laws. *Hutcheson* involved union picketing of Anheuser-Busch and a call for a boycott of

[33]312 U.S. 219 (1941).

Anheuser-Busch products as a result of a dispute over work-assignment decisions. The Court ruled that such conduct was legal as long as it was not done in concert with nonlabor groups.

The scope of the labor relations exemption from the antitrust laws was further clarified by the Supreme Court in *Amalgamated Meat Cutters v. Jewel Tea Co.*[34] In that case, the union and a group of grocery stores negotiated restrictions on the hours its members would work, since the contract required the presence of union butchers for fresh meat sales. The effect of the agreement was to restrict the hours during which the grocery stores could sell fresh (rather than prepackaged) meat. Jewel Tea argued that such a restriction of competition among the grocery stores violated the Sherman Antitrust Act. The Supreme Court held that since the union was pursuing its legitimate interests—that is, setting hours of work through a collective bargaining relationship—and did not act in concert with one group of employers to impose restrictions on another group of employers, the contract did not violate the Sherman Act.

Despite the broad scope of the antitrust exemption for labor relations activities, several cases have held unions in violation of the antitrust laws. In *United Mine Workers v. Pennington*,[35] the union agreed with one group of mine operators to impose wage and pension demands on a different group of mines. The union and the first group of mine owners were held by the Court to have been aware that the second group, composed of smaller mining operations, would be unable to meet the demands and could be forced to cease operations. The Supreme Court stated that if the union had agreed with the first group of employers in order to eliminate competition from the smaller mines, the union would be in violation of the antitrust laws. Although the union, acting alone, could attempt to force the smaller mines to agree to its demands, the union lost its exemption from the antitrust laws when it combined with one group of employers to force demands on the second group.

In *Connell Construction Co. v. Plumbers Local 100*,[36] a union attempted to force a general contractor to agree to hire only plumbing subcontractors who had contracts with the union. The general contractor did not itself employ any plumbers, and the union did not represent the employees of the general contractor. The effect of the union demand would be to restrict competition among plumbing subcontractors. Nonunion firms, and even unionized firms that had contracts with other unions, would be denied access to plumbing jobs. The Supreme Court held that the union conduct was not exempt from the antitrust laws because the union did not have a collective bargaining relationship with Connell, the general contractor. Although a union may attempt to impose restrictions on employers with whom it has a bargaining relationship, it may not attempt to impose such restrictions on employers outside that bargaining relationship.

In *Brown v. Pro Football, Inc.*,[37] the U.S. Supreme Court held that the nonstatutory exemption from the antitrust laws continued past the expiration of the collective agreement and the point of impasse and lasted as long as a collective bargaining relationship existed. The Court therefore upheld the legality of salary restrictions imposed by the members of a multiemployer bargaining unit—the teams of the National Football League—unilaterally after the expiration of their collective agreement and after bargaining in good faith to impasse.

---

[34] 381 U.S. 676 (1965).

[35] 381 U.S. 657 (1965).

[36] 421 U.S. 616 (1975).

[37] 518 U.S. 231 (1996).

The NFL rule requiring a player to wait for at least three full football seasons after high school graduation before being eligible to enter the NFL draft was held to be within the non-statutory exemption from the antitrust laws in *Clarett v. National Football League.*[38] In summary, then, the parties are generally exempt from the antitrust laws when they act alone to pursue legitimate concerns within the context of a collective bargaining relationship. If a union agrees with one group of employers to impose demands on another group or if it attempts to impose work restrictions on employers outside a collective bargaining relationship, it is subject to the antitrust laws.

Concept *Summary* » 15.3

Union Bargaining and Antitrust Law

Union Activity Exempt from Antitrust Law

- Unions pursuing legitimate labor concerns in the context of a collective bargaining relationship
- Unions acting in self-interest and not combining with non-labor groups

Union Activity Subject to Antitrust Law

- Unions attempting to impose restrictions outside of a collective bargaining relationship
- Unions agreeing with one group of employers to impose restrictions on another group of employers

The WORKING Law

NBA and Players' Union Asked to Repeal Minimum Age Rule for Players

Tennessee Congressman Steve Cohen has asked the National Basketball Association and the NBA Players Union to repeal their rule requiring that players must be at least nineteen years old and be at least one year out of high school. The rule was adopted in 2005 and is part of the collective agreement between the NBA and the players' union. The agreement expires in 2011 and NBA Commission David Stern has indicated that he would like to see the minimum age raised to twenty years of age. The NBA defended the rule as increasing the chances that incoming players will have the requisite experience, maturity, and life skills to perform at a high level. Congressman Cohen, who represents the Memphis area, noted that the University of Memphis basketball team lost players Derrick Rose and Tyreke Evans, who each played one season before declaring their intention to turn professional. Cohen also pointed out that some of the NBA's biggest stars, Kobe Bryant, LeBron James, Kevin Garnett, Rashard Lewis, and Dwight Howard went directly to the NBA from high school (before the current rule was adopted). Dan Wasserman, spokesman for the NBA players' union, said that he expected the age rule to be a main issue in negotiations for a new collective agreement.

Sources: Pete Thamel, "Congressman Asks NBA and Union to Rescind Age Minimum for Players," *The New York Times on the Web*, June 4, 2009; Frederic J. Frommer, "NBA Defends Age Minimum to Congress," *The Associated Press*, July 20, 2009.

---

[38] 369 F.3d 124 (2d Cir. 2004).

CHAPTER REVIEW

» Key Terms

collective bargaining	« 455	*mandatory bargaining subjects*	« 466	*mass layoffs*	« 474
impasse	« 464	*permissive bargaining subjects*	« 471	*failing firm exception*	« 474

» Summary

- The duty to bargain in good faith arises under Section 9(a) of the NLRA because of a union's status as exclusive bargaining agent. When a union demonstrates the support of a majority of the employees in the bargaining unit, both the union and the employer are required to bargain in good faith, as defined in Section 8(d).
- The NLRB presumptions regarding the union's majority status require that the employer recognize and bargain with the union for at least one year following the union's victory in a representation election or for a reasonable period of time following a voluntary recognition of the union by the employer. If the parties have negotiated a collective bargaining agreement, the presumption of union majority support continues for the length of the collective agreement or for the first three years of the agreement if it is for a longer term. After the expiration of the collective agreement, the employer must demonstrate a good faith doubt as to the union's majority support, based on some objective evidence, to refuse to bargain with the union.
- Bargaining in good faith, as defined in Section 8(d), requires that the parties meet and discuss matters with an open mind to explore the basis of an agreement. The parties are not required to make concessions or to reach an agreement.
- The NLRB has classified bargaining subject matter as either mandatory, permissive, or illegal. Attempts to negotiate illegal subjects, or taking an illegal subject to impasse, are a violation of the duty to bargain in good faith. Mandatory subjects are those that directly affect the wages, hours, and terms and conditions of employment of the employees in the bargaining unit; the parties are required to discuss such issues and, after reaching impasse, may strike or lock out over mandatory subjects. Permissive subjects are those that are neither mandatory nor illegal; while the parties are free to discuss these matters, they cannot take permissive subjects to impasse.
- The NLRB's remedies for violations of the duty to bargain in good faith are limited to cease-and-desist orders; the NLRB cannot order parties to reach an agreement, nor can it impose contractual terms on the parties.

» Problems

Questions

1. Under what circumstances may an employer whose employees are unionized bargain legally with individual employees?
2. Must an employer refuse to bargain with either union when two unions are seeking to represent the employer's workers? Explain your answer.
3. What are mandatory bargaining subjects? What is the significance of an item being classified as a mandatory bargaining subject?
4. When is an employer required to provide financial information to a union?
5. What conduct by unions is subject to the antitrust laws?

Case Problems

6. During bargaining, the employer reached an impasse on (a) a detailed "management rights" clause, (b) a broad "zipper" clause, (c) a waiver-of-past-practices provision, and (d) a no-strike provision. The employer's final economic offer consisted of an increase of ten cents per hour for seven of the nine bargaining unit employees and a wage review for the remaining two.

   Based on these facts, the NLRB concluded that the employer had engaged in mere surface bargaining and condemned the employer's final proposals as "terms which no self respecting union could be expected to accept." The company appealed the case to the Ninth Circuit.

   If you had sat on the panel at the appellate court level, would you have agreed or disagreed with the board's conclusions? See *NLRB v. Tomco Communications, Inc.* [567 F.2d 871, 97 L.R.R.M. 2660 (9th Cir. 1978)].

7. The personnel department at an electrical utility had a policy of giving all new employees a "psychological aptitude test." The union demanded access to the test questions, answers, and individual scores for the employees in the bargaining unit. The union pointed out that among similar types of information that the NLRB had ordered disclosed in other cases were seniority lists, employees' ages, names and addresses of successful and unsuccessful job applicants, information about benefits received by retirees under employer's pension and insurance plans, information on employee grievances, and information on possible loss of work due to a proposed leasing arrangement.

   The company claimed that if it released the information the union sought, its test security program would be severely compromised. Furthermore, employee confidence in the confidentiality of the testing program would be shattered.

   How do you think the NLRB would rule in this case? See *Detroit Edison Co. v. NLRB* [440 U.S. 301, 100 L.R.R.M. 2728 (1979)].

8. During negotiations for renewing the collective agreement, the union representing the employees at Mercy Hospital presented a proposal that the hospital cafeteria be open for all employees from the hours of 6:30 A.M.–8:00 P.M. and 2:00 A.M.–4:00 A.M. The cafeteria had been open for those hours for the past ten years, but the hospital had considered closing it overnight. The union argued that there were approximately 175 employees working the overnight shift, and many of them used the cafeteria for lunch and breaks. The hospital responded that the cafeteria had been losing money during the 2:00 A.M.–4:00 A.M. operations. The union proposal was made on May 15, 2007; on May 19, without any notice to and discussions with the union, the hospital closed the cafeteria overnight. The hospital installed additional vending machines and provided a toaster and microwave for use by the employees. The union filed an unfair labor practice complaint with the NLRB over the hospital's closing of the cafeteria overnight.

   How should the NLRB rule on the complaint? Was the hospital required to bargain with the union over the decision to close the cafeteria overnight? Why? See *Mercy Hospital of Buffalo* [311 NLRB 869 (1993)].

9. Sonat Marine was engaged in the business of transporting petroleum and petrochemical products. The Seafarers International Union (SIU) represented two separate bargaining units of Sonat's employees. One unit consisted of licensed employees—that is, the tugboat masters, mates, and pilots. In 2004, Sonat advised the union that it intended to withdraw recognition of the SIU as the bargaining representative of these licensed personnel at the expiration of the current collective-bargaining agreement. Sonat's stated reason was that it had determined that these personnel were supervisors who were not subject to the NLRA as employees. The union demanded information on the factual basis for Sonat's position. Sonat refused to provide a response.

   The union filed an unfair labor practice charge, asserting that Sonat was not bargaining in good faith. Was the union right? See *Sonat Marine, Inc.* [279 NLRB 100 (1986)].

10. Pratt-Farnsworth, Inc., a unionized construction contractor in New Orleans, owned a nonunion subsidiary, Halmar. During negotiations of a new collective bargaining agreement with Pratt-Farnsworth, the Carpenters' Union demanded that the company provide information concerning Halmar's business activities; the union was suspicious that the subsidiary was being used by the parent to siphon off work that could have been done by union members.

    If you represented the union, what arguments would you make to support your demand for information? If you were on the company's side, how would you respond? See *Carpenters Local 1846 v. Pratt-Farnsworth, Inc.* [690 F.2d 489, 111 L.R. R.M. 2787 (5th Cir. 1982)].

11. The company and the union commenced collective bargaining in April 2003. After four sessions, the company submitted, on June 15, a contract package for union ratification. Two days later, the union's membership rejected the package. No strike ensued.

    Following rejection, the union's chief negotiator contacted the company and pointed out four stumbling blocks to ratification: union security, wages, overtime pay, and sickness and accident benefits. On July 7, the company resubmitted its original contract package unchanged. The union agreed to put it to a second ratification vote. However, before the vote took place, the company's president withdrew the package from the bargaining table. His reasoning was that the union's failure to strike indicated that the company had earlier overestimated the union's economic power. When in subsequent bargaining sessions the company proposed wages and benefits below those in the original package, the union charged it with bad-faith bargaining.

    How should the NLRB have ruled on this complaint? See *Pennex Aluminum Corp.* [271 NLRB 1205 (1984)].

12. For more than thirty years without challenge by the union, the Brod & McClung-Pace Co.'s bargaining unit employees performed warranty work at customers' facilities. Then the international union altered its constitution to forbid its members to do such warranty work. Pursuant to this constitutional change, the local union, which was subject to the international's constitution, sought a midterm modification of its collective bargaining agreement with the company to eliminate the warranty work. When the firm refused, the union sought to achieve a unilateral change by threatening its members with court-collectible fines if they continued to perform the work.

    Did the union violate the NLRA? If so, how? See *Sheet Metal Workers Int'l. Ass'n., Local 16* [270 NLRB 116 (1984)].

13. After five sessions of multiemployer bargaining, the Carpenters' Union and the Lake Charles District of the Associated General Contractors of Louisiana reached a new agreement. However, the printed contract inadvertently omitted a "weather clause," which was to state that an employee who reported for work but was sent home because of inclement weather would get four hours' pay, and an employee sent home because of weather after having started work would get paid only for hours actually worked, but not less than two hours. When the omission was discovered, the contract was already ratified and signed. The union refused to add the clause. The company then asked to reopen bargaining over the

wage and reporting clauses that were affected by the omission. The union refused. Who, if anyone, has committed an unfair labor practice? See *International Brotherhood of Carpenters Local 1476* [270 NLRB 1432 (1984)].

14. The production workers at Molded Products Co., represented by the Allied Workers Union, went on strike in June 2002, after their collective agreement expired. The strike lasted two months, and during the strike, almost half of the 150 workers crossed the picket line and returned to work. When the strike ended, the company recalled sixty of the strikers and operated with a work force of 135. Some of the workers then circulated a petition stating that they no longer wished to be represented by the union, and seventy of the workers signed it. The company then notified the union that it was withdrawing recognition and refused to bargain with the union over renewing the collective agreement. The union filed a complaint with the NLRB, arguing that the company's withdrawal of recognition violated Sections 8(a)(1) and (5).

    How should the NLRB rule on the complaint? Why? Explain your answer. See *Quazite Div. of Morrison Molded Fiberglass Co. v. NLRB* [87 F.3d 493 (D.C. Cir. 1996)].

15. Plymouth Stamping, an automotive parts company located in Michigan, decided to contract out its parts assembly operations in response to deteriorating sales and financial conditions. It notified the union on February 11, 2008, of its plans to subcontract. The notice stated that the operation would be discontinued as of February 15, that the assembly operation employees would be either laid off or transferred, and that the action was necessary "due to economic and business reasons." The union requested a meeting, which was held on February 14, 2008. At this meeting, the company explained that the action was the result of a number of factors, including declining sales, noncompetitive wage rates, burdensome state taxes, and high workers' compensation costs. The company, in response to a question concerning possible ways to retain the jobs, stated that the union would have to accept substantial wage cuts, a cost-of-living freeze, a reduction in some benefits, and a modification in work rules. The union requested that the company delay any action until at least the following week; the company, while stating that its decision was not final, requested a reply from the union by February 15 as to whether it would agree to concessions. The union failed to respond by February 15, and over the weekend (February 16 and 17), the company moved its assembly equipment to a plant in Ohio. Meanwhile, unbeknownst to the company, the union, in a letter dated February 14, had requested information regarding the specifics of the decision. The company received the union's letter on February 20. The company responded to the union's letter on March 11; it stated that the decision was not irreversible and that it was prepared to discuss the matter with the union. The company repeated that the decision to subcontract was taken because "assembly operations are labor intensive and the costs (wages/benefits) associated with supporting this labor group have made the company noncompetitive." On March 1, the company entered into a formal leasing agreement with the subcontracting company; the lease allowed the company to terminate the lease and repossess the equipment and gave the subcontractor the option to purchase the equipment. The subcontractor purchased the equipment on July 1, 1980. The union filed an unfair labor practice complaint with the NLRB, charging the company with violations of Sections 8(a)(1) and 8(a)(5) for failing to bargain over a mandatory subject of bargaining and making a unilateral change in a mandatory subject without bargaining to impasse.

    How should the NLRB decide the union's complaint? What would have been the effect of the WARN law if it had applied to this case? See *NLRB v. Plymouth Stamping Division, Eltec Corp.* [870 F.2d 1112 (6th Cir. 1989)].

Hypothetical Scenarios

16. During the negotiations between the employer, Spina Mfg., and the union representing Spina's employees, the union representative noted that the company did not have an Employee Assistance Program (EAP), although it did have a drug and

alcohol policy. Parker, Spina's manager replied that the company's health insurance program addressed such employee issues and said that he did not favor instituting an EAP program. After a fatal employee accident in the workplace, Parker contacted TriCity Family Services, a local social services agency, to launch an EAP program for employees. Parker did not notify the union about the EAP before agreeing with TriCity to set up the program. At the next negotiation session, Parker gave the union representatives a brochure and related information about the EAP program, and told them that he instituted the program as result of the workplace accident. At the negotiation session held the next day, Parker asked the union representatives whether they had read the EAP information. The union representatives answered that they had not yet done so. The union did not offer a counterproposal to the EAP established by Parker. The union filed an unfair labor practice charge with the NLRB, alleging that the employer's unilateral decision to create the EAP was in violation of Section 8(a)(5). Spina's managers responded that its actions in creating the EAP were motivated solely by the desire to provide the employees with immediate grief counseling in light of the death of one of their fellow employees in the workplace accident. They also said that they did notify the union that they were willing to discuss and negotiate the program during their ongoing negotiations. Did Spina's unilateral creation of the EAP violate Section 8(a)(5)? Explain your answer.

17. Rodgers Graphics, a commercial printer, refused to bargain with the Communications Workers of America, Local 14, after its collective bargaining agreement expired. The company claimed that it had a good faith reasonable doubt of the union's majority status, based on the following facts:

    - The company's president, Doyle McDonald, gathered from frequent conversations with various employees that the employees were not happy with the union.
    - Cynthia Termath, an employee who served as one of two union stewards, told McDonald that most employees had lost confidence in the union, did not think it was representing them well, no longer wanted the union to represent them, and were generally dissatisfied with it. Termath gained her information from her conversations with about sixty other employees.
    - Ignacio Burgos, the other union steward, also told McDonald that the employees were dissatisfied with the union.
    - Company managers informed McDonald that there was a "lack of interest" in the union among employees.

    Does Rodgers' refusal to bargain with the union violate Sections 8(a)(1) and 8(a)(5) of the NLRA? Explain your answer.

18. Lakeland Bus Lines, Inc. is a private bus company whose drivers are represented by the Amalgamated Transit Union, Local 164. The parties' collective agreement expired on January 31, 2007. In February, when negotiations on a new agreement stalled, the company gave a final offer to the union. On the same day, Lakeland's president sent a letter to the bargaining unit employees detailing the company's bargaining position and its financial difficulties. The union then requested that the company provide financial information to verify that it could not afford any contract terms that exceeded the costs of its final offer. Company representatives refused to furnish any of the requested information. Lakeland's employees subsequently rejected the company's final offer, and the company unilaterally implemented the terms of its final offer. The union filed unfair labor practice charges with the NLRB, claiming that Lakeland had failed to bargain in good faith by refusing to provide financial information requested by the union and by unilaterally imposing the terms of its final offer. How should the NLRB rule on the union's complaint? Why?

19. Callahan Construction Co. and the Carpenters' Union had concluded negotiations for a new collective agreement covering Callahan's employees, when the union representative informed Callahan that the union would not agree to the final contract wage proposal unless the employer joined the Green Builders Association and agreed to promote energy-efficient and environmentally friendly construction

techniques. Does the union's demand violate the duty to bargain in good faith? Explain your answer.

20. Local No. 580 of the Teamsters Union was certified by the NLRB as the exclusive bargaining representative for the employees of Adams Potato Chip Co. At subsequent negotiations for a collective agreement covering the employees, the union negotiators indicated that they would accept the company's proposal if the company agreed to change its offer of three weeks' vacation for workers with at least fifteen years of service to three weeks' vacation after ten years of service. The company's lead negotiator agreed to the change and the parties held that the negotiations were completed. The company president later refused to sign the written agreement, claiming that the company negotiator lacked authority to agree to the change in vacation policy. Has the company violated Section 8(a)(5)? Explain.

Picketing and Strikes

Collective bargaining involves economic conflict: Each party to the negotiations seeks to protect its economic interests by extracting concessions from the other side. Both union and management back up their demands with the threat of pressure tactics that would inflict economic harm upon the other party. If the negotiations reach an impasse, the union may go on strike, or the employer may lock out to force concessions. This chapter discusses the limitations placed on the use of such pressure tactics.

Pressure Tactics

Pressure Tactics
Union pressure tactics involve strikes and calls for boycotts, while employers may resort to lockouts.

Picketing
Placing persons outside an employer's premises to convey information to the public via words, signs, or distributing literature.

Patrolling
The movement of persons back and forth around an employer's premises.

Pressure tactics include:

- Picketing
- Patrolling
- Strikes
- Boycotts by unions
- Lockouts by employers

Picketing is the placing of persons outside the premises of an employer to convey information to the public. The information may be conveyed by words, signs, or the distribution of literature. Picketing is usually accompanied by ***patrolling***, which is the movement of persons back and forth around the premises of an employer. A ***strike*** (see p. 488 for definition)—the organized withholding of labor by workers—is the traditional weapon by which workers attempt to pressure employers. If the strike is successful, the economic harm resulting from the cessation of production will force the employer to accede to the union's demands. Strikes are usually accompanied by picketing and patrolling as means of enforcing the strike. Unions may also instigate a *boycott* of the employer's product to increase the economic pressure upon the employer.

Strike
The organized withholding of labor by workers—the traditional weapon by which workers attempt to pressure employers.

Employers are free to replace employees who go on strike. If the strike is an economic strike, replacement may be permanent. Employers are also free to lock out the employees—that is, to intentionally withhold work from them—to force the union to make concessions. An employer may resort to a lockout only after bargaining in good faith to an impasse. However, the bargaining dispute must be over a mandatory bargaining subject. Limitations on the right of an employer to lock out were discussed in Chapter 14 in the cases of *NLRB v. Brown* and *American Shipbuilding v. NLRB*.

Strikes may be economic strikes or unfair labor practice strikes. (The rights of the striking workers to reinstatement and their protection under the National Labor Relations Act [NLRA] were discussed in Chapter 14.) Strikes in violation of contractual no-strike clauses may give rise to union liability for damages and to judicial "back-to-work" orders. The enforcement of no-strike clauses is discussed in Chapter 17. The focus in this chapter is on economic strikes and picketing. When the word "strike" is used, it refers to an economic strike unless otherwise specified.

Strikes in the Health-Care Industry

Section 8(g) of the NLRA provides that any union must give written notice of any strike, picketing or any other concerted refusal to work against any health-care institution at least ten days prior to the beginning of the strike or picketing. The notice must be given to the employer and to the Federal Mediation and Conciliation Service and must indicate the date and time the strike or picketing will commence. The purpose of this notice requirement is to allow the health-care institution to make arrangements for patient care that could be affected by the strike or picketing. The notice may be extended by the written agreement of both the union and the health-care employer. A union that unilaterally delays the start of a strike beyond the time specified in the written notice violates Section 8(g). Employees who engage in a strike in violation of the notice requirements of Section 8(g) lose their status as employees under the NLRA, and may be discharged for such conduct, as in *Minnesota Licensed Practical Nurses Assn.*[1] However, in *Civil Service Employees Association, Local 1000 v. National Labor Relations Board*,[2] employees who participated in peaceful picketing at a health-care institution without giving the appropriate notice, did not lose status as employees under the NLRA because they were not engaged in a strike.

The Legal Protection of Strikes

There is no constitutional right to strike. In fact, courts have traditionally held strikes to be criminal conspiracies (see Chapter 12). Constitutional restrictions, however, apply only to government activity; private sector strikes generally raise no constitutional issues. Strikes by private sector employees are regulated by the NLRA and are protected activity under Section 7 of the act. For public sector employees, there may be no right to strike (see Chapter 19).

[1]406 F.3d 1020 (8th Cir. 2005).

[2]569 F.3d 88 (2d Cir. 2009).

Although there is no recognized constitutional right to strike, there is a constitutional right to picket. The courts have held that picketing involves the expression and communication of opinions and ideas and is therefore protected under the First Amendment's freedom of speech. In *Thornhill v. Alabama*,[3] the Supreme Court held a state statute that prohibited all picketing, including even peaceful picketing, to be unconstitutional. Courts did, however, recognize that picketing involves conduct apart from speech so that there may be some reason for limitations upon the conduct of picketing. In *Teamsters Local 695 v. Vogt*,[4] the Supreme Court held that picketing, because it involves speech plus patrolling, may be regulated by the government more readily than pure speech activity.

The Norris–La Guardia Act

As you recall from Chapter 12, the Norris–La Guardia Act, passed in 1932, severely restricted the ability of federal courts to issue injunctions in labor disputes. The act did not "protect" strikes; it simply restricted the ability of federal courts to issue injunctions. The act defines "labor dispute" very broadly to cover disputes even when the parties are not in an employer–employee relationship. Furthermore, the dispute need not be the result of economic concerns, as illustrated by the following case.

case 16.1 »

JACKSONVILLE BULK TERMINALS V. ILA

457 U.S. 702 (1982)

Facts: On January 4, 1980, President Carter announced a trade embargo against the Soviet Union in response to the USSR's invasion of Afghanistan. In response, the International Longshoremen's Association (ILA) announced that its members would not handle any cargo bound to, or coming from, the Soviet Union or carried on Russian ships. As a result, the ILA affiliated union refused to load cargo bound for the Soviet Union aboard three ships at the shipping terminal operated by Jacksonville Bulk Terminals, Inc. (JBT) at the Port of Jacksonville, Florida. The employer consequently filed suit under Section 301(a) of the NLRA. The employer alleged that the union's work stoppage violated the collective bargaining agreement between the union and JBT, and requested that the court issue an injunction against the work stoppage. The trial court issued a preliminary injunction against the work stoppage, reasoning that the anti-injunction provisions of the Norris–LaGuardia Act did not apply because the work stoppage was politically motivated. On appeal, the U.S. Court of Appeal for the Fifth Circuit reversed the trial court. The employer then appealed to the U.S. Supreme Court.

Issue: Does the anti-injunction provision of the Norris–LaGuardia Act prevent a court from issuing an injunction against a works stoppage that is politically motivated?

Decision: Section 4 of the Norris–La Guardia Act provides in part:

> No court of the United States shall have jurisdiction to issue any restraining order or temporary or permanent injunction in any case involving or growing out of any labor dispute to prohibit any person or persons participating or interested in such dispute ... from doing, whether singly or in concert, any of the following acts: a) Ceasing or refusing to perform any work or to remain in any relation of employment....

[3] 310 U.S. 88 (1940).

[4] 354 U.S. 284 (1957).

Congress adopted this broad prohibition to remedy the growing tendency of federal courts to enjoin strikes by narrowly construing the Clayton Act's labor exemption from the Sherman Act's prohibition against conspiracies to restrain trade. The Supreme Court has consistently given the anti-injunction provisions of the Norris–La Guardia Act a broad interpretation, recognizing exceptions only in limited situations where necessary to accommodate the Act to specific federal legislation or paramount congressional policy.

The employer here argued that the Norris–La Guardia Act does not apply in this case because of the union's political motivation underlying the work stoppage means that this controversy is not a "labor dispute" as defined by the Norris–La Guardia Act. Section 13(c) of the Act broadly defines the term labor dispute to include "any controversy concerning terms or conditions of employment." The employer's argument has no basis in the plain language of the Norris–La Guardia Act.

The critical element in determining whether the provisions of the Norris–La Guardia Act apply is whether "the employer–employee relationship is the matrix of the controversy." In this case, the employer and the union representing its employees are the disputants, and their dispute concerns the interpretation of the labor contract that defines their relationship. Therefore, the employer–employee relationship is "the matrix" of this controversy. The Norris–La Guardia Act does not exempt labor disputes that spring from political protests and therefore the plain language of the Norris–La Guardia Act prevents the federal courts from enjoining the union's work stoppage in this case. The Supreme Court affirmed the court of appeals decision vacating the injunction issued by the trial court.

«

The Norris–La Guardia Act applied only to federal courts, but a number of states passed similar legislation restricting the issuance of labor injunctions by their courts.

Some exceptions to the Norris–La Guardia restrictions have been recognized. Sections 10(j) and 10(l) of the NLRA authorize the National Labor Relations Board (NLRB) to seek injunctions against unfair labor practices. Section 10(h) of the NLRA provides that Norris–La Guardia does not apply to actions brought under Sections 10(j) and (l) or to actions to enforce NLRB orders in the courts. The Supreme Court upheld this exemption in the case of *Bakery Sales Drivers, Local 33 v. Wagshal.*[5] The ability to initiate or maintain an action for an injunction under Sections 10(j) or (l) is restricted to the NLRB, according to *Solien v. Misc. Drivers & Helpers Union, Local 610.*[6] Another exception to the Norris–La Guardia restrictions has been recognized when a union strikes over an issue that is subject to arbitration. That exception is discussed in Chapter 17.

The National Labor Relations Act

The National Labor Relations Act, as mentioned earlier, makes strikes protected activity. The NLRA also contains several provisions that deal with picketing. Section 8(b)(4) outlaws secondary boycotts, and Section 8(b)(7) prohibits recognitional picketing in some situations. In *NLRB v. Drivers, Chauffeurs, Helpers Local 639,*[7] the Supreme Court held that the NLRB may not regulate peaceful picketing that does not run afoul of Section 8(b)(4) or Section 8(b)(7). Section 8(b)(1)(A) may be used to prohibit union violence on the picket line, but it does not extend to peaceful picketing. As a result, NLRB regulation of picketing under the NLRA is limited to specific situations such as recognition picketing or secondary picketing.

[5]333 U.S. 437 (1948).

[6]440 F.2d 124 (8th Cir. 1971), *cert. denied*, 403 U.S. 905 (1971), *rehearing denied*, 405 U.S. 996 (1972).

[7]362 U.S. 274 (1960).

State Regulation of Picketing

Although the NLRB role in regulating picketing is limited, the states enjoy a major role in the legal regulation of picketing. *Thornhill v. Alabama*, mentioned earlier, prohibited the states from banning all picketing, including peaceful picketing. In *Teamsters Local 695 v. Vogt*, also mentioned earlier, the Supreme Court held that the states may regulate picketing when it conflicts with valid state interests. The state interest in protecting the safety of its citizens and enforcing the criminal law justifies state regulation of violent picketing. State courts may issue injunctions against acts of violence by strikers, but an outright ban on all picketing because of violence can be justified only when "the fear generated by past violence would survive even though future picketing might be wholly peaceful" according to the Supreme Court in *Milk Wagon Drivers, Local 753 v. Meadowmoor Dairies, Inc.*[8]

State courts may also issue injunctions against *mass picketing*—picketing in which pickets march so closely together that they block access to the plant—even though it is peaceful, as in *Westinghouse Electric Co. v. U.E., Local 410.*[9] Picketing intended to force an employer to join a conspiracy in violation of state antitrust laws may be enjoined by a state court, according to *Giboney v. Empire Storage & Ice Co.*[10] According to *Linn v. United Plant Guard Workers Local 114,*[11] state courts may also enjoin the use of language by pickets that constitutes fraud, misrepresentation, libel, or inciting a breach of the peace.

All of these cases involved picketing activity on public property. Can trespass laws be used to prohibit peaceful picketing on private property? That is the question addressed by the following case.

case 16.2 » HUDGENS V. NLRB

424 U.S. 507 (1976)

Stewart, J.

The petitioner, Scott Hudgens, is the owner of the North DeKalb Shopping Center, located in suburban Atlanta, Ga. The center consists of a single large building with an enclosed mall. Surrounding the building is a parking area which can accommodate 2,640 automobiles. The shopping center houses 60 retail stores leased to various business. One of the lessees is the Butler Shoe Co. Most of the stores, including Butler's, can be entered only from the interior mall.

In January 1971, warehouse employees of the Butler Shoe Co. went on strike to protest the company's failure to agree to demands made by their union in contract negotiations. The strikers decided to picket not only Butler's warehouse but its nine retail stores in the Atlanta area as well, including the store in the North DeKalb Shopping Center. On January 22, 1971, four of the striking warehouse employees entered the center's enclosed mall carrying placards which read: "Butler Shoe Warehouse on Strike, AFL-CIO, Local 315." The general manager of the shopping center informed the employees that they could not picket within the mall or on the parking lot and threatened them with arrest if they did not leave. The employees departed but returned

[8]312 U.S. 287 (1941).

[9]139 N.J. Eq. 97 (1946).

[10]336 U.S. 490 (1949).

[11]383 U.S. 53 (1966).

a short time later and began picketing in an area of the mall immediately adjacent to the entrances of the Butler store. After the picketing had continued for approximately 30 minutes, the shopping center manager again informed the pickets that if they did not leave they would be arrested for trespassing. The pickets departed.

The union subsequently filed with the Board an unfair labor practice charge against Hudgens, alleging interference with rights protected by Section 7 of the Act. Relying on this Court's decision in *Food Employees v. Logan Valley Plaza*, the Board entered a cease-and-desist order against Hudgens, reasoning that because the warehouse employees enjoyed a First Amendment right to picket on the shopping center property, the owner's threat of arrest violated Section 8(a)(1) of the Act. Hudgens filed a petition for review in the Court of Appeals for the Fifth Circuit. Soon thereafter this Court decided *Lloyd Corp. v. Tanner, and Central Hardware Co. v. NLRB*, and the Court of Appeals remanded the case to the Board for reconsideration in light of those two decisions.

The Board, in turn, remanded to an Administrative Law Judge, who made findings of fact, recommendations, and conclusions to the effect that Hudgens had committed an unfair labor practice by excluding the pickets. This result was ostensibly reached under the statutory criteria set forth in *NLRB v. Babcock & Wilcox Co.*, a case which held that union organizers who seek to solicit for union membership may intrude on an employer's private property if no alternative means exist for communicating with the employees. But the Administrative Law Judge's opinion also relied on the Court's constitutional decision in *Logan Valley* for a "realistic view of the facts." The Board agreed with the findings and recommendations of the Administrative Law Judge, but departed somewhat from his reasoning. It concluded that the pickets were within the scope of Hudgens' invitation to members of the public to do business at the shopping center, and that it was, therefore, immaterial whether or not there existed an alternative means of communicating with the customers and employees of the Butler store.

Hudgens again petitioned for review in the Court of Appeals for the Fifth Circuit, and there the Board changed its tack and urged that the case was controlled not by Babcock & Wilcox, but by *Republic Aviation Corp. v. NLRB*, a case which held that an employer commits an unfair labor practice if he enforces a no-solicitation rule against employees on his premises who are also union organizers, unless he can prove that the rule is necessitated by special circumstances. The Court of Appeals enforced the Board's cease-and-desist order but on the basis of yet another theory. While acknowledging that the source of the pickets' rights was Section 7 of the Act, the Court of Appeals held that the competing constitutional and property right considerations discussed in *Lloyd Corp. v. Tanner*, "burde[n] the General Counsel with the duty to prove that other locations less intrusive upon Hudgens' property rights than picketing inside the mall were either unavailable or ineffective," and that the Board's General Counsel had met that burden in this case.

In this Court the petitioner Hudgens continues to urge that *Babcock & Wilcox Co.* is the controlling precedent, and that under the criteria of that case the judgment of the Court of Appeals should be reversed. The respondent union agrees that a statutory standard governs, but insists that, since the Section 7 activity here was not organizational as in *Babcock* but picketing in support of a lawful economic strike, an appropriate accommodation of the competing interests must lead to an affirmance of the Court of Appeals' judgment. The respondent Board now contends that the conflict between employee picketing rights and employer property rights in a case like this must be measured in accord with the commands of the First Amendment, pursuant to the Board's asserted understanding of *Lloyd Corp. v. Tanner*, and that the judgment of the Court of Appeals should be affirmed on the basis of that standard.

As the above recital discloses, the history of this litigation has been a history of shifting positions on the part of the litigants, the Board, and the Court of Appeals. It has been a history, in short, of considerable confusion, engendered at least in part by decisions of this Court that intervened during the course of the litigation. In the present posture of the case the most basic question is whether the respective rights and liabilities of the parties are to be decided under the criteria of the National Labor Relations Act alone, under a First Amendment standard, or under some combination of the two. It is to that question, accordingly, that we now turn.

It is, of course, a commonplace that the constitutional guarantee of free speech is a guarantee only against abridgment by government, federal or state.... [T]he rights and liabilities of the parties in this case are dependent exclusively upon the National Labor Relations Act. Under the Act the task of the Board, subject to review by the courts, is to resolve conflicts between Section 7 rights and private property rights, "and to seek a proper accommodation between the two." What is "a proper accommodation" in any situation may largely depend upon the content and the context of the Section 7 rights being asserted. The task of the Board and the reviewing courts under the Act, therefore, stands in conspicuous contrast to the duty of a court in applying the standards of the First Amendment, which requires "above all else" that expression must not be restricted by government "because of its message, its ideas, its subject matter, or its content."

In the *Central Hardware* case, and earlier in the case of *NLRB v. Babcock & Wilcox Co.*, the Court considered the nature of the Board's task in this area under the Act. Accommodation between employees' Section 7 rights and employers' property rights, the Court said in Babcock & Wilcox, "must be obtained with as little destruction of one as is consistent with the maintenance of the other."

Both *Central Hardware and Babcock & Wilcox* involved organizational activity carried on by nonemployees on the employers' property. The context of the Section 7 activity in the present case was different in several respects which may or may not be relevant in striking the proper balance. First, it involved lawful economic strike activity rather than organizational activity. Second, the Section 7 activity here was carried on by Butler's employees (albeit not employees of its shopping center store), not by outsiders. Third, the property interests impinged upon in this case were not those of the employer against whom the Section 7 activity was directed, but of another.

The *Babcock & Wilcox* opinion established the basic objective under the Act: accommodation of Section 7 rights and private property rights "with as little destruction of one as is consistent with the maintenance of the other." The locus of that accommodation, however, may fall at differing points along the spectrum depending on the nature and strength of the respective Section 7 rights and private property rights asserted in any given context. In each generic situation, the primary responsibility for making this accommodation must rest with the Board in the first instance....

For the reasons stated in this opinion, the judgment is vacated and the case is remanded to the Court of Appeals with directions to remand to the National Labor Relations Board, so that the case may be there considered under the statutory criteria of the National Labor Relations Act alone.

It is so ordered.

Case Questions

1. With whom does the union have the dispute? Where is the union picketing? Who seeks to prevent the union from picketing there? What is the purpose of the union's picketing there?
2. According to the *Babcock & Wilcox* decision (see Chapter 14), what factors should the court consider in determining whether a union can picket on private property?
3. Are the picketers employees of Butler Shoe Co.? How does the picketing affect the employer's property rights? Explain.

Concept *Summary* » 16.1

Regulation of Picketing

- The Norris–LaGuardia Act prohibits the federal courts from issuing injunctions in labor disputes
- The National Labor Relations Act allows the NLRB to seek injunctions in federal courts in certain situations:
  - The NLRB *must* seek an injunction when a complaint alleges violations of:
    - Section 8(b)(4)
    - Section 8(b)(7)
    - Section 8(e)
  - Section 10(j) provides that the NLRB *may* seek an injunction in other unfair labor practice cases
- State courts *may* issue injunctions against picketing in certain situations:
  - Violent picketing
  - Mass picketing
  - Use of picket signs involving language that constitutes fraud, misrepresentation, libel, or inciting a breach of the peace

Picketing Under the NLRA

As has been noted, Sections 8(b)(4) and 8(b)(7) of the NLRA prohibit certain kinds of picketing. Peaceful picketing is protected activity under the NLRA. However, violent picketing and mass picketing, as well as threatening conduct by the picketers, are not protected under Section 7. Employees who engage in such conduct may be disciplined or discharged by the employer and may also be subject to injunctions, criminal charges, and civil tort suits. Section 8(b)(7) regulates picketing by unions for organizational or recognitional purposes. Section 8(b)(4) deals with secondary boycotts—certain union pressure tactics aimed at employers that are not involved in a labor dispute with the union.

Section 8(b)(7): Recognitional and Organizational Picketing

Section 8(b)(7) was added to the NLRA by the 1959 Landrum-Griffin Act. It prohibits recognitional picketing by an uncertified union in certain situations. Section 8(b)(7) contains the following provisions:

> [It is an unfair practice for a labor organization] (7) to picket or cause to be picketed, or threaten to picket or cause to be picketed, any employer where an object thereof is forcing or requiring an employer to recognize or bargain with a labor organization as the representative of his employees, or forcing or requiring the employees of an employer to accept or select such labor organization as their collective-bargaining representative, unless such labor organization is currently certified as the representative of such employees:
>
> (A) where the employer has lawfully recognized in accordance with this Act any other labor organization and a question concerning representation may not appropriately be raised under Section 9(c) of this Act,
>
> (B) where within the preceding twelve months a valid election under Section 9(c) of this Act has been conducted, or
>
> (C) where such picketing has been conducted without a petition under Section 9(c) being filed within a reasonable period of time not to exceed thirty days from the commencement of such picketing: *Provided*, That when such a petition has been filed the Board shall forthwith, without regard to the provisions of Section 9(c)(1) or the absence of a showing of a substantial interest on the part of the labor organization, direct an election in such unit as the Board finds to be appropriate and shall certify the results thereof: *Provided further*, That nothing in this subparagraph (C) shall be construed to prohibit any picketing or other publicity for the purpose of truthfully advising the public (including consumers) that an employer does not employ members of, or have a contract with, a labor organization, unless an effect of such picketing is to induce any individual employed by any other person in the course of his employment, not to pick up, deliver or transport any goods or not to perform any services.
>
> Nothing in this paragraph (7) shall be construed to permit any act which would otherwise be an unfair labor practice under this Section 8(b).

The interpretation of Section 8(b)(7) and its application to recognitional picketing are the subjects of the following case.

case 16.3 » **SMITLEY v. NLRB**

327 F.2d 351 (U.S. Court of Appeals, 9th Cir. 1964)

[After the NLRB dismissed a complaint that the union had violated Section 8(b)(7)(C), the company sought judicial review of the Board's decision.]

Duniway, J.

The findings of the Board as to the facts are not attacked. It found, in substance, that the unions picketed the cafeteria for more than thirty days before filing a representation petition under Section 9(c) of the act, that an object of the picketing was to secure recognition, that the purpose of the picketing was truthfully to advise the public that petitioners employed nonunion employees or had no contract with the unions, and that the picketing did not have the effect of inducing any stoppage of deliveries or services to the cafeteria by employees of any other employer.... We conclude that the views of the Board, as stated after its second consideration of the matter, are correct, and that the statute has not been violated....

It will be noted that Subdivision (7) of Subsection (b), Section 8, starts with the general prohibition of picketing "where an object thereof is forcing or requiring an employer to recognize or bargain with a labor organization" (this is often called recognitional picketing) "... or forcing or requiring the employees of an employer to accept or select such labor organization...." (this is often called organizational picketing), "... unless such labor organization is currently certified as the representative of such employees: ..." This is followed by three subparagraphs, (A), (B), and (C). Each begins with the same word, "where." (A) deals with the situation "where" the employer has lawfully recognized another labor organization and a question of representation cannot be raised under Section 9(c). (B) refers to the situation "where," within the preceding 12 months, a valid election under Section 9(c) has been conducted. (C) with which we are concerned, refers to a situation "where" there has been no petition for an election under Section 9(c) filed within a reasonable period of time, not to exceed thirty days, from the commencement of the picketing. Thus, Section 8(b)(7) does not purport to prohibit all picketing having the named "object" of recognitional or organizational picketing. It limits the prohibition of such picketing to three specific situations.

There are no exceptions or provisos in subparagraphs (A) and (B), which describe two of those situations. There are, however, two provisos in subparagraph (C). The first sets up a special procedure for an expedited election under Section 9(c). The second is one with which we are concerned. It is an exception to the prohibition of "such picketing," i.e., recognitional or organizational picketing, being a proviso to a prohibition of such picketing "where" certain conditions exist....

... We think that, in substance, the effect of the second proviso to subparagraph (C) is to allow recognitional or organizational picketing to continue if it meets two important restrictions: (1) it must be addressed to the public and be truthful and (2) it must not induce other unions to stop deliveries or services. The picketing here met those criteria....

[The court affirmed the Board's dismissal of the complaint.]

Case Questions

1. Why was the union picketing the cafeteria? How long had it been picketing?
2. What kind of picketing is allowed under the proviso to Section 8(b)(7)(C)? What two conditions must be met for picketing to fall under the proviso's protection?
3. Does the picketing in this case fall under the proviso? Explain.

If a union pickets in violation of Section 8(b)(7)(C), the employer may request that the NLRB hold an expedited election. The NLRB will determine the appropriate bargaining unit and hold an election. No showing of interest on the part of the union is necessary. The NLRB will certify the results of the election; if the union is certified, the employer must bargain with it. If the union loses, continued picketing will violate Section 8(b)(7)(B). Why? Section 10(1) requires the board to seek an injunction against the picketing when it issues a complaint for an alleged Section 8(b)(7) violation. In *International Transp. Serv. v. NLRB*,[12] a union picketing to force the employer to recognize a one-person bargaining unit was held to violate Section 8(b)(7)(C) because the NRLB will not accept petitions for certification of one-person units, so the union could not file a petition for an election within a reasonable period of time.

As *Smitley* emphasizes, not all recognitional picketing violates Section 8(b)(7). The proviso in Section 8(b)(7)(C) allows recognitional picketing directed at the public to inform

[12] 449 F.3d 160 (D.C. Cir. 2006).

them that the picketed employer does not have a contract with the union. Such picketing for publicity may continue beyond thirty days, unless it causes other employees to refuse to work.

Picketing to protest substandard wages paid by an employer, as long as the union does not have a recognitional object, is not subject to Section 8(b)(7). Such picketing may continue indefinitely and is not unlawful, even if it has the effect of disrupting deliveries to the employer, according to *Houston Building & Construction Trades Council.*[13] Similarly, picketing to protest unfair practices by the employer, when there is no recognitional objective, is not prohibited, according to *UAW Local 259.*[14]

Concept *Summary* » 16.2

Recognitional Picketing

Section 8(b)(7) – Recognitional Picketing

- Picketing to force an employer to recognize a union as representative of its employees when:
  - another union has been legally recognized;
  - a representation election has been held within the last 12 months; or
  - the union pickets for a reasonable period of time without filing a petition for an election
- Exceptions: Publicity or picketing to advise the public that an employer does not have a contract with a labor organization

The WORKING Law

Striking Bakery Workers Continue Picketing

The workers at the Stella D'Oro cookie factory in the Bronx's Riverdale neighborhood went on strike August 13, 2008, and have manned a picket line outside the factory every day from 6 a.m. until 10 p.m. The workers are members of Local 50 of the Bakery, Confectionary, Tobacco Workers and Grain Millers International Union. The strike began when negotiations between the union and the employer, Brynwood Partners, broke down. The company wanted to reduce the workers' hourly wages by $1 each year for the next five years, to eliminate the twelve sick days and eight of the twelve holidays for the workers, to end payment of overtime for working Saturday, to require the workers to contribute 20 percent toward their health-care costs, and to replace the pension plan with a 401(k) plan.

[13] 136 NLRB 321 (1962).

[14] 133 NLRB 1468 (1961).

The company has hired replacement workers and continues to produce cookies, breadsticks, and biscotti.

The union has called for a boycott of all Stella D'Oro products to support the strikers. The union has filed unfair labor practice charges with the NLRB, alleging that the employer has not bargained in good faith by refusing to provide financial information to the union after claiming inability to pay and by unilaterally changing pay and benefits, and has refused to reinstate the strikers after the union made an unconditional offer to return to work. In a decision issued June 30, 2009, an Administrative Law Judge held that the company had violated Sections 8(a)(1), (3), and (5).

Source: Mike Jaccarino, "Strikers Won't Crumble," *Daily News*, June 14, 2009, p. 30; Stella D'Oro Biscuit Company, Inc., Case No.2-CA-38960, June 30, 2009.

Section 8(b)(4): Secondary Boycotts

Section 8(b)(4), which deals with secondary boycotts, is one of the most complex provisions of the NLRA. Section 8(b)(4) contains the following provisions:

> [It is an unfair practice for a labor organization] (4) (i) to engage in, or to induce or encourage any individual employed by any person engaged in commerce or in an industry affecting commerce to engage in, a strike or refusal in the course of his employment to use, manufacture, process, transport, or otherwise handle or work on any goods, articles, materials, or commodities or to perform any services; or (ii) to threaten, coerce, or restrain any person engaged in commerce or in an industry affecting commerce, where in either case an object thereof is:
>
> (A) forcing or requiring any employer or self-employed person to join any labor or employer organization to enter into any agreement which is prohibited by Section 8(e);
>
> (B) forcing or requiring any person to cease using, selling, handling, transporting, or otherwise dealing in the products of any other producer, processor, or manufacturer, or to cease doing business with any other person, or forcing or requiring any other employer to recognize or bargain with a labor organization as the representative of his employees unless such labor organization has been certified as the representative of such employees under the provisions of Section 9: Provided, That nothing contained in this clause (B) shall be construed to make unlawful, where not otherwise unlawful, any primary strike or primary picketing;
>
> (C) forcing or requiring any employer to recognize or bargain with a particular labor organization as the representative of his employees if another labor organization has been certified as the representative of such employees under the provisions of Section 9;
>
> (D) forcing or requiring any employer to assign particular work to employees in a particular labor organization or in a particular trade, craft, or class rather than to employees in another labor organization or in another trade, craft, or class, unless such employer is failing to conform to an order or certification of the Board determining the bargaining representative for employees performing such work:
>
> Provided, That nothing contained in this Subsection (b) shall be construed to make unlawful a refusal by any person to enter upon the premises of any employer (other than his own employer), if the employees of such employer are engaged in a strike ratified or approved by a representative of such employees whom such employer is required under this Act: Provided further, That for the purposes of this paragraph (4) only, nothing contained in such paragraph shall be construed to prohibit publicity, other than picketing, for the purpose of truthfully advising the public, including consumers and members of a labor organization, that a product or products are produced by an employer with whom the labor organization has a primary dispute and are distributed by another employer, as long as such publicity does not have an effect of inducing any individual employed by any person other than the primary employer in the course of his employment to refuse to pick up, deliver, or transport any goods, or not to perform any services, at the establishment of the employer engaged in such distributions....

When considering Section 8(b)(4), the courts and the Board generally consider the intention behind the provisions rather than its literal wording. The intention is to protect employers who are not involved in a dispute with a union from being pressured by that union. For example, if the union representing the workers of a toy manufacturing company goes on strike, it is free to picket the manufacturer (the primary employer). But if the union pickets the premises of a wholesaler who distributes the toys of the primary employer, such picketing may be secondary and prohibited by Section 8(b)(4)(B). Whether the picketing is prohibited depends on whether the union's picketing has the objective of trying to force the wholesaler to cease doing business with the manufacturer.

Most secondary picketing situations, however, are more complicated than this simple example. For instance, if the primary employer's location of business is mobile, such as a cement-mix delivery truck, is the union allowed to picket a construction site where the cement truck is making a delivery? What if the union has a dispute with a subcontractor on a construction site? Can it picket the entire construction site?

Primary picketing by a union is against an employer with which it has a dispute. Section 8(b)(4) does not prohibit such picketing, even though it is intended to persuade customers to cease doing business with the primary employer. It is important, therefore, to identify which employer is the primary employer—the employer with whom the union has the dispute. It is helpful to consider three questions when confronting a potential secondary picketing situation.

- With whom does the union have the dispute? This question identifies the primary employer.
- Is the union picketing at the primary employer's premises or at the site of a neutral employer?
- What is the object of the union's picketing? If the union is picketing at a secondary employer to force that employer to cease doing business with the primary employer, then it is illegal. But if the picketing is intended only to inform the public that the secondary employer handles the primary product, it is legal.

The objective of the picketing is the key to its legality: Does the picketing have an objective prohibited by Section 8(b)(4)?

Ambulatory Situs Picketing
Union picketing that follows the primary employer's mobile business.

Ambulatory *Situs* Picketing

When the primary employer's business location is mobile, picketing by a union following that mobile location is called ***ambulatory situs picketing***. The following NLRB decision sets out the conditions under which the union may engage in ambulatory *situs* picketing.

case 16.4 »

Sailors' Union of the Pacific and Moore Dry Dock Co.

92 NLRB 547 (NLRB, 1950)

Facts: Samsoc, a shipping company, contracted with Kaiser Gypsum to ship gypsum from Mexico in the ship *Phopho*. Samsoc replaced the *Phopho* crew with a foreign crew. The union demanded bargaining rights for the ship, but Samsoc refused. The union therefore requested permission from Moore to post pickets alongside the ship at the dry dock, but Moore refused. The union then posted pickets at the entrances to the dry dock. The signs carried by the picketers clearly indicated that the union's dispute was with the ship and not with the dry dock company. When the pickets were posted, the dry-dock workers refused to work on the ship but did perform other work. The dry-dock company filed an unfair practice charge with the NLRB, alleging that the union's picketing at the dry dock violated Section 8(b)(4)(B).

Issue: Does picketing directed against the primary employer, but taking place at a secondary location, violate Section 8(b)(4)(B)?

Decision: Picketing at the premises of the primary employer is traditionally recognized as primary action, even though it is intended to induce and encourage third persons to cease doing business with the picketed employer. The *Phopho* was the place of employment of the seamen, and it was the *situs* of the dispute between Samsoc and the union over working conditions aboard the vessel. If Samsoc, the ship's owner, had its own dock at which the *Phopho* had been docked while undergoing conversion by Moore Dry Dock employees, it is clear that picketing by the union at the dock site would be primary picketing, even though the union might have expected that the picketing would be more effective in persuading Moore employees not to work on the ship. In the case here, however, the *Phopho* was not tied up at its own dock, but at Moore's dock, and the union picketing was going on in front of the gates at Moore's premises. The location of the primary employer is not limited to a fixed location—here it is ambulatory. Thus, the *situs* may come to rest temporarily at the premises of another employer. How can the union picket to follow the *situs* while it is stationed at the premises of a secondary employer, if the only way to picket is in front of the secondary employer's premises? The situation requires balancing the right of a union to picket at the site of its dispute against the right of a secondary employer to be free from picketing in a controversy in which it is not directly involved.

The NLRB rules for ensuring that the picketing at the secondary location is legally permitted primary picketing are as follows:

- The union's picketing at the secondary location is limited to the times when the *situs* of the labor dispute is located at the secondary employer's premises;
- at the time of the picketing, the primary employer is engaged in its normal business at the *situs*;
- the picketing is limited to places reasonably close to the location of the *situs*; and
- the picketing clearly discloses that the union's dispute is with the primary employer and not the secondary employer.

All these conditions were met in the present case:

- During the entire period of the union's picketing at Moore's shipyard, the *Phopho* was tied up at a dock there;
- while the ship was at the dry dock, its crew was engaged in getting the ship ready for sea, which is part of the normal business of a ship, so the *Phopho* was engaged in its normal business;
- when Moore refused to allow the union to place pickets alongside the ship, the union posted its pickets at the shipyard entrance which was as close to the *Phopho* as they could get under the circumstances; and
- the union's picketing and other conduct clearly indicated that its dispute was solely with the primary employer, the owners of the *Phopho*.

The NLRB therefore dismissed the unfair labor practice complaint because it held that the union's picketing at Moore's premises was primary in nature, and did not violate Section 8(b)(4)(B).

«

Reserved Gate Picketing: Secondary Employees at the Primary Site

The *Moore Dry Dock* case deals with the legality of picketing at a secondary, or neutral, location. What about the legality of picketing that affects secondary employees at a primary site? The following case, also called the *General Electric* case, deals with that situation.

case 16.5 » Local 761, International Union of Electrical Radio & Machineworkers [General Electric] v. NLRB

366 U.S. 667 (1961)

Facts: General Electric Corporation operates a huge plant known as Appliance Park near Louisville, Kentucky, where it manufactures household appliances. The lot on which the plant is located is surrounded by a large drainage culvert, and access to the lot is limited to five roadways, known as gates, that cross the culvert. At any given time, there are employees of various contractors present at the GE plant. Those employees perform a variety of tasks:

- some do construction work on new buildings;
- some install and repair ventilating and heating equipment;
- some engage in retooling and rearranging operations necessary to the manufacture of new models; and
- others do general maintenance work.

In order to isolate the GE employees from the effects of any labor disputes involving the contractors, GE requires that the employees of the contractors use Gate 3-A; Gate 3-A is limited to use only by the contractors and GE employees are not permitted to use it. A large sign has been posted at the gate which states: *"Gate 3-A for Employees of Contractors Only—G.E. Employees Use Other Gates,"* and guards at the gate enforce the ban on GE employees using the gate.

The union representing the GE employees went on strike against GE, and initially placed pickets at all gates, including Gate 3-A. The signs carried by the pickets at all gates read: "Local 761 on Strike G.E. Unfair." Because of the picketing at Gate 3-A, almost all of the employees of independent contractors refused to enter the company premises. GE filed a complaint with the NLRB, alleging that union's picketing at Gate 3-A, used exclusively by the employees of the contractors, violated Section 8(b)(4)(ii)(B). The ALJ hearing the complaint recommended that the complaint be dismissed because the picketing at Gate 3-A was primary in nature.

The NLRB reversed the ALJ's decision and held that, because only the employees of the independent contractors used Gate 3-A, the union's object in picketing there was encourage those employees to engage in a concerted refusal to work "with an object of forcing the independent contractors to cease doing business with the Company," in violation of Section 8(b)(4)(ii)(B). On review, the Court of Appeals for the District of Columbia granted enforcement of the Board's order. The union then appealed to the U.S. Supreme Court.

Issue: Does the union picketing at the gate used only by the employees of the contractors violate Section 8(b)(4)(ii)(B)?

Decision: Section 8(b)(4)(B) of the National Labor Relations Act provided that it shall be an unfair labor practice for a labor organization:

> to engage in, or to induce or encourage the employees of any employer to engage in, a strike or a concerted refusal in the course of their employment to use, manufacture, process, transport, or otherwise handle or work on any goods, articles, materials, or commodities or to perform any services, where an object thereof is: [(B)] forcing or requiring … any employer or other person … to cease doing business with any other person.…

The Supreme Court noted that Section 8(b)(4)(B) could not be literally construed because to do so would ban most primary strikes. Congress included a proviso in Section 8(b)(4)(B) that states "*Provided*, That nothing in this clause (B) shall be construed to make unlawful, where not otherwise unlawful, any primary strike or picketing." The prohibition in Section 8(b)(4)(B) is directed toward secondary boycotts, which involve union pressure or sanctions directed not at the primary employer, who is a party to the dispute, but at some third party who has no involvement in the dispute. A union involved in a strike with the primary employer is free to use persuasion, including picketing, not only on the primary employer and his employees, but also on secondary employers who were customers or suppliers of the primary employer, and persons dealing with them, and even employees of secondary employers, as long as the union does not "induce or encourage the employees of any [other] employer to engage in a strike or a concerted refusal in the course of their employment." Section 8(b)(4)(B) does not speak generally of secondary boycotts, but rather condemns specific union conduct directed to specific objectives: inducing employees to engage in a strike or concerted refusal, of which an object must be to force or require their employer or another person to cease doing business with a third person.

While the distinction between legitimate "primary activity" and prohibited "secondary activity," is critical, it is not always a "bright line." The objectives of any picketing include a desire to influence others from withholding from the employer their services or trade; but primary picketing which induces secondary employees to respect a primary picket line is not the equivalent of picketing that has an object of inducing those employees to engage in concerted conduct against their employer in order to force him to refuse to deal with the struck employer. Under the *Moore Dry Dock* analysis, whether picketing at a gate used exclusively by employees of independent contractors who work at the primary employer's premises depends upon the type of work that is being performed by those employees who use the separate gate. The NLRB has only applied the separate gate analysis to situations where the independent workers were performing tasks unconnected to the normal operations of the struck employer, usually construction work on the buildings of the primary employer. The Court of Appeals of the Second Circuit upheld the NLRB application of Section 8(b)(4)(B) to a separate-gate situation. The court there held that

> there must be a separate gate marked and set apart from other gates; and the work done by the employees who use the separate gate must be unrelated to the normal operations of the primary employer, and the work must be of a kind that would not, if done when the plant were engaged in its regular operations, necessitate curtailing those operations.

The Supreme Court adopted the analysis of the Second Circuit, but in this case, neither the NLRB nor the court of appeals considered whether the employees who used Gate 3-A performed work necessary to the normal operations of General Electric. If that is so, then the gate would not be considered a separate gate, and the mixed use of the gate would allow the striking union to picket that gate as part of its actions directed against the primary employer. The Supreme Court therefore remanded the case to the NLRB to consider whether the work performed by the employees using Gate 3-A was related to the normal operations of GE, the primary employer.

«

Common *Situs* Picketing

Common Situs Picketing
Union picketing of an entire construction site.

The *General Electric* case made the nature of the work performed by the secondary employees at the primary site the key to whether the union may target secondary employees with picketing. In the construction industry, subcontractors and the general contractor are all working on the same project: erecting a building. Does this mean a union that has a dispute with the general contractor may picket the entire construction site (such picketing is known as ***common situs picketing***)? Should the NLRB apply the *General Electric* separate gate approach to picketing at construction sites, or does the legality of common *situs* picketing require a different approach? In *Building and Construction Trades Council of New Orleans, AFL-CIO and Markwell and Hartz, Inc.*,[15] the NLRB held that the *Moore Dry Dock* approach applied to common *situs* picketing. The following case illustrates the application of the *Moore Dry Dock* doctrine to a case of common *situs* picketing.

case 16.6 » International Union of Operating Engineers, Local 150, AFL-CIO v. NLRB

47 F.3d 218 (7th Cir. 1995)

Coffin, Circuit Judge

Local 150 of the International Union of Operating Engineers, AFL-CIO, seeks review of a decision by the National Labor Relations Board (Board) that the Union violated the secondary boycott provisions of the National Labor Relations Act (NLRA), Section 8(b)(4)(i), (ii)(B). The Board, which cross-petitions for enforcement of its order, found that the Union … picketed neutral gates at a multi-employer workplace in an effort to force the uninvolved employers to pressure the struck employer into settling the dispute more quickly.…

[15] 155 NLRB 319 (1965).

LTV Steel operates a large steel making plant in East Chicago, Indiana. Located on the grounds of the 1,150-acre facility are two companies that serve as subcontractors to LTV for the processing and disposal of slag, a by-product of the steelmaking process. The strike at issue in this case was aimed at one of those companies, Edward C. Levy Co. (Levy), whose collective bargaining agreement with Local 150 expired at the end of September 1991. Employees of the other slag processing firm, the Heckett Division of Harsco Corp. (Heckett), also are represented by Local 150....

The LTV plant has three entrances, designated as the East Bridge gate, the West Bridge gate, and the Burma Road gate. The East and West Bridge gates are the entrances normally used for access to the facility by employees and vendors. The ALJ found that the Burma Road entrance is used only in strike situations, as part of a so-called "reserved gate" system. Such a system is common where employers share a site but only one is experiencing labor strife. One entrance is "reserved" for the exclusive use of traffic related to the struck firm, and all picketing must be directed there. This system is designed to keep neutral parties out of the dispute, and avoids the need for them to cross picket lines.

The strike against Levy began on October 12, 1991, and ended on October 18. On the first day of the strike, LTV posted signs at each of the three gates. All of them identified the East and West Bridge gates as "neutral" gates reserved for the use of LTV Steel and all persons having business with the company, except for anyone connected with Levy. The signs directed Levy's traffic to the Burma Road gate, "which has been reserved solely and exclusively for Levy's employees, their suppliers, their delivery men, their subcontractors and all others having business with Levy." LTV expected the Union to picket only at this gate.

It is undisputed that no one from LTV gave written notice, or any other formal notification, of the gate arrangement to the Union, which established picket lines on public property near each of the three gates. The signs posted by LTV at the East and West Bridge gates could be seen by the picketers, but the words probably were not visible. Two company officials testified, however, that they told picketers at both the East and West Bridge locations on October 12 that a Levy gate had been set up at the Burma Road entrance and that the picketing should be confined to that location. An LTV security officer also testified that he informed four picketers near the East Bridge gate entrance that they would have to picket at Burma Road....

Burma Road ... is a distinctly non-road-like path that lies between the Amoco Oil gate and the EJ & E property. A large pole placed there by Amoco usually blocks the entrance to Burma Road from Front Street, but this was removed at LTV's request during the strike. The truck traffic generated by Levy made the location of the road "obvious" as the strike progressed.

Burma Road is central to this case because the Board maintains that, once the Levy reserved gate was established, the Union was legally permitted to picket only at that location. The Union claims that it ... received no notice of the reserved gate system....

Also of significance is the role of Heckett's employees during the strike. Heckett and Levy are direct competitors and, consequently, there apparently was some concern on the part of the Union about whether LTV would look to Heckett for help during a strike by Levy. Heckett's employees, meanwhile, were concerned about what the Union expected of them if a strike were called against Levy; their contract had a no-strike provision and they feared losing their jobs if they did not report to work.... Several Heckett employees testified that they were told either before the strike, or at its outset, that a neutral gate would be set up. On two occasions, however, Union officials at least implicitly urged members to respect picket signs established at their worksite, thereby disdaining the reserved gate system....

About 53 of the 69 Union members employed by Heckett worked during the strike. On October 14, during the strike, the Union filed internal charges against them for "refus[ing] to honor the picket line," in violation of the Union's by-laws.

... the Board found that various of the Union's actions constituted unfair labor practices under the NLRA: (1) picketing at neutral gates; (2) distributing pamphlets encouraging employees of neutral employers to stay out of work; (3) bringing internal charges against members employed by a neutral employer; and (4) applying to employees of a neutral employer the Union bylaw barring members from working on a job where a strike has been called.

The Union challenges only the finding that it violated the NLRA by picketing at the East and West Bridge gates....

The question before us, therefore, is whether substantial evidence in the record supports the Board's finding that the Union's picketing ran afoul of the NLRA's secondary boycott provisions. Union conduct violates section 8(b)(4) of the NLRA "if any object of that activity is to exert improper influence on secondary or neutral parties...." Whether the Union was motivated by a secondary objective is a question of fact, and is to be determined through examination of "the totality of [the] union's conduct in [the] given situation."

... Because not all union conduct that interferes with uninvolved employers is banned, the distinction between permissible "primary" activity and unlawful "secondary" activity "is often more nice than obvious." This is particularly true where the primary and secondary employers occupy a common work site. As an evidentiary tool for determining the dispositive point—the union's intent—the NLRB has adopted the so-called *Moore Dry Dock* standards. Under these standards, a union's picketing is presumed to be lawful primary activity if (1) it is "strictly limited to times when the situs of the dispute is located on the secondary employer's premises"; (2) "the primary employer is engaged in its normal business at the situs"; (3) it is "limited to places reasonably close to the location of the situs"; and (4) it "discloses clearly that the dispute is with the primary employer."

The third [*Moore Dry Dock*] standard is the one of significance in this case. When an employer implements a valid reserved gate system, and a union continues to picket a gate designated exclusively for neutrals, a violation of the third Dry Dock criterion is established because the picketing is not limited to the "location" of the dispute as permissibly confined. This gives rise to a presumption of illegitimate, secondary intent. The question remains, however, "a factual inquiry into the union's actual state of mind under the totality of the circumstances."

... Under these standards, we have little difficulty affirming the Board's determination that the Union violated section 8(b)(4) by intentionally enmeshing neutrals in its dispute with Levy. The ALJ's most crucial finding, that the Union knew about the reserved gate system, yet "consciously chose" to ignore it, is amply supported by the record. The evidence recounted by the ALJ showed that Union officials anticipated the establishment of a reserved gate system and had indicated to some Heckett employees that the Union itself was working toward setting up a safe gate. In addition, Union officials knew that Levy was using the Burma Road entrance, and it is undisputed that [the Burma Road] gate was used only during strikes as part of a reserved gate system. Thus, the fact that the Union sent pickets to Burma Road by itself reflects knowledge that a reserved gate system was in place. Moreover, while the wording on the signs posted at the East and West Bridge gates may not have been visible to picketers and supervising Union officials, they certainly could see that signs had been posted and so must have realized that the anticipated reserved gates had been designated. Indeed, LTV officials testified that they told Union members at both the East and West Bridge gates to move to the Levy gate at Burma Road....

The Union contends that, in the absence of formal notice of a reserved gate system, it may not be penalized for failing to confine its picketing to the Burma Road location. We acknowledge that it would be better if employers gave written or other formal notice of such a system, even when it appears that the Union must have gained actual knowledge through an informal method. In these circumstances, however, we cannot say that the ALJ improperly imposed responsibility on the Union based, among other factors, on its having received sufficient notice of the system.... Moreover, misuse of the reserved gate system was not the only evidence of the Union's intent to engage in secondary activity. As the Board found, the Union unlawfully distributed pamphlets to Heckett employees advising them that they had the right not to work "no matter how many gates the employer sets up." In addition, on the first day of the strike, a picketer who identified himself as picket captain, told LTV's labor relations manager that a Union official had directed that all three gates be picketed and that the Union's "intent was to impact not only Levy employees but Heckett employees, iron workers and other employees." This intent also was reflected in statements made by Union official Cisco at a November meeting, in which he suggested that the strike would have been shorter if the Heckett employees had not crossed the picket line. Finally, the fact that the Union brought charges against those employees for crossing the line lends further support to the finding of a secondary objective.

... In sum, we believe the ALJ permissibly found that the Union received adequate notice of a validly established reserved gate system, and "chose to ignore it." This conclusion, particularly when taken together with the Union's distribution of leaflets encouraging Heckett employees to honor the picket line, the disciplinary action against the 53 employees who did work, and the statements made by Union representatives, provides more than substantial evidence to support the Board's determination that Local 150's picketing activity was intended to implicate secondary parties and thus was unlawful under section 8(b)(4).

The Union's petition for review is therefore denied, and the Board's cross-application for enforcement of its order is granted.

Case Questions

1. Was the union ever formally notified by LTV about the reserved gate arrangement set up in response to the strike against Levy? Did the court determine that the union was aware of the reserved gate arrangement? Why?

2. What is the relevance of the third *Moore Dry Dock* standard—the requirement that the union picketing be limited to places reasonably close to the *situs* of the dispute (the operations of the struck employer, Levy)? Where was the *situs* of Levy's operations in this case?

3. What is the significance of the union's efforts to get Heckett employees to honor the picket line against Levy? What is the significance of the union's efforts to discipline the Heckett employees who crossed the picket line?

The NLRB had adopted a requirement that a union notifying an employer of its intention to engage in common *situs* picketing must affirmatively declare its intention to conform with the requirements of *Moore Dry Dock*, but that requirement was rejected by the U.S. Court of Appeals for the Ninth Circuit in United Ass'n of Journeymen, Local 32 v. NLRB,[16] and by the U.S. Court of Appeals for the D.C. Circuit in *Sheet Metal Workers' Int. Ass'n, Local 15 v. NLRB.*[17]

Ally Doctrine

Not all union picketing directed against employers other than the primary employer is prohibited. The secondary boycott prohibitions were intended to protect neutral employers from union pressure. If any employer is not neutral—because it is performing the work normally done by the workers of the primary employer, who are now on strike—may the union picket that other employer? That is the issue addressed in the following case.

case 16.7 » NLRB v. Business Machine & Office Appliance Mechanics Conference Board, IUE, Local 459 [Royal Typewriter Co.]

228 F.2d 553 (2d Cir. 1955), cert. denied, 351 U.S. 962 (1956)

Lumbard, J.

This case arose out of a labor dispute between the Royal Typewriter Company and the Business Machine and Office Appliance Mechanics Conference Board, Local 459, IUECIO, the certified bargaining agent of Royal's typewriter mechanics and other service personnel. The National Labor Relations Board now seeks enforcement of an order directing the Union to cease and desist from certain picketing and to post appropriate notices....

On about March 23, 1954, the Union, being unable to reach agreement with Royal on the terms of a contract, called the Royal service personnel out on strike. The service employees customarily repair typewriters either at Royal's branch offices or at its customers' premises. Royal has several arrangements under which it is obligated to render service to its customers. First, Royal's warranty on each new machine obligates it to provide free inspection and repair for one year. Second, for a fixed periodic fee Royal contracts to service machines not under warranty. Finally, Royal is committed to repairing typewriters rented from it or loaned by it to replace machines undergoing repair. Of course, in addition Royal provides repair service on call by non-contract users.

During the strike Royal differentiated between calls from customers to whom it owed a repair obligation and others.

[16]912 F.2d 1108, 1110 (9th Cir.1990).

[17]491 F.3d 429 (D.C. Cir. 2007).

Royal's office personnel were instructed to tell the latter to call some independent repair company listed in the telephone directory. Contract customers, however, were advised to select such an independent from the directory to have the repair made, and to send a receipted invoice to Royal for reimbursement for reasonable repairs within their agreement with Royal. Consequently many of Royal's contract customers had repair services performed by various independent repair companies. In most instances the customer sent Royal the unpaid repair bill and Royal paid the independent company directly. Among the independent companies paid directly by Royal for repairs made for such customers were Typewriter Maintenance and Sales Company and Tytell Typewriter Company....

During May, 1954, the Union picketed four independent typewriter repair companies who had been doing work covered by Royal's contracts pursuant to the arrangement described above. The Board found this picketing unlawful with respect to Typewriter Maintenance and Tytell. Typewriter Maintenance was picketed for about three days and Tytell for several hours on one day. In each instance the picketing, which was peaceful and orderly, took place before entrances used in common by employees, deliverymen and the general public. The signs read substantially as follows (with the appropriate repair company name inserted):

> NOTICE TO THE PUBLIC ONLY EMPLOYEES OF ROYAL TYPEWRITER COMPANY ON STRIKE TYTELL TYPEWRITER COMPANY EMPLOYEES ARE BEING USED AS STRIKEBREAKERS BUSINESS MACHINE & OFFICE APPLIANCE MECHANICS UNION, LOCAL 459, IUE-CIO

Both before and after this picketing, which took place in mid-May, Tytell and Typewriter Maintenance did work on Royal accounts and received payment directly from Royal. Royal's records show that Typewriter Maintenance's first voucher was passed for payment by Royal on April 20, 1954, and Tytell's first voucher was passed for payment on May 3, 1954. After these dates each independent serviced various of Royal's customers on numerous occasions and received payment directly from Royal....

On the above facts the Trial Examiner and the Board found that ... the repair company picketing violated Section 8 (b)(4) of the National Labor Relations Act.... We are of the opinion that the Board's finding with respect to the repair company picketing cannot be sustained. The independent repair companies were so allied with Royal that the Union's picketing of their premises was not prohibited by Section 8(b)(4).

We approve the "ally" doctrine which had its origin in a well reasoned opinion by Judge Rifkind in the *Ebasco case, Douds v. Architects, Engineers, Chemists & Technicians, Local 231*. Ebasco, a corporation engaged in the business of providing engineering services, had a close business relationship with Project, a firm providing similar services. Ebasco subcontracted some of its work to Project and when it did so Ebasco supervised the work of Project's employees and paid Project for the time spent by Project's employees on Ebasco's work plus a factor for overhead and profit. When Ebasco's employees went on strike, Ebasco transferred a greater percentage of its work to Project, including some jobs that had already been started by Ebasco's employees. When Project refused to heed the Union's requests to stop doing Ebasco's work, the Union picketed Project and induced some of Project's employees to cease work. On these facts Judge Rifkind found that Project was not "doing business" with Ebasco within the meaning of Section 8(b)(4) and that the Union had therefore not committed an unfair labor practice under that Section. He reached this result by looking to the legislative history of the Taft-Hartley Act and to the history of the secondary boycotts which it sought to outlaw. He determined that Project was not a person "wholly unconcerned in the disagreement between an employer and his employees" such as Section 8(b)(4) was designed to protect....

Here there was evidence of only one instance where Royal contacted an independent (Manhattan Typewriter Service, not named in the complaint) to see whether it could handle some of Royal's calls. Apart from that incident there is no evidence that Royal made any arrangement with an independent directly. It is obvious, however, that what the independents did would inevitably tend to break the strike. As Judge Rifkind pointed out in the *Ebasco* case: "The economic effect on Ebasco's employees was precisely that which would flow from Ebasco's hiring strikebreakers to work on its own premises...."

Moreover, there is evidence that the secondary strikes and boycotts sought to be outlawed by Section 8(b)(4) were only those which had been unlawful at common law. And although secondary boycotts were generally unlawful, it has been held that the common law does not proscribe union activity designed to prevent employers from doing the farmed-out work of a struck employer. Thus the picketing of the independent typewriter companies was not the kind of a secondary activity which Section 8(b)(4) of the Taft-Hartley Act was designed to outlaw. Where an employer is attempting to avoid the economic impact of a strike by securing the services of others to do his work, the striking union obviously has a great interest, and we think a proper interest in preventing those services from being rendered. This interest is more fundamental than the interest in bringing pressure on customers of the primary employer. Nor are those who render such services completely uninvolved in the primary strike. By doing the work of the primary employer they secure benefits themselves at the same time that they aid the primary employer. The ally employer may easily extricate himself from the dispute and insulate himself from picketing by refusing to do that work. A case may arise where the ally employer is unable to determine that the work he is doing is "farmed-out." We need not decide whether the picketing of such an employer would be lawful, for that is not the situation here. The existence of the strike, the receipt of checks from Royal, and the picketing itself certainly put the independents on notice that some of the work they were doing might be work farmed-out by Royal. Wherever they worked on new Royal machines they were probably aware that such machines were covered by a Royal warranty. But in any event, before working on a Royal machine they could have inquired of the customer whether it was covered by a Royal contract and refused to work on it if it was. There is no indication that they made any effort to avoid doing Royal's work. The Union was justified in picketing them in order to induce them to make such an effort. We therefore hold that an employer is not within the protection of Section 8(b)(4) when he knowingly does work which would otherwise be done by the striking employees of the primary employer and where this work is paid for by the primary employer pursuant to an arrangement devised and originated by him to enable him to meet his contractual obligations.

Enforcement denied.

Case Questions

1. Against whom was the union on strike? Why did the union picket the independent typewriter repair shops?
2. Was the union's picketing at the independent repair shops primary or secondary? Explain your answer.
3. What is the rationale for the "ally" exception to the secondary picketing prohibitions of Section 8(b)(4)? How does that rationale apply to the facts in this case? Explain.

Publicity: "Consumer" Picketing

The second proviso to Section 8(b)(4) allows the union to use "... publicity, other than picketing, for the purpose of truthfully advising the public" that the secondary employer is handling the product of the primary employer. Such publicity is legal unless it has the effect of inducing other employees to refuse to perform their services at the secondary employer's location. This proviso allows the union to distribute handbills addressed to the public, asking for the public to support the union in its strike by refusing to buy the primary product or by refraining from shopping at the secondary employer.

In the case of *NLRB v. Fruit and Vegetable Packers, Local 760 (Tree Fruits)*,[18] the Supreme Court held that the publicity proviso did not, by negative implication, prohibit peaceful picketing by a union at a supermarket that sold apples packed by the employer against whom the union was on strike. The union's picketing was directed at consumers and asked only that they refuse to buy the apples; it did not ask them to refrain from shopping at the market. The Supreme Court found that such picketing was not prohibited because it was directed at the primary product rather than the neutral supermarket.

In *Tree Fruits*, the primary product, the apples, was only one of many products sold by the supermarket. May the union engage in consumer picketing when the secondary employer sells only one product—the primary product? In *NLRB v. Retail Store Employees Union, Local 1001,*

[18] 377 U.S. 58 (1964).

Retail Clerks Int. Association (Safeco),[19] the union striking against Safeco Title Insurance Co. conducted consumer picketing of local title companies, asking consumers to cancel their Safeco policies. The local title companies sold title insurance, performed escrow services, and conducted title searches; over 90 percent of their gross income was derived from the sale of Safeco title insurance. The Supreme Court held that the consumer picketing was in violation of Section 8(b)(4) because, unlike that in *Tree Fruits*, it was "reasonably calculated to induce customers not to patronize the neutral parties at all.... Product picketing that reasonably can be expected to threaten neutral parties with ruin or substantial loss simply does not square with the language or the purpose of Section 8(b)(4)(ii)(B)." The Court also stated that if "secondary picketing were directed against a product representing a major portion of a neutral's business, but significantly less than that represented by a single dominant product.... The critical question would be whether, by encouraging customers to reject the struck product, the secondary appeal is reasonably likely to threaten the neutral party with ruin or substantial loss."

The effect of the *Safeco* decision is to restrict *consumer picketing* (also known as *product picketing*) to situations in which the primary product accounts for less than a substantial portion of the business of the neutral party at whose premises the picketing takes place. Other problems under consumer picketing have involved cases in which the primary product has become mixed with the product of the neutral or secondary employer. In such merged product cases, the public is unable to separate the primary product from the secondary product; hence, a call to the public to avoid the primary product becomes, in effect, a call to avoid the secondary employer's product altogether. For example, if a union representing striking bakery workers pickets a fast-food restaurant, urging customers not to eat the sandwich buns supplied by the struck bakery, the effect of the union's consumer picketing may be to urge consumers to boycott the restaurant totally, according to *Teamsters Local 327*.[20] In *Kroger Co. v. NLRB*,[21] the union representing striking paper workers picketed grocery stores, asking consumers to refrain from using paper bags to pack their groceries. The picketing was held to violate Section 8(b)(4) because the bags had lost their separate identity and had become "merged" with the products (groceries) of the neutral grocery stores.

ethical DILEMMA

CONSUMER AND PUBLICITY PICKETING

You are the human resources manager for FoodMart, a regional grocery retailer. The FoodMart employees are members of the Retail Clerks Union, and FoodMart and the union are engaged in negotiations to renew their collective agreement. The retail grocery business is extremely competitive, and a number of low-cost, low-overhead chains compete directly with FoodMart. The employees of the low-cost grocery chains are not unionized, and their wages are barely above the minimum wage. FoodMart employees'

[19] 447 U.S. 607 (1980).

[20] 170 NLRB 91 (1968), *enforced* 411 F.2d 147 (6th Cir. 1969).

[21] 647 F.2d 634 (6th Cir. 1980).

wages average around $9.25 per hour, and FoodMart also offers generous benefit packages, including medical insurance and pensions. As a result, FoodMart's labor costs are much higher than the low-cost chains, and FoodMart has seen its profit margins decline. FoodMart had considered proposing wage and benefit reductions to the union; the union had publicly vowed not to agree to any wage concessions.

To avoid a strike, the CEO suggests that you offer the union a guarantee not to reduce wages and benefits if the union agrees to begin a campaign of consumer and publicity picketing and handbilling in front of the low-cost grocery stores—to inform the public how the low-cost chains treat their employees. What arguments can you make in favor of such a proposal? What arguments can you make against it? Should you make such an offer to the union? Prepare a memo to the CEO outlining the positive and negative aspects of the proposal, and recommending a course of action, with appropriate supporting reasons.

The Publicity Proviso

The publicity proviso of Section 8(b)(4) purports to allow publicity, other than picketing, for the purposes of truthfully advising the public that the products of the employer against whom the union is striking are being distributed by another employer. How far does that proviso go in allowing consumer appeals by a union? This question is addressed by the following Supreme Court decision.

case 16.8 » Edward J. DeBartolo Corp. v. Florida Gulf Coast Building Trades Council

485 U.S. 568 (1988)

Facts: The Florida Gulf Coast Building Trades Council, a group of construction unions, engaged in handbilling at the entrances to a shopping mall in Tampa, Florida, to protest the presence of High Construction Co., a nonunion contractor constructing a department store in the mall. The handbilling was peaceful. The union's handbills asked mall customers not to shop at any of the stores in the mall "until the Mall's owner publicly promises that all construction at the Mall will be done using contractors who pay their employees fair wages and fringe benefits." The handbills made clear that the union was seeking only a consumer boycott against the other mall tenants, not a secondary strike by the employees of the mall tenants.

DeBartolo, the mall owner, tried to get the union to change the language of the handbills to state that the union's dispute did not involve DeBartolo or the mall lessees other than Wilson, and to get the union to limit its distribution to the immediate vicinity of construction site. DeBartolo then filed a complaint with the NLRB, charging the union with engaging in unfair labor practices under Section 8(b)(4) of the NLRA.

The NLRB's General Counsel issued a complaint—which the NLRB eventually dismissed—concluding that the handbilling was protected by the publicity proviso of Section 8(b)(4). The Court of Appeals for the Fourth Circuit affirmed the Board, but the Supreme Court reversed, holding that the handbilling did not fall within the proviso's limited scope of exempting "publicity intended to inform the public that the primary employer's product is 'distributed by' the secondary employer" because DeBartolo and the other tenants, as opposed to Wilson, did not distribute products of High. The Court remanded the case to the NLRB for a determination whether the handbilling was in violation of Section 8(b)(4), and, if so, whether it was protected by the First Amendment.

On remand, the NLRB held that the union's handbilling was in violation of Section 8 (b)(4)(ii)(B), reasoning that "handbilling and other activity urging a consumer boycott constituted coercion." Because it held that the handbilling was prohibited by Section 8(b)(4), the NLRB also held that it was not necessary to consider whether the handbilling was protected by the First Amendment. On review, the court of appeals held that the handbilling was protected by the First Amendment, and refused to enforce the NLRB order. DeBartolo again appealed to the U.S. Supreme Court.

Issue: Is peaceful handbilling a violation of Section 8(b)(4), or is the handbilling protected by the First Amendment?

Decision: The Supreme Court noted that the handbills here truthfully revealed the existence of a labor dispute and urged potential customers of the mall not to patronize the retailers doing business in the mall. The handbilling was peaceful, and no picketing or patrolling was involved; it was expressive activity arguing that substandard wages should be opposed by abstaining from shopping in a mall where such wages were paid. The court of appeals was correct that the NLRB's interpretation of Section 8(b)(4)(ii) raises concerns under the First Amendment.

The Court noted that the main issue here was whether the handbilling must be held to "threaten, coerce, or restrain any person" to cease doing business with another, within the meaning of Section 8(b)(4)(ii)(B). The Court stated that more than mere persuasion is necessary to prove a violation of 8(b)(4)(ii), which requires a showing of threats, coercion, or restraints. The Court held that the handbills involved in this case did not constitute "threats, coercion or restraints." There was no suggestion that the handbills had any coercive effect on customers of the mall. There was no violence, picketing, or patrolling and only an attempt to persuade customers not to shop in the mall. The NLRB here found that the handbilling "coerced" mall tenants, explaining that "[a]ppealing to the public not to patronize secondary employers is an attempt to inflict economic harm on the secondary employers by causing them to lose business … such appeals constitute 'economic retaliation' and are therefore a form of coercion." The Court noted, however, that its decision in *Tree Fruits* held that any kind of handbilling, picketing, or other appeals to a secondary employer to cease doing business with the employer involved in the labor dispute was not "coercion" within the meaning of Section 8 (b)(4)(ii)(B) just because it has some economic impact on the neutral. *Tree Fruits* involved a union picking a retailer, asking the public not to buy a product produced by the primary employer and sold by the retailer. The impact of this picketing was not coercion within the meaning of Section 8(b)(4) even though, if the appeal succeeded, the retailer would lose revenue. *Tree Fruits* held that Congress did not intend to prohibit all peaceful consumer picketing at secondary sites.

It is also clear that the language of Section 8(b)(4)(ii), standing alone, does not give any indication that handbilling, without picketing, "coerces" secondary employers. The loss of customers because they read a handbill urging them not to patronize a business, and not because they are intimidated by a line of picketers, is the result of mere persuasion, and the neutral who reacts is doing no more than what its customers honestly want it to do.

Section 8(b)(4) should not be read as prohibiting publicity that does not involve picketing, and that includes making appeals to customers of a retailer as they approach the store, to urge a complete boycott of the retailer because he handles products produced by nonunion shops. Interpreting Section 8(b)(4) as not reaching the handbilling involved in this case is necessary to avoid raising the question of the constitutionality of a prohibition on otherwise peaceful publicity. The Supreme Court affirmed the decision of the court of appeals.

Sheet Metal Workers Int. Assoc., Local 15 v. NLRB[22] held that union conduct including leafleting, staging a mock funeral procession, and displaying a huge inflatable rat to protest the use of nonunion labor at a construction site was protected by the First Amendment, as with the *DeBartolo* decision. A union distributing handbills and displaying a huge banner reading "labor dispute" on public property outside firms that were employing nonunion contractors was not picketing and did not violate Section 8(b)(4)(ii)(B), according to *Overstreet v. United Brotherhood of Carpenters and Joiners of America, Local Union No. 1506.*[23] The case of *Int. Longshoremen's Association v. NLRB*[24] involved requests by U.S. union officials to Japanese unions asking for support in a dispute with nonunion shipping firms. The Japanese unions responded by stating that they would refuse to unload any cargo that had been loaded by

[22]491 F.3d 429 (D.C. Cir. 2007).

[23]409 F.3d 1199 (9th Cir. 2005).

[24]56 F.3d 205 (D.C. Cir. 1995).

nonunion workers. The U.S. Court of Appeals for the D.C. Circuit held that the Japanese unions were not acting as agents of the U.S. unions, and the U.S. unions' requests for support did not violate Section 8(b)(4). But not all union handbilling or publicity activity is protected. In *Warshawsky & Co. v. NLRB*,[25] union handbilling directed at employees of neutral subcontractors and intended to induce them to walk off the job was held to be an effort to induce a secondary boycott in violation of Section 8(b)(4); and a union protesting the use of nonunion carpenters at a residential complex by using a sound system to broadcast a protest message at excessive volume levels was held to violate Section 8(b)(4)(ii)(B) in *Metropolitan Regional Council of Philadelphia (Society Hill Towers)*.[26]

Section 8(b)(4)(D): Jurisdictional Disputes

Section 8(b)(4)(D) prohibits a union from picketing an employer in order to force that employer to assign work to that union. If the picketing union is not entitled to that work by reason of a certification or NLRB order, such picketing violates Section 8(b)(4)(D). For example, the union representing plasterers and the union representing stonemasons on the construction site of an apartment complex both might demand the right to lay the ceramic tiles in hallways and bathrooms. If either union picketed to force such assignment of the work, it would be a violation of Section 8(b)(4)(D).

When a Section 8(b)(4)(D) complaint is filed with the Board, Section 10(k) requires that the Board give the parties involved ten days to settle the dispute. If the parties are unable to settle the jurisdictional dispute in ten days, the Board must then make an assignment of the work in dispute. Once the Board awards the work, the successful union may picket to force the employer to live up to the Board order. Section 10(l) requires that the Board seek an injunction against the picketing when a complaint alleging a violation of Section 8(b)(4)(D) is filed.

Concept *Summary* » 16.3

SECONDARY PICKETING

Section 8(b)(4) – Secondary Picketing

- Picketing to pressure a neutral party—one with whom the union does not have a dispute—with the object to:
  - Force an employer to join a labor organization
  - Force any person to cease doing business with another person
  - Force an employer to recognize a union when another union has been certified as bargaining representative
  - Force an employer to assign work to employees of one union rather than another
- Exceptions:
  - Individuals are allowed to refuse to cross a picket line
  - Publicity, other than picketing, to advise the public the products of the primary employer are being distributed by another employer

[25] 182 F.3d 948 (D.C. Cir. 1999).

[26] 335 NLRB 814 (2001), *enforced by* 50 Fed. Appx. 88 (3d Cir. 2002).

Section 8(e): Hot Cargo Clauses

Hot Cargo Clauses
Provisions in collective bargaining agreements that purport to permit employees to refuse to handle the product of any employer involved in a labor dispute.

Hot cargo clauses are provisions in collective bargaining agreements purporting to permit employees to refuse to handle the product of any employer involved in a labor dispute. Section 8(e), inserted into the NLRA as one of the 1959 Landrum-Griffin amendments, prohibits the negotiation and enforcement of such clauses:

> (e) It shall be an unfair labor practice for any labor organization and any employer to enter into any contract or agreement, express or implied, whereby such employer ceases or refrains or agrees to cease or refrain from handling, using, selling, transporting or otherwise dealing in any of the products of any other employer, or to cease doing business with any other person, and any contract or agreement entered into heretofore or hereafter containing such an agreement shall be to such extent unenforcble and void: *Provided*, That nothing in this subsection (e) shall apply to an agreement between a labor organization and an employer in the construction industry relating to the contracting or subcontracting of work to be done at the site of the construction, alteration, painting, or repair of a building, structure, or other work: *Provided further*, That for the purposes of this subsection (e) and section 8(b)(4)(B) the terms "any employer," "any person engaged in commerce or an industry affecting commerce,""any person" when used in relation to the terms "any other producer, processor, or manufacturer," "any employer," or "any other person" shall not include persons in the relation of a jobber, manufacturer, contractor, or subcontractor working on the goods or premises of the jobber or manufacturer or performing parts of an integrated process of production in the apparel and clothing industry: *Provided further*, That nothing in this Act shall prohibit the enforcement of any agreement which is within the foregoing exception.

It can be seen that the provisos to Section 8(e) exempt the garment industry and the construction industry from its provisions. The garment industry is completely exempted; the construction industry is exempted to the extent of allowing unions to negotiate hot cargo clauses that relate to work normally done at the work site.

The objective of Section 8(e) is to prohibit language in a collective agreement that purports to authorize conduct that is prohibited by Section 8(b)(4), such as refusing to handle goods produced by a nonunion employer or by an employer who is being struck by a different union. The courts have allowed contract language that authorizes conduct that is primary, such as refusing to cross a primary picket line and refusing to perform the work normally done by the employees of an employer who is the target of a primary strike. One issue that has been problematic under Section 8(e) is whether work preservation clauses outside the construction industry are prohibited by Section 8(e). The courts have consistently held that when unions seek to retain the right to perform work that they have traditionally done or to acquire work that is similar to work they have traditionally done, and such activity to enforce the clauses is directed against the employer with the right of control over the working conditions at issue, such activity is primary. In *NLRB v. International Longshoremen's Association.*[27] the Supreme Court considered a union rule penalizing shippers who used prepacked containers to ship cargo that had traditionally been loaded and unloaded by union members at the docks. The Court held that, even though the use of containers had eliminated most of the traditional loading work done by longshoremen, the language that sought to preserve such "unnecessary" work was a legitimate work preservation clause under Sections 8(e) and 8(b)(4). The union's objective through the language was the preservation of work similar in nature to that traditionally performed by the longshoremen, and the employers had the power to control the assignment of such work. A neutrality agreement, by which an employer agrees that

[27] 473 U.S. 61 (1985).

all business entities it controls will allow unions access for organizing and to recognize the union if a majority of employees sign authorization cards, was not in violation of Section 8(e) because it did not require the employer to cease doing business with any company refusing to accept the neutrality agreement, according to *Heartland Ind. Partners LLC.*[28]

Remedies for Secondary Activity

As mentioned, the NLRB is required to seek an immediate injunction against the picketing when a complaint alleging a violation of Section 8(b)(4), Section 8(b)(7), or Section 8(e) is filed. The injunction is intended to prevent the activity in question until its legality can be determined. If the Board holds the conduct illegal, it will issue a cease-and-desist order against it.

Section 303 of the NLRA also provides that any person suffering harm to business or property by reason of activity that violates Section 8(b)(4) may sue in federal court to recover damages for the injuries sustained and legal fees. Either the primary or secondary employer may sue under Section 303, and they may file a suit regardless of whether an unfair labor practice charge has been filed with the NLRB.

National Emergencies

Sections 206 to 210 of the NLRA, which were added by the Taft-Hartley Act of 1947, provide for injunctions forestalling strikes when they threaten the national health or safety. When a strike or threatened strike poses such a threat, the president is authorized to appoint a board of inquiry to report on the issues involved in the dispute. The U.S. attorney general can secure an injunction to forestall the strike for up to eighty days, while the Federal Mediation and Conciliation Service (FMCS) attempts to resolve the dispute. The parties are not bound by the FMCS recommendations, and if no agreement is reached, the NLRB is required to poll the employees to determine if they will accept the employer's last offer. If the last offer is rejected, the injunction is dissolved, and the president may refer the issue to Congress for "appropriate action."

The emergency provisions of the Taft-Hartley Act have been invoked only rarely in recent years. President George W. Bush's action to stop a lockout of longshoremen in West Coast ports in October 2002 was the first use of the Taft-Hartley emergency provisions since 1978. The emergency provisions allow the president to delay a strike but do not address the causes of the strike. As a result, the dispute remains despite the invocation of the emergency provisions, and the strike or lockout may resume after the delay period under the injunction expires.

[28] 348 NLRB 1081 (2006).

CHAPTER REVIEW

» Key Terms

pressure tactics	« 487	***strike***	« 487	***common situs picketing***	« 501
picketing	« 487	***ambulatory situs picketing***	« 498	***hot cargo clauses***	« 511
patrolling	« 487				

» Summary

- When collective bargaining fails to produce an agreement in a labor dispute, either party may resort to pressure tactics to try to force the other side to settle the dispute. Union pressure involves strikes and calls for a boycott, while employers may resort to lockouts. The right to strike is not constitutionally guaranteed, but a strike is protected activity under the NLRA. Picketing, which usually accompanies a strike, is subject to several controls under the NLRA and related legislation.
- The Norris–La Guardia Act restricts the ability of the federal courts to issue injunctions against union conduct in a labor dispute; the term *labor dispute* is defined broadly in the Norris–La Guardia Act and includes strikes that are politically motivated. State courts can regulate violent picketing or picketing in violation of state laws, but when an unfair labor practice complaint has been filed concerning the legality of union picketing on private property, the *Babcock & Wilcox* approach should be used to decide the issue.
- The NLRA prohibits recognitional picketing, but publicity picketing directed to inform the public of a labor dispute is protected. Similarly, secondary picketing—union picketing directed at neutral employers who are not involved in the labor dispute—is an unfair labor practice. Exceptions to the prohibition on secondary picketing include consumer picketing and other publicity activities, such as handbilling; employers who are allies of the struck employer may also be picketed by the union involved in the labor dispute.
- Hot cargo clauses—contract language that would allow unions to engage in secondary activity—are illegal under Section 8(e) of the NLRA; exceptions to Section 8(e) allow work preservation clauses and exclude the garment industry from the prohibitions of both Section 8(e) and Section 8(b)(4).
- Remedies for illegal secondary activity include injunctions under Section 10(l) and civil suits for damages under Section 303 of the NLRA.

» Problems

Questions

1. In what situations can the states regulate picketing? Explain your answer.
2. What is recognitional or organization picketing? Under what circumstances is it prohibited by the NLRA?
3. What is primary picketing? What is secondary picketing? What factors determine the legality of picketing against neutral employers?
4. What is the ally doctrine? How does it affect the legality of picketing under Section 8(b)(4)?
5. What is a hot cargo clause? Why are hot cargo clauses prohibited by the NLRA?

Case Problems

6. Plaintiff owned and operated a supermarket in Springfield, Missouri. The defendant union neither represented, nor did it claim to want to organize, the supermarket's clerks. Nevertheless, the union sporadically picketed the supermarket, claiming that the impetus for its picketing was that the supermarket paid substandard wages.

   Initially, the union picketed in the public street, but subsequently, it moved onto the supermarket's sidewalk. After the supermarket filed a trespass complaint with the local police, the pickets moved back to the street but simultaneously filed an unfair labor practice charge with the NLRB. The Board issued a complaint, asserting that the supermarket violated Section 8(a)(1) of the NLRA by ordering the pickets off the sidewalk.

   The supermarket's owners initiated a lawsuit, seeking an injunction to keep the pickets off the sidewalk and also to stop other alleged picketing activities. The plaintiffs alleged that the pickets called customers "scab shoppers," took down license numbers of customers' cars, and misstated on their placards that the plaintiff was an Arizona company, coming in from out of state, when in fact it was a Missouri corporation.

   In what kind of picketing was the union engaging? What was the theory on which the NLRB issued its complaint on behalf of the union, and how do you think it will fare before an administrative law judge?

   Does the issuance of that complaint by the Board preempt the Missouri state court from enjoining any of the picketers' activities? All of their activities? Is your answer any different if the Section 8(a)(1) charge is ultimately sustained by the ALJ who hears the case? See *Smitty's Super Markets v. Local 322* [637 S.W.2d 148, 116 L.R.R.M. 3393 (Missouri Ct. Apps. (1982)].
7. Theater Techniques, Inc. (TTI) was a supplier of theatrical props and scenery for Broadway shows. TTI had a subcontract with Nolan Studios to paint scenery and props provided by TTI. Nolan Studios' employees were represented by Local 829, United Scenic Artists, whose collective agreement gave the union jurisdiction over the sculpting and painting of props. When some props from TTI arrived at Nolan already fabricated, the union employees refused to paint them unless Nolan paid a premium rate for the work. Nolan did not inform the union that TTI had contractual control over the disputed work, but Nolan did file a complaint with the NLRB, charging the union with violating Section 8(b)(4)(B) by refusing to handle the props from TTI to force Nolan to stop doing business with TTI.

   How should the Board decide the unfair labor practice complaint filed by Nolan? Explain your answer. See *United Scenic Artists, Local 829 v. NLRB* [762 F.2d 1027 (D.C. Cir. 1985)].
8. Local 366 of the Brewery, Bottling, Can & Allied Industrial Union called a strike against the Coors bottling plant in Golden, Colorado. Local 366 was affiliated with the AFL-CIO and received nationwide union support for a boycott of Coors beer during the strike.

   During the course of this protracted labor dispute, Coors made an agreement with KQED, a broadcasting station in the San Francisco Bay Area, under which the brewer would provide financial support and volunteers for a Coors Day portion of the station's annual fund-raising telethon.

Prior to the telethon, an article appeared in the *San Francisco Bay Guardian*, which stated that Coors "is notorious for antiunion activities during a ... strike" and had long been "the subject of a labor-backed nationwide boycott." Following the appearance of the article, the coordinator of the Northern California Chapter of the Coors Boycott Committee met with the KQED general manager to inform him of the swelling opposition to Coors Day, allegedly warning him not to stumble into a "shooting war" and that he could not guarantee the safety of the teleauction volunteers. KQED subsequently canceled Coors Day, and Coors sued the coordinator and other union supporters for damages.

Was the boycott group a labor organization under the jurisdiction of the NLRA? If so, did the boycott group violate the NLRA? Did it violate the federal antitrust laws? Did it violate any state laws? If so, would a state court have had jurisdiction of the case? See *Adolph Coors Co. v. Wallace* [570 F. Supp. 202, 115 L.R.R.M. 3100 (N.D. Cal. 1984)].

9. Delta Air Lines subcontracted the janitorial work of its offices at the Los Angeles International Airport to the National Cleaning Company. National entered into a collective bargaining agreement with the Hospital and Service Employees Union, Local 399. Delta later lawfully terminated its contract with National and made a new contract with Statewide Maintenance Company, a nonunion employer. Consequently, National fired five of the six janitors who had cleaned Delta's offices.

   In furtherance of its recognitional dispute with Statewide Maintenance, the union began distributing handbills at Delta's L.A. airport facilities in front of the downtown Los Angeles office. One or two persons usually distributed the flyers at each facility. The handbilling caused no interruptions in deliveries or refusals by Delta's employees to do their work.

   There were four handbills altogether. The first stated, "Please do not fly Delta Airlines. Delta Airlines unfair. Does not provide AFL-CIO conditions of employment. (signed by union)." The other side said, "It takes more than money to fly Delta. It takes nerve. Let's look at the accident record." There followed a list of fifty-five accidents involving Delta over the years, along with the total number of deaths and injuries.

   The second handbill, distributed a week later, contained all the information on side two of the first handbill but not the information from side one.

   The third handbill, another week later, again consisted of two sides. Side one said:

   > Please Do Not Fly Delta Airlines. This airline has caused members of Service Employees Union, Local 399, AFL-CIO, at Los Angeles International Airport, to become unemployed. In their place they have contracted with a maintenance company which does not provide Local 399 wages, benefits and standards. We urge all union members to protest Delta's action to the Delta office in your region. If you are concerned about the plight of fellow union members ... Please Do Not Fly Delta Airlines.

   Side two contained the same accident information as the previous two broadsides.

   Handbill four contained the same accident information as the prior three, with the following prefatory statement:

   > As members of the public and in order to protect the wages and conditions of Local 399 members and to publicize our primary dispute with the Statewide Building Maintenance Company, we wish to call to the attention of the consuming public certain information about Delta Airlines from the official records of the Civil Aeronautics Board of the United States Government.

   Simultaneous with the handbilling activities, the union published copies of flyers one and three in two union newspapers, along with an advertisement stating singly, "Do Not Fly Delta."

   Analyze each of the four handbills. What, if anything, in each constituted an illegal secondary boycott? What, if anything, was protected by the NLRA's publicity proviso? Is the same true with respect to the newspaper ads? See *Service Employees Local 399 v. NLRB* [117 L.R.R.M. 2717, 743 F.2d 1417 (9th Cir. 1984)].

10. Shortly after the Soviet invasion of Afghanistan in 1979, the United States imposed an embargo on

exports to the Soviet Union. However, some grain shipments were exempted from the embargo. Nevertheless, the International Longshoremen's Association (ILA), apparently disagreeing with the exemptions, adopted a resolution that its longshoremen would not handle any goods exported to or arriving from the Soviet Union.

Sovfracht Chartering Corporation, a Soviet government maritime agency, chartered a Belgian ship (*The Belgium*) to transport exempt and duly licensed grain from Houston to Russia. The Houston stevedore companies had to hire all longshoremen from ILA hiring halls. When TTT Stevedores, an employer party to an ILA collective bargaining agreement, sought to load the Soviet-bound grain on board *The Belgium*, it was informed that the ILA local would not provide any of its members to do the work. When informed of this decision, Sovfracht canceled *The Belgium*'s stop in Houston.

Was the ILA guilty of a secondary boycott? If so, against whom? What arguments can be made that this action was not illegal activity under the NLRA? See *ILA v. NLRB* [723 F.2d 963, 115 L.R. R.M. 2093 (D.C. Cir. 1983)].

11. The Iron Workers Union had been engaged in organizing the employees of Stokrr's Multi-Ton Corporation. When Stokrr's refused to recognize the union, the union called a strike of the company's employees. Perkins Trucking Company handled and transported Stokrr's products. Three days into the strike, pickets gathered around a Perkins truck as it attempted to make a pickup at the Stokrr's facility. One of the union pickets jumped on the running board of the Perkins truck and yelled at the driver, "We're going to rape your wife.... I'm going to break your legs." The picket then pointed at the driver's face and stated, "Just remember what I look like, because I know who you are. I'm going to get you.... [W]e're going to get all your trucks, you run a lot of them." At that point, the police assisted the Perkins truck through the picket line to the loading dock.

    Sometime later, eight to twelve strikers arrived at the Perkins terminal at 7 A.M. carrying placards. But they engaged in no picketing of the terminal facility; they stood around, five to ten feet from the terminal gate. They told the assistant shop steward of the union at Perkins that they were "individuals" trying to gain information for their "personal use" and that they wanted to know if Perkins was handling any of Stokrr's freight. They were told that Perkins had not handled any Stokrr's freight for "the last couple of weeks." At about 8 A.M., the strikers departed.

    Based on these facts, could it be said that Perkins was an ally of Stokrr's? What provisions of the NLRA, if any, did the union violate? See *Iron Workers, Local 455*, [243 NLRB 340, 102 L.R. R.M. 1109 (1979)].

12. Caruso was sole proprietor of Linoleum & Carpet City in Spokane, Washington. He also owned a parking lot a quarter of a mile from his business. Periodically, delivery trucks blocked access to the lot.

    On October 26, Caruso found a beer truck and a van blocking the entrance to his lot. Caruso called a tow truck to have the vehicles removed. (He had first called the owner, whose name was on the truck, and asked him to remove it.) The driver of the van settled his share of the tow truck costs, but Contos, the driver of the truck, refused to pay his share. Contos told Caruso he would report him to the Teamsters Union and the union would "break" him.

    On November 9, an article was published in the *Washington Teamster*. The article, titled "Don't Patronize Carpet City in Spokane," was printed once on the front page of the teamster paper and twice more in substantially the same form on page 5. It continued to state that the owner harassed laboring people who used his parking lot. It was signed Teamsters Union, Local 690.

    Soon after publication of the first three articles, people began calling Linoleum & Carpet City and stating that they would not shop there. Sales dropped dramatically, and the following May, Caruso relocated his business hoping to minimize his losses.

    Assess the union's activities in light of the NLRA. Are there any unfair labor practices? Are there any common law counts that Caruso could pursue against the union for destroying his business? If so, does he face a preemption problem? See *Caruso v. Teamsters Local 690* [120 L.R.R.M. 2233 (Wash. S.C. 1983)].

13. Zellers worked as an elevator installer; he was a member of Local 123 of the Elevator Constructors. Zellers was employed by Eggers Construction Co. and was working at a neutral construction site. The elevator construction crew was directed to use a separate, neutral gate at the work site because another union had set up a picket line at a different gate at the work site. When he saw the other picket line, Zellers refused to enter the work site, even though there was no picket line at the gate he was required to use. Because of his refusal to enter the gate, Zellers was suspended by Eggers. The Elevator Constructors Union filed a grievance protesting the suspension of Zellers. Eggers then filed an unfair labor practice complaint with the NLRB, alleging that the union filing the grievance was in violation of Section 8(b)(4) because it sought to authorize Zellers' refusal to work in order to force the general contractor to get rid of the employer subject to the strike by the other union.

    How should the board rule on Eggers' unfair labor practice complaint? Explain your answer. See *NLRB v. Elevator Constructors* [134 L.R.R.M. 2137 (8th Cir. 1990)].

14. The Truck Drivers' Union was engaged in a primary labor dispute with Piggyback Services, Inc., a nonunion employer. The dispute began when the Santa Fe Railroad awarded Piggyback a subcontract to ramp and deramp intermodal freight (freight carried inside trailers and containers on railroad flatcars) at Santa Fe's Richmond, California, rail terminal. That work had been performed by union members for a wholly owned subsidiary of Santa Fe. Piggyback had initially agreed to hire the former union workers, but later reneged on that promise, and the union began picketing and distributing handbills at Santa Fe's Richmond rail terminal.

    In an effort to insulate itself from the union's labor dispute with Piggyback, Santa Fe designated a gate, Gate 1, as the sole entrance to the Richmond facility for employees, customers, visitors, and suppliers of Piggyback. Santa Fe also posted signs at four other entrances to the Richmond facility, designated as Gate 2, Gate 3, Gate 4, and Gate 5, stating that these "neutral" gates were reserved for the exclusive use of Santa Fe's employees, customers, visitors, and suppliers, and that Gate 1 was available only for Piggyback's employees, customers, visitors, and suppliers.

    Although Piggyback employees entered only through Gate 1, and the union fully acknowledged that it had no labor dispute with Santa Fe, the union began picketing at the four neutral gates. Handbills distributed by the union at neutral locations urged neutral employees and customers entering the Santa Fe railway yard to either honor the picket line or, alternatively, to cease all work related to Piggyback's day-to-day operations. The union sent letters to the presidents of the seven unions that represented Santa Fe employees. The letters requested that union members employed by Santa Fe not perform work directly related to Piggyback's operations at the Richmond terminal. A similar letter was sent by the union to United Parcel Services (UPS), Santa Fe's primary unionized intermodal trucking customer.

    The UPS drivers and other Santa Fe customers honored the picket line by refusing to deliver intermodal freight to the Richmond terminal. In response, Santa Fe established a drop-off site about a mile-and-a-half from Gate 3 for use by UPS and other Santa Fe customers. Although no Piggyback employees were stationed at the UPS drop-off site, the union expanded its activity to that location. The union also picketed at the two railroad spur lines where intermodal freight cars entered the railway yard.

    Santa Fe filed an unfair labor practice complaint with the NLRB, alleging that the union picketing violated Section 8(b)(4). How should the NLRB rule on the complaint? Why? Explain your answer. See *NLRB v. General Truck Drivers, Warehousemen, Helpers and Automotive Employees of Contra Costa County, Local No. 315* [20 F.3d 1017 (9th Cir. 1994)].

15. Rainbow, a tour bus company based in Honolulu, provides ground transportation services to various tourist agencies in the Honolulu area. In 2006, Steven Kolt became a part owner and president of the company and adopted its present name.

    Rainbow had been a nonunion business. In the latter part of that year and early the next year, some employees began inquiring into joining a union.

Soon thereafter, the union picketed the Rainbow yard. Approximately thirty to forty pickets were involved. The pickets were somewhat threatening and unruly and temporarily blocked ingress and egress to the Rainbow yard. Rainbow immediately sought to enjoin the picketing in Hawaii state court and the union agreed before the state court judge to reduce the number of pickets to two.

Rainbow then commenced the lawsuit that is the subject of this appeal. Rainbow brought two counts. The first alleged violations cognizable under Section 303 of the Labor Management Relations Act. The second count, a pendent state law claim, alleged the union had engaged in unlawful mass picketing that tortiously interfered with Rainbow's employment contracts and resulted in a loss of business.

The union and two former Rainbow employees filed unfair labor practice charges with the NLRB. They alleged Rainbow had unlawfully interfered with its employees' Section 7 rights by threatening and terminating several of them. Rainbow answered that the union had engaged in activity violative of Sections 8(b)(1)(A) (coercing employees in the exercise of their Section 7 rights); (b)(4) (illegal secondary conduct); and (b)(7) (illegal recognitional picketing when no petition had been timely filed). The NLRB consolidated the complaints, and a hearing was held from July 6 to July 13, 2007.

The ALJ entered his decision on March 29, 2008. The NLRB affirmed the ALJ's findings and adopted his order with minor modifications. The NLRB rejected Rainbow's claims and found for the union.

Does the NLRB's decision in favor of the union mean that Rainbow cannot recover damages in this case? Or is there a theory of recovery on which it should be permitted to proceed? See *Rainbow Coaches v. Hawaii Teamsters* [704 F.2d 1443, 113 L.R.R.M. 2383 (9th Cir. 1983)].

Hypothetical Scenarios

16. The United Brotherhood of Carpenters has a dispute with Brady Contracting over Brady's use of nonunion employees on construction jobs. The union claims that Brady's wages and benefits are below the area standards paid by unionized contractors. Brady is currently constructing several retail stores in the Phoenix area. The union sent letters to the various retail store owners, urging them not to work with Brady until Brady agreed to pay area standard wages and benefits. The union also informed the retailers that the union would begin an "aggressive public information campaign" against Brady, including displaying banners at the retail stores. The union then set up protests at several retail stores—it displayed large banners reading "Shame on [the name of the retailer]" and "Labor Dispute." The banners were displayed on public property about twenty feet from the retail store. Union members also distributed handbills that explained that the union's dispute was with Brady and not the retailer. Brady and two retailers filed unfair labor practice charges with the NLRB. Does the union conduct here violate Section 8(b)(4)? Explain your answer.
17. Midwest Moving Co. is a nonunion commercial moving and storage business. The International Brotherhood of Teamsters, Local 55, has been trying, without any success, to organize Midwest's employees. Midwest signed a contract to relocate Morgan Stanley's local office to an office building in downtown Chicago. The union learns of the upcoming job and notifies the building owner that it intends to picket at the building when Midwest employees are present there. The building owner informed the union that Midwest would be required to use the loading dock at the rear of the building, and would only have access to the loading dock after 6:00 P.M. and before 8:00 A.M. the next day. Shortly before 6:00 P.M, several union members began distributing handbills on the sidewalk in front of the building, and as the Midwest trucks approached, several other union members carrying picket signs began to walk back and forth in the alley near the loading dock at the rear of the building. The picketing was peaceful, but Midwest complained that the picketing made it difficult for the Midwest trucks to approach the loading dock. The building owner and Midwest both filed complaints about the picketing with the NLRB. Is the union picketing here primary or secondary? Why? Is the picketing in violation of Section 8(b)(4)? Explain.

18. Local 15 of the United Food and Commercial Workers Union went on strike against Gold Medal Bakery when negotiations for a new contract reached an impasse. The bakery's cookies are sold at FoodCo grocery stores in the Syracuse area. The union posts members holding signs saying "Don't Buy Gold Medal Cookies" and "Don't Eat Scab Cookies" in front of the local FoodCo stores. As a result of the union actions, sales of Gold Medal Cookies fall sharply. FoodCo files an unfair labor practice charge against the union with the NLRB. Is the union's conduct legal under the NLRA? Explain.
19. State Electric, a nonunion contractor, is doing the electrical work at the construction site of a church. The employees of a number of other contractors are also working at the construction site. The Electricians' Union begins picketing the construction site, but pickets at all gates into the site even though State Electric employees are restricted to Gate 1. When the union begins picketing, the employees of the other contractors at the site refuse to work. Has the union violated Section 8(b)(4)? Explain. What, if any, actions should the union take to make sure the picketing is legal? Why?
20. Speedy Delivery, Inc. is a local parcel delivery service. Its drivers are represented by Local 33 of the Service Employees International Union. The Teamsters Union, Local 747 approaches the manager of Speedy Delivery and demands that the company recognize it as the bargaining representative for its employees. When the manager refuses, the Teamsters begin picketing around Speedy Delivery's warehouse and garage. The picketing causes several UPS and FedEx truck drivers to refuse to make deliveries to Speedy Delivery. Does the Teamster's picketing violate the NLRA? If so, which section? Why?

CHAPTER 17

The Enforcement and Administration of the Collective Agreement

The signing of a collective agreement by a union and an employer may mark the end of the bargaining process; it is also the beginning of a continuing relationship between them. The agreement creates rights for and imposes obligations on both parties. The parties are bound to uphold the terms of the contract for its duration. How can union and management ensure that the "other side" will honor the contract? What means are available to enforce the contract in the event of a breach by either side? How can disputes over the interpretation of the agreement be resolved? This chapter discusses the means available for the enforcement and administration of the collective agreement.

Section 301 of the National Labor Relations Act (NLRA) provides that suits for violations of contracts between an employer and a labor union may be brought in federal and state courts. Therefore, either the union or employer could bring a lawsuit over the other side's failure to live up to the contract. However, lawsuits are a cumbersome means of resolving most contract disputes; they are also expensive and time consuming. For these reasons, lawsuits are impractical for resolving disputes over how collective agreements should be interpreted or applied.

Either party to the agreement could resort to pressure tactics to try to resolve a contract dispute. The union could go on strike or the employer could lock out the employees to force the other side to live up to the contract. The employer generally is not willing to lock out employees and cease production over minor matters. Nor are union members likely to strike, lose wages, and risk being replaced over insignificant issues.

Arbitration

Arbitration
The settlement of disputes by a neutral adjudicator chosen by the parties.

Because of the shortcomings of both lawsuits and pressure tactics as a way to resolve contract disputes, the parties usually agree, as a part of their collective agreement, to establish their own process for resolving disputes peacefully. The peaceful settlement process usually involves ***arbitration***. Arbitration is the settlement of disputes by a neutral adjudicator chosen by the parties to the dispute. It provides a means to resolve contractual disputes relatively inexpensively and expeditiously. Arbitration also provides flexibility because the parties are free to tailor the arbitration process to suit their particular situation. The parties generally incorporate arbitration as the final step of the grievance procedure. In return for the agreement by each party to arbitrate their dispute, they give up their right to strike or lock out over such issues.

Interest Arbitration Versus Rights Arbitration

In a labor relations setting, arbitration may be used either to settle a dispute over the creation of a new collective agreement or over the interpretation and administration of an existing agreement. When arbitration is used to create a new agreement (or renew an existing one), it is known as ***interest arbitration***—the parties seek to protect their economic interests through favorable contract terms. Interest arbitration is common in the public sector, where employees are generally prohibited from striking. Interest arbitration replaces pressure tactics as a means to resolve the negotiating impasse in the public sector. It is much less common in the private sector.

Interest Arbitration
Arbitration that is used to create a new collective agreement or to renew an existing agreement.

If the dispute involves interpreting an existing agreement rather than creating a new one, the arbitration to resolve it is known as ***rights arbitration***. Rights arbitration is the means to define the rights and obligations of each party under the agreement. It is very common in both the public and private sectors. Even though rights arbitration is not required by the NLRA, more than 90 percent of all collective agreements provide for rights arbitration as the means to resolve disputes over the interpretation and/or application of the collective agreement. This chapter is concerned with rights arbitration, and unless otherwise specified, the term *arbitration* refers to rights arbitration.

Rights Arbitration
Arbitration to resolve a dispute involving the interpretation or application of an existing collective agreement; arbitration that defines the rights and obligations of each party under the agreement.

Rights Arbitration and the Grievance Process

Rights arbitration is generally used as the final step in the ***grievance process***—a process set up to deal with complaints under the collective agreement. Like rights arbitration, the grievance process is created by the parties to the agreement. It is not required by statute. Because it is voluntarily created by the parties under the collective agreement, the grievance process can be tailored to fit their particular situation or desires.

Grievance Process
The process set up by a collective agreement to deal with complaints that arise under the collective agreement.

A ***grievance*** is simply a complaint that either party to the agreement is not living up to the obligations of the agreement. Most grievances are filed by employees complaining about the actions of the employer (or its agents), but management may also file grievances under the agreement.

Grievance
A complaint that one party to a collective agreement is not living up to the obligations of the agreement.

Grievance procedures vary widely; the parties to an agreement can devise whatever procedure is best suited to their purposes. The following is an example of a four-step grievance procedure, with arbitration as the final step:

ARTICLE XIII: GRIEVANCE PROCEDURE

SECTION 1. Any grievance or dispute between the Company and the Union involving the interpretation or application of any terms of this Agreement shall be adjusted according to the following procedure:

Step One: The employee who believes he has suffered a grievance or been unjustly treated may raise the alleged grievance with his Foreman or Assistant Foreman in an attempt to settle the same. The said employee may be accompanied or represented if he so desires by the Steward. The Foreman shall have two (2) working days to settle the grievance.

Step Two: If the matter is not satisfactorily settled in Step One, it may be taken to the Second Step by the Union's reducing it to writing, on a mutually agreed upon form provided by the Company. Any grievance taken to the Second Step must be signed by a Steward, a Chief Steward, or a Local Union Committee member. Two (2) copies will be delivered to the Supervisor, who will sign and date the grievance upon receipt of it. A meeting will be arranged within four (4) working days following receipt of the form, between the Supervisor, Plant Superintendent, Grievant, Steward, or in his absence, Chief Steward. A written answer shall be given within four (4) working days from the date of the meeting even though an oral decision is given at the meeting. If the answer is not received during the time period, the grievance shall be deemed settled in favor of the grievant or Union.

Step Three: The Steward, or Chief Steward in his absence, may appeal the Second Step decision by completing the "Appeal to Third Step" portion of the grievance form and by delivering the same to the Industrial Relations Department within five (5) working days (excluding Saturday and Sunday) after the decision in the Second Step. The Industrial Relations Department shall arrange a meeting within five (5) working days (excluding Saturday and Sunday) following receipt of the appeal, between the representative designated by the Company, the Shop Grievance Committee, and the International Representative. A written answer shall be given within five (5) working days (excluding Saturday and Sunday) from the date of the meeting even though an oral decision is given at the meeting. Any failure by either party to meet the time limits required shall deem the grievance settled in favor of the other party.

Step Four: Any grievance or dispute involving the interpretation or application of this Agreement, which has not been satisfactorily settled in the foregoing steps, may, at the request of either party, be submitted to an arbitrator or arbitration board selected as hereinafter provided, by written notice delivered to the other party within four (4) calendar weeks subsequent to the decision in Step Three. Any failure, by either party, to meet such time limits shall be deemed a waiver of the grievance. Unless the parties mutually agree upon arbitration by the State Board of Mediation and Arbitration, the matter shall be referred to the American Arbitration Association for arbitration under its rules. The fees and expenses of the arbitrator thus selected shall be divided equally between the parties.

SECTION 2. The arbitration board or the arbitrator is not authorized to add to, modify, or take away from the express terms of this Agreement and shall be limited to the interpretation or application of the provisions of the Agreement of the determination as to whether there is a violation of it. Any decision of the arbitration board or the arbitrator within the scope of the above authority shall be final and binding on both parties.

SECTION 3. Time limits above set forth must be complied with strictly.

SECTION 4. The Company or the Union may institute a grievance at Step Three on any matter concerning general application, and process it through Step Four.

It can be seen that the actual grievance procedure is a series of meetings between union and management representatives. As the grievance remains unresolved and moves through the various steps of the procedure, the rank of the representatives involved increases. Either party may request that a grievance unresolved at Step Three be submitted to arbitration.

Concept *Summary* » 17.1

Rights Arbitration vs. Interest Arbitration

Rights Arbitration	Interest Arbitration
Used to resolve disputes over the enforcement of a collective agreement—to determine the rights and obligations of the parties under the collective agreement	Used to create or renew the terms of a collective agreement
Arbitration clause is *quid pro quo* for a union agreeing not to strike during the term of the agreement	Used in the public sector to resolve contract disputes involving employees who are prohibited from striking

The Courts and Arbitration

As noted, arbitration as a means to resolve grievances is a voluntary mechanism; the parties to the contract have agreed to use it. But what happens if either party refuses to submit a dispute to arbitration? What remedies are available to the party seeking arbitration? The following case deals with an attempt to use Section 301 of the NLRA to force management to arbitrate a union grievance.

As *Lincoln Mills* indicates, if the parties have agreed to arbitration as a means of resolving disputes, the courts will require them to use it. What is voluntary about arbitration, then, is its existence—whether the agreement provides for arbitration. Once the parties have agreed to use arbitration, the courts will enforce that agreement.

What should the role of the court be when it is asked to order that a dispute be arbitrated or when it is asked to enforce an arbitration award? Those issues were addressed by the Supreme Court in three cases that came to be known as the *Steelworkers Trilogy*. In *United Steelworkers of America v. Warrior & Gulf Navigation Co.*,[1] the Supreme Court held that when a court is asked to order arbitration under Section 301, an order to arbitrate the grievance should not be denied "unless it may be said with positive assurance that the arbitration clause is not susceptible of an interpretation that covers the asserted dispute. Doubts should be resolved in favor of coverage." In a more recent decision, the Supreme Court again affirmed the holding of *Warrior & Gulf Navigation*. In *AT&T Technologies v. Communications Workers of America*,[2] the Court held that it is the role of the courts, not that of the arbitrators, to resolve questions of whether a grievance is subject to arbitration.

The collective agreement's arbitration clause may also affect the right of individual employees to bring employment discrimination suits. (See the discussion on this topic in Chapter 8.) In *Alexander v. Gardner Denver Co.*,[3] the Supreme Court held that an employee who had lost in arbitration under the collective agreement was still able to bring a Title VII suit in court. The Court held that the arbitration dealt with the employee's rights under the

[1]363 U.S. 574 (1960).

[2]475 U.S. 643 (1986).

[3]415 U.S. 147 (1974).

case 17.1 »

Textile Workers Union of America v. Lincoln Mills of Alabama
353 U.S. 448 (1957)

Facts: The Textile Workers Union entered into a collective bargaining agreement with the employer, Lincoln Mills. The agreement provided that there would be no strikes or work stoppages, and contained a grievance procedure. The last step in the grievance procedure was arbitration, which could be invoked by either party. The union processed several grievances concerning work loads and work assignments through the various steps in the grievance procedure, but the employer denied them. The union then requested arbitration, and the employer refused. The union then filed suit under Section 301 of the NLRA to compel the employer to arbitrate the grievances. The trial court ordered the employer to arbitrate the grievances under the arbitration provisions of the collective bargaining agreement. The employer appealed, and the court of appeals reversed the trial court decision. The union then appealed to the U.S. Supreme Court.

Issue: Does Section 301 authorize a court to order the parties to a collective agreement to arbitrate a grievance?

Decision: The Court looked to the wording of Section 301, which provides:

> (a) Suits for violation of contracts between an employer and a labor organization representing employees in an industry affecting commerce as defined in this chapter, or between any such labor organizations, may be brought in any district court of the United States having jurisdiction of the parties, without respect to the amount in controversy or without regard to the citizenship of the parties.

Previous decisions involving Section 301 hold that Section 301(a) authorizes federal courts to fashion a body of federal law for the enforcement of collective bargaining agreements, including enforcing of promises to arbitrate grievances under collective bargaining agreements. The agreement to arbitrate grievance disputes, contained in this collective bargaining agreement, should be enforced. The agreement to arbitrate grievances is the *quid pro quo* for an agreement not to strike. Section 301 expresses a federal policy that federal courts should enforce these agreements to arbitrate in order to ensure that industrial peace can be promoted. In enforcing agreements to arbitrate under Section 301, the courts should to apply substantive federal law, fashioned from the policy of the national labor laws. The Court also noted that the Norris–La Guardia Act, which restricts federal courts issuing injunctions in labor disputes, does not apply to suits seeking to order arbitration under Section 301. The Supreme Court reversed the decision of the court of appeals and remanded the case. «

collective agreement, which were distinct from the employee's statutory rights under Title VII. In *Wright v. Universal Marine Supply*,[4] the Supreme Court held that the arbitration clause of a collective agreement must contain a "clear and unmistakable waiver" of the individual employee's rights to sue, in order to waive individual employee's right to sue over employment discrimination claims. More recently, the Supreme Court decided the case of *14 Penn Plaza v. Pyett*,[5] involving age discrimination claims filed by employees covered by a collective agreement that included an arbitration clause specifically covering any claims under Title VII, the Age Discrimination in Employment Act, and other EEO legislation. The Court held that

[4]525 U.S. 70 (1998). Applying the holding in *Wright*, the U.S. Court of Appeals for the Sixth Circuit held that an employee who had arbitrated a claim of employment discrimination was not prevented from bringing a court suit over the same discrimination claim because the collective agreement's general nondiscrimination clause was not a "clear and unmistakable waiver," in *Kennedy v. Superior Printing Co.*, 215 F.3d 650 (6th Cir. 2000).

[5]129 S.Ct. 1456 (2009).

the employees were required to arbitrate their age discrimination claims. The Court noted that *Alexander* did not apply where the collective bargaining agreement's arbitration provision expressly included statutory claims as well as contractual claims arising under the terms of the collective agreement. The effect of the decision in *14 Penn Plaza v. Pyett* may be limited, however, because the Court specifically refrained from holding that employees must arbitrate their statutory EEO claims when the union controls access to arbitration and could prevent the employees from pursuing their EEO claims through arbitration.

The limited role of the court ordering arbitration was emphasized in *United Steelworkers v. American Mfg. Co.*,[6] the second case in the trilogy. In that case, the Supreme Court held that

> [t]he function of the court … is confined to ascertaining whether the party seeking arbitration is making a claim which on its face is governed by the contract. Whether the moving party is right or wrong is a question of contract interpretation for the arbitrator…. *The courts, therefore, have no business weighing the merits of the grievance.* [emphasis added]

The duty to arbitrate arises from the collective agreement between the parties, but does the duty to arbitrate continue to exist after the expiration of the collective agreement? In *Litton Financial Printing Div., Litton Business Systems v. NLRB*,[7] the Supreme Court held that the duty to arbitrate continues after the expiration of the agreement if the grievance arises "under the agreement." In other words:

- it involves facts and occurrences that arose prior to expiration;
- it concerns postexpiration action that infringes a right accrued or vested under the agreement; or
- it involves disputed contract rights that survive the expiration of the collective agreement.

When one of the parties refuses to comply with the arbitrator's award or decision after the grievance has been arbitrated, the other party may seek to have the award judicially enforced. What is the role of the court that is asked to enforce the arbitration decision? This was the subject of the final case in the trilogy, *United Steelworkers v. Enterprise Wheel & Car Co.*[8] In that case, the Supreme Court held that the court is required to enforce the arbitrator's decision unless it is clear to the court that the arbitrator has exceeded the authority given to him or her by the collective agreement. The Court stated that "the question of interpretation of the collective agreement is a question for the arbitrator. It is the arbitrator's construction which was bargained for; and so far as the arbitrator's decision concerns the construction of the contract, the courts have no business overruling him because their interpretation of the contract is different from his." In *Major League Baseball Players Association v. Garvey*,[9] the Supreme Court emphasized that even when the court vacates an arbitration award, the court must remand the issue back to arbitration for resolution rather than settling the merits of the dispute according to the court's own judgment.

Under the *Enterprise Wheel & Car* decision, the court should refuse to enforce an arbitration decision that violates the law. How should the court react when an employer claims that an arbitration decision conflicts with the "policy" behind the law?

---

[6]363 U.S. 564 (1960).

[7]501 U.S. 190 (1991).

[8]363 U.S. 593 (1960).

[9]532 U.S. 504 (2001).

case 17.2 » EASTERN ASSOCIATED COAL CORPORATION v. UNITED MINE WORKERS OF AMERICA, DISTRICT 17

531 U.S. 57 (2000)

Justice Breyer delivered the opinion of the Court.

... Eastern Associated Coal Corp., and respondent, United Mine Workers of America, are parties to a collective-bargaining agreement with arbitration provisions. The agreement specifies that, in arbitration, in order to discharge an employee, Eastern must prove it has "just cause." Otherwise the arbitrator will order the employee reinstated. The arbitrator's decision is final.

James Smith worked for Eastern as a member of a road crew, a job that required him to drive heavy trucklike vehicles on public highways. As a truck driver, Smith was subject to Department of Transportation (DOT) regulations requiring random drug testing of workers engaged in "safety-sensitive" tasks.

In March 1996, Smith tested positive for marijuana. Eastern sought to discharge Smith. The union went to arbitration, and the arbitrator concluded that Smith's positive drug test did not amount to "just cause" for discharge. Instead the arbitrator ordered Smith's reinstatement, provided that Smith (1) accept a suspension of 30 days without pay, (2) participate in a substance-abuse program, and (3) undergo drug tests at the discretion of Eastern (or an approved substance-abuse professional) for the next five years.

Between April 1996 and January 1997, Smith passed four random drug tests. But in July 1997 he again tested positive for marijuana. Eastern again sought to discharge Smith. The union again went to arbitration, and the arbitrator again concluded that Smith's use of marijuana did not amount to "just cause" for discharge, in light of two mitigating circumstances. First, Smith had been a good employee for 17 years. And, second, Smith had made a credible and "very personal appeal under oath ... concerning a personal/family problem which caused this one time lapse in drug usage."

The arbitrator ordered Smith's reinstatement provided that Smith (1) accept a new suspension without pay, this time for slightly more than three months; (2) reimburse Eastern and the union for the costs of both arbitration proceedings; (3) continue to participate in a substance-abuse program; (4) continue to undergo random drug testing; and (5) provide Eastern with a signed, undated letter of resignation, to take effect if Smith again tested positive within the next five years.

Eastern brought suit in federal court seeking to have the arbitrator's award vacated, arguing that the award contravened a public policy against the operation of dangerous machinery by workers who test positive for drugs. The District Court, while recognizing a strong regulation-based public policy against drug use by workers who perform safety-sensitive functions, held that Smith's conditional reinstatement did not violate that policy. And it ordered the award's enforcement.

The Court of Appeals for the Fourth Circuit affirmed on the reasoning of the District Court. [Eastern appealed to the U.S. Supreme Court.] ...

Eastern claims that considerations of public policy make the arbitration award unenforceable.... Eastern does not claim here that the arbitrator acted outside the scope of his contractually delegated authority. Hence we must treat the arbitrator's award as if it represented an agreement between Eastern and the union as to the proper meaning of the contract's words "just cause." ... We must then decide whether a contractual reinstatement requirement would fall within the legal exception that makes unenforceable "a collective bargaining agreement that is contrary to public policy." The Court has made clear that any such public policy must be "explicit," "well defined," and "dominant." It must be "ascertained 'by reference to the laws and legal precedents and not from general considerations of supposed public interests.'" And, of course, the question to be answered is not whether Smith's drug use itself violates public policy, but whether the agreement to reinstate him does so. To put the question more specifically, does a contractual agreement to reinstate Smith with specified conditions run contrary to an explicit, well-defined, and dominant public policy, as ascertained by reference to positive law and not from general considerations of supposed public interests? ...

We agree, in principle, that courts' authority to invoke the public policy exception is not limited solely to instances where the arbitration award itself violates positive law. Nevertheless, the public policy exception is narrow and must satisfy the principles set forth in ... *Misco*. Moreover, in a case like the one before us, where two political branches have created a detailed regulatory regime in a specific field, courts should approach with particular caution pleas to divine further public policy in that area.

Eastern asserts that a public policy against reinstatement of workers who use drugs can be discerned from an examination of that regulatory regime, which consists of the Omnibus

Transportation Employee Testing Act of 1991 and DOT's implementing regulations. The Testing Act … requires the Secretary of Transportation to promulgate regulations requiring "testing of operators of commercial motor vehicles for the use of a controlled substance." It mandates suspension of those operators who have driven a commercial motor vehicle while under the influence of drugs. And DOT's implementing regulations set forth sanctions applicable to those who test positive for illegal drugs.

In Eastern's view, these provisions embody a strong public policy against drug use by transportation workers in safety-sensitive positions and in favor of random drug testing in order to detect that use. Eastern argues that reinstatement of a driver who has twice failed random drug tests would undermine that policy—to the point where a judge must set aside an employer-union agreement requiring reinstatement.

Eastern's argument, however, loses much of its force when one considers further provisions of the Act that make clear that the Act's remedial aims are complex. The Act says that "rehabilitation is a critical component of any testing program".… Neither the Act nor the regulations forbid an employer to reinstate in a safety-sensitive position an employee who fails a random drug test once or twice. The congressional and regulatory directives require only that the above-stated prerequisites to reinstatement be met.

Moreover, when promulgating these regulations, DOT decided not to require employers either to provide rehabilitation or to "hold a job open for a driver" who has tested positive, on the basis that such decisions "should be left to management/driver negotiation." That determination reflects basic background labor law principles, which caution against interference with labor-management agreements about appropriate employee discipline.…

We believe that these expressions of positive law embody several relevant policies. As Eastern points out, these policies include Testing Act policies against drug use by employees in safety-sensitive transportation positions and in favor of drug testing. They also include a Testing Act policy favoring rehabilitation of employees who use drugs. And the relevant statutory and regulatory provisions must be read in light of background labor law policy that favors determination of disciplinary questions through arbitration when chosen as a result of labor-management negotiation.

The award before us is not contrary to these several policies, taken together. The award does not condone Smith's conduct or ignore the risk to public safety that drug use by truck drivers may pose. Rather, the award punishes Smith by suspending him for three months, thereby depriving him of nearly $9,000 in lost wages; it requires him to pay the arbitration costs of both sides; it insists upon further substance-abuse treatment and testing; and it makes clear (by requiring Smith to provide a signed letter of resignation) that one more failed test means discharge.

The award violates no specific provision of any law or regulation. It is consistent with DOT rules requiring completion of substance-abuse treatment before returning to work, for it does not preclude Eastern from assigning Smith to a non-safety-sensitive position until Smith completes the prescribed treatment program. It is consistent with the Testing Act's … driving license suspension requirements, for those requirements apply only to drivers who, unlike Smith, actually operated vehicles under the influence of drugs. The award is also consistent with the Act's rehabilitative concerns, for it requires substance-abuse treatment and testing before Smith can return to work.…

Regarding drug use by persons in safety-sensitive positions, then, Congress has enacted a detailed statute. And Congress has delegated to the Secretary of Transportation authority to issue further detailed regulations on that subject. Upon careful consideration, including public notice and comment, the Secretary has done so. Neither Congress nor the Secretary has seen fit to mandate the discharge of a worker who twice tests positive for drugs. We hesitate to infer a public policy in this area that goes beyond the careful and detailed scheme Congress and the Secretary have created.

We recognize that reasonable people can differ as to whether reinstatement or discharge is the more appropriate remedy here. But both employer and union have agreed to entrust this remedial decision to an arbitrator. We cannot find in the Act, the regulations, or any other law or legal precedent an "explicit,""well defined,""dominant" public policy to which the arbitrator's decision "runs contrary." We conclude that the lower courts correctly rejected Eastern's public policy claim.

The judgment of the Court of Appeals is **affirmed**.

Case Questions

1. Why did the arbitrator order the reinstatement of Smith? What penalties did Smith suffer as a result of testing positive for drug use?
2. What does the employer use to define the public policy it claims requires that Smith be discharged? Does the Court read those materials as defining the same public policy as claimed by the employer?
3. Does the Court enforce the arbitrator's award here? Why?

In *Paperworkers v. Misco, Inc.*,[10] the Supreme Court held that a court may refuse to enforce an arbitration award only if the award violates "explicit" public policy as defined by reference to legislation and court decisions rather than "general considerations of supposed public interests." In the following case, an employer argues that an arbitration award reinstating an employee who had failed a drug test should not be enforced because it violates public policy.

Judicial Enforcement of No-Strike Clauses

The decisions in the *Steelworkers Trilogy* emphasized that arbitration was a substitute for industrial strife. The *Lincoln Mills* decision stated that the employer's agreement to arbitrate disputes is the quid pro quo for the union's agreement not to strike over arbitrable disputes.

No-Strike Clause
A provision in a collective agreement by which the union agrees not to strike over disputes of interpretation of the agreement during the term of the agreement.

Many agreements contain ***no-strike clauses*** by which the union agrees not to strike over disputes of interpretation of the agreement during the term of the agreement. In *Teamsters Local 174 v. Lucas Flour*,[11] the Supreme Court held that a no-strike clause will be implied by the court, even when the agreement itself is silent on the matter, if the agreement contains an arbitration provision. The implied no-strike clause covers any dispute that is subject to arbitration under the agreement.

If the collective agreement contains an express no-strike clause, or even an implied one under *Lucas Flour*, can a federal court enforce that clause by enjoining a strike in violation of the no-strike clause? What about the antiinjunction provisions of the Norris–La Guardia Act? This issue was presented to the Supreme Court in *Boys Markets, Inc. v. Retail Clerks Union, Local 770.*[12] The Court in *Boys Markets* held that the Norris–La Guardia Act did not prevent a federal court from issuing an injunction to stop a strike over an issue that was subject to the arbitration clause of a collective agreement.

Injunctions under the doctrine of *Boys Markets* may also be issued against employers for breaches of the collective agreement that threaten the arbitration process. In *Oil, Chemical and Atomic Workers International Union, Local 2–286 v. Amoco Oil Co.*,[13] the court affirmed an injunction preventing an employer's unilateral implementation of a drug testing program, pending the outcome of arbitration to determine the employer's right to institute such a program under the collective bargaining agreement.

The decision in *Boys Markets* allowing federal courts to enjoin strikes in violation of no-strike clauses does not mean that a union may never go on strike during the term of a collective agreement. The *Boys Markets* holding is limited to strikes over issues subject to arbitration under the agreement. In *Jacksonville Bulk Terminals, Inc. v. Int. Longshoremen's Ass'n.*,[14] the Supreme Court refused to enjoin a refusal by longshoremen to handle cargo destined for the Soviet Union in protest over the Soviet invasion of Afghanistan. The Court held that the strike was over a political dispute that was not arbitrable under the collective

---

[10]484 U.S. 29 (1987).

[11]369 U.S. 95 (1962).

[12]398 U.S. 235 (1970).

[13]885 F.2d 697 (10th Cir. 1989).

[14]457 U.S. 702 (1982).

agreement. The policy behind that decision was first set out in the Supreme Court decision of *Buffalo Forge Co. v. United Steelworkers of America*,[15] which held that the use of an injunction to stop a strike, as in *Boys Markets*, is appropriate only when the cause of the strike is a dispute that is subject to arbitration under the collective agreement.

Concept *Summary* » 17.2

Courts and Arbitration

- The courts will enforce a no-strike clause where the dispute is subject to the arbitration clause
- The courts will enforce an agreement to arbitrate unless the grievance is clearly not within the scope of the arbitration agreement
- When ordering arbitration, the court is not to rule on the merits of the grievance
- The courts are required to enforce an arbitration award unless the arbitrator has exceeded her/his authority under the collective agreement or violates explicit public policy

Remedies for Breach of No-Strike Clauses

As the preceding cases demonstrate, an employer may enjoin strikes that violate a no-strike clause when the strike is over an arbitrable issue. But even when an injunction will not be issued, an employer may still recover damages for breach of the no-strike clause through a suit under Section 301. In the *Lucas Flour* case, the Supreme Court upheld a damage award for a strike in violation of the implied no-strike clause.

Section 301 Suits The Supreme Court had held that suits under Section 301 are governed by the appropriate state statutes of limitations, according to *UAW v. Hoosier Cardinal Corp.*[16] More recently, in *DelCostello v. Teamsters*,[17] the Court held that suits under Section 301 by an individual employee against the employer for breach of the collective agreement and against the union for breach of the duty of fair representation were subject to the six-month limitation period under Section 10(b) of the NLRA.

Section 301, while allowing damage suits for breach of no-strike clauses, places some limitations upon such suits. Section 301(b) specifies that "any money judgment against a labor organization in a district court of the United States shall be enforceable only against the organization as an entity and its assets, and shall not be enforceable against any individual member or his assets." In *Atkinson v. Sinclair Refining Co.*,[18] the Supreme Court held that Section 301 does not authorize damage suits against individual union officials when their union is liable for violating a no-strike clause. In *Complete Auto Transit, Inc. v. Reis*,[19] the Court held that individual employees are not liable for damages from a wildcat strike not

[15] 428 U.S. 397 (1975).

[16] 383 U.S. 696 (1966).

[17] 462 U.S. 151 (1983).

[18] 370 U.S. 238 (1962).

[19] 451 U.S. 401 (1981).

authorized by their union in breach of the collective agreement. If the employer cannot recover damages from the individuals responsible for such a strike, what other steps can the employer take against those individuals?

In *Carbon Fuel Co. v. United Mine Workers*,[20] the Supreme Court held that an international union was not liable for damages resulting from a strike by one of its local unions when the international had neither instigated, authorized, supported, nor encouraged the strike. Why would the employer seek damages from the international when the local had gone on strike?

The result of the *Complete Auto Transit and Carbon Fuel* cases is to deprive the employer of the right to recover damages from either the union or the individual union members when a strike by the individual union members is not authorized by the union. The remedy of damages is available to the employer only when the union has called or authorized the strike in breach of the collective agreement.

When the employer can pursue arbitration over the union violation of the agreement, the court will stay a suit for damages pending arbitration according to the Supreme Court decision in *Drake Bakeries Inc. v. Bakery Workers Local 50*.[21] The employer's obligation to arbitrate such disputes continues despite the union's breach of its contractual obligations, according to *Packinghouse Workers Local 721 v. Needham Packing Co.*[22]

Section 301 and Other Remedies Can a court hear a suit alleging a breach of contract under Section 301 even though the contract is silent about judicial remedies? In *Groves v. Ring Screw Works*,[23] the collective agreement provided for arbitration in discharge cases only upon agreement of both parties. It also provided that if a grievance was not resolved through the grievance procedure, the union could go on strike over the issue. Two employees who were discharged by the employer filed suit for wrongful discharge in state court; their union joined the suits as a plaintiff. The employer argued that the union could not file suit because the contract did not require arbitration. The Supreme Court reversed the court of appeals. The Court unanimously held that a contract giving the union the right to strike or the employer the right to lock out does not automatically strip federal courts of the authority to resolve contractual disputes. The union was not precluded from filing suit against the employer to enforce the contract, even though the contract was silent about judicial remedies.

Section 301 Preemption of Other Remedies In *Allis-Chalmers Corp. v. Leuck*,[24] the Supreme Court held that if the resolution of a state law claim depends on the interpretation of a collective agreement, the application of the state law is preempted by federal law. A suit under state law alleging bad-faith handling of a disability benefits claim was preempted by Section 301 because the collective agreement set out provisions for handling disability claims. In *I.B.E.W. v. Hechler*,[25] the Supreme Court held that an employee's tort suit against the union for failure to provide a safe place to work was precluded by Section 301 because her claim was "nothing more than a breach of the union's federal duty of fair representation." However, where state law

[20]444 U.S. 212 (1979).

[21]370 U.S. 254 (1962).

[22]376 U.S. 247 (1964).

[23]498 U.S. 168 (1990).

[24]471 U.S. 202 (1985).

[25]481 U.S. 851 (1987).

remedies exist independently of any collective agreement and do not require interpretation of the agreement, the state law remedy is not preempted. In *Lingle v. Norge Division of Magic Chef, Inc.*,[26] the Supreme Court held that an employee who was discharged for filing a workers' compensation claim could file suit under state law for compensation and punitive damages. Her suit was not preempted by Section 301.

California law requires that employers pay discharged employees all wages owed to them immediately at the time of the discharge. The California State commissioner of labor interpreted that law as not applying to employees covered by a collective agreement containing an arbitration clause. In *Livadas v. Bradshaw*,[27] the U.S. Supreme Court held that the commissioner's interpretation was preempted by Section 301 because it denied employees benefits for engaging in activity—pursuing arbitration and other remedies under the collective agreement—protected under federal labor law.

The NLRB and Arbitration

As the preceding cases have demonstrated, the courts favor the policy of voluntary resolution of disputes between labor and management. The courts will therefore refrain from deciding issues that are subject to arbitration, instead deferring to the arbitrator's resolution of such issues. If a grievance under an agreement involves conduct that may also be an unfair labor practice under the NLRA, what is the role of the National Labor Relations Board (NLRB)? Should the Board, like the courts, defer to arbitration? Or should the Board decide the issue to ensure that the parties' statutory rights are protected? The following case applies to these issues.

case 17.3 »

UNITED TECHNOLOGIES
268 NLRB No. 83 (NLRB, 1984)

Facts: The union alleged that the employer, United Technologies, violated Section 8(a)(1) by threatening an employee, Sherfield, with disciplinary action if she persisted in processing a grievance to the second step. At the hearing before an NLRB ALJ, the employer denied that it had violated Section 8(a)(1) and argued that, because the dispute fell under the grievance arbitration provisions of the collective bargaining agreement, it should be submitted to arbitration rather than be resolved by the NLRB. The employer urged the Board to defer the exercise of its unfair labor practice jurisdiction to the grievance arbitration under the collective agreement. The ALJ, relying on *General American Transportation Corp.*, rejected the employer's arguments because the employer's conduct constituted an alleged violation of Section 8(a)(1). The employer then sought review of the ALJ's decision before the NLRB.

Issue: When should the NLRB defer to arbitration under the relevant collective agreement rather than proceed under the unfair labor practice procedures under the NLRA?

Decision: The NLRB noted that arbitration had gained widespread acceptance as a means of resolving labor disputes and occupies a firmly established place in federal labor policy. The preference for arbitration recognizes that the parties to a collective bargaining agreement are in the best position to resolve, with the help of a neutral third party if necessary, disputes concerning the correct interpretation of their contract. In line with recognition, courts and administrative agencies have developed the concept of deference to the arbitration process so that courts support, rather than interfere with, the arbitration process. The NLRB has played a key role in supporting arbitration.

[26] 486 U.S. 399 (1988).

[27] 512 U.S. 107 (1994).

The NLRB first expressed that position in *Collyer Insulated Wire*, where the NLRB dismissed a complaint alleging unilateral changes in wages and working conditions in violation of Section 8(a)(5) in deference to the parties' grievance-arbitration machinery. The *Collyer* majority articulated several factors favoring deferral:

- the dispute arose within the confines of a long and productive collective bargaining relationship;
- there was no claim of employer animosity to the employees' exercise of protected rights;
- the parties' contract provided for arbitration in a very broad range of disputes;
- the arbitration clause clearly encompassed the dispute at issue;
- the employer had asserted its willingness to utilize arbitration to resolve the dispute; and
- the dispute was eminently well suited to resolution by arbitration.

In these circumstances, deferral to the arbitration process gives full effect to the parties' agreement to submit disputes to arbitration. The *Collyer* deferral policy was holding the parties to their agreement to arbitrate by directing them to avoid substituting the NLRB's processes for that under their collective agreement.

In *National Radio*, the NLRB extended its deferral policy under *Collyer* to cases involving allegations of violations of Section 8(a)(3). Following *National Radio*, the NLRB routinely dismissed complaints alleging violations of Section 8(a)(3) and (1) in deference to arbitration. However, in *General American Transportation*, the NLRB later changed its position and adopted a different standard for deferral to arbitration, declining to defer cases alleging violations of Sections 8(a)(1) and (3) and 8(b)(1)(A) and (2).

The current NLRB majority decided to again adopt the *Collyer* standards for deferral and to reject the position of *General American Transportation*. The NLRB held that the dispute in this case was well suited for deferral: it centered on an allegedly threatening statement made by a foreman to an employee and a shop steward during a first-step grievance meeting. The statement is alleged to be a violation of Section 8 (a)(1), but it is also clearly subject to the broad grievance-arbitration provision of the collective bargaining agreement, and the employer has expressed its willingness to arbitrate the dispute. The NLRB therefore decided to defer the dispute to the arbitration under the collective agreement rather than proceed with the unfair labor practice proceedings.

«

When the Board has deferred an unfair labor practice charge to arbitration, should the Board automatically uphold the arbitrator's decision? This question is addressed in the following case.

case 17.4 »

Olin Corp.

268 NLRB No. 86 (NLRB, 1984)

Facts: Olin Corp. and the union representing Olin's production and maintenance employees were parties to a collective bargaining agreement that contained the following provision:

> Article XIV—Strikes and Lockouts During the life of the Agreement, the Company will not conduct a lockout at the Plant and neither the Local Union nor the International Union, nor any officer or representative of either, will cause or permit its members to cause any strike, slowdown or stoppage (total or partial) of work or any interference, directly or indirectly, with the full operation of the plant.

On December 17, 1980 the company suspended two pipefitters for refusing to perform a job that they felt was more appropriately work that should have been done by millwrights. In response to the suspension, the union staged a "sick out" during which approximately 43 employees left work that day with medical excuses. Olin gave formal written reprimands to 39 of the employees who had engaged in the sick out. In a letter dated December 29, Olin notified union president Spatorico that he was discharged based on his entire record and in particular for threatening the sick out, participating in the sick out, and failing to prevent it. The union filed a grievance over Spatorico's discharge, and the grievance was taken to arbitration.

The arbitrator found that a sick out had occurred at Olin's facility, that Spatorico "at least partially caused or participated" in it, and that he failed to try to stop it until after it had occurred. The arbitrator concluded that Spatorico's conduct contravened his obligation under article XIV of the collective bargaining agreement, and stated, "Union officers implicitly have an affirmative duty not to cause strikes which are in violation of the clause, not to participate in such strikes and to try to stop them when they occur." The arbitrator upheld the discharge.

As part of the grievance, the union complained that the discharge was an unfair labor practice in violation of Sections 8(a)(1) and 8(a)(3). Noting that the unfair labor practice charges had been referred to arbitration, the arbitrator found "no evidence that the company discharged the grievant for his legitimate Union activities." The union filed unfair labor practice charges with the NLRB.

The ALJ refused to defer to the arbitration award, on the grounds that the arbitrator did not consider the unfair labor practice charges "in any serious way." The ALJ determined that the arbitrator was not competent to decide the unfair labor practice issue because the arbitration award was limited to interpretation of the contract. The ALJ also determined that the arbitrator did not explicitly refer to the statutory right and the waiver questions raised by the unfair labor practice charge. On the merits of the case, however, the ALJ agreed with the arbitrator's conclusion, holding that Spatorico's "participation in the strike was inconsistent with his contractual obligation to attempt to stop the illegal strike. The judge concluded that article XIV of the collective bargaining agreement was sufficiently clear and therefore, "Spatorico exposed himself to the greater liability" and that Olin did not violate Section 8(a)(3) and (1) by discharging him while merely reprimanding other employees. The union sought NLRB review of the ALJ decision.

Issue: Should the NLRB defer to the arbitrator's decision and refuse to hear the unfair labor practice charges filed by the union?

Decision: The NLRB agreed with the ALJ that the union's unfair labor practice complaint should be dismissed. However, the NLRB did not rule on the merits of the unfair labor practice complaint because it would defer to the arbitrator's award, in accord with the legal rules set out in the NLRB decision in *Spielberg Mfg. Co.* In that decision, the NLRB held that it would defer to an arbitration award where:

- the proceedings appear to have been fair and regular;
- all parties have agreed to be bound by the arbitration; and
- the decision of the arbitrator is not clearly repugnant to the purposes and policies of the Act.

The NLRB decision in *Raytheon Co.* added the further condition that the arbitrator considered the merits of the unfair labor practice issue. The NLRB stated that national labor policy strongly favors the voluntary arbitration of disputes.

In light of the prior NLRB decisions, and the federal labor policy favoring arbitration, the NLRB adopted the following conditions for deferral to arbitration awards. The NLRB would find that an arbitrator has adequately considered the unfair labor practice if:

- the contractual issue being arbitrated is factually parallel to the unfair labor practice issue; and
- the arbitrator was presented generally with the facts relevant to resolving the unfair labor practice.

Any differences that may exist between the contractual and statutory standards of review should be considered by the NLRB as part of its determination under the *Spielberg* standards of whether an award is "clearly repugnant" to the act. In determining whether the arbitration award was "clearly repugnant" to the purposes and policies of the NLRA, the NLRB stated that it would not require that the arbitrator's award to be totally consistent with Board precedent. The NLRB will defer to the arbitration award unless the award is "palpably wrong,"—that is, unless the arbitrator's decision is not susceptible to an interpretation consistent with the act. The party seeking to have the NLRB refuse to defer, and instead to consider the merits of the case, has the burden of showing that the standards for deferral have not been met. That means that the party seeking to have the NLRB ignore the determination of the arbitrator has the burden of affirmatively demonstrating the defects in the arbitral process or award. As to the present case, the NLRB held that the arbitration proceeding here has met the standards for deferral, and that the arbitrator adequately considered the unfair labor practice issue.

Several courts of appeals have rejected the NLRB's broad deferral policy under *United Technologies* and *Olin*. In *Taylor v. NLRB*,[28] the court stated that the Board's deferral policy inappropriately divests the Board of its unfair labor practice jurisdiction under Section 10(b) of the NLRA. The court held that the policy of presuming every arbitration proceeding addresses every possible unfair labor practice issue overlooks situations when the contractual and statutory issues may be factually parallel but involve differing elements of proof or questions of factual relevance. In *Hammondtree v. NLRB*,[29] the court held that an employee may not be forced to give up the right to have the Board adjudicate an unfair labor practice claim simply because the employer and union have established parallel contractual provisions and procedures for resolving the claim. Only where the employee waives unfair labor practice rights or the claim rests on otherwise arbitrable matters may the Board defer to arbitration.

Concept *Summary* » 17.3

The NLRB and Arbitration

- The NLRB will refer a dispute to arbitration when:
  - the dispute arose within the confines of a long and productive collective bargaining relationship;
  - there was no claim of employer animosity to the employees' exercise of protected rights;
  - the parties' contract provided for arbitration in a very broad range of disputes;
  - the arbitration clause clearly encompassed the dispute at issue;
  - the employer had asserted its willingness to utilize arbitration to resolve the dispute; and
  - the dispute was eminently well suited to resolution by arbitration
- The NLRB will enforce defer to an arbitration award when:
  - the proceedings appear to have been fair and regular;
  - all parties have agreed to be bound by the arbitration;
  - the decision of the arbitrator is not clearly repugnant to the purposes and policies of the Act;
  - the arbitrator considered the merits of the unfair labor practice issue:
    - the contractual issue arbitrated was factually parallel to the unfair labor practice issue; and
    - the arbitrator was presented generally with the facts relevant to resolving the unfair labor practice

---

[28] 786 F.2d 1516 (11th Cir. 1986).

[29] 894 F.2d 438 (D.C. Cir. 1990).

Changes in the Status of Employers

Successor Employers

When a new employer takes over a unionized firm, what is the obligation of the successor employer to recognize the union, to adhere to the collective agreement, and to arbitrate grievances that arose under the collective agreement?

In *John Wiley & Sons, Inc. v. Livingston,*[30] the Supreme Court held that the successor employer must arbitrate a grievance arising under the collective agreement where there was a "substantial continuity of identity in the business enterprise" and the employer retained a majority of the employees from the former unionized work force. The union in Wiley sought only to force the new employer to arbitrate; it did not seek to force the employer to bargain with it. In *NLRB v. Burns International Security Services, Inc.*,[31] the Supreme Court dealt with a case where the union sought to force the new employer to recognize the union and to abide by the collective agreement. The Supreme Court held that the successor employer was not bound by the prior collective agreement but was required to recognize and bargain with the union because it had retained enough employees from the prior, unionized work force to constitute a majority of the new employer's work force.

What factors should be considered when determining whether a "substantial continuity of identity" of the operation exists, and at what point in the hiring process does the presence of a union's supporters constituting a majority of the work force trigger the duty to bargain with the union? The Supreme Court addressed these issues in the following case.

case 17.5 »

Fall River Dyeing & Finishing Corp. v. NLRB

482 U.S. 27 (1987)

Blackmun, J.

... For over 30 years before 1982, Sterlingwale operated a textile dyeing and finishing plant in Fall River, Massachusetts. Its business consisted basically of two types of dyeing, called, respectively, "converting" and "commission." Under the converting process, which in 1981 accounted for 60 to 70 percent of its business, Sterlingwale bought unfinished fabrics for its own account, dyed and finished them, and then sold them to apparel manufacturers. In commission dyeing, which accounted for the remainder of its business, Sterlingwale dyed and finished fabrics owned by customers according to their specifications. The financing and marketing aspects of converting and commission dyeing are different. Converting requires capital to purchase fabrics and a sales force to promote the finished products. The production process, however, is the same for both converting and commission dyeing.

In the late 1970s the textile-dyeing business, including Sterlingwale's, began to suffer from adverse economic conditions and foreign competition. After 1979, business at Sterlingwale took a serious turn for the worse because of the loss of its export market, and the company reduced the number of its employees. Finally, in February 1982, Sterlingwale laid off all its production employees, primarily because it no longer had the capital to continue the converting business. It retained a skeleton crew of workers and supervisors to ship out the goods remaining on order and to maintain the corporation's building and machinery. In the months following

[30]376 U.S. 543 (1964).

[31]406 U.S. 272 (1972).

the layoff, Leonard Ansin, Sterlingwale's president, liquidated the inventory of the corporation and, at the same time, looked for a business partner with whom he could "resurrect the business." …

For almost as long as Sterlingwale had been in existence, its production and maintenance employees had been represented by the United Textile Workers of America, AFL-CIO, Local 292 (Union).

In late summer 1982, however, Sterlingwale finally went out of business. It made an assignment for the benefit of its creditors [who held] … a first mortgage on most of Sterlingwale's real property and … a security interest on Sterlingwale's machinery and equipment….

During this same period, a former Sterlingwale employee and officer, Herbert Chace, and Arthur Friedman, president of one of Sterlingwale's major customers … formed petitioner Fall River Dyeing & Finishing Corp. Chace, who had resigned from Sterlingwale in February 1982, had worked there for 27 years, had been vice-president in charge of sales at the time of his departure, and had participated in collective bargaining with the Union during his tenure at Sterlingwale. Chace and Friedman formed petitioner with the intention of engaging strictly in the commission-dyeing business and of taking advantage of the availability of Sterlingwale's assets and workforce. Accordingly, Friedman [acquired] … Sterlingwale's plant, real property, and equipment, and [sold] them to petitioner. Petitioner also obtained some of Sterlingwale's remaining inventory at the liquidator's auction. Chace became petitioner's vice-president in charge of operations and Friedman became its president. In September 1982, petitioner began operating out of Sterlingwale's former facilities and began hiring employees…. Petitioner's initial hiring goal was to attain one full shift of workers, which meant from 55 to 60 employees. Petitioner planned to "see how business would be" after this initial goal had been met and, if business permitted, to expand to two shifts. The employees who were hired first spent approximately four to six weeks in start-up operations and an additional month in experimental production.

By letter dated October 19, 1982, the Union requested petitioner to recognize it as the bargaining agent for petitioner's employees and to begin collective bargaining. Petitioner refused the request, stating that, in its view, the request had "no legal basis." At that time, 18 of petitioner's 21 employees were former employees of Sterlingwale. By November of that year, petitioner had employees in a complete range of jobs, had its production process in operation, and was handling customer orders; by mid-January 1983, it had attained its initial goal of one shift of workers. Of the 55 workers in this initial shift, a number that represented over half the workers petitioner would eventually hire, 36 were former Sterlingwale employees. Petitioner continued to expand its workforce, and by mid-April 1983 it had reached two full shifts. For the first time, ex-Sterlingwale employees were in the minority but just barely so (52 or 53 out of 107 employees).

Although petitioner engaged exclusively in commission dyeing, the employees experienced the same conditions they had when they were working for Sterlingwale. The production process was unchanged and the employees worked on the same machines, in the same building, with the same job classifications, under virtually the same supervisors. Over half the volume of petitioner's business came from former Sterlingwale customers, …

On November 1, 1982, the Union filed an unfair labor practice charge with the Board, alleging that in its refusal to bargain petitioner had violated Section 8(a)(1) and (5) of the National Labor Relations Act. After a hearing, the Administrative Law Judge (ALJ) decided that, on the facts of the case, petitioner was a successor to Sterlingwale…. Thus, in the view of the ALJ, petitioner's duty to bargain rose in mid-January because former Sterlingwale employees then were in the majority and because the Union's October demand was still in effect. Petitioner thus committed an unfair labor practice in refusing to bargain. In a brief decision and order, the Board, with one member dissenting, affirmed this decision. The Court of Appeals for the First Circuit, also by a divided vote, enforced the order….

… [I]n *NLRB v. Burns International Security Services, Inc.*, this Court first dealt with the issue of a successor employer's obligation to bargain with a union that had represented the employees of its predecessor…. These presumptions [of majority support developed in Burns are based not so much on an absolute certainty that the union's majority status will not erode following certification, as on a particular policy decision. The overriding policy of the NLRA is "industrial peace." The presumptions of majority support further this policy by "promot[ing] stability in collective-bargaining relationships, without impairing the free choice of employees." In essence, they enable a union to concentrate on obtaining and fairly administering a collective-bargaining agreement without worrying that, unless it produces immediate results, it will lose majority support and will be decertified…. The presumptions also remove any temptation on the part of the employer to avoid good-faith bargaining in the hope that, by delaying, it will undermine the union's support among the employees….

The rationale behind the presumptions is particularly pertinent in the successorship situation and so it is understandable that the Court in Burns referred to them. During a transition between employers, a union is in a peculiarly vulnerable position. It has no formal and established bargaining relationship with the new employer, is uncertain about the new employer's plans, and cannot be sure if or when the new employer must bargain with it. While being concerned with the future of its members with the new employer, the union also must protect whatever rights still exist for its members under the collective bargaining agreement with the predecessor employer. Accordingly, during this unsettling transition period, the union needs the presumptions of majority status to which it is entitled to safeguard its members' rights and to develop a relationship with the successor.

The position of the employees also supports the application of the presumptions in the successorship situation. If the employees find themselves in a new enterprise that substantially resembles the old, but without their chosen bargaining representative, they may well feel that their choice of a union is subject to the vagaries of an enterprise's transformation.... Without the presumptions of majority support and with the wide variety of corporate transformations possible, an employer could use a successor enterprise as a way of getting rid of a labor contract and of exploiting the employees' hesitant attitude towards the union to eliminate its continuing presence.

In addition to recognizing the traditional presumptions of union majority status, however, the Court in Burns was careful to safeguard "the rightful prerogative of owners independently to rearrange their businesses." If the new employer makes a conscious decision to maintain generally the same business and to hire a majority of its employees from the predecessor, then the bargaining obligation of Section 8(a)(5) is activated. This makes sense when one considers that the employer intends to take advantage of the trained workforce of its predecessor....

We now hold that a successor's obligation to bargain is not limited to a situation where the union in question has been recently certified. Where, as here, the union has a rebuttable presumption of majority status, this status continues despite the change in employers. And the new employer has an obligation to bargain with that union so long as the new employer is in fact a successor of the old employer and the majority of its employees were employed by its predecessor.

We turn now to the three rules, as well as to their application to the facts of this case, that the Board has adopted for the successorship situation.

In Burns we approved the approach taken by the Board and accepted by courts with respect to determining whether a new company was indeed the successor to the old. This approach, which is primarily factual in nature and is based upon the totality of the circumstances of a given situation, requires that the Board focus on whether the new company has "acquired substantial assets of its predecessor and continued, without interruption or substantial change the predecessor's business operations." Hence, the focus is on whether there is "substantial continuity" between the enterprises. Under this approach, the Board examines a number of factors: whether the business of both employers is essentially the same; whether the employees of the new company are doing the same jobs in the same working conditions under the same supervisors; and whether the new entity has the same production process, produces the same products, and basically has the same body of customers.... In conducting the analysis, the Board keeps in mind the question whether "those employees who have been retained will understandably view their job situations as essentially unaltered." ...

[W]e find that the Board's determination that there was "substantial continuity" between Sterlingwale and petitioner and that petitioner was Sterlingwale's successor is supported by substantial evidence in the record. Petitioner acquired most of Sterlingwale's real property, its machinery and equipment, and much of its inventory and materials. It introduced no new product line. Of particular significance is the fact that, from the perspective of the employees, their jobs did not change. Although petitioner abandoned converting dyeing in exclusive favor of commission dyeing, this change did not alter the essential nature of the employees' jobs because both types of dyeing involved the same production process. The job classifications of petitioner were the same as those of Sterlingwale; petitioner's employees worked on the same machines under the direction of supervisors most of whom were former supervisors of Sterlingwale. The record, in fact, is clear that petitioner acquired Sterlingwale's assets with the express purpose of taking advantage of its predecessor's workforce....

For the reasons given above, this is a case where the other factors suggest "substantial continuity" between the companies despite the 7-month hiatus. Here, moreover, the extent of the hiatus between the demise of Sterlingwale and the start-up of petitioner is somewhat less than certain. After the February layoff, Sterlingwale retained a skeleton crew of supervisors and employees that continued to ship goods to customers and to maintain the plant. In addition, until the assignment for the benefit of the creditors late in the summer, Ansin was seeking to resurrect the business or to find a buyer for Sterlingwale. The Union was aware of these efforts. Viewed from the employees' perspective, therefore, the hiatus may have been much less than seven months. Although petitioner hired the employees through advertisements, it often relied on recommendations from supervisors, themselves formerly employed by Sterlingwale, and intended the advertisements to reach the former Sterlingwale workforce. Accordingly, we hold that, under settled law, petitioner was a successor to Sterlingwale. We thus must consider if and when petitioner's duty to bargain arose.

In *Burns*, the Court determined that the successor had an obligation to bargain with the union because a majority of its employees had been employed by Wackenhut. The "triggering" fact for the bargaining obligation was this composition of the successor's workforce. The Court, however, did not have to consider the question when the successor's obligation to bargain arose: Wackenhut's contract expired on June 30 and Burns began its services with a majority of former Wackenhut guards on July 1. In other situations, as in the present case, there is a start-up period by the new employer while it gradually builds its operations and hires employees. In these situations, the Board, with the approval of the Courts of Appeals, has adopted the "substantial and representative complement" rule for fixing the moment when the determination as to the composition of the successor's workforce is to be made. If, at this particular moment, a majority of the successor's employees had been employed by its predecessor, then the successor has an obligation to bargain with the union that represented these employees. In deciding when a "substantial and representative complement" exists in a particular employer transition, the Board examines a number of factors. It studies "whether the job classifications designated for the operation were filled or substantially filled and whether the operation was in normal or substantially normal production." In addition, it takes into consideration "the size of the complement on that date and the time expected to elapse before a substantially larger complement would be at work … as well as the relative certainty of the employer's expected expansion." …

We conclude … that in this situation the successor is in the best position to follow a rule the criteria of which are straightforward. The employer generally will know with tolerable certainty when all its job classifications have been filled or substantially filled, when it has hired a majority of the employees it intends to hire, and when it has begun normal production. Moreover, the "full complement" standard advocated by petitioner is not necessarily easier for a successor to apply than is the "substantial and representative complement." In fact, given the expansionist dreams of many new entrepreneurs, it might well be more difficult for a successor to identify the moment when the "full complement" has been attained, which is when the business will reach the limits of the new employer's initial hopes, than it would be for this same employer to acknowledge the time when its business has begun normal production—the moment identified by the "substantial and representative complement" rule. We therefore hold that the Board's "substantial and representative complement" rule is reasonable in the successorship context. Moreover, its application to the facts of this case is supported by substantial record evidence. The Court of Appeals observed that by mid-January petitioner "had hired employees in virtually all job classifications, had hired at least fifty percent of those it would ultimately employ in the majority of those classifications, and it employed a majority of the employees it would eventually employ when it reached full complement." At that time petitioner had begun normal production. Although petitioner intended to expand to two shifts, and, in fact, reached this goal by mid-April, that expansion was contingent expressly upon the growth of the business. Accordingly, as found by the Board and approved by the Court of Appeals, mid-January was the period when petitioner reached its "substantial and representative complement." Because at that time the majority of petitioner's employees were former Sterlingwale employees, petitioner had an obligation to bargain with the Union then.

We also hold that the Board's "continuing demand" rule is reasonable in the successorship situation. The successor's duty to bargain at the "substantial and representative complement" date is triggered only when the union has made a bargaining demand. Under the "continuing demand" rule, when a union has made a premature demand that has been rejected by the employer, this demand remains in force until the moment when the employer attains the "substantial and representative complement."

Such a rule, particularly when considered along with the "substantial and representative complement" rule, places a minimal burden on the successor and makes sense in light of the union's position. Once the employer has concluded that it has reached the appropriate complement, then, in order to determine whether its duty to bargain will be triggered, it has only to see whether the union already has made a demand for bargaining. Because the union has no established relationship with the successor and because it is unaware of the successor's plans for its operations and hiring, it is likely that, in many cases, a union's bargaining demand will be premature. It makes no sense to require the union repeatedly to renew its bargaining demand in the hope of having it correspond with the "substantial and representative complement" date, when, with little trouble, the employer can regard a previous demand as a continuing one.

The reasonableness of the "continuing demand" rule is demonstrated by the facts of this case. Although the Union had asked Ansin to inform it about his plans for Sterlingwale so that it could become involved in the employer transition, the Union learned about this transition only after it had become a *fait accompli*. Without having any established relationship with petitioner, it therefore is not surprising that the Union's October bargaining demand was premature. The Union, however, made clear after this demand that, in its view, petitioner had a bargaining obligation: the Union filed an unfair labor practice in November. Petitioner responded by denying that it had any duty to bargain. Rather than being a successor confused about when a bargaining obligation might arise, petitioner took an initial position—and stuck with it—that it never would have any bargaining obligation with the Union.

The judgment of the Court of Appeals is affirmed.

It is so ordered.

Case Questions

1. What is the NLRB's "substantial and representative complement" rule? How does it apply to the facts in this case? Explain.
2. What factors does the NLRB consider when determining if there is a "substantial continuity" of operation between the former employer and a successor employer? How do those factors apply to the facts here?
3. What is the NLRB's "continuing demand" rule? How does it apply to the facts in this case? Explain.

Following *Fall River Dyeing*, a court held that an employer who assumed operation of a steel mill that had been closed for two years and that had drastically reduced the number of employees and restructured job classifications was not a successor employer because of the lack of a substantial continuity of operation with the former employer, according to *CitiSteel USA v. NLRB*.[32] However, a two-year hiatus in operations did not preclude the NLRB from holding that the new employer was a successor in *Pennsylvania Transformer Technology, Inc. v. NLRB*.[33]

An employer that intends to rehire most of the employees from the predecessor firm may lawfully recognize the union that represented the previous firm's workers, and negotiate with the union over the terms upon which it will hire those workers, according to *Road & Rail Services., Inc.*[34] Where a successor employer has rehired most of the employees from the previous employer, it is a violation of Section 8(a)(5) for the successor employer to unilaterally change the terms of employment for the individuals it hires from the previous employer, as held by *Rosedev Hospitality, Secaucus LP*.[35] A successor employer who discriminatorily refuses to rehire the unionized employees from the prior firm violates Section 8(a)(3), according to *Planned Bldg. Servs. Inc.*[36]

[32] 53 F.3d 350 (D.C. Cir. 1995).

[33] 254 F.3d 217 (2001).

[34] 348 NLRB No. 77 (2006).

[35] 349 NLRB 202 (2007).

[36] 347 NLRB 670 (2006).

ethical DILEMMA

To Retain or Not to Retain?

Immense Multinational Business (IMB) is planning to purchase the entire plant, assets, and operation of CastCo, a small manufacturing company. The employees at CastCo are represented by the International Molders Union, but IMB's employees are not unionized. IMB plans to maintain most of the operations at CastCo and is considering whether to retain the former CastCo employees as well. What are the benefits of retaining the former CastCo production workers? Are there any arguments against retaining the CastCo workers? Are there any legal restrictions on the decision whether to retain the CastCo workers? How should IMB proceed here?

You, the recently promoted director of human resources for IMB's manufacturing operations, are asked by the CEO to prepare a memo discussing these issues and recommending a course of action. Be sure to support your recommendation.

In *Trafford Dist. Center v. NLRB*,[37] where a company formed after a bankrupt employer surrendered its assets was determined by the NLRB to be an "alter ego" of the original employer, the successor firm was held to violate Sections 8(a)(1) and 8(a)(5) when it refused to honor the terms of the union's collective agreement with the predecessor employer.

A successor employer can be held liable for the remedy of an unfair labor practice committed by the old employer. In *NLRB v. Winco Petroleum*,[38] a successor was held subject to a bargaining order remedy even though the successor itself was not guilty of a refusal to bargain.

The incumbent union in a successorship situation is entitled to a rebuttable presumption of continuing majority status, but that presumption does not preclude a petition for a representation or decertification election or an otherwise valid challenge to the union's majority status, according to *MV Transportation*.[39]

Bankruptcy and the Collective Agreement

The prior cases dealt with the obligations of successor employers. When an employer experiencing financial difficulties seeks protection from creditors under the bankruptcy laws, can the employer also reject the collective agreement?

When a corporation files a petition for the protection of the bankruptcy laws, the financial obligations of the corporation are suspended pending the resolution of the issue by the bankruptcy courts. What happens when a unionized employer files a petition for bankruptcy? Is the employer required to adhere to the terms and conditions of the collective agreement? In the case of *NLRB v. Bildisco & Bildisco*,[40] the Supreme Court held that an employer who

---

[37] 478 F.3d 172 (3d Cir. 2007).

[38] 668 F.2d 973 (8th Cir. 1982).

[39] 337 NLRB 770 (2002).

[40] 465 U.S. 513 (1984).

files for reorganization under Chapter 11 of the Bankruptcy Act does not violate Section 8(a)5 by unilaterally changing the terms of the collective agreement after filing the bankruptcy petition. The Court also held that the bankruptcy court may allow the employer to reject the collective agreement if the court finds that the agreement "burdens the estate" of the employer and if "the equities balance in favor of rejecting the labor contract."

Following the Supreme *Court's Bildisco* decision, Congress amended the Bankruptcy Code to deal with the rejection of a collective agreement. The changes, enacted in Public Law 98-353 (1984), 11 U.S.C. Section 1113, allow the employer petitioning for bankruptcy protection to reject the collective agreement only when the following conditions are met:

1. The employer has made a proposal for contractual modifications, necessary to permit reorganization and treating all interested parties equitably, to the union.
2. The employer must provide the union with such relevant information as is necessary to evaluate the proposal.
3. The employer must offer to "confer in good faith in attempting to reach mutually satisfactory modifications."
4. The bankruptcy court finds that the union has rejected the employer's proposal "without good cause."
5. The court concludes that "the balance of equities clearly favors rejection" of the agreement.

The bankruptcy court is required to hold a hearing on the employer's petition within fourteen days and to issue its determination on the rejection issue within thirty days after the hearing.

The WORKING Law

Reorganizations of GM and Chrysler give UAW a Unique Role as Union and Investor

General Motors and Chrysler both emerged from bankruptcy in the summer of 2009. General Motors and Chrysler had struggled for years in the face of declining sales, increased foreign competition, and soaring retiree healthcare and benefit costs. In 2007, General Motors agreed with the United Auto Workers to transfer the company's healthcare liabilities to a union-run trust (a Voluntary Employee Beneficiary Association, or VEBA) and to reduce wages and benefits for new employees. But the general economic crisis of 2008 and 2009 caused a drastic fall in auto sales, and dried up credit for would-be customers. General Motors lost $80 billion from 2005–2009. In May 2009, the UAW agreed to accept wage and benefit concessions and to eliminate restrictive work rules as part of the reorganization of the company, and also agreed to take General Motors stock in lieu of half of the $20.4 billion that General Motors owed to the VEBA. The union also agreed to similar concessions at Chrysler, and agreed not to go on strike against General Motors or Chrysler until 2015.

As a result of the reorganization in bankruptcy, a new corporation, the Vehicle Acquisitions Holding LLC, was created to assume most of the assets of the former company. This "new General Motors" is owned by the U.S. and Canadian governments and the UAW. The liabilities of the "old General Motors" were retained by General Motors, which will eventually be liquidated under the bankruptcy courts. In return for bailouts from the U.S. Treasury of about $50 billion, the U.S. government received a 60.8 percent ownership stake in "new General Motors," and the Canadian government received 11.7 percent in return for providing $9.5 billion. The UAW-operated VEBA received 17.5 percent, with warrants to purchase an additional 2.5 percent, $6.5 billion worth of preferred stock, and a note for $6.5 billion. The unsecured bondholders received a 10 percent stake in return for having lent the company $27 billion. Challenges to the General Motors by some bondholders to the bankruptcy reorganization were rejected by the Bankruptcy Court of the Southern District of New York in *In re General Motors Corp.*[1]

General Motors offered its workers a buyout and early retirement program in an effort to reduce its workforce. Workers who agreed to retire would be given cash payments of between $20,000 to $115,000, with the largest payouts going to workers with at least twenty years of service who agreed to give up retirement benefits other than pensions. The retiring workers would also receive a voucher worth $25,000 toward the purchase of a new vehicle. As of August 2009, about 6,000 employees had agreed to the buyout, but because that fell short of General Motor's target of shedding nearly 14,000 workers, layoffs may be necessary.

In the case of Chrysler, the shares have been divided as follows:

- The VEBA received 55 percent
- The U.S. government received 10 percent in return for providing a bailout of $25.5 billion
- The Italian automaker Fiat, in return for agreeing to operate the reorganized Chrysler, will receive 20 percent of the shares, which could increase to 35 percent if the new firm reaches certain goals set by the U.S. Treasury

The reorganization agreements of Chrysler and General Motors placed the UAW in an unusual position—acting as a union representing the firms' employees, but also serving as a major investor in the firms. The alternative to the union's acceptance of the reorganization plans would most likely have been liquidation of the firms, which would mean huge job losses.

Some analysts predict that the UAW's new role would make the union more willing to work with management to increase profitability—a higher stock price would provide the VEBA with billions more to cover retiree healthcare costs in the years ahead. But other industry experts feel it will be difficult for the union to give up its traditional focus on preserving jobs for its members rather than increasing profits and share price. The financial future of the union and its members will depend upon the stock performance of Chrysler and General Motors. It remains to be seen whether the UAW would be willing to go on strike against either of the companies, if the strike could affect the price of the shares of stock held by the VEBA to cover the healthcare costs of retirees.

Sources: "The Bankruptcy of General Motors: A Giant Falls," *The Economist*, June 4, 2009; "GM Nears Bankruptcy: Chapter 11 Beckons," *The Economist*, May 21, 2009; "Chrysler and General Motors: End Game," *The Economist*, April 30, 2009; David Kiley, "A Mucky Road

[1] 407 B.R. 463 (Bkrtcy. S.D.N.Y. 2009).

for the UAW," *Business Week*, May 11, 2009; "Rescue Plan Would Give U.S. Most of GM's Stock," The Washington Post, May 27, 2009; Nick Bunkley, "Union Workers at G.M. Ratify Concessions," *The New York Times*, May 30, 2009; Steven Greenhouse, "G.M.'s New Owners, Labor and Government, Adjust to Roles," *The New York Times*, June 2, 2009; Michael J. de la Merced, "Court Ruling Clears Path for New G.M," *The New York Times*, July 6, 2009; Nick Bunkley, "After 6,000 Take Buyouts, G.M. to Lay Off Thousands," *The New York Times*, August 4, 2009.

The provisions of Section 1113 apply to employers under the NLRA and also to employers under the Railway Labor Act, such as railroads and airlines. In addition to the bankruptcy filings of Chrysler and General Motors, fluctuating oil prices and the economic crisis have caused numerous airlines to go through Chapter 11 bankruptcy proceedings, including:

- Aloha Airlines
- ATA Airlines
- Comair
- Delta Air Lines
- Frontier Airlines
- Era Aviation
- Hawaiian Airlines
- Independence Air
- Mesaba Airlines
- Northwest Airlines
- United Airlines
- U.S. Airways

The results have been significant wage and benefit reductions for the labor unions involved. The Northwest pilots agreed to a pay cut of 24 percent over a 5 1/2 year contract. A bankruptcy court approved the imposition of a proposal lowering the Northwest flight attendants' take-home pay by up to 40 percent. The Delta pilots agreed to a new contract with a 14 percent pay cut, in addition to concessions in a 2004 agreement in which Delta's pilots had agreed to a 33 percent wage cut. The following case addresses the question of whether a union rejected the proposals of a bankrupt employer "without good cause" as required under Section 1113 in order for the employer to reject the collective agreement.

case 17.6 » In re Bruno's Supermarkets, LLC

2009 WL 1148369 (Bankr.N.D.Ala. April 27, 2009) Memorandum Opinion

Benjamin Cohen, United States Bankruptcy Judge

The matters before the Court are: (1) the Debtor's Motion to Reject Collective Bargaining Agreements Pursuant to Section 1113, filed March 9, 2009 and (2) the Objection of United Food and Commercial Workers Union Local 1657 to Debtor's Motion to Reject Collective Bargaining Agreements Pursuant to Section 1113.

I. Background

Bruno's began as a family-owned grocery business in 1933. It remained family-owned until 1995 when it was acquired by Kohlberg Kravis Roberts & Co.... [after several sales, it was purchased by] Lone Star Fund V (U.S.), L.P. ("Lone Star Five"), a private equity firm based in Dallas, Texas.

Bruno's and the United Food & Commercial Workers Union Local 1657 have had a relationship since the family-owned days. That relationship continued with the company's three purchasers.

Bruno's and the Union have four current collective bargaining agreements (CBAs) covering employees in various stores.... Each of these CBAs has what is commonly referred to as a "successorship clause." A successorship clause makes the CBA binding on a "successor" employer, that is, a later purchaser. All of Bruno's CBAs with the three non-family owners have included these successorship clauses.... The successorship clause in each of the four current CBAs reads in part:

> In the event that any or part of the assets of the employer are sold to a purchaser as a going concern, the Employer shall require the purchaser as a condition of the sale to recognize the Union, and assume all obligations of the Employer under this Collective Bargaining Agreement as of the sale closing date.

Bruno's filed the current Chapter 11 bankruptcy on February 5, 2009 ... the parties ... agree that ... a sale of all, or a substantial part of, Bruno's stores as an ongoing business is all that will save the company from liquidation.

II. The Parties' Positions

Bruno's position is that no one will purchase all, or a substantial part of, its stores for an ongoing business so long as a sale is conditioned on accepting the CBAs with the successorship clauses. Bruno's argues that not only will no one purchase the stores with an attached Union contract containing a successorship clause, but also that a CBA with a successorship clause would, "absolutely prevent a sale, lead to liquidation, and ultimately result in nearly 4000 lost jobs."

Bruno's contends that the evidence is "uncontroverted" that potential purchasers, "will not purchase with the CBAs in place." ... Bruno's has repeatedly expressed to the UFCW the need for successorship clause removal. Yet the UFCW has, without good cause, refused to remove the clause. Because Bruno's has established all nine requirements for § 1113 relief, the Court should grant Bruno's Motion, keep the sales process alive, and provide employees the opportunity to retain their jobs.... The Union's initial position was that it opposed any modification of the successorship clauses. Since March 13, 2009, its position has been that while it rejects Bruno's proposal to eliminate the successorship clause, it offers for the current successorship clauses to be modified to relieve a buyer from assuming the current CBAs, if the buyer agrees to negotiate with the Union to reach a new agreement with a successorship clause.

The Union summarized its position: ... the relief sought is premature and thus not necessary to the Debtor's reorganization under the appropriate standard inasmuch as a potential purchaser may appear and, consistent with the sale schedule, negotiate an acceptable agreement with the Union. Finally, a consensual labor agreement is necessary to preserve the value of the estate's assets which would be undermined by the threat of a strike should the agreements be rejected. A union's right to strike after a bankruptcy court approves rejection of a collective bargaining agreement is clear, and here the Union reserves its rights to do so absent an acceptable negotiated agreement with a purchaser or purchasers.

III. Applicable Law

Section 1113 of the Bankruptcy Code allows a debtor to reject a collective bargaining agreement under certain conditions. Courts agree that there are nine elements that must be satisfied to meet those section 1113 conditions....

The nine elements a debtor must satisfy before it may reject a CBA are:

1. The debtor in possession must make a proposal to the Union to modify the collective bargaining agreement.
2. The proposal must be based on the most complete and reliable information available at the time of the proposal.
3. The proposed modifications must be necessary to permit the reorganization of the debtor.
4. The proposed modifications must assure that all creditors, the debtor and all of the affected parties are treated fairly and equitably.
5. The debtor must provide to the Union such relevant information as is necessary to evaluate the proposal.
6. Between the time of the making of the proposal and the time of the hearing on approval of the rejection of the existing collective bargaining agreement, the debtor must meet at reasonable times with the Union.
7. At the meetings the debtor must confer in good faith in attempting to reach mutually satisfactory modifications of the collective bargaining agreement.
8. The Union must have refused to accept the proposal without good cause.
9. The balance of the equities must clearly favor rejection of the collective bargaining agreement.

Bruno's bears the burden of proving all of these nine elements by a preponderance of the evidence. If it does not, this Court may not allow it to reject its collective bargaining agreements....

The general issue is: Did Bruno's prove all nine elements by a preponderance of the evidence? The dispositive issue is: Did the Union have good cause to refuse Bruno's proposal to remove the successorship clauses from the four current collective bargaining agreements?

V. Additional Findings of Fact

The core dispute between Bruno's and the Union is whether anyone will purchase Bruno's assets as a going business if that purchase includes the successorship clauses in the parties' four current collective bargaining agreements.

Bruno's contends that no one will unless those clauses are removed or the CBAs are rejected outright. Bruno's argues that if neither occurs, no one will purchase the property as an ongoing business.

The Union disagrees but does not insist that a buyer assume the current contracts. As an alternative, it offers that a buyer agree to negotiate with the Union and enter into a new agreement with a new successorship clause....

Again, this Court must ask, if there will be bidders at an auction even if the CBAs are in force, or there will be buyers who are "willing to negotiate and willing to participate in the development of a collective bargaining agreement ...," how many would there be if the potential buyers knew that the buyer would not be required to assume the current CBAs but instead could negotiate a new agreement with the Union?

... As discussed earlier, Bruno's must prove all of the nine elements listed above. If it fails on any one, the Court may not approve its request to reject the collective bargaining agreements. As discussed in detail below, the Court finds that Bruno's did not prove element number eight. Therefore, Bruno's did not prove all nine elements, and the Court may not approve Bruno's request to reject the current CBAs.

Element number eight is, "The Union must have refused to accept the proposal without good cause." The immediate question is: What is "good cause?"

B. Good Cause

One of the most often cited opinions defining "good cause" is *New York Typographical Union No. 6 v. Maxwell Newspapers, Inc. (In re Maxwell Newspapers, Inc.)*, 981 F.2d 85 (2nd Cir. 1992).... [in that case] Judge Richard J. Cardamone explained:

> What "good cause" means is difficult to answer in the abstract apart from the moorings of a given case. A more constructive and perhaps more answerable inquiry is why this term is in the statute. We think good cause serves as an incentive to the debtor trying to have its labor contract modified to propose in good faith only those changes necessary to its successful reorganization, while protecting it from the union's refusal to accept the changes without a good reason.
>
> To that end, the entire thrust of § 1113 is to ensure that well-informed and good faith negotiations occur in the market place, not as part of the judicial process. Reorganization procedures are designed to encourage such a negotiated voluntary modification. Knowing that it cannot turn down an employer's proposal without good cause gives the union an incentive to compromise on modifications of the collective bargaining agreement, so as to prevent its complete rejection. Because the employer has the burden of proving its proposals are necessary, the union is protected from an employer whose proposals may be offered in bad faith.
>
> Thus, for example, a union will not have good cause to reject an employer's proposal that contains only those modifications essential for the debtor's reorganization, that is, the union's refusal to accept it will be held to be without good cause. On the other hand, as we have noted, where the union makes compromise proposals during the negotiating process that meet its needs while preserving the debtor's savings, its rejection of the debtor's proposal would be with good cause.

In re Northwest Airlines Corp., 346 B.R. 307 (Bankr. S.D.N.Y. Jun 29, 2006) includes a good general definition of "good cause" and explains the relationship of the "good cause" concept to section 1113. It reads:

> After the requirements of § 1113(b) are met, § 1113(c)(2) conditions the rejection of a collective bargaining agreement on a union's refusal to accept a debtor's proposal "without good cause." Although "good cause" is not defined in the Bankruptcy Code, it is closely related to the requirements of § 1113(b)(1) described above, as well as the requirement under § 1113(b)(2) that the parties negotiate in good faith.
>
> In terms of § 1113, the burden on the parties to negotiate is best analyzed under § 1113(c)(2), which permits rejection of the agreement only if the union has rejected the debtor's proposal without good cause. If the union seeks to negotiate compromises that meet its needs while preserving the debtor's required savings, it would be unlikely that its rejection of the proposal could be found to be lacking good cause. If, on the other hand, the union refuses to compromise, it is as unlikely it could be found to have acted with good cause.

The court added:

> Once a debtor establishes that its proposal is necessary, fair and in good faith, the union must produce sufficient evidence to justify its refusal to accept the debtor's proposal. If a union demands provisions that are not economically feasible and offers no alternatives that would permit the debtor to reorganize, the court will find that the union acted without good cause ...

C. Application of the "Good Cause" Standards

Applying these legal standards to the evidence, the Court finds that the Union had "good cause" to reject Bruno's proposal that the successorship clauses should be removed from the four current CBAs.

After the parties exchanged and discussed different proposals, their final positions were these. Bruno's position was that the successorship clauses should be eliminated. The Union's position was that the successorship clauses should remain. The parties were completely at odds. They were at an impasse. To break this deadlock the Union modified its proposal. It made a counterproposal that a buyer would not be required to assume the current CBAs with the successorship clauses, if the buyer agreed to negotiate with the Union to reach a new agreement with a successorship clause....

The Union's counterproposal Clearly successorship clauses are very important to potential purchasers.... [Bruno's witnesses had] testified that no potential buyer had approached Bruno's and offered to purchase the stores as an ongoing business and at the same time agreed to assume the four current CBAs....

To support its position, Bruno's argued that the successorship clauses will, "absolutely prevent a sale, lead to liquidation, and ultimately result in nearly 4000 lost jobs." ... [But one of Bruno's witnesses also testified] "We have bidders who have indicated for a small number of stores that they would be willing to negotiate with the Union. We have not had bidders who have indicated that they would be willing to assume the collective bargaining agreement. To the extent that it's in place, it will impact, may impact in totality the number of bidders who show up. Um, but, that's not to suggest that none of those bidders is willing to negotiate and willing to participate in the development of a collective bargaining agreement per se."

Documentary evidence and testimony supports these conclusions.... The documentary evidence from those "offers" confirms that there is room for compromise.... of the two offers Bruno's had at the time, both were willing to accept the now Union position that neither would be required to assume the current CBAs, but that they would negotiate with the Union later to reach a CBA. That is precisely the Union's current position and the proposal the Union offered to Bruno's when the Union refused Bruno's proposal. Therefore, while the Union's counterproposal may not be the total solution to these parties' problems, it cannot be said that the Union refused Bruno's proposal "without good cause," even where the Union insists that any new contract include a successorship clause. That is the evidence. As such, that evidence supports the conclusion that the Union's counterproposal was legitimate and was something that at least two potential buyers considered.

In addition, the evidence confirms that there is a real difference between assuming a current CBA with a successorship clause and renegotiating a new CBA with a new successorship clause. Mr. Glanzer, the Union's expert, testified that there are degrees of successorship clauses. The current ones are "middle-of-the-road." That testimony demonstrates that there are differences that leave the door open for a new CBA with a different successorship clause. Maybe the Union thinks it can renegotiate a new CBA with a more stringent successorship clause. Maybe a buyer thinks it can renegotiate a new CBA with a less stringent successorship clause. There are clearly many possibilities.

In either event, section 1113's purpose is to require the parties to negotiate. This Court's duty is to review those negotiations. The specific part of those negotiations under review here is the Union's refusal of Bruno's proposal that the successorship clauses be eliminated. The issue is whether that refusal was made "without good cause." For the reasons stated above, the Court finds that it was not.

In summary, the Union made a counterproposal that was a positive step in resolving this very difficult situation for Bruno's, its employees, its creditors, and its landlords.... When the Union attempted to compromise, it did what the law required it to do. That is what this Court has considered in determining the Union's "good cause," not which proposal or counterproposal is better.

Therefore, the answer to the question the Court asked above is yes. There is a real difference between the Union's original proposal and its counterproposal. That counterproposal met the legal standards described above. Based on those conclusions, the Court finds that the Union acted with good cause when it refused Bruno's proposal to eliminate the successorship clauses from the four current collective bargaining agreements....

VII. Conclusion

The issue is not whether Bruno's position is right and the Union's is wrong, or vice versa. The issue is not whether collective bargaining agreements are good or bad. The issue is whether Bruno's proved, by a preponderance of the evidence, that the Union refused Bruno's proposal "without good cause." The Court finds that it did not. In contrast, the Court finds that the Union met the legal standards discussed above and did prove, by a preponderance of the evidence, that it refused Bruno's proposal with good cause. A separate order will be entered in conformity with this Memorandum Opinion...

Case Questions

1. What are the procedural requirements that an employer must meet in order to reject a collective bargaining agreement under Section 1113?
2. What proposal has the bankrupt employer made to the union here? How did the union respond? Did the union modify its position regarding the employer's proposal? Explain.
3. How does the court here define "good cause"? Has the union here rejected the employer's proposal here without good cause? Explain.

In *Wheeling Pittsburgh Steel Corp. v. United Steelworkers*,[41] the Third Circuit Court of Appeals held that it was an error to allow the employer to void the collective agreement where the employer did not give any persuasive rationale for asking the unionized employees to take disproportionate cuts for a five-year period without any provision for improvement if the employer's position improved. In *Teamsters Local 807 v. Carey Trans.*,[42] the Second Circuit Court of Appeals upheld rejection of the agreement where unionized employees were expected to take cuts greater than those for nonunion employees because the union wages were 60 percent higher than industry average, whereas the other employees' compensation was barely competitive.

The NLRB has made it clear that filing a petition for bankruptcy protection does not affect the employer's obligation to recognize and bargain with the union, according to *Airport Bus Service.*[43] In *Willis Elec.*,[44] the NLRB held that an employer unilaterally abrogating an agreement without obtaining bankruptcy court relief is guilty of violating Section 8(a)(5); economic necessity is not a defense for such conduct. In *NLRB v. Superior Forwarding, Inc.*,[45] the court of appeals held that a bankruptcy court may enjoin the NLRB from proceeding with hearings on unfair labor practice charges that arise from an employer's unilateral modification of a collective agreement, when the unfair labor practice proceedings would threaten the assets of the employer.

---

[41] 791 F.2d 1074 (1986).

[42] 816 F.2d 82 (1987).

[43] 273 NLRB 561 (1984).

[44] 269 NLRB 1145 (1984).

[45] 762 F.2d 695 (8th Cir. 1985).

Bankruptcy and Retiree Benefits

From the 1950's through the 1970's, employers were willing to negotiate with unions for generous healthcare benefit provisions for retired employees; this was particularly true in the automobile and steel industries. But from the 1980's on, the costs of such retiree benefits, known as "legacy costs" became a significant financial burden on the employers. The steel and automobile industries began to face strong competition from foreign firms, the costs of medical care increased substantially, and the number of retirees grew. It was estimated that the costs of retiree healthcare benefits added $1,400 to the cost of each car produced by General Motors,[46] while the European and Japanese were not saddled with such legacy costs. The huge retiree medical costs added to the other financial problems that forced General Motors and Chrysler into bankruptcy.[47] In many cases, firms facing bankruptcy unilaterally stopped paying the retiree benefits. In response such actions, Congress amended the Bankruptcy Code to include Section 1114, which creates a procedure for modification or rejection of retiree benefit obligations similar to that under Section 1113 for the rejection of collective agreements. Section 1114[48] requires that the bankrupt employer make a proposal for modification to the representative of the retirees (either a labor union, or a committee appointed by the trustee in bankruptcy). The employer must also provide the retirees' representative with the information upon which the proposal is based and demonstrating the necessity of the modification for the reorganization of the employer. The employer must negotiate in good faith with the representative over the proposed modification. If the representative does not agree to the modification, the employer can ask the bankruptcy court to order the modification. Before the court can order the modification, the employer must convince the court that the modification is necessary to permit the reorganization of the employer, that the proposed modification treats all affected parties fairly and equitably, and that the retirees' representative refused to accept the proposal without good cause.

In the case of General Motors, the company and the United Auto Workers Union agreed to have the retiree benefits assumed by a VEBA. However, some of the retirees of some subsidiaries of the "old General Motors" were represented by other unions (non-UAW unions), and were not included in the agreement setting up the VEBA. As part of its emergence from bankruptcy, the productive assets of the former General Motors Corporation were purchased by a newly created firm ("new General Motors"), while the liabilities, including those for retiree benefits, remained with the "old General Motors." The non-UAW unions objected to the proposal for the "new General Motors" to emerge from bankruptcy, because the "new General Motors" would only agree to pay reduced benefits to their retirees. The bankruptcy court, in *In re General Motors Corp.*,[49] held that the obligation to comply with the requirements of Section 1114 applied only to the bankrupt employer ("old General

---

[46] "The Bankruptcy of General Motors: A Giant Falls," *The Economist*, June 4, 2009.

[47] As noted in the "Working Law" feature in this chapter, the companies eventually agreed with the United Auto Workers Union to have a union-operated trust, known as a Voluntary Employee Beneficiary Association, or VEBA, assume the responsibility of paying future retiree medical benefits in return for a huge cash payment from the firms.

[48] 11 U.S.C. § 1114.

[49] 407 B.R. 463 (Bkrtcy. S.D.N.Y. 2009).

Motors" in this case) and not the corporation purchasing the productive assets of the firm ("new General Motors"). The court stated that "old General Motors" had complied with the requirements of Section 1114. If, in the future, "old General Motors" fails to comply with its obligations under the modification, the unions could ask the court to take appropriate action. The court noted:

> The Court fully realizes that UAW retirees will get a better result, after all is said and done, than … [non-UAW] Retirees will, but that is not by reason of any violation of the Code or applicable caselaw. It is because as a matter of reality, the Purchaser ["new GM"] needs a properly motivated workforce to enable New GM to succeed, requiring it to enter into satisfactory agreements with the UAW—which includes arrangements satisfactory to the UAW for UAW retirees. And the Purchaser is not similarly motivated, in triaging its expenditures, to assume obligations for retirees of unions whose members, with little in the way of exception, no longer work for GM.
>
> The Court has also considered … that in pre-bankruptcy planning, GM and the U.S. Treasury focused on the duties to … [non-UAW] Retirees, and made a conscious decision that … [non-UAW] retirees would not be offered as good a deal as others…. The U.S. Treasury, in making hard decisions about where to spend its money and make New GM as viable as possible, made business decisions that it was entitled to make, and the fact that there were so few … [non-UAW] employees still working for GM was an understandable factor in that decision. The Court's responsibility is not to make fairness judgments as to those decisions, but merely to gauge those decisions under applicable law.[50]

[50]407 B.R. 463 at 512.

CHAPTER REVIEW

» Key Terms

arbitration	« 521	***rights arbitration***	« 522	***grievance***	« 522
interest arbitration	« 522	***grievance process***	« 522	***no-strike clauses***	« 529

» Summary

- Arbitration is the usual method by which the parties to a collective agreement enforce that agreement. The existence of an arbitration clause is voluntary; the NLRA does not require that the parties include an arbitration clause in the agreement. But if the parties do agree to an arbitration clause, it becomes legally enforceable through Section 301 of the NLRA, and arbitration becomes the preferred means of interpreting and enforcing the agreement. When asked to order arbitration, a court should not consider the merits of the grievance but rather only whether the grievance is within the scope of the arbitration clause. When asked to enforce an arbitration award under Section 301, the court should not substitute its judgment for that of the arbitrator but rather only consider whether the arbitrator acted within the scope of his or her authority under the agreement. Courts should refuse to enforce an arbitration award only when the arbitrator exceeded the authority granted under the agreement or when the arbitration award violates "clear and explicit public policy."
- Section 301 also allows a court to enforce a no-strike clause in a collective agreement; despite the Norris–La Guardia Act, a court may grant an injunction to stop a strike that is over an issue subject to arbitration under a collective agreement. Suits under Section 301 may be used to seek damages for violations of the agreement, including the no-strike clause. Remedies under Section 301 may preempt any state law remedies or actions that involve the interpretation or application of the collective agreement.
- The NLRB will defer unfair labor practice complaints to arbitration under the requirements set out in *United Technologies* and will recognize arbitration decisions as resolving unfair labor practice charges when the conditions set out in the *Olin* case are met.
- Successor employers may be required to recognize and bargain with the union that had represented the employees of the former employer when there is a substantial continuity of operation and the employees from the former unionized employer make up a majority of the successor's employees. Section 1113 of the Bankruptcy Code sets out the procedure to be followed by an employer seeking to reject a collective agreement after having filed a petition for bankruptcy protection with the bankruptcy court.

» Problems

Questions

1. What is rights arbitration? What is interest arbitration? Why is arbitration used to resolve contract disputes between unions and employers?
2. When will a court enforce a contractual promise to arbitrate disputes over the interpretation and application of a collective agreement? When should a course refuse to enforce an arbitrator's decision?
3. What remedies are available to an employer against workers striking in violation of a no-strike clause? Against a union striking in violation of a no-strike clause?
4. When will the NLRB defer consideration of an unfair labor practice complaint to arbitration?
5. When is a successor employer obligated to recognize and bargain with the union representing the employees of the former employer?

Case Problems

6. An employee of the Du Pont Company's plant in East Chicago attacked his supervisor and another employee and destroyed some company equipment all for no apparent reason. He was discharged by the company. He was subsequently arrested and spent thirty days under observation in a hospital psychiatric ward. Two psychiatrists subsequently testified in court that the employee was temporarily insane at the time of the incident, and therefore, he was acquitted of the criminal charges. They also testified that the worker had recovered and was not likely to suffer another mental breakdown.

   Following his acquittal, the worker's discharge was challenged by the union on the ground that the employee was not responsible for the assaults due to temporary mental incapacity. Therefore, argued the union, he was not dismissed for "just cause" as called for under the "security of employment" clause in the collective bargaining agreement.

   The company refused to reinstate the employee, and the union moved the grievance to arbitration. The arbitrator ruled in the union's favor and ordered the grievant reinstated to his job. Du Pont filed suit in a federal court in Indiana to overturn the arbitrator's ruling.

   If you represented the company in front of the federal judge, what arguments would you make for overturning the arbitrator's award? If you represented the union, what counterarguments would you make in response? How should the judge have ruled? See *E. I. Du Pont De Nemours & Co. v. Grasselli Employees Independent Ass'n. of E. Chicago* [790 F.2d 611 (7th Cir. 1986)].
7. The labor contract between the West Penn Power Company of Arnold, Pennsylvania, and System Local No. 102 of the Utility Workers of America included a provision that employees engaged in the construction or maintenance of power lines would not be required to work outdoors during "inclement weather" and that the responsible supervisor would determine when weather conditions were too severe for outdoor work.

   The no-strike clause in the labor agreement required the union and its officers to make a "sincere, active effort to have work resumed at a normal rate" if the employees engaged in a wildcat strike or refused to carry out job assignments.

   One day in November, seven employees, including the union's president and vice president, ceased working due to weather conditions, despite their supervisor's repeated orders to keep on working. West Penn subsequently suspended the five rank-and-file employees for five days each, but discharged the two union officers for "their refusal to proceed with a work assignment and to make an active effort as (union officers) to have work resumed by other union employees."

   An arbitration panel sustained the union president's discharge, while reducing the vice president's termination to a thirty-day suspension. Both men responded by filing unfair labor practice charges with the NLRB.

   What do you think was the basis for the unfair labor practice charges filed by the two union officials? How should the NLRB respond? Should it defer to arbitration in this case? If not, how should it rule on the unfair labor practice charges? What remedy should it impose if it finds the two men were wrongfully discharged? See *West Penn Power Co.* [274 NLRB No. 1160 (1985)].

8. Safeway Stores, Inc., discharged a journeyman meat cutter for disobeying an order and threatening a supervisor with physical harm. United Food and Commercial Workers Local 400 filed a grievance on behalf of the employee, and a few days later, representatives of the company and the union met to discuss the grievance. Unable to reach an informal resolution, the union submitted the grievance to arbitration.

   The arbitrator found that the grievant was guilty of disobeying a direct order and that he had compounded his offense by threatening his supervisor with bodily harm. However, the arbitrator refused to sustain the discharge because he also found that the company had not fully disclosed to the union or the grievant all the reasons for the discharge. At the grievance meeting, the company had stated that the reason for the discharge was the incident of insubordination. But during the arbitration hearing, the personnel director testified that his decision to discharge the grievant was based not only on his acts of insubordination but also on his past disciplinary record and a newspaper clipping he had seen concerning the grievant's conviction for assault and battery of his former girlfriend.

   The company refused to abide by the arbitrator's decision and sought to have it overturned in the U.S. District Court for the District of Columbia.

   If you had been the federal judge sitting in this case, would you have affirmed or overturned the arbitrator's award? See *Safeway Stores, Inc. v. United Food and Commercial Workers Local 400* [621 F.Supp. 1233 (D.D.C. 1985)].

9. *The Cleveland Press* and *The Plain Dealer*, the two daily newspapers in Cleveland, Ohio, were part of a multiemployer bargaining group that had signed a collective bargaining agreement with the Cleveland Typographical Union, Local 53. The contract stated that each covered employee was entitled to "a regular full-time job … for the remainder of his working life."

   When the *Cleveland Press* went out of business, eighty-nine former Press employees sued the parent company, E. W. Scripps Company, and *The Plain Dealer* to enforce the lifetime employment guarantee in their collective bargaining agreement. In addition to their Section 301 action, the plaintiffs also charged that the two defendants had conspired to create a daily newspaper monopoly in the city of Cleveland. The defendants replied, among other defenses, that the plaintiffs had no standing to sue on this second basis.

   Should the federal judge enforce the contract guarantee of lifetime jobs? If you say yes, what kind of a remedy should the judge fashion? What evidence do you see to support the plaintiffs' antitrust allegation? If defendants violated the Sherman Act, what impact should this have on their case? See *Province v. Cleveland Press Publishing Co.* [787 F.2d 1047 (6th Cir. 1986)].

10. Nolde Bros. Bakery's collective bargaining agreement with the Bakery & Confectionery Workers Union, Local 358, provided that any grievance between the parties was subject to binding arbitration. During negotiations over the renewal of the agreement, the union gave notice of its intention to cancel the existing agreement. Negotiations continued for several days past the termination date, and the union threatened to strike. The employer informed the union that it was permanently closing its plant. The employer paid the employees their accrued wages and vacation pay but refused to pay severance pay as called for in the collective agreement. The employer argued that its duty to pay severance pay and its duty to arbitrate the claim for severance pay expired with the collective agreement. The union sued under Section 301 to force the employer to arbitrate the question of whether the employer was required to pay severance pay.

    How should the court decide the union's suit? Is the employer required to arbitrate the matter? Explain your answer. See *Nolde Bros. v. Bakery & Confectionery Workers Local 358* [430 U.S. 243 (1977)].

11. The Grissom family owned and operated a motor lodge and restaurant franchised by the Howard Johnson Co.; they employed fifty-three employees, who were represented by the Hotel & Restaurant Employees Union. The Grissoms sold their business to the Howard Johnson Co. Howard Johnson hired forty-five employees, nine of whom were former employees of the Grissoms. The union requested that Howard Johnson recognize it and meet the obligations of the prior collective agreement, but Howard Johnson refused. The union then sought arbitration of the question of the successor's obligations under the agreement; it filed a suit under Section 301 to compel Howard Johnson to arbitrate.

    Is Howard Johnson required to recognize and bargain with the union? Is Howard Johnson required to arbitrate the question of the successor's obligation? Explain your answer. See *Howard Johnson Co. v. Hotel & Restaurant Employees Detroit Local Joint Board* [417 U.S. 249 (1974)].

12. The underlying dispute in this case arose when Waller Brothers, which operates a stone quarry engaged in removing and processing stone and packing the stone in boxes for shipment, purchased an "Instapak" machine, which sprays protective padding around the stone being packed for shipment. Before the purchase of the Instapak, the stone was packed with strips of synthetic material as padding. Employees called "craters" pack the stone for shipment.

    The union claims that it was entitled to negotiate a new wage rate for an Instapak machine operator, whereas the company maintains that the operation of the machine is only a function of the crater job classification, which is subject to a previously negotiated wage rate. The company takes the position that both the no-strike clause and the provision for mandatory grievance arbitration contained in the collective bargaining agreement apply to this dispute. The union for its part relies on the portion of the contract that provides that wage rates are not subject to arbitration and that the union expressly reserves the right to strike in the event of a disagreement on wages.

    If the union calls a strike and the company goes into court seeking a Boys Markets injunction, should the court grant or deny it? See *Waller Bros. Stone Co. v. District 23* [620 F.2d 132 (6th Cir. 1980)].

13. HMC Management Corp., an apartment rental and management company, discharged two of its employees for substandard work performance. The employees, represented by the Carpenters Union, filed grievances. The employer subsequently decided to rehire one of the employees but not the other one. When the grievance filed by the employee who was not rehired was arbitrated, the arbitrator acknowledged that the employer had sufficient reason to discharge the two employees but held that the employer had acted improperly when it rehired one employee but not the other. The arbitrator ordered that the employer reinstate the other employee. The employer filed suit in federal court to have the arbitration award vacated.

    Should the court enforce or vacate the arbitrator's decision? Explain your answer. See *HMC Mgt. Corp. v. Carpenters District Council* [750 F.2d 1302 (5th Cir. 1985)].

14. The appellate court judge who wrote the decision of the three-judge panel in this case began his opinion as follows:

    > Coffin, Chief Judge—This tempest has beenbrewed in a very small teapot. The dispute which precipitated the filing in this court of more than 80 pages of briefs and an extensive appendix began on July 30, 1974, when appellee Anheuser-Busch posted a notice prohibiting employees at its Merrimack, New Hampshire, brewery from wearing tank-top shirts on the job. Tank-tops are sleeveless shirts which leave exposed the shoulders, arms and underarms of the wearer. Beginning on July 31, when three employees were sent home after refusing to doff their tank-tops for other shirts, the emotional temperature rose, with over a dozen more employees, including shop stewards, being sent home a few days later. The issue peaked by August 14, when thirteen of the eighteen employees in the Brewery Department wore tank-tops, refused to put on other shirts, and went home. Approximately thirty employees in the Maintenance Department wore tank-tops on August 15. On August 16 no maintenance employees reported for work and production at the brewery was halted.

    The brewery filed a lawsuit in federal district court seeking injunctive relief and damages against the employees' union on the grounds that the collective bargaining agreement contained a no-strike clause and an arbitration clause.

The union responded that (1) the employees' actions were individual, not concerted, activity; (2) the employees were entitled to wear the tank-tops pending arbitration of the controversy; and (3) the employer should not be permitted to hide behind a *Boys Markets* injunction after management's over-reaction had itself precipitated the crisis.

How do you think the court ruled in this dispute? See *Anheuser-Busch v. Teamsters Local 633* [511 F.2d 1097 (1st Cir.)], *cert. denied* [423 U.S. 875(1975)].

15. Stikes, an employee of Chevron Corp., was discharged for refusing to allow the employer to search her car under a company antidrug policy, adopted in 1984, that required workers to submit to random searches of person and property. Stikes was a member of the bargaining unit represented by the Oil, Chemical and Atomic Workers Union; the collective agreement covering the bargaining unit provided for arbitration of discharge cases. Rather than submit a grievance over her discharge, Stikes filed a suit against Chevron in the state court. The suit charged Chevron with wrongful discharge, intentional infliction of emotional distress, unfair business practice, and violation of rights to privacy under the state constitution. Chevron argued that the suit was preempted by Section 301 because it was a suit to enforce the collective agreement.

    Does Stikes have a right to sue under state law over her discharge, or is her suit preempted by Section 301? Explain your answer. See *Stikes v. Chevron USA Inc.* [914 F.2d 1265 (9th Cir. 1990)].

Hypothetical Scenarios

16. The employees of Robinson Ford Sales, a local auto dealer, are represented by Local 303 of the United Automobile Workers Union. Because of slumping sales, the dealership announces that it must change the medical insurance provided to the employees under the collective agreement by doubling the co-pays and deductibles that the employees are required to pay. The union objects that the change violates the collective agreement, and demands that the dealership submit the dispute to arbitration under the collective agreement arbitrations procedures. The dealership refuses to do so, and the union files suit under Section 301 of the NLRA to force the employer to submit the dispute to arbitration. The trial court refuses to order Robinson to arbitrate the dispute, holding that Robinson's reduced business was a legitimate reason for making the changes. The union then appeals to the federal court of appeals. Should the court of appeals order the employer to arbitrate the dispute? What factors should the court consider when deciding whether to order arbitration?

17. West World Holding, Inc. owned an office building in Boise. The maintenance and cleaning employees for the building were represented by Service Employees International Union, Local 32, and the union and employer had a collective agreement governing the terms and conditions of employment for those employees. West World sold the building to Maiden LLC, a Denver-based real estate company, on August 27, 2007. Maiden announced that it would retain all maintenance and cleaning employees who had worked for West World. Local 32 then requested that Maiden bargain with the union over whether to continue to adhere to the terms of collective agreement with West World. Maiden refused to recognize the union, and made unilateral changes to the terms and conditions of employment for the workers. The union filed an unfair labor practice charge against Maiden over its refusal to recognize the union. How should the NLRB rule—is Maiden required to recognize and bargain with the union? Is Maiden bound by the previous collective agreement? Explain your answer.

18. Crucible Metals Foundry makes structural steel for the construction industry, but has been losing orders because new construction has been affected by the lack of availability credit funding. Crucible is forced to file for reorganization under Chapter 11 of the Bankruptcy Code. Crucible submits a proposal to the union representing its production workers that would eliminate the pension and medical insurance benefits that the employees and retirees presently enjoy under the current collective agreement.

Crucible argues that the costs of those programs are prohibitively expensive and the firm can no longer afford them. The union is reluctant to agree to the proposal. What steps must Crucible pursue to reject the requirements of the collective agreement?

19. Sievers, a union steward at Spina Manufacturing Co., was fired when he filed a grievance over the employer's change to its overtime pay policies. Sievers argued that the action was in violation of the collective agreement and also violated the federal Fair Labor Standards Act. The union filed unfair labor practice charges with the NLRB, claiming that the discharge was a violation of Sections 8(a)(1) and (3) of the NLRA. The employer argued that dispute over the discharge should be arbitrated under the collective agreement's arbitration provisions, and that the NLRB should defer the dispute to arbitration. Should the NLRB refer the dispute to arbitration? What factors will the NLRB consider in making it decision?

20. Michaels, a police officer with the Shelbyville Police Department, was dismissed for violating the city's sexual harassment policy. Michaels and the union representing the police officers, filed a grievance over the discharge, and ultimately submitted the grievance to arbitration under the collective agreement covering police officers. The arbitrator held that Michaels had violated the sexual harassment policy, but because of Michaels' previously unblemished record, reduced the discharge to a suspension without pay for three months. The city objected to the arbitration award, and brings an action in the federal district court to have the arbitrator's decision vacated. What factors should the court consider in deciding this case? How should the court decide? Why?

The Rights of Union Members

Unions, as bargaining agents representing bargaining units of employees, have significant power and control over individual employees. Those employees are precluded from dealing with the employer on matters of wages and working conditions; the employees must go through the union in dealing with the employer. Because employees are dependent on the union, they must be protected from the arbitrary or unreasonable exercise of union power. This chapter explores the legal controls of unions to protect the rights of union members.

Protection of the Rights of Union Members

Duty of Fair Representation
Legal duty on the part of the union to represent fairly all members of the bargaining unit.

The legal controls on unions are the result of actions by the courts, the National Labor Relations Board (NLRB), and Congress. The courts and the NLRB have imposed a ***duty of fair representation*** on the part of the union—an obligation to represent fairly all members of the bargaining unit. Congress has legislated a *union members' "bill of rights"* to guarantee that union internal procedures are fair and has prohibited certain practices by unions that interfere with employees' rights under the National Labor Relations Act (NLRA).

In 1947, the Taft-Hartley Act added a list of union unfair labor practices to the NLRA, which included the following:

- Section 7 was amended to give employees the right to refrain from engaging in concerted activity, as well as the right to engage in such activity.
- Section 8(b)(1)(A) prohibits union activity that interferes with, restrains, or coerces employees in the exercise of their Section 7 rights.
- Section 8(b)(2) prohibits unions from causing an employer to discriminate against employees in terms and conditions of employment because they are not union members.
- Section 8(b)(5) protects employees from unreasonable union dues and initiation fees.

The Landrum-Griffin Act of 1959 added the union member's bill of rights to the NLRA. Those provisions will be discussed in detail later in this chapter.

The Union's Duty of Fair Representation

The duty of fair representation is a judicially created obligation on the part of the union to represent fairly all employees in the bargaining unit. The duty was developed by the courts because of the union's role as exclusive bargaining agent for the bargaining unit. The initial cases dealing with the duty of fair representation arose under the Railway Labor Act; subsequent cases applied the duty to unions under the NLRA as well. In the following case, the Supreme Court developed the concept of the duty of fair representation.

case 18.1 » STEELE V. LOUISVILLE & NASHVILLE R.R.

323 U.S. 192 (1944)

Stone, C.J.

The question is whether the Railway Labor Act ... imposes on a labor organization, acting by authority of the statute as the exclusive bargaining representative of a craft or class of railway employees, the duty to represent all the employees in the craft without discrimination because of their race, and, if so, whether the courts have jurisdiction to protect the minority of the craft or class from the violation of such obligation.

... Petitioner, a Negro, is a locomotive fireman in the employ of respondent railroad, suing on his own behalf and that of his fellow employees who, like petitioner, are Negro firemen employed by the Railroad. Respondent Brotherhood, a labor organization, is as provided under Section 2, Fourth of the Railway Labor Act, the exclusive bargaining representative of the craft of firemen employed by the Railroad and is recognized as such by it and the members of the craft. The majority of the firemen employed by the Railroad are white and are members of the Brotherhood, but a substantial minority are Negroes who, by the constitution and ritual of the Brotherhood, are excluded from its membership. As the membership of the Brotherhood constitutes a majority of all firemen employed on respondent Railroad and as under Section 2, Fourth, the members, because they are the majority, have chosen the Brotherhood to represent the craft, petitioner and other Negro firemen on the road have been required to accept the Brotherhood as their representative for the purposes of the Act.

On March 28, 1940, the Brotherhood, purporting to act as representative of the entire craft of firemen, without informing the Negro firemen or giving them opportunity to be heard, served a notice on respondent Railroad and on twenty other railroads operating principally in the southeastern part of the United States. The notice announced the Brotherhood's desire to amend the existing collective bargaining agreement in such a manner as ultimately to exclude all Negro firemen from the service. By established practice on the several railroads so notified only white firemen can be promoted to serve as engineers, and the notice proposed that only "promotable," i.e., white, men should be employed as firemen or assigned to new runs or jobs or permanent vacancies in established runs or jobs.

On February 18, 1941, the railroads and the Brotherhood, as representative of the craft, entered into a new agreement which provided that not more than 50 percent of the firemen in each class of service in each seniority district of a carrier should be Negroes; that until such percentage should be reached all new runs and all vacancies should be filled by white men; and that the agreement did not sanction the employment of Negroes in any seniority district in which they were not working....

... [W]e think that Congress, in enacting the Railway Labor Act and authorizing a labor union, chosen by a majority of a craft, to represent the craft, did not intend to confer plenary power upon the union to sacrifice, for the benefit of its members, rights of the minority of the craft, without imposing on it any duty to protect the minority. Since petitioner and the other Negro members of the craft are not members of the Brotherhood or eligible for membership, the authority to act for them is derived not from their action or consent but wholly from the command of the Act....

Section 2, Second, requiring carriers to bargain with the representative so chosen, operates to exclude any other from representing a craft. The minority members of a craft are thus deprived by the statute of the right, which they would otherwise possess, to choose a representative of their own, and its members cannot bargain individually on behalf of themselves as to matters which are properly the subject of collective bargaining....

The fair interpretation of the statutory language is that the organization chosen to represent a craft is to represent all its members, the majority as well as the minority, and it is to act for and not against those whom it represents. It is a principle of general application that the exercise of a granted power to act in behalf of others involves the assumption toward them of a duty to exercise the power in their interest and behalf, and that such a grant of power will not be deemed to dispense with all duty toward those for whom it is exercised unless so expressed.

We think that the Railway Labor Act imposes upon the statutory representative of a craft at least as exacting a duty to protect equally the interests of the members of the craft as the Constitution imposes upon a legislature to give equal protection to the interests of those for whom it legislates. Congress has seen fit to clothe the bargaining representative with powers comparable to those possessed by a legislative body both to create and restrict the rights of those whom it represents, but it also imposed on the representative a corresponding duty. We hold that the language of the Act to which we have referred, read in the light of the purposes of the Act, expresses the aim of Congress to impose on the bargaining representative of a craft or class of employees the duty to exercise fairly the power conferred upon it in behalf of all those for whom it acts, without hostile discrimination against them.

This does not mean that the statutory representative of a craft is barred from making contracts which may have unfavorable effects on some of the members of the craft represented. Variations in terms of the contract based on differences relevant to the authorized purposes of the contract in conditions to which they are to be applied, such as differences in seniority, the type of work performed, the competence and skill with which it is performed, are within the scope of the bargaining representation of a craft, all of whose members are not identical in their interest or merit. Without attempting to mark the allowable limits of differences in the terms of contracts based on differences of conditions to which they apply, it is enough for present purposes to say that the statutory power to represent a craft and to make contracts as to wages, hours and working conditions does not include the authority to make among members of the craft discriminations not based on such relevant differences. Here the discriminations based on race alone are obviously irrelevant and invidious. Congress plainly did not undertake to authorize the bargaining representative to make such discriminations....

The representative which thus discriminates may be enjoined from so doing, and its members may be enjoined from taking the benefit of such discriminatory action. No more is the Railroad bound by or entitled to take the benefit of a contract which the bargaining representative is prohibited by the statute from making. In both cases the right asserted, which is derived from the duty imposed by the statute on the bargaining representative, is a federal right implied from the statute and the policy which it has adopted....

So long as a labor union assumes to act as the statutory representative of a craft, it cannot rightly refuse to perform the duty, which is inseparable from the power of representation conferred upon it, to represent the entire membership of the craft. While the statute does not deny to such a bargaining labor organization the right to determine eligibility to its membership, it does require the union, in collective bargaining and in making contracts with the carrier, to represent non-union or minority union members of the craft without hostile discrimination, fairly, impartially, and in good faith. Wherever necessary to that end, the union is required to consider requests of non-union members of the craft and expressions of their views with respect to collective bargaining with the employer and to give to them notice of and opportunity for hearing upon its proposed action....

We conclude that the duty which the statute imposes on a union representative of a craft to represent the interests of all its members stands on no different footing and that the statute contemplates resort to the usual judicial remedies of injunction and award of damages when appropriate for breach of that duty.

The judgment is accordingly reversed and remanded....
So ordered.

Case Questions

1. Is Steele a member of the union? Why?

2. To what conduct by the union and the railroad did Steele object?

3. To which employees does the union owe a duty of fair representation? What is the source of the union's duty of fair representation?

The *Steele* case held that the duty of fair representation arose out of the union's exclusive bargaining agent status under Section 2, Ninth, of the Railway Labor Act. In *Syres v. Oil Workers Local 23*,[1] the Supreme Court held that the duty of fair representation also extended to unions granted bargaining agent status under Section 9(a) of the NLRA.

Unions, in representing employees, must make decisions that affect different employees in different ways. For example, in negotiating a contract, the union must decide whether to seek increased wages or improved benefits—trade-offs must be made in fashioning contract proposals. Older employees may be more concerned with pensions, whereas younger employees may be more concerned with increased wages. Should the courts monitor the union's negotiation proposals to ensure that all workers are fairly represented? In *Ford Motor Co. v. Huffman*,[2] the Supreme Court held that unions should be given broad discretion by the courts in negotiation practices; the courts should ensure only that the union operates "in good faith and honesty of purpose in the exercise of its discretion."

ethical DILEMMA

Union Membership Benefits and Costs

You are the human resource manager of the Springfield plant of Immense Multinational Business; the plant production employees are represented by a union, and the collective agreement has a union shop clause requiring employees in the bargaining unit to join the union and to maintain their membership in good standing.

You have just hired a new production employee, Waylon Smithers, who asks you if he is required to join the union. He also asks you what benefits he may receive by becoming a union member and what the negative aspects of union membership are. How should you respond to him? Prepare a short memo outlining your response to his questions, supporting your comments with appropriate references.

The courts also give unions some leeway in exercising their contractual duties. In *Steelworkers v. Rawson*,[3] the Supreme Court held that the allegations that the union had been negligent in its duty under the collective agreement to conduct safety inspections did not amount to a breach of the duty of fair representation because mere negligence, even in the performance of a contractual duty, does not amount to a breach of the duty of fair representation. However, a union's negligent failure to follow hiring hall rules may be a breach of the duty of fair representation, according to *Jacoby v. NLRB*.[4]

[1] 350 U.S. 892 (1955).

[2] 345 U.S. 330 (1953).

[3] 495 U.S. 362 (1990).

[4] 233 F.3d 611 (D.C. Cir. 2000).

Although the courts allow unions broad latitude in negotiations, they may be more concerned with union decisions involving individual employee grievances. In *Vaca v. Sipes*,[5] the Supreme Court held that an individual does not have an absolute right to have a grievance taken to arbitration, but the union must make decisions about the merits of a grievance in good faith and in a nonarbitrary manner.

In *Vaca*, the union refused to arbitrate the employee's grievance. If the union decides to arbitrate the grievance but mishandles the employee's claim, does it violate the duty of fair representation? What if the union gives the grievance only perfunctory handling? The following case addresses these questions.

case 18.2 »

Hines v. Anchor Motor Freight, Inc.

424 U.S. 554 (1976)

Facts: Two truck drivers employed by Anchor Motor Freight, Inc., were discharged for allegedly submitting expense claims in excess of the actual costs of their motel rooms. The relevant collective agreement provided that discharge required just cause. At a grievance meeting between the union and the employer, the employer presented the following:

- the motel receipts submitted by the employees that showed charges in excess of the rates shown on the motel's registration cards;
- a notarized statement of the motel clerk asserting the accuracy of the registration cards; and
- an affidavit of the motel owner affirming that the registration cards were accurate and that inflated receipts had been supplied to the employees.

The union claimed petitioners were innocent and opposed the discharges. The grievance over the discharge was then submitted to arbitration under the collective agreement. The two employees suggested that the union investigate the motel, but the union responded that "there was nothing to worry about" and that they need not hire their own attorney.

At the arbitration hearing, Anchor presented its case. Then both the union and employees were afforded an opportunity to present their case. The employees denied the claim of dishonesty, but neither they nor the union presented any other evidence contradicting the documents presented by the company. The arbitration panel upheld the discharges.

The employees then retained an attorney and sought rehearing based on a statement by the motel owner that the discrepancy between the receipts and the registration cards could have been attributable to the motel clerk's recording on the cards less than what was actually paid and pocketing the difference between the amount receipted and the amount recorded. The arbitration panel unanimously denied rehearing "because there was no new evidence presented which would justify reopening this case." It was later discovered that the motel clerk was in fact the culprit.

The discharged employees filed suit against both the union and the employer. They alleged that because their discharge was not for good cause, the employer was in violation of the collective agreement. They also alleged that the union violated its duty of fair representation by arbitrarily failing to make an effort to investigate the employer's charges of dishonesty. The union relied upon the decision of the arbitration panel, and the employer claimed that the employees had been properly discharged for just cause. The employer also claimed that the employees, diligently and in good faith represented by the union, had unsuccessfully resorted to the grievance and arbitration machinery provided by the contract, and that the adverse decision of the arbitration panel was binding upon the union and employees under the collective agreement.

During pretrial discovery proceedings, the motel clerk revealed that he had falsified the records and had pocketed the difference between the sums shown on the receipts and the registration cards. The trial court granted summary judgment for the employer and the union on the ground that the decision of the arbitration panel was final and binding on the

[5] 386 U.S. 171 (1967).

employees and that they had failed to show that the union had acted arbitrarily, or in bad faith. The court stated that the union's conduct of the investigation and arbitration may have demonstrated bad judgment on the part of the union, but it was insufficient to prove a breach of the duty of fair representation.

The employees then appealed to the U.S. Court of Appeals, which reversed the decision of the trial court and held that the employees had presented sufficient evidence to support a finding of bad faith or arbitrary conduct on the part of the union. An appeal was taken to the U.S. Supreme Court.

Issue: Can the union be sued for breach of the duty of fair representation when the employer's discharge of the employees was held by the arbitration panel not to be in violation of the collective agreement?

Decision: The Supreme Court noted that, in order to prevail against either the employer or the union, the employees must show not only that their discharge was in violation of the collective agreement requirement of just cause, but must also carry the burden of demonstrating a breach of the duty of fair representation by the union. Such a showing requires more than just demonstrating mere errors in judgment. The employees are not entitled to relitigate their discharge merely because they offer newly discovered evidence that the charges against them were false and that in fact they were fired without cause. The grievance processes cannot be expected to be error-free. The finality provision of the collective agreement regarding arbitration has sufficient force to surmount occasional instances of mistake.

However, an arbitration decision may be reopened where the employees' representation by the union has been dishonest, in bad faith or discriminatory. Here, in order to prevail, the employees must show that the arbitration decision was in error because it was undermined by the union's breach of the duty of fair representation. If they can make such a showing, then they are entitled to remedies against both the employer for violating the collective agreement and the union for breach of the duty of fair representation. The employer is not immunized from liability for discharge without just cause by reason of the union's breach of the duty of fair representation.

The Supreme Court reversed the court of appeals' decision affirming the dismissal of the suit against the employer.

«

Union Dues and the Duty of Fair Representation

Union Shop
A union security provision in a collective agreement that requires employees to become union members within thirty days of their employment.

Agency Shop
A union security provision in a collective agreement that requires employees to pay union dues and fees, but does not require that they become union members.

A union owes a duty of fair representation to all employees in the bargaining unit it represents, whether or not the employees are members of the union. As you recall from Chapter 14, Section 8(a)(3) allows the employer and union to agree on a union security clause (unless there is a state "right-to-work" law that prohibits mandatory union membership or union dues). Union security clauses generally involve either a ***union shop*** clause, which requires employees to become union members within thirty days of their employment, or an ***agency shop*** clause, which requires employees to pay union dues and fees. Negotiating a union security clause that incorporates the language of Section 8(a)(3) of the NLRA is not a violation of the union's duty of fair representation, as held in *Marquez v. Screen Actors Guild.*[6] An employer who unilaterally ceases to deduct union dues from employees under a union security clause violates Sections 8(a)(1) and 8(a)(5), according to *NLRB v. Oklahoma Fixture Co.*[7] Where the collective agreement contains a union shop agreement, a proviso to Section 8 (a)(3) states that an employer may not discharge an employee for failing to join the union if union membership is denied for a reason other than failure to pay union dues or fees. In

[6]525 U.S. 33 (1998).

[7]332 F.3d 1284 (10th Cir. 2003).

NLRB v. General Motors Corp.,[8] the Supreme Court held that the effect of that proviso is to reduce an employee's obligation under a union shop clause to "a financial core"—that is, simply to pay union dues and fees. According to the Supreme Court's decision in *Communications Workers of America v. Beck*,[9] unions may not use the dues or fees of employees who are not union members to pay for union activities not related to collective bargaining. Such employees are entitled to a reduction in dues and fees by the percentage of union expenditures that go for non–collective bargaining expenses. Employees who are not union members may not be charged for the portion of union dues spent on organizing activities outside the appropriate bargaining unit, according to *United Food and Commercial Workers Union, Local 1036 v. NLRB*.[10] However, in *Lehnert v. Ferris Faculty Ass'n*,[11] the Supreme Court held that employees who are not union members but are subject to an agency fee provision under a collective agreement can be charged a pro rata share of the costs of union activities related to bargaining, litigation, preparation for a strike, and other union activities that may not directly benefit members of bargaining unit; they are not required to pay the costs of lobbying activity by the union. In *Chicago Teachers Union, Local No. 1 v. Hudson*,[12] the Supreme Court held that the union is required to provide objecting members with information relating to the union expenditures on collective bargaining and political activities and must include an adequate explanation of the basis of dues and fees. The objecting members must also be provided with a reasonable opportunity to challenge, before an impartial decision maker, the amount of the dues or fees; the union must hold in escrow the disputed amounts pending the resolution of the challenges. Unions may require that disputes over the amount of agency fees charged to nonmembers be arbitrated. However, the objecting nonmembers, unless they have specifically agreed to arbitrate their dispute, are not required to exhaust the arbitration process before filing suit in federal court, as held in *Air Line Pilots Association v. Miller*.[13] A state law that requires public sector unions to get affirmative authorization of the use of agency shop fees for political purposes does not violate the unions' First Amendment rights, according to the Supreme Court decision in *Davenport v. Washington Education Association*.[14] In *Ysursa v. Pocatello Education Ass'n*,[15] the Supreme Court upheld the constitutionality of an Idaho state law that prohibited public sector employees from authorizing voluntary payroll deductions for union political activities.

---

[8]373 U.S. 734 (1963).

[9]487 U.S. 735 (1988).

[10]249 F.3d 1115 (2001).

[11]500 U.S. 507 (1991).

[12]475 U.S. 292 (1986).

[13]523 U.S. 866 (1998).

[14]551 U.S. 177 (2007).

[15]129 S.Ct. 1093 (2009).

case 18.3 » International Brotherhood of Teamsters, Local 776, AFL-CIO (Carolina Freight Carriers Corporation)

324 NLRB 1154 (NLRB 1997)

Michael O. Miller, ALJ

... Since before 1994, the Employer had recognized Respondent [union] (and the Teamsters National Freight Industry Negotiating Committee) as the exclusive collective-bargaining representative of its employees in a unit appropriate for collective-bargaining purposes. The collective-bargaining agreement includes a "Union Shop" clause which ... "[a]ll present employees who are not members of the Local union and all employees who are hired hereafter [to] become and remain members in good standing of the Local Union as a condition of employment on and after the thirty-first (31st) day following the beginning of their employment...."

It further provides that an employee "who has failed to acquire, or thereafter maintain, membership in the Union ... shall be terminated seventy-two (72) hours after his Employer has received written notice from ... the Local Union."

... Carolina hired Timothy Blosser on May 2, 1994, as a casual dock laborer. As a casual, he had no set or guaranteed hours; his schedule was determined each week....

The following case illustrates how the NLRB applies the Beck decision.

On May 27, the Union sent Blosser a registered letter outlining what it asserted were his union membership and financial obligations. That letter stated:

Our Constitution states that after thirty (30) calendar days, you are required to join the Local Union.... Your initiation fee is $200.00 plus the first month's dues which is two times your hourly rate, plus one dollar ($1.00) assessment for the death benefit....

According to our records, your first day of employment at Carolina Freight was May 2, 1994. Therefore, per the terms of our agreement with Carolina Freight and as outlined above, you are hereby notified that you must come into the Local Union office and join and/or become a member in good standing in the Local Union on, but not before June 2, 1994.

Upon failure to comply on this date, we shall contact your employer to inform him that you are not eligible to work. If you have any questions regarding Teamsters Local Union No. 776 or are no longer employed by the above-mentioned company, please feel free to call.

The letter omitted any reference to employee rights to opt out of full membership or pay less than the full amount of dues.

On June 1, Blosser responded to the Union's demand ... he described, as a violation of the duty of fair representation, a union's maintenance and application of a union-security clause requiring membership in good standing without advising the unit employees that their obligation was limited to the payment of uniform initiation fees and dues.

... Blosser asserted that nonmembers "do not have to pay a fee equal to union dues," that they "can only be required to pay a fee that equals their share of what the union can prove is its costs of collective bargaining, contract administration, and grievance adjustment with their employer."

... The Union replied on June 3, notifying Blosser that "the fees established by our auditor is [sic] 87% of the two times the hourly rate, and $1.00 for the death benefit, plus the $200.00 initiation fee." Accordingly, the dues, he was told, would be $26.10 per month. He had, he was told, seven days to comply before the employer would be informed not to assign him work.

The correspondence continued. Blosser replied, insisting that, "before the union demands fees, an independent accountant's verification of the union's cost of collective bargaining, NOT the union's interpretation" must be provided. Because no such verification had been provided, Blosser asserted that no payment could be demanded and that he would await receipt of that verification. He also asserted that the initiation fee should similarly be reduced by the appropriate percentage, 87 percent according to the Union's calculation. Finally, he requested a copy of the collective bargaining agreement.

On June 20, the Union sent Blosser the "latest auditor's verification of the core fees," those for 1993, noting that the computations of the core fees using the 1994 financial information was [sic] in process. The computation showed the Union's expenses and the portion of those expenses, if any, which were chargeable under Beck. It concluded that the expenses chargeable to protesting members amounted to 86.7 percent of the total expenses.

Blosser was also told that copies of the National Master Freight Agreement and the supplement applicable to Carolina are "given to all members when they become members of the Union." A hope was expressed that his dues and initiation fee would be received within 72 hours.

On June 24, the Union sent Blosser a computer-generated letter reiterating his obligation to pay the initiation fee and dues. The sums demanded were the full dues and initiation fee; there was no reference to any adjustments.... It also reiterated his obligation to "become a member in good standing" with no reference to his right to choose financial core membership and it threatened to notify his employer that he was ineligible to work if he did not comply within 72 hours.

Blosser wrote back on June 27, asserting that he was entitled to the independent auditor's complete audit or his complete review, as well as his opinion letter, for the Local's expenses as well as those of the Union's District and National levels, where some of the dues money goes. He also threatened to file an additional unfair labor practice charge if he did not get a copy of the collective-bargaining agreement, to which he claimed entitlement as a member of the unit.

On June 29, the Union gave him a copy of the contract. The other information he sought, the Union stated, was "being investigated as to the legality;" he was promised a subsequent response. Blosser never became a member of the [union]; neither did he pay it any fees or dues. He voluntarily left Carolina's employ on June 29.

... The union-security clause in Respondent's collective-bargaining agreement requires all employees "to become and remain members in good standing." On May 27, and on June 24, the Union demanded that Blosser "join and/or become a member in good standing in the Local Union." At no time was he told that he had a right to be and remain a nonmember. By failing to so inform him, Respondent breached the duty of fair representation owed to him as a member of the bargaining unit and thereby violated Section 8(b)(1)(A)....

As set forth [by the NLRB] in *California Saw & Knife Works* (1995), a union, when it seeks to enforce a union-security clause, is required to inform the employees [who choose not to join the union] of their rights under Beck. Thus, they must tell the employees that they are not required to pay the full dues and fees, give those employees information upon which to intelligently decide whether to object, and apprise them of the union's internal procedures for filing objections. Respondent did none of those when it made repeated demands upon Blosser that he join the Union and pay dues. It thus failed in its duty of fair representation, in violation of Section 8 (b)(1)(A).

In its various demands that he pay the dues and the initiation fee and join the Union, Respondent gave Blosser only three to seven days in which to decide and act, on pain of the loss of his job if he failed to comply. At the times it did so, Respondent had not yet provided him with the Beck notifications to which he was entitled. General Counsel argues that by failing to give Blosser a reasonable time within which to satisfy his dues obligation, Respondent further breached its duty of fair representation.

... the complaint further alleges this conduct more generally as unlawful restraint and coercion. I agree. By threatening to cause his termination if he did not join the Union in an unreasonably short time and without the information necessary for him to reasonably decide whether to assume objector status, Respondent has restrained and coerced him in violation of Section 8(b)(1)(A).

Respondent's repeated demands upon Blosser continued to seek payment of the full $200 initiation fee, even after it acknowledged that some portion of the dues were [sic] not chargeable to objectors as representational expenses.... The complaint expressly raised the issue of the Union's attempt to collect the full initiation fee from Blosser. Respondent offered no evidence that funds derived from initiation fees were expended differently than those derived from periodic dues and presented no argument on brief that initiation fees should be exempt from the Beck apportionment. Accordingly, I find that by seeking to require Blosser, a nonmember objector, to pay the full initiation fee, Respondent breached its duty of fair representation and thereby violated Section 8(b)(1)(A).

In its computation of "core fees," the Union included, as chargeable to objecting employees, its organizing expenses. The complaint alleges that by the inclusion of such expenses the Union has breached its duty of fair representation.... It is axiomatic that the organizing of other bargaining units, at least within the same industry and/or geographical area, strengthens a union's hand in bargaining with the employer of objecting employees. Successful organization of the employees of an employer's competitors precludes that employer from arguing, at the bargaining table, that the lesser wages and benefits paid by his union-free competition prevents him from granting wage and benefit increases sought by the union which represents his employees. It also tends to increase the support which his employees will receive should they find it necessary to engage in economic action, such as a strike. Organizing of other employees thus inures "to the benefit of the members of the local union by virtue of their membership in the parent organization."

Moreover, in order to avoid the "free rider" problem ... it is essential that a union be permitted to charge objecting nonmembers for its expenses in organizing other units. The bargaining unit in which the objector finds him or herself has already been organized. The expense of that organizational effort was borne by the union (and its members in previously organized units) sometime in the past; it can no longer be charged to current employees. Only by permitting a union to pass along the cost of its current organizing efforts to the members of its already organized units can it equitably recoup those expenses.

It may be that some organizing expenses are too remote, in terms of industry or geography, to pose more than a theoretical benefit to the objector's bargaining unit. However… I find that organizing expenses are not "necessarily nonchargeable … as a matter of law" and recommend dismissal of this allegation.

… Having found that the Respondent has engaged in certain unfair labor practices, I find that it must be ordered to cease and desist and to take certain affirmative action designed to effectuate the policies of the Act.…

[On review by the NLRB, the Board affirmed the judge's rulings, findings, and conclusions and adopted the recommended Order.]

Case Questions

1. What information does the NLRB require a union to provide to employees who choose not to become members? What information did the union provide to Blosser?
2. Why is the union allowed to include organizing expenses in the expenses chargeable to nonmembers? What is the "free rider" problem?
3. How was the union's conduct coercive? What unfair labor practices did the union commit? Explain.

Shortly after taking office in 2001, President George W. Bush signed Executive Order 13201,[16] which applied to all firms doing business with the federal government. The order required those firms to post notices in the workplace informing employees subject to a union security agreement that they have the right to refuse to pay the portion of their union dues that is expended for activities unrelated to collective bargaining, contract administration, or grievance adjustment. However, on January 30, 2009, President Barack Obama issued Executive Order 13496,[17] which revoked Executive Order 13201. The new Executive Order requires employers to post a notice, the content of which will be established by the Secretary of Labor, informing employees of their rights under the National Labor Relations Act.

The WORKING Law

Executive Order 13496: Notification of Employee Rights under Federal Labor Laws

On August 3, 2009, the Department of Labor published a notice of proposed rulemaking (NPRM) seeking comments on proposed 29 CFR Part 471.[1] Proposed Part 471 implements Executive Order (E.O.) 13496, signed by President Barack Obama on January 30, 2009 (74 FR 6107, February 4, 2009).[2]

[1] See http://edocket.access.gpo.gov/2009/pdf/E9-17577.pdf

[2] See http://edocket.access.gpo.gov/2009/pdf/E9-2485.pdf

[16] 66 FR 11221, 2001 WL 169257 (Feb. 17, 2001).

[17] 74 FR 6107, 2009 WL 248091 (Jan. 30, 2009).

E.O.13496 requires federal contractors and subcontractors to post a required notice in their workplaces informing employees of their rights under federal labor laws, and provides that the requirement to post the employee notice be included in federal contracts and subcontracts.

The proposed regulation implements E.O. 13496 by prescribing the form and content of the notice, which incorporates employee rights under the National Labor Relations Act (NLRA). The proposed regulation also includes enforcement procedures and provisions regarding sanctions, penalties, and remedies that may be imposed for violations. Federal government contracting departments and agencies are obliged to include the notice requirements in every government contract, except collective bargaining agreements entered into by a federal agency, contracts for purchases under the Simplified Acquisition Threshold, and in those cases where the Secretary exempts a contracting department or agency pursuant to the Executive Order. The proposed regulation requires government contractors to include the contract clause in all subcontracts.

The provisions of the proposed contract clause include the text of the required notice, enforcement procedures, and an explanation of the sanctions, penalties, and remedies that may be imposed if the contractor or subcontractor fails to comply with its obligations.

The notice required by E.O. 13496 and the proposed regulation outlines the fundamental rights regarding union activity and collective bargaining that employees have under the NLRA, provides examples of conduct that is illegal under the NLRA, and provides contact information in the event that an employee suspects that the law has been violated.

Enforcement responsibilities for proposed Part 471 are shared by two agencies. The Office of Federal Contract Compliance Programs (OFCCP) is responsible for investigation and conciliation, and that agency will refer violations to the Office of Labor-Management Standards (OLMS) for enforcement. The sanctions, penalties, and remedies under proposed Part 471 include the debarring of federal contractors and subcontractors from future federal contracts and subcontracts.

E.O. 13496 also revoked E.O. 13201, which required Federal contractors and subcontractors to post a notice (the "Beck poster") informing their employees of rights concerning payment of union dues or fees.[3] The Department published a final rule on March 30, 2009, rescinding the regulations at 29 CFR Part 470, which had implemented the Beck poster provisions (74 FR 14045).[4] OLMS has removed all material from its Web site relating to E.O. 13201.

E.O. 13496 advances the Administration's goal of promoting economy and efficiency of federal government procurement by ensuring that workers employed in the private sector as a result of federal government contracts are informed of their rights to engage in union activity and collective bargaining. Knowledge of such basic statutory rights promotes stable labor-management relations, thus reducing costs to the federal government.

[Note: the provisions of the Executive Order regarding submission of comments have been omitted.]

Source: http://www.dol.gov/esa/olms/regs/compliance/lrposter_highlights.htm (last accessed Sept. 14, 2009).

---

[3]See E.O. 13496, Section 13.

[4]See http://edocket.access.gpo.gov/2009/pdf/E9-6926.pdf

Liability for Breach of the Duty of Fair Representation

Most cases involving the duty of fair representation arise from action by the employer; after the employee has been disciplined or discharged, the union's alleged breach of the duty compounds the problem.

How should the damages awarded in such a case be divided between the employer and the union? Which party should bear primary liability? In *Vaca v. Sipes*,[18] the Supreme Court held that an employer cannot escape liability for breach of the collective agreement just because the union has breached its duty of fair representation.

Where the employee has established a breach of the collective agreement by the employer and a breach of the duty of fair representation by the union, the employer and the union must share liability. In *Bowen v. U.S. Postal Service*,[19] the Supreme Court held that the employer is liable for back pay for the discharge of an employee in breach of the collective agreement, whereas the union breaching the duty of fair representation by refusing to grieve the discharge is responsible for any increase in damages suffered by the employee as a result of the breach of the duty of fair representation. In *Chauffeurs, Teamsters and Helpers, Local No. 391 v. Terry*,[20] the Supreme Court held that to recover damages against both the employer and the union, the employee must prove both that the employer's actions violated the collective agreement and that the union's handling of the grievance breached the duty of fair representation.

The NLRB has held that when an employee has established that the union improperly refused to process a grievance or handled it in a perfunctory manner, the Board is prepared to resolve doubts about the merits of the grievance in favor of the employee, according to *Rubber Workers Local 250 (Mack-Wayne Enclosures)*.[21]

Enforcing the Duty of Fair Representation

In *Miranda Fuel Co.*,[22] the NLRB held that a breach of the duty of fair representation by a union was a violation of Section 8(b)(1)(A) of the NLRA. The Board reasoned that "Section 7 … gives employees the right to be free from unfair or irrelevant or invidious treatment by their exclusive bargaining agent in matters affecting their employment." Although the Court of Appeals for the Second Circuit refused to enforce the Board's order in *Miranda*,[23] other courts of appeals have affirmed NLRB findings of Section 8(b)(1)(A) violations in subsequent duty of fair representation cases. The NLRB continues to hold that breach of the duty of fair representation by a union is an unfair labor practice.

The NLRB does not have exclusive jurisdiction over claims of the breach of the duty of fair representation; federal courts also may exercise jurisdiction over such claims according to the Supreme Court in *Breininger v. Sheet Metal Workers Local 6*.[24] The cases developing the duty of fair representation that we have seen so far have involved lawsuits filed against both the union and the employer. Such suits are filed under Section 301 of the NLRA and may be filed

---

[18] 386 U.S. 171 (1967).

[19] 459 U.S. 212 (1983).

[20] 494 U.S. 558 (1990).

[21] 279 NLRB 1074 (1986).

[22] 140 NLRB 181 (1962).

[23] 326 F.2d 172 (1963).

[24] 493 U.S. 67 (1989).

either in state or federal courts and are subject to federal labor law, not state contract law. In *Steelworkers v. Rawson*,[25] the Supreme Court held that a wrongful death suit brought under state law against a union by the heirs of miners killed in an underground fire was preempted by Section 301. According to the Supreme Court in *Chauffeurs, Teamsters and Helpers, Local No. 391 v. Terry*, an employee who seeks back pay as a remedy for a union's violation of the duty of fair representation is entitled to a jury trial.

In *DelCostello v. Teamsters*,[26] the Supreme Court held that the time limit for bringing a suit under Section 301 alleging a breach of the duty of fair representation is six months. In cases where the employee is required to exhaust internal procedures, the six-month time limit does not begin to run until those procedures have been exhausted, according to *Frandsen v. BRAC*.[27] A suit against a union for failing to enforce an arbitration award is an action for breach of the duty of fair representation and is subject to the six-month limitations period, as held by *Carrion v. Enterprise Association, Metal Trades Branch Local Union 638*.[28]

Exhausting Internal Remedies

We have seen that the duty of fair representation may be enforced by either a Section 301 suit or a Section 8(b)(1)(A) unfair labor practice proceeding. Before either action can be initiated, however, the employee alleging breach of the duty of fair representation must attempt to exhaust internal remedies that may be available.

Because most complaints of breaches of the duty of fair representation result from employer actions, such as discharge or discipline, which are then compounded by the union's breach of its duty, the affected employee may have the right to file a grievance under the collective bargaining agreement to challenge the employer's actions. When contractual remedies—the grievance procedure and arbitration—are available to the employee, he or she must first attempt to use those procedures. This means that the employee must file a grievance and attempt to have it processed through to arbitration before filing a Section 301 suit or a Section 8(b)(1)(A) complaint. The requirement of exhausting contractual remedies flows from the policy of fostering voluntary settlement of disputes. This policy is behind the court's deferral to arbitration (recall the *Steelworkers Trilogy* from Chapter 17) and the NLRB deferral to arbitration (recall the *United Technologies* and the *Olin Corp*. cases from Chapter 17).

The requirement of exhausting contractual remedies is not absolute. In *Glover v. St. Louis–San Francisco Railway*,[29] the Supreme Court held that employees need not exhaust contract remedies when the union and employer are cooperating in the violation of employee rights. In such cases, attempts to get the union to file a grievance or to process it through to arbitration would be an exercise in futility.

Aside from contractual remedies, an employee may have available internal union procedures to deal with complaints against the union. Some union constitutions provide for review of complaints of alleged mistreatment of union members by union leaders. For example, if local union officials refuse to submit the employee's grievance to arbitration, the

---

[25]495 U.S. 362 (1990).

[26]462 U.S. 151 (1983).

[27]782 F.2d 674 (7th Cir. 1986).

[28]227 F.3d 29 (2d Cir. 2000).

[29]393 U.S. 324 (1969).

employee may appeal that decision to the membership of the local. An appeal to the international union leadership may also be available. Should an employee be required to exhaust such internal union remedies before filing a suit or unfair practice complaint alleging breach of the duty of fair representation?

In *Clayton v. United Auto Workers*,[30] the Supreme Court held that an employee is not required to exhaust internal union remedies when the internal union appeals procedure cannot result in reactivation of the employee's grievance or award the complete relief sought by the employee. In such cases, the employee may file a Section 301 suit or a Section 8(b)(1)(A) complaint without exhausting the internal union remedies. If such remedies could provide the relief sought by the employee, they must be pursued before filing under Section 301 or Section 8(b)(1)(A).

If the alleged breach of the duty of fair representation involves claims of discrimination based on race, sex, religion, or national origin, the affected employees may also have legal remedies under Title VII of the Civil Rights Act of 1964. Just as in *Alexander v. Gardner-Denver* (see Chapter 8), the remedies under Title VII are separate from any remedies under Section 301 or Section 8(b)(1)(A). The affected employees may then file a complaint with the Equal Employment Opportunity Commission under Title VII as well as filing under Section 301 and/or Section 8(b)(1)(A).

Remedies available under an action for breach of the duty of fair representation depend on whether the employee pursues the claim under Section 301 or Section 8(b)(1)(A). Under Section 301, an action against both the employer and the union can be brought. An employee may recover monetary damages (but not punitive damages) and legal fees and may get an injunction (such as ordering the union to arbitrate the grievance or ordering the employer to reinstate the employee). Under Section 8(b)(1)(A), the NLRB can order the union to

- pay compensation for lost wages, benefits, and legal fees;
- arbitrate the grievance; and
- "cease and desist" from further violations.

If the employee's complaint involves action by both the employer and the union, Section 301 would be preferable; if only the union is involved, either Section 301 or Section 8(b)(1)(A) is appropriate.

Concept *Summary* » 18.1

The Duty of Fair Representation

- Unions must not act arbitrarily, discriminatorily or in bad faith when representing members of the bargaining unit
- Enforced through Section 8(b)(1)(A) or Section 301
  - Section 8(b)(1)(A)—NLRB unfair labor practice action against the union
  - Section 301—suits in court against union and/or employer
  - Must first exhaust internal remedial procedures unless they do not provide the remedies sought

[30] 451 U.S. 679 (1981).

Rights of Union Members

In addition to being protected by the duty of fair representation, union members have certain rights against the union guaranteed by statute. The union members' bill of rights under the Labor Management Reporting and Disclosure Act and Section 8(b)(1) establishes those rights.

Union Discipline of Members

Section 8(b)(1)(A) prohibits union actions that restrain, coerce, or interfere with employee rights under Section 7. Section 8(b)(1)(A), however, does provide that "This paragraph shall not impair the right of a labor organization to prescribe its own rules with respect to the acquisition or retention of membership therein."

In *NLRB v. Allis-Chalmers Mfg. Co.*,[31] the Supreme Court held that a union could impose fines against members who crossed a picket line and worked during an authorized strike. In *NLRB v. Boeing Co.*,[32] the Supreme Court held that a union may file suit in a state court to enforce fines imposed against members. However, if union members legally resign from the union before crossing the picket line and return to work during a strike, the union cannot impose fines against them, as held by the Supreme Court in *NLRB v. Textile Workers Granite State Joint Board*.[33] Where the process used by a union to determine the amount of fines levied against members does not allow the fines to be apportioned between the members' conduct before and after they resigned from the union, the NLRB will rescind the entire amount of the fines, according to *Sheet Metal Workers Ass'n*.[34]

In response to the *Textile Workers Granite State Joint Board* decision, a number of unions adopted rules that limited the right of members to resign from the union during a strike. Such rules violate section 8(b)(1)(A) according to the Supreme Court decision in *Pattern Makers' League of North America v. NLRB*.[35] Where workers in a right-to-work state resign from the union but continue to work in the bargaining unit, and later decide to rejoin the union, a union rule requiring them to pay a "reinitiation" fee equal to the amount of union dues that they would have paid had they remained in the union did not violate Section 8(b)(1)(A), as held in *Lee v. NLRB*.[36]

Union Members' Bill of Rights

The Labor Management Reporting and Disclosure Act (LMRDA) seeks to ensure that union members are guaranteed certain rights when subjected to internal union proceedings. Section 101 of the LMRDA is commonly called the union members' bill of rights.

---

[31] 388 U.S. 175 (1967).

[32] 412 U.S. 67 (1973).

[33] 409 U.S. 213 (1972).

[34] 338 NLRB 116 (2002).

[35] 473 U.S. 95 (1985).

[36] 325 F.3d 749 (6th Cir. 2003).

Union Disciplinary Procedures

Procedural safeguards against improper disciplinary action are provided by Section 101(a) (5), which states:

> No member of any labor organization may be fined, suspended, expelled, or otherwise disciplined except for nonpayment of dues by such organization or by any officer thereof unless such member has been (A) served with written specific charges; (B) given a reasonable time to prepare his defense; (C) afforded a full and fair hearing.

Section 102 of the LMRDA allows any person whose rights under the act have been violated to bring a civil suit in the federal courts for such relief as may be appropriate. In *Wooddell v. International Brotherhood of Electrical Workers, Local 71*,[37] the Supreme Court held that a union member suing under the LMRDA, alleging discrimination against him by the union in job referrals through the union hiring hall, was entitled to a jury trial.

When a union member alleges that his or her rights have been violated by union disciplinary action, what standards should the court apply to determine if the union procedure was reasonable? This question was addressed by the following case.

case 18.4 »

Boilermakers v. Hardeman

401 U.S. 233 (1971)

Facts: George Hardeman was a boilermaker, and a member of Local Lodge 112 of the International Brotherhood of Boilermakers. He went to the union hiring hall to see Herman Wise, business manager of the local, who was the official responsible for referring workers for jobs. An employer who was a friend of Hardeman had promised to ask for him by name for a job. He sought an assurance from Wise that he would be referred for the job, but Wise refused to make a definite commitment. Hardeman threatened violence if no work was forthcoming in the next few days. Hardeman returned to the hiring hall the next day and waited for a referral, but there was none. He returned to the hiring hall the next day, and when Wise came out of his office, Hardeman handed him a copy of a telegram asking for Hardeman by name. As Wise was reading the telegram, Hardeman began punching him in the face.

The union brought disciplinary charges against Hardeman. He was tried on charges of creating dissension and working against the interest and harmony of the local, and of threatening and using force to restrain an officer of the lodge from properly discharging the duties of his office. The trial committee found him guilty of the charges, and the local sustained the finding and voted his expulsion for an indefinite period. Hardeman then sought an internal union appeal of this action, but the verdict and the penalty were upheld. Five years later, Hardeman filed suit against the union, alleging that it violated Section 101(a)(5) by denying him a full and fair hearing in the union disciplinary proceedings. After a jury trial, Hardeman was awarded damages of $152,150. On appeal, the U.S. Court of Appeals for the Fifth Circuit affirmed the trial decision. The union then appealed to the U.S. Supreme Court.

Issue: What standards should the courts use to review whether union disciplinary procedures are reasonable under Section 101(a)?

Decision: The union claimed that the NLRB had exclusive jurisdiction over the subject matter of this lawsuit because it involves an allegation of discrimination against Hardeman in job referrals, which is arguably an unfair labor practice under Sections 8(b)(1)(A) and 8(b)(2) of the NLRA and that the federal courts must defer to the exclusive competence of the NLRB. The Court rejected that claim, holding that Hardeman's suit alleged that his expulsion was unlawful under Section 101(a)(5), and he sought compensation for

[37] 502 U.S. 93 (1991).

the consequences of the claimed wrongful expulsion. The issue presented by Hardeman's suit was whether the union disciplinary proceedings had denied him a full and fair hearing within the meaning of Section 101(a)(5)(c). Congress explicitly referred claims under Section 101(a)(5) not to the NLRB, but to the federal district courts, as stated in Section 102. The internal union procedures resulted in Hardeman being convicted on both charges, and he was expelled from the union.

When the trial court was considering Hardeman's suit against the union, the trial judge held that whether Hardeman was rightfully or wrongfully expelled was a question of law for the judge to determine. The judge assumed that the transcript of the union disciplinary hearing contained evidence adequate to support conviction of using threats or force against an officer of the union, but held that there was no evidence in the transcript to support the charge of creating dissension and working against the interest and harmony of the local.

Because the union tribunal had returned only a general verdict, and since one of the charges was thought to be supported by no evidence whatsoever, the trial judge held that Hardeman had been deprived of the full and fair hearing guaranteed by Section 101(a)(5), and the court of appeals affirmed. The Supreme Court disagreed, holding that neither the language nor the legislative history of Section 101(a)(5) could justify the substitution of judicial authority for the union's authority to interpret its regulations when determining whether the scope of offenses warrant discipline of union members. The Court stated that Section 101(a)(5) was not intended to authorize courts to determine the scope of offenses for which a union may discipline its members, and it is not appropriate for a court to construe the union's written disciplinary rules in order to determine whether particular conduct may be punished at all. Here, Hardeman was given a detailed statement of the facts relating to the fight which formed the basis for the disciplinary action against him, which complied with the notice requirement of Section 101(a)(5). Section 101(a)(5)(c) guarantees union members a "full and fair" disciplinary hearing, and the parties and the lower federal courts are in full agreement that this guarantee requires the charging party to provide some evidence at the disciplinary hearing to support the charges made. The courts have repeatedly held that conviction on charges unsupported by any evidence is a denial of due process, and Section 101(a)(5)(c) imports a similar requirement into union disciplinary proceedings. In this case, there is no question that the charges were adequately supported "some evidence."

The Supreme Court reversed the court of appeals' decision affirming the trial court verdict.

To have a valid claim under Section 101(a)(5) and Section 102, the union member must have been subjected to discipline by the union. In *Breininger v. Sheet Metal Workers Local 6*,[38] the Supreme Court held that Breininger's suit over the union's failure to refer him under a hiring hall agreement because he supported a political rival of the union business manager did not state a claim under the LMRDA. The Court held that the failure to refer him was not "discipline" within the meaning of the act. Where a union pursuing disciplinary action against a member did not allow the member to record the disciplinary hearing and allowed a biased decision-maker to sit as a member of the hearing board, the union was held to have violated the LMRDA due process requirements, according to *Knight v. Longshoremen, ILA*.[39]

Free Speech and Association

Whereas Section 101(a)(5) guarantees union members' procedural rights in union disciplinary proceedings, the other provisions of Section 101(a) provide for other basic rights in participating in union activities. These rights take precedence over any provisions of union constitutions or bylaws that are inconsistent with Section 101 rights. Section 101(b) states that any such inconsistent provisions shall have no effect.

[38] 493 U.S. 67 (1989).

[39] 457 F.3d 331 (3d Cir. 2006).

Section 101(a)(2) provides for the rights of freedom of speech and assembly for union members. Every union member has the right to meet and assemble with other members and to express any views or opinions, subject to the union's reasonable rules for the conduct of meetings. As long as any item of business is properly before a union meeting, a union member may express his or her views on that item of business. The latitude given to union members to express their opinions at union meetings is very broad. Any restrictions on such expression must be reasonable and required for the orderly conducting of union meetings. Violations of these rights give rise to civil liability. In *Hall v. Cole*,[40] a union member was expelled from the union after introducing a series of resolutions alleging undemocratic actions and questionable policies by union officials. The union claimed such resolutions violated a rule against "deliberate and malicious vilification with regard to the execution or duties of any office." The member filed suit under Section 102, alleging violations of his rights guaranteed by Section 101(a)(2). The Supreme Court upheld the trial decision ordering that the member be reinstated in the union and awarding him $5,500 in legal fees.

In *Sheet Metal Workers International Association v. Lynn*,[41] an elected business agent of the union filed suit under Section 102 over his removal from office because of statements he made at a union meeting opposing a dues increase sought by the union trustee. The Supreme Court held that his removal from office constituted a violation of the free speech provisions of Section 101(a)(2).

In *United Steelworkers of America v. Sadlowski*,[42] the Supreme Court held that a union rule prohibiting contributions from nonmembers in campaigns for union offices did not violate a union member's right of free speech and assembly under Section 101(a)(2), even though it had the effect of making a challenge to incumbent union officers much more difficult.

The courts have recognized some other limits on union members' rights of free speech and assembly. A union member cannot preach "dual unionism"—that is, advocate membership in another union during his union's meeting. Furthermore, the remarks of a union member are subject to libel and slander laws. The right of free assembly does not protect a group of members who engage in a wildcat strike that violates the union's no-strike agreement with the employer.

Right to Participate in Union Affairs

The right of union members to participate in all membership business, such as meetings, discussions, referendums, and elections, is guaranteed by Section 101(a)(1) of the LMRDA. This right to participate is subject to the reasonable rules and regulations of the union's constitution and bylaws. Any provisions that are inconsistent with these rights are of no effect by reason of Section 101(b).

The provisions of the LMRDA allow a union to require that members exhaust internal union remedies before pursuing external action for violation of the rights granted by the LMRDA. Section 101(a)(4) does provide, however, that the internal union proceedings cannot last longer than four months. If the proceedings take longer than four months, the member is not required to pursue them before instituting external proceedings.

[40]412 U.S. 1 (1973).

[41]488 U.S. 347 (1989).

[42]457 U.S. 102 (1982).

Election Procedures

Title IV of the LMRDA requires that union elections be conducted according to certain democratic procedures. Section 401 sets the following requirements:

- National and international labor organizations must elect their officers at least every five years
- Every local union must hold elections at least every three years
- Elections shall be by secret ballot or at a convention of delegates chosen by secret ballot
- There must be advance notice of the election, freedom of choice among candidates, and publication and one year's preservation of the election results
- Dues and assessments cannot be used to support anyone's candidacy
- Every candidate has the right to inspect lists of members' names and addresses
- Each candidate has the right to have observers at polling places and at the counting of the ballots

In the case of *International Organization for Masters, Mates & Pilots v. Brown,*[43] the Supreme Court held that labor unions must cooperate with all reasonable requests from candidates for union office to distribute campaign literature despite union rules restricting such requests. In that case, the Court decided that a union refusal to provide a membership list to a candidate because of a union rule prohibiting preconvention mailings was in violation of the LMRDA.

The election provisions of the LMRDA also prohibit unduly restrictive eligibility requirements that enable incumbents to become entrenched in office. Such eligibility requirements are the subject of the following case.

case 18.5 » HERMAN V. LOCAL 1011, UNITED STEELWORKERS OF AMERICA

207 F.3d 924 (7th Cir. 2000), cert. denied, 531 U.S. 1010 (2000)

Posner, Chief Judge

Section 401(e) of the Labor-Management Reporting and Disclosure Act [LMRDA] makes all union members in good standing eligible to run for office in the union's elections subject to "reasonable qualifications uniformly imposed." The constitution of the steelworkers international union conditions eligibility for local office on the member's having attended at least eight of the local's monthly meetings (or been excused from attendance at them, in which event he must have attended one-third of the meetings from which he was not excused) within the two years preceding the election. Noting that the rule disqualifies 92 percent of the almost 3,000 members of Local 1011 of the steelworkers union, the district judge, at the behest of the Secretary of Labor ... declared the rule void.

The Act's aim was to make the governance of labor unions democratic. The democratic presumption is that any adult member of the polity, which in this case is a union local, is eligible to run for office....

As an original matter we would think it, not absurd, but still highly questionable, to impose a meeting-attendance requirement on aspirants for union office, at least in the absence of any information, which has not been vouchsafed us, regarding the character of these meetings. All we know is that they are monthly and that the union's constitution requires that all expenditure and other decisions of the union's hierarchy be approved at these meetings; yet despite the formal power that the attendants exercise, only a tiny percentage of the union's membership bothers to attend—on average no more than 3 percent (fewer than 90 persons). We are not told

[43] 498 U.S. 466 (1991).

whether an agenda or any other material is distributed to the membership in advance of the meeting to enable members to decide whether to attend and to enable them to participate intelligently if they do attend. We do not know how long the meetings last or what information is disseminated at them orally or in writing to enable the attenders to cast meaningful, informed votes. For all we know the only attenders are a tiny coterie of insiders not eager to share their knowledge with the rest of the union's members....

All we know for sure about this case, so far as bears on the reasonableness of the meeting-attendance requirement, is that the requirement disqualifies the vast majority of the union's members, that it requires members who have not been attending meetings in the past to decide at least eight months before an election that they may want to run for union office (for remember that the meetings are monthly and that a candidate must have attended at least eight within the past two years unless he falls within one of the excuse categories), and that the union itself does not take the requirement very seriously, for it allows members who have attended no meetings to run for office, provided that they fall into one of the excuse categories. The categories are reasonable in themselves—service with the armed forces, illness, being at work during the scheduled time of the meeting, and so forth—and they expand the pool of eligibles from 95 union members to 242, of whom 53 attended not a single meeting. But if the meeting-attendance requirement were regarded as a vital condition of effective officership, equivalent in importance to the LMRDA's requirement that the candidate be a union member in good standing, the fact that a member was without fault in failing to satisfy it would not excuse the failure.... So many of the union's members are excused from the meeting-attendance requirement that there could be an election for officers of Local 1011 at which none of the candidates satisfied the requirement.

The requirement is paternalistic. Union members should be capable of deciding for themselves whether a candidate for union office who had not attended eight, or five, or for that matter any meetings within the past two years should by virtue of his poor attendance forfeit the electorate's consideration. The union's rule is antidemocratic in deeming the electors incompetent to decide an issue that is in no wise technical or esoteric—what weight to give to a candidate's failure to have attended a given number of union meetings in the recent past.... And since most union members interested in seeking an office in the union are likely to attend meetings just to become known ... the rule is superfluous.

... Under conditions of pervasive apathy, a requirement of attending even a single meeting might disqualify the vast bulk of the membership. That is true here. Only 14 percent of the members attended even one meeting within the last two years. Yet the Department of Labor does not argue that therefore even a one-meeting requirement would be unreasonable.

... We think the proper approach, and one that is consistent with the case law ... is to deem a condition of eligibility that disqualifies the vast bulk of the union's membership from standing for union office presumptively unreasonable. The union must then present convincing reasons, not merely conjectures, why the condition is either not burdensome or though burdensome is supported by compelling need. This approach distinguishes ... between impact and burden. A requirement that to be eligible to be a candidate a member of the union have attended one meeting of the union in his lifetime would not be burdensome even though it might disqualify a large fraction of the union membership simply because very few members took any interest in the governance of the union. That defense is unavailable here, however. Requiring attendance at eight meetings in two years imposes a burden because it compels the prospective candidate not only to sacrifice what may be scarce free time to sit through eight meetings, but also, if he is disinclined to attend meetings for any reason other than to be able to run for union office, to make up his mind whether to run many months before the election.

The burden is great enough in this case to place the onus of justification on the union. The only justification offered is that the requirement of attending eight meetings in two years encourages union members who might want to run for office, perhaps especially opponents of the incumbents, to attend union meetings (since otherwise they may not be eligible to run), thus bolstering attendance at the meetings and fostering participatory democracy. The slight turnout at the meetings suggests that this goal, though worthy, cannot be achieved by the means adopted; the means are not adapted to the end, suggesting that the real end may be different. So far as appears, the union has given no consideration to alternative inducements to attend meetings that would not involve disqualifying from office more than nine-tenths of its members.... Under the rule challenged in this case, a union member who wanted to be sure of qualifying for eligibility to run for office might have to start attending meetings as much as a year in advance of the election, because he might miss one or more meetings for reasons that the union does not recognize as excusing (such as vacation or family leave) and because the union might cancel one or more meetings. And yet a year before the election an issue that might move a union member to incur the time and expense of running for office might not even be on the horizon....

The district court was right to invalidate the meeting-attendance requirement as unreasonable, and the judgment is therefore.

AFFIRMED.

Case Questions

1. What does the election rule require of members who want to run for union office? Why would the union impose such a requirement?
2. Why has the Secretary of Labor (Herman) challenged the election-eligibility rule?
3. What does the court mean by distinguishing "between impact and burden" of the challenged rule? How does the court's approach apply to the rule at issue in this case?

Concept *Summary* » 18.2

The Union Members Bill of Rights

- Rules regarding acquisition and retention of membership must be reasonable
- Union internal disciplinary procedure requirements
  - Must provide specific written charges
  - Must allow a reasonable time to prepare defense
  - Must provide for a full and fair hearing
- Union members are accorded freedom of speech and association
- Union members have the right to participate in union meetings, discussions, referenda, and elections
- Requirements for union election procedures
  - National unions must hold elections for officers at least every five years
  - Local unions must hold elections at least every three years
  - Elections must be by secret ballot or at a convention of delegates chosen by secret ballot
  - Advance notice of elections, a choice of candidates and preservation of election results for at least one year
  - Union dues or assessments cannot be used to support any candidacy
  - Candidates have the right to a list of members' names and addresses, and to have observers present at polling places and the counting of the ballots

Other Restrictions on Unions

Duties of Union Officers

The provisions of the LMRDA and the Taft-Hartley amendments to the NLRA imposed a number of duties on union officers to eliminate financial corruption and racketeering and to safeguard union funds. All officials handling union money must be bonded, and persons convicted of certain criminal offenses are barred from holding union office for five years.

Unions are also subjected to annual reporting requirements by the LMRDA. The union reports, filed with the Secretary of Labor, must contain the following information:

- the name and the title of each officer;
- the fees and dues required of members;
- provisions for membership qualification and issuing work permits;
- the process for electing and removing officers;
- disciplinary standards for members;
- details of any union benefit plans; and
- authorization rules for bargaining demands, strikes, and contract ratification.

Any changes in the union constitution, bylaws, or rules must be reported. In addition, detailed financial information must be reported annually; these financial reports must contain information on the following:

- assets and liabilities at the beginning and end of the fiscal year;
- union receipts and their sources;
- salaries paid by the union in excess of $10,000 total;
- any loans by the union in excess of $250; and
- any other union disbursements.

All reports and information filed with the Secretary of Labor must also be made available to union members.

Union officials must report any security or financial interest in, or any benefit received from, any employer whose employees are represented by the union and anything of value received from any business dealing connected with the union. The LMRDA imposes on union officers a duty to refrain from dealing with the union as an adverse party in any manner connected with their duties and to refrain from holding or acquiring any personal or pecuniary interest that conflicts with the interests of the union, according to *Chathas v. Local 134 I.B.E.W.*[44] Employers are required to make annual reports of any expenditures or transactions with union representatives and payments to employees or consultants for the purpose of influencing organizational or bargaining activities.

Welfare and Pension Plans

Section 302 of the Taft-Hartley Act, along with the Employee Retirement Income Security Act (ERISA), controls the operation and administration of employee welfare and pension plans. Persons administering such funds must handle them to protect the interests of all employees. Union officials serving as trustees or administrators of such funds may receive only one full-time salary. They must also be careful to keep their roles as trustee and union official separated.

[44] 233 F.3d 508 (7th Cir. 2000), *cert. denied,* 533 U.S. 949 (2001).

Section 304 of the Taft-Hartley Act, along with the federal election laws, control union political contributions and expenditures. Union dues or assessments may not be used to fund political expenditures. However, the union may establish a separate political fund if it is financed by voluntary contributions from union members. Members must be kept informed of the use of such funds and must not be subject to any reprisals in connection with the collection of contributions. State laws may affect public sector unions; a law requiring public sector unions to get affirmative authorization of the use of agency shop fees for political purposes was valid and did not violate the unions' First Amendment rights, as held by *Davenport v. Washington Education Association*.[45]

---

[45]551 U.S. 177 (2007).

CHAPTER REVIEW

» Key Terms

duty of fair representation	« 557	***union shop***	« 562	***agency shop***	« 562

» Summary

- The duty of fair representation was developed by the Supreme Court to ensure that unions protected the rights of the employees they represent. The NLRB has determined that a breach of the duty of fair representation is an unfair labor practice in violation of Section 8(b)(1)(A) of the NLRA. Section 301 may also be used to bring a suit for breach of duty of fair representation in the courts. Although unions have some leeway to exercise judgment as to how to represent their members, actions that are discriminatory, arbitrary, or in bad faith are violations of the duty of fair representation.
- Unions owe the duty of fair representation to all employees in the bargaining unit, not just to union members. Employees subject to a union security clause may not be terminated for failing to join the union, as long as membership is denied to them for reasons other than failure to pay union dues or fees. Nonmembers who pay union dues and fees are entitled to a reduction in those dues and fees reflecting union expenditures on matters not related to collective bargaining. Failure to inform such employees of their rights, or to allow them the reductions, is a violation of the duty of fair representation.
- Unions are entitled to make and enforce reasonable rules for internal discipline and maintenance of membership; however, unions cannot enforce such rules against employees who resign from the union. Rules that restrict the right of employees to resign from the union may violate Section 8(b)(1)(A).
- The Labor Management Reporting and Disclosure Act (LMRDA) sets out a bill of rights for union members, guaranteeing them certain procedural rights for internal union proceedings. Union officials must comply with the financial and reporting requirements of the LMRDA, and elections for union officers are subject to the requirements of Section 401 of the LMRDA.

» Problems

Questions

1. What is meant by the duty of fair representation? What standard of conduct by a union is required by the duty of fair representation? Who is protected by the duty of fair representation? What remedies are available for a breach of the duty of fair representation?
2. What is the union member's bill of rights?
3. Can bargaining unit employees who are not union members be required to pay union dues and fees? What information must the union provide to such employees?
4. When can a union enforce its disciplinary rules against employees who resign from the union?

When can a union restrict the right of members to resign? Explain your answers.

5. What restrictions are placed on union officers by the Taft-Hartley Act and the Labor Management Reporting and Disclosure Act amendments to the NLRA?

Case Problems

6. An employee joined the United States Postal Service (USPS) in 1975 as a part-time substitute rural carrier near Spokane, Washington. In 1976, the employee was given a full-time rural route. He obtained this route under a provision in the collective bargaining agreement giving senior part-timers first priority for new full-time routes.

   City delivery carriers and managers were jealous of the employee for obtaining this route, the court relates. He began to experience harassment from some of his co-workers, and in addition, the route he worked was overburdened. In January 1978, the employee and another man were arrested and charged with stealing equipment from a railroad yard. He pled guilty and received a suspended sentence. The theft was reported in the local press.

   USPS fired the employee, asserting that the conviction meant he no longer was entrusted to safeguard mail or postal funds. He filed a grievance, but the shop steward declined to represent him. The union's steward fulfilled this task instead. When decisions at lower steps were negative, the union considered arbitration. However, the union's general counsel advised against arbitration on the ground that there was little likelihood of success.

   Based on these facts, do you think the union fulfilled its duty of fair representation to the discharged postal worker? See *Johnson v. U.S. Postal Service and National Rural Letter Carriers Association* [756 F.2d 1461 (9th Cir. 1985)].

7. After being on sick leave for half a year because of high blood pressure, Owens attempted to return to work. Owens's family physician had approved his return to work, but Owens's employer's company physician felt that Owens's blood pressure was too high to return, and the employer discharged him. Owens filed a grievance over his discharge, which the union processed through the grievance procedure in the collective agreement. In preparation for taking Owens's grievance to arbitration, the union had Owens examined by another physician. That doctor also believed that Owens should not return to work. In light of its doctor's opinion, the union decided not to take Owens's grievance to arbitration. Owens demanded that his grievance be arbitrated, but the union refused. Owens then sued the union and the employer in state court, alleging breach of the collective agreement and of the duty of fair representation.

   How should the court decide Owens's claims against the union? Against the employer? Explain your answers. See *Vaca v. Sipes* [368 U.S. 171 (1967)].

8. Beginning in 1973, an employer's employees had been represented by Local P-706 of the then Amalgamated Meat Cutters Union. In December 1978, an employee filed a decertification petition in Case 11–RD–284, and the parties entered into a stipulated election agreement. Shortly thereafter, a notice was posted or mailed by the Meat Cutters announcing a meeting on December 30, 1978. Of the 176 unit employees, 16 attended the meeting and voted 15–1 for what was orally described as a "merger." On January 11, 1979, the NLRB election was held. Local P-706 remained the sole recipient of the 158 valid ballots cast. On May 4, 1979, the board issued its Decision and Certification of Representative to Local P-706, overruling, *inter alia,* the employer's objection, which contended that the Meat Cutters' holding of the merger vote had interfered with the election.

   Prior to the Board's decision, however, the following events had taken place. Since Local P-706 was an amalgamated local, the merger process was completed on February 17 when the employees of the other employers voted. The employer's employees were expressly excluded from this vote. The February 17 tally was in favor of merger, as of course was the combined tally of the December 30, 1978, and February 17 votes. Pursuant to these votes, sometime in March, Local P-706 surrendered its charter to the Meat Cutters and admittedly became defunct. The board, which was then considering challenges and objections in the decertification proceeding, was not informed of this action.

On July 6, Local 525 filed a petition in Case 11–AC–14 seeking to amend Local P-706's certification to reflect its merger into Local 525. On September 18, the regional director granted the employer's motion to dismiss on the ground that the December 30, 1978, merger vote was procedurally defective because the employees had not been given adequate notice of the union meeting at which the merger vote occurred. Local 525 did not request review of the regional director's decision.

With a view to devising the "quickest way to settle the matter" and thereby remedy the deficiency of the December 30, 1978, vote, Local 525 sent a September 27 letter to all employees of the employer who had either been members of the then defunct Local P-706 or who had since signed membership cards for Local 525. The letter informed the recipients of an October 21 meeting whose sole purpose would be to vote again on the merger issue. This letter indicated that only "Union Members" would be eligible to vote. Of the 176 unit employees, 67 members were sent letters, of which 52 were received. The October 21 vote was 14–0 in favor of merger. Local 525 then petitioned the NLRB to be certified as the employees' collective bargaining representative.

How should the NLRB have ruled on this petition? See *Fast Food Merchandisers and Food & Commercial Workers, Local 525* [274 NLRB 143 (1985)].

9. The plaintiff, Joan Taschner, worked for Thrift-Rack, Inc. in its warehouse for nine years, from 1973 until September 1982. Teamsters Local Union 384 was at all times relevant to this action the exclusive bargaining representative for the employees of Thrift-Rack.

   In September 1982, the plaintiff successfully cross-bid for an outside job of driver-salesperson. While working outside as a driver, she developed a severe neurodermatitis condition and allergic reaction, requiring a doctor's supervision and medication. As a result, she was unable to perform her outside job as a driver.

   The plaintiff twice requested Thrift-Rack to transfer her to her prior warehouse position, which was still open, or to any other warehouse position. The company, however, rejected her requests on grounds that the plaintiff claims were not provided for in the collective agreement and that were in violation of past practice.

   In response to the company's refusal to transfer her, the plaintiff filed a grievance with Local 384. That grievance was denied by the union agent, James Hill, on grounds that no cross-bidding was allowed, that there were two separate seniority lists for union members who were employed by the company, and that an employee must be working in a unit to be allowed to bid for a job in that unit. Plaintiff requested to take her grievance to arbitration, but that request was denied by Hill. Subsequently, the warehouse position was awarded to another employee with less seniority, no experience, and lower qualifications than the plaintiff possessed.

   On November 2, 1982, Thrift-Rack again refused the plaintiff's request to transfer to any warehouse position, although there were still warehouse jobs open, some of which may not have been bid upon by warehouse workers. The company refused to give her any work, informing her that there was no work available for her and to go home. Thereafter, the plaintiff called Thrift-Rack every day for about one week. She reported that she was still on medication and could not drive, but that she was available for any other work. She specifically requested transfer to any position in the warehouse. Thrift-Rack continued to refuse to transfer her to any position in the warehouse.

   What recourse did the plaintiff have against her union? See *Taschner v. Hill* [589 F. Supp. 127, 118 L.R.R.M. 2044 (E.D. Pa. 1984)].

10. Plaintiff Feist received a Coast Guard license as a third assistant engineer in 1974 and was accepted into the applicant program of the Merchant Engineers' Beneficial Association (MEBA) in 1975. From 1975 on, he served aboard vessels as a licensed third engineer, completed additional schooling, and worked the required number of days to achieve what is known as Group I status. The plaintiff paid all

MEBA dues and had satisfied the requirement of a $2,500 initiation fee for membership. The plaintiff claims that in May 1979 he was informed that the District Investigating Committee had voted to deny him membership in the MEBA. Plaintiff's application was denied a second time on September 7, 1979, and again on February 13, 1981. Plaintiff filed suit against the MEBA, alleging that he had satisfied the requirements of membership in the MEBA and had been wrongfully denied membership status and the right to a full hearing, all in violation of the LMRDA.

Acceptance into membership of the MEBA is governed by Article 3 of the National Constitution, Articles 3 and 4 of the District Constitution, and Rules and Regulations No. 3, promulgated by the National Executive Committee. Rules and Regulations No. 3 states, in pertinent part, "The MEBA reserves the absolute right in its own discretion, for any reason whatsoever (a) at any time prior to acceptance into membership to terminate any applicant's status as such, or (b) to reject the application for membership." The plaintiff sued the union, demanding that he be admitted to membership.

How should the federal court have ruled on the plaintiff's demand? See *Feist v. Engineers' Beneficial Ass'n.* [118 L.R.R.M. 2419 (E.D. La. 1983)].

11. The plaintiffs were boilermakers by trade and also union members. When boilermakers were needed on a construction job, an agreement between the parent union and participating building contractors called "Southeastern States Articles of Agreement" provided that the contractor would request that the union provide the workers and would employ those sent by the union if they were qualified. The controversy resulted from an incident in which the plaintiff boilermakers, upon arriving at the work site, found it picketed by a large and belligerent group from another trade, the pipefitters. It was agreed, for the purposes of the case, that the pipefitters' acts and presence were illegal. The referred boilermakers made no attempt to pass through the picket line, and this impasse continued unbroken for several days. After the weekend had passed, a replacement group of boilermakers appeared at the work site in a large body, led by the business agent. The newly recruited boilermakers went right through the line, but the pipefitters, along with the plaintiff boilermakers who had respected the picket lines the previous week, continued to hold off, standing apart. Soon thereafter, an official of the contractor came out from the job site and handed termination notices to all in that group, asserting absenteeism as the ground.

The record reflects a fear by the union that it would be in serious trouble if it could not improve its record of complying with its agreements with employers, and this incident of course involved not honoring illegal picket lines and thereby making the boilermakers abettors of illegal conduct by others.

The preceding situation is dealt with in a series of documents that were in evidence. The previously mentioned Articles of Agreement provide as follows:

> 1.4.4. There will be no recognition of any unauthorized or illegal picket line established by any person or organization, and the international and local officers of the Union will immediately upon being informed that such a situation exists, order all employees to cross such picket line.
>
> The Joint Referral Committee Standards entered into by employers and union provides that a registrant is not to be referred for employment from the out-of-work list for ninety days after:
>
> 4. Involvement in any unauthorized strike, work stoppage, slowdown, or any other activity having the effect of disrupting the job....
>
> 6. Insistence on recognizing illegal or unauthorized picket lines.

This ninety-day exclusion from referral was often called "benching" in the record of this case.

The employer demanded in writing that the rules be applied to seven men, including the plaintiffs herein, and accordingly, the Union Rules Committee notified all business agents nationwide, effectively blacklisting the offenders. One of the men was obliged to quit a job he had found in Florida. At the time of trial, the three plaintiffs did not yet have work as boilermakers, though the ninety days had long since expired. They were restored to the bottom of the out-of-work list—not to their previous seniority.

Evaluate the discipline handed out to these boilermakers and the manner in which it was meted. Why were they disciplined? Were they accorded due process of law? See *Turner v. Boilermakers Local 455* [755 F.2d 866 (11th Cir. 1985)].

12. On February 23, 1983, Gerald Forrest, a union member, addressed to Carroll Koepplinger, president of the defendant union, a letter setting forth the basis of his objections to the December 1982 election. The local received Forrest's letter and filed it. Forrest did not receive a response from the union, and pursuant to the LMRDA, he thereafter filed a timely complaint with the U.S. Department of Labor. The Department of Labor conducted an investigation of the allegations of Forrest's complaint and found probable cause to believe that violations of Title IV had occurred.

    At the time of the election, 378 members belonged to the local. They were employed by approximately eighteen employers spread geographically in the states of Illinois and Iowa. Eight separate nomination meetings were held and were generally conducted by Koepplinger. Following the nomination meetings, the Local 518 secretary reviewed the list of the nominees to determine the eligibility of each in accordance with the union requirements. One of those requirements was that no member could be nominated to any office unless the individual had been a member of the local or international union continuously for five years immediately preceding his or her nomination. As a result of that requirement, four nominees were ruled ineligible to run for office.

    The shop stewards distributed the ballots to union members in their shops while the members were working. The instruction sheet did not contain any instructions for shop stewards with respect to the procedure to be followed in issuing ballots. At least two of the shop stewards who distributed ballots were themselves candidates for union office (one of the two was unopposed). After collecting all the voted ballots, the stewards returned the package to the secretary of the local. The voted ballots were stored in an unlocked filing cabinet in the union hall. The secretary took leave of absence from the local from approximately December 23, 1982, to January 3, 1983, during which time Koepplinger had sole responsibility for the conduct of the election.

    Koepplinger selected December 30, 10:00 A.M., to tally the ballots. Koepplinger was present at the local union hall during the tally but in a different room from where the tally took place. The candidates were not affirmatively advised of the time and place of the election tally, and no observers were present. It is unclear whether any candidates had actual notice of the counting. The court requested affidavits from the parties on this question. Only the plaintiff filed affidavits. Those affidavits state that the affiants were never advised of the tally by anyone from the local. They do not answer the question of whether actual notice occurred.

    The referendum committee that counted the ballots did not count or reconcile the number of unused ballots and the number of voted ballots to account for all of the official printed ballots. After the election, the local maintained all the election records except for the unvoted ballots. Koepplinger threw these away approximately three weeks after the election tally as part of an office cleanup.

    According to the election records, there were 328 voted ballots. There were fifteen elected officers, of which three were contested races.

    Should the court overturn this election? See *Donovan v. Graphic Arts Union* [118 L.R.R.M. 2093 (C.D. Ill. 1984)].

13. Suit was filed as a class action by ten employees of the Kroger Company. These employees claimed that Teamsters International and Teamsters Local 327, which represented their bargaining unit, breached the union's duty to represent all members of the collective bargaining unit fairly. The employees also charged that Kroger conspired with the union to "reduce" the conditions and benefits of their employment. More specifically, the plaintiffs claimed that Local 327 failed to represent the members of the union fairly in negotiating a collective bargaining agreement with Kroger, with the result that the union "bargained away substantial benefits relating primarily to seniority." The complaint charged the International Union with failing to furnish a skilled negotiator to aid in the negotiations when requested to do so by the negotiating committee.

The complaint also alleged that the business agent and president of Local 327 conspired with Kroger in formulating an agreement that contained terms and conditions that were contrary to union policies and that diminished the rights of the plaintiffs and the class they sought to represent (all the unit members in two Kroger warehouses in the Nashville, Tennessee, area). The complaint further alleged that Local 327 and its business agent and president fraudulently changed the results of a membership vote on the proposed collective bargaining agreement to reflect ratification when in fact the proposed agreement had been rejected. Finally, the complaint asserted that the agreement negotiated by Local 327 and Kroger contained a provision that discriminated against female members of the unit by prescribing a lower wage scale for the unit employees in one of the warehouses than for the employees in the other. Virtually all employees in the warehouse with the lower wage rate were women.

Did the union breach its duty of fair representation? See *Storey v. Teamsters Local 327* [759 F.2d 517, 118 L.R.R.M. 3273 (6th Cir. 1985)].

14. In 1983, General Motors Corporation signed a collective bargaining agreement with the International Brotherhood of Electrical Workers, under the wage provisions of which new employees joining the bargaining unit were to be paid at a different (lower) hourly rate than current members. A so-called two-tier wage scale resulted from the arbitration of a Postal Service dispute that same year. Since then, a number of other unions have accepted two-tier systems as concessions in their collective bargaining agreements. Labor negotiators commonly refer to such two-tier wage concessions as "selling the unborn."

    Can you articulate an argument on behalf of these "unborn" (new employees) that two-tier labor contracts violate the union's duty of fair representation? Do you see an Equal Employment Opportunity implication to such an agreement? See "IRRA Panelists Address Two-Tier Implications for Fair Representation and Equal Opportunity" [No. 1 DLR A–5 (1985)].

15. Fontana, the president of the National Association of Letter Carriers, Branch 1100, attended a union seminar in Las Vegas, Nevada. Another union officer in attendance reported back to other Branch officers that Fontana had failed to attend classes at the seminar and had charged personal expenses on his union credit cards. The Branch officers subsequently accused Fontana of misappropriating union funds. Political tensions grew, and Fontana filed numerous charges against other officers for insubordination and violations of the Branch's by-laws. Those other Branch officers brought charges against Fontana, and the Branch membership found Fontana guilty and removed him as Branch president. Fontana retained his membership in the Branch.

    Several months later, three Branch members filed additional charges against Fontana, charging him with "misconduct based on his disrupting the Branch by repeatedly filing frivolous charges against other members", and "misuse of his position of influence." The written charges did not cite any specific incidents or actions, but rather made only general allegations. Committees were appointed to investigate these charges and present reports of their findings to the Branch membership. One month later, the Branch membership found Fontana guilty of the additional charges and suspended his membership. Fontana appealed the decision to the national union, and the national's Committee on Appeals reversed Fontana's suspension with respect to the charges, but continued the suspension, however, because he had failed to pay union dues while the appeal was pending. On May 10, 1994, Fontana brought suit in federal court against the Branch, individual members of the Branch, and the national union under the LMRDA. Did the union's disciplinary procedures here satisfy the requirements under Section 101(a)(5) of the LMRDA? Explain your answer. See *Johnson v. National Ass'n of Letter Carriers Branch 1100* [182 F.3d 1071 (Cal. 1999)].

Hypothetical Scenarios

16. Local 1357 of the International Brotherhood of Electrical Workers (IBEW) found Kellerman, the Business Manager and Financial Secretary of the local, guilty of spending $80,499.92 without proper documentation and authorization, in violation of the IBEW Constitution, the local's bylaws, rules, and policies. Kellerman was barred from holding office for five years and ordered him to make restitution of $80,499.92 to the local or face expulsion from the union. Three years later, Kellerman announced his intention to seek election as Business Manager of the local. The local election committee ruled that he was not eligible for election because the five year restriction on his holding office had not expired. Kellerman sued the local union, alleging that the restriction on his eligibility to run for office violated the LMRDA. How should the court rule on Kellerman's suit? Why?
17. Darryl Green worked as a utility worker for National Edison, and was a member of Local 222 of the Utility Workers of America Union. The collective agreement between National Edison and the union provided that employees who have been employed for one year or longer can only be discharged for just cause, but employees with less than one year's service are probationary workers and can be discharged at will. On March 12, 2007, while still a probationary employee, Green was disciplined for being away from his work area without permission on two occasions. As penalty for those violations, consistent with the collective agreement, the employer extended Green's probationary period. Several months later, on two consecutive days, Green left work early without permission. The employer terminated Green because he was still a probationary employee, and had violated the employer's work rules.

    Green filed a grievance challenging his discharge, and the local union pursued the grievance through the preliminary stages of the grievance procedure under the collective agreement. The employer denied the grievance and refused to reinstate Green. Green then asked the local union to take his grievance to arbitration, the final step of the grievance procedure. At a meeting of the local, Green presented his request for arbitration, but the membership of the local voted not to take his grievance to arbitration. Green appealed that decision to the national union, which upheld the local decision not to arbitrate his grievance. Green then filed suit against both the employer and the local and national unions. He alleged that the employer violated the collective bargaining agreement by terminating his employment without just cause, and that the local and national unions had breached their duties of fair representation by not submitting his grievance to arbitration. How should the court rule on his suit against the employer and the unions? Explain your answer.
18. Martin and Harris are employed by Stith Mfg. Co., but are not members of the union that represents the Stith production workers. However, they are required to pay an agency fee to the union under the collective agreement between the union and the employer. A portion of the agency fees they pay go into a "strike pay" fund that is used to support workers who go on strike. When negotiations to renew the expiring collective agreement break down, the union votes to go on strike. Harris and Martin oppose the strike, and continue working during the strike. They also refuse to pay the portion of the agency fee that goes to the strike pay fund. Can the union require that they pay the portion of the agency fee that is paid into the strike pay fund? Explain your answer.
19. Under a labor agreement governing construction work at jobsites in California, Steamfitters Local Union No. 342 had the exclusive right to dispatch workers to contractor Contra Costa Electric. Shears, a member of the union for 27 years, was registered for employment through the union's hiring hall. Because of his skills and experience, his name was placed on the highest priority "A" list, meaning that he would be among the first employees dispatched for any job. Due to an innocent computer filing error, the union mistakenly dispatched several lower-priority individuals ahead of Shears. When it discovered the error, the union immediately dispatched Shears to the jobsite. Shears filed an unfair labor practice charge with the NLRB, claiming that

the union breached its duty of fair representation to him by failing to dispatch him to the job site earlier. How should the NLRB rule on his complaint? Why? Explain your answer.

20. McKelvie was hired as a production worker by Onondaga Pottery Works. The employer has a collective agreement with the Ceramic Workers Union that contains a union shop provision. McKelvie is glad to have a job after being unemployed for several months, but she strongly objects to joining the union and paying union dues. She asks you for advice—can she be forced to join the union? Can she be forced to pay union dues? Explain your answers.

Public Sector Labor Relations

The rights of public sector employees to organize and bargain collectively are relatively recent legal developments. The National Labor Relations Act (NLRA) excludes employees of the federal, state, and local governments from its coverage. Only in the last few decades have Congress, the executive branch, and the states adopted legal provisions allowing public employees some rights to organize and bargain collectively. This chapter examines the legal provisions that enable public employees to engage in labor relations activities. Labor relations legislation affecting the federal sector is examined in some detail, and certain aspects of state legislation are also considered.

Government as Employer

Although many labor relations issues in the public sector are similar to those in the private sector, there are also significant differences. Actions taken by government employers with regard to their employees may raise issues of the constitutional rights of those employees. Both the U.S. Constitution and the various state constitutions regulate and limit government action affecting citizens. Because public sector workers are both citizens and employees, their constitutional rights must be respected by their employers. The public sector employer may therefore be limited in its attempts to discipline or regulate its employees by constitutional provisions. The private sector employer faces no similar constitutional problems.

Another area in which public sector labor relations differs from that of the private sector involves the idea of sovereignty. The government, as government, is sovereign; it cannot vacate or delegate its sovereignty. The government may be obligated by law to perform certain functions and provide certain services, and government officials are given authority to take such actions and make such decisions as are necessary to perform those functions. Collective bargaining involves sharing decision-making power between the employer and the union; the employer and the union jointly determine working conditions, rates of pay, benefits, and so on. For the public sector employer, collective bargaining may involve delegating to the union the authority relating to the employer's statutory obligations. Bargaining may also affect the financial condition of the employer, requiring tax increases or cutbacks in the level of public services provided by the government employer. Because of this concern over sharing or delegating government sovereignty with the union, public sector labor relations statutes may narrowly define "terms and conditions" of employment and limit the matters that are subject to collective bargaining to avoid the government employer abdicating its legal authority. In the federal government, for example, most employees have their wages set by statute. Collective bargaining in the federal service is precluded from dealing with any matter that is "provided for by Federal statute." Some state public sector labor relations statutes do not provide for collective bargaining at all but rather for consultation or "meeting and conferring" on working conditions.

A third area in which public sector employment differs from the private sector deals with the right to strike. The right to strike is protected by Section 7 of the NLRA for private sector workers. Public sector workers, in general, do not have the right to strike. The activities of the government employer are usually vital to the public interest. Disruptions of these activities because of labor disputes could imperil the welfare of the public. For that reason, the right to strike by public sector workers may be prohibited (as in the federal government and most states) or be limited to certain employees whose refusal to work would not endanger the public safety or welfare (as in several states).

The following case involves a challenge to the prohibitions of strikes by federal employees. The union representing postal clerks argues that such a prohibition violates their members' constitutional rights to strike.

case 19.1 » Postal Clerks v. Blount

325 F. Supp. 879 (U.S.D.C., D.C. 1971), aff'd, 404 U.S. 802 (1971)

This action was brought by the United Federation of Postal Clerks (hereafter sometimes referred to as "Clerks"), an unincorporated public employee labor organization which consists primarily of employees of the Post Office Department, and which is the exclusive bargaining representative of approximately 305,000 members of the clerk craft employed by defendant. Defendant Blount is the Postmaster General of the United States. The Clerks seek declaratory and injunctive relief invalidating portions of 5 U.S.C. Section 7311, 18 U.S. C. Section 1918, an affidavit required by 5 U.S.C. Section 3333 to implement the above statutes, and Executive Order 11491. The Government, in response, filed a motion to dismiss or in the alternative for summary judgment, and plaintiff filed its opposition thereto and cross motion for summary judgment....

5 U.S.C. Section 7311(3) prohibits an individual from accepting or holding a position in the federal government or in the District of Columbia if he

> (3) participates in a strike ... against the Government of the United States or the government of the District of Columbia....

Paragraph C of the appointment affidavit required by 5 U.S.C. Section 3333, which all federal employees are required to execute under oath, states:

> I am not participating in any strike against the Government of the United States or any agency thereof, and I will not so participate while an employee of the Government of the United States or any agency thereof.

18 U.S.C. Section 1918, in making a violation of 5 U.S.C. Section 7311 a crime, provides:

> Whoever violates the provision of Section 7311 of Title 5 that an individual may not accept or hold a position in the Government of the United States or the government of the District of Columbia if he ...

> (3) participates in a strike, or asserts the right to strike, against the Government of the United States or the District of Columbia ... shall be fined not more than $1,000 or imprisoned not more than one year and a day, or both.

Section 2(e)(2) of Executive Order 11491 exempts from the definition of a labor organization any group which:

> asserts the right to strike against the Government of the United States or any agency thereof, or to assist or participate in such strike, or imposes a duty or obligation to conduct, assist or participate in such a strike.

Section 19(b)(4) of the same Executive Order makes it an unfair labor practice for a labor organization to:

> call or engage in a strike, work stoppage, or slowdown; picket any agency in a labor-management dispute; or condone any such activity by failing to take affirmative action to prevent or stop it; ...

Plaintiff contends that the right to strike is a fundamental right protected by the Constitution, and that the absolute prohibition of such activity by 5 U.S.C. Section 7311(3), and the other provisions set out above thus constitutes an infringement of the employees' First Amendment rights of association and free speech and operates to deny them equal protection of the law. Plaintiff also argues that the language to "strike" and "participate in a strike" is vague and overbroad and therefore violative of both the First Amendment and the Due Process Clause of the Fifth Amendment. For the purposes of this opinion, we will direct our attention to the attack on the constitutionality of 5 U.S.C. Section 7311(3), the key provision being challenged....

At common law no employee, whether public or private, had a constitutional right to strike in concert with his fellow workers. Indeed, such collective action on the part of employees was often held to be a conspiracy. When the right of private employees to strike finally received full protection, it was by statute, Section 7 of the National Labor Relations Act, which "took this conspiracy weapon away from the employer in employment relations which affect interstate commerce" and guaranteed to employees in the private sector the right to engage in concerted activities for the purpose of collective bargaining. It seems clear that public employees stand on no stronger footing in this regard than private employees and that in the absence of a statute, they too do not possess the right to strike. The Supreme Court has spoken approvingly of such a restriction, and at least one federal district court has invoked the provisions of a predecessor statute, 5 U.S.C. Section 118p-r, to enjoin a strike by government employees. Likewise, scores of state cases have held that state employees do not have a right to engage in concerted work stoppages in the absence of legislative authorization. It is fair to conclude that, irrespective of the reasons given, there is a unanimity of opinion on the part of courts and legislatures that government employees do not have the right to strike.

Congress has consistently treated public employees as being in a different category than private employees. The National Labor Relations Act and the Labor-Management Relations Act of 1947 (Taft-Hartley) both defined "employer" as not including any governmental or political subdivisions, and thereby indirectly withheld the protections of Section 7 from governmental employees. Congress originally enacted the no-strike provision separately from other restrictions on employee activity by attaching riders to appropriations bills which prohibited strikes by government employees....

Given the fact that there is no constitutional right to strike, it is not irrational or arbitrary for the Government to condition employment on a promise not to withhold labor collectively, and to prohibit strikes by those in public employment, whether because of the prerogatives of the sovereign, some sense of higher obligation associated with public service, to assure the continuing functioning of the Government without interruption, to protect public health and safety, or for other reasons. Although plaintiff argues that the provisions in question are unconstitutionally broad in covering all Government employees regardless of the type or importance of the work they do, we hold that it makes no difference whether the jobs performed by certain public employees are regarded as "essential" or "nonessential," or whether similar jobs are performed by workers in private industry who do have the right to strike protected by statute. Nor is it relevant that some positions in private industry are arguably more affected with a public interest than are some positions in the Government service....

Furthermore, it should be pointed out that the fact that public employees may not strike does not interfere with their rights which are fundamental and constitutionally protected. The right to organize collectively and to select representatives for the purposes of engaging in collective bargaining is such a fundamental right. But, as the Supreme Court noted in *Local 232 v. Wisconsin Employment Relations Board*, "The right to strike, because of its more serious impact upon the public interest, is more vulnerable to regulation than the right to organize and select representatives for lawful purposes of collective bargaining which this Court has characterized as a 'fundamental right' and which, as the Court has pointed out, was recognized as such in its decisions long before it was given protection by the National Labor Relations Act."

Executive Order 11491 recognizes the right of federal employees to join labor organizations for the purpose of dealing with grievances, but that Order clearly and expressly defines strikes, work stoppages and slowdowns as unfair labor practices. As discussed above, that Order is the culmination of a longstanding policy. There certainly is no compelling reason to imply the existence of the right to strike from the right to associate and bargain collectively. In the private sphere, the strike is used to equalize bargaining power, but this has universally been held not to be appropriate when its object and purpose can only be to influence the essentially political decisions of Government in the allocation of its resources. Congress has an obligation to ensure that the machinery of the Federal Government continues to function at all times without interference. Prohibition of strikes by its employees is a reasonable implementation of that obligation.

Accordingly, we hold that the provisions of the statute, the appointment affidavit and the Executive Order, as construed above, do not violate any constitutional rights of those employees who are members of plaintiff's union. The Government's motion to dismiss the complaint is granted.

Order to be presented.

Case Questions

1. Do public sector employees have a constitutional right to strike? Is the right to strike protected at common law?
2. Does the right of employees to organize and join unions for purposes of collective bargaining include the right to strike?
3. Are the legislative prohibitions against strikes by federal employees constitutional? What is the rationale behind such prohibitions?

Concept *Summary* » 19.1

Characteristics of Public Sector Labor Relations

- Public employers must respect their employees' constitutional rights
- Public employers have sovereignty as government entities
  - May restrict the scope of collective bargaining that affects their statutory obligations
- Dispute resolution involves mediation and interest arbitration
  - Most public employees do not have the right to strike

Federal Government Labor Relations

Historical Background

It is not clear exactly when federal employees began negotiating over the terms of their employment, but informal bargaining began as long ago as 1883. In that year, the Pendleton Act, known as the Civil Service Act, was passed. It granted Congress the sole authority to set wages, hours, and other terms and conditions of federal employment. This act led to informal bargaining and congressional lobbying by federal employees seeking higher wages and better working conditions.

In 1906, President Theodore Roosevelt halted the informal bargaining by issuing an executive order forbidding federal employees or their associations from soliciting increases in pay, either before Congress, its committees, or before the heads of the executive agencies. Employees violating the order faced dismissal.

In the years following the executive order, Congress passed several laws that gave limited organization rights to some federal workers. The Lloyd–La Follette Act of 1912 gave postal workers the right to join unions. In 1920, the federal government negotiated the terms of a contract with the union representing construction workers building the government-sponsored Alaskan Railroad.

It was not until 1962, with the issuing of Executive Order 10988 by President Kennedy, that large numbers of federal employees were given the right to organize. The executive order recognized the right of federal workers to organize and to present their views on terms and conditions of employment to the agencies for which they worked.

Executive Order 10988 was supplemented by Executive Order 11491, which was issued in 1969 by President Nixon. That order placed the entire program of employee-management relations under the supervision and control of the Federal Labor Relations Council.

The Federal Service Labor-Management Relations Law of 1978, which was enacted as part of the Civil Service Reform Act of 1978, was the first comprehensive enactment covering labor relations in the federal government. The Federal Service Labor-Management Relations Act (FSLMRA) took effect in January 1979.

The Federal Service Labor-Management Relations Act

Federal Labor Relations Authority (FLRA) The federal agency created under the Federal Service Labor-Management Relations Act to administer federal employee labor relations.

The FSLMRA, which was modeled after the NLRA, established a permanent structure for labor relations in the federal public sector. It created the ***Federal Labor Relations Authority (FLRA)*** to administer the act, and it granted federal employees the right to organize and bargain collectively. It also prohibited strikes and other defined unfair practices.

Coverage

The FSLMRA covers federal employees who are employed by a federal agency or who have ceased to work for the agency because of an unfair labor practice. Most federal agencies are covered, but some are specifically exempted. The following agencies are excluded from FSLMRA coverage:

- the FBI
- the CIA
- the National Security Agency
- the General Accounting Office
- the Tennessee Valley Authority
- the FLRA
- the Federal Service Impasses Panel

Furthermore, any agency that the president determines is investigative in nature or has a primary function of intelligence and would thus not be amenable to FSLMRA coverage because of national security may be excluded. The FSLMRA also excludes certain employees from coverage, including:

- noncitizens working outside the United States for federal agencies;
- supervisory and management employees;
- certain foreign service officers; and
- any federal employee participating in an illegal strike.

The Thurmond Act of 1969 prohibits military personnel from belonging to a union. That act makes it a felony for enlisted personnel to join a union or for military officers or their representatives to recognize or bargain with a union. The Thurmond Act does not apply to civilian employees of the military.

Employees covered by the FSLMRA are granted the right to form, join, or assist any labor organization or to refrain from such activity freely and without reprisal. Employees may act as representatives of a labor organization and present views of the organization to the heads of agencies, the executive branch, and Congress.

Postal Service Employees

The employees of the U.S. Postal Service are not subject to the FSLMRA. The Postal Service Reorganization Act, which created the U.S. Postal Service as an independent agency, provides that postal service employees are subject to the NLRA, with some limitations. The National Labor Relations Board (NLRB) is authorized to determine appropriate bargaining units, hold representation elections, and enforce the unfair labor practice provisions of the NLRA for postal service employees. The postal service unions bargain with the U.S. Postal Service over wages, hours, and conditions of employment, but postal service workers are not permitted to strike. Instead, the Postal Service Reorganization Act provides for fact-finding and binding arbitration if an impasse exists after 180 days from the start of bargaining. Supervisory and managerial employees of the Postal Service are not subject to the NLRA provisions.

Administration

The FSLMRA created the FLRA, which assumed the duties of the Federal Labor Relations Council created by Executive Order 11491. The FLRA is the central authority responsible for the administration of the FSLMRA.

The FLRA is composed of three members who are nominated by the president and confirmed by the Senate. The members serve five-year terms. The FLRA is empowered to do the following:

- Determine the appropriateness of units for representation
- Supervise or conduct elections to determine if a labor organization has been selected as the exclusive representative by majority of the employees in the appropriate unit
- Resolve issues relating to the duty to bargain in good faith
- Resolve complaints of unfair labor practices

The FLRA has the authority to hold hearings and issue subpoenas. It may order any agency or union to cease and desist from violating the provisions of the FSLMRA, and it can enlist the federal courts in proceedings against unions that strike illegally. The FLRA may take any remedial actions it deems appropriate in carrying out the policies of the act.

Representation Issues

Under the FSLMRA, a union becomes the exclusive representative of an appropriate unit of employees when it has been selected by a majority of votes cast in a representation election. When selected, the union becomes the sole representative of the employees in the unit and is authorized to negotiate the terms and conditions of employment of the employees in the unit. The union must fairly represent all employees in the unit without discrimination or regard to union membership. The FLRA is authorized to settle questions relating to issues of representation, such as the determination of the appropriate unit and the holding of representation elections.

Appropriate Representation Units The FLRA is empowered to determine the appropriateness of a representation unit of federal employees. The FLRA ensures the employees the fullest possible freedom in exercising their rights under the FSLMRA in determining the unit, and it ensures a clear and identifiable community of interest among the employees in the unit to promote effective dealing with the agency involved. The FLRA may determine the appropriateness of a unit on an agency, plant, installation, functional, or other basis.

Units may not include:

- Any management or supervisory employees
- Confidential employees
- Employees engaged in personnel work except those in a purely clerical capacity
- Employees doing investigative work that directly affects national security
- Employees administering the FSLMRA
- Employees primarily engaged in investigation or audit functions relating to the work of individuals whose duties affect the internal security of an agency

Any employees engaged in administering any provision of law relating to labor-management relations may not be represented by a labor organization that is affiliated with an organization representing other individuals under the act. An appropriate unit may include professional and nonprofessional employees only if the professional employees, by majority vote, approve their inclusion.

Representation Elections The procedures for representation elections under the FSLMRA closely resemble those for elections under the NLRA. The act allows for the holding of consent elections to determine the exclusive representative of a bargaining unit. It also provides that the FLRA may investigate the question of representation, including holding an election, if a petition is filed by any person alleging that 30 percent of the employees in a unit wish to be represented by a union for the purpose of collective bargaining. In addition, when a petition alleging that 30 percent of the members of a bargaining unit no longer wish to be represented by their exclusive representative union, the FLRA will investigate the representation question.

If the FLRA finds reasonable cause to believe that a representation question exists, it will provide, upon reasonable notice, an opportunity for a hearing. If, on the basis of the hearing, the FLRA finds that a question of representation does exist, it will conduct a representation election by secret ballot. An election will not be held if the unit has held a valid election within the preceding twelve months.

When an election is scheduled, a union may intervene and be placed on the ballot if it can show that it is already the unit's exclusive representative or that it has the support of at least 10 percent of the employees in the unit. The election is by secret ballot, with the employees choosing between the union(s) and "no representation." If no choice receives a majority of votes cast, a runoff election is held between the two choices receiving the highest number of votes. The results of the election are certified; if a union receives a majority of votes cast, it becomes the exclusive representative of the employees in the unit.

A union that has obtained exclusive representation status is entitled to be present at any formal discussions between the agency and unit employees concerning grievances, personnel policies and practices, or other conditions of employment. The exclusive representative must also be given the opportunity to be present at any examination of an employee in the unit in connection with an agency investigation that the employee reasonably believes may result in disciplinary action, provided that he or she has requested such representation. (This right is the equivalent of the *Weingarten rights* established by the NLRB for organized employees in the private sector. See Chapter 14.)

Consultation Rights If the employees of an agency have not designated any union as their exclusive representative on an agency-wide basis, a union that represents a substantial number of agency employees may be granted consultation rights. Consultation rights entitle the union to be informed of any substantive change in employment conditions proposed by the agency. The union is to be permitted reasonable time to present its views and recommendations regarding the proposed changes. The agency must consider the union recommendations before taking final action, and it must provide the union with written reasons for taking the final action.

Collective Bargaining

The FSLMRA requires that agencies and exclusive representatives of agency employees meet and negotiate in good faith. Good faith is defined as approaching the negotiations with a sincere resolve to reach a collective bargaining agreement, meeting at reasonable times and convenient places as frequently as may be necessary, and being represented at negotiations by duly authorized representatives prepared to discuss and negotiate on any condition of employment.

In *National Federation of Federal Employees, Local 1309 v. Dept. of the Interior,*[1] the Supreme Court held that the FLRA had the power to determine whether federal employers were required to engage in "midterm" bargaining—bargaining during the term of a collective agreement over subjects that were not included in the agreement. The FLRA, on remand from the Supreme Court, decided that the FSLMRA required employers to engage in midterm bargaining and the refusal to do so was an unfair labor practice under the FSLMRA.[2]

Conditions of Employment The act defines "conditions of employment" as including personnel policies, practices, and matters—whether established by rule, regulation, or otherwise—that affect working conditions. However, the act excludes the following from being defined as conditions of employment:

- Policies relating to prohibited political activity
- Matters relating to the classification of any position
- Policies or matters that are provided for by federal statute

---

[1]526 U.S. 86 (1999).

[2]*U.S. Dept. of the Interior v. National Federation of Federal Employees, Local 1309*, 56 FLRA 45, *reconsideration denied*, 56 FLRA 279 (2000).

Wages Wages for most federal employees are not subject to collective bargaining because they are determined by statute. Federal "blue-collar" employees are paid under the coordinated Federal Wage System, which provides for pay comparable to pay for similar jobs in the private sector. Federal "white-collar" employees are paid under the General Schedule (GS), and increases and changes in GS pay scales are made by presidential order. However, in *Fort Stewart Schools v. Federal Labor Relations Authority*,[3] the Supreme Court considered the question of whether schools owned and operated by the U.S. Army were required to negotiate with the union representing school employees over mileage reimbursement, paid leave, and a salary increase. The school declined to negotiate, claiming that the proposals were not subject to bargaining under the FSLMRA. The school claimed that "conditions of employment" under the FSLMRA included any matter insisted upon as a prerequisite to accepting employment but did not include wages. The Supreme Court upheld an order of the FLRA that the school was required to bargain over wages and fringe benefits. Whereas the wages of most federal employees are set by law under the GS of the Civil Service Act, the school employees' wages are exempted from the GS. Wages for the school employees, therefore, were within the conditions of employment over which the school was required to bargain. Section 7106 of the FSLMRA, which provides that "nothing in this chapter shall affect the authority of any management official of any agency to determine the ... budget ... of the agency...." did not exempt wages and fringe benefits from the duty to bargain. Agency management seeking to avail themselves of that provision to avoid bargaining over a proposal must demonstrate that the proposal would result in significant and unavoidable increases in costs.

Management Rights The FSLMRA contains a very strong management-rights clause, which also restricts the scope of collective bargaining. According to that clause, collective bargaining is not to affect the authority of any management official or any agency to determine the mission, budget, organization, number of employees, or the internal security practices of the agency. In addition, management's right to hire, assign, direct, lay off, retain or suspend, reduce in grade or pay, or take disciplinary action against any employee is not subject to negotiation. Decisions to assign work, contract out work, or select candidates to fill positions are not subject to negotiation. The act also precludes bargaining over any actions necessary to carry out the mission of the agency during emergencies.

The duty to bargain extends to matters that are the subject of any rule or regulation as long as the particular rule or regulation is not government-wide. However, if the agency determines there is a compelling need for such a regulation, it can refuse to bargain over that regulation. The exclusive representative must be given an opportunity to show that no compelling need exists for the regulation. Disputes over the existence of a compelling need are to be resolved by the FLRA.

The agency's duty to bargain includes the obligation to furnish, upon request by the exclusive representative, data and information normally maintained by the agency. Such data must be reasonably available and necessary for full and proper discussion of subjects within the scope of bargaining. Data related to the guidance, training, advice, or counsel of management or supervisors relating to collective bargaining are excluded from the obligation to provide information. The duty to bargain in good faith also includes the duty to execute a written document embodying the terms of agreement, if either party so requests.

---

[3] 495 U.S. 641 (1990).

Impasse Settlement

Federal Service Impasse Panel
Federal body created under the Federal Service Labor-Management Relations Act to resolve impasses in collective bargaining in the federal service.

The FSLMRA created the ***Federal Service Impasse Panel***, which is authorized to take any actions necessary to resolve an impasse in negotiations. The Federal Mediation and Conciliation Service, created by the Taft-Hartley Act, also assists in the resolution of impasses by providing mediation services for the parties. If the mediation efforts fail to lead to an agreement, either party may request that the Federal Service Impasse Panel consider the dispute. The panel may either recommend procedures for resolving the impasse or assist the parties in any other way it deems appropriate. The formal impasse resolution procedures may include hearings, fact-finding, recommendations for settlement, or directed settlement. The parties may also seek binding arbitration of the impasse with the approval of the panel.

Grievance Arbitration The FSLMRA provides that all collective agreements under it must contain a grievance procedure. The grievance procedure must provide for binding arbitration as the final step in resolving grievances. If arbitration is invoked, either party may appeal the arbitrator's decision to the FLRA for review within thirty days of the granting of the award. Upon review, the FLRA may overturn the arbitrator's award only if it is contrary to a law, rule, or regulation, or is inconsistent with the standards for review of private sector awards by the federal courts (see Chapter 17). If no appeal is taken from the arbitrator's award within thirty days of the award, the arbitrator's award is final and binding.

When a grievance involves matters that are subject to a statutory review procedure, the employee may choose to pursue the complaint through the statutory procedure or through the negotiated grievance procedure. Examples would be grievances alleging discrimination in violation of Title VII of the Civil Rights Act of 1964, where the grievor can elect to pursue the complaint through the grievance process or through the procedure under Title VII. Performance ratings, demotions, and suspensions or removals that are subject to Civil Service review procedures may be pursued either through the civil service procedures or the grievance procedure.

Unfair Labor Practices

The FSLMRA prohibits unfair labor practices by agencies and unions. The unfair labor practices defined in the act are similar to those defined by Sections 8(a) and 8(b) of the NLRA.

Agency Unfair Practices

Unfair labor practices by agencies under the FSLMRA include:

- Interfering with or restraining the exercise of employees' rights under the act
- Encouraging or discouraging union membership by discrimination in conditions of employment
- Sponsoring or controlling a union
- Disciplining or discriminating against an employee for filing a complaint under the act
- Refusing to negotiate in good faith
- Refusing to cooperate in impasse procedures

It is also an unfair labor practice for an agency to enforce any rule or regulation that conflicts with a preexisting collective bargaining agreement.

Union Unfair Labor Practices

Union unfair labor practices under the FSLMRA include:

- Interfering with or restraining the exercise of employees' rights under the act
- Coercing or fining a member for the purpose of impeding job performance
- Discriminating against an employee on the basis of race, color, creed, national origin, gender, age, civil service status, political affiliation, marital status, or disability
- Refusing to negotiate in good faith
- Refusing to cooperate in impasse procedures

It is also an unfair labor practice for a union to call or condone a strike, work slowdown, or stoppage or to picket the agency if the picketing interferes with the agency's operations. Informational picketing that does not interfere with agency operations is allowed.

Unfair Labor Practice Procedures

When a complaint alleging unfair labor practices is filed with the FLRA, the General Counsel's Office of the FLRA investigates the complaint and attempts to reach a voluntary settlement. If no settlement is reached and the investigation uncovers evidence that the act has been violated, a complaint is issued. The complaint contains a notice of the charge and sets a date for a hearing before the FLRA. The party against whom the complaint is filed has the opportunity to file an answer to the complaint and to appear at the hearing to contest the charges.

If the FLRA finds, by a preponderance of evidence, that a violation has occurred, it will issue written findings and an appropriate remedial order. FLRA decisions are subject to judicial review by the federal courts of appeals.

Unfair Labor Practice Remedies

The FLRA has broad authority for fashioning remedial orders for unfair labor practices. Remedial orders may include cease-and-desist orders, reinstatement with back pay, renegotiation of the agreement between the parties with retroactive effect, or any other actions deemed necessary to carry out the purposes of the act.

When a union has been found by the FLRA to have intentionally engaged in a strike or work stoppage in violation of the act, the FLRA may revoke the exclusive representation status of the union or take any other disciplinary action deemed appropriate. Employees engaging in illegal strikes are subject to dismissal. The FLRA may also seek injunctions, restraining orders, or contempt citations in the federal courts against striking unions.

The following case involves the review of an FLRA order revoking the exclusive representation status of the air traffic controllers' union because of its involvement in an illegal strike.

case 19.2 »

Professional Air Traffic Controllers Org. v. FLRA

685 F.2d 547 (D.C. Cir. 1982)

Facts: The Professional Air Traffic Controllers Organization (PATCO) was the exclusive bargaining representative for air traffic controllers employed by the Federal Aviation Administration (FAA) since the early 1970s. PATCO and the FAA began negotiations for a new contract in early 1981, and a tentative agreement was reached in June. That proposed agreement was overwhelmingly rejected in a vote by the PATCO membership. Following the rejection, the parties resumed negotiations in late July, and PATCO announced a strike deadline of August 3, 1981. When the negotiations failed to reach an agreement, PATCO went on strike against the FAA on August 3, 1981. Of the 9,304 air traffic controllers scheduled to work on August 3, only 2,308 reported for work, resulting in a significantly reduction in the number of private and commercial flights in the U.S. President Reagan warned the strikers that if they did not return to work by August 5, they would be terminated. Approximately 11,000 air traffic controllers were fired.

In addition, the FAA filed an unfair labor practice charge against PATCO with the Federal Labor Relations Authority (FLRA). An FLRA regional director issued a complaint on the unfair labor practice charge, alleging that the strike was prohibited by federal law and seeking revocation of PATCO's certification under the Civil Service Reform Act. The FLRA held that PATCO had called or participated in an illegal strike, and revoked PATCO's certification as exclusive bargaining representative of the air traffic controllers. PATCO then sought judicial review of the FLRA decision before the U.S. Court of Appeals for the D.C. Circuit.

Issue: Did PATCO engage in an illegal strike and should PATCO's certification have been revoked?

Decision: Federal employees have long been forbidden from striking against their employer, the federal government. Section 7311(2) of Title 5 of the U.S. Code prohibits a person who "participates in a strike … against the Government of the United States" from accepting or holding a position in the federal government. Violating that prohibition is a criminal offense. Newly hired federal employees are required to execute an affidavit attesting that they have not struck and will not strike against the government.

In addition, since the beginning of formal collective bargaining between federal employee unions and the federal government, unions have been required under Executive Order No. 10988 to disavow using the strike as an economic weapon. Since 1969, striking has been expressly designated a union unfair labor practice. The Civil Service Reform Act, passed in 1978, added a new provision,[1] that authorized the FLRA to "revoke the exclusive recognition status" of a recognized union, or "take any other appropriate disciplinary action" against any labor organization, when that union has called, participated in or condoned a strike, work stoppage or slowdown against a federal agency in a labor-management dispute.

Here, the FLRA held that PATCO had called or participated in a strike in violation of federal law, and revoked PATCO's status as exclusive bargaining representative for the air traffic controllers. The court of appeals held that the FLRA was fully justified in taking official notice of proceedings in the District Court for the District of Columbia that found PATCO and its President, Robert Poli, in contempt of court for violating the restraining order against the strike. Before the FLRA, PATCO offered no evidence to indicate that it even attempted to end the strike. The court of appeals therefore affirmed the FLRA finding that the strike was an unfair labor practice.

The court then considered whether the FLRA properly exercised its discretion under the Act to revoke the exclusive recognition status of PATCO. The FLRA has substantial discretion under Section 7120(f) to decide whether or not to revoke the certification of a union found guilty by the FLRA of striking or condoning a strike against the government. On judicial review of the FLRA's exercise of its remedial discretion, the court has a limited role. The court will uphold the remedial orders of the FLRA "unless it can be shown that the order is a patent attempt to achieve ends other than those which can fairly be said to effectuate the policies of the Act." Here, the court of appeals had little trouble deciding that the FLRA did not abuse its discretion. The FLRA could take official notice that PATCO has repeatedly violated legal prohibitions against striking and other job actions in the past. PATCO openly defied the restraining orders and injunctions directed at the strike of August 3, 1981. PATCO made no attempt to end the strike. Even after the striking controllers had been terminated and

[1]5 U.S.C. § 7120(f).

the FLRA had ordered revocation of its exclusive recognition status, PATCO failed to satisfy the FLRA request that it end the strike and promise to abide by the no-strike provisions of the Civil Service Reform Act. PATCO was a repeat offender that has willfully ignored statutory proscriptions and judicial injunctions. The court affirmed the FLRA order finding PATCO had violated the legal prohibitions against strikes by federal employees, and revoking PATCO's certification as exclusive bargaining representative of the federal air traffic controllers.

«

Judicial Review of FLRA Decisions

As the *PATCO* case illustrates, final orders, other than bargaining unit determinations and arbitration awards, are subject to review in the federal courts of appeals. The party seeking review has ten days from the issuance of the FLRA decision to file a petition for review with the court of appeals for the appropriate circuit. Unless specifically authorized by the appeals court, the filing of a petition for review does not operate to stay the FLRA order.

Upon review, the court may affirm, enforce, modify, or set aside the FLRA order. Findings of fact by the FLRA are deemed conclusive if they are supported by substantial evidence. The order of the court of appeals is subject to discretionary review by the Supreme Court.

Concept *Summary* » 19.2

THE FEDERAL SERVICE LABOR MANAGEMENT RELATIONS ACT

- Covers employees of most federal agencies, but some agencies are exempted
- Administered by the Federal Labor Relations Authority (FLRA)
- Duty to bargain in good faith—but statutory management rights clause restricts scope of bargaining
- Impasses in negotiations resolved through mediation or Federal Service Impasse Panel or arbitration
- Imposes mandatory grievance arbitration
- Defines unfair labor practices by agencies and unions
- Prohibits strikes, work stoppages or work slowdowns by employees and unions

The Hatch Act

The Hatch Act[4] prohibits certain political activity by federal employees. Federal employees are prevented from taking an active part in the management of political campaigns or from running for office in a partisan political campaign. The act also restricts federal employees from

[4]5 U.S.C. §7321 *et seq.*

engaging in political activity while on the job. The purpose of the restrictions on the political activities of federal employees is to:

- avoid the appearance of political bias in government actions;
- prevent the coercion of federal employees to engage in political action or to support political positions; and
- avoid politicizing the federal civil service.

The Hatch Act's restrictions on political activity by federal employees were held to be constitutional in *Burrus v. Vegliante*.[5] That case also held that the American Postal Workers Union's use of bulletin boards in nonpublic areas of post offices to display political materials violated the Hatch Act prohibitions against political activities on the job. Most states have legislation similar to the Hatch Act to restrict political activities by state government employees.

Union Security Provisions

A union that is granted exclusive representation rights under the FSLMRA must accept, as a member, any unit employee who seeks membership. A union may not require union membership as a condition of employment. This means that the collective agreement may not contain a closed shop or union shop provision. For the government employer to require that employees join a union in order to retain their jobs would violate the employees' constitutional rights of association protected by the First Amendment (or Fourteenth Amendment if the employer is a state or local government agency).

Agency shop provisions, which require that an employee pay union dues or fees but do not require union membership, do not raise the same constitutional problems. However, if the employee's dues money is spent by the union on matters other than those relating to collective bargaining or representation issues, the employee is, in effect, forced to contribute to causes and for purposes that he or she may oppose. Does this "forced contribution" violate the employee's constitutional rights?

In *Abood v. Detroit Board of Education*,[6] the Supreme Court held that union expenditures for expression of political views, in support of political candidates, or for advancement of ideological causes not related to its duties as bargaining agent can be financed only from dues or assessments paid by employees who do not object to advancing such ideas and who are not coerced into doing so. To do otherwise violates the First Amendment rights of the employees who object to such expenditures. The Court held that employees who object to political expenditures by the union are entitled to a refund of that portion of their dues payments that represents the proportion that union political expenditures bear to the total union expenditures. A state law requiring public sector unions to get affirmative authorization of the use of agency shop fees for political purposes was valid and did not violate the unions' First Amendment rights, according to *Davenport v. Washington Education Association*.[7] In *Ysursa v.*

---

[5]336 F.2d 82 (2d Cir. 2003).

[6]431 U.S. 209 (1977).

[7]551 U.S. 177 (2007).

Pocatello Education Association,[8] the Supreme Court held that a state law prohibiting the use of payroll deductions of public employees for political purposes was not in violation of the First Amendment.

In *Chicago Teachers Union, Local No. 1 v. Hudson*,[9] the Supreme Court addressed the procedures that the union must make available for employees who object to union expenditures of their dues or fees. The Court held that the union is required to provide objecting members with information relating to the union expenditures on collective bargaining and political activities and must include an adequate explanation of the basis of dues and fees. The members must also be provided a reasonably prompt opportunity to challenge—before an impartial decision maker—the amount of the dues or fees, and the union must hold in escrow the amounts in dispute pending the resolution of the challenges by the members.

The *Abood* and *Chicago Teachers Union* cases hold that individuals who object to a union's political activities are not required to pay that portion of union dues and fees that fund such nonbargaining activities. What standards should a court use to determine which union expenditures are related to its collective bargaining activities? The Supreme Court considered this question in the case of *Lehnert v. Ferris Faculty Association*.[10] The Court set out three criteria for determining which activities can be funded by dues and fees of objecting individuals:

- The activity must be germane to collective bargaining
- It must be justified by the government's interest in promoting labor peace and avoiding "free riders" who benefit from union activities without paying for union services
- It must not significantly add to the burdening of free speech inherent in allowing a union shop or agency shop provision

Using these criteria, the *Lehnert* Court held that the teachers' union could not charge objecting individuals for lobbying, electoral activities, or political activities beyond the limited context of contract implementation or negotiation. In addition, the union could not charge for expenses incurred in conducting an illegal work stoppage or for litigation expenses unless the litigation concerned the individual's own bargaining unit. The union could charge objecting individuals for:

- national union programs and publications designed to disseminate information germane to collective bargaining;
- information services concerning professional development, job opportunities, and miscellaneous matters that benefited all teachers, even though they may not directly concern members of the individual's bargaining unit;
- participation by local delegates at state or national union meetings at which representation policies and bargaining strategies are developed; and
- expenses related to preparation for a strike.

---

[8]129 S.Ct. 1093 (2009).

[9]475 U.S. 292 (1986).

[10]500 U.S. 507 (1991).

The Court also held that the union could not charge the objecting individuals for public relations efforts designed to enhance the reputation of the teaching profession generally because such efforts were not directly connected to the union's collective bargaining function.

It should be noted that private sector employees have the same right to object to political expenditures by their unions; in *Communications Workers of America v. Beck*,[11] (see Chapter 18), the Supreme Court stated that

> We conclude that Section 8(a)(3) … authorizes the exaction [from nonmembers or objecting employees] of only those fees and dues necessary to "performing the duties of an exclusive representative of the employees in dealing with the employer on labor-management issues."

The FSLMRA provides that union dues may be deducted from an employee's pay only if authorized by the employee. The employer may not charge a service fee for deductions to either the employee or the union. Employee authorizations for dues deduction may not be revoked for a period of one year from their making.

Federal Labor Relations and National Security

The terrorist attacks of September 11, 2001, brought about a profound government emphasis on protecting national security. President George W. Bush, responding to pressure from Congress, created the Department of Homeland Security (DHS) and gave it responsibility for a broad range of institutions and organizations within the federal government, including Customs and Border Protection, Citizen and Immigration Services, the U.S. Coast Guard, and the Transportation Security Administration. As part of the administrative reorganization involved with the creation of DHS, the Bush administration sought to increase management flexibility and control over employees and working conditions. The Homeland Security Act of 2002 authorized the Secretary of Homeland Security and the director of the Office of Personnel Management to adopt regulations to create a human resource management system. The act also stated that any regulations adopted had to "ensure that employees may organize, bargain collectively and participate through labor organizations of their choosing in decisions which affect them.…" Pursuant to the authority granted under the Homeland Security Act, DHS adopted the "Department of Homeland Security Human Resources Management System," a human resource management system that restricted bargaining over personnel actions and limited the role of the FLRA in handling labor relations matters. The unions representing the affected DHS employees challenged the human resource management system as violating the legislative requirement to protect collective bargaining rights and illegally restricting the statutory authority of the FLRA and the Merit System Protection Board (MSPB), which administers the federal civil service system and regulations.

The Department of Defense (DoD) also sought more flexibility and control in its human resource management system for its civilian employees. The National Defense Authorization Act for Fiscal Year 2004 authorized DoD to establish a "National Security Personnel System" (NSPS) to restructure labor relations between management and employees. That act also provided that NSPS would supersede all collective bargaining agreements for the bargaining units in the DoD until 2009. Several unions representing the DoD civilian employees challenged the resulting NSPS as going beyond the legislative authority granted to DoD.

---

[11] 487 U.S. 735 (1988).

The WORKING Law

Airport Screeners Seek Bargaining Rights

The legislation that established the Transportation Security Administration (TSA), the federal agency in the Department of Homeland Security that employs some 45,000 officers who work as airport screeners, states that the Administrator of the TSA has the authority to decide whether or not to allow its employees to engage in collective bargaining. The Bush Administration took the position that collective bargaining rights for TSA employees would weaken travel security protection by adding an additional layer of procedures to TSA operations, and would limit the agency's ability to respond quickly in emergencies because it would be required to negotiate changes in security procedures with unions representing its employees. Proponents for collective bargaining rights argue that collective bargaining can ensure that the agency is run more effectively, and that current TSA employees complain of hostile work environments, favoritism, and fear of retaliation by managers for reports of violations of regulations. They also point out that staffing levels at some airports are very low, so that employees are required to work through break times, work extra shifts, and work on scheduled days off. A survey of the "Best Places to Work" in the federal government for 2009 ranked the TSA near the bottom of federal agencies, although the ratings for employee job satisfaction for the TSA had increased by nearly 23 percent.

While the TSA legislation currently does not allow for collective bargaining, it does permit employees to join unions, and both the American Federation of Government Employees (AFGE) and the National Treasury Employees Union (NTEU) have been signing up members among the employees at airports around the country. If the new TSA administrator does grant permission for collective bargaining, those unions will probably petition for an election to determine which union will have representation rights. In July, 2009, officials from the TSA held meetings with the leaders of the AFGE and NTEU. Topics discussed included leave policies, disciplinary actions, and the TSA's pay-for-performance system. The meeting with the AFGE included eight airport screeners from around the country. AFGE President John Gage said that the screeners "shared real-life experiences of what it means to work on the front line for airport security." The unions are also pressing Congress to change the law to allow TSA employees to engage in collective bargaining, and the House of Representatives Homeland Security Committee approved a bill, the Transportation Security Workforce Enhancement Act, that would establish bargaining rights. Despite opposition from some Republicans, the prospects for passage of the legislation by both the House and Senate look good. During the presidential campaign, then-candidate Obama expressed support for allowing TSA employees to engage in collective bargaining, stating that TSA had the "unfettered ability to deny its workforce even the most basic labor rights and protections." But the now-President Obama has not yet appointed an administrator for TSA. Janet Napolitano, Secretary of the Department of Homeland Security (DHS), has indicated that she would ask the DHS general counsel to review whether she has the authority under existing legislation to grant collective bargaining rights to TSA employees.

Sources: Steve Vogel, "At TSA, A Waiting Game for Bargaining Rights," *The Washington Post*, April 2, 2009; Steve Vogel and Joe Davidson, "SA Unions to Use Rankings as Bargaining Chip," Washingtonpost.com, May 22, 2009; Joe Davidson, "Airport Screeners a Step Closer to Bargaining Rights," Washingtonpost.com. July 10, 2009; Joe Davidson, "Labor-Management Talks a First for TSA," Washingtonpost.com, July 24, 2009.

The following two decisions of the U.S. Court of Appeals for the District of Columbia involve the legal challenges to the DHS and the DoD human resources management systems by the unions representing their employees.

case 19.3 » National Treasury Employees Union v. Michael Chertoff, Secretary, United States Department of Homeland Security

452 F.3d 839 (D.C.Cir. 2006)

Edwards, Senior Circuit Judge

When Congress enacted the Homeland Security Act of 2002 ("HSA" or the "Act") and established the Department of Homeland Security ("DHS" or the "Department"), it provided that "the Secretary of Homeland Security may, in regulations prescribed jointly with the Director of the Office of Personnel Management, establish, and from time to time adjust, a human resources management system." [5 U.S.C. § 9701 (Supp. II 2002)] Congress made it clear, however, that any such system "shall—(1) be flexible; (2) be contemporary; (3) not waive, modify, or otherwise affect [certain existing statutory provisions relating to … merit hiring, equal pay, whistleblowing, and prohibited personnel practices], [and] (4) ensure that employees may organize, bargain collectively, and participate through labor organizations of their own choosing in decisions which affect them, subject to any exclusion from coverage or limitation on negotiability established by law." The Act also mandated that DHS employees receive "fair treatment in any appeals that they bring in decisions relating to their employment." Section 9701 does not mention "Chapter 71," which codifies the Federal Services Labor-Management Statute and delineates the framework for collective bargaining for most federal sector employees.

In February 2005, the Department and Office of Personnel Management ("OPM") issued regulations establishing a human resources management system … [the] Department of Homeland Security Human Resources Management System ("Final Rule" or "HR system"). The Final Rule … defines the scope and process of collective bargaining for affected DHS employees, channels certain disputes through the Federal Labor Relations Authority ("FLRA" or the "Authority"), creates an in-house Homeland Security Labor Relations Board ("HSLRB"), and assigns an appellate role to the Merit Systems Protection Board ("MSPB") in cases involving penalties imposed on DHS employees.

Unions representing many DHS employees filed a complaint in [District of Columbia] District Court … challeng[ing] aspects of the Final Rule.… the District Court found that the regulations would not ensure collective bargaining, would fundamentally and impermissibly alter FLRA jurisdiction, and would create an appeal process at MSPB that is not fair. Based on these rulings, the District Court enjoined DHS from implementing [certain sections] … of the regulations. However, the District Court rejected the Unions' claims that the regulations impermissibly restricted the scope of bargaining and that DHS lacked authority to give MSPB an intermediate appellate function in cases involving mandatory removal offenses.… The case is now before this court on appeal by the Government and cross-appeal by the Unions. We affirm in part and reverse in part.

We hold that the regulations fail in two important respects to "ensure that employees may … bargain collectively," as the HSA requires. First, we agree with the District Court that the Department's attempt to reserve to itself the right to unilaterally abrogate lawfully negotiated and executed agreements is plainly unlawful. If the Department could unilaterally abrogate lawful contracts, this would nullify the Act's specific guarantee of collective bargaining rights, because the agency cannot "ensure" collective bargaining without affording employees the right to negotiate binding agreements.

Second, we hold that the Final Rule violates the Act insofar as it limits the scope of bargaining to employee-specific personnel matters. The regulations effectively eliminate all meaningful bargaining over fundamental working conditions (including even negotiations over procedural protections), thereby committing the bulk of decisions concerning conditions of employment to the Department's exclusive discretion. In no sense can such a limited scope of bargaining be viewed as consistent with the Act's mandate that DHS "ensure" collective-bargaining rights for its employees. The Government argues that the HSA does not require the Department to adhere to the terms of Chapter 71 and points out that the Act states that the HR system must be "flexible," and from this concludes that a drastically limited scope of bargaining is fully justified. This contention is specious. Although the HSA does not compel the Government to adopt the terms of Chapter 71 as such, Congress did not say that Chapter 71 is irrelevant to an understanding of how DHS is to comply with its obligations under the Act. "Collective bargaining" is a term of art and Chapter 71 gives guidance to its meaning. It is also noteworthy that the HSA requires that the HR system be "contemporary" as well as flexible. We know of no contemporary system of *collective bargaining* that limits the scope of bargaining to employee-specific personnel matters, as does the HR system, and the Government cites to none. We therefore reverse the District Court on this point.

We affirm the District Court's judgment that the Department exceeded its authority in attempting to conscript FLRA into the HR system. The Authority is an independent administrative agency, operating pursuant to its own organic statute and long-established procedures. Although the Department was free to avoid FLRA altogether, it chose instead to impose upon the Authority a completely novel appellate function, defining FLRA's jurisdiction and dictating standards of review to be applied by the Authority. In essence, the Final Rule attempts to co-opt FLRA's administrative machinery, prescribing new practices in an exercise of putative authority that only Congress possesses. Nothing in the HSA allows DHS to disturb the operations of FLRA....

The allowance of unilateral contract abrogation and the limited scope of bargaining under DHS's Final Rule plainly violate the statutory command in the HSA that the Department "ensure" collective bargaining for its employees. We therefore vacate any provisions of the Final Rule that betray this command. DHS's attempt to co-opt FLRA's administrative machinery constitutes an exercise of power far outside the Department's statutory authority. We therefore affirm the District Court's decision to vacate the provisions of the Final Rule that encroach on the Authority.

The judgments of the District Court are affirmed in part and reversed in part, and the case is hereby remanded for further proceedings consistent with this opinion.

So ordered.

case 19.4 » American Federation of Government Employees, AFL-CIO v. Robert M. Gates, Secretary of Defense

486 F.3d 1316 (D.C. Cir. 2007)

Kavanaugh, Circuit Judge

This case arises out of a contentious dispute over the collective-bargaining rights of hundreds of thousands of civilian employees of the Department of Defense. Our limited judicial task is to determine whether the Department of Defense has acted consistently with its statutory authority in promulgating certain regulations. The primary legal question we must decide is whether the National Defense Authorization Act for Fiscal Year 2004 authorizes DoD to curtail collective-bargaining rights that DoD's civilian employees otherwise possess under the Civil Service Reform Act of 1978. We hold that the National Defense

Authorization Act grants DoD *temporary* authority to curtail collective bargaining for DoD's civilian employees. By its terms, the Act authorizes DoD to curtail collective bargaining through November 2009. But after November 2009, with certain specified exceptions, DoD again must ensure collective bargaining consistent with the Civil Service Reform Act of 1978. We reverse the District Court's judgment, and we uphold the DoD regulations at issue in this appeal....

To put together the pieces of the statutory puzzle in this case, one must first appreciate the difference between Chapter 71 and Chapter 99 of Title 5 of the U.S. Code. Chapter 71 of Title 5 codifies the Civil Service Reform Act of 1978 and establishes the right of federal civilian employees, including civilian employees at the Department of Defense, "to engage in collective-bargaining with respect to conditions of employment through representatives chosen by employees." The Act generally requires agency management to "meet and negotiate" in good faith with recognized unions over conditions of employment "for the purposes of arriving at a collective-bargaining agreement." The Act exempts various matters from collective bargaining, such as hiring, firing, suspending, paying, and reducing the pay of employees. Therefore, the Civil Service Reform Act ensures collective-bargaining for federal employees, albeit more limited than the collective bargaining rights for private employees.

Chapter 99 of Title 5 codifies a section of the National Defense Authorization Act for Fiscal Year 2004 and sets out a new labor relations framework for Department of Defense employees. Chapter 99 differs from the Chapter 71 model in several respects. In particular, Section 9902(a) of Chapter 99 establishes procedures for DoD, in coordination with the Office of Personnel Management, to "establish, and from time to time adjust, a human resources management system for some or all of the organizational or functional units of the Department of Defense." The "human resources management system" is called the "National Security Personnel System." Within the National Security Personnel System, the Act authorizes DoD to establish a "labor relations system" to structure bargaining between management and employees....

After Congress enacted the National Defense Authorization Act in November 2003, DoD began developing the National Security Personnel System. On February 14, 2005, DoD published a proposed system in the Federal Register. After various DoD employee representatives submitted comments, DoD held several meetings with employee representatives in the spring of 2005. On November 1, 2005, DoD promulgated final regulations setting up the National Security Personnel System....

The regulations curtail the scope of Chapter 71 collective bargaining in several ways relevant to this appeal:

- The regulations permit certain DoD officials to issue "implementing issuances" to abrogate any provision of an existing collective bargaining agreement or effectively take any topic off the table for future bargaining purposes. DoD may also promulgate "issuances" that take topics off the table. (Issuances and implementing issuances are documents issued to carry out DoD policies; implementing issuances relate to the National Security Personnel System, while issuances relate to any DoD policy.) Under the regulations, both issuances and implementing issuances can have prospective effect, but only implementing issuances can abrogate existing collective bargaining agreements.
- The regulations broaden the scope of "management rights"—that is, actions that management can take without collective bargaining—beyond the management rights already provided in Chapter 71. In particular, the regulations permit DoD "to take whatever other actions may be necessary to carry out the Department's mission."
- The regulations curtail bargaining over (i) the procedures DoD must follow when exercising management rights and (ii) the "appropriate arrangements" that DoD must make for employees affected by exercises of management rights.
- The regulations limit collective-bargaining rights over pay and benefits for employees of certain DoD units known as "non-appropriated fund instrumentalities." These employees' compensation is not set by statute and is therefore traditionally subject to collective bargaining....

[S]ubsection (m) of Section 9902 grants DoD expansive authority to curtail collective bargaining through November 2009.... After November 2009, however, the authority in subsection (m) runs out, and collective bargaining under Chapter 71 again will structure the Department's labor relations ... In effect, therefore, the Act sets up a temporary, experimental period through November 2009 during which DoD has broad leeway to restructure its labor relations system. But after November 2009, assuming that Congress has not amended the statute in the meantime, the Chapter 71 collective-bargaining requirements ... again will apply and govern labor relations for DoD's civilian workers (subject to targeted exceptions).

... In sum, we hold that the plain language of the National Defense Authorization Act authorizes DoD to curtail collective bargaining for DoD's civilian employees through November 2009. For purposes of our analysis, we find the relevant statutory terms plain.... Because we conclude that the National Defense Authorization Act authorizes DoD to curtail collective bargaining, we reverse the contrary judgment of the District Court....

We reverse the judgment of the District Court and uphold the DoD regulations at issue in this appeal.

So ordered.

Case Questions

1. As noted, the court of appeals held that the DHS regulations were invalid, but upheld the DoD regulations. Because the intent and the effects of the regulations in both cases were similar, how can you explain the different results in the two decisions?
2. In the DHS decision, what reasons did the court give for holding that the regulations failed to ensure the rights of the employees to bargain collectively?
3. In the DoD case, how did the NSPS limit the scope of collective bargaining for the civilian employees? Were the restrictions on collective bargaining legal? Explain.

Note that the National Defense Authorization Act for Fiscal Year 2008[12] amended Section 9902 to eliminate subsection (m), and to require that the DoD bargain collectively within the National Security Personnel System (NSPS). The amended legislation also ensures that no collective bargaining agreement is superseded under the NSPS.

State Public Sector Labor Relations Legislation

In 1954, Wisconsin adopted a public employee labor relations law covering state, county, and municipal employees. Since that first legal provision for state public sector labor relations, approximately forty states have adopted provisions relating to public sector labor relations. The various state laws differ widely in their treatment of issues such as employee coverage, impasse resolution procedures, and restrictions on the scope of bargaining. Because of the diversity of statutes, it is not possible to discuss them in detail; thus, the remaining portion of this chapter discusses certain general features of state public sector labor relations statutes.

Coverage of State Laws

As noted, approximately forty states have provisions for some labor relations activity by state or local employees. Most of those states have adopted statutes that provide for organizing rights and for collective bargaining by public employees. Some states that have no statutes dealing with public sector labor relations allow voluntary collective bargaining by public employees based on court decisions. Other states, while not restricting the rights of public employees to join unions, prohibit collective bargaining by public employees based on statutory prohibitions or court decisions.

In states that have public sector labor relations statutes, the pattern of coverage of those statutes varies. Some statutes cover all state and local employees. Others may cover only local or only state employees. Some states have several statutes, with separate statutes covering teachers, police, and firefighters. Some states also allow for the enactment of municipal labor relations legislation. New York City, for example, has established an Office of Collective Bargaining by passage of a city ordinance.

[12]Pub.L. No. 110-181, § 1106 (2008).

The courts have generally held that there is no constitutionally protected right to bargain collectively. For that reason, the courts have upheld restrictions or prohibitions on the right to bargain. The right to join unions or to organize, however, has been held to be protected by the constitutional freedom of association under the First and Fourteenth Amendments. Because the right to organize is constitutionally protected, restrictions on that right of public employees have consistently been struck down by the courts.

But while public employees in general may have the right to organize, many states exclude supervisors and managerial or confidential employees from unionizing. Other states may allow those employees to organize but provide for bargaining units separate from other employees. The courts have generally upheld exclusions of managerial, supervisory, and confidential employees from organizing and bargaining.

Representation Issues

Most of the state statutes authorizing public sector labor relations provide for exclusive bargaining representatives of the employees. The statutes generally create a Public Employee Relations Board (PERB) to administer the act and to determine representation issues and unfair labor practice complaints.

Bargaining Units

Determining appropriate bargaining units is generally the function of the PERB agency created by the particular statute. Some statutes provide for bargaining by all categories of public employees, whereas other statutes may specifically define appropriate units, such as teachers within a particular school district. When the PERB is entrusted with determining the appropriate unit, it generally considers community interest factors such as the nature of work, similarity of working conditions, efficiency of administration, and the desires of the employees. Some statutes require determination based on efficiency of administration. Police and law enforcement officers and firefighters are generally in separate district-wide units (or statewide units for state law enforcement officers). Faculty at public universities may be organized in statewide units or may bargain on an institution unit basis. In general, PERB agencies seek to avoid a proliferation of small units.

Representation Elections

The procedures for holding representation elections for units of public employees generally resemble those under the FSLMRA and the NLRA. The union seeking representation rights petitions the PERB requesting an election. The union must demonstrate some minimum level of employee support within the unit. If the parties fail to reach agreement on the bargaining unit definition, the eligibility of employees to vote, and the date and other details of the election, the PERB settles such issues after holding hearings on them.

The elections are by secret ballot, and the results are certified by the PERB. Either party may file objections to the election with the PERB; the PERB then reviews the challenges and possibly orders a new election when the challenges are upheld.

Bargaining

As noted, a majority of states have provisions requiring, or at least permitting, some form of collective bargaining. Some statutes may use the term “meet and confer” rather than collective bargaining, but in actual operation, the process is not substantially different from collective bargaining.

The scope of bargaining subjects may be restricted to protect the statutory authority of, or to ensure the provision of essential functions by, the public employer. The public employer may also be legally prohibited from agreeing with the union on particular subjects. For example, state law may require a minimum number of evaluations of employees annually, and the employer may not agree to fewer evaluations.

Public sector labor relations statutes generally have broad management-rights clauses. As a result, the subjects of "wages, hours and other terms and conditions" of employment may be defined more narrowly than is the case in the private sector under the NLRA.

The state PERBs generally classify subjects for bargaining as mandatory, permissive, and illegal subjects. Mandatory topics involve the narrowly defined matters relating to wages, hours, and other terms and conditions of employment. Permissive subjects generally are those related to government policy, the employer's function, or matters of management rights. Illegal subjects may include matters to which the employer is precluded by law from agreeing. Some states may prohibit bargaining over certain items that may be classified as permissive in other states.

In *Central State University v. A.A.U.P., Central State Chapter*,[13] the U.S. Supreme Court upheld the constitutionality of an Ohio law that required state public universities to set instructional workloads for professors and exempted those workloads from collective bargaining. The following case deals with whether a public employer's attempts to exempt parts of a collective agreement from being subject to arbitration as required by state law violate the duty to bargain in good faith.

case 19.5 » City of Bethany v. The Public Employees Relations Board

904 P.2d 604 (Ok. Sup. Ct. 1995)

Facts: The International Association of Firefighters, Local 2085 (the Union) and the City of Bethany (City) began negotiating for a collective bargaining agreement for the 1987–88 fiscal year. During the negotiations, the City proposed that certain issues would not be subject to arbitration under the new contract. In response, the Union argued that the Oklahoma Fire and Police Arbitration Act (FPAA) required that every item of a contract must be arbitrable, and declared an impasse on June 10, 1987. In August, the Union filed an unfair labor practice charge against the City with the state Public Employees Relations Board (PERB).

After a hearing, the PERB found that the FPAA did not allow parties to negotiate for the removal of a class of grievances, issues, or penalties from the arbitration process, and that the City had committed an unfair labor practice. PERB issued a cease and desist order directing the City to cease and desist from bargaining in bad faith by proposing and insisting upon illegal bargaining proposals. The City then filed a petition for judicial review of the PERB decision, and challenged the constitutionality of the arbitration provisions of the FPAA. The District Court affirmed the PERB, and upheld the constitutionality of FPAA, and the City appealed to the Oklahoma Supreme Court.

Issue: Is the FPAA requirement that matters be subject to arbitration constitutional, and has the City committed an unfair labor practice by seeking to exempt some issues from arbitration?

[13]526 U.S. 124 (1999).

Decision: Arbitration is the prime vehicle for resolving a dispute concerning the interpretation of a collective bargaining agreement formed under the FPAA. The legislation requires an arbitration clause be included in all collective bargaining agreements entered into under the Act. Although the FPAA permits the parties to adopt different grievance procedures, it does require that all disputes over any terms contained in the collective bargaining agreement be subject to final and binding grievance arbitration.

Under the Act, unions and employers are obligated to meet and negotiate in good faith over issues concerning wages, hours, grievances, working conditions and other terms and conditions of employment. These items are mandatory subjects of bargaining and neither party is compelled to agree to a proposal or required to make a concession regarding such items during the negotiation process.

The court then examined the principles underlying the legislative policy requiring mandatory arbitration:

- The prohibition against strikes by firefighters and police officers is not contained in the state constitution, but is found only in the FPAA. The state legislature explicitly balanced the requirement that collective bargaining agreements contain a no-strike provision with the requirement that the agreements also provide for grievance arbitration. To invalidate the grievance arbitration requirement would destroy that public policy decision.
- The FPAA states that any dispute over the "interpretation or application of any provision" of the collective bargaining agreement is subject to grievance arbitration. Neither side can bargain to exclude certain contractual provisions from mandatory grievance arbitration.
- When the parties cannot agree to a grievance arbitration procedure, they may resort to the statutory procedures for selecting impasse arbitrators and use those procedures for selecting a grievance arbitration panel.
- The statute mandates "final" grievance arbitration, whatever procedure is used to select the arbitrators; the parties are bound by the arbitration results.

Given the policy underlying the statutory requirement for grievance arbitration statute, the duty of the parties to an agreement to bargain in good faith becomes clear. The parties are free to bargain with respect to the "mechanics" and "procedures" of the grievance procedure. They may insist on their positions on these issues and press them to impasse.

What the parties may not do is create a two-tier grievance system under which some grievances are arbitrable and others are not. Such an approach would undermine the careful balance the legislature has struck in the statute: grievance arbitration in exchange for no-strike pledges by the unions representing public safety workers. The logic of such a two-tier regime would ultimately lead to the implication that firefighters and police officers could lawfully strike over non-arbitrable grievances. The duty to bargain in good faith is violated when a party insists upon contract terms which would be illegal if incorporated in the collective bargaining agreement. A party may not insist at the negotiating table upon terms which would modify statutory requirements for collective bargaining agreements, and the parties covered by the FPAA violate their duty to bargain in good faith when they assert positions in negotiations that would, if accepted, require the other side to agree to terms contrary to those mandated by statute. The court affirmed the decision of the trial court upholding the PERB rulings.

«

Bargaining and Open-Meeting Laws

Open-Meeting ("Sunshine") Laws
Laws that require that meetings of public bodies be open to the public.

Some states have adopted ***open-meeting, or "sunshine," laws*** that require meetings of public bodies be open to the public. Such laws could present a problem for collective bargaining by public employers because they may allow members of the general public to take part in the bargaining process. In some states, such as Ohio, collective bargaining is exempted from the open-meeting law. In other states, however, the right of the public to participate in the bargaining is legally protected.

Impasse Resolution Procedure

Because most state laws restrict or prohibit strikes by public employees, they must provide some alternative means for resolving bargaining impasses. Most statutes provide for a process that includes fact-finding, mediation, and ultimately, interest arbitration.

Mediation is generally the first step in the impasse resolution process. The mediator may be appointed by the PERB at the request of either party. The mediator attempts to offer suggestions and to reduce the number of issues in dispute.

If the mediation is unsuccessful, fact-finding is the second step. Each party presents its case to the fact-finder, who will issue a report defining the issues in dispute and establishing the reasonableness of each side's position. The fact-finder's report may be released to the public in an attempt to bring the pressure of public opinion upon the parties to force a settlement.

If no resolution is reached after mediation and fact-finding, the statutes generally provide for interest arbitration (see Chapter 18). The arbitration may be either voluntary or compulsory, and it may be binding or nonbinding. Compulsory, binding arbitration is generally found in statutes dealing with employees who provide essential services, such as firefighters and police. Nonbinding arbitration awards may be disregarded by the public employer if it so chooses. Binding arbitration awards bind both parties to the arbitrator's settlement of the dispute.

In several states, the arbitration of bargaining disputes has been challenged as being an illegal delegation of the public employer's legal authority to the arbitrator. Most state courts have upheld the legality of arbitration; examples are Maine, Michigan, Minnesota, New York, Oklahoma, Pennsylvania, and Washington. In some states, however, courts have held compulsory arbitration to be illegal. Such was the case in Colorado, South Dakota, Texas, and Utah.

Some statutes allow for judicial review of arbitration awards, generally on grounds of whether the award is unreasonable, arbitrary, or capricious.

Strikes by State Workers

Most state public sector labor relations statutes prohibit strikes by public employees. Statutes in other states, such as Hawaii, Michigan, Pennsylvania, and Vermont, allow strikes by employees whose jobs do not immediately affect the public health, safety, and welfare. Still other states' statutes allow for strikes in situations in which the public employer refuses to negotiate or to abide by an arbitration award.

Penalties for illegal strikes vary from state to state. New York's Taylor Law, which prohibits all strikes by public employees, provides for fines and the loss of dues check-off provisions for unions involved in illegal strikes. Employees who participate in illegal strikes in New York may face probation, loss of job, and loss of pay. The court may issue injunctions or restraining orders against illegal strikes.

Disciplining public sector employees, even those who have taken part in illegal strikes, may pose constitutional problems for the public sector employer. The employer must ensure that any disciplinary procedure ensures the employees "due process," including adequate notice of and an opportunity to participate in a hearing on the proposed penalty.

Public Employees and First Amendment Free Speech Rights

ethical DILEMMA

Religion in City Hall

You are the director of human resources for the City of Rochester. The city's employees are represented by the Rochester City Employees Association (RCEA). One of the employees at city hall is a devout fundamentalist Christian who frequently asks other employees, particularly non-Christian employees, if they are willing to be "born again" and to pray with her. A number of employees have complained to you, and the union threatens to file a grievance over her behavior.

The state civil service law gives the city the right to impose and enforce reasonable disciplinary rules. The RCEA demands that the city impose a rule prohibiting city employees from engaging in religious conduct on the job and from harassing other employees over matters of religion. You are concerned about the constitutionality of such a rule and of imposing discipline on an employee for religious behavior.

After reading this section, what are the potential constitutional problems raised by the proposed rule? What arguments can you make in favor of the proposed rule? What arguments can you make against it? Prepare a memo discussing these issues for the mayor and city council and recommend whether the city should adopt the rule.

The employment practices of public employers may also be matters of public concern— citizens and taxpayers may want to express their views on matters such as benefits for domestic partners, family leave, pension benefits and even workforces. Public employees have a dual role—they are employees who are affected by such practices or policies, and they are also citizens (and taxpayers). Do the public employees, as citizens, have the right to speak out on matters relating to their employer's practices? Can a public employer prohibit its employees from speaking out on such issues? Does the First Amendment freedom of speech protect those employees from disciplinary action by the employer? The following two cases involve the question of whether or not a school board can allow a teacher to comment at a public meeting on matters currently being negotiated with the teachers' union, and whether an employee of a district attorney who reports concerns about improper actions by other employees to his supervisor is protected by the First Amendment.

case 19.6 » City of Madison Joint School District No. 8 v. Wisconsin Employment Relations Commission

429 U.S. 167 (1976)

Burger, C.J.

The question presented on this appeal from the Supreme Court of Wisconsin is whether a State may constitutionally require that an elected board of education prohibit teachers, other than union representatives, to speak at open meetings, at which public participation is permitted, if such speech is addressed to the subject of pending collective-bargaining negotiations.

The Madison Board of Education and Madison Teachers, Inc. (MTI), a labor union, were parties to a collective-bargaining agreement during the calendar year of 1971. In January 1971 negotiations commenced for renewal of the agreement and MTI submitted a number of proposals. One among them called for the inclusion of a so-called "fair share" clause, which would require all teachers, whether members of MTI or not, to pay union dues to defray the costs of collective bargaining. Wisconsin law expressly permits inclusion of "fair share" provisions in municipal employee collective-bargaining agreements. Another proposal presented by the union was a provision for binding arbitration of teacher dismissals. Both of these provisions were resisted by the school board. The negotiations deadlocked in November 1971 with a number of issues still unresolved, among them "fair share" and arbitration.

During the same month, two teachers, Holmquist and Reed, who were members of the bargaining unit, but not members of the union, mailed a letter to all teachers in the district expressing opposition to the "fair share" proposal. Two hundred teachers replied, most commenting favorably on Holmquist and Reed's position. Thereupon a petition was drafted calling for a one-year delay in the implementation of "fair share" while the proposal was more closely analyzed by an impartial committee. The petition was circulated to teachers in the district on December 6, 1971. Holmquist and Reed intended to present the results of their petition effort to the school board and the MTI at the school board's public meeting that same evening.

Because of the stalemate in the negotiations, MTI arranged to have pickets present at the school board meeting. In addition, 300 to 400 teachers attended in support of the union's position. During a portion of the meeting devoted to expression of opinion by the public, the president of MTI took the floor and spoke on the subject of the ongoing negotiations. He concluded his remarks by presenting to the board a petition signed by 1,300–1,400 teachers calling for the expeditious resolution of the negotiations. Holmquist was next given the floor, after John Matthews, the business representative of MTI, unsuccessfully attempted to dissuade him from speaking. Matthews had also spoken to a member of the school board before the meeting and requested that the board refuse to permit Holmquist to speak. Holmquist stated that he represented "an informal committee of 72 teachers in 49 schools" and that he desired to inform the board of education, as he had already informed the union, of the results of an informational survey concerning the "fair share" clause. He then read the petition which had been circulated to the teachers in the district that morning and stated that in the 31 schools from which reports had been received, 53 percent of the teachers had already signed the petition.

Holmquist stated that neither side had adequately addressed the issue of "fair share" and that teachers were confused about the meaning of the proposal. He concluded by saying: "Due to this confusion, we wish to take no stand on the proposal itself, but ask only that all alternatives be presented clearly to all teachers and more importantly to the general public to whom we are all responsible. We ask simply for communication, not confrontation." The sole response from the school board was a question by the president inquiring whether Holmquist intended to present the board with the petition. Holmquist answered that he would. Holmquist's presentation had lasted approximately 2 ½ minutes.

Later that evening, the board met in executive session and voted a proposal acceding to all of the union's demands with the exception of "fair share." During a negotiating session the following morning, MTI accepted the proposal and a contract was signed on December 14, 1971.

In January 1972, MTI filed a complaint with the Wisconsin Employment Relations Commission (WERC) claiming that the board had committed a prohibited labor practice by permitting Holmquist to speak at the December 6 meeting. MTI claimed that in so doing the board had engaged in negotiations with a member of the bargaining unit other than the exclusive collective-bargaining representative, in violation of Wis. Stat. Sections 111.70(3)(a)(1), (4) (1973). Following a hearing the Commission concluded that the board was guilty of the prohibited labor practice and ordered that it "immediately cease and desist from permitting employees, other than representatives of Madison Teachers Inc., to appear and speak at meetings of the Board of Education, on matters subject to collective bargaining between it and Madison Teachers, Inc." The Commission's action was affirmed by the Circuit Court of Dane County.

The Supreme Court of Wisconsin affirmed. The court recognized that both the Federal and State Constitutions protect freedom of speech and the right to petition the government, but noted that these rights may be abridged in the face of "a clear and present danger that [the speech] will bring about the substantive evils that [the legislature] has a right to prevent." The court held that abridgment of the speech in this case was justified in order "to avoid the dangers attendant upon relative chaos in labor management relations."

The Wisconsin court perceived "clear and present danger" based upon its conclusion that Holmquist's speech before the school board constituted "negotiation" with the board. Permitting such "negotiation," the court reasoned, would undermine the bargaining exclusivity guaranteed the majority union under Wis. Stat. Section 111.70(3)(a)(4) (1973). From that premise it concluded that teachers' First Amendment rights could be limited. *Assuming, arguendo,* that such a "danger" might in some circumstances justify some limitation of First Amendment rights, we are unable to read this record as presenting such danger as would justify curtailing speech.

The Wisconsin Supreme Court's conclusion that Holmquist's terse statement during the public meeting constituted negotiation with the board was based upon its adoption of the lower court's determination that, "[e]ven though Holmquist's statement superficially appears to be merely a 'position statement,' the court deems from the total circumstances that it constituted 'negotiating.'" This cryptic conclusion seems to ignore the ancient wisdom that calling a thing by a name does not make it so. Holmquist did not seek to bargain or offer to enter into any bargain with the board, nor does it appear that he was authorized by any other teachers to enter into any agreement on their behalf. Although his views were not consistent with those of MTI, communicating such views to the employer could not change the fact that MTI alone was authorized to negotiate and to enter into a contract with the board.

Moreover the school board meeting at which Holmquist was permitted to speak was open to the public. He addressed the school board not merely as one of its employees but also as a concerned citizen, seeking to express his views on an important decision of his government. We have held that teachers may not be "compelled to relinquish the First Amendment rights they would otherwise enjoy as citizens to comment on matters of public interest in connection with the operation of the public schools in which they work." ... Where the State has opened a forum for direct citizen involvement, it is difficult to find justification for excluding teachers who make up the overwhelming proportion of school employees and who are most vitally concerned with the proceedings. It is conceded that any citizen could have presented precisely the same points and provided the board with the same information as did Holmquist.

Regardless of the extent to which true contract negotiations between a public body and its employees may be regulated—an issue we need not consider at this time—the participation in public discussion of public business cannot be confined to one category of interested individuals. To permit one side of a debatable public question to have a monopoly in expressing its views to the government is the antithesis of constitutional guarantees. Whatever its duties as an employer, when the board sits in public meetings to conduct public business and hear the views of citizens, it may not be required to discriminate between speakers on the basis of their employment, or the content of their speech....

The WERC's order is not limited to a determination that a prohibited labor practice had taken place in the past; it also restrains future conduct. By prohibiting the school board from "permitting employees ... to appear and speak at meetings of the Board of Education" the order constitutes an indirect, but effective, prohibition on persons such as Holmquist from communicating with their government. The order would have a substantial impact upon virtually all communication between teachers and the school board. The order prohibits speech by teachers "on matters subject to collective bargaining." As the dissenting opinion below noted, however, there is virtually no subject concerning the operation of the school system that could not also be characterized as a potential subject of collective bargaining. Teachers not only constitute the overwhelming bulk of employees of the school system, but they are the very core of that system; restraining teachers' expressions to the board on matters involving the operation of the schools would seriously impair the board's ability to govern the district....

The judgment of the Wisconsin Supreme Court is reversed, and the case is remanded to that court for further proceedings not inconsistent with this opinion.

Reversed and remanded.

Case Questions

1. Why did the Wisconsin Supreme Court characterize Holmquist's statement as constituting negotiation? Did the U.S. Supreme Court agree with that characterization? Why?
2. Was Holmquist addressing the school board in his capacity as an employee, as a concerned citizen, or as both? Why is it relevant here? Explain your answer.
3. When can the First Amendment rights of the freedom of speech and the right to petition the government be limited? Were those circumstances applicable to the facts in this case? Explain.

The *City of Madison* decision recognized that public employees are also citizens who enjoy First Amendment protection of freedom of speech—they may not be prohibited from speaking out in a public forum on matters of public interest, even if those matters relate to labor relations policies affecting those employees. But how far does the First Amendment protection extend. Does it cover all work-related speech of public employees? That is the question addressed by the Supreme Court in the following case.

case 19.7 »

Garcetti v. Ceballos
547 U.S. 410 (2006)

Facts: Richard Ceballos was a deputy district attorney for the Los Angeles County District Attorney's Office. In February 2000, a defense attorney contacted Ceballos about a pending criminal case and told him that there were inaccuracies in an affidavit used to obtain a critical search warrant. The attorney informed Ceballos that he had filed a motion to challenge the warrant, and asked Ceballos to review the case. Ceballos determined the affidavit contained serious misrepresentations. He informed his supervisors and prepared a memo explaining his concerns and recommending dismissal of the case. A meeting was held to discuss Ceballos' concerns about the affidavit. The meeting allegedly became heated, and Ceballos was criticized for his handling of the case. The supervisor decided to proceed with the prosecution, and at a hearing on the motion to challenge the warrant, Ceballos was called by the defense and testified about his observations about the affidavit. The trial court rejected the challenge to the warrant.

Ceballos claimed that in the aftermath of these events he was subjected to a series of retaliatory employment actions, including reassignment to a trial deputy position, transfer to another courthouse, and denial of a promotion. Ceballos initiated an employment grievance, but the grievance was denied. Ceballos then filed suit, claiming that his employer had violated the First and Fourteenth Amendments by retaliating against him based on his memo. The trial court granted the employer's motion for summary judgment, but on appeal, the U.S. Court of Appeals for the Ninth Circuit reversed the trial court, holding that Ceballos allegations of wrongdoing in his memorandum constituted protected speech under the First Amendment. The employer appealed to the U.S. Supreme Court.

Issue: Does the First Amendment protect a government employee from discipline based on speech made pursuant to the employee's official duties?

Decision: The court of appeals held that Ceballos' memo was "inherently a matter of public concern," but did not consider whether the speech was made in Ceballos' capacity as a citizen or as part of his professional duties. The Supreme Court, however, stated that there were two questions to ask to determine whether constitutional protection is accorded to speech by a public employee.

The first question is whether the employee spoke as a citizen on a matter of public concern. If the employee is not speaking as a citizen, but rather in the course of official duties, the employee's speech is not protected by the First Amendment. If the employee is speaking as a citizen, then the possibility of a First Amendment claim arises. In that case, the court considers the second question, whether the government employer had an adequate justification for treating the employee differently from any other member of the general public. Government has broader discretion to restrict speech when it is acting in its role as employer, but any restrictions it can impose must be directed at speech that has some potential to affect the employer's operations. When public employees speak out, they may express views that contravene governmental policies or impair the proper performance of governmental functions.

At the same time, the First Amendment limits the ability of a public employer to impose restrictions on employees in their capacities as private citizens. So long as employees are speaking as citizens about matters of public concern, the employer can only impose speech restrictions that are necessary for their employers to operate efficiently and effectively. However, when public employees make statements pursuant to their official duties, the employees are not speaking as citizens for First Amendment purposes, and the Constitution does not protect their communications from employer discipline.

In this case, Ceballos believed the affidavit used to obtain a search warrant contained serious misrepresentations, and he conveyed his opinion and recommendation in a memo to his supervisor. His expressions were made pursuant to his duties as a calendar deputy, not as a citizen, and his conduct was not protected by the First Amendment. The Supreme Court reversed the decision of the court of appeals. «

CHAPTER REVIEW

» Key Terms

Federal Labor Relations Authority (FLRA) « 593

federal service impasse panel « 598

open-meeting, or "sunshine," laws « 612

» Summary

- Labor relations in the public sector differ from those in the private sector in several ways: (1) government employees are also citizens who have certain rights under the federal and appropriate state constitutions, which may limit disciplinary procedures by government employers; (2) government sovereignty requires that the scope of collective bargaining be restricted; and (3) the right of public employees to strike may be limited or completely prohibited. While legislation in some states permits certain public employees to strike, federal government employees are prohibited from striking. A union that authorizes or conducts a strike against the federal government may have its status as exclusive bargaining representative revoked, and federal employees who go on strike are subject to discharge.
- The Federal Service Labor-Management Relations Act (FSLMRA) regulates federal labor relations; it grants federal employees the right to join or assist unions. Certain federal employees, including members of the armed forces and those involved in intelligence work or national security matters, are excluded from coverage of the FSLMRA. The FSLMRA requires employers and unions to negotiate in good faith, but the act also contains a broad management-rights clause and restricts the scope of collective bargaining subjects. The Federal Labor Relations Authority (FLRA) administers the FSLMRA; the FLRA determines appropriate representation units, conducts representation elections, and hears complaints of unfair labor practices under the FSLMRA.
- State public sector labor relations legislation varies widely; some states grant certain public employees the right to strike, and most states require that employers negotiate, or "meet and confer," with the unions representing public employees. The scope of collective bargaining under state public sector legislation is generally restricted by broad management-rights clauses. State public sector labor relations laws are generally administered by a state Public Employee Relations Board (PERB), which conducts representation elections and decides unfair labor practice complaints.

» Problems

Questions

1. In what ways does the role of government as employer raise constitutional issues not found in the private sector?
2. Which federal employees are covered by the FSLMRA? Which federal agencies are excluded from the act's coverage?
3. What restrictions are placed on the scope of collective bargaining under the FSLMRA? What procedures are available for impasse settlement under the FSLMRA?
4. What legal issues are raised by union security clauses in the public sector? Explain why these issues arise.
5. To what extent may states restrict the right of state public employees to join unions? To what extent may the right of state public sector employees to bargain collectively be restricted?

Case Problems

6. In April 1978, public employee Dorothea Yoggerst heard an unconfirmed report that her boss, the director of the Illinois Governor's Office of Management and Human Development, had been discharged. While still at work, she asked a co-worker, "Did you hear the good news?"

   Yoggerst was orally reprimanded by her supervisor. Subsequently, a written memorandum of the reprimand was placed in her personnel file. Two months later, she resigned her job, citing this alleged infringement of her First Amendment right of free speech as her reason for leaving. Yoggerst sued four defendants, including the supervisor who reprimanded her and the personnel director.

   An earlier case heard by the Supreme Court, *Connick v. Myers*, involved the firing of a public employee for distributing to her co-workers a questionnaire that challenged the trustworthiness of her superiors. In that case, the high court enunciated a two-prong test: (1) Did the speech in question address a matter of public concern? (2) How did the employee's right to speak her mind compare to the government's interest in efficient operations? The U.S. Court of Appeals applied this same test in the *Yoggerst* case.

   How do you think the courts ruled in these two cases? See *Yoggerst v. Hedges and McDonough* [739 F.2d 293 (7th Cir. 1984)]; *Connick v. Myers* [461 U.S. 138 (1983)], and *Garcetti v. Ceballos* [547 U.S. 410 (2006)].
7. The Toledo Police Patrolmen's Association is the union representing the employees of the Toledo, Ohio, police department. Several police department employees objected to the amount of agency fees that they were required to pay because they reflected union political expenditures. The union had charged objectors an agency fee that was equal to 100 percent of the regular union dues. The union claimed that its collective bargaining expenditures were $166,020 annually, whereas the dues collected amounted to only $162,138 annually, but the union refused to make its financial records available to the objecting employees. The employees filed suit in federal court, asking the court to order the union to provide financial information and to submit to an audit to verify the procedure used to determine the agency fees.

   How should the court rule on the employees' suit? See *Tierney v. City of Toledo* [917 F.2d 927 (6th Cir. 1990)].
8. The federal Department of Health and Human Services (H&HS) decided to institute a total ban on smoking in all of its facilities. The National Treasury Employees Union, which represents the H&HS employees, demanded that the agency bargain with it over the decision. The agency refused, arguing that the decision was not subject to bargaining under the FSLMRA.

   How should the Federal Labor Relations Authority rule on the union's claim? See *Dept. of*

Health and Human Services Family Support Admin. v. Federal Labor Relations Authority [920 F.2d 45 (D.C. Cir. 1990)].

9. A group of twenty community college faculty instructors in Minnesota refused to join the Minnesota Community College Faculty Association. Under state law, faculty unions were given the exclusive right to engage in discussions with administrators about matters of academic policy. The twenty nonmembers argued that this exclusive representation policy violated principles of free speech and academic freedom enshrined in the First Amendment.

   How should the Supreme Court respond? See *Minn. State Bd. for Community Colleges v. Knight* [465 U.S. 271 (1984)].

10. Marjorie Rowland began working at Stebbins High School in Yellow Springs, Ohio, in August 1974. The school principal subsequently asked her to resign when it was learned that she had stated she was bisexual. When she refused, the school suspended her but was forced to rehire her by a preliminary injunction issued by a federal district judge. The administration assigned her to a job with no student contact and, when her contract expired, refused to renew it. Rowland sued.

    How do you think the court would rule on Rowland's suit? Why? See *Rowland v. Mad River Local School District* [730 F.2d 444 (6th Cir. 1984)].

11. On September 22, 1978, all eighteen employees of the public works, fire, and finance departments of the City of Gridley, California, went on strike following the breakdown in negotiations over a new collective bargaining agreement. The city notified the union that it regarded the strike as illegal and immediately revoked the union's certification as collective bargaining representative. The city's labor relations officer notified the employees that they would be fired if they did not return to work at their next regular shift. The city council met in emergency session on a Saturday and voted to terminate the employees. On Sunday, the union notified the city that all employees would return to their jobs on Monday. The city refused to reinstate them.

    Although the city council had earlier declared that "participation by any employee in a strike … is unlawful and shall subject the employee to disciplinary action, up to and including discharge," the union challenged the city's actions on the basis that (1) the discharged employees had been entitled to a hearing, and (2) the sanction of revoking recognition was contrary to the purpose of California's public employee relations laws—that is, to permit the employees to have responsibilities of their own choosing.

    The case reached the California Supreme Court. How do you think the court ruled? See *IBEW Local 1245 v. City of Gridley* [34 Cal.3d 191 (Supr. Ct. Cal. 1983)].

12. Student Services Inc. was a nonprofit organization that operated a bookstore, bowling alley, vending machines, and other services at Edinboro State College in Pennsylvania. The Retail Clerks Union filed a petition with the Pennsylvania Labor Relations Board seeking a Public Employees Relations Act. After several hearings, an election was held and the union won. The board subsequently certified the union.

    The company challenged the board's jurisdiction, stating that it was not a part of the state college and therefore was a private employer covered by the NLRA. The bookstore, bowling alley, and other services were housed rent-free in a building owned by the Commonwealth of Pennsylvania and situated on the college campus. Pennsylvania law defines a "public employer" in pertinent part as "any nonprofit organization or institution and any charitable, religious, scientific, literary, recreational, health, educational or welfare institution receiving grants or appropriations from local, State or Federal governments."

    How should the court have ruled on Student Services' status? See *In the Matter of Employees of Student Services, Inc.* [495 Pa. 42, 432 A.2d 189 (Pa. 1981)].

13. The Combined Federal Campaign (CFC) is an annual charitable fund-raising drive conducted in the federal workplace during working hours largely through the voluntary efforts of federal employees.

Participating organizations confine their fund-raising activities to a thirty-word statement submitted by them for inclusion in the campaign literature.

Volunteer federal employees distribute to their co-workers literature describing the campaign and the participants, along with pledge cards. Designated funds are paid directly to the specified recipient.

The CFC is a relatively recent idea. Prior to 1957, charitable solicitation in the federal workplace occurred on an ad hoc basis. Federal managers received requests from dozens of organizations seeking endorsements and the right to solicit contributions from federal employees at their work sites. In facilities where solicitation was permitted, weekly campaigns were commonplace.

In 1957, President Eisenhower established the forerunner of the CFC to bring order to the solicitation process and to ensure truly voluntary giving by federal employees. The order established an advisory committee and set forth general procedures and standards for a uniform fund-raising program. It permitted no more than three charitable solicitations annually and established a system requiring prior approval by a committee on fund-raising for participation by "voluntary health and welfare" agencies.

A number of organizations joined in challenging these criteria, including the NAACP Legal Defense and Educational Fund, Inc., the Sierra Club Legal Defense Fund, the Puerto Rican Legal Defense and Education Fund, the Federally Employed Women Legal Defense and Education Fund, the Indian Law Resource Center, the Lawyers Committee for Civil Rights under Law, and the Natural Resources Defense Council. Each of the groups attempts to influence public policy through one or more of the following means: political activity, advocacy, lobbying, and litigation on behalf of others.

On what grounds did these organizations challenge the regulations? How do you think the Supreme Court ruled? See *Cornelius v. NAACP Legal Defense and Educational Fund* [473 U.S. 788 (1985)].

14. The Indianapolis city government pressed theft charges against a former employee, Michael McGraw, when his supervisor discovered that he had used the computer to keep customer lists and payment records for his private business—the sale to co-workers and others of Nature-Slim, a liquid diet supplement for people who want to lose weight. The city decided to press charges for theft after it was unsuccessful in blocking McGraw's application for unemployment compensation benefits. The discharge of McGraw was not related to the alleged misuse of the computer. A jury convicted McGraw on two counts of theft.

    The state criminal code defines a thief in the following terms: "A person who knowingly or intentionally exerts unauthorized control over property of another person with intent to deprive the other of any part of its value, or use, commits theft, a class D felony."

    Should McGraw's conviction be permitted to stand? Suppose the conviction is overturned. Should he be reinstated? See *Indiana v. McGraw* [480 N.E.2d 552 (Ind. 1985)].

15. The legislature of the state of Iowa, concerned about the proliferation of drugs in American society and their alleged availability even inside the nation's prisons, passed a law allowing prison officials to conduct random blood and urinalysis tests on state correction officers. The law allowed testing without any reasonable suspicion that the officers to be tested were in fact users or under the influence of any controlled substance. A total of 1,750 officers filed a class-action suit challenging the law as a search and seizure without a warrant and as a violation of their due process rights.

    How should the federal court rule? See *McDonell v. Hunter* [809 F.2d 1302 (8th Cir. 1987)].

Hypothetical Scenarios

16. The school teachers and teachers' aides in the Syracuse City School District, in Syracuse, New York, are represented by the Syracuse United Teachers, a union affiliated with the New York

State United Teachers. The teachers' union and the Syracuse School District have not had a contract for three years, and negotiations have been at an impasse. The School District has proposed eliminating seventy-five teacher positions and 200 teachers' aide positions because of declining tax revenues. The teachers' union calls for a one-day strike on the first day of the school year to protest the proposed job cuts. What legal remedies, if any, can the Syracuse School District pursue against the teachers and against the teachers' union? Explain. Would your answers be different if the public school district were located in Vermont rather than in New York? Why?

17. Houseman and Harmon have a contract with the Kentucky State Police to train forensic lab specialists. The state police received a large federal grant as part of the economic stimulus package, and decided to use the grant to train more forensic lab specialists for the police crime lab. Rather than solicit bids from companies interested in conducting the training, the state police awarded a no-bid contract to National Forensic Science Center, a Florida company. Houseman and Harmon wrote a letter to the director of the police crime lab criticizing the no-bid contract as overpriced and a waste of taxpayers' money. They also sent a copy of the letter to the local newspaper, which did a story on the no-bid contract. The director of the crime lab then suspended Houseman and Harmon. They claimed that their suspension was in retaliation for their letter about the no-bid contract, and was in violation of their First Amendment rights. Was it? Explain.

18. The nonprofessional employees at the federal Government Services Administration Center are represented by the National Federation of Federal Employees Union, Local 144. The depot had provided child-care services for both military and civilian employees through an on-site day-care center. The staff at the day-care center were members of Local 144, and many other union members sent their children to the day-care center. In April 2009, the depot's director of personnel sent a letter to all employees informing them that the day-care center would be closed in three months. The union then notified the director that it was requesting negotiations over the decision to close the day-care center. The director responded that the decision was not subject to bargaining under the Federal Service Labor-Management Relations Act. The union then filed an unfair labor practice complaint with the FLRA. Was the refusal to bargain over the closure of the day-care center a violation of the FSLMRA? Explain.

19. The staff auditors and clerks at the federal Internal Revenue Service Processing Center in Andover, Massachusetts are represented by the National Treasury Employees Union. During the months of February, March, and April, the employees are required to work twelve-hour shifts to process the huge volume of income tax returns. In January, 2009, the director of the processing center notifies the employees that as of February 15, they will be required to work double shifts. The union officials plan a "sick-out" to protest—the workers will take turns calling in sick and refuse to work at least one day a week. Does the union's action violate federal law? What, if any, actions can be taken against the union? What, if any, actions can be taken against the employees? Explain.

20. During contract negotiations, the faculty union representing the professors at Springfield State University, a public university located in Springfield, Ohio, presented the school administration with a demand that the teaching load for faculty be limited to no more than three courses per semester. The college administration refused to bargain over the proposal because it involves a matter of inherent management rights. Must the university administration bargain over teaching loads for faculty? Explain your answer.

PART 4

EMPLOYMENT LAW ISSUES

Occupational Safety and Health

Observing that increased responsibilities and anemic staffing have hampered Uncle Sam's ability to protect workers, President Barack Obama pledged in the first months of his presidency to step up federal enforcement of workplace safety. Obama's first budget, released in late February 2009, and passed in substantial part in early April 2009, increased funding to the Occupational Safety and Health Administration (OSHA).

"For the past eight years, the department's labor law enforcement agencies have struggled with growing workloads and shrinking staff," the 134-page budget proposal said. "The president's budget seeks to reverse this trend, restoring the department's ability to meet its responsibilities to working Americans under the more than 180 worker protection laws it enforces."

The funding increase was aimed at enabling OSHA to "vigorously enforce workplace safety laws and whistleblower protections, and ensure the safety and health of American workers," according to the White House document. (The extra money also was intended to beef up enforcement of wage and hour regulations, and to enforce equal opportunity aspects of federal contracting.)

AFL-CIO Director for Safety and Health Peg Seminario told news media that Obama's proposal represented "a welcome change in direction from the policies of President George W. Bush, who repeatedly proposed cutting or freezing OSHA's budget."[1]

By contrast, Randy Johnson, a vice president at the U.S. Chamber of Commerce, and who worked for OSHA in the Reagan administration, commented that "money ought to be spent educating employers about workplace safety rather than trying to monitor every job site."

"Maybe if they provided more money to the poultry industry for education they would have been able to prevent those injuries,"[2] asserted Johnson, referring to the avian flu scare.

The number of federal OSHA compliance officers has declined by about 35 percent since 1980, even though the nation's employment generally has risen dramatically during the same three decades. OSHA agents annually inspect only about 1 percent of all U.S. workplaces.

[1] http://www.aflcio.org/issues/safety/

[2] http://www.uschamber.com/issues/index/labor/osha_reform.htm

Twenty-four states have accepted Congress's invitation to enact their own workplace safety programs, leaving it to the federal agency to try to oversee safety in the remaining twenty-six, plus the American territories—notably Puerto Rico, the Virgin Islands, and Guam. Federal funding assistance for the state-run OSHA programs dramatically trails inflation, rising only about 1 percent in the aggregate since 2001.

Congresswoman Lynn Woolsey, a California Democrat who chairs of the House's work force protection panel, commented that Obama's proposal "signals a new day" for workers.

"The health and safety of our workers is absolutely paramount, but under President Bush, enforcement of safety violations had been hindered by out-of-date regulations and inadequate funding," she asserted. "Simply put, OSHA in recent years has failed in its obligation to protect our workers."[3]

On April 3, 2009, Congress passed a $3.5 trillion budget that largely tracked the president's proposals. The Department of Labor's share totaled a bit more than $13 billion. Bottom line: Look for a more active OSHA during the three years immediately ahead.

Policy and Processes of the Occupational Safety and Health Act

The Occupational Safety and Health Act (OSH Act) was enacted by Congress in 1970. The statute has two broad goals:

- To assure safe and healthful working conditions for working men and women
- To provide a framework for research, education, training, and information in the field of occupational safety and health

The act requires employers to furnish their employees a workplace that is free from recognized hazards that cause, or are likely to cause, serious injury or death. A recognized hazard is one that is known to be hazardous, taking into account the standard of knowledge of the industry.

The act also requires that employers meet the various health and safety standards set under the act and keep records of injuries, deaths, accidents, illnesses, and particular hazards.

The Occupational Safety and Health Act applies to all employees who work for an employer that is engaged in a business affecting interstate commerce. This broad coverage reaches almost all employers and employees in the United States and its territories, with some exceptions. The act does not apply to the federal and state governments in their capacity as employers, nor does it apply to domestic servants or self-employed persons.

The act contains no specific industry-wide exemptions. However, if other federal agencies exercise statutory authority to prescribe or enforce standards or regulations affecting occupational safety or health, the Occupational Safety and Health Act does not apply. For this exemption to operate, it must be shown that the working conditions of the affected employees are covered by another federal statute that has the protection of employees as one of its purposes. The other agency must also have exercised its jurisdiction to make regulations or standards applying to specific working conditions that would otherwise be covered by the act. An example of such a situation involves the workers on offshore oil platforms. Their working

[3]http://woolsey.house.gov/

conditions were governed by health and safety regulations enacted and enforced by both the U.S. Coast Guard and the U.S. Geological Survey. In *Marshall v. Nichols*,[4] the court held that the Occupational Safety and Health Administration was precluded from exerting its jurisdiction over offshore oil platforms because of the coverage by the Coast Guard and the Geological Survey.

Administration and Enforcement

The Occupational Safety and Health Act created three federal agencies for administration and enforcement. The Occupational Safety and Health Administration (OSHA) is the primary agency created for enforcement of the act. An independent agency within the Department of Labor, it has the authority to:

- promulgate standards;
- conduct inspections of workplaces;
- issue citations for violations; and
- recommend penalties.

OSHA acts on behalf of the Secretary of Labor.

The National Institute of Occupational Safety and Health (NIOSH) is an agency created to conduct research and promote the application of the research results to ensure that no worker will suffer diminished health, reduced functional capacity, or decreased life expectancy as a result of his or her work experience.

The Occupational Safety and Health Review Commission (OSHRC) is a quasi-judicial agency created to adjudicate contested enforcement actions of OSHA. Whereas OSHA may issue citations and recommend penalties for violations of the act, only OSHRC can actually assess and enforce the penalties. The decisions of OSHRC can be appealed to the U.S. courts of appeals. OSHRC has three members appointed by the president for overlapping six-year terms and a number of administrative law judges who have career tenure.

Standards, Feasibility, and Variances

To reach the goal of providing hazard-free workplaces for all employees, the act provides for the setting of standards regulating the health and safety of working conditions. The Secretary of Labor is granted authority under the act to promulgate occupational safety and health standards through OSHA. The act provides for the issuance of three kinds of standards: interim standards, permanent standards, and emergency standards.

- *Interim standards* are those that the Secretary of Labor had power to issue for the first two years following the effective date of the act. These standards were generally modeled on various preexisting industry consensus standards. The Secretary, in adopting previously accepted national consensus standards, was not required to hold public hearings or any other formal proceedings.
- *Permanent standards* are both newly created standards and revised interim standards. These standards are developed by OSHA and NIOSH and are frequently based on suggestions made by interested parties, such as employers, employees, states and other

[4] 486 F. Supp. 615 (E.D. Texas 1980).

political subdivisions, and labor unions. The Secretary of Labor is also empowered to appoint an advisory committee to assist in the promulgation of permanent standards. This committee has ninety days from its date of appointment, unless a longer or shorter period is prescribed by the Secretary, to make its recommendations regarding a proposed rule.

After OSHA has developed a proposed rule that promulgates, modifies, or revokes an occupational safety or health standard, the Secretary must publish a notice in the *Federal Register*. Included in this notice must be a statement of the reasons for adopting a new standard, changing an existing standard, or revoking a prior standard. Interested parties are then allowed thirty days after publication to submit written data, objections, or comments relating to the proposed standards. If the interested party files written objections and requests a public hearing concerning these objections, the Secretary must publish a notice in the *Federal Register* specifying the time and place of the hearing and the standard to which the objection has been filed.

Within sixty days after the expiration of the period for comment or after the completion of any hearing, the Secretary must issue a rule promulgating, modifying, or revoking the standard or make a determination that the rule should not be issued. If adopted, the rule must state its effective date. This date must ensure a sufficient period for affected employers and employees to be informed of the existence of the standard and of its terms.

- The Secretary of Labor may, under special circumstances, avoid the procedures just described by issuing temporary *emergency standards*. These standards are issued when the Secretary believes that employees are exposed to grave dangers from substances or agents determined to be toxic or physically harmful. Actual injury does not have to occur before a temporary emergency standard can be promulgated, although there must be a genuinely serious emergency.

  Emergency standards take effect immediately upon publication in the *Federal Register*. After publication, the Secretary must then follow the procedure for formally adopting a permanent standard to make the emergency standard into a permanent standard. That new permanent standard must be issued within six months after its publication as an emergency standard.

Appeals of Standards After a standard has been promulgated by the Secretary, any person adversely affected by it can file a challenge to the validity of the standard. Such challenges must be filed with the appropriate federal court of appeals before the sixtieth day after the issuance of the standard.

Upon reviewing the standard, the court of appeals will uphold the standard if it is supported by substantial evidence. The Secretary must demonstrate that the standard was in response to a significant risk of material health impairment.

Feasibility The act grants the Secretary authority to issue standards dealing with toxic materials or harmful physical agents. A standard must be one that most adequately assures, to the extent feasible and on the basis of the best available evidence, that no employee will suffer material impairment of health or functional capacity, even if the employee has regular exposure to the hazard. The feasibility of a standard must be examined from two perspectives: technological feasibility and economic feasibility. Further, OSHA can force an industry to develop and diffuse new technology to satisfy precise permissible exposure limits to toxic materials or harmful physical agents that have never before been attained, if OSHA can present substantial evidence showing that companies acting vigorously and in good faith can develop the technology. The standard also must satisfy the requirement of economic feasibility.

Burden of Proof The Secretary must carry the burden of proving both technological and economic feasibility when promulgating and enforcing standards governing toxic materials and harmful physical agents. However, the Secretary does not have to establish that the cost of a standard bears a reasonable relationship to its benefits, as established in the case of *American Textile Mfr.'s Inst. v. Donovan.*[5]

In general, the Secretary bears the burden of proving by "substantial evidence on the record considered as a whole" that the cited employer violated the act. The prima facie case which the Secretary must prove to make an OSHA citation "stick" is well illustrated in the following case.

case 20.1 » Trinity Industries, Inc. v. Occupational Safety and Health Review Commission

206 F.3d 539 (5th Cir. 2000)

Reynaldo G. Garza, Circuit Judge

Background

Trinity Industries operates plants that manufacture and repair railcars. Trinity also "lines" new "hopper" railcars by spraying their insides with a chemical coating designed to seal and protect the interior of a railcar. Absent proper ventilation, this lining process has the potential to create a hazardous atmosphere inside the railcar. A hazardous atmosphere is defined as one that is oxygen deficient or which contains toxic levels of a hazardous gas or dust of flammable vapors in excess of ten percent of the lower flammable limit (LFL) or lower explosive limit (LEL). At issue in this case are citations issued against Trinity based on an OSHA inspector's finding that the atmosphere inside at least one of Trinity's railcars exceeded ten percent of the LEL during the lining process.

Trinity designed a ventilation system to prevent the build up of a hazardous atmosphere, consisting of a ventilation duct on top of the railcar which pulls air out of the railcar, thus forcing fresh air to be drawn into the railcar through its bottom opening. The entire process exchanges all of the air in the railcar with air from outside the railcar every minute.

Railcars are "confined spaces" per OSHA regulations. OSHA's standard for employee entry into confined spaces governs work activities in confined spaces. A confined space is "permit required" if it contains, or has the potential to contain, a hazardous atmosphere.... [The applicable regulation], however, allows alternative methods of compliance if the confined space only contains a "potentially hazardous atmosphere," and if continuous ventilation alone is sufficient to maintain safe conditions. According to Trinity, ... the employer need not comply with the costly and time consuming requirements set forth in [the remainder of the regulation].

Over a ten-year period ending with his departure from the company, Trinity's former corporate and environmental director, Jerry Riddles, tested the inside of more than a thousand railcars during the actual lining operation while the cars were ventilated. The levels of combustible and toxic vapors inside the railcars were tested with direct reading instruments placed inside the railcars. During this testing, Riddles never received a reading above ten percent of the LEL no matter which lining material was used. Based on this testing, Trinity concluded that its railcar lining operation was governed by subpart (c) rather than by subpart (d), and that its ventilation system maintained safe conditions inside the railcars during the lining operations.

The alleged violation in this case occurred at a plant in Bessemer, Alabama. Riddles tested about sixty cars at this plant as part of his ten-year program. The Bessemer plant safety directors also tested the cars periodically and found no hazardous atmosphere inside the cars during the lining process. However, during a subsequent OSHA inspection, an inspector detected levels of flammable vapor at 24–26 percent of the LEL. Notably, all of his measurements were taken

[5] 101 S.Ct. 2478 (1981).

from outside the railcar. Apparently, the reading instruments were placed at the opening at the bottom of the railcar where outside air is pulled in, presumably measuring the air being pulled into the car rather than directly measuring the air in the car. The inspector conceded that these readings did not tell him "the actual concentrations inside the hopper car." Trinity suggested that open paint cans in the area may have been the source for the high readings outside of the railcar, but denied that the readings were evidence of concentrations inside the railcar.

Based on these readings from outside the railcar, the Secretary of Labor found that there was a hazardous atmosphere inside the railcars despite Trinity's ventilation system.... Trinity was cited for, *inter alia*, failure to comply with [the regulation].

Trinity appealed the citation to an Administrative Law Judge (ALJ) who noted that there was "no evidence to dispute Trinity's claim that, under usual conditions, the ventilation system maintained flammable vapors below ten percent of the LEL," but concluded that the OSHA test established the existence of a hazardous atmosphere at the time of the inspection and therefore that the lining operation did not qualify for the ... exception.

Trinity then petitioned the Commission for review on the grounds that the ALJ's decision was inconsistent and illogical, and that the ALJ had affirmed the confined space citation without requiring the Secretary to prove that Trinity knew or should have known of the violations. On review, the Commission held that the inspector's tests showed at least a "potential" for the atmosphere inside the cars to be hazardous when ventilated. The Commission also held that Trinity was not eligible for the ... exception and affirmed the citations as violations.... Notably, the Commission declined to consider the knowledge issue, finding that it need not be addressed since it was not raised in the petition for review. On appeal, Trinity argues that even if there was a hazardous atmosphere inside the railcar (or the potential for one), there is no basis for finding that Trinity knew or should have known of this condition and thus the citations must be dismissed.

Discussion

...

Since the Commission declined to address the issue of knowledge, we will conduct *de novo* review of whether the evidence of knowledge is sufficient to sustain the violation. To prove the knowledge element of its burden, the Secretary must show that the employer knew of, or with exercise of reasonable diligence could have known of the non-complying condition. When the Secretary alleges that a contaminant is present in impermissible levels, but the employer shows that it had made measurements and determined that the concentration was not excessive, the burden is on the Secretary to show that the employer's failure to discover the excessive concentration resulted from a failure to exercise reasonable diligence. Thus, in this case, the Secretary must show that Trinity knew or should have known that its ventilation was not maintaining an atmosphere below ten percent of the LEL during the lining operation.

Trinity argues that the uncontroverted evidence consists of sworn testimony describing more than a thousand tests which demonstrated that its ventilation system was maintaining an atmosphere below ten percent of LEL during the lining operation. These tests were explicitly credited by the ALJ. The Secretary responds that the OSHA inspection demonstrates that Trinity was out of compliance on the day in question. Additionally, we note that the Secretary alleges that there are issues over the documentation of the tests on which Trinity relied, worker imperfection in maintaining the ventilation system, and general sloppiness, all of which are alleged to demonstrate a lack of reasonable diligence on Trinity's part. However, the most thorough evidence of the vapor levels remains the extensive testing conducted by Trinity as described by sworn testimony of the railroad safety experts who conducted the tests. On the basis of this evidence, we find that the Secretary failed in its burden of proving that Trinity knew or should have known that the levels in the railcars were improper. Therefore, we VACATE the citations issued against Trinity.

Conclusion

The citations issued against Trinity by the Secretary of Labor are hereby **VACATED**.

Case Questions

1. Why should the Secretary of Labor be required to prove that the employer had knowledge of a noncomplying condition? Wouldn't a safer workplace result from holding employers strictly liable for conditions that do not comply with OSHA regulations?

2. How might the Secretary of Labor have proven that the employer had knowledge of the noncomplying condition in this case?
3. How did the OSHA investigator's testing technique differ from that of the employer's own safety manager? Which technique do you feel was more appropriate?
4. Should courts second-guess the OSHA's experts when it comes to determining whether unsafe conditions exist in a workplace? Or in determining the appropriate burden of proof to place on the Secretary of Labor, should judges defer to the agency's judgment in these matters?

Variances If an employer, or a class of employers, believes that the OSHA standard is inappropriate to its particular situation, an exemption, or variance, may be sought. This variance may be temporary or permanent.

- A *temporary variance* may be granted when the employer is unable to comply with a standard by its effective date because of the unavailability of professional or technological personnel or of materials or equipment necessary to come into compliance with the standard. The employer must show that all possible actions have been taken to protect employees and that all actions necessary for compliance are being undertaken. A temporary variance can be granted only after the affected employees have been given notice of the request and an opportunity for a hearing. Temporary variances can be granted for a one-year period and may then be renewed for two six-month periods.
- *Permanent variances* are granted when the employer establishes by a preponderance of the evidence that its particular procedures provide as safe and healthful a workplace as the OSHA standard would provide. The affected employees must be informed of the request for the permanent variance and may request a hearing. If the variance is granted, either the employees or OSHA may petition to modify or revoke the variance.

The Secretary of Labor also has authority to issue experimental variances involving new or improved techniques to safeguard worker safety or health.

Concept *Summary* » 20.1

OSHA's Organizational Structure and Standards

Administration and enforcement:

- Occupational Health and Safety Administration: Enforcement
- National Institute of Occupational Safety and Health: Research
- Occupational Safety and Health Review Commission: Adjudication

Standards of enforcement:

- Standards: Interim, permanent, emergency
- Standards may be challenged in federal court
- Secretary of Labor has burden of proving standard's feasibility
- Variances may be allowed to employers under appropriate circumstances

Employee Rights

In addition to being granted the right to a workplace free from recognized hazards, employees under the Occupational Safety and Health Act are protected from retaliation or discrimination by their employer because they have exercised any rights granted by the act. Section 11(c)(1) of the act provides that:

> No person shall discharge or in any manner discriminate against any employee because such employee has filed any complaint or instituted or caused to be instituted any proceeding under or related to this Act or has testified or is about to testify in any such proceeding or because of the exercise by such employee on behalf of himself or others of any right afforded by this Act.

Pursuant to Section 11(c)(1), the Secretary of Labor has adopted a regulation that protects employees from discrimination because they refuse to work in the face of a dangerous condition. The right to refuse can be exercised when employees are exposed to a dangerous condition posing the risk of serious injury or death and when there is insufficient time, due to the nature of the hazard, to resort to the regular statutory procedures for enforcement. When possible, the employees should attempt to have the employer correct the hazardous condition before exercising their right to refuse. The dangerous condition triggering the employees' refusal must be of such a nature that a reasonable person, under the circumstances facing the employees, would conclude that there is a real danger of death or serious injury. However, as the following case excerpt illustrates, a worker refuses to perform his duties at his own peril, should OSHA find he behaved unreasonably.

case 20.2 »

Wood v. Department of Labor

275 F.3d 107 (D.C. Cir. 2001)

Facts: Wood was employed as a senior electrician by United Engineers and Constructors (UE&C) at the Johnston Atoll Chemical Agent Disposal System (JACADS). JACADS is a facility consisting of several chemical weapons incinerators located on the Johnston Atoll in the Pacific Ocean. The facility is operated by UE&C pursuant to a U.S. Army contract to dismantle and destroy the lethal chemical weapons stockpile stored on the island. Due to the type of weapons handled at JACADS, the working conditions at the facility are probably as dangerous as any undertaken in the world. According to his complaint, before working at JACADS, Wood was employed at the Pine Bluff Arsenal in Arkansas, where he gained extensive experience in the field of chemical weapons destruction, making over 1,000 "toxic entries" with various levels of protective clothing and respirators.

Upon his arrival at JACADS in 1990, Wood discovered that management and many of his co-employees failed to appreciate the dangers associated with the destruction of chemical weapons. In particular, he found basic safety equipment and training, the norm at Pine Bluff, inadequate at JACADS. As a result, Wood began making a number of safety complaints about conditions at the facility. In November 1990, Wood's concerns were confirmed when an investigation conducted by the Occupational Safety and Health Administration resulted in the issuance of a "serious" citation for two violations.

Subsequently, Wood and his supervisors had a number of clashes regarding safety issues at JACADS. The supervisors saw many of Wood's allegations as scare tactics, intended to frighten his co-workers. The disputes culminated in Wood's refusal to work in a toxic area because UE&C had not provided him with new corrective lenses for the facepiece of his protective mask. Because he had already received a final reprimand for refusal to work, Wood was discharged for insubordination on February 4, 1991. Wood filed a complaint with OSHA, which investigated and found that under the particular circumstances that day, Wood was not entitled to refuse to work. Wood appealed OSHA's decision in federal court.

Issue: Was Wood's termination a retaliatory discharge, which the Department of Labor was required to rectify?

Decision: Only the Secretary of Labor is authorized to "determine" whether the "subsection has been violated." The Secretary has delegated to the Assistant Secretary for Occupational Safety and Health "the authority and assigned responsibility for administering the safety and health programs and activities of the Department of Labor ... under ... the Occupational Safety and Health Act of 1970." Using this authority, the Assistant Secretary for Occupational Safety and Health determined in this case on May 3, 1996 that Wood's refusal to work was *not* protected activity under section 11(c)(2) and therefore UE&C did *not* violate the Act by discharging him. The threshold requirement of section 11(c)(2) not having been met, Wood as a matter of law was unable to make out a retaliatory discharge claim.

Even where the employee has a legitimate reason for refusing the work order, the remedy for illegal discipline may be moot for all practical purposes. In the words of the Transport Workers Union:

> A word of caution: Don't expect quick action on '11(c)' complaints. The procedure is lengthy and can take as much as two or three years. For this reason, workers who have been fired, disciplined or suffered other discrimination should file a grievance under the union contract. If more than one worker was involved in the safety-related activity which we believe was the real reason the action that was taken against them, they may be able to get the action corrected by contacting the National Labor Relations Board. Workers should talk to their union representative about this procedure.[6]

The U.S. is not the only nation that attempts to afford workers this right of refusal. Other industrialized nations may have better approaches to the problem. Canada, for example, has a fairly detailed approach, which is embodied in the employer policy in the sample policy below:

Carlton University's Policy

Work Refusal Procedures

The Occupational Health and Safety Act of Ontario provides employees the right to refuse work for safety reasons. These procedures follow the requirements of the Act.

Right to Refuse Work

Under the Occupational Health and Safety Act, a worker may refuse to work or do particular work if he/she has reason to believe that,

Any equipment, machine, device or thing he/she is to use or operate is likely to endanger himself/herself or another worker.

The physical condition of the workplace in which he/she works or is to work is likely to endanger himself/herself.

Any equipment, machine, device or thing he/she is to operate or the physical condition of the workplace in which he/she works is in contravention of the Act and such contravention is likely to endanger himself/herself or another worker.

[6] http://www.twu.org/default.asp?contentID=716

Procedures for Work Refusal

First Stage Refusal

(a) Upon refusing to do unsafe work, the worker must immediately report the circumstances of the refusal to the supervisor. The supervisor should contact the Department of University Safety.

(b) The supervisor must immediately investigate the report in the presence of the worker and a worker representative from the [Joint Occupational Health and Safety Committee]. The worker representative must be made available and must attend the investigation without delay; time spent by this representative is deemed to be work time, for which the person shall be paid at his/her regular or premium rate, as may be proper. If these workers are not available, a worker selected because of his/her knowledge, experience and training should be called.

The worker representatives from the Joint Occupational Health and Safety Committee to be contacted for a work refusal are the certified members:

Colleen Neely, CUASA 520-2600 ext. 8198

Troy Giles, Physical Plant 520-2600 ext. 3668

(c) Until the investigation is completed, the worker must remain in a safe place near the work station.

(d) During the investigation, supervisors must record as many details as possible regarding the refusal, using the attached Employer's Report.

(e) The Ministry of Labour is only called if the refusal progresses to the second stage.

Second Stage Refusal

(a) If the worker is dissatisfied with the results of the investigation and has reasonable grounds to believe that the circumstances are still such that the work is dangerous, then he/she may continue to refuse to work.

(b) Upon the continuance of the worker's refusal to work, the supervisor should notify the Department of University Safety, who will immediately notify a Ministry of Labour Officer. Until the ministry is notified, the work cannot be reassigned to another worker and the worker must remain near the work station.

(c) The Ministry of Labour Officer will investigate the work refusal in the presence of the employer, the worker and the worker's representative.

(d) Pending the investigation and decision of the officer,

(i) The worker must continue to remain at a safe place near the work station during his/her normal working hours unless the supervisor assigns the worker reasonable alternative work during those hours, or, if such an assignment is not practicable, the supervisor may give the worker other directions (which may include being sent home).

(ii) No other worker shall be assigned to the work that is being investigated unless that worker has been advised of the other worker's refusal and reasons for it, in the presence of the worker representative, and has signed a statement of being advised of the refusal.

(e) Supervisors must take great care that they do not intentionally penalize any worker for exercising, or seeking to exercise their rights under the Act.

(f) After the investigation, the officer will decide whether the machine, device, thing or workplace is likely to endanger the worker or another person. This decision will be given in writing, as soon as practical, to the employer, the worker and the worker's representative.

(g) If the inspector does not consider the refusal to be based on reasonable grounds, the worker is expected to return to work. If, however, the worker maintains that he/she has reasonable grounds for refusing such work, the inspector cannot order a return to work. If, however, no reasonable grounds exist for such further refusal, the worker may be subject to disciplinary action by the employer.

Employer Reprisals Prohibited

If a worker has acted in compliance with the Act, its regulations or an order made under them, the employer (or any person acting on its behalf) may not, because the worker so acted,

(a) Dismiss or threaten to dismiss the worker;

(b) Discipline or threaten to discipline the worker;

(c) Impose any penalty on the worker;

(d) Intimidate or coerce a worker.

If a worker complains that the employer (or a person acting on its behalf) has improperly taken any of these actions, he/she may file a grievance.

Work refusals can be avoided with a workplace commitment to health and safety, advising workers of hazards, providing safety training, and keeping the lines of communication open to encourage an atmosphere where workers feel free to raise health and safety concerns at any time, knowing management will treat them seriously.

Supervisor Notification to Human Resources and University Safety

Before imposing discipline or sending workers home during or after a work refusal, supervisors must consult with the Director of Human Resources and the Director of University Safety.

Canada's procedures are more complex and detailed than those under the U.S. Occupational Safety and Health Act, raising the question in light of the *Wood* case of which approach accords employees greater protection.

Concept *Summary* » 20.2

Refusal to Work

- Employee may refuse to obey a work order, if the order poses a reasonable threat to the employee's health and safety
- Right to refuse is not uniquely American; other nations also recognize this right, e.g., Canada
- Retaliation for reasonable refusal is prohibited
- Terminated employee may challenge discharge in federal agencies and courts

Inspections, Investigations, and Recordkeeping

OSHA's occupational safety and health standards are enforced through physical inspections of workplaces. Practical realities in enforcing the act have forced OSHA to prioritize the inspection process. Thus, inspections are targeted in the following order:

- First to the investigation of complaints of imminent danger,
- then to investigation of fatal and catastrophic accidents,
- then to investigation of complaints filed by employees alleging hazardous working conditions,
- then to investigation of high-hazard industries, and finally,
- random general investigations.

Recordkeeping Requirements

OSHA relies on several sources of information to determine when and where inspections will occur. First, employers with eight or more employees are required under the act to keep records of and to make periodic reports to OSHA on occupational injuries and illnesses. Occupational injuries must be recorded if they involve or result in:

- death;
- loss of consciousness;
- medical treatment other than minor first aid;
- one or more lost workdays;
- the restriction of work or motion; or
- transfer to another job.

Second, the employer is required to maintain accurate records of employee exposures to potentially toxic materials or harmful physical agents required to be monitored under the act. Third, any employee or representative of an employee who believes that a violation of a safety or health standard exists that threatens physical harm, or believes that an imminent danger exists, may request an inspection.

Inspections

The compliance officer conducting the inspection may enter without delay and at reasonable times any factory, business establishment, construction site, or workplace covered by the act. This inspection may include all pertinent conditions, structures, machines, apparatus, devices, equipment, and materials on the inspection site. The office is also given authority to question privately any employer, owner, operator, agent, or employee.

The act allows the employer and a representative authorized by the employees to accompany the inspector during the physical inspection of the work site.

In *Marshall v. Barlow's Inc.*,[7] the Supreme Court held that an employer subject to an OSHA inspection may insist upon a search warrant. As a result of *Marshall v. Barlow's*, the compliance officer now must request permission to enter the workplace or other area that is

[7] 436 U.S. 307, 1973.

to be the subject of the search. If the employer refuses entry or forbids the continuation of an inspection, the compliance officer must terminate the inspection or confine it to those areas where no objection has been raised. Following such a refusal, an ex parte application for an inspection warrant can be obtained from either a U.S. district judge or a U.S. magistrate.

ethical DILEMMA

When the OSHA Inspection Finds That the Endangered Workers Are Illegally in the U.S.

The following story appeared in the national newspaper *USA TODAY* on June 7, 2006:

> NEW ORLEANS (AP)—They are the backbone of post–Hurricane Katrina reconstruction: Workers who converge at dawn and wait to be picked up for 14-hour shifts of hauling debris, ripping out drywall and nailing walls.
>
> But because many are in the country illegally, immigrant workers rebuilding New Orleans are especially vulnerable to exploitation, according to a study released Tuesday by professors at Tulane University and the University of California at Berkeley.
>
> The illegal immigrants often work in hazardous conditions without protective gear and earn far less than their legal counterparts, the study said. Nearly one-third of the illegal immigrants interviewed by researchers reported working with harmful substances and in dangerous conditions, while 19% said they were not given any protective equipment.
>
> Illegal immigrants also were paid significantly less—if at all—earning on average $10 per hour, compared with $16.50 for documented workers, the study said.
>
> "What is fundamentally unfair is these are workers who have responded to a national priority to rebuild this city and yet whose rights are being violated," said Laurel Fletcher, director of Berkeley's International Human Rights Law Clinic and one of the study's co-authors.
>
> Under federal labor law, illegal immigrants are afforded the same health and safety protections as documented workers. Regardless of their legal status, laborers can sue most employers under the Fair Labor Standards Act for violation of the minimum wage law and overtime regulations, the researchers said.
>
> The federal Occupational Safety and Health Administration said it has conducted more than 7,000 on-site inspections in the New Orleans area. The U.S. Department of Labor said it was concerned about wage and safety violations and had hurried to establish a Gulf Coast office.

- Do you agree that illegal immigrant workers should receive the same protections under the federal Occupational Safety and Health Act as American workers and legal immigrants?
- If OSHA inspects a site for safety violations and the inspector suspects that illegal workers are employed at the site, should s/he be required to report this suspicion to the U.S. Immigration and Customs Enforcement (ICE) agency?
- What if the OSHA inspection was prompted by a call or complaint from one of the illegal workers? Does this change your answer?

Source: http://www.usatoday.com/news/nation/2006-06-07-immigrant-workers_x.htm

Sometimes the legitimacy of the inspection becomes entwined with the even knottier question of overlapping jurisdiction. For example, the U.S. Coast Guard—now a part of the new cabinet-level Department of Homeland Security created by the Homeland Security Act in 2003—enjoys jurisdiction over the navigable waterways and vessels sailing those waters. In the following case, fatal injuries aboard an oil exploration barge led to a Coast Guard investigation of the accident. Neither the Coast Guard nor OSHA had ever before inspected the vessel, and in fact, under USCG regulations, no regular inspections were required. On the basis of the investigation results, OSHA cited the vessel's owners for violations of the Occupational Safety and Health Act. Ultimately, it fell to the U.S. Supreme Court to ascertain whether OSHA has jurisdiction to piggyback onto a Coast Guard inspection/investigation and sanction the offending employer under the OSH Act and its implementing regulations.

case 20.3 » Chao v. Mallard Bay Drilling, Inc.

534 U.S. 235 (U.S. Supreme Court 2002)

Stevens, J.

Respondent operates a fleet of barges used for oil and gas exploration. On April 9, 1997, one of those barges, "Rig 52," was towed to a location in the territorial waters of Louisiana, where it drilled a well over two miles deep. On June 16, 1997, when the crew had nearly completed drilling, an explosion occurred, killing four members of the crew and injuring two others. Under United States Coast Guard regulations, the incident qualified as a "marine casualty" because it involved a commercial vessel operating "upon the navigable waters of the United States."

Pursuant to its statutory authority, the Coast Guard conducted an investigation of the casualty. The resulting report was limited in scope to what the Guard described as "purely vessel issues," and noted that the Guard "does not regulate mineral drilling operations in state waters, and does not have the expertise to adequately analyze all issues relating to the failure of an oil/natural gas well." The Coast Guard determined that natural gas had leaked from the well, spread throughout the barge, and was likely ignited by sparks in the pump room. The report made factual findings concerning the crew's actions, but did not accuse respondent of violating any Coast Guard regulations. Indeed, the report noted the limits of the Coast Guard's regulation of vessels such as Rig 52: The report explained that, although Rig 52 held a Coast Guard Certificate of Documentation, it had "never been inspected by the Coast Guard." In Coast Guard terminology, Rig 52 was an "uninspected vessel," as opposed to one of the 14 varieties of "inspected vessels" subject to comprehensive Coast Guard regulation.

Based largely on information obtained from the Coast Guard concerning this incident, the Occupational Safety and Health Administration (OSHA) cited respondent for three violations of the Occupational Safety and Health Act of 1970 (OSH Act or Act), implementing regulations. The citations alleged that the respondent failed promptly to evacuate employees on board the drilling rig; failed to develop and implement an emergency response plan to handle anticipated emergencies; and failed to train employees in emergency response. Respondent did not deny the charges, but challenged OSHA's jurisdiction to issue the citations on two grounds: that Rig 52 was not a "workplace" within the meaning of sec. 4(a) of the Act; and that sec. 4(b)(1) of the Act pre-empted OSHA occupational safety and health on vessels in navigable waters....

Congress has assigned a broad and important mission to the Coast Guard. Its governing statute provides, in part:

> The Coast Guard ... shall administer laws and promulgate and enforce regulations for the promotion of safety of life and property on and under the high seas and waters subject to the jurisdiction of the United States covering all matters not specifically delegated by law to some other executive department ... 14 U.S.C. 2 (2000 ed.).

Under this provision, the Guard possesses authority to promulgate and enforce regulations promoting the safety of vessels anchored in state navigable waters, such as Rig 52. As mentioned above, however, in defining the Coast Guard's regulatory authority, Congress has divided the universe of vessels into two classes: "inspected vessels" and "uninspected vessels." ... Congress has listed 14 types of vessels that are "subject to inspection" by the Guard pursuant to a substantial body of rules mandated by Congress....

The parties do not dispute that OSHA's regulations have been pre-empted with respect to inspected vessels, because the Coast Guard has broad statutory authority to regulate the occupational health and safety of workers aboard inspected vessels, and it has exercised that authority. Indeed, the Coast Guard and OSHA signed a "Memorandum of Understanding" (MOU) on March 17, 1983, evidencing their agreement that, as a result of the Guard's exercise of comprehensive authority over inspected vessels, OSHA "may not enforce the OSH Act with respect to the working conditions of seamen aboard inspected vessels." The MOU recognizes that the exercise of the Coast Guard's authority—and hence the displacement of OSHA jurisdiction—extends not only to those working conditions on inspected vessels specifically discussed by Coast Guard regulations, but to all working conditions on inspected vessels, including those "not addressed by the specific regulations."

... Uninspected vessels such as Rig 52, however, present an entirely different regulatory situation. Nearly all of the Coast Guard regulations responsible for displacing OSHA's jurisdiction over inspected vessels, as described in the MOU, do not apply to uninspected vessels like Rig 52. Rather, in the context of uninspected vessels, the Coast Guard's regulatory authority—and exercise thereof—is more limited. With respect to uninspected vessels, the Coast Guard regulates matters related to marine safety, such as fire extinguishers, life preservers, engine flame arrestors, engine ventilation, and emergency locating equipment. Because these general marine safety regulations do not address the occupational safety and health concerns faced by inland drilling operations on uninspected vessels, they do not pre-empt OSHA's authority under sec. 4(b)(1) in this case....

We think it equally clear that Rig 52 was a "workplace" as that term is defined in sec. 4(a) of the Act. The vessel was located within the geographic area described in the definition: "a State," namely Louisiana. Nothing in the text of sec. 4(a) attaches any significance to the fact that the barge was anchored in navigable waters. Rather, the other geographic areas described in sec 4(a) support a reading of that provision that includes a State's navigable waters...

Accordingly, the judgment of the Court of Appeals is **reversed**.

Case Questions

1. Why didn't the Coast Guard conduct inspections of vessels such as Rig 52?
2. Since the Coast Guard has chosen not to inspect such vessels, should OSHA inspect them? Does it have the legal right to inspect them under this Supreme Court decision?
3. Since neither the USCG nor OSHA chose to inspect Rig 52 in the past, is it fair to fine the owners of the vessel for OSH Act violations?
4. Since OSHA piggybacked its citations and penalties upon another agency's investigation/inspection, should the cited owners/employers have objected that OSHA's decision was based on inadmissible or unreliable information?

The WORKING Law

New Health and Safety Challenges in the 21st Century Workplace

Environmental health and safety concerns have taken on new urgency in our post-9/11 world of terrorist threats. Shortly after the attacks on the World Trade Center and the Pentagon, anthrax spores were discovered in U.S. post offices from Connecticut to Washington, D.C. Even the U.S. congressional postal facility was contaminated, and a number of people died from exposure to anthrax.

One frequently articulated reason that the Bush administration decided to extend its "War on Terrorism" to Saddam Hussein's regime in Iraq was alleged intelligence information that the Middle Eastern dictator was developing chemical and biological weapons of mass destruction.

When, simultaneous with the U.S. invasion of Iraq, an epidemic involving a hitherto unheard-of virus began in southern China, Hong Kong, and Singapore, memories of the fall 2001 anthrax incidents led to renewed fears of biological attacks on the United States. Employers in so-called "clean" industries, such as international finance, found themselves faced with quarantining employees returning from business in the Far East during the late winter and into the spring and summer of 2003. "SARS," which stands for severe acute respiratory syndrome, became the newest acronym in the news media, as thousands were stricken, hundreds died, and cases popped up in Toronto and elsewhere in North America.

More recently, avian flu has reared its ugly head as a potential pandemic threat, albeit to date it has largely been limited to Asia and its ability to leap from one human victim to another has not been demonstrated. Nonetheless, savvy employers are preparing to handle the potential threat posed by avian flu.

Avian Flu

The direst prediction to date was made in the October 2005 issue of *National Geographic:* "Sooner or later a deadly virus that can jump from birds to people will sweep the globe."[1] In an article titled "Tracking the Next Killer Flu," author Tim Appenzeller reported on the death of a Vietnamese child, and then stated, "Ngoan's death and more than 50 others in Southeast Asia over the past two years have raised alarms worldwide. Affected countries are struggling to take action; other nations are sending aid and advisers while stockpiling drugs and developing vaccines at home. And scientists have stepped up their research into the fateful traffic of disease between animals and people."

Appenzeller's article goes on to cite the opinion of Dr. Robert Webster of the St. Jude Children's Research Hospital in Memphis, who has studied flu viruses for some forty years. "This virus," said Dr. Webster, "right from scratch is probably the worst influenza virus, in terms of being highly pathogenic, that I've ever seen or worked with." But, he added, "It can make that first step across [from bird to human], but then it doesn't spread easily from human to human. Thank God. Or else we'd be in big trouble."

Ultimately, the experts agree that we will "be in big trouble." The November 2005 issue of *Vanity Fair* concurred with *National Geographic*'s bottom line, stating flatly, "Every virologist we interviewed said the same thing: A pandemic will occur."[2] In October 2005, the Associated Press reported the first recorded appearance of avian flu in Europe—in Turkey and Romania, to be precise. According to the October 15 AP Wire Service Report, "Romanian authorities called for calm ... as they quarantined an eastern region where tests confirmed Europe's first appearance of a deadly strain of bird flu that has devastated flocks and killed dozens of people in Asia."[3] The news report went on to say that, "[A]fter the deadly H5N1 virus was confirmed in Turkey on Europe's doorstep, European Union experts agreed that steps should be taken to limit contact between domestic fowl and wild birds." The hypothesis was that migrating wild fowl had carried the disease to Turkey and eastern Romania.

According to the Centers for Disease Control:[4]

> *On February 19, 2004, the Canadian Food Inspection Agency announced an outbreak of avian influenza A (H7N3) in poultry in the Fraser Valley region of British Columbia. Culling operations and other measures were performed in an effort to control the spread of the virus. Health Canada reported two cases of laboratory-confirmed influenza A (H7): one in a person involved in culling operations on March 13–14, and the other in a poultry worker who had close contact with poultry on March 22–23. Both patients developed conjunctivitis (eye infection) and other flu-like symptoms. Their illnesses resolved after treatment with the antiviral medication oseltamivir.*

---

[1] Appenzeller, Tim. "Tracking the Next Killer Flu." *National Geographic*. October 2005. Available online at http://ngm.nationalgeographic.com/ngm/0510/feature1/index.html.

[2] Prochnau, William; Parker, Laura. "The Waiting Plague; For the epidemiologists at the Centers for Disease Control and Prevention and the World Health Organization, avian flu is potentially the greatest killer in history." *Vanity Fair*. 01 Nov 2005.

[3] Mutler, Alison. "Romania Officials Urge Calm on Bird Flu." *AP Online*. 15 Oct 2005. Available online at http://www.highbeam.com/doc/1P1-114186975.html.

[4] Available online at http://www.cdc.gov/flu/avian/outbreaks/past.htm

Although these are the only laboratory-confirmed cases of avian influenza A (H7) in humans during this outbreak in Canada, approximately 10 other poultry workers exhibited conjunctival and/or upper respiratory symptoms after having contact with poultry. Use of personal protective equipment is mandatory for all persons involved in culling activities, and compliance with prescribed safety measures is monitored. Epidemiologic, laboratory, and clinical evaluation is ongoing, as is surveillance for signs of avian influenza in exposed persons. There is currently no evidence of person-to-person transmission of avian influenza from this outbreak. For more information about this outbreak, visit the Canadian Food Inspection Agency website at http://www.inspection.gc.ca/english/anima/heasan/disemala/avflu/situatione.shtml

In February 2004, an outbreak of highly pathogenic avian influenza (HPAI) A (H5N2) was detected and reported in a flock of 7,000 chickens in south-central Texas. This was the first outbreak of HPAI in the United States in 20 years.

In February 2004, an outbreak of low pathogenic avian influenza (LPAI) A (H7N2) was reported on 2 chicken farms in Delaware and in four live bird markets in New Jersey supplied by the farms. In March 2004, surveillance samples from a flock of chickens in Maryland tested positive for LPAI H7N2. It is likely that this was the same strain.

OSHA's Recommendations

OSHA offers the following guidance for farm and poultry workers and others at risk of coming into contact with avian flu:[5]

1. All persons who have been in close contact with the infected animals, contact with contaminated surfaces, or after removing gloves, should wash their hands frequently. Hand hygiene should consist of washing with soap and water for 15–20 seconds or the use of other standard hand-disinfection procedures as specified by state government, industry, or USDA outbreak-response guidelines.
2. All workers involved in the culling, transport, or disposal of avian influenza-infected poultry should be provided with appropriate personal protective equipment:
   - Protective clothing capable of being disinfected or disposed, preferably coveralls plus an impermeable apron or surgical gowns with long cuffed sleeves plus an impermeable apron;
   - Gloves capable of being disinfected or disposed; gloves should be carefully removed and discarded or disinfected and hands should be cleaned;
   - Respirators: the minimum recommendation is a disposable particulate respirator (e.g., N95, N99 or N100) used as part of a comprehensive respiratory protection program. The elements of such a program are described in 29 CFR 1910.134. Workers should be fit tested for the model and size respirator they wear and be trained to fit-check for face-piece to face seal;
   - Goggles;
   - Boots or protective foot covers that can be disinfected or disposed.
3. Environmental clean up should be carried out in areas of culling, using the same protective measures as above.
4. Unvaccinated workers should receive the current season's influenza vaccine to reduce the possibility of dual infection with avian and human influenza viruses.
5. Workers should receive an influenza antiviral drug daily for the duration of time during which direct contact with infected poultry or contaminated surfaces occurs. The choice of antiviral drug should be based on sensitivity testing when

[5]See http://www.osha.gov/dts/shib/shib121304.pdf

possible. In the absence of sensitivity testing, a neuramindase inhibitor (oseltamavir) is the first choice since the likelihood is smaller that the virus will be resistant to this class of antiviral drugs than to amantadine or rimantadine.

6. Potentially exposed workers should monitor their health for the development of fever, respiratory symptoms, and/or conjunctivitis (i.e., eye infections) for 1 week after last exposure to avian influenza-infected or exposed birds or to potentially avian influenza-contaminated environmental surfaces. Individuals who become ill should seek medical care and, prior to arrival, notify their health care provider that they may have been exposed to avian influenza.

Concept *Summary* » 20.3

Inspections and RecordKeeping

- OSHA annually inspects thousands of workplaces
- Employers must maintain records of work-related injuries for OSHA inspection
- If an employer refuses entry, the OSHA inspector must get a search warrant from a federal judge
- Illegal immigrants are entitled to the same health and safety protections as American workers
- An ethical dilemma may exist when an OSHA inspector, in the workplace to insure workers' health and safety, discovers that some workers are illegal aliens

Citations, Penalties, Abatement, and Appeal

De Minimis Violation
A technical violation, but so insignificant as to require no fine or remediation.

When an inspection leads to the discovery of a violation of a standard under the act, the employer is issued either a written citation describing the particular nature of the violation or a notice of *de minimis* violations. A ***de minimis violation*** is one that has no direct or immediate relationship to the health or safety of the workers or the workplace affected, and no citations or proposed penalties are issued.

If a citation is issued, the employer must be notified by certified mail within a reasonable time, but in no event longer than six months after the identification of the violation, of any proposed penalty to be assessed. The employer then has fifteen working days within which to notify OSHA that it intends to contest the citation or the proposed penalty. If the employer does not contest, the citation becomes final and is not subject to appeal or review.

The citation must set a reasonable time for the abatement of the violation, usually not to exceed thirty days. The employer is required to post the citation, or a copy, prominently at or near each place the violation occurred. The employees or representatives of the employees may file a notice challenging the period of time set in the citation for the abatement.

If the employer challenges the citation, the penalty assessed, or the period for abatement, a hearing is held before an administrative law judge, who makes findings of fact and conclusions of law that either affirm, modify, or vacate the citation. This order becomes final thirty days after it is filed with OSHA unless, within that time, a member of OSHRC exercises the statutory right to direct review by the full commission. Any party to the proceeding may file a petition requesting this discretionary review. A final order of the commission may be appealed to the appropriate U.S. court of appeals.

The penalty and citation may be separately challenged by the employer. However, if only the penalty is contested, the violation is not subject to review.

When the citation and proposed penalty are contested, the employer has an absolute defense to the citation if it can prove that compliance to the standard is impossible. A showing that the standards are merely impractical or difficult to meet will not excuse performance.

In the event the violation is not corrected within the allowed time, the employer is notified by certified mail of the failure to abate and of the proposed penalty. This notice and proposed penalty are final unless, here again, the employer files a notice of contest within fifteen working days. If the order is not contested, it is deemed a final order and is not subject to judicial review.

If the employer has made a good-faith effort to comply with the abatement requirements of the initial citation but the abatement has not occurred because of factors beyond the reasonable control of the employer, a petition for modification of abatement can be filed. If OSHA or an employee objects to the requested extension or modification, a hearing is held before OSHRC.

If the employer files a petition for modification, the petition must state in detail the steps taken by the employer to abate the hazard, the additional time necessary to abate, the reasons additional time is necessary, including unavailability of technical or professional personnel or equipment, and interim steps being taken to protect employees.

If the employer fails to correct a cited violation after it has become final, a fine may be imposed of not more than $1,000 per day. If the violation is found to be willful, a repeat violation, or results in the death of an employee, OSHA can impose fines of up to $70,000. In the past, OSHA had a practice of imposing a large fine and then allowing the offender to negotiate a reduction in the fine. In 1990, Congress amended the act to prohibit OSHA from reducing a fine for a willful violation below $7,000. The act also provides for criminal penalties of up to six months imprisonment, with the maximum increased to twelve months for a repeat violation.

Concept *Summary* » 20.4

Citations, Penalties, Abatement, and Appeal

- A citation is an OHSA charge that an employer has committed a serious or a *de minimus* violation of the Occupational Safety and Health Act
- A citation, like a traffic ticket, will include a penalty, usually a fine that varies in amount with the seriousness of the violation
- The citation also will require the employer to abate, i.e., eliminate the hazard within a specified time frame
- The employer may appeal the citation, if it disagrees with OSHA

Workplace Violence

Workplace violence has emerged as an important safety concern in the 21st century. Its most extreme form—homicide—is the second leading cause of fatal occupational injury in the United States. Every year, almost 1,000 workers are murdered and about 1.5 million are assaulted in their places of employment. Concern about workplace violence has intensified exponentially in the wake of the terrorist attacks and anthrax events of autumn 2001. Businesses based primarily in office buildings, which once thought themselves above and beyond the workplace safety concerns of heavy industry and hermetically sealed from the violent intrusions endemic to convenience food stores and other retail establishments, now find themselves in need of policies and procedures to deal with all manner of threats from inside and outside their organizations. Most large businesses have felt compelled to go so far as to develop evacuation plans in anticipation of the day when it is their high-rise office building or corporate office park that is the target of a terrorist attack or a biological or chemical incursion.

Workplace violence can be classified as follows:

- Violence by emotionally enraged persons
- Violence by an angry spouse or relative of an employee
- Random acts of violence
- Violence against law enforcement or security
- Terrorism and hate crimes

Persons who commit workplace violence often share one or more of the following characteristics:

- A history of violence
- Psychosis
- Romantic obsession
- Chemical dependence
- Depression
- Paranoia or pathological blaming
- Impaired neurological functioning
- Elevated frustration with the work environment
- Interest in or obsession with weapons
- Personality disorder

Other documented indicators of a potential for workplace violence are the following:

- Alcohol abuse
- Drug abuse
- Impaired judgment
- Emotional difficulties
- Financial problems
- Legal problems
- Strained family relations
- Occupational failure
- Threats
- Absenteeism
- Deterioration of personal appearance, attitude, and behavior
- Deterioration of interpersonal relations
- Inefficiency

Documenting Behavior

Incidents of workplace violence or possible violent behavior should be documented as follows:

- Record incidents promptly
- Indicate date, time, and location
- Detail the behavior
- List all persons and work products involved
- Identify the performance standards and disciplinary rules violated
- Record the consequences of the action
- Record management's response
- Record the employee's reaction to management's response

A Supervisor's Response

Supervisors should respond as follows to indicators of potential workplace violence:

- Don't try to diagnose the behavior personally
- Don't discuss drinking unless it occurs on the job
- Don't moralize
- Don't be misled by sympathy-evoking tactics
- Don't cover up for a friend
- Don't put the individual into an isolated work area
- Don't ignore the problem or the signs of trouble
- Do remember that chemical dependence is progressive and likely will only get worse over time
- Do bring to the attention of suspected employees the company's employee assistance program
- Do make it clear that your organization is concerned with job performance and that, if performance does not improve, the job is in jeopardy
- Do explain that the employee must make the personal decision to seek help
- Do emphasize that the employee assistance program is confidential

Prevention

The following should be done to prevent workplace violence:

- Develop a written policy
- Form a crisis management team
- Develop policies on counseling, suspension, and termination
- Immediately investigate all incidents, such as threats
- Contact specialists for assistance
- Be flexible: Revise plans, policies, and procedures as information develops

Evacuation Plans

In the words of labor lawyer Louis Lessig of the New Jersey law firm Brown & Connery, "Employers of all sizes are now drafting and revising emergency evacuation procedures. But, in order to adequately prepare, it is necessary to know in advance which employees, if any, will need assistance."[8] In line with Lessig's observation, the EEOC recently released guidelines concerning the creation of emergency plans that comply with the Americans with Disabilities Act. The guide lists three ways in which employers can obtain the information Lessig says they need:

- The employer can ask about a new hire's needs in this regard after making an offer of employment and prior to the commencement of work
- The employer is allowed to send out periodic surveys to all employees to ascertain such special needs; however, self-identification must be strictly voluntary and be used only in conjunction with construction of the emergency plan
- The employer may ask all employees with declared disabilities if they will require such special assistance in the event of an evacuation of the work site.

---

[8]See http://www.lessig.org/blog/

Also worth noting is the ADA provision that while, in general, medical information must be maintained in confidentiality, relevant information can be provided by the employer to:

- Health-care workers
- Emergency coordinators
- Floor captains
- A colleague designated to provide the special assistance required

Packages and Mail

Although the East Coast anthrax scare is behind us and there have been no publicized repetitions, employees should still be alert. The OSHA offers the following guidelines.

GENERAL MAIL HANDLING	THINGS THAT SHOULD TRIGGER SUSPICION
• Be observant for suspicious envelopes and packages • Open all mail with a letter opener or by the method least likely to disturb the contents • Do not blow into envelopes • Do not shake or pour out the contents • Keep hands away from nose and mouth • Wash hands after handling the mail	• Discoloration, crystallization, strange odor, or oil stains • Powder or residue • Protruding wires or aluminum foil • Excessive tape or string • Unusual size or unusual weight for its size • Lopsided or oddly shaped envelope • Postmark that does not match return address • Restrictive endorsement such as Personal or Confidential

In the wake of the many workplace-violence incidents of the past two decades, many employers have adopted "zero-tolerance polices," when it comes to worker violence or threats of violence. Other employers, perhaps subscribing to the old adage that "every dog is entitled to one bite," will give an employee who exhibits violent or threatening behavior but does no immediate harm a second chance before terminating him. Regardless of the policy or approach, the employer faces a dilemma, since the terminated employee may be expected to challenge his firing, pointing when possible to an alleged discriminatory motive on the part of his supervisor or the company's HR office, as exemplified by the following case.

case 20.4 »

Anders v. Waste Management of Wisconsin

463 F.3d 670 (7th Cir. 2006)

Anders, an African-American male, was a unionized "roll-off" waste-hauler employed at Waste Management's facility in Franklin, Wisconsin. His supervisor during the period of time relevant to this case was Manager Dave Koch, who was, in turn, supervised by District Manager William Snow. Over Snow was Regional Manager Dennis Drephal. Waste Management's regional management facility, where Drephal worked, however, was in Menomonee Falls, Wisconsin, thirty miles from Franklin.

As a roll-off driver, Anders had no pre-determined route. Each morning when he reported to work he was handed a route slip that detailed his itinerary for that day. This arrangement was company policy and was set forth in Anders's labor agreement. When he arrived at the Franklin facility on November 12, 2002, he was handed his route slip by supervisor John Pena. Anders claims that after receiving the slip he was told by a co-worker that the stops on his route had been serviced the day before. He claims [that if] that were the case, the routes would not need to be serviced again the next day, and that this would negatively affect his incentive pay. Waste Management policy, however, states that a driver should attend to his route even if he believes it was serviced the day before. The reason behind this rule is that some customers intentionally scheduled back to back service.

Acting under the belief that his route would not need to be serviced again, Anders decided to leave work. Claiming that he was feeling sick—*that is*, sleepy, shaky, and experiencing a headache, he told Pena that he was going home. Shortly after Anders left the facility, however, Bob O'Brien told Pena that he overheard Anders say he was "going up to get [Regional Manager] Dennis Drephal and then he was coming down to get [Manager] Dave [Koch]." Pena immediately had someone from the Franklin facility call the Menomonee Falls office and notify them of Anders's intentions.

Despite having told Pena that he was not feeling well and needed to go home, Anders drove the thirty miles to the Menomonee Falls office. Upon his arrival, he was met in the facility parking lot by John Schiller, who had received the warning call from Pena. According to Schiller, Anders wanted to talk to Drephal because he was unhappy with his route assignments and supervisors, Koch and Snow. Schiller told Anders that it was not acceptable for him to have walked off the job, and that he could wait inside the building for Drephal to arrive.

Anders went inside briefly, but soon returned to the parking lot. He claimed that as he waited for Drephal he began to shake, and his head and chest started hurting; so he went outside to get some fresh air. In the meantime, Schiller called Drephal, who told him to have Snow talk to Anders. After Schiller located Snow, the two men were on their way to meet Anders when another employee told them that he was outside lying on his car. Given that this was November, Schiller went to bring Anders back inside. This did not go as planned. After a few minutes had passed, and Schiller had not yet returned, Snow and Sam Phillips walked out to the parking lot where they saw Anders first pound his fists into his car and then smash his cellular telephone into the ground. Anders became short of breath, and someone called the paramedics. At this point, Schiller went to lead Anders back into the building.

As Anders was being escorted into the building he attempted to attack Snow. At first he simply leered at Snow, but he then clenched his fists, lowered his shoulder into an aggressive stance, and charged. Snow was, to say the least, afraid. Schiller, who witnessed the entire event, had to position himself between the two men. Anders, Schiller said, was "mad as hell" while in the parking lot, briefly calmed down before heading back to the facility, and then became "very violent" upon seeing Snow. Phillips, who also witnessed the event, described Anders as having moved toward Snow "with aggression," causing him to move back and exclaim "don't come after me." Anders acknowledged that he did walk toward Snow, and that his behavior could have been interpreted as threatening.

This was not Anders's first aggressive incident in the workplace. His personnel records reflect that he received other disciplinary violations in 2002. Particularly, on October 24, he lost his temper with Koch after receiving a tardy notice. Both Koch and Pena testified that after being given the notice Anders threw his jacket to the ground and yelled at Koch in an insubordinate and boisterous manner. Anders does not dispute that this disagreement occurred.

These combined actions violated Waste Management's Rules and Regulations, which Anders acknowledged receiving and understanding upon starting work in 1996.

Rule 7 prohibits fighting, assaulting, or otherwise endangering any employee. Rule 11 prohibits insubordination, and the refusal or failure to follow Company procedures or to complete work assignments. Further, in 2001, Anders acknowledged receiving and understanding the Company's Code of Conduct, which included its Workplace Violence policy. The policy states, in relevant part, that Waste Management "does not tolerate violent behavior at [its] workplaces, whether committed by or against [their] employees. These behaviors are prohibited: making threatening remarks, causing physical injury to someone else, intentionally damaging someone else's property, and/or acting aggressively in a way that causes someone else to fear they could be injured."

Anders was subsequently fired from Waste Management. It is undisputed that Drephal was the final decision-maker. In choosing to fire Anders, Drephal considered the events of November 12 as described by Pena, Snow, Schiller, and Phillips. Additionally, Supervisor Tom Dixon told Drephal that Anders had been involved in an altercation with another employee, and Maintenance Manager Brian Schlomann informed Drephal that Anders had been short with him on a prior occasion. Further, Snow informed Drephal that Anders commented to him on November 6, that "if things did not improve at Waste Management someone was going to get hurt."

Anders claimed that he suffered from "panic, anxiety, depression disorder" (panic disorder). The disorder, he submits, was the cause of his behavior on November 12. Further, he claims that he requested leave under the FMLA on November 6, 2002, but that Waste Management denied the request. Snow testified that he and Anders did speak on November 6 regarding Anders's health. During the conversation, he told Anders that the company would give him time off to see a doctor if it was needed. Snow said that Anders also wanted to talk about routes and compensation that day, and that he had to remind Anders the routes were not assigned to specific drivers and that the incentive compensation was bound to fluctuate. Snow also noted that, between August and November, the overall haul volume decreased, and that numerous drivers experienced a drop-off in their incentive pay scheme. Regarding Anders's claim that he informed the company of his condition, Snow said Anders did not report experiencing headaches or sleeplessness that day.

Anders's union elected not to challenge Waste Management's employment decision. Article 11 of his labor agreement explicitly stated that "[a]ny employee desiring a leave of absence from his employment shall secure written permission from both the Union and the Employer." Anders sought no such permission. Further, Anders testified that prior to his termination he had not been advised by a physician that he was in need of a leave of absence.

After being terminated from Waste Management, Anders was hired by an industry competitor, City Wide Disposal. In 2003, Waste Management acquired City Wide's assets and hired a number of their employees. Anders was not re-hired. This decision, Waste Management claims, was a standard application of company policy based on the same review that led them to fire Anders in the first place....

II. Analysis

A. Race Discrimination

We examine first Anders's claim that Waste Management fired him on the basis of race. This portion of our review includes his arguments for relief under Title VII, § 1981, and the WFEA. At the outset, we note that the relevant examination is the same for both Title VII and § 1981. Therefore, we subject all three claims to the same review.

Given the scope of the record before us, Anders fails to establish either that he was meeting his employer's legitimate expectations, or that he was treated differently from similarly situated employees. On the former point, the inquiry must focus on Anders's performance at the time of his dismissal. It cannot be disputed that his behavior on November 12 failed to meet Waste Management's "legitimate expectations" as established by its Code of Conduct and Workplace Violence policy. That morning, Anders walked off the job site at Franklin, drove nearly 30 miles to confront his managers, and then attempted to attack Snow in front of numerous employees. Even considering Anders's contention that Pena gave him permission to leave the facility, this permission was conditioned on the fact that he said he was ill and wanted to go home. This, again, is not what he did. It was only the beginning of his aggressive and violent conduct. And while Anders's claims that his behavior was not intended to be threatening, he acknowledged that it may have been interpreted as such. This lone claim of misinterpretation is not sufficient to create a genuine issue of material fact when compared to the testimony of Pena, Snow, Schiller, and Phillips.

When considering the latter issue, his failure to establish that he was treated less favorably than similarly situated employees of a different race, we look to many different factors. While Anders claims on appeal that there were four white, comparable Waste Management employees who engaged in analogous acts of aggression, the record is devoid of any information as to the specifics of their actions, their supervisor, or any mitigating circumstances. And so,

Anders's claim of race discrimination must fail, too. We consider next his claim under the ADA.

B. Americans with Disabilities Act

For Anders to establish a claim of disability discrimination, he must first demonstrate that he is disabled within the meaning of the ADA and the WFEA. To prove this fact he can show that he has "(1) a physical or mental impairment that substantially limits him in one or more major life activities ...; (2) a record of such an impairment; or (3)[is] regarded [by the employer] as having such an impairment." 42 U.S.C. § 12102 (2)(A)-(C). If his condition does not meet one of these categories, he is not disabled under the ADA. Similarly, the WFEA requires a demonstration of "a physical or mental impairment which makes achievement unusually difficult or limits the capacity to work." § 111.32(8)(a). Anders is unable to satisfy the requirements of either statute.

Even considering the facts in a light most favorable to his claim, we see that Anders's panic disorder lasted, at most, from sometime around November 6 until shortly after November 12. After it was diagnosed he testified, "things ... panned out greatly," and he could do his job "110 percent." As the Supreme Court ruled in *Toyota Motor Mfg., Ky. v. Williams*, a short-term impairment such as this does not rise to the level of disability as defined by the ADA. Instead, Anders must have demonstrated that the impairment limited a major life activity on a permanent or long-term basis. Additionally, Anders's inability to meet the requirements of the ADA renders his argument on appeal, that Waste Management failed to accommodate his disability, moot. There was simply nothing to accommodate.

Likewise, under the WFEA, Anders carries the burden of establishing that his condition is a handicap.... Again, even when viewed in the most favorable light, Anders's few experiences with his panic disorder do not indicate such a condition.

C. Family and Medical Leave Act

Having rejected Anders's race discrimination and ADA claims, we turn next to his argument that Waste Management denied him medical leave on November 6 and after November 12, 2002. We agree that summary judgment was appropriate here, too.

The FMLA entitles eligible employees "to a total of 12 workweeks of leave during any 12-month period ... [b] ecause of a serious health condition that makes the employee unable to perform the functions of the position of such employee." 29 U.S.C. § 2612(a)(1)(D). As a threshold matter, Anders can not demonstrate that his claimed anxiety disorder rendered him unable to perform the duties of his position prior to November 12, 2002. The record before us shows that his one stand-out incident, the October 24 confrontation with Koch, stemmed from his being penalized for tardiness. Other than this, the facts show that he appeared for work on a regular basis and without incident.

Regarding his claim that Waste Management denied him FMLA leave on November 6, the record shows that Anders merely indicated he was not feeling well. Nothing that he said to Snow that day would have put Waste Management on notice that FMLA applied, thus placing them in a position to deny his request. Additionally, Anders himself had no idea that such leave was necessary. In his deposition he stated that, as of that date, he had not seen a physician regarding his condition. Nor had he requested leave through the Waste Management human resources department or his labor union. These scant facts raise no genuine issue appropriate for trial.

We are left then, with Anders's behavior on November 12. But again, he cannot demonstrate that his inability to perform the duties of his job were the result of a serious health condition. While he claims on appeal that he left work that morning because he was not feeling well, he used the opportunity not to seek medical assistance, but, instead, to drive thirty miles to the Menomonee Falls office to confront his manager. It was this deliberate and aggressive act that yielded his termination, not his panic disorder. Indeed, his medical records from later that day indicate he was "angry at a supervisor at work" and was experiencing "current homicidal/ assaultive ideation." The FMLA "was designed to help working men and women balance the conflicting demands of work and personal life," it was not intended to excuse violence in the work place. While we recognize that *Palmer* addressed an ADA claim, and thus is not directly on point, we find its reasoning instructive: there we declined to place the defendant employer on the razor's edge: "in jeopardy of violating the [law] if it fired such an employee, yet in jeopardy of being deemed negligent if it retained him and he hurt someone."

D. Failure to Re-Hire

Anders's last substantive point is that the district court erred in dismissing his Title VII race retaliation claim. He argues that Waste Management chose not to rehire him following their acquisition of City Wide because he had filed a complaint with the Equal Employment Opportunity Commission. But Anders has not pointed to any direct evidence of retaliation, nor has he shown that after filing the charge only he, and not any similarly situated employee who did not file a charge, was subjected to an adverse action even though he was performing his job in a satisfactory manner. Again, summary judgment was appropriate.

. . .

III. Conclusion

For the foregoing reasons, the decision of the district court is **Affirmed**.

Case Questions

1. On the facts recited by the Court of Appeals, do you believe that the plaintiff was behaving rationally at the time of his altercation?
2. Why did the court find that the plaintiff was not disabled for purposes of ADA protection?
3. Why do you think the plaintiff's union declined to pursue a grievance on his behalf?
4. Of what value to the defendant was the existence of a workplace violence policy at the time of the incident? Do you think the case would have come out any differently if no such policy had been in place?
5. How do you think the plaintiff would have fared, had the employer called the police at the time of the incident and pressed charges? Would the employer have avoided this lawsuit if it had called in the police?

Concept *Summary* » 20.5

Workplace Violence

- Incidents of workplace violence have become increasingly common in the U.S.
- In the 21st century, employers must adopt policies and procedures aimed at protecting employees from violence
- Employees themselves must be aware of and trained in practices and procedures to detect and respond to threats
- The employer's dilemma is that in protecting employees from potentially violent co-workers, they run the risk of discrimination-based suits from terminated employees, who deny they posed a threat

CHAPTER REVIEW

» Key Terms

de minimis violation « 642

» Summary

- The Occupational Safety and Health Act was enacted by Congress in response to the large number of workplace deaths, diseases, and injuries occurring in the United States every year. Scholars and critics disagree about how effective the OSH Act has been in reducing or preventing such occurrences.
- The OSH Act empowers the Occupational Safety and Health Administration to promulgate rules and set standards for workplace safety. These rules are subject to challenge in our federal courts.
- The Occupational Safety and Health Administration is also empowered to enforce the law and the regulations by means of workplace inspections and citations. Its agents are not required to meet the same strict search warrant requirements imposed upon police officers by the Fourth Amendment to the U.S. Constitution. Furthermore, while OSHA's jurisdiction can sometimes become entangled with that of other agencies, such as the Environmental Protection Agency and the U.S. Coast Guard, recent case law suggests that in this post-9/11 world of heightened health and safety concerns, the U.S. Supreme Court is prepared to allow OSHA a substantial amount of leverage in conducting inspections and enforcing the OSH Act and its implementing regulations.
- Not only is OSHA's jurisdiction over workplace safety not exclusive, but in some major areas—workplace smoking being a very significant one—private litigation has played a significant role in securing employee rights and recompensing employee injuries.
- In addition to employee-to-employee violence and third-party threats, such as terrorism, the risk posed by flu pandemics and other health hazards involved in conducting global business are all too real. An employee returning from a trip abroad or a customer coming from overseas can infect a firm's entire workforce, quite literally putting the organization out of business. No company can afford to be blasé about such possibilities today. Both OSHA and the CDC are acutely concerned with anticipating and, if necessary, meeting such challenges. Another emerging area of OSHA concern is workplace violence, a complicated issue that implicates multiple government agencies, professions, and causes. Here, too, the September 11, 2001 terrorist attacks and the anthrax crisis that followed have led many corporations to develop policies and procedures for dealing with a wide range of health and safety threats that might come from within as well as from outside their workplaces, including in the case of many larger corporations and organizations, detailed work site evacuation plans.

» Problems

Questions

1. What agencies were created by the Occupational Safety and Health Act, and what are the roles of those agencies?
2. Describe the procedures used to create permanent standards under OSHA.
3. When can employees exercise the right to refuse to work under OSHA without fear of reprisal?
4. What is the purpose of workplace inspections under OSHA? What is the effect of the Barlow's case on that purpose?
5. What procedures must be followed in issuing a citation under OSHA? What penalties may be imposed for violations of OSHA?

Case Problems

6. An employee filed a complaint with the Occupational Safety and Health Administration, accusing her employer—a printing plant—of assorted safety violations. A few days after filing the complaint, she held a lunchtime meeting with her co-workers in an effort to get them to protest their work conditions. Later that same afternoon, she was called to her supervisor's office where she was fired.

   The Department of Labor brought this action, claiming that the employee's termination was retaliatory. The company contended that during the meeting with her supervisor, the employee became loud, abusive, and even threatened him.

   If the threatening and abusive language can be proven, should this constitute an independent reason for the discharge, such that the DOL's claim of retaliatory firing should be defeated? Does the lunchtime meeting with her co-workers implicate any other federal labor statute in your consideration of this case? Does this consideration change the outcome? See *Herman v. Crescent Publishing Group, Inc.* [2000 WL 1371311 (S.D.N.Y.)].
7. The U.S. Department of Labor's Wage and Hour Division audited an employer and determined that the company had committed violations of the minimum wage and overtime provisions of the federal Fair Labor Standards Act (see Chapter 22). The company wished to appeal this determination.

   The firm's human resources director called the main number of the Department of Labor's offices in the corporation's home city. She was put through to an official in the OSHA office in the local federal building. This OSHA official, responding to the human resources director's inquiry, advised her that she need not count weekends and holidays when calculating the deadline date for filing her company's appeal. It turned out that this information was incorrect, and as a result, the appeal was dismissed by the Wage and Hour Division's appellate office as untimely.

   Should a court order the Department of Labor to honor the appeal, since one of its agencies gave the human resources manager the incorrect information upon which her company relied to its detriment? What are the policy considerations pro and con regarding such a ruling? Is there a constitutional issue involved in this case? See *Atlantic Adjustment Co. v. U.S. Dept. of Labor* [90 F. Supp.2d 627 (E.D. Pa. 2000)].
8. Following an explosion and fire at an employer's petrochemical facility, OSHA investigators interviewed numerous employees of the company. While OSHA's investigation was still pending, the company sent the agency a Freedom of Information Act (FOIA) request, asking for transcriptions of all witness statements taken by the investigators. When OSHA declined to provide these statements, the company sued, seeking a writ of mandamus that would require the agency to comply with the FOIA request.

   What policy considerations favor requiring OSHA to provide the company with copies of these statements? What policy considerations are against requiring disclosure? Do these policy considerations change in any way as the underlying case progresses from the investigative to later stages in OSHA's procedures? Are there constitutional considerations involved? See *Cooper Cameron Corp. v. U.S. Dept. of Labor* [118 F. Supp.25 757 (S.D. Texas 2000)];

see also *Freedom of Information Act* [5 U.S.C. 552 (West 2000)].

9. Because the availability of new plots was becoming very limited, a cemetery company in a major metropolitan area began selling single plots wherein a husband and wife ultimately would be interred one on top of the other. When the first spouse died, a grave was excavated to a depth sufficient to leave room for the future interment of the surviving spouse. To "square off" the corners of the grave, a member of the cemetery's grounds crew would enter the newly dug grave with a spade or trowel to perform the task.

   One of the groundskeepers filed a complaint with OSHA claiming that it was unsafe to work in the graves without shoring. An inspector from OSHA decided that the double graves were deep enough to require proper shoring before a grave-digger enters them to square them off. The cemetery's general manager replied that no other cemetery's procedure included shoring and that if required to do so, his company would become uncompetitive.

   What recourse does the general manager have? (This case problem is drawn from the experience of one of the authors in legal practice.)

10. Employees of the state's Department of Environmental Management (DEM) complained to the state's attorney general that their agency was not properly implementing the requirements of the federal Solid Waste Disposal Act. DEM fired them after it learned of their complaint.

    The Solid Waste Disposal Act contains a whistle-blower protection clause. See 42 U.S.C. 6971 (West 2000). The employees sued in federal court to collect damages from the state under this provision. The state moved to dismiss the action on the basis of its sovereign immunity.

    What is sovereign immunity and when do you think a state should be able to rely upon this legal principle to avoid liability? Should the fact that this case creates a potential clash between state and federal government influence the court's decision on whether or not to dismiss the action? See *Rhode Island v. United States* [16 BNA IER Cases 1258 (D.R.I. 2000)].

11. Sami Al-Arian was a tenured professor of computer engineering at the University of South Florida. Early in 2002, the university terminated his employment, citing his public statements, reported by the media and broadcast on TV, in support of Islamic *jihad*. The university claimed in terminating Al-Arian that he posed a threat to the safety of other university employees.

    Do you think the university was justified in firing the Palestinian professor? What arguments could you make in favor of his reinstatement if you were his attorney? Did OSHA have any jurisdiction in this case? Would OSHA have had grounds to issue a citation for a safety violation if the university had failed to fire the professor and his presence on campus had in fact resulted in a violent third-party action that killed or injured university employees? See *U.S. v. Al-Arian* [308 F.Supp.2d 1322 (M.D.Fla. 2004)].

12. About one year later, Al-Arian was charged by federal law enforcement officials with raising money to support a terrorist organization, Palestinian Islamic Jihad, allegedly responsible for more than 100 murders in Israel and the Israeli-occupied territories.

    Does this indictment strengthen the university's case for firing Al-Arian? Is your answer the same whether or not the university knew of these indictable activities prior to the indictment? See *West's Termination of Employment Bulletin*, May 2003, at 11.

13. We have seen in this chapter that OSHA shares responsibility for workplace health and safety with a variety of other federal agencies (such as the U.S. Coast Guard), as well as state and local governmental bodies and even private rights of action (as in the secondhand smoke cases). In this case, the Teamsters Union was endeavoring to unionize the Overnite Transportation Company's Bedford, Illinois, facility. In furtherance of those organizing efforts, Teamster-paid pickets appeared at the work site armed with ax handles disguised as picket signs. In the ensuing confrontation, some of the company's employees, mainly security guards, were injured.

    Which governmental body should have jurisdiction over this case: OSHA, the National Labor Relations Board, the U.S. District Court, or an appropriate state court? See *Overnite Transportation Co. v. International Brotherhood of Teamsters,*

Chauffeurs, Warehousemen and Helpers of America [773 N.E.2d 26 (Ill. App. 2002)].

14. Plaintiff drove a bus for defendant Diversified Paratransit, Inc., which was in the business of transporting developmentally disabled adults and children from their homes and care providers to various day-care centers and schools. One such adult client harassed the plaintiff regularly, including exposing himself to her and ultimately grabbing her and trying to kiss her. Her complaints to her employer were largely ignored. Following the incident involving physical contact, she quit her job.

    Does the plaintiff have the right to file an OSHA complaint in this case? Does she have a private right of action to sue her employer? If so, what is her legal theory? Does the lawsuit have any OSHA preemption problems? See *Salazar v. Diversified Paratransit, Inc.* [126 Cal. Rptr.2d 475 (Cal. App. 2002)].

15. The plaintiff in this case was employed by United Engineers and Constructors at its chemical weapons incinerator on the Johnston Atoll in the South Pacific. Due to the types of weapons handled at the facility, the court observed, "the working conditions ... are probably as dangerous as any undertaken in the world." Plaintiff had previously been employed at the Pine Bluff Arsenal in Arkansas, where he had made more than 1,000 "toxic entries"—that is, entries into a contaminated area of a plant, requiring protective clothing and other precautions. Upon his arrival at the atoll, he concluded that the company's managers and his co-workers failed to appreciate the risks they were running. In particular, he concluded that the basic training and the safety equipment were both inadequate. Consequently, he began complaining. His complaints were vindicated by the subsequent issuance of two "serious" citations by OSHA following the agency's inspection of the facility in reaction to plaintiff's complaints. The citations related to unapproved respirators and the standby-team's use of improper equipment. (A "serious" violation means that the hazard poses a "substantial probability of death or serious physical harm.")

    Disputes between plaintiff and his superiors continued. The situation came to a climax when plaintiff refused to work in a toxic area because the company had failed to provide him with a new set of corrective lenses for his face mask. Plaintiff was discharged for insubordination. He again filed an OSH Act complaint, and the agency's regional investigator made an initial finding that the complaint had merit. However, after several local attempts to amicably resolve the dispute, the case was forwarded to the OSHA regional solicitor in San Francisco with a recommendation that the case be adjudicated. However, the regional solicitor decided to dismiss the case due to a possible jurisdictional dispute with the U.S. Army, which conducted its own inspection/investigation but failed to act. Instead, the army turned the file over to the Department of Labor, where OSHA gave the case one final review but still refused to take adjudicative action.

    Based on these facts, what are the policy considerations in favor and against allowing the plaintiff to pursue a lawsuit against OSHA, seeking a writ of mandamus from a federal judge, and requiring OSHA to adjudicate plaintiff's retaliation claim against the employer? See *Wood v. Department of Labor* [275 F.3d 107 (D.C. Cir. 2001)].

Hypothetical Scenarios

16. The Hot Zone Thermometer Company manufactured outdoor thermometers in a small factory in the Bronx. The company employed illegal aliens of various backgrounds to do the assembly work. This work, among other things, involved injecting liquid mercury into the glass tubes, sealing the tubes, and affixing them to the wooden frames of the twelve-inch devices. Inevitably, workers came into contact with the mercury. The owners of the company knew how dangerous mercury is, but declined to provide protective equipment, such as rubber gloves and masks, or even to warn the workers. On a tip, OSHA and ICE raided the factory. ICE arrested the illegal workers. OSHA cited the company for serious violations. The story was front-page news in the tabloid *New York Post*. The New York district attorney has decided it would really help her reelection campaign, if she prosecuted the owners of Hot Zone under the city's criminal code.

Do you think that the DA should be allowed to prosecute the owners criminally, or should health and safety enforcement such as this be limited to the citations and fines permitted under the Occupational Safety and Health Act? If you believe that criminal prosecutions should be permitted under some circumstances, where would you draw that line?

17. Columbia Iron & Steel, Inc. operates a foundry, where pipes and other plumbing fixtures are cast. Much of the raw material used in the manufacturing process comes from scrap metal or all kinds, including galvanized pipe containing zinc. While overexposure to zinc fumes can result in the so-called "zinc shakes," this is a temporary condition. When a worker appears in the plant's clinic with zinc shakes, the doctor typically prescribes a week of sick leave, after which the employee is cleared to return to work. However, women workers are a different story. While not absolutely proven, it is widely accepted in the medical profession that exposure to zinc in the early stages of pregnancy can result in spontaneous abortion or severe birth defects. Consequently, the company has a rule against women of childbearing age working in the "hot end" of the foundry, where exposure to zinc fumes is likely to occur. However, hot end work pays much better than quality assurance and packing work at the cold end of the plant. A number of young women working in the foundry contend that it should be left up to them whether or not to risk exposure to zinc by working in the hot end of the plant, if they are otherwise qualified to do the work.

    What is your view of their position? If OSHA has regulations that apply to iron foundries, and if those regulations do not address the potential risk that concerns the company, how does this affect your answer? If the women are willing to wave any rights they may have against the company in the event that their reproductive systems are harmed in the hot end, what are the public policy considerations pro and con permitting such a waiver?

18. Geraldine Jones is a clerk in the Sack-of-Suds convenience store. She works on the night shift alone. OSHA has issued recommendations for prevention of workplace violence, many of which relate directly to Jones's situation. However, the OSHA publication specifically states,

> These recommendations are **not** a new standard or regulation and do not create any new OSHA duties. Under the Occupational Safety and Health Act of 1970 (the OSH Act, or the Act), the extent of an employer's obligation to address workplace violence is governed by the General Duty Clause. The fact that a measure is recommended in this document but not adopted by an employer is not evidence of a violation of the General Duty Clause. The recommendations provide information about possible workplace violence prevention strategies. They describe a variety of tools that may be useful to employers designing a violence prevention program.

The Sack-of-Suds owners decline to provide any training or protection for employees such as Jones. The company's iron-clad rule for clerks is that no more than $50 is to be kept in the register at any one time. All other cash is to be stuffed through the slot in a floor safe, which Jones is unable to open. One night an armed robber entered her store and demanded the money. When Jones could only produce a little less that $50 from her cash drawer, the thief became infuriated, beating Jones severely.

    If Jones complains to OSHA, will the agency be able to make a citation and fine stick against the company on these facts?

19. The High-Flier Aircraft Company manufactures small aircraft in a plant which features a fifty-foot high, arced roof; this accommodates an overhead crane to move the aircraft fuselages from one end of the assembly line to the other. During the recent economic downturn, orders for executive jets for corporate CEOs have been way down. Grateful for an order for a top-of-the-line plane from a *Fortune 500* company, High-Flier's employees are determined to produce a top-flight aircraft within the short timeline provided in the sales contract. Consequently, when the crane breaks down and the line is forced to stop, Fred Smith, the plant's head maintenance mechanic, is determined to repair the crane without wasting the time involved in following the normal maintenance procedure, which requires lowering the boom to floor level. Instead, Fred climbs to the top of the crane. Finding no

convenient place to fix a safety line, he goes to work "without a net," so to speak. He slips and falls to his death. When OSHA propose to cite the company for Fred's death and impose a significant fine, the company appeals on the ground that Fred failed to follow plant procedure, but instead took it upon himself to risk his life at the top of the crane.

What should the federal court rule in this case?

20. Responding to a call alleging safety violations from a janitorial employee at the Toddler Togs garment factory, an OSHA inspector drives up to the back of the factory. A group of workers on break is sitting around on the loading dock, smoking and eating snacks. The inspector introduces himself. One of the employees identifies herself as the caller. She invites him to come into the shipping area, where he sees several violations, which he subsequently cites. The plant manager first learns of the inspection when he receives the citations via certified mail.

Is the inspection legal? If the plant manager learns the identity of the janitor involved, are there legal grounds for disciplining her?

CHAPTER 21

The Employee's Safety Nets: *Unemployment and Workers' Compensation, Social Security, and Retirement Plans*

Not until the 1900s, and for a substantial number of Americans not even until the 1930s, did the government assist workers affected by unemployment, on-the-job injury, work-related disability, or old age. Until that time, Americans (like workers around the world then and millions even today) relied on their families, ethnic communities, churches, and social clubs for aid when their incomes were temporarily or permanently disrupted. For instance, Irish coal miners in Pennsylvania in the 1870s might have belonged to the Ancient Order of Hibernians, a benevolent society with a fund dedicated to assisting the widows and orphans of miners killed in the "pits." Increasingly, too, workers organized and looked to their unions for help in times of trouble. But before Congress passed the National Labor Relations Act (NLRA) in 1935, most unions were mere shadows of what they would later become.

Federal Employment Liability Act (FELA) A federal law designed to protect and compensate railroad workers injured on the job.

Congress did occasionally become involved in the welfare of employees in private industry, even before the groundbreaking legislation of the 1930s. The Railway Labor Act (governing labor relations), which was passed in 1926, and the ***Federal Employment Liability Act (FELA)***, which was passed in 1908, predate the NLRA and workers' compensation laws, respectively. The FELA was enacted in recognition of the incredible number of casualties in the railroad industry (about 25,000 deaths annually around the turn of the last century) and of the virtual hopelessness of injured workers trying to sue their employers in those days.

Suppose a railroad worker in 1900 was hit by a railcar that rolled in deadly silence down the track because of a faultily set brake. The injured, perhaps permanently disabled, worker might hold the railroad responsible and seek to sue it for money damages. To do so, he would first have to find a lawyer willing to take the case. Having little or no savings, he might find it difficult to obtain an attorney prepared to take on one of the great financial juggernauts of the era. If he did, he faced a daunting set of defenses that the railroad company could raise. The railroad's lawyers most likely would first argue that the hapless employee, by taking the job, had assumed the risk of injury. They would then seek to establish that he somehow had been contributorily negligent, such as by not being alert while in the rail yard. Finally, they would invoke the fellow-servant doctrine; that is, they would say that he was not injured by their client, "the railroad," but by a co-worker who had negligently failed to set the brake properly.

As you can see, any worker who recovered what his injuries deserved from the railroad had to have been both very persistent and very lucky. For most workers, or their widows and orphans, the alternative was one of the forms of charity previously mentioned, perhaps in combination with some modest form of public dole. But being employed in the key industry of industrialized America, railroad workers were the first who were able to exert unified pressure to better their circumstances. Theirs was the first major industry to be organized by several railway brotherhoods, such as the Brotherhood of Railway Clerks. Once organized, they successfully lobbied for passage of the FELA.

Although the FELA still requires an injured railroad worker to file suit in a federal or state court, it substantially reduces the burden of proof placed upon the employee/plaintiff, while depriving the railroad/defendant of some of its most potent defenses. Thus, injured employees generally win their cases under the FELA, which is still in force today.

Not until the New Deal era of the 1930s did such legislation become widespread in the United States. The Pennsylvania Superior Court summarized the development of such U.S. laws in a 1946 unemployment compensation decision, *Bliley Electric Company v. Unemployment Compensation Board of Review*:[1]

> The statute, almost ten years old, introduced into our law a new concept of social obligation, extended the police power of the State into a virgin field, and created a body of rights and duties unknown to the common law. England was the first common law country to operate a similar system, and its experience began as an experiment in 1911. Its law, revised as trial exposed error, became the basis for the American unemployment compensation system, although in detail there are vast variances between the American and British systems. Wisconsin passed an act in 1932, but it required the enactment of the Social Security Act by Congress on August 14, 1935 to induce other states to adopt the system. All of the states have enacted conforming legislation, and their statutes include the basic requirements laid down by the Act of Congress, but they differ widely and sharply in respect to the details, which Congress left open to state legislation.

The model for the genesis of unemployment benefits identified by the Pennsylvania Superior Court also matches the historical pattern for social security and workers' compensation. Although the roots of these laws can be traced to the second decade of the 20th century (just a bit behind England and Germany), the widespread availability of these important benefits is indebted to President Franklin Roosevelt's New Deal.

All three social welfare programs—social security pensions, workers' compensation, and unemployment compensation—descend from a common history and came into being about the same time. A major distinction between unemployment and workers' compensation versus social security is that the states have primary responsibility for the first two (with some notable exceptions), whereas social security is a federally supervised program applied uniformly across the country. But despite this difference, plus many distinctions between the various states' systems of unemployment or workers' compensation, the common threads, like the common ancestry, make it possible to discuss each of these forms of worker welfare in general terms. Wherever you wind up working in the United States, you will find that state's systems readily recognizable.

Last but not least in this chapter is the Employee Retirement Income Security Act (ERISA), a latecomer to the "security net" outlined above. In 1974, the act was passed by Congress in response to numerous instances of pension fund mismanagement and abuse. Retired employees had their pension benefits reduced or terminated because their pension plan had been inadequately funded or depleted through mismanagement. In other instances, employees retiring after as many as twenty years or more of service with an employer were

---

[1]45 A.2d 898, 901 (1946).

ineligible for pensions because of complex and strict eligibility requirements. ERISA is intended to prevent such abuses and to protect the interests of employees and their beneficiaries in employee benefit plans.

Unemployment Compensation

The economic crisis of late 2008, extending well into 2009, starkly underlined the significance of unemployment compensation. The national unemployment rate approached 10 percent in the depths of the severe recession, a level unseen since the "stagflation" days of the 1970s. Most of the job casualties of this downturn were able to collect weekly unemployment compensation checks for anywhere from twenty-six to fifty-two weeks, depending upon the individual states' laws, financial circumstances, and the availability of federal bailout supplements to state funds.

Unemployment Compensation Benefits paid to employees out of work through no fault of their own and who are available for suitable work if and when it becomes available.

Willful Misconduct The high level of fault that disqualifies an out-of-work worker from unemployment benefits.

However, not every out-of-work employee was entitled to this benefit. Eligibility for ***unemployment compensation*** requires that the "idleness" occur in a specific set of circumstances: The employee must be out of work through no fault of his or her own and be available for suitable work if and when it becomes available.

The concept of fault is an attenuated one; that is, only a high level of fault, termed ***willful misconduct***, will serve to disqualify the out-of-work worker from these benefits. Incompetence is considered to be an unfortunate condition, not a basis for affixing guilt, under this branch of employment law. So although an at-will employee, or even one protected by a "good cause" provision in a labor contract, may properly be dismissed for poor performance, that alone will not disqualify him or her from receiving unemployment benefits.

"Willful misconduct" is an issue of constant debate and redefinition in the unemployment compensation systems of our fifty states. For example, is absenteeism "misconduct"? If it is, when is it "willful"? The employee who is "excessively" (itself a tough term to define) absent or tardy may be lazy, or he/she may have children to get to day care or a bus to catch that is unreliable. In the latter instance, the employee can probably still be discharged but most likely will not be denied benefits until she/he can find another job.

Even if the conduct is clearly willful and wrong, it still may not be enough to disqualify the applicant for unemployment benefits. If, for instance, the misconduct is not readily discernible to the average worker and the employer failed to promulgate a rule or give a warning for prior infractions, an unemployment referee may be reluctant to deny benefits.

Besides being guilty of willful misconduct, a claimant may be denied benefits if he/she voluntarily quit the job. Under normal conditions, an employee cannot quit his job and then apply for unemployment benefits. In other words, when a worker is discontented, he/she is expected to stick with his/her current job until he/she finds another—not quit and collect benefits pending reemployment.

However, in some compelling circumstances, the law will allow an employee to leave the employment. In these cases, the quit is considered involuntary because it amounts to a constructive discharge from the job. Some such cases have involved extreme instances of sexual or racial harassment by the employee's immediate supervisor to the extent that the boards and courts held that no worker should be required to submit to such abuse or risk denial of unemployment compensation. Others have concerned an employee's extreme allergic reaction to substances in the workplace. In all such cases, the employee must remain available for alternative jobs that the state employment agency might direct him or her to apply for. (In some instances, such as when an allergy is so severe and general that the employee cannot work at all, workers' compensation might be the more appropriate remedy.)

Litigating Unemployment Claims

Unemployment compensation litigation usually starts with a terminated worker's application for benefits. The unemployment claim is usually evaluated in the first instance by an unemployment office or agency in the area where the worker resides. Regardless of whether the decision is favorable or unfavorable, an appeal is possible. The worker's motive for appealing an unfavorable decision is obvious. But why would an employer challenge the grant of benefits to someone it had let go? The answer is that unemployment benefits are paid for by a tax on the wages of the workers and an equal levy on the employer's total payroll. In most jurisdictions, this tax is variable, rising and falling with the particular company's experience in drawing upon the state fund. Consequently, if undeserving dischargees are permitted to receive benefits, the employer will experience a gradual increase in these payroll taxes.

Challenged decisions go to a referee and from there can usually be appealed into the state court system. A case can potentially go all the way to a state's supreme court, which typically reviews a few selected cases of special significance each year.

Some organizations and their HR operations consider eligibility for unemployment compensation to be a ministerial matter to be administered by a low- or mid-level staffer on a case-by-case basis. Other, more sophisticated employers recognize that unemployment compensation claims must be considered within the context of the company's total human resource strategy. These executives understand that unemployment compensation claims can:

- impact the organization's bottom line (as when substantial turn over accompanied by increased claims substantially enlarges the company's payroll taxes);
- create a record which is helpful to the claimant when later pursuing a discrimination or other type of wrongful discharge claim against the corporation; and
- be included in a severance/release agreement between the company and an employee departing under less than amicable circumstances.

However, using the terminated employee's potential eligibility for unemployment benefits, and the company's ability to oppose the former employee's claim, presents some danger to the employer who abuses this leverage. The case below illustrates this risk.

case 21.1 » Label Systems Corp. v. Aghamohammadi

270 Conn. 291, 852 A.2d 703 (Connecticut Supreme Court, 2004)

This appeal arose out of a dispute between two former employees, the defendants, Samad Aghamohammadi and Pamela Markham, and their former employer, the plaintiff, Label Systems Corporation (Label Systems), as well as its president, Kenneth P. Felis. Label Systems commenced this action against the defendants, who counterclaimed against Label Systems and filed a third-party complaint against Felis. A jury found the defendants liable for conversion (theft), and awarded Label Systems compensatory and punitive damages. In addition, the jury found Label Systems and

Felis liable for vexatious litigation in relation to a prior action, and awarded the defendants compensatory damages. The trial court rendered judgment in accordance with the jury's verdict. The plaintiffs appealed, and the defendants cross-appealed to the Appellate Court. The state supreme court took jurisdiction under a special jurisdictional statute.

The jury had rendered its verdict on the following facts in evidence: Label Systems, a corporation located in Bridgeport, was in the business of manufacturing and producing, among other things, labels, stickers and holograms. The defendants were a married couple, both of whom were employed by Label Systems. Aghamohammadi, an immigrant from Iran, began his employment with Label Systems in 1985, and advanced to the position of head of the finishing department. In that capacity, Aghamohammadi was responsible for the examination and inspection of finished products for defects, packaging finished products for shipment and shipping products to customers. Markham began her employment at Label Systems in 1982, and served as the office manager and bookkeeper, where she was primarily responsible for paying Label Systems' bills, managing its finances, and overseeing its medical plan. Both defendants were regarded as valuable and trusted employees by Felis. During their employment, the defendants were provided with a company car, which they used for their commute from Waterbury to Bridgeport. In November, 1992, while driving the company car, their sole means of transportation, the defendants were rear-ended by another car. Subsequently, the defendants received a check in the amount of $1095.01 from the other driver's insurance company. Because Markham was nearing the end of a difficult pregnancy, her first, the defendants did not want to be without the car, and they chose to delay having it repaired until after her delivery. Accordingly, the defendants cashed the insurance check and deposited the proceeds into their personal checking account. In early 1993, Felis equipped the defendants' house with computer equipment so that Markham could work from home after the baby was born, and he built and furnished a nursery in the office for Markham to use after she returned to work.

On February 15, 1993, upon their arrival at work, the defendants were met outside by Felis and other members of his staff. Felis gave the defendants letters of termination that accused them of willful and felonious misconduct in the course of their employment, terminated their employment, and refused to allow them to enter the facility to collect their personal belongings.

The defendants surrendered the company car to Felis, and departed in an awaiting limousine, which had been arranged by Felis. Later that evening, Aghamohammadi was arrested based upon Felis' claim that Aghamohammadi had threatened him when receiving his letter of termination. Label Systems immediately stopped paying a salary to both defendants, and terminated their health insurance.

On February 23, 1993, Markham gave birth to the defendants' first child. On March 10, 1993, Label Systems filed a three-count complaint against the defendants, alleging conversion, breach of duties of loyalty and appropriation of trade secrets. The defendants had requested unemployment benefits immediately following their termination, and on April 7, 1993, over the objection of Label Systems, separate awards of unemployment benefits were made to both defendants. The defendants were unable to extend their health insurance at their own expense, however, because of the alleged willful and felonious misconduct underlying the termination of their employment. On April 22, 1993, Felis, on behalf of Label Systems, appealed from the decisions awarding unemployment benefits to the defendants, claiming that the defendants were terminated for willful and felonious misconduct, and, therefore, that they were precluded from receiving such benefits. Over the course of the next four months, three separate hearings were held in which the plaintiffs offered testimony and evidence in support of their claim of willful and felonious misconduct by the defendants. On August 18, 1993, after the third hearing, both appeals were unilaterally withdrawn by the plaintiffs.

In April, 1994, in response to the withdrawal of the appeals, the defendants counterclaimed against Label Systems, and filed a third-party complaint against Felis, both of which alleged vexatious litigation, abuse of process, intentional infliction of emotional distress, negligent infliction of emotional distress, slander per se, slander, interference with contractual relations, wrongful discharge and intentional interference with prospective contractual relations. In July, 2001, the actions proceeded to trial, where the jury found the defendants liable for conversion, rejected all of Label Systems' remaining claims, and awarded Label Systems $50 in compensatory damages. In addition, the jury found that the defendants had converted Label Systems' property under circumstances warranting punitive damages, in an amount to be set by the trial court according to the prior agreement of the parties. In regard to the counterclaims and third-party complaint, the jury found the plaintiffs liable for vexatious litigation, rejected all of the remaining claims, and awarded Markham $160,000 and Aghamohammadi $60,000 in compensatory damages. These awards were doubled automatically pursuant to General Statutes § 52-568 (1), which provides for the doubling of damages for groundless or vexatious actions. The trial court denied several post-trial motions filed by both parties, awarded Label Systems $19,460.17 in punitive damages, and rendered judgment in accordance with the jury's verdict. This appeal followed....

In regard to the appeal from Markham's award, the plaintiffs advanced two reasons supporting their belief, prior to the time of termination, that Markham had engaged in willful and felonious misconduct. First was Felis' belief that Markham had met with Henry J. Behre, Jr., a former employee of Label Systems, and provided him with confidential company information to assist him with his arbitration action then pending against Label Systems for back wages. As the trial court properly noted, however, the jury reasonably could have credited Markham's testimony that she had never disclosed any confidential information to Behre, as well as Behre's testimony that Felis had disclosed the information to Behre in earlier conversations. In addition, it was well within the province of the jury not to credit the testimony of Felis. Second was Felis' belief that Markham had leaked information to Behre concerning a financial investment made in Label Systems by RPM, Inc. (RPM). The jury reasonably could have declined to credit this testimony, and instead credit the testimony of Behre that Felis not only told him of RPM's investment in Label Systems, but that the letter that had terminated his employment relationship with Label Systems had the logo of both companies at the top of the page, thereby making the relationship between the companies obvious. This letter was admitted into evidence, and the jury was able to examine it firsthand. Indeed, Felis testified that in 1992, RPM had circulated a memo to all of its operating companies, including Label Systems, that highlighted RPM's concern with having its logo directly next to each individual operating company's logo on items such as stationery and invoices.

In regard to the appeal from Aghamohammadi's award, Felis testified that, at the time of Aghamohammadi's termination, Felis believed that Aghamohammadi was responsible for an alleged shortage of materials at Label Systems, and that Aghamohammadi was a partner with Behre in an undisclosed business venture, Mecca Trading and Shipping (Mecca). With respect to Mecca, Aghamohammadi testified that he had disclosed Mecca to Felis previously, had offered to make Felis a partner in the business, and that Felis allowed him to make limited use of Label Systems equipment and facilities in his spare time for activities relating to Mecca. To the contrary, Felis testified that Aghamohammadi never disclosed Mecca's existence to him, and that he discovered Mecca's existence just prior to terminating the defendants. It was entirely reasonable, therefore, for the jury to credit Aghamohammadi's testimony over Felis' testimony. With respect to the alleged shortage of materials, Aghamohammadi testified that he was not responsible for any alleged shortage, and that he never stole or misappropriated any material from Label Systems. Indeed, Felis testified that he could not identify whether the alleged shortages occurred with raw product, partially finished product or finished product.

In sum, our review of the record reveals that there was sufficient evidence from which the jury could 'reasonably and legally have reached their conclusion.' Accordingly, we conclude that the trial court did not abuse its discretion in denying the plaintiffs' motion for a directed verdict on the vexatious litigation claim....

In regard to Aghamohammadi, the jury reasonably could have credited his testimony that the initiation of the appeal, the accusation of willful and felonious misconduct, and the concomitant threatened loss of benefits, collectively caused him such emotional harm as to give up all hope of being successful in the United States, and to plead with his wife to move back to his native country of Iran. Thus, we agree with the trial court that Aghamohammadi's feelings, 'as he expressed and visibly displayed them to the jury,' reasonably supported the jury's award of $60,000 and that the jury's award 'reflects a thoughtful exercise of judgment and discretion.'

The award of $120,000 to Markham, while certainly more substantial than the award to Aghamohammadi, also is reasonably supported by the evidence presented at trial. Specifically, viewed in the light most favorable to Markham, the jury reasonably could have found that she had endured mental and emotional suffering due to the vexatious appeal of the unemployment awards for the same reasons as we discussed with regard to Aghamohammadi. In addition, the jury could have found that the emotional damage to Markham was exacerbated, in comparison to Aghamohammadi, by virtue of the fact that she recently had given birth and had a prior history of depression. Indeed, Markham's testimony provided reasonable support for the jury's conclusion that the appeal deeply distressed her, both while the appeal was pending and for a long period after it was withdrawn summarily. If the jury thought Markham was embellishing her testimony, or exaggerating the impact the appeal had on her well-being, it could have rejected her claim or awarded her a smaller amount in damages. In its memorandum of decision, however, the trial court noted that when 'the court saw her give that testimony, it knew at once that the jury would be moved by it.' Accordingly, while we agree that the damages awarded to Markham were 'ample,' we nevertheless are unable to conclude that the trial court abused its discretion by denying the plaintiffs' motion for remittitur [reduction].

Case Questions

1. Were the defendants, husband and wife, guilty of any wrong doing?
2. If so, why, then, were they awarded unemployment compensation in the first place?
3. Do you agree that the plaintiffs were guilty of "vexatious litigation" when they opposed the defendants' unemployment compensation claim?
4. Why did the plaintiffs oppose the defendants' unemployment compensation? Was their motive purely personal animosity or were they pursuing a broader corporate strategy with regard to the defendants or in terms of overall company HR policy?
5. In retrospect, given the length and outcome of the litigation, what advice would you have given the company?

Concept *Summary* » 21.1

UNEMPLOYMENT COMPENSATION

- Typically administered by the states, not the federal government
- Intended to assist employees out of work through no fault of their own
- Disqualifications for an out-of-work employee include:
  - Willful misconduct
  - Voluntary quitting
- Litigating unmeritorious claims:
  - Keeps payroll taxes down
  - May prevent subsequent wrongful discharge claims

Workers' Compensation

Workers' Compensation
Benefits awarded an employee when injuries are work related.

Workers' compensation, as it has been instituted in virtually every state, is a statutory tradeoff. As noted earlier in the case of the injured railway worker, the employer loses several highly successful defenses to the injured employee's claim: assumption of risk, contributory negligence, and the fellow-servant doctrine. In return, employers get immunity from suits by injured employees, with some limited exceptions. Typically, the exceptions are failure to carry the requisite compensation insurance; intentional, as opposed to accidental, injuries to employees; and those rare circumstances in which the employer—a hospital, for example—deals with, and harms, the employee in its capacity as a third-party provider of a service and not as employer.

For the worker, typical compensation schemes permit easy access to benefits, relatively simple adjudication of disputed claims, plus the possibility of an additional, perhaps more substantial, recovery in a related third-party tort action against, say, the manufacturer of the machine that caused the work-related injury. Employers and insurance carriers often complain about fraudulent claims, usually involving hard-to-disprove back injuries. Perhaps the only possible response to claims of fraud is that any system conceived and run by human beings will be subject to some abuses. The concept of workers' compensation is eminently fair, and in practice, it has spared millions of injured workers and their families untold hardship.

To be eligible for workers' compensation, an employee's injury must be work related. Sometimes factual circumstances make it difficult to determine whether the worker's injury or illness is really work related and therefore covered by workers' compensation or falls outside the exclusive jurisdiction of the act. Some examples include:

- Injuries intentionally inflicted upon one employee by another
- Injuries occurring when the employee is "on the road," especially if the trip began from the employee's home
- Chronic illnesses such as lung disease, especially if contributing factors include workplace hazards (e.g., dust) in combination with personal behavior (e.g., smoking)

One of the most difficult issues for the courts in recent years has been *in utero* injury to a fetus as the result of the mother's on-the-job accident. Should workers' compensation be the child's exclusive remedy, just as it is the mother's, or should the parents be able to sue for larger damages on the child's behalf?

Some state legislatures and courts have answered this question in the affirmative, as shown in the Ethical Dilemma offered below. This dilemma arises from a long tradition in Anglo-Saxon law, climaxed by the U.S. Supreme Court's 1973 abortion decision that generally denies legal standing to fetuses as full-fledged human beings. But what to do, then, if the fetus is injured "on the job," but survives to become a full-fledged "person" in the eyes of the law?

ethical DILEMMA

IN UTERO WORKPLACE INJURIES

In *Meyer v. Burger King Corporation,*[1] Sonrise Management, Inc. (Sonrise) was the management company for a Burger King Corporation restaurant located in Lacey, Washington. Verona Meyer (Verona) was employed by Sonrise at this Burger King. On April 26, 1995, Verona was working her shift at the restaurant. She was approximately 35 weeks pregnant at the time. While in the course and scope of her employment on that day, she lost her footing and struck her lower abdomen on the corner of a table known as the "Whopper board." Later that evening, Verona went to the hospital and delivered her baby, Patricia. Verona and Gary Meyer, her husband, claimed that blunt trauma to Verona's abdomen from the Whopper board had caused an abruption of the placenta, in which the placenta partially detached from Verona's uterine wall. The Meyers further claimed that, because of the placental abruption, there was a loss of oxygen to Patricia while she was *in utero*, and this loss of oxygen in turn resulted in Patricia being born several hours later with severe injuries.

In April 1998, the Meyers, on behalf of themselves and their daughter, Patricia, filed suit against Sonrise for negligence. The complaint alleged that both Verona and Patricia were injured in the course of Verona's employment because of unsafe working conditions. The Meyers claimed damages for Patricia's injuries, which allegedly included permanent mental and physical disabilities, and for their own subsequent losses due to destruction of the parent/child relationship.

The Washington state supreme court wrote, "We must determine whether the exclusionary provision of the [Workers' Compensation] Act bars Patricia's claims and those of her parents. This is a question of law which we review *de novo.*"

The court then reviewed how numerous "sister" courts around the nation have dealt with this difficult issue:

- "The most analogous representative case is *Cushing ex rel. Brewer v. Time Saver Stores, Inc.,*[2] where the Louisiana Court of Appeals held the exclusivity provision of Louisiana's workers' compensation statute did not bar a child's claim for damages for prenatal injuries suffered as a result of the mother's fall at work.[3] In that case, the mother was performing recordkeeping duties in the store's back room. The room was without furniture, so the woman was compelled to sit on boxes and use crates and plywood as a surface for an adding machine. The boxes shifted, the mother fell, and the adding machine fell on her abdomen, causing an abruption of the placenta. Her baby was born prematurely 12 days later with severe birth defects, including permanent brain damage. The Louisiana court reasoned the exclusivity provision of the statute barred actions that depend on the injuries of the employee, such as loss of support or loss of consortium (i.e., because the mother/father or husband/wife suffered an injury, the family suffered a loss based upon that injury). The *Cushing* court found the child's injuries in no way derived from the mother's injuries because '[w] hether mom is there to continue bringing home a pay check or to participate in the child's life has no relevance to this child's alleged brain damage.'[4] The court held the workers' compensation statute was not intended to nor does it purport to affect the rights of an employee's child who is injured on the employer's job site."
- "The Colorado Supreme Court reached the same conclusion in *Pizza Hut of Am., Inc. v. Keefe,*[5] In that case, the court reasoned the fact the mother and child were injured in the same event does not render the damage to the child derivative of the mother's injury because the child's right of action arises out of the child's own personal injuries and not merely the personal injuries suffered by the mother.[6] When the employee's child is *born*, it stands in the same position as any other nonemployee member of the public. Workers' compensation laws would not bar a claim by a child who was injured while visiting his or her parent in the workplace. Therefore, the exclusivity provisions of workers' compensation statutes do not bar claims by a nonemployee child who sustains prenatal injuries in the workplace, as it does not bar claims asserted by third party victims.[7] A nonemployee's injury is neither collateral nor derivative of an employee's injury merely because both resulted from the same negligent conduct by the employer. Thus, a child still in the womb can sustain independent injuries arising from the same event allegedly caused by the negligence of the employer."
- "Most recently, the Hawaii Supreme Court reached a similar conclusion. In *Omori v. Jowa Hawai'i Co.,*[8] a pregnant employee who worked at a convenience store had her water break prematurely. Her doctor ordered her to stop working. However, the convenience store manager refused to allow her time off. Her job included lifting boxes, stacking shelves, and various cleaning duties. Allegedly, as a consequence of being forced to continue working, the mother suffered a premature rupture of the membrane and the child was born prematurely with severe physical injuries. The mother brought suit on behalf

of the child for his injuries and also for loss of consortium with the child. The court found the child's injuries were independent of any injury to the worker and held Hawaii's workers' compensation statute *did not bar* a child from bringing an action against the mother's employer for prenatal injuries, *nor* a claim by the parents for loss of consortium."[9]

The Washington Supreme Court, following the lead of these other courts, declined to limit the child's remedy to the provisions of the Workers' Compensation Act. In a concurring opinion, one justice attempted to square the decision with the U.S. Supreme Court's 1974 [*Roe*] precedent, which ruled that an unborn fetus lacks legal rights. "The common thread throughout all these cases is a limited recognition of a *person's* retroactive right to recover for prenatal injuries. The United States Supreme Court has likewise upheld recovery for prenatal injuries for children later born alive, while clarifying that 'the unborn have never been recognized in the law as persons in the whole sense.'[10] While upholding Patricia's right to a remedy because she is a person exercising her retroactive right to recover for prenatal injuries, we do not recognize a fetus as a 'person[ ] in the whole sense' and thus do not affect the jurisprudence established under *Roe*."

The justices, besides reconciling *Roe*, expressly rejected the employer's arguments that:

- the fetus's injury occurred simultaneously with the mother's,
- the company could not bar pregnant employees form the workplace without committing illegal discrimination, and
- it could not take steps to protect the unborn child in the way that it could guard against injury to its customers' children.

---

[1]144 Wash.2d 160, 26 P.3d 925 (2001).

[2]552 So.2d 730 (La.Ct.App.1989).

[3]*Id.* at 731–32.

[4]*Id.* at 732.

[5]900 P.2d 97 (Colo.1995).

[6]*Id.* at 101.

[7]*Id.* at 101.

[8]91 Hawai'i 157, 981 P.2d 714 (Ct.App.1999).

[9]*Id.* at 717–19.

[10]*Roe v. Wade*, 410 U.S. 113, 161-162, 93 S.Ct. 705, 35 L.Ed.2d 147 (1973).

Federal Preemption of Workers' Compensation Claims

Although workers' compensation has been left primarily to the states to administer, the system does brush up against various federal acts for compensating workers for whom Congress now deems, or at some time in the past considered, deserving of special protection. Railroad workers have long had recourse to the FELA; sailors come under the Jones Act[2]; and many other maritime workers are covered by the Longshoremen's and Harbor Workers'

---

[2]46 U.S.C. Section 688.

Compensation Act.[3] U.S. government workers have their own Federal Employees Compensation Act.[4] In all cases, these acts supersede state workers' compensation laws.

The FELA has given rise to some difficult litigation. Suppose a railroad subsidiary is a trucking company that picks up and delivers goods to the railroad's freight yard, where the subsidiary's drivers are supervised by the railroad yardmaster. Does this make the railroad a joint employer of the driver? If so, can a driver injured at the yard claim workers' compensation benefits against the trucking subsidiary and then turn around and sue the railroad for even more money, such as for pain and suffering, under the FELA? The answer to this question typically turns on the railroad's right to control the driver's activities, as well as the legal relationship between the two companies.

A similar problem can arise when a worker contends that although the employer's liability under state law is limited to paying workers' compensation, separate employer liability exists under a preemptive federal law. In the 1990 case of *Adams Fruit Co., Inc. v. Barrett*,[5] the Supreme Court held that workers could bring suit for violations of specific federal legislation despite the fact that they had received benefits under the state workers' compensation law. The Court held that the specific federal legislation superseded the exclusivity provisions of the state workers' compensation law.

On the other hand, although ERISA (discussed in detail later in this chapter) has sweeping preemptive impact on most state laws, it specifically exempts state workers' compensation laws from its preemptive powers.

Concept *Summary* » 21.2

Workers' Compensation

- The fifty states administer workers' compensation laws
- Employers give up common law defenses
- Employees give up right to sue for tort damages
- Applicability is limited to job-related injuries
    - Sometimes its difficult to determine whether an injury is actually job related
- Some federal laws preempt workers' compensation laws
    - ERISA is not one of them

Social Security

Nearly one in every seven Americans receives social security benefits. The Social Security system was originally entitled "old age and survivor's insurance" (OASI), and the notion that it really was insurance was a significant component of Franklin Roosevelt's success in selling

[3] 33 U.S.C. Section 901, *et seq.*

[4] 5 U.S.C. Section 1801.

[5] 494 U.S. 638, 58 U.S.L.W. 4367.

the program to Congress and the country. During the decades that followed, the Social Security system rode out recurrent crises, as the baby boomers born after World War II retired in ever larger numbers, and the deficit-ridden federal government borrowed from the Social Security fund. Today, at least for the foreseeable future, Social Security remains relatively sound, even in the face of the record deficits being run by Uncle Sam in an effort to reverse the financial meltdown of late 2008/early 2009. The system's benefits fall into three major categories—retirement insurance benefits, Medicare, and disability.

Retirement Insurance Benefits

The original and still the main purpose of social security is to provide partial replacement of earnings when a worker decides it is time to retire. Although benefits have increased substantially in the last two decades, both in relative and absolute terms, this retirement benefit was never intended to totally replace what that worker was earning prior to retirement. And yet, for many Americans over sixty-five, social security is the main, or even the only, source of income. This is true in part because the other major piece of federal legislation dealing with pensions, ERISA, goes a long way toward protecting an employee's accrued pension benefits. But, as you will learn, ERISA does not require an employer to establish a pension plan for its employees in the first place. And many workers still do not have significant pension plans where they work. Social security is often the only safety net when it is no longer possible to continue working.

Monthly benefits are payable to a retired insured worker from age sixty-two onward. Under some circumstances, a spouse or children may also be eligible. For a person to be "fully insured" by social security, he or she must accrue a minimum of forty quarters (that is, ten years) of contributions. These contributions are shared by the employer and the employee, who has no choice but to have the tax taken directly out of each paycheck, until a maximum amount of taxable income (for social security purposes only) has been earned in a calendar year.

Medicare

In addition to basic benefits, retired Americans receive a form of health insurance under the social security system. Medicare benefits cover a portion of the costs of hospitalization and the medical expenses of insured workers and their spouses age sixty-five and older, as well as younger disabled workers in some circumstances. This insurance is divided into two parts, designated by the federal bureaucracy as A and B.

Part A is hospital insurance for inpatient hospital care, inpatient skilled nursing care, and hospice care. Part B is supplementary medical insurance, which helps defray the costs of doctors' services and other medical expenses not covered by part A.

A worker who applies for social security benefits and is receiving them at age sixty-five is automatically covered under part A. The same is true for someone who has been receiving social security disability benefits (discussed briefly below) for at least twenty-four months. Part B is not entirely free. One-fourth of the premium is paid by the beneficiary, whereas the other three-fourths are covered by the federal government's general revenues.

Disability

Under the social security system, a worker is considered disabled when a severe physical or mental impairment prevents that person from working for a year or more or is expected to result in the victim's death. The disability does not have to be work related (as is the case for workers' compensation disability), but it must be total. In other words, if the injured or ailing worker can do some sort of work, though not necessarily the same work as before the disability, then this program probably will not apply. Under some circumstances, a disabled worker's spouse, children, or surviving family members are also eligible for benefits.

Just as older workers must accrue forty quarters of credit to be fully insured, so too, younger people must earn some social security credits to qualify for disability benefits. For instance, before reaching age twenty-four, a member of the work force would need six credits (six quarters of work subject to social security tax) during the preceding three years. A worker who becomes disabled between ages thirty-one and forty-two must be credited with twenty quarters on his or her account.

After twenty-four months of disability, Medicare is made available, just as in the case of retired Americans. Additionally, the social security system provides services intended to get disabled people back into the work force and off the benefit rolls. Usually, vocational rehabilitation services are provided by state rehabilitation agencies in cooperation with the federal Social Security Administration. The law provides that disability benefits can continue during a nine-month return-to-work trial period. Generally, if the trial is successful, benefits will be continued during a three-month "adjustment period" and then stopped.

Related to this aspect of the social security system is supplemental security income, a program financed by general funds from the U.S. Treasury (not social security taxes) and aimed at aiding legally blind, elderly, or partially disabled workers.

Such benefits are difficult to obtain, as exemplified by the following case, in which the Court of Appeals affirms the administrative law judge (ALJ)'s denial of benefits. As a general rule, benefits will be denied if the claimant is found capable of doing almost any job that is available in the U.S. economy, whether or not the job relates to his/her prior career. Furthermore, the courts are inclined to accord great deference to the expertise of ALJs, who deal with these claims day in and day out.

case 21.2 »

Wall v. Astrue

2009 WL 522867 U.S. Court of Appeals (10th Cir. 2009)

Facts: Claimant Joan Wall was born in February 1942. She most recently worked as a telemarketer for MCI from October 1997 to April 1998 and as a customer service representative for Telequest from April 1998 to October 1999. Wall suffered injury in August 1995 when a Cadillac struck the rear end of the vehicle she was driving. She was injured again in an August 1999 fall in a flooded restroom at work. She neither sought nor engaged in substantial work after late 1999.

Wall filed an application for supplemental social security benefits based on disability in October 2001. In February 2002, the Social Security Administration initially denied her claim, concluding that even if she was precluded from performing her past relevant work, she could still perform other work in the national economy. Wall subsequently received a hearing before an ALJ in May 2003. In October of that year, the ALJ concluded Wall was not disabled under the meaning of the Social Security Act (SSA). In January 2005, the Appeals Council denied her request for review. Accordingly, the ALJ's decision stood as the Social Security Administration's final decision for purposes of appeal.

Issue: Did the ALJ commit a reversible error in deciding that Wall, while unable to perform her previous occupation, could still find suitable work?

Decision: The appellate court panel ruled that the ALJ had done his duty in developing a full record of Wall's alleged disability, which she claimed was a cognitive impairment. In other words, Wall had been the full measure of "due process of law" to which she was entitled in pursuing her claim. The judges also concluded that, while another ALJ might have come out differently on the case, substantial evidence in the hearings record supported this ALJ's decision. That being so, the judges affirmed the ALJ's decision.

Concept *Summary* » 21.3

SOCIAL SECURITY

- A federally funded and administered program initiated during the New Deal
- Consists of three parts:
  - Pensions
  - Medical benefits
  - Long-term disability insurance

Employee Retirement Income Security Act (ERISA)

Employee Retirement Income Security Act (ERISA)
An act that sets standards for pension plans including fiduciary conduct, information disclosure, plan taxation, and remedies for employees.

The ***Employee Retirement Income Security Act,*** known as ***ERISA***, imposes standards of conduct and responsibility upon pension fund fiduciaries (persons having authority or control over the management of pension fund assets). The act also requires that pension plan administrators disclose relevant financial information to employees and the government. The act sets certain minimum standards that pension plans must meet to qualify for preferential tax treatment, and it provides legal remedies to employees and their beneficiaries in the event of violations.

The provisions of ERISA apply to employee benefit plans established by employers. The act recognizes two types of benefit plans: welfare plans and pension plans. Welfare plans usually provide participating employees and their beneficiaries with medical coverage, disability benefits, death benefits, vacation pay, and/or unemployment benefits. Welfare plans may also include apprenticeship programs, prepaid legal services, day care centers, and scholarship funds. Pension plans are defined as including any plan intended to provide retirement income to employees and resulting in deferral of income for such employees.

ERISA's main focus is on pension plans. It seeks to ensure that all employees covered by pension plans receive the benefits due them under the plans. ERISA does not require an employer to provide a pension plan for its employees. However, if a pension plan is offered, ERISA sets the minimum standards and requirements that the pension plan must meet.

The provisions of ERISA do not apply to employee benefit plans that are established by federal, state, or local government employers. Nor does the act apply to plans covering employees of tax-exempt churches or to plans maintained solely for the purpose of complying with state workers' compensation, unemployment compensation, or disability insurance laws. Neither does ERISA apply to plans maintained outside the United States primarily for the benefit of nonresident aliens. But these exemptions are relatively narrow; ERISA's reach is very broad.

The two main features of ERISA—the imposition of standards for fiduciary conduct and responsibility and the setting of minimum standards for pension plan requirements—have different bases for their coverage. The fiduciary duties and conduct standards apply to any employee benefit plan established or maintained by an employer engaged in interstate commerce or in an industry or activity affecting interstate commerce. They also apply to plans established and maintained by unions representing employees engaged in an industry or activity affecting interstate commerce.

The minimum standards for pension plans must be met for the employee pension plans to qualify for preferential tax treatment. Because such tax treatment enables an employer to deduct contributions to qualified benefit plans immediately but does not consider the payments as income to participating employees until they receive the payments after retirement, most employers seek to "qualify" their plans by complying with ERISA's minimum standards. Such compliance, however, is not required. Some employers who view the ERISA requirements as too stringent have chosen not to qualify their pension and other benefit plans for preferential tax treatment. Those employers are still subject to the fiduciary duties of ERISA if they are engaged in, or affect, interstate commerce (which today includes the vast majority of enterprises).

Preemption

Despite the broad preemptive power that the federal courts have given to ERISA, as originally recognized and explained by the U.S. Supreme Court in *Shaw v. Delta Airlines, Inc.*[6] several courts have allowed plaintiffs raising claims of discrimination in employee benefit plans to pursue them under state antidiscrimination laws. The following case stands as a recent example of such an exception from ERISA's broad reach. The case is doubly interesting in that, once the court allows the plaintiff to sue outside ERISA's framework, he runs headlong into a complicated set of state statutes, which regulate Health Management Organizations (HMOs) and motor vehicle accident insurance claims.

case 21.3 »

Wirth v. Aetna U.S. Healthcare

2006 WL 3360457 (U.S. Ct. Appeals, 3d Cir. November 21, 2006)

Rendell, Circuit Judge

On appeal, Jonathan Wirth contends that the Employee Retirement and Income Security Act of 1974 ("ERISA"), 29 U.S.C. § § 1001 *et seq.*, does not preempt his state law claims against Aetna U.S. Healthcare ("Aetna") and, therefore, that the District Court erred in granting removal of his suit from state to federal court. Wirth also contends that, even if removal was proper, the District Court erred in holding that Pennsylvania's Health Maintenance Organization Act ("HMO Act") exempts Aetna from Wirth's claim under Pennsylvania's Motor Vehicle Financial Responsibility Law ("MVFRL"). We have jurisdiction to review his challenge under 28 U.S.C. § 1291.

. . .

I. Factual and Procedural Background

Wirth was injured in a motor vehicle accident caused by a third party tortfeasor. His treatment for those injuries was covered under an HMO healthcare agreement issued by

[6] 463 U.S. 85 (1983).

Aetna.[1] Wirth recovered a settlement from the third party tortfeasor; subsequently, Aetna, who claimed it was acting within its contractual rights, asserted a subrogation lien to recover monies from that settlement. Wirth paid Aetna $2,066.90 to release its lien and then filed a class action suit in state court alleging, *inter alia*, unjust enrichment and violation of section 1720 of the MVFRL, which provides that in "actions arising out of the maintenance or use of a motor vehicle, there shall be no right of subrogation or reimbursement from a claimant's tort recovery with respect to ... benefits paid or payable by a program, group contract or other arrangement." 75 Pa. Cons.Stat. § 1720.

Aetna removed the suit to federal court, contending that Wirth's claims were simply to "recover benefits due to him under the terms of his plan," 29 U.S.C. § 1132(a)(1)(B), and therefore fell within the scope of section 502(a)(1)(B) of ERISA. As such, Aetna argued that Wirth's claims evoked the doctrine of "complete preemption," which holds that certain federal laws so thoroughly occupy a field of regulatory interest that any claim brought within the field, however stated in the complaint, constitutes a federal claim and therefore bestows a federal court with jurisdiction. See *Metro. Life Ins. Co. v. Taylor*, 481 U.S. 58, 63-64 (1987). The District Court agreed, finding that ERISA was such a thoroughly robust regulatory regime, and denied Wirth's motion to remand.

After concluding it had subject matter jurisdiction over the action, the District Court proceeded to consider the specific allegations of Wirth's complaint. There, Wirth averred that, by laying claim to any portion of his tort recovery, Aetna had violated the anti-subrogation provision found at Section 1720 of the MVFRL. Aetna countered, contending that section 1720 was inapplicable to an HMO like itself because the HMO Act provides that HMOs will not be governed by a state law that regulates insurance "unless such law specifically and in exact terms applies to such health maintenance organization." 40 Pa. Cons.Stat. § 1560(a). Aetna urged that subrogation was permissible because section 1720 does not employ the term "health maintenance organization," and is therefore not specifically applicable to HMOs. The District Court agreed, finding that "there is nothing in § 1720 which specifically and in exact terms applies to HMOs," and dismissed Wirth's claims.

On appeal, Wirth challenges both the District Court's conclusion that his claims are completely preempted by section 502(a) of ERISA—the basis for the District Court's jurisdictionover the action—as well as the Court's interpretation of sections 1720 of the MVFRL and 1560(a) of the HMO Act.

[1] However, remember that under ERISA it is illegal to fire an employee for the express purpose of preventing him or her from reaping the benefits of the plan. See *Le v. Applied Biosystems* [886 F. Supp. 717 (N.D. Cal. 1995)].

II. Subject Matter Jurisdiction Claim: Preemption Under Section 502(a)

Wirth argues that the removal of his lawsuit to federal court, and the reclassification of his state law claim as an ERISA action, was error....

Under § 502(a), a participant in an ERISA-covered plan may bring a civil action to "recover benefits due to him under the terms of his plan, to enforce his rights under the terms of the plan, or to clarify his rights to future benefits under the terms of the plan." 29 U.S.C. § 1132(a)(1)(B). Wirth contends that because his claims are neither for "benefits due" nor to "enforce rights" under the Aetna plan, ERISA does not provide a civil enforcement mechanism for Wirth to challenge or defend against Aetna's liens and, therefore, that the District Court erred in granting removal of the case from state to federal court....

On appeal in *Levine*, we considered, *inter alia*, "whether plaintiffs' unjust enrichment claims for monies taken pursuant to subrogation and reimbursement provisions in their ERISA health plans are claims for 'benefits due' within the meaning of ERISA section 502(a)." ...

As we noted in our Interim Opinion, our holding in *Levine* applies squarely to the present facts and precludes Wirth's argument that seeking recovery of the $2,066.90 paid to extinguish Aetna's lien is not tantamount to seeking recovery of "benefits due" to him. Here, as in *Levine*, the actions undertaken by the insurer resulted in diminished benefits provided to the plaintiff insureds. That the bills and coins used to extinguish Aetna's lien are not literally the same as those used to satisfy its obligation to cover Wirth's injuries is of no import, "the benefits are under something of a cloud." *Arana*, 338 F.3d at 438. For these reasons, we reiterate the holding of our Interim Opinion: Wirth's claims against Aetna are completely preempted by ERISA and there was no error in the District Court's conclusion that it had jurisdiction over this matter.

III. Interpretation of Pennsylvania Law

Wirth argues that, even if the District Court was correct in exercising jurisdiction over this claim, it erred in finding that Pennsylvania's HMO Act exempted Aetna from complying with the anti-subrogation provision found in section 1720 of the MVFRL. In interpreting state law, as we must here, "the decisions of the state's highest court constitute the authoritative source" of guiding precedent. *Conn. Mutual Life Ins. Co. v. Wyman*, 718 F.2d 63, 65 (3d Cir.1983). However, when the question is a novel one "or where applicable state precedent is ambiguous, absent or incomplete, we must determine or predict how the highest state court would rule." *Rolick v. Collins Pine Co.*, 925 F.2d 661, 664 (3d Cir.1991).

Is an HMO exempt, by virtue of Pennsylvania's HMO Act, 40 Pa. Cons. Stat. § 1560(a), from complying with the anti-subrogation provision found in section 1720 of the MVFRL?

The Pennsylvania Supreme Court granted our petition and, in an August 22, 2006 Opinion, answered the question in the affirmative, reasoning as the District Court did in its ruling. See *Wirth v. Aetna U.S. Healthcare*, 904 A.2d 858 (Pa.2006). 75Pa.Cons.Stat. § 1720.[2]

The Pennsylvania Supreme Court considered Wirth's two primary arguments in support of his position that the MVFRL "specifically and in exact terms" refers to HMOs: (1) that the "broad term 'program, group contract or other arrangement' [found in the MVFRL] includes HMOs as well as every conceivable type of healthcare arrangement"; and (2) that "the phrase 'program, group contract or other arrangement' is a specific and exact term that 'applies' to HMO plans." *Wirth*, 904 A.2d at 861 (internal quotations omitted).

The Court rejected both of these contentions, finding the MVFRL's language to be neither sufficiently specific nor exact to demonstrate the General Assembly's intent to bring HMOs within the ambit of the MVFRL. To reach this conclusion, the Court first examined a series of Pennsylvania statutes "that on their face arguably apply to HMOs," *Id.* at 862, and found that when "the General Assembly wishes to make insurance statutes applicable to HMOs, it does so by using the terms 'health maintenance organization' or 'HMO' or by specifically referring to the HMO Act. Furthermore, when it intends to include HMOs within general terms such as 'insurer' or 'managed care plan,' it does so 'specifically and in exact terms.'" *Id.* at 863–64. As was clear to the Pennsylvania Supreme Court, as well as to the District Court, the MVFRL does not include the terms "health maintenance organization" or "HMO" and, therefore, does not "specifically and in exact terms" set out to reach such entities.

Secondly, the Court examined the language of the MVFRL and found that though "the definition of 'program, group contract or other arrangement' in Section 1719 is not exclusive, it contains nothing specific or explicit with respect to HMOs ..." *Id.* at 864. Therefore, the Court concluded that the MVFRL's failure to *specifically mention* HMOs clearly indicated "that Section 1720 does not apply to HMOs." *Id.* at 865.

Additionally, the Court considered Wirth's contention that "to the extent that the HMO Act and the MVFRL are in conflict, the anti-subrogation provision of the MVFRL should control over the earlier adopted HMO Act." *Id.* Although the Court granted that "last-in-time" is an accepted way of reconciling two conflicting statutes, it nevertheless found that no conflict existed between the HMO Act and the MVFRL because the HMO Act's express language contemplated the application of future statutes to HMOs and, in doing so, clearly dictated that HMOs would be exempt from those laws unless they specifically stated otherwise. *Id.* For these reasons, the Court found it clear that "in this instance the Legislature intended that statutes promulgated after [the HMO Act's enactment in] 1972 would not apply to HMOs unless they so provided in specific and exact terms." *Id.* Notwithstanding this requirement for specificity in the future, the General Assembly thereafter did not specifically include HMOs. *Id.* at 863–65.

Finally, the Court addressed Wirth's public policy argument that "prohibiting subrogation furthers the goals of the MVFRL of reducing the cost of automobile insurance and providing complete compensation for individuals injured in motor vehicle accidents." The Court found it unnecessary to investigate the General Assembly's legislative intent because of the clear and unambiguous language of the HMO Act. *Id.* at 865–66.

In holding that "an HMO is exempt from complying with the anti-subrogation provision of the MVFRL," *Id.* at 866, the Pennsylvania Supreme Court clearly and directly answered our certified question. Because the Court's opinion on matters of Pennsylvania state law constitutes precedent that we are bound to follow, *Conn. Mutual Life Ins. Co.*, 718F.2d at 65, we will affirm the District Court's ruling that Aetna was within its contractual rights to seek subrogation from Appellant.

IV. Conclusion

For the reasons set forth, we will affirm the order of the District Court.

[2]Though we will not rescribe the full text of the Court's decision here, as it is available as a published precedential opinion, we do summarize its essential points so that we may elucidate our reasons for affirming the District Court.

Case Questions

1. What is the Motor Vehicle Financial Responsibility Law and why is it relevant to this case?
2. How does Pennsylvania's HMO Act figure into the court's decision in this case?
3. If the U.S. district court was correct about total ERISA preemption applying here, why does the federal appeals court care what the Pennsylvania Supreme Court said?
4. What does the term "subrogation" mean and why is it relevant in this case?
5. What was the plaintiff's public policy argument in this case and how did the court of appeals respond to it?

Fiduciary Responsibility

ERISA imposes standards of conduct and responsibility on fiduciaries of benefit plans established or maintained by employers and unions engaged in or affecting interstate commerce. The act requires that all such plans must be in writing and must designate at least one named fiduciary who has the authority to manage and control the plan's operation and management. The plan must also provide a written procedure for establishing and carrying out a funding policy that is consistent with the plan's objectives and with ERISA's requirements. The written provisions must also specify the basis on which contributions to the fund and payments from the fund will be made. Finally, the written plan must describe the procedure for allocation of responsibility for administering and operating the benefit plan.

ERISA requires that all assets of the benefit plan must be held in trust for the benefit of participating employees and their beneficiaries. The plan must establish a procedure for handling claims on the fund by participants and their beneficiaries. Any individual with a claim against the fund must exhaust these internal procedures before seeking legal remedies from the courts.

Fiduciary

Fiduciary
Any person exercising discretionary authority over benefit plan administration, management, or disposition of plan assets; or who renders investment advice regarding the plan.

ERISA defines a ***fiduciary*** as including any person exercising discretionary authority or control respecting the management of the benefit plan, or disposition of plan assets; or who renders, or has authority or responsibility to render, investment advice (for which he or she is compensated) with respect to any money or property of the plan; or who has any discretionary authority or responsibility in the administration of the plan. Persons not normally considered fiduciaries, such as consultants or advisers, *may* be found to be fiduciaries when their expertise is used in a managerial, administrative, or advisory capacity by the plan.

The WORKING Law

The 2008 Amendments to ERISA Respond to Financial Crisis

In December 23, 2008, President George W. Bush signed the Worker, Retiree, and Employer Recovery Act of 2008 ("WRERA"). The WRERA makes technical corrections to the Pension Protection Act of 2006 ("PPA") and amends the PPA, the Internal Revenue Code ("Code"), the Employee Retirement Income Security Act of 1974 ("ERISA"), and the Age Discrimination in Employment Act of 1967 ("ADEA"). Among other things, the WRERA suspends the Required Minimum Distribution ("RMD") rules for 2009 for 401(k), 403(b), governmental 457(f) and other defined contribution plans and individual retirement accounts ("IRA's") (but not for defined benefit pension plans). This suspension is a direct reaction by Congress to the "meltdown" in the financial markets, mentioned above under our discussion of Social Security, and its devastating effect on retirement accounts. The act allows participants, who have reached the age when they are required to begin withdrawing funds from their retirement accounts, to postpone selling their investments at current depressed values. (Generally, Section 401(a)(9) of the Code requires participants to begin receiving distributions from a qualified plan no later than April 1 following the year in which the participant reaches age 70.)

Concept *Summary* » 21.4

ERISA

- ERISA
  - regulates employee benefits, especially pensions
  - does not require an employer to provide any employee benefits, not even pensions
  - has wide preemptive power but does not preempt all state laws
    - State banking, insurance, and workers' compensation laws are generally not preempted
  - imposes strict fiduciary duties on employers and plan administrators
- 2008 amendments to ERISA seek primarily to provide relief to retirees who must draw upon their diminished pension funds

CHAPTER REVIEW

» Key Terms

Federal Employment Liability Act (FELA) « 657

unemployment compensation « 659

willful misconduct « 659

workers' compensation « 663

Employee Retirement Income Security Act (ERISA) « 670

fiduciary « 674

» Summary

- The American worker's safety net consists primarily of unemployment compensation, workers' compensation, Social Security, and retirement plans.
- Employees who lose their jobs through no willful fault of their own are entitled to unemployment compensation benefits while they look for alternative employment. Unemployment compensation is administered at the state level and is funded by payroll taxes imposed on employers and employees alike.
- Workers' compensation benefits are mandated by state law and provide medical insurance and income supplements for employees who are injured on the job. Workers injured while commuting to and from work are not covered. The advantage to the employer is that covered employees cannot sue their employers for negligence, but rather must be content with the benefits prescribed by the state system.
- Social Security is a federal program that provides minimum pension benefits for retirees, as well as benefits for permanently disabled workers. The program, dating from the New Deal of the 1930s, is funded by taxes on employers and employees. Participation is mandatory.
- In sharp contrast to unemployment, workers' compensation, and Social Security, neither the federal nor the state governments require private employers to provide pensions. However, if an employer does provide a pension plan, it is regulated by ERISA. Additionally, this sweeping federal law also regulated many other employee benefit plans.

» Problems

Questions

1. Many Western nations provide their citizens with health insurance. Many, too, mandate employee pensions, as do our own federal and state governments, for their own employees. Should the United States Congress (a) create a system of national health insurance and/or (b) require all employers to provide pensions for their employees?
2. In view of the fact that in 2008–09 many pension plans lost 50 percent or more of their value, do you believe that ERISA has been proven to be an ineffective law?
3. Most state workers' compensation laws do not apply to injuries sustained when employees are commuting to and from work. What are the pros and cons of this rule?
4. Are there any arguments to be made for eliminating the rule that employees who are guilty of willful misconduct are ineligible for unemployment compensation benefits? New Jersey law only applies this ineligibility to the first six weeks of unemployment. What do you think of this rule?
5. Do you think that the Social Security system is economically sustainable in the 21st century?

Case Problems

6. Plaintiff was fired by his employer, along with a co-worker, as a result of a fistfight that the two of them conducted on the company's premises. The plaintiff subsequently sued the employer for wrongful discharge, claiming that he was only defending himself and that the state's public policy favoring victim compensation in cases of violent crime created a cause of action. The state also has a well-established common-law rule favoring at-will employment.

   What are the arguments for and against a wrongful discharge cause of action in this case? (Review Chapter 2, if necessary, in answering this question.)

   Is the plaintiff entitled to receive unemployment compensation benefits under this set of facts? How does your answer to this question affect your answer to the question above, if at all?

   Are the plaintiff's injuries arguably compensable under the state's workers' compensation act? How should the workers' compensation act be factored into the court's consideration of the plaintiff's public policy wrongful discharge claim? See *Quebedeaux v. Dow Chemical Company* [820 So.2d 542 (La. Supreme 2002)].
7. Plaintiff/employee suffered mental/emotional trauma but no physical injuries as the result of an armed robbery that occurred in the store while the plaintiff was on the job. Her posttraumatic stress disorder was manifest by nausea, cramps, confusion, and the side effects of her prescribed medication. She sued her employer for negligence in failing to maintain appropriate security measures in the store.

   What are the arguments for and against an employer defense of workers' compensation exclusivity with regard to plaintiff's injuries? How should the court rule? See *Rivers v. Grimsley Oil Company, Inc.* [842 So.2d 975 (Fla. App. 2003)].
8. Plaintiff was injured on the job when she was attacked by a co-worker. She sued the employer on the basis of negligent hiring and negligent supervision. The employer sought dismissal of the lawsuit on the ground that the attack was a work-related accident that is covered by the exclusivity provisions of workers' compensation and that workers' compensation benefits should be the plaintiff's sole remedy in this case.

   What are the arguments for and against the employer's defense? How should the court rule? See *Caple v. Bullard Restaurants, Inc.* [152 N.C. App. 421, 567 S.E.2d 828 (2002)].
9. Plaintiff/truck driver was fired after he tested positive for use of marijuana on the job. Under applicable federal interstate trucking regulations, the driver had the right to a second test at the employer's expense within seventy-two hours of the positive result. The employer failed to advise the employee of this right. However, the employee paid for his own test, which came up negative. The employer then refused to consider the results of that second test and let the discharge stand.

When the plaintiff applies for unemployment compensation, if the referee considers only the employer's evidence of a positive drug test, should the plaintiff be found guilty of willful misconduct and denied benefits? Should the referee allow the plaintiff/employee to submit evidence of his personally purchased drug test? How much weight should the referee give this test? See *Southwood Door Company v. Burton* [847 SO.2d 833 (Miss. Supreme 2003)].

10. A terminated sales representative claimed he was fired because he was HIV-positive. The company contended that he was let go due to intentional disrespect for his supervisors and contravention of company rules. On appeal of the unemployment referee's decision, the state superior court ruled that plaintiff's supervisor knew nothing of his health condition. This ruling became a final judgment on the unemployment compensation claim, which therefore was denied due to plaintiff's willful misconduct.

    Should this judgment collaterally stop the plaintiff from relitigating his disability discrimination claim against the former employer under the state's antidiscrimination statute? See *Shields v. Bellsouth Advertising and Publishing Co.* [273 Ga. 774, 545 S.E.2d 898 (Ga. Supreme 2001)].

11. Plaintiff suffered a heart attack. He applied for Social Security disability Insurance (SSDI). His claim was initially rejected, but he appealed and was successful on appeal. The social security administrative law judge found that plaintiff was unable to perform the work he had done in the past. During the pendency of this social security claim, plaintiff was also a part of an unfair labor practice complaint against his employer. The National Labor Relations Board administrative law judge found that plaintiff and his co-workers had been the victims of their employer's unfair labor practices and therefore would ordinarily be entitled to back-pay awards for any periods of unemployment related to the unfair labor practices. However, the employer contended that plaintiff should not be eligible for any back pay under the National Labor Relations Act because he had a total-disability claim concurrently pending with the Social Security Administration and would not have reported for work during the pendency of that claim anyway. What do you think? See *Performance Friction Corporation*, [335 NLRB No. 86, 2001 WL 1126575 (NLRB)].

12. A medical center sued a major insurance company in state court, contending that the insurance carrier had breached its contract with the center's hospital by failing to reimburse it for the full contractual amounts when the hospital rendered services to the carrier's insured patients. The insurance company removed the case to federal district court, claiming that the controversy was essentially federal in nature, involving a welfare benefit plan regulated by ERISA. The medical center moved to have the case remanded to state court, pointing out that ERISA exempts from its coverage, among other things, insurance contracts. Who is right? See *Lakeview Medical Center v. Aetna Health Management, Inc.* [2000 WL 1727553 (E.D. La.)].

13. The administrator of a major corporation's employee benefit plans filed suit, seeking to preempt claims by obtaining a declaratory judgment that certain sales personnel were not actually employees and therefore were not entitled to benefits under the plans. The personnel in question performed sales services for the marketing subsidiary of the parent corporation. The evidence showed that these personnel were paid neither wages nor salaries, but instead earned fees by selling magazine subscriptions. These salespeople claimed they were subject to substantial supervision such as:

    - review of sales presentations;
    - review of correspondence;
    - occasional accompaniment by managers to meetings with clients; and
    - management direction on the handling of clients.

    They were required to file periodic reports, but were not required to work any particular hours or any particular number of hours in a week. Nor did they have to obtain advance approval to take a vacation. The company claims they are independent contractors and therefore not entitled to employee benefits. What do you say? See *Administrative Committee of Time Warner, Inc. v. Biscardi*, [2000 WL 1721168 (S.D.N.Y.)].

14. Cypress Mountain Coals Corporation entered into a collective bargaining agreement with the United Mine Workers of America under which the company agreed, among other things, to add disability pensions to its existing obligations under the union's multiemployer pension plan. The plan documents were silent as to whether or not an injured employee could qualify if his disability was not exclusively caused by a mining accident. A year after the collective agreement was consummated, Cypress employee Donald Miller was injured in a mine accident. But when he applied for a disability pension, the company denied his application, contending that his disability was partly caused by preexisting conditions. The union sued Cypress for breach of the collective agreement and the pension plan.

    Which law should the court apply in determining this controversy, the NLRA or ERISA, or both? Is state workers' compensation law implicated here in any way? And what about the collective bargaining agreement's grievance/arbitration clause? (In considering this last question, review Chapter 1, if necessary.) See *United Mine Workers of America v. Cypress Mountain Coals Corp.* [171 BNA LRRM 2512 (6th Cir. 2002)].

15. Petitioner Metropolitan Life Insurance Company (MetLife) is an administrator and the insurer of Sears, Roebuck & Company's long-term disability insurance plan, which is governed by the Employee Retirement Income Security Act of 1974 (ERISA). The plan gives MetLife (as administrator) discretionary authority to determine the validity of an employee's benefits claim and provides that MetLife (as insurer) will pay the claims. Respondent Wanda Glenn, a Sears employee, was granted an initial twenty-four months of benefits under the plan following a diagnosis of a heart disorder. MetLife encouraged her to apply for, and she began receiving, Social Security disability benefits based on an agency determination that she could do no work. But when MetLife itself had to determine whether she could work, in order to establish eligibility for extended plan benefits, it found her capable of doing sedentary work and denied her the benefits.

    In challenging Met Life's decision, Glenn contends that the court should consider Met Life's conflict of interest as both the administrator and the payor under the plan. Do you agree? If so, how much weight should the judge give this factor in assigning burdens of proof? See *Metropolitan Life Insurance Company v. Glenn*, 128 S.Ct. 2343 (2008).

Hypothetical Situations

16. A ski instructor, and member of the ski patrol in the Oregon Cascades resort region, was married to a woman who was HIV-positive. When she developed full-fledged AIDS, she applied for and was awarded Social Security disability benefits. After the instructor's employer learned of his wife's total-disability status under the Social Security program and the cause of her disability, it demanded that the plaintiff submit to a blood test to ascertain whether he was HIV-positive. When he refused, he was fired. What rights do you think the plaintiff has under federal employment laws based on these facts?

17. A discharged U.S. Navy officer filed claims for back pay and reinstatement, claiming that he was wrongfully discharged after he refused, on religious grounds, to sign reenlistment papers that required him to use his Social Security number as his personal military identification number. He argued that the Navy erroneously listed his discharge as "voluntary" and that in fact he was constructively discharged. Should the officer be reinstated with back pay?

18. Plaintiff was employed in one of the defendant's stores. She suffered a back injury and made a workers' compensation claim. When she was partially recovered, she returned to the store on a light-duty assignment that allowed her to work four hours per day. Upon her return, co-workers made fun of her injury and mocked her limitations, sometimes implying by their barbs that the injury was faked. The plaintiff sued for disability discrimination under the state's antidiscrimination statute, retaliation under the state's workers' compensation act, and intentional infliction of emotional distress.

How should a court rule on each of these claims as against plaintiff's employer? Does it make a difference whether the store manager was aware of her co-workers' behavior? Whether she complained to higher company officials about it? Whether the manager took part in the behavior?

If a court finds retaliation for pursuing a workers' compensation claim, should this finding insulate the employer from liability under the state's antidiscrimination statute? Under state tort law?

19. In March 2009, the entire United States was in a furor over the fact that the beleaguered insurance giant AIG, which had just received hundreds of millions of dollars in bailout money from the U.S. government, had paid out $165 million in performance and retention bonuses to key executives. If you were attorney general of the United States, how would you have advised President Obama with regard to recovering these funds? Are the employee benefits covered by ERISA? Did the CEO of AIG have a fiduciary duty with regard to these funds under ERISA to the employees who claimed they were entitled to the bonuses? Did the CEO have a fiduciary duty to the U.S., which owned 79 percent of AIG at that time?

20. Suppose that a unionized employee is fired on the grounds that her disability is work related and therefore, even with reasonable accommodations, she cannot perform the fundamental duties of her position. The terminated employee subsequently files for and receives disability benefits under the Social Security Act. She also files a grievance through her union under the grievance/arbitration provision of the collective bargaining agreement and she files a disability discrimination claim in state court. You are the HR director of the company. Advise the CEO on how to respond to these actions. Consider and deal with the following issues:

- Does the former employee's successful receipt of Social Security disability benefits preclude her claim of having a non-job-related disability?
- Is this claim essentially a workers' compensation matter, subject to the exclusive remedies of the state workers' compensation act?
- Does it matter whether or not she received unemployment compensation benefits when she was first fired?
- Can the employer require her to submit her claim to arbitration, as her exclusive remedy?
- Does ERISA figure into this case in any way?

The Fair Labor Standards Act

Since the Fair Labor Standards Act (FLSA) was first enacted in 1938, the temptation may be to view FLSA issues such as minimum wages, overtime entitlements, and even child labor as long-settled and of little immediate importance in 21st century America.

But to the contrary, globalization has put new pressure on American free enterprise, which all too often has succumbed to the lure of faraway places where sweatshops can be established to replace high-wage, frequently unionized factories in the United States or to the temptation to hire illegal aliens to staff sweatshops here in our own cities (see Chapter 5). "Globalization" has been described by one noted labor historian as follows:

> Globalization has been used to describe a variety of developments including the spread of popular music, movies and fashion, the increasing ease of global communication and transportation, the rapid international diffusion of new technologies and the increasingly international scope of large corporations.... Many of the Western nations ha[ve] reached the late stage of development and huge private corporations in partnership with governments range across the globe seeking industrial markets, investment areas, trading partners and ... sources of cheap labor and raw materials.... Finally, in the midst of this ... globalization ... a third wave is looming, a global information economy, the emergence and dominance of the information sector—the sector that produces, manipulates, processes, distributes and markets information products—a sector now controlled by the wealthy nations.[1]

Even more fundamentally, while slavery was abolished by the United States by a bloody Civil War and the subsequent Thirteenth Amendment to the Constitution, slavery and trafficking of human beings throughout the world exacerbate the worst symptoms of globalization. The U.S. Department of State has recently estimated that at least 700,000 beings are annually trafficked across international borders to be enslaved in sweatshops, on vast construction projects, on plantations, and in brothels.[2] A CIA study claimed that 50,000 people are trafficked across U.S. borders every year. These numbers still stand today. Anthony M. DeStefano of *Newsday* has written, "I believe that the tendency to see human trafficking

[1]Dr. Joseph Gowaskie, Rider University, Lawrenceville, N.J., unpublished paper quoted with permission.

[2]"Trafficking in Persons Report," U.S. State Department, July 2001, http://www.state.gov.

primarily as sex trafficking has muddled U.S. thinking about the intricacies of human migration.... Terrible cases have emerged involving trafficked immigrant laborers trapped in sweatshop industries ranging from garment manufacturing to farming and poultry processing. Other cases involve domestic workers kept as virtual indentured servants...."[3]

Faced with such facts and figures, Americans can no longer take for granted the sanctity of the minimum wage, their entitlement to premium pay or compensatory time off for hours worked in excess of 40 per week, or that child and/or "sweated" labor is an historical artifact to be experienced only in the display cases of the Smithsonian Institution's Museum of American History. To the contrary, a thorough understanding and appreciation of the FLSA have assumed new urgency in the new millennium.

Background of the FLSA

In 1931, Congress passed the Davis-Bacon Act, which provides that contractors working on government construction projects must pay the prevailing wage rates in the geographic area, as determined by the secretary of labor. The Davis-Bacon Act is still in force.

The federal government attempted the general regulation of wages and hours through the National Industrial Recovery Act (NIRA). NIRA, passed in 1933, was an attempt to improve general conditions during the Great Depression. NIRA provided for the development of "codes of fair competition" for various industries. The codes, to be developed by trade associations within each industry, would specify the minimum wages to be paid, the maximum hours to be worked, and limitations on child labor. When approved by the president, the codes would have the force of law. The Supreme Court held that the NIRA was an unconstitutional delegation of congressional power in the 1935 case of *Schecter Poultry Corp. v. U.S.*[4]

In 1936, the Walsh-Healy Act was passed. Like the Davis-Bacon Act, it regulates working conditions for government contractors. The Walsh-Healy Act sets minimum standards for wages for contractors providing at least $10,000 worth of goods to the federal government. It also requires that hours worked in excess of forty per week be paid at time-and-a half the regular rate of pay. The Walsh-Healy Act, like Davis-Bacon, is also still in force.

In 1937, the Supreme Court was presented with a case that challenged the legality of a Washington state law that set a minimum wage for women. In several prior cases, the court had held minimum wage laws to be unconstitutional, as it had done with the NIRA. Though the *West Coast Hotel* case is now sixty-five years old, the principles it enunciates are as pertinent to the body of employment law as they ever were.

[3]Anthony M. DeStefano, *The War on Human Trafficking* (New Brunswick, NJ: Rutgers University Press 2007), p. xxi.

[4]295 U.S. 495 (1935).

case 22.1 »

WEST COAST HOTEL CO. v. PARRISH

300 U.S. 379 (1937)

Facts: This case questioned of the constitutionality of a minimum wage law of the State of Washington. The act, entitled "Minimum Wages for Women," authorized the fixing of minimum wages for women and minors. It provided:

> SECTION 1. The welfare of the State of Washington demands that women and minors be protected from conditions of labor which have a pernicious effect on their health and morals. The State of Washington, therefore, exercising herein its police and sovereign power declares that inadequate wages and unsanitary conditions of labor exert such pernicious effect.
>
> SEC. 2. It shall be unlawful to employ women or minors in any industry or occupation within the State of Washington under conditions of labor detrimental to their health or morals; and it shall be unlawful to employ women workers in any industry within the State of Washington at wages which are not adequate for their maintenance.
>
> SEC. 3. There is hereby created a commission to be known as the "Industrial Welfare Commission" for the State of Washington, to establish such standards of wages and conditions of labor for women and minors employed within the State of Washington, as shall be held hereunder to be reasonable and not detrimental to health and morals, and which shall be sufficient for the decent maintenance of women.

The appellant was in the hotel business. The appellee Elsie Parrish was employed as a chambermaid and (with her husband) brought this suit to recover the difference between the wages paid her and the minimum wage fixed pursuant to the state law. The minimum wage was $14.50 per week of 48 hours. The appellant challenged the act as repugnant to the due process clause of the Fourteenth Amendment of the Constitution of the United States. The Supreme Court of the State, reversing the trial court, sustained the statute and directed judgment for the plaintiffs. West Coast Hotel appealed to the U.S. Supreme Court.

Issue: In reviewing the case, the Court was required to revisit one of its long-standing precedents, *Adkins v. Children's Hospital*,[1] in which New York's minimum wage for women had been struck down, and ask whether this case was wrongly decided and therefore ought to be overruled.

Decision: The Court explained that the principle which must control its decision was the due process clause of the Fourteenth Amendment, which in effect applies the analogous due process clause of the Fifth Amendment (which limits the federal government) to the states. The due process violation alleged by those attacking minimum wage regulations for women was deprivation of freedom of contract. "What is this freedom?" the Court inquired. The Constitution does not speak of freedom of contract. It speaks of liberty and prohibits the deprivation of liberty without due process of law. In prohibiting that deprivation, the Constitution does not recognize an absolute and uncontrollable liberty. Liberty under the Constitution is subject to the restraints of due process, just as the states themselves are subject to the due process limitation on its legislation. State regulation of private enterprise, if it is reasonable in relation to its subject matter, and is adopted in the interests of the community, meets the due process standard.

The Court then went on to ask, rhetorically, "What can be closer to the public interest than the health of women and their protection from unscrupulous and overreaching employers?" The answer was that the protection of women is a legitimate goal of the exercise of state power. The legislature of the state was clearly entitled to consider the situation of women in employment, the fact that they are in the class receiving the least pay, that their bargaining power is relatively weak, and that they are the ready victims of those who would take advantage of their necessitous circumstances. The legislature then was entitled to adopt measures to reduce the evils of the "sweating system," the exploiting of workers at wages so low as to be insufficient to meet the bare cost of living, thus making their very helplessness the occasion of a most injurious competition. The legislature had the right to consider that its minimum wage requirements would be an important aid in carrying out its policy of protection.

Perhaps feeling that such a "radical" (in the eyes of conservatives) decision required a "belt and suspenders," the

---

[1] 261 U.S. 525 (1923).

majority added an additional "compelling consideration," which they said recent economic experience (i.e., the Great Depression) had brought into a strong light. The exploitation of a class of workers who are in an unequal position with respect to bargaining power and are thus relatively defenseless against the denial of a living wage is not only detrimental to their health and well-being but casts a direct burden for their support upon the community. What these workers lose in wages the taxpayers were called upon to pay through public assistance (at that time called "the dole").

The majority opinion ended by overruling an earlier case that had held that minimum wage laws violated the due process clauses and therefore were unconstitutional. "Our conclusion is that the case of *Adkins v. Children's Hospital*, should be, and it is, overruled. The judgment of the Supreme Court of the State of Washington is Affirmed."

Origin and Purpose of the Fair Labor Standards Act

The *Schecter Poultry* decision and the *West Coast Hotel* case were the main factors behind the FLSA. The *Schecter* case, which struck down the National Industrial Recovery Act, forced the federal government to attempt direct regulation of hours and wages in general. The *West Coast Hotel* case demonstrated that some regulation of working conditions was viewed by the Supreme Court as a valid exercise of government power.

After the *West Coast Hotel* decision, President Roosevelt told Congress, "All but the hopelessly reactionary will agree that to conserve our primary resources of manpower, Government must have some control over maximum hours, minimum wages, the evil of child labor, and the exploitation of unorganized labor."

The FLSA was passed by Congress and signed into law on June 25, 1938. The Supreme Court held the FLSA to be constitutional in the 1941 case of *U.S. v. Darby Lumber Co.*[5] The FLSA, as amended over the years, continues in force today. It is the essential, although unglamorous, foundation for more recent federal regulation of working conditions through OSHA, ERISA, and even ADEA. The FLSA deals with four areas: minimum wages, overtime pay provisions, child labor, and equal pay for equal work. (The Equal Pay Act is an amendment to the FLSA. See Chapter 7 for a discussion of the provisions of the Equal Pay Act.)

Coverage

The FLSA, as amended, provides for three bases of coverage. Employees who are engaged in interstate commerce, including both import and export, are covered. In addition, employees who are engaged in the production of goods for interstate commerce are subject to the FLSA. The "production" of goods includes "any closely related process or occupation directly essential" to the production of goods for interstate commerce. Finally, all employees employed in an "enterprise engaged in" interstate commerce are subject to the FLSA, regardless of the relationship of their duties to commerce or the production of goods for commerce. This basis, the "enterprise" test, is subject to minimum dollar-volume limits for certain types of businesses. Employees of small employers would have to qualify for FLSA coverage under one of the other two bases of coverage. Employers and employees not covered by FLSA are

[5]312 U.S. 100.

generally subject to state laws, similar to the FLSA, which regulate minimum wages and maximum hours of work.

In 1966, the FLSA was extended to cover some federal employees and to include state and local hospitals and educational institutions. In 1974, FLSA coverage was extended to most federal employees, to state and local government employees, and to private household domestic workers.

The Congressional Accountability Act of 1995[6] extended the coverage of Fair Labor Standards Act to the employees of the House of Representatives, the Senate, the Capitol Guide Service, the Capitol Police, the Congressional Budget Office, the Office of the Architect of the Capitol, the Office of the Attending Physician, and the Office of Technology Assessment.

The extension of FLSA coverage to state and local government employees spawned a controversy under provisions of the U.S. Constitution. In the 1976 decision of *National League of Cities v. Usery*,[7] the Supreme Court held that federal regulation of the working conditions of state and local government employees infringed upon state sovereignty. The question was addressed again, in 1985, by the Supreme Court in *Garcia v. San Antonio Metropolitan Transit Authority*,[8] which overruled *National League of Cities*, stating, "we perceive nothing in the overtime and minimum-wage requirements of the FLSA … that is destructive of state sovereignty or violative of any constitutional provision." One event that helped persuade the court to overrule *National League of Cities* a mere nine years after it was decided was an intervening congressional amendment of the FLSA permitting states and municipalities to provide their nonexempt employees with compensatory time off in lieu of overtime pay.

This FLSA amendment generated even more litigation. The Supreme Court felt compelled to speak yet again on this contentious problem of federal regulation of public employers' wage and hour obligations. This time, the Justices were asked to determine whether a public employer, faced with a potential obligation to pay off accrued compensatory time in cash could force its employees to take time off.

case 22.2 » Christensen v. Harris County

120 S. Ct. 1655 (2000)

Thomas, Justice

Under the Fair Labor Standards Act of 1938 (FLSA), States and their political subdivisions may compensate their employees for overtime by granting them compensatory time or "comp time," which entitles them to take time off work with full pay. If the employees do not use their accumulated compensatory time, the employer is obligated to pay cash compensation under certain circumstances. Fearing the fiscal consequences of having to pay for accrued compensatory time, Harris County adopted a policy requiring its employees to schedule time off in order to reduce the amount of accrued compensatory time. Employees of the Harris County Sheriff's Department sued, claiming that the FLSA prohibits such a policy. The Court of Appeals rejected their claim. Finding that nothing in the FLSA or its implementing regulations prohibits an employer from compelling the use of compensatory time, we affirm.

---

[6]Pub. L. 104-1, 109 Stat. 3 (January 23, 1995).

[7]426 U.S. 833.

[8]469 U.S. 528.

I

A

The FLSA generally provides that hourly employees who work in excess of 40 hours per week must be compensated for the excess hours at a rate not less than 1½ times their regular hourly wage. Although this requirement did not initially apply to public-sector employers, Congress amended the FLSA to subject States and their political subdivisions to its constraints, at first on a limited basis, and then more broadly. States and their political subdivisions, however, did not feel the full force of this latter extension until our decision in *Garcia v. San Antonio Metropolitan Transit Authority*, 426 U.S. 833, which overruled our holding in *National League of Cities v. Usery*, 426 U.S. 833, that the FLSA could not constitutionally restrain traditional governmental functions.

In the months following Garcia, Congress acted to mitigate the effects of applying the FLSA to States and their political subdivisions, passing the Fair Labor Standards Amendments of 1985. Those amendments permit States and their political subdivisions to compensate employees for overtime by granting them compensatory time at a rate of 1½ hours for every hour worked. To provide this form of compensation, the employer must arrive at an agreement or understanding with employees that compensatory time will be granted instead of cash compensation.

The FLSA expressly regulates some aspects of accrual and preservation of compensatory time. For example, the FLSA provides that an employer must honor an employee's request to use compensatory time within a "reasonable period" of time following the request, so long as the use of the compensatory time would not "unduly disrupt" the employer's operations. The FLSA also caps the number of compensatory time hours that an employee may accrue. After an employee reaches that maximum, the employer must pay cash compensation for additional overtime hours worked. In addition, the FLSA permits the employer at any time to cancel or "cash out" accrued compensatory time hours by paying the employee cash compensation for unused compensatory time. And the FLSA entitles the employee to cash payment for any accrued compensatory time remaining upon the termination of employment.

B

Petitioners are 127 deputy sheriffs employed by respondents Harris County, Texas, and its sheriff, Tommy B. Thomas (collectively, Harris County). It is undisputed that each of the petitioners individually agreed to accept compensatory time, in lieu of cash, as compensation for overtime.

As petitioners accumulated compensatory time, Harris County became concerned that it lacked the resources to pay monetary compensation to employees who worked overtime after reaching the statutory cap on compensatory time accrual and to employees who left their jobs with sizable reserves of accrued time. As a result, the county began looking for a way to reduce accumulated compensatory time. It wrote to the United States Department of Labor's Wage and Hour Division, asking "whether the Sheriff may schedule non-exempt employees to use or take compensatory time."

The Acting Administrator of the Division replied:

> "[I]t is our position that a public employer may schedule its nonexempt employees to use their accrued FLSA compensatory time as directed if the prior agreement specifically provides such a provision....
>
> "Absent such an agreement, it is our position that neither the statute nor the regulations permit an employer to require an employee to use accrued compensatory time." Opinion Letter from Dept. of Labor, Wage and Hour Div. (Sept. 14, 1992), 1992 WL 845100 (Opinion Letter).

After receiving the letter, Harris County implemented a policy under which the employees' supervisor sets a maximum number of compensatory hours that may be accumulated. When an employee's stock of hours approaches that maximum, the employee is advised of the maximum and is asked to take steps to reduce accumulated compensatory time. If the employee does not do so voluntarily, a supervisor may order the employee to use his compensatory time at specified times.

Petitioners sued, claiming that the county's policy violates the FLSA because §207(o)(5)—which requires that an employer reasonably accommodate employee requests to use compensatory time—provides the exclusive means of utilizing accrued time in the absence of an agreement or understanding permitting some other method. The District Court agreed, granting summary judgment for petitioners and entering a declaratory judgment that the county's policy violated the FLSA. The Court of Appeals for the Fifth Circuit reversed, holding that the FLSA did not speak to the issue and thus did not prohibit the county from implementing its compensatory time policy.

II

Both parties, and the United States as *amicus curiae*, concede that nothing in the FLSA expressly prohibits a State or subdivision thereof from compelling employees to utilize accrued compensatory time. Petitioners and the United States, however, contend that the FLSA implicitly prohibits such a practice in the absence of an agreement or understanding authorizing compelled use.

Title 29 U.S.C. §207(o)(5) provides:

> An employee ...
> (A) who has accrued compensatory time off ..., and
>
> (B) who has requested the use of such compensatory time, shall be permitted by the employee's employer to use such time within a reasonable period after making the request if the use of the compensatory time does not unduly disrupt the operations of the public agency.

Petitioners and the United States rely upon the canon *expressio unius est exclusio alterius*, contending that the express grant of control to employees to use compensatory time, subject to the limitation regarding undue disruptions of workplace operations, implies that all other methods of spending compensatory time are precluded.

We find this reading unpersuasive. We accept the proposition that "[w]hen a statute limits a thing to be done in a particular mode, it includes a negative of any other mode." But that canon does not resolve this case in petitioners' favor. The "thing to be done" as defined by §207(o)(5) is not the expenditure of compensatory time, as petitioners would have it. Instead, §207(o)(5) is more properly read as a minimal guarantee that an employee will be able to make some use of compensatory time when he requests to use it. As such, the proper *expressio unius* inference is that an employer may not, at least in the absence of an agreement, deny an employee's request to use compensatory time for a reason other than that provided in §207(o)(5). The canon's application simply does not prohibit an employer from telling an employee to take the benefits of compensatory time by scheduling time off work with full pay.

In other words, viewed in the context of the overall statutory scheme, §207(o)(5) is better read not as setting forth the exclusive method by which compensatory time can be used, but as setting up a safeguard to ensure that an employee will receive timely compensation for working overtime. Section 207(o)(5) guarantees that, at the very minimum, an employee will get to use his compensatory time (i.e., take time off work with full pay) unless doing so would disrupt the employer's operations. And it is precisely this concern over ensuring that employees can timely "liquidate" compensatory time that the Secretary of Labor identified in her own regulations governing §207(o)(5):

> "Compensatory time cannot be used as a means to avoid statutory overtime compensation. An employee has the right to use compensatory time earned and must not be coerced to accept more compensatory time than an employer can realistically and in good faith expect to be able to grant within a reasonable period of his or her making a request for use of such time."

At bottom, we think the better reading of §207(o)(5) is that it imposes a restriction upon an employer's efforts to prohibit the use of compensatory time when employees request to do so; that provision says nothing about restricting an employer's efforts to require employees to use compensatory time. Because the statute is silent on this issue and because Harris County's policy is entirely compatible with §207(o)(5), petitioners cannot prove that Harris County has violated §207.

Our interpretation of §207(o)(5)—one that does not prohibit employers from forcing employees to use compensatory time—finds support in two other features of the FLSA. First, employers remain free under the FLSA to decrease the number of hours that employees work. An employer may tell the employee to take off an afternoon, a day, or even an entire week. Thus, under the FLSA an employer is free to require an employee to take time off work, and an employer is also free to use the money it would have paid in wages to cash out accrued compensatory time. The compelled use of compensatory time challenged in this case merely involves doing both of these steps at once. It would make little sense to interpret §207(o)(5) to make the combination of the two steps unlawful when each independently is lawful.

III

In an attempt to avoid the conclusion that the FLSA does not prohibit compelled use of compensatory time, petitioners and the United States contend that we should defer to the Department of Labor's opinion letter, which takes the position that an employer may compel the use of compensatory time only if the employee has agreed in advance to such a practice. [A] court must give effect to an agency's regulation containing a reasonable interpretation of an ambiguous statute.

Here, however, we confront an interpretation contained in an opinion letter, not one arrived at after, for example, a formal adjudication or notice-and-comment rulemaking. Interpretations such as those in opinion letters—like interpretations contained in policy statements, agency manuals, and enforcement guidelines, all of which lack the force of law—do not warrant … deference. Instead, interpretations contained in formats such as opinion letters are "entitled to respect" … but only to the extent that those interpretations have the "power to persuade." As explained above, we find unpersuasive the agency's interpretation of the statute at issue in this case.

Of course, the framework of deference … does apply to an agency interpretation contained in a regulation. But in this case the Department of Labor's regulation does not address the issue of compelled compensatory time. The regulation provides only that "[t]he agreement or understanding [between the employer and employee] may include other provisions governing the preservation, use, or cashing out of compensatory time so long as these provisions are consistent with [§207 (o)]." Nothing in the regulation even arguably requires that an employer's compelled use policy must be included in an agreement. The text of the regulation itself indicates that its command is permissive, not mandatory.

…

As we have noted, no relevant statutory provision expressly or implicitly prohibits Harris County from pursuing its policy of forcing employees to utilize their compensatory time. In its opinion letter siding with the petitioners, the Department of Labor opined that "it is our position that neither the statute nor the regulations permit an employer to require an employee to use accrued compensatory time." Opinion Letter. But this view is exactly backwards. Unless the FLSA prohibits respondents from adopting its policy, petitioners cannot show that Harris County has violated the FLSA. And the FLSA contains no such prohibition. The judgment of the Court of Appeals is affirmed.

It is so ordered.

Case Questions

1. Why do you suppose the FLSA amendment, permitting states and municipalities to give their employees compensatory time off in lieu of paying overtime pay, helped persuade the Supreme Court that the FLSA unconstitutionally infringed upon state sovereignty? How does this amendment relate to the age-old constitutional principle that "the power to tax is the power to destroy"?
2. Explain the reasoning as to why the FLSA does not forbid public employers from forcing their employees to take compensatory time off, even when those employees would prefer not to do so.
3. Why should a public employee mind being ordered to take some time off?
4. Suppose that Harris County had lost this case. Could the county, in order to prevent its employees from accumulating more compensatory time, lay them off? If so, would this in effect force such employees to fall back on their accumulated comp time anyway?
5. If such employees were represented by a labor union, what should the union's position appropriately be with respect to this controversy? In light of the court's ruling, what provisions might that union try to negotiate into the relevant collective bargaining agreement to provide its members with as much discretion in their use of comp time as legally possible?

«

Concept *Summary* » 22.1

Background and Jurisdiction of the FLSA

- New Deal legislation, enacted after Supreme Court reversed its position on the constitutionality of minimum wage laws
- Remains a vital part of U.S. employment and labor law system in light of human trafficking and sweat-shop persistence in 21st century
- Regulates:
    - Minimum wages
    - Overtime pay

- Child labor
- Equal pay for equal work

- Applies to public as well as private sector workers
  - But public employers may provide compensatory time in lieu of overtime pay

Minimum Wages

Minimum Wage
The wage limit, set by the government, under which an employer is not allowed to pay an employee.

The government regulation of the ***minimum wage*** is an attempt to reduce poverty and bring the earnings of workers closer to the cost of living. The setting of the minimum wage was also an attempt to maintain the purchasing power of the public to lift the country out of the economic depths of the Great Depression.

The concept of a minimum wage may seem simple: The employer may not pay employees less than the minimum wage per hour. In 1938, the minimum wage was set at $0.25 per hour, and it was raised to $0.40 per hour through the next seven years. The federal minimum wage for covered nonexempt employees is $7.25 per hour effective July 24, 2009.

Although the concept of the minimum wage seems simple, administering it may present some problems because of the wide variation in methods of compensating employees. For example, many employees are paid on an hourly basis, whereas others receive a weekly or monthly salary. Waiters and waitresses often rely on tips from customers for a large percentage of their earnings. Machinists and sewing machine operators are usually paid on a "piece-rate" basis; that is, they earn a certain amount of money for each piece completed. Salespeople usually earn a commission, which may or may not be supplemented by a base salary. Musicians may be paid a flat rate per engagement, and umpires or referees may be paid by the game.

Such atypical compensation methods are subject to regulations developed by the administrator of the Wage and Hour Division of the Department of Labor (DOL). The regulations are designed to ensure that all workers receive at least the minimum wage. If a worker is a "tipped worker"—that is, one who receives tips from customers—the employer is allowed to reduce the minimum wage paid to that worker by up to 40 percent, with the difference to be made up by tips received. The earnings of workers who are paid on a piece-rate basis must average out to at least the minimum wage; the time period over which the earnings are averaged cannot be longer than a single workweek. This means that the earnings of such an employee may be less than the minimum wage for any single hour, as long as the total earnings for the week average out to the minimum wage. Some persons being paid for the work may not even be viewed as employees at all for purposes of Fair Labor Standards Act coverage. In the following case, the state was using convict labor. Prisoners were paid a modest amount of money, which they could use to purchase minor "luxury" items.

case 22.3 »

Lockett v. Neubauer
2005 WL 3557780 (D.Kan.2005)

Plaintiff sues numerous defendants including the Kansas Department of Corrections (KDOC), the Kansas Secretary of Corrections (SOC), the Warden at EDCF, and Aramark Correctional Services, Inc., (hereinafter Aramark). Plaintiff complains that he and other inmates working for Aramark are receiving 40 to 60 cents per hour rather than minimum wage. He asserts Aramark is required by the Fair Labor Standards Act, 29 U.S.C. 201, *et seq.* (FLSA), to pay minimum wage. He alleges either Aramark pays less than required by the FLSA, or pays the proper amount to "revolving fund of KDOC/EDCF" who has then "distributed less than FLSA requires" to the inmate workers. He also claims defendants have "fixed the books" to show minimum wages are paid to inmates, he has not consented to the "keeping" of his minimum wage pay, and he is being subjected to slave labor in violation of the 13 Amendment. Plaintiff asserts defendants' denial of minimum wage is without due process and in violation of the equal protection clause. In addition to the FLSA, he cites Kansas regulations, civil rights statutes and constitutional provisions as legal authority for his claim.

As factual support, plaintiff alleges he began working for Aramark on September 11, 2002. He states that Aramark contracts with KDOC and EDCF. He also states that in 2004 his Aramark supervisor told him Aramark pays minimum wage to the EDCF/KDOC, who then pay "prison wages" to inmates. Plaintiff argues his prison employment is within the purview of the FLSA because his employment records are maintained by and in the sole possession of Aramark. He further alleges Aramark has "exclusive power" to select, hire, fire, and supervise inmates; controls schedules, duties and conditions of employment; and determines rates and method of pay. He seeks declaratory, injunctive, and monetary relief including back pay with interest.

Discussion

Since plaintiff's complaint was filed pro se, it has been held "to less stringent standards than formal pleadings drafted by lawyers."... Nevertheless, a pro se complaint, like any other, must present a claim upon which relief can be granted by the court.... For purposes of this 1915A screening, the court has accepted as true allegations of fact set forth in plaintiff's complaint.

FLSA Claim

The claims raised in the complaint are also subject to being dismissed as against all defendants in either capacity for failure to state a claim. Plaintiff was previously advised that his claims are substantially similar to those determined in this district in *Moore v. McKee*, 2003 WL 22466160 (D. Kan., Sept. 5, 2003, unpublished). The plaintiff in *Moore*, a state prisoner, brought suit against two officers of Aramark, "the corporation which provides food services at the prison," alleging they violated the FLSA, "breached a contract, and violated his constitutional rights by failing to pay him minimum wage for his services." On defendants' motion to dismiss, the district court accepted plaintiff's allegations that Aramark had contracted with KDOC to pay no less than minimum wage but to pay such wages to KDOC and not the individual inmates, and that plaintiff was being paid less than minimum wage. The court granted defendants' motion, holding that "plaintiff cannot maintain such a claim because inmates are not employees' under the FLSA." *Id* at *2 ... Plaintiff was granted time to show cause why this action should not be dismissed for the reasons stated in *Moore* and this court's show cause order. He has filed Plaintiff's Response to Show Cause. Having considered all the materials filed, the court finds as follows.

Plaintiff's claim that he is entitled to relief under the Fair Labor Standards Act is legally frivolous. The FLSA provides that "[e]very employer shall pay to each of his employees ... not less than" minimum wage.... The Act defines "employee" as "any individual employed by an employer."... The term "employer" includes "any person acting directly or indirectly in the interest of an employer in relation to an employee and includes a public agency."... The term "employ" means "to suffer or permit to work."... Over time Congress has exempted specified classes of workers from FLSA's coverage and broadened coverage of others. Prisoner laborers have never been on the exempted or covered lists.

Plaintiff argues he is an employee as defined in the FLSA, and reasons that prisoners are not among the workers expressly exempted by the statute. The plain language of the statute is too general to be helpful in this case. Neither Congress nor the United States Supreme Court has declared whether prisoner workers are covered by FLSA. Most federal district and appellate courts deciding similar cases have held the FLSA does not apply to prisoner laborers.... Cases holding that prisoner laborers were not "employees" under FLSA have generally involved inmates working within the prison for prison authorities or for private employers.... Most courts opined in dicta that prisoners are not categorically always barred from being "employees" covered by FLSA.

The rare cases where courts found the FLSA covered inmate labor involved prisoners working outside the prison directly for private employers.... Plaintiff cites these two cases as authority for his claims. However, their facts are distinguishable from plaintiff's case in that he is not working outside the prison, or directly employed by a private enterprise. Moreover, the rationales in these two cases are not as persuasive and have been called into question by later opinions in the Second, Fifth and other Circuits.

Plaintiff's exhibit of the Warden's response to his administrative grievance at EDCF provides in relevant part:

Employment in food service as a job assignment in this correctional facility does not constitute private prison based employment....

As a food service worker you were given a work assignment. That work assignment and compensation are governed by IMPP 10-109 (Inmate Work Assignments).

The reasoning in cases finding prisoner laborers not covered by FLSA is much more persuasive. First, the Thirteenth Amendment excludes convicted criminals from its prohibition of involuntary servitude, so prisoners may be required to work without any compensation.... Since there is no federal constitutional right to compensation for prisoner labor; pay is "by the grace of the state."... Second, the relationship between the KDOC and "a prisoner is far different from a traditional employer-employee relationship."... It is clear from Kansas law that the KDOC retains ultimate control over its prisoners in work release programs. The KDOC's "control" over plaintiff is far greater than an employer's and "does not stem from any remunerative relationship or bargained-for exchange of labor for consideration, but from incarceration itself."... In short, plaintiff is not in a true economic employer-employee relationship with Aramark or the KDOC, so the FLSA does not cover him....

Plaintiff contends the four factors of the economic reality test must be applied to determine his claims, and cites Watson and Carter. Under the Ninth Circuit test, a court inquired: "whether the alleged employer (1) had the power to hire and fire the employees, (2) supervised and controlled employee work schedules or conditions of employment, (3) determined the rate and method of payment, and (4) maintained employment records." *Bonnette v. California Health & Welfare Agency*, 704 F.2d 1465, 1470 (9 Cir.1983) (no longer good law). However, even those courts applying the economic reality test have generally held prisoners are not "employees" entitled to minimum wage under the FLSA.... More significantly, this district and the Tenth Circuit Court of Appeals have held that the Bonnette economic test does not apply to prisoners.... As the Seventh and Ninth Circuits reasoned, the traditional factors of the "economic reality" test "fail to capture the true nature of [most prison employment] relationship[s], for essentially they presuppose a free labor situation." *Vanskike*, 974 F.2d at 809; *see Hale*, 993 F.3d at 1394 (quoting *Vanskike*). The Seventh Circuit explained:

Prisoners are essentially taken out of the national economy upon incarceration. When they are assigned work within the prison for purposes of training and rehabilitation, they have not contracted with the government to become its employees....

Vanskike, 974 F.2d at 810.

The Ninth Circuit further explained in Hale:

[t]he case of inmate labor is different from [the] type of situation where labor is exchanged for wages in a free market. Convicted criminals do not have the right freely to sell their labor and are not protected by the Thirteenth Amendment against involuntary servitude.

Hale, 993 F.2d at 1394; *Vanskike*, 974 F.2d at 809 (Thirteenth Amendment's specific exclusion of prisoner labor supports the idea that a prisoner performing required work for the prison is actually engaged in involuntary servitude, not employment).

This court agrees with the majority of courts that the "policies underlying the FLSA ... have limited application in the separate world of prison."... Requiring the payment of minimum wage for a prisoner's work in prison would not further the fundamental goal of the FLSA to ensure workers' welfare and standard of living since a prison inmate's basic needs are met irrespective of inability to pay. The second purpose of the Act—to prevent unfair competition—is protected by other statutes, regulations and contract provisions. For example, with respect to prison-made goods, the Ashurst-Sumners Act, 18 U.S.C. §§ 1761-62, penalizes their transportation in commerce. However, governments are rationally permitted to use the fruits of prisoner labor. Plaintiff does not make goods distributed outside the prison, but is assigned to work in food service at the prison. Plaintiff is not subject to FLSA simply because non-inmates could be hired to do his job.

Case Questions

1. How did the plaintiff's status as a convict and prisoner affect the court's decision?
2. How did the impact, or lack of impact, on the larger economy affect the court's decision?
3. Might prisoner rehabilitation be improved by requiring prisons to pay FLSA minimum wages in all cases?
4. What objections might a state's taxpayers legitimately have to a state being forced to pay prisoners the minimum wage?
5. Should a prisoner's receipt of free room and board be considered by courts in such cases?

As seen in *Lockett*, another tricky issue with which the DOL and courts have wrestled is the time required for an employee to prepare to perform the job and the time required to end the day's performance. This issue has arisen, for instance:

- Where the shifts of incoming and outgoing retail clerks must effectuate a transfer of the store's cash register between their shifts;
- Where miners and factory workers must don uniforms or equipment in a locker room at the start of their shifts and perhaps shower and change at the end of their workdays.

A closely related and equally thorny issue is when time spent by an employee waiting to work or "on call" is compensable and when it is not. Both of these issues arose in the *Hiner* case.

case 22.4 »

Hiner v. Penn-Harris-Madison School Corporation

256 F. Supp. 2d 854 (N.D. Indiana 2003)

Facts: The plaintiffs were twenty bus operators employed by a school district. They filed a claim for unpaid overtime compensation pursuant to the FLSA and the Indiana Wage Statute on October 15, 2001. The drivers' typical daily schedule was as follows. Most drove two daily routes, the first, or secondary school route, delivers secondary students to and from school, while the second, or elementary school route, delivers elementary students. Both routes occurred in the morning and afternoon with some drivers driving additional mid-day routes in between their other responsibilities.

Prior to embarking on their secondary student routes, the drivers were required to conduct pretrip bus inspection. After dropping off the secondary students, they had a period of "down-time" until beginning their elementary school routes. The period of down-time varied for each driver, ranging anywhere from twelve minutes to one hour. Under their collective bargaining agreement, they were paid for their down-time in addition to a paid morning break which was included as part of their morning route. Following their morning breaks/down-time, the drivers began picking up elementary school students. The time at which the drivers began their elementary routes varies depending on individual elementary schools' start times. Following their elementary routes, the drivers had another period of down-time until some drivers began their mid-day routes.

As in the morning, they picked up secondary students first, conducted their routes, and returned to the elementary schools for their elementary routes. Their pay began ten minutes prior to student dismissal for the first student pick-up and ended with the last student drop-off. Their employment agreement only paid them from their first morning pick-up until their final afternoon drop-off. They were not compensated for the time it took them to drive to their first morning pick-up and from their final afternoon drop-off.

Issue: Whether the drivers' daily bus inspections and all pre- and postroute drive time should be included as hours worked for purposes of overtime compensation under the FLSA.

Decision: The court began by referring to a federal statute, known as the Portal-to-Portal Act, which eliminates from minimum wage and overtime a lot of preliminary and after-shift activities that do not involve any of the principal work activities from "hours worked"—such as commuting to and from work.

By contrast, two examples of what is meant by an integral part of the principal activity are:

> (1) in connection with the operation of a lathe, an employee will frequently, at the commencement of the workday, oil, grease, or clean the machine, or install a new cutting tool;
>
> (2) in the case of a garment worker in a textile mill, who is required to report 30 minutes before other employees report to commence their principal activities, and who during such 30 minutes distributes clothing or parts of clothing at the workbenches of other employees and gets machines in readiness for operation by other employees.

Such activities are an integral part of the principal activity, and are subject to the FLSA's minimum wage and overtime requirements.

In this case, the defendant conceded that the mandatory inspections, as well as the plaintiffs' pre- and postroute driving time, constituted hours worked under the FLSA. The plaintiffs' motion for partial summary judgment therefore was granted in part. But because the Court had insufficient evidence to determine the length of each individual plaintiff's pre- and postroute drive time, as well as the duration of an individual plaintiff's inspections, the federal judge felt unable to grant or deny the plaintiffs' motion for partial summary judgment as to each individual plaintiff's monetary entitlement.

The judge then turned to the waiting-time aspects of the case. In determining whether on-call time is compensable, the key question is whether the time is spent predominantly for the employer's benefit or primarily for the benefit of the employee. The court noted that an individual plaintiff's compensated down-time is not considered working time under the FLSA in cases where an individual employee's down-time exceeds twenty minutes and the employee is not required to perform services for his/her, but is instead free to use his/her down-time for personal pursuits.

Here again, the judge refused to grant the summary judgment in full, because, while the guiding legal principle was clear, the facts regarding each individual plaintiff remained to be established on a case-by-case basis. In other words, a trial probably was the most efficient way to hear from each plaintiff on this issue.

«

Concept *Summary* » 22.2

MINIMUM WAGE

- The minimum wage is the lowest amount that an employer may pay per hour to employees who are paid by the hour
- This minimum has risen steadily since the FLSA was first enacted and reached $7.25 per hour on July 24, 2009
- Issues regarding eligibility for minimum wages include:
  - Whether the workers actually are "employees" under the FLSA (as with incarcerated prisoners)
  - Whether waiting and down time are compensable hours of work

Overtime Pay

Overtime Pay
Employees covered by the FLSA are entitled to overtime pay, at one-and-a-half times their regular pay rate, for hours worked in excess of forty hours per workweek.

Workweek
A term the FLSA uses to signify seven consecutive days; the law does not require that the workweek start or end on any particular day of the calendar week.

In addition to being entitled to earn the minimum wage, employees covered by the FLSA are entitled to ***overtime pay*** at one-and-a-half times their regular pay rate, for hours worked in excess of forty hours per ***workweek***.

The term workweek has special significance under the FLSA. It is a "term of art" with a fairly precise meaning. A workweek consists of seven consecutive days, but the law does not require that the workweek start or end on any particular day of the calendar week. For instance, a workweek may run from Tuesday to Monday or from Friday to Thursday. The starting day of the workweek may be changed from time to time, provided that the purpose of the change is not to avoid the requirements of the law (such as avoiding the payment of overtime to a group of workers).

As with the minimum wage, regulations have been developed to compute the hourly wages of workers paid by commission, piece-rate, and so forth for the purpose of calculating overtime pay. A more difficult question is deciding whether certain hours, not strictly part of working hours, should be included in working time for the calculation of wages and overtime. The Portal to Portal Act of 1947, which amended the FLSA, provides that preliminary or postwork activities are to be included in compensable time only if they are called for under contract or industry custom or practice.

ethical DILEMMA

Convenience Store Clerk's Conundrum

College sophomore Suzy Smart works part-time in the Handi Mart convenience store near campus. The manager at Handi Mart requires that each clerk arrive fifteen minutes prior to the start of the shift so that the clerk going off duty can review the sales figures and cash status with the replacement before leaving. The clerk going off duty punches her timecard after this review, but the oncoming clerk is not allowed to clock in until the review is completed and she has agreed that the sales and cash figures are accurate. Sometimes this exercise takes more than fifteen minutes; no matter how long it takes, the clerk coming on duty may not punch her timecard and start earning wages until the process is completed.

This semester, Suzy is taking a course on labor and employment law. After reading the text chapter concerning minimum wage and overtime rules under the FLSA, she realizes that the store manager is violating the law by not allowing the oncoming clerk to punch the time clock as soon as she arrives. She brings this up with the store manager.

The store manager tells Suzy that he is not allowed by the parent corporation of Handi Mart to compensate two clerks for the same period of time, no matter how brief, because this is classified by the corporation as a "single coverage" store. Furthermore, he adds ominously, if Suzy complains to the Wage and Hour Division of the U.S. DOL, he probably will be forced by the company to lay off Suzy and the other part-timers and cover the evening shifts himself. "You may get everyone a few dollars in back pay," he adds, "but you'll also cost everybody their jobs. Remember, some of your co-workers are single parents who need this extra income to make ends meet." Should Suzy file a minimum wage complaint with the U.S. DOL?

Exemptions from Overtime and Minimum Wage Provisions

Exempt Employees
Employees whose hours of work and compensation are not stipulated by the FLSA.

Not all employees under the FLSA are entitled to overtime pay or subject to the minimum wage. The FLSA sets out four general categories of employees, who are exempt from the minimum wage and overtime requirements of the statute. Such ***exempt employees*** include: executives, administrators, professionals, and outside salespeople.

Executive Employees

The regulations under the FLSA provide the following test:

(1) Employee is compensated on a salary basis at a rate of not less than $455 per week (or $380 per week, if employed in American Samoa by an employer other than the Federal Government), exclusive of board, lodging, or other facilities;

(2) Her/his primary duty is management of the enterprise in which the employee is employed or of a customarily recognized department or subdivision thereof;

(3) S/he customarily and regularly directs the work of two or more other employees; and

(4) S/he has the authority to hire or fire other employees or to make suggestions and recommendations as to the hiring, firing, advancement, promotion or any other change of status of other employees are given particular weight.[9]

Administrative Employees

The regulations under the FLSA set out the following test:

(1) Employee is compensated on a salary or fee basis at a rate of not less than $455 per week (or $380 per week, if employed in American Samoa by an employer other than the Federal Government), exclusive of board, lodging, or other facilities;

(2) Her/his primary duty is the performance of office or non-manual work directly related to the management or general business operations of the employer or the employer's customers; and

(3) Her/his primary duty includes the exercise of discretion and independent judgment with respect to matters of significance.[10]

Professional Employees

Employees in bona fide professional positions are exempted from the FLSA's overtime and minimum wage provisions if they meet the following test:

(1) Employee is compensated on a salary or fee basis at a rate of not less than $455 per week (or $380 per week, if employed in American Samoa by an employer other than the Federal Government), exclusive of board, lodging, or other facilities; and

(2) Her/his primary duty is the performance of work:

    (a) Requiring knowledge of an advanced type in a field of science or learning customarily acquired by a prolonged course of specialized intellectual instruction; or

    (b) Requiring invention, imagination, originality, or talent in a recognized field of artistic or creative endeavor.[11]

Outside Salespeople

The regulations under the FLSA exempt outside salespeople from both the overtime and minimum wage provisions. To be exempt, the following requirements must be met:

(1) Employee's primary duty is:

    (a) making sales within the meaning of section 3(k) of the Act, or

    (b) obtaining orders or contracts for services or for the use of facilities for which a consideration will be paid by the client or customer; and

---

[9]http://www.dol.gov/dol/allcfr/ESA/Title_29/Part_541/29CFR541.100.htm

[10]http://www.dol.gov/dol/allcfr/ESA/Title_29/Part_541/29CFR541.200.htm

[11]http://www.dol.gov/dol/allcfr/ESA/Title_29/Part_541/29CFR541.300.htm

(2) S/he is customarily and regularly engaged away from the employer's place or places of business in performing such primary duty.

   (a) The term "primary duty" is defined at Section 541.700. In determining the primary duty of an outside sales employee, work performed incidental to and in conjunction with the employee's own outside sales or solicitations, including incidental deliveries and collections, shall be regarded as exempt outside sales work. Other work that furthers the employee's sales efforts also shall be regarded as exempt work including, for example, writing sales reports, updating or revising the employee's sales or display catalogue, planning itineraries and attending sales conferences.

   (b) The requirements of subpart G (salary requirements) of this part do not apply to the outside sales employees described in this section.[12]

An employer, which wants to pay a category of employees a salary and treat them as falling outside the minimum wage and overtime rules, cannot end its inquiry with the FLSA, however. When Congress determines that the federal government should regulate some aspect of our lives, it also decides whether the new federal statute will preempt the field, or whether (alternatively) the fifty states may continue to play a role. In such enterprises as TV and radio broadcasting and airline travel, Uncle Sam has taken over regulating almost all activities. In others, such as ERISA (see Chapter 21), Congress has claimed the largest part of pension and benefits regulation, leaving only insurance and banking to state laws. But in some important areas of employment law, such as job discrimination (see Chapters 6–10), Congress actually has encouraged the states to supplement federal efforts with their own laws. The same is true for the FLSA. The states may supplement the federal wage and hours laws and regulations, provided state law expands the rights accorded to workers by the federal scheme.

Sometimes state involvement in wage and hour issues can make the law quite confusing. For instance, what if workers from New Mexico and Arizona are sent to do a job in California? Which law should apply, if the federal law and the laws of the several states provide differing rights with respect to overtime pay? This issue troubled the U.S. Court of Appeals for the Ninth Circuit in 2008 and 2009. In 2008, the court awarded overtime pay to such out-of-state workers.[13] Then on February 17, 2009, the court thought better of its decision, withdrew it, and certified the case to the California Supreme Court for its opinion. As one law firm observed in its newsletter, "[T]he court had held in the now-withdrawn opinion that non-California residents who perform work in California are entitled to overtime pay under the California Labor Code—regardless of the overtime laws in their home states—and may also assert claims under California's unfair competition law, Business and Professions Code Section 17200. The court based this conclusion, in part, on a determination that California had a sufficient interest in protecting employees working within its borders, even if these employees are not residents of California.

"In conjunction with the withdrawal of this decision, the Ninth Circuit has sought guidance from the California Supreme Court on three questions central to the case:

(1) Do the California Labor Code's overtime provisions apply to out-of-state employees working overtime in California for a California-based employer in the circumstances of this case?

---

[12]http://www.dol.gov/dol/allcfr/ESA/Title_29/Part_541/29CFR541.500.htm

[13]Sullivan *v. Oracle Corporation*, 547 F.3d 1177 (9th Cir. 2008).

(2) Does California's Business and Professions Code Section 17200 apply to the overtime work described in question one?

(3) Does California's Business and Professions Code Section 17200 apply to out-of-state employees performing overtime work outside California for a California-based employer where the employer violates the overtime provisions of the federal Fair Labor Standards Act (which, unlike the California Labor Code, does not require overtime pay for more than eight hours worked in a day, but only for more than 40 hours worked in a week)?

"The Ninth Circuit's request reflects the uncertainty of California law."[14]

Concept *Summary* » 22.3

Overtime Pay

- Employees who are paid by the hour generally are entitled to one-and-a-half times their hourly rates for work in excess of forty hours in a single workweek
- Exemptions from the minimum wage and overtime roles:
  - Salaried employees who earn at least the minimum weekly salary specified by the U.S. Department of Labor and who are bona fide executives, administrators or professionals
  - Outside sales people, who are paid mainly by commissions
- The FLSA allows the states to regulate wages and hours, including overtime provisions, provided the state rules are more generous to employees than the federal law
- The blend of federal and state jurisdiction over wage and hour matters, such as overtime entitlements, can create confusing legal issues

Limitations on Child Labor

The problems of child labor are graphically demonstrated by photographs from the late 19th and early 20th centuries showing children who had spent their youth toiling in coal mines or factories. The children, often immigrants, were subjected to the same hazardous conditions and occupational diseases as were their parents. They received little or no formal education. Their wages were usually meager and, as a result, drove down the wages of adult workers who held the same, or similar, jobs.

[14]http://www.seyfarth.com/index.cfm/fuseaction/publications.publications_detail/object_id/737082be-721d-43ac-8a40-cd025b6fc61e/

The social and economic problems of child labor were recognized by government; many states passed legislation attempting to limit child labor. Those early laws were restricted in their effectiveness, though, and the number of children employed continued to rise until about 1910. Congress made several attempts to enact federal limitations on child labor. In 1916, a law prohibiting the shipment in interstate commerce of goods produced by factories or mines employing child labor was passed. The Supreme Court, however, in the 1918 case of *Hammer v. Dagenhart*,[15] held that the law was unconstitutional because it exceeded the limited power granted to the federal government under the commerce clause of the Constitution.

National Industrial Recovery Act (NIRA) An act primarily designed to regulate and revitalize industry; promoted fair trade practices.

The ***National Industrial Recovery Act (NIRA)*** provided that the codes of fair competition for each industry could limit child labor, but in 1935, the NIRA was held unconstitutional by the Supreme Court in *Schecter Poultry v. U.S.* In 1936, the Walsh-Healy Act prohibited contractors under government contracts from using child labor to produce, manufacture, or furnish materials for the contract. The Fair Labor Standards Act of 1938 at last provided for general federal regulation of child labor.

While the FLSA's prohibitions and limitations on child labor are by and large taken for granted in the United States, we now all live and compete in a global marketplace. Many nations either do not share American wage and hour standards or do not enforce such laws, even if they are "on the books." Furthermore, if such a country fails to require the payment of a living wage, it usually also fails to enforce health and safety standards, and probably persecutes labor leaders who are attempting to force reforms by organizing the exploited workers. The following "Working Law" section presents the testimony of a Colombian labor leader concerning the origin of all those lovely flowers that we see for sale on thousands of street corners in our major cities. Since her testimony summarizes a plethora of inter-related abuses, it could as readily appear in one of several other chapters of this textbook. We offer it here by way of sharp contrast to the complex safety net of U.S. wage and hour rules and regulations. By doing so, we hope to suggest how fragile American workers' seemingly well-entrenched rights really are.

The WORKING Law

The Straight Story About Those Awful Overseas Sweatshops

Written Testimony Submitted by

Beatriz Fuentes, President
Sintrasplendor union at Splendor Flowers
Bogotá, Colombia

Before the
Committee on Commerce, Science, and Transportation,
United States Senate

February 14, 2007

[15] 247 U.S. 1.

Introduction

I am the president of the Sintrasplendor union, which was founded in November 2004 at the Splendor Flowers plantation in Colombia, a farm belonging to the multinational Dole. I have more than ten years of experience working in the Colombian cut flower industry. For Valentine's Day, the day when more Americans buy cut flowers from Colombia than any other day of the year, I have traveled to the U.S. to share my testimony about the poor working conditions that exist in many Colombian flower plantations, and which I have experienced firsthand over the past decade.

My coworkers and I have witnessed the limitations of Colombian labor law enforcement, and voluntary initiatives in addressing these serious labor rights violations. New, enforceable strategies are needed to effectively guarantee workers' rights in this industry.

Occupational Health and Safety

Flower workers are inadequately protected against occupational hazards. In the greenhouses, we are exposed on a daily basis to highly toxic chemicals, without sufficient protection. We are also exposed to extreme temperatures, and we work long hours doing repetitive tasks. These conditions cause serious health problems including allergies, respiratory problems, eye problems, spinal problems, and carpal tunnel syndrome.

I have had a problem with carpal tunnel syndrome for the past five years, due to the fact that I have had to spend 8–10 hours straight cutting stems with scissors. Most workers are assigned to one job for several months at a time, frequently causing repetitive motion injuries. Currently, we must trim 300–400 flowers per hour.

On July 14, 2005, there was a tragic accident on one of the company buses on which we ride to work every day. On that day, as on most days, the bus was excessively overloaded. We had asked them to fix this problem but they hadn't done anything about it. Several workers were killed or injured. I was on this bus when the accident occurred.

Forced Pregnancy Testing

It is also common for flower plantations to require female job applicants to take a pregnancy test to demonstrate that they are not pregnant, which is illegal. Or they ask if we are planning on having more children, and if we have had an operation. The management does not do this out of concern that the pregnant women are exposed to the same toxic pesticides as all of the other workers. They do it because they don't want to pay the maternity leave or the other benefits legally due to pregnant workers.

Union Busting

Colombia is the most dangerous country in the world to be a trade union leader. Compared to other sectors, the cut flower industry fortunately has not experienced the same extreme level of trade union violence. Other forms of retaliation against unions remain all too common, however, and we hope that the violence will not escalate.

My coworkers and I founded a new independent union at Splendor Flowers, called Sintrasplendor, in November 2004. We were motivated to form a union because of the worsening conditions at Splendor. The company began assigning more and more flowerbeds to each worker, making the workload intolerable. Over the past ten years, the workload has doubled from 15–20 flowerbeds up to 30–40 flowerbeds per worker. This means more backbreaking labor for no more pay. Lately the company has been firing sick workers and old workers. They also announced that they would soon turn some jobs over to subcontractors, which means that those workers will lose the little job stability that they currently have. The company was writing up its own collective agreements and making the workers sign them, without even giving them a chance to voice their opinions. We hoped that a union would enable us to present a petition to the company, and therefore negotiate improved working conditions, guaranteed overtime pay, and salary increases.

Sintrasplendor was the first independent union to be successfully established in a Dole-owned flower company in Colombia. When Sintrasplendor received its registration from the Ministry of Social Protection, the company presented a list of objections, asking the Ministry to revoke the registration. Splendor Flowers used various forms of persecution against the independent union, including assigning extra work on days when the Sintrasplendor had planned assemblies and other union-related activities.

The company invited in another union and signed a collective bargaining agreement with them almost immediately. The agreement said that any worker who joined the company union, Sinaltraflor, would be rewarded with 40,000 pesos (approximately US$20). The company wanted the majority of workers to join Sinaltraflor, because they could then negotiate with Sinaltraflor instead of with Sintrasplendor. The company even lent one of its buses to take workers to a Sinaltraflor meeting, during working hours. Company representatives pressured workers not to join Sintrasplendor. When we distributed flyers in the plantation to explain to workers why we had formed an independent union, the company prohibited workers from reading them. According to Colombian law, it is legal to read this kind of flyer inside the workplace, during lunchtime or a break.

The Colombian government recognized our union as a legal entity in 2005. Nevertheless, the company still has not sat down to negotiate with us.

On October 12, 2006 Dole announced that it would close the Corzo farm at Splendor Flowers. We believe that the motivation behind this closure is that the company did not want to provide basic rights and decent work conditions to its workers. Clearly, we can not trust our local laws to protect our labor rights—including our right to organize—but rather we need new and enforceable international legal tools to ensure these rights.

Splendor-Corzo will officially close in mid 2007 after the company completes the necessary legal processes. Corzo is the larger of the two farms at Splendor Flowers. Dole justifies the closure of Splendor-Corzo by saying that it has "historically produced products with limited/seasonal demand and have high costs." However, in 2001, Splendor Flowers was the second most successful flower company in Colombia, reaching 19 million dollars in sales. Dole has not provided evidence that Splendor is a losing enterprise. It appears that the plantation closure is a response to the growing support for Sintrasplendor. Splendor management has been offering workers compensation to get them to resign. This past weekend, they fired over 200 workers. Of more than 2000 workers employed at this plantation in

2006, only 150 remain. We are worried that Dole will soon announce the closure of La Fragancia, the other plantation where an independent union has successfully been established.

Lack of Recourse to Labor Authorities

Colombian workers who want to file complaints about labor rights violations are often discouraged because governmental institutions like the Ministry of Labor take so long to resolve these cases. For example, in early 2005, my union filed several complaints before a labor judge, regarding occupational health problems and violations of the right to organize. Almost two years have passed and none of these cases has been resolved. Meanwhile, a month and a half ago the company filed a request with the Ministry of Labor to approve the mass firing of all workers at Splendor Flowers, so they can close the farm. The decision is expected to be released next week. Apparently, justice comes faster for companies than for workers.

Conclusion

Because of the low wages in this sector and the long working hours, I have very little time to spend with my two young children, and lack the money to give them a decent education. The realities of the flower industry have contributed to social instability and disintegration of many families in the flower-growing region of Colombia.

We need effective legal mechanisms to ensure that these companies give us safe, healthy, and decent workplaces. Thank you for allowing me to share this testimony, and I hope you take it into account in the consideration of S. 367.

Source: "Overseas Sweatshop Abuses, Their Impact on U.S. Workers, and the Need for Anti-Sweatshop Legislation," Betty Fuentes, Colombian flower plantation worker and labor activist, Wednesday, February 14, 2007.[1]

---

[1]http://commerce.senate.gov/public/index.cfm?FuseAction=Hearings.Testimony&Hearing_ID=13b987c2-7cb1-4772-9b72-481947ce2d28&Witness_ID=beca49f9-bb76-41df-813e-14540f0f6f60.

The FLSA and Child Labor

The FLSA does not prohibit all child labor; rather, it proscribes only "oppressive" child labor. The act prohibits the interstate shipment of goods from establishments employing oppressive child labor. It also prohibits oppressive child labor in any enterprise with two or more employees engaged in the production of goods for interstate commerce. The definition of "oppressive child labor" is crucial to the administration of the act. The act defines oppressive child labor by using age restrictions and identifying hazardous occupations.

Employing minors under age eighteen in any occupation identified as hazardous by the secretary of labor is prohibited. At present, a number of occupations have been identified as hazardous by the secretary of labor, including the following:

- coal mining or mining other than coal;
- occupations in or about plants manufacturing explosives or articles containing explosive components;

- occupations involving operation of motor-driven hoisting apparatus;
- logging or saw milling occupations;
- occupations involving exposure to radioactive substances;
- occupations of motor-vehicle operator or helper;
- occupations involving operation of power-driven woodworking machines;
- occupations involving operation of power-driven metalworking, forming, punching, or shearing machines;
- occupations in or about slaughtering or meatpacking plants or rendering plants;
- occupations involving the manufacture of brick, tile, or related products;
- occupations involving the operation of circular saws, handsaws, and guillotine shears;
- occupations involving wrecking, demolition, and ship-breaking.

Minors aged sixteen to eighteen may work in certain nonhazardous occupations, and minors aged fourteen to sixteen may be employed in non-manufacturing or nonmining occupations for limited hours outside school hours. Minors under age fourteen can be employed only in agriculture under specific limitations and with parental consent.

The regulations limiting work by minors aged fourteen to sixteen further specify that the minors' hours between 7 A.M. and 7 P.M. may not exceed eighteen hours per week when school is in session or forty hours per week when school is not in session; nor may they exceed three hours per day when school is in session or eight hours per day when school is not in session.

Specific exemptions from the category of oppressive child labor include the employment of:

- newspaper carriers who are engaged in delivering papers to consumers;
- minors who are hired as actors or performers in movies, radio, television, or theatrical productions; and
- minors who are employed by their parents, or persons standing in the place of parents, in occupations other than manufacturing, mining, or others identified as hazardous by the secretary of labor.

Although child labor cases have become relatively rare in recent years, the DOL strictly enforces the FLSA provision, as the following case illustrates.

case 22.5 »

CHAO V. VIDTAPE, INC

196 F. Supp. 2d 281 (E.D.N.Y. 2002)

Facts: The Secretary of Labor commenced this lawsuit on May 1, 1998, after an investigation of the labor practices of the defendants. The court held a bench trial on April 23, 2001 to May 1, 2001, and the parties gave summations on October 18, 2001. At the conclusion of the trial, the court granted a judgment in favor of the Secretary on March 29, 2002.

Wilber Amaya testified that he was fourteen years old when Vidtape hired him to pack videos and boxes using a "hand truck." At his interview, he presented his INS work permit ... which indicated that Amaya was born on September 2, 1982. Amaya worked ten hour days, six days a week, during the months when school was in session. Vidtape terminated Amaya after the Department of Labor began its investigation. The court credited his testimony.

Issue: If young Wilber's testimony is taken to be true, as it was by the judge, did the defendant's violate the FLSA's child labor restrictions?

Decision: In employing Wilber Amaya, the defendants violated the act's child labor provision. Section 212(c) provides that "no employer shall employ any oppressive child labor in commerce or in the production of goods for commerce or in any enterprise engaged in commerce or the production of goods for commerce." "Oppressive child labor" is defined as a "condition of employment under which ... any employee under the age of sixteen is employed by an employer ... in any occupation." Children between the age of 14 and 16 cannot be employed for more than three hours a day, 18 hours per week when school is in session, and 8 hours a day, 40 hours a week when school is not in session. The regulations also state that minors are not permitted to work in occupations that involve manufacturing of goods.

Although the defendants asserted as an affirmative defense that Wilber was hired at the request of a relative and that defendants were not aware that they had violated child labor law, intent or willfulness is not an element of this offense.

The defendants also violated the so-called "hot goods" provision of the law by manufacturing products in violation of the act. The "hot goods" provision in section 215(a)(1) provides that it is unlawful for any person to "transport, ... ship, ... deliver or sell in commerce ... any goods in the production of which any employee was employed" in violation of minimum wage, overtime or child labor restrictions. The remedy for violating this provision is an injunction, ordering Vidtape from continuing its illegal behavior.

Concept Summary » 22.4

CHILD LABOR

- The FLSA does not forbid all child labor
- Rather, the FLSA regulates when and how children may be employed
- The FLSA and its regulations pay particular attention to child labor in dangerous industries and involving dangerous equipment
- Sweatshops, including those that use child labor, persist in the U.S. and abroad, posing a continuing challenge to U.S. law enforcement officials and wage and hour regulators

Enforcement and Remedies Under the FLSA

The FLSA is enforced by the Department of Labor (DOL). The Wage and Hour Division of the DOL performs inspections and investigations and issues rules and regulations. The Secretary of Labor is authorized to file suit on behalf of employees seeking to collect wages and overtime and may also recover liquidated damages in an amount equal to the amount of wages owed. The Secretary may also seek injunctions against violations of the act. Criminal proceedings for willful violations may be instituted by the Department of Justice.

Employees may file suit to recover back wages and overtime plus liquidated damages in an equal amount. They may also seek reinstatement and may recover legal fees. The statute of limitations for violations is two years; for willful violations it is extended to three years. The Supreme Court discussed the definition of "willful" in *McLaughlin v. Richland Shoe Co.*[16] The Court defined "willful" as "that the employer either knew or showed reckless disregard as to whether its conduct was prohibited by the FLSA." Employees generally may not release employers for less than the full amount owing, nor may employees waive their rights to compensation under the act.

[16] 486 U.S. 128 (1988).

The child labor prohibitions are enforced by the prohibition of interstate shipment of goods produced by child labor and by fines. Fines may also be levied against employers who keep inadequate wage and hour records.

The following case involves a discussion of the standard used by the court in determining whether to award liquidated damages in addition to back pay.

case 22.6 »

Mogilevsky v. Bally Total Fitness Corporation

2003 WL 21098646 (U.S. District Court, D. Mass. 2003)

Facts: The plaintiff brought claims regarding unpaid wages against his former employer pursuant to the FLSA and the common law. The court held a bench trial (i.e., without a jury) on his claims in September 2002.

The hours in question accrued between January 1998 and December 1999. Mogilevsky filed his action on May 18, 2001. The FLSA sets forth a two-year statute of limitations, unless the employer's violation was willful, in which case the statute of limitations is extended to three years.

The Supreme Court has stated that an employer's violation is willful within the meaning of the Fair Labor Standards Act when it can be shown that the employer knew, or recklessly disregarded, that it was acting in violation of the Act. At the trial, the evidence showed that, although Bally's failure to pay Mogilevsky his proper wages may well have been negligent, that failure might not rise to the level of reckless disregard, given the lack of clarity in Mogilevsky's own records and his unorthodox approach to scheduling training sessions.

Issue: Based on the trial evidence, what should be the length of time for which the plaintiff can claim unpaid wages, two years or longer?

Decision: The federal judge ruled that the appropriate statute of limitations period for Mogilevsky's claims was two years.

But the judge went on to observe that a question remained as to whether Mogilevsky could recover for the hours accrued prior to May 18, 1999, on some alternative legal theory. With respect to these hours, said His Honor, Bally could potentially be held liable under Mogilevsky's common law breach of contract claim, which carries a six-year statute of limitations.

However, the court ruled that a common law breach of contract claim was inapplicable here. The documents that Mogilevsky cited as giving rise to this "contract"—the Employee Information and Acknowledgment Form and the Employee Handbook—simply contained what are essentially promises to adhere to federal and state law regarding payment of overtime wages. The judge didn't feel that these employer policies created a separate, common law contractual right. (See Chapter 2.)

«

Concept *Summary* » 22.5

FLSA Enforcement

- U.S. Department of Labor is charged with enforcing the FLSA
- The DOL's Wage and Hour Division is the component of the cabinet-level department which specifically creates and enforces the regulations that operationalize the FLSA's broad principles
- The Wage and Hour Division can investigate violations and sue on behalf of employees
- A private right of action is available for aggrieved workers
    - Remedies include liquidated damages and attorney fees

CHAPTER REVIEW

» Key Terms

minimum wage	« 689	***workweek***	« 693	***National Industrial Recovery Act (NIRA)***	« 698
overtime pay	« 693	***exempt employees***	« 694		

» Summary

- The Fair Labor Standards Act (FLSA) is the primary federal law governing minimum wages, overtime compensation, and child labor in the United States. It does not preempt similar state laws that provide employees with greater protections in these key categories. The FLSA has been declared by the Supreme Court not to be an unconstitutional taking of employers' property or an unconstitutional interference with the right to make contracts.
- Minimum hourly wages need not be paid to bona fide executives, administrators, professionals, and outside salespeople, who typically receive salaries and commissions. Hourly workers, who are entitled to at least the federal minimum wage, cannot be penalized by deductions for tools, uniforms, or cash register losses.
- Executives, administrators, professionals, and outside salespeople also are not entitled to overtime pay. Hourly employees are entitled to at least one-and-a-half times their regular hourly pay rates for all hours over forty in any workweek.
- FLSA child labor provisions limit the use of children and teens in dangerous workplaces. Since the law does not extend to American corporations' activities outside the United States and its territories, critics of corporate practices in third-world countries recently have accused a number of major corporations of exploiting child labor, as well as workers generally, in offshore operations.

» Problems

Questions

1. What are the main provisions of the FLSA? What are the bases of coverage for the FLSA?
2. Does the FLSA require the payment of overtime? Under what circumstances?
3. What are the major exceptions from the overtime and minimum wage requirements of the FLSA? What are the tests used to determine whether an employee falls under one of those exemptions?
4. What is meant by "oppressive child labor"? What is the significance of oppressive child labor under the FLSA?

5. What remedies are available for violations of the minimum wage and overtime provisions of the FLSA? What penalties may be imposed for violations of the child labor prohibitions?

Case Problems

6. The employer is a not-for-profit corporation that provides services to mentally retarded and developmentally disabled individuals. It operates residential group homes for its clientele. Each such geographically separate house is under the sole charge of a house manager. The house manager's job includes (1) managing the house's budget; (2) hiring and managing other employees at the house; and (3) maintaining employment records. However, these house managers also perform nonmanagerial tasks such as transporting clients, assisting them with bathing and dressing, and numerous other chores normally performed by their subordinates.

   Should these house managers be classified as exempt executive employees for purposes of minimum wage and overtime pay under the FLSA? See *Department of Labor, Wage and Hour Division, Opinion Letter of July 14, 2000* [2000 WL 1537209].

7. Company A sells airtime and infomercials on television. It employs telephone callers at $9 per hour. Company B, which is owned by the same parent company, does telephone collection calling of its clients' debtors, paying the same hourly rate of $9.

   Employee C works forty hours per week for Company A. He also is employed evenings for a total of ten hours per week for Company B.

   Should Company B be required to pay Employee C time-and-one-half for overtime compensation? See *Department of Labor, Wage and Hour Division, Opinion Letter of July 14, 2000, Attachment 1* [2000 WL 1537209].

8. A volunteer ambulance company contracts with a for-profit corporation to provide drivers and emergency medical technicians (EMTs). The for-profit company then bills the volunteer ambulance company for the services of these employees. Sometimes, however, these very same drivers and EMTs provide their services to the volunteer ambulance company as volunteers in their off-duty hours.

   Should the volunteer ambulance company be required to pay these drivers and EMTs either minimum wages and/or overtime compensation for their "volunteer" hours? See *Department of Labor, Wage and Hour Division, Opinion Letter of May 22, 2000* [2000 WL 1537253].

9. The employer established a performance-based bonus plan under which workers who were not exempt from the minimum wage and overtime provisions of the FLSA were evaluated on various productivity criteria. At year's end, some of the company's top performers were given lump-sum, one-time bonuses. Who received the bonuses and in what amounts were determinations made by the CEO in her sole discretion. The company was under no advance contractual obligation to give any bonuses or to give any particular employees a bonus.

   Should the employer be permitted to exclude these lump-sum bonuses when calculating a recipient's hourly rate of pay for purposes of determining whether she or he has been receiving the proper amount when entitled to overtime compensation? See *Department of Labor, Wage and Hour Division, Opinion Letter of May 19, 2000* [2000 WL 1537273].

10. A company allowed its employees to take a half-hour lunch break. However, the break was uncompensated, and the employees were not permitted to leave the employer's premises during the break. Nevertheless, these employees did leave their positions on the production line and eat in an employee lunchroom. They also went outdoors at their discretion.

    Should the employer be required under the FLSA to compensate these hourly production workers for their thirty-minute lunch breaks? What about maintenance workers who might be recalled early from their lunch breaks if an equipment breakdown required it? See *Brown v. Howard Industries, Inc.* [116 F.Supp.2d [PN764 (S.D. Miss. 2000)].

11. Pursuant to the FLSA exception, which allows public employers to give their hourly workers compensatory time in lieu of overtime pay, a town provided its police officers with compensatory time credits in place of overtime premiums. However, when police officers tried to "cash in"

their compensatory entitlements, the chief of police—following the instructions of the town council—approved such requests only when a police officer's absence on "comp time" did not require the town to pay a replacement officer overtime/comp time.

Should the town be permitted to restrict the police officers' enjoyment of their comp time entitlements in this fashion? See *Canney v. Town of Brookline* [2000 WL 1612703 (D. Mass.)].

12. The employee, an immigrant, filed a claim with state's labor commission, claiming unpaid overtime entitlements. The employer then reported her immigration status to the Immigration and Naturalization Service (now the Bureau of Citizenship and Immigration Services in the Department of Homeland Security), which upon investigation found that the employee in fact was in violation of INS regulations.

    Should the employee be permitted to pursue a lawsuit against the employer, alleging retaliation in violation of Section 215(a)(3) of the FLSA, which makes it illegal to punish an employee for exercising her rights under the FLSA? Does your answer change if the Immigration Control and Enforcement (ICE) agency fails to find that the employee is working in violation of ICE regulations? What if the reporting employer honestly believed in good faith that the violation existed?

    What are the competing public policy considerations for and against permitting such a lawsuit under these two different sets of facts? See *Contreras v. Corinthian Vigor Insurance Brokerage, Inc.* [2000 WL 1521369 (N.D. Cal.)].

13. The employee was employed as a "floating" pharmacist by a small chain of drug stores. As the floater, he was shifted from store to store to fill in for ill and vacationing regular pharmacists. He was paid an hourly wage of $27 but no overtime, even though he sometimes worked more than forty hours in a single week.

    When he sued for his unpaid overtime compensation, the company contended that he is a professional employee and therefore not entitled to overtime compensation under the FLSA. Is the company correct? What different or additional facts, if any, might cause you to change your answer? See *Iheanacho v. Safeway, Inc.* [2000 WL 1364239 (D. Oregon)].

14. A university provided free housing for its male security guards but not for its female guards. The university claimed that its purpose was to ensure round-the-clock availability of public safety officers on the campus in case of emergencies, and therefore, the housing was for its benefit and convenience and not an added form of compensation to the male officers. University officials also claimed that it would be unduly expensive to try to make the facilities coed to accommodate the female guards.

    The female guards brought suit under the Equal Pay Act provisions of the FLSA (see Chapter 4). Who should win? See *Stewart v. S.U.N.Y. Maritime College* [2000 WL 1218379 (S.D.N.Y.)].

15. A local bus company makes its money by transporting passengers to and from the local train station and to bus depots, where they catch interstate buses. The company runs no buses outside state lines but is strictly local. Nevertheless, the company is regulated by the U.S. Department of Transportation. The FLSA exempts interstate transportation activities.

    The local bus company admits it never pays its drivers overtime compensation when they exceed forty hours of work in a week. But it argues that it is exempt because it is engaged in interstate transportation.

    Do you agree? See *United Transportation Local Union 759 v. Orange Newark Elizabeth Bus, Inc.* [111 F.Supp.2d 514 (D.N.J. 2000)].

Hypothetical Scenarios

16. Clara is the supervisor in charge of a fast-food restaurant. She has six cooks, dishwashers and waitresses under her supervision. However, she herself often has to cook at the grill, load and run the dishwasher, and even occasionally wait on tables, during particularly busy times or when workers call in sick. She is paid a weekly salary of $500. Do you think she should be exempt from the FLSA's minimum wage and overtime provisions?

17. Jerry is a security officer. He is paid by the hour to help protect celebrities. A typical evening shift involves riding in the limousine with a famous performer, accompanying her into the arena where she is performing, then sitting around backstage,

while the show is going proceeding. While the performer is on stage, Jerry and his fellow guards have no particular duties to perform. They usually play cards or watch the concert. However, they are not allowed to leave the performance venue. They continue to wear their Bluetooth head sets and must respond immediately, if called upon to do so. Should they continue to receive their hourly wages for the time they are just sitting around backstage?

18. Cindy is a saleswoman. Four days a week she is "in the field," making sales calls. A typical work day, Monday through Thursday, begins with her reviewing her schedule at her kitchen table over her morning coffee. She then spends the rest of her days making her calls, returning home in the late afternoon, where she does about an hour's worth of paperwork, submitting orders electronically to the home office. On Fridays, however, she is required to report to the home office, where she attends a mandatory sales meeting and works at her desk the remainder of the day. Is Cindy an outside salesperson who is exempt form the minimum wage and overtime provisions of the FLSA? Does your answer apply to Fridays, too?

19. Henry is an avid adherent of a religious cult, which requires members to turn over all their property to the church elders. He lives in a communal setting owned and maintained by the church, which provides his food and clothing. He is required to work a ten-hour day in one of several church-affiliated enterprises. He is paid nothing for this work. Is the church violating the FLSA where Henry is concerned? Does the fact that he does the work not only voluntarily but gladly affect your answer?

20. Maggie is ten years old. Her parents are legal migrant farm workers. While her parents are picking fruit in the fields, the agri-business which employs them provides day care for children such as Maggie. However, Maggie and the other children are often required to work in the farm kitchens, preparing meals, including operating such electrical equipment such as meat slicers, as they help prepare the meals that are then delivered to the workers in the fields. Is Maggie's work subject to the FLSA's child labor provisions? How about the FLSA's minimum wage requirements?

Civil Rights Act of 1964

42 U.S.C. §2000e et seq., as amended by the Civil Rights Act of 1991, P.L. 102–166

Title VII—Nondiscrimination in Employment

Section 701. Definitions

For the purposes of this subchapter—

(a) The term "person" includes one or more individuals, governments, governmental agencies, political subdivisions, labor unions, partnerships, associations, corporations, legal representatives, mutual companies, joint-stock companies, trusts, unincorporated organizations, trustees, trustees in cases under Title 11, or receivers.

(b) The term "employer" means a person engaged in an industry affecting commerce who has fifteen or more employees for each working day in each of twenty or more calendar weeks in the current or preceding calendar year, and any agent of such a person, but such term does not include (1) the United States, a corporation wholly owned by the Government of the United States, an Indian tribe, or any department or agency of the District of Columbia subject by statute to procedures of the competitive service (as defined in section 2102 of Title 5) or (2) a bona fide private membership club (other than a labor organization) which is exempt from taxation under section 501(c) of Title 26, except that during the first year after March 24, 1972, persons having fewer than twenty-five employees (and their agents) shall not be considered employers.

(c) The term "employment agency" means any person regularly undertaking with or without compensation to procure employees for an employer or to procure for employees opportunities to work for an employer and includes an agent of such a person.

(d) The term "labor organization" means a labor organization engaged in an industry affecting commerce, and any agent of such an organization, and includes any organization of any kind, any agency, or employee representation committee, group, association, or plan so engaged in which employees participate and which exists for the purpose, in whole or in part, of dealing with employers concerning grievances, labor disputes, wages, rates of pay, hours, or other terms or conditions of employment, and any conference, general committee, joint or system board, or joint council so engaged which is subordinate to a national or international labor organization.

(e) A labor organization shall be deemed to be engaged in an industry affecting commerce if (1) it maintains or operates a hiring hall or hiring office which procures employees for an employer or procures for employees opportunities to work for an employer; or (2) the number of its members (or, where it is a labor organization composed of other labor organizations or their representatives, if the aggregate number of the members of such other labor organization) is (A) twenty-five or more during the first year after March 24, 1972, or (B) fifteen or more thereafter, and such labor organization—

(1) is the certified representative of employees under the provisions of the National Labor Relations Act, as amended, or the Railway Labor Act, as amended;

(2) although not certified, is a national or international labor organization or a local labor organization recognized or acting as the representative of employees of an employer or employers engaged in an industry affecting commerce; or

(3) has chartered a local labor organization or subsidiary body which is representing or actively seeking to represent employees of employers within the meaning of paragraph (1) or (2); or

(4) has been chartered by a labor organization representing or actively seeking to represent employees within the meaning of paragraph (1) or (2) has the local or subordinate body through which such employees may enjoy membership or become affiliated with such labor organization; or

(5) is a conference, general committee, joint or system board, or joint council subordinate to a national or international labor organization, which includes a labor organization engaged in an industry affecting commerce within the meaning of any of the preceding paragraphs of this subsection.

(f) The term "employee" means an individual employed by an employer, except that the term "employee" shall not include any person elected to public office in any State or political subdivision of any State by the qualified voters thereof, or any person chosen by such officer to be on such officer's personal staff, or an appointee on the policy making level or an immediate adviser with respect to the exercise of the constitutional or legal powers of the office. The exemption set forth in the preceding sentence shall not include employees subject to the civil service laws of a State government, governmental agency or political subdivision.

With respect to employment in a foreign country, such term includes an individual who is a citizen of the United States.

(g) The term "commerce" means trade, traffic, commerce, transportation, transmission, or communication among the several States; or between a State and any place outside thereof; or within the District of Columbia, or a possession of the United States; or between points in the same State but through a point outside thereof.

(h) The term "industry affecting commerce" means any activity, business, or industry in commerce or in which a labor dispute would hinder or obstruct commerce or the free flow of commerce and includes any activity or industry "affecting commerce" within the meaning of the Labor-Management Reporting and Disclosure Act of 1959, and further includes any governmental industry, business, or activity.

(i) The term "State" includes a State of the United States, the District of Columbia, Puerto Rico, the Virgin Islands, American Samoa, Guam, Wake Island, the Canal Zone, and Outer Continental Shelf lands defined in the Outer Continental Shelf Lands Act.

(j) The term "religion" includes all aspects of religious observance and practice, as well as belief, unless an employer demonstrates that he is unable to reasonably accommodate to an employee's or prospective employee's religious observance or practice without undue hardship on the conduct of the employer's business.

(k) The terms "because of sex" or "on the basis of sex" include, but are not limited to, because of or on the basis of pregnancy, childbirth, or related medical conditions; and women affected by pregnancy, childbirth, or related medical conditions shall be treated the same for all employment-related purposes, including receipt of benefits under fringe benefit programs, as other persons not so affected but similar in their ability or inability to work and nothing in section 2000e-2(h) of this title shall be interpreted to permit otherwise. This subsection shall not require an employer to pay for health insurance benefits for abortion, except where the life of the mother would be endangered if the fetus were carried to term, or except where medical complications have arisen from an abortion: Provided, That nothing herein shall preclude an employer from providing abortion benefits or otherwise affect bargaining agreements in regard to abortion.

(l) The term "complaining party" means the Commission, the Attorney General, or a person who may bring an action or proceeding under this title.

(m) The term "demonstrates" means meets the burdens of production and persuasion.

(n) The term "respondent" means an employer, employment agency, labor organization, joint labor-management committee controlling apprenticeship or other training or retraining program, including an on-the-job training program, or Federal entity subject to section 717.

Section 702. Subchapter not applicable to employment of aliens outside state and individuals for performance of activities of religious corporations, associations, educational institutions, or societies

(a) This subchapter shall not apply to an employer with respect to the employment of aliens outside any State, or to a religious corporation, association, educational institution, or society with respect to the employment of individuals of a particular religion to perform work connected with the carrying on by such corporation, association, educational institution, or society of its activities.

(b) It shall not be unlawful under section 703 or 704 for an employer (or a corporation controlled by an employer), labor organization, employment agency, or joint management committee controlling apprenticeship or other training or retraining (including on-the-job training programs) to take any action otherwise prohibited by such section, with respect to an employee in a workplace in a foreign country if compliance with such section would cause such employer (or such corporation), such organization, such agency, or such committee to violate the law of the foreign country in which such workplace is located.

(c) (1) If an employer controls a corporation whose place of incorporation is a foreign country, any practice prohibited by section 703 or 704 engaged in by such corporation shall be presumed to be engaged in by such employer.

(2) Sections 703 and 704 shall not apply with respect to the foreign operations of an employer that is a foreign person not controlled by an American employer.

(3) For purposes of this subsection, the determination of whether an employer controls a corporation shall be based on—

(A) the interrelation of operations;

(B) the common management;

(C) the centralized control of labor relations; and

(D) the common ownership or financial control, of the employer and the corporation.

Section 703. Unlawful employment practices

(a) It shall be an unlawful employment practice for an employer—

(1) to fail or refuse to hire or to discharge any individual, or otherwise to discriminate against any individual with respect to his compensation, terms, conditions, or privileges of employment, because of such individual's race, color, religion, sex, or national origin; or

(2) to limit, segregate, or classify his employees or applicants for employment in any way which would deprive or tend to deprive any individual of employment opportunities or otherwise adversely affect his status as an employee, because of such individual's race, color, religion, sex, or national origin.

(b) It shall be an unlawful employment practice for an employment agency to fail or refuse to refer for employment, or otherwise to discriminate against, any individual because of his race, color, religion, sex, or national origin, or to classify or refer for employment any individual on the basis of his race, color, religion, sex, or national origin.

(c) It shall be an unlawful employment practice for a labor organization—

(1) to exclude or to expel from its membership, or otherwise to discriminate against, any individual because of his race, color, religion, sex, or national origin;

(2) to limit, segregate, or classify its membership or applicants for membership or to classify or fail or refuse to refer for employment any individual, in any way which would deprive or tend to deprive any individual of employment opportunities, or would limit such employment opportunities or otherwise adversely affect his status as an employee or as an applicant for employment, because of such individual's race, color, religion, sex, or national origin; or

(3) to cause or attempt to cause an employer to discriminate against an individual in violation of this section.

(d) It shall be an unlawful employment practice for any employer, labor organization, or joint labor-management committee controlling apprenticeship or other training or retraining, including on-the-job training programs to discriminate against any individual because of his race, color, religion, sex, or national origin in admission to, or employment in, any program established to provide apprenticeship or other training.

(e) Notwithstanding any other provision of this subchapter, (1) it shall not be an unlawful employment practice for an employer to hire and employ employees, for an employment agency to classify, or refer for employment any individual, for a labor organization to classify its membership or to classify or refer for employment any individual, or for an employer, labor organization, or joint labor-management committee controlling apprenticeship or other training or retraining programs to admit or employ any individual in any such program, on the basis of his religion, sex, or national origin in those certain instances where religion, sex, or national origin is a bona fide occupational qualification reasonably necessary to the normal operation of that particular business or enterprise, and (2) it shall not be an unlawful employment practice for a school, college, university, or other educational institution or institution of learning to hire and employ employees of a particular religion if such school, college, university, or other educational institution or institution of learning is, in whole or in substantial part, owned, supported, controlled, or managed by a particular religion or by a particular religious corporation, association, or society, or if the curriculum of such school, college, university, or other educational institution or institution of learning is directed toward the propagation of a particular religion.

(f) As used in this subchapter, the phrase "unlawful employment practice" shall not be deemed to include any action or measure taken by an employer, labor organization, joint labor-management committee, or employment agency with respect to an individual who is a member of the Communist Party of the United States or of any other organization required to register as a Communist-action or Communist-front organization by final order of the

Subversive Activities Control Board pursuant to the Subversive Activities Control Act of 1950.

(g) Notwithstanding any other provision of this title, it shall not be an unlawful employment practice for an employer to fail or refuse to hire and employ an individual for any position, for an employer to discharge an individual from any position, or for an employment agency to fail or refuse to refer any individual for employment in any position, or for a labor organization to fail or refuse to refer any individual for employment in any position, if—

  (1) the occupancy of such position, or access to the premises in or upon which any part of the duties of such position is performed or is to be performed, is subject to any requirement imposed in the interest of the national security of the United States under any security program in effect pursuant to or administered under any statute of the United States or any Executive order of the President; and

  (2) such individual has not fulfilled or has ceased to fulfill that requirement.

(h) Notwithstanding any other provision of this subchapter, it shall not be an unlawful employment practice for an employer to apply different standards of compensation, or different terms, conditions, or privileges of employment pursuant to a bona fide seniority or merit system, or a system which measures earnings by quantity or quality of production or to employees who work in different locations, provided that such differences are not the result of an intention to discriminate because of race, color, religion, sex, or national origin; nor shall it be an unlawful employment practice for an employer to give and to act upon the results of any professionally developed ability test provided that such test, its administration or action upon the results is not designed, intended or used to discriminate because of race, color, religion, sex or national origin. It shall not be an unlawful employment practice under this subchapter for any employer to differentiate upon the basis of sex in determining the amount of the wages or compensation paid or to be paid to employees of such employer if such differentiation is authorized by the provisions of section 206(d) of Title 29.

(i) Nothing contained in this subchapter shall apply to any business or enterprise on or near an Indian reservation with respect to any publicly announced employment practice of such business or enterprise under which a preferential treatment is given to any individual because he is an Indian living on or near a reservation.

(j) Nothing contained in this subchapter shall be interpreted to require any employer, employment agency, labor organization, or joint labor-management committee subject to this subchapter to grant preferential treatment to any individual or to any group because of the race, color, religion, sex, or national origin of such individual or group on account of an imbalance which may exist with respect to the total number of percentage of persons of any race, color, religion, sex, or national origin employed by any employer, referred or classified for employment by an employment agency or labor organization, admitted to membership or classified by any labor organization, or admitted to, or employed in, any apprenticeship or other training program, in comparison with the total number or percentage of persons of such race, color, religion, sex, or national origin in any community, State, section, or other area, or in the available work force in any community, State, section, or other area.

(k) (1) (A) An unlawful employment practice based on disparate impact is established under this title only if—

      (i) a complaining party demonstrates that a respondent uses a particular employment practice that causes a disparate impact on the basis of race, color, religion, sex, or national origin and the respondent fails to demonstrate that the challenged practice is job related for the position in question and consistent with business necessity; or

      (ii) the complaining party makes the demonstration described in subparagraph (C) with respect to an alternative employment practice and the respondent refuses to adopt such alternative employment practice.

    (B) (i) With respect to demonstrating that a particular employment practice causes a disparate impact as described in subparagraph (A)(i), the complaining party shall demonstrate that each particular challenged employment practice causes a disparate impact, except that if the complaining party can demonstrate to the court that the elements of a respondent's decision-making process are not capable of separation for analysis, the decision-making process may be analyzed as one employment practice.

      (ii) If the respondent demonstrates that a specific employment practice does not cause the disparate impact, the respondent shall not be required to demonstrate that such practice is required by business necessity.

(C) The demonstration referred to by subparagraph (A)(ii) shall be in accordance with the law as it existed on June 4, 1989, with respect to the concept of "alternative employment practice."

(2) A demonstration that an employment practice is required by business necessity may not be used as a defense against a claim of intentional discrimination under this title.

(3) Notwithstanding any other provision of this title, a rule barring the employment of an individual who currently and knowingly uses or possesses a controlled substance, as defined in schedules I and II of section 102(6) of the Controlled Substances Act (21 U.S.C. 802(6)), other than the use or possession of a drug taken under the supervision of a licensed health care professional, or any other use or possession authorized by the Controlled Substances Act or any other provision of Federal law, shall be considered an unlawful employment practice under this title only if such rule is adopted or applied with an intent to discriminate because of race, color, religion, sex, or national origin.

(l) It shall be an unlawful employment practice for a respondent, in connection with the selection or referral of applicants or candidates for employment or promotion, to adjust the scores of, use different cutoff scores for, or otherwise alter the results of, employment related tests on the basis of race, color, religion, sex, or national origin.

(m) Except as otherwise provided in this title, an unlawful employment practice is established when the complaining party demonstrates that race, color, religion, sex, or national origin was a motivating factor for any employment practice, even though other factors also motivated the practice.

(n) (1) (A) Notwithstanding any other provision of law, and except as provided in paragraph (2), an employment practice that implements and is within the scope of a litigated or consent judgment or order that resolves a claim of employment discrimination under the Constitution or Federal civil rights laws may not be challenged under the circumstances described in subparagraph (B).

(B) A practice described in subparagraph (A) may not be challenged in a claim under the Constitution or Federal civil rights laws—

(i) by a person who, prior to the entry of the judgment or order described in subparagraph (A), had—

(I) actual notice of the proposed judgment or order sufficient to apprise such person that such judgment or order might adversely affect the interests and legal rights of such person and that an opportunity was available to present objections to such judgment or order by a future date certain; and

(II) a reasonable opportunity to present objections to such judgment or order; or

(ii) by a person whose interests were adequately represented by another person who had previously challenged the judgment or order on the same legal grounds and with a similar factual situation, unless there has been an intervening change in law or fact.

(2) Nothing in this subsection shall be construed to—

(A) alter the standards for intervention under rule 24 of the Federal Rules of Civil Procedure or apply to the rights of parties who have successfully intervened pursuant to such rule in the proceeding in which the parties intervened;

(B) apply to the rights of parties to the action in which a litigated or consent judgment or order was entered, or of members of a class represented or sought to be represented in such action, or of members of a group on whose behalf relief was sought in such action by the Federal Government;

(C) prevent challenges to a litigated or consent judgment or order on the ground that such judgment or order was obtained through collusion or fraud, or is transparently invalid or was entered by a court lacking subject matter jurisdiction; or

(D) authorize or permit the denial to any person of the due process of law required by the Constitution.

(3) Any action not precluded under this subsection that challenges an employment consent judgment or order described in paragraph (1) shall be brought in the court, and if possible before the judge, that entered such judgment or order. Nothing in this subsection shall preclude a transfer of such action pursuant to section 1404 of title 28, United States Code.

Section 704. Other unlawful employment practices

(a) It shall be an unlawful employment practice for an employer to discriminate against any of his employees or applicants for employment, for an employment agency, or joint labor-management committee controlling apprenticeship or other training or retraining, including on-the-job training programs, to discriminate against any individual, or for a labor organization to discriminate against any member thereof or applicant for membership, because he has opposed any practice made an unlawful employment practice by this subchapter, or because he has made a charge, testified, assisted, or participated in any manner in an investigation, proceeding, or hearing under this subchapter.

(b) It shall be an unlawful employment practice for an employer, labor organization, employment agency, or joint labor-management committee controlling apprenticeship or other training or retraining, including on-the job training programs, to print or publish or cause to be printed or published any notice or advertisement relating to employment by such an employer or membership in or any classification or referral for employment by such a labor organization, or relating to any classification or referral for employment by such an employment agency, or relating to admission to, or employment in, any program established to provide apprenticeship or other training by such a joint labor-management committee, indicating any preference, limitation, specification, or discrimination, based on race, color, religion, sex, or national origin, except that such a notice or advertisement may indicate a preference, limitation, specification, or discrimination based on religion, sex, or national origin when religion, sex, or national origin is a bona fide occupational qualification for employment.

Section 705. Equal Employment Opportunity Commission

(a) There is hereby created a Commission to be known as the Equal Employment Opportunity Commission, which shall be composed of five members, not more than three of whom shall be members of the same political party. Members of the Commission shall be appointed by the President by and with the advice and consent of the Senate for a term of five years. Any individual chosen to fill a vacancy shall be appointed only for the unexpired term of the member whom he shall succeed, and all members of the Commission shall continue to serve until their successors are appointed and qualified, except that no such member of the Commission shall continue to serve (1) for more than sixty days when the Congress is in session unless a nomination to fill such vacancy shall have been submitted to the Senate, or (2) after the adjournment sine die of the session of the Senate in which such nomination was submitted. The President shall designate one member to serve as Chairman of the Commission, and one member to serve as Vice Chairman. The Chairman shall be responsible on behalf of the Commission for the administrative operations of the Commission, and, except as provided in subsection (b) of this section, shall appoint, in accordance with the provisions of Title 5 governing appointments in the competitive service, such officers, agents, attorneys, administrative law judges, and employees as he deems necessary to assist it in the performance of its functions and to fix their compensation in accordance with the provisions of chapter 51 and subchapter III of chapter 53 of Title 5, relating to classification and General Schedule pay rates: Provided, That assignment, removal, and compensation of administrative law judges shall be in accordance with sections 3105, 3344, 5372, and 7521 of Title 5.

(b) (1) There shall be a General Counsel of the Commission appointed by the President, by and with the advice and consent of the Senate, for a term of four years. The General Counsel shall have responsibility for the conduct of litigation as provided in sections 2000e-5 and 2000e-6 of this title. The General Counsel shall have such other duties as the Commission may prescribe or as may be provided by law and shall concur with the Chairman of the Commission on the appointment and supervision of regional attorneys. The General Counsel of the Commission on the effective date of this Act shall continue in such position and perform the functions specified in this subsection until a successor is appointed and qualifies.

(2) Attorneys appointed under this section may, at the direction of the Commission, appear for and represent the Commission in any case in court, provided that the Attorney General shall conduct all litigation to which the Commission is a party in the Supreme Court pursuant to this subchapter.

(c) A vacancy in the Commission shall not impair the right of the remaining members to exercise all the powers of the Commission and three members thereof shall constitute a quorum.

(d) The Commission shall have an official seal which shall be judicially noticed.

(e) The Commission shall at the close of each fiscal year report to the Congress and to the President concerning the action it has taken, and the moneys it has disbursed. It shall make such further reports on the cause of and means of eliminating discrimination and such recommendations for further legislation as may appear desirable.

(f) The principal office of the Commission shall be in or near the District of Columbia, but it may meet or exercise any or all its powers at any other place. The Commission may establish such regional or State offices as it deems necessary to accomplish the purpose of this subchapter.

(g) The Commission shall have power—

(1) to cooperate with and, with their consent, utilize regional, State, local, and other agencies, both public and private, and individuals;

(2) to pay to witnesses whose depositions are taken or who are summoned before the Commission or any of its agents the same witness and mileage fees as are paid to witnesses in the courts of the United States;

(3) to furnish to persons subject to this subchapter such technical assistance as they may request to further their compliance with this subchapter or an order issued thereunder;

(4) upon the request of (i) any employer, whose employees, or some of them, or (ii) any labor organization, whose members or some of them, refuse or threaten to refuse to cooperate in effectuating the provisions of this subchapter, to assist in such effectuation by conciliation or such other remedial action as is provided by this subchapter;

(5) to make such technical studies as are appropriate to effectuate the purposes and policies of this subchapter and to make the results of such studies available to the public;

(6) to intervene in a civil action brought under section 2000e-5 of this title by an aggrieved party against a respondent other than a government, governmental agency or political subdivision.

(h) (1) The Commission shall, in any of its educational or promotional activities, cooperate with other departments and agencies in the performance of such educational and promotional activities.

(2) In exercising its powers under this title, the Commission shall carry out educational and out-reach activities (including dissemination of information in languages other than English) targeted to—

(A) individuals who historically have been victims of employment discrimination and have not been equitably served by the Commission; and

(B) individuals on whose behalf the Commission has authority to enforce any other law prohibiting employment discrimination, concerning rights and obligations under this title or such law, as the case may be.

(i) All offices, agents, attorneys, and employees of the Commission shall be subject to the provisions of section 7324 of Title 5, notwithstanding any exemption contained in such section.

(j) (1) The Commission shall establish a Technical Assistance Training Institute, through which the Commission shall provide technical assistance and training regarding the laws and regulations enforced by the Commission.

(2) An employer or other entity covered under this title shall not be excused from compliance with the requirements of this title because of any failure to receive technical assistance under this subsection.

(3) There are authorized to be appropriated to carry out this subsection such sums as may be necessary for fiscal year 1992.

Section 706. Enforcement provision

(a) Power of Commission to prevent unlawful employment practices The Commission is empowered, as hereinafter provided, to prevent any person from engaging in any unlawful employment practice as set forth in section 2000e-2 or 2000e-3 of this title.

(b) Charges by persons aggrieved or member of Commission of unlawful employment practices by employers, etc.; filing; allegations; notice to respondent; contents of notice; investigation by Commission; contents of charges; prohibition on disclosure of charges; determination of reasonable cause; conference, conciliation, and persuasion for elimination of unlawful practices; prohibition on disclosure of informal endeavors to end unlawful practices; use of evidence in subsequent proceedings; penalties for disclosure of information; time for determination of reasonable cause

Whenever a charge is filed by or on behalf of a person claiming to be aggrieved, or by a member of the Commission, alleging that an employer, employment agency, labor organization, or joint labor-management committee controlling apprenticeship or other training or retraining, including on-the-job training programs, has engaged in an unlawful employment practice, the Commission shall serve a notice of the charge (including the date, place and circumstances of the alleged unlawful employment practice) on such employer, employment agency, labor organization, or joint labor-management committee (hereinafter referred to as the "respondent") within ten days, and shall make an investigation thereof. Charges shall be in writing under oath or affirmation and shall contain such information and be in such form as the Commission requires. Charges shall not be made public by the Commission. If the Commission determines after such investigation that there is not reasonable cause to believe that the charge is true, it shall dismiss the charge and promptly notify the person claiming to be aggrieved and the respondent of its action. In determining whether reasonable cause exists, the Commission shall accord substantial weight to final findings and orders made by State or local authorities in proceedings commenced under State or local law pursuant to the requirements of subsections (c) and (d) of this section. If the Commission determines after such investigation that there is reasonable cause to believe that the charge is true, the Commission shall endeavor to eliminate any such alleged unlawful employment practice by informal methods of conference, conciliation, and persuasion. Nothing said or done during and as a part of such informal endeavors may be made public by the Commission, its officers or employees, or used as evidence in a subsequent proceeding without the written consent of the persons concerned. Any person who makes public information in violation of this subsection shall be fined not more than $1,000 or imprisoned for not more than one year, or both. The Commission shall make its determination on reasonable cause as promptly as possible and, so far as practicable, not later than one hundred and twenty days from the filing of the charge or, where applicable under subsection (c) or (d) of this section, from the date upon which the Commission is authorized to take action with respect to the charge.

(c) State or local enforcement proceedings; notification of State or local authority; time for filing charges with Commission; commencement of proceedings

In the case of an alleged unlawful employment practice occurring in a State, or political subdivision of a State, which has a State or local law prohibiting the unlawful employment practice alleged and establishing or authorizing a State or local authority to grant or seek relief from such practice or to institute criminal proceedings with respect thereto upon receiving notice thereof, no charge may be filed under subsection (a) of this section by the person aggrieved before the expiration of sixty days after proceedings have been commenced under the State or local law, unless such proceedings have been earlier terminated, provided that such sixty-day period shall be extended to one hundred and twenty days during the first year after the effective date of such State or local law. If any requirement for the commencement of such proceedings is imposed by a State or local authority other than a requirement of the filing of a written and signed statement of the facts upon which the proceeding is based, the proceeding shall be deemed to have been commenced for the purposes of this subsection at the time such statement is sent by registered mail to the appropriate State or local authority.

(d) State or local enforcement proceedings; notification of State or local authority; time for action on charges by Commission

In the case of any charge filed by a member of the Commission alleging an unlawful employment practice occurring in a State or political subdivision of a State which has a State or local law prohibiting the practice alleged and establishing or authorizing a State or local authority to grant or seek relief from such practice or to institute criminal proceedings with respect thereto upon receiving notice thereof, the Commission shall, before taking any action with respect to such charge, notify the appropriate State or local officials and, upon request, afford them a reasonable time, but not less than sixty days (provided that such sixty-day period shall be extended to one hundred and twenty days during the first year after the effective day of such State or local law), unless a shorter period is requested, to act under such State or local law to remedy the practice alleged.

(e) Time for filing charges; time for service of notice of charge on respondent; filing of charge by Commission with State or local agency; seniority system

(1) A charge under this section shall be filed within one hundred and eighty days after the alleged unlawful employment practice occurred and notice of the charge (including the date, place and circumstances of the alleged unlawful employment practice) shall be served upon the person against whom such charge is made within ten days thereafter, except that in a case of an unlawful employment practice with respect to which the person aggrieved has initially instituted proceedings with a State or local agency with authority to grant or seek relief from such practice or to institute criminal proceedings with respect thereto upon receiving notice thereof, such charge shall be filed by or on behalf of the person aggrieved within three hundred days after the alleged unlawful employment practice occurred, or within thirty days after receiving notice that the State or local agency has terminated the proceedings under the State or local law, whichever is earlier, and a copy of such charge shall be filed by the Commission with the State or local agency.

(2) For purposes of this section, an unlawful employment practice occurs, with respect to a seniority system that has been adopted for an intentionally discriminatory purpose in violation of this subchapter (whether or not that discriminatory purpose is apparent on the face of the seniority provision),

when the seniority system is adopted, when an individual becomes subject to the seniority system, or when a person aggrieved is injured by the application of the seniority system or provision of the system.

(3) (A) For purposes of this section, an unlawful employment practice occurs, with respect to discrimination in compensation in violation of this title, when a discriminatory compensation decision or other practice is adopted, when an individual becomes subject to a discriminatory compensation decision or other practice, or when an individual is affected by application of a discriminatory compensation decision or other practice, including each time wages, benefits, or other compensation is paid, resulting in whole or in part from such a decision or other practice.

(B) In addition to any relief authorized by section 1977A of the Revised Statutes (42 U.S.C. 1981a), liability may accrue and an aggrieved person may obtain relief as provided in subsection (g)(1), including recovery of back pay for up to two years preceding the filing of the charge, where the unlawful employment practices that have occurred during the charge filing period are similar or related to unlawful employment practices with regard to discrimination in compensation that occurred outside the time for filing a charge.

(f) Civil action by Commission, Attorney General, or person aggrieved; preconditions; procedure; appointment of attorney; payment of fees, costs, or security; intervention; stay of Federal proceedings; action for appropriate temporary or preliminary relief pending final disposition of charge; jurisdiction and venue of United States courts; designation of judge to hear and determine case; assignment of case for hearing; expedition of case; appointment of master

(1) If within thirty days after a charge is filed with the Commission or within thirty days after expiration of any period of reference under subsection (c) or (d) of this section, the Commission has been unable to secure from the respondent a conciliation agreement acceptable to the Commission, the Commission may bring a civil action against any respondent not a government, governmental agency, or political subdivision named in the charge. In the case of a respondent which is a government, governmental agency, or political subdivision, if the Commission has been unable to secure from the respondent a conciliation agreement acceptable to the Commission, the Commission shall take no further action and shall refer the case to the Attorney General who may bring a civil action against such respondent in the appropriate United States district court. The person or persons aggrieved shall have the right to intervene in a civil action brought by the Commission or the Attorney General in a case involving a government, governmental agency, or political subdivision. If a charge filed with the Commission pursuant to subsection (b) of this section is dismissed by the Commission, or if within one hundred and eighty days from the filing of such charge or the expiration of any period of reference under subsection (c) or (d) of this section, whichever is later, the Commission has not filed a civil action under this section or the Attorney General has not filed a civil action in a case involving a government, governmental agency, or political subdivision, or the Commission has not entered into a conciliation agreement to which the person aggrieved is a party, the Commission, or the Attorney General in a case involving a government, governmental agency, or political subdivision, shall so notify the person aggrieved and within ninety days after the giving of such notice a civil action may be brought against the respondent named in the charge (A) by the person claiming to be aggrieved or (B) if such charge was filed by a member of the Commission, by any person whom the charge alleges was aggrieved by the alleged unlawful employment practice. Upon application by the complainant and in such circumstances as the court may deem just, the court may appoint an attorney for such complainant and may authorize the commencement of the action without the payment of fees, costs, or security. Upon timely application, the court may, in its discretion, permit the Commission, or the Attorney General in a case involving a government, governmental agency, or political subdivision, to intervene in such civil action upon certification that the case is of general public importance. Upon request, the court may, in its discretion, stay further proceedings for not more than sixty days pending the termination of State or local proceedings described in subsection (c) or (d) of this section or further efforts of the Commission to obtain voluntary compliance.

(2) Whenever a charge is filed with the Commission and the Commission concludes on the basis of a preliminary investigation that prompt judicial action is necessary to carry out the purposes of this Act, the

Commission, or the Attorney General in a case involving a government, governmental agency, or political subdivision, may bring an action for appropriate temporary or preliminary relief pending final disposition of such charge. Any temporary restraining order or other order granting preliminary or temporary relief shall be issued in accordance with rule 65 of the Federal Rules of Civil Procedure. It shall be the duty of a court having jurisdiction over proceedings under this section to assign cases for hearing at the earliest practicable date and to cause such cases to be in every way expedited.

(3) Each United States district court and each United States court of a place subject to the jurisdiction of the United States shall have jurisdiction of actions brought under this subchapter. Such an action may be brought in any judicial district in the State in which the unlawful employment practice is alleged to have been committed, in the judicial district in which the employment records relevant to such practice are maintained and administered, or in the judicial district in which the aggrieved person would have worked but for the alleged unlawful employment practice, but if the respondent is not found within any such district, such an action may be brought within the judicial district in which the respondent has his principal office. For purposes of sections 1404 and 1406 of Title 28 *[United States Code]*, the judicial district in which the respondent has his principal office shall in all cases be considered a district in which the action might have been brought.

(4) It shall be the duty of the chief judge of the district (or in his absence, the acting chief judge) in which the case is pending immediately to designate a judge in such district to hear and determine the case. In the event that no judge in the district is available to hear and determine the case, the chief judge of the district, or the acting chief judge, as the case may be, shall certify this fact to the chief judge of the circuit (or in his absence, the acting chief judge) who shall then designate a district or circuit judge of the circuit to hear and determine the case.

(5) It shall be the duty of the judge designated pursuant to this subsection to assign the case for hearing at the earliest practicable date and to cause the case to be in every way expedited. If such judge has not scheduled the case for trial within one hundred and twenty days after issue has been joined, that judge may appoint a master pursuant to rule 53 of the Federal Rules of Civil Procedure.

(g) Injunctions; appropriate affirmative action; equitable relief; accrual of back pay; reduction of back pay; limitations on judicial orders

(1) If the court finds that the respondent has intentionally engaged in or is intentionally engaging in an unlawful employment practice charged in the complaint, the court may enjoin the respondent from engaging in such unlawful employment practice, and order such affirmative action as may be appropriate, which may include, but is not limited to, reinstatement or hiring of employees, with or without back pay (payable by the employer, employment agency, or labor organization, as the case may be, responsible for the unlawful employment practice), or any other equitable relief as the court deems appropriate. Back pay liability shall not accrue from a date more than two years prior to the filing of a charge with the Commission. Interim earnings or amounts earnable with reasonable diligence by the person or persons discriminated against shall operate to reduce the back pay otherwise allowable.

(2) (A) No order of the court shall require the admission or reinstatement of an individual as a member of a union, or the hiring, reinstatement, or promotion of an individual as an employee, or the payment to him of any back pay, if such individual was refused admission, suspended, or expelled, or was refused employment or advancement or was suspended or discharged for any reason other than discrimination on account of race, color, religion, sex, or national origin or in violation of section 2000e-3(a) of this Title.

(B) On a claim in which an individual proves a violation under section 2000e-2(m) of this title and a respondent demonstrates that the respondent would have taken the same action in the absence of the impermissible motivating factor, the court—

(i) may grant declaratory relief, injunctive relief (except as provided in clause (ii)), and attorney's fees and costs demonstrated to be directly attributable only to the pursuit of a claim under section 2000e-2(m) of this title; and

(ii) shall not award damages or issue an order requiring any admission, reinstatement, hiring, promotion, or payment, described in subparagraph (A).

(h) Provisions of chapter 6 of Title 29 not applicable to civil actions for prevention of unlawful practices

The provisions of chapter 6 of title 29 shall not apply with respect to civil actions brought under this section.

(i) Proceedings by Commission to compel compliance with judicial orders In any case in which an employer, employment agency, or labor organization fails to comply with an order of a court issued in a civil action brought under this section, the Commission may commence proceedings to compel compliance with such order.

(j) Appeals

Any civil action brought under this section and any proceedings brought under subsection (i) of this section shall be subject to appeal as provided in sections 1291 and 1292, Title 28.

(k) Attorney's fee; liability of Commission and United States for costs

In any action or proceeding under this subchapter the court, in its discretion, may allow the prevailing party, other than the Commission or the United States, a reasonable attorney's fee (including expert fees) as part of the costs, and the Commission and the United States shall be liable for costs the same as a private person.

Section 707. Civil actions by Attorney General

(a) Whenever the Attorney General has reasonable cause to believe that any person or group of persons is engaged in a pattern or practice of resistance to the full enjoyment of any of the rights secured by this subchapter, and that the pattern or practice is of such a nature and is intended to deny the full exercise of the rights herein described, the Attorney General may bring a civil action in the appropriate district court of the United States by filing with it a complaint (1) signed by him (or in his absence the Acting Attorney General), (2) setting forth facts pertaining to such pattern or practice, and (3) requesting such relief, including an application for a permanent or temporary injunction, restraining order or other order against the person or persons responsible for such pattern or practice, as he deems necessary to insure the full enjoyment of the rights herein described.

(b) The district courts of the United States shall have and shall exercise jurisdiction of proceedings instituted pursuant to this section, and in any such proceeding the Attorney General may file with the clerk of such court a request that a court of three judges be convened to hear and determine the case. Such request by the Attorney General shall be accompanied by a certificate that, in his opinion, the case is of general public importance. A copy of the certificate and request for a three-judge court shall be immediately furnished by such clerk to the chief judge of the circuit (or in his absence, the presiding circuit judge of the circuit) in which the case is pending. Upon receipt of such request it shall be the duty of the chief judge of the circuit or the presiding circuit judge, as the case may be, to designate immediately three judges in such circuit, of whom at least one shall be a circuit judge and another of whom shall be a district judge of the court in which the proceeding was instituted, to hear and determine such case, and it shall be the duty of the judges so designated to assign the case for hearing at the earliest practicable date, to participate in the hearing and determination thereof, and to cause the case to be in every way expedited. An appeal from the final judgment of such court will lie to the Supreme Court.

In the event the Attorney General fails to file such a request in any such proceeding, it shall be the duty of the chief judge of the district (or in his absence, the acting chief judge) in which the case is pending immediately to designate a judge in such district to hear and determine the case. In the event that no judge in the district is available to hear and determine the case, the chief judge of the district, or the acting chief judge, as the case may be, shall certify this fact to the chief judge of the circuit (or in his absence, the acting chief judge) who shall then designate a district or circuit judge of the circuit to hear and determine the case.

It shall be the duty of the judge designated pursuant to this section to assign the case for hearing at the earliest practicable date and to cause the case to be in every way expedited.

(c) Effective two years after March 24, 1972, the functions of the Attorney General under this section shall be transferred to the Commission, together with such personnel, property, records, and unexpended balances of appropriations, allocations, and other funds employed, used, held, available, or to be made available in connection with such functions unless the President submits, and neither House of Congress vetoes, a reorganization plan pursuant to chapter 9 of Title 5, inconsistent with the provisions of this subsection. The Commission shall carry out such functions in accordance with subsections (d) and (e) of this section.

(d) Upon the transfer of functions provided for in subsection (c) of this section, in all suits commenced pursuant to this section prior to the date of such transfer, proceedings shall continue without abatement, all court orders and decrees shall remain in effect, and the Commission shall be substituted as a party for the United States of America, the Attorney General, or the Acting Attorney General, as appropriate.

(e) Subsequent to March 24, 1972, the Commission shall have authority to investigate and act on a charge of a pattern or practice of discrimination, whether filed by or on behalf of a person claiming to be aggrieved or by a member of the Commission. All such actions shall be conducted in accordance with the procedures set forth in section 2000e-5 of this title.

Section 708. Effect on state laws

Nothing in this subchapter shall be deemed to exempt or relieve any person from any liability, duty, penalty, or punishment provided by any present or future law of any State or political subdivision of a State, other than any such law which purports to require or permit the doing of any act which would be an unlawful employment practice under this subchapter.

Section 709. Investigations

(a) In connection with any investigation of a charge filed under section 2000e-5 of this title, the Commission or its designated representative shall at all reasonable times have access to, for the purposes of examination, and the right to copy any evidence of any person being investigated or proceeded against that relates to unlawful employment practices covered by this subchapter and is relevant to the charge under investigation.

(b) The Commission may cooperate with State and local agencies charged with the administration of State fair employment practices laws and, with the consent of such agencies, may, for the purpose of carrying out its functions and duties under this subchapter and within the limitation of funds appropriated specifically for such purpose, engage in and contribute to the cost of research and other projects of mutual interest undertaken by such agencies, and utilize the services of such agencies and their employees, and, notwithstanding any other provision of law, pay by advance or reimbursement such agencies and their employees for services rendered to assist the Commission in carrying out this subchapter. In furtherance of such cooperative efforts, the Commission may enter into written agreements with such State or local agencies and such agreements may include provisions under which the Commission shall refrain from processing a charge in any cases or class of cases specified in such agreements or under which the Commission shall relieve any person or class of persons in such State or locality from requirements imposed under this section. The Commission shall rescind any such agreement whenever it determines that the agreement no longer serves the interest of effective enforcement of this subchapter.

(c) Every employer, employment agency, and labor organization subject to this subchapter shall (1) make and keep such records relevant to the determinations of whether unlawful employment practices have been or are being committed, (2) preserve such records for such periods, and (3) make such reports therefrom as the Commission shall prescribe by regulation or order, after public hearing, as reasonable, necessary, or appropriate for the enforcement of this subchapter or the regulations or orders thereunder. The Commission shall, by regulation, require each employer, labor organization, and joint labor-management committee subject to this subchapter which controls an apprenticeship or other training program to maintain such records as are reasonably necessary to carry out the purposes of this subchapter, including, but not limited to, a list of applicants who wish to participate in such program, including the chronological order in which applications were received, and to furnish to the Commission upon request, a detailed description of the manner in which persons are selected to participate in the apprenticeship or other training program. Any employer, employment agency, labor organization, or joint labor-management committee which believes that the application to it of any regulation or order issued under this section would result in undue hardship may apply to the Commission for an exemption from the application of such regulation or order, and, if such application for an exemption is denied, bring a civil action in the United States district court for the district where such records are kept. If the Commission or the court, as the case may be, finds that the application of the regulation or order to the employer, employment agency, or labor organization in question would impose an undue hardship, the Commission or the court, as the case may be, may grant appropriate relief. If any person required to comply with the provisions of this subsection fails or refuses to do so, the United States district court for the district in which such person is found, resides, or transacts business, shall, upon application of the Commission, or the Attorney General in a case involving a government, governmental agency or political subdivision, have jurisdiction to issue to such person an order requiring him to comply.

(d) In prescribing requirements pursuant to subsection (c) of this section, the Commission shall consult with other interested State and Federal agencies and shall endeavor to coordinate its requirements with those adopted by such agencies. The Commission shall furnish upon request and without cost to any State or local agency charged with the administration of a fair employment practice law information obtained pursuant to subsection (c) of this section from any employer, employment agency, labor organization, or joint labor-management committee subject to the jurisdiction of such agency. Such information shall be furnished on condition that it not be made public by the recipient agency prior to the institution of a proceeding under State or local law involving such information. If this condition is violated by a recipient agency, the Commission may decline to honor subsequent requests pursuant to this subsection.

(e) It shall be unlawful for any officer or employee of the Commission to make public in any manner whatever any information obtained by the Commission pursuant to its authority under this section prior to the institution of any proceeding under this subchapter involving such information. Any officer or employee of the Commission who shall make public in any manner whatever any information in violation of this subsection shall be guilty of a misdemeanor and upon conviction thereof, shall be fined not more than $1,000, or imprisoned not more than one year.

Section 710. Conduct of hearings and investigations pursuant to section 161 of Title 29

For the purpose of all hearings and investigations conducted by the Commission or its duly authorized agents or agencies, section 161 of Title 29 shall apply.

Section 711. Posting of notices; penalties

(a) Every employer, employment agency, and labor organization, as the case may be, shall post and keep posted in conspicuous places upon its premises where notices to employees, applicants for employment, and members are customarily posted a notice to be prepared or approved by the Commission setting forth excerpts from, or summaries of, the pertinent provisions of this subchapter and information pertinent to the filing of a complaint.

(b) A willful violation of this section shall be punishable by a fine of not more than $100 for each separate offense.

Section 712. Veterans' special rights or preference

Nothing contained in this subchapter shall be construed to repeal or modify any Federal, State, territorial, or local law creating special rights or preference for veterans.

Section 713. Regulations; conformity of regulations with administrative procedure provisions; reliance on interpretations and instructions of commission

(a) The Commission shall have authority from time to time to issue, amend, or rescind suitable procedural regulations to carry out the provisions of this subchapter. Regulations issued under this section shall be in conformity with the standards and limitations of subchapter II of chapter 5 of Title 5.

(b) In any action or proceeding based on any alleged unlawful employment practice, no person shall be subject to any liability or punishment for or on account of (1) the commission by such person of an unlawful employment practice if he pleads and proves that the act or omission complained of was in good faith, in conformity with, and in reliance on any written interpretation or opinion of the Commission, or (2) the failure of such person to publish and file any information required by any provision of this subchapter if he pleads and proves that he failed to publish and file such information in good faith, in conformity with the instructions of the Commission issued under this subchapter regarding the filing of such information. Such a defense, if established, shall be a bar to the action or proceeding, notwithstanding that (A) after such act or omission, such interpretation or opinion is modified or rescinded or is determined by judicial authority to be invalid or of no legal effect, or (B) after publishing or filing the description and annual reports, such publication or filing is determined by judicial authority not to be in conformity with the requirements of this subchapter.

Section 714. Application to personnel of commission of sections 111 and 1114 of Title 18; punishment for violation of section 1114 of Title 18

The provisions of sections 111 and 1114, Title 18, shall apply to officers, agents, and employees of the Commission in the performance of their official duties. Notwithstanding the provisions of sections 111 and 1114 of Title 18, whoever in violation of the provisions of section 1114 of such title kills a person while engaged in or on account of the performance of his official functions under this Act shall be punished by imprisonment for any term of years or for life.

Section 715. Equal Employment Opportunity Coordinating Council; establishment; composition; duties; report to President and Congress

The Equal Employment Opportunity Commission shall have the responsibility for developing and implementing agreements, policies, and practices designed to maximize effort, promote efficiency, and eliminate conflict, competition, duplication and inconsistency among the operations, functions and jurisdictions of the various departments, agencies and branches of the Federal Government responsible for the implementation and enforcement of equal employment opportunity legislation, orders, and policies. On or before October 1 of each year, the

Equal Employment Opportunity Commission shall transmit to the President and to the Congress a report of its activities, together with such recommendations for legislative or administrative changes as it concludes are desirable to further promote the purposes of this section.

Section 716. Presidential conferences; acquaintance of leadership with provisions for employment rights and obligations; plans for fair administration; membership

The President shall, as soon as feasible after July 2, 1964, convene one or more conferences for the purpose of enabling the leaders of groups whose members will be affected by this subchapter to become familiar with the rights afforded and obligations imposed by its provisions, and for the purpose of making plans which will result in the fair and effective administration of this subchapter when all of its provisions become effective. The President shall invite the participation in such conference or conferences of (1) the members of the President's Committee on Equal Employment Opportunity, (2) the members of the Commission on Civil Rights, (3) representatives of State and local agencies engaged in furthering equal employment opportunity, (4) representatives of private agencies engaged in furthering equal employment opportunity, and (5) representatives of employers, labor organizations, and employment agencies who will be subject to this subchapter.

Section 717. Employment by federal government

(a) All personnel actions affecting employees or applicants for employment (except with regard to aliens employed outside the limits of the United States) in military departments as defined in section 102 of Title 5, in executive agencies as defined in section 105 of Title 5 (including employees and applicants for employment who are paid from nonappropriated funds), in the United States Postal Service and the Postal Rate Commission, in those units of the Government of the District of Columbia having positions in the competitive service, and in those units of the legislative and judicial branches of the Federal Government having positions in the competitive service, and in the Library of Congress shall be made free from any discrimination based on race, color, religion, sex, or national origin.

(b) Except as otherwise provided in this subsection, the Equal Employment Opportunity Commission shall have authority to enforce the provisions of subsection (a) of this section through appropriate remedies, including reinstatement or hiring of employees with or without back pay, as will effectuate the policies of this section, and shall issue such rules, regulations, orders and instructions as it deems necessary and appropriate to carry out its responsibilities under this section. The Equal Employment Opportunity Commission shall—

(1) be responsible for the annual review and approval of a national and regional equal employment opportunity plan which each department and agency and each appropriate unit referred to in subsection (a) of this section shall submit in order to maintain an affirmative program of equal employment opportunity for all such employees and applicants for employment;

(2) be responsible for the review and evaluation of the operation of all agency equal employment opportunity programs, periodically obtaining and publishing (on at least a semiannual basis) progress reports from each such department, agency, or unit; and

(3) consult with and solicit the recommendations of interested individuals, groups, and organizations relating to equal employment opportunity.

The head of each such department, agency, or unit shall comply with such rules, regulations, orders, and instructions which shall include a provision that an employee or applicant for employment shall be notified of any final action taken on any complaint of discrimination filed by him thereunder. The plan submitted by each department, agency, and unit shall include, but not be limited to—

(A) provision for the establishment of training and education programs designed to provide a maximum opportunity for employees to advance so as to perform at their highest potential; and

(B) a description of the qualifications in terms of training and experience relating to equal employment opportunity for the principal and operating officials of each such department, agency, or unit responsible for carrying out the equal employment opportunity program and of the allocation of personnel and resources proposed by such department, agency, or unit to carry out its equal employment opportunity program. With respect to employment in the Library of Congress, authorities granted in this subsection to the Equal Employment Opportunity Commission shall be exercised by the Librarian of Congress.

(c) Within 90 days of receipt of notice of final action taken by a department, agency, or unit referred to in subsection (a) of this section, or by the Equal Employment Opportunity Commission upon an appeal from a decision or order of such department, agency, or unit on a complaint of discrimination based on race, color, religion, sex or national origin, brought pursuant to subsection (a) of this section, Executive Order 11478 or any succeeding Executive orders, or after one hundred and eighty days from the filing of the initial charge with the department, agency, or unit or with the Equal Employment Opportunity Commission on appeal from a decision or order of such department, agency, or unit until such time as final action may be taken by a department, agency, or unit, an employee or applicant for employment, if aggrieved by the final disposition of his complaint, or by the failure to take final action on his complaint, may file a civil action as provided in section 2000e-5 of this title, in which civil action the head of the department, agency, or unit, as appropriate, shall be the defendant.

(d) The provisions of section 2005e-5 (f) through (k) of this title, as applicable, shall govern civil actions brought hereunder, and the same interest to compensate for delay in payment shall be available as in cases involving nonpublic parties.

(e) Nothing contained in this Act shall relieve any Government agency or official of its or his primary responsibility to assure nondiscrimination in employment as required by the Constitution and statutes or of its or his responsibilities under Executive Order 11478 relating to equal employment opportunity in the Federal Government.

Section 718. Procedure for denial, withholding, termination, or suspension of government contract subsequent to acceptance by government of affirmative action plan of employer; time of acceptance of plan

No Government contract, or portion thereof, with any employer, shall be denied, withheld, terminated, or suspended, by any agency or officer of the United States under any equal employment opportunity law or order, where such employer has an affirmative action plan which has previously been accepted by the Government for the same facility within the past twelve months without first according such employer full hearing and adjudication under the provisions of section 554 of Title 5, and the following pertinent sections: Provided, That if such employer has deviated substantially from such previously agreed to affirmative action plan, this section shall not apply: Provided further, That for the purposes of this section an affirmative action plan shall be deemed to have been accepted by the Government at the time the appropriate compliance agency has accepted such plan unless within forty-five days thereafter the Office of Federal Contract Compliance has disapproved such plan.

Text of Title 42 U.S.C. Section 1981

42 U.S.C. Section 1981, as amended by the Civil Rights Act of 1991, P.L. 102–166

Equal Rights under the Law

Section 1981.

(a) All persons within the jurisdiction of the United States shall have the same right in every State and Territory to make and enforce contracts, to sue, be parties, give evidence, and to the full and equal benefit of all laws and proceedings for the security of persons and property as is enjoyed by white citizens, and shall be subject to like punishment, pains, penalties, taxes, licenses, and exactions of every kind, and to no other.

(b) For purposes of this section, the term "make and enforce contracts" includes the making, performance, modification, and termination of contracts, and the enjoyment of all benefits, privileges, terms, and conditions of the contractual relationship.

(c) The rights protected by this section are protected against impairment by nongovernmental discrimination and impairment under color of State law.

Damages in Cases of Intentional Discrimination in Employment

Section 1981a.

(a) Right of Recovery

(1) Civil rights. In an action brought by a complaining party under section 706 or 717 of the Civil Rights Act of 1964 against a respondent who engaged in unlawful intentional discrimination (not an employment practice that is unlawful because of its disparate impact) prohibited under section 703, 704, or 717 of the Act, and provided that the complaining party cannot recover under section 1977 of the Revised Statutes (42 U.S.C. 1981), the complaining party may recover compensatory and punitive damages as allowed in subsection (b), in addition to any relief authorized by section 706(g) of the Civil Rights Act of 1964, from the respondent.

(2) Disability. In an action brought by a complaining party under the powers, remedies, and procedures set forth in section 706 or 717 of the Civil Rights Act of 1964 (as provided in section 107(a) of the Americans with Disabilities Act of 1990 (42 U.S. C. 12117(a)), and section 505(a)(1) of the Rehabilitation Act of 1973 (29 U.S.C. 794a(a) (1)), respectively) against a respondent who engaged in unlawful intentional discrimination (not an employment practice that is unlawful because of its disparate impact) under section 501 of the Rehabilitation Act of 1973 (29 U.S.C. 791) and the regulations implementing section 501, or who violated the requirements of section 501 of the Act or the regulations implementing section 501 concerning the provision of a reasonable accommodation, or section 102 of the Americans with Disabilities Act of 1990 (42 U.S.C. 12112), or committed a violation of section 102(b)(5) of the Act, against an individual, the complaining party may recover compensatory and punitive damages as allowed in subsection (b), in addition to any relief authorized by section 706(g) of the Civil Rights Act of 1964, from the respondent.

(3) Reasonable accommodation and good faith effort. In cases where a discriminatory practice involves the provision of a reasonable accommodation pursuant to section 102(b)(5) of the Americans with Disabilities Act of 1990 or regulations implementing

section 501 of the Rehabilitation Act of 1973, damages may not be awarded under this section where the covered entity demonstrates good faith efforts, in consultation with the person with the disability who has informed the covered entity that accommodation is needed, to identify and make a reasonable accommodation that would provide such individual with an equally effective opportunity and would not cause an undue hardship on the operation of the business.

(b) Compensatory and Punitive Damages
   (1) Determination of punitive damages. A complaining party may recover punitive damages under this section against a respondent (other than a government, government agency or political subdivision) if the complaining party demonstrates that the respondent engaged in a discriminatory practice or discriminatory practices with malice or with reckless indifference to the federally protected rights of an aggrieved individual.
   (2) Exclusions from compensatory damages. Compensatory damages awarded under this section shall not include backpay, interest on backpay, or any other type of relief authorized under section 706(g) of the Civil Rights Act of 1964.
   (3) Limitations. The sum of the amount of compensatory damages awarded under this section for future pecuniary losses, emotional pain, suffering, inconvenience, mental anguish, loss of enjoyment of life, and other nonpecuniary losses, and the amount of punitive damages awarded under this section, shall not exceed, for each complaining party—
      (A) in the case of a respondent who has more than 14 and fewer than 101 employees in each of 20 or more calendar weeks in the current or preceding calendar year, $50,000;
      (B) in the case of a respondent who has more than 100 and fewer than 201 employees in each of 20 or more calendar weeks in the current or preceding calendar year, $100,000; and
      (C) in the case of a respondent who has more than 200 and fewer than 501 employees in each of 20 or more calendar weeks in the current or preceding calendar year, $200,000; and
      (D) in the case of a respondent who has more than 500 employees in each of 20 or more calendar weeks in the current or preceding calendar year, $300,000.
   (4) Construction. Nothing in this section shall be construed to limit the scope of, or the relief available under, section 1977 of the Revised Statutes (42 U.S.C. 1981).

(c) Jury Trial. If a complaining party seeks compensatory or punitive damages under this section—
   (1) any party may demand a trial by jury; and
   (2) the court shall not inform the jury of the limitations described in subsection (b)(3).

(d) Definitions. As used in this section:
   (1) Complaining party. The term "complaining party" means—
      (A) in the case of a person seeking to bring an action under subsection (a)(1), the Equal Employment Opportunity Commission, the Attorney General, or a person who may bring an action or proceeding under title VII of the Civil Rights Act of 1964 (42 U.S.C. 2000e et seq.); or
      (B) in the case of a person seeking to bring an action under subsection (a)(2), the Equal Employment Opportunity Commission, the Attorney General, a person who may bring an action or proceeding under section 505 (a)(1) of the Rehabilitation Act of 1973 (29 U.S.C. 794a(a)(1)), or a person who may bring an action or proceeding under title I of the Americans with Disabilities Act of 1990 (42 U.S.C. 12101 et seq.).
   (2) Discriminatory practice. The term "discriminatory practice" means the discrimination described in paragraph (1), or the discrimination or the violation described in paragraph (2), of subsection (a).

Extracts from the Age Discrimination in Employment Act

29 U.S.C. Section 621 et seq., as amended by P.L. 99–592 (1986); P.L. 101–433 (1990); P.L. 102–166 (1991); P.L. 104–208 (1996) and

Congressional Statement of Findings and Purpose

Section 621.

(a) The Congress hereby finds and declares that—
  (1) in the face of rising productivity and affluence, older workers find themselves disadvantaged in their efforts to retain employment, and especially to regain employment when displaced from jobs;
  (2) the setting of arbitrary age limits regardless of potential for job performance has become a common practice, and certain otherwise desirable practices may work to the disadvantage of older persons;
  (3) the incidence of unemployment, especially long-term unemployment with resultant deterioration of skill, morale, and employer acceptability is, relative to the younger ages, high among older workers; their numbers are great and growing; and their employment problems grave;
  (4) the existence in industries affecting commerce, of arbitrary discrimination in employment because of age, burdens commerce and the free flow of goods in commerce.

(b) It is therefore the purpose of this chapter to promote employment of older persons based on their ability rather than age; to prohibit arbitrary age discrimination in employment; to help employers and workers find ways of meeting problems arising from the impact of age on employment.

Section 623. Prohibition of age discrimination

(a) Employer practices It shall be unlawful for an employer—
  (1) to fail or refuse to hire or to discharge any individual or otherwise discriminate against any individual with respect to his compensation, terms, conditions, or privileges of employment, because of such individual's age;
  (2) to limit, segregate, or classify his employees in any way which would deprive or tend to deprive any individual of employment opportunities or otherwise adversely affect his status as an employee, because of such individual's age; or
  (3) to reduce the wage rate of any employee in order to comply with this chapter.

(b) Employment agency practices

It shall be unlawful for an employment agency to fail or refuse to refer for employment, or otherwise to discriminate against, any individual because of such individual's age, or to classify or refer for employment any individual on the basis of such individual's age.

(c) Labor organization practices

It shall be unlawful for a labor organization—
  (1) to exclude or to expel from its membership, or otherwise to discriminate against, any individual because of his age;
  (2) to limit, segregate, or classify its membership, or to classify or fail or refuse to refer for employment any individual, in any way which would deprive or tend to deprive any individual of employment opportunities or would limit such employment opportunities or otherwise adversely affect his status as an employee or as an applicant for employment, because of such individual's age;
  (3) to cause or attempt to cause an employer to discriminate against an individual in violation of this section.

(d) Opposition to unlawful practices; participation in investigations, proceedings, or litigation

It shall be unlawful for an employer to discriminate against any of his employees or applicants for employment, for an employment agency to discriminate against any individual, or for a labor organization to discriminate against any member thereof or applicant for membership, because such individual, member or applicant for membership has opposed any practice made unlawful by this section, or because such individual, member or applicant for membership has made a charge, testified, assisted, or participated in any manner in an investigation, proceeding, or litigation under this chapter.

(e) Printing or publication of notice or advertisement indicating preference, limitation, etc.

It shall be unlawful for an employer, labor organization, or employment agency to print or publish, or cause to be printed or published, any notice or advertisement relating to employment by such an employer or membership in or any classification or referral for employment by such a labor organization, or relating to any classification or referral for employment by such an employment agency, indicating any preference, limitation, specification, or discrimination, based on age.

(f) Lawful practices; age as occupational qualification; other reasonable factors; laws of foreign workplace; seniority system; employee benefit plans; discharge or discipline for good cause

It shall not be unlawful for an employer, employment agency, or labor organization—

(1) to take any action otherwise prohibited under subsections (a), (b), (c), or (e) of this section where age is a bona fide occupational qualification reasonably necessary to the normal operation of the particular business, or where the differentiation is based on reasonable factors other than age, or where such practices involve an employee in a workplace in a foreign country, and compliance with such subsections would cause such employer, or a corporation controlled by such employer, to violate the laws of the country in which such workplace is located;

(2) to take any action otherwise prohibited under subsection (a), (b), (c), or (e) of this section

(A) to observe the terms of a bona fide seniority system that is not intended to evade the purposes of this chapter, except that no such seniority system shall require or permit the involuntary retirement of any individual specified by section 631(a) of this title because of the age of such individual; or

(B) to observe the terms of a bona fide employee benefit plan—

(i) where, for each benefit or benefit package, the actual amount of payment made or cost incurred on behalf of an older worker is no less than that made or incurred on behalf of a younger worker, as permissible under section 1625.10, title 29, Code of Federal Regulations (as in effect on June 22, 1989); or

(ii) that is a voluntary early retirement incentive plan consistent with the relevant purpose or purposes of this chapter. Notwithstanding clause (i) or (ii) of subparagraph (B), no such employee benefit plan or voluntary early retirement incentive plan shall excuse the failure to hire any individual, and no such employee benefit plan shall require or permit the involuntary retirement of any individual specified by section 631(a) of this title, because of the age of such individual. An employer, employment agency, or labor organization acting under subparagraph (A), or under clause (i) or (ii) of subparagraph (B), shall have the burden of proving that such actions are lawful in any civil enforcement proceeding brought under this chapter; or

(3) to discharge or otherwise discipline an individual for good cause.

(g) Repealed. [Pub. L. 101–239, Title VI, § 6202(b)(3)(C)(i), Dec. 19, 1989, 103 Stat. 2233]

(h) Practices of foreign corporations controlled by American employers; foreign employers not controlled by American employers; factors determining control

(1) If an employer controls a corporation whose place of incorporation is in a foreign country, any practice by such corporation prohibited under this section shall be presumed to be such practice by such employer.

(2) The prohibitions of this section shall not apply where the employer is a foreign person not controlled by an American employer.

(3) For the purpose of this subsection the determination of whether an employer controls a corporation shall be based upon the—

(A) interrelation of operations,

(B) common management,

(C) centralized control of labor relations, and

(D) common ownership or financial control, of the employer and the corporation.

(i) Employee pension benefit plans; cessation or reduction of benefit accrual or of allocation to employee account; distribution of benefits after attainment of normal retirement age; compliance; highly compensated employees

(1) Except as otherwise provided in this subsection, it shall be unlawful for an employer, an employment agency, a labor organization, or any combination thereof to establish or maintain an employee pension benefit plan which requires or permits

(A) in the case of a defined benefit plan, the cessation of an employee's benefit accrual, or the reduction of the rate of an employee's benefit accrual, because of age, or

(B) in the case of a defined contribution plan, the cessation of allocations to an employee's account, or the reduction of the rate at which amounts are allocated to an employee's account, because of age.

(2) Nothing in this section shall be construed to prohibit an employer, employment agency, or labor organization from observing any provision of an employee pension benefit plan to the extent that such provision imposes (without regard to age) a limitation on the amount of benefits that the plan provides or a limitation on the number of years of service or years of participation which are taken into account for purposes of determining benefit accrual under the plan.

(3) In the case of any employee who, as of the end of any plan year under a defined benefit plan, has attained normal retirement age under such plan—

(A) if distribution of benefits under such plan with respect to such employee has commenced as of the end of such plan year, then any requirement of this subsection for continued accrual of benefits under such plan with respect to such employee during such plan year shall be treated as satisfied to the extent of the actuarial equivalent of in-service distribution of benefits, and

(B) if distribution of benefits under such plan with respect to such employee has not commenced as of the end of such year in accordance with section 1056(a)(3) of this title and section 401 (a)(14)(C) of Title 26, and the payment of benefits under such plan with respect to such employee is not suspended during such plan year pursuant to section 1053(a)(3)(B) of this title or section 411(a)(3)(B) of Title 26, then any requirement of this subsection for continued accrual of benefits under such plan with respect to such employee during such plan year shall be treated as satisfied to the extent of any adjustment in the benefit payable under the plan during such plan year attributable to the delay in the distribution of benefits after the attainment of normal retirement age.

The provisions of this paragraph shall apply in accordance with regulations of the Secretary of the Treasury. Such regulations shall provide for the application of the preceding provisions of this paragraph to all employee pension benefit plans subject to this subsection and may provide for the application of such provisions, in the case of any such employee, with respect to any period of time within a plan year.

(4) Compliance with the requirements of this subsection with respect to an employee pension benefit plan shall constitute compliance with the requirements of this section relating to benefit accrual under such plan.

(5) Paragraph (1) shall not apply with respect to any employee who is a highly compensated employee (within the meaning of section 414(q) of Title 26) to the extent provided in regulations prescribed by the Secretary of the Treasury for purposes of precluding discrimination in favor of highly compensated employees within the meaning of subchapter D of chapter 1 of Title 26.

(6) A plan shall not be treated as failing to meet the requirements of paragraph (1) solely because the subsidized portion of any early retirement benefit is disregarded in determining benefit accruals.

(7) Any regulations prescribed by the Secretary of the Treasury pursuant to clause (v) of section 411(b) (1) (H) of Title 26 and subparagraphs (C) and (D) of section 411(b)(2) of Title 26 shall apply with respect to the requirements of this subsection in the same manner and to the same extent as such regulations apply with respect to the requirements of such sections 411(b)(1)(H) and 411(b)(2) of Title 26.

(8) A plan shall not be treated as failing to meet the requirements of this section solely because such plan provides a normal retirement age described in section 1002(24)(B) of this title and section 411(a)(8)(3) of Title 26.

(9) For purposes of this subsection—

(A) The terms "employee pension benefit plan", "defined benefit plan", "defined contribution plan", and "normal retirement age" have the meanings provided such terms in section 1002 of this title.

(B) The term "compensation" has the meaning provided by section 414(s) of Title 26.

(j) Employment as firefighter or law enforcement officer It shall not be unlawful for an employer which is a State, a political subdivision of a State, an agency or instrumentality of a State or a political subdivision of a State, or an interstate agency to fail or refuse to hire or to discharge any individual because of such individual's age if such action is taken—

(1) with respect to the employment of an individual as a firefighter or as a law enforcement officer, the employer has complied with section 3(d) (2) of the Age Discrimination in Employment Amendments of 1996 if the individual was discharged after the date described in such section, and the individual has attained—

(A) the age of hiring or retirement, respectively, in effect under applicable State or local law on March 3, 1983; or

(B) (i) if the individual was not hired, the age of hiring in effect on the date of such failure or refusal to hire under applicable State or local law enacted after September 30, 1996; or

(ii) if applicable State or local law was enacted after September 30, 1996, and the individual was discharged, the higher of—

(I) the age of retirement in effect on the date of such discharge under such law; and

(II) age 55; and

(2) pursuant to a bona fide hiring or retirement plan that is not a subterfuge to evade the purposes of this chapter.

(k) Seniority system or employee benefit plan; compliance A seniority system or employee benefit plan shall comply with this chapter regardless of the date of adoption of such system or plan.

(l) Lawful practices; minimum age as condition of eligibility for retirement benefits; deductions from severance pay; reduction of long-term disability benefits

Notwithstanding clause (i) or (ii) of subsection (f)(2)(B) of this section—

(1) it shall not be a violation of subsection (a), (b), (c), or (e) of this section solely because—

(A) an employee pension benefit plan (as defined in section 1002 (2) of this title) provides for the attainment of a minimum age as a condition of eligibility for normal or early retirement benefits; or

(B) a defined benefit plan (as defined in section 1002(35) of this title) provides for—

(i) payments that constitute the subsidized portion of an early retirement benefit; or

(ii) social security supplements for plan participants that commence before the age and terminate at the age (specified by the plan) when participants are eligible to receive reduced or unreduced old-age insurance benefits under title II of the Social Security Act (42 U.S.C. 401 et seq.), and that do not exceed such old-age insurance benefits.

(2) (A) It shall not be a violation of subsection (a), (b), (c), or (e) of this section solely because following a contingent event unrelated to age—

(i) the value of any retiree health benefits received by an individual eligible for an immediate pension;

(ii) the value of any additional pension benefits that are made available solely as a result of the contingent event unrelated to age and following which the individual is eligible for not less than an immediate and unreduced pension; or

(iii) the values described in both clauses (i) and (ii); are deducted from severance pay made available as a result of the contingent event unrelated to age.

(B) For an individual who receives immediate pension benefits that are actuarially reduced under subparagraph (A)(i), the amount of the deduction available pursuant to subparagraph (A)(i) shall be reduced by the same percentage as the reduction in the pension benefits.

(C) For purposes of this paragraph, severance pay shall include that portion of supplemental unemployment compensation benefits (as described in section 501 (c)(17) of Title 26) that—

(i) constitutes additional benefits of up to 52 weeks;

(ii) has the primary purpose and effect of continuing benefits until an individual becomes eligible for an immediate and unreduced pension; and

(iii) is discontinued once the individual becomes eligible for an immediate and unreduced pension.

(D) For purposes of this paragraph and solely in order to make the deduction authorized under this paragraph, the term "retiree health benefits" means benefits provided pursuant to a group health plan covering retirees, for which (determined as of the contingent event unrelated to age)—
   (i) the package of benefits provided by the employer for the retirees who are below age 65 is at least comparable to benefits provided under title XVIII of the Social Security Act (42 U.S.C. 1395 et seq.);
   (ii) the package of benefits provided by the employer for the retirees who are age 65 and above is at least comparable to that offered under a plan that provides a benefit package with one-fourth the value of benefits provided under title XVIII of such Act; or
   (iii) the package of benefits provided by the employer is as described in clauses (i) and (ii).

(E) (i) If the obligation of the employer to provide retiree health benefits is of limited duration, the value for each individual shall be calculated at a rate of $3,000 per year for benefit years before age 65, and $750 per year for benefit years beginning at age 65 and above.
   (ii) If the obligation of the employer to provide retiree health benefits is of unlimited duration, the value for each individual shall be calculated at a rate of $48,000 for individuals below age 65, and $24,000 for individuals age 65 and above.
   (iii) The values described in clauses (i) and (ii) shall be calculated based on the age of the individual as of the date of the contingent event unrelated to age. The values are effective on October 16, 1990, and shall be adjusted on an annual basis, with respect to a contingent event that occurs subsequent to the first year after October 16, 1990, based on the medical component of the Consumer Price Index for all-urban consumers published by the Department of Labor.
   (iv) If an individual is required to pay a premium for retiree health benefits, the value calculated pursuant to this subparagraph shall be reduced by whatever percentage of the overall premium the individual is required to pay.

(F) If an employer that has implemented a deduction pursuant to subparagraph (A) fails to fulfill the obligation described in subparagraph (E), any aggrieved individual may bring an action for specific performance of the obligation described in subparagraph (E). The relief shall be in addition to any other remedies provided under Federal or State law.

(3) It shall not be a violation of subsection (a), (b), (c), or (e) of this section solely because an employer provides a bona fide employee benefit plan or plans under which long-term disability benefits received by an individual are reduced by any pension benefits (other than those attributable to employee contributions)—
   (A) paid to the individual that the individual voluntarily elects to receive; or
   (B) for which an individual who has attained the later of age 62 or normal retirement age is eligible.

(m) Voluntary retirement incentive plans

Notwithstanding subsection (f)(2)(b) of this section, it shall not be a violation of subsection (a), (b), (c), or (e) of this section solely because a plan of an institution of higher education (as defined in section 1001 of Title 20) offers employees who are serving under a contract of unlimited tenure (or similar arrangement providing for unlimited tenure) supplemental benefits upon voluntary retirement that are reduced or eliminated on the basis of age, if—
   (1) such institution does not implement with respect to such employees any age-based reduction or cessation of benefits that are not such supplemental benefits, except as permitted by other provisions of this chapter;
   (2) such supplemental benefits are in addition to any retirement or severance benefits which have been offered generally to employees serving under a contract of unlimited tenure (or similar arrangement providing for unlimited tenure), independent of any early retirement or exit-incentive plan, within the preceding 365 days; and
   (3) any employee who attains the minimum age and satisfies all non-age-based conditions for receiving a benefit under the plan has an opportunity lasting not less than 180 days to elect to retire and to receive the

maximum benefit that could then be elected by a younger but otherwise similarly situated employee, and the plan does not require retirement to occur sooner than 180 days after such election.

Administration

Section 625. The Secretary shall have the power—

(a) to make delegations, to appoint such agents and employees, and to pay for technical assistance on a fee for service basis, as he deems necessary to assist him in the performance of his functions under this chapter;

(b) to cooperate with regional, State, local, and other agencies, and to cooperate with and furnish technical assistance to employers, labor organizations, and employment agencies to aid in effectuating the purposes of this chapter.

Recordkeeping, Investigation, and Enforcement

Section 626.

(a) Attendance of witnesses; investigations, inspections, records, and homework regulations

The Equal Employment Opportunity Commission shall have the power to make investigations and require the keeping of records necessary or appropriate for the administration of this chapter in accordance with the powers and procedures provided in sections 209 and 211 of this title *[sections 9 and 11 of the Fair Labor Standards Act of 1938, as amended]*.

(b) Enforcement; prohibition of age discrimination under fair labor standards; unpaid minimum wages and unpaid overtime compensation; liquidated damages; judicial relief; conciliation, conference, and persuasion

The provisions of this chapter shall be enforced in accordance with the powers, remedies, and procedures provided in sections 211(b), 216 (except for subsection (a) thereof), and 217 of this title *[sections 11(b), 16 (except for subsection (a) thereof), and 17 of the Fair Labor Standards Act of 1938, as amended]*, and subsection (c) of this section. Any act prohibited under section 623 of this title *[section 4]* shall be deemed to be a prohibited act under section 215 of this title *[section 15 of the Fair Labor Standards Act of 1938, as amended]*. Amounts owing to a person as a result of a violation of this chapter shall be deemed to be unpaid minimum wages or unpaid overtime compensation for purposes of sections 216 and 217 of this title *[sections 16 and 17 of the Fair Labor Standards Act of 1938, as amended]*: *Provided*, That liquidated damages shall be payable only in cases of willful violations of this chapter. In any action brought to enforce this chapter the court shall have jurisdiction to grant such legal or equitable relief as may be appropriate to effectuate the purposes of this chapter, including without limitation judgments compelling employment, reinstatement or promotion, or enforcing the liability for amounts deemed to be unpaid minimum wages or unpaid overtime compensation under this section. Before instituting any action under this section, the Equal Employment Opportunity Commission shall attempt to eliminate the discriminatory practice or practices alleged, and to effect voluntary compliance with the requirements of this chapter through informal methods of conciliation, conference, and persuasion.

(c) Civil actions; persons aggrieved; jurisdiction; judicial relief; termination of individual action upon commencement of action by Commission; jury trial

(1) Any person aggrieved may bring a civil action in any court of competent jurisdiction for such legal or equitable relief as will effectuate the purposes of this chapter: *Provided*, That the right of any person to bring such action shall terminate upon the commencement of an action by the Equal Employment Opportunity Commission to enforce the right of such employee under this chapter.

(2) In an action brought under paragraph (1), a person shall be entitled to a trial by jury of any issue of fact in any such action for recovery of amounts owing as a result of a violation of this chapter, regardless of whether equitable relief is sought by any party in such action.

(d) (1) Filing of charge with Commission; timeliness; conciliation, conference, and persuasion

No civil action may be commenced by an individual under this section until 60 days after a charge alleging unlawful discrimination has been filed with the Equal Employment Opportunity Commission. Such a charge shall be filed—

(A) within 180 days after the alleged unlawful practice occurred; or

(B) in a case to which section 633(b) of this title applies, within 300 days after the alleged unlawful practice occurred, or within 30 days after receipt by the individual of notice of termination of proceedings under State law, whichever is earlier.

(2) Upon receiving such a charge, the Commission shall promptly notify all persons named in such charge as

prospective defendants in the action and shall promptly seek to eliminate any alleged unlawful practice by informal methods of conciliation, conference, and persuasion.

(3) For purposes of this section, an unlawful practice occurs, with respect to discrimination in compensation in violation of this Act, when a discriminatory compensation decision or other practice is adopted, when a person becomes subject to a discriminatory compensation decision or other practice, or when a person is affected by application of a discriminatory compensation decision or other practice, including each time wages, benefits, or other compensation is paid, resulting in whole or in part from such a decision or other practice.

(e) Reliance on administrative rulings; notice of dismissal or termination; civil action after receipt of notice

Section 259 of this title *[section 10 of the Portal to Portal Act of 1947]* shall apply to actions under this chapter. If a charge filed with the Commission under this chapter is dismissed or the proceedings of the Commission are otherwise terminated by the Commission, the Commission shall notify the person aggrieved. A civil action may be brought under this section by a person defined in section 630(a) of this title *[section 11(a)]* against the respondent named in the charge within 90 days after the date of the receipt of such notice.—

(f) Waiver

(1) An individual may not waive any right or claim under this chapter unless the waiver is knowing and voluntary. Except as provided in paragraph (2), a waiver may not be considered knowing and voluntary unless at a minimum—

(A) the waiver is part of an agreement between the individual and the employer that is written in a manner calculated to be understood by such individual, or by the average individual eligible to participate;

(B) the waiver specifically refers to rights or claims arising under this chapter;

(C) the individual does not waive rights or claims that may arise after the date the waiver is executed;

(D) the individual waives rights or claims only in exchange for consideration in addition to anything of value to which the individual already is entitled;

(E) the individual is advised in writing to consult with an attorney prior to executing the agreement;

(F) (i) the individual is given a period of at least 21 days within which to consider the agreement; or

(ii) if a waiver is requested in connection with an exit incentive or other employment termination program offered to a group or class of employees, the individual is given a period of at least 45 days within which to consider the agreement;

(G) the agreement provides that for a period of at least 7 days following the execution of such agreement, the individual may revoke the agreement, and the agreement shall not become effective or enforceable until the revocation period has expired;

(H) if a waiver is requested in connection with an exit incentive or other employment termination program offered to a group or class of employees, the employer (at the commencement of the period specified in subparagraph (F)) informs the individual in writing in a manner calculated to be understood by the average individual eligible to participate, as to—

(i) any class, unit, or group of individuals covered by such program, any eligibility factors for such program, and any time limits applicable to such program; and

(ii) the job titles and ages of all individuals eligible or selected for the program, and the ages of all individuals in the same job classification or organizational unit who are not eligible or selected for the program.

(2) A waiver in settlement of a charge filed with the Equal Employment Opportunity Commission, or an action filed in court by the individual or the individual's representative, alleging age discrimination of a kind prohibited under section 623 or 633a of this title *[section 4 or 15]* may not be considered knowing and voluntary unless at a minimum—

(A) subparagraphs (A) through (E) of paragraph (1) have been met; and

(B) the individual is given a reasonable period of time within which to consider the settlement agreement.

(3) In any dispute that may arise over whether any of the requirements, conditions, and circumstances set forth in subparagraph (A), (B), (C), (D), (E), (F), (G), or (H) of paragraph (1), or subparagraph (A) or

(B) of paragraph (2), have been met, the party asserting the validity of a waiver shall have the burden of proving in a court of competent jurisdiction that a waiver was knowing and voluntary pursuant to paragraph (1) or (2).

(4) No waiver agreement may affect the Commission's rights and responsibilities to enforce this chapter. No waiver may be used to justify interfering with the protected right of an employee to file a charge or participate in an investigation or proceeding conducted by the Commission.

Notices to Be Posted

Section 627. Every employer, employment agency, and labor organization shall post and keep posted in conspicuous places upon its premises a notice to be prepared or approved by the Commission setting forth information as the Commission deems appropriate to effectuate the purposes of this chapter.

Rules and Regulations; Exemptions

Section 628. In accordance with the provisions of subchapter II of chapter 5 of Title 5, the Equal Employment Opportunity Commission may issue such rules and regulations as it may consider necessary or appropriate for carrying out this chapter, and may establish such reasonable exemptions to and from any or all provisions of this chapter as it may find necessary and proper in the public interest.

Criminal Penalties

Section 629. Whoever shall forcibly resist, oppose, impede, intimidate or interfere with a duly authorized representative of the Equal Employment Opportunity Commission while it is engaged in the performance of duties under this chapter shall be punished by a fine of not more than $500 or by imprisonment for not more than one year, or by both: *Provided*, however, That no person shall be imprisoned under this section except when there has been a prior conviction hereunder.

Definitions

Section 630. For the purposes of this chapter—

(a) The term "person" means one or more individuals, partnerships, associations, labor organizations, corporations, business trusts, legal representatives, or any organized groups of persons.

(b) The term "employer" means a person engaged in an industry affecting commerce who has twenty or more employees for each working day in each of twenty or more calendar weeks in the current or preceding calendar year: *Provided*, That prior to June 30, 1968, employers having fewer than fifty employees shall not be considered employers. The term also means (1) any agent of such a person, and (2) a State or political subdivision of a State and any agency or instrumentality of a State or a political subdivision of a State, and any interstate agency, but such term does not include the United States, or a corporation wholly owned by the Government of the United States.

(c) The term "employment agency" means any person regularly undertaking with or without compensation to procure employees for an employer and includes an agent of such a person; but shall not include an agency of the United States.

(d) The term "labor organization" means a labor organization engaged in an industry affecting commerce, and any agent of such an organization, and includes any organization of any kind, any agency, or employee representation committee, group, association, or plan so engaged in which employees participate and which exists for the purpose, in whole or in part, of dealing with employers concerning grievances, labor disputes, wages, rates of pay, hours, or other terms or conditions of employment, and any conference, general committee, joint or system board, or joint council so engaged which is subordinate to a national or international labor organization.

(e) A labor organization shall be deemed to be engaged in an industry affecting commerce if (1) it maintains or operates a hiring hall or hiring office which procures employees for an employer or procures for employees opportunities to work for an employer, or (2) the number of its members (or, where it is a labor organization composed of other labor organizations or their representatives, if the aggregate number of the members of such other labor organization) is fifty or more prior to July 1, 1968, or twenty-five or more on or after July 1, 1968, and such labor organization—

(1) is the certified representative of employees under the provisions of the National Labor Relations Act, as amended, or the Railway Labor Act, as amended; or

(2) although not certified, is a national or international labor organization or a local labor organization recognized or acting as the representative of employees of an employer or employers engaged in an industry affecting commerce; or

(3) has chartered a local labor organization or subsidiary body which is representing or actively seeking to represent employees of employers within the meaning of paragraph (1) or (2); or

(4) has been chartered by a labor organization representing or actively seeking to represent employees within

the meaning of paragraph (1) or (2) as the local or subordinate body through which such employees may enjoy membership or become affiliated with such labor organization; or

(5) is a conference, general committee, joint or system board, or joint council subordinate to a national or international labor organization, which includes a labor organization engaged in an industry affecting commerce within the meaning of any of the preceding paragraphs and this subsection.

(f) The term "employee" means an individual employed by any employer except that the term "employee" shall not include any person elected to public office in any State or political subdivision of any State by the qualified voters thereof, or any person chosen by such officer to be on such officer's personal staff, or an appointee on the policy-making level or an immediate adviser with respect to the exercise of the constitutional or legal powers of the office. The exemption set forth in the preceding sentence shall not include employees subject to the civil service laws of a State government, governmental agency, or political subdivision.

(g) The term, "commerce" means trade, traffic, commerce, transportation, transmission, or communication among the several States; or between a State and any place outside thereof; or within the District of Columbia, or a possession of the United States; or between points in the same State but through a point outside thereof.

(h) The term "industry affecting commerce" means any activity, business, or industry in commerce or in which a labor dispute would hinder or obstruct commerce or the free flow of commerce and includes any activity or industry "affecting commerce" within the meaning of the Labor-Management Reporting and Disclosure Act of 1959.

(i) The term "State" includes a State of the United States, the District of Columbia, Puerto Rico, the Virgin Islands, American Samoa, Guam, Wake Island, the Canal Zone, and Outer Continental Shelf lands defined in the Outer Continental Shelf Lands Act.

(j) The term "firefighter" means an employee, the duties of whose position are primarily to perform work directly connected with the control and extinguishment of fires or the maintenance and use of firefighting apparatus and equipment, including an employee engaged in this activity who is transferred to a supervisory or administrative position.

(k) The term "law enforcement officer" means an employee, the duties of whose position are primarily the investigation, apprehension, or detention of individuals suspected or convicted of offenses against the criminal laws of a State, including an employee engaged in this activity who is transferred to a supervisory or administrative position. For the purpose of this subsection, "detention" includes the duties of employees assigned to guard individuals incarcerated in any penal institution.

(l) The term "compensation, terms, conditions, or privileges of employment" encompasses all employee benefits, including such benefits provided pursuant to a bona fide employee benefit plan.

Age Limits

Section 631.

(a) The prohibitions in this chapter shall be limited to individuals who are at least 40 years of age.

(b) In the case of any personnel action affecting employees or applicants for employment which is subject to the provisions of section 633a of this title, the prohibitions established in section 633a of this title shall be limited to individuals who are at least 40 years of age.

(c) (1) Nothing in this chapter shall be construed to prohibit compulsory retirement of any employee who has attained 65 years of age who, for the 2-year period immediately before retirement, is employed in a bona fide executive or a high policymaking position, if such employee is entitled to an immediate nonforfeitable annual retirement benefit from a pension, profit-sharing, savings, or deferred compensation plan, or any combination of such plans, of the employer of such employee, which equals, in the aggregate, at last $44,000.

(2) In applying the retirement benefit test of paragraph (1) of this subsection, if any such retirement benefit is in a form other than a straight life annuity (with no ancillary benefits), or if employees contribute to any such plan or make rollover contributions, such benefit shall be adjusted in accordance with regulations prescribed by the Secretary, after consultation with the Secretary of the Treasury, so that the benefit is the equivalent of a straight life annuity (with no ancillary benefits) under a plan to which employees do not contribute and under which no rollover contributions are made.

(d) Nothing in this Act shall be construed to prohibit compulsory retirement of any employee who has attained 70 years of age, and who is serving under a contract of unlimited tenure (or similar arrangement providing for unlimited tenure) at an institution of higher education.

Annual Report to Congress

Section 632. *[Repealed]*

Federal–State Relationship

Section 633.

(a) Nothing in this chapter shall affect the jurisdiction of any agency of any State performing like functions with regard to discriminatory employment practices on account of age except that upon commencement of action under this chapter such action shall supersede any State action.

(b) In the case of an alleged unlawful practice occurring in a State which has a law prohibiting discrimination in employment because of age and establishing or authorizing a State authority to grant or seek relief from such discriminatory practice, no suit may be brought under section 626 of this title before the expiration of sixty days after proceedings have been commenced under the State law, unless such proceedings have been earlier terminated: *Provided*, That such sixty-day period shall be extended to one hundred and twenty days during the first year after the effective date of such State law. If any requirement for the commencement of such proceedings is imposed by a State authority other than a requirement of the filing of a written and signed statement of the facts upon which the proceeding is based, the proceeding shall be deemed to have been commenced for the purposes of this subsection at the time such statement is sent by registered mail to the appropriate State authority.

Nondiscrimination on Account of Age in Federal Government Employment

Section 633a.

(a) Federal agencies affected

All personnel actions affecting employees or applicants for employment who are at least 40 years of age (except personnel actions with regard to aliens employed outside the limits of the United States) in military departments as defined in section 102 of Title 5 *[5 U.S.C. § 102]*, in executive agencies as defined in section 105 of Title 5 *[5 U.S.C. § 105]* (including employees and applicants for employment who are paid from nonappropriated funds), in the United States Postal Service and the Postal Regulatory Commission, in those units in the government of the District of Columbia having positions in the competitive service, and in those units of the judicial branch of the Federal Government having positions in the competitive service, in the Smithsonian Institution, and in the Government Printing Office, the Government Accountability Office, and the Library of Congress shall be made free from any discrimination based on age.

(b) Enforcement by Equal Employment Opportunity Commission and by Librarian of Congress in the Library of Congress; remedies; rules, regulations, orders, and instructions of Commission: compliance by Federal agencies; powers and duties of Commission; notification of final action on complaint of discrimination; exemptions: bona fide occupational qualification

Except as otherwise provided in this subsection, the Equal Employment Opportunity Commission is authorized to enforce the provisions of subsection (a) of this section through appropriate remedies, including reinstatement or hiring of employees with or without backpay, as will effectuate the policies of this section. The Equal Employment Opportunity Commission shall issue such rules, regulations, orders, and instructions as it deems necessary and appropriate to carry out its responsibilities under this section. The Equal Employment Opportunity Commission shall—

(1) be responsible for the review and evaluation of the operation of all agency programs designed to carry out the policy of this section, periodically obtaining and publishing (on at least a semiannual basis) progress reports from each department, agency, or unit referred to in subsection (a) of this section;

(2) consult with and solicit the recommendations of interested individuals, groups, and organizations relating to nondiscrimination in employment on account of age; and

(3) provide for the acceptance and processing of complaints of discrimination in Federal employment on account of age.

The head of each such department, agency, or unit shall comply with such rules, regulations, orders, and instructions of the Equal Employment Opportunity Commission which shall include a provision that an employee or applicant for employment shall be notified of any final action taken on any complaint of discrimination filed by him thereunder. Reasonable exemptions to the provisions of this section may be established by the Commission but only when the Commission has established a maximum age requirement on the basis of a determination that age is a bona fide occupational qualification necessary to the performance of the duties of the position. With respect to employment in the Library of Congress, authorities granted in this subsection to the Equal Employment Opportunity Commission shall be exercised by the Librarian of Congress.

(c) Civil actions; jurisdiction; relief

Any person aggrieved may bring a civil action in any Federal district court of competent jurisdiction for such legal or equitable relief as will effectuate the purposes of this chapter.

(d) Notice to Commission; time of notice; Commission notification of prospective defendants; Commission elimination of unlawful practices

When the individual has not filed a complaint concerning age discrimination with the Commission, no civil action may be commenced by any individual under this section until the individual has given the Commission not less than thirty days' notice of an intent to file such action. Such notice shall be filed within one hundred and eighty days after the alleged unlawful practice occurred. Upon receiving a notice of intent to sue, the Commission shall promptly notify all persons named therein as prospective defendants in the action and take any appropriate action to assure the elimination of any unlawful practice.

(e) Duty of Government agency or official

Nothing contained in this section shall relieve any Government agency or official of the responsibility to assure nondiscrimination on account of age in employment as required under any provision of Federal law.

(f) Applicability of statutory provisions to personnel action of Federal departments, etc.

Any personnel action of any department, agency, or other entity referred to in subsection (a) of this section shall not be subject to, or affected by, any provision of this chapter, other than the provisions of sections 7(d)(3) and 631(b) of this title *[section 12(b)]* and the provisions of this section.

(g) Study and report to President and Congress by Equal Employment Opportunity Commission; scope

(1) The Equal Employment Opportunity Commission shall undertake a study relating to the effects of the amendments made to this section by the Age Discrimination in Employment Act Amendments of 1978, and the effects of section 631(b) of this title *[section 12(b)]*.

(2) The Equal Employment Opportunity Commission shall transmit a report to the President and to the Congress containing the findings of the Commission resulting from the study of the Commission under paragraph (1) of this subsection. Such report shall be transmitted no later than January 1, 1980.

Extracts from the Family and Medical Leave Act

29 U.S.C. Section 2611 et seq.

Section 2611. Definitions

As used in this subchapter:

(1) Commerce

The terms "commerce" and "industry or activity affecting commerce" mean any activity, business, or industry in commerce or in which a labor dispute would hinder or obstruct commerce or the free flow of commerce, and include "commerce" and any "industry affecting commerce", as defined in paragraphs (1) and (3) of section 142 of this title.

(2) Eligible employee

(A) In general

The term "eligible employee" means an employee who has been employed—

(i) for at least 12 months by the employer with respect to whom leave is requested under section 2612 of this title; and

(ii) for at least 1,250 hours of service with such employer during the previous 12-month period.

(B) Exclusions

The term "eligible employee" does not include—

(i) any Federal officer or employee covered under subchapter V of chapter 63 of Title 5; or

(ii) any employee of an employer who is employed at a worksite at which such employer employs less than 50 employees if the total number of employees employed by that employer within 75 miles of that worksite is less than 50.

(C) Determination

For purposes of determining whether an employee meets the hours of service requirement specified in subparagraph (A)(ii), the legal standards established under section 207 of this title shall apply.

(3) Employ; employee; State

The terms "employ", "employee", and "State" have the same meanings given such terms in subsections (c), (e), and (g) of section 203 of this title.

(4) Employer

(A) In general

The term "employer"—

(i) means any person engaged in commerce or in any industry or activity affecting commerce who employs 50 or more employees for each working day during each of 20 or more calendar workweeks in the current or preceding calendar year;

(ii) includes—

(I) any person who acts, directly or indirectly, in the interest of an employer to any of the employees of such employer; and

(II) any successor in interest of an employer;

(iii) includes any "public agency", as defined in section 203(x) of this title; and

(iv) includes the Government Accountability Office and the Library of Congress.

(B) Public agency

For purposes of subparagraph (A)(iii), a public agency shall be considered to be a person engaged in commerce or in an industry or activity affecting commerce.

(5) Employment benefits

The term "employment benefits" means all benefits provided or made available to employees by an employer, including group life insurance, health insurance, disability insurance, sick leave, annual leave, educational benefits, and pensions, regardless of whether such benefits are provided by a practice or written policy of an employer or through an "employee benefit plan", as defined in section 1002(3) of this title.

(6) Health care provider

The term "health care provider" means—

(A) a doctor of medicine or osteopathy who is authorized to practice medicine or surgery (as appropriate) by the State in which the doctor practices; or

(B) any other person determined by the Secretary to be capable of providing health care services.

(7) Parent

The term "parent" means the biological parent of an employee or an individual who stood in loco parentis to an employee when the employee was a son or daughter.

(8) Person

The term "person" has the same meaning given such term in section 203(a) of this title.

(9) Reduced leave schedule

The term "reduced leave schedule" means a leave schedule that reduces the usual number of hours per workweek, or hours per workday, of an employee.

(10) Secretary

The term "Secretary" means the Secretary of Labor.

(11) Serious health condition

The term "serious health condition" means an illness, injury, impairment, or physical or mental condition that involves—

(A) inpatient care in a hospital, hospice, or residential medical care facility; or

(B) continuing treatment by a health care provider.

(12) Son or daughter

The term "son or daughter" means a biological, adopted, or foster child, a stepchild, a legal ward, or a child of a person standing in loco parent is, who is—

(A) under 18 years of age; or

(B) 18 years of age or older and incapable of self-care because of a mental or physical disability.

(13) Spouse

The term "spouse" means a husband or wife, as the case may be.

(14) Covered active duty

The term covered "active duty" means—

(A) in the case of a member of a regular component of the Armed Forces, duty during the deployment of the member with the Armed Forces to a foreign country; and

(B) in the case of a member of a reserve component of the Armed Forces, duty during the deployment of the member with the Armed Forces to a foreign country under a call or order to active duty under a provision of law referred to in section 101(a)(13)(B) of title 10, United States Code.

(15) Covered servicemember

The term "covered servicemember" means—

(A) a member of the Armed Forces (including a member of the National Guard or Reserves) who is undergoing medical treatment, recuperation, or therapy, is otherwise in outpatient status, or is otherwise on the temporary disability retired list, for a serious injury or illness; or

(B) a veteran who is undergoing medical treatment, recuperation, or therapy, for a serious injury or illness and who was a member of the Armed Forces (including a member of the National Guard or Reserves) at any time during the period of 5 years preceding the date on which the veteran undergoes that medical treatment, recuperation, or therapy.

(16) Outpatient status

The term "outpatient status", with respect to a covered servicemember, means the status of a member of the Armed Forces assigned to—

(A) a military medical treatment facility as an outpatient; or

(B) a unit established for the purpose of providing command and control of members of the Armed Forces receiving medical care as outpatients.

(17) Next of kin

The term "next of kin", used with respect to an individual, means the nearest blood relative of that individual.

(18) Serious injury or illness

The term "serious injury or illness"—

(A) in the case of a member of the Armed Forces (including a member of the National Guard or Reserves), means an injury or illness that was incurred by the member in line of duty on active duty in the Armed Forces (or existed before the beginning of the member's active duty and was aggravated by service in line of duty on active duty in the Armed Forces) and that may render the member medically unfit to perform the duties of the member's office, grade, rank, or rating; and

(B) in the case of a veteran who was a member of the Armed Forces (including a member of the National Guard or Reserves) at any time during a period described in paragraph (15)(B), means a qualifying (as defined by the Secretary of Labor) injury or illness that was incurred by the member in line of duty on active duty in the Armed Forces (or existed before the beginning of the member's active duty and was aggravated by service in line of duty on active duty in the Armed Forces) and that manifested itself before or after the member became a veteran.

(19) Veteran

The term 'veteran' has the meaning given the term in section 101 of title 38, United States Code.

Section 2612. Leave requirement

(a) In general

(1) Entitlement to leave

Subject to section 2613 of this title, an eligible employee shall be entitled to a total of 12 workweeks of leave during any 12-month period for one or more of the following:

(A) Because of the birth of a son or daughter of the employee and in order to care for such son or daughter.

(B) Because of the placement of a son or daughter with the employee for adoption or foster care.

(C) In order to care for the spouse, or a son, daughter, or parent, of the employee, if such spouse, son, daughter, or parent has a serious health condition.

(D) Because of a serious health condition that makes the employee unable to perform the functions of the position of such employee.

(E) Because of any qualifying exigency (as the Secretary shall, by regulation, determine) arising out of the fact that the spouse, or a son, daughter, or parent of the employee is on covered active duty (or has been notified of an impending call or order to covered active duty) in the Armed Forces in support of a contingency operation.

(2) Expiration of entitlement

The entitlement to leave under subparagraphs (A) and (B) of paragraph (1) for a birth or placement of a son or daughter shall expire at the end of the 12-month period beginning on the date of such birth or placement.

(3) Servicemember family leave

Subject to section 2613 of this title, an eligible employee who is the spouse, son, daughter, parent, or next of kin of a covered servicemember shall be entitled to a total of 26 workweeks of leave during a 12-month period to care for the servicemember. The leave described in this paragraph shall only be available during a single 12-month period.

(4) Combined leave total

During the single 12-month period described in paragraph (3), an eligible employee shall be entitled to a combined total of 26 workweeks of leave under paragraphs (1) and (3). Nothing in this paragraph shall be construed to limit the availability of leave under paragraph (1) during any other 12-month period.

(b) Leave taken intermittently or on reduced leave schedule

(1) In general

Leave under subparagraph (A) or (B) of subsection (a)(1) of this section shall not be taken by an employee intermittently or on a reduced leave schedule unless the employee and the employer of the employee agree otherwise. Subject to paragraph (2), subsection (e)(2) of this section, and subsection (b)(5) or (f) (as appropriate) of section 2613 of this of this title, leave under subparagraph (C) or (D) of subsection (a)(1) of this section or under subsection (a)(3) of this section may be taken intermittently or on a reduced leave schedule when medically necessary. Subject to subsection (e)(3) of this section and section 2613 (f) of this title, leave under subsection (a)(1)(E) of this section may be taken intermittently or on a reduced leave schedule. The taking of leave intermittently or on a reduced leave schedule pursuant to this paragraph shall not result in a reduction in the total amount of leave to which the employee is entitled under subsection (a) of this section beyond the amount of leave actually taken.

(2) Alternative position

If an employee requests intermittent leave, or leave on a reduced leave schedule, under subparagraph (C) or (D) of subsection (a)(1) of this section or under subsection (a)(3) of this section, that is foreseeable based on planned medical treatment, the employer may require such employee to transfer temporarily to an available alternative position offered by the employer for which the employee is qualified and that—

(A) has equivalent pay and benefits; and

(B) better accommodates recurring periods of leave than the regular employment position of the employee.

(c) Unpaid leave permitted

Except as provided in subsection (d) of this section, leave granted under subsection (a) may consist of unpaid leave. Where an employee is otherwise exempt under regulations issued by the Secretary pursuant to section 213(a)(1) of this title, the compliance of an employer with this subchapter by providing unpaid leave shall not affect the exempt status of the employee under such section.

(d) Relationship to paid leave

(1) Unpaid leave

If an employer provides paid leave for fewer than 12 workweeks (or 26 workweeks in the case of leave provided under subsection (a)(3) of this section), the additional weeks of leave necessary to attain the 12 workweeks (or 26 workweeks, as appropriate) of leave required under this subchapter may be provided without compensation.

(2) Substitution of paid leave

(A) In general

An eligible employee may elect, or an employer may require the employee, to substitute any of the accrued paid vacation leave, personal leave, or family leave of the employee for leave provided under subparagraph (A), (B), (C), or (E) of subsection (a)(1) of this section for any part of the 12-week period of such leave under such subsection.

(B) Serious health condition

An eligible employee may elect, or an employer may require the employee, to substitute any of the accrued paid vacation leave, personal leave, or medical or sick leave of the employee for leave provided under subparagraph (C) or (D) of subsection (a)(1) of this section for any part of the 12-week period of such leave under such subsection, except that nothing in this subchapter shall require an employer to provide paid sick leave or paid medical leave in any situation in which such employer would not normally provide any such paid leave. An eligible employee may elect, or an employer may require the employee, to substitute any of the accrued paid vacation leave, personal leave, family leave, or medical or sick leave of the employee for leave provided under subsection (a)(3) of this section for any part of the 26-week period of such leave under such subsection, except that nothing in this subchapter requires an employer to provide paid sick leave or paid medical leave in any situation in which the employer would not normally provide any such paid leave.

(e) Foreseeable leave

(1) Requirement of notice

In any case in which the necessity for leave under subparagraph (A) or (B) of subsection (a)(1) of this section is foreseeable based on an expected birth or placement, the employee shall provide the employer with not less than 30 days' notice, before the date the leave is to begin, of the employee's intention to take leave under such subparagraph, except that if the date of the birth or placement requires leave to begin in less than 30 days, the employee shall provide such notice as is practicable.

(2) Duties of employee

In any case in which the necessity for leave under subparagraph (C) or (D) of subsection (a)(1) of this section or under subsection (a)(3) of this section is foreseeable based on planned medical treatment, the employee—

(A) shall make a reasonable effort to schedule the treatment so as not to disrupt unduly the operations of the employer, subject to the approval of the health care provider of the employee or the health care provider of the son, daughter, spouse, parent, or covered servicemember of the employee, as appropriate; and

(B) shall provide the employer with not less than 30 days' notice, before the date the leave is to begin, of the employee's intention to take leave under such subparagraph, except that if the date of the treatment requires leave to begin in less than 30 days, the employee shall provide such notice as is practicable.

(3) Notice for leave due to covered active duty of family member

In any case in which the necessity for leave under subsection (a)(1)(E) of this section is foreseeable, whether because the spouse, or a son, daughter, or parent, of the employee is on covered active duty, or because of notification of an impending call or order to covered active duty in support of a contingency operation, the employee shall provide such notice to the employer as is reasonable and practicable.

(f) Spouses employed by same employer

(1) In general

In any case in which a husband and wife entitled to leave under subsection (a) of this section are employed by the same employer, the aggregate number of workweeks of leave to which both may be entitled may be limited to 12 workweeks during any 12-month period, if such leave is taken—

(A) under subparagraph (A) or (B) of subsection (a)(1) of this section; or

(B) to care for a sick parent under subparagraph (C) of such subsection.

(2) Servicemember family leave

(A) In general

The aggregate number of workweeks of leave to which both that husband and wife may be entitled under subsection (a) of this section may be limited to 26 workweeks during the single 12-month period described in subsection (a)(3) of this section if the leave is—

(i) leave under subsection (a)(3) of this section; or

(ii) a combination of leave under subsection (a)(3) of this section and leave described in paragraph (1).

(B) Both limitations applicable

If the leave taken by the husband and wife includes leave described in paragraph (1), the limitation in paragraph (1) shall apply to the leave described in paragraph (1).

Section 2613. Certification

(a) In general

An employer may require that a request for leave under subparagraph (C) or (D) of paragraph (1) or paragraph (3) of section 2612(a) of this title be supported by a certification issued by the health care provider of the eligible employee or of the son, daughter, spouse, or parent of the employee, or of the next of kin of an individual in the case of leave taken under such paragraph (3), as appropriate. The employee shall provide, in a timely manner, a copy of such certification to the employer.

(b) Sufficient certification

Certification provided under subsection (a) of this section shall be sufficient if it states—

(1) the date on which the serious health condition commenced;

(2) the probable duration of the condition;

(3) the appropriate medical facts within the knowledge of the health care provider regarding the condition;

(4) (A) for purposes of leave under section 2612(a)(1)(C) of this title, a statement that the eligible employee is needed to care for the son, daughter, spouse, or parent and an estimate of the amount of time that such employee is needed to care for the son, daughter, spouse, or parent; and

(B) for purposes of leave under section 2612(a)(1)(D) of this title, a statement that the employee is unable to perform the functions of the position of the employee;

(5) in the case of certification for intermittent leave, or leave on a reduced leave schedule, for planned medical treatment, the dates on which such treatment is expected to be given and the duration of such treatment;

(6) in the case of certification for intermittent leave, or leave on a reduced leave schedule, under section 2612(a)(1)(D) of this title, a statement of the medical necessity for the intermittent leave or leave on a reduced leave schedule, and the expected duration of the intermittent leave or reduced leave schedule; and

(7) in the case of certification for intermittent leave, or leave on a reduced leave schedule, under section 2612(a)(1)(C) of this title, a statement that the employee's intermittent leave or leave on a reduced leave schedule is necessary for the care of the son, daughter, parent, or spouse who has a serious health condition, or will assist in their recovery, and the expected duration and schedule of the intermittent leave or reduced leave schedule.

(c) Second opinion

(1) In general

In any case in which the employer has reason to doubt the validity of the certification provided under subsection (a) of this section for leave under subparagraph (C) or (D) of section 2612(a)(1) of this title, the employer may require, at the expense of the employer, that the eligible employee obtain the opinion of a second health care provider designated or approved by the employer concerning any information certified under subsection (b) of this section for such leave.

(2) Limitation

A health care provider designated or approved under paragraph (1) shall not be employed on a regular basis by the employer.

(d) Resolution of conflicting opinions

(1) In general

In any case in which the second opinion described in subsection (c) of this section differs from the opinion in the original certification provided under subsection (a) of this section, the employer may require, at the expense of the employer, that the employee obtain the opinion of a third health care provider designated or approved jointly by the employer and the employee concerning the information certified under subsection (b) of this section.

(2) Finality

The opinion of the third health care provider concerning the information certified under subsection (b) of this section shall be considered to be final and shall be binding on the employer and the employee.

(e) Subsequent recertification

The employer may require that the eligible employee obtain subsequent recertifications on a reasonable basis.

(f) Certification related to covered active duty or call to active duty

An employer may require that a request for leave under section 2612(a)(1)(E) of this title be supported by a certification issued at such time and in such manner as the Secretary may by regulation prescribe. If the Secretary issues a regulation requiring such certification, the employee shall provide, in a timely manner, a copy of such certification to the employer.

Section 2614. Employment and benefits protection

(a) Restoration to position

(1) In general

Except as provided in subsection (b) of this section, any eligible employee who takes leave under section 2612 of this title for the intended purpose of the leave shall be entitled, on return from such leave—

(A) to be restored by the employer to the position of employment held by the employee when the leave commenced; or

(B) to be restored to an equivalent position with equivalent employment benefits, pay, and other terms and conditions of employment.

(2) Loss of benefits

The taking of leave under section 2612 of this title shall not result in the loss of any employment benefit accrued prior to the date on which the leave commenced.

(3) Limitations

Nothing in this section shall be construed to entitle any restored employee to—

(A) the accrual of any seniority or employment benefits during any period of leave; or

(B) any right, benefit, or position of employment other than any right, benefit, or position to which the employee would have been entitled had the employee not taken the leave.

(4) Certification

As a condition of restoration under paragraph (1) for an employee who has taken leave under section 2612(a)(1)(D) of this title, the employer may have a uniformly applied practice or policy that requires each such employee to receive certification from the health care provider of the employee that the employee is able to resume work, except that nothing in this paragraph shall supersede a valid State or local law or a collective bargaining agreement that governs the return to work of such employees.

(5) Construction

Nothing in this subsection shall be construed to prohibit an employer from requiring an employee on leave under section 2612 of this title to report periodically to the employer on the status and intention of the employee to return to work.

(b) Exemption concerning certain highly compensated employees

(1) Denial of restoration

An employer may deny restoration under subsection (a) of this section to any eligible employee described in paragraph (2) if—

(A) such denial is necessary to prevent substantial and grievous economic injury to the operations of the employer;

(B) the employer notifies the employee of the intent of the employer to deny restoration on such basis at the time the employer determines that such injury would occur; and

(C) in any case in which the leave has commenced, the employee elects not to return to employment after receiving such notice.

(2) Affected employees

An eligible employee described in paragraph (1) is a salaried eligible employee who is among the highest paid 10 percent of the employees employed by the employer within 75 miles of the facility at which the employee is employed.

(c) Maintenance of health benefits

(1) Coverage

Except as provided in paragraph (2), during any period that an eligible employee takes leave under section 2612 of this title, the employer shall maintain coverage under any "group health plan" (as defined in section 5000(b)(1) of Title 26) for the duration of such leave at the level and under the conditions coverage would have been provided if the employee had continued in employment continuously for the duration of such leave.

(2) Failure to return from leave

The employer may recover the premium that the employer paid for maintaining coverage for the employee under such group health plan during any period of unpaid leave under section 2612 of this title if—

(A) the employee fails to return from leave under section 2612 of this title after the period of leave to which the employee is entitled has expired; and

(B) the employee fails to return to work for a reason other than—

(i) the continuation, recurrence, or onset of a serious health condition that entitles the employee to leave under subparagraph (C) or (D) of section 2612(a)(1) of this title or under section 2612(a)(3) of this title; or

(ii) other circumstances beyond the control of the employee.

(3) Certification

(A) Issuance

An employer may require that a claim that an employee is unable to return to work because of the continuation, recurrence, or onset of the serious health condition described in paragraph (2)(B)(i) be supported by—

(i) a certification issued by the health care provider of the son, daughter, spouse, or parent of the employee, as appropriate, in the case of an employee unable to return to work because of a condition specified in section 2612(a)(1)(C) of this title;

(ii) a certification issued by the health care provider of the eligible employee, in the case of an employee unable to return to work because of a condition specified in section 2612(a)(1)(D) of this title; or

(iii) a certification issued by the health care provider of the servicemember being cared for by the employee, in the case of an employee unable to return to work because of a condition specified in section 2612(a)(3) of this title.

(B) Copy

The employee shall provide, in a timely manner, a copy of such certification to the employer.

(C) Sufficiency of certification

(i) Leave due to serious health condition of employee

The certification described in subparagraph (A)(ii) shall be sufficient if the certification states that a serious health condition prevented the employee from being able to perform the functions of the position of the employee on the date that the leave of the employee expired.

(ii) Leave due to serious health condition of family member

The certification described in subparagraph (A)(i) shall be sufficient if the certification states that the employee is needed to care for the son, daughter, spouse, or parent who has a serious health condition on the date that the leave of the employee expired.

Section 2615. Prohibited acts

(a) Interference with rights

(1) Exercise of rights

It shall be unlawful for any employer to interfere with, restrain, or deny the exercise of or the attempt to exercise, any right provided under this subchapter.

(2) Discrimination

It shall be unlawful for any employer to discharge or in any other manner discriminate against any individual for opposing any practice made unlawful by this subchapter.

(b) Interference with proceedings or inquiries

It shall be unlawful for any person to discharge or in

any other manner discriminate against any individual because such individual—

(1) has filed any charge, or has instituted or caused to be instituted any proceeding, under or related to this subchapter;

(2) has given, or is about to give, any information in connection with any inquiry or proceeding relating to any right provided under this subchapter; or

(3) has testified, or is about to testify, in any inquiry or proceeding relating to any right provided under this subchapter.

Section 2616. Investigative authority

(a) In general

To ensure compliance with the provisions of this subchapter, or any regulation or order issued under this subchapter, the Secretary shall have, subject to subsection (c) of this section, the investigative authority provided under section 211(a) of this title.

(b) Obligation to keep and preserve records

Any employer shall make, keep, and preserve records pertaining to compliance with this subchapter in accordance with section 211(c) of this title and in accordance with regulations issued by the Secretary.

(c) Required submissions generally limited to annual basis

The Secretary shall not under the authority of this section require any employer or any plan, fund, or program to submit to the Secretary any books or records more than once during any 12-month period, unless the Secretary has reasonable cause to believe there may exist a violation of this subchapter or any regulation or order issued pursuant to this subchapter, or is investigating a charge pursuant to section 2617(b) of this title.

(d) Subpoena powers

For the purposes of any investigation provided for in this section, the Secretary shall have the subpoena authority provided for under section 209 of this title.

Section 2617. Enforcement

(a) Civil action by employees

(1) Liability

Any employer who violates section 2615 of this title shall be liable to any eligible employee affected—

(A) for damages equal to—

(i) the amount of—

(I) any wages, salary, employment benefits, or other compensation denied or lost to such employee by reason of the violation; or

(II) in a case in which wages, salary, employment benefits, or other compensation have not been denied or lost to the employee, any actual monetary losses sustained by the employee as a direct result of the violation, such as the cost of providing care, up to a sum equal to 12 weeks (or 26 weeks, in a case involving leave under section 2612 (a)(3) of this title) of wages or salary for the employee;

(ii) the interest on the amount described in clause (i) calculated at the prevailing rate; and

(iii) an additional amount as liquidated damages equal to the sum of the amount described in clause (i) and the interest described in clause (ii), except that if an employer who has violated section 2615 of this title proves to the satisfaction of the court that the act or omission which violated section 2615 of this title was in good faith and that the employer had reasonable grounds for believing that the act or omission was not a violation of section 2615 of this title, such court may, in the discretion of the court, reduce the amount of the liability to the amount and interest determined under clauses (i) and (ii), respectively; and

(B) for such equitable relief as may be appropriate, including employment, reinstatement, and promotion.

(2) Right of action

An action to recover the damages or equitable relief prescribed in paragraph (1) may be maintained against any employer (including a public agency) in any Federal or State court of competent jurisdiction by any one or more employees for and in behalf of—

(A) the employees; or

(B) the employees and other employees similarly situated.

(3) Fees and costs

The court in such an action shall, in addition to any judgment awarded to the plaintiff, allow a reasonable attorney's fee, reasonable expert witness fees, and other costs of the action to be paid by the defendant.

(4) Limitations

The right provided by paragraph (2) to bring an action by or on behalf of any employee shall terminate—

(A) on the filing of a complaint by the Secretary in an action under subsection (d) of this section in which restraint is sought of any further delay in the payment of the amount described in paragraph (1)(A) to such employee by an employer responsible under paragraph (1) for the payment; or

(B) on the filing of a complaint by the Secretary in an action under subsection (b) of this section in which a recovery is sought of the damages described in paragraph (1)(A) owing to an eligible employee by an employer liable under paragraph (1), unless the action described in subparagraph (A) or (B) is dismissed without prejudice on motion of the Secretary.

(b) Action by Secretary

(1) Administrative action

The Secretary shall receive, investigate, and attempt to resolve complaints of violations of section 2615 of this title in the same manner that the Secretary receives, investigates, and attempts to resolve complaints of violations of sections 206 and 207 of this title.

(2) Civil action

The Secretary may bring an action in any court of competent jurisdiction to recover the damages described in subsection (a)(1)(A) of this section.

(3) Sums recovered

Any sums recovered by the Secretary pursuant to paragraph (2) shall be held in a special deposit account and shall be paid, on order of the Secretary, directly to each employee affected. Any such sums not paid to an employee because of inability to do so within a period of 3 years shall be deposited into the Treasury of the United States as miscellaneous receipts.

(c) Limitation

(1) In general

Except as provided in paragraph (2), an action may be brought under this section not later than 2 years after the date of the last event constituting the alleged violation for which the action is brought.

(2) Willful violation

In the case of such action brought for a willful violation of section 2615 of this title, such action may be brought within 3 years of the date of the last event constituting the alleged violation for which such action is brought.

(3) Commencement

In determining when an action is commenced by the Secretary under this section for the purposes of this subsection, it shall be considered to be commenced on the date when the complaint is filed.

(d) Action for injunction by Secretary

The district courts of the United States shall have jurisdiction, for cause shown, in an action brought by the Secretary—

(1) to restrain violations of section 2615 of this title, including the restraint of any withholding of payment of wages, salary, employment benefits, or other compensation, plus interest, found by the court to be due to eligible employees; or

(2) to award such other equitable relief as may be appropriate, including employment, reinstatement, and promotion.

(e) Solicitor of Labor

The Solicitor of Labor may appear for and represent the Secretary on any litigation brought under this section.

(f) Government Accountability Office and Library of Congress

In the case of the Government Accountability Office and the Library of Congress, the authority of the Secretary of Labor under this subchapter shall be exercised respectively by the Comptroller General of the United States and the Librarian of Congress.

Section 2618. Special rules concerning employees of local educational agencies

(a) Application

(1) In general

Except as otherwise provided in this section, the rights (including the rights under section 2614 of this title, which shall extend throughout the period of leave of any employee under this section), remedies, and procedures under this subchapter shall apply to—

(A) any "local educational agency" (as defined in section 7801 of Title 20) and an eligible employee of the agency; and

(B) any private elementary or secondary school and an eligible employee of the school.

(2) Definitions

For purposes of the application described in paragraph (1):

(A) Eligible employee

The term "eligible employee" means an eligible employee of an agency or school described in paragraph (1).

(B) Employer

The term "employer" means an agency or school described in paragraph (1).

(b) Leave does not violate certain other Federal laws

A local educational agency and a private elementary or secondary school shall not be in violation of the Individuals with Disabilities Education Act (20 U.S.C. 1400 et seq.), section 794 of this title or title VI of the Civil Rights Act of 1964 (42 U.S.C. 2000d et seq.), solely as a result of an eligible employee of such agency or school exercising the rights of such employee under this subchapter.

(c) Intermittent leave or leave on reduced schedule for instructional employees

(1) In general

Subject to paragraph (2), in any case in which an eligible employee employed principally in an instructional capacity by any such educational agency or school requests leave under subparagraph (C) or (D) of section 2612(a)(1) of this title or under section 2612(a)(3) of this title that is foreseeable based on planned medical treatment and the employee would be on leave for greater than 20 percent of the total number of working days in the period during which the leave would extend, the agency or school may require that such employee elect either—

(A) to take leave for periods of a particular duration, not to exceed the duration of the planned medical treatment; or

(B) to transfer temporarily to an available alternative position offered by the employer for which the employee is qualified, and that—

(i) has equivalent pay and benefits; and

(ii) better accommodates recurring periods of leave than the regular employment position of the employee.

(2) Application

The elections described in subparagraphs (A) and (B) of paragraph (1) shall apply only with respect to an eligible employee who complies with section 2612(e)(2) of this title.

(d) Rules applicable to periods near conclusion of academic term

The following rules shall apply with respect to periods of leave near the conclusion of an academic term in the case of any eligible employee employed principally in an instructional capacity by any such educational agency or school:

(1) Leave more than 5 weeks prior to end of term

If the eligible employee begins leave under section 2612 of this title more than 5 weeks prior to the end of the academic term, the agency or school may require the employee to continue taking leave until the end of such term, if—

(A) the leave is of at least 3 weeks duration; and

(B) the return to employment would occur during the 3-week period before the end of such term.

(2) Leave less than 5 weeks prior to end of term

If the eligible employee begins leave under subparagraph (A), (B), or (C) of section 2612(a)(1) of this title or under section 2612(a)(3) of this tile during the period that commences 5 weeks prior to the end of the academic term, the agency or school may require the employee to continue taking leave until the end of such term, if—

(A) the leave is of greater than 2 weeks duration; and

(B) the return to employment would occur during the 2-week period before the end of such term.

(3) Leave less than 3 weeks prior to end of term

If the eligible employee begins leave under subparagraph (A), (B), or (C) of section 2612(a)(1) of this title or under section 2612(a)(3) of this title during the period that commences 3 weeks prior to the end of the academic term and the duration of the leave is greater than 5 working days, the agency or school may require the employee to continue to take leave until the end of such term.

(e) Restoration to equivalent employment position

For purposes of determinations under section 2614(a)(1)(B) of this title (relating to the restoration of an eligible employee to an equivalent position), in the case of a local educational agency or a private elementary or secondary school, such determination shall be made on the basis of established school board policies and practices, private school policies and practices, and collective bargaining agreements.

(f) Reduction of amount of liability

If a local educational agency or a private elementary or secondary school that has violated this subchapter proves to the satisfaction of the court that the agency, school, or department had reasonable grounds for believing that the underlying act or omission was not a violation of this subchapter, such court may, in the discretion of the court, reduce the amount of the liability provided for under section 2617(a)(1)(A) of this title to the amount and interest determined under clauses (i) and (ii), respectively, of such section.

Section 2619. Notice

(a) In general

Each employer shall post and keep posted, in conspicuous places on the premises of the employer where notices to employees and applicants for employment are customarily posted, a notice, to be prepared or approved by the Secretary, setting forth excerpts from, or summaries of, the pertinent provisions of this subchapter and information pertaining to the filing of a charge.

(b) Penalty

Any employer that willfully violates this section may be assessed a civil money penalty not to exceed $100 for each separate offense.

* * *

Section 2651. Effect on other laws

(a) Federal and State antidiscrimination laws

Nothing in this Act or any amendment made by this Act shall be construed to modify or affect any Federal or State law prohibiting discrimination on the basis of race, religion, color, national origin, sex, age, or disability.

(b) State and local laws

Nothing in this Act or any amendment made by this Act shall be construed to supersede any provision of any State or local law that provides greater family or medical leave rights than the rights established under this Act or any amendment made by this Act.

Section 2652. Effect on existing employment benefits

(a) More protective

Nothing in this Act or any amendment made by this Act shall be construed to diminish the obligation of an employer to comply with any collective bargaining agreement or any employment benefit program or plan that provides greater family or medical leave rights to employees than the rights established under this Act or any amendment made by this Act.

(b) Less protective

The rights established for employees under this Act or any amendment made by this Act shall not be diminished by any collective bargaining agreement or any employment benefit program or plan.

Section 2653. Encouragement of more generous leave policies

Nothing in this Act or any amendment made by this Act shall be construed to discourage employers from adopting or retaining leave policies more generous than any policies that comply with the requirements under this Act or any amendment made by this Act.

Section 2654. Regulations

The Secretary of Labor shall prescribe such regulations as are necessary to carry out subchapter I of this chapter and this subchapter not later than 120 days after February 5, 1993.

Extracts from the Americans with Disabilities Act

42 U.S.C. §§ 12101–12211

SEC. 12101. *[Section 2] Findings and Purposes*

(a) Findings. —The Congress finds that—

(1) physical or mental disabilities in no way diminish a person's right to fully participate in all aspects of society, yet many people with physical or mental disabilities have been precluded from doing so because of discrimination; others who have a record of a disability or are regarded as having a disability also have been subjected to discrimination;

(2) historically, society has tended to isolate and segregate individuals with disabilities, and, despite some improvements, such forms of discrimination against individuals with disabilities continue to be a serious and pervasive social problem;

(3) discrimination against individuals with disabilities persists in such critical areas as employment, housing, public accommodations, education, transportation, communication, recreation, institutionalization, health services, voting, and access to public services;

(4) unlike individuals who have experienced discrimination on the basis of race, color, sex, national origin, religion, or age, individuals who have experienced discrimination on the basis of disability have often had no legal recourse to redress such discrimination;

(5) individuals with disabilities continually encounter various forms of discrimination, including outright intentional exclusion, the discriminatory effects of architectural, transportation, and communication barriers, overprotective rules and policies, failure to make modifications to existing facilities and practices, exclusionary qualification standards and criteria, segregation, and relegation to lesser services, programs, activities, benefits, jobs, or other opportunities;

(6) census data, national polls, and other studies have documented that people with disabilities, as a group, occupy an inferior status in our society, and are severely disadvantaged socially, vocationally, economically, and educationally;

(7) the Nation's proper goals regarding individuals with disabilities are to assure equality of opportunity, full participation, independent living, and economic self-sufficiency for such individuals; and

(8) the continuing existence of unfair and unnecessary discrimination and prejudice denies people with disabilities the opportunity to compete on an equal basis and to pursue those opportunities for which our free society is justifiably famous, and costs the United States billions of dollars in unnecessary expenses resulting from dependency and nonproductivity.

(b) Purpose. —It is the purpose of this chapter—

(1) to provide a clear and comprehensive national mandate for the elimination of discrimination against individuals with disabilities;

(2) to provide clear, strong, consistent, enforceable standards addressing discrimination against individuals with disabilities;

(3) to ensure that the Federal Government plays a central role in enforcing the standards established in this chapter on behalf of individuals with disabilities; and

(4) to invoke the sweep of congressional authority, including the power to enforce the fourteenth amendment and to regulate commerce, in order to address the major areas of discrimination faced day to day by people with disabilities.

SEC. 12102. *[Section 3] Definitions*

As used in this chapter:

(1) Disability. —The term "disability" means, with respect to an individual—

(A) a physical or mental impairment that substantially limits one or more major life activities of such individual;

(B) a record of such an impairment; or

(C) being regarded as having such an impairment (as described in paragraph (3)).

(2) Major life activities

(A) In general

For purposes of paragraph (1), major life activities include, but are not limited to, caring for oneself, performing manual tasks, seeing, hearing, eating, sleeping, walking, standing, lifting, bending, speaking, breathing, learning, reading, concentrating, thinking, communicating, and working.

(B) Major bodily functions

For purposes of paragraph (1), a major life activity also includes the operation of a major bodily function, including but not limited to, functions of the immune system, normal cell growth, digestive, bowel, bladder, neurological, brain, respiratory, circulatory, endocrine, and reproductive functions.

(3) Regarded as having such an impairment

For purposes of paragraph (1)(C):

(A) An individual meets the requirement of "being regarded as having such an impairment" if the individual establishes that he or she has been subjected to an action prohibited under this chapter because of an actual or perceived physical or mental impairment whether or not the impairment limits or is perceived to limit a major life activity.

(B) Paragraph (1)(C) shall not apply to impairments that are transitory and minor. A transitory impairment is an impairment with an actual or expected duration of 6 months or less.

(4) Rules of construction regarding the definition of disability

The definition of "disability" in paragraph (1) shall be construed in accordance with the following:

(A) The definition of disability in this chapter shall be construed in favor of broad coverage of individuals under this chapter, to the maximum extent permitted by the terms of this chapter.

(B) The term "substantially limits" shall be interpreted consistently with the findings and purposes of the ADA Amendments Act of 2008.

(C) An impairment that substantially limits one major life activity need not limit other major life activities in order to be considered a disability.

(D) An impairment that is episodic or in remission is a disability if it would substantially limit a major life activity when active.

(E) (i) The determination of whether an impairment substantially limits a major life activity shall be made without regard to the ameliorative effects of mitigating measures such as—

(I) medication, medical supplies, equipment, or appliances, low-vision devices (which do not include ordinary eyeglasses or contact lenses), prosthetics including limbs and devices, hearing aids and cochlear implants or other implantable hearing devices, mobility devices, or oxygen therapy equipment and supplies;

(II) use of assistive technology;

(III) reasonable accommodations or auxiliary aids or services; or

(IV) learned behavioral or adaptive neurological modifications.

(ii) The ameliorative effects of the mitigating measures of ordinary eyeglasses or contact lenses shall be considered in determining whether an impairment substantially limits a major life activity.

(iii) As used in this subparagraph—

(I) the term "ordinary eyeglasses or contact lenses" means lenses that are intended to fully correct visual acuity or eliminate refractive error; and

(II) the term "low-vision devices" means devices that magnify, enhance, or otherwise augment a visual image.

SEC. 12103. *[Section 4] Additional Definitions*

As used in this chapter:

(1) Auxiliary aids and services. —The term "auxiliary aids and services" includes—

(A) qualified interpreters or other effective methods of making aurally delivered materials available to individuals with hearing impairments;

(B) qualified readers, taped texts, or other effective methods of making visually delivered materials available to individuals with visual impairments;

(C) acquisition or modification of equipment or devices; and

(D) other similar services and actions.

(2) State. —The term "State" means each of the several States, the District of Columbia, the Commonwealth of Puerto Rico, Guam, American Samoa, the Virgin Islands of the United States, the Trust Territory of the Pacific Islands, and the Commonwealth of the Northern Mariana Islands.

Subchapter I [Title I] — Employment

SEC. 12111. *[Section 101] Defenses*

As used in this subchapter:

(1) Commission. —The term "Commission" means the Equal Employment Opportunity Commission established by section 2000e-4 of this title *[section 705 of the Civil Rights Act of 1964]*.

(2) Covered entity. —The term "covered entity" means an employer, employment agency, labor organization, or joint labor management committee.

(3) Direct threat. —The term "direct threat" means a significant risk to the health or safety of others that cannot be eliminated by reasonable accommodation.

(4) Employee. —The term "employee" means an individual employed by an employer. With respect to employment in a foreign country, such term includes an individual who is a citizen of the United States.

(5) Employer. —

- (A) In general. —The term "employer" means a person engaged in an industry affecting commerce who has 15 or more employees for each working day in each of 20 or more calendar weeks in the current or preceding calendar year, and any agent of such person, except that, for two years following the effective date of this subchapter, an employer means a person engaged in an industry affecting commerce who has 25 or more employees for each working day in each of 20 or more calendar weeks in the current or preceding year, and any agent of such person.
- (B) Exceptions. —The term "employer" does not include—
    - (i) the United States, a corporation wholly owned by the government of the United States, or an Indian tribe; or
    - (ii) a bona fide private membership club (other than a labor organization) that is exempt from taxation under section 501(c) of Title 26 *[the Internal Revenue Code of 1986]*.

(6) Illegal use of drugs. —

- (A) In general. —The term "illegal use of drugs" means the use of drugs, the possession or distribution of which is unlawful under the Controlled Substances Act [21 U.S.C. 801 et seq.]. Such term does not include the use of a drug taken under supervision by a licensed health care professional, or other uses authorized by the Controlled Substances Act or other provisions of Federal law.
- (B) Drugs. —The term "drug" means a controlled substance, as defined in schedules I through V of section 202 of the Controlled Substances Act [21 U.S.C. 812].

(7) Person, etc. —The terms "person", "labor organization", "employment agency", "commerce", and "industry affecting commerce", shall have the same meaning given such terms in section 2000e of this title *[section 701 of the Civil Rights Act of 1964]*.

(8) Qualified individual. —The term "qualified individual" means an individual who, with or without reasonable accommodation, can perform the essential functions of the employment position that such individual holds or desires. For the purposes of this subchapter, consideration shall be given to the employer's judgment as to what functions of a job are essential, and if an employer has prepared a written description before advertising or interviewing applicants for the job, this description shall be considered evidence of the essential functions of the job.

(9) Reasonable accommodation. —The term "reasonable accommodation" may include—

- (A) making existing facilities used by employees readily accessible to and usable by individuals with disabilities; and
- (B) job restructuring, part-time or modified work schedules, reassignment to a vacant position, acquisition or modification of equipment or devices, appropriate adjustment or modifications of examinations, training materials or policies, the provision of qualified readers or interpreters, and other similar accommodations for individuals with disabilities.

(10) Undue hardship. —

- (A) In general. —The term "undue hardship" means an action requiring significant difficulty or expense, when considered in light of the factors set forth in subparagraph (B).
- (B) Factors to be considered. —In determining whether an accommodation would impose an undue hardship on a covered entity, factors to be considered include—
    - (i) the nature and cost of the accommodation needed under this chapter;
    - (ii) the overall financial resources of the facility or facilities involved in the provision of the reasonable accommodation; the number of

persons employed at such facility; the effect on expenses and resources, or the impact otherwise of such accommodation upon the operation of the facility;

(iii) the overall financial resources of the covered entity; the overall size of the business of a covered entity with respect to the number of its employees; the number, type, and location of its facilities; and

(iv) the type of operation or operations of the covered entity, including the composition, structure, and functions of the workforce of such entity; the geographic separateness, administrative, or fiscal relationship of the facility or facilities in question to the covered entity.

SEC. 12112. *[Section 102] Discrimination*

(a) General rule. —No covered entity shall discriminate against a qualified individual on the basis of disability in regard to job application procedures, the hiring, advancement, or discharge of employees, employee compensation, job training, and other terms, conditions, and privileges of employment.

(b) Construction. —As used in subsection (a) of this section, the term "discriminate against a qualified individual on the basis of disability" includes—

(1) limiting, segregating, or classifying a job applicant or employee in a way that adversely affects the opportunities or status of such applicant or employee because of the disability of such applicant or employee;

(2) participating in a contractual or other arrangement or relationship that has the effect of subjecting a covered entity's qualified applicant or employee with a disability to the discrimination prohibited by this subchapter (such relationship includes a relationship with an employment or referral agency, labor union, an organization providing fringe benefits to an employee of the covered entity, or an organization providing training and apprenticeship programs);

(3) utilizing standards, criteria, or methods of administration—

(A) that have the effect of discrimination on the basis of disability; or

(B) that perpetuate the discrimination of others who are subject to common administrative control;

(4) excluding or otherwise denying equal jobs or benefits to a qualified individual because of the known disability of an individual with whom the qualified individual is known to have a relationship or association;

(5) (A) not making reasonable accommodations to the known physical or mental limitations of an otherwise qualified individual with a disability who is an applicant or employee, unless such covered entity can demonstrate that the accommodation would impose an undue hardship on the operation of the business of such covered entity; or

(B) denying employment opportunities to a job applicant or employee who is an otherwise qualified individual with a disability, if such denial is based on the need of such covered entity to make reasonable accommodation to the physical or mental impairments of the employee or applicant;

(6) using qualification standards, employment tests or other selection criteria that screen out or tend to screen out an individual with a disability or a class of individuals with disabilities unless the standard, test or other selection criteria, as used by the covered entity, is shown to be job-related for the position in question and is consistent with business necessity; and

(7) failing to select and administer tests concerning employment in the most effective manner to ensure that, when such test is administered to a job applicant or employee who has a disability that impairs sensory, manual, or speaking skills, such test results accurately reflect the skills, aptitude, or whatever other factor of such applicant or employee that such test purports to measure, rather than reflecting the impaired sensory, manual, or speaking skills of such employee or applicant (except where such skills are the factors that the test purports to measure).

(c) Covered entities in foreign countries. —

(1) In general. —It shall not be unlawful under this section for a covered entity to take any action that constitutes discrimination under this section with respect to an employee in a workplace in a foreign country if compliance with this section would cause such covered entity to violate the law of the foreign country in which such workplace is located.

(2) Control of corporation

(A) Presumption. —If an employer controls a corporation whose place of incorporation is a foreign country, any practice that constitutes discrimination under this section and is engaged in by such corporation shall be presumed to be engaged in by such employer.

(B) Exception. —This section shall not apply with respect to the foreign operations of an employer that is a foreign person not controlled by an American employer.

(C) Determination. —For purposes of this paragraph, the determination of whether an employer controls a corporation shall be based on—

(i) the interrelation of operations;

(ii) the common management;

(iii) the centralized control of labor relations; and

(iv) the common ownership or financial control, of the employer and the corporation.

(d) Medical examinations and inquiries. —

(1) In general. —The prohibition against discrimination as referred to in subsection (a) of this section shall include medical examinations and inquiries.

(2) Pre-employment. —

(A) Prohibited examination or inquiry. —Except as provided in paragraph (3), a covered entity shall not conduct a medical examination or make inquiries of a job applicant as to whether such applicant is an individual with a disability or as to the nature or severity of such disability.

(B) Acceptable inquiry. —A covered entity may make pre-employment inquiries into the ability of an applicant to perform job-related functions.

(3) Employment entrance examination. —A covered entity may require a medical examination after an offer of employment has been made to a job applicant and prior to the commencement of the employment duties of such applicant, and may condition an offer of employment on the results of such examination, if—

(A) all entering employees are subjected to such an examination regardless of disability;

(B) information obtained regarding the medical condition or history of the applicant is collected and maintained on separate forms and in separate medical files and is treated as a confidential medical record, except that—

(i) supervisors and managers may be informed regarding necessary restrictions on the work or duties of the employee and necessary accommodations;

(ii) first aid and safety personnel may be informed, when appropriate, if the disability might require emergency treatment; and

(iii) government officials investigating compliance with this chapter shall be provided relevant information on request; and (C) the results of such examination are used only in accordance with this subchapter.

(4) Examination and inquiry. —

(A) Prohibited examinations and inquiries. —A covered entity shall not require a medical examination and shall not make inquiries of an employee as to whether such employee is an individual with a disability or as to the nature or severity of the disability, unless such examination or inquiry is shown to be job-related and consistent with business necessity.

(B) Acceptable examinations and inquiries. —A covered entity may conduct voluntary medical examinations, including voluntary medical histories, which are part of an employee health program available to employees at that work site. A covered entity may make inquiries into the ability of an employee to perform job-related functions.

(C) Requirement. —Information obtained under subparagraph (B) regarding the medical condition or history of any employee are subject to the requirements of subparagraphs (B) and (C) of paragraph (3).

SEC. 12113. *[Section 103] Defenses*

(a) In general. —It may be a defense to a charge of discrimination under this chapter that an alleged application of qualification standards, tests, or selection criteria that screen out or tend to screen out or otherwise deny a job or benefit to an individual with a disability has been shown to be job-related and consistent with business necessity, and such performance cannot be accomplished by reasonable accommodation, as required under this subchapter.

(b) Qualification standards. —The term "qualification standards" may include a requirement that an individual shall not pose a direct threat to the health or safety of other individuals in the workplace.

(c) Qualification standards and tests related to uncorrected vision. —Notwithstanding section 12102(4)(E)(ii) of this title, a covered entity shall not use qualification standards, employment tests, or other selection criteria based on an individual's uncorrected vision unless the standard, test, or other selection criteria, as used by the covered entity, is shown to be job-related for the position in question and consistent with business necessity.

(d) Religious entities. —

(1) In general. —This subchapter shall not prohibit a religious corporation, association, educational institution, or society from giving preference in employment to individuals of a particular religion to perform work connected with the carrying on by such corporation, association, educational institution, or society of its activities.

(2) Religious tenets requirement. —Under this subchapter, a religious organization may require that all applicants and employees conform to the religious tenets of such organization.

(e) List of infectious and communicable diseases. —

(1) In general. —The Secretary of Health and Human Services, not later than 6 months after July 26, 1990 *[the date of enactment of this Act]*, shall—

(A) review all infectious and communicable diseases which may be transmitted through handling the food supply;

(B) publish a list of infectious and communicable diseases which are transmitted through handling the food supply;

(C) publish the methods by which such diseases are transmitted; and

(D) widely disseminate such information regarding the list of diseases and their modes of transmissibility to the general public. Such list shall be updated annually.

(2) Applications. —In any case in which an individual has an infectious or communicable disease that is transmitted to others through the handling of food, that is included on the list developed by the Secretary of Health and Human Services under paragraph (1), and which cannot be eliminated by reasonable accommodation, a covered entity may refuse to assign or continue to assign such individual to a job involving food handling.

(3) Construction. —Nothing in this chapter shall be construed to preempt, modify, or amend any State, county, or local law, ordinance, or regulation applicable to food handling which is designed to protect the public health from individuals who pose a significant risk to the health or safety of others, which cannot be eliminated by reasonable accommodation, pursuant to the list of infectious or communicable diseases and the modes of transmissibility published by the Secretary of Health and Human Services.

SEC. 12114. *[Section 104] Illegal Use of Alcohol and Drugs*

(a) Qualified individual with a disability. —For purposes of this subchapter, a qualified individual with a disability shall not include any employee or applicant who is currently engaging in the illegal use of drugs, when the covered entity acts on the basis of such use.

(b) Rules of construction. —Nothing in subsection (a) of this section shall be construed to exclude as a qualified individual with a disability an individual who—

(1) has successfully completed a supervised drug rehabilitation program and is no longer engaging in the illegal use of drugs, or has otherwise been rehabilitated successfully and is no longer engaging in such use;

(2) is participating in a supervised rehabilitation program and is no longer engaging in such use; or

(3) is erroneously regarded as engaging in such use, but is not engaging in such use; except that it shall not be a violation of this chapter for a covered entity to adopt or administer reasonable policies or procedures, including but not limited to drug testing, designed to ensure that an individual described in paragraph (1) or (2) is no longer engaging in the illegal use of drugs.

(c) Authority of covered entity. —

A covered entity—

(1) may prohibit the illegal use of drugs and the use of alcohol at the workplace by all employees;

(2) may require that employees shall not be under the influence of alcohol or be engaging in the illegal use of drugs at the workplace;

(3) may require that employees behave in conformance with the requirements established under the Drug Free Workplace Act of 1988 (41 U.S.C. 701 et seq.);

(4) may hold an employee who engages in the illegal use of drugs or who is an alcoholic to the same qualification standards for employment or job performance and behavior that such entity holds other employees, even if any unsatisfactory performance or behavior is related to the drug use or alcoholism of such employee; and (5) may, with respect to Federal regulations regarding alcohol and the illegal use of drugs, require that—

(A) employees comply with the standards established in such regulations of the Department of Defense, if the employees of the covered entity are employed in an industry subject to such regulations, including complying with regulations (if any) that apply to employment in sensitive positions in such an industry, in the case of employees of the covered entity who are employed in such positions (as defined in the regulations of the Department of Defense);

(B) employees comply with the standards established in such regulations of the Nuclear Regulatory Commission, if the employees of the covered entity are employed in an industry subject to such regulations, including complying with regulations (if any) that apply to employment in sensitive positions in such an industry, in the case of employees of the covered entity who are employed in such positions (as defined in the regulations of the Nuclear Regulatory Commission); and

(C) employees comply with the standards established in such regulations of the Department of Transportation, if the employees of the covered entity are employed in a transportation industry subject to such regulations, including complying with such regulations (if any) that apply to employment in sensitive positions in such an industry, in the case of employees of the covered entity who are employed in such positions (as defined in the regulations of the Department of Transportation).

(d) Drug testing. —

(1) In general. —For purposes of this subchapter, a test to determine the illegal use of drugs shall not be considered a medical examination.

(2) Construction. —Nothing in this subchapter shall be construed to encourage, prohibit, or authorize the conducting of drug testing for the illegal use of drugs by job applicants or employees or making employment decisions based on such test results.

(e) Transportation employees. —Nothing in this subchapter shall be construed to encourage, prohibit, restrict, or authorize the otherwise lawful exercise by entities subject to the jurisdiction of the Department of Transportation of authority to—

(1) test employees of such entities in, and applicants for, positions involving safety sensitive duties for the illegal use of drugs and for on duty impairment by alcohol; and

(2) remove such persons who test positive for illegal use of drugs and on duty impairment by alcohol pursuant to paragraph (1) from safety sensitive duties in implementing subsection (c) of this section.

SEC. 12115. *[Section 105] Posting Notices*

Every employer, employment agency, labor organization, or joint labor management committee covered under this subchapter shall post notices in an accessible format to applicants, employees, and members describing the applicable provisions of this chapter, in the manner prescribed by section 2000e-10 of this title *[section 711 of the Civil Rights Act of 1964]*.

SEC. 12116. *[Section 106] Regulations*

Not later than 1 year after July 26, 1990 *[the date of enactment of this Act]*, the Commission shall issue regulations in an accessible format to carry out this subchapter in accordance with subchapter II of chapter 5 of title 5 *[United States Code]*.

SEC. 12117. *[Section 107] Enforcement*

(a) Powers, remedies, and procedures. —The powers, remedies, and procedures set forth in sections 2000e-4, 2000e-5, 2000e-6, 2000e-8, and 2000e-9 of this title *[sections 705, 706, 707, 709 and 710 of the Civil Rights Act of 1964]* shall be the powers, remedies, and procedures this subchapter provides to the Commission, to the Attorney General, or to any person alleging discrimination on the basis of disability in violation of any provision of this chapter, or regulations promulgated under section 12116 of this title *[section 106]*, concerning employment.

(b) Coordination. —The agencies with enforcement authority for actions which allege employment discrimination under this subchapter and under the Rehabilitation Act of 1973 *[29 U.S.C. 701 et seq.]* shall develop procedures to ensure that administrative complaints filed under this subchapter and under the Rehabilitation Act of 1973 are dealt with in a manner that avoids duplication of effort and prevents imposition of inconsistent or conflicting standards for the same requirements under this subchapter and the Rehabilitation Act of 1973. The Commission, the Attorney General, and the Office of Federal Contract Compliance Programs shall establish such coordinating mechanisms (similar to provisions contained in the joint regulations promulgated by the Commission and the Attorney General at part 42 of title 28 and part 1691 of title 29, Code of Federal Regulations, and the Memorandum of Understanding between the Commission and the Office of Federal Contract Compliance Programs dated January 16, 1981 (46 Fed. Reg. 7435, January 23, 1981)) in regulations implementing this subchapter and Rehabilitation Act of 1973 not later than 18 months after July 26, 1990 *[the date of enactment of this Act]*.

[42 USC § 2000e-5 note](a) AMERICANS WITH DISABILITIES ACT OF 1990. — The amendments made by section 3 *[Lilly Ledbetter Fair Pay Act of 2009, PL 111-2, 123 Stat. 5]* shall apply to claims of discrimination in compensation brought under title I and section 503 of the Americans with Disabilities Act of 1990 (42 U.S.C. 12111 et seq., 12203), pursuant to section 107(a) of such Act (42 U.S.C. 12117(a)), which adopts the powers, remedies, and procedures set forth in section 706 of the Civil Rights Act of 1964 (42 U.S.C. 2000e-5).

SUBCHAPTER IV [Title V] - MISCELLANEOUS PROVISIONS

SEC. 12201. *[Section 501] Construction*

(a) In general. —Except as otherwise provided in this chapter, nothing in this chapter shall be construed to apply a lesser standard than the standards applied under Title V of the Rehabilitation Act of 1973 (29 U.S.C. 790 et seq.) or the regulations issued by Federal agencies pursuant to such title.

(b) Relationship to other laws. —Nothing in this chapter shall be construed to invalidate or limit the remedies, rights, and procedures of any Federal law or law of any State or political subdivision of any State or jurisdiction that provides greater or equal protection for the rights of individuals with disabilities than are afforded by this chapter. Nothing in this chapter shall be construed to preclude the prohibition of, or the imposition of restrictions on, smoking in places of employment covered by subchapter I of this chapter [title I], in transportation covered by subchapter II or III of this chapter *[title II or III]*, or in places of public accommodation covered by subchapter III of this chapter *[title III]*.

(c) Insurance. —Subchapters I through III of this chapter *[titles I through III]* and title IV of this Act shall not be construed to prohibit or restrict—

(1) an insurer, hospital or medical service company, health maintenance organization, or any agent, or entity that administers benefit plans, or similar organizations from underwriting risks, classifying risks, or administering such risks that are based on or not inconsistent with State law; or

(2) a person or organization covered by this chapter from establishing, sponsoring, observing or administering the terms of a bona fide benefit plan that are based on underwriting risks, classifying risks, or administering such risks that are based on or not inconsistent with State law; or

(3) a person or organization covered by this chapter from establishing, sponsoring, observing or administering the terms of a bona fide benefit plan that is not subject to State laws that regulate insurance.

Paragraphs (1), (2), and (3) shall not be used as a subterfuge to evade the purposes of subchapter I and III of this chapter *[titles I and III]*.

(d) Accommodations and services. —Nothing in this chapter shall be construed to require an individual with a disability to accept an accommodation, aid, service, opportunity, or benefit which such individual chooses not to accept.

(e) Benefits under State worker's compensation laws

Nothing in this chapter alters the standards for determining eligibility for benefits under State worker's compensation laws or under State and Federal disability benefit programs.

(f) Fundamental alteration

Nothing in this chapter alters the provision of section 12182(b)(2)(A)(ii) of this title, specifying that reasonable modifications in policies, practices, or procedures shall be required, unless an entity can demonstrate that making such modifications in policies, practices, or procedures, including academic requirements in postsecondary education, would fundamentally alter the nature of the goods, services, facilities, privileges, advantages, or accommodations involved.

(g) Claims of no disability

Nothing in this chapter shall provide the basis for a claim by an individual without a disability that the individual was subject to discrimination because of the individual's lack of disability.

(h) Reasonable accommodations and modifications

A covered entity under subchapter I of this chapter, a public entity under subchapter II of this chapter, and any person who owns, leases (or leases to), or operates a place of public accommodation under subchapter III of this chapter, need not provide a reasonable accommodation or a reasonable modification to policies, practices, or procedures to an individual who meets the definition of disability in section 12102(1) of this title solely under subparagraph (C) of such section.

SEC. 12202. *[Section 502] State Immunity*

A State shall not be immune under the eleventh amendment to the Constitution of the United States from an action in Federal or State court of competent jurisdiction for a violation of this chapter. In any action against a State for a violation of the requirements of this chapter, remedies (including remedies both at law and in equity) are available for such a violation to the same extent as such remedies are available for such a violation in an action against any public or private entity other than a State.

SEC. 12203. *[Section 503] Prohibition Against Retaliation and Coercion*

(a) Retaliation. —No person shall discriminate against any individual because such individual has opposed any act or practice made unlawful by this chapter or because such individual made a charge, testified, assisted, or participated in any manner in an investigation, proceeding, or hearing under this chapter.

(b) Interference, coercion, or intimidation. —It shall be unlawful to coerce, intimidate, threaten, or interfere with any individual in the exercise or enjoyment of, or on account of his or her having exercised or enjoyed, or on account of his or her having aided or encouraged any other individual in the exercise or enjoyment of, any right granted or protected by this chapter.

(c) Remedies and procedures. —The remedies and procedures available under sections 12117, 12133, and 12188 of this title *[sections 107, 203 and 308]* shall be available to aggrieved persons for violations of subsections (a) and (b) of this section, with respect to subchapter I, subchapter II and subchapter III, respectively, of this chapter *[title I, title II and title III, respectively]*.

[42 USC § 2000e-5 note]

(a) AMERICANS WITH DISABILITIES ACT OF 1990. —The amendments made by section 3 *[Lilly Ledbetter Fair Pay Act of 2009, PL 111-2, 123 Stat. 5]* shall apply to claims of discrimination in compensation brought under title I and section 503 of the Americans with Disabilities Act of 1990 (42 U.S.C. 12111 et seq., 12203), pursuant to section 107(a) of such Act (42 U.S.C. 12117(a)), which adopts the powers, remedies, and procedures set forth in section 706 of the Civil Rights Act of 1964 (42 U.S.C. 2000e-5).

SEC. 12205. *[Section 505] Attorney's Fees*

In any action or administrative proceeding commenced pursuant to this chapter, the court or agency, in its discretion, may allow the prevailing party, other than the United States, a reasonable attorney's fee, including litigation expenses, and costs, and the United States shall be liable for the foregoing the same as a private individual.

TRANSVESTITES

SEC. 12208. *[Section 509]*

For the purposes of this chapter, the term "disabled" or "disability" shall not apply to an individual solely because that individual is a transvestite.

COVERAGE OF CONGRESS AND THE AGENCIES OF THE LEGISLATIVE BRANCH

SEC. 12209. *[Section 510]*

(a) Coverage of the Senate. —

(1) Commitment to Rule XLII. —The Senate reaffirms its commitment to Rule XLII of the Standing Rules of the Senate which provides as follows:

"No member, officer, or employee of the Senate shall, with respect to employment by the Senate or any office thereof—

"(a) fail or refuse to hire an individual;

"(b) discharge an individual; or

"(c) otherwise discriminate against an individual with respect to promotion, compensation, or terms, conditions, or privileges of employment on the basis of such individual's race, color, religion, sex, national origin, age, or state of physical handicap."

(2) Matters other than employment. —

(A) In general. —The rights and protections under this chapter shall, subject to subparagraph (B), apply with respect to the conduct of the Senate regarding matters other than employment.

(B) Remedies. —The Architect of the Capitol shall establish remedies and procedures to be utilized with respect to the rights and protections provided pursuant to subparagraph (A). Such remedies and procedures shall apply exclusively, after approval in accordance with subparagraph (C).

(C) Proposed remedies and procedures. —For purposes of subparagraph (B), the Architect of the Capitol shall submit proposed remedies and procedures to the Senate Committee on Rules and Administration. The remedies and procedures shall be effective upon the approval of the Committee on Rules and Administration.

(3) Exercise of rulemaking power. —Notwithstanding any other provision of law, enforcement and adjudication of the rights and protections referred to in paragraph (2)(A) shall be within the exclusive jurisdiction of the United States Senate. The provisions of paragraph (1), (2) are enacted by the Senate as an exercise of the rulemaking power of the Senate, with full recognition of the right of the Senate to change its rules, in the same manner, and to the same extent, as in the case of any other rule of the Senate.

(b) Coverage of the House of Representatives. —
  (1) In general. —Notwithstanding any other provision of this chapter or of law, the purposes of this chapter shall, subject to paragraphs (2) and (3), apply in their entirety to the House of Representatives.
  (2) Employment in the House. —
    (A) Application. —The rights and protections under this chapter shall, subject to subparagraph (B), apply with respect to any employee in an employment position in the House of Representatives and any employing authority of the House of Representatives.
    (B) Administration. —
      (i) In general. —In the administration of this paragraph, the remedies and procedures made applicable pursuant to the resolution described in clause (ii) shall apply exclusively.
      (ii) Resolution. —The resolution referred to in clause (i) is House Resolution 15 of the One Hundred First Congress, as agreed to January 3, 1989, or any other provision that continues in effect the provisions of, or is a successor to, the Fair Employment Practices Resolution (House Resolution 558 of the One Hundredth Congress, as agreed to October 4, 1988).
    (C) Exercise of rulemaking power. —The provisions of subparagraph (B) are enacted by the House of Representatives as an exercise of the rulemaking power of the House of Representatives, with full recognition of the right of the House to change its rules, in the same manner, and to the same extent as in the case of any other rule of the House.
  (3) Matters other than employment. —
    (A) In general. —The rights and protections under this chapter shall, subject to subparagraph (B), apply with respect to the conduct of the House of Representatives regarding matters other than employment.
    (B) Remedies. —The Architect of the Capitol shall establish remedies and procedures to be utilized with respect to the rights and protections provided pursuant to subparagraph (A). Such remedies and procedures shall apply exclusively, after approval in accordance with subparagraph (C).
    (C) Approval. —For purposes of subparagraph (B), the Architect of the Capitol shall submit proposed remedies and procedures to the Speaker of the House of Representatives. The remedies and procedures shall be effective upon the approval of the Speaker, after consultation with the House Office Building Commission.

(c) Instrumentalities of Congress. —
  (1) In general. —The rights and protections under this chapter shall, subject to paragraph (2), apply with respect to the conduct of each instrumentality of the Congress.
  (2) Establishment of remedies and procedures by instrumentalities. —The chief official of each instrumentality of the Congress shall establish remedies and procedures to be utilized with respect to the rights and protections provided pursuant to paragraph (1). Such remedies and procedures shall apply exclusively, except for the employees who are defined as Senate employees, in section 201(c)(1) of the Civil Rights Act of 1991.
  (3) Report to Congress. —The chief official of each instrumentality of the Congress shall, after establishing remedies and procedures for purposes of paragraph (2), submit to the Congress a report describing the remedies and procedures.
  (4) Definition of instrumentalities. —For purposes of this section, instrumentalities of the Congress include the following: the Architect of the Capitol, the Congressional Budget Office, the General Accounting Office, the Government Printing Office, the Library of Congress, the Office of Technology Assessment, and the United States Botanic Garden.
  (5) Construction. —Nothing in this section shall alter the enforcement procedures for individuals with disabilities provided in the General Accounting Office Personnel Act of 1980 *[31 U.S.C. 731 et seq.]* and regulations promulgated pursuant to that Act.

SEC. 12210. *[Section 511] Illegal Use of Drugs*

(a) In general. —For purposes of this chapter, the term "individual with a disability" does not include an individual who is currently engaging in the illegal use of drugs, when the covered entity acts on the basis of such use.

(b) Rules of construction. —Nothing in subsection (a) of this section shall be construed to exclude as an individual with a disability an individual who—
  (1) has successfully completed a supervised drug rehabilitation program and is no longer engaging

in the illegal use of drugs, or has otherwise been rehabilitated successfully and is no longer engaging in such use;

(2) is participating in a supervised rehabilitation program and is no longer engaging in such use; or

(3) is erroneously regarded as engaging in such use, but is not engaging in such use; except that it shall not be a violation of this chapter for a covered entity to adopt or administer reasonable policies or procedures, including but not limited to drug testing, designed to ensure that an individual described in paragraph (1) or (2) is no longer engaging in the illegal use of drugs; however, nothing in this section shall be construed to encourage, prohibit, restrict, or authorize the conducting of testing for the illegal use of drugs.

(c) Health and other services. —Notwithstanding subsection (a) of this section and section 12211(b)(3) of this title *[section 512(b)(3)]*, an individual shall not be denied health services, or services provided in connection with drug rehabilitation, on the basis of the current illegal use of drugs if the individual is otherwise entitled to such services.

(d) Definition of illegal use of drugs. —

(1) In general. —The term "illegal use of drugs" means the use of drugs, the possession or distribution of which is unlawful under the Controlled Substances Act (21 U.S.C. 812). Such term does not include the use of a drug taken under supervision by a licensed health care professional, or other uses authorized by the Controlled Substances Act or other provisions of Federal law.

(2) Drugs

The term "drug" means a controlled substance, as defined in schedules I through V of section 202 of the Controlled Substances Act *[21 U.S.C. 812]*.

SEC. 12211. *[Section 512] Definitions*

(a) Homosexuality and bisexuality. —For purposes of the definition of "disability" in section 12102(2) of this title *[section 3(2)]*, homosexuality and bisexuality are not impairments and as such are not disabilities under this chapter.

(b) Certain conditions. —Under this chapter, the term "disability" shall not include—

(1) transvestism, transsexualism, pedophilia, exhibitionism, voyeurism, gender identity disorders not resulting from physical impairments, or other sexual behavior disorders;

(2) compulsive gambling, kleptomania, or pyromania; or

(3) psychoactive substance use disorders resulting from current illegal use of drugs.

Extracts from the Rehabilitation Act

29 U.S.C. §705, §§791–794a

SEC. 791. [Section 501] Employment of Individuals with Disabilities

(a) Interagency Committee on Employees who are Individuals with Disabilities; establishment; membership; co-chairmen; availability of other Committee resources; purpose and functions

There is established within the Federal Government an Interagency Committee on Employees who are Individuals with Disabilities (hereinafter in this section referred to as the "Committee"), comprised of such members as the President may select, including the following (or their designees whose positions are Executive Level IV or higher): the Chairman of the Equal Employment Opportunity Commission (hereafter in this section referred to as the "Commission"), the Director of the Office of Personnel Management, the Secretary of Veterans Affairs, the Secretary of Labor, the Secretary of Education, and the Secretary of Health and Human Services. Either the Director of the Office of Personnel Management and the Chairman of the Commission shall serve as co-chairpersons of the Committee or the Director or Chairman shall serve as the sole chairperson of the Committee, as the Director and Chairman jointly determine, from time to time, to be appropriate. The resources of the President's Committees on Employment of People with Disabilities and on Mental Retardation shall be made fully available to the Committee. It shall be the purpose and function of the Committee (1) to provide a focus for Federal and other employment of individuals with disabilities, and to review, on a periodic basis, in cooperation with the Commission, the adequacy of hiring, placement, and advancement practices with respect to individuals with disabilities, by each department, agency, and instrumentality in the executive branch of Government and the Smithsonian Institution, and to insure that the special needs of such individuals are being met; and (2) to consult with the Commission to assist the Commission to carry out its responsibilities under subsections (b), (c), and (d) of this section. On the basis of such review and consultation, the Committee shall periodically make to the Commission such recommendations for legislative and administrative changes as it deems necessary or desirable. The Commission shall timely transmit to the appropriate committees of Congress any such recommendations.

(b) Federal agencies; affirmative action program plans

Each department, agency, and instrumentality (including the United States Postal Service and the Postal Regulatory Commission) in the executive branch and the Smithsonian Institution shall, within one hundred and eighty days after September 26, 1973, submit to the Commission and to the Committee an affirmative action program plan for the hiring, placement, and advancement of individuals with disabilities in such department, agency, instrumentality, or Institution. Such plan shall include a description of the extent to which and methods whereby the special needs of employees who are individuals with disabilities are being met. Such plan shall be updated annually, and shall be reviewed annually and approved by the Commission, if the Commission determines, after consultation with the Committee, that such plan provides sufficient assurances, procedures and commitments to provide adequate hiring, placement, and advancement opportunities for individuals with disabilities.

(c) State agencies; rehabilitated individuals, employment

The Commission, after consultation with the Committee, shall develop and recommend to the Secretary for referral to the appropriate State agencies, policies and procedures which will facilitate the hiring, placement, and advancement in employment of individuals who have received rehabilitation services under State vocational rehabilitation programs, veterans' programs, or any other program for individuals with disabilities, including the promotion of job opportunities for such individuals. The Secretary shall encourage such State agencies to adopt and implement such policies and procedures.

(d) Report to Congressional committees

The Commission, after consultation with the Committee, shall, on June 30, 1974, and at the end of each subsequent fiscal year, make a complete report to the appropriate committees of the Congress with respect to the practices of and achievements in hiring, placement, and advancement of individuals with disabilities by each department, agency, and instrumentality and the Smithsonian Institution and the effectiveness of the affirmative action programs required by subsection (b) of this section, together with recommendations as to legislation which have been submitted to the Commission under subsection (a) of this section, or other appropriate action to insure the adequacy of such practices. Such report shall also include an evaluation by the Committee of the effectiveness of the activities of the Commission under subsections (b) and (c) of this section.

(e) Federal work experience without pay; non-Federal status

An individual who, as a part of an individualized plan for employment under a State plan approved under this chapter, participates in a program of unpaid work experience in a Federal agency, shall not, by reason thereof, be considered to be a Federal employee or to be subject to the provisions of law relating to Federal employment, including those relating to hours of work, rates of compensation, leave, unemployment compensation, and Federal employee benefits.

(f) Federal agency cooperation; special consideration for positions on President's Committee on Employment of People with Disabilities

(1) The Secretary of Labor and the Secretary of Education are authorized and directed to cooperate with the President's Committee on Employment of People with Disabilities in carrying out its functions.

(2) In selecting personnel to fill all positions on the President's Committee on Employment of People with Disabilities, special consideration shall be given to qualified individuals with disabilities.

(g) Standards used in determining violation of section

The standards used to determine whether this section has been violated in a complaint alleging nonaffirmative action employment discrimination under this section shall be the standards applied under title I of the Americans with Disabilities Act of 1990 (42 U.S.C. 12111 et seq.) and the provisions of sections 501 through 504, and 510, of the Americans with Disabilities Act of 1990 (42 U.S.C. 12201-12204 and 12210), as such sections relate to employment.

[42 U.S.C. § 2000e-5 note]

(b) REHABILITATION ACT OF 1973.— The amendments made by section 3 *[Lilly Ledbetter Fair Pay Act of 2009, PL 111-2, 123 Stat. 5]* shall apply to claims of discrimination in compensation brought under sections 501 and 504 of the Rehabilitation Act of 1973 (29 U.S.C. 791, 794), pursuant to—

(1) sections 501(g) and 504(d) of such Act (29 U.S.C. 791(g), 794(d)), respectively, which adopt the standards applied under title I of the Americans with Disabilities Act of 1990 *[42 U.S.C. 12101 et seq.]* for determining whether a violation has occurred in a complaint alleging employment discrimination; and

(2) paragraphs (1) and (2) of section 505(a) of such Act (29 U.S.C. 794a(a)) (as amended by subsection (c)).

SEC. 793 [Section 503] Employment under Federal contracts

(a) Amount of contracts or subcontracts; provision for employment and advancement of qualified individuals with disabilities; regulations

Any contract in excess of $10,000 entered into by any Federal department or agency for the procurement of personal property and nonpersonal services (including construction) for the United States shall contain a provision requiring that the party contracting with the United States shall take affirmative action to employ and advance in employment qualified individuals with disabilities. The provisions of this section shall apply to any subcontract in excess of $10,000 entered into by a prime contractor in carrying out any contract for the procurement of personal property and nonpersonal services (including construction) for the United States. The President shall implement the provisions of this section by promulgating regulations within ninety days after September 26, 1973.

(b) Administrative enforcement; complaints; investigations; departmental action

If any individual with a disability believes any contractor has failed or refused to comply with the provisions of a contract with the United States, relating to employment of individuals with disabilities, such individual may file a complaint with the Department of Labor. The Department shall promptly investigate such complaint and shall take such action thereon as the facts and circumstances warrant, consistent with the terms of such contract and the laws and regulations applicable thereto.

(c) Waiver by President; national interest special circumstances for waiver of particular agreements; waiver by Secretary of Labor of affirmative action requirements

(1) The requirements of this section may be waived, in whole or in part, by the President with respect to a particular contract or subcontract, in accordance with guidelines set forth in regulations which the President shall prescribe, when the President determines that special circumstances in the national interest so require and states in writing the reasons for such determination.

(2) (A) The Secretary of Labor may waive the requirements of the affirmative action clause required by regulations promulgated under subsection (a) of this section with respect to any of a prime contractor's or subcontractor's facilities that are found to be in all respects separate and distinct from activities of the prime contractor or subcontractor related to the performance of the contract or subcontract, if the Secretary of Labor also finds that such a waiver will not interfere with or impede the effectuation of this chapter.

(B) Such waivers shall be considered only upon the request of the contractor or subcontractor. The Secretary of Labor shall promulgate regulations that set forth the standards used for granting such a waiver.

(d) Standards used in determining violation of section

The standards used to determine whether this section has been violated in a complaint alleging nonaffirmative action employment discrimination under this section shall be the standards applied under title I of the Americans with Disabilities Act of 1990 (42 U.S.C. 12111 et seq.) and the provisions of sections 501 through 504, and 510, of the Americans with Disabilities Act of 1990 (42 U.S.C. 12201-12204 and 12210), as such sections relate to employment.

(e) Avoidance of duplicative efforts and inconsistencies

The Secretary shall develop procedures to ensure that administrative complaints filed under this section and under the Americans with Disabilities Act of 1990 [42 U.S.C.A. § 12101 et seq.] are dealt with in a manner that avoids duplication of effort and prevents imposition of inconsistent or conflicting standards for the same requirements under this section and the Americans with Disabilities Act of 1990 [42 U.S.C.A. § 12101 et seq.].

SEC. 794. [Section 504] Nondiscrimination under Federal grants and programs

(a) Promulgation of rules and regulations

No otherwise qualified individual with a disability in the United States, as defined in section 705(20) of this title, shall, solely by reason of her or his disability, be excluded from the participation in, be denied the benefits of, or be subjected to discrimination under any program or activity receiving Federal financial assistance or under any program or activity conducted by any Executive agency or by the United States Postal Service. The head of each such agency shall promulgate such regulations as may be necessary to carry out the amendments to this section made by the Rehabilitation, Comprehensive Services, and Developmental Disabilities Act of 1978. Copies of any proposed regulation shall be submitted to appropriate authorizing committees of the Congress, and such regulation may take effect no earlier than the thirtieth day after the date on which such regulation is so submitted to such committees.

(b) "Program or activity" defined

For the purposes of this section, the term "program or activity" means all of the operations of—

(1) (A) a department, agency, special purpose district, or other instrumentality of a State or of a local government; or

(B) the entity of such State or local government that distributes such assistance and each such department or agency (and each other State or local government entity) to which the assistance is extended, in the case of assistance to a State or local government;

(2) (A) a college, university, or other postsecondary institution, or a public system of higher education; or

(B) a local educational agency (as defined in section 7801 of Title 20), system of vocational education, or other school system;

(3) (A) an entire corporation, partnership, or other private organization, or an entire sole proprietorship—

(i) if assistance is extended to such corporation, partnership, private organization, or sole proprietorship as a whole; or

(ii) which is principally engaged in the business of providing education, health care, housing, social services, or parks and recreation; or

(B) the entire plant or other comparable, geographically separate facility to which Federal financial assistance is extended, in the case of any other corporation, partnership, private organization, or sole proprietorship; or

(4) any other entity which is established by two or more of the entities described in paragraph (1), (2), or (3); any part of which is extended Federal financial assistance.

(c) Significant structural alterations by small providers

Small providers are not required by subsection (a) of this section to make significant structural alterations to their existing facilities for the purpose of assuring program accessibility, if alternative means of providing the services are available. The terms used in this subsection shall be construed with reference to the regulations existing on March 22, 1988.

(d) Standards used in determining violation of section

The standards used to determine whether this section has been violated in a complaint alleging employment discrimination under this section shall be the standards applied under title I of the Americans with Disabilities Act of 1990 (42 U.S.C. 12111 et seq.) and the provisions of sections 501 through 504, and 510, of the Americans with Disabilities Act of 1990 (42 U.S.C. 12201 to 12204 and 12210), as such sections relate to employment.

SEC. 794a. [Section 505] Remedies and Attorney's Fees

(a) (1) The remedies, procedures, and rights set forth in section 717 of the Civil Rights Act of 1964 (42 U.S.C. 2000e-16), including the application of sections 706(f) through 706(k) (42 U.S.C. 2000e-5 (f) through (k)) (and the application of section 706(e) (3) (42 U.S.C. 2000e-5(e)(3)) to claims of discrimination in compensation), shall be available, with respect to any complaint under section 791 of this title, to any employee or applicant for employment aggrieved by the final disposition of such complaint, or by the failure to take final action on such complaint. In fashioning an equitable or affirmative action remedy under such section, a court may take into account the reasonableness of the cost of any necessary work place accommodation, and the availability of alternatives therefore or other appropriate relief in order to achieve an equitable and appropriate remedy.

(2) The remedies, procedures, and rights set forth in title VI of the Civil Rights Act of 1964 (42 U.S.C. 2000d et seq.) (and in subsection (e)(3) of section 706 of such Act (42 U.S.C. 2000e-5), applied to claims of discrimination in compensation) shall be available to any person aggrieved by any act or failure to act by any recipient of Federal assistance or Federal provider of such assistance under section 794 of this title.

(b) In any action or proceeding to enforce or charge a violation of a provision of this subchapter, the court, in its discretion, may allow the prevailing party, other than the United States, a reasonable attorney's fee as part of the costs.

SEC. 705 [Section 7] Definitions

For the purposes of this chapter:

* * *

(10) Drug and illegal use of drugs

(A) Drug

The term "drug" means a controlled substance, as defined in schedules I through V of section 202 of the Controlled Substances Act (21 U.S.C. 812).

(B) The term "illegal use of drugs" means the use of drugs, the possession or distribution of which is unlawful under the Controlled Substances Act *[21 U.S.C. 801 et seq.]*. Such term does not include the use of a drug taken under supervision by a licensed health care professional, or other uses authorized by the Controlled Substances Act *[21 U.S.C. 801 et seq.]* or other provisions of Federal law.

* * *

(20) Individual with a disability

(B) Certain programs; limitations on major life activities

Subject to subparagraphs (C), (D), (E), and (F), the term "individual with a disability" means, for purposes of sections 701, 711, and 712 of this title and subchapters II, IV, V, and VII of this chapter [29 U.S.C. §§ 760 et seq., 780 et seq., 790 et seq., and 796 et seq.], any person who has a disability as defined in section 12102 of Title 42.

(C) Rights and advocacy provisions

(i) In general; exclusion of individuals engaging in drug use

For purposes of subchapter V of this chapter [29 U.S.C. § 790 et seq.], the term "individual with a disability" does not include an individual who is currently engaging in the illegal use of drugs, when a covered entity acts on the basis of such use.

(ii) Exception for individuals no longer engaging in drug use

Nothing in clause (i) shall be construed to exclude as an individual with a disability an individual who—

(I) has successfully completed a supervised drug rehabilitation program and is no longer engaging in the illegal use of drugs, or has otherwise been rehabilitated successfully and is no longer engaging in such use;

(II) is participating in a supervised rehabilitation program and is no longer engaging in such use; or

(III) is erroneously regarded as engaging in such use, but is not engaging in such use; except that it shall not be a violation of this chapter [29 U.S.C. § 701 et seq.] for a covered entity to adopt or administer reasonable policies or procedures, including but not limited to drug testing, designed to ensure that an individual described in subclause (I) or (II) is no longer engaging in the illegal use of drugs.

* * *

(E) Rights provisions; exclusion of individuals on basis of homosexuality or bisexuality

For the purposes of sections 791, 793, and 794 of this title—

(i) for purposes of the application of subparagraph (B) to such sections, the term "impairment" does not include homosexuality or bisexuality; and

(ii) therefore the term "individual with a disability" does not include an individual on the basis of homosexuality or bisexuality.

(F) Rights provisions; exclusion of individuals on basis of certain disorders

For the purposes of sections 791, 793, and 794 of this title, the term "individual with a disability" does not include an individual on the basis of—

(i) transvestism, transsexualism, pedophilia, exhibitionism, voyeurism, gender identity disorders not resulting from physical impairments, or other sexual behavior disorders;

(ii) compulsive gambling, kleptomania, or pyromania; or

(iii) psychoactive substance use disorders resulting from current illegal use of drugs.

Text of the Genetic Information Nondiscrimination Act

42 U.S.C. §§ 2000ff–2000ff-11, Pub. L. No. 110-233 (2008)

Prohibiting Employment Discrimination on the Basis of Genetic Information

§ 2000ff. Definitions

In this chapter:

(1) Commission

The term "Commission" means the Equal Employment Opportunity Commission as created by section 2000e-4 of this title.

(2) Employee; employer; employment agency; labor organization; member

(A) In general

The term "employee" means—

(i) an employee (including an applicant), as defined in section 2000e(f) of this title;

(ii) a State employee (including an applicant) described in section 2000e-16c(a) of this title;

(iii) a covered employee (including an applicant), as defined in section 1301 of Title 2;

(iv) a covered employee (including an applicant), as defined in section 411(c) of Title 3; or

(v) an employee or applicant to which section 2000e-16(a) of this title applies.

(B) Employer

The term "employer" means—

(i) an employer (as defined in section 2000e(b) of this title);

(ii) an entity employing a State employee described in section 2000e-16c(a) of this title;

(iii) an employing office, as defined in section 1301 of Title 2;

(iv) an employing office, as defined in section 411(c) of Title 3; or

(v) an entity to which section 2000e-16(a) of this title applies.

(C) Employment agency; labor organization

The terms "employment agency" and "labor organization" have the meanings given the terms in section 2000e of this title.

(D) Member

The term "member", with respect to a labor organization, includes an applicant for membership in a labor organization.

(3) Family member

The term "family member" means, with respect to an individual—

(A) a dependent (as such term is used for purposes of section 1181(f)(2) of Title 29 of such individual, and

(B) any other individual who is a first-degree, second-degree, third-degree, or fourth-degree relative of such individual or of an individual described in subparagraph (A).

(4) Genetic information

(A) In general

The term "genetic information" means, with respect to any individual, information about—

(i) such individual's genetic tests,

(ii) the genetic tests of family members of such individual, and

(iii) the manifestation of a disease or disorder in family members of such individual.

(B) Inclusion of genetic services and participation in genetic research

Such term includes, with respect to any individual, any request for, or receipt of, genetic services, or participation in clinical research which includes genetic services, by such individual or any family member of such individual.

(C) Exclusions

The term "genetic information" shall not include information about the sex or age of any individual.

(5) Genetic monitoring

The term "genetic monitoring" means the periodic examination of employees to evaluate acquired modifications to their genetic material, such as chromosomal damage or evidence of increased occurrence of mutations, that may have developed in the course of employment due to exposure to toxic substances in the workplace, in order to identify, evaluate, and respond to the effects of or control adverse environmental exposures in the workplace.

(6) Genetic services

The term "genetic services" means—

(A) a genetic test;

(B) genetic counseling (including obtaining, interpreting, or assessing genetic information); or

(C) genetic education.

(7) Genetic test

(A) In general

The term "genetic test" means an analysis of human DNA, RNA, chromosomes, proteins, or metabolites, that detects genotypes, mutations, or chromosomal changes.

(B) Exceptions

The term "genetic test" does not mean an analysis of proteins or metabolites that does not detect genotypes, mutations, or chromosomal changes.

§ 2000ff-1. Employer practices

(a) Discrimination based on genetic information

It shall be an unlawful employment practice for an employer—

(1) to fail or refuse to hire, or to discharge, any employee, or otherwise to discriminate against any employee with respect to the compensation, terms, conditions, or privileges of employment of the employee, because of genetic information with respect to the employee; or

(2) to limit, segregate, or classify the employees of the employer in any way that would deprive or tend to deprive any employee of employment opportunities or otherwise adversely affect the status of the employee as an employee, because of genetic information with respect to the employee.

(b) Acquisition of genetic information

It shall be an unlawful employment practice for an employer to request, require, or purchase genetic information with respect to an employee or a family member of the employee except—

(1) where an employer inadvertently requests or requires family medical history of the employee or family member of the employee;

(2) where—

(A) health or genetic services are offered by the employer, including such services offered as part of a wellness program;

(B) the employee provides prior, knowing, voluntary, and written authorization;

(C) only the employee (or family member if the family member is receiving genetic services) and the licensed health care professional or board certified genetic counselor involved in providing such services receive individually identifiable information concerning the results of such services; and

(D) any individually identifiable genetic information provided under subparagraph (C) in connection with the services provided under subparagraph (A) is only available for purposes of such services and shall not be disclosed to the employer except in aggregate terms that do not disclose the identity of specific employees;

(3) where an employer requests or requires family medical history from the employee to comply with the certification provisions of section 2613 of Title 29 or such requirements under State family and medical leave laws;

(4) where an employer purchases documents that are commercially and publicly available (including newspapers, magazines, periodicals, and books, but not including medical databases or court records) that include family medical history;

(5) where the information involved is to be used for genetic monitoring of the biological effects of toxic substances in the workplace, but only if—

(A) the employer provides written notice of the genetic monitoring to the employee;

(B) (i) the employee provides prior, knowing, voluntary, and written authorization; or

(ii) the genetic monitoring is required by Federal or State law;

(C) the employee is informed of individual monitoring results;

(D) the monitoring is in compliance with—

(i) any Federal genetic monitoring regulations, including any such regulations that may be promulgated by the Secretary of Labor pursuant to the Occupational Safety and Health Act of 1970 (29 U.S.C. 651 et seq.), the Federal Mine Safety and Health Act of 1977 (30 U.S.C. 801 et seq.), or the Atomic Energy Act of 1954 (42 U.S.C. 2011 et seq.); or

(ii) State genetic monitoring regulations, in the case of a State that is implementing genetic monitoring regulations under the authority of the Occupational Safety and Health Act of 1970 (29 U.S.C. 651 et seq.); and

(E) the employer, excluding any licensed health care professional or board certified genetic counselor that is involved in the genetic monitoring program, receives the results of the monitoring only in aggregate terms that do not disclose the identity of specific employees; or

(6) where the employer conducts DNA analysis for law enforcement purposes as a forensic laboratory or for purposes of human remains identification, and requests or requires genetic information of such employer's employees, but only to the extent that such genetic information is used for analysis of DNA identification markers for quality control to detect sample contamination.

(c) Preservation of protections

In the case of information to which any of paragraphs (1) through (6) of subsection (b) applies, such information may not be used in violation of paragraph (1) or (2) of subsection (a) or treated or disclosed in a manner that violates section 2000ff-5 of this title.

§ 2000ff-2. Employment agency practices

(a) Discrimination based on genetic information

It shall be an unlawful employment practice for an employment agency—

(1) to fail or refuse to refer for employment, or otherwise to discriminate against, any individual because of genetic information with respect to the individual;

(2) to limit, segregate, or classify individuals or fail or refuse to refer for employment any individual in any way that would deprive or tend to deprive any individual of employment opportunities, or otherwise adversely affect the status of the individual as an employee, because of genetic information with respect to the individual; or

(3) to cause or attempt to cause an employer to discriminate against an individual in violation of this chapter.

(b) Acquisition of genetic information

It shall be an unlawful employment practice for an employment agency to request, require, or purchase genetic information with respect to an individual or a family member of the individual except—

(1) where an employment agency inadvertently requests or requires family medical history of the individual or family member of the individual;

(2) where—

(A) health or genetic services are offered by the employment agency, including such services offered as part of a wellness program;

(B) the individual provides prior, knowing, voluntary, and written authorization;

(C) only the individual (or family member if the family member is receiving genetic services) and the licensed health care professional or board certified genetic counselor involved in providing such services receive individually identifiable information concerning the results of such services; and

(D) any individually identifiable genetic information provided under subparagraph (C) in connection with the services provided under subparagraph (A) is only available for purposes of such services and shall not be disclosed to the employment agency except in aggregate terms that do not disclose the identity of specific individuals;

(3) where an employment agency requests or requires family medical history from the individual to comply with the certification provisions of section 2613 of Title 29 or such requirements under State family and medical leave laws;

(4) where an employment agency purchases documents that are commercially and publicly available (including newspapers, magazines, periodicals, and books, but not including medical databases or court records) that include family medical history; or

(5) where the information involved is to be used for genetic monitoring of the biological effects of toxic substances in the workplace, but only if—

(A) the employment agency provides written notice of the genetic monitoring to the individual;

(B) (i) the individual provides prior, knowing, voluntary, and written authorization; or

(ii) the genetic monitoring is required by Federal or State law;

(C) the individual is informed of individual monitoring results;

(D) the monitoring is in compliance with—
   (i) any Federal genetic monitoring regulations, including any such regulations that may be promulgated by the Secretary of Labor pursuant to the Occupational Safety and Health Act of 1970 (29 U.S.C. 651 et seq.), the Federal Mine Safety and Health Act of 1977 (30 U.S.C. 801 et seq.) , or the Atomic Energy Act of 1954 (42 U.S.C. 2011 et seq.); or
   (ii) State genetic monitoring regulations, in the case of a State that is implementing genetic monitoring regulations under the authority of the Occupational Safety and Health Act of 1970 (29 U.S.C. 651 et seq.); and

(E) the employment agency, excluding any licensed health care professional or board certified genetic counselor that is involved in the genetic monitoring program, receives the results of the monitoring only in aggregate terms that do not disclose the identity of specific individuals.

(c) Preservation of protections

In the case of information to which any of paragraphs (1) through (5) of subsection (b) applies, such information may not be used in violation of paragraph (1), (2), or (3) of subsection (a) or treated or disclosed in a manner that violates section 2000ff-5 of this title.

§ 2000ff-3. Labor organization practices

(a) Discrimination based on genetic information

It shall be an unlawful employment practice for a labor organization—

(1) to exclude or to expel from the membership of the organization, or otherwise to discriminate against, any member because of genetic information with respect to the member;

(2) to limit, segregate, or classify the members of the organization, or fail or refuse to refer for employment any member, in any way that would deprive or tend to deprive any member of employment opportunities, or otherwise adversely affect the status of the member as an employee, because of genetic information with respect to the member; or

(3) to cause or attempt to cause an employer to discriminate against a member in violation of this chapter.

(b) Acquisition of genetic information

It shall be an unlawful employment practice for a labor organization to request, require, or purchase genetic information with respect to a member or a family member of the member except—

(1) where a labor organization inadvertently requests or requires family medical history of the member or family member of the member;

(2) where—
   (A) health or genetic services are offered by the labor organization, including such services offered as part of a wellness program;
   (B) the member provides prior, knowing, voluntary, and written authorization;
   (C) only the member (or family member if the family member is receiving genetic services) and the licensed health care professional or board certified genetic counselor involved in providing such services receive individually identifiable information concerning the results of such services; and
   (D) any individually identifiable genetic information provided under subparagraph (C) in connection with the services provided under subparagraph (A) is only available for purposes of such services and shall not be disclosed to the labor organization except in aggregate terms that do not disclose the identity of specific members;

(3) where a labor organization requests or requires family medical history from the members to comply with the certification provisions of section 2613 of Title 29 or such requirements under State family and medical leave laws;

(4) where a labor organization purchases documents that are commercially and publicly available (including newspapers, magazines, periodicals, and books, but not including medical databases or court records) that include family medical history; or

(5) where the information involved is to be used for genetic monitoring of the biological effects of toxic substances in the workplace, but only if—
   (A) the labor organization provides written notice of the genetic monitoring to the member;
   (B) (i) the member provides prior, knowing, voluntary, and written authorization; or
      (ii) the genetic monitoring is required by Federal or State law;
   (C) the member is informed of individual monitoring results;
   (D) the monitoring is in compliance with—
      (i) any Federal genetic monitoring regulations, including any such regulations that

may be promulgated by the Secretary of Labor pursuant to the Occupational Safety and Health Act of 1970 (29 U.S.C. 651 et seq.), the Federal Mine Safety and Health Act of 1977 (30 U.S.C. 801 et seq.), or the Atomic Energy Act of 1954 (42 U.S.C. 2011 et seq.); or

(ii) State genetic monitoring regulations, in the case of a State that is implementing genetic monitoring regulations under the authority of the Occupational Safety and Health Act of 1970 (29 U.S.C. 651 et seq.); and

(E) the labor organization, excluding any licensed health care professional or board certified genetic counselor that is involved in the genetic monitoring program, receives the results of the monitoring only in aggregate terms that do not disclose the identity of specific members.

(c) Preservation of protections

In the case of information to which any of paragraphs (1) through (5) of subsection (b) applies, such information may not be used in violation of paragraph (1), (2), or (3) of subsection (a) or treated or disclosed in a manner that violates section 2000ff-5 of this title.

§ 2000ff-4. Training programs

(a) Discrimination based on genetic information

It shall be an unlawful employment practice for any employer, labor organization, or joint labor-management committee controlling apprenticeship or other training or retraining, including on-the-job training programs—

(1) to discriminate against any individual because of genetic information with respect to the individual in admission to, or employment in, any program established to provide apprenticeship or other training or retraining;

(2) to limit, segregate, or classify the applicants for or participants in such apprenticeship or other training or retraining, or fail or refuse to refer for employment any individual, in any way that would deprive or tend to deprive any individual of employment opportunities, or otherwise adversely affect the status of the individual as an employee, because of genetic information with respect to the individual; or

(3) to cause or attempt to cause an employer to discriminate against an applicant for or a participant in such apprenticeship or other training or retraining in violation of this chapter.

(b) Acquisition of genetic information

It shall be an unlawful employment practice for an employer, labor organization, or joint labor-management committee described in subsection (a) to request, require, or purchase genetic information with respect to an individual or a family member of the individual except—

(1) where the employer, labor organization, or joint labor-management committee inadvertently requests or requires family medical history of the individual or family member of the individual;

(2) where—

(A) health or genetic services are offered by the employer, labor organization, or joint labor-management committee, including such services offered as part of a wellness program;

(B) the individual provides prior, knowing, voluntary, and written authorization;

(C) only the individual (or family member if the family member is receiving genetic services) and the licensed health care professional or board certified genetic counselor involved in providing such services receive individually identifiable information concerning the results of such services; and

(D) any individually identifiable genetic information provided under subparagraph (C) in connection with the services provided under subparagraph (A) is only available for purposes of such services and shall not be disclosed to the employer, labor organization, or joint labor-management committee except in aggregate terms that do not disclose the identity of specific individuals;

(3) where the employer, labor organization, or joint labor-management committee requests or requires family medical history from the individual to comply with the certification provisions of section 2613 of Title 29 or such requirements under State family and medical leave laws;

(4) where the employer, labor organization, or joint labor-management committee purchases documents that are commercially and publicly available (including newspapers, magazines, periodicals, and books, but not including medical databases or court records) that include family medical history;

(5) where the information involved is to be used for genetic monitoring of the biological effects of toxic substances in the workplace, but only if—

(A) the employer, labor organization, or joint labor-management committee provides written notice of the genetic monitoring to the individual;

(B) (i) the individual provides prior, knowing, voluntary, and written authorization; or

(ii) the genetic monitoring is required by Federal or State law;

(C) the individual is informed of individual monitoring results;

(D) the monitoring is in compliance with—

(i) any Federal genetic monitoring regulations, including any such regulations that may be promulgated by the Secretary of Labor pursuant to the Occupational Safety and Health Act of 1970 (29 U.S.C. 651 et seq.), the Federal Mine Safety and Health Act of 1977 (30 U.S.C. 801 et seq.), or the Atomic Energy Act of 1954 (42 U.S.C. 2011 et seq.); or

(ii) State genetic monitoring regulations, in the case of a State that is implementing genetic monitoring regulations under the authority of the Occupational Safety and Health Act of 1970 (29 U.S.C. 651 et seq.); and

(E) the employer, labor organization, or joint labor-management committee, excluding any licensed health care professional or board certified genetic counselor that is involved in the genetic monitoring program, receives the results of the monitoring only in aggregate terms that do not disclose the identity of specific individuals; or

(6) where the employer conducts DNA analysis for law enforcement purposes as a forensic laboratory or for purposes of human remains identification, and requests or requires genetic information of such employer's apprentices or trainees, but only to the extent that such genetic information is used for analysis of DNA identification markers for quality control to detect sample contamination.

(c) Preservation of protections

In the case of information to which any of paragraphs (1) through (6) of subsection (b) applies, such information may not be used in violation of paragraph (1), (2), or (3) of subsection (a) or treated or disclosed in a manner that violates section 2000ff-5 of this title.

§ 2000ff-5. Confidentiality of genetic information

(a) Treatment of information as part of confidential medical record

If an employer, employment agency, labor organization, or joint labor-management committee possesses genetic information about an employee or member, such information shall be maintained on separate forms and in separate medical files and be treated as a confidential medical record of the employee or member. An employer, employment agency, labor organization, or joint labor-management committee shall be considered to be in compliance with the maintenance of information requirements of this subsection with respect to genetic information subject to this subsection that is maintained with and treated as a confidential medical record under section 12112(d)(3)(B) of this title.

(b) Limitation on disclosure

An employer, employment agency, labor organization, or joint labor-management committee shall not disclose genetic information concerning an employee or member except—

(1) to the employee or member of a labor organization (or family member if the family member is receiving the genetic services) at the written request of the employee or member of such organization;

(2) to an occupational or other health researcher if the research is conducted in compliance with the regulations and protections provided for under part 46 of title 45, Code of Federal Regulations;

(3) in response to an order of a court, except that—

(A) the employer, employment agency, labor organization, or joint labor-management committee may disclose only the genetic information expressly authorized by such order; and

(B) if the court order was secured without the knowledge of the employee or member to whom the information refers, the employer, employment agency, labor organization, or joint labor-management committee shall inform the employee or member of the court order and any genetic information that was disclosed pursuant to such order;

(4) to government officials who are investigating compliance with this chapter if the information is relevant to the investigation;

(5) to the extent that such disclosure is made in connection with the employee's compliance with the certification provisions of section 2613 of Title 29 or such requirements under State family and medical leave laws; or

(6) to a Federal, State, or local public health agency only with regard to information that is described in section 2000ff(4)(A)(iii) of this title and that

concerns a contagious disease that presents an imminent hazard of death or life-threatening illness, and that the employee whose family member or family members is or are the subject of a disclosure under this paragraph is notified of such disclosure.

(c) Relationship to HIPAA regulations

With respect to the regulations promulgated by the Secretary of Health and Human Services under part C of title XI of the Social Security Act (42 U.S.C. 1320d et seq.) and section 264 of the Health Insurance Portability and Accountability Act of 1996 (42 U. S.C. 1320d-2 note), this chapter does not prohibit a covered entity under such regulations from any use or disclosure of health information that is authorized for the covered entity under such regulations. The previous sentence does not affect the authority of such Secretary to modify such regulations.

§ 2000ff-6. Remedies and enforcement

(a) Employees covered by title VII of the Civil Rights Act of 1964

(1) In general

The powers, procedures, and remedies provided in sections 705, 706, 707, 709, 710, and 711 of the Civil Rights Act of 1964 (42 U.S.C. 2000e-4 et seq.) to the Commission, the Attorney General, or any person, alleging a violation of title VII of that Act (42 U.S.C. 2000e et seq.) shall be the powers, procedures, and remedies this chapter provides to the Commission, the Attorney General, or any person, respectively, alleging an unlawful employment practice in violation of this chapter against an employee described in section 2000ff(2)(A)(i) of this title, except as provided in paragraphs (2) and (3).

(2) Costs and fees

The powers, remedies, and procedures provided in subsections (b) and (c) of section 1988 of this title, shall be powers, remedies, and procedures this chapter provides to the Commission, the Attorney General, or any person, alleging such a practice.

(3) Damages

The powers, remedies, and procedures provided in section 1981a of this title, including the limitations contained in subsection (b)(3) of such section 1981a, shall be powers, remedies, and procedures this chapter provides to the Commission, the Attorney General, or any person, alleging such a practice (not an employment practice specifically excluded from coverage under section 1981a(a)(1) of this title).

(b) Employees covered by Government Employee Rights Act of 1991

(1) In general

The powers, remedies, and procedures provided in sections 2000e-16b and 2000e-16c of this title to the Commission, or any person, alleging a violation of section 2000e-16b(a)(1) of this title shall be the powers, remedies, and procedures this chapter provides to the Commission, or any person, respectively, alleging an unlawful employment practice in violation of this chapter against an employee described in section 2000ff(2)(A)(ii) of this title, except as provided in paragraphs (2) and (3).

(2) Costs and fees

The powers, remedies, and procedures provided in subsections (b) and (c) of section 1988 of this title, shall be powers, remedies, and procedures this chapter provides to the Commission, or any person, alleging such a practice.

(3) Damages

The powers, remedies, and procedures provided in section 1981a of this title, including the limitations contained in subsection (b)(3) of such section 1981a, shall be powers, remedies, and procedures this chapter provides to the Commission, or any person, alleging such a practice (not an employment practice specifically excluded from coverage under section 1981a(a)(1) of this title).

(c) Employees covered by Congressional Accountability Act of 1995

(1) In general

The powers, remedies, and procedures provided in the Congressional Accountability Act of 1995 (2 U.S.C. 1301 et seq.) to the Board (as defined in section 101 of that Act (2 U.S.C. 1301)), or any person, alleging a violation of section 201(a)(1) of that Act (42 U.S.C. 1311(a)(1)) shall be the powers, remedies, and procedures this chapter provides to that Board, or any person, alleging an unlawful employment practice in violation of this chapter against an employee described in section 2000ff(2)(A)(iii) of this title, except as provided in paragraphs (2) and (3).

(2) Costs and fees

The powers, remedies, and procedures provided in subsections (b) and (c) of section 1988 of this title, shall be powers, remedies, and procedures this chapter provides to that Board, or any person, alleging such a practice.

(3) Damages

The powers, remedies, and procedures provided in section 1981a of this title, including the limitations contained in subsection (b)(3) of such section 1981a, shall be powers, remedies, and procedures this chapter provides to that Board, or any person, alleging such a practice (not an employment practice specifically excluded from coverage under section 1981a(a)(1) of this title).

(4) Other applicable provisions

With respect to a claim alleging a practice described in paragraph (1), title III of the Congressional Accountability Act of 1995 (2 U.S.C. 1381 et seq.) shall apply in the same manner as such title applies with respect to a claim alleging a violation of section 201(a)(1) of such Act (2 U.S.C. 1311 (a)(1)).

(d) Employees covered by of Title 3

(1) In general

The powers, remedies, and procedures provided in of Title 3 to the President, the Commission, the Merit Systems Protection Board, or any person, alleging a violation of section 411(a)(1) of that title, shall be the powers, remedies, and procedures this chapter provides to the President, the Commission, such Board, or any person, respectively, alleging an unlawful employment practice in violation of this chapter against an employee described in section 2000ff(2)(A)(iv) of this title, except as provided in paragraphs (2) and (3).

(2) Costs and fees

The powers, remedies, and procedures provided in subsections (b) and (c) of section 1988 of this title, shall be powers, remedies, and procedures this chapter provides to the President, the Commission, such Board, or any person, alleging such a practice.

(3) Damages

The powers, remedies, and procedures provided in section 1981a of this title, including the limitations contained in subsection (b)(3) of such section 1981a, shall be powers, remedies, and procedures this chapter provides to the President, the Commission, such Board, or any person, alleging such a practice (not an employment practice specifically excluded from coverage under section 1981a(a)(1) of this title).

(e) Employees covered by section 717 of the Civil Rights Act of 1964

(1) In general

The powers, remedies, and procedures provided in section 717 of the Civil Rights Act of 1964 (42 U.S.C. 2000e-16) to the Commission, the Attorney General, the Librarian of Congress, or any person, alleging a violation of that section shall be the powers, remedies, and procedures this title provides to the Commission, the Attorney General, the Librarian of Congress, or any person, respectively, alleging an unlawful employment practice in violation of this chapter against an employee or applicant described in section 2000ff(2)(A)(v) of this title, except as provided in paragraphs (2) and (3).

(2) Costs and fees

The powers, remedies, and procedures provided in subsections (b) and (c) of section 1988 of this title, shall be powers, remedies, and procedures this chapter provides to the Commission, the Attorney General, the Librarian of Congress, or any person, alleging such a practice.

(3) Damages

The powers, remedies, and procedures provided in section 1981a of this title, including the limitations contained in subsection (b)(3) of such section 1981a, shall be powers, remedies, and procedures this chapter provides to the Commission, the Attorney General, the Librarian of Congress, or any person, alleging such a practice (not an employment practice specifically excluded from coverage under section 1981a(a)(1) of this title).

(f) Prohibition against retaliation

No person shall discriminate against any individual because such individual has opposed any act or practice made unlawful by this chapter or because such individual made a charge, testified, assisted, or participated in any manner in an investigation, proceeding, or hearing under this chapter. The remedies and procedures otherwise provided for under this section shall be available to aggrieved individuals with respect to violations of this subsection.

(g) Definition

In this section, the term "Commission" means the Equal Employment Opportunity Commission.

§ 2000ff-7. Disparate impact

(a) General rule

Notwithstanding any other provision of this Act, "disparate impact", as that term is used in section 2000e-2(k) of this title, on the basis of genetic information does not establish a cause of action under this Act.

(b) Commission

On the date that is 6 years after May 21, 2008, there shall be established a commission, to be known as the Genetic Nondiscrimination Study Commission (referred to in this section as the "Commission") to review the developing science of genetics and to make recommendations to Congress regarding whether to provide a disparate impact cause of action under this Act.

(c) Membership

(1) In general

The Commission shall be composed of 8 members, of which—

(A) 1 member shall be appointed by the Majority Leader of the Senate;

(B) 1 member shall be appointed by the Minority Leader of the Senate;

(C) 1 member shall be appointed by the Chairman of the Committee on Health, Education, Labor, and Pensions of the Senate;

(D) 1 member shall be appointed by the ranking minority member of the Committee on Health, Education, Labor, and Pensions of the Senate;

(E) 1 member shall be appointed by the Speaker of the House of Representatives;

(F) 1 member shall be appointed by the Minority Leader of the House of Representatives;

(G) 1 member shall be appointed by the Chairman of the Committee on Education and Labor of the House of Representatives; and

(H) 1 member shall be appointed by the ranking minority member of the Committee on Education and Labor of the House of Representatives.

(2) Compensation and expenses

The members of the Commission shall not receive compensation for the performance of services for the Commission, but shall be allowed travel expenses, including per diem in lieu of subsistence, at rates authorized for employees of agencies under subchapter I of of Title 5, while away from their homes or regular places of business in the performance of services for the Commission.

(d) Administrative provisions

(1) Location

The Commission shall be located in a facility maintained by the Equal Employment Opportunity Commission.

(2) Detail of Government employees

Any Federal Government employee may be detailed to the Commission without reimbursement, and such detail shall be without interruption or loss of civil service status or privilege.

(3) Information from Federal agencies

The Commission may secure directly from any Federal department or agency such information as the Commission considers necessary to carry out the provisions of this section. Upon request of the Commission, the head of such department or agency shall furnish such information to the Commission.

(4) Hearings

The Commission may hold such hearings, sit and act at such times and places, take such testimony, and receive such evidence as the Commission considers advisable to carry out the objectives of this section, except that, to the extent possible, the Commission shall use existing data and research.

(5) Postal services

The Commission may use the United States mails in the same manner and under the same conditions as other departments and agencies of the Federal Government.

(e) Report

Not later than 1 year after all of the members are appointed to the Commission under subsection (c)(1), the Commission shall submit to Congress a report that summarizes the findings of the Commission and makes such recommendations for legislation as are consistent with this Act.

(f) Authorization of appropriations

There are authorized to be appropriated to the Equal Employment Opportunity Commission such sums as may be necessary to carry out this section.

§ 2000ff-8. Construction

(a) In general

Nothing in this chapter shall be construed to—

(1) limit the rights or protections of an individual under any other Federal or State statute that provides equal or greater protection to an individual than the rights or protections provided for under this chapter, including the protections of an individual under the Americans with Disabilities Act of 1990 (42 U.S.C. 12101 et seq.) (including coverage afforded to individuals under section 102 of such Act (42 U.S.C. 12112)), or under the Rehabilitation Act of 1973 (29 U.S.C. 701 et seq.);

(2) (A) limit the rights or protections of an individual to bring an action under this chapter against an employer, employment agency, labor organization, or joint labor-management committee for a violation of this chapter; or

(B) provide for enforcement of, or penalties for violation of, any requirement or prohibition applicable to any employer, employment agency, labor organization, or joint labor-management committee subject to enforcement for a violation under—

(i) the amendments made by title I of this Act;

(ii) (I) subsection (a) of section 1181 of Title 29 as such section applies with respect to genetic information pursuant to subsection (b)(1)(B) of such section;

(II) section 1182(a)(1)(F) of Title 29; or

(III) section 1182(b)(1) of Title 29 of such Act as such section applies with respect to genetic information as a health status-related factor;

(iii) (I) subsection (a) of section 300gg of this title as such section applies with respect to genetic information pursuant to subsection (b)(1)(B) of such section;

(II) section 300gg-1(a)(1)(F) of this title; or

(III) section 300gg-1(b)(1) of this title as such section applies with respect to genetic information as a health status-related factor; or

(iv) (I) subsection (a) of section 9801 of Title 26 as such section applies with respect to genetic information pursuant to subsection (b)(1)(B) of such section;

(II) section 9802(a)(1)(F) of such title; or

(III) section 9802(b)(1) of such title as such section applies with respect to genetic information as a health status-related factor;

(3) apply to the Armed Forces Repository of Specimen Samples for the Identification of Remains;

(4) limit or expand the protections, rights, or obligations of employees or employers under applicable workers' compensation laws;

(5) limit the authority of a Federal department or agency to conduct or sponsor occupational or other health research that is conducted in compliance with the regulations contained in part 46 of title 45, Code of Federal Regulations (or any corresponding or similar regulation or rule);

(6) limit the statutory or regulatory authority of the Occupational Safety and Health Administration or the Mine Safety and Health Administration to promulgate or enforce workplace safety and health laws and regulations; or

(7) require any specific benefit for an employee or member or a family member of an employee or member under any group health plan or health insurance issuer offering group health insurance coverage in connection with a group health plan.

(b) Genetic information of a fetus or embryo

Any reference in this chapter to genetic information concerning an individual or family member of an individual shall—

(1) with respect to such an individual or family member of an individual who is a pregnant woman, include genetic information of any fetus carried by such pregnant woman; and

(2) with respect to an individual or family member utilizing an assisted reproductive technology, include genetic information of any embryo legally held by the individual or family member.

(c) Relation to authorities under title I

With respect to a group health plan, or a health insurance issuer offering group health insurance coverage in connection with a group health plan, this title does not prohibit any activity of such plan or issuer that is authorized for the plan or issuer under any provision of law referred to in clauses (i) through (iv) of subsection (a)(2)(B).

§ 2000ff-9. Medical Information That Is Not Genetic Information

An employer, employment agency, labor organization, or joint labor-management committee shall not be considered to be in violation of this chapter based on the use, acquisition, or disclosure of medical information that is not genetic information about a manifested disease, disorder, or pathological condition of an employee or member, including a manifested disease, disorder, or pathological condition that has or may have a genetic basis.

§ 2000ff-10. Regulations

Not later than 1 year after May 21, 2008, the Commission shall issue final regulations to carry out this chapter.

§ 2000ff-11. Authorization of Appropriations

There are authorized to be appropriated such sums as may be necessary to carry out this chapter (except for section 2000ff-7 of this title).

Text of the National Labor Relations Act

49 Stat. 449–57 (1935), as amended by 61 Stat. 136–52 (1947), 65 Stat. 601 (1951), 72 Stat. 945 (1958), 73 Stat. 525–42 (1959), 84 Stat. 930 (1970), 88 Stat. 395–97 (1974), 88 Stat. 1972 (1975), 94 Stat. 347 (1980), 94 Stat. 3452 (1980); 29 U.S.C. Section 151 et seq.

Findings and Policies

Section 1. The denial by some employers of the right of employees to organize and the refusal by some employers to accept the procedure of collective bargaining lead to strikes and other forms of industrial strife or unrest, which have the intent or the necessary effect of burdening or obstructing commerce by (a) impairing the efficiency, safety, or operation of the instrumentalities of commerce; (b) occurring in the current of commerce; (c) materially affecting, restraining, or controlling the flow of raw materials or manufactured or processed goods from or into the channels of commerce, or the prices of such materials or goods in commerce; or (d) causing diminution of employment and wages in such volume as substantially to impair or disrupt the market for goods flowing from or into the channels of commerce.

The inequality of bargaining power between employees who do not possess full freedom of association or actual liberty of contract, and employers who are organized in the corporate or other forms of ownership association substantially burdens and affects the flow of commerce, and tends to aggravate recurrent business depressions by depressing wage rates and the purchasing power of wage earners in industry and by preventing the stabilization of competitive wage rates and working conditions within and between industries.

Experience has proved that protection by law of the right of employees to organize and bargain collectively safeguards commerce from injury, impairment, or interruption, and promotes the flow of commerce by removing certain recognized sources of industrial strife and unrest, by encouraging practices fundamental to the friendly adjustment of industrial disputes arising out of differences as to wages, hours, or other working conditions, and by restoring equality of bargaining power between employers and employees.

Experience has further demonstrated that certain practices by some labor organizations, their officers, and members have the intent or the necessary effect of burdening or obstructing commerce by preventing the free flow of goods in such commerce through strikes and other forms of industrial unrest or through concerted activities which impair the interest of the public in the free flow of such commerce. The elimination of such practices is a necessary condition to the assurance of the rights herein guaranteed.

It is hereby declared to be the policy of the United States to eliminate the causes of certain substantial obstructions to the free flow of commerce and to mitigate and eliminate these obstructions when they have occurred by encouraging the practice and procedure of collective bargaining and by protecting the exercise by workers of full freedom of association, self-organization, and designation of representatives of their own choosing, for the purpose of negotiating the terms and conditions of their employment or other mutual aid or protection.

Definitions

Section 2. When used in this Act—

(a) (1) The term "person" includes one or more individuals, labor organizations, partnerships, associations, corporations, legal representatives, trustees, trustees in cases under Title II of the United States Code or receivers.

(2) The term "employer" includes any person acting as an agent of an employer, directly or indirectly, but shall not include the United States or any wholly

owned Government corporation, or any Federal Reserve Bank, or any State or political subdivision thereof, or any person subject to the Railway Labor Act, as amended from time to time, or any labor organization (other than when acting as an employer), or anyone acting in the capacity of officer or agent of such labor organization.

(3) The term "employee" shall include any employee, and shall not be limited to the employees of a particular employer, unless the Act explicitly states otherwise, and shall include any individual whose work has ceased as a consequence of, or in connection with, any current labor dispute or because of any unfair labor practice, and who has not obtained any other regular and substantially equivalent employment, but shall not include any individual employed as an agricultural laborer, or in the domestic service of any family or person at his home, or any individual employed by his parent or spouse, or any individual having the status of an independent contractor, or any individual employed as a supervisor, or any individual employed by an employer subject to the Railway Labor Act, as amended from time to time, or by any other person who is not an employer as herein defined.

(4) The term "representatives" includes any individual or labor organization.

(5) The term "labor organization" means any organization of any kind, or any agency or employee representation committee or plan, in which employees participate and which exists for the purpose, in whole or in part, of dealing with employers concerning grievances, labor disputes, wages, rates of pay, hours of employment, or conditions of work.

(6) The term "commerce" means trade, traffic, commerce, transportation, or communication among the several States, or between the District of Columbia or any Territory of the United States and any State or other Territory, or between any foreign country and any State, Territory, or the District of Columbia, or within the District of Columbia or any Territory, or between points in the same State but through any other State or any Territory or the District of Columbia or any foreign country.

(7) The term "affecting commerce" means in commerce, or burdening or obstructing commerce or the free flow of commerce, or having led or tending to lead to a labor dispute burdening or obstructing commerce or the free flow of commerce.

(8) The term "unfair labor practice" means any unfair labor practice listed in section 8.

(9) The term "labor dispute" includes any controversy concerning terms, tenure or conditions of employment, or concerning the association or representation of persons in negotiating, fixing, maintaining, changing, or seeking to arrange terms or conditions of employment, regardless of whether the disputants stand in the proximate relation of employer and employee.

(10) The term "National Labor Relations Board" means the National Labor Relations Board provided for in section 3 of this Act.

(11) The term "supervisor" means any individual having authority, in the interest of the employer, to hire, transfer, suspend, lay off, recall, promote, discharge, assign, reward, or discipline other employees, or responsibly to direct them, or to adjust their grievances, or effectively to recommend such action, if in connection with the foregoing the exercise of such authority is not of a merely routine or clerical nature, but requires the use of independent judgment.

(12) The term "professional employee" means—

(A) any employee engaged in work (i) predominantly intellectual and varied in character as opposed to routine mental, manual, mechanical, or physical work; (ii) involving the consistent exercise of discretion and judgment in its performance; (iii) of such a character that the output produced or the result accomplished cannot be standardized in relation to a given period of time; (iv) requiring knowledge of an advanced type in a field of science or learning customarily acquired by a prolonged course of specialized intellectual instruction and study in an institution of higher learning or a hospital, as distinguished from a general academic education or from an apprenticeship or from training in the performance of routine mental, manual, or physical processes; or

(B) any employee, who (i) has completed the courses of specialized intellectual instruction and study described in clause (iv) or paragraph (a), and (ii) is performing related work under the supervision of a professional person to qualify himself to become a professional employee as defined in paragraph (a).

(13) In determining whether any person is acting as an "agent" of another person so as to make such other person responsible for his acts, the question of whether the specific acts performed were actually authorized or subsequently ratified shall not be controlling.

(14) The term "health care institution" shall include any hospital, convalescent hospital, health maintenance organization, health clinic, nursing home, extended care facility, or other institution devoted to the care of sick, infirm, or aged person.

National Labor Relations Board

Section 3.

(a) The National Labor Relations Board (hereinafter called the "Board") created by this Act prior to its amendment by the Labor Management Relations Act, 1947, is hereby continued as an agency of the United States, except that the Board shall consist of five instead of three members, appointed by the President by and with the advice and consent of the Senate. Of the two additional members so provided for, one shall be appointed for a term of five years and the other for a term of two years. Their successors, and the successors of the other members, shall be appointed for terms of five years each, excepting that any individual chosen to fill a vacancy shall be appointed only for the unexpired term of the member whom he shall succeed. The President shall designate one member to serve as Chairman of the Board. Any member of the Board may be removed by the President, upon notice and hearing, for neglect of duty or malfeasance in office, but for no other cause.

(b) The Board is authorized to delegate to any group of three or more members any or all the powers which it may itself exercise. The Board is also authorized to delegate to its regional directors its power under section 9 to determine the unit appropriate for the purpose of collective bargaining, to investigate and provide for hearings, and determine whether a question of representation exists, and to direct an election or take a secret ballot under subsection (c) or (e) of section 9 and certify the results thereof, except that upon the filing of a request therefor with the Board by any interested person, the Board may review any action of a regional director delegated to him under this paragraph, but such a review shall not, unless specifically ordered by the Board, operate as a stay of any action taken by the regional director. A vacancy in the Board shall not impair the right of the remaining members to exercise all of the powers of the Board, and three members of the Board shall, at all times, constitute a quorum of the Board, except that two members shall constitute a quorum of any group designated pursuant to the first sentence hereof. The Board shall have an official seal which shall be judicially noted.

(c) The Board shall at the close of each fiscal year make a report in writing to Congress and to the President stating in detail the cases it has heard, the decisions it has rendered, and an account of all moneys it has disbursed.

(d) There shall be a General Counsel of the Board who shall be appointed by the President, by and with the advice and consent of the Senate, for a term of four years. The General Counsel of the Board shall exercise general supervision over all attorneys employed by the Board (other than trial examiners and legal assistants to Board members) and over the officers and employees in the regional offices. He shall have final authority, on behalf of the Board, in respect to the investigation of charges and issuance of complaints under section 10, and in respect of the prosecution of such complaints before the Board, and shall have such other duties as the Board may prescribe or as may be provided by law. In case of a vacancy in the office of the General Counsel the President is authorized to designate the officer or employee who shall act as General Counsel during such vacancy, but no person or persons so designated shall so act (1) for more than forty days when the Congress is in session unless a nomination to fill such vacancy shall have been submitted to the Senate, or (2) after the adjournment *sine die* of the session of the Senate in which such nomination was submitted.

Section 4.

(a) Each member of the Board and the General Counsel of the Board shall receive a salary of $12,000 a year, shall be eligible for reappointment, and shall not engage in any other business, vocation, or employment. The Board shall appoint an executive secretary, and such attorneys, examiners, and regional directors, and such other employees as it may from time to time find necessary for the proper performance of its duties. The Board may not employ any attorneys for the purpose of reviewing transcripts of hearings or preparing drafts of opinions except that any attorney employed for assignment as a legal assistant to any Board member may for such Board member review such transcripts and prepare such drafts. No trial examiner's report shall be reviewed, either before or after its publication, by any person other than a member of the Board or his legal assistant, and no trial examiner shall advise or consult with the Board with respect to exceptions taken to his findings, rulings, or recommendations. The Board may establish or utilize such regional, local, or other agencies, and utilize such voluntary and uncompensated services, as may from time to time be needed. Attorneys appointed under this section may, at the direction of the Board, appear for and represent the Board in any case in court. Nothing in this Act shall be construed to authorize the Board to appoint individuals for the purpose of conciliation or mediation, or for economic analysis.

(b) All of the expenses of the Board, including all necessary traveling and subsistence expenses outside the District of Columbia incurred by the members or employees of the Board under its orders, shall be allowed and paid on the presentation of itemized vouchers therefor approved by the Board or by any individual it designates for that purpose.

Section 5. The principal office of the Board shall be in the District of Columbia, but it may meet and exercise any or all of its powers at any other place. The Board may, by one or more of its members or by such agents or agencies as it may designate, prosecute any inquiry necessary to its functions in any part of the United States. A member who participates in such an inquiry shall not be disqualified from subsequently participating in a decision of the Board in the same case.

Section 6. The Board shall have authority from time to time to make, amend, and rescind, in the manner prescribed by the Administrative Procedure Act, such rules and regulations as may be necessary to carry out the provisions of this Act.

Rights of Employees

Section 7. Employees shall have the right to self-organization, to form, join, or assist labor organizations, to bargain collectively through representatives of their own choosing, and to engage in other concerted activities for the purpose of collective bargaining or other mutual aid or protection, and shall also have the right to refrain from any or all such activities except to the extent that such right may be affected by an agreement requiring membership in a labor organization as a condition of employment as authorized in section 8(a)(3).

Section 8.

(a) It shall be an unfair labor practice for an employer;

(1) to interfere with, restrain, or coerce employees in the exercise of the rights guaranteed in section 7;

(2) to dominate or interfere with the formation or administration of any labor organization or contribute financial or other support to it: *Provided,* That subject to rules and regulations made and published by the Board pursuant to section 6, an employer shall not be prohibited from permitting employees to confer with him during working hours without loss of time or pay.

(3) by discrimination in regard to hire or tenure of employment or any term or condition of employment to encourage or discourage membership in any labor organization: *Provided,* That nothing in this Act, or in any other statute of the United States, shall preclude an employer from making an agreement with a labor organization (not established, maintained, or assisted by any action defined in section 8(a) of this Act as an unfair labor practice) to require as a condition of employment membership therein on or after the thirtieth day following the beginning of such employment or the effective date of such agreement, whichever is the later, (i) if such labor organization is the representative of the employees as provided in section 9(a), in the appropriate collective-bargaining unit covered by such agreement when made, and (ii) unless following an election held as provided in section 9(3) within one year preceding the effective date of such agreement, the Board shall have certified that at least a majority of the employees eligible to vote in such election have voted to rescind the authority of such labor organization to make such an agreement: *Provided further,* That no employer shall justify any discrimination against any employee for nonmembership in a labor organization (A) if he has reasonable grounds for believing that such membership was not available to the employee on the same terms and conditions generally applicable to other members, or (B) if he has reasonable grounds for believing that membership was denied or terminated for reasons other than the failure of the employee to tender the periodic dues and the initiation fees uniformly required as a condition of acquiring or retaining membership;

(4) to discharge or otherwise discriminate against an employee because he has filed charges or given testimony under this Act;

(5) to refuse to bargain collectively with the representatives of his employees, subject to the provisions of section 9(a).

(b) It shall be an unfair labor practice for a labor organization or its agents—

(1) to restrain or coerce (A) employees in the exercise of the rights guaranteed in section 7: *Provided,* That this paragraph shall not impair the right of a labor organization to prescribe its own rules with respect to the acquisition or retention of membership therein; or (B) an employer in the selection of his representatives for the purpose of collective bargaining or the adjustment of grievances;

(2) to cause or attempt to cause an employer to discriminate against an employee in violation of subsection (a)(3) or to discriminate against an employee with

respect to whom membership in such organization has been denied or terminated on some ground other than his failure to tender the periodic dues and the initiation fees uniformly required as a condition of acquiring or retaining membership;

(3) to refuse to bargain collectively with an employer, provided it is the representative of his employees subject to the provisions of section 9(a);

(4) (i) to engage in, or to induce or encourage any individual employed by any person engaged in commerce or in an industry affecting commerce to engage in, a strike or a refusal in the course of his employment to use, manufacture, process, transport, or otherwise handle or work on any goods, articles, materials, or commodities or to perform any services; or (ii) to threaten, coerce, or restrain any person engaged in commerce or in an industry affecting commerce, where in either case an object thereof is:

(A) forcing or requiring any employer or self-employed person to join any labor or employer organization or to enter into any agreement which is prohibited by section 8(e);

(B) forcing or requiring any person to cease using, selling, handling, transporting, or otherwise dealing in the products of any other producer, processor, or manufacturer, or to cease doing business with any other person, or forcing or requiring any other employer to recognize or bargain with a labor organization as the representative of his employees unless such labor organization has been certified as the representative of such employees under the provisions of section 9: *Provided*, That nothing contained in this clause (B) shall be construed to make unlawful, where not otherwise unlawful, any primary strike or primary picketing;

(C) forcing or requiring any employer to recognize or bargain with a particular labor organization as the representative of his employees if another labor organization has been certified as the representative of such employees under the provisions of section 9;

(D) forcing or requiring any employer to assign particular work to employees in a particular labor organization or in a particular trade, craft, or class rather than to employees in another labor organization or in another trade, craft, or class, unless such employer is failing to conform to an order or certification of the Board determining the bargaining representative for employees performing such work: *Provided*, That nothing contained in this subsection (b) shall be construed to make unlawful a refusal by any person to enter upon the premises of any employer (other than his own employer), if the employees of such employer are engaged in a strike ratified or approved by a representative of such employees whom such employer is required to recognize under this Act: *Provided further*, That for the purposes of this paragraph (4) only, nothing contained in such paragraph shall be construed to prohibit publicity, other than picketing, for the purpose of truthfully advising the public, including consumers and members of a labor organization, that a product or products are produced by an employer with whom the labor organization has a primary dispute and are distributed by another employer, as long as such publicity does not have an effect of inducing any individual employed by any person other than the primary employer in the course of his employment to refuse to pick up, deliver, or transport any goods, or not to perform any services, at the establishment of the employer engaged in such distribution;

(5) to require of employees covered by an agreement authorized under subsection (a)(3) the payment, as a condition precedent to becoming a member of such organization, of a fee in an amount which the Board finds excessive or discriminatory under all the circumstances. In making such a finding, the Board shall consider, among other relevant factors, the practices and customs of labor organizations in the particular industry, and the wages currently paid to the employees affected;

(6) to cause or attempt to cause an employer to pay or deliver or agree to pay or deliver any money or other thing of value, in the nature of an exaction for services which are not performed or not to be performed; and

(7) to picket or cause to be picketed, or threaten to picket or cause to be picketed, any employer where an object thereof is forcing or requiring an employer to recognize or bargain with a labor organization as the representative of his employees, or forcing or requiring the employees of an employer to accept or select such labor organization as their collective bargaining representative, unless such labor organization is currently certified as the representative of such employees:

(A) where the employer has lawfully recognized in accordance with this Act any other labor organization and a question concerning representation may not appropriately be raised under section 9(c) of this Act,

(B) where within the preceding twelve months a valid election under section 9(c) of this Act has been conducted, or

(C) where such picketing has been conducted without a petition under section 9(c) being filed within a reasonable period of time not to exceed thirty days from the commencement of such picketing: *Provided,* That when such a petition has been filed the Board shall forthwith, without regard to the provisions of section 9(c)(1) or the absence of a showing of a substantial interest on the part of the labor organization, direct an election in such unit as the Board finds to be appropriate and shall certify the results thereof: *Provided further,* That nothing in this subparagraph (C) shall be construed to prohibit any picketing or other publicity for the purpose of truthfully advising the public (including consumers) that an employer does not employ members of, or have a contract with, a labor organization, unless an effect of such picketing is to induce any individual employed by any other person in the course of his employment, not to pick up, deliver or transport any goods or not to perform any services.

(C) Nothing in this paragraph (7) shall be construed to permit any act which would otherwise be an unfair labor practice under this section 8(b).

(c) The expressing of any views, argument, or opinion, or the dissemination thereof, whether in written, printed, graphic, or visual form, shall not constitute or be evidence of an unfair labor practice under any of the provisions of this Act, if such expression contains no threat of reprisal or force or promise of benefit.

(d) For the purposes of this section, to bargain collectively is the performance of the mutual obligation of the employer and the representative of the employees to meet at reasonable times and confer in good faith with respect to wages, hours, and other terms and conditions of employment, or the negotiation of an agreement or any question arising thereunder, and the execution of a written contract incorporating any agreement reached if requested by either party, but such obligation does not compel either party to agree to a proposal or require the making of a concession: *Provided,* That where there is in effect a collective-bargaining contract covering employees in an industry affecting commerce, the duty to bargain collectively shall also mean that no party to such contract shall terminate or modify such contract, unless the party desiring such termination or modification—

(1) serves a written notice upon the party to the contract of the proposed termination or modification sixty days prior to the expiration date thereof, or in the event such contract contains no expiration date, sixty days prior to the time it is proposed to make such termination or modification;

(2) offers to meet and confer with the other party for the purpose of negotiating a new contract or a contract containing the proposed modifications;

(3) notifies the Federal Mediation and Conciliation Service within thirty days after such notice of the existence of a dispute, and simultaneously therewith notifies any State or Territorial agency established to mediate and conciliate disputes within the State or Territory where the dispute occurred, provided no agreement has been reached by that time; and

(4) continues in full force and effect, without resorting to strike or lockout, all the terms and conditions of the existing contract for a period of sixty days after such notice is given or until the expiration date of such contract, whichever occurs later.

The duties imposed upon employers, employees, and labor organizations by paragraphs (2), (3), and (4) shall become inapplicable upon an intervening certification of the Board, under which the labor organization or individual, which is a party to the contract, has been superseded as or ceased to be the representative of the employees subject to the provisions of section 9(a), and the duties so imposed shall not be construed as requiring either party to discuss or agree to any modification of the terms and conditions contained in a contract for a fixed period, if such modification is to become effective before such terms and conditions can be reopened under the provisions of the contract. Any employee who engages in a strike within any notice period specified in this subsection, or who engages in any strike with the appropriate period specified in subsection (g) of this section, shall lose his status as an employee of the employer engaged in the particular labor dispute, for the purposes of sections 8, 9, and 10 of this Act, as amended, but such loss of status for such employee shall terminate if and when he is reemployed by such employer. Whenever the collective bargaining involves employees of a health care institution, the provisions of this section 8(d) shall be modified as follows:

(A) The notice of section 8(d)(1) shall be ninety days; the notice of section 8(d)(3) shall be sixty days; and the contract period of section 8(d)(4) shall be ninety days.

(B) Where the bargaining is for an initial agreement following certification or recognition, at least thirty days' notice of the existence of a dispute shall be given by the labor organization to the agencies set forth in section 8(d)(3).

(C) After notice is given to the Federal Mediation and Conciliation Service under either clause (A) or (B) of this sentence, the Service shall promptly communicate with the parties and use its best efforts, by mediation and conciliation, to bring them to agreement. The parties shall participate fully and promptly in such meetings as may be undertaken by the Service for the purpose of aiding in a settlement of the dispute.

(e) it shall be an unfair labor practice for any labor organization and any employer to enter into any contract or agreement, express or implied, whereby such employer ceases or refrains or agrees to cease or refrain from handling, using, selling, transporting or otherwise dealing in any of the products of any other employer, or to cease doing business with any other person, and any contract or agreement entered into heretofore or hereafter containing such an agreement shall be to such extent unenforceable and void: *Provided,* That nothing in this subsection (e) shall apply to an agreement between a labor organization and an employer in the construction industry relating to the contracting or subcontracting of work to be done at the site of the construction, alteration, painting, or repair of a building, structure, or other work: *Provided further,* That for the purposes of this subsection (e) and section 8(b)(4)(B) the terms "any employer," "any person engaged in commerce or in industry affecting commerce," and "any person" when used in relation to the terms "any other producer, processor, or manufacturer," "any other employer," or "any other person" shall not include persons in the relation of a jobber, manufacturer, contractor, or subcontractor working on the goods or premises of the jobber or manufacturer or performing parts of an integrated process of production in the apparel and clothing industry: *Provided further,* That nothing in this Act shall prohibit the enforcement of any agreement which is within the foregoing exception.

(f) It shall not be an unfair labor practice under subsections (a) and (b) of this section for an employer engaged primarily in the building and construction industry to make an agreement covering employees engaged (or who, upon their employment, will be engaged) in the building and construction industry with a labor organization of which building and construction employees are members (not established, maintained, or assisted by any action defined in section 8(a) of this Act as an unfair labor practice) because (1) the majority status of such labor organization has not been established under the provisions of section 9 of this Act prior to the making of such agreement, or (2) such agreement requires as a condition of employment, membership in such labor organization after the seventh day following the beginning of such employment or the effective date of the agreement, whichever is later, or (3) such agreement requires the employer to notify such labor organization of opportunities for employment with such employer, or gives such labor organization an opportunity to refer qualified applicants for such employment, or (4) such agreement specifies minimum training or experience qualifications for employment or provides for priority in opportunities for employment based upon length of service with such employer, in the industry or in the particular geographical area: *Provided,* That nothing in this subsection shall set aside the final proviso to section 8 (a)(3) of this Act: *Provided further,* That any agreement which would be invalid, but for clause (1) of this subsection, shall not be a bar to a petition filed pursuant to section 9(c) or 9(e).

(g) A labor organization before engaging in any strike, picketing, or other concerted refusal to work at any health care institution shall, not less than ten days prior to such action, notify the institution in writing and the Federal Mediation and Conciliation Service of that intention, except that in the case of bargaining for an initial agreement following certification or recognition the notice required by this subsection shall not be given the expiration of the period specified in clause (B) of the last sentence of section 8(d) of this Act. The notice shall state the date and time that such action will commence. The notice, once given, may be extended by the written agreement of both parties.

Representatives and Elections

Section 9.

(a) Representatives designated or selected for the purposes of collective bargaining by the majority of the employees in a unit appropriate for such purposes, shall be the exclusive representatives of all the employees in such unit for the purposes of collective bargaining in respect to rates of pay, wages, hours or employment, or other conditions of employment: *Provided,* That any individual employee or a group of employees shall have the right at any time to present grievances to their employer and to have such grievances adjusted, without the intervention of the bargaining representative, as long as the adjustment is not inconsistent with the terms of a collective-bargaining contract or agreement then in effect: *Provided further,* That the bargaining representative has been given opportunity to be present at such adjustment.

(b) The Board shall decide in each case whether, in order to assure to employees the fullest freedom in exercising the rights guaranteed by this Act, the unit appropriate for the purposes of collective bargaining shall be the employer unit, craft unit, plant unit, or subdivision thereof: Provided, That the Board shall not (1) decide that any unit is appropriate for such purposes if such unit includes both professional employees and employees who are not professional employees unless a majority of such professional employees vote for inclusion in such unit; or (2) decide that any craft unit is inappropriate for such purposes on the ground that a different unit has been established by a prior Board determination, unless a majority of the employees in the proposed craft unit votes against separate representation; or (3) decide that any unit is appropriate for such purposes if it includes, together with other employees, any individual employed as a guard to enforce against employees and other persons rules to protect property of the employer or to protect the safety of persons on the employer's premises; but no labor organization shall be certified as the representative of employees in a bargaining unit of guards if such organization admits to membership, or is affiliated directly or indirectly with an organization which admits to membership, employees other than guards.

(c) (1) Wherever a petition shall have been filed, in accordance with such regulations as may be prescribed by the Board—

(A) by an employee or group of employees or any individual or labor organization acting in their behalf alleging that a substantial number of employees (i) wish to be represented for collective bargaining and that their employer declines to recognize their representative as the representative defined in section 9(a), or (ii) assert that the individual or labor organization, which has been certified or is being recognized by their employer as the bargaining representative, is no longer a representative as defined in section 9(a); or

(B) by an employer, alleging that one or more individuals or labor organizations have presented to him a claim to be recognized as the representative defined in section 9(a): the Board shall investigate such petition and if it has reasonable cause to believe that a question of representation affecting commerce exists shall provide for an appropriate hearing upon due notice. Such hearing may be conducted by an officer or employee of the regional office, who shall not make any recommendations with respect thereto. If the Board finds upon the record of such hearing that such a question of representation exists, it shall direct an election by secret ballot and shall certify the results thereof.

(2) In determining whether or not a question of representation affecting commerce exists, the same regulations and rules of decision shall apply irrespective of the identity of the person filing the petition or the kind of relief sought and in no case shall the Board deny a labor organization a place on the ballot by reason of an order with respect to such labor organization or its predecessor not issued in conformity with section 10(c).

(3) No election shall be directed in any bargaining unit or any subdivision within which, in the preceding twelve-month period, a valid election shall have been held. Employees engaged in an economic strike who are not entitled to reinstatement shall be eligible to vote under such regulations as the Board shall find are consistent with the purposes and provisions of this Act in any election conducted within twelve months after the commencement of the strike. In any election where none of the choices on the ballot receives a majority, a run-off shall be conducted, the ballot providing for a selection between the two choices receiving the largest and second largest number of valid votes cast in the election.

(4) Nothing in this section shall be construed to prohibit the waiving of hearings by stipulation for the purpose of a consent election in conformity with regulations and rules of decision of the Board.

(5) In determining whether a unit is appropriate for the purposes specified in subsection (b) the extent to which the employees have organized shall not be controlling.

(d) Whenever an order of the Board made pursuant to section 10(c) is based in whole or in part upon facts certified following an investigation pursuant to subsection (c) of this section and there is a petition for the enforcement or review of such order, such certification and the record of such investigation shall be included in the transcript of the entire record required to be filed under section 10(e) or 10(f), and thereupon the decree of the court enforcing, modifying, or setting aside in whole or in part the order of the Board shall be made and entered upon the pleadings, testimony, and proceedings set forth in such transcript.

(e) (1) Upon the filing with the Board, by 30 per centum or more of the employees in a bargaining unit covered by an agreement between their employer and a labor organization made pursuant to section 8(a)(3), of a petition alleging they desire that such authority be rescinded, the Board shall take a secret ballot of the employees in such unit and certify the results thereof to such labor organization and to the employer.

(2) No election shall be conducted pursuant to this subsection in any bargaining unit or any subdivision within which, in the preceding twelve-month period, a valid election shall have been held.

Prevention of Unfair Labor Practices

Section 10.

(a) The Board is empowered, as hereinafter provided, to prevent any person from engaging in any unfair labor practice (listed in section 8) affecting commerce. This power shall not be affected by any other means of adjustment or prevention that has been or may be established by agreement, law, or otherwise: *Provided,* That the Board is empowered by agreement with any agency of any State or Territory to cede to such agency jurisdiction over any cases in any industry (other than mining, manufacturing, communications, and transportation except where predominantly local in character) even though such cases may involve labor disputes affecting commerce, unless the provision of the State or Territorial statute applicable to the determination of such cases by such agency is inconsistent with the corresponding provision of this Act or has received a construction inconsistent therewith.

(b) Whenever it is charged that any person has engaged in or is engaging in any such unfair labor practice, the Board, or any agent or agency designated by the Board for such purposes, shall have power to issue and cause to be served upon such person a complaint stating the charges in that respect, and containing a notice of hearing before the Board or a member thereof, or before a designated agent or agency, at a place therein fixed, not less than five days after the serving of said complaint: *Provided,* That no complaint shall issue based upon any unfair labor practice occurring more than six months prior to the filing of the charge with the Board and the service of a copy thereof upon the person against whom such charge is made, unless the person aggrieved thereby was prevented from filing such charge by reason of service in the armed forces, in which event the six-month period shall be computed from the day of his discharge. Any such complaint may be amended by the member, agent, or agency conducting the hearing or the Board in its discretion at any time prior to the issuance of an order based thereon. The person so complained of shall have the right to file an answer to the original or amended complaint and to appear in person or otherwise and give testimony at the place and time fixed in the complaint. In the discretion of the member, agent, or agency conducting the hearing or the Board, any other person may be allowed to intervene in the said proceeding and to present testimony. Any such proceeding shall, so far as practicable, be conducted in accordance with the rules of evidence applicable in the district courts of the United States under the rules of civil procedure for the district courts of the United States, adopted by the Supreme Court of the United States pursuant to the Act of June 19, 1934 (U.S.C., title 28, secs. 723-B, 723-C).

(c) The testimony taken by such member, agent, or agency or the Board shall be reduced to writing and filed with the Board. Thereafter, in its discretion, the Board upon notice may take further testimony or hear argument. If upon the preponderance of the testimony taken the Board shall be of the opinion that any person named in the complaint has engaged in or is engaging in any such unfair labor practice, then the Board shall state its findings of fact and shall issue and cause to be served on such person an order requiring such person to cease and desist from such unfair labor practice, and to take such affirmative action including reinstatement of employees with or without back pay, as will effectuate the policies of this Act: *Provided,* That where an order directs reinstatement of an employee, back pay may be required of the employer or labor organization, as the case may be, responsible for the discrimination suffered by him: And *provided further,* That in determining whether a complaint shall issue alleging a violation of section 8(a) (1) or section 8(a)(2), and in deciding such cases, the same regulations and rules of decision shall apply irrespective of whether or not the labor organization affected is affiliated with a labor organization national or international in scope. Such order may further require such person to make reports from time to time showing the extent to which it has complied with the order. If upon the preponderance of the testimony taken the Board shall not be of the opinion that the person named in the complaint has engaged in or is engaging in any such unfair labor practice, then the Board shall state its findings of fact and shall issue an order dismissing the said complaint. No order of the Board shall require the reinstatement of any individual as an employee who has been suspended or discharged, or the payment to him of any back pay, if such individual was suspended or discharged for cause. In case the evidence is presented before a member of the Board, or before an examiner or examiners thereof, such member, or such examiner or examiners, as the case may be, shall issue and cause to be served on the parties to the proceeding a proposed report, together with a recommended order, which shall be filed with the Board, and if no exceptions are filed within twenty days after service thereof upon such parties, or within such further period as the Board may authorize, such recommended order shall become the order of the Board and become effective as therein prescribed.

(d) Until the record in the case shall have been filed in a court, as hereinafter provided, the Board may at any time, upon reasonable notice and in such manner as it shall deem proper, modify or set aside, in whole or in part, any finding or order made or issued by it.

(e) The Board shall have power to petition any court of appeals of the United States, or if all the courts of appeals to which application may be made are in vacation, any district court of the United States, within any circuit or district, respectively, wherein the unfair labor practice in question occurred or wherein such person resides or transacts business, for the enforcement of such order and for appropriate temporary relief or restraining order, and shall file in the court the record in the proceedings, as provided in section 2112 of title 28, United States Code. Upon the filing of such petition, the court shall cause notice thereof to be served upon such person, and thereupon shall have jurisdiction of the proceeding and of the question determined therein, and shall have power to grant such temporary relief or restraining order as it deems just and proper, and to make and enter a decree enforcing, modifying, and enforcing as so modified, or setting aside in whole or in part the order of the Board. No objection that has not been urged before the Board, its member, agent, or agency, shall be considered by the court, unless the failure or neglect to urge such objection shall be excused because of extraordinary circumstances. The findings of the Board with respect to questions of fact if supported by substantial evidence on the record considered as a whole shall be conclusive. If either party shall apply to the court for leave to adduce additional evidence and shall show to the satisfaction of the court that such additional evidence is material and that there were reasonable grounds for the failure to adduce such evidence in the hearing before the Board, its member, agent, or agency, the court may order such additional evidence to be taken before the Board, its member, agent, or agency, and to be made a part of the record. The Board may modify its findings as to the facts, or make new findings, by reason of additional evidence so taken and filed, and it shall file such modified or new findings, which findings with respect to question of fact if supported by substantial evidence on the record considered as a whole shall be conclusive, and shall file its recommendations, if any, for the modification or setting aside of its original order. Upon the filing of the record with it the jurisdiction of the court shall be exclusive and its judgment and decree shall be final, except that the court shall be subject to review by the appropriate United States court of appeals if application was made to the district court as hereinabove provided, and by the Supreme Court of the United States upon writ of certiorari or certification as provided in section 1254 of title 28.

(f) Any person aggrieved by a final order of the Board granting or denying in whole or in part the relief sought may obtain a review of such order in any circuit court of appeals of the United States in the circuit wherein the unfair labor practice in question was alleged to have been engaged in or wherein such person resides or transacts business, or in the United States Court of Appeals for the District of Columbia, by filing in such court a written petition praying that the order of the Board be modified or set aside. A copy of such petition shall be forthwith transmitted by the clerk of the court to the Board, and thereupon the aggrieved party shall file in the court the record in the proceeding, certified by the Board, as provided in section 2112 of title 28, United States Code. Upon the filing of such petition, the court shall proceed in the same manner as in the case of an application by the Board under subsection (e) of this section, and shall have the same jurisdiction to grant to the Board such temporary relief or restraining order as it deems just and proper, and in like manner to make and enter a decree enforcing, modifying, and enforcing as so modified, or setting aside in whole or in part the order of the Board; the findings of the Board with respect to questions of fact if supported by substantial evidence on the record considered as a whole shall in like manner be conclusive.

(g) The commencement of proceedings under subsection (e) or (f) of this section shall not, unless specifically ordered by the court, operate as a stay of the Board's order.

(h) When granting appropriate temporary relief or a restraining order, or making and entering a decree enforcing, modifying, and enforcing as so modified, or setting aside in whole or in part an order of the Board, as provided in this section, the jurisdiction of courts sitting in equity shall not be limited by the Act entitled "An Act to amend the Judicial Code and to define and limit the jurisdiction of courts sitting in equity, and for other purposes," approved March 23, 1932 (U.S.C., Supp. VII, title 29, secs. 101–115).

(i) Petitions filed under this Act shall be heard expeditiously, and if possible within ten days after they have been docketed.

(j) The Board shall have power, upon issuance of a complaint as provided in subsection (b) charging that any person has engaged in or is engaging in an unfair labor practice, to petition any district court of the United States (including the District Court of the United States for the District of Columbia), within any district wherein the unfair labor practice in question is alleged to have occurred or wherein such person resides or transacts business, for appropriate temporary relief or restraining order. Upon the filing of any such petition the court shall cause notice thereof to be served upon such person, and thereupon shall have jurisdiction to grant to the Board such temporary relief or restraining order as it deems just and proper.

(k) Whenever it is charged that any person has engaged in an unfair labor practice within the meaning of paragraph (4)(D) of section 8(b), the Board is empowered and directed to hear and determine the dispute out of which such unfair labor practice shall have arisen, unless, within ten days after notice that such charge has been filed, the parties to such dispute submit to the Board satisfactory evidence that they have adjusted, or agreed upon methods for the voluntary adjustment of, the dispute. Upon compliance by the parties to the dispute with the decision of the Board or upon such voluntary adjustment of the dispute, such charge shall be dismissed.

(l) Whenever it is charged that any person has engaged in an unfair labor practice within the meaning of paragraph (4) (A), (B), or (C) of section 8(b), or section 8(e) of section 8(b)(7), the preliminary investigation of such charge shall be made forthwith and given priority over all other cases except cases of like character in the office where it is filed or is referred. If, after such investigation, the officer or regional attorney to whom the matter may be referred has reasonable cause to believe such charge is true and that a complaint should issue, he shall, on behalf of the Board, petition any district court of the United States (including the District Court of the United States for the District of Columbia) within any district where the unfair labor practice in question has occurred, is alleged to have occurred, or wherein such person resides or transacts business, for appropriate injunctive relief pending the final adjudication of the Board with respect to such matter. Upon the filing of any such petition the district court shall have jurisdiction to grant such injunctive relief or temporary restraining order as it deems just and proper, not withstanding any other provision of law: *Provided further,* That no temporary restraining order shall be issued without notice unless a petition alleges that substantial and irreparable injury to the charging party will be unavoidable and such temporary restraining order shall be effective no longer than five days and will become void at the expiration of such period: *Provided further,* That such officer or regional attorney shall not apply for any restraining order under section 8(b)(7) if a charge against the employer under section 8(a)(2) has been filed and after the preliminary investigation, he has reasonable cause to believe that such charge is true and that a complaint should issue. Upon filing of any such petition the courts shall cause notice thereof to be served upon any person involved in the charge and such person, including the charging party, shall be given an opportunity to appear by counsel and present any relevant testimony: *Provided further,* That for the purposes of this subsection district courts shall be deemed to have jurisdiction of a labor organization (1) in the district in which such organization maintains its principal office, or (2) in any district in which its duly authorized officers or agents are engaged in promoting or protecting the interests of employee members. The service of legal process upon such officer or agent shall constitute service upon the labor organization and make such organization a party to the suit. In situations where such relief is appropriate the procedure specified herein shall apply to charges with respect to section 8(b)(4)(D).

(m) Whenever it is charged that any person has engaged in an unfair labor practice within the meaning of subsection (a)(3) or (b)(2) of section 8, such charge shall be given priority over all other cases except cases of like character in the office where it is filed or to which it is referred and cases given priority under subsection (l).

Investigatory Powers

Section 11. For the purpose of all hearings and investigations, which, in the opinion of the Board, are necessary and proper for the exercise of the powers vested in it by section 9 and section 10—

(a) (1) The Board, or its duly authorized agents or agencies, shall at all reasonable times have access to, for the purpose of examination, and the right to copy any evidence of any person being investigated or proceeded against that relates to any matter under investigation or in question. The Board, or any member thereof, shall upon application of any party to such proceedings, forthwith issue to such party subpoenas requiring the attendance and testimony of witnesses or the production of any evidence in such proceeding or investigation requested in such application. Within five days after the service of a subpoena on any person requiring the production of any evidence in his possession or under his control, such person may petition the Board to revoke, and the Board shall revoke, such subpoena if in its opinion the evidence whose production is required does not relate to any matter under investigation, or any matter in question in such proceedings, or if in its opinion such subpoena does not describe with sufficient particularity the evidence whose production is required. Any member of the Board, or any agent or agency designated by the Board for such purposes, may administer oaths and affirmations, examine witnesses, and receive evidence. Such attendance of witnesses and the production of such evidence may be required from any place in the United States or any Territory or possession thereof, at any designated place of hearing.

(2) In case of contumacy or refusal to obey a subpoena issued to any person, any district court of the United States or the United States courts of any Territory or possession, or the District Court of the United States for the District of Columbia, within the jurisdiction of which the inquiry is carried on or within the jurisdiction of which said person guilty of contumacy or refusal to obey is found or resides or transacts business, upon application by the Board shall have jurisdiction to issue to such person an order requiring such person to appear before the Board, its member, agent, or agency, there to produce evidence if so ordered, or there to give testimony touching the matter under investigation or in question; and any failure to obey such order of the court may be punished by said court as a contempt thereof.

(3) Repealed.

(4) Complaints, orders and other process and papers of the Board, its member, agent, or agency, may be served either personally or by registered or certified mail or by telegraph or by leaving a copy thereof at the principal office or place of business of the person required to be served. The verified return by the individual so serving the same setting forth the manner of such service shall be proof of the same, and the return post office receipt or telegraph receipt therefor when registered or certified and mailed or telegraphed as aforesaid shall be proof of service of the same. Witnesses summoned before the Board, its member, agent, or agency, shall be paid the same fees and mileage that are paid witnesses in the courts of the United States, and witnesses whose depositions are taken and the persons taking the same shall severally be entitled to the same fees as are paid for like services in the courts of the United States.

(5) All process of any court to which application may be made under this Act may be served in the judicial district where the defendant or other person required to be served resides or may be found.

(6) The several departments and agencies of the Government, when directed by the President, shall furnish the Board, upon its request, all records, papers, and information in their possession relating to any matter before the Board.

Section 12. Any person who shall willfully resist, prevent, impede, or interfere with any member of the Board or any of its agents or agencies in the performance of duties pursuant to this Act shall be punished by a fine of not more than $5,000 or by imprisonment for not more than one year, or both.

Limitations

Section 13. Nothing in this Act, except as specifically provided for herein, shall be construed so as either to interfere with or impede or diminish in any way the right to strike, or to affect the limitations or qualifications on that right.

Section 14.

(a) Nothing herein shall prohibit any individual employed as a supervisor from becoming or remaining a member of a labor organization, but no employer subject to this Act shall be compelled to deem individuals defined herein as supervisors as employees for the purpose of any law, either national or local, relating to collective bargaining.

(b) Nothing in this Act shall be construed as authorizing the execution or application of agreements requiring membership in a labor organization as a condition of employment in any State or Territory in which such execution or application is prohibited by State or Territorial law.

(c) (1) The Board, in its discretion, may, by rule of decision or by published rules adopted pursuant to the Administrative Procedure Act, decline to assert jurisdiction over any labor dispute involving any class or category of employers, where, in the opinion of the Board, the effect of such labor dispute on commerce is not sufficiently substantial to warrant the exercise of its jurisdiction: *Provided,* That the Board shall not decline to assert jurisdiction over any labor dispute over which it would assert jurisdiction under the standards prevailing upon August 1, 1959.

(2) Nothing in this Act shall be deemed to prevent or bar any agency or the courts of any State or Territory (including the Commonwealth of Puerto Rico, Guam, and the Virgin Islands), from assuming and asserting jurisdiction over labor disputes over which the Board declines, pursuant to paragraph (1) of this subsection, to assert jurisdiction.

Section 15. Wherever the application of the provisions of section 272 of chapter 10 of the Act entitled "An Act to establish a uniform system of bankruptcy throughout the United States," approved July 1, 1898, and Acts amendatory thereof and supplementary thereto (U.S.C., title 11, sec. 672), conflicts with the application of the provisions of this Act, this Act shall prevail: Provided, That in any situation where the provisions of this Act cannot be validly enforced, the provisions of such other Acts shall remain in full force and effect.

Section 16. If any provision of this Act, or the application of such provision to any person or circumstances, shall be held invalid, the remainder of this Act, or the application of such provision to persons or circumstances other than those as to which it is held invalid, shall not be affected thereby.

Section 17. This Act may be cited as the "National Labor Relations Act."

Section 18. No petition entertained, no investigation made, no election held, and no certification issued by the National Labor Relations Board, under any of the provisions of section 9 of the National Labor Relations Act, as amended, shall be invalid by reason of the failure of the Congress of Industrial Organizations to have complied with the requirements of section 9(f), (g), or (h) of the aforesaid Act prior to December 22, 1949, or by reason of the failure of the American Federation of Labor to have complied with the provisions of section 9(f), (g), or (h) of the aforesaid Act prior to November 7, 1947: *Provided,* That no liability shall be imposed under any provision of this Act upon any person for failure to honor any election or certificate referred to above, prior to the effective date of this amendment: *Provided, however,* That this proviso shall not have the effect of setting aside or in any way affecting judgments or decrees heretofore entered under section 10(e) or (f) and which have become final.

Individuals with Religious Convictions

Section 19. Any employee who is a member of and adheres to established and traditional tenets or teachings of a bona fide religion, body, or sect which has historically held conscientious objections to joining or financially supporting labor organizations shall not be required to join or financially support any labor organization as a condition of employment; except that such employee may be required in a contract between such employees' employer and a labor organization in lieu of periodic dues and initiation fees, to pay sums equal to such dues and initiation fees to a nonreligious nonlabor organization charitable fund exempt from taxation under section 501(c)(3) of title 26 of the Internal Revenue Code, chosen by such employee from a list of at least three such funds, designated in such contract or if the contract fails to designate such funds, then to any such fund chosen by the employee. If such employee who holds conscientious objections pursuant to this section requests the labor organization to use the grievance-arbitration procedure on the employee's behalf, the labor organization is authorized to charge the employee for the reasonable cost of using such procedure.

Text of the Labor Management Relations Act

61 Stat. 136–52 (1947), as amended by 73 Stat. 519ff (1959), 83 Stat. 133 (1969), 87 Stat. 314 (1973), 88 Stat. 396–97 (1974); 29 U.S.C. Sections 141–97

AN ACT

To amend the National Labor Relations Act, to provide additional facilities for the mediation of labor disputes affecting commerce, to equalize legal responsibilities of labor organizations and employers, and for other purposes.

Be it enacted by the Senate and House of Representatives of the United States of America in Congress assembled.

Short Title and Declaration of Policy

Section 1.

(a) This Act may be cited as the "Labor Management Relations Act, 1947,"

(b) Industrial strife which interferes with the normal flow of commerce and with the full production of articles and commodities for commerce, can be avoided or substantially minimized if employers, employees, and labor organizations each recognize under law one another's legitimate rights in their relations with each other, and above all recognize under law that neither party has any right in its relations with any other to engage in acts or practices which jeopardize the public health, safety, or interest.

It is the purpose and policy of this Act, in order to promote the full flow of commerce, to prescribe the legitimate rights of both employees and employers in their relations affecting commerce, to provide orderly and peaceful procedures for preventing the interference by either with the legitimate rights of the other, to protect the rights of individual employees in their relations with labor organizations whose activities affect commerce, to define and proscribe practices on the part of labor and management which affect commerce and are inimical to the general welfare, and to protect the rights of the public in connection with labor disputes affecting commerce.

TITLE I

Amendments of National Labor Relations Act

Section 101. The National Labor Relations Act is hereby amended to read as follows:

(The text of the National Labor Relations Act as amended appears on Appendix A, supra.)

Effective Date of Certain Changes

Section 102. [Omitted.]

Section 103. [Omitted.]

Section 104. [Omitted.]

TITLE II

Conciliation of Labor Disputes in Industries Affecting Commerce; National Emergencies

Section 201. That it is the policy of the United States that—

(a) sound and stable industrial peace and the advancement of the general welfare, health, and safety of the Nation and of the best interest of employers and employees can most satisfactorily be secured by the settlement of issues between employers and employees through the processes of conference and collective bargaining between employers and the representatives of their employees;

(b) the settlement of issues between employers and employees through collective bargaining may be advanced by making available full and adequate governmental facilities for conciliation, mediation, and voluntary arbitration to aid and encourage employers and the representatives of their employees to reach and maintain agreements concerning rates of pay, hours, and working conditions, and to make all reasonable efforts to settle their differences by mutual agreement reached through conferences and collective bargaining or by such methods as may be provided for in any applicable agreement for the settlement of disputes; and

(c) certain controversies which arise between parties to collective-bargaining agreements may be avoided or minimized by making available full and adequate governmental facilities for furnishing assistance to employers and the representatives of their employees in formulating for inclusion within such agreements provision for adequate notice of any proposed changes in the terms of such agreements, for the final adjustment of grievances or questions regarding the application or interpretation of such agreements, and other provisions designed to prevent the subsequent arising of such controversies.

Section 202.

(a) There is hereby created an independent agency to be known as the Federal Mediation and Conciliation Service (herein referred to as the "Service," except that for sixty days after the date of the enactment of this Act such term shall refer to the Conciliation Service of the Department of Labor). The Service shall be under the direction of a Federal Mediation and Conciliation Director (hereinafter referred to as the "Director"), who shall be appointed by the President by and with the advice and consent of the Senate. The Director shall receive compensation at the rate of $12,000 per annum. The Director shall not engage in any other business, vocation, or employment.

(b) The Director is authorized, subject to the civil-service laws, to appoint such clerical and other personnel as may be necessary for the execution of the functions of the Service, and shall fix their compensations in accordance with the Classification Act of 1923, as amended, and may, without regard to the provisions of the civil-service laws and the Classification Act of 1923, as amended, appoint and fix the compensation of such conciliators and mediators as may be necessary to carry out the functions of the Service. The Director is authorized to make such expenditures for supplies, facilities, and services as he deems necessary. Such expenditures shall be allowed and paid upon presentation of itemized vouchers therefor approved by the Director or by any employee designated by him for that purpose.

(c) The principal office of the Service shall be in the District of Columbia, but the Director may establish regional offices convenient to localities in which labor controversies are likely to arise. The Director may by order, subject to revocation at any time, delegate any authority and discretion conferred upon him by this Act to any regional director, or other officer or employee of the Service. The Director may establish suitable procedures for cooperation with State and local mediation agencies. The Director shall make an annual report in writing to Congress at the end of the fiscal year.

(d) All mediation and conciliation functions of the Secretary of Labor or the United States Conciliation Service under section 8 of the Act entitled "An Act to create a Department of Labor," approved March 4, 1913 (U.S. C., title 29, sec. 51), and all functions of the United States Conciliation Service under any other law are hereby transferred to the Federal Mediation and Conciliation Service, together with the personnel and records of the United States Conciliation Service. Such transfer shall take effect upon the sixtieth day after the date of enactment of this Act. Such transfer shall not affect any proceedings pending before the United States Conciliation Service or any certification, order, rule, or regulation theretofore made by it or by the Secretary of Labor. The Director and the Service shall not be subject in any way to the jurisdiction or authority of the Secretary of Labor or any official or division of the Department of Labor.

Functions of the Service

Section 203.

(a) It shall be the duty of the Service, in order to prevent or minimize interruptions of the free flow of commerce growing out of labor disputes, to assist parties to labor disputes in industries affecting commerce to settle such disputes, through conciliation and mediation.

(b) The Service may proffer its services in any labor dispute in any industry affecting commerce, either upon its own motion or upon the request of one or more of the parties to the dispute, whenever in its judgment such dispute threatens to cause a substantial interruption of commerce. The Director and the Service are directed to avoid attempting to mediate disputes which would have only a minor effect on interstate commerce if State or other conciliation services are available to the parties. Whenever the Service does proffer its services in any dispute, it shall be the duty of the Service promptly to put itself in communication with the parties and to use its best efforts, by mediation and conciliation, to bring them to agreement.

(c) If the Director is not able to bring the parties to agreement by conciliation within a reasonable time, he shall seek to induce the parties voluntarily to seek other means of settling the dispute without resort to strike, lockout, or other coercion, including submission to the employees in the bargaining unit of the employer's last offer of settlement for approval or rejection in a secret ballot. The failure or refusal of either party to agree to any procedure suggested by the Director shall not be deemed a violation of any duty or obligation imposed by this Act.

(d) Final adjustment by a method agreed upon by the parties is hereby declared to be the desirable method for settlement of grievance disputes arising over the application or interpretation of an existing collective-bargaining agreement. The Service is directed to make its conciliation and mediation services available in the settlement of such grievance disputes only as a last resort and in exceptional cases.

(e) The Service is authorized and directed to encourage and support the establishment and operation of joint labor management activities conducted by plant, area, and industrywide committees designed to improve labor management relationships, job security and organizational effectiveness, in accordance with the provisions of section 205A.

Section 204.

(a) In order to prevent or minimize interruptions of the free flow of commerce growing out of labor disputes, employers and employees and their representatives, in any industry affecting commerce, shall—

  (1) exert every reasonable effort to make and maintain agreements concerning rates of pay, hours, and working conditions, including provision for adequate notice of any proposed change in the terms of such agreements;

  (2) whenever a dispute arises over the terms or application of a collective-bargaining agreement and a conference is requested by a party or prospective party thereto, arrange promptly for such a conference to be held and endeavor in such conference to settle such dispute expeditiously; and

  (3) in case such dispute is not settled by conference, participate fully and promptly in such meetings as may be undertaken by the Service under this Act for the purpose of aiding a settlement of the dispute.

Section 205.

(a) There is hereby created a National Labor-Management Panel which shall be composed of twelve members appointed by the President, six of whom shall be selected from among persons outstanding in the field of management and six of whom shall be selected from among persons outstanding in the field of labor. Each member shall hold office for a term of three years, except that any member appointed to fill a vacancy occurring prior to the expiration of the term for which his predecessor was appointed shall be appointed for the remainder of such term, and the terms of office of the members first taking office shall expire, as designated by the President at the time of appointment, four at the end of the first year, four at the end of the second year, and four at the end of the third year after the date of appointment. Members of the panel, when serving on business of the panel, shall be paid compensation at the rate of $25 per day, and shall also be entitled to receive an allowance for actual and necessary travel and subsistence expenses while so serving away from their places of residence.

(b) It shall be the duty of the panel, at the request of the Director, to advise in the avoidance of industrial controversies and the manner in which mediation and voluntary adjustment shall be administered, particularly with reference to controversies affecting the general welfare of the country.

Section 205A.

(a) (1) The Service is authorized and directed to provide assistance in the establishment and operation of plant, area and industrywide labor management committees which—

  (A) have been organized jointly by employers and labor organizations representing employees in that plant, area, or industry; and

  (B) are established for the purpose of improving labor management relationships, job security, organizational effectiveness, enhancing economic development or involving workers in decisions affecting their jobs including improving communication with respect to subjects of mutual interest and concern.

(2) The Service is authorized and directed to enter into contracts and to make grants, where necessary or appropriate, to fulfill its responsibilities under this section.

(b) (1) No grant may be made, no contract may be entered into and no other assistance may be provided under the provisions of this section to a plant labor management committee unless the employees in that plant are represented by a labor organization and there is in effect at that plant a collective bargaining agreement.

(2) No grant may be made, no contract may be entered into and no other assistance may be provided under the provisions of this section to an area or industrywide labor management committee unless its participants include any labor organizations certified or recognized as the representative of the employees of an employer participating in such committee. Nothing in this clause shall prohibit participation in an area or industrywide committee by an employer whose employees are not represented by a labor organization.

(3) No grant may be made under the provisions of this section to any labor management committee which the Service finds to have as one of its purposes the discouragement of the exercise of rights contained in section 7 of the National Labor Relations Act (29 U.S.C. 157), or the interference with collective bargaining in any plant, or industry.

(c) The Service shall carry out the provisions of this section through an office established for that purpose.

(d) There are authorized to be appropriated to carry out the provisions of this section $10,000,000 for the fiscal year 1979, and such sums as may be necessary thereafter.

(e) Nothing in this section or the amendments made by this section shall affect the terms and conditions of any collective bargaining agreement whether in effect prior to or entered into after the date of enactment of this section.

National Emergencies

Section 206. Whenever in the opinion of the President of the United States, a threatened or actual strike or lock-out affecting an entire industry or a substantial part thereof engaged in trade, commerce, transportation, transmission, or communication among the several States or with foreign nations, or engaged in the production of goods for commerce, will, if permitted to occur or to continue, imperil the national health or safety, he may appoint a board of inquiry to inquire into the issues involved in the dispute and to make a written report to him within such time as he shall prescribe. Such report shall include a statement of the facts with respect to the dispute, including each party's statement of its position but shall not contain any recommendations. The President shall file a copy of such report with the Service and shall make its contents available to the public.

Section 207.

(a) A board of inquiry shall be composed of a chairman and such other members as the President shall determine, and shall have power to sit and act in any place within the United States and to conduct such hearings either in public or in private, as it may deem necessary or proper, to ascertain the facts with respect to the causes and circumstances of the dispute.

(b) Members of a board of inquiry shall receive compensation at the rate of $50 for each day actually spent by them in the work of the board, together with necessary travel and subsistence expenses.

(c) For the purpose of any hearing or inquiry conducted by any board appointed under this title, the provisions of section 9 and 10 (relating to the attendance of witnesses and the production of books, papers, and documents) of the Federal Trade Commission Act of September 16, 1914, as amended (U.S.C. 19, title 15, secs. 49 and 50, as amended), are hereby made applicable to the powers and duties of such board.

Section 208.

(a) Upon receiving a report from a board of inquiry the President may direct the Attorney General to petition any district court of the United States having jurisdiction of the parties to enjoin such strike or lock-out or the continuing thereof, and if the court finds that such threatened or actual strike or lockout—

  (i) affects an entire industry or a substantial part thereof engaged in trade, commerce, transportation, transmission, or communication among the several States or with foreign nations, or engaged in the production of goods for commerce, and

  (ii) if permitted to occur or to continue, will imperil the national health or safety, it shall have jurisdiction to enjoin any such strike or lockout, or the continuing thereof, and to make such other orders as may be appropriate.

(b) In any case, the provisions of the Act of March 23, 1932, entitled "An Act to amend the Judicial Code and to define and limit the jurisdiction of courts sitting in equity, and for other purposes," shall not be applicable.

(c) The order or orders of the court shall be subject to review by the appropriate circuit court of appeals and by the Supreme Court upon writ of certiorari or certification as provided in sections 239 and 240 of the Judicial Code, as amended (U.S.C., title 29, secs. 346 and 347).

Section. 209.

(a) Whenever a district court has issued an order under section 208 enjoining acts or practices which imperil or threaten to imperil the national health or safety, it shall be the duty of the parties to the labor dispute giving rise to such order to make every effort to adjust and settle their differences, with the assistance of the Service created by this Act. Neither party shall be under any duty to accept, in whole or in part, any proposal of settlement made by the Service.

(b) Upon the issuance of such order, the President shall reconvene the board of inquiry which has previously reported with respect to the dispute. At the end of a sixty-day period (unless the dispute has been settled by that time), the board of inquiry shall report to the President the current position of the parties and the effort which has been made for settlement, and shall include a statement by each party of its position and a statement of the employer's last offer of settlement. The President shall make such report available to the public. The National Labor Relations Board, within the succeeding fifteen days, shall take a secret ballot of the employees of each employer involved in the dispute on the question of whether they wish to accept the final offer of settlement made by their employer as stated by him and shall certify the results thereof to the Attorney General within five days thereafter.

Section 210. Upon the certification of the results of such ballot or upon a settlement being reached, whichever happens sooner, the Attorney General shall move the court to discharge the injunction, which motion shall then be granted and the injunction discharged. When such motion is granted, the President shall submit to the Congress a full and comprehensive report of the proceedings, including the findings of the board of inquiry and the ballot taken by the National Labor Relations Board, together with such recommendations as he may see fit to make for consideration and appropriate action.

Compilation of Collective-Bargaining Agreements, Etc.

Section. 211.

(a) For the guidance and information of interested representatives of employers, employees, and the general public, the Bureau of Labor Statistics of the Department of Labor shall maintain a file of copies of all available collective-bargaining agreements and other available agreements and actions thereunder settling or adjusting labor disputes. Such file shall be open to inspection under appropriate conditions prescribed by the Secretary of Labor, except that no specific information submitted in confidence shall be disclosed.

(b) The Bureau of Labor Statistics in the Department of Labor is authorized to furnish upon request of the Service, or employers, employees, or their representatives, all available data and factual information which may aid in the settlement of any labor dispute, except that no specific information submitted in confidence shall be disclosed.

Exemption of Railway Labor Act

Section 212. The provisions of this title shall not be applicable with respect to any matter which is subject to the provisions of the Railway Labor Act, as amended from time to time.

Conciliation of Labor Disputes in the Health Care Industry

Section 213.

(a) If, in the opinion of the Director of the Federal Mediation and Conciliation Service a threatened or actual strike or lockout affecting a health care institution will, if permitted to occur or to continue, substantially interrupt the delivery of health care in the locality concerned, the Director may further assist in the resolution of the impasse by establishing within 30 days after the notice to the Federal Mediation and Conciliation Service under clause (A) of the last sentence of section 8(d) (which is required by clause (3) of such section 8(d)), or within 10 days after the notice under clause (B), an impartial Board of Inquiry to investigate the issues involved in the dispute and to make a written report thereon to the parties within fifteen (15) days after the establishment of such a Board. The written report shall contain the findings of fact together with the Board's recommendations for settling the dispute. Each such Board shall be composed of such number of individuals as the Director may deem desirable. No member appointed under this section shall have any interest or involvement in the health care institutions or the employee organizations involved in the dispute.

(b) (1) Members of any board established under this section who are otherwise employed by the Federal Government shall serve without compensation but shall be reimbursed for travel, subsistence, and other necessary expenses incurred by them in carrying out its duties under this section.

(2) Members of any board established under this section who are not subject to paragraph (1) shall receive compensation at a rate prescribed by the Director but not to exceed the daily rate prescribed for GS-18 of the General Schedule under section 5332 of title 5, United States Code, including travel for each day they are engaged in the performance of their duties under this section and shall be entitled to reimbursement for travel, subsistence, and other necessary

expenses incurred by them in carrying out their duties under this section.

(c) After the establishment of a board under subsection (a) of this section and for 15 days after any such board has issued its report, no change in the status quo in effect prior to the expiration of the contract in the case of negotiations for a contract renewal, or in effect prior to the time of the impasse in the case of an initial bargaining negotiation, except by agreement, shall be made by the parties to the controversy.

TITLE III

Suits by and against Labor Organizations

Section 301.

(a) Suits for violation of contracts between an employer and a labor organization representing employees in an industry affecting commerce as defined in this Act, or between any such labor organizations, may be brought in any district court of the United States having jurisdiction of the parties, without respect to the amount in controversy or without regard to the citizenship of the parties.

(b) Any labor organization which represents employees in an industry affecting commerce as defined in this Act and any employer whose activities affect commerce as defined in this Act shall be bound by the acts of its agents. Any such labor organization may sue or be sued as an entity and in behalf of the employees whom it represents in the courts of the United States. Any money judgment against a labor organization in a district court of the United States shall be enforceable only against the organization as an entity and against its assets, and shall not be enforceable against any individual member or his assets.

(c) For the purposes of actions and proceedings by or against labor organizations in the district courts of the United States, district courts shall be deemed to have jurisdiction of a labor organization (1) in the district in which such organization maintains its principal offices, or (2) in any district in which its duly authorized officers or agents are engaged in representing or acting for employee members.

(d) The service of summons, subpoena, or other legal process of any court of the United States upon an officer or agent of a labor organization, in his capacity as such, shall constitute service upon the labor organization.

(e) For the purpose of this section, in determining whether any person is acting as an "agent" of another person so as to make such other person responsible for his acts, the question of whether the specific acts performed were actually authorized or subsequently ratified shall not be controlling.

Restrictions on Payments to Employee Representatives

Section 302.

(a) It shall be unlawful for any employer or association of employers or any person who acts as a labor relations expert, adviser, or consultant to an employer or who acts in the interest of an employer to pay, lend, or deliver, or agree to pay, lend, or deliver, any money or other thing of value—
   (1) to any representative of any of his employees who are employed in an industry affecting commerce; or
   (2) to any labor organization, or any officer or employee thereof, which represents, seeks to represent, or would admit to membership, any of the employees of such employer who are employed in an industry affecting commerce;
   (3) to any employee or group or committee of employees of such employer employed in an industry affecting commerce in excess of their normal compensation for the purpose of causing such employee or group or committee directly or indirectly to influence any other employees in the exercise of the right to organize and bargain collectively through representation of their own choosing; or
   (4) to any officer or employee of a labor organization engaged in an industry affecting commerce with intent to influence him in respect to any of his actions, decisions, or duties as a representative of employees or as such officer or employee of such labor organization.

(b) (1) It shall be unlawful for any person to request, demand, receive, or accept, or agree to receive or accept, any payment, loan, or delivery of any money or other thing of value prohibited by subsection (a).
   (2) It shall be unlawful for any labor organization, or for any person acting as an officer, agent, representative, or employee of such labor organization, to demand or accept from the operator of any motor vehicle (as defined in part II of the Interstate Commerce Act) employed in the transportation of property in commerce, or the employer of any such operator, any money or other thing of value payable to such organization or to an officer, agent, representative or employee thereof as a fee or charge for the unloading, or the connection with the unloading, of the cargo of such vehicle: *Provided,* That nothing in this paragraph shall be construed to make unlawful any payment by an employer to any of his employees as compensation for their services as employees.

(c) The provisions of this section shall not be applicable

(1) in respect to any money or other thing of value payable by an employer to any of his employees whose established duties include acting openly for such employer in matters of labor relations or personnel administration or to any representative of his employees, or to any officer or employee of a labor organization, who is also an employee or former employee of such employer, as compensation for, or by reason of, his service as an employee of such employer;

(2) with respect to the payment or delivery of any money or other thing of value in satisfaction of a judgment of any court or a decision or award of an arbitrator or impartial chairman or in compromise, adjustment, settlement, or release of any claim, complaint, grievance or dispute in the absence of fraud or duress;

(3) with respect to the sale or purchase of an article or commodity at the prevailing market price in the regular course of business;

(4) with respect to money deducted from the wages of employees in payment of membership dues in a labor organization: Provided, That the employer has received from each employee, on whose account such deductions are made, a written assignment which shall not be irrevocable for a period of more than one year, or beyond the termination date of the applicable collective agreement, whichever occurs sooner;

(5) with respect to money or other thing of value paid to a trust fund established by such representative, for the sole and exclusive benefit of the employees of such employer, and their families and dependents (or of such employees, families, and dependents jointly with the employees of other employers making similar payments, and their families and dependents): *Provided,* That (A) such payments are held in trust for the purpose of paying, either from principal or income or both, for the benefit of employees, their families and dependents, for medical or hospital care, pensions on retirement or death of employees, compensation for injuries or illness resulting from occupational activity or insurance to provide any of the foregoing, or unemployment benefits or life insurance, disability and sickness insurance, or accident insurance; (B) the detailed basis on which such payments are to be made is specified in a written agreement with the employer, and employees and employers are equally represented in the administration of such fund, together with such neutral persons as the representatives of the employers and the representatives of employees may agree upon and in the event the employer and employee groups deadlock on the administration of such fund and there are no neutral persons empowered to break such deadlock, such agreement provides that the two groups shall agree on an impartial umpire to decide such dispute, or in event of their failure to agree within a reasonable length of time, an impartial umpire to decide such dispute shall, on petition of either group, be appointed by the district court of the United States for the district where the trust fund has its principal office, and shall also contain provisions for an annual audit of the trust fund, a statement of the results of which shall be available for inspection by interested persons at the principal office of the trust fund and at such other places as may be designated in such written agreement; and (C) such payments as are intended to be used for the purpose of providing pensions or annuities for employees are made to a separate trust which provides that the funds held therein cannot be used for any purpose other than paying such pensions or annuities;

(6) with respect to money or other thing of value paid by any employer to a trust fund established by such representative for the purpose of pooled vacation, holiday, severance or similar benefits, or defraying costs of apprenticeship or other training program: *Provided,* That the requirements of clause (B) of the proviso to clause (5) of this subsection shall apply to such trust funds;

(7) with respect to money or other thing of value paid by any employer to a pooled or individual trust fund established by such representative for the purpose of (A) scholarships for the benefit of employees, their families, and dependents for study at educational institutions, or (B) child care centers for preschool and school age dependents of employees: *Provided,* That no labor organization or employer shall be required to bargain on the establishment of any such trust fund, and refusal to do so shall not constitute an unfair labor practice: *Provided further,* That the requirements of clause (B) of the proviso to clause (5) of this subsection shall apply to such trust funds;

(8) with respect to money or any other thing of value paid by any employer to a trust fund established by such representative for the purpose of defraying the costs of legal services for employees, their families, and dependents for counsel or plan of their

choice: Provided, That the requirements of clause (B) of the proviso to clause (5) of this subsection shall apply to such trust funds: Provided further, That no such legal services shall be furnished: (A) to initiate any proceeding directed (i) against any such employer or its officers or agents except in workman's compensation cases, or (ii) against such labor organization, or its parent or subordinate bodies, or their officers or agents, or (iii) against any other employer or labor organization, or their officers or agents, in any matter arising under the National Labor Relations Act, as amended, or this Act; and (B) in any proceeding where a labor organization would be prohibited from defraying the costs of legal services by the provisions of the Labor-Management Reporting and Disclosure Act of 1959; or

(9) with respect to money or other things of value paid by an employer to a plant, area or industrywide labor management committee established for one or more of the purposes set forth in section 5(b) of the Labor Management Cooperation Act of 1978.

(d) Any person who willfully violates any of the provisions of this section shall, upon conviction thereof, be guilty of a misdemeanor and be subject to a fine of not more than $10,000 or to imprisonment for not more than one year, or both.

(e) The district courts of the United States and the United States courts of the Territories and possessions shall have jurisdiction, for cause shown, and subject to the provisions of section 17 (relating to notice to opposite party) of the Act entitled "An Act to supplement existing laws against unlawful restraints and monopolies, and for other purposes," approved October 15, 1914, as amended (U.S.C., title 28, sec. 381), to restrain violations of this section, without regard to the provisions of sections 6 and 20 of such Act of October 15, 1914, as amended (U.S.C., title 15, sec. 17 and title 29, sec. 52), and the provisions of the Act entitled "An Act to amend the Judicial Code to define and limit the jurisdiction of courts sitting in equity, and for other purposes," approved March 23, 1932 (U.S.C., title 29, secs. 101–115).

(f) This section shall not apply to any contract in force on the date of enactment of this Act, until the expiration of such contract, or until July 1, 1948, whichever first occurs.

(g) Compliance with the restrictions contained in subsection (c)(5)(B) upon contributions to trust funds, otherwise lawful, shall not be applicable to contributions to such trust funds established by collective agreement prior to January 1, 1946, nor shall subsection (c)(5)(A) be construed as prohibiting contributions to such trust funds if prior to January 1, 1947, such funds contained provisions for pooled vacation benefits.

Boycotts and Other Unlawful Combinations

Section 303.

(a) It shall be unlawful, for the purpose of this section only, in an industry or activity affecting commerce, for any labor organization to engage in any activity or conduct defined as an unfair labor practice in section 8(b)(4) of the National Labor Relations Act, as amended.

(b) Whoever shall be injured in his business or property by reason of any violation of subsection (a) may sue therefore in any district court of the United States subject to the limitations and provisions of section 301 hereof without respect to the amount in controversy, or in any other court having jurisdiction of the parties, and shall recover the damages by him sustained and the cost of the suit.

Restriction on Political Contributions

Section 304. Section 313 of the Federal Corrupt Practices Act, 1925 (U.S.C., 1940 edition, title 2, sec. 251; Supp. V, title 50, App., sec. 1509), as amended, is amended to read as follows:

Section 313. It is unlawful for any national bank, or any corporation organized by authority of any law of Congress to make a contribution or expenditure in connection with any election to any political office, or in connection with any primary election or political convention or caucus held to select candidates for any political office, or for any corporation whatever, or any labor organization to make a contribution or expenditure in connection with any election at which Presidential and Vice Presidential electors or a Senator or Representative in, or a Delegate or Resident Commissioner to Congress are to be voted for, or in connection with any primary election or political convention or caucus held to select candidates for any of the foregoing offices, or for any candidate, political committee, or other person to accept or receive any contribution prohibited by this section. Every corporation or labor organization which makes any contribution or expenditure in violation of this section shall be fined not more than $5,000; and every officer or director of any corporation, or officer of any labor organization, who consents to any contribution or expenditure by the corporation or labor organization, as the case may be, in violation of this section shall be fined not more than $1,000 or imprisoned for not more than one year, or both. For the purposes of this section, "labor organization" means any organization of any kind, or any agency or employee representation committee or plan, in which employees participate and which exists for the purpose, in whole or in part, of dealing with employers concerning grievances, labor disputes, wages, rates of pay, hours of employment, or conditions of work.

Strikes by Government Employees

Section 305. [Repealed by Ch. 690, 69 Stat. 624, effective August 9, 1955. Sec. 305 made it unlawful for government employees to strike and made strikers subject to immediate discharge, forfeiture of civil-service status, and three-year blacklisting for federal employment.]

TITLE IV

Creation of Joint Committee to Study and Report on Basic Problems Affecting Friendly Labor Relations and Productivity

Section 401. There is hereby established a joint congressional committee to be known as the Joint Committee on Labor-Management Relations (hereafter referred to as the committee), and to be composed of seven Members of the Senate Committee on Labor and Public Welfare, to be appointed by the President pro tempore of the Senate, and seven Members of the House of Representatives Committee on Education and Labor, to be appointed by the Speaker of the House of Representatives. A vacancy in membership of the committee, shall not affect the powers of the remaining members to execute the functions of the committee, and shall be filled in the same manner as the original selection. The committee shall select a chairman and a vice chairman from among its members.

Section 402. The committee, acting as a whole or by subcommittee shall conduct a thorough study and investigation of the entire field of labor-management relations, including but not limited to—

(a) (1) the means by which permanent friendly cooperation between employers and employees and stability of labor relations may be secured throughout the United States;

(2) the means by which the individual employee may achieve a greater productivity and higher wages, including plans for guaranteed annual wages, incentive profit-sharing and bonus systems;

(3) the internal organization and administration of labor unions, with special attention to the impact on individuals of collective agreements requiring membership in unions as a condition of employment;

(4) the labor relations policies and practices of employers and associations of employers;

(5) the desirability of welfare funds for the benefit of employees and their relation to the social-security system;

(6) the methods and procedures for best carrying out the collective-bargaining processes, with special attention to the effects of industrywide or regional bargaining upon the national economy;

(7) the administration and operation of existing Federal laws relating to labor relations; and

(8) such other problems and subjects in the field of labor-management relations as the committee deems appropriate.

Section 403. The committee shall report to the Senate and the House of Representatives not later than March 15, 1948, the results of its study and investigation, together with such recommendations as to necessary legislation and such other recommendations as it may deem advisable, and shall make its final report not later than January 2, 1949.

Section 404. The committee shall have the power, without regard to the civil-service laws and the Classification Act of 1923, as amended, to employ and fix the compensation of such officers, experts, and employees as it deems necessary for the performance of its duties, including consultants who shall receive compensation at a rate not to exceed $35 for each day actually spent by them in the work of the committee, together with their necessary travel and subsistence expenses. The committee is further authorized with the consent of the head of the department or agency concerned, to utilize the services, information, facilities, and personnel of all agencies in the executive branch of the Government and may request the governments of the several States, representatives of business, industry, finance, and labor, and such other persons, agencies, organizations, and instrumentalities as it deems appropriate to attend its hearings and to give and present information, advice, and recommendations.

Section 405. The committee, or any subcommittee thereof, is authorized to hold such hearings; to sit and act at such times and places during the sessions, recesses, and adjourned periods of the Eightieth Congress; to require by subpoena or otherwise the attendance of such witnesses and the production of such books, papers, and documents; to administer oaths; to take such testimony; to have such printing and binding done; and to make such expenditures within the amount appropriated therefor as it deems advisable. The cost of stenographic services in reporting such hearings shall not be in excess of 25 cents per one hundred words. Subpoenas shall be issued under the signature of the chairman or vice chairman of the committee and shall be served by any person designated by them.

Section 406. The members of the committee shall be reimbursed for travel, subsistence, and other necessary expenses incurred by them in the performance of the duties vested in the committee, other than expenses in connection with meetings of the committee held in the District of Columbia during such times as the Congress is in session.

Section 407. There is hereby authorized to be appropriated the sum of $150,000, or so much thereof as may be necessary, to carry out the provisions of this title, to be disbursed by the Secretary of the Senate on vouchers signed by the chairman.

TITLE V

Definitions

Section 501. When used in this Act—

(a) (1) The term "industry affecting commerce" means any industry or activity in commerce or in which a labor dispute would burden or obstruct commerce or tend to burden or obstruct commerce or the free flow of commerce.

(2) The term "strike" includes any strike or other concerted stoppage of work by employees (including a stoppage by reason of the expiration of a collective-bargaining agreement) and any concerted slow-down or other concerted interruption of operations by employees.

(3) The terms "commerce," "labor disputes," "employer," "employee," "labor organization," "representative," "person," and "supervisor" shall have the same meaning as when used in the National Labor Relations Act as amended by this Act.

Saving Provision

Section 502. Nothing in this Act shall be construed to require an individual employee to render labor or service without his consent, nor shall anything in this Act be construed to make the quitting of his labor by an individual employee an illegal act; nor shall any court issue any process to compel the performance by an individual of such labor or service, without his consent; nor shall the quitting of labor by an employee or employees in good faith because of abnormally dangerous conditions for work at the place of employment of such employee or employees be deemed a strike under this Act.

Separability

Section 503. If any provision of this Act, or the application of such provision to any person or circumstance, shall be invalid, the remainder of this Act, or the application of such provision to persons or circumstances other than those as to which it is held invalid, shall not be affected thereby.

Text of the Labor-Management Reporting and Disclosure Act of 1959

73 Stat. 519 (1959), as amended, 79 Stat. 888 (1965), 88 Stat. 852 (1974); 29 U.S.C. Sections 401–531

SHORT TITLE

Section 1. This Act may be cited as the "Labor-Management Reporting and Disclosure Act of 1959."

Declaration of Findings, Purposes, and Policy

Section 2.

(a) The Congress finds that, in the public interest, it continues to be the responsibility of the Federal Government to protect employees' rights to organize, choose their own representatives, bargain collectively, and otherwise engage in concerted activities for their mutual aid or protection; that the relations between employers and labor organizations and the millions of workers they represent have a substantial impact on the commerce of the Nation; and that in order to accomplish the objective of a free flow of commerce it is essential that labor organizations, employers, and their officials adhere to the highest standards of responsibility and ethical conduct in administering the affairs of their organizations, particularly as they affect labor-management relations.

(b) The Congress further finds, from recent investigations in the labor and management fields, that there have been a number of instances of breach of trust, corruption, disregard of the rights of individual employees, and other failures to observe high standards of responsibility and ethical conduct which require further and supplementary legislation that will afford necessary protection of the rights and interests of employees and the public generally as they relate to the activities of labor organizations, employers, labor relations consultants, and their officers and representatives.

(c) The Congress, therefore, further finds and declares that the enactment of this Act is necessary to eliminate or prevent improper practices on the part of labor organizations, employers, labor relations consultants, and their officers and representatives which distort and defeat the policies of the Labor Management Relations Act, 1947, as amended, and the Railway Labor Act, as amended, and have the tendency or necessary effect of burdening or obstructing commerce by (1) impairing the efficiency, safety, or operation of the instrumentalities of commerce; (2) occurring in the current of commerce; (3) materially affecting, restraining, or controlling the flow of raw materials or manufactured or processed goods into or from the channels of commerce, or the prices of such materials or goods in commerce; or (4) causing diminution of employment and wages in such volume as substantially to impair or disrupt the market for goods flowing into or from the channels of commerce.

Definitions

Section 3. For the purposes of titles I, II, III, IV, V (except section 505), and VI of this Act—

(a) "Commerce" means trade, traffic, commerce, transportation, transmission, or communication among the several States or between any State and any place outside thereof.

(b) "State" includes any State of the United States, the District of Columbia, Puerto Rico, the Virgin Islands, American Samoa, Guam, Wake Island, the Canal Zone, and Outer Continental Shelf lands defined in the Outer Continental Shelf Lands Act (43 U.S.C. §§ 1331–1343).

(c) "Industry affecting commerce" means any activity, business, or industry in commerce or in which a labor dispute would hinder or obstruct commerce or the free flow of commerce and includes any activity or industry "affecting commerce" within the meaning of the Labor Management Relations Act, 1947, as amended, or the Railway Labor Act, as amended.

(d) "Person" includes one or more individuals, labor organizations, partnerships, associations, corporations, legal representatives, mutual companies, joint-stock companies, trusts, unincorporated organizations, trustees, trustees in bankruptcy, or receivers.

(e) "Employer" means any employer or any group or association of employers engaged in an industry affecting commerce (1) which is, with respect to employees engaged in an industry affecting commerce, an employer within the meaning of any law of the United States relating to the employment of any employees or (2) which may deal with any labor organization concerning grievances, labor disputes, wages, rates of pay, hours of employment, or conditions of work, and includes any person acting directly or indirectly as an employer or as an agent of an employer in relation to an employee but does not include the United States or any corporation wholly owned by the Government of the United States or any State or political subdivision thereof.

(f) "Employee" means any individual employed by an employer, and includes any individual whose work has ceased as a consequence of, or in connection with, any current labor dispute or because of any unfair labor practice or because of exclusion or expulsion from a labor organization in any manner or for any reason inconsistent with the requirements of this Act.

(g) "Labor dispute" includes any controversy concerning terms, tenure, or conditions of employment, or concerning the association or representation of persons in negotiating, fixing, maintaining, changing, or seeking to arrange terms or conditions of employment, regardless of whether the disputants stand in the proximate relation of employer and employee.

(h) "Trusteeship" means any receivership, trusteeship, or other method of supervision or control whereby a labor organization suspends the autonomy otherwise available to a subordinate body under its constitution or bylaws.

(i) "Labor organization" means a labor organization engaged in an industry affecting commerce and includes any organization of any kind, any agency, or employee representation committee, group, association, or plan so engaged in which employees participate and which exists for the purpose, in whole or in part, of dealing with employers concerning grievances, labor disputes, wages, rates of pay, hours, or other terms or conditions of employment, and any conference, general committee, joint or system board, or joint council so engaged which is subordinate to a national or international labor organization, other than a State or local central body.

(j) A labor organization shall be deemed to be engaged in an industry affecting commerce if it—

(1) is the certified representative of employees under the provisions of the National Labor Relations Act, as amended, or the Railway Labor Act, as amended; or

(2) although not certified, is a national or international labor organization or a local labor organization recognized or acting as the representative of employees of an employer or employers engaged in an industry affecting commerce; or

(3) has chartered a local labor organization or subsidiary body which is representing or actively seeking to represent employees of employers within the meaning of paragraph (1) or (2), or

(4) has been chartered by a labor organization representing or actively seeking to represent employees within the meaning of paragraph (1) or (2) as the local or subordinate body through which such employees may enjoy membership or become affiliated with such labor organization; or

(5) is a conference, general committee, joint or system board, or joint council, subordinate to a national or international labor organization, which includes a labor organization engaged in an industry affecting commerce within the meaning of any of the preceding paragraphs of this subsection, other than a State or local central body.

(k) "Secret ballot" means the expression by ballot, voting machine, or otherwise, but in no event by proxy, of a choice with respect to any election or vote taken upon any matter, which is cast in such a manner that the person expressing such choice cannot be identified with the choice expressed.

(l) "Trust in which a labor organization is interested" means a trust or other fund or organization (1) which was created or established by a labor organization, or one or more of the trustees or one or more members of the governing body of which is selected or appointed by a labor organization, and (2) a primary purpose of which is to provide benefits for the members of such labor organization or their beneficiaries.

(m) "Labor relations consultant" means any person who, for compensation, advises or represents an employer, employer organization, or labor organization concerning employee organizing, concerted activities, or collective bargaining activities.

(n) "Officer" means any constitutional officer, any person authorized to perform the functions of president, vice president, secretary, treasurer, or other executive functions of a labor organization, and any member of its executive board or similar governing body.

(o) "Member" or "member in good standing", when used in reference to a labor organization, includes any person who has fulfilled the requirements for membership in such organization, and who neither has voluntarily withdrawn from membership nor has been expelled or suspended from membership after appropriate proceedings consistent with lawful provisions of the constitution and bylaws of such organization.

(p) "Secretary" means the Secretary of Labor.

(q) "Officer, agent, shop steward, or other representative", when used with respect to a labor organization, includes elected officials and key administrative personnel, whether elected or appointed (such as business agents, heads of departments or major units, and organizers who exercise substantial independent authority), but does not include salaried nonsupervisory professional staff, stenographic, and service personnel.

(r) "District court of the United States" means a United States district court and a United States court of any place subject to the jurisdiction of the United States.

TITLE I—BILL OF RIGHTS OF MEMBERS OF LABOR ORGANIZATIONS

Bill of Rights

Section 101.

(a) (1) *Equal Rights.*—Every member of a labor organization shall have equal rights and privileges within such organization to nominate candidates, to vote in elections or referendums of the labor organization, to attend membership meetings, and to participate in the deliberations and voting upon the business of such meetings, subject to reasonable rules and regulations in such organization's constitution and bylaws.

(2) *Freedom of Speech and Assembly.*—Every member of any labor organization shall have the right to meet and assemble freely with other members; and to express any views, arguments, or opinions; and to express at meetings of the labor organization his views, upon candidates in an election of the labor organization or upon any business properly before the meeting, subject to the organization's established and reasonable rules pertaining to the conduct of meetings: *Provided,* That nothing herein shall be construed to impair the right of a labor organization to adopt and enforce reasonable rules as to the responsibility of every member toward the organization as an institution and to his refraining from conduct that would interfere with its performance of its legal or contractual obligations.

(3) *Dues, Initiation Fees, and Assessments.*—Except in the case of a federation of national or international labor organizations, the rates of dues and initiation fees payable by members of any labor organization in effect on the date of enactment of this Act shall not be increased, and no general or special assessment shall be levied upon such members, except—

(A) in a case of a local labor organization, (i) by majority vote by secret ballot of the members in good standing voting at a general or special membership meeting, after reasonable notice of the intention to vote upon such question, or (ii) by majority vote of the members in good standing voting in a membership referendum conducted by secret ballot; or

(B) in the case of a labor organization, other than a local labor organization or a federation of national or international labor organizations, (i) by majority vote of the delegates voting at a regular convention, or at a special convention of such labor organization held upon not less than thirty days' written notice to the principal office of each local or constituent labor organization entitled to such notice, or (ii) by majority vote of the members in good standing of such labor organization voting in a membership referendum conducted by secret ballot, or (iii) by majority vote of the members of the executive board or similar governing body of such labor organization, pursuant to express authority contained in the constitution and bylaws of such labor organization: *Provided,* That such action on the part of the executive board or similar governing body shall be effective only until the next regular convention of such labor organization.

(4) *Protection of the Right to Sue.*—No labor organization shall limit the right of any member thereof to institute an action in any court, or in a proceeding before any administrative agency, irrespective of whether or not the labor organization or its officers are named as defendants or respondents in such action or proceeding, or the right of any member of a labor organization to appear as a witness in any

judicial, administrative, or legislative proceeding, or to petition any legislature or to communicate with any legislator: Provided, That any such member may be required to exhaust reasonable hearing procedures (but not to exceed a four-month lapse of time) within such organization, before instituting legal or administrative proceedings against such organizations or any officer thereof: And provided further, That no interested employer or employer association shall directly or indirectly finance, encourage, or participate in, except as a party, any such action, proceeding, appearance, or petition.

(5) *Safeguards Against Improper Disciplinary Action.*— No member of any labor organization may be fined, suspended, expelled, or otherwise disciplined except for nonpayment of dues by such organization or by any officer thereof unless such member has been (A) served with written specific charges; (B) given a reasonable time to prepare his defense; (C) afforded a full and fair hearing.

(b) Any provision of the constitution and bylaws of any labor organization which is inconsistent with the provisions of this section shall be of no force or effect.

Civil Enforcement

Section 102. Any person whose rights secured by the provisions of this title have been infringed by any violation of this title may bring a civil action in a district court of the United States for such relief (including injunctions) as may be appropriate. Any such action against a labor organization shall be brought in the district court of the United States for the district where the alleged violation occurred, or where the principal office of such labor organization is located.

Retention of Existing Rights

Section 103. Nothing contained in this title shall limit the rights and remedies of any member of a labor organization under any State or Federal law or before any court or other tribunal, or under the constitution and bylaws of any labor organization.

Right to Copies of Collective Bargaining Agreements

Section 104. It shall be the duty of the secretary or corresponding principal officer of each labor organization, in the case of a local labor organization, to forward a copy of each collective bargaining agreement made by such labor organization with any employer to any employee who requests such a copy and whose rights as such employee are directly affected by such agreement, and in the case of a labor organization other than a local labor organization, to forward a copy of any such agreement to each constituent unit which has members directly affected by such agreement; and such officer shall maintain at the principal office of the labor organization of which he is an officer copies of any such agreement made or received by such labor organization, which copies shall be available for inspection by any member or by any employee whose rights are affected by such agreement. The provisions of section 210 shall be applicable in the enforcement of this section.

Information as to Act

Section 105. Every labor organization shall inform its members concerning the provisions of this Act.

TITLE II—REPORTING BY LABOR ORGANIZATIONS, OFFICERS AND EMPLOYEES OF LABOR ORGANIZATIONS, AND EMPLOYERS

Report of Labor Organizations

Section 201.

(a) Every labor organization shall adopt a constitution and bylaws and shall file a copy thereof with the Secretary, together with a report, signed by its president and secretary or corresponding principal officers, containing the following information—

(1) the name of the labor organization, its mailing address, and any other address at which it maintains its principal office or at which it keeps the records referred to in this title;

(2) the name and title of each of its officers;

(3) the initiation fee or fees required from a new or transferred member and fees for work permits required by the reporting labor organization;

(4) the regular dues or fees or other periodic payments required to remain a member of the reporting labor organization; and

(5) detailed statements, or references to specific provisions of documents filed under this subsection which contain such statements, showing the provision made and procedures followed with respect to each of the following: (A) qualifications for or restrictions on membership, (B) levying of assessments, (C) participation in insurance or other benefit plans, (D) authorization for disbursement of funds of the

labor organization, (E) audit of financial transactions of the labor organization, (F) the calling of regular and special meetings, (G) the selection of officers and stewards and of any representatives to other bodies composed of labor organizations' representatives, with a specific statement of the manner in which each officer was elected, appointed, or otherwise selected, (H) discipline or removal of officers or agents for breaches of their trust, (I) imposition of fines, suspensions and expulsions of members, including the grounds for such action and any provision made for notice, hearing, judgment on the evidence, and appeal procedures, (J) authorization for bargaining demands, (K) ratification of contract terms, (L) authorization for strikes, and (M) issuance of work permits. Any change in the information required by this subsection shall be reported to the Secretary at the time the reporting labor organization files with the Secretary the annual financial report required by subsection (b).

(b) Every labor organization shall file annually with the Secretary a financial report signed by its president and treasurer or corresponding principal officers containing the following information in such detail as may be necessary accurately to disclose its financial condition and operations for its preceding fiscal year—
   (1) assets and liabilities at the beginning and end of the fiscal year;
   (2) receipts of any kind and the sources thereof;
   (3) salary, allowances, and other direct or indirect disbursements (including reimbursed expenses) to each officer and also to each employee who, during such fiscal year, received more than $10,000 in the aggregate from such labor organization and any other labor organization affiliated with it or with which it is affiliated, or which is affiliated with the same national or international labor organization;
   (4) direct and indirect loans made to any officer, employee, or member, which aggregated more than $250 during the fiscal year, together with a statement of the purpose, security, if any, and arrangements for repayment;
   (5) direct and indirect loans to any business enterprise, together with a statement of the purpose, security, if any, and arrangements for repayment; and
   (6) other disbursements made by it including the purpose thereof; all in such categories as the Secretary may prescribe.

(c) Every labor organization required to submit a report under this title shall make available the information required to be contained in such report to all of its members, and every such labor organization and its officers shall be under a duty enforceable at the suit of any member of such organization in any State court of competent jurisdiction or in the district court of the United States for the district in which such labor organization maintains its principal office, to permit such member for just cause to examine any books, records, and accounts necessary to verify such report. The court in such action may, in its discretion, in addition to any judgment awarded to the plaintiff or plaintiffs, allow a reasonable attorney's fee to be paid by the defendant, and costs of the action.

Report of Officers and Employees of Labor Organizations

Section 202.

(a) Every officer of a labor organization and every employee of a labor organization (other than an employee performing exclusively clerical or custodial services) shall file with the Secretary a signed report listing and describing for his preceding fiscal year—
   (1) any stock, bond, security, or other interest, legal or equitable, which he or his spouse or minor child directly or indirectly held in, and any income or any other benefit with monetary value (including reimbursed expenses) which he or his spouse or minor child derived directly or indirectly from, an employer whose employees such labor organization represents or is actively seeking to represent, except payments and other benefits received as a bona fide employee of such employer;
   (2) any transaction in which he or his spouse or minor child engaged, directly or indirectly, involving any stock, bond, security, or loan to or from, or other legal or equitable interest in the business of an employer whose employees such labor organization represents or is actively seeking to represent;
   (3) any stock, bond, security, or other interest, legal or equitable, which he or his spouse or minor child directly or indirectly held in, and any income or any other benefit with monetary value (including reimbursed expenses) which he or his spouse or minor child directly or indirectly derived from, any business a substantial part of which consists of buying from, selling or leasing to, or otherwise dealing with, the business of an employer whose employees such labor organization represents or is actively seeking to represent;
   (4) any stock, bond, security, or other interest, legal or equitable, which he or his spouse or minor child

directly or indirectly held in, and any income or any other benefit with monetary value (including reimbursed expenses) which he or his spouse or minor child directly or indirectly derived from, a business any part of which consists of buying from, or selling or leasing directly or indirectly to, or otherwise dealing with such labor organization;

(5) any direct or indirect business transaction or arrangement between him or his spouse or minor child and any employer whose employees his organization represents or is actively seeking to represent, except work performed and payments and benefits received as a bona fide employee of such employer and except purchases and sales of goods or services in the regular course of business at prices generally available to any employee of such employer; and

(6) any payment of money or other thing of value (including reimbursed expenses) which he or his spouse or minor child received directly or indirectly from any employer or any person who acts as a labor relations consultant to an employer, except payments of the kinds referred to in section 302(c) of the Labor Management Relations Act, 1947, as amended.

(b) The provisions of paragraphs (1), (2), (3), (4), and (5) of subsection (a) shall not be construed to require any such officer or employee to report his bona fide investments in securities traded on a securities exchange registered as a national securities exchange under the Securities Exchange Act of 1934, in shares in an investment company registered under the Investment Company Act of 1940, or in securities of a public utility holding company registered under the Public Utility Holding Company Act of 1935, or to report any income derived therefrom.

(c) Nothing contained in this section shall be construed to require any officer or employee of a labor organization to file a report under subsection (a) unless he or his spouse or minor child holds or has held an interest, has received income or any other benefit with monetary value or a loan, or has engaged in a transaction described therein.

Report of Employers

Section 203.

(a) Every employer who in any fiscal year made—

(1) any payment or loan, direct or indirect, of money or other thing of value (including reimbursed expenses), or any promise or agreement therefor, to any labor organization or officer, agent, shop steward, or other representative of a labor organization, or employee of any labor organization, except (A) payments or loans made by any national or State bank, credit union, insurance company, savings and loan association or other credit institution and (B) payments of the kind referred to in section 302(c) of the Labor Management Relations Act, 1947, as amended;

(2) any payment (including reimbursed expenses) to any of his employees, or any group or committee of such employees, for the purpose of causing such employee or group or committee of employees to persuade other employees to exercise or not to exercise, or as to the manner of exercising, the right to organize and bargain collectively through representatives of their own choosing unless such payments were contemporaneously or previously disclosed to such other employees;

(3) any expenditure, during the fiscal year, where an object thereof, directly or indirectly, is to interfere with, restrain, or coerce employees in the exercise of the right to organize and bargain collectively through representatives of their own choosing, or is to obtain information concerning the activities of employees or a labor organization in connection with a labor dispute involving such employer, except for use solely in conjunction with an administrative or arbitral proceeding or a criminal or civil judicial proceeding;

(4) any agreement or arrangement with a labor relations consultant or other independent contractor or organization pursuant to which such person undertakes activities where an object thereof, directly or indirectly, is to persuade employees to exercise or not to exercise, or persuade employees as to the manner of exercising, the right to organize and bargain collectively through representatives of their own choosing, or undertakes to supply such employer with information concerning the activities of employees or a labor organization in connection with a labor dispute involving such employer, except information for use solely in conjunction with an administrative or arbitral proceeding or a criminal or civil judicial proceeding; or

(5) any payment (including reimbursed expenses) pursuant to an agreement or arrangement described in subdivision (4); shall file with the Secretary a report, in a form prescribed by him, signed by its president and treasurer or corresponding principal officers showing in detail the date and amount of

each such payment, loan, promise, agreement, or arrangement and the name, address, and position, if any, in any firm or labor organization of the person to whom it was made and a full explanation of the circumstances of all such payments, including the terms of any agreement or understanding pursuant to which they were made.

(b) Every person who pursuant to any agreement or arrangement with an employer undertakes activities where an object thereof is, directly or indirectly—

(1) to persuade employees to exercise or not to exercise, or persuade employees as to the manner of exercising, the right to organize and bargain collectively through representatives of their own choosing; or

(2) to supply an employer with information concerning the activities of employees or a labor organization in connection with a labor dispute involving such employer, except information for use solely in conjunction with an administrative or arbitral proceeding or a criminal or civil judicial proceeding;

shall file within thirty days after entering into such agreement or arrangement a report with the Secretary, signed by its president and treasurer or corresponding principal officers, containing the name under which such person is engaged in doing business and the address of its principal office, and a detailed statement of the terms and conditions of such agreement or arrangement. Every such person shall file annually, with respect to each fiscal year during which payments were made as a result of such an agreement or arrangement, a report with the Secretary, signed by its president and treasurer or corresponding principal officers, containing a statement (A) of its receipts of any kind from employers on account of labor relations advice or services, designating the sources thereof, and (B) of its disbursements of any kind, in connection with such services and the purposes thereof. In each such case such information shall be set forth in such categories as the Secretary may prescribe.

(c) Nothing in this section shall be construed to require any employer or other person to file a report covering the services of such person by reason of his giving or agreeing to give advice to such employer or representing or agreeing to represent such employer before any court, administrative agency, or tribunal of arbitration or engaging or agreeing to engage in collective bargaining on behalf of such employer with respect to wages, hours, or other terms or conditions of employment or the negotiation of an agreement or any question arising thereunder.

(d) Nothing contained in this section shall be construed to require an employer to file a report under subsection (a) unless he has made an expenditure, payment, loan, agreement, or arrangement of the kind described therein. Nothing contained in this section shall be construed to require any other person to file a report under subsection (b) unless he was a party to an agreement or arrangement of the kind described therein.

(e) Nothing contained in this section shall be construed to require any regular officer, supervisor, or employee of an employer to file a report in connection with services rendered to such employer nor shall any employer be required to file a report covering expenditures made to any regular officer, supervisor, or employee of an employer as compensation for service as a regular officer, supervisor, or employee of such employer.

(f) Nothing contained in this section shall be construed as an amendment to, or modification of the rights protected by, section 8(c) of the National Labor Relations Act, as amended.

(g) The term "interfere with, restrain, or coerce" as used in this section means interference, restraint, and coercion which, if done with respect to the exercise of rights guaranteed in section 7 of the National Labor Relations Act, as amended, would, under section 8(a) of such Act, constitute an unfair labor practice.

Attorney-Client Communications Exempted

Section 204. Nothing contained in this Act shall be construed to require an attorney who is a member in good standing of the bar of any State, to include in any report required to be filed pursuant to the provisions of this Act any information which was lawfully communicated to such attorney by any of his clients in the course of a legitimate attorney-client relationship.

Reports Made Public Information

Section 205.

(a) The contents of the reports and documents filed with the Secretary pursuant to sections 201, 202, 203, and 211 shall be public information, and the Secretary may publish any information and data which he obtains pursuant to the provisions of this title. The Secretary may use the information and data for statistical and research purposes, and compile and publish such studies, analyses, reports, and surveys based thereon as he may deem appropriate.

(b) The Secretary shall by regulation make reasonable provision for the inspection and examination, on the request of any person, of the information and data contained in any report or other document filed with him pursuant to section 201, 202, 203, or 211.

(c) The Secretary shall by regulation provide for the furnishing by the Department of Labor of copies of reports or other documents filed with the Secretary pursuant to this title, upon payment of a charge based upon the cost of the service. The Secretary shall make available without payment of a charge, or require any person to furnish, to such State agency as is designated by law or by the Governor of the State in which such person has his principal place of business or headquarters, upon request of the Governor of such State, copies of any reports and documents filed by such person with the Secretary pursuant to section 201, 202, 203, or 211, or of information and data contained therein. No person shall be required by reason of any law of any State to furnish to any officer or agency of such State any information included in a report filed by such person with the Secretary pursuant to the provisions of this title, if a copy of such report, or of the portion thereof containing such information, is furnished to such officer or agency. All moneys received in payment of such charges fixed by the Secretary pursuant to this subsection shall be deposited in the general fund of the Treasury.

Retention of Records

Section 206. Every person required to file any report under this title shall maintain records on the matters required to be reported which will provide in sufficient detail the necessary basic information and data from which the documents filed with the Secretary may be verified, explained or clarified, and checked for accuracy and completeness, and shall include vouchers, worksheets, receipts, and applicable resolutions, and shall keep such records available for examination for a period of not less than five years after the filing of the documents based on the information which they contain.

Effective Date

Section 207.

(a) Each labor organization shall file the initial report required under section 201(a) within ninety days after the date on which it first becomes subject to this Act.

(b) Each person required to file a report under section 201 (b), 202, 203(a), or the second sentence of 203(b), or section 211 shall file such report within ninety days after the end of each of its fiscal years; except that where such person is subject to section 201(b), 202, 203(a), the second sentence of 203(b), or section 211, as the case may be, for only a portion of such a fiscal year (because the date of enactment of this Act occurs during such person's fiscal year or such person becomes subject to this Act during its fiscal year) such person may consider that portion as the entire fiscal year in making such report.

Rules and Regulations

Section 208. The Secretary shall have authority to issue, amend, and rescind rules and regulations prescribing the form and publication of reports required to be filed under this title and such other reasonable rules and regulations (including rules prescribing reports concerning trusts in which a labor organization is interested) as he may find necessary to prevent the circumvention or evasion of such reporting requirements. In exercising his power under this section the Secretary shall prescribe by general rule simplified reports for labor organizations or employers for whom he finds that by virtue of their size a detailed report would be unduly burdensome, but the Secretary may revoke such provision for simplified forms of any labor organization or employer if he determines, after such investigation as he deems proper and due notice and opportunity for a hearing, that the purposes of this section would be served thereby.

Criminal Provisions

Section 209.

(a) Any person who willfully violates this title shall be fined not more than $10,000 or imprisoned for not more than one year, or both.

(b) Any person who makes a false statement or representation of a material fact, knowing it to be false, or who knowingly fails to disclose a material fact, in any document, report, or other information required under the provisions of this title shall be fined not more than $10,000 or imprisoned for not more than one year, or both.

(c) Any person who willfully makes a false entry in or willfully conceals, withholds, or destroys any books, records, reports, or statements required to be kept by any provision of this title shall be fined not more than $10,000 or imprisoned for not more than one year, or both.

(d) Each individual required to sign reports under sections 201 and 203 shall be personally responsible for the filing of such reports and for any statement contained therein which he knows to be false.

Civil Enforcement

Section 210. Whenever it shall appear that any person has violated or is about to violate any of the provisions of this title, the Secretary may bring a civil action for such relief (including injunctions) as may be appropriate. Any such action may be brought in the district court of the United States where the violation occurred or, at the option of the parties, in the United States District Court for the District of Columbia.

Surety Company Reports

Section 211. Each surety company which issues any bond required by this Act or the Welfare and Pension Plans Disclosure Act shall file annually with the Secretary, with respect to each fiscal year during which any such bond was in force, a report, in such form and detail as he may prescribe by regulation, filed by the president and treasurer or corresponding principal officers of the surety company, describing its bond experience under each such Act, including information as to the premiums received, total claims paid, amounts recovered by way of subrogation, administrative and legal expenses and such related data and information as the Secretary shall determine to be necessary in the public interest and to carry out the policy of the Act. Notwithstanding the foregoing, if the Secretary finds that any such specific information cannot be practicably ascertained or would be uninformative, the Secretary may modify or waive the requirements for such information.

TITLE III—TRUSTEESHIPS

Reports

Section 301.

(a) Every labor organization which has or assumes trustee-ship over any subordinate labor organization shall file with the Secretary within thirty days after the date of the enactment of this Act or the imposition of any such trusteeship, and semiannually thereafter, a report, signed by its president and treasurer or corresponding principal officers, as well as by the trustees of such subordinate labor organization, containing the following information: (1) the name and address of the subordinate organization; (2) the date of establishing the trusteeship; (3) a detailed statement of the reason or reasons for establishing or continuing the trusteeship; and (4) the nature and extent of participation by the membership of the subordinate organization in the selection of delegates to represent such organization in regular or special conventions or other policy-determining bodies and in the election of officers of the labor organization which has assumed trusteeship over such subordinate organization. The initial report shall also include a full and complete account of the financial condition of such subordinate organization as of the time trusteeship was assumed over it. During the continuance of a trusteeship the labor organization which has assumed trusteeship over a subordinate labor organization shall file on behalf of the subordinate labor organization the annual financial report required by section 201(b) signed by the president and treasurer or corresponding principal officers of the labor organization which has assumed such trusteeship and the trustees of the subordinate labor organization.

(b) The provisions of sections 201(c), 205, 206, 208, and 210 shall be applicable to reports filed under this title.

(c) Any person who willfully violates this section shall be fined not more than $10,000 or imprisoned for not more than one year, or both.

(d) Any person who makes a false statement or representation of a material fact, knowing it to be false, or who knowingly fails to disclose a material fact, in any report required under the provisions of this section or willfully makes any false entry in or willfully withholds, conceals, or destroys any documents, books, records, reports, or statements upon which such report is based, shall be fined not more than $10,000 or imprisoned for not more than one year, or both.

(e) Each individual required to sign a report under this section shall be personally responsible for the filing of such report and for any statement contained therein which he knows to be false.

Purposes for which a Trusteeship May Be Established

Section 302. Trusteeships shall be established and administered by a labor organization over a subordinate body only in accordance with the constitution and bylaws of the organization which has assumed trusteeship over the subordinate body and for the purpose of correcting corruption or financial malpractice, assuring the performance of collective bargaining agreements or other duties of a bargaining representative, restoring democratic procedures, or otherwise carrying out the legitimate objects of such labor organization.

Unlawful Acts Relating to Labor Organization under Trusteeship

Section 303.

(a) During any period when a subordinate body of a labor organization is in trusteeship, it shall be unlawful (1) to count the vote of delegates from such body in any convention or election of officers of the labor organization unless the delegates have been chosen by secret ballot in an election in which all the members in good standing of such subordinate body were eligible to participate, or (2) to transfer to such organization any current receipts or other funds of the subordinate body except the normal per capita tax and assessments payable by subordinate bodies not in trusteeship: *Provided,* That nothing herein contained shall prevent the distribution of the assets of a labor organization in accordance with its constitution and bylaws upon the bona fide dissolution thereof.

(b) Any person who willfully violates this section shall be fined not more than $10,000 or imprisoned for not more than one year, or both.

Enforcement

Section 304.

(a) Upon the written complaint of any member or subordinate body of a labor organization alleging that such organization has violated the provisions of this title (except section 301) the Secretary shall investigate the complaint and if the Secretary finds probable cause to believe that such violation has occurred and has not been remedied he shall, without disclosing the identity of the complainant, bring a civil action in any district court of the United States having jurisdiction of the labor organization for such relief (including injunctions) as may be appropriate. Any member or subordinate body of a labor organization affected by any violation of this title (except section 301) may bring a civil action in any district court of the United States having jurisdiction of the labor organization for such relief (including injunctions) as may be appropriate.

(b) For the purpose of actions under this section, district courts of the United States shall be deemed to have jurisdiction of a labor organization (1) in the district in which the principal office of such labor organization is located, or (2) in any district in which its duly authorized officers or agents are engaged in conducting the affairs of the trusteeship.

(c) In any proceeding pursuant to this section a trusteeship established by a labor organization in conformity with the procedural requirements of its constitution and bylaws and authorized or ratified after a fair hearing either before the executive board or before such other body as may be provided in accordance with its constitution or bylaws shall be presumed valid for a period of eighteen months from the date of its establishment and shall not be subject to attack during such period except upon clear and convincing proof that the trusteeship was not established or maintained in good faith for a purpose allowable under section 302. After the expiration of eighteen months the trusteeship shall be presumed invalid in any such proceeding and its discontinuance shall be decreed unless the labor organization shall show by clear and convincing proof that the continuation of the trusteeship is necessary for a purpose allowable under section 302. In the latter event the court may dismiss the complaint or retain jurisdiction of the cause on such conditions and for such period as it deems appropriate.

Report to Congress

Section 305. The Secretary shall submit to the Congress at the expiration of three years from the date of enactment of this Act a report upon the operation of this title.

Complaint by Secretary

Section 306. The rights and remedies provided by this title shall be in addition to any and all other rights and remedies at law or in equity: Provided, That upon the filing of a complaint by the Secretary the jurisdiction of the district court over such trusteeship shall be exclusive and the final judgment shall be res judicata.

TITLE IV—ELECTIONS

Terms of Office; Election Procedures

Section 401.

(a) Every national or international labor organization, except a federation of national or international labor organizations, shall elect its officers not less often than once every five years either by secret ballot among the members in good standing or at a convention of delegates chosen by secret ballot.

(b) Every local labor organization shall elect its officers not less often than once every three years by secret ballot among the members in good standing.

(c) Every national or international labor organization, except a federation of national or international labor organizations, and every local labor organization, and its officers, shall be under a duty, enforceable at the suit of any bona fide candidate for office in such labor organization in the district court of the United States in which such labor organization maintains its principal office, to comply with all reasonable requests of any candidate to distribute by mail or otherwise at the candidate's expense campaign literature in aid of such person's candidacy to all members in good standing of such labor organization and to refrain from discrimination in favor of or against any candidate with respect to the use of lists of members, and whenever such labor organizations or its officers authorize the distribution by mail or otherwise to members of campaign literature on behalf of any candidate or of the labor organization itself with reference to such election, similar distribution at the request of any other bona fide candidate shall be made by such labor organization and its officers, with equal treatment as to the expense of such distribution. Every bona fide candidate shall have the right, once within 30 days prior to an election of a labor organization in which he is a candidate, to inspect a list containing the names and last known addresses of all members of the labor organization who are subject to a collective bargaining agreement requiring membership therein as a condition of employment, which list shall be maintained and kept at the principal office of such labor organization by a designated official thereof. Adequate safeguards to insure a fair election shall be provided, including the right of any candidate to have an observer at the polls and at the counting of the ballots.

(d) Officers of intermediate bodies, such as general committees, system boards, joint boards, or joint councils, shall be elected not less often than once every four years by secret ballot among the members in good standing or by labor organization officers representative of such members who have been elected by secret ballot.

(e) In any election required by this section which is to be held by secret ballot a reasonable opportunity shall be given for the nomination of candidates and every member in good standing shall be eligible to be a candidate and to hold office (subject to section 504 and to reasonable qualifications uniformly imposed) and shall have the right to vote for or otherwise support the candidate or candidates of his choice, without being subject to penalty, discipline, or improper interference or reprisal of any kind by such organization or any member thereof. Not less than fifteen days prior to the election notice thereof shall be mailed to each member at his last known home address. Each member in good standing shall be entitled to one vote. No member whose dues have been withheld by his employer for payment to such organization pursuant to his voluntary authorization provided for in a collective bargaining agreement, shall be declared ineligible to vote or be a candidate for office in such organization by reason of alleged delay or default in the payment of dues. The votes cast by members of each local labor organization shall be counted, and the results published, separately. The election officials designated in the constitution and bylaws or the secretary, if no other official is designated, shall preserve for one year the ballots and all other records pertaining to the election. The election shall be conducted in accordance with the constitution and bylaws of such organization insofar as they are not inconsistent with the provisions of this title.

(f) When officers are chosen by a convention of delegates elected by secret ballot, the convention shall be conducted in accordance with the constitution and bylaws of the labor organization insofar as they are not inconsistent with the provisions of this title. The officials designated in the constitution and bylaws or the secretary, if no other is designated, shall preserve for one year the credentials of the delegates and all minutes and other records of the convention pertaining to the election of officers.

(g) No moneys received by any labor organization by way of dues, assessment, or similar levy, and no moneys of an employer shall be contributed or applied to promote the candidacy of any person in an election subject to the provisions of this title. Such moneys of a labor organization may be utilized for notices, factual statements of issues not involving candidates, and other expenses necessary for the holding of an election.

(h) If the Secretary, upon application of any member of a local labor organization, finds after hearing in accordance with the Administrative Procedure Act that the constitution and bylaws of such labor organization do not provide an adequate procedure for the removal of an elected officer guilty of serious misconduct, such officer may be removed, for cause shown and after notice and hearing, by the members in good standing voting in a secret ballot conducted by the officers of such labor organization in accordance with its constitution and bylaws insofar as they are not inconsistent with the provisions of this title.

(i) The Secretary shall promulgate rules and regulations prescribing minimum standards and procedures for determining the adequacy of the removal procedures to which reference is made in subsection (h).

Enforcement

Section 402.

(a) A member of a labor organization—
   (1) who has exhausted the remedies available under the constitution and bylaws of such organization and of any parent body or
   (2) who has invoked such available remedies without obtaining a final decision within three calendar months after their invocation,

   may file a complaint with the Secretary within one calendar month thereafter alleging the violation of any provision of section 401 (including violation of the constitution and bylaws of the labor organization pertaining to the election and removal of officers). The challenged election shall be presumed valid pending a final decision thereon (as hereinafter provided) and in the interim the affairs of the organization shall be conducted by the officers elected or in such other manner as its constitution and bylaws may provide.

(b) The Secretary shall investigate such complaint and, if he finds probable cause to believe that a violation of this title has occurred and has not been remedied, he shall, within sixty days after the filing of such complaint, bring a civil action against the labor organization as an entity in the district court of the United States in which such labor organization maintains its principal office to set aside the invalid election, if any, and to direct the conduct of an election in hearing and vote upon the removal of officers under the supervision of the Secretary and in accordance with the provisions of this title and such rules and regulations as the Secretary may prescribe. The court shall have power to take such action as it deems proper to preserve the assets of the labor organization.

(c) If, upon a preponderance of the evidence after a trial upon the merits, the court finds—
   (1) that an election has not been held within the time prescribed by section 401, or
   (2) that the violation of section 401 may have affected the outcome of an election the court shall declare the election, if any, to be void and direct the conduct of a new election under supervision of the Secretary and, so far as lawful and practicable, in conformity with the constitution and bylaws of the labor organization. The Secretary shall promptly certify to the court the names of the persons elected, and the court shall thereupon enter a decree declaring such persons to be the officers of the labor organization. If the proceeding is for the removal of officers pursuant to subsection (h) of section 401, the Secretary shall certify the results of the vote and the court shall enter a decree declaring whether such persons have been removed as officers of the labor organization.

(d) An order directing an election, dismissing a complaint, or designating elected officers of a labor organization shall be appealable in the same manner as the final judgment in a civil action, but an order directing an election shall not be stayed pending appeal.

Application of Other Laws

Section 403. No labor organization shall be required by law to conduct elections of officers with greater frequency or in a different form or manner than is required by its own constitution or bylaws, except as otherwise provided by this title. Existing rights and remedies to enforce the constitution and bylaws of a labor organization with respect to elections prior to the conduct thereof shall not be affected by the provisions of this title. The remedy provided by this title for challenging an election already conducted shall be exclusive.

Effective Date

Section 404. The provisions of this title shall become applicable—

(a) (1) ninety days after the date of enactment of this Act in the case of a labor organization whose constitution and bylaws can lawfully be modified or amended by action of its constitutional officers or governing body, or
   (2) where such modification can only be made by a constitutional convention of the labor organization, not later than the next constitutional convention of such labor organization after the date of enactment of this Act, or one year after such date, whichever is sooner. If no such convention is held within such one-year period, the executive board or similar governing body empowered to act for such labor organization between conventions is empowered to make such interim constitutional changes as are necessary to carry out the provisions of this title.

TITLE V—SAFEGUARDS FOR LABOR ORGANIZATIONS

Fiduciary Responsibility of Officers of Labor Organizations

Section 501.

(a) The officers, agents, shop stewards, and other representatives of a labor organization occupy positions of trust in relation to such organization and its members as a group. It is, therefore, the duty of each such person, taking into account the special problems and functions of a labor organization, to hold its money and property solely for the benefit of the organization and its members and to manage, invest, and expend the same in accordance with its constitution and bylaws and any resolutions of the governing bodies adopted thereunder, to refrain from dealing with such organizations as an adverse party or in behalf of an adverse party in any matter connected with his duties and from holding or acquiring any pecuniary or personal interest which conflicts with the interests of such organization, and to account to the organization for any profit received by him in whatever capacity in connection with transactions conducted by him or under his direction on behalf of the organization. A general exculpatory provision in the constitution and bylaws of such a labor organization or a general exculpatory resolution of a governing body purporting to relieve any such person of liability for breach of the duties declared by this section shall be void as against public policy.

(b) When any officer, agent, shop steward, or representative of any labor organization is alleged to have violated the duties declared in subsection (a) and the labor organization or its governing board or officers refuse or fail to sue or recover damages or secure an accounting or other appropriate relief within a reasonable time after being requested to do so by any member of the labor organization, such member may sue such officer, agent, shop steward, or representative in any district court of the United States or in any State court of competent jurisdiction to recover damages or secure an accounting or other appropriate relief for the benefit of the labor organization. No such proceeding shall be brought except upon leave of the court obtained upon verified application and for good cause shown which application may be made ex parte. The trial judge may allot a reasonable part of the recovery in any action under this subsection to pay the fees of counsel prosecuting the suit at the instance of the member of the labor organization and to compensate such member for any expenses necessarily paid or incurred by him in connection with the litigation.

(c) Any person who embezzles, steals, or unlawfully and willfully abstracts or converts to his own use, or the use of another, any of the moneys, funds, securities, property, or other assets of a labor organization of which he is an officer, or by which he is employed, directly or indirectly, shall be fined not more than $10,000 or imprisoned for not more than five years, or both.

Bonding

Section 502.

(a) Every officer, agent, shop steward, or other representative or employee of any labor organization (other than a labor organization whose property and annual financial receipts do not exceed $5,000 in value), or of a trust in which a labor organization is interested, who handles funds or other property thereof shall be bonded to provide protection against loss by reason of acts of fraud or dishonesty on his part directly or through connivance with others. The bond of each such person shall be fixed at the beginning of the organization's fiscal year and shall be in an amount not less than 10 per centum of the funds handled by him and his predecessor or predecessors, if any, during the preceding fiscal year, but in no case more than $500,000. If the labor organization or the trust in which a labor organization is interested does not have a preceding fiscal year, the amount of the bond shall be, in the case of a local labor organization, not less than $1,000, and in the case of any other labor organization or of a trust in which a labor organization is interested, not less than $10,000. Such bonds shall be individual or schedule in form, and shall have a corporate surety company as surety thereon. Any person who is not covered by such bonds shall not be permitted to receive, handle, disburse, or otherwise exercise custody or control of the funds or other property of a labor organization or of a trust in which a labor organization is interested. No such bond shall be placed through an agent or broker or with a surety company in which any labor organization or any officer, agent, shop steward, or other representative of a labor organization has any direct or indirect interest. Such surety company shall be a corporate surety which holds a grant of authority from the Secretary of the Treasury under the Act of July 30, 1947 (6 U.S.C. 6–13), as an acceptable surety on Federal bonds: Provided, That when in the opinion of the Secretary a labor organization has made other bonding arrangements which would provide the protection required by this section at comparable cost or less, he may exempt such labor organization from placing a bond through a surety company holding such grant of authority.

(b) Any person who willfully violates this section shall be fined not more than $10,000 or imprisoned for not more than one year, or both.

Making of Loans; Payment of Fines

Section 503.

(a) No labor organization shall make directly or indirectly any loan or loans to any officer or employee of such organization which results in a total indebtedness on the part of such officer or employee to the labor organization in excess of $2,000.

(b) No labor organization or employer shall directly or indirectly pay the fine of any officer or employee convicted of any willful violation of this Act.

(c) Any person who willfully violates this section shall be fined not more than $5,000 or imprisoned for not more than one year, or both.

Prohibition Against Certain Persons Holding Office

Section 504.

(a) No person who is or has been a member of the Communist Party or who has been convicted of, or served any part of a prison term resulting from his conviction of, robbery, bribery, extortion, embezzlement, grand larceny, burglary, arson, violation of narcotics laws, murder, rape, assault with intent to kill, assault which inflicts grievous bodily injury, or a violation of title II or III of this Act, or conspiracy to commit any such crimes, shall serve—
   (1) as an officer, director, trustee, member of any executive board or similar governing body, business agent, manager, organizer, or other employee (other than as an employee performing exclusively clerical or custodial duties) of any labor organization, or
   (2) as a labor relations consultant to a person engaged in an industry or activity affecting commerce, or as an officer, director, agent, or employee (other than as an employee performing exclusively clerical or custodial duties) of any group or association of employers dealing with any labor organization, during or for five years after the termination of his membership in the Communist Party, or for five years after such conviction or after the end of such imprisonment, unless prior to the end of such five-year period, in the case of a person so convicted or imprisoned, (A) his citizenship rights, having been revoked as a result of such conviction, have been fully restored, or (B) the Board of Parole of the United States Department of Justice determines that such person's service in any capacity referred to in clause (1) or (2) would not be contrary to the purposes of this Act. Prior to making any such determination the Board shall hold an administrative hearing and shall give notice of such proceeding by certified mail to the State, County, and Federal prosecuting officials in the jurisdiction or jurisdictions in which such person was convicted. The Board's determination in any such proceeding shall be final. No labor organization or officer thereof shall knowingly permit any person to assume or hold any office or paid position in violation of this subsection.

(b) Any person who willfully violates this section shall be fined not more than $10,000 or imprisoned for not more than one year, or both.

(c) For the purposes of this section, any person shall be deemed to have been "convicted" and under the disability of "conviction" from the date of the judgment of the trial court or the date of the final sustaining of such judgment on appeal, whichever is the later event, regardless of whether such conviction occurred before or after the date of enactment of this Act.

TITLE VI—MISCELLANEOUS PROVISIONS

Investigations

Section 601.

(a) The Secretary shall have power when he believes it necessary in order to determine whether any person has violated or is about to violate any provision of this Act (except title I or amendments made by this Act to other statutes) to make an investigation and in connection therewith he may enter such places and inspect such records and accounts and question such persons as he may deem necessary to enable him to determine the facts relative thereto. The Secretary may report to interested persons or officials concerning the facts required to be shown in any report required by this Act and concerning the reasons for failure or refusal to file such a report or any other matter which he deems to be appropriate as a result of such an investigation.

(b) For the purpose of any investigation provided for in this Act, the provisions of sections 9 and 10 (relating to the attendance of witnesses and the production of books, papers, and documents) of the Federal Trade Commission Act of September 16, 1914, as amended (15 U.S.C. 49, 50), are hereby made applicable to the jurisdiction, powers, and duties of the Secretary or any officers designated by him.

Extortionate Picketing

Section 602.

(a) It shall be unlawful to carry on picketing on or about the premises of any employer for the purpose of, or as part of any conspiracy or in furtherance of any plan or purpose for, the personal profit or enrichment of any individual (except a bona fide increase in wages or other employee benefits) by taking or obtaining any money or other thing of value from such employer against his will or with his consent.

(b) Any person who willfully violates this section shall be fined not more than $10,000 or imprisoned not more than twenty years, or both.

Retention of Rights under Other Federal and State Laws

Section 603.

(a) Except as explicitly provided to the contrary, nothing in this Act shall reduce or limit the responsibilities of any labor organization or any officer, agent, shop steward, or other representative of a labor organization, or of any trust in which a labor organization is interested, under any other Federal law or under the laws of any State, and, except as explicitly provided to the contrary, nothing in this Act shall take away any right or bar any remedy to which members of a labor organization are entitled under such other Federal law or law of any State.

(b) Nothing contained in titles I, II, III, IV, V, or VI of this Act shall be construed to supersede or impair or otherwise affect the provisions of the Railway Labor Act, as amended, or any of the obligations, rights, benefits, privileges, or immunities of any carrier, employee, organization, representative, or person subject thereto; nor shall anything contained in said titles (except section 505) of this Act be construed to confer any rights, privileges, immunities, or defenses upon employers, or to impair or otherwise affect the rights of any person under the National Labor Relations Act, as amended.

Effect on State Laws

Section 604. Nothing in this Act shall be construed to impair or diminish the authority of any State to enact and enforce general criminal laws with respect to robbery, bribery, extortion, embezzlement, grand larceny, burglary, arson, violation of narcotics laws, murder, rape, assault with intent to kill, or assault which inflicts grievous bodily injury, or conspiracy to commit any of such crimes.

Service of Process

Section 605. For the purposes of this Act, service of summons, subpoena, or other legal process of a court of the United States upon an officer or agent of a labor organization in his capacity as such shall constitute service upon the labor organization.

Administrative Procedure Act

Section 606. The provisions of the Administrative Procedure Act shall be applicable to the issuance, amendment, or rescission of any rules or regulations, or any adjudication, authorized or required pursuant to the provisions of this Act.

Other Agencies and Departments

Section 607. In order to avoid unnecessary expense and duplication of functions among Government agencies, the Secretary may make such arrangements or agreements for cooperation or mutual assistance in the performance of his functions under this Act and the functions of any such agency as he may find to be practicable and consistent with law. The Secretary may utilize the facilities or services of any department, agency, or establishment of the United States or of any State or political subdivision of a State, including the services of any of its employees, with the lawful consent of such department, agency, or establishment; and each department, agency, or establishment of the United States is authorized and directed to cooperate with the Secretary and, to the extent permitted by law, to provide such information and facilities as he may request for his assistance in the performance of his functions under this Act. The Attorney General or his representative shall receive from the Secretary for appropriate action such evidence developed in the performance of his functions under this Act as may be found to warrant consideration for criminal prosecution under the provisions of this Act or other Federal law.

Criminal Contempt

Section 608. No person shall be punished for any criminal contempt allegedly committed outside the immediate presence of the court in connection with any civil action prosecuted by the Secretary or any other person in any court of the United States under the provisions of this Act unless the facts constituting such criminal contempt are established by the verdict of the jury in a proceeding in the district court of the United States, which jury shall be chosen and empaneled in the manner prescribed by the law governing trial juries in criminal prosecutions in the district courts of the United States.

Prohibition on Certain Discipline by Labor Organization

Section 609. It shall be unlawful for any labor organization, or any officer, agent, shop steward, or other representative of a labor organization, or any employee thereof to fine, suspend, expel, or otherwise discipline any of its members for exercising any right to which he is entitled under the provisions of this Act. The provisions of section 102 shall be applicable in the enforcement of this section.

Deprivation of Rights under Act by Violence

Section 610. It shall be unlawful for any person through the use of force or violence, or threat of the use of force or violence, to restrain, coerce, or intimidate, or attempt to restrain, coerce, or intimidate any member of a labor organization for the purpose of interfering with or preventing the exercise of any right to which he is entitled under the provisions of this Act. Any person who willfully violates this section shall be fined not more than $1,000 or imprisoned for not more than one year, or both.

Separability Provisions

Section 611. If any provision of this Act, or the application of such provision to any person or circumstances, shall be held invalid, the remainder of this Act or the application of such provision to persons or circumstances other than those as to which it is held invalid, shall not be affected thereby.

GLOSSARY

A

Academic Freedom The college professors' right to take unpopular positions in the classroom and in scholarly work without fear of reprisals by the university.

Administrative Law Judges (ALJs) Formerly called trial examiners, these judges are independent of both the Board and the general counsel.

Affirmative Action Plans Programs which involve giving preference in hiring or promotion to qualified female or minority employees.

After-Acquired Evidence Evidence, discovered after an employer has taken an adverse employment action, that the employer uses to justify the action taken.

Agency Shop A union security provision in a collective agreement that requires employees to pay union dues and fees, but does not require that they become union members.

Agency Shop Agreement Agreement requiring employees to pay union dues, but not requiring them to join the union.

Alien Tort Claims Act Federal statute which provides a cause of action for aggrieved aliens in U.S. courts.

Ambulatory Situs Picketing Union picketing that follows the primary employer's mobile business.

Arbitration The settlement of disputes by a neutral adjudicator chosen by the parties.

Authorization Cards Cards signed by employees indicating that they authorize the union to act as the employees' bargaining agent and to seek an election on behalf of the employees.

B

Bargaining Unit Group of employees being represented by a union.

Bennett Amendment The provision of Section 703(h) that allows pay differentials between employees of different sexes when the pay differential is due to seniority, merit pay, productivity-based pay, or a factor other than sex.

Bona Fide Occupational Qualification (BFOQ) An exception to the civil rights law that allows an employer to hire employees of a specific gender, religion, or national origin when business necessity—the safe and efficient performance of the particular job—requires it.

Business Necessity The safe and efficient performance of the business or performance of a particular job requires that employees be of a particular sex, religion or national origin.

C

Captive-Audience Speeches Meetings or speeches held by the employer during working hours, which employees are required to attend.

Closed Shop An employer who agrees to hire only those employees who are already union members.

Collective Bargaining Process by which a union and employer meet and confer with respect to wages, hours, and other terms and conditions of employment.

Common Law Judge-made law as opposed to statutes and ordinances enacted by legislative bodies.

Common Situs Picketing Union picketing of an entire construction site.

Comparable Worth A standard of equal pay for jobs of equal value; not the same as equal pay for equal work.

Confidential Employees Persons whose job involves access to confidential labor relations information.

Consent Election Election conducted by the regional office giving the regional director final authority over any disputes.

Construct Validity A method of demonstrating that an employment selection device selects employees based on the traits and characteristics that are required for the job in question.

Content Validity A method of demonstrating that an employment selection device reflects the content of the job for which employees are being selected.

Contract Bar Rule A written labor contract bars an election during the life of the bargaining agreement, subject to the "open-season" exception.

Contract Compliance Program Regulations which provide that all firms having federal government contracts or subcontracts exceeding $10,000 must include a no-discrimination clause in the contract.

Conventions International laws, usually sponsored by the United nations or other multi-national organizations, to which a number of nations agree to adhere.

Criminal Conspiracy A crime that may be committed when two or more persons agree to do something unlawful.

Criterion-Related Validity A method of demonstrating that an employment selection device correlates with the skills and knowledge required for successful job performance.

D

De Minimis Violation A technical violation, but so insignificant as to require no fine or remediation.

Decertification Petition Petition stating that a current bargaining representative no longer has the support of a majority of the employees in the bargaining unit.

Defamation An intentional, false, and harmful communication.

Depressions Severe declines in economic activity.

Dicta Opinions of a judge or appellate panel of judges that are tangential to the rule, holding, and decision which are at the core of the judicial pronouncement.

Disparate Impact The discriminatory effect of apparently neutral employment criteria.

Disparate Treatment When an employee is treated differently from others due to race, color, religion, gender or national origin.

Drug Testing Testing of human blood and/or urine for the presence of controlled/illegal substances.

Duty of Fair Representation Legal duty on the part of the union to represent fairly all members of the bargaining unit.

E

Eavesdropping Surreptitiously listening to others' conversations.

Economic Strike A strike over economic issues such as a new contract or a grievance.

Election of Remedies A litigant's choice of solutions for a perceived wrong; for example, a plaintiff may have a choice between money damages and a court order of restitution.

Employee Assistance Program (EAP) Includes a range of psychological, health, fitness and legal services aimed at helping employees solve problems that interfere with job performance.

Employee Free Choice Act Bill which, if enacted, will make it easier for unions to organize workers.

Employee Retirement Income Security Act (ERISA) An act that sets standards for pension plans including fiduciary conduct, information disclosure, plan taxation, and remedies for employees.

Employment-at-Will Both the employee and the employer are free to unilaterally terminate the relationship at any time and for any legally permissible reason, or for no reason at all.

English-Only Rules Employer work rules requiring that employees speak English in the workplace during working hours.

Equal Pay Act of 1963 Federal legislation that requires that men and women performing substantially equal work be paid equally.

Ex Parte Proceedings Court hearings in which one party, usually the defendant, is not present and is not able to take part.

Excelsior List A list of the names and addresses of the employees eligible to vote in a representation election.

Exempt Employees Employees whose hours of work and compensation are not stipulated by the FLSA.

Express Contract A contract in which the terms are explicitly stated, usually in writing but perhaps only verbally, and often in great detail. In interpreting such a contract, the judge and/or the jury is asked only to determine what the explicit terms are and to interpret them according to their plain meaning.

F

Failing Firm Exception An exception to the WARN notice requirement for layoffs that occurs when the employer can demonstrate that giving the required notice would prevent the firm from obtaining capital or business necessary to maintain the operation of the firm.

Featherbedding The practice of getting paid for services not performed or not to be performed.

Federal Employment Liability Act (FELA) A federal law designed to protect and compensate railroad workers injured on the job.

Federal Labor Relations Authority (FLRA) The federal agency created under the Federal Service Labor-Management Relations Act to administer federal employee labor relations.

Federal Service Impasse Panel Federal body created under the Federal Service Labor-Management Relations Act to resolve impasses in collective bargaining in the federal service.

Fiduciary Any person exercising discretionary authority over benefit plan administration, management, or disposition of plan assets; or who renders investment advice regarding the plan.

Forty-Eight-Hour Rule NLRB requirement that a party filing a petition for a representation election must provide evidence to support the petition within 48 hours of the filing.

Four-Fifths Rule A mathematical formula developed by the EEOC to demonstrate disparate impact of a facially neutral employment practice on selection criteria.

Front Pay Monetary damages awarded to a plaintiff instead of re-instatement or hiring.

G

Genetic Testing Examination of chromosomes, genes and proteins in human cells in a search for defects.

Global Corporate Responsibility Philosophy which says that corporations should behave as good global citizens.

Global Unions International labor organizations, which typically attempt to organize employees of globalized industries.

Globalization The integration of national economies into a worldwide economy, due to trade, investment, migration and information technology.

Good Cause A substantial reason, not arbitrary or capricious or illegally discriminatory.

Grievance A complaint that one party to a collective agreement is not living up to the obligations of the agreement.

Grievance Process The process set up by a collective agreement to deal with complaints that arise under the collective agreement.

H

Health-Insurance Reform Effort by the Obama Administration and Congress to solve the problems of high cost and limited coverage of the US health insurance system.

Hiring Halls A job-referral mechanism operated by unions whereby unions refer members to prospective employers.

Honesty Tests Employment tests used by employers as a screening device to evaluate employees or applicants on various workplace behaviors such as truthfulness, perceptions about employee theft, admissions of theft, and drug use.

Hostile Environment Harassment Harassment which may not result in economic detriment to the victim, but which subjects the victim to unwelcome conduct or comments and may interfere with the employee's work performance.

Hot Cargo Clauses Provisions in collective bargaining agreements that purport to permit employees to refuse to handle the product of any employer involved in a labor dispute.

I

Immigration Reform and Control Act (IRCA) of 1986 The most recent major overhaul of U.S immigration law.

Impasse A deadlock in negotiations.

Implied Contract A contractual relationship, the terms and conditions of which must be inferred from the contracting parties' behavior toward one another.

Independent Contractor A person working as a separate business entity.

Individual Employee Rights Rights enjoyed by workers as individuals, as against collective rights secured by unionization; sources are statutes and court decisions.

Information Technology The study, design, development, implementation, support or management of computer-based information systems.

In-House Unions Unions created and controlled by the employer.

Injunction A court order to provide remedies prohibiting some action or commanding the righting of some wrongdoing.

Intentional Infliction of Emotional Distress Purposely outrageous conduct causing emotional harm.

Interest Arbitration Arbitration that is used to create a new collective agreement or to renew an existing agreement.

L

Laboratory Conditions The conditions under which a representative election is held; the NLRB tries to ensure that neither the employer nor the union unduly affects the employees' free choice.

Libel A written falsehood.

Lilly Ledbetter Fair Pay Act Statute that extends time in which an employee may file suit under several federal employment statutes.

Lockout An employer's temporary withdrawal of employment to pressure employees to agree to the employer's bargaining proposals.

M

Malice Knowledge or reckless disregard of the falsity of a communication.

Managerial Employees Persons involved in the formulation or effectuation of management policies.

Mandatory Bargaining Subjects Those matters that vitally affect the terms and conditions of employment of the employees in the bargaining unit; the parties must bargain in good faith over such subjects.

Mass Layoffs Layoffs creating an employment loss during any thirty-day period for 500 or more employees or for fifty or more employees who constitute at least one-third of the full-time labor force at a unit of the facility.

Minimum Wage The wage limit, set by the government, under which an employer is not allowed to pay an employee.

N

National Industrial Recovery Act (NIRA) An act primarily designed to regulate and revitalize industry; promoted fair trade practices.

Negligent Hiring When an employer hires an employee that the employer knows (or should have known through reasonable checks) could cause injury to others.

Negligent Infliction of Emotional Distress Carelessly outrageous conduct causing emotional harm.

Networks Group of computers, all inter-connected to one another.

Nonsuspect Class A basis of discrimination, classification, or differential by government action which is neutral with regard to race, color, gender, religion or national origin, and which is related to legitimate government interests. Examples of nonsuspect classes are age, veteran status, or personal achievement.

North American Free Trade Agreement (NAFTA) Treaty among Canada, the US and Mexico to foster free trade across their national borders.

No-Strike Clause A provision in a collective agreement by which the union agrees not to strike over disputes of interpretation of the agreement during the term of the agreement.

O

Open-Meeting ("Sunshine") Laws Laws that require that meetings of public bodies be open to the public.

Overtime Pay Employees covered by the FLSA are entitled to overtime pay, at one-and-a-half times their regular pay rate, for hours worked in excess of forty hours per workweek.

P

Patrolling The movement of persons back and forth around an employer's premises.

Permissive Bargaining Subjects Those matters that are neither mandatory or illegal; the parties may, but are not required to, bargain over such subjects.

Picketing Placing persons outside an employer's premises to convey information to the public by words, signs, or distributing literature.

Pregnancy Discrimination Act of 1978 An act that amended Title VII to include pregnancy discrimination in the definition of sex discrimination.

Pressure Tactics Union pressure tactics involve strikes and calls for boycotts, while employers may resort to lockouts.

Prima Facie Case A case "on the face of it" or "at first sight"; often used to establish that if a certain set of facts is proven, then it is apparent that another fact is established.

Protected Health Information (PHI) Information specifically identified by federal law as subject to privacy protection.

Public Policy Exception Although the employee is employed at-will, termination is illegal if a clear and significant mandate of law (statutory or common) is damaged if the firing is permitted to stand unchallenged.

Q

Qualified Individual with a Disability An individual with a disability who is able to perform, with reasonable accommodation, the requirements of the job in question, despite the disability.

Qualified Privilege Immunity from a suit in the absence of malice.

Quid Pro Quo Harassment Harassment where the employee's response to the harassment is considered in granting employment benefits.

R

Racketeer Influenced and Corrupt Organizations Act (RICO) A federal law designed to criminally penalize those that engage in illegal activities as part of an ongoing criminal organization (e.g., the mafia).

Reasonable Suspicion Justifiably suspecting a person, based on facts or circumstances, of inappropriate or criminal activities.

Recessions Periodic economic downturns.

Retaliatory Demotion Reduction in rank, salary, or job title as a punishment.

Rights Arbitration Arbitration to resolve a dispute involving the interpretation or application of an existing collective agreement; arbitration that defines the rights and obligations of each party under the agreement.

Right-to-Work Laws Laws which prohibit union security agreements.

Runaway Shop Situation in which an employer closes in one location and opens in another to avoid unionization.

S

Seniority The length of service on the job.

Sexual Harassment Unwelcome sexual advances, requests for sexual favors, or other verbal or physical conduct of a sexual nature that the employee is required to accept as a condition of employment, the employee's response to such conduct is used as a basis for employment decisions, or such conduct creates a hostile working environment.

Slander A spoken falsehood.

Strict Liability Plaintiff prevails without proving negligence.

Strict Scrutiny Test A constitutional analysis used by courts hearing equal protection claims involving governmental discrimination based on a "suspect class." This test requires the government to demonstrate that the discriminatory treatment was necessary to achieve a compelling government purpose and that the governmental action was "narrowly tailored" to achieve the compelling purpose.

Strike The organized withholding of labor by workers—the traditional weapon by which workers attempt to pressure employers.

Substance Abuse Long-term use or dependance on alcohol or drugs.

Supervisor Person with authority to direct, hire, fire, or discipline employees in the interests of the employer.

Surveillance Monitoring of behavior.

Suspect Class A basis of discrimination, classification, or differential treatment—such as race, color, gender, religion or national origin—by government action, for which there is little legitimate justification for treating persons because of such characteristics.

System Administrators Persons employed by an organization's IT department to manage and oversee a network of computers.

T

Title VII of the Civil Rights Act of 1964 Legislation that outlawed discrimination in terms and conditions of employment based on race, color, sex, religion or national origin.

Tort A private or civil wrong or injury, caused by one party to another, either intentionally or negligently.

Tortious Interference with Contract Unprivileged intrusion into a contractual relationship.

Trade Secrets Proprietary information protected by common law or state statute.

Twenty-Four-Hour Silent Period The twenty-four-hour period prior to the representation election, during which the parties must refrain from formal campaign meetings.

U

Undue Hardship An accommodation that requires significant difficulty or expense for the employer.

Unemployment Compensation Benefits paid to employees out of work through no fault of their own and who are available for suitable work if and when it becomes available.

Unfair Labor Practice Strike A strike to protest employer unfair practices.

Unfair Labor Practices (ULPs) Actions by employers or unions that interfere with the rights of employees under the National Labor Relations Act.

Uniform Guidelines on Employee Selection Regulations adopted by the EEOC and other federal agencies that provide for methods of demonstrating a disparate impact and for validating employee selection criteria.

Union Security Agreements Contract provisions requiring employees to join the union or pay union dues.

Union Shop A union security provision in a collective agreement that requires employees to become union members within thirty days of their employment.

Union Shop Agreement Agreement requiring employees to join the union after a certain period of time.

Union Shop Clause Clause in an agreement requiring all present and future members of a bargaining unit to be union members.

V

Voluntary Recognition An employer agreeing to recognize a union with majority support as the exclusive bargaining agent for the workers in the bargaining unit, without holding a certification election.

W

Weingarten Rights The right of employees to have a representative of their choice present at meetings that may result in disciplinary action against the employees.

Whipsaw Strikes Strikes by a union selectively pitting one firm in an industry against the other firms.

Whistleblowers Employees who report or attempt to report employer wrongdoing or actions threatening public health or safety to government authorities.

Willful Misconduct The high level of fault that disqualifies an out-of-work worker from unemployment benefits.

Workers' Compensation Benefits awarded an employee when injuries are work related.

Workweek A term the FLSA uses to signify seven consecutive days; the law does not require that the workweek start or end on any particular day of the calendar week.

Writ of Certiorari A court order requiring the court below to certify the record of a case and send it up on appeal.

Y

Yellow-Dog Contracts Employment contracts requiring employees to agree not to join a union.

INDEX OF CASES

INDEX OF SUBJECTS

C

D

E

F

G

H

I

J

K

L

M

N

O

P

Q

R

S

T

U

V

W

Y